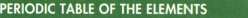

PERIODIC TABLE OF THE ELEMENTS

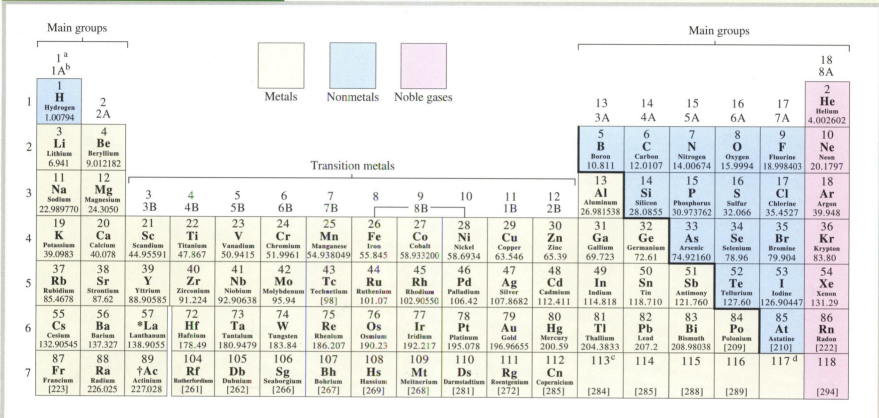

Metals | Nonmetals | Noble gases

Period	1[a] 1A[b]	2 2A	3 3B	4 4B	5 5B	6 6B	7 7B	8 8B	9 8B	10 8B	11 1B	12 2B	13 3A	14 4A	15 5A	16 6A	17 7A	18 8A
1	1 **H** Hydrogen 1.00794																	2 **He** Helium 4.002602
2	3 **Li** Lithium 6.941	4 **Be** Beryllium 9.012182											5 **B** Boron 10.811	6 **C** Carbon 12.0107	7 **N** Nitrogen 14.00674	8 **O** Oxygen 15.9994	9 **F** Fluorine 18.998403	10 **Ne** Neon 20.1797
3	11 **Na** Sodium 22.989770	12 **Mg** Magnesium 24.3050											13 **Al** Aluminum 26.981538	14 **Si** Silicon 28.0855	15 **P** Phosphorus 30.973762	16 **S** Sulfur 32.066	17 **Cl** Chlorine 35.4527	18 **Ar** Argon 39.948
4	19 **K** Potassium 39.0983	20 **Ca** Calcium 40.078	21 **Sc** Scandium 44.95591	22 **Ti** Titanium 47.867	23 **V** Vanadium 50.9415	24 **Cr** Chromium 51.9961	25 **Mn** Manganese 54.938049	26 **Fe** Iron 55.845	27 **Co** Cobalt 58.933200	28 **Ni** Nickel 58.6934	29 **Cu** Copper 63.546	30 **Zn** Zinc 65.39	31 **Ga** Gallium 69.723	32 **Ge** Germanium 72.61	33 **As** Arsenic 74.92160	34 **Se** Selenium 78.96	35 **Br** Bromine 79.904	36 **Kr** Krypton 83.80
5	37 **Rb** Rubidium 85.4678	38 **Sr** Strontium 87.62	39 **Y** Yttrium 88.90585	40 **Zr** Zirconium 91.224	41 **Nb** Niobium 92.90638	42 **Mo** Molybdenum 95.94	43 **Tc** Technetium [98]	44 **Ru** Ruthenium 101.07	45 **Rh** Rhodium 102.90550	46 **Pd** Palladium 106.42	47 **Ag** Silver 107.8682	48 **Cd** Cadmium 112.411	49 **In** Indium 114.818	50 **Sn** Tin 118.710	51 **Sb** Antimony 121.760	52 **Te** Tellurium 127.60	53 **I** Iodine 126.90447	54 **Xe** Xenon 131.29
6	55 **Cs** Cesium 132.90545	56 **Ba** Barium 137.327	57 ***La** Lanthanum 138.9055	72 **Hf** Hafnium 178.49	73 **Ta** Tantalum 180.9479	74 **W** Tungsten 183.84	75 **Re** Rhenium 186.207	76 **Os** Osmium 190.23	77 **Ir** Iridium 192.217	78 **Pt** Platinum 195.078	79 **Au** Gold 196.96655	80 **Hg** Mercury 200.59	81 **Tl** Thallium 204.3833	82 **Pb** Lead 207.2	83 **Bi** Bismuth 208.98038	84 **Po** Polonium [209]	85 **At** Astatine [210]	86 **Rn** Radon [222]
7	87 **Fr** Francium [223]	88 **Ra** Radium 226.025	89 **†Ac** Actinium 227.028	104 **Rf** Rutherfordium [261]	105 **Db** Dubnium [262]	106 **Sg** Seaborgium [266]	107 **Bh** Bohrium [267]	108 **Hs** Hassium [269]	109 **Mt** Meitnerium [268]	110 **Ds** Darmstadtium [281]	111 **Rg** Roentgenium [272]	112 **Cn** Copernicium [285]	113[c] [284]	114 [285]	115 [288]	116 [289]	117[d]	118 [294]

Main groups: 1–2 and 13–18. Transition metals: 3–12.

*Lanthanide series	58 **Ce** Cerium 140.116	59 **Pr** Praseodymium 140.90765	60 **Nd** Neodymium 144.24	61 **Pm** Promethium [145]	62 **Sm** Samarium 150.36	63 **Eu** Europium 151.964	64 **Gd** Gadolinium 157.25	65 **Tb** Terbium 158.92534	66 **Dy** Dysprosium 162.50	67 **Ho** Holmium 164.93032	68 **Er** Erbium 167.26	69 **Tm** Thulium 168.93421	70 **Yb** Ytterbium 173.04	71 **Lu** Lutetium 174.967
†Actinide series	90 **Th** Thorium 232.0381	91 **Pa** Protactinium 231.03588	92 **U** Uranium 238.0289	93 **Np** Neptunium 237.048	94 **Pu** Plutonium [244]	95 **Am** Americium [243]	96 **Cm** Curium [247]	97 **Bk** Berkelium [247]	98 **Cf** Californium [251]	99 **Es** Einsteinium [252]	100 **Fm** Fermium [257]	101 **Md** Mendelevium [258]	102 **No** Nobelium [259]	103 **Lr** Lawrencium [262]

Atomic masses in brackets are the masses of the longest-lived or most important isotope of certain radioactive elements.

[a] The labels on top (1, 2, 3 ... 18) are the group numbers recommended by the International Union of Pure and Applied Chemistry (IUPAC).

[b] The labels on the bottom (1A, 2A, ... 8A) are the group numbers commonly used in the United States and the ones we use in this text.

[c] The names and symbols of elements 113 and above have not been assigned.

[d] Discovered in 2010, element 117 is under review by IUPAC.

Further information is available at the Web site of WebElements™.

TABLE OF ATOMIC MASSES BASED ON CARBON-12

Name	Symbol	Atomic Number	Atomic Mass	Name	Symbol	Atomic Number	Atomic Mass
Actinium	Ac	89	227.028	Meitnerium	Mt	109	(268)
Aluminum	Al	13	26.9815	Mendelevium	Md	101	(258)
Americium	Am	95	(243)	Mercury	Hg	80	200.59
Antimony	Sb	51	121.760	Molybdenum	Mo	42	95.94
Argon	Ar	18	39.948	Neodymium	Nd	60	144.24
Arsenic	As	33	74.9216	Neon	Ne	10	20.1797
Astatine	At	85	(210)	Neptunium	Np	93	237.048
Barium	Ba	56	137.327	Nickel	Ni	28	58.6934
Berkelium	Bk	97	(247)	Niobium	Nb	41	92.9064
Beryllium	Be	4	9.01218	Nitrogen	N	7	14.0067
Bismuth	Bi	83	208.980	Nobelium	No	102	(259)
Bohrium	Bh	107	(267)	Osmium	Os	76	190.23
Boron	B	5	10.811	Oxygen	O	8	15.9994
Bromine	Br	35	79.904	Palladium	Pd	46	106.42
Cadmium	Cd	48	112.411	Phosphorus	P	15	30.9738
Calcium	Ca	20	40.078	Platinum	Pt	78	195.078
Californium	Cf	98	(251)	Plutonium	Pu	94	(244)
Carbon	C	6	12.0107	Polonium	Po	84	(209)
Cerium	Ce	58	140.116	Potassium	K	19	39.0983
Cesium	Cs	55	132.905	Praseodymium	Pr	59	140.908
Chlorine	Cl	17	35.4527	Promethium	Pm	61	(145)
Chromium	Cr	24	51.9961	Protactinium	Pa	91	231.036
Cobalt	Co	27	58.9332	Radium	Ra	88	226.025
Copernicium	Cn	112	(285)	Radon	Rn	86	(222)
Copper	Cu	29	63.546	Rhenium	Re	75	186.207
Curium	Cm	96	(247)	Rhodium	Rh	45	102.906
Darmstadtium	Ds	110	(281)	Roentgenium	Rg	111	(272)
Dubnium	Db	105	(262)	Rubidium	Rb	37	85.4678
Dysprosium	Dy	66	162.50	Ruthenium	Ru	44	101.07
Einsteinium	Es	99	(252)	Rutherfordium	Rf	104	(261)
Erbium	Er	68	167.26	Samarium	Sm	62	150.36
Europium	Eu	63	151.964	Scandium	Sc	21	44.9559
Fermium	Fm	100	(257)	Seaborgium	Sg	106	(266)
Fluorine	F	9	18.9984	Selenium	Se	34	78.96
Francium	Fr	87	(223)	Silicon	Si	14	28.0855
Gadolinium	Gd	64	157.25	Silver	Ag	47	107.868
Gallium	Ga	31	69.723	Sodium	Na	11	22.9898
Germanium	Ge	32	72.61	Strontium	Sr	38	87.62
Gold	Au	79	196.967	Sulfur	S	16	32.066
Hafnium	Hf	72	178.49	Tantalum	Ta	73	180.948
Hassium	Hs	108	(269)	Technetium	Tc	43	(98)
Helium	He	2	4.00260	Tellurium	Te	52	127.60
Holmium	Ho	67	164.930	Terbium	Tb	65	158.925
Hydrogen	H	1	1.00794	Thallium	Tl	81	204.383
Indium	In	49	114.818	Thorium	Th	90	232.038
Iodine	I	53	126.904	Thulium	Tm	69	168.934
Iridium	Ir	77	192.217	Tin	Sn	50	118.710
Iron	Fe	26	55.845	Titanium	Ti	22	47.867
Krypton	Kr	36	83.80	Tungsten	W	74	183.84
Lanthanum	La	57	138.906	Uranium	U	92	238.029
Lawrencium	Lr	103	(262)	Vanadium	V	23	50.9415
Lead	Pb	82	207.2	Xenon	Xe	54	131.29
Lithium	Li	3	6.941	Ytterbium	Yb	70	173.04
Lutetium	Lu	71	174.967	Yttrium	Y	39	88.9059
Magnesium	Mg	12	24.3050	Zinc	Zn	30	65.39
Manganese	Mn	25	54.9380	Zirconium	Zr	40	91.224

Atomic masses in this table are relative to carbon-12 and limited to six significant figures, although some atomic masses are known more precisely. For certain radioactive elements the numbers listed (in parentheses) are the mass numbers of the most stable isotopes.

Chemistry
FOR CHANGING TIMES

THIRTEENTH EDITION

John W. Hill
University of Wisconsin–River Falls

Terry W. McCreary
Murray State University

Doris K. Kolb

PEARSON

Boston Columbus Indianapolis New York San Francisco Upper Saddle River
Amsterdam Cape Town Dubai London Madrid Milan Munich Paris Montréal Toronto
Delhi Mexico City São Paulo Sydney Hong Kong Seoul Singapore Taipei Tokyo

Editor in Chief: Adam Jaworski
Senior Marketing Manager: Jonathan Cottrell
Senior Project Editor: Jennifer Hart
VP/Executive Director, Development: Carol Trueheart
Development Editor: Donald Gecewicz
Media Producer: Kristin Mayo
Assistant Editor: Coleen McDonald
Editorial Assistant: Fran Falk
Marketing Assistant: Nicola Houston
Managing Editor, Chemistry and Geosciences: Gina M. Cheselka
Senior Project Manager, Production: Beth Sweeten
Production Management, Full Service: Thistle Hill Publishing Services, LLC
Compositor: Cenveo Publisher Services/Nesbitt Graphics, Inc.
Senior Technical Art Specialist: Connie Long
Illustrator: Precision Graphics
Design Manager: Derek Bacchus
Interior/Cover Designer: tani hasegawa
Photo Manager: Maya Melenchuk
Photo Researcher: Eric Schrader
Text Permissions Manager: Beth Wollar
Text Permissions Researchers: Jenny Bevington
Operations Specialist: Jeff Sargent
Cover Photo Credit: Nicky Linzey/Dreamstime

Credits and acknowledgments borrowed from other sources and reproduced, with permission, in this textbook appear on the appropriate page within the text or on page PC-1.

Library of Congress Cataloging-in-Publication-Data

Hill, John William, 1933–
Chemistry for changing times / John W. Hill, Terry W. McCreary, Doris K. Kolb.
p. cm.
Includes bibliographical references and index.
ISBN-13: 978-0-321-75087-7
ISBN-10: 0-321-75087-X
1. Chemistry—Textbooks. I. McCreary, Terry Wade, 1955– II. Kolb, Doris K. III. Title.
QD33.2.H54 2013
540–dc23

2011041338

www.pearsonhighered.com

ISBN-10: 032175087X; ISBN-13: 9780321750877

2 3 4 5 6 7 8 9 10—DOW—17 16 15 14 13

Brief Contents

Green Chemistry *v*
Contents *vi*
Preface *xiii*
To the Student *xxi*
About the Authors *xxii*
Highlights of the Thirteenth Edition *xxii*

1 Chemistry 1
2 Atoms 41
3 Atomic Structure 61
4 Chemical Bonds 89
5 Chemical Accounting 125
6 Gases, Liquids, Solids . . . and Intermolecular Forces 152
7 Acids and Bases 175
8 Oxidation and Reduction 201
9 Organic Chemistry 229
10 Polymers 266
11 Nuclear Chemistry 295
12 Chemistry of Earth 331
13 Air 350
14 Water 385
15 Energy 411
16 Biochemistry 454
17 Food 494
18 Drugs 530
19 Fitness and Health 585
20 Chemistry Down on the Farm . . . and in the Garden and on the Lawn 613
21 Household Chemicals 643
22 Poisons 680

Appendix: Review of Measurement and Mathematics *A-1*
Glossary *A-18*
Answers *A-26*
Credits *C-1*
Index *I-1*

The thirteenth edition of *Chemistry for Changing Times* is pleased to present the green chemistry essays listed below. The topics have been carefully chosen to introduce students to the concepts of green chemistry—a new approach to designing chemicals and chemical transformations that are beneficial for human health and the environment. The green chemistry essays in this edition highlight cutting-edge research by chemists, molecular scientists, and engineers to explore the fundamental science and practical applications of chemistry that is "benign by design." These examples emphasize the responsibility of chemists for the consequences of the new materials they create and the importance of building a sustainable chemical enterprise.

Chapter 1 Green Chemistry
Jennifer L. Young
ACS Green Chemistry Institute®
Robert Peoples
ACS Green Chemistry Institute®

Chapter 2 It's Elemental
Lallie C. McKenzie
Chem11 LLC

Chapter 3 Clean Energy from Solar Fuels
Scott Cummings
Kenyon College

Chapter 4 Green Chemistry and Chemical Bonds
John C. Warner
Warner Babcock Institute for Green Chemistry
Amy S. Cannon
Beyond Benign

Chapter 5 Atom Economy
Margaret Kerr
Worcester State University

Chapter 6 Supercritical Fluids
Doug Raynie
South Dakota State University

Chapter 7 Sustainability: It's Basic (and Acidic)
Irv Levy
Gordon College

Chapter 8 Green Oxidation Catalysts
Colin P. Horwitz
GreenOx Catalysts, Inc.

Chapter 9 The Art of Organic Synthesis: Green Chemists Find a Better Way
Thomas E. Goodwin
Hendrix College

Chapter 10 Greener Polymers
Jennifer L. Young
ACS Green Chemistry Institute®

Chapter 11 Green Remediation of Nuclear Waste
Bevin W. Parks-Lee
Industrial Organic Chemist

Chapter 12 We're Going to Need a Bigger Earth . . .
Denyce K. Wicht
Suffolk University

Chapter 13 It's Not Easy Being Green
Irv Levy
Gordon College

Chapter 14 Porous Materials in Water Remediation
Randall Hicks
Wheaton College (Norton, MA)

Chapter 15 Have We Got the Energy?
Michael Heben
University of Toledo

Chapter 16 Green Chemistry and Biochemistry
David A. Vosburg
Harvey Mudd College

Chapter 17 Greener Ways to Isolate Nutrients from Food
David M. Brown
Davidson College

Chapter 18 Green Pharmaceuticals
Joseph Fortunak
Howard University

Chapter 19 Your Fitness Benefits the Planet
Doris Lewis
Suffolk University

Chapter 20 Safer Pesticides through Green Chemistry
Amy S. Cannon
Beyond Benign

Chapter 21 Practicing Green Chemistry at Home
Marty Mulvihill
University of California–Berkeley

Chapter 22 Fishing for a Greener World
Siba Das
Oregon State University
Robert L. Tanguay
Oregon State University

Contents

Preface xiii
To the Student xxi
About the Authors xxii

1 Chemistry 1

1.1 Science and Technology: The Roots of Knowledge 2
1.2 Changing Perceptions and Changing Practices 3
1.3 Science: Reproducible, Testable, Tentative, Predictive, and Explanatory 5
1.4 Science and Technology: Risks and Benefits 8
1.5 Chemistry: Its Central Role 10
1.6 Solving Society's Problems: Scientific Research 11
1.7 Chemistry: A Study of Matter and Its Changes 13
1.8 Classification of Matter 16
1.9 The Measurement of Matter 20
1.10 Density 25
1.11 Energy: Heat and Temperature 28
1.12 Critical Thinking 32

Summary 34 • Review Questions 35 • Problems 36 • Additional Problems 38 • Collaborative Group Projects 40

2 Atoms 41

2.1 Atoms: Ideas from the Ancient Greeks 42
2.2 Scientific Laws: Conservation of Mass and Definite Proportions 43
2.3 John Dalton and the Atomic Theory of Matter 47
2.4 Mendeleev and the Periodic Table 51
2.5 Atoms and Molecules: Real and Relevant 53

Summary 56 • Review Questions 57 • Problems 58 • Additional Problems 59 • Collaborative Group Projects 60

3 Atomic Structure 61

3.1 Electricity and the Atom 62
3.2 Serendipity in Science: X-Rays and Radioactivity 65
3.3 Three Types of Radiation 66
3.4 Rutherford's Experiment: The Nuclear Model of the Atom 68
3.5 The Atomic Nucleus 69
3.6 Electron Arrangement: The Bohr Model 73
3.7 Electron Arrangement: The Quantum Model 77
3.8 Electron Configurations and the Periodic Table 81

Summary 85 • Review Questions 86 • Problems 87 • Additional Problems 88 • Collaborative Group Projects 88

4 Chemical Bonds 89

4.1 The Art of Deduction: Stable Electron Configurations 90
4.2 Lewis (Electron-Dot) Symbols 91
4.3 The Reaction of Sodium and Chlorine 92
4.4 Using Lewis Symbols for Ionic Compounds 94
4.5 Formulas and Names of Binary Ionic Compounds 98
4.6 Covalent Bonds: Shared Electron Pairs 100
4.7 Unequal Sharing: Polar Covalent Bonds 102
4.8 Polyatomic Molecules: Water, Ammonia, and Methane 105
4.9 Polyatomic Ions 106
4.10 Rules for Writing Lewis Formulas 108
4.11 Molecular Shapes: The VSEPR Theory 113
4.12 Shapes and Properties: Polar and Nonpolar Molecules 116

Summary 119 • **Review Questions** 121 • **Problems** 121 • **Additional Problems** 123 • **Collaborative Group Projects** 124

5 Chemical Accounting 125

5.1 Chemical Sentences: Equations 126
5.2 Volume Relationships in Chemical Equations 129
5.3 Avogadro's Number and the Mole 131
5.4 Molar Mass: Mole-to-Mass and Mass-to-Mole Conversions 134
5.5 Solutions 141

Summary 146 • **Review Questions** 147 • **Problems** 147 • **Additional Problems** 149 • **Collaborative Group Projects** 151

6 Gases, Liquids, Solids . . . and Intermolecular Forces 152

6.1 Solids, Liquids, and Gases 153
6.2 Comparing Ionic and Molecular Substances 156
6.3 Forces between Molecules 157
6.4 Forces in Solutions 159
6.5 Gases: The Kinetic–Molecular Theory 161
6.6 The Simple Gas Laws 162
6.7 The Ideal Gas Law 169

Summary 171 • **Review Questions** 172 • **Problems** 172 • **Additional Problems** 173 • **Collaborative Group Projects** 174

7 Acids and Bases 175

7.1 Acids and Bases: Experimental Definitions 176
7.2 Acids, Bases, and Salts 178
7.3 Acidic and Basic Anhydrides 183
7.4 Strong and Weak Acids and Bases 185
7.5 Neutralization 186

7.6 The pH Scale 188
7.7 Buffers and Conjugate Acid–Base Pairs 191
7.8 Acids and Bases in Industry and in Daily Life 192
Summary 196 • Review Questions 197 • Problems 197 • Additional Problems 199 • Collaborative Group Projects 200

8 Oxidation and Reduction 201

8.1 Oxidation and Reduction: Three Views 202
8.2 Oxidizing and Reducing Agents 206
8.3 Electrochemistry: Cells and Batteries 208
8.4 Corrosion and Explosion 213
8.5 Oxygen: An Abundant and Essential Oxidizing Agent 215
8.6 Some Common Reducing Agents 218
8.7 Oxidation, Reduction, and Living Things 223
Summary 224 • Review Questions 225 • Problems 226 • Additional Problems 227 • Collaborative Group Projects 228

9 Organic Chemistry 229

9.1 Aliphatic Hydrocarbons 230
9.2 Aromatic Compounds: Benzene and Its Relatives 238
9.3 Chlorinated Hydrocarbons: Many Uses, Some Hazards 239
9.4 The Functional Group 241
9.5 Alcohols, Phenols, and Ethers 244
9.6 Aldehydes and Ketones 249
9.7 Carboxylic Acids and Esters 251
9.8 Nitrogen-Containing Compounds: Amines and Amides 256
Summary 259 • Review Questions 261 • Problems 261 • Additional Problems 264 • Collaborative Group Projects 265

10 Polymers 266

10.1 Polymerization: Making Big Molecules Out of Little Ones 267
10.2 Polyethylene: From the Battle of Britain to Bread Bags 268
10.3 Addition Polymerization: One + One + One + . . . Gives One! 272
10.4 Rubber and Other Elastomers 276
10.5 Condensation Polymers 279
10.6 Properties of Polymers 284
10.7 Plastics and the Environment 285
Summary 290 • Review Questions 291 • Problems 292 • Additional Problems 292 • Collaborative Group Projects 294

11 Nuclear Chemistry 295

11.1 Natural Radioactivity 296
11.2 Nuclear Equations 298
11.3 Half-Life and Radioisotopic Dating 303
11.4 Artificial Transmutation 307
11.5 Uses of Radioisotopes 308
11.6 Penetrating Power of Radiation 313
11.7 Energy from the Nucleus 315
11.8 Nuclear Bombs 319
11.9 Uses of Nuclear Energy 322

Summary 325 • Review Questions 327 • Problems 328 • Additional Problems 329 • Collaborative Group Projects 330

12 Chemistry of Earth 331

12.1 Spaceship Earth: The Materials Manifest 332
12.2 Silicates and the Shapes of Things 334
12.3 Metals and Ores 338
12.4 Earth's Dwindling Resources 342

Summary 346 • Review Questions 347 • Problems 347 • Additional Problems 348 • Collaborative Group Projects 349

13 Air 350

13.1 Earth's Atmosphere: Divisions and Composition 351
13.2 Chemistry of the Atmosphere 352
13.3 Pollution through the Ages 355
13.4 Automobile Emissions 360
13.5 Photochemical Smog: Making Haze while the Sun Shines 362
13.6 Acid Rain: Air Pollution —> Water Pollution 365
13.7 The Inside Story: Indoor Air Pollution 367
13.8 Stratospheric Ozone: Earth's Vital Shield 370
13.9 Carbon Dioxide and Climate Change 373
13.10 Who Pollutes? Who Pays? 378

Summary 381 • Review Questions 382 • Problems 382 • Additional Problems 384 • Collaborative Group Projects 384

14 Water 385

14.1 Water: Some Unique Properties 386
14.2 Water in Nature 388
14.3 Chemical and Biological Contamination 391
14.4 Water: Who Uses It and How Much? 394
14.5 Groundwater Contamination —> Tainted Tap Water 397
14.6 Making Water Fit to Drink 399
14.7 Wastewater Treatment 404

Summary 407 • Review Questions 408 • Problems 408 • Additional Problems 409 • Collaborative Group Projects 410

15 Energy 411

15.1 Energy: Starring Our Sun 412
15.2 Energy and Chemical Reactions 415
15.3 The Laws of Thermodynamics 418
15.4 Power: People, Horses, and Fossils 421
15.5 Coal: The Carbon Rock of Ages 423
15.6 Natural Gas and Petroleum 426
15.7 Convenient Energy 432
15.8 Nuclear Energy 434
15.9 Renewable Energy Sources 439

Summary 449 • Review Questions 450 • Problems 451 • Additional Problems 452 • Collaborative Group Projects 453

16 Biochemistry 454

16.1 Energy and the Living Cell 455
16.2 Carbohydrates: A Storehouse of Energy 457
16.3 Fats and Other Lipids 460
16.4 Proteins: Polymers of Amino Acids 463
16.5 Structure and Function of Proteins 469
16.6 Nucleic Acids: Parts, Structure, and Function 476
16.7 RNA: Protein Synthesis and the Genetic Code 481
16.8 The Human Genome 483

Summary 487 • Review Questions 489 • Problems 489 • Additional Problems 491 • Collaborative Group Projects 493

17 Food 494

17.1 Carbohydrates in the Diet 495
17.2 Fats and Cholesterol 498
17.3 Proteins: Muscle and Much More 504
17.4 Minerals, Vitamins, and Other Essentials 506
17.5 Starvation, Fasting, and Malnutrition 511
17.6 Food Additives 512
17.7 Problems with Our Food 520

Summary 524 • Review Questions 525 • Problems 526 • Additional Problems 527 • Collaborative Group Projects 529

18 Drugs 530

18.1 Scientific Drug Design 531
18.2 Pain Relievers: From Aspirin to Oxycodone 532
18.3 Drugs and Infectious Diseases 540
18.4 Chemicals against Cancer 548
18.5 Hormones: The Regulators 551
18.6 Drugs for the Heart 559

18.7 Drugs and the Mind 561
18.8 Drugs and Society 577

Summary 579 • Review Questions 581 • Problems 581 • Additional Problems 582 • Collaborative Group Projects 583

19 Fitness and Health 585

19.1 Calories: Quantity and Quality 586
19.2 Vitamins, Minerals, Fluids, and Electrolytes 588
19.3 Weight Loss: Diets and Exercise 593
19.4 Measuring Fitness 596
19.5 Some Muscular Chemistry 600
19.6 Drugs, Athletic Performance, and the Brain 604

Summary 609 • Review Questions 610 • Problems 610 • Additional Problems 611 • Collaborative Group Projects 612

20 Chemistry Down on the Farm . . . and in the Garden and on the Lawn 613

20.1 Farming with Chemicals: Fertilizers 615
20.2 The War against Pests 622
20.3 Herbicides and Defoliants 631
20.4 Sustainable Agriculture 634
20.5 Some Malthusian Mathematics 636

Summary 639 • Review Questions 640 • Problems 640 • Additional Problems 641 • Collaborative Group Projects 642

21 Household Chemicals 643

21.1 Cleaning with Soap 644
21.2 Synthetic Detergents 649
21.3 Laundry Auxiliaries: Softeners and Bleaches 655
21.4 All-Purpose and Special-Purpose Cleaning Products 657
21.5 Solvents, Paints, and Waxes 661
21.6 Cosmetics: Personal Care Chemicals 663

Summary 676 • Review Questions 677 • Problems 677 • Additional Problems 678 • Collaborative Group Projects 679

22 Poisons 680

22.1 Natural Poisons 681
22.2 Poisons and How They Act 683
22.3 More Chemistry of the Nervous System 688
22.4 The Lethal Dose 691
22.5 The Liver as a Detox Facility 692
22.6 Carcinogens and Teratogens 694
22.7 Hazardous Wastes 699

Summary 703 • Review Questions 704 • Problems 704 • Additional Problems 705 • Collaborative Group Projects 705

Appendix: Review of Measurement and Mathematics A-1
Glossary A-18
Answers A-26
Credits C-1
Index I-1

Preface

Chemistry for Changing Times is now in its thirteenth edition. Times have changed immensely since the first edition appeared in 1972 and are changing more rapidly than ever—especially in the vital areas of biochemistry, the environment, energy, materials, drugs, and health and nutrition. This book has changed accordingly. We have thoroughly updated the text and integrated green chemistry throughout it, with a new or revised green chemistry essay in each chapter, as well as learning objectives and end-of-chapter problems correlated to each essay. In preparing this new edition, we have responded to suggestions from users and reviewers of the twelfth edition, and we have used our own writing, teaching, and life experiences. The text has been fully revised and updated to reflect the latest scientific developments in a fast-changing world.

New to This Edition

- We have incorporated a complete list of learning objectives at the beginning of each chapter and section-specific objectives at the beginning of each section. Another list placed just before the end-of-chapter problems correlates the learning objectives with particular problems. This will assist students in studying as well as aiding professors in assigning homework and assessing students' mastery of topics.
- We have reorganized sections within chapters to reflect the links between learning objectives and end-of-chapter questions both in the text and in MasteringChemistry®. In addition, Self-Assessment Questions at the end of each section will help facilitate student learning. These multiple-choice items provide immediate feedback to test students' understanding of the material.
- Green chemistry coverage has been increased and is now integrated into the text:
  - All essays have been carefully reviewed and have been rewritten extensively or replaced entirely.
  - Each essay identifies the principles of green chemistry that are applied in it.
  - Each end-of-chapter summary now includes a section on the green chemistry essay.
  - Learning objectives related to green chemistry have been added to each chapter and are linked to end-of-chapter problems in the textbook and to MasteringChemistry problems.
  - In each chapter, there are two to five end-of-chapter problems that relate to the green chemistry essay.
  - Chapter references have been added to the green chemistry essays when applicable.
- We have revised more than 25% of the end-of-chapter problems. Several of the worked-out examples and their accompanying exercises have also been modified or revised.
- The text has been enhanced with a new design. Each chapter starts with a compelling image and a set of questions called "Have You Ever Wondered?" These real-life questions will engage students in the chapter's content. Answers to the questions are found in the margins within the chapter, near the related text content. Those questions and answers are color-coded for connectivity.
- Critical Thinking Exercises have been revised or replaced in all chapters, with at least 25% being new or modified. These exercises require the student

to apply information and concepts learned from the chapter in both concrete and abstract fashion.

- Collaborative Group Projects, which follow the end-of-chapter problems, have been revised or replaced in all chapters. These projects make it easy for instructors who want to encourage collaborative work and to make group assignments for PowerPoint or poster presentations. These projects can extend the students' learning of chemistry far beyond the textbook.

To the Instructor

Our knowledge base has expanded enormously since this book's first edition, never more so than in the last few years. We have faced tough choices in deciding what to include and what to leave out. We now live in what has been called the Information Age. Unfortunately, information is not knowledge; the information may or may not be valid. Our focus, more than ever, is on helping students evaluate information. May we all someday gain the gift of wisdom.

A major premise is that a chemistry course for students who are not majoring in science should be quite different from the course offered to science majors. It must present basic chemical concepts with intellectual honesty, but it need not—probably should not—focus on esoteric theories or rigorous mathematics. It should include lots of modern everyday applications. The textbook should be appealing to look at, easy to understand, and interesting to read.

Three-fourths of the legislation considered by the U.S. Congress involves questions having to do with science or technology, yet only rarely does a scientist or engineer enter politics. Most of the people who make important decisions regarding our health and our environment are not trained in science, but it is critical that these decision makers be scientifically literate. In the judicial system, decisions often depend on scientific evidence, but judges and jurors frequently have little education in the sciences. A chemistry course for students who are not science majors should emphasize practical applications of chemistry to problems involving such things as environmental pollution, radioactivity, energy sources, and human health. The students who take liberal arts chemistry courses include future teachers, business leaders, lawyers, legislators, accountants, artists, journalists, jurors, and judges.

Objectives

Our main objectives for a chemistry course for students who are not majoring in science are as follows:

- To attract lots of students from a variety of disciplines. If students do not enroll in the course, we can't teach them.
- To help students learn so that they may become productive, creative, ethical, and engaged citizens.
- To use topics of current interest to illustrate chemical principles. We want students to appreciate the importance of chemistry in the real world.
- To relate chemical problems to the everyday lives of our students. Chemical problems become more significant to students when they can see a personal connection.
- To instill in students an appreciation for chemistry as an open-ended learning experience. We hope that our students will develop a curiosity about science and will want to continue learning throughout their lives.
- To acquaint students with scientific methods. We want students to be able to read about science and technology with some degree of critical judgment. This is especially important because many scientific problems are complex and controversial.
- To show students, by addressing the concepts of sustainability and green chemistry, that chemists seek better, safer, and more environmentally friendly processes and products.

- To help students become literate in science. We want our students to develop a comfortable knowledge of science so that they find news articles relating to science interesting rather than intimidating.

Applications

Periodically through the text, the reader will find *boxed* features. These essays focus on interesting, relevant applications of the chemistry covered in a particular chapter or section and include the following:

- What Science Is Not; Beyond the Alchemists' Wildest Dreams; Risks of Death; Nanoworld (Chapter 1)
- Recycling (Chapter 2)
- A Compound by Any Other Name . . . ; Useful Applications of Free Radicals (Chapter 4)
- Why Doesn't Stomach Acid Dissolve the Stomach? (Chapter 7)
- Photochromic Glass (Chapter 8)
- Salicylates: Pain Relievers Based on Salicylic Acid (Chapter 9)
- The Many Forms of Carbon; Conducting Polymers: Polyacetylene (Chapter 10)
- Cell Phones and Microwaves and Power Lines, Oh My! (Chapter 11)
- Energy Return on Energy Invested; Hydrogen in Your Future (Car) (Chapter 15)
- Infectious Prions: Deadly Protein; Enzymes as Green Catalysts; DNA Profiling; Genetically Modified Organisms (Chapter 16)
- It's a Drug! No, It's a Food! No, It's . . . a Dietary Supplement! Nanoscience in Foods (Chapter 17)
- Chemistry, Allergies, and the Common Cold; Vaccine or No Vaccine? Diabetes; Love, Trust, Sexual Fidelity, and Chemistry (Chapter 18)
- Improving Athletic Performance through Chemistry; Chemistry of Sports Materials (Chapter 19)
- Fritz Haber; Development of Insect Resistance (Chapter 20)
- Personal Cleanliness; Hazards of Mixing Cleaners; Antiaging Creams and Lotions; Nanoparticles in Cosmetics; Aromatherapy (Chapter 21)
- Renaissance Poisoners; Getting Rid of "Toxins"; Chemistry and Counterterrorism (Chapter 22)

In addition, short *It DOES Matter!* items are presented in the margins. These features briefly discuss a specific application or phenomenon and show students that the material being studied does relate to the world in which we live.

Visualization

Visual material adds greatly to the general appeal of a textbook. For that reason, new photographs and diagrams have been added throughout this book. Color diagrams can be highly instructive, and colorful photographs relating to descriptive chemistry do much to enhance the learning process. We have added and revised illustrations that use both microscopic (molecular) and macroscopic (visual) views to help students visualize chemical phenomena. Some of the figure captions feature questions that focus students' attention on the concept illustrated in the figure.

Readability

Over the years, students have told us that they have found this textbook easy to read. The language is simple, and the style is conversational. Explanations are clear and easy to understand. The friendly tone of the book has been maintained in this edition. Since the format and the amount of open space on a page also contribute to readability, we have made conscious improvements in the design of this edition. For example, some of the margin notes that appeared in previous editions have been incorporated directly into the text to reduce crowding and improve the flow.

Units of Measurement

The United States continues to use the traditional English system for many kinds of measurements even though the metric system has long been used internationally. A modern version of the metric system, the Système International (SI), is now widely used, especially by scientists. So what units should be used in a text for liberal arts students? In presenting chemical principles, we use primarily metric units. In other parts of the book, we use those units that the students are most likely to encounter elsewhere in the same context.

Chemical Structures

The structures of many complicated molecules are presented in the text, especially in the later chapters. These structures are presented mainly to emphasize that they are actually known and to illustrate the fact that substances with similar properties often have similar structures. In many of the structures, functional groups or specific molecular features have been emphasized with color. For example, basic functional groups are usually shown in blue, acidic ones in red, and neutral in green. Students should not feel that they must learn all these structures, but they should take the time to look at them. We hope that they will come to recognize familiar features in these molecules.

Chapter Summaries and Glossary

Each chapter summary, with key terms highlighted in blue, provides a quick review. A list that follows the summary recaps the Learning Objectives and correlates them to the end-of-chapter problems. This correlation can help an instructor to make assignments. The Glossary gives definitions of terms that appear in boldface throughout the text and are highlighted in the chapter summaries, as well as some other terms frequently encountered.

Questions and Problems

Worked-out Examples and accompanying exercises are given within most chapters. Each Example carefully guides students through the process for solving a particular type of problem. It is then followed by one or more exercises that allow students to check their comprehension right away. Many Examples are followed by two exercises, labeled A and B. The goal in an A exercise is to apply to a similar situation the method outlined in the Example. In a B exercise, students must often combine that method with other ideas previously learned. Many of the B exercises provide a context closer to that in which chemical knowledge is applied, and they thus serve as a bridge between the worked Examples and the more challenging problems at the end of the chapter. The A and B exercises provide a simple way for the instructor to assign homework that is closely related to the Examples. Answers to all the in-chapter exercises are given in the Answers section at the back of the book.

Answers to all odd-numbered end-of-chapter problems, identified by blue numbers, are given in the Answers section at the back of the book. The end-of-chapter problems include the following:

- Review Questions for the most part simply ask for a recall of material in the chapter.
- A set of matched-pair problems is arranged according to subject matter in each chapter.

- Additional Problems are not grouped by type. Some of these are more challenging than the matched-pair problems and often require a synthesis of ideas from more than one chapter. Others pursue an idea further than is done in the text or introduce new ideas.
- Many colleges and universities now emphasize group learning as well as individual assignments. The Collaborative Group Projects permit an instructor to easily assign group work in an open-ended context; most of these projects can have multiple directions and multiple focus points.

Supplementary Materials

The most important learning aid is the teacher. In order to make the instructor's job easier and enrich the education of students, we have provided a variety of supplementary materials.

Instructor Resources

MasteringChemistry® with Pearson eText

www.masteringchemistry.com

MasteringChemistry® from Pearson has been designed and refined with a single purpose in mind: to help educators create that moment of understanding with their students. The Mastering platform delivers engaging, dynamic learning opportunities—focused on instructors' course objectives and responsive to each student's progress—that are proven to help students absorb course material and understand difficult concepts. By complementing their teaching with our engaging technology and content, instructors can be confident that their students will arrive at that moment—the moment of true understanding.

- The MasteringChemistry® tutorial system helps students figure out where they are going wrong when problem solving by providing answer-specific feedback and coaching. By offering feedback specific to wrong answers given, MasteringChemistry® tutorials coach 92% of students to the correct answer.
- The program enables professors to compare their class performance against the national average on specific questions or topics. At a glance, professors can see class distribution of grades, time spent, most difficult problems, most difficult steps, and even the most common answer.
- Pearson eText gives students access to the text whenever and wherever they can access the Internet. The eText pages look exactly like the printed text, and include powerful interactive and customization functions. This does not include the actual bound book.

Instructor Resource DVD

(0321767772) This DVD provides an integrated collection of resources to help instructors make efficient and effective use of their time. It features all artwork from the text, including figures and tables in PDF format for high-resolution printing, as well as four prebuilt PowerPoint™ presentations. The first presentation contains the images embedded within PowerPoint slides. The second includes a complete lecture outline that the instructor can modify. The final two presentations contain worked "in-chapter" sample exercises and questions to be used with classroom response systems. This DVD also contains movies, animations, and electronic files of the Instructor's Resource Manual, as well as the Test Item File.

Printed Test Bank

(0321767780) This test bank contains over 2500 multiple choice, true/false, and matching questions.

Instructor Manual (download only)

(0321767802) Organized by chapter, this useful guide includes objectives, lecture outlines, and references to figures and solved problems, as well as teaching tips.

Instructor Manual for Lab Manual (download only)

(0321767756) An online resource, the Instructor Manual for the Lab Manual provides instructors with useful tips, lab notes, and answers to lab report questions and pre- and post-lab questions.

Test Bank for WebCT (download only)

(0321767683) The WebCT Test Bank contains test bank questions for import into WebCT Learning System.

Test Bank for Blackboard (download only)

(0321767691) The Blackboard Test Bank contains test bank questions for import into Blackboard Learning System.

Student Resources

MasteringChemistry® with Pearson eText

www.masteringchemistry.com

MasteringChemistry® from Pearson has been designed and refined with a single purpose in mind: to help educators create that moment of understanding with their students. The Mastering platform delivers engaging, dynamic learning opportunities—focused on instructors' course objectives and responsive to each student's progress—that are proven to help students absorb course material and understand difficult concepts. By complementing their teaching with our engaging technology and content, instructors can be confident that their students will arrive at that moment—the moment of true understanding.

Study Guide and Selected Solutions Manual

(0321767810) The Study Guide and Selected Solutions Manual assists students with the text material. It contains learning objectives, chapter outlines, key terms, additional problems with self-tests and answers, and answers to the odd-numbered problems in the text.

Chemical Investigations for Changing Times

(0321767799) This resource contains 66 laboratory experiments and is specifically referenced to *Chemistry for Changing Times*.

Acknowledgments

Through the last four decades, we have greatly benefited from hundreds of helpful reviews. It would take far too many pages to list all of those reviewers here. Many of you have contributed to the flavor of the book and helped us minimize our errors. Please know that your contributions are deeply appreciated. For the thirteenth edition, we are grateful for challenging reviews from the following reviewers:

Reviewers of the Thirteenth Edition

Debe Bell, *Metro State College*
Mark Blazer, *Shasta College*
Kirsten Casey, *Anne Arundel Community College*
Alice Harper, *Berry College*
Alton Hassell, *Baylor University*
Donna K. Howell, *Park University*
David Lippman, *University of Texas, Austin*
James L. Marshall, *University of North Texas*

Douglas Mulford, *Emory University*

David S. Newman, *Bowling Green State University*

Charlotte A. Ovechka, *University of St. Thomas*

James K. Owen, *The Art Institute of Tennessee*

Christine Seppanen, *Riverland Community College*

Michael Dennis Seymour, *Hope College*

Shirish K. Shah, *Towson University*

Julianne Smist, *Springfield College*

Mona Uppal, *Tarrant County College, NE*

Paloma Valverde, *Wentworth Institute of Technology*

Matthew E. Wise, *University of Colorado, Boulder*

Accuracy Reviewers

Edie Banner, *Florida Southern College*

Rill Reuter, *Winona State University*

Bradley Sieve, *Northern Kentucky University*

Green Chemistry Contributors

We are enormously grateful to Jennifer Young, former manager of the American Chemical Society's Green Chemistry Institute®, who coordinated the development of the new and revised green chemistry essays and correlated the content of these essays. We thank her for her dedication to this project. We also thank the team of green chemists listed below who contributed the green essays and helped to integrate the each essay's content into the chapter with learning objectives, end-of-chapter problems, summaries, and section references.

David Brown, *Davidson College*

Amy Cannon, *Beyond Benign*

Scott Cummings, *Kenyon College*

Joseph Fortunak, *Howard University*

Tom Goodwin, *Hendrix College*

Michael Heben, *University of Toledo*

Randall Hicks, *Wheaton College*

Colin Horwitz, *GreenOx Catalysts*

Margaret Kerr, *Worcester State University*

Irv Levy, *Gordon College*

Doris Lewis, *Suffolk University*

Lallie C. McKenzie, *Chem11 LLC*

Martin Mulvihill, *University of California–Berkeley*

Bevin Parks-Lee

Bob Peoples, *ACS Green Chemistry Institute*

Douglas Raynie, *South Dakota State University*

Robert Tanguay, *Oregon State University*

David Vosburg, *Harvey Mudd College*

John Warner, *Warner Babcock Institute*

Denyce Wicht, *Suffolk University*

Jennifer Young, *ACS Green Chemistry Institute*

Reviewers of Previous Editions

Michelle Boucher, *Utica College*

Roxanne Finney, *Skagit Valley College*

Luther Giddings, *Salt Lake Community College*

Todd Hamilton, *Georgetown College*

Alton Hassell, *Baylor University*

Scott Hewitt, *California State University, Fullerton*

Sherell Hickman, *Brevard Community College, Cocoa*

Beth Hixon, *Tulsa Community College*

James L. Klino, *SUNY College of Agriculture and Technology, Cobleskill*

Meghan Knapp, *Georgetown College*

Kim Loomis, *Century College*

Jeremy Mason, *Texas Technical University*

Lois Schadenwald, *Normandale Community College*

Joseph Sinski, *Bellarmine University*

Kelli M. Slunt, *University of Mary Washington*

Jie Song, *University of Michigan, Flint*

Wayne M. Stalick, *University of Central Missouri*

Durwin Striplin, *Davidson College*

Shashi Unnithan, *Front Range Community College*

Edward Vitz, *Kutztown University*

Dan Wacks, *University of Redlands*

Elizabeth Wallace, *Western Oklahoma State College*

Matthew E. Wise, *University of Colorado, Boulder*

We also appreciate the many people who have called, written, or e-mailed with corrections and other helpful suggestions. Cynthia S. Hill prepared much of the original material on biochemistry, food, and health and fitness.

We owe a special debt of gratitude to Doris K. Kolb (1927–2005), who was an esteemed coauthor from the seventh through the eleventh editions. Doris and her husband Ken were friends and helpful supporters long before Doris joined the author team. She provided much of the spirit and flavor of the book. Doris's contributions to *Chemistry for Changing Times*—and indeed to all of chemistry and chemical education—will live on for many years to come, not only in her publications, but in the hearts and minds of her many students, colleagues, and friends.

Throughout her career as a teacher, scientist, community leader, poet, and much more, Doris was blessed with a wonderful spouse, colleague, and companion, Kenneth E. Kolb. Over the years, Ken did chapter reviews, made suggestions, and gave invaluable help for many editions. All who knew Doris miss her greatly. Those of us who had the privilege of working closely with her miss her wisdom and wit most profoundly. Let us all dedicate our lives, as Doris did hers, to making this world a better place.

We also want to thank our colleagues at the University of Wisconsin–River Falls, Murray State University, and Bradley University for all their help and support through the years.

We also owe a debt of gratitude to the many creative people at Pearson who have contributed their talents to this edition. Jennifer Hart, our chemistry project editor, has been a delight to work with, providing valuable guidance throughout the project. She showed extraordinary skill and diplomacy in coordinating all the many facets of this project. Development Editor Donald Gecewicz contributed greatly to this project, especially in challenging us to be better authors in every way. We treasure his many helpful suggestions of new material and better presentation of all the subject matter. We are grateful to Editor in Chief Adam Jaworski for his overall guidance and to production Project Manager Beth Sweeten for her diligence and patience in bringing all the parts together to yield a finished work. We are indebted to our copy editor, Jane Hoover, whose expertise helped improve the consistency of the text; and to proofreaders and accuracy checkers Rill Reuter, Brad Sieve, and Edie Banner, whose sharp eyes caught many of our errors and typos. We also salute our photo researcher, Eric Schrader, who vetted hundreds of images in the search for quality photographic illustrations.

John W. Hill owes a very special kind of thanks to his wonderful spouse, Ina, who over the years has done typing, library research, and so many other things that allow him time to concentrate on writing. Most of all, he is grateful for her boundless patience, unflagging support, understanding, and enduring love. He is also grateful to his beloved daughter Cindy for her help with the house and the yard and so many other things. Terry W. McCreary would like to thank his wife, Geniece, and children, Corinne and Yvette, for their unflagging support, understanding, and love.

Finally, we also thank all those many students whose enthusiasm has made teaching such a joy. It is gratifying to have students learn what you are trying to teach them, but it is a supreme pleasure to find that they want to learn even more. And, of course, we are grateful to all of you who have made so many helpful suggestions. We welcome and appreciate all your comments, corrections, and criticisms.

John W. Hill
jwhill602@comcast.net

Terry W. McCreary
terry.mccreary@murraystate.edu

Doris K. Kolb

To the Student

Tell me, what is it you plan to do
with your one wild and precious life?

—American poet Mary Oliver (b. 1935)
"The Summer Day," from *New and Selected Poems*
(Boston, MA: Beacon Press, 1992)

Welcome to Our Chemical World!

Life is largely a do-it-yourself job, but others can help you make your life better. We hope to help by showing how chemistry can enhance your understanding of the world around you. You do not need to exclude chemistry from your learning experiences. Chemistry is fun. Through this book, we would like to share with you some of the excitement of chemistry and some of the joy of learning about it. Learning chemistry will enrich your life—now and long after this course is over—through a better understanding of the natural world, the technological questions now confronting us, and the choices you will face as a citizen in a scientific and technological society.

Learning chemistry involves thinking logically, critically, and creatively. Skills gained in this course can be exceptionally useful in many aspects of your life. You will learn how to use the language of chemistry: symbols, formulas, and equations. More important, you will learn how to obtain meaning from information. The most important thing you will learn is how to learn. Memorized material quickly fades into oblivion unless it is arranged on a framework of understanding.

Chemistry Directly Affects Our Lives

How does the human body work? How does aspirin cure headaches, reduce fevers, and lessen the chance of a heart attack or stroke? How does penicillin kill bacteria without harming our healthy body cells? Is ozone a good thing or a threat to our health? Are iron supplement pills poisonous? Do we really face climate change, and if so, how severe will it be? Do humans contribute to climate change, and if so, to what degree? Why do most weight-loss diets seem to work in the short run but fail in the long run? Why do our moods swing from happy to sad? Can a chemical test on urine predict possible suicide attempts? Chemists have found answers to questions such as these and continue to seek the knowledge that will unlock still other secrets of our universe. As these mysteries are resolved, the direction of our lives often changes—sometimes dramatically. We live in a chemical world—a world of drugs, biocides, food additives, fertilizers, fuels, detergents, cosmetics, and plastics. We live in a world with toxic wastes, polluted air and water, and dwindling petroleum reserves. Knowledge of chemistry will help you better understand the benefits and hazards of this world and will enable you to make intelligent decisions in the future.

We Are All Chemically Dependent

Even in the womb we are chemically dependent. We need a constant supply of oxygen, water, glucose, amino acids, triglycerides, and a multitude of other chemical substances.

Our bodies are intricate chemical factories. They are durable but delicate systems. Innumerable chemical reactions that allow our bodies to function properly occur constantly within us. Thinking, learning, exercising, feeling happy or sad, putting on too much weight or not gaining enough, and virtually all life processes are made possible by these chemical reactions. Everything that we ingest is part of a complex process that determines whether our bodies work effectively or not. The consumption of some substances can initiate chemical reactions that will stop body functions. Other substances, if consumed, can cause permanent handicaps, and still others can make living less comfortable. A proper balance of the right foods provides the chemicals that fuel the reactions we need in order to function at our best. The knowledge of chemistry that you will soon be gaining will help you better understand how your body works so that you will be able to take proper care of it.

Changing Times

We live in a world of increasingly rapid change. It has been said that the only constant is change itself. At present, we are facing some of the greatest problems that humans have ever encountered, and these dilemmas confronting us seem to have no perfect solutions. We are sometimes forced to make a best choice among only bad alternatives, and our decisions often provide only temporary solutions to our problems. Nevertheless, if we are to choose properly, we must understand what our choices are. Mistakes can be costly, and they cannot always be rectified. It is easy to pollute, but cleaning up pollution once it is there is enormously expensive. We can best avoid mistakes by collecting as much information as possible and evaluating it carefully before making critical decisions. Science is a means of gathering and evaluating information, and chemistry is central to all the sciences.

Chemistry and the Human Condition

Above all else, our hope is that you will learn that the study of chemistry need not be dull and difficult. Rather, it can enrich your life in so many ways—through a better understanding of your body, your mind, your environment, and the world in which you live. After all, the search to understand the universe is an essential part of what it means to be human. We offer you a challenge first issued by American educator Horace Mann (1796–1859) in his 1859 address at Antioch College: "Be ashamed to die until you have won some victory for humanity."

About the Authors

John W. Hill

Hill received his Ph.D. from the University of Arkansas. As an organic chemist, he has published more than 50 papers, most of which have an educational bent. He has authored or coauthored several introductory-level chemistry textbooks, all of which have been published in multiple editions. He has also presented over 60 papers at national conferences, many relating to science education. He has received several awards for outstanding teaching and has long been active in the American Chemical Society, both locally and nationally. Now professor emeritus at the University of Wisconsin–River Falls, Hill authored the first edition of *Chemistry for Changing Times* in 1972. Revising and updating this book has been a major focus of his life for four decades.

Terry W. McCreary

McCreary received his B.S. from St. Francis University, his M.S. from the University of Georgia, and his Ph.D. from Virginia Tech. He has taught chemistry at Murray State University since 1988, and was presented with the Regents Excellence in Teaching Award in 2008. He is a member of the American Chemical Society and the Kentucky Academy of Science and has served as technical editor for the *Journal of Pyrotechnics*. In his spare time, he designs, builds, and flies rockets with the Tripoli Rocketry Association; he was elected president of the association in 2010. McCreary is the author of several laboratory manuals; *General Chemistry* with John Hill, Ralph Petrucci, and Scott Perry; and *Experimental Composite Propellant*, a fundamental treatise on the preparation and properties of solid rocket propellant.

About Our Sustainability Initiatives

Pearson recognizes the environmental challenges facing this planet, as well as acknowledges our responsibility in making a difference.

This book is carefully crafted to minimize environmental impact. The materials used to manufacture this book originated from sources committed to responsible forestry practices. The paper is FSC® certified. The binding, cover, and paper come from facilities that minimize waste, energy consumption, and the use of harmful chemicals.

Pearson closes the loop by recycling every out-of-date text returned to our warehouse. Along with developing and exploring digital solutions to our market's needs, Pearson has a strong commitment to achieving carbon-neutrality. As of 2009, Pearson became the first carbon- and climate-neutral publishing company. Since then, Pearson remains strongly committed to measuring, reducing, and offsetting our carbon footprint.

The future holds great promise for reducing our impact on Earth's environment, and Pearson is proud to be leading the way. We strive to publish the best books with the most up-to-date and accurate content, and to do so in ways that minimize our impact on Earth. To learn more about our initiatives, please visit **www.pearson.com/responsibility**.

PEARSON

MasteringChemistry®

www.masteringchemistry.com

NEW for this edition! MasteringChemistry is designed with a single purpose: to help students reach the moment of understanding. The Mastering online homework and tutoring system delivers self-paced tutorials that provide students with individualized coaching set to instructors' course objectives. MasteringChemistry helps students arrive better prepared for lecture and lab.

Engaging Experiences

MasteringChemistry promotes interactivity and active learning in Liberal Arts Chemistry. Research shows that Mastering's immediate feedback and tutorial assistance help students understand and master concepts and skills in Chemistry—allowing them to retain more knowledge and perform better in this course and beyond.

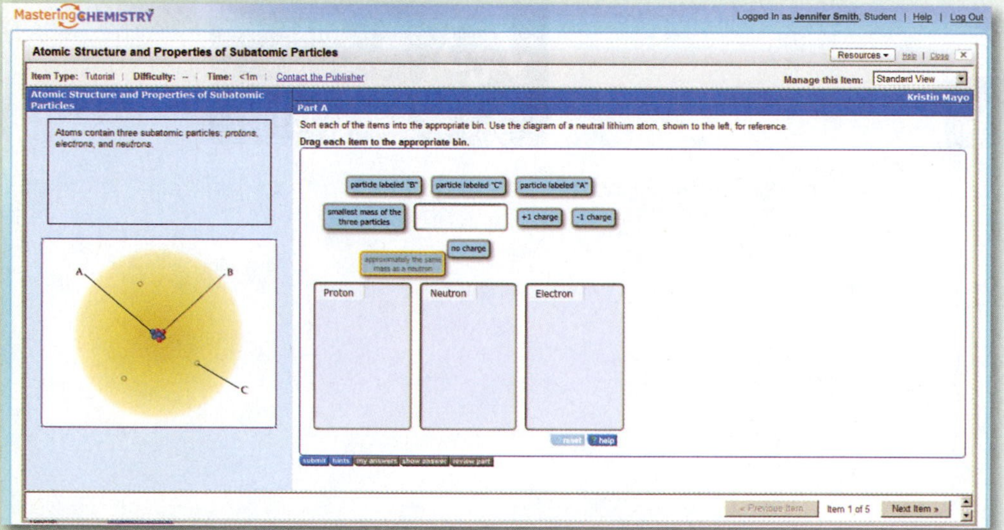

Student Tutorials

MasteringChemistry is the only system to provide instantaneous feedback to the most common wrong answers. Students can submit an answer and receive immediate, error-specific feedback, as well as request hints (simpler sub-problems).

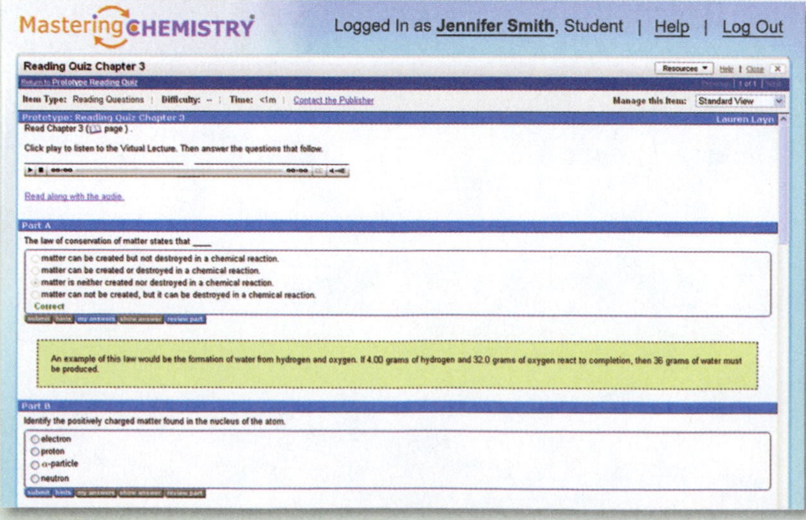

Reading Quizzes

Reading Quizzes give instructors the opportunity to assign reading, and test students on their comprehension of chapter content.

Annotation Function allows students to take notes.

Google®-based search function.

Highlight Function lets students highlight what they want to remember.

Zoom lets students zoom in and out for better viewing.

Hyperlinks link to quizzes, tests, activities, and animations.

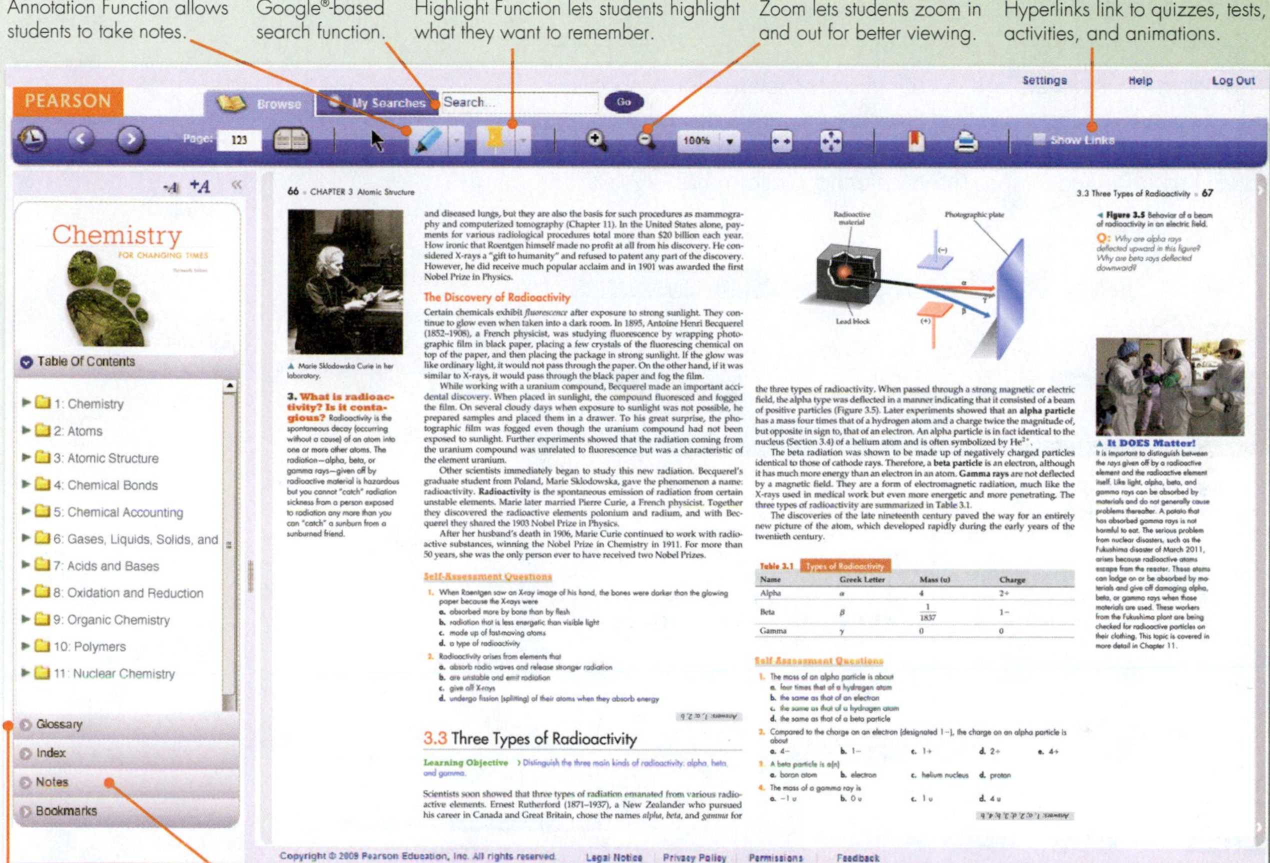

Interactive Glossary provides pop-up definitions and terms.

Instructor Notes allow instructors to share his or her notes and highlights with the class.

Pearson eText

Pearson eText gives students access to the text whenever and wherever they can access the Internet. The eText pages look exactly like the printed text, and include powerful interactive and customization functions. Users can create notes, highlight text in different colors, create bookmarks, zoom, click hyperlinked words and phrases to view definitions, and view as a single page or as two pages. Pearson eText also offers a full text search and the ability to save and export notes.

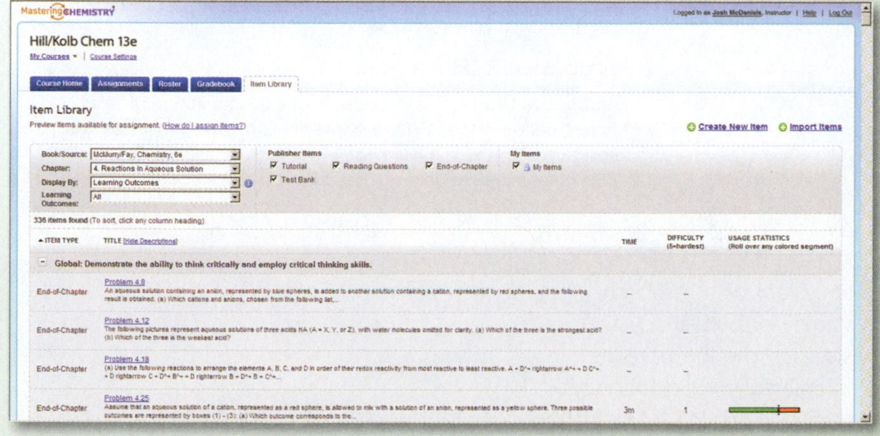

NEW! Learning Objectives

Learning Objectives appear in each section of **Chemistry for Changing Times** and at the beginning and end of the chapter. These objectives bring the main goals of each section to the foreground, and are linked to end-of-chapter problems in the text and in MasteringChemistry. These learning objectives give focus points to each section and will increase efficiencies in teaching and learning.

MasteringChemistry®

www.masteringchemistry.com

A Trusted Partner

The Mastering platform was developed by scientists for science students and instructors, and has a proven history with more than 10 years of student use. Mastering currently has more than 1.5 million active registrations with active users in 50 states and in 41 countries. The Mastering platform has 99.8% server reliability.

Gradebook

Every assignment is automatically graded. At a glance, shades of red highlight vulnerable students and challenging assignments.

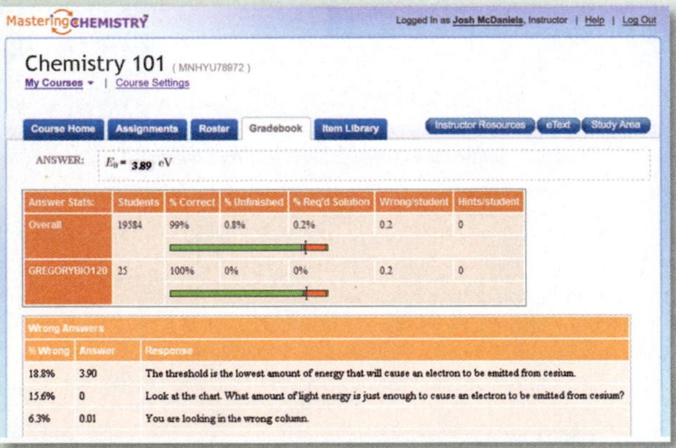

Student Performance Data

With a single click, Student Performance Data provides at-a-glance statistics on each class as well as national results. Wrong-answer summaries give insight into students' misconceptions and facilitate just-in-time teaching adjustments.

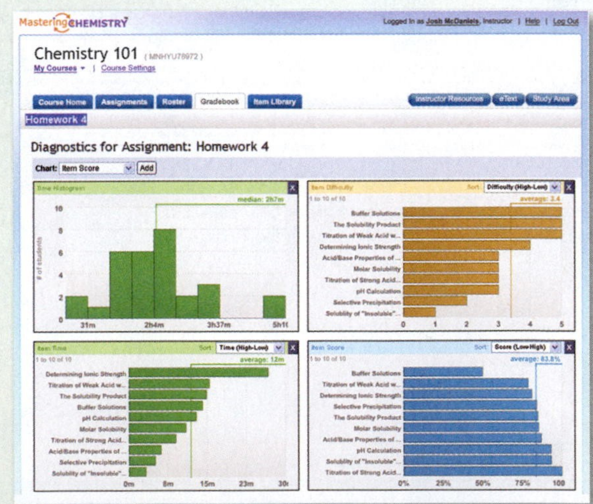

Gradebook Diagnostics

Gradebook Diagnostics provide unique insight into class and student performance. With a single click, charts summarize the most difficult problems, vulnerable students, grade distribution, and score improvement over the duration of the course.

Proven Results

The Mastering platform is the only online homework system with research showing that it improves student learning. A wide variety of published papers, based on NSF-sponsored research and tests, illustrate the benefits of the Mastering program. Results documented in scientifically valid efficacy papers are available at www.masteringchemistry.com/site/results

Green Chemistry Emphasis

The concept of green chemistry has been expanded in the **Thirteenth Edition,** and is integrated throughout with a framework incorporating the 12 Principles of Green Chemistry. Each chapter contains a green essay which identifies the principles that are applied in that essay. Chapters are further enhanced by the inclusion of green chemistry content within the learning objectives as well as the end-of-chapter summaries and questions.

Irvin Levy, *Gordon College*

Sustainability: It's Basic (and Acidic)

Green chemistry is a part of sustainable chemistry. Sustainability, often defined as "meeting the needs of the present generation without compromising the ability of future generations to meet their needs," is much in the news these days. Green chemistry is one of the critical means of attaining sustainability. Understanding of acids and bases has led to greener, more sustainable methods for producing consumer products. Two important examples are soap and renewable biofuels.

Soap traditionally has been made from fats left from cooking meats and from vegetable oils. Fats and oils contain substances composed of three long chains of carbon atoms connected to a central set of three carbon atoms, an arrangement called a *triglyceride* (Chapter 16). To make soap, the fats are heated and mixed with lye solution (aqueous sodium hydroxide—a base). Each mole of triglyceride reacts with three moles of base to produce three moles of soap and one mole of the byproduct glycerol (also called glycerin). Soaps are salts (Section 7.2) of carboxylic acids that usually have a long chain of carbon atoms. An example of a typical soap is sodium palmitate. Its chemical formula is shown here.

$$CH_3(CH_2)_{14}COO^-Na^+$$

The byproduct glycerol has a number of uses, including as a moisturizing ingredient in soap. Chemists at Gordon College (Wenham, MA) found that adding glycerol to the fats and oils traditionally used in soap-making decreased the quantity of starting materials required for soap production. Much more glycerol byproduct is produced industrially than can be used by the soap industry, however, so the search continues for other green uses for glycerol.

The chemistry of biodiesel fuel production (also see Chapter 15) is much like that of soap-making. In both processes, bases are used and glycerol is formed. With the use of methanol (CH_3OH) in place of water and a catalytic amount of base, though, the triglycerides are converted to compounds called *esters* (Section 9.7). An example of a typical biodiesel molecule is shown here.

$$CH_3(CH_2)_{14}COOCH_3$$

Although the long chains of carbon atoms in biodiesel often are the same as in soap molecules, biodiesel molecules have a different group on one end of the chain. Compare these compounds to a typical diesel molecule from petroleum that does not contain any atoms other than carbon and hydrogen.

$$CH_3(CH_2)_{14}CH_3$$

What do soap, biodiesel, and glycerol have to do with sustainability and green chemistry? The first principle of green chemistry encourages the prevention of waste. Sometimes wastes also are harmful to the environment. Wouldn't it be better to redirect apparently useless materials into something useful?

Consider this: Each year billions of gallons of fats and oils are used to fry foods. Fryer oils degrade fairly quickly in commercial kitchens. For many years the used oils were carted off by disposal companies as waste. Today, much of that used oil is converted into biodiesel fuel, providing an alternative fuel that doesn't deplete fossil petroleum reserves. This approach satisfies the green chemistry principle of using renewable resources while providing new use for what was once considered waste. And it gets better! Petroleum diesel fuel is hazardous to humans and toxic to the environment. Biodiesel is much safer.

Acids also are involved in green processes such as cleaning. For example, polylactic acid (PLA) is a type of biodegradable and renewable plastic made from chemicals derived from corn (see Green Chemistry essay, Chapter 10). PLA plastic, made by companies such as NatureWorks, is found in many consumer materials, such as plastic cups. Research at Simmons College in Boston has led to a new way to convert used PLA cups into an antimicrobial cleaning solution containing lactic acid ($CH_3CHOHCOOH$). The shredded plastic is mixed with alcohol and base to break down the polymer to sodium lactate ($CH_3CHOHCOONa$). The basic sodium lactate solution is neutralized with acid to form the lactic acid cleaner, which is useful for wiping away soap scum.

In the quest for sustainability, acids and bases are an essential part of the toolbox that will continue to be used as chemists search for better ways to prevent waste and use renewable starting materials. You might argue that sustainability is basic—not to mention acidic.

182

Green Chemistry Essays

Green Chemistry essays, written by experts in the field, include topics that have been carefully chosen to introduce students to one or more of the 12 Principles of Green Chemistry. The Principles that are applied in the essays are clearly identified, and references to the chapter are included when applicable.

SUMMARY

Section 7.1—Acids taste sour, turn litmus red, and react with active metals to form hydrogen. Bases taste bitter, turn litmus blue, and feel slippery to the skin. Acids and bases react to form salts and water. An **acid–base indicator** such as litmus has different colors in acid and in base and is used to determine whether solutions are acidic or basic.

Section 7.2—According to Arrhenius's definition, an *acid* produces hydrogen ions (H^+, also called protons) in aqueous solution, and a *base* produces hydroxide ions (OH^-). **Neutralization** is the combination of H^+ and OH^- to form water. The anion and cation that were associated with H^+ and OH^- ions combine to form an ionic **salt**. In the more general Brønsted–Lowry acid–base theory, an **acid** is a proton donor and a **base** is a proton acceptor. When a Brønsted–Lowry acid dissolves in water, the H_2O molecules pick up H^+ to form hydronium ions (H_3O^+). A Brønsted–Lowry base in water accepts a proton from a water molecule, forming OH^-.

Section 7.3—Some nonmetal oxides (such as CO_2 and SO_3) are **acidic anhydrides** in that they react with water to form acids. Some metal oxides (such as Li_2O and CaO) are **basic anhydrides**; they react with water to form bases.

Section 7.4—A **strong acid** is one that ionizes completely in water to form H^+ ions and anions. A **weak acid** ionizes only slightly in water; most of the acid exists as intact molecules. Common strong acids are sulfuric, hydrochloric, and nitric acids. Likewise, a **strong base** is completely ionized in water, and a **weak base** is only slightly ionized. Sodium hydroxide and potassium hydroxide are common strong bases.

Section 7.5—The reaction between an acid and a base is called *neutralization*. In aqueous solution, it is the combination of H^+ and OH^- that forms water. The other anions and cations form an ionic salt.

Section 7.6—The **pH** scale indicates the degree of acidity or basicity; pH is defined as $pH = -\log[H^+]$, where $[H^+]$ is the molar concentration of hydrogen ion. A pH of 7 ($[H^+] = 1 \times 10^{-7}$ M) is neutral; pH values lower than 7 represent increasing acidity, and pH values greater than 7 represent increasing basicity. A change in pH of one unit represents a tenfold change in $[H^+]$.

Section 7.7—A pair of compounds or ions that differ by one proton (H^+) is called a **conjugate acid–base pair**. A **buffer solution** is a mixture of a weak acid and its conjugate base or a weak base and its conjugate acid. A buffer maintains a nearly constant pH when a small amount of a strong acid or a strong base is added.

Section 7.8—An antacid is a base such as sodium bicarbonate, magnesium hydroxide, aluminum hydroxide, or calcium carbonate that is taken to relieve hyperacidity. Overuse of some antacids can make the blood too alkaline (basic), a condition called **alkalosis**. **Acid rain** is rain with a pH less than 5.6. The acidity is due to sulfur oxides and nitrogen oxides from natural sources as well as industrial air pollution and automobile exhaust fumes. Acid rain can have serious effects on plant and animal life. Sulfuric acid is the number one chemical produced in the United States and is used for making fertilizers and other industrial chemicals. Hydrochloric acid is used for rust removal and etching mortar and concrete. Lime (calcium oxide) is made from limestone and is the cheapest and most widely used base. It is an ingredient in plaster and cement and is used in agriculture. Sodium hydroxide is used to make many industrial products, as well as soap. Amm onia is a weak base produced mostly for use as fertilizer. Concentrated strong acids and bases are corrosive poisons that can cause serious burns. Living cells have an optimal pH that is necessary for the proper functioningof proteins.

Green chemistry Base is used to convert renewable fats and oils into products such as soaps and biofuels. Treatment with acid can decompose special plastics (such as polylactic acid, PLA) into a useful antimicrobial cleaner. Application of the "12 Principles of Green Chemistry" can guide us to find practical uses for materials that were once considered waste.

End-of-Chapter Summaries

Each end-of-chapter summary now includes a section summarizing the green chemistry within each chapter essay.

Learning Objectives

› Distinguish between acids and bases using their chemical and physical properties. (7.1)	Problems 1, 26, 27
› Explain how an acid–base indicator works. (7.1)	Problem 2
› Identify Arrhenius and Brønsted–Lowry acids and bases. (7.2)	Problems 4, 12–22, 59
› Write a balanced equation for a neutralization or an ionization. (7.2)	Problems 8, 39–46, 60, 67
› Identify acidic and basic anhydrides, and write equations showing their reactions with water. (7.3)	Problems 7, 29, 30
› Define and identify strong and weak acids and bases. (7.4)	Problems 5, 9, 10, 31–38, 61
› Identify the reactants and predict the products in a neutralization reaction. (7.5)	
› Describe the relationship between the pH of a solution and its acidity or basicity. (7.6)	Problems 47–54
› Find the molar concentration of hydrogen ion, $[H^+]$, from a pH value or the pH value from $[H^+]$. (7.6)	
› Write the formula for the conjugate base of an acid or for the conjugate acid of a base. (7.7)	Problems 55, 56
› Describe the action of a buffer. (7.7)	Problem 65
› Describe everyday uses of acids and bases and how they affect daily life. (7.8)	Problems 11, 57, 58
› Write equations for the production of soap and of biofuel.	Problem 73
› Describe ways by which acids and bases can contribute to greener production of consumer products.	Problems 71, 72, 74

Learning Objectives

Learning Objectives for each section in the text and related to green chemistry have been added to every chapter. They are linked to end-of-chapter problems in the textbook and to MasteringChemistry problems.

51. What is the hydrogen ion concentration of a solution that has a pH of 3?
52. What is the hydrogen ion concentration of a solution that has a pH of 11?
53. Milk of magnesia has a hydrogen ion concentration between 1.0×10^{-10} M and 1.0×10^{-11} M. What two whole-number values is the pH of milk of magnesia between?
54. Oven cleaner has a pH between 13 and 14. What two whole-number values of x should be used in 1.0×10^{-x} M to express the range of hydrogen ion concentration?

Conjugate Acid–Base Pairs

55. In the following reaction in aqueous solution, identify **(a)** which of the reactants is the acid and which is the base, **(b)** the conjugate base of the acid, and **(c)** the conjugate acid of the base.
$$HNO_3(aq) + NH_3(aq) \longrightarrow NO_3^-(aq) + NH_4^+(aq)$$
56. In the following reaction in aqueous solution, identify **(a)** which of the reactants is the acid and which is the base, **(b)** the conjugate base of the acid, and **(c)** the conjugate acid of the base.
$$CH_3CH_2COOH + H_2O \longrightarrow CH_3CH_2COO^- + H_3O^+$$

Antacids

57. Mylanta liquid has 200 mg of $Al(OH)_3$ and 200 mg of $Mg(OH)_2$ per teaspoonful. Write the equation for the neutralization of stomach acid [represented as HCl(aq)] by each of these substances.
58. What is the Brønsted–Lowry base in each of the following compounds, which are ingredients in antacids?
    a. $NaHCO_3$
    b. $Mg(OH)_2$
    c. $MgCO_3$
    d. $CaCO_3$

End-of-Chapter Questions

In each chapter, two to five end-of-chapter problems relate to the green chemistry in that chapter.

Focus on Relevance

Abundant applications and examples fill each chapter of this edition, and material is updated throughout to mirror the latest scientific developments in a fast-changing world. Compelling visuals and features such as "It DOES Matter!" highlight current events and enable students to relate to the text more readily.

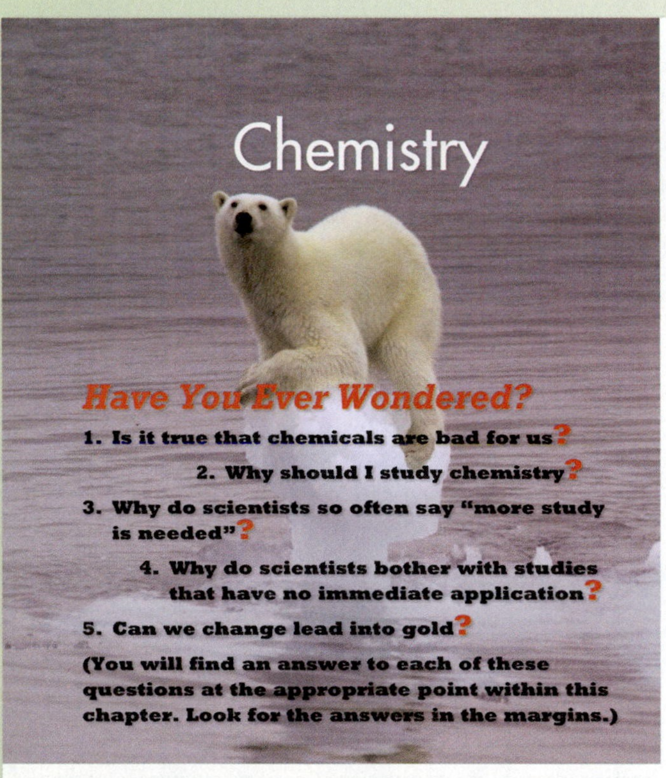

Chemistry
Have You Ever Wondered?
1. Is it true that chemicals are bad for us?
2. Why should I study chemistry?
3. Why do scientists so often say "more study is needed"?
4. Why do scientists bother with studies that have no immediate application?
5. Can we change lead into gold?
(You will find an answer to each of these questions at the appropriate point within this chapter. Look for the answers in the margins.)

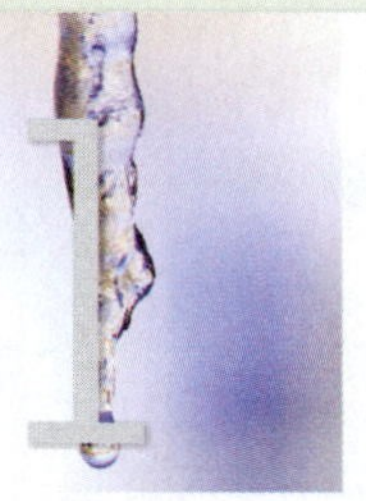

Learning Objectives

- Distinguish science from technology. (1.1)
- Define *alchemy* and *natural philosophy*. (1.1)
- Briefly describe the contributions of Bacon, Galileo, and Carson to the changing perceptions of science. (1.2)
- Define *green chemistry* and *sustainable chemistry*. (1.2)
- Define *hypothesis, scientific law, scientific theory*, and *scientific model*, and explain their relationships in science. (1.3)
- Explain what a variable is, and describe how variables introduce uncertainty. (1.3)
- Define *risk* and *benefit*, and give an example of each. (1.4)
- Estimate a desirability quotient, given information about benefits and risks. (1.4)
- Give an example of a use of chemistry in your daily life and in society at large. (1.5)
- Distinguish basic research from applied research. (1.6)
- Distinguish mass from weight, physical change from chemical change, and physical properties from chemical properties. (1.7)
- Classify matter according to state and as mixture, substance, compound, and/or element. (1.8)
- Assign proper units of measurement to observations, and manipulate units in conversions. (1.9)
- Calculate the density, mass, or volume of an object given the other two quantities. (1.10)
- Distinguish between heat and temperature. (1.11)
- Explain how the different temperature scales are related. (1.11)
- Use critical thinking to evaluate claims and statements. (1.12)
- Define green chemistry.
- Describe how *green chemistry* reduces risk and prevents environmental problems.

1

A Science for All Seasons Chemistry pervades every aspect of our lives. Look around you. Everything you see is made of chemicals: the food we eat, the air we breathe, the clothes we wear, the medicines we take, the vehicles we ride in, and the buildings we live and work in.

Everything we *do* also involves chemistry. Whenever we eat a sandwich, bathe, drive a car, listen to music, or ride a bicycle, we use chemistry. Even when we are asleep, chemical reactions go on constantly throughout our bodies.

Chemistry also affects society as a whole. Developments in health and medicine involve a lot of chemistry. The astounding advances in

Chemistry is everywhere, not just in laboratories. Chemistry occurs in soil and rocks, in waters, in clouds, and in us. Knowledge of chemistry enhances our understanding of climate change, helps to provide food for Earth's increasing population, and is crucial to the development and production of sustainable fuels.

Have You Ever Wondered? Questions

"Have You Ever Wondered?" chapter-opening questions reflect real-life queries that may arise in students' minds and are related to the chapter content. Answers are included at appropriate locations within the chapter.

▲ **It DOES Matter!**
Polyethylene with a molecular mass from two to six million, called *ultra-high-molecular-weight polyethylene (UHMWPE)*, is used to make fibers 10 times stronger than steel and around 40% stronger than Kevlar (see Problem 30 on page 292) for use in body armor. Most modern skis are coated with UHMWPE on the bottom surface.

It DOES Matter! Boxes

A stronger emphasis on relevance is found in the "It DOES Matter!" boxes. There are approximately 10% more "It DOES Matter!" boxes in the Thirteenth Edition.

Cell Phones and Microwaves and Power Lines, Oh My!

There are many types of radiation. *Ionizing* radiation that comes from decaying atomic nuclei is highly energetic and can damage tissue, as discussed above. *Electromagnetic* radiation has many forms—visible light, radio waves, television broadcast waves, microwaves, ultraviolet light, military ULF (ultra-low-frequency), and others. A few types of electromagnetic radiation—X-rays and gamma rays—have enough energy to ionize tissue, and ultraviolet light has been strongly implicated in *melanoma* (skin cancer). But what about microwaves and radio waves, which don't have nearly as much energy? Although very large amounts of microwaves can cause burns (by heating), there is no conclusive evidence that low levels of microwaves pose significant threat to human health. A 2006 study involving almost half a million Danish citizens failed to show a relationship between cell phone use and cancer, though some scientists consider this study inconclusive. However, higher levels of radio frequencies over long periods of time *may* be a different matter. In May 2011, the World Health Organization (WHO) classified heavy cell phone use—30 minutes of talking daily for ten years—as possible posing an increased risk of *glioma*, a type of brain cancer. The WHO's press release was very cautious, stating that "there could be some risk … therefore we need to keep a close watch for a link between cell phones and cancer risk." For low levels of exposure to non-ionizing electromagnetic radiation, the hazard appears to be difficult to measure, let alone assess.

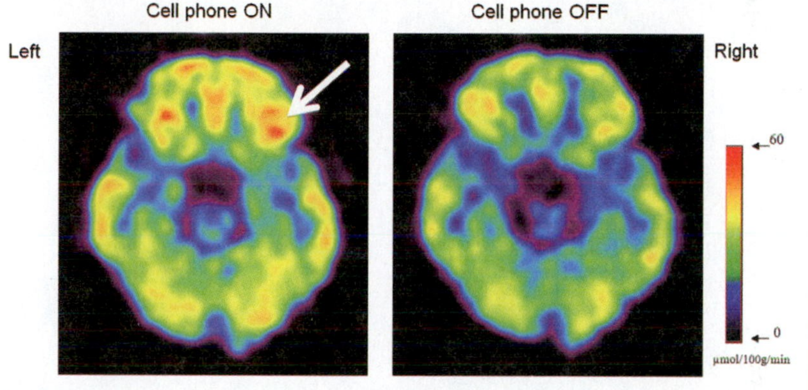

▲ A brain scan shows slight differences when a cell phone held to the ear is on (left) and off (right).

Current Environmental and Relevant Applications

These applications include many interesting and relevant topics to help students connect chemistry to the world around them.

Self-Assessment Questions

1. Consider how the qualities *discrete* and *continuous* apply to materials at the macroscopic (visible to the unaided eye) level. Which of the following is continuous?

a. apple juice
b. a ream of paper
c. a bowl of cherries
d. chocolate chips

2. The view that matter is continuous rather than atomic prevailed for centuries because it was

a. actually correct
b. not considered important
c. not tested by experiment
d. tested and found to be true

Answers: 1, a; 2, c

Self-Assessment Questions

Self-Assessment Questions appear in each section as a concept check for students as they progress through the chapter.

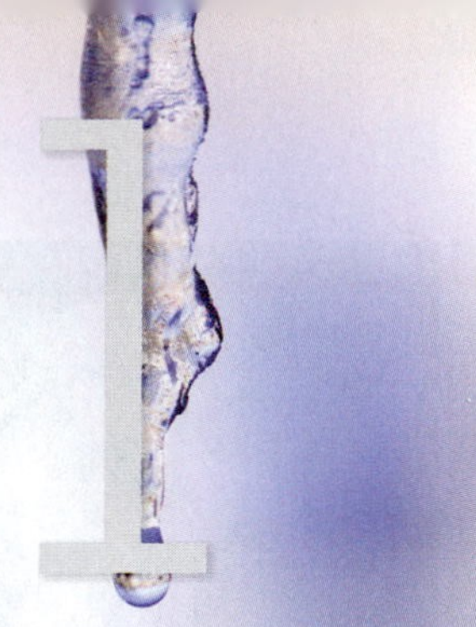

Chemistry

Have You Ever Wondered?

1. Is it true that chemicals are bad for us?
2. Why should I study chemistry?
3. Why do scientists so often say "more study is needed"?
4. Why do scientists bother with studies that have no immediate application?
5. Can we change lead into gold?

(You will find an answer to each of these questions at the appropriate point within this chapter. Look for the answers in the margins.)

A Science for All Seasons

Chemistry pervades every aspect of our lives. Look around you. Everything you see is made of chemicals: the food we eat, the air we breathe, the clothes we wear, the medicines we take, the vehicles we ride in, and the buildings we live and work in.

Everything we *do* also involves chemistry. Whenever we eat a sandwich, bathe, drive a car, listen to music, or ride a bicycle, we use chemistry. Even when we are asleep, chemical reactions go on constantly throughout our bodies.

Chemistry also affects society as a whole. Developments in health and

Chemistry is everywhere, not just in laboratories. Chemistry occurs in soil and rocks, in waters, in clouds, and in us. Knowledge of chemistry enhances our understanding of climate change, helps to provide food for Earth's increasing population, and is crucial to the development and production of sustainable fuels.

Learning Objectives

- Distinguish science from technology. (1.1)
- Define *alchemy* and *natural philosophy*. (1.1)
- Briefly describe the contributions of Bacon, Galileo, and Carson to the perceptions of science. (1.2)
- Define *hypothesis, scientific law, scientific theory,* and *scientific model*, and explain their relationships in science. (1.3)
- Define *risk* and *benefit*, and give an example of each. (1.4)
- Estimate a desirability quotient from benefit and risk data. (1.4)
- Give an example of a use of chemistry in your daily life and in society at large. (1.5)
- Distinguish basic research from applied research. (1.6)
- Differentiate: mass and weight; physical and chemical change; physical and chemical properties. (1.7)
- Classify matter according to state and as mixture, substance, compound, and/or element. (1.8)
- Assign proper units of measurement to observations, and manipulate units in conversions. (1.9)
- Calculate the density, mass, or volume of an object given the other two quantities. (1.10)
- Distinguish between heat and temperature. (1.11)
- Explain how the temperature scales are related. (1.11)
- Use critical thinking to evaluate claims and statements. (1.12)
- Define green chemistry.
- Describe how *green chemistry* reduces risk and prevents environmental problems.

▲ Organic foods are not chemical-free. In fact, they are made entirely of chemicals!

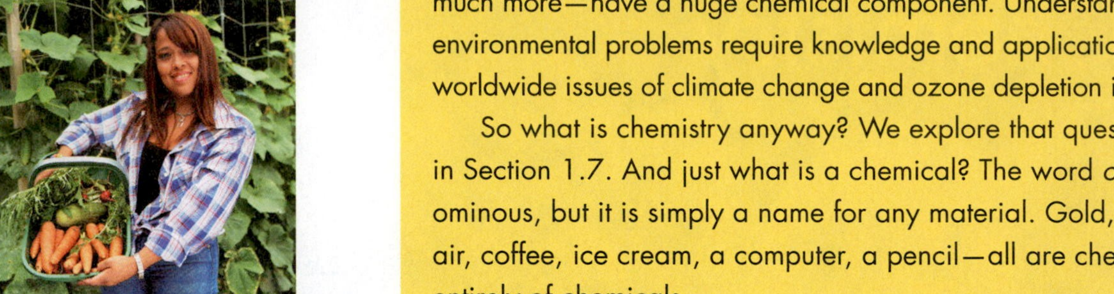

medicine involve a lot of chemistry. The astounding advances in biotechnology—decoding the human genome, developing new drugs, improving nutrition, and much more—have a huge chemical component. Understanding and solving environmental problems require knowledge and application of chemistry. The worldwide issues of climate change and ozone depletion involve chemistry.

So what is chemistry anyway? We explore that question in some detail in Section 1.7. And just what is a chemical? The word *chemical* may sound ominous, but it is simply a name for any material. Gold, water, salt, sugar, air, coffee, ice cream, a computer, a pencil—all are chemicals or are made entirely of chemicals.

Material things undergo changes. Sometimes these changes occur naturally—maple leaves turn yellow and red in autumn. Often, we change material things intentionally, to make them more useful, as when we light a candle or cook an egg. Most of these changes are accompanied by changes in energy. For example, when we burn gasoline, the process releases energy that we can use to propel an automobile.

▲ A century ago, contaminated drinking water was often the cause of outbreaks of cholera. Modern water treatment uses chemicals to remove solid matter and kill disease-causing bacteria, making water safe to drink.

Your own body is a marvelous chemical factory. It takes the food you eat and turns it into skin, bones, blood, and muscle, while also generating energy for all your activities. This amazing chemical factory operates continuously 24 hours a day for as long as you live. Chemistry affects your own life every moment, and it also transforms society as a whole. Chemistry shapes our civilization.

1. Is it true that chemicals are bad for us? Everything you can see, smell, taste, or touch is either a chemical or is made of chemicals. Chemicals are neither good nor bad in themselves. They can be put to good use, bad use, or anything in between.

2. Why should I study chemistry? Chemistry is a part of many areas of study and affects everything you do. Knowledge of chemistry helps you to understand many facets of modern life.

1.1 Science and Technology: The Roots of Knowledge

Learning Objectives › Distinguish science from technology › Define *alchemy* and *natural philosophy*.

Chemistry is a *science*, but what is science? **Science** is an accumulation of knowledge about nature and our physical world and of theories that we use to explain that knowledge. Let's examine the roots of science. Our study of the material universe has two interrelated facets: the *technological* (or *factual*) and the *philosophical* (or *theoretical*).

Technology is the application of knowledge for practical purposes. It arose long before science, originating in prehistoric times. Early people used fire to bring about chemical changes. They cooked food, baked pottery, and smelted ores to produce metals such as copper. They made beer and wine by fermentation and obtained dyes and drugs from plants. These tasks—and many others—were accomplished without an understanding of the scientific principles involved.

About 2500 years ago, Greek philosophers were among the first to formulate *theories* of chemistry—rational explanations of the behavior of matter. Those philosophers generally did not test their theories by experimentation. Nevertheless, their view of nature—attributed mainly to Aristotle—dominated Western thinking about the workings of the material world for the next 20 centuries.

The experimental roots of chemistry are in **alchemy**, a mixture of chemistry and magic that flourished in Europe during the Middle Ages, from about C.E. 500 to 1500. Alchemists searched for a "philosophers' stone" that would turn cheaper metals into gold and for an elixir that would bring eternal life. Although alchemists never achieved these goals, they discovered many new chemical substances and perfected techniques such as distillation and extraction that are still used today. Modern chemists inherited from the alchemists an abiding interest in human health and the quality of life.

Technology also developed rapidly during the late Middle Ages in Europe, though its progress was hampered by the Aristotelian philosophy that still prevailed. The beginnings of modern science are more recent, however, and coincide with the emergence of the experimental method. What we now call science grew out of **natural philosophy**—philosophical speculation about nature. Science had its true beginnings in the seventeenth century, when astronomers, physicists, and physiologists began to rely on experimentation.

▲ Aristotle (384–322 B.C.E.), Greek philosopher and tutor of Alexander the Great, believed that we could understand nature through logic. The idea of experimental science did not triumph over Aristotelian logic until about C.E. 1500.

Beyond the Alchemists' Wildest Dreams

Modern chemists can transform matter in ways that would astound the alchemists. They can change ordinary salt into lye and laundry bleach. They can convert sand into transistors and computer chips. And they can turn crude oil into plastics, fibers, pesticides, drugs, detergents, and a host of other products. Many products of modern chemistry are much more valuable than the glittering metal that the alchemists vainly sought. For example, a form of carbon called *nanotubes* (see the box on page 25) has thousands of potential uses but is extremely expensive to make. A kilogram of purified nanotubes costs more than $2,500,000, while a kilogram of gold will set you back only about $50,000.

Self-Assessment Questions

Match each term in the left column with the best definition or explanation of it in the right column.

1. alchemy
2. natural philosophy
3. science
4. technology

a. application of knowledge for practical purposes
b. grew out of Greek philosophy, alchemy, and natural philosophy
c. a mixture of chemistry and magic
d. philosophical speculation about nature

Answers: 1, c; 2, d; 3, b; 4, a

▲ Alchemists made many positive contributions to chemistry. This illustration from the 1512 edition of Hieronymus Brunschwig's *Liber de arte distillandi* (On the art of distilling) shows a distillation apparatus. *(Source: Donald and Mildred Othmer Collection)*

1.2 Changing Perceptions and Changing Practices

Learning Objectives › Briefly describe the contributions of Bacon, Galileo, and Carson to the perceptions of science.

Science is ever-changing. Francis Bacon, a philosopher who practiced law and served as a judge, was among the first to argue that science should be experimental. His dream was that science could solve the world's problems and enrich human life with new inventions, thereby increasing happiness and prosperity. Bacon was not a scientist, and it was left to others to bring about the birth of modern science. Notable

▲ Francis Bacon (1561–1626), English philosopher and Lord Chancellor to King James I.

among these was the Italian Galileo Galilei (1564–1642). Galileo developed a vastly improved telescope and advanced the science of astronomy through observations such as sunspots, the moons of Jupiter, and the phases of Venus. He also did experiments and made many other observations that led many to call him the father of modern science.

The science of chemistry also has changed over the years. Early people used plant, animal, and mineral materials much as they occurred in nature. They later learned to modify materials to better meet their needs—for example, baking clay to make ceramic materials, cooking food to make it more digestible, and obtaining metals from ores. For most of human history, people exploited resources such as metals and petroleum and gave little thought to ever running out of such resources. An environmental movement arose in the 1970s as people became increasingly aware that reckless use of resources not only caused appalling pollution but would lead in the end to severe shortages. Rachel Carson, a biologist, was an early proponent of environmental awareness. The main theme of her book *Silent Spring* (1962) was that our use of chemicals to control insects was threatening to destroy all life, including ourselves. People in the pesticide industry and their allies roundly denounced Carson as a "propagandist," while some scientists rallied to support her. By the late 1960s, however, the threatened extinction of several species of birds and the disappearance of fish from many rivers, lakes, and areas of the ocean caused many scientists to move into Carson's camp. Popular support for Carson's views became overwhelming.

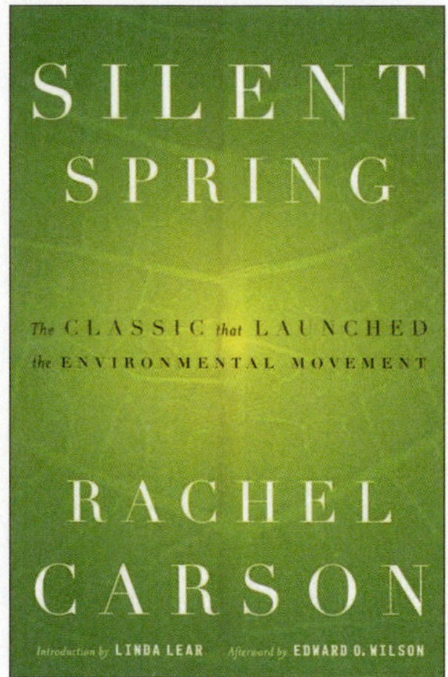

▲ Rachel Carson's *Silent Spring* was one of the first publications to point out a number of serious environmental issues.

In response to growing public concern, chemists developed the concept of **green chemistry**, which uses materials and processes that are intended to prevent or reduce pollution at its source. This approach was further extended in the first decade of the twenty-first century to include the idea of sustainability. **Sustainable chemistry** is designed to meet the needs of the present generation without compromising the needs of future generations. Sustainability preserves resources and aspires to produce environmentally friendly products from renewable resources.

Some chemicals can indeed cause problems, especially when misused, but many others have extremely helpful uses. Chemicals are used to kill bacteria that cause dreadful diseases, to relieve pain and suffering, to increase food production, to provide fuel for heating, cooling, lighting, and transportation, and to provide materials for building our machines, making our clothing, and constructing our houses. Chemistry has provided ordinary people with luxuries that were not available even to the mightiest rulers in ages past. Chemicals are essential to our lives—life itself would be impossible without chemicals.

Self-Assessment Questions

Select the best answer or response.

1. Francis Bacon thought that science would
   a. destroy life on Earth
   b. increase human happiness and prosperity
   c. find a way to turn lead to gold
   d. produce toxic chemicals
2. The main theme of Rachel Carson's *Silent Spring* was that life on Earth would be destroyed by
   a. botulism
   b. nuclear war
   c. overpopulation
   d. pesticides
3. Galileo has been called the father of modern science because he
   a. anticipated environmental problems
   b. made observations and did experiments
   c. thought that science would destroy life on Earth
   d. tried to use science to get rich
4. A goal of green chemistry is to
   a. produce cheap green dyes
   b. provide great wealth for corporations
   c. reduce pollution
   d. turn deserts into forests and grasslands

5. Which best exemplifies sustainable chemistry?
   a. Toluene, extracted from coal, is used to make TNT, an explosive.
   b. Paper is made from hardwood trees.
   c. Minerals mined in South America are used in China to make LCD screens.
   d. Plastic bottles are made from both petroleum and recycled plastic.

Answers: 1, b; 2, d; 3, b; 4, c; 5, b

1.3 Science: Reproducible, Testable, Tentative, Predictive, and Explanatory

Learning Objectives › Define *hypothesis, scientific law, scientific theory,* and *scientific model,* and explain their relationships in science.

We have defined science, but science has *characteristics* that distinguish it from other studies.

Scientists often disagree about what is and what will be, but does that make science merely a guessing game in which one guess is as good as another? Not at all. Science is based on observations and experimental tests of our assumptions. However, it is not a collection of unalterable facts; we cannot force nature to fit our preconceived ideas. Science is good at correcting errors, but it is not especially good at establishing truths. Science is an unfinished work. The things we have learned from science fill millions of books and scholarly journals, but what we know pales in comparison to what we do not yet know.

Scientific Data Must Be Reproducible

Scientists collect data by making careful observations. Data reported by a scientist must also be observable by other scientists. The data must be *reproducible.* Careful measurements are required, conditions are thoroughly controlled and described, and scientific work is not fully accepted until it has been verified by other scientists.

Observations, though, are just the beginning of the intellectual processes of science. There are many different paths to scientific discovery, and there is no general set of rules. Science is not a straightforward process for cranking out discoveries.

Scientific Hypotheses Are Testable

Scientists do not merely state what they feel may be true. They develop *testable* **hypotheses** (educated guesses) as tentative explanations of observed data. They test these hypotheses by designing and performing experiments. Experimentation distinguishes science from the arts and humanities. In the humanities, people still argue about some of the same questions that were being debated thousands of years ago: What is truth? What is beauty? These arguments persist because the proposed answers cannot be tested and confirmed objectively.

Like artists and poets, scientists are often imaginative and creative. The tenets of science, however, are *testable.* Experiments can be devised to answer most scientific questions. Ideas can be tested and thereby either verified or rejected. For example, it was long thought that exercise caused muscles to tire and become sore from a buildup of lactic acid. Recent findings suggest instead that lactic acid *delays* muscle tiredness and that the cause of tired, sore muscles may be related to other factors, including leakage of calcium ions inside muscle cells, which weakens contractions. Through many experiments, scientists have established a firm foundation of knowledge, allowing each new generation to build on the past.

Scientific Laws Summarize Observations

Large amounts of scientific data can sometimes be summarized in brief statements called **scientific laws.** For example, Robert Boyle (1627–1691), an Irishman, conducted

3. Why do scientists so often say "more study is needed"?
More data help scientists refine a hypothesis so that it is better defined, clearer, or more applicable.

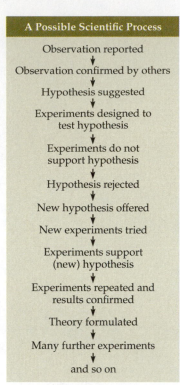

A Possible Scientific Process

Observation reported
↓
Observation confirmed by others
↓
Hypothesis suggested
↓
Experiments designed to test hypothesis
↓
Experiments do not support hypothesis
↓
Hypothesis rejected
↓
New hypothesis offered
↓
New experiments tried
↓
Experiments support (new) hypothesis
↓
Experiments repeated and results confirmed
↓
Theory formulated
↓
Many further experiments
↓
and so on

many experiments on gases. In each experiment, he found that the volume of the gas decreased when the pressure applied to the gas was increased.

Many scientific laws can be stated mathematically. For example, Boyle's law can be written as $PV = k$, where P is the pressure on a gas, V is its volume, and k is a constant number. If P is doubled, V will be cut in half. Scientific laws are *universal*. Under the specified conditions, they hold everywhere in the observable universe.

Scientific Theories Are Tentative and Predictive

Scientists organize the knowledge they accumulate on a framework of detailed explanations called theories. A **theory** represents the best current explanation for a phenomenon, but it is always *tentative*. In the future, a theory may have to be modified or even discarded as a result of new observations, for the body of knowledge that is science is rapidly growing and always changing.

Theories provide organization for scientific knowledge, but they are also useful for their *predictive* value. Predictions based on theories are tested by further experiments. Theories that make successful predictions are usually widely accepted by the scientific community. A theory developed in one area is often found to apply in others.

Scientific Models Are Explanatory

Scientists often use models to help *explain* complicated phenomena. A *scientific model* uses tangible items or pictures to represent invisible processes. For example, the invisible particles of a gas can be visualized as billiard balls, as marbles, or as dots or circles on paper. We know that when a glass of water is left standing for a period of time, the water disappears through the process of evaporation (Figure 1.1). Scientists explain evaporation with a theory, the kinetic–molecular theory, which proposes that a liquid is composed of tiny particles called *molecules* that are in constant motion. (This theory is discussed further in Chapter 6; here it is used simply as an example.) In the bulk of the liquid, these molecules are held together by forces of attraction. The molecules collide with one another like billiard balls on a playing table. Sometimes, a "hard break" of billiard balls causes one ball to fly off the table. Likewise, some of the molecules of a liquid gain enough energy through collisions to break the attraction to their neighbors, escape from the liquid, and disperse among the widely spaced molecules in air. The water in the glass gradually disappears. This model gives us more than a name for evaporation; it gives us an understanding of the phenomenon.

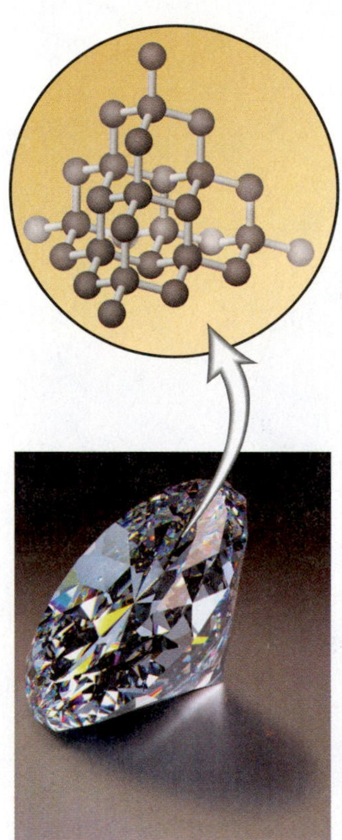

▲ A molecular model of diamond shows the tightly linked, rigid structure that explains why diamonds are so hard.

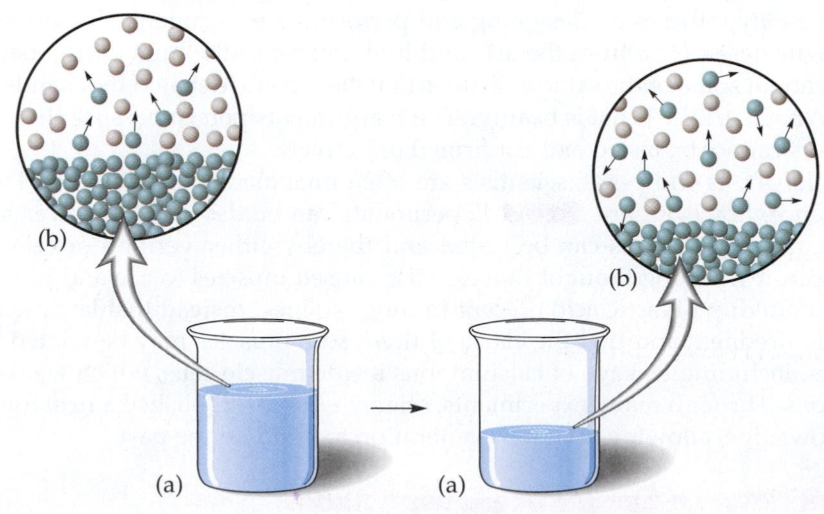

● = Water molecule
● = Air (nitrogen or oxygen) molecule

▶ **Figure 1.1** The evaporation of water. (a) When a container of water is left standing open to the air, the water slowly disappears. (b) Scientists explain evaporation in terms of the motion of molecules.

What Science Is Not

Responsible news media generally try to be fair, presenting both sides of an issue regardless of where the prevailing evidence lies. In science, the evidence often indicates that one side is simply wrong. Scientists strive for accuracy, not balance. The idea of a flat Earth is not given equal credence to a (roughly) spherical Earth. Only ideas that have survived experimental testing or that can be tested by experiment are considered valid. Ideas that are beautiful, elegant, or even sacrosanct can be invalidated by experimental data.

Science is not a democratic process. Majority rule does not determine what constitutes sound science. Science does not accept notions that are proven false or remain untested by experiment.

When doing experiments, developing theories, and constructing models, it is important to note that a *correlation* between two items is not necessarily evidence that one *causes* the other. For example, many people suffer from allergies in the fall when goldenrod is in bloom. However, research has shown that the main cause of these allergies is ragweed pollen. There is a correlation between the blooming of goldenrod and autumnal allergies, but goldenrod pollen is not the cause. Ragweed happens to bloom at the same time.

The Limitations of Science

Some people say that we could solve many of our problems if we would only attack them using the methods of science. Why can't the procedures of the scientist be applied to social, political, ethical, and economic problems? And why do scientists disagree over environmental, social, and political issues?

Disagreement often results from the inability to control *variables*. A **variable** is something that can change over the course of an experiment. If, for example, we wanted to study in the laboratory how the volume of a gas varies with changes in pressure, we could hold constant such factors as temperature and the amount and kind of gas. If, on the other hand, we wanted to determine the effect of low levels of a particular pollutant on the health of a human population, we would find it almost impossible to control such variables as individuals' diets, habits, and exposure to other substances, all of which affect health. Although we could make observations, formulate hypotheses, and conduct experiments on the health effect of the pollutant, interpretation of the results would be difficult and subject to disagreement.

Self-Assessment Questions

Select the best answer or response.

1. To gather information to support or discredit a hypothesis, a scientist
   a. conducts experiments b. consults an authority
   c. establishes a scientific law d. formulates a scientific theory
2. The statement that mass is always conserved when chemical changes occur is an example of a scientific
   a. experiment b. hypothesis
   c. law d. theory
3. A successful theory
   a. can be used to make predictions b. eventually becomes a scientific law
   c. is not subject to further testing d. is permanently accepted as true
4. Which of the following is *not* a hypothesis?
   a. All solutions of seaborgium (element 106) are blue.
   b. Copernicum (element 112) will have properties similar to those of mercury.
   c. Extrasensory perception works only when no negative forces are present.
   d. Water reacts with seaborgium to form hydrogen gas.
5. A possible explanation for a collection of observations is called a(n)
   a. experiment b. law
   c. myth d. theory

6. Social problems are difficult to solve because it is difficult to
   a. control variables
   b. discount paranormal events
   c. form hypotheses
   d. formulate theories

Answers: 1, a; 2, c; 3, a; 4, c; 5, d; 6, a

1.4 Science and Technology: Risks and Benefits

Learning Objectives › Define *risk* and *benefit*, and give an example of each. › Estimate a desirability quotient from benefit and risk data.

Most people recognize that society has benefited from science and technology, but many seem not to realize that there are risks associated with every technological advance. How can we determine when the benefits outweigh the risks? One approach, called **risk–benefit analysis**, involves the estimation of a desirability quotient (DQ).

$$DQ = \frac{\text{Benefits}}{\text{Risks}}$$

A *benefit* is anything that promotes well-being or has a positive effect. Benefits may be economic, social, or psychological. A *risk* is any hazard that leads to loss or injury. Some of the risks associated with modern technology have led to disease, death, economic loss, and environmental deterioration. Risks and benefits may involve one individual, a group, or society as a whole.

▲ **It DOES Matter!**
For most people of northern European ancestry, milk is a wholesome food; its benefits far outweigh its risks. Other ethnic groups have high rates of lactose intolerance among adults, and the desirability quotient for milk is much smaller.

Every technological advance has both benefits and risks. Most people recognize the benefits of the automobile. But driving a car involves risk—individual risks of injury or death in a traffic accident and societal risks such as pollution and climate change. Most people consider the benefits of driving a car to outweigh the risks.

Weighing the benefits and risks connected with a product is more difficult when considering a group of people. For example, pasteurized low-fat milk is a safe, nutritious beverage for many people of northern European descent. However, a few people in this group can't tolerate lactose, the sugar in milk. And some are allergic to milk proteins. For these individuals, drinking milk can be harmful. But milk allergies and lactose intolerance are relatively uncommon among people of northern European descent, so the benefits of milk are large and the risks are small, resulting in a large DQ. However, adults of other ethnic backgrounds often are lactose-intolerant, and for them, milk has a small DQ. Thus, milk is not always suitable for use in programs to relieve malnutrition.

The artificial sweetener aspartame is the most highly studied of all food additives. There is little evidence that use of an artificial sweetener helps with efforts to lose weight. (Aspartame may provide some benefit to diabetics, however, because sugar consumption presents a large risk to them.) There are anecdotal reports of problems due to use of the sweetener, but these have not been confirmed in controlled studies. To most people, the risk involved in using aspartame is small. This leads to an uncertain DQ—and, it seems, to endless debate over the product's safety.

Other technologies provide large benefits and present large risks. For these technologies, too, the DQ is uncertain. An example is the conversion of coal to liquid fuels. Most people find liquid fuels to be very beneficial in transportation, home heating, and industry. There are great risks associated with coal conversion, however, including risks to coal mine workers, air and water pollution, and the exposure of conversion plant workers to toxic chemicals. The result, again, is an uncertain DQ and political controversy.

There are yet other problems in risk–benefit analysis. Some technologies benefit one group of people while presenting a risk to another. For example, gold plating and gold wires in computers and other consumer electronics benefit the consumer, providing greater reliability and longer life. But when the devices are scrapped, small-scale attempts to recover the gold often produce serious pollution in the area of recovery. Difficult political decisions are needed in such cases.

Other technologies provide current benefits but present future risks. For example, although nuclear power now provides useful electricity, improperly stored wastes from nuclear power plants might present hazards for centuries. Thus, the use of nuclear power is controversial.

Science and technology obviously involve *both* risks and benefits. The determination of benefits is almost entirely a social judgment. Although risk assessment also involves social and personal decisions, it can often be greatly aided by scientific investigation.

CONCEPTUAL Example 1.1 Risk–Benefit Analysis

Heroin is thought by some to be more effective than other drugs for the relief of severe pain. For example, heroin is a legal prescription drug in the United Kingdom. People can become addicted to heroin with continued use in as little as three days, and recreational use often renders addicts unable to function in society. Do a risk–benefit analysis of the use of heroin in treating the pain of **(a)** a young athlete with a broken leg and **(b)** a terminally ill cancer patient.

Solution

a. The heroin would provide the benefit of pain relief, but its use for such purposes has been judged to be too risky by the U.S. Food and Drug Administration. The DQ is low.

b. The heroin would provide the benefit of pain relief. The risk of addiction in a dying person is irrelevant. Heroin is banned for any purpose in the United States. The DQ is uncertain. (Both answers involve judgments that are not clearly scientific; people can differ in their assessments of each.)

■ EXERCISE 1.1A

Chloramphenicol is a powerful antibacterial drug that often destroys bacteria unaffected by other drugs. It is highly dangerous to some individuals, however, causing fatal aplastic anemia in about 1 in 30,000 people. Do a risk–benefit analysis of administering chloramphenicol to **(a)** sick farm animals, whose milk or meat might contain residues of the drug, and **(b)** a person with Rocky Mountain spotted fever facing a high probability of death or permanent disability.

■ EXERCISE 1.1B

The drug thalidomide was introduced in the 1950s as a sleeping aid. It was found to be a *teratogen*, a substance that causes birth defects, and was removed from the market after children in Europe whose mothers took it during pregnancy were born with deformed limbs. Recently, thalidomide has been investigated as an effective treatment for the lesions caused by leprosy and for Kaposi's sarcoma (a form of cancer often suffered by AIDS patients). Do a risk-benefit analysis of prescribing thalidomide to **(a)** all women and **(b)** women with AIDS.

Self-Assessment Questions

Select the best answer or response.

1. Our perception of risk is
  a. always based on sound science **b.** always higher than actual risk
  c. always lower than actual risk **d.** often different from actual risk

2. Among the following, the highest risk of death (see Table 1.1) is associated with
  a. airplane accident **b.** car accident
  c. cigarettes **d.** radon

Answers: 1, d; 2, c

Risks of Death

Our perception of risk often differs from the actual risk we face. Some people fear flying but readily assume the risk of an automobile trip. The odds of dying from various causes are listed in Table 1.1.

Table 1.1 Approximate Lifetime Risks of Death in the United States

Action	Lifetime Risk[a]	Approximate Lifetime Odds	Details/Assumptions
All causes	1	1 in 1	We all die of something.
Cigarettes	0.25	1 in 4	Cigarette smoking, 1 pack/day
Heart disease	0.20	1 in 5	Heart attacks, congestive heart failure
All cancers	0.14	1 in 7	All cancers
Motor vehicles	0.011	1 in 88	Death in motor vehicle accident
Home accidents	0.010	1 in 100	Home accident death
Radon	0.0030	1 in 300	Radon in homes, cancer deaths
Background radiation	0.0010	1 in 1000	Sea level background radiation, cancers
Peanut butter (aflatoxin)	0.00060	1 in 1700	4 tablespoons peanut butter per day
Airplane accidents	0.0002	1 in 5000	Death in aircraft crashes
Terrorist attack[b]	0.00077	1 in 1300	One 9/11-level attack per year
Terrorist attack[c]	0.000077	1 in 13,000	One 9/11-level attack every 10 years

[a]The odds of dying of a particular cause in a given year are calculated by dividing the population by the number of deaths by that cause in that year. Lifetime odds of dying of a specific cause are calculated by dividing the one-year odds by the life expectancy of a person born in that year.

[b]Unlikely scenario

[c]More reasonable scenario

1.5 Chemistry: Its Central Role

Learning Objective › Give an example of a use of chemistry in your daily life and in society at large.

Science is a unified whole. Common scientific laws apply everywhere and on all levels of organization. The various areas of science interact and support one another. Accordingly, chemistry is not only useful in itself but also fundamental to other scientific disciplines. The application of chemical principles has revolutionized biology and medicine, has provided materials for powerful computers used in mathematics, and has profoundly influenced other fields such as psychology. The social goals of better health, nutrition, and housing are dependent to a large extent on the knowledge and techniques of chemists. Many modern materials have been developed by chemists, and even more amazing materials are in the works. Recycling of basic materials—paper, glass, and metals—involves chemical processes. Chemistry is indeed a central science (Figure 1.2). There is no area of our daily lives that is not affected by chemistry.

Chemistry is also important to the *economy* of industrial nations. In the United States, the chemical industry makes thousands of consumer products, including personal-care products, agricultural products, plastics, coatings, soaps, and detergents. It produces 80% of the materials used to make medicines. The U.S. chemical industry is one of the country's largest industries, with sales of more than $675 billion per year, and it accounts for 10% of all U.S. exports. It employs 800,000 workers, including scientists, engineers, and technicians, and it generates nearly 11% of all U.S. patents. And despite widespread fear of chemicals, workers in the chemical industry are five times safer than the average worker in the U.S. manufacturing sector.

◀ **Figure 1.2** Chemistry has a central role among the sciences.

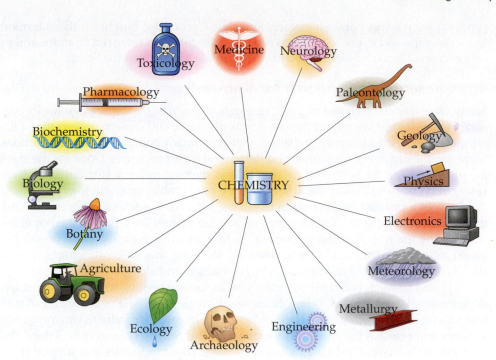

Self-Assessment Question

Select the best answer or response.

1. Chemistry is called the central science because
   - **a.** the chemical industry is based mainly in the U.S. Midwest
   - **b.** it is the core course in all college curricula
   - **c.** it is fundamental to other scientific disciplines
   - **d.** the source of many environmental problems
2. The U.S. chemical industry is
   - **a.** patently unsafe
   - **b.** the source of nearly all pollution
   - **c.** the source of many consumer products
   - **d.** unimportant to the U.S. economy

Answers: 1, c; 2, c

1.6 Solving Society's Problems: Scientific Research

Learning Objective › Distinguish basic research from applied research.

Chemistry is a powerful force in shaping society today. Chemical research not only plays a pivotal role in other sciences but it also has a profound influence on society as a whole. Chemists, like other scientists, do one of two categories of research: *applied research* or *basic research*. The two often overlap, and it isn't always possible to label a particular project as one or the other.

Applied Research

Some chemists test polluted soil, air, and water. Others analyze foods, fuels, cosmetics, detergents, and drugs. Still others synthesize new substances for use as drugs or pesticides or formulate plastics for new applications. These activities are examples of **applied research**—work oriented toward the solution of a particular problem in an industry or the environment.

Among the most monumental accomplishments in applied research were those of George Washington Carver. Born in slavery, Carver attended Simpson College and later graduated from Iowa State University. A botanist and agricultural chemist, Carver taught and did research at Tuskegee Institute. He developed over 300 products from peanuts, from peanut butter to hand cleaner to insulating board. He created other new

▲ George Washington Carver (1864–1943), research scientist, in his laboratory at Tuskegee Institute.

products from sweet potatoes, pecans, and clay. Carver also taught southern farmers to rotate crops and to use legumes to replenish the nitrogen removed from the soil by cotton crops. Carver's work helped to revitalize the economy of the South.

Basic Research: The Search for Knowledge

Many chemists are involved in **basic research,** the search for knowledge for its own sake. Some chemists work out the fine points of atomic and molecular structure. Others measure the intricate energy changes that accompany complex chemical reactions. Some synthesize new compounds and determine their properties. Done for the sheer joy of unraveling the secrets of nature and discovering order in our universe, basic research is characterized by the absence of any predictable, marketable product.

4. Why do scientists bother with studies that have no immediate application? The results of basic research may not have an immediate practical use; however, basic research extends our understanding of the world and can be considered an investment in the future.

Lack of a product doesn't mean that basic research is useless. Far from it! Findings from basic research often *are* applied at a later time. This may be the hope, but it is not the main goal of the researcher. In fact, most of our modern technology is based on results obtained in basic research. Without this base of factual information, technological innovation would be haphazard and slow.

Applied research is carried out mainly by industries seeking to gain a competitive edge by developing a novel, better, or more salable product. The ultimate aim of such research is usually profit for the stockholders. Basic research is conducted mainly at universities and research institutes. Most support for this research comes from federal and state governments and foundations, although some larger industries also support it.

An example of basic research that was later applied to improving human welfare is the work of Gertrude Elion (1918–1999) and George Hitchings (1905–1998), who studied compounds called *purines* in an attempt to understand their role in the chemistry of the cell. Their basic research at Burroughs Wellcome Research Laboratories in North Carolina led to the discovery of a number of valuable new drugs that facilitate organ transplants and treat various diseases such as gout, malaria, herpes, and cancer. Elion and Hitchings shared the 1988 Nobel Prize in Physiology or Medicine, and in 1991 Elion became the first woman to be inducted into the National Inventors Hall of Fame.

Another example involves the work of two physicists. In 1930, Otto Stern (1888–1969) and Walther Gerlach (1889–1979) determined that certain atomic nuclei (Chapter 3) have a property called *spin,* which causes these nuclei to act as tiny magnets. Isidor Isaac Rabi (1898–1988) later developed a method for recording the magnetic properties of atomic nuclei. For their basic research in studying and measuring these minuscule magnetic fields, Stern and Rabi won the Nobel Prize in Physics in 1943 and 1944, respectively. In the 1940s, teams led by Edward M. Purcell and Felix Bloch used nuclear spins to work out the structure of complicated molecules. Their technique, called *nuclear magnetic resonance* (NMR), has become a major tool of chemists for determining molecular structure. Purcell and Bloch shared the Nobel Prize in Physics in 1952 for their research. Still later, in the 1960s, Paul Lauterbur, Peter Mansfield, and other scientists applied the principles of NMR to performing scans of the human body. This noninvasive diagnostic technique, called *magnetic resonance imaging* (MRI), has replaced many exploratory surgical operations and made other surgical procedures much more precise. Lauterbur and Mansfield won the 2003 Nobel Prize in Physiology or Medicine for their work.

▲ **It DOES Matter!**
Gertrude Elion won a Nobel Prize for her basic research on purines. Her work has led to many applications in pharmaceuticals and medicine. Many important modern applications started out with basic research.

Importance of Basic Research

"There are two compelling reasons why society must support basic science. One is substantial: The theoretical physics of yesterday is the nuclear defense of today; the obscure synthetic chemistry of yesterday is curing disease today. The other reason is cultural. The essence of our civilization is to explore and analyze the nature of man and his surroundings. As proclaimed in the Bible in the Book of Proverbs: 'Where there is no vision, the people perish.'"

Arthur Kornberg (1918–2007), American biochemist and recipient of Nobel Prize in Physiology or Medicine, 1959

Self-Assessment Question

Classify each of the following as (a) basic research or (b) applied research.

1. A chemist tries to develop a new antibiotic similar to ampicillin.
2. A team of scientists tries to genetically engineer a variety of rice that contains vitamin A.
3. A scientist seeks to extract biologically active compounds from sea sponges.
4. Scientists identify adrenal hormones and determine their structure and biological effects.

Answers: 1, b; 2, b; 3, a; 4, a

1.7 Chemistry: A Study of Matter and Its Changes

Learning Objective › Differentiate: mass and weight; physical and chemical change; and physical and chemical properties.

Chemistry is often defined as the study of matter and the changes it undergoes. Because the entire physical universe is made up of matter and energy, the field of chemistry extends from atoms to stars, from rocks to living organisms. Now let's look at matter a little more closely.

Matter is the stuff that makes up all material things. It is anything that occupies space and has mass. Matter has *mass*; you can weigh it. Wood, sand, water, air, and people have mass and are therefore matter. **Mass** is a measure of the quantity of matter that an object contains. The greater the mass of an object, the more difficult it is to change its velocity. You can easily deflect a tennis ball coming toward you at 30 meters per second (m/s), but you would have difficulty stopping a cannonball of the same size moving at the same speed. A cannonball has more mass than a tennis ball of equal size.

The mass of an object does not vary with location. An astronaut has the same mass on the moon as on Earth. In contrast, **weight** measures a force. On Earth, it measures the force of attraction between our planet and the mass in question. On the moon, where gravity is one-sixth that on Earth, an astronaut weighs only one-sixth as much as on Earth (Figure 1.3). Weight varies with gravity; mass does not.

▲ **Figure 1.3** Astronaut John W. Young leaps from the lunar surface, where gravity pulls at him with only one-sixth as much force as on Earth.

Q: *If an astronaut has a mass of 72 kg, what would be his mass on the moon? If an astronaut weighs 180 lb on Earth, what would he weigh on the moon?*

CONCEPTUAL Example 1.2 Mass and Weight

Gravity on the planet Mercury is 0.376 times that on Earth. **(a)** What would be the mass on Mercury of a person who has a mass of 62.5 kilograms (kg) on Earth? **(b)** What would be the weight on Mercury of a person who weighs 124 pounds (lb) on Earth?

Solution

a. The person's mass would be the same as on Earth (62.5 kg). The quantity of matter has not changed.

b. The person would weigh only $0.376 \times 124 \text{ lb} = 46.6 \text{ lb}$; the force of attraction between Mercury and the person would be only 0.376 times that between Earth and the person.

■ EXERCISE 1.2

At the surface of Venus, the force of gravity is 0.903 times that at Earth's surface. **(a)** What would be the mass of a 1.00-kg object on Venus? **(b)** How much would a man who weighs 198 lb on Earth weigh on the surface of Venus?

▶ **Figure 1.4** A comparison of the physical properties of two elements. Copper (left), obtained as pellets, can be hammered into thin foil or drawn into wire. Iodine (right) consists of brittle gray crystals that crumble into a powder when struck.

Q: *What additional physical properties of copper and iodine are apparent from the photographs?*

Physical and Chemical Properties

We can use our knowledge of chemistry to change matter to make it more useful. Chemists can change crude oil into gasoline, plastics, pesticides, drugs, detergents, and thousands of other products. Changes in matter are accompanied by changes in energy. Often, we change matter to extract part of its energy. For example, we burn gasoline to get energy to propel our automobiles.

To distinguish between samples of matter, we can compare their properties (Figure 1.4). A **physical property** of a substance is a characteristic or behavior that can be observed or measured without generating new types of matter. Color, odor, and hardness are physical properties (Table 1.2). A **chemical property** describes how a substance reacts with other types of matter—how its basic building blocks can change (Table 1.3).

A **physical change** involves an alteration in the physical appearance of matter without changing its chemical identity or composition. An ice cube can melt to form a liquid, but it is still water. Melting is a physical change, and the temperature at which it occurs—the melting point—is a physical property.

A **chemical change** involves a change in the chemical identity of matter into other substances that are chemically different. In exhibiting a chemical property, matter undergoes a chemical change. At least one substance in the original matter is replaced by one or more new substances. Iron metal reacts with oxygen from the air to form rust (iron oxide). When sulfur burns in air, sulfur, which is made up of

Table 1.2 Some Examples of Physical Properties

Property	Examples
Temperature	0 °C for ice water, 100 °C for boiling water.
Mass	A nickel weighs 5 g. A penny weighs 2.5 g.
Color	Sulfur is yellow. Bromine is reddish-brown.
Taste	Acids are sour. Bases are bitter.
Odor	Benzyl acetate smells like jasmine. Hydrogen sulfide smells like rotten eggs.
Boiling point	Water boils at 100 °C. Ethyl alcohol boils at 78.5 °C.
Hardness	Diamond is exceptionally hard. Sodium metal is soft.
Density	1.00 g/mL for water, 19.3 g/cm^3 for gold.

Table 1.3 Some Examples of Chemical Properties

Substance	Typical Chemical Property
Iron	rusts (combines with oxygen to form iron oxide).
Carbon	burns (combines with oxygen to form carbon dioxide).
Silver	tarnishes (combines with sulfur to form silver sulfide).
Nitroglycerin	explodes (decomposes to produce a mixture of gases).
Carbon monoxide	is toxic (combines with hemoglobin, causing anoxia).
Neon	is inert (does not react with anything).

one type of atom, and oxygen (from air), which is made up of another type of atom, combine to form sulfur dioxide, which is made up of molecules that have sulfur and oxygen atoms in the ratio 1:2. (A *molecule* is a group of atoms bound together as a single unit. You'll learn more about atoms and molecules later.)

It is difficult at times to determine whether a change is physical or chemical, but we can decide on the basis of what happens to the composition or structure of the matter involved. *Composition* refers to the types of atoms that are present and their relative proportions, and *structure* to the arrangement of those atoms with respect to one another or in space. A chemical change results in a change in composition or structure, whereas a physical change does not.

CONCEPTUAL Example 1.3 Chemical Change and Physical Change

Which of the following events involve chemical changes and which involve physical changes?

a. You trim your fingernails.
b. Lemon juice converts milk to curds and whey.
c. Molten aluminum is poured into a mold, where it solidifies.
d. Sodium chloride (table salt) is broken down into sodium metal and chlorine gas

Solution

We examine each change and determine whether there has been a change in composition or structure. In other words, we ask, "Have any substances that are chemically different been created?" If so, the change is chemical; if not, it is physical.

a. Physical change: The composition of a fingernail is not changed by cutting.
b. Chemical change: The compositions of curds and whey are different from the composition of milk.
c. Physical change: Whether it is solid or liquid, aluminum is the same substance with the same composition.
d. Chemical change: New substances, sodium and chlorine, are formed.

■ EXERCISE 1.3A

Which of the following events involve chemical changes and which involve physical changes?

a. Gasoline vaporizes from an open container.
b. Magnesium metal burns in air to form a white powder called *magnesium oxide*.
c. A dull knife is sharpened with a whetstone.

■ EXERCISE 1.3B

Which of the following events involve chemical changes and which involve physical changes?

a. A steel wrench left out in the rain becomes rusty.
b. A stick of butter melts.
c. Charcoal briquettes are burned.
d. Peppercorns are ground into flakes.

Self-Assessment Questions

Select the best answer or response.

1. Which of the following is *not* an example of matter?
   a. gasoline fumes b. ether fumes c. gold d. a sentiment
2. Which of the following is an example of matter?
   a. air b. a prayer c. a thought d. yellow light
3. Two identical items are taken from Earth to Mars, where they have
   a. both the same mass and the same weight as on Earth
   b. neither the same mass nor the same weight as on Earth
   c. the same mass but not the same weight as on Earth
   d. the same weight but not the same mass as on Earth
4. What kind of change does not alter the identity of a material?
   a. chemical b. physical c. physical state d. temperature
5. Bending glass tubing in a hot flame involves
   a. applied research b. a chemical change
   c. an experiment d. a physical change
6. Transforming liquid water into steam involves
   a. removing energy from the water b. a change in chemical makeup
   c. a chemical change d. a physical change
7. Which of the following is a chemical property?
   a. iodine vapor is purple b. copper tarnishes
   c. salt dissolves in water d. balsa wood is easily carved
8. Which of the following is an example of a physical change?
   a. A cake is baked from flour, baking powder, sugar, eggs, shortening, and milk.
   b. Milk left outside a refrigerator overnight turns sour.
   c. Sheep are sheared, and the wool is spun into yarn.
   d. Spiders eat flies and make silk.
9. Which of the following is an example of a chemical change?
   a. An egg is broken and poured into an eggnog mix.
   b. A tree is pruned, shortening some branches.
   c. A tree is watered and fertilized, and it grows larger.
   d. Frost forms on a cold windowpane.

Answers: 1, d; 2, a; 3, c; 4, b; 5, d; 6, d; 7, b; 8, c; 9, c

1.8 Classification of Matter

Learning Objective › Classify matter according to state and as mixture, substance, compound, and/or element.

In this section, we examine three of the many ways of classifying matter. First, we look at the physical forms or *states of matter*.

The States of Matter

There are three familiar states of matter: solid, liquid, and gas (Figure 1.5). They can be classified by bulk properties (a *macro* view) or by arrangement of the particles that comprise them (a *molecular*, or *micro*, view). A **solid** object maintains its shape and volume regardless of its location. A **liquid** occupies a definite volume but assumes the shape of the portion of a container that it occupies. If you have 355 milliliters (mL) of a soft drink, you have 355 mL whether the soft drink is in a can, in a bottle, or, through a mishap, on the floor—which demonstrates another property of liquids. Unlike solids, liquids flow readily. A **gas** maintains neither shape nor volume. It expands to fill completely whatever container it occupies. Gases flow and are easily compressed. For example, enough air for many minutes of breathing can be compressed into a steel tank for SCUBA diving.

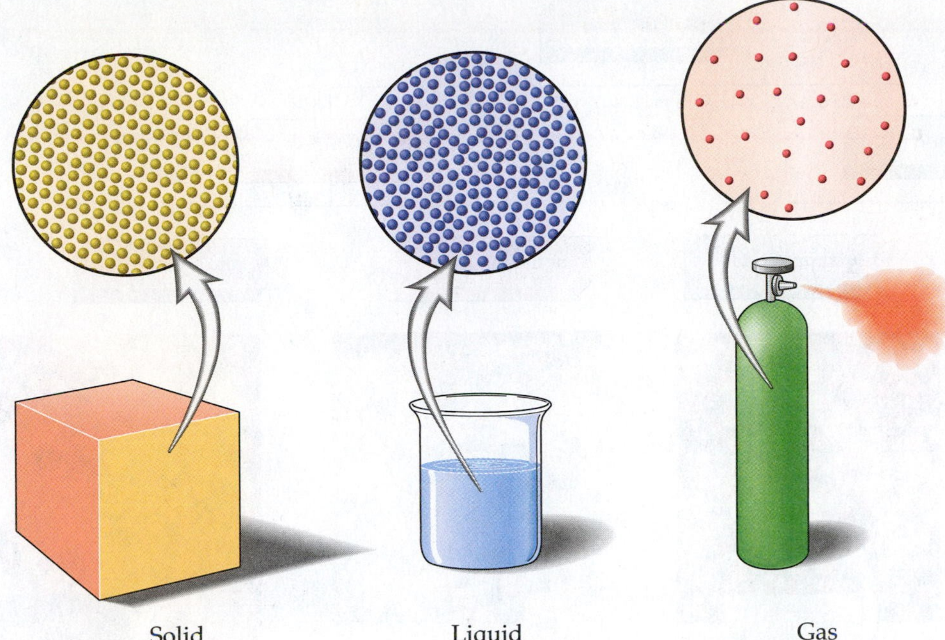

◀ **Figure 1.5** The kinetic–molecular theory can be used to interpret (or explain) the bulk properties of *solids*, *liquids*, and *gases*. In solids, the particles are close together and in fixed positions. In liquids, the particles are close together, but they are free to move about. In gases, the particles are far apart and are in rapid random motion.

Q: *Based on this figure, why does a quart of water vapor weigh so much less than a quart of liquid water?*

Bulk properties of *solids*, *liquids*, and *gases* are explained using the kinetic–molecular theory. In solids, the particles are close together and in fixed positions. In liquids, the particles are close together, but they are free to move about. In gases, the particles are far apart and are in rapid random motion. We discuss the states of matter in more detail in Chapter 5.

Substances and Mixtures

Matter can be either pure or mixed (Figure 1.6). Pure matter is considered to be a **substance**, defined as having a definite, or fixed, composition that does not vary from one sample to another. Pure gold (24-karat gold) consists entirely of gold atoms; it is a substance. All samples of pure water are comprised of molecules consisting of two hydrogen atoms and one oxygen atom; water is a substance.

The composition of a **mixture** of two or more substances is variable. The substances retain their identities. They do not change chemically; they simply mix. Mixtures can be separated by physical means. Mixtures can be either *homogeneous* or *heterogeneous*. All parts of a homogeneous mixture have the same composition (Section 6.4) and the same appearance. A saline solution—a solution of salt in water—is a homogeneous mixture. The proportions of salt and water can vary from one solution to another, but the water is still water and the salt remains salt. The two substances can be separated by physical means. For example, the water can be boiled away, leaving the salt behind.

Sand and water form a heterogeneous mixture. The appearance is not the same throughout. The grains of sand are different from the liquid water. Most things we deal with each day are heterogeneous mixtures. All you have to do is look at a computer, a book, a pen, or a person to see that different parts of those mixtures have different compositions (your hair is quite different from your skin, for example).

Elements and Compounds

A *substance* is either an element or a compound. An **element** is one of the fundamental substances from which all material things are constructed. Elements cannot be broken down into simpler substances by any chemical process. There are more than 100 known elements, of which this book deals with only about a third, which are listed on the inside front cover. Oxygen, carbon, sulfur, aluminum, and iron are familiar elements.

A **compound** is a substance made up of two or more elements chemically combined in a fixed ratio. For example, water is a compound because it has fixed

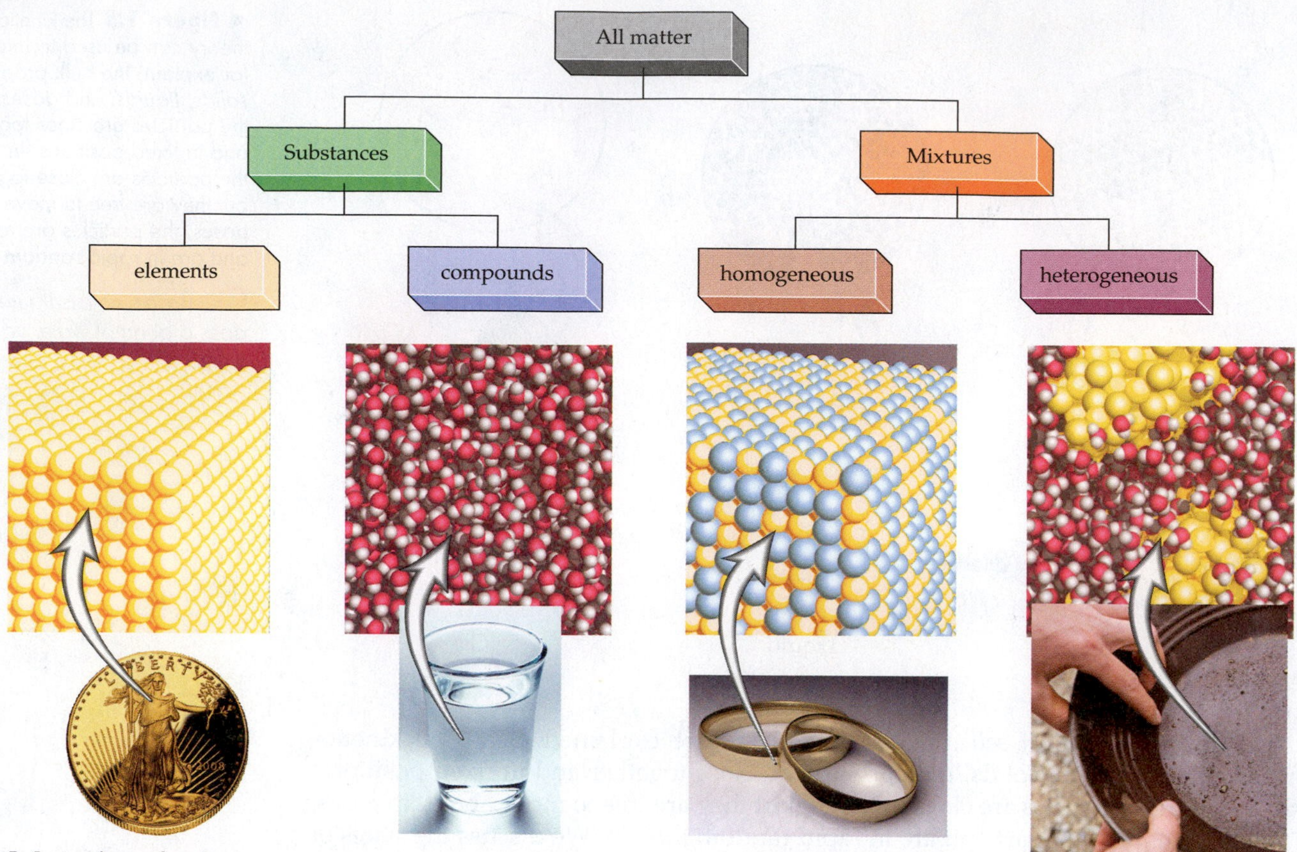

▲ **Figure 1.6** A scheme for classifying matter. The "molecular-level" views are of gold, an *element*; water, a *compound*; 12-karat gold, a *homogeneous mixture* of silver and gold; and the contents of a prospector's pan, a *heterogeneous mixture* of gold flakes in water.

proportions of hydrogen (H) and oxygen (O). Aluminum oxide (the "sand" on sandpaper), carbon dioxide, and iron disulfide (FeS_2, "fool's gold") are other compounds.

Because elements are so fundamental to our study of chemistry, we find it useful to refer to them in a shorthand form. Each element can be represented by a **chemical symbol** made up of one or two letters derived from the name of the element. Symbols for the elements are listed in the Table of Atomic Masses (inside front cover). The first letter of a symbol is always capitalized. The second (if there are two) is always lowercase. (It makes a difference. For example, Co is the symbol for cobalt, a metallic element, but CO is the formula for carbon monoxide, a poisonous compound.)

The elements' symbols are the alphabet of chemistry. Most are based on the English names of the elements, but a few are based on Latin names (Table 1.4).

5. Can we change lead into gold? One element cannot be changed into another element by chemical reactions. An element cannot be created or destroyed, although an element can be extracted from a mixture or compound containing the element.

A chemical symbol in a formula stands for one atom of the element. If more than one atom is included in a formula, a subscript number is used after the symbol. For example, the formula H_2 represents two atoms of hydrogen, and the formula CH_4 stands for one atom of carbon and four atoms of hydrogen. Mixtures do not have such formulas because a mixture does not have a fixed composition.

CONCEPTUAL Example 1.4 Elements and Compounds

Which of the following represent elements and which represent compounds?

C Cu HI BN In HBr

Solution

The periodic table shows that C, Cu, and In represent elements (each is a single symbol). HI, BN, and HBr are each composed of two symbols and represent compounds.

■ EXERCISE 1.4A

Which of the following represent elements and which represent compounds?

He CuO No NO KF Os

■ EXERCISE 1.4B

How many *different* elements are represented in the list in Exercise 1.4A?

Table 1.4 Some Elements with Symbols Derived from Latin Names

Usual English Name	Latin Name	Symbol	Spanish Name[b]	French Name[b]
Copper	cuprum	Cu	cobre	cuivre
Gold	aurum	Au	oro	or
Iron	ferrum	Fe	hierro	fer
Lead	plumbum	Pb	plomo	plomb
Mercury	hydrargyrum	Hg	mercurio	mercure
Potassium	kalium[a]	K	potasio	potassium
Silver	argentum	Ag	plata	argent
Sodium	natrium[a]	Na	sodio	sodium
Tin	stannum	Sn	estaño	étain

[a]The elements potassium and sodium were unknown in ancient times. The names *kalium* and *natrium* are the names that were used then for the compounds potassium carbonate and sodium carbonate.

[b]Note that element names in Spanish and French are often close to the Latin names.

Atoms and Molecules

An **atom** is the smallest characteristic part of an element. Each element is composed of atoms of a particular kind. For example, the element copper is made up of copper atoms, and gold is made up of gold atoms. All copper atoms are alike in a fundamental way and are different from gold atoms.

The smallest characteristic part of most compounds is a molecule. A **molecule** is a group of atoms bound together as a unit. All the molecules of a given compound have the same atoms in the same proportions. For example, all water molecules have two hydrogen (H) atoms and one oxygen (O) atom, as indicated by the formula (H_2O). We will discuss atoms in some detail in Chapter 2, and much of the focus of many later chapters is on molecules.

Self-Assessment Questions

1. Which state of matter has neither a definite volume nor a definite shape?
a. gas **b.** homogeneous
c. liquid **d.** solid

2. Which of the following is a mixture?
a. carbon **b.** copper
c. silver **d.** soda water

3. Which of the following is *not* an element?
a. aluminum **b.** brass
c. lead **d.** sulfur

4. A compound can be separated into its elements
a. by chemical means **b.** by mechanical means
c. by physical means **d.** using a magnet

5. The smallest part of an element is a(n)
a. atom **b.** corpuscle
c. mass **d.** molecule

6. The symbol for potassium is
a. K **b.** P
c. Pm **d.** Po

7. Br is the symbol for
a. beryllium **b.** boron
c. brass **d.** bromine

Answers: 1, a; 2, d; 3, b; 4, a; 5, a; 6, a; 7, d

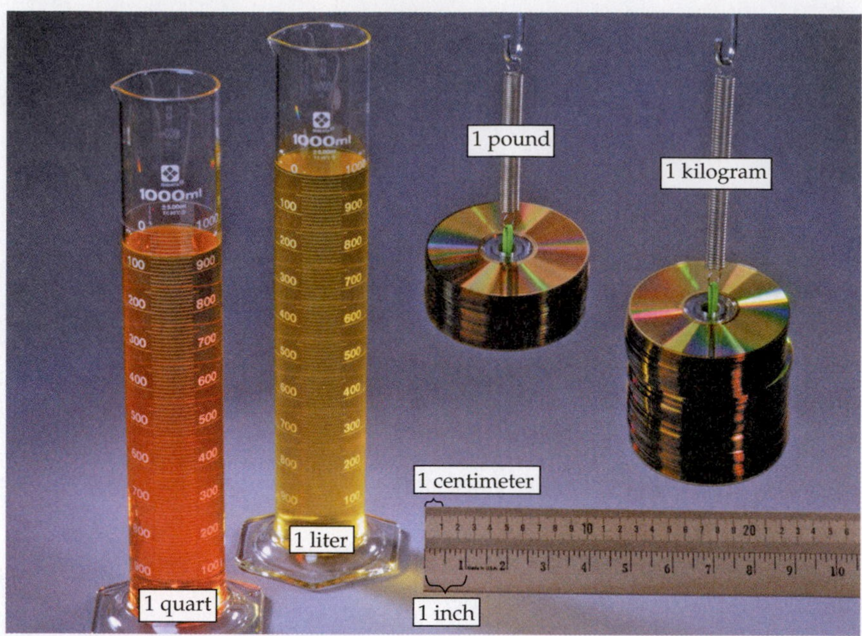

▶ **Figure 1.7** Comparisons of metric and customary units of measure. The meter stick is 100 centimeters long and is slightly longer than the yardstick below it (1 m = 1.0936 yd).

Q: *From this figure, approximately how many pounds are in a kilogram? Which two units are closer in size, the inch and centimeter or the quart and the liter?*

1.9 The Measurement of Matter

Learning Objective › Assign proper units of measurement to observations, and manipulate units in conversions.

Accurate measurements of such properties as mass, volume, time, and temperature are essential to the compilation of dependable scientific data. Such data are of critical importance in all science-related fields. Measurements of temperature and blood pressure are routinely made in medicine, and modern medical diagnosis depends on a whole battery of other measurements, including careful chemical analyses of blood and urine.

The measurement system agreed on by scientists since 1960 is the *International System of Units*, or **SI units** (from the French *Système Internationale*), a modernized version of the metric system established in France in 1791. Most countries use metric measures in everyday life. In the United States these units are used mainly in science laboratories, although they are increasingly being used in commerce, especially in businesses with an international component. The contents of most bottled beverages are given in metric units, and metric measurements are also common in sporting events. Figure 1.7 compares some metric and customary units.

Because SI units are based on the decimal system, it is easy to convert from one unit to another. All measured quantities can be expressed in terms of the seven base units listed in Table 1.5. We use the first six in this text.

Table 1.5 The Seven SI Base Units

Physical Quantity	Name of Unit	Symbol of Unit
Length	meter[a]	m
Mass	kilogram	kg
Time	second	s
Temperature	kelvin	K
Amount of substance	mole	mol
Electric current	ampere	A
Luminous intensity	candela	cd

[a]Spelled *metre* in most countries.

Exponential Numbers: Powers of Ten

Scientists deal with objects smaller than atoms and as large as the universe. We usually use exponential notation to describe the sizes of such objects. A number is in *exponential notation* when it is written as the product of a coefficient and a power of 10, such as 1.6×10^{-19} or 35×10^6. A number is said to be expressed in *scientific notation* when the coefficient has a value between 1 and 10. Appendix A.2 provides a more detailed discussion of scientific notation.

An electron has a diameter of about 10^{-15} meter (m) and a mass of about 10^{-30} kilogram (kg). At the other extreme, a galaxy typically measures about 10^{23} m across and has a mass of about 10^{41} kg. It is difficult even to imagine numbers so small and so large. The accompanying figure offers some perspectives on size.

Because measurements using the basic SI units can be of awkward magnitude, we often use exponential numbers. However, it is sometimes more convenient to use prefixes (Table 1.6) to indicate units larger and smaller than the base unit. The following examples show how prefixes and powers of ten are interconverted.

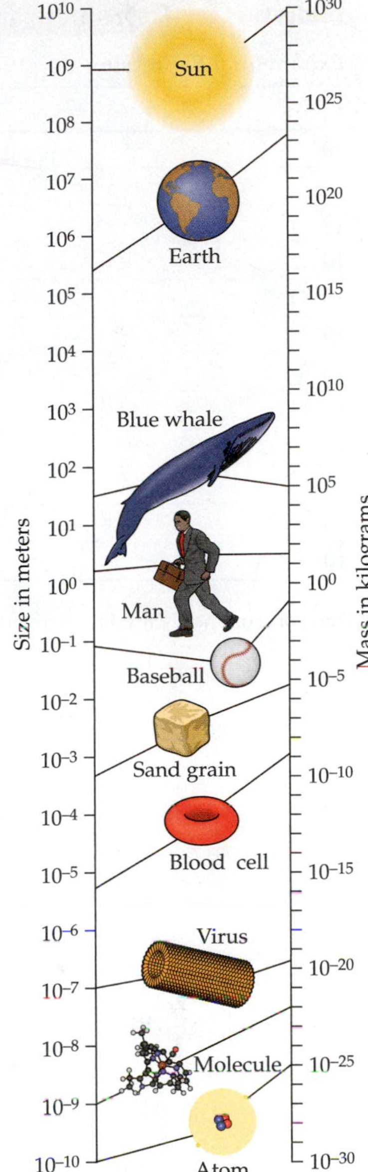

▲ Comparison of very large and very small objects is much easier with exponential notation.

Example 1.5 Prefixes and Powers of Ten

Convert each of the following measurements to a unit that replaces the power of ten by a prefix.

a. 2.89×10^{-6} g **b.** 4.30×10^{3} m

Solution

Our goal is to replace each power of ten with the appropriate prefix from Table 1.6. For example, $10^{-3} = 0.0001$ corresponds to milli(unit). (It doesn't matter what the unit is; here we are dealing only with the prefixes.)

a. 10^{-6} corresponds to the prefix *micro-*, that is, $10^{-6} \times$ (unit) = micro (unit); so we have 2.89 μg

b. 10^{3} corresponds to the prefix *kilo-*, that is, $10^{3} \times$ (unit) = kilo (unit); so we have 4.30 km

■ EXERCISE 1.5

Convert each of the following measurements to a unit that replaces the power of ten by a prefix.

a. 7.24×10^{3} g **b.** 4.29×10^{-6} m **c.** 7.91×10^{-3} s
d. 2.29×10^{-2} g **e.** 7.90×10^{6} m

Example 1.6 Prefixes and Powers of Ten

Use scientific notation to express each of the following measurements in terms of an SI base unit.

a. 4.12 cm **b.** 947 ms **c.** 3.17 nm

Solution

a. Our goal is to find the power of ten that relates the given unit to the SI base unit. That is, centi (base unit) = $10^{-2} \times$ (base unit)

$$4.12 \text{ cm} = 4.12 \text{ centimeter} = 4.12 \times 10^{-2} \text{ m}$$

b. To change millisecond (ms) to the base unit second, we replace the prefix *milli-* by 10^{-3}. To obtain an answer in conventional scientific notation, we also need to replace the coefficient 947 by 9.47×10^2. The result of these two changes is

$$9.47 \text{ ms} = 9.47 \times 10^{-3}\text{s} = 9.47 \times 10^{2} \times 10^{-3}\text{s} = 9.47 \times 10^{-1}\text{s}$$

c. To change nanometer (nm) to the base unit meter, we replace the prefix *nano-* by 10^{-9}. The answer in exponential form is 3.17×10^{-9} m.

Table 1.6 Approved Numerical Prefixes[a]

Exponential Expression	Decimal Equivalent	Prefix	Pronounced	Symbol
10^{12}	1,000,000,000,000	*tera-*	TER-uh	T
10^{9}	1,000,000,000	*giga-*	GIG-uh	G
10^{6}	1,000,000	*mega-*	MEG-uh	M
10^{3}	1,000	*kilo-*	KIL-oh	k
10^{2}	100	*hecto-*	HEK-toe	h
10^{1}	10	*deka-*	DEK-uh	da
10^{-1}	0.1	*deci-*	DES-ee	d
10^{-2}	0.01	*centi-*	SEN-tee	c
10^{-3}	0.001	*milli-*	MIL-ee	m
10^{-6}	0.000001	*micro-*	MY-kro	μ
10^{-9}	0.000000001	*nano-*	NAN-oh	n
10^{-12}	0.000000000001	*pico-*	PEE-koh	p
10^{-15}	0.000000000000001	*femto-*	FEM-toe	f

[a]The most commonly used prefixes are shown in color.

▪ EXERCISE 1.6

Use scientific notation to express each of the following measurements in terms of an SI base unit.

a. 7.45 nm **b.** 5.25 μs **c.** 1.415 km
d. 2.06 mm **e.** 6.19×10^{6} mm

Mass

The SI base unit for mass is the **kilogram (kg)**, about 2.2 pounds (lb). This base unit is unusual in that it already has a prefix. A more convenient mass unit for most laboratory work is the gram (g).

$$1 \text{ kg} = 10^3 \text{ g} = 1000 \text{ g} \qquad \text{or} \qquad 1 \text{ g} = 0.001 \text{ kg} = 10^{-3} \text{ kg}$$

The milligram (mg) is a suitable unit for small quantities of materials, such as some drug dosages.

$$1 \text{ mg} = 10^{-3} \text{ g} = 0.001 \text{ g}$$

Chemists can now detect masses in the microgram (μg), nanogram (ng), picogram (pg), and even smaller ranges.

Length, Area, and Volume

The SI base unit of length is the **meter (m)**, a unit about 10% longer than 1 yard (yd). The kilometer (km) is used to measure distances along highways.

$$1 \text{ km} = 1000 \text{ m}$$

In the laboratory, we usually find lengths smaller than the meter to be more convenient. For example, we use the centimeter (cm), which is about the width of a typical calculator button, or the millimeter (mm), which is about the thickness of the cardboard backing in a notepad.

$$1 \text{ cm} = 0.01 \text{ m} \qquad 1 \text{ mm} = 0.001 \text{ m}$$

For measurements at the atomic and molecular level, we use the micrometer (μm), the nanometer (nm), and the picometer (pm). For example, a hemoglobin molecule, which is nearly spherical, has a diameter of 5.5 nm or 5500 pm, and the diameter of a sodium atom is 372 pm.

The units for area and volume are derived from the base unit of length. The SI unit of area is the square meter (m^2), but we often find square centimeters (cm^2) or square millimeters (mm^2) to be more convenient for laboratory work.

$$1\ cm^2 = (10^{-2}\ m)^2 = 10^{-4}\ m^2 \qquad 1\ mm^2 = (10^{-3}\ m)^2 = 10^{-6}\ m^2$$

Similarly, the SI unit of volume is the cubic meter (m^3), but two units more likely to be used in the laboratory are the cubic centimeter (cm^3 or cc) and the cubic decimeter (dm^3). A cubic centimeter is about the volume of a sugar cube, and a cubic decimeter is slightly larger than 1 quart (qt).

$$1\ cm^3 = (10^{-2}\ m)^3 = 10^{-6}\ m^3 \qquad 1\ dm^3 = (10^{-1}\ m)^3 = 10^{-3}\ m^3$$

The cubic decimeter is commonly called a liter. A **liter (L)** is 1 cubic decimeter or 1000 cubic centimeters.

$$1\ L = 1\ dm^3 = 1000\ cm^3$$

The milliliter (mL) or cubic centimeter is frequently used in laboratories. A milliliter is about one "squirt" from a medicine dropper.

$$1\ mL = 1\ cm^3$$

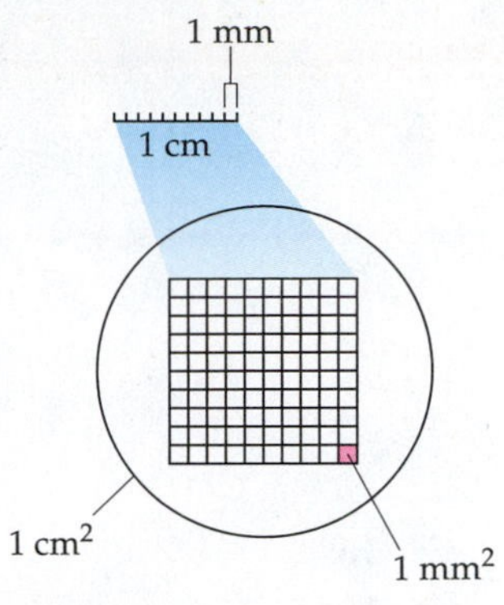

▲ Units of area such as mm^2 and cm^2 are derived from units of length.

Q: *How many mm are in 1 cm? How many mm^2 are in 1 cm^2?*

Time

The SI base unit for measuring intervals of time is the second (s). Extremely short time periods are expressed using SI prefixes: millisecond (ms), microsecond (μs), nanosecond (ns), and picosecond (ps).

$$1\ ms = 10^{-3}\ s \qquad 1\ \mu s = 10^{-6}\ s \qquad 1\ ns = 10^{-9}\ s \qquad 1\ ps = 10^{-12}\ s$$

Long time intervals, in contrast, are usually expressed in traditional, non-SI units: minute (min), hour (h), day (d), and year (y).

$$1\ min = 60\ s \qquad 1\ h = 60\ min \qquad 1\ d = 24\ h \qquad 1\ y = 365\ d$$

Problem Solving: Estimation

Many chemistry problems require calculations that yield numerical answers. When you use a calculator, it will always give you an answer—but the answer may not be correct. You may have punched a wrong number or used the wrong function. You can learn to estimate answers so you can tell whether your calculated answers are reasonable. At times an estimated answer is good enough, as the following Example and Exercises illustrate. This ability to estimate answers can be important in everyday life as well as in a chemistry course. Note that estimation does *not* require a detailed calculation. Only a rough calculation—or none at all—is required.

Example 1.7 Mass, Length, Area, Volume

Without doing detailed calculations, determine which of the following is a reasonable **(a)** mass (weight) and **(b)** height for a typical two-year-old child.

Mass:	10 mg	10 g	10 kg	100 g
Height:	85 mm	85 cm	850 cm	8.5 m

Solution

a. In customary units, a two-year-old child should weigh about 20–25 lb. Since 1 kg is a little more than 2 lb, the only reasonable answer is 10 kg.

b. In customary units, a two-year-old child should be about 30–36 in. tall. Since 1 cm is a little less than 0.5 in., the answer must be a little more than twice that range, or a bit over 60–72 cm. Thus the only reasonable answer is 85 cm.

■ EXERCISE 1.7A

Without doing a detailed calculation, determine which of the following is a reasonable area for the front cover of your textbook.

$500\ mm^2$ $50\ cm^2$ $500\ cm^2$ $50\ m^2$

■ EXERCISE 1.7B

Without doing a detailed calculation, determine which of the following is a reasonable volume for your textbook.

$1600\ mm^3$ $16\ cm^3$ $1600\ cm^3$ $1.6\ m^3$

Problem Solving: Unit Conversions

It is easy to convert from one metric unit to another using the *unit conversion* method of problem solving. If you are not familiar with this method, you should study it now in Appendix A.3, which also discusses the conversion of common units to metric units. You can find a discussion of *significant figures*, a way of indicating the precision of measurements, in Appendix A.4. In the following problems and throughout the text, we will simply carry three digits in most calculations.

Example 1.8 Unit Conversions

Convert **(a)** 1.83 kg to grams and **(b)** 729 μL to milliliters.

Solution

a. We start with the given quantity, 1.83 kg, and use the equivalence 1 kg = 1000 g to form a conversion factor (see Appendix A.3) that allows us to cancel the unit kg and end with the unit g.

$$1.83\ \cancel{kg} \times \frac{1000\ g}{1\ \cancel{kg}} = 1830\ g$$

b. Here we start with the given quantity, 729 μL, and use the equivalences $10^6\ \mu L = 1\ L$ and $10^3\ mL = 1\ L$ to form conversion factors that allow us to cancel the unit μL and end with the unit mL.

$$729\ \cancel{\mu L} \times \frac{1\ \cancel{L}}{10^6\ \cancel{\mu L}} \times \frac{1000\ mL}{1\ \cancel{L}} = 0.729\ mL$$

■ EXERCISE 1.8

Convert **(a)** 0.755 m to millimeters, **(b)** 205.6 mL to liters, **(c)** 0.206 g to micrograms, and **(d)** 7.38 cm to millimeters.

Self-Assessment Questions

1. The SI unit of length is the
   a. foot **b.** kilometer **c.** pascal **d.** meter
2. The SI unit of mass is the
   a. dram **b.** gram **c.** grain **d.** kilogram
3. The prefix that means 10^{-6} is
   a. centi- **b.** deci- **c.** micro- **d.** milli-
4. A meter is about 10% longer than a(n)
   a. foot **b.** inch **c.** mile **d.** yard
5. One cubic centimeter is equal to one
   a. deciliter **b.** dram **c.** liter **d.** milliliter
6. One quart is slightly less than one
   a. deciliter **b.** kiloliter **c.** liter **d.** milliliter

Nanoworld

For over two centuries, chemists have been able to rearrange atoms to make molecules, which have dimensions in the *picometer* (10^{-12} m) range. This ability has led to revolutions in the design of drugs, plastics, and many other materials. Over the last several decades, scientists have made vast strides in handling materials with dimensions in the *micrometer* (10^{-6} m) range. The revolution in electronic devices—computers, cell phones, and so on—was spurred by the ability of scientists to produce computer chips by photolithography on a micrometer scale.

Now many scientists focus on *nanotechnology*. The prefix *nano-* means one-billionth (10^{-9}). Nanotechnology bridges the gap between picometer-sized molecules and micrometer-sized electronics. A nanometer-sized object contains just a few hundred to a few thousand atoms or molecules, and such objects often have different properties than large objects of the same substance. For example, bulk gold is yellow, but a ring made up of nanometer-sized gold particles appears red. Carbon in the form of graphite (pencil lead) is quite weak and soft, but carbon nanotubes can be 100 times stronger than steel. Nanotubes, so called because of their size (only one 10,000th the thickness of a human hair) and their shape (hollow tube), have thousands of potential uses but are extremely expensive to make. Scientists can now manipulate matter on every scale, from nanometers to meters, greatly increasing the scope of materials design. We will examine some of the many practical applications of nanotechnology in subsequent chapters.

7. A rope is 5.775 cm long. What is its length in millimeters?
- **a.** 0.05775 mm
- **b.** 0.5775 mm
- **c.** 5.775 mm
- **d.** 57.75 mm

8. Which of the following has a mass of roughly 1 g?
- **a.** an ant
- **b.** an orange
- **c.** a peanut
- **d.** a watermelon

9. Which of the following has a thickness of roughly 1 cm?
- **a.** a brick
- **b.** a cell phone
- **c.** a knife blade
- **d.** this textbook

10. Which of the following has a volume of roughly 250 mL (0.250 L)?
- **a.** 1 cup
- **b.** 1 gallon
- **c.** 1 pint
- **d.** 1 tablespoon

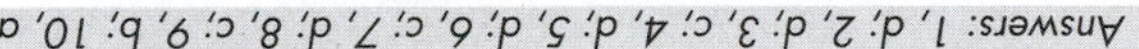

Answers: 1, d; 2, d; 3, c; 4, d; 5, d; 6, c; 7, d; 8, c; 9, b; 10, a

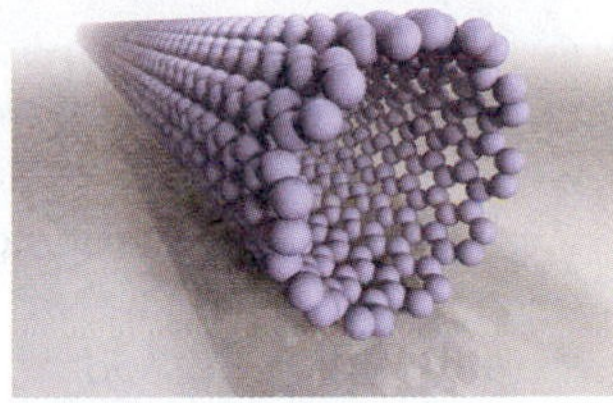

▲ Molecular view of a carbon nanotube—stronger than steel and more expensive than gold.

1.10 Density

Learning Objective › Calculate the density, mass, or volume of an object given the other two quantities.

In everyday life, we might speak of lead as "heavy" or aluminum as "light," but such descriptions are imprecise at best. Scientists use the term *density* to describe this important property. The **density**, *d*, of a substance is the quantity of mass, *m*, per unit of volume, *V*.

$$d = \frac{m}{V}$$

For substances that don't mix, such as oil and water, the concept of density allows us to predict which will float on the other. It isn't just the mass of each material, but the *mass per unit volume*—the density—that determines the result. Density is the property that explains why oil (lower density) floats on water (higher density) in a bottle of Italian salad dressing. Figure 1.8 shows other examples.

We can rearrange the equation for density to give

$$m = d \times V \qquad \text{and} \qquad V = \frac{m}{d}$$

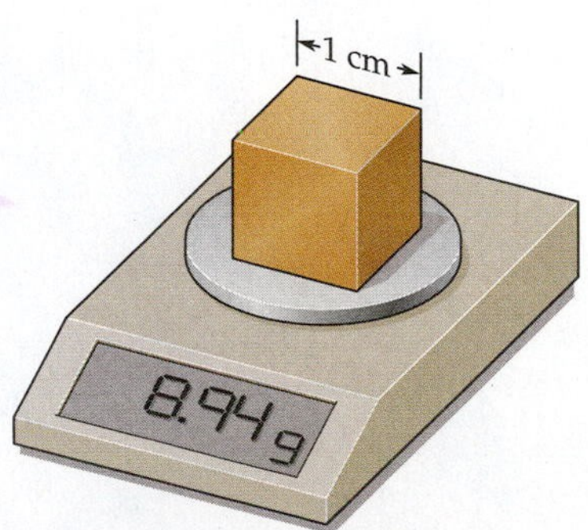

▲ One cubic centimeter of copper weighs 8.94 g, so the density of copper is 8.94 g/cm^3.

Q: *What is the mass of 2 cm^3 of copper? What is the density 2 cm^3 of copper?*

▲**Figure 1.8** At room temperature, the density of water is 1.00 g/mL. A coin sinks in water, but a cork floats on water.

Q: *Is the density of these coins less than, equal to, or greater than 1.00 g/mL? Is the density of the corks less than, equal to, or greater than 1.00 g/mL?*

You can do your own demonstration of a density difference. Make a classic French vinaigrette salad dressing by adding 10 mL of red wine vinegar to 30–40 mL of extra virgin olive oil. Add seasonings such as salt, pepper, oregano, thyme, Dijon mustard, and garlic. Which material, oil or vinegar, forms the top layer? Enjoy!

Table 1.7 Densities of Some Common Substances at Specified Temperatures

Substance*	Density	Temperature
Solids		
Copper (Cu)	8.94 g/cm^3	25 °C
Gold (Au)	19.3 g/cm^3	25 °C
Magnesium (Mg)	1.738 g/cm^3	20 °C
Water (ice) (H_2O)	0.917 g/cm^3	0 °C
Liquids		
Ethanol (CH_3CH_2OH)	0.789 g/mL	20 °C
Hexane ($CH_3CH_2CH_2CH_2CH_2CH_3$)	0.660 g/mL	20 °C
Mercury (Hg)	13.534 g/mL	25 °C
Urine (a mixture)	1.003–1.030 g/mL	25 °C
Water (H_2O)	0.998 g/mL	0 °C
	1.000 g/mL	4 °C
	0.998 g/mL	20 °C

*Formulas are provided for possible future reference.

These equations are useful for calculations. Densities of some common substances are listed in Table 1.7. They are customarily reported in grams per milliliter (g/mL) for liquids and grams per cubic centimeter (g/cm^3) for solids. Values listed in the table are used in some of the following Examples and Exercises and in some of the end-of-chapter problems.

As with problems involving mass, length, area, and volume (page 23), it is often sufficient to estimate answers to problems involving densities, for example, in determining relative volumes of materials or whether or not a material will float or sink in water. Such estimation is illustrated in the following Example and Exercises. Note again that estimation does *not* require a detailed calculation.

Example 1.9 Mass, Volume, and Density

Answer the following without doing detailed calculations. **(a)** Which has the greater volume, a 50.0-g block of copper or a 50.0-g block of gold? **(b)** Which has the greater mass, 225 mL of ethanol or 225 mL of hexane?

Solution

a. From Table 1.7, we see that the density of gold (19.3 g/cm^3) is greater than that of copper (8.94 g/cm^3). A block of copper thus has to be larger in volume than a block of gold of the same mass. A 50.0-g block of copper has a greater volume than a 50.0-g block of gold.

b. From Table 1.7, we see that the density of ethanol (0.789 g/mL) is greater than that of hexane (0.660 g/mL). Because ethanol is more dense (that is, it has more mass in each unit of volume), 225 mL of it has a greater mass than does 225 mL of hexane.

■ EXERCISE 1.9A

Without doing a detailed calculation, determine which has the greater volume, a 500.0-g block of ice or a 500.0-g block of magnesium.

■ EXERCISE 1.9B

Wood does not dissolve in water and will float on water if its density is less than that of water. Padauk ($d = 0.86\ g/cm^3$) and ebony ($d = 1.2\ g/cm^3$) are tropical woods. Which will float on water and which will sink in water? What will padauk and ebony do in ethyl alcohol?

When we need a numerical answer, we can use the relationship of mass and volume to density to form conversion factors. Then we use the unit conversion method of problem solving.

Example 1.10 Density from Mass and Volume

What is the density of iron if 156 g of iron occupies a volume of 20.0 cm^3?

Solution

The given quantities are

$$m = 156 \text{ g} \quad \text{and} \quad V = 20.0 \text{ cm}^3$$

We use the equation that defines density.

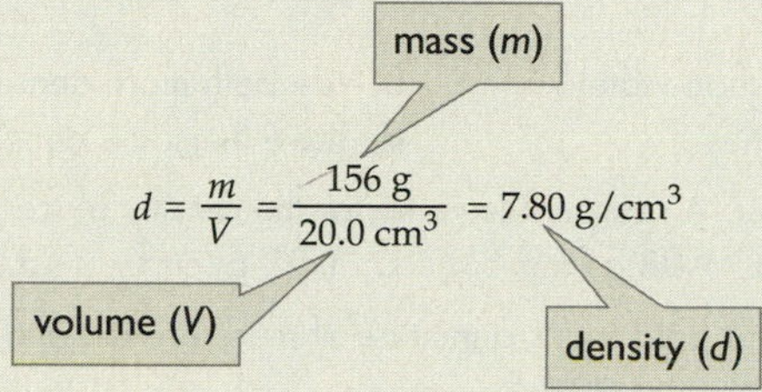

■ EXERCISE 1.10A

What is the density, in grams per milliliter, of a salt solution if 210 mL has a mass of 234 g?

■ EXERCISE 1.10B

What is the density, in grams per cubic centimeter, of a metal alloy if a cube of it that measures 2.00 cm on an edge has a mass of 94.3 g?

Example 1.11 Mass from Density and Volume

What is the mass in grams of 1.00 L of gasoline if its density is 0.703 g/mL?

Solution

We can express the given density as a ratio, 0.703 g/1.00 mL, and use it as a conversion factor. We also need the factor 1000 mL/1 L to convert liters to milliliters.

$$m = d \times V = \frac{0.703 \text{ g}}{1 \text{ mL}} \times 1 \text{ L} \times \frac{1000 \text{ mL}}{1 \text{ L}} = 703 \text{ g}$$

■ EXERCISE 1.11A

What is the mass in grams of 250.0 mL of glycerol, which has a density of 1.264 g/mL at 20 °C?

■ EXERCISE 1.11B

What is the mass in kilograms of the ethanol that fills a 16-gallon "gas tank"? (1 gallon = 3.78 L; also see Table 1.7)

Example 1.12 Volume from Mass and Density

What volume in milliliters is occupied by 461 g of mercury? (See Table 1.7.)

Solution

Here we can express the inverse of the density as a ratio, 1 mL/13.534 g, and use it as a conversion factor.

$$V = 461 \text{ g} \times \frac{1 \text{ mL}}{13.534 \text{ g}} = 34.1 \text{ mL}$$

■ EXERCISE 1.12A

What volume in cubic centimeters is occupied by a 25.8-g piece of magnesium? (See Table 1.7.)

■ EXERCISE 1.12B

You need 875 g of hexane. Will it fit in a 1.00-L container? (See Table 1.7.)

Self-Assessment Questions

1. The density of a wood plank floating on a lake is
a. less than that of air **b.** less than that of water
c. more than that of water **d.** the same as that of water

2. A pebble and a lead sinker both sink when dropped into a pond. This shows that the two objects
a. are both less dense than water **b.** are both more dense than water
c. have different densities **d.** have the same density

3. Ice floats on liquid water. A reasonable value for the density of ice is
a. 0.92 g/cm^3 **b.** 1.08 g/cm^3 **c.** 1.98 g/cm^3 **d.** 4.90 g/cm^3

4. A prospector panning for gold swirls a mixture of mud, gravel, and water in a pan. He looks for gold at the bottom because gold
a. dissolves in water and sinks **b.** has a high density and sinks
c. is less dense than rocks **d.** is repelled by the other minerals

5. Which of the following metals will sink in a pool of mercury (d = 13.534 g/cm^3)?
a. aluminum (d = 2.6 g/cm^3) **b.** iron (d = 7.9 g/cm^3)
c. lead (d = 11.34 g/cm^3) **d.** uranium (d = 19.5 g/cm^3)

6. If the volume of a rock is 80.0 cm^3 and its mass is 160.0 g, its density is
a. 0.03 g/cm^3 **b.** 0.50 g/cm^3 **c.** 2.0 g/cm^3 **d.** 128 g/cm^3

Answers: 1, b; 2, b; 3, a; 4, b; 5, d; 6, c

1.11 Energy: Heat and Temperature

Learning Objectives › Distinguish between heat and temperature. › Explain how the temperature scales are related.

The physical and chemical changes that matter undergoes are almost always accompanied by changes in energy. **Energy** is required to make something happen that wouldn't happen by itself. Energy is the ability to change matter, either physically or chemically.

Two important concepts in science that are related, and sometimes confused, are *temperature* and *heat*. When two objects at different temperatures are brought together, heat flows from the warmer to the cooler object until both are at the same temperature. **Heat** is energy on the move, the energy that flows from a warmer object to a cooler one. **Temperature** is a measure of how hot or cold an object is. Temperature tells us the direction in which heat will flow. Heat flows from more energetic (higher-temperature) to less energetic (lower-temperature) atoms or molecules. For example, if you touch a hot test tube, heat will flow from the tube to your hand. If the tube is hot enough, your hand will be burned.

The SI base unit of temperature is the **kelvin (K)**. For laboratory work, we often use the more familiar **Celsius scale**. On this temperature scale, the freezing point of water is 0 degrees Celsius (°C) and the boiling point is 100 °C. The interval between these two reference points is divided into 100 equal parts, each a *degree Celsius*. The Kelvin scale is called an *absolute scale* because its zero point is the coldest temperature possible, or absolute zero. (This fact was determined by theoretical considerations and has been confirmed by experiment, as we will see in Chapter 6.) The zero point on the Kelvin scale, 0 K, is equal to −273.15 °C, which we often round to −273 °C. A kelvin is the same size as a degree Celsius, so the freezing point of water on the Kelvin scale is 273 K. The Kelvin scale has no negative temperatures, and we don't use a degree sign with the K. To convert from degrees Celsius to kelvins, simply add 273.15 to the Celsius temperature.

$$K = {}^{\circ}C + 273.15$$

Example 1.13 Temperature Conversions

Diethyl ether boils at 36 °C. What is the boiling point of this liquid on the Kelvin scale?

Solution

$$K = {}^{\circ}C + 273.15$$
$$K = 36 + 273.15 = 309\ K$$

■ EXERCISE 1.13A

What is the boiling point of ethanol (78 °C) expressed in kelvins?

■ EXERCISE 1.13B

At atmospheric pressure, liquid nitrogen boils at −196 °C. Express that temperature in kelvins.

The Fahrenheit temperature scale is widely used in the United States. Figure 1.9 compares the three temperature scales. Note that on the Fahrenheit scale, there are 180 Fahrenheit degrees between the freezing point and the boiling point of water. On the Celsius scale there are 100 Celsius degrees between these two points. Thus, one Celsius degree equals 1.8 Fahrenheit degrees. Conversions between Fahrenheit and Celsius temperatures use this relationship, which is discussed in Appendix A.5.

The SI-derived unit of energy is the **joule (J)**, but the **calorie (cal)** is the more familiar unit in everyday life.

$$1\ cal = 4.184\ J$$

A calorie is the amount of heat required to raise the temperature of 1 g of water by 1 °C.

The "calorie" used for expressing the energy content of foods is actually a **kilocalorie (kcal)**.

$$1000\ cal = 1\ kcal = 4184\ J$$

A dieter might be aware that a banana split contains 1500 "calories." If the dieter realized that this was really 1500 *kilo*calories, or 1,500,000 calories, giving up the banana split might be easier! The concept of heat is discussed further in Appendix A.5.

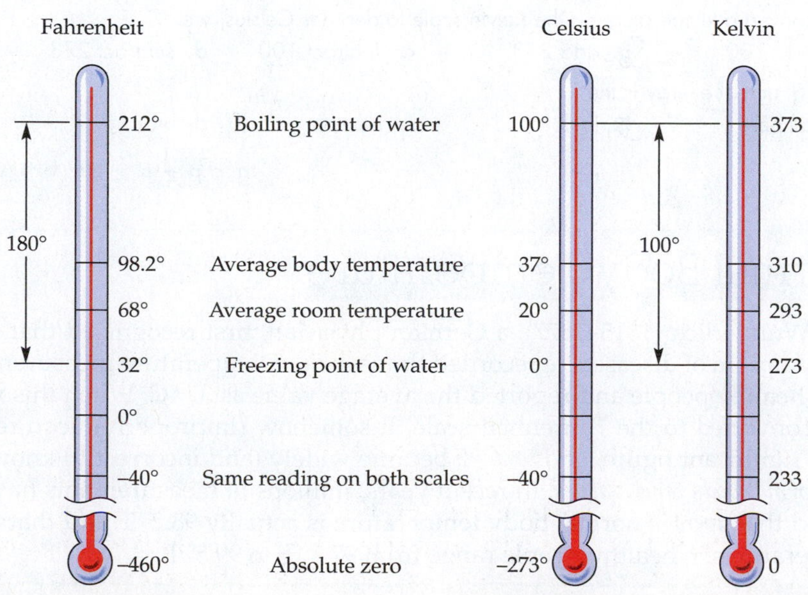

◄ **Figure 1.9** A comparison of the Fahrenheit, Celsius, and Kelvin temperature scales.

▶ **Figure 1.10** Temperature and heat are different phenomena. Both the tub and the pool are at roughly the same temperature—about 40 °C—but it took much more heat to warm the pool to that temperature than it did the tub of water.

Example 1.14 Energy Conversions

When 1.00 g of gasoline burns, it yields about 10.3 kcal of energy. What is this quantity of energy in kilojoules (kJ)?

Solution

$$10.3\ \cancel{\text{kcal}} \times \frac{1000\ \cancel{\text{cal}}}{1\ \cancel{\text{kcal}}} \times \frac{4.184\ \cancel{\text{J}}}{1\ \cancel{\text{cal}}} \times \frac{1\ \text{kJ}}{1000\ \cancel{\text{J}}} = 43.1\ \text{kJ}$$

■ EXERCISE 1.14A

Each day the average European woman consumes food with an energy content of 7525 kJ. What is this daily intake in kilocalories (food calories)?

■ EXERCISE 1.14B

It takes about 12 kJ of energy to melt a single ice cube. How much energy in kilocalories does it take to melt a tray of 12 ice cubes?

Self-Assessment Questions

1. Heat is
   - a. an element
   - b. the energy flow from a hot object to a cold one
   - c. a measure of energy intensity
   - d. a temperature above room temperature
2. The SI scale for temperature is known as the
   - a. Celsius scale
   - b. Fahrenheit scale
   - c. Kelvin scale
   - d. Richter scale
3. Water freezes at
   - a. 0 °C
   - b. 0 °F
   - c. 273 °C
   - d. 373 K
4. To convert a temperature on the Kelvin scale to degrees Celsius, we
   - a. add 100
   - b. add 273
   - c. subtract 100
   - d. subtract 273
5. The SI unit of energy is the
   - a. ampere
   - b. joule
   - c. newton
   - d. watt

Answers: 1, b; 2, c; 3, a; 4, d; 5, b

Normal Body Temperature

Carl Wunderlich (1815–1877), a German physician, first recognized that fever is a symptom of disease. He recorded thousands of temperature measurements from healthy people and reported the average value as 37 °C. When this value was converted to the Fahrenheit scale, it somehow (improperly) acquired an extra significant figure, and 98.6 °F became widely (and incorrectly) known as the *normal body temperature*. In recent years, millions of measurements have revealed that *average* normal body temperature is actually 98.2 °F and that body temperatures in healthy people range from 97.7 °F to 99.5 °F.

GREEN CHEMISTRY

Principles 1, 2, 3, 4, 5, 6, 7, 8, 9, 10, 11, 12

Jennifer L. Young and Robert Peoples, *ACS Green Chemistry Institute®*

Green chemistry is the design of chemical products and processes that reduce or eliminate the generation and use of hazardous substances. To put this definition into practice, chemists follow the twelve principles of green chemistry, which are listed in the inside front cover. Overall, green chemistry is about preventing waste, using nonhazardous chemicals, conserving energy, using renewable resources, and making products that degrade after use. The goal of green chemistry is to minimize the harmful impacts of substances on human health and the environment by using safer alternatives. As you will learn in each chapter, green chemistry applies to all chemistry areas and concepts, and pervades all types of chemistry.

Green chemistry was developed about 20 years ago as a new, holistic way of thinking about chemicals and chemistry—considering the sources of chemicals, where they will end up, and what impact they will have on human beings and the planet. The proven twelve principles are in commercial practice around the world, and a growing number of products on store shelves have been made by green chemistry.

Green chemistry is as rigorous as traditional chemistry. The scientific method involving hypotheses, laws, theories, and models (Section 1.3) still applies in green chemistry. Because some concepts of green chemistry are still relatively new, especially compared to other chemistry ideas that have been around for centuries, many students and even professional chemists are learning about green chemistry for the first time. Green chemistry is a hard science and a new science that will be critical for developing future technologies that are safe for people and the planet.

This chapter discusses the risk associated with science (Section 1.5). Risk includes both hazard and exposure; reducing either one reduces risk. Protective equipment and other safety measures can prevent exposure of workers, the public, and the environment to hazardous chemicals. However, there is always a possibility that the protection will fail (because of human error or acts of nature), causing exposure to the materials. Green chemistry, on the other hand, aims to dramatically reduce risk by using chemicals that are inherently safer and less hazardous. When selecting chemicals to use in a product or process, chemists consider the physical and chemical properties (Section 1.7). Green chemists also evaluate other properties, including toxicity toward human beings and degradability in the environment.

The world faces a growing number of environmental problems, some of which have been caused by chemicals. However, green chemistry can provide solutions and minimize future problems by avoiding hazardous materials and preventing pollution. You will read about many green chemistry technologies and solutions throughout this book. Each chapter contains a green chemistry essay that presents some of the latest technologies in areas such as biofuels, plastics, medicine, and food.

Many companies are using green chemistry to design new products and processes. Companies that make or use chemicals are choosing to use less energy, create less waste, and select chemicals and solvents that are less hazardous. They are making these decisions based on green chemistry, not only because it's the right thing to do but also because these actions save money and make good business sense. Between 1996 and 2011, 82 professors, small businesses, and large companies were presented with the Presidential Green Chemistry Challenge Award (PGCCA). These awards have recognized advances in pest control, plastics, medicines, fuel, paints, electronics, textiles, cosmetics, cleaning products, and a wide range of other areas that depend on chemistry. Several of the award-winning technologies are featured throughout this book.

The future of this planet and its growing number of inhabitants will all depend on clean energy, water, air, food, medicine, and technology. You can contribute to sustainability through the products you purchase, recycling, conserving energy, and even through your career choices. Green chemistry is essential to a sustainable future!

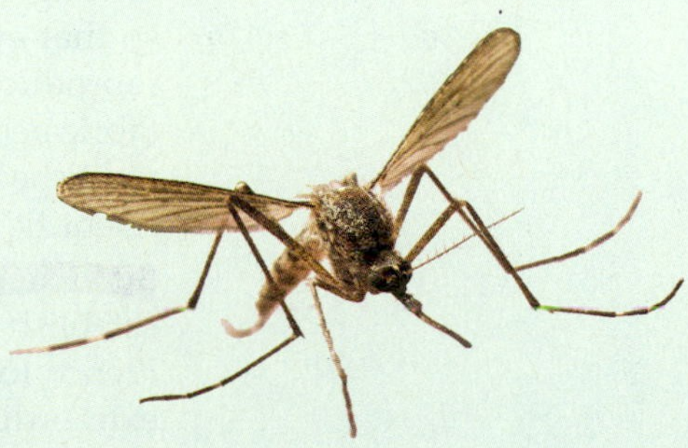

▲ Natular™ is a greener mosquito larvicide, developed by Clarke, for which the company won a 2010 PGCCA. Mosquitoes are much more than a summer annoyance; they spread malaria, yellow fever, and other diseases, and their control is a huge issue worldwide. Natular™ is a new, environmentally more responsible weapon in this control.

1.12 Critical Thinking

Learning Objective › Use critical thinking to evaluate claims and statements.

One of the hallmarks of science is the ability to think critically—to evaluate statements and claims in a rational, objective fashion. For example, a diet-plan advertisement shows people who have lost a lot of weight. Somewhere in the ad, in tiny print, you may find a statement such as "results may vary" or "results not typical." Such ads also often advise combining the plan with diet and exercise. Does an ad like this prove that a diet plan works? You can use critical thinking to evaluate the ad's claim. Critical thinking involves gathering facts, assessing them, using logic to reach a conclusion, and then evaluating the conclusion. The ability to think critically can be learned, and it will serve you well in everyday life as well as in science courses. Critical thinking is important for workers in all types of professions and employees in all kinds of industries. We will use an approach adapted from one developed by James Lett.[1] This approach is outlined below and followed by several examples.

You can use the acronym **FLaReS** (ignore the vowels) to remember four principles used to test a claim: *f*alsifiability, *l*ogic, *r*eplicability, and *s*ufficiency.

- **Falsifiability:** Can any conceivable evidence show the claim to be false? It must be possible to think of evidence that would prove the claim false. A hypothesis that cannot be falsified is of no value. Science cannot prove anything true in an absolute sense, although it can provide overwhelming evidence. Science *can* prove something false.
- **Logic:** Any argument offered as evidence in support of a claim must be sound. An argument is sound if its conclusion follows inevitably from its premises and if its premises are true. It is unsound if a premise is false, and it is unsound if there is a single exception in which the conclusion does not necessarily follow from the premises.
- **Replicability:** If the evidence for a claim is based on an experimental result, it is necessary that the evidence be replicable in subsequent experiments or trials. Scientific research is almost always reviewed by other qualified scientists. The peer-reviewed research is then published in a form that enables others to repeat the experiment. Sometimes bad science slips through the peer-review process, but such results eventually fail the test of replicability. For example, in May 2005 the journal *Science* published research by Korean biomedical scientist Hwang Woo-suk in which he claimed to have tailored embryonic stem cells so that every patient could receive custom treatment. Others were unable to reproduce Hwang's findings, and evidence emerged that he had intentionally fabricated results. *Science* retracted the article in January 2006. Research results published in media that are not peer reviewed have little or no standing in the scientific community—nor should you rely on them.
- **Sufficiency:** The evidence offered in support of a claim must be adequate to establish the truth of that claim, with these stipulations: (1) The burden of evidence for any claim rests on the claimant, (2) extraordinary claims demand extraordinary evidence, and (3) evidence based on an authority figure or on testimony is never adequate.

If a claim passes all four FLaReS tests, then it *might* be true. On the other hand, it could still be proven false. However, if a claim fails even one of the FLaReS tests, it is likely to be false. The FLaReS method is a good starting point for evaluating the myriad claims that you will find on the Internet and elsewhere.We apply one or more of the FLaReS principles to evaluate a claim in each of the following examples.

[1]Lett used the acronym FiLCHeRS (ignore the vowels) as a mnemonic for six rules: *f*alsifiability, *l*ogic, *c*omprehensiveness, *h*onesty, *r*eplicability, and *s*ufficiency. See Lett, James, "A Field Guide to Critical Thinking," *The Skeptical Inquirer*, Winter 1990, pp. 153–160.

CRITICAL THINKING  EXAMPLES

1.1 A practitioner claims outstanding success in curing cancer with a vaccine made from a patient's own urine. However, the vaccine works only if the patient's immune system is still sufficiently strong. Is the claim falsifiable?

Solution

No. The practitioner can always say that the patient's immune system was no longer sufficiently strong.

1.2 A website claims, "The medical-industrial complex suppresses natural treatments because they cure the patient. A cured patient no longer needs a doctor, and the doctor loses income." Is the claim logical?

Solution

No. Doctors do not cure all patients. Many remain ill and some die.

1.3 Many "psychics" claim to be able to predict the future. These predictions are often made near the end of one year and concern the next year. Apply all the FLaReS tests to evaluate this claim.

Solution

1. Is the claim falsifiable? Yes. You could write down a prediction and then check it yourself at the end of the year.
2. Is the claim logical? No. If psychics could really predict the future, they could readily win lotteries, ward off all kinds of calamities by providing advance warning, and so on.
3. Is the claim reproducible? No. Psychics often make broad, general predictions, such as "tornadoes will hit Oklahoma in April and May." (It would be a rare year when there were no tornadoes in Oklahoma in those months.) The psychics later make claim-specific references to "hits" while ignoring "misses." Here are some past predictions of Sylvia Browne, a self-proclaimed world-famous psychic: Bill Bradley would be elected U.S. president in 2000; Michael Jackson would be found guilty in his 2005 child molestation trial (he was acquitted); a cure for breast cancer would be found by the end of 1999. None of the well-known psychics, including Browne, James Van Praagh, John Edward, and the Jamison sisters (Terry and Linda), predicted the terrorist attacks on the United States on September 11, 2001.
4. Is the claim sufficient? No. Any such claim is extraordinary; it would require extraordinary evidence. The burden of proof for the claim rests on the claimant.

CRITICAL THINKING EXERCISES

Apply knowledge that you have gained in this chapter and one or more of the FLaReS principles to evaluate the following statements or claims.

1.1 An alternative health practitioner claims that a nuclear power plant releases radiation at a level so low that it cannot be measured, but that this radiation is harmful to the thyroid gland. He sells a thyroid extract that he claims can prevent the problem.

1.2 A doctor claims that she can cure a patient of arthritis by simply massaging the affected joints. If she has the patient's complete trust, she can cure the arthritis within a year. Several of her patients have testified that the doctor has cured their arthritis.

1.3 German physicist Jan Hendrik Schön of Bell Labs claimed in 2001 that he had produced a molecular scale transistor. Others scientists noted that his data contained irregularities. Attempts to perform experiments similar to Schön's did not give similar results.

1.4 A mercury-containing preservative called thiomersal was used to prevent bacterial and fungal contamination in vaccines from the 1930s until its use was phased out starting in 1999. In the United States, a widespread concern arose that these vaccines caused autism. There was no such concern in the United Kingdom, although the vaccine with the same preservative was used there. Is the concern valid?

1.5 A woman claims that she has memorized the New Testament. She offers to quote any chapter of any book entirely from memory.

1.6 The label on a bag of Morton solar salt crystals has the statement "No chemicals or additives."

SUMMARY

Section 1.1—**Technology** is the practical application of knowledge, while **science** is an accumulation of knowledge about nature and our physical world along with our explanations of that knowledge. The roots of chemistry lie in **natural philosophy**, philosophical speculation about nature, and in **alchemy**, a mixture of chemistry and magic practiced in Europe in the Middle Ages.

Section 1.2—**Green chemistry** uses materials and processes that are intended to prevent or reduce pollution at its source. **Sustainable chemistry** is designed to meet the needs of the present generation without compromising the needs of future generations.

Section 1.3—Science is *reproducible, testable, predictive, explanatory,* and *tentative.* In one common scientific method, a set of confirmed observations about nature may lead to a **hypothesis**—a tentative explanation of the observations. A **scientific law** is a brief statement that summarizes large amounts of data. If a hypothesis stands up to testing and further experimentation, it may become a **theory**—the best current explanation for a phenomenon. A theory is always tentative and can be rejected if it does not continue to stand up to further testing. A valid theory can be used to predict new scientific facts. Scientists disagree over social and political issues partly because of the inability to control **variables**, factors that can change during an experiment.

Section 1.4—Science and technology have provided many benefits for our world, but they have also introduced new risks. A **risk–benefit analysis** can help us decide which outweighs the other.

Section 1.5—Chemistry is fundamental to other scientific disciplines and plays a central role in society and daily life.

Section 1.6—Most chemists are involved in some kind of research. The purpose of **applied research** is to make useful products or to solve a particular problem, while **basic research** is carried out simply to obtain new knowledge or to answer a fundamental question. Basic research often also leads to a useful product or process.

Section 1.7—**Chemistry** is the study of matter and the changes it undergoes. **Matter** is anything that has mass and takes up space. **Mass** is a measure of the amount of matter in an object, while **weight** represents the gravitational force of attraction for an object. **Physical properties** of matter can be observed without making new substances. When **chemical properties** are observed, new substances are formed. A **physical change** does not entail a change in chemical composition. A **chemical change** does involve such a change.

Section 1.8—Matter can be classified according to physical state. A **solid** has definite shape and volume. A **liquid** has definite volume but takes the shape of its container. A **gas** takes both the shape and the volume of its container. Matter also can be classified according to composition. A **substance** always has the same composition, no matter how it is made or where it is found. A **mixture** can have different compositions depending on how it is prepared. Substances are either elements or compounds. An **element** is composed of atoms of one type, an **atom** being the smallest characteristic particle of an element. There are over a hundred elements, each of which is represented by a **chemical symbol** consisting of one or two letters derived from the element's name. A **compound** is made up of two or more elements, chemically combined in a fixed ratio. Most compounds exist as **molecules**, groups of atoms bound together as a unit.

Section 1.9—Scientific measurements are expressed with **SI units**, which comprise an agreed-on standard version of the metric system. Base units include the **kilogram (kg)** for mass and the **meter (m)** for length. Although it is not the SI standard unit of volume, the **liter (L)** is widely used. Prefixes make basic units larger or smaller by factors of ten.

Section 1.10—**Density** can be thought of as "how heavy something is for its size." It is the amount of mass per unit volume.

$$d = \frac{m}{V}$$

Density can be used as a conversion factor. The density of water is almost exactly 1 g/mL.

Section 1.11—When matter undergoes a physical or chemical change, a change in **energy** is involved. Energy is the *ability* to cause these changes. **Heat** is energy flow from a warmer object to a cooler one. **Temperature** is a measure of how hot or cold an object is. The **kelvin (K)** is the SI base unit of temperature, but the **Celsius scale (°C)** is more commonly used. On the Celsius scale, water boils at 100 °C and freezes at 0 °C. The SI unit of heat is the **joule (J)**. A more familiar unit, the **calorie (cal)**, is the amount of heat needed to raise the temperature of 1 g of water by 1 °C. The food "calorie" is actually a **kilocalorie (kcal)**, or 1000 calories.

Section 1.12—Claims may be tested by applying critical thinking. The acronym **FLaReS** represents four principles used to test a claim: *f*alsifiability, *l*ogic, *r*eplicability, and *s*ufficiency.

Green chemistry Green chemistry means preventing waste, using nonhazardous chemicals and renewable resources, conserving energy, and making products that degrade after use. Developed about 20 years ago, green chemistry takes into account the sources and ultimate destinations of chemicals, and the impact they will have on humans and the planet.

Learning Objectives

› Distinguish science from technology. (1.1)	Problem 1
› Define *alchemy* and *natural philosophy*. (1.1)	Problems 43, 44
› Briefly describe the contributions of Bacon, Galileo, and Carson to the perceptions of science. (1.2)	Problem 2
› Define *hypothesis, scientific law, theory,* and *scientific model*, and explain their relationships in science. (1.3)	Problems 3, 71, 72, 74, 75

› Define *risk* and *benefit*, and give an example of each. (1.4)	Problem 5
› Estimate a desirability quotient from benefit and risk data. (1.4)	Problems 7, 13–18
› Give an example of a use of chemistry in your daily life and in society at large. (1.5)	Problems 15, 72
› Distinguish basic research from applied research. (1.6)	Problems 8, 9
› Differentiate: mass and weight; physical and chemical change; and physical and chemical properties. (1.7)	Problems 29–32
› Classify matter in three ways. (1.8)	Problems 33–44
› Assign proper units of measurement to observations, and manipulate units in conversions. (1.9)	Problems 10–12, 19–28, 45–52, 69, 70, 73, 78–80
› Calculate the density, mass, or volume of an object given the other two quantities. (1.10)	Problems 53–64, 76, 77, 81–83, 85–88
› Distinguish between heat and temperature. (1.11)	Problems 67, 68
› Explain how the temperature scales are related. (1.11)	Problems 65, 66
› Use critical thinking to evaluate claims and statements. (1.12)	Problem 6, Critical Thinking 1.1–1.6
› Define green chemistry.	Problem 89
› Describe how green chemistry reduces risk and prevents environmental problems.	Problems 90–92

REVIEW QUESTIONS

1. State five distinguishing characteristics of science. Which characteristic best serves to distinguish science from other disciplines?
2. Why is Galileo regarded by some as the father of modern science?
3. Why can't scientific methods always be used to solve social, political, ethical, and economic problems?
4. How does technology differ from science?
5. What is risk–benefit analysis?
6. What sorts of judgments go into **(a)** the evaluation of benefits and **(b)** the evaluation of risks?
7. What is a DQ? What does a large DQ mean? Why is it often difficult to estimate a DQ?
8. What derived units of **(a)** mass and **(b)** length are commonly used in the laboratory?
9. What is the SI-derived unit for volume? What volume units are more often used in the laboratory?
10. Following is an incomplete table of SI prefixes, their symbols, and their meanings. Fill in the blank cells. The first row is completed as an example.

Prefix	Symbol	Definition
tera-	T	10^{12}
______	M	______
centi-	______	______
______	μ	______
milli-	______	______
______	______	10^{-1}
______	K	______
nano-	______	______

11. Identify the following research projects as either applied or basic.
    a. A Virginia Tech chemist tests a method for analyzing coal powder in less than a minute, before the powder goes into a coal-fired energy plant.
    b. A Purdue engineer develops a method for causing aluminum to react with water to generate hydrogen for automobiles.
    c. A worker at University of Illinois Urbana-Champaign examines the behavior of atoms at high temperatures and low pressures.
12. Identify the following work as either applied research or basic research.
    a. An engineer determines the strength of a titanium alloy that will be used to construct notebook-computer cases.
    b. A biochemist runs experiments to determine how oxygen binds to the blood cells of lobsters.
    c. A biologist determines the number of eagles that nest annually in Kentucky's Land Between the Lakes area over a six-year period.

PROBLEMS

A Word of Advice *You cannot learn to work problems by reading them or by watching your instructor work them, just as you cannot become a piano player solely by reading about piano-playing skills or by attending performances. Working problems will help you improve your understanding of the ideas presented in the chapter and your ability to synthesize concepts as well as allow you to practice your estimation skills. Plan to work through the great majority of these problems.*

Risk–Benefit Analysis

13. Penicillin kills bacteria, thus saving the lives of thousands of people who otherwise might die of infectious diseases. Penicillin causes allergic reactions in some people, which can lead to death if the resulting condition is not treated. Do a risk–benefit analysis of the use of penicillin by society as a whole.
14. Do a risk–benefit analysis of the use of penicillin by a person who is allergic to it. (See Problem 13.)
15. Paints used on today's automobiles are often composed of two components and harden several hours after mixing. One component is an *isocyanate* that can sensitize a person, causing an allergic reaction, if it is breathed (even in small amounts) over a long time period. Do a risk-benefit analysis of the use of these paints by **(a)** an automotive factory worker and **(b)** a hobbyist who is restoring a 1965 Mustang. How might the DQ for both of these people be increased?
16. X-rays are widely used in medicine and dentistry. Do a risk-benefit analysis for **(a)** a dental patient who has one set of x-rays done per year and **(b)** a dentist who stays in the room with a patient while x-rays are taken, three times each day.
17. Synthetic food colorings make food more attractive and increase sales. A few such dyes are suspected *carcinogens* (cancer inducers). Who derives most of the benefits from the use of food colorings? Who assumes most of the risk associated with use of these dyes?
18. The virus called HIV causes AIDS, a devastating and often deadly disease. Several drugs are available to treat HIV infection, but all are expensive. Used separately and in combination, these drugs have resulted in a huge drop in AIDS deaths. An expensive new drug shows promise for treating HIV/AIDS patients, especially in preventing passage of the HIV virus from a pregnant woman to her fetus. What is the DQ for administering this drug to **(a)** a man who thinks he may be infected with HIV, **(b)** a pregnant woman who is HIV positive, and **(c)** an unborn child whose mother has AIDS?

Mass and Weight

19. Which are realistic masses for a cellular telephone and a laptop computer, respectively?

    100 mg, 100 g   100 g, 100 mg   100 g, 2 kg   1 kg, 2 kg

20. In Europe, A2 sized paper measures 594 mm × 420 mm. Is this larger or smaller than the standard 8½ in. × 11 in. paper used in the United States?
21. Two samples are weighed under identical conditions in a laboratory. Sample A weighs 1.00 lb and Sample B weighs 2.00 lb. Does Sample B have twice the mass of Sample A?
22. Sample X on the moon has exactly the same mass as Sample Y on Earth. Do the two samples weigh the same? Explain.

Length, Area, and Volume

23. Which of the following is a reasonable volume for a teacup?

    25 mL   250 mL   2.5 L   25 L

24. Which of the following is a reasonable approximation for the area of a credit card?

    $4\ cm^2$ $40\ cm^2$ $400\ cm^2$ $4\ m^2$

25. Earth's oceans contain $3.50 \times 10^8\ mi^3$ of water and cover an area of $1.40 \times 10^8\ mi^2$. What is the volume of ocean water in cubic kilometers?
26. What is the area of Earth's oceans in square kilometers? See Problem 25.
27. Consider the two tubes shown below. The aluminum tube has an outside diameter of 0.998 in. and an inside diameter of 0.782 in. Without doing a detailed calculation, determine whether the aluminum tube will fit inside another aluminum tube with an inside diameter of 26.3 mm.

28. Which one(s) of the following could be the inside diameter of the paper tube shown above (with Problem 27): 19.9 mm; 24.9 mm, 18.7 mm?

Physical and Chemical Properties and Changes

29. Identify the following as physical or chemical properties.
    a. Zinc metal can be shaped into many different forms by hammering.
    b. Silver metal tarnishes, forming black silver sulfide.
    c. Sodium metal is soft enough to cut with a butter knife.
    d. Gold melts at 1064 °C.
30. Identify the following as physical or chemical properties.
    a. Milk chocolate melts in the mouth.
    b. A laser printer prints faster than an inkjet printer.
    c. Titanium chips burn with a brilliant white light.
    d. Yogurt is made by allowing a bacterial culture to ferment in warm milk.

31. Identify the following changes as physical or chemical.
    a. Bits of yellow plastic are melted and forced into a mold to make a yellow toy.
    b. Waste oil from restaurants is converted to biodiesel fuel that burns differently from cooking oil.
    c. Orange juice is prepared by adding three cans of water to one can of orange-juice concentrate.

32. Identify the following changes as physical or chemical.
    a. Bacteria are killed by chlorine added to a swimming pool.
    b. Brown print is created in an inkjet printer by mixing cyan, magenta, and yellow inks.
    c. Sugar is dissolved in water to make syrup.

Substances and Mixtures

33. Identify each of the following as a substance or a mixture.
    a. helium gas used to fill a balloon
    b. the juice squeezed from an orange
    c. distilled water
    d. carbon dioxide gas

34. Identify each of the following as a substance or a mixture.
    a. hydrogen peroxide, H_2O_2
    b. oxygen
    c. smog
    d. a carrot
    e. blueberry pancakes
    f. cellophane tape

35. Which of the following mixtures are homogeneous and which are heterogeneous?
    a. copper water pipe b. distilled water
    c. liquid oxygen d. chicken noodle soup

36. Which of the following mixtures are homogeneous and which are heterogeneous?
    a. gasoline
    b. Italian salad dressing
    c. rice pudding
    d. an intravenous glucose solution

37. Every sample of the sugar glucose (no matter where on Earth it comes from) consists of 8 parts (by mass) oxygen, 6 parts carbon, and 1 part hydrogen. Is glucose a substance or a mixture? Explain.

38. An advertisement for shampoo says, "Pure shampoo, with nothing artificial added." Is this shampoo a substance or a mixture? Explain.

Elements and Compounds

39. Which of the following represent elements and which represent compounds?
    a. H b. He c. HF d. Hf

40. Which of the following represent elements and which represent compounds?
    a. Li b. CO c. Cf d. CF_4

41. Without consulting tables, name each of the following.
    a. Al b. Ca c. Cl d. Ag

42. Without consulting tables, write a symbol for each of the following.
    a. oxygen b. phosphorus
    c. sodium d. helium

43. In his 1789 textbook, *Traité élémentaire de Chimie*, Antoine Lavoisier (Chapter 2) listed 33 known elements, one of which was baryte. Which of the following observations best shows that baryte cannot be an element?
    a. Baryte is insoluble in water.
    b. Baryte melts at 1580 °C.
    c. Baryte has a density of 4.48 g/cm^3.
    d. Baryte is formed in hydrothermal veins and around hot springs.
    e. Baryte is formed as a solid when sulfuric acid and barium hydroxide are mixed.
    f. Baryte is formed as a sole product when a particular metal is burned in oxygen.

44. In 1774 Joseph Priestley isolated a gas that he called "dephlogisticated air." Which of the following observations best shows that dephlogisticated air is an element?
    a. Dephlogisticated air combines with charcoal to form "fixed air."
    b. Dephlogisticated air combines with "inflammable air" to form water.
    c. Dephlogisticated air combines with a metal to form a solid called a "calx."
    d. Dephlogisticated air has never been separated into simpler substances.
    e. Dephlogisticated air and "mephitic air" are the main components of the atmosphere.

The Metric System: Measurement and Unit Conversion

45. Change the unit for each of the following measurements by replacing the power of ten with an appropriate SI prefix.
    a. 8.01×10^{-6} g b. 7.9×10^{-3} L
    c. 1.05×10^{3} m

46. Use exponential notation to express each of the following measurements in terms of an SI base unit.
    a. 45 mg b. 125 ns c. 10.7 μL

47. Carry out the following conversions.
    a. 37.4 mL to L b. 1.55×10^2 km to m
    c. 0.198 g to mg d. 1.19 m^2 to cm^2
    e. 78 μs to ms

48. Carry out the following conversions.
    a. 546 mm to m
    b. 65 ns to μs
    c. 87.6 mg to kg
    d. 46.3 dm^3 to L
    e. 181 pm to μm

49. Indicate which is the larger unit in each pair.
    a. mm or cm b. kg or g c. dL or μL

50. Indicate which is the larger unit in each pair.
    a. L or cm^3 b. dm^3 or mL c. μs or ps

51. How many millimeters are there in 1.00 cm? In 1.83 m?

52. How many milliliters are there in 1.00 cm^3? In 15.3 cm^3?

Density

(You may need data from Table 1.7 for some of these problems.)

53. What is the density, in grams per milliliter, of **(a)** a salt solution if 37.5 mL has a mass of 43.75 g and **(b)** 2.75 L of the liquid glycerol, which has a mass of 3465 g?

54. What is the density, in grams per milliliter, of **(a)** a sulfuric acid solution if 10.00 mL has a mass of 15.04 g and **(b)** a 10.0-cm^3 block of plastic with a mass of 9.23 g?

55. What is the mass, in grams, of **(a)** 125 mL of castor oil, a laxative, which has a density of 0.962 g/mL and **(b)** 477 mL of blood plasma, with $d = 1.027$ g/mL?

56. What is the mass, in grams, of **(a)** 30.0 mL of the liquid propylene glycol, a moisturizing agent for foods, which has a density of 1.036 g/mL at 25 °C and **(b)** 1.000 L of mercury at 25 °C?

57. What is the volume of **(a)** 227 g of hexane (in milliliters) and **(b)** a 454-g block of ice (in cubic centimeters)?

58. What is the volume of **(a)** a 475-g piece of copper (in cubic centimeters) and **(b)** a 253-g sample of mercury (in milliliters)?

59. Suppose you put 40 mL of mercury, 40 mL of hexane, and 80 mL of water in the 250-mL beaker shown here. The three liquids do not mix with one another. Provide a sketch that shows the relative locations and depths of the three liquids in the container.

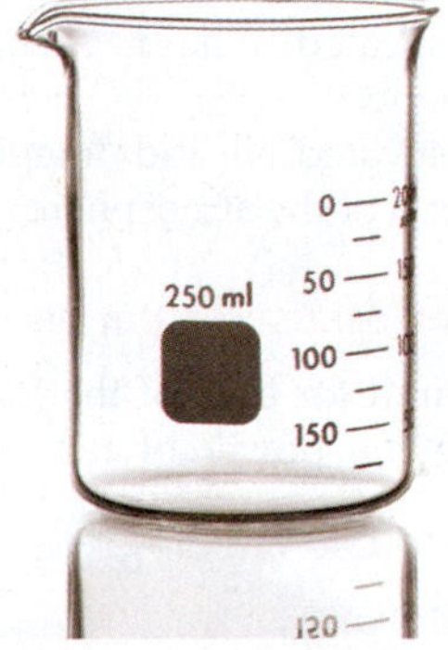

60. A piece of red maple wood ($d = 0.49$ g/cm^3), a piece of balsa wood ($d = 0.11$ g/cm^3), a copper coin, a gold coin, and a piece of ice are dropped into the mixture of Problem 59. Where will each solid end up in the beaker?

61. A metal stand specifies a maximum load of 450 lb. Will it support an aquarium that weighs 59.5 lb and is filled with 37.9 L of seawater ($d = 1.03$ g/mL)?

62. E85 fuel is a mixture of 85% ethanol and 15% gasoline by volume. What mass in kilograms of E85 ($d = 0.758$ g/mL) can be contained in a 14.0-gal tank?

63. An artist wants to produce a pot with a mass of 2.45 kg. She starts with wet clay that loses 10.9% of its mass after firing. The wet clay has a density of 1.60 g/cm^3. What should be the diameter of a sphere of wet clay that she starts with? (*Hint*: The volume of a sphere is $4\pi r^3/3$ where r is the radius.)

64. Air has an average density of about 1.29 g/L. What is the mass in grams of the air inside a car that has a volume of about 2550 L?

Energy: Heat and Temperature

65. Convert 195 K to degrees Celsius.

66. Normal body temperature is about 37 °C. What is this temperature in kelvins?

67. The label on a 100-mL container of orange juice packaged in New Zealand reads in part, "energy . . . 161 kJ." What is that value in kilocalories (food "calories")?

68. To vaporize 1.00 g of sweat (water) from your skin, the water must absorb 584 calories. What is that value in kilojoules?

ADDITIONAL PROBLEMS

69. A certain chemistry class is 1.00 microcentury (μcen) long. What is its length in minutes?

70. A unit of beauty, a *helen*, thought to have been invented by British mathematician W.A.H. Rushton, is based on Helen of Troy (from Christopher Marlowe's translation of Homer's *Iliad*), who is widely known as having "the face that launched a thousand ships." How many ships could be launched by a face with 1.00 millihelen of beauty?

71. English chemist William Henry studied the amounts of gases absorbed by water at different temperatures and under different pressures. In 1803, he stated a formula, $p = k_{H}c$, which related the concentration of the dissolved gas at a constant temperature to the partial pressure of that gas in equilibrium with that liquid. This relationship describes a scientific
    a. hypothesis
    b. law
    c. observation
    d. theory

72. Which of the following activities involve chemistry?
    a. cooking breakfast
    b. eating breakfast
    c. riding a bicycle to classes
    d. working on a laptop computer
    e. sleeping

73. American writer Cullen Murphy coined a unit of fame, the warhol, based on artist Andy Warhol's claim that "everyone will be famous for fifteen minutes."

$$1 \text{ warhol} = 15 \text{ min of fame}$$

Entertainer Herbert Khaury (stage name Tiny Tim) was famous, starting in 1962, for about 200 kilowarhols. How long was that in years?

For Problems 74 and 75, classify each of the numbered statements as (a) an experiment, (b) a hypothesis, (c) a scientific law, (d) an observation, or (e) a theory. (It is not necessary to understand the science involved to do these problems.)

74. Many scientific advances of the nineteenth century came from the study of gases. (1) For example, Joseph Gay-Lussac reacted hydrogen and oxygen to produce water vapor and he reacted nitrogen and oxygen to form either dinitrogen oxide (N_2O) or nitrogen monoxide (NO). Gay-Lussac found that hydrogen and oxygen react in a 2:1 volume ratio and that nitrogen and oxygen can react in 2:1 or 1:1 volume ratios, depending on the product. (2) In 1808 Gay-Lussac published a paper in which he stated that the relative volumes of gases in a chemical reaction are present in the ratio of small integers provided that all gases are measured at the same temperature and pressure. (3) In 1811 Amedeo Avogadro proposed that equal volumes of all gases measured at the same temperature and pressure contain the same number of molecules. (4) By the middle of the century, Rudolf Clausius, James Clerk Maxwell, and others had developed a detailed rationalization of the behavior of gases in terms of molecular motions.

75. Potassium bromate acts as a conditioner in flour dough. Flour contains a protein called *gluten*. Proteins consist of amino-acid units linked in long chains. (1) Dough to which potassium bromate has been added rises better, producing a lighter, larger volume loaf. (2) Potassium bromate acts by oxidizing the gluten and cross-linking tyrosine (an amino acid) units of the protein molecules, enabling the dough to retain gas better. (3) A scientist wonders if sodium bromate might cross-link separate tyrosine molecules, forming a dimer (a molecule consisting of two subunits). (4) She adds sodium bromate to a solution of tyrosine. (5) She notes that a precipitate (solid falling out of solution) is formed.

76. A glass container weighs 48.462 g. A sample of 8.00 mL of antifreeze solution is added, and the container and the antifreeze together weigh 60.562 g. Calculate the density of the antifreeze solution.

77. A rectangular block of balsa wood ($d = 0.11 \text{ g/cm}^3$) measures 7.6 cm $\times$ 7.6 cm $\times$ 94 cm. What is the mass of the block in grams?

78. Arrange the following in order of increasing length (shortest first): (1) a 1.21-m chain, (2) a 75-in. board, (3) a 3-ft 5-in. rattlesnake, (4) a yardstick.

79. Arrange the following in order of increasing mass (lightest first): (1) a 5-lb bag of potatoes, (2) a 1.65-kg cabbage, (3) 2500 g of sugar.

80. One of the people in the photo has a mass of 47.2 kg and a height of 1.53 m. Which one is it likely to be?

81. Some metal chips having a volume of 3.29 cm^3 are placed on a piece of paper and weighed. The combined mass is found to be 18.43 g. The paper itself weighs 1.21 g. Calculate the density of the metal.

82. A 10.5-inch (26.7-cm) iron skillet has a mass of 7.00 lb (3180 g). How many cubic centimeters of iron does it contain? (See Table 1.7.)

83. A 5.79-mg piece of gold is hammered into gold leaf of uniform thickness with an area of 44.6 cm^2. What is the thickness of the gold leaf? (See Table 1.7.)

84. Suppose that you were assigned to determine the effect of saturated fat intake in mice. List three specific variables that would exist in such an experiment, and suggest a way to minimize each variable.

85. What is the mass, in metric tons, of a cube of gold that is 36.1 cm on each side? (1 metric ton = 1000 kg) (See Table 1.7.)

86. A collection of gold-colored metal beads has a mass of 425 g. The volume of the beads is found to be 48.0 cm^3. Using the given densities and those in Table 1.7, identify the metal: bronze ($d = 9.87 \text{ g/cm}^3$), copper, gold, or nickel silver ($d = 8.86 \text{ g/cm}^3$).

87. The density of a planet can be approximated from its radius and estimated mass. Calculate the approximate average density, in grams per cubic centimeter, of **(a)** Jupiter, which has a radius of about 7.0×10^4 km and a mass of 1.9×10^{27} kg; **(b)** Earth, radius of 6.4×10^3 km and mass of 5.98×10^{24} kg; and **(c)** Saturn, radius 5.82×10^4 km and mass of 5.68×10^{26} kg. The volume of a sphere is $4\pi r^3/3$ where r = radius. How does the density of each planet compare to that of water?

88. The extrasolar planet HAT-P-1 orbits a star 450 light-years from Earth. The planet has about half the mass of Jupiter, and its radius is about 1.38 times that of Jupiter (see Problem 87). Calculate the approximate average density, in grams per cubic centimeter, of HAT-P-1. How does this density compare to that of water?

89. Define green chemistry.

90. List six of the Twelve Principles of Green Chemistry.

91. How does green chemistry reduce risk? (choose one)
   a. by reducing hazard and exposure
   b. by avoiding the use of chemicals
   c. by increasing exposures to higher levels
   d. by reducing human errors

92. For companies implementing green chemistry, how does green chemistry save money?
   a. by lowering costs
   b. by using less energy
   c. by creating less waste
   d. all of the above

COLLABORATIVE GROUP PROJECTS

Prepare a PowerPoint, poster, or other presentation (as directed by your instructor) to share with the class.

1. The Global University Leadership Forum has developed a Sustainable Campus Charter by which a school's core mission is aligned with sustainable development, facilities, research, and education. Is your school committed to sustainability? If so, in what way is it working toward sustainability? If not, consult with administrative, faculty, and student groups on how to get such a program started.

2. Prepare a brief biographical report on one of the following.
   a. Francis Bacon
   b. Rachel Carson
   c. Galileo
   d. George Washington Carver

(The following problem is best done in a group of four students.)

3. Make copies of the following form. Student 1 should write a word from the list in the first column of the form and its definition in the second column. Then, she or he should fold the first column under to hide the word and pass the sheet to Student 2, who uses the definition to determine what word was defined and place that word in the third column. Student 2 then folds the second column under to hide it and passes the sheet to Student 3, who writes a definition for the word in the third column and then folds the third column under and passes the form to Student 4. Finally, Student 4 writes the word corresponding to the definition given by Student 3.

   Compare the word in the last column with that in the first column. Discuss any differences in the two definitions. If the word in the last column differs from that in the first column, determine what went wrong in the process.
   a. hypothesis
   b. theory
   c. mixture
   d. substance

Text Entry	Student 1	Student 2	Student 3	Student 4
Word	Definition	Word	Definition	Word

Atoms

Have You Ever Wondered?

1. How small are atoms?
2. If we can't see atoms, how do we know they exist?
3. Why is it often difficult to destroy hazardous wastes?
4. Is light made of atoms?
5. Why is the table of elements called the "periodic table"?
6. What's the difference between atoms and molecules?

Learning Objectives

- Explain the ancient Greeks' ideas about the characteristics of matter. (2.1)
- Describe the significance of the laws of conservation of mass and definite proportions. (2.2)
- Calculate the amounts of elements from the composition of a compound. (2.2)
- Explain why the idea that matter is made of atoms is a theory. (2.3)
- Understand how atomic theory explains the law of conservation of mass. (2.3)
- Describe how the elements are arranged in the periodic table and why the arrangement is important. (2.4)
- Distinguish atoms from molecules. (2.5)
- Identify elements that could be classified as hazardous or rare.
- Explain how green chemistry can change technologies that rely on hazardous or rare elements.

Are They for Real?

We hear something about atoms almost every day. The twentieth century saw the start of the so-called Atomic Age. The terms *atomic power*, *atomic energy*, and *atomic bomb* are a part of our ordinary vocabulary. But just what are atoms?

Every material thing in the world is made up of atoms, tiny particles that are much, much too small to see even with the finest optical microscope. The smallest speck of matter that can be detected by the human eye is made up of many billions of atoms. There are more than 10^{22} (10,000,000,000,000,000,000,000) atoms in a penny. Imagine that the

At the heart of every tablet computer (above), printer, telephone, television, MP3 player, and virtually every other electronic device lies a wafer of silicon (above right) in one or more integrated circuits (ICs or "chips"). The silicon used for electronics must be so pure that these devices were not possible until zone-refining purification was developed, about sixty years ago. Silicon is an *element*, made of a single type of atom. For making ICs, only about one atom of impurity can be present for every billion atoms of silicon. But how do we even know that atoms exist? The false-color image at the right shows individual silicon atoms in a hexagonal arrangement, using a recently developed technique called *scanning tunneling microscopy*. However, the behavior of matter led scientists to the atomic nature of matter over two hundred years ago. In this chapter, we will see some of that history, and we will explore the properties of atoms.

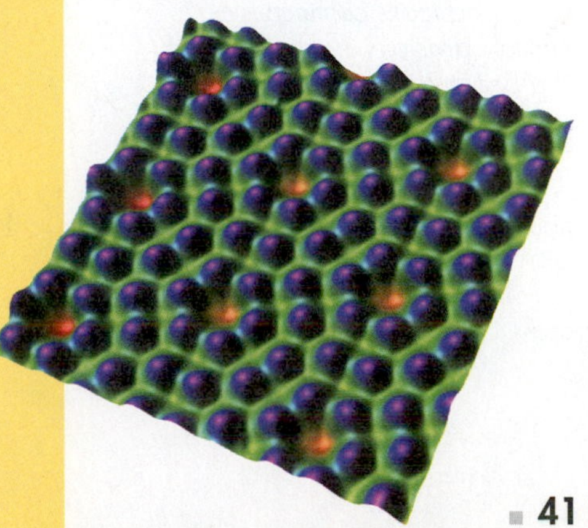

1. How small are atoms? Atoms are so small that the smallest particle of matter visible to your eye contains more atoms than you could count in a lifetime!

atoms in a penny were enlarged until they were barely visible, like tiny grains of sand. The atoms in a single penny would then make enough "sand" to cover the entire state of Texas several feet deep. Comparing an atom to a penny is like comparing a grain of sand to a Texas-size sandbox.

Why should we care about something as tiny as an atom? Because our world is made up of atoms, and atoms are a part of all we do. *Everything* is made of atoms, including you and me. And because chemistry is the study of the behavior of matter, it observes the behavior of atoms. The behavior and interactions of atoms determine the behavior and interactions of matter.

Atoms are not all alike. Each element has its own kind of atom. On Earth, about 90 elements occur in nature. About two dozen more have been synthesized by scientists. As far as we know, the entire universe is made up of these same few elements. An **atom** is the smallest particle that is characteristic of a given element.

▲ A marble statue of Democritus, who first formulated the atomic nature of matter.

2.1 Atoms: Ideas from the Ancient Greeks

Learning Objective › Explain the ancient Greeks' ideas about the characteristics of matter.

A pool of water can be separated into drops, and then each drop can be split into smaller and smaller drops. Suppose that you could keep splitting the drops into still smaller ones even after they became much too small to see. Would you ever reach a point at which a tiny drop could no longer be separated into smaller droplets of water? Is water infinitely divisible, or would you eventually come to a particle that, if divided, would no longer be water?

The Greek philosopher Leucippus, who lived in the fifth century B.C.E., and his pupil Democritus (ca. 460–ca. 370 B.C.E.) might well have discussed this question as they strolled along the beach by the Aegean Sea. Leucippus reasoned that there must ultimately be tiny particles of water that could not be divided further. After all, from a distance the sand on the beach looked continuous, but closer inspection showed it to be made up of tiny grains (Figure 2.1).

Democritus expanded on Leucippus's idea. He called the particles *atomos* (meaning "cannot be cut"), from which we derive the modern name *atom* for the tiny, discrete particle of an element. Democritus thought that each kind of atom was distinct in shape and size (Figure 2.2). He thought that real substances were

▶ **Figure 2.1** A sandy beach.

Q: *Sand looks continuous—infinitely divisible—when you look at a beach from a distance. Is it really continuous? Water looks continuous, even when viewed up close. Is it really continuous? Is a cloud continuous? Is air?*

mixtures of various kinds of atoms. The Greeks at that time believed that there were four basic elements: earth, air, fire, and water. These "elements" were related by four "principles"—hot, moist, dry, and cold—as shown in Figure 2.3. These ideas seem strange to us today, but they persisted for two millennia.

Four centuries after Democritus, the Roman poet Lucretius (ca. 95–ca. 55 B.C.E.) wrote a long didactic poem (a poem meant to teach), *On the Nature of Things*, in which he presented strong arguments for the atomic nature of matter. Unfortunately, a few centuries earlier, the famous Greek philosopher Aristotle (ca. 384–ca. 322 B.C.E.) had declared that matter was continuous (infinitely divisible) rather than discrete (consisting of tiny indivisible particles). The people of that time had no way to determine which view was correct. To most of them, Aristotle's continuous view of matter seemed more logical and reasonable, and so it prevailed for 2000 years, even though it was wrong.

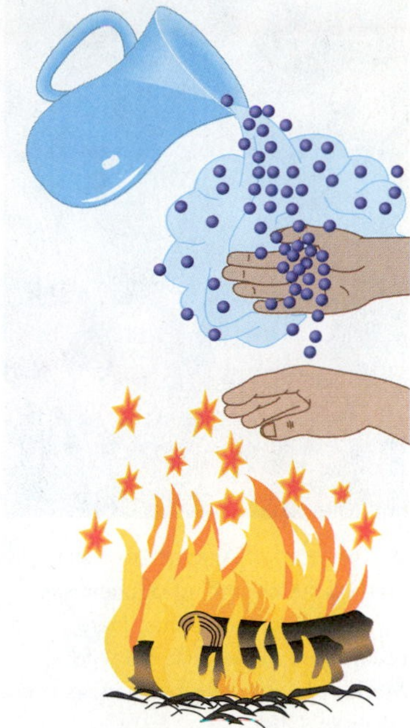

▲ **Figure 2.2** Democritus imagined that "atoms" of water might be smooth, round balls and that atoms of fire might have sharp edges.

Self-Assessment Questions

1. Consider how the qualities *discrete* and *continuous* apply to materials at the macroscopic (visible to the unaided eye) level. Which of the following is continuous?
   - **a.** apple juice
   - **b.** a ream of paper
   - **c.** a bowl of cherries
   - **d.** chocolate chips
2. The view that matter is continuous rather than atomic prevailed for centuries because it was
   - **a.** actually correct
   - **b.** not considered important
   - **c.** not tested by experiment
   - **d.** tested and found to be true

Answers: 1, a; 2, c

2.2 Scientific Laws: Conservation of Mass and Definite Proportions

Learning Objectives › Describe the significance of the laws of conservation of mass and definite proportions. › Calculate the amounts of elements from the composition of a compound.

The eighteenth century saw the triumph of careful observation and measurement in chemistry. Antoine Lavoisier (1743–1794) perhaps did more than anyone to establish chemistry as a quantitative science. He found that when a chemical reaction was carried out in a closed container, the total mass of the system was not changed. Perhaps the most important chemical reaction that Lavoisier performed was decomposition of a red compound containing mercury to form metallic mercury and a gas he named *oxygen*. Both Carl Wilhelm Scheele (1742–1786), a Swedish apothecary, and Joseph Priestley (1733–1804), a Unitarian minister who later fled England and settled in America in 1794, had carried out the same reaction earlier, but Lavoisier was the first to weigh all the substances present before and after the reaction. He was also the first to interpret the reaction correctly.

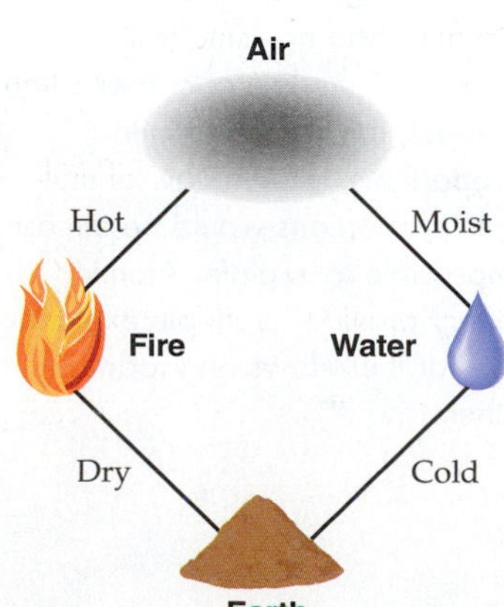

▲ **Figure 2.3** The Greek view of matter was that there were only four elements (in bold) connected by four "principles."

The Law of Conservation of Mass

Lavoisier carried out many quantitative experiments. He found that when coal was burned, it united with oxygen to form carbon dioxide. He experimented with animals, observing that when a guinea pig breathed, oxygen was consumed and carbon dioxide was formed. Lavoisier therefore concluded that respiration was related

▲ The work of Antoine Lavoisier marked the beginning of chemistry as a quantitative science. Here, Lavoisier is shown with his wife, Marie, in a painting by Jacques Louis David in 1788.

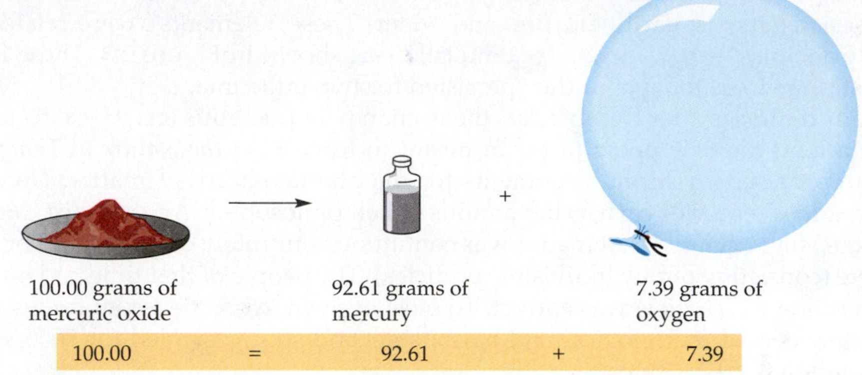

▲ **Figure 2.4** Although mercuric oxide (a red solid) has none of the properties of mercury (a silver liquid) or oxygen (a colorless gas), when 100.00 g of mercuric oxide is decomposed by heating, the products are 92.61 g of mercury and 7.39 g of oxygen. Properties are completely changed in this reaction, but there is no change in mass.

Q: *When 10.00 g of mercuric oxide decomposes, 0.739 g of oxygen forms. What mass of mercury forms?*

to combustion. In each of these reactions, he found that matter was *conserved*—the amount remained constant.

Lavoisier summarized his findings as the **law of conservation of mass**, which states that matter is neither created nor destroyed during a chemical change (Figure 2.4). The total mass of the reaction products is always equal to the total mass of the reactants (starting materials). We will discuss chemical reactions in more detail beginning with Chapter 4. For now, some simple examples and discussion will illustrate the conservation of mass.

Scientists by this time had abandoned the Greek idea of the four elements and were almost universally using Robert Boyle's working definition of an element presented in his book *The Sceptical Chymist* (published in 1661). Boyle said that a supposed *element* must be tested. If a substance could be broken down into simpler substances, it was not an element. The simpler substances might be elements and should be regarded as such until the time (if it ever came) when they in turn could be broken down into still simpler substances. On the other hand, two or more elements might combine to form a more complex substance called a *compound*.

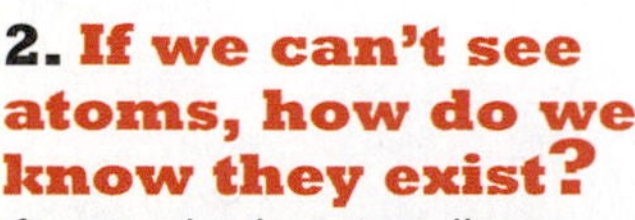

2. If we can't see atoms, how do we know they exist?

If matter had no "smallest particles," the law of conservation of mass, the law of definite proportions, and the law of multiple proportions would be almost impossible to explain. Atomic theory provides a simple explanation for these laws and for many others.

Using Boyle's definition, Lavoisier included a table of elements in his book *Elementary Treatise on Chemistry*. (The table included some substances that we now know to be compounds, as well as light and heat, which are actually forms of energy.) Lavoisier was the first to use systematic names for chemical elements. He is often called the "father of modern chemistry," and his book is usually regarded as the first chemistry textbook.

The law of conservation of mass is the basis for many chemical calculations. This law states that we cannot create materials from nothing. We can make new materials only by changing the way atoms are combined. For example, we can obtain iron metal from iron ore only because the ore contains iron atoms. Furthermore, we cannot get rid of wastes by the destruction of matter. We must put wastes somewhere. However, through chemical reactions, we can change some kinds of potentially hazardous wastes to less harmful forms. Such transformations of matter from one form to another are what chemistry is all about.

The Law of Definite Proportions

By the end of the eighteenth century, Lavoisier and other scientists noted that many substances were compounds, composed of two or more elements. Each compound had the same elements in the same proportions, regardless of where

(a)

(b)

(c)

▲ **Figure 2.5** The compound known as *basic copper carbonate* has the formula $Cu_2(OH)_2CO_3$ and occurs in nature as the mineral *malachite* **(a)**. It is formed as a patina on copper roofs **(b)**. It can also be synthesized in the laboratory **(c)**. Regardless of its source, basic copper carbonate always has the same composition. Analysis of this compound led Proust to formulate the law of definite proportions.

it came from or who prepared it. The painstaking work of Joseph Louis Proust (1754–1826) convinced most chemists of the general validity of these observations. In one set of experiments, for example, Proust found that basic copper carbonate, whether prepared in the laboratory or obtained from natural sources, was always composed of 57.48% by mass copper, 5.43% carbon, 0.91% hydrogen, and 36.18% oxygen (Figure 2.5).

To summarize these and many other experiments, Proust formulated a new scientific law in 1799. The **law of definite proportions** states that a compound always contains the same elements in certain definite proportions and in no others. (This generalization is also sometimes called the *law of constant composition*.)

An early illustration of the law of definite proportions is found in the work of the noted Swedish chemist J. J. Berzelius, illustrated in Figure 2.6. Berzelius heated a quantity (say, 10.00 g) of lead with various amounts of sulfur to form lead sulfide. Lead is a soft, grayish metal, and sulfur is a yellow solid. Lead sulfide is a shiny, black solid. Therefore, it was easy to tell when all the lead had reacted. Excess sulfur was washed away with carbon disulfide, a solvent that dissolves sulfur but not lead sulfide. As long as he used at least 1.55 g of sulfur with 10.00 g of lead, Berzelius got exactly 11.55 g of lead sulfide. Any sulfur in excess of 1.55 g was left over; it did not react. If Berzelius used more than 10.00 g of lead with 1.55 g of sulfur, he got 11.55 g of lead sulfide, with some lead left over.

▲ Jöns Jacob Berzelius (1779–1848) was the first person to prepare an extensive list of atomic weights. Published in 1828, it agrees remarkably well with most of today's accepted values.

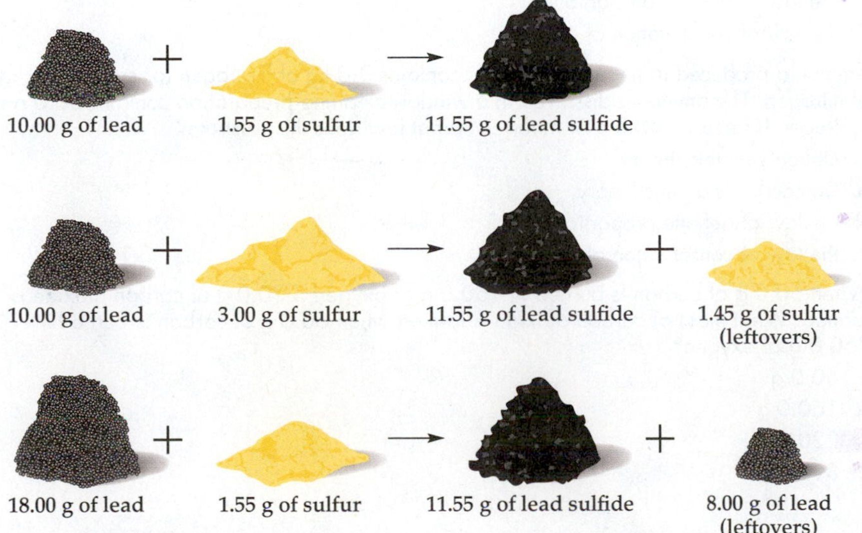

◀ **Figure 2.6** An example showing how Berzelius's experiments illustrate the law of definite proportions.

Q: *What mass of sulfur can react completely with 20.00 g of lead? What mass of lead sulfide forms?*

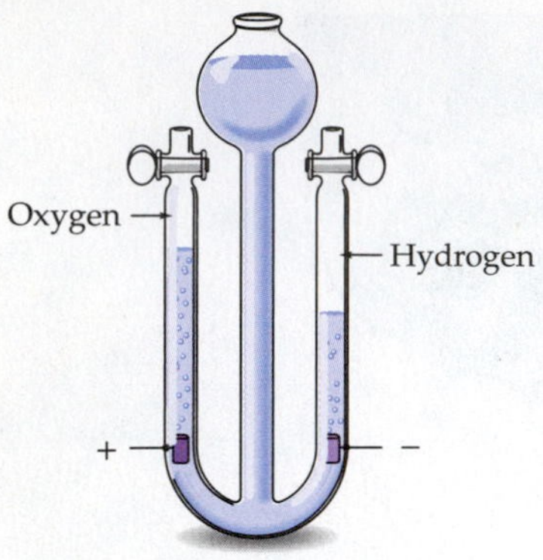

▲ **Figure 2.7** Electrolysis of water. Hydrogen and oxygen are always produced in a volume ratio of 2 : 1.

Q: *If 24 cubic feet of hydrogen gas is produced by electrolysis, how much oxygen gas will be produced?*

The law of definite proportions is further illustrated by the electrolysis of water. In 1783, Henry Cavendish (1731–1810), a wealthy, eccentric English nobleman, found that water forms when hydrogen burns in oxygen. (It was Lavoisier, however, who correctly interpreted the experiment and who first used the names *hydrogen* and *oxygen.*) Later, in 1800, the English chemists William Nicholson and Anthony Carlisle decomposed water into hydrogen and oxygen gases by passing an electric current through the water (Figure 2.7). (The Italian scientist Alessandro Volta had invented the chemical battery only six weeks earlier.) The two gases are always produced in a 2:1 volume ratio. Although this is a volume ratio and Berzelius's experiment gave a mass ratio, both substantiate the law of definite proportions. This scientific law led to rapid developments in chemistry and dealt a death blow to the ancient Greek idea of water as an element.

The law of definite proportions is the basis for chemical formulas (Chapter 4), such as H_2O for water. Constant composition also means that substances have constant properties. Pure water always dissolves salt or sugar, and at normal pressure it always freezes at 0 °C and boils at 100 °C.

Self-Assessment Questions

1. In any chemical change, compared to the mass of the reactants, the mass of the products is
a. always equal
b. always greater
c. always less
d. often different

2. In an experiment in which 36.04 g of liquid water is decomposed into hydrogen gas and oxygen gas, the total mass of the products is
a. 0 g
b. 18.02 g
c. 36.04 g
d. uncertain

3. The ancient Greeks thought that water was an element. In 1800, Nicholson and Carlisle decomposed water into hydrogen and oxygen. Their experiment proved that
a. electricity causes decomposition
b. the Greeks were correct
c. hydrogen and oxygen are elements
d. water is not an element

4. The fact that salt (sodium chloride) from any place on Earth is always 39.34% sodium and 60.66% chlorine by mass illustrates
a. Dalton's atomic theory
b. Democritus's atomic theory
c. the law of definite proportions
d. the law of conservation of mass

5. Ammonia produced in an industrial plant contains 3.0 kg of hydrogen for every 14.0 kg of nitrogen. The ammonia dissolved in a window-cleaning preparation contains 30.0 g of hydrogen for every 140.0 g of nitrogen. What law does this illustrate?
a. Dalton's atomic theory
b. Democritus's atomic theory
c. the law of definite proportions
d. the law of conservation of mass

6 When 60.0 g of carbon is burned in 160.0 g of oxygen, 220.0 g of carbon dioxide is formed. What mass of carbon dioxide is formed when 60.0 g of carbon is burned in 750.0 g of oxygen?
a. 60.0 g
b. 160.0 g
c. 220.0 g
d. 810.0 g

Answers: 1, a; 2, c; 3, d; 4, c; 5, c; 6, c

2.3 John Dalton and the Atomic Theory of Matter

Learning Objectives › Explain why the idea that matter is made of atoms is a theory. › Understand how atomic theory explains the law of conservation of mass.

Lavoisier's law of conservation of mass and Proust's law of definite proportions were repeatedly verified by experiment. This work led to attempts to develop theories to explain these laws.

In 1803, John Dalton, an English schoolteacher, proposed a model to explain the accumulating experimental data. By this time, the composition of a number of substances was known with a fair degree of accuracy. (To avoid confusion, we will use modern values, terms, and examples rather than those actually used by Dalton.) For example, all samples of water have an oxygen-to-hydrogen mass ratio of 7.94:1.00. Similarly, all samples of ammonia have a nitrogen-to-hydrogen mass ratio of 4.63:1.00 (14:3). Dalton explained these unvarying ratios by assuming that matter is made of atoms.

As Dalton continued his work, he discovered another law that his theory would have to explain. Proust had stated that a compound contains elements in certain proportions and only those proportions. Dalton's new law, called the **law of multiple proportions**, stated that elements might combine in *more* than one set of proportions, with each set corresponding to a different compound. For example, carbon combines with oxygen in a mass ratio of 1.00:2.66 (or 3.00:8.00) to form carbon dioxide, a gas that is a product of respiration and of the burning of coal or wood. But Dalton found that carbon also combines with oxygen in a mass ratio of 1.00:1.33 (or 3.00:4.00) to form carbon monoxide, a poisonous gas produced when a fuel is burned in the presence of a limited air supply.

▲ John Dalton (1766–1844), who, in addition to developing the atomic theory, carried out important investigations of the behavior of gases. All of his contributions to science were made in spite of the fact that he was color-blind.

Dalton then used his **atomic theory** to explain the various laws. Following are the important points of Dalton's atomic theory, with some modern modifications that we will consider later.

Dalton's Atomic Theory	Modern Modifications
1. All matter is composed of extremely small particles called atoms.	1. Dalton assumed atoms to be indivisible. This isn't quite true, as we will see in Chapter 3.
2. All atoms of a given element are alike, but atoms of a given element differ from the atoms of any other element.	2. Dalton assumed that all the atoms of a given element were identical in all respects, including mass. We now know this to be incorrect, as we will see on page 48.
3. Compounds are formed when atoms of different elements combine in fixed proportions.	3. Unmodified. The numbers of each kind of atom in simple compounds usually form a simple ratio. For example, the ratio of carbon atoms to oxygen atoms is 1:1 in carbon monoxide and 1:2 in carbon dioxide.
4. A chemical reaction involves a *rearrangement* of atoms. No atoms are created, destroyed, or broken apart in a chemical reaction.	4. Unmodified for *chemical* reactions. Atoms are broken apart in *nuclear* reactions. We will discuss chemical reactions in Chapter 5 and nuclear reactions in Chapter 11.

3. Why is it often difficult to destroy hazardous wastes?

Hazardous wastes that are compounds or mixtures can be converted to other compounds or mixtures—but the elements from those compounds or mixtures are still present and may be hazardous as well. For example, insecticide containing arsenic oxide can be broken down into the elements arsenic and oxygen—but the element arsenic is poisonous and can't be broken down into something else.

Explanations Using Atomic Theory

Dalton's theory clearly explains the difference between elements and compounds. *Elements* are composed of only one kind of atom. For example, a sample of the element phosphorus contains only phosphorus atoms. *Compounds* are made up of two

▶ **Figure 2.8** The law of definite proportions and the law of conservation of mass interpreted in terms of Dalton's atomic theory.

Q: *If 20 molecules of fluorine and 28 molecules of hydrogen react, how many molecules of HF can form? Which element is left over? How many molecules of the leftover element are there?*

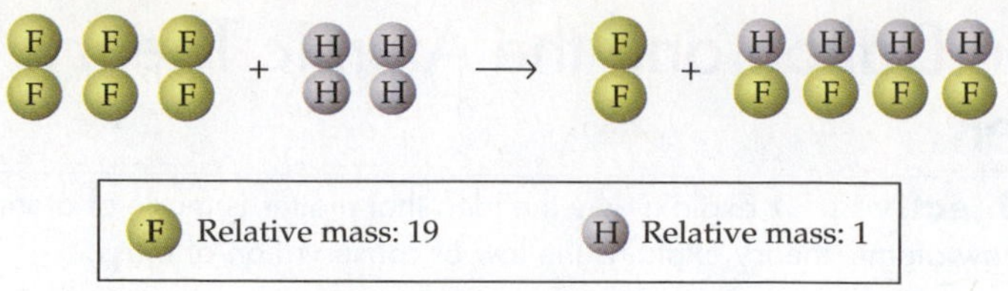

or more kinds of atoms chemically combined in definite proportions. (We will see exactly what *kind* means in Section 3.5.)

Dalton set up a table of relative atomic masses based on hydrogen having a mass of 1. Many of Dalton's atomic masses were inaccurate, as we might expect because of the equipment available at that time. The masses we use today are relative atomic masses, usually called simply *atomic masses*. Historically, these relative masses were determined by comparison with a standard mass, a technique called *weighing*. For this historical reason, these relative masses are often called *atomic weights*. You will find a table of atomic masses on the inside front cover of this book. We will use these modern values in some examples showing how Dalton's atomic theory explains the various laws.

To explain the law of definite proportions, Dalton's reasoning went something like this: Why should 1.0 g of hydrogen always combine with 19 g of fluorine? Why shouldn't 1.0 g of hydrogen also combine with 18 g, or 20 g, or any other mass of fluorine? If an atom of fluorine has a mass 19 times that of a hydrogen atom, the compound formed by the union of one atom of each element would have to consist of 1 part by mass of hydrogen and 19 parts by mass of fluorine. Matter must be atomic for the law of definite proportions to be valid (Figure 2.8).

Atomic theory also explains the law of conservation of mass. When fluorine atoms combine with hydrogen atoms to form hydrogen fluoride, the atoms are merely rearranged. Matter is neither lost nor gained; the mass does not change.

Finally, atomic theory explains the law of multiple proportions. For example, 1.00 g of carbon combines with 1.33 g of oxygen to form carbon monoxide or with 2.66 g of oxygen to form carbon dioxide. Carbon dioxide has twice the mass of oxygen per gram of carbon as carbon monoxide does. This is because one atom of carbon combines with *one* atom of oxygen to form carbon monoxide, whereas one atom of carbon combines with *two* atoms of oxygen to form carbon dioxide.

Using modern values, we assign an oxygen atom a relative mass of 16.0 and a carbon atom a relative mass of 12.0. One atom of carbon combined with one atom of oxygen (in carbon monoxide) means a mass ratio of 12.0 parts carbon to 16.0 parts oxygen, or 3.00 : 4.00. One atom of carbon combined with two atoms of oxygen (in carbon dioxide) gives a mass ratio of 12.0 parts carbon to $2 \times 16.0 = 32.0$ parts oxygen, or 3.00 : 8.00. Because all oxygen atoms have the same average mass, and all carbon atoms have the same average mass, the ratio of oxygen in carbon dioxide to oxygen in carbon monoxide is 8.00 to 4.00 or 2 : 1. The same law holds true for other compounds formed from the same two elements. Table 2.1 shows another example of the law of multiple proportions, involving nitrogen and oxygen.

▲ **It DOES Matter!**
A molecule with one carbon (C) atom and two oxygen (O) atoms is carbon dioxide (CO_2), a gas that you exhale and that provides the "fizz" in soft drinks. Cooled to about −80 °C, it becomes dry ice (shown above), used to keep items frozen during shipping. But a molecule with one less O atom is deadly carbon monoxide, CO. Just 0.2% CO in the air is enough to kill. Unfortunately, most fuels produce a little CO when they burn, which is why a car engine should never be left running in a closed garage.

Dalton also invented a set of symbols (Figure 2.9) to represent the different kinds of atoms. These symbols have since been replaced by modern symbols of one or two letters (inside front cover).

Isotopes: Atoms of an Element with Different Masses

As we have noted, Dalton's second assumption, that all atoms of an element are alike, has been modified. Atoms of an element can have different masses, and such atoms are called *isotopes*. For example, most carbon atoms have a relative atomic

Table 2.1 The Law of Multiple Proportions

Compound	Representation[a]	Mass of N per 1.000 g of O	Ratio of the Masses of N[b]
Nitrous oxide		1.750 g	(1.750 ÷ 0.4375) = 4.000
Nitric oxide		0.8750 g	(0.8750 ÷ 0.4375) = 2.000
Nitrogen dioxide		0.4375 g	(0.4375 ÷ 0.4375) = 1.000

[a] (blue sphere) = nitrogen atom and (red sphere) = oxygen atom

[b] We obtain the ratio of the masses of N that combine with a given mass of O by dividing each quantity in the third column by the smallest (0.4375 g).

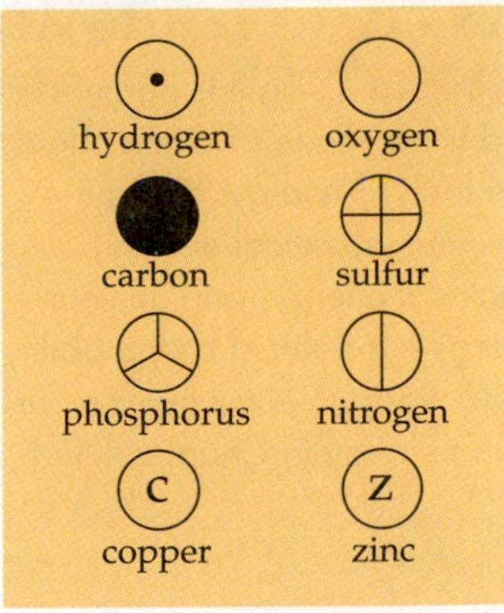

▲ **Figure 2.9** Some of Dalton's symbols for the elements.

Q: *Using Dalton's symbols, draw diagrams for sulfur dioxide and sulfur trioxide. (Place the sulfur atom in the center and arrange the oxygen atoms around it.) What law do these two compounds illustrate?*

mass of 12 (carbon-12), but 1.1% of carbon atoms have a relative atomic mass of 13 (carbon-13). We discuss isotopes in more detail in Chapter 3.

Problem Solving: Mass and Atom Ratios

We can use proportions, such as those determined by Dalton, to calculate the amount of a substance needed to combine with (or form) a given quantity of another substance. To learn how to do this, let's look at some examples.

CONCEPTUAL Example 2.1 Mass Ratios

Hydrogen gas for fuel cells can be made by decomposing *methane* (CH_4), the main component of natural gas. The decomposition gives carbon (C) and hydrogen (H) in a ratio of 3.00 parts by mass of carbon to 1.00 part by mass of hydrogen. How much hydrogen can be made from 90.0 g of methane?

Solution

We can express the ratio of parts by mass in any units we choose—pounds, grams, kilograms—as long as it is the same for both elements. Using grams as the units, we see that 3.00 g of C and 1.00 g of H would be produced if 4.00 g of CH_4 were decomposed. To convert g CH_4 to g H, we need a conversion factor that includes 1.00 g H and 4.00 g CH_4.

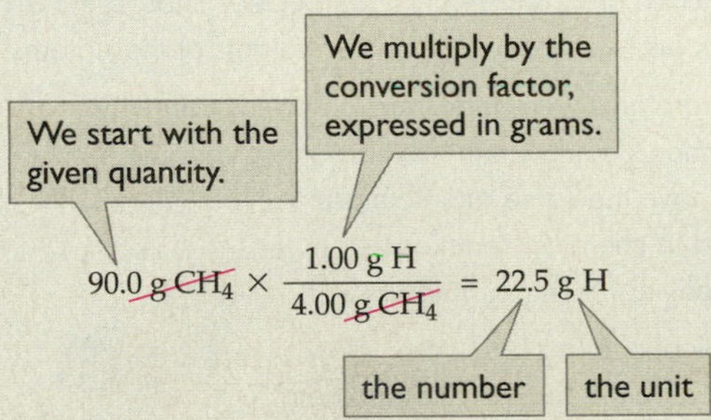

$$90.0\ \text{g CH}_4 \times \frac{1.00\ \text{g H}}{4.00\ \text{g CH}_4} = 22.5\ \text{g H}$$

■ EXERCISE 2.1A

The gas ammonia can be decomposed to give 3.00 parts by mass of hydrogen and 14.0 parts by mass of nitrogen. What mass of nitrogen is obtained if 10.2 g of ammonia is decomposed?

■ EXERCISE 2.1B

Nitrous oxide, sometimes called "laughing gas," can be decomposed to give 7.00 parts by mass of nitrogen and 4.00 parts by mass of oxygen. What mass of nitrogen is obtained if enough nitrous oxide is decomposed to yield 36.0 g of oxygen?

4. Is light made of atoms? Light is not matter and is not made of atoms. Light is a form of *energy*. Energy—including chemical energy, electrical energy, and nuclear energy—is defined as the ability to do work. We will learn more about energy in Chapter 15.

CONCEPTUAL Example 2.2 Atom Ratios

Hydrogen sulfide gas can be decomposed to give sulfur and hydrogen in a mass ratio of 16.0:1.00. If the relative mass of sulfur is 32.0 when the mass of hydrogen is taken to be 1.00, how many hydrogen atoms are combined with each sulfur atom in the gas?

Solution

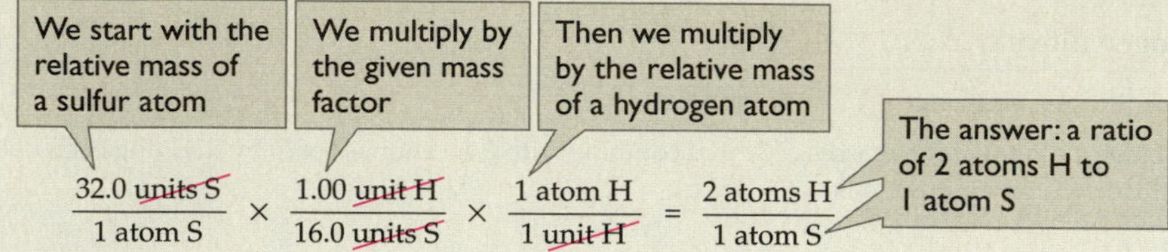
We start with the relative mass of a sulfur atom
We multiply by the given mass factor
Then we multiply by the relative mass of a hydrogen atom
The answer: a ratio of 2 atoms H to 1 atom S

$$\frac{32.0 \text{ units S}}{1 \text{ atom S}} \times \frac{1.00 \text{ unit H}}{16.0 \text{ units S}} \times \frac{1 \text{ atom H}}{1 \text{ unit H}} = \frac{2 \text{ atoms H}}{1 \text{ atom S}}$$

■ EXERCISE 2.2

Phosphine gas can be decomposed to give phosphorus and hydrogen in a mass ratio of 10.3:1.00. If the relative mass of phosphorus is 31.0 when the mass of hydrogen is taken to be 1.00, how many hydrogen atoms are combined with each phosphorus atom in the gas?

Despite some inaccuracies, Dalton's atomic theory was a great success. Why? Because it served—and still serves—to explain a large amount of experimental data. It also successfully predicted how matter would behave under a wide variety of circumstances. Dalton arrived at his atomic theory by basing his reasoning on experimental findings, and with modest modification, the theory has stood the test of time and of modern, highly sophisticated instrumentation. Formulation of so successful a theory was quite a triumph for a Quaker schoolteacher in 1803.

Self-Assessment Questions

1. Two compounds, ethylene and acetylene, both contain only carbon and hydrogen. A sample of acetylene contains 92.26 g of C and 7.74 g H. An ethylene sample contains 46.13 g of C and 7.74 g H. If the formula for acetylene is C_2H_2, the formula for ethylene is
   a. CH **b.** C_2H
   c. CH_3 **d.** C_2H_4
2. According to Dalton, elements are distinguished from each other by
   a. density in the solid state **b.** nuclear charge
   c. shapes of their atoms **d.** weights of their atoms
3. Dalton postulated that atoms were indestructible to explain why
   a. the same two elements can form more than one compound
   b. no two elements have the same atomic mass
   c. mass is conserved in chemical reactions
   d. nuclear fission (splitting) is impossible
4. Dalton viewed chemical change as
   a. a change of atoms from one type into another
   b. creation and destruction of atoms
   c. a rearrangement of atoms
   d. a transfer of electrons
5. How many types of atoms are present in a given compound?
   a. at least two **b.** hundreds
   c. three or more **d.** depends on the mass of the compound
6. Hydrogen and carbon combine in a 4.0:12.0 mass ratio to form methane. If every molecule of methane contains 4 H atoms and 1 C atom, an atom of carbon must have a mass that is
   a. $\frac{4}{12}$ times the mass of a hydrogen atom **b.** 4 times the mass of a hydrogen atom
   c. $\frac{12}{3}$ times the mass of a hydrogen atom **d.** 12 times the mass of a hydrogen atom

Questions 7–9 refer to the following figures:

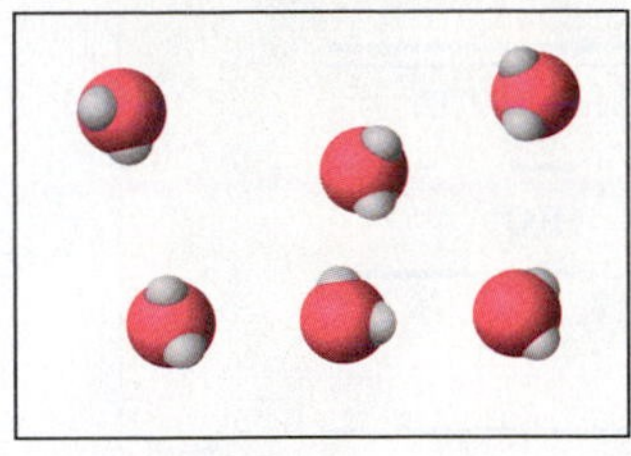
(a)

(b)

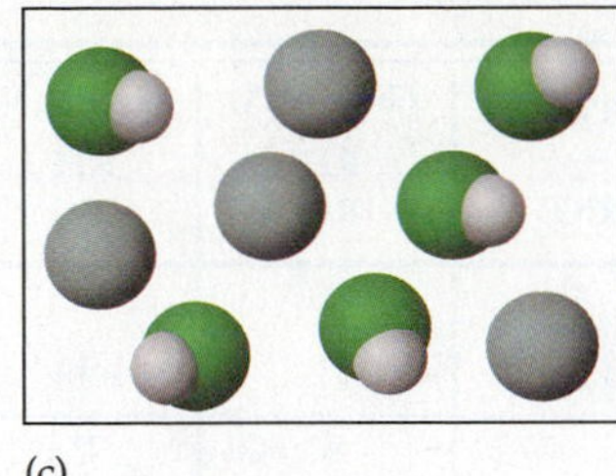
(c)

7. Which figure represents an element?
8. Which figure represents a compound?
9. Which figure represents a mixture?

Answers: 1, d; 2, d; 3, c; 4, c; 5, a; 6, d; 7, b; 8, a; 9, c

2.4 Mendeleev and the Periodic Table

Learning Objective › Describe how the elements are arranged in the periodic table and why the arrangement is important.

During the eighteenth and nineteenth centuries, new elements were discovered with surprising frequency. By 1830 there were 55 known elements, all with different properties that demonstrated no apparent order. Dalton had set up a table of relative atomic masses in his 1808 book *A New System of Chemical Philosophy*. Dalton's rough values were improved in subsequent years, notably by Berzelius, who, in 1828, published a table of atomic weights containing 54 elements. Most of Berzelius's values agree well with modern values.

Relative Atomic Masses

Although it was impossible to determine actual masses of atoms in the nineteenth century, chemists were able to determine relative atomic masses by measuring the amounts of various elements that combined with a given mass of another element. Dalton's atomic masses were based on an atomic mass of 1 for hydrogen. As more accurate atomic masses were determined, this standard was replaced by one in which the atomic mass of naturally occurring oxygen was assigned a value of 16.0000. Because the isotopic composition of oxygen varies a bit depending on its source, the oxygen standard was replaced in 1961 by a more logical one based on a single isotope of carbon, carbon-12. Adoption of this new standard caused little change in atomic masses. These relative atomic masses are usually expressed in **atomic mass units (amu)**, commonly referred to today simply as *units* (*u*).

In December 2010, the atomic masses for eleven elements were adjusted slightly. Although their atomic masses had not actually changed, the isotopic composition of these elements varies slightly from location to location. For example, boron's atomic mass is now listed in some sources as 10.806–10.821 u. Most periodic tables still list a single value, however, which is accurate enough for most purposes.

▲ Dmitri Mendeleev, the Russian chemist who arranged the 63 known elements into a periodic table similar to the one we use today, was considered one of the great teachers of his time. Unable to find a suitable chemistry textbook, he wrote his own, *The Principles of Chemistry*. Mendeleev also studied the nature and origin of petroleum and made many other contributions to science. Element 101 is named mendelevium (Md) in his honor.

Mendeleev's Periodic Table

Various attempts were made to arrange the elements in some sort of systematic fashion. The most successful arrangement—one that soon became widely accepted by chemists—was published in 1869 by Dmitri Ivanovich Mendeleev (1834–1907), a Russian chemist. Mendeleev's **periodic table** arranged the 63 elements known at the time primarily in order of increasing atomic mass. However, his first consideration in this table was an element's *properties*. He placed silver, gold, and several other

Tabelle II.

Reihen	Gruppe I. — R^2O	Gruppe II. — RO	Gruppe III. — R^2O^3	Gruppe IV. RH^4 RO^2	Gruppe V. RH^3 R^2O^5	Gruppe VI. RH^2 RO^3	Gruppe VII. RH R^2O^7	Gruppe VIII. — RO^4
1	H = 1							
2	Li = 7	Be = 9,4	B = 11	C = 12	N = 14	O = 16	F = 19	
3	Na = 23	Mg = 24	Al = 27,3	Si = 28	P = 31	S = 32	Cl = 35,5	
4	K = 39	Ca = 40	— = 44	Ti = 48	V = 51	Cr = 52	Mn = 55	Fe = 56, Co = 59, Ni = 59, Cu = 63.
5	(Cu = 63)	Zn = 65	— = 68	— = 72	As = 75	Se = 78	Br = 80	
6	Rb = 85	Sr = 87	?Yt = 88	Zr = 90	Nb = 94	Mo = 96	— = 100	Ru = 104, Rh = 104, Pd = 106, Ag = 108.
7	(Ag = 108)	Cd = 112	In = 113	Sn = 118	Sb = 122	Te = 125	J = 127	
8	Cs = 133	Ba = 137	?Di = 138	?Ce = 140	—	—	—	— — — —
9	(—)	—	—	—	—	—	—	
10	—	—	?Er = 178	?La = 180	Ta = 182	W = 184	—	Os = 195, Ir = 197, Pt = 198, Au = 199.
11	(Au = 199)	Hg = 200	Ti = 204	Pb = 207	Bi = 208	—	—	
12	—	—	—	Th = 231	—	U = 240	—	— — — —

der chemischen Elemente.

▲ **Figure 2.10** Mendeleev's periodic table. In this 1898 version, he wrongly "corrected" the atomic weight of tellurium to be less than that of iodine.

metals slightly out of order. This allowed sulfur, selenium, and tellurium, which have similar chemical properties, to appear in the same column. This rearrangement also put iodine in the same column as chlorine and bromine, which it resembles chemically.

5. Why is the table of elements called the "periodic table"?

Periodic indicates that something occurs regularly. The physical and chemical properties of the elements are periodic. That is, many of those properties are similar for elements in a given column of the table.

To place elements in groups with similar properties, Mendeleev also had to leave gaps in his table. Instead of considering these blank spaces as defects, he boldly predicted the existence of elements yet undiscovered. Further, he even predicted the properties of some of the missing elements. For example, three of the missing elements were soon discovered and named scandium, gallium, and germanium. As can be seen in Table 2.2, Mendeleev's predictions for germanium were amazingly successful. This remarkable predictive value led to wide acceptance of Mendeleev's table.

The modern periodic table (inside front cover) contains 118 elements, some of which have reportedly been observed or synthesized but have not yet been verified or named. Each element is represented by a box in the periodic table, as shown in Figure 2.11. We will discuss the periodic table and its theoretical basis in Chapter 3.

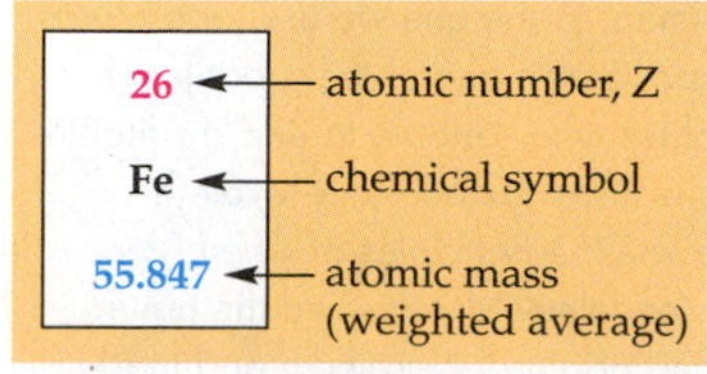

▲ **Figure 2.11** Representation of an element on the modern periodic table.

Table 2.2 Properties of Germanium: Predicted and Observed

Property	Predicted by Mendeleev for Eka-Silikon (1871)	Observed by Winkler for Germanium (1886)
Atomic mass	72	72.6
Density (g/cm^3)	5.5	5.47
Color	Dirty gray	Grayish white
Density of oxide (g/cm^3)	EsO_2: 4.7	GeO_2: 4.703
Boiling point of chloride	$EsCl_4$: below 100 °C	$GeCl_4$: 86 °C

CONCEPTUAL Example 2.3 Predicting Periodic Properties

In 1829, Johann Dobereiner, a German chemist, published his observations that there were several groups of three elements that were quite similar. In each case, the middle element seemed to be halfway between the other two in atomic mass, reactivity, and other properties. One such group, which he called *alkali formers*, was lithium, sodium, and potassium. Show that the relative atomic mass of the middle element in this triad is close to the average of the relative atomic masses of the other two elements.

Solution

The atomic mass of lithium (Li) is 6.941 u and that of potassium (K) is 39.098 u. The average of the two is (6.941 u + 39.098 u) ÷ 2 = 22.795 u, quite close to the modern value for sodium (Na) of 22.989 u.

■ EXERCISE 2.3

Another of Dobereiner's triads was the *salt formers* chlorine, bromine, and iodine. Show that the relative atomic mass of the middle element in this triad is close to the average of the relative atomic masses of the other two elements.

Self-Assessment Questions

1. Which of the following is *not* true of Mendeleev's periodic table?
   a. It includes new elements that he had just discovered.
   b. The elements are arranged generally in order of increasing atomic mass.
   c. He left gaps for predicted new elements.
   d. He placed some heavier elements before lighter ones.
2. Relative masses in the modern periodic table are based on the value for
   a. the carbon-12 isotope
   b. the hydrogen atom
   c. naturally occurring oxygen
   d. the oxygen-16 isotope
3. The number of elements known today is approximately
   a. 12
   b. 100
   c. 1000
   d. 30 million

Answers: 1, a; 2, a; 3, b

2.5 Atoms and Molecules: Real and Relevant

Learning Objective › Distinguish atoms from molecules.

Are atoms real? Certainly they are real as a concept, a highly useful concept. And scientists today can observe computer-enhanced images of individual atoms. These portraits provide powerful (though still indirect) evidence that atoms exist.

Are atoms relevant? Much of modern science and technology—including the production of new materials and the technology of pollution control—is based on the concept of atoms. We have seen that atoms are conserved in chemical reactions. Thus, material things—things made of atoms—can be recycled, for the atoms are not destroyed no matter how we use them. The one way we might "lose" a material from a practical standpoint is to spread its atoms so thinly that it would take too much time and energy to put them back together again. The essay on recycling (page 54) describes a real-world example of such loss.

Now back to Leucippus and Democritus and their musings on that Greek beach. We now know that if we keep dividing drops of water, we will ultimately obtain a small particle—called a *molecule*—that is still water. A **molecule** is a group of atoms chemically bonded, or connected, to one another. Molecules are represented by chemical formulas. The symbol H represents an *atom* of hydrogen. The formula

▲ An image of atoms of manganese obtained using STM.

6. What's the difference between atoms and molecules? A molecule is made of atoms that are combined in fixed proportions. A carbon atom is the smallest particle of the element carbon, and a carbon dioxide molecule is the smallest particle of the compound carbon dioxide. As you have probably figured out, molecules can be broken down into their atoms.

Recycling

Because it is an element, iron cannot be created or destroyed, but that does not mean it always exists in its elemental state. Let's consider two different pathways for the recycling of iron.

1. Hematite, an iron ore, is obtained from a mine and converted into pig iron, which is used to make steel cans. Once discarded, the cans rust. Iron ions (ions are explained in Chapter 4) slowly leach from the rust into groundwater and eventually wind up in the ocean. These dissolved ions can be absorbed by and incorporated into marine plants. Marine creatures that eat the plants will in turn absorb and incorporate iron ions. The original iron atoms are now widely separated in space. Some of them might even become part of the hemoglobin in your blood. The iron has been recycled, but it will never again resemble the original pig iron.

2. Iron ore is taken from a mine and converted to pig iron and then into steel. The steel is used in making an automobile, which is driven for a decade and then sent to the junkyard. There it is compacted and sent to a recycling plant, where the steel is recovered and ultimately used again in a new automobile. Once the iron was removed from its ore, it was conserved in its elemental metallic form. In this form of recycling, the iron continues to be useful for a long time.

H_2 represents a *molecule* of hydrogen, which is composed of two hydrogen atoms. The formula H_2O represents a molecule of water, which is composed of two hydrogen atoms and one oxygen atom. If we divide a water molecule, we will obtain *two atoms* of hydrogen and *one atom* of oxygen.

And if we divide those atoms . . . but that is a story for another time.

Dalton regarded the atom as indivisible, as did his successors up until the discovery of radioactivity in 1895. We examine the evolving concept of the atom in Chapter 3.

Self-Assessment Questions

1. We can recycle materials because atoms
   a. always combine in the same way
   b. are conserved
   c. are indivisible
   d. combine in multiple portions
2. A molecule is
   a. a collection of like atoms
   b. conserved in chemical reactions
   c. a group of atoms chemically bonded to one another
   d. indivisible

Answers: 1, b; 2, c

GREEN CHEMISTRY

Principles 3, 7, 10

Lallie C. McKenzie, *Chem11 LLC*

It's Elemental

In this chapter, you learned that everything is made up of atoms and that atoms are the smallest particles of an element. Although the universe is composed of an uncountable number of compounds and mixtures, the basic building blocks of these are elements. The periodic table (inside front cover) organizes the elements by relative mass and, more importantly, by their predictable chemical properties.

What do elements have to do with green chemistry? When chemists design products and processes, they take advantage of the entire periodic table, including elements used rarely or not at all in nature or in our bodies. It is important to think about possible impacts of the chosen elements on human health and on the environment. Two important factors to evaluate are inherent hazard and natural abundance. Hazard can be different for the element itself or when it is in a compound, so the element's form can determine whether it causes harm. For example, sodium is very reactive with water, but sodium chloride is a compound that we eat. Also, as you learned from the law of conservation of mass (Section 2.2), elements cannot be created or destroyed. Therefore, the amounts of these materials on the planet are limited and may be scarce.

Green Chemistry Principles 3, 7, and 10 apply to products and processes that involve hazardous and rare elements. Understanding the impacts of toxic elements and compounds on human health and the environment lets us reduce or eliminate their use by developing safer alternatives. Also, designing new technologies that rely on abundant elements can prevent depletion of resources. Finally, reclaiming materials after use is critical if they can cause harm or are scarce.

The use of lead and mercury, two particularly hazardous elements, has been reduced through green chemistry. These elements are known to harm many of the systems of the human body and can impact children's development. Although lead and mercury are important in many products, the urgent need to limit exposure to them has led to their replacement with safer alternatives. For example, lead in paints has been replaced with titanium dioxide, compounds with lower toxicity now substitute for lead stabilizers in plastics, and new lead-free chemicals are being used instead of traditional solder in electronics. In addition, recent developments have reduced the liquid mercury required in fluorescent lighting, and mercury-based thermometers and switches have been replaced with electronic or non-hazardous versions. Because coal-fired power plants emit mercury, advances in alternative energy sources also reduce our exposure to this element.

Many current technologies may be limited by their need for scarce elements. For example, the permanent magnets in computer hard drives, wind turbines, and hybrid cars are mainly made of neodymium and dysprosium. Green chemistry can promote new opportunities. Although almost all of the elements are found in the Earth's crust, eight account for more than 98% of the total. In fact, almost three-fourths of the crust is comprised of two elements, silicon and oxygen. Besides being scarce, some elements, such as rare earth metals like cerium, yttrium, neodymium, and lanthanum, are drawn from a single source and can be difficult to separate from other materials. Current supplies are much lower than needed to support projected growth.

Approaches based on earth-abundant elements (such as silicon, iron, and aluminum) would support technology and protect resources. As discussed in the essay on page 54, atoms of a material can be reclaimed directly through recycling processes or spread through the environment. If released, hazardous materials can impact health and the environment, so recycling of these elements should be a priority. Reclaimed raw materials reduce the demand for natural resources—notably, scarce elements. Green chemistry supports the design of materials where the individual elemental components can be recycled easily.

Green chemistry approaches are especially important when products and processes present health or environmental risks. Identifying and replacing hazardous and rare elements can lead to greener technologies and a sustainable future for everyone.

◀ New technologies have led to mercury-free efficient lightbulbs like this one. These products save energy and do not contain toxic elements used in traditional fluorescent lighting.

CRITICAL THINKING  EXERCISES

Apply knowledge that you have gained in this chapter and one or more of the FLaReS principles (Chapter 1) to evaluate the following statements or claims.

2.1 In a science fiction movie, a woman proceeds through nine months of pregnancy in minutes. She takes in no nutrients during this time. She dies during labor and an emergency C-section is performed to save the child. The child lives for only a matter of hours, rapidly aging, and dies a withered old man. A classmate claims that the movie is based on a documented, secret alien encounter.

2.2 A health-food store has a large display of bracelets made of copper metal. Some people claim that wearing such a bracelet will protect the wearer from arthritis or rheumatoid diseases.

2.3 An old cookbook claims that cooking acidic food, such as spaghetti sauce, in an iron pot provides more nutrients than cooking the same food in an aluminum pot.

2.4 A company markets a device it calls a "water enerоxizer." It claims the device can supply so much energy to drinking water that the mass of oxygen in the water is increased, thereby providing more oxygen to the body.

SUMMARY

Section 2.1—The concept of atoms was first suggested in ancient Greece by Leucippus and Democritus. However, this idea was rejected for almost 2000 years in favor of Aristotle's view that matter was continuous in nature.

Section 2.2—The **law of conservation of mass** resulted from careful experiments by Lavoisier and others, who weighed all the reactants and products for a number of chemical reactions and found that no change in mass occurred. Boyle said that a proposed element must be tested. If it could be broken down into simpler substances, it was not an element. The **law of definite proportions** (law of constant composition) was formulated by Proust, based on his experiments and on those of Berzelius. It states that a given compound always contains the same elements in exactly the same proportions by mass.

Section 2.3—In 1803, Dalton explained the laws of definite proportions and conservation of mass with his **atomic theory**, which had four main points: (1) Matter is made up of tiny particles called atoms; (2) atoms of the same element are alike; (3) compounds are formed when atoms of different elements combine in certain proportions; and (4) during chemical reactions, atoms are rearranged, not destroyed. Dalton also discovered the **law of multiple proportions**, which states that different elements might combine in two or more different sets of proportions, each set corresponding to a different compound. His atomic theory also explained this new law. These laws can be used to perform calculations to find the amounts of elements that combine or are present in a compound or reaction. In more than two centuries atomic theory has undergone only minor modification.

Section 2.4—Berzelius published a table of atomic weights in 1828, and his values agree well with modern ones. In 1869, Mendeleev published his version of the **periodic table**, a systematic arrangement of the elements that allowed him to predict the existence and properties of undiscovered elements. In the modern periodic table, each element is listed, along with its symbol and the average mass of an atom of that element in **atomic mass units**, which are very tiny units of mass.

Section 2.5—Because atoms are conserved in chemical reactions, matter (which is made of atoms) can always be recycled. Atoms can be lost, in effect, if they are scattered in the environment. A **molecule** is a group of atoms chemically bonded together. Just as an atom is the smallest particle of an element, a modecule is the smallest particle of most compounds.

Green chemistry When chemists design products and processes, potential impacts on human health and the environment of the incorporated elements should be considered. Identifying and replacing toxic and rare elements can lead to greener technologies and enhance sustainability.

Learning Objectives

› Explain the ancient Greeks' ideas about the characteristics of matter. (2.1)	Problems 1–3
› Describe the significance of the laws of conservation of mass and definite proportions. (2.2)	Problems 6, 10, 15–28, 45, 48
› Calculate the amounts of elements from the composition of a compound. (2.2)	Problems 41–43, 46, 49–51
› Explain why the idea that matter is made of atoms is a theory. (2.3)	Problem 8
› Understand how atomic theory explains the law of conservation of mass. (2.3)	Problem 11, 35–40, 44, 47

› Describe how the elements are arranged in the periodic table and why the arrangement is important. (2.4)	Problem 50
› Distinguish atoms from molecules. (2.5)	Problem 12
› Identify elements that can be classified as hazardous or rare.	Problem 52
› Explain how green chemistry can change technologies that rely on hazardous or rare elements.	Problems 53, 54

REVIEW QUESTIONS

1. Distinguish between **(a)** the atomic view and the continuous view of matter and **(b)** the ancient Greek definition of an element and the modern one.
2. What was Democritus's contribution to atomic theory? Why did the idea that matter was continuous (rather than atomic) prevail for so long? What discoveries finally refuted the idea?
3. Consider the following *macroscopic* (visible to the unaided eye) objects. Which are best classified as *discrete* (like Democritus's description of matter) and which are *continuous* (like Aristotle's description)?
   a. people **b.** cloth
   c. calculators **d.** milk chocolate
   e. M&M's candies
4. Describe Lavoisier's contribution to the development of modern chemistry.
5. How did Boyle define an element?
6. State the law of definite proportions, and illustrate it using the compound zinc sulfide, ZnS.
7. State the law of multiple proportions. For a fixed mass of the first element in each of the following compounds, what is the relationship between (ratio of) the
   a. masses of oxygen in ClO_2 and in ClO?
   b. masses of fluorine in ClF_3 and ClF?
   c. masses of oxygen in P_4O_6 and P_4O_{10}?
8. Outline the main points of Dalton's atomic theory.
9. In the figure, the blue spheres represent phosphorus atoms, and the red ones represent oxygen atoms. The box labeled "Initial" represents a mixture. Which one of the other three boxes (A, B, or C) could *not* represent that mixture after a chemical reaction occurred? Explain briefly.

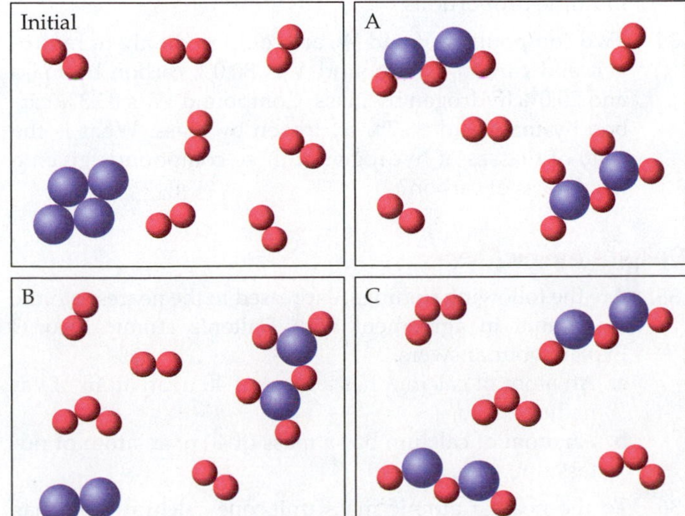

10. Fructose (fruit sugar) is always composed of 40.0% carbon, 53.3% oxygen, and 6.7% hydrogen regardless of the fruit that it comes from. What law does this illustrate?
11. Use Dalton's atomic theory to explain each of the following laws and give an example that illustrates each law.
    a. conservation of mass
    b. definite proportions
    c. multiple proportions
12. Lavoisier considered *alumina* an element. In 1825, the Danish chemist Hans Christian Oersted isolated aluminum metal by reacting aluminum chloride with potassium. Later experiments showed that alumina is formed by reacting aluminum metal with oxygen. What did these experiments prove?
13. What law does the following list of compounds illustrate? N_2O, NO, NO_2, N_2O_4
14. What did each of the following contribute to the development of modern chemistry?
    a. J. J. Berzelius
    b. Henry Cavendish
    c. Joseph Proust
    d. Dmitri Mendeleev

PROBLEMS

Conservation of Mass

15. If 45.0 g of vinegar is added to 5.0 g of baking soda in an open beaker, the total mass after reaction is less than 50.0 g. The vinegar bubbles and fizzes during the reaction. Has the law of conservation of mass been violated? Explain.

16. An iron nail dissolves in a solution of hydrochloric acid. The nail disappears. Have the iron atoms been destroyed? If so, how? If not, where are they?

17. Water is about 11.2% hydrogen and 88.8% oxygen by weight. If you fill a container with 11.2 g of hydrogen and 88.8 g of oxygen, does that vessel contain water? Explain.

18. Many reactions seem to violate the law of conservation of mass. For example, **(a)** when an iron object rusts, the rusty object has a greater mass than before, and **(b)** when a piece of charcoal burns, the remaining material (ash) has less mass than the charcoal. Explain these observations, and suggest an experiment that would demonstrate that mass is conserved in each case.

19. Acetylene, used for welding, contains 24.02 g of carbon for every 2.02 g of hydrogen. If you have 78.5 g of carbon that can be converted to acetylene, what mass of hydrogen will be needed for the conversion?

20. Nitrous oxide (N_2O, "laughing gas") contains 28.01 g of nitrogen in every 44.01 g of nitrous oxide. What mass of nitrous oxide can be formed from 48.7 g of nitrogen?

21. A student in a chemistry class calculates the mass of titanium(IV) oxide (which contains only titanium and oxygen) that can be formed from 37.7 g of titanium and 20.1 g of oxygen. Her calculated answer is 59.8 g of titanium(IV) oxide. Explain to the student why her answer is impossible.

22. A student heats 2.796 g of zinc powder with 2.414 g of sulfur. He reports that he obtains 4.169 g of zinc sulfide and recovers 1.041 g of unreacted sulfur. Show by calculation whether or not his results obey the law of conservation of mass.

23. When 1.00 g zinc and 0.80 g sulfur are allowed to react, all the zinc is used up, 1.50 g of zinc sulfide is formed, and some unreacted sulfur remains. What is the mass of *unreacted* sulfur (choose one)?
    a. 0.20 g
    b. 0.30 g
    c. 0.50 g
    d. impossible to determine from this information alone

24. A city has to come up with a plan to dispose of its solid wastes. The solid wastes consist of many different kinds of materials, and the materials are comprised of many different kinds of atoms. The options for disposal include burying the wastes in a landfill, incinerating them, and dumping them at sea. Which method, if any, will get rid of the atoms that make up the wastes? Which method, if any, will immediately change the chemical form of the wastes?

Definite Proportions

25. When 18.02 g of water is decomposed by electrolysis, 16.00 g of oxygen and 2.02 g of hydrogen are formed. According to the law of definite proportions, what masses, in grams, of **(a)** hydrogen and **(b)** oxygen will be formed by the electrolysis of 775 g of water?

26. Hydrogen from the decomposition of water has been promoted as the fuel of the future (Chapter 15). What mass of water, in kilograms, would have to be electrolyzed to produce 125 kg of hydrogen? (See Problem 25.)

27. Given a plentiful supply of air, 3.0 parts carbon will react with 8.0 parts oxygen by mass to produce carbon dioxide. Use this mass ratio to calculate the mass of carbon required to produce 14 kg of carbon dioxide.

28. When 31 g of phosphorus reacts with oxygen, 71 g of an oxide of phosphorus is the product. What mass of phosphorus is needed to produce 39 g of this product?

Multiple Proportions

29. Carbon combines with oxygen in a mass ratio of 1.000:2.664 to form carbon dioxide (CO_2) and in a mass ratio of 1.000:1.332 to form carbon monoxide (CO). A third carbon-oxygen compound, called carbon suboxide, is 52.96% C by mass and 47.04% O by mass. Show that these compounds follow the law of multiple proportions.

30. A compound containing only oxygen and rubidium has 0.187 g of O per 1.00 g of Rb. The relative atomic masses are 16.0 for O and 85.5 for Rb. What is a possible O-to-Rb mass ratio for a different oxide of rubidium (choose one)?
    a. 8.0:85.5 **b.** 16.0:85.5
    c. 32.0:85.5 **d.** 16.0:171

31. A sample of an oxide of tin with the formula SnO consists of 0.742 g of tin and 0.100 g of oxygen. A sample of another oxide of tin consists of 0.555 g of tin and 0.150 g of oxygen. What is the formula of the second oxide?

32. Consider three oxides of nitrogen, X, Y, and Z. Oxide X has an oxygen-to-nitrogen mass ratio of 2.28:1.00, oxide Y has an oxygen-to-nitrogen mass ratio of 1.14:1.00, and oxide Z has an oxygen-to-nitrogen mass ratio of 0.57:1.00. What is the whole-number ratio of masses of oxygen in these compounds given a fixed mass of nitrogen?

33. Sulfur forms two compounds with fluorine, T and U. Compound T has 0.447 g of sulfur combined with 1.06 g of fluorine; compound U has 0.438 g of sulfur combined with 1.56 g of fluorine. Show that these data support the law of multiple proportions.

34. Two compounds, V and W, are composed only of hydrogen and carbon. Compound V is 80.0% carbon by mass and 20.0% hydrogen by mass. Compound W is 83.3% carbon by mass and 16.7% hydrogen by mass. What is the ratio of masses of hydrogen in these compounds given a fixed mass of carbon?

Dalton's Atomic Theory

35. Are the following findings, expressed to the nearest atomic mass unit, in agreement with Dalton's atomic theory? Explain your answers.
    a. An atom of calcium has a mass of 40 u; an atom of vanadium, 50 u.
    b. An atom of calcium has a mass of 40 u; an atom of potassium, 40 u.

36. To the nearest atomic mass unit, one calcium atom has a mass of 40 u and another calcium atom has a mass of

44 u. Do these findings support or contradict Dalton's atomic theory? Explain.

37. An atom of uranium splits into two smaller atoms when struck by a particle called a *neutron*. Do these findings support or contradict Dalton's atomic theory? Explain.

38. According to Dalton's atomic theory, when elements react, their atoms combine in (choose one)
    a. a simple whole-number ratio that is unique for each set of elements
    b. exactly a 1:1 ratio
    c. one or more simple whole-number ratios
    d. pairs
    e. random proportions

39. Hydrogen and oxygen combine in a mass ratio of about 1:8 to form water. If every water molecule consists of two atoms of hydrogen and one atom of oxygen, what fraction or multiple of the mass of a hydrogen atom is the mass of an oxygen atom?
    a. $\frac{1}{16}$ **b.** $\frac{1}{8}$ **c.** 8 times **d.** 16 times

40. The elements fluorine and nitrogen combine in a mass ratio of 57:14 to form a compound. If every molecule of the compound consists of three atoms of fluorine and one atom of nitrogen, what fraction or multiple of the mass of a fluorine atom is the mass of a nitrogen atom?
    a. $\frac{19}{14}$ **b.** 3 times **c.** $\frac{14}{19}$ **d.** 14 times

Chemical Compounds

41. A blue solid called *azulene* is thought to be a pure compound. Analyses of three samples of the material yield the following results.

	Mass of Sample	Mass of Carbon	Mass of Hydrogen
Sample 1	1.000 g	0.937 g	0.0629 g
Sample 2	0.244 g	0.229 g	0.0153 g
Sample 3	0.100 g	0.094 g	0.0063 g

Could the material be a pure compound?

42. A colorless liquid is thought to be a pure compound. Analyses of three samples of the material yield the following results.

	Mass of Sample	Mass of Carbon	Mass of Hydrogen
Sample 1	1.000 g	0.862 g	0.138 g
Sample 2	1.549 g	1.295 g	0.254 g
Sample 3	0.988 g	0.826 g	0.162 g

Could the material be a pure compound? Explain.

ADDITIONAL PROBLEMS

43. When 0.2250 g of magnesium is heated with 0.5331 g of nitrogen in a closed container, the magnesium is completely converted to 0.3114 g of magnesium nitride. What mass of unreacted nitrogen must remain?

44. Gasoline can be approximated by the formula C_8H_8. An environmental advocate points out that burning one gallon (about 7 lb) of gasoline produces about 19 lb of carbon dioxide, a greenhouse gas that raises the temperature of the atmosphere. Explain this seeming contradiction of the law of conservation of mass.

45. A compound of uranium and fluorine is used to generate uranium for nuclear power plants. The gas can be decomposed to yield 2.09 parts by mass of uranium for every 1 part by mass of fluorine. If the relative mass of a uranium atom is 238 and the relative mass of a fluorine atom is 19, calculate the number of fluorine atoms that are combined with one uranium atom.

46. Two experiments were performed in which sulfur was burned completely in pure oxygen gas, producing sulfur dioxide and leaving some unreacted oxygen. In the first experiment, burning 0.312 g of sulfur produced 0.623 g of sulfur dioxide. In the second experiment, 1.305 g of sulfur was burned. What mass of sulfur dioxide was produced?

47. In an experiment illustrated at right, about 15 mL of hydrochloric acid solution was placed in a flask and approximately 3 g of sodium carbonate was put into a balloon. The opening of the balloon was then carefully stretched over the top of the flask, taking care not to allow the sodium carbonate to fall into the acid in the flask. The flask was placed on an electronic balance, and the mass of the flask and its contents was found to be 38.61 g. The sodium carbonate was then slowly shaken into the acid. The balloon began to fill with gas. When the reaction was complete, the mass of the flask and its contents, including the gas in the balloon, was found to be 38.61 g. What law does this experiment illustrate? Explain.

48. In one experiment, 3.06 g hydrogen was allowed to react with an excess of oxygen to form 27.35 g water. In a second experiment, electric current broke down a sample of water into 1.45 g hydrogen and 11.51 g oxygen. Are these results consistent with the law of definite proportions? Show why or why not.

49. Use Figure 2.4 to calculate the mass of mercuric oxide that would be needed to produce 100.0 g of mercury metal.

50. Gold chloride, $AuCl_3$, is formed when gold metal is dissolved in *aqua regia*, a highly corrosive mixture of acids. Determine the mass ratio of gold to chlorine in gold chloride:
  a. based on Mendeleev's values from his periodic table (Figure 2.10)
  b. based on values in the modern periodic table in the inside front cover of this book

51. See Table 2.1. Another compound of nitrogen and oxygen contains 0.5836 g of nitrogen per 1.000 g of oxygen. Calculate the ratio of mass of N in this compound to mass of N in nitrogen dioxide. What *whole-number* ratio does this value represent?

52. Identify whether the following elements are hazardous, rare, or neither.
  a. silicon
  b. neodymium
  c. mercury
  d. oxygen
  e. lead

53. Give two examples of how green chemistry has helped to reduce the use of lead in consumer products.

54. Why is it important to recycle mercury-based fluorescent lightbulbs instead of putting them in landfills?

COLLABORATIVE GROUP PROJECTS

Prepare a PowerPoint, poster, or other presentation (as directed by your instructor) to share with the class.

1. Prepare a brief biographical report on one of the following.
   a. Henry Cavendish **b.** Joseph Proust
   c. John Newlands **d.** Lothar Meyer
   e. Dmitri Mendeleev **f.** John Dalton
   g. Antoine Lavoisier **h.** Marie-Anne Pierrette Paulze
2. Prepare a brief report on early Greek contributions to and ideas in the field of science, focusing on the work of one of the following: Aristotle, Leucippus, Democritus, Thales, Anaximander, Anaximenes of Miletus, Heraclitus, Empedocles, or another Greek philosopher of the time before 300 B.C.E.
3. Prepare a brief report on the *phlogiston theory*. Describe what the theory was, how it explained changes in mass when something is burned, and why it was finally abandoned.
4. Write a brief essay on recycling of one of the following: metals, paper, plastics, glass, food wastes, or grass clippings. Contrast a recycling method that maintains the properties of an element with one that changes them.

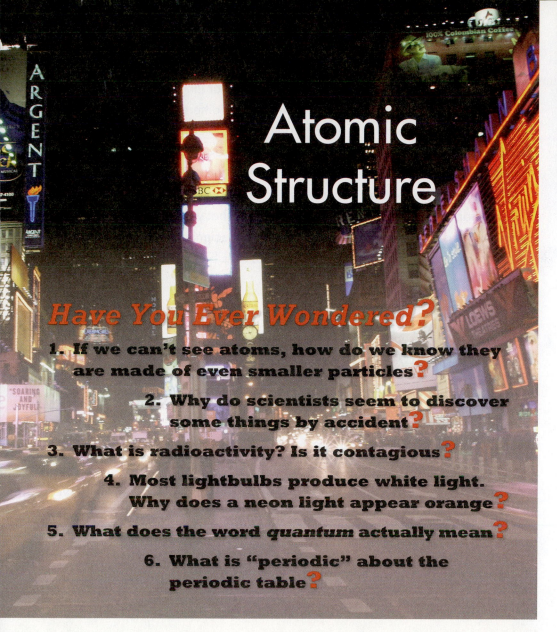

Atomic Structure

Have You Ever Wondered?

1. If we can't see atoms, how do we know they are made of even smaller particles?
2. Why do scientists seem to discover some things by accident?
3. What is radioactivity? Is it contagious?
4. Most lightbulbs produce white light. Why does a neon light appear orange?
5. What does the word *quantum* actually mean?
6. What is "periodic" about the periodic table?

Images of the Invisible

Atoms are exceedingly tiny particles, much too small to see even with an optical microscope. It is true that scientists can obtain images of individual atoms, but they use special instruments such as the scanning tunneling microscope (STM, page 53). Even so, we can see only outlines of atoms and their arrangements in a substance. If atoms are so small, how can we possibly know anything about their inner structures?

Although scientists have never examined the interior of an atom directly, they have been able to obtain a great deal of *indirect* information. By designing clever experiments and exercising their powers of deduction, scientists have constructed an amazingly detailed model of what an atom's interior must be like.

Neon lights—the signature of entertainment, restaurants, bars, and the big city. Interestingly enough, most of the flickering illumination seen at the Radio City Music Hall, on Times Square, and in Las Vegas is not from the element neon. The liquid fire of real neon lights is a characteristic orange-red color, and neon cannot be made to glow in any other color. Other colors are created by coating the inside of the tubing with a *phosphor* that glows in a specific color when current is applied to the tube. But why will neon only give off orange-red light? The answer lies in the structure of its atoms—the subject of this chapter.

Learning Objectives

- Explain the electrical properties of an atom. (3.1)
- Describe how the properties of electricity explain the structure of atoms. (3.1)
- Describe the experiments that led to the discovery of X-rays and an explanation of radioactivity. (3.2)
- Distinguish the three main kinds of radioactivity: alpha, beta, and gamma. (3.3)
- Sketch the nuclear model of the atom, and identify its parts. (3.4)
- List the particles that make up the nucleus of an atom, and give their relative masses and electric charges. (3.5)
- Identify elements and isotopes from their nuclear particles. (3.5)
- Define *quantum*. (3.6)
- Arrange the electrons in a given atom in energy levels (shells). (3.6)
- Relate the idea of a quantum of energy to an orbital. (3.7)
- Write an electron configuration (in subshell notation) for a given atom. (3.7)
- Describe how an element's electron configuration relates to its location in the periodic table. (3.8)
- Distinguish the conversion of solar energy into electrical energy in a solar cell from the conversion of solar energy into the chemical-bond energy of a solar fuel.
- Explain why splitting water into the elements hydrogen and oxygen requires an energy input and producing water by the reaction of hydrogen and oxygen releases energy.

Why do we care about the structure of particles as tiny as atoms? The reason is that the arrangement of various parts of atoms determines the properties of different kinds of matter. Only by understanding atomic structure can we learn how atoms combine to make millions of different substances. With such knowledge, we can modify and synthesize materials to meet our needs more precisely. Knowledge of atomic structure is even essential to good health care. Many medical diagnoses are based on chemical analyses that have been developed from our understanding of atomic structure.

Perhaps of greater interest to you is the fact that your understanding of chemistry (as well as much of biology and other sciences) depends, at least in part, on your knowledge of atomic structure. Let's begin by going back to the time of John Dalton.

▲ In addition to Michael Faraday's work in electrochemistry, he also devised methods for liquefying gases such as chlorine and invented the electrical transformer.

3.1 Electricity and the Atom

Learning Objectives › Explain the electrical properties of an atom. › Describe how the properties of electricity explain the structure of atoms.

Dalton, who set forth his atomic theory in 1803, regarded the atom as hard and indivisible. However, it wasn't long before evidence accumulated to show that matter has electrical properties. Indeed, the electrolytic decomposition of water by Nicholson and Carlisle in 1800 (Section 2.2) had already indicated this. Electricity played an important role in unraveling the structure of the atom.

Static electricity has been known since ancient times, but continuous electric current was born with the nineteenth century. In 1800, Alessandro Volta invented an electrochemical cell much like a modern battery. If the poles of such a cell are connected by a wire, current flows through the wire. The current is sustained by chemical reactions inside the cell. Volta's invention soon was applied in many areas of science and everyday life.

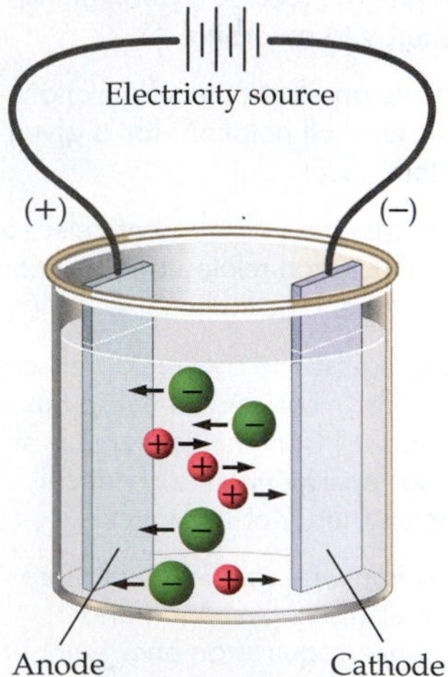

▲ **Figure 3.1** An electrolysis apparatus. The electricity source (for example, a battery) directs electrons through wires from the anode to the cathode. Cations (+) are attracted to the cathode (−), and anions (−) are attracted to the anode (+). This migration of ions is the flow of electricity through the solution.

Electrolysis

Soon after Volta's invention, Humphry Davy (1778–1829), a British chemist, built a powerful battery that he used to pass electricity through molten (melted) salts. Davy quickly discovered several new elements. In 1807, he liberated highly reactive potassium metal from molten potassium hydroxide. Shortly thereafter, he produced sodium metal by passing electricity through molten sodium hydroxide. Within a year, Davy had also produced magnesium, strontium, barium, and calcium metals for the first time. The science of electrochemistry was born. (We will study electrochemistry in more detail in Chapter 8.)

Davy's protégé, Michael Faraday (1791–1867), greatly extended this new science. Lacking in formal education, Faraday consulted others to define many of the terms we still use today. His physician, Whitlock Nicholl (1786–1838), helped coin the term **electrolysis** for chemical reactions caused by electricity (Figure 3.1) and the name **electrolyte** for a compound that conducts electricity when melted or dissolved in water. English classical scholar William Whewell (1794–1866) suggested the names for the parts of the electrolytic apparatus. The carbon rods or metal strips inserted into a molten compound or a solution to carry the electric current are called **electrodes**. The electrode that bears a positive charge is the **anode**, and the negatively charged electrode is the **cathode**. The entities that carry the electric current through a melted compound or a solution are called *ions*. An **ion** is an atom or a group of atoms bonded together that has an electric charge. An ion with a negative charge is an **anion**; it travels toward the anode. A positively charged ion is a **cation**; it moves toward the cathode.

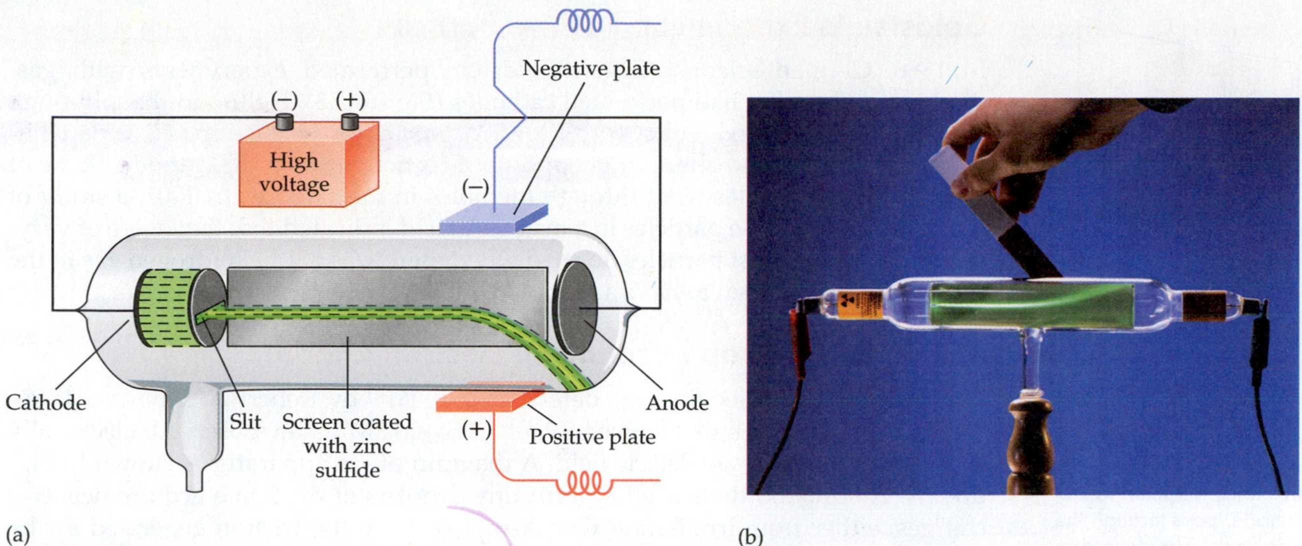

▲ **Figure 3.2** Thomson's apparatus, showing deflection of the cathode rays (a beam of electrons). Cathode rays are invisible but can be observed because they produce a green fluorescence when they strike a zinc sulfide–coated screen. The diagram (a) shows deflection of the beam in an electric field. The photograph (b) shows the deflection in a magnetic field. Cathode rays travel in straight lines unless some kind of external field is applied.

Faraday's work established that atoms have electrical properties, but further details of atomic structure had to wait several decades for more powerful sources of electricity and better vacuum pumps.

1. If we can't see atoms, how do we know they are made of even smaller particles? The existence of electrons and other subatomic particles was deduced from the behavior of electricity. The existence and behavior of the subatomic particles make atoms behave the way they do.

Cathode-Ray Tubes

In 1875, William Crookes (1832–1919), an English chemist, was able to construct a low-pressure gas-discharge tube that would allow electricity to pass through it. His experiment is shown in Figure 3.2. Crookes's tube is the antecedent of neon tubes used for signs and of cathode-ray tubes used in old television sets and computer monitors. Metal electrodes are sealed in the tube, which is connected to a vacuum pump so that most of the air can be removed from it. A beam of current produces a green fluorescence when it strikes a screen coated with zinc sulfide. This beam, which seems to leave the cathode and travel to the anode, was called a **cathode ray**.

Thomson's Experiment: Mass-to-Charge Ratio

Considerable speculation arose about the nature of cathode rays, and many experiments were undertaken. Were these rays beams of particles, or did they consist of a wavelike form of energy much like visible light? The answer came (as scientific answers should) from an experiment performed by the English physicist Joseph John Thomson in 1897. Thomson showed that cathode rays were deflected in an electric field (look again at Figure 3.2a). The beam was attracted to the positive plate and repelled by the negative plate. Thomson concluded that cathode rays consisted of negatively charged particles. His experiments also showed that the particles were the same regardless of the materials from which the electrodes were made or the type of gas in the tube. He concluded that these negative particles are part of all kinds of atoms. Thomson named these negatively charged units **electrons**. Cathode rays, then, are beams of electrons emanating from the cathode of a gas-discharge tube.

Cathode rays are deflected in magnetic fields as well as in electric fields. The greater the charge on a particle, the more it is deflected in an electric (or magnetic) field. The heavier the particle, the less it is deflected by a force. By measuring the amount of deflection in fields of known strength, Thomson was able to calculate the *ratio* of the mass of the electron to its charge. (He could not measure either the mass or the charge separately.) Thomson was awarded the Nobel Prize in Physics in 1906.

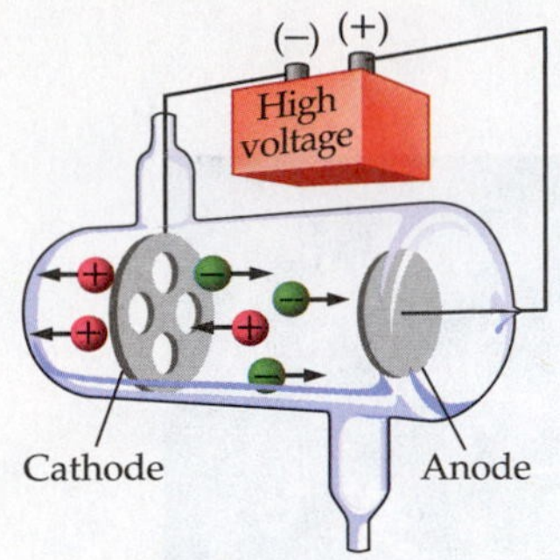

▲ **Figure 3.3** Goldstein's apparatus for the study of positive particles. This apparatus, with holes in the cathode, is a modification of the cathode-ray tube in Figure 3.2. Some positive ions, attracted toward the cathode, pass through the holes in the cathode. The deflection of these particles (not shown) in a magnetic field can be studied in the region to the left of the cathode.

Goldstein's Experiment: Positive Particles

In 1886, German scientist Eugen Goldstein performed experiments with gas-discharge tubes that had perforated cathodes (Figure 3.3). He found that although electrons were formed and sped off toward the anode as usual, positive particles were also formed and shot in the opposite direction, toward the cathode. Some of these positive particles went through the holes in the cathode. In 1907, a study of the deflection of these particles in a magnetic field indicated that they were of varying mass. The lightest particles, formed when there was a little hydrogen gas in the tube, were later shown to have a mass 1837 times that of an electron.

Millikan's Oil-Drop Experiment: Electron Charge

The charge on the electron was determined in 1909 by Robert A. Millikan (1868–1953), a physicist at the University of Chicago. Millikan observed electrically charged oil drops in an electric field. A diagram of his apparatus is shown in Figure 3.4. A spray bottle is used to form tiny droplets of oil. Some acquire negative charges, either from irradiation with X-rays or from the friction generated as the particles rub against the opening of the spray nozzle and against each other. (The charge is static electricity, just like the charge you get from walking across a nylon carpet.) Either way, the droplets acquire one or more extra electrons.

Some of the oil droplets pass into a chamber where they can be viewed through a microscope. The negative plate at the bottom of the chamber repels the negatively charged droplets, and the positive plate attracts them. By manipulating the charge on each plate and observing the behavior of the droplets, the charge on each droplet can be determined. Millikan took the smallest possible difference in charge between two droplets to be the charge of an individual electron. For his research, he received the Nobel Prize in Physics in 1923.

From Millikan's value for the charge and Thomson's value for the mass-to-charge ratio, the mass of the electron was readily calculated. That mass was found to be only 9.1×10^{-28} g. To have a mass of 1 g would require more than 1×10^{27} electrons—that's a 1 followed by 27 zeros, or a billion billion billion electrons. More important, the electron's mass is much *smaller* than that of the lightest atom. This means that electrons are much smaller than atoms.

You can find out more about numbers like 9.1×10^{-28} and 1×10^{27} in the Appendix. However, in practice, we seldom use the actual mass and charge of the electron. For many purposes, the electron is considered the unit of electrical charge. The charge is shown as a superscript minus sign (meaning $^{1-}$). In indicating charges on ions, we use $^{-}$ to indicate a net charge due to one "extra" electron, $^{2-}$ to indicate a charge due to two "extra" electrons, and so on.

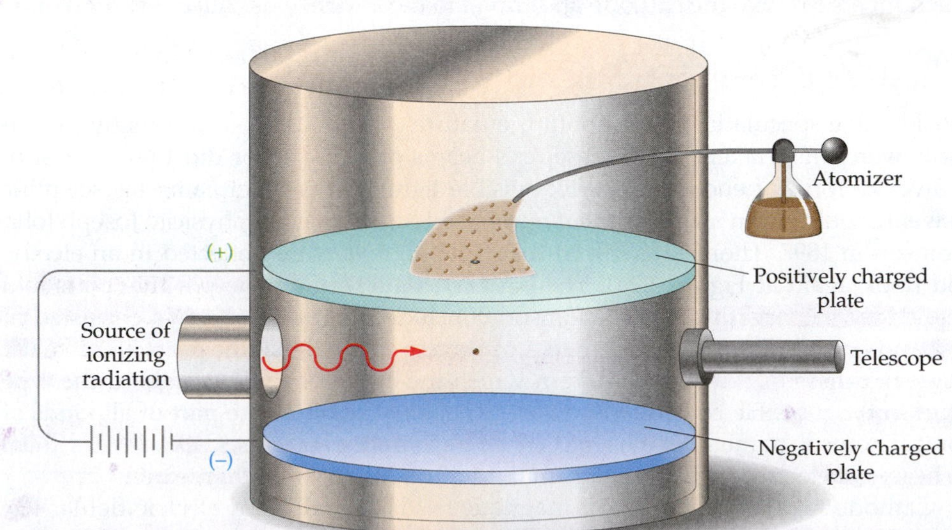

▲ **Figure 3.4** The Millikan oil-drop experiment. Oil drops irradiated with X-rays pick up electrons and become negatively charged. Their fall due to gravity can be balanced by adjusting the voltage of the electric field. The charge on the oil drop can be determined from the applied voltage and the mass of the oil drop. The charge on each drop is that of some whole number of electrons.

Self-Assessment Questions

1. The use of electricity to cause a chemical reaction is called
   a. anodizing b. corrosion c. electrolysis d. hydrolysis
2. During electrolysis of molten sodium hydroxide, chloride anions move to the
   a. anode, which is negatively charged
   b. anode, which is positively charged
   c. cathode, which is negatively charged
   d. cathode, which is positively charged
3. Cathode rays are *not*
   a. composed of negatively charged particles
   b. composed of particles with a mass of 1 u
   c. deflected by electric fields
   d. the same from element to element
4. Thomson used a cathode-ray tube to discover that cathode rays
   a. are deflected by an electric field
   b. are radiation similar to X-rays
   c. could ionize air inside the tube
   d. could ionize the air outside the far end of the tube
5. When J. J. Thomson discovered the electron, he measured its
   a. atomic number b. charge c. mass d. mass-to-charge ratio
6. In his oil-drop experiment, Millikan determined the charge of an electron by
   a. measuring the diameters of the tiniest drops
   b. noting that the drops had either a certain minimum charge or multiples of that charge
   c. using an atomizer that could spray out individual electrons
   d. viewing the smallest charged drops microscopically and noting that they had one extra electron

Answers: 1, c; 2, b; 3, b; 4, a; 5, d; 6, b

3.2 Serendipity in Science: X-Rays and Radioactivity

Learning Objective › Describe the experiments that led to the discovery of X-rays and an explanation of radioactivity.

Let's take a look at two serendipitous discoveries of the last years of the nineteenth century that profoundly changed the world and are related to atomic structure.

2. Why do scientists seem to discover some things by accident? *Serendipity*—a "happy accident" like drilling for water and striking oil—happens to everyone at times. Scientists, however, are trained observers. When something unexpected happens, they often wonder why and investigate. The same accident might happen to an untrained person and go unnoticed (though often even scientists miss important finds at first). Or, if noticed, its significance might not be grasped.

Roentgen: The Discovery of X-Rays

In 1895, German scientist Wilhelm Conrad Roentgen (1845–1923) was working in a dark room, studying the glow produced in certain substances by cathode rays. To his surprise, he noted this glow on a chemically treated piece of paper some distance from the cathode-ray tube. The paper even glowed when a wall separated the tube from the paper; this type of ray could travel through walls. When he waved his hand between the radiation source and the glowing paper, he was able to see an image of the bones of his hand in darker shades on the paper. He called these mysterious rays **X-rays**. He found in general that X-rays were absorbed more by bone or other hard and fairly dense materials than by soft, less dense tissues.

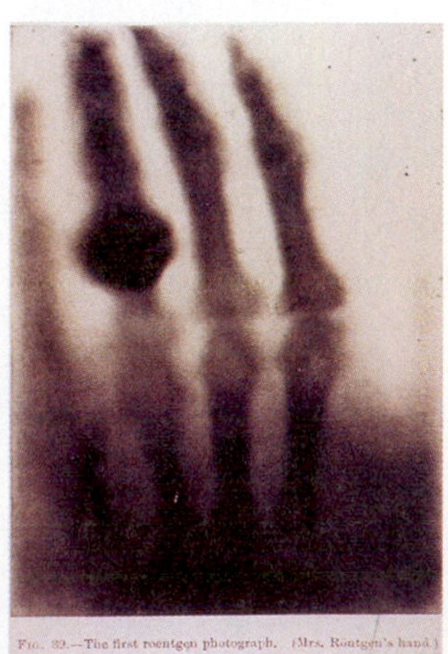

▲ X-rays were used in medicine shortly after they were discovered by Wilhelm Roentgen in 1895. In fact, the first known X-ray photograph is the one seen here—of Mrs. Roentgen's hand!

X-rays are a form of electromagnetic radiation—energy with electric and magnetic components. Among other types, electromagnetic radiation also includes visible light, radio waves, microwaves, infrared radiation, ultraviolet light, and gamma rays (Section 3.3). These forms differ in energy, with radio waves lowest in energy, followed by microwaves, infrared radiation, visible light, ultraviolet light, X-rays, and gamma rays.

Today, X-rays are one of the most widely used tools in the world for medical diagnosis. Not only are they employed for examining decayed teeth, broken bones,

▲ Marie Sklodowska Curie in her laboratory.

3. What is radioactivity? Is it contagious? Radioactivity is the spontaneous decay (occurring without a cause) of an atom into one or more other atoms. The radiation—alpha, beta, or gamma rays—given off by radioactive material is hazardous but you cannot "catch" radiation sickness from a person exposed to radiation any more than you can "catch" a sunburn from a sunburned friend.

and diseased lungs, but they are also the basis for such procedures as mammography and computerized tomography (Chapter 11). In the United States alone, payments for various radiological procedures total more than $20 billion each year. How ironic that Roentgen himself made no profit at all from his discovery. He considered X-rays a "gift to humanity" and refused to patent any part of the discovery. However, he did receive much popular acclaim and in 1901 was awarded the first Nobel Prize in Physics.

The Discovery of Radioactivity

Certain chemicals exhibit *fluorescence* after exposure to strong sunlight. They continue to glow even when taken into a dark room. In 1895, Antoine Henri Becquerel (1852–1908), a French physicist, was studying fluorescence by wrapping photographic film in black paper, placing a few crystals of the fluorescing chemical on top of the paper, and then placing the package in strong sunlight. If the glow was like ordinary light, it would not pass through the paper. On the other hand, if it was similar to X-rays, it would pass through the black paper and fog the film.

While working with a uranium compound, Becquerel made an important accidental discovery. When placed in sunlight, the compound fluoresced and fogged the film. On several cloudy days when exposure to sunlight was not possible, he prepared samples and placed them in a drawer. To his great surprise, the photographic film was fogged even though the uranium compound had not been exposed to sunlight. Further experiments showed that the radiation coming from the uranium compound was unrelated to fluorescence but was a characteristic of the element uranium.

Other scientists immediately began to study this new radiation. Becquerel's graduate student from Poland, Marie Sklodowska, gave the phenomenon a name: radioactivity. **Radioactivity** is the spontaneous emission of radiation from certain unstable elements. Marie later married Pierre Curie, a French physicist. Together they discovered the radioactive elements polonium and radium, and with Becquerel they shared the 1903 Nobel Prize in Physics.

After her husband's death in 1906, Marie Curie continued to work with radioactive substances, winning the Nobel Prize in Chemistry in 1911. For more than 50 years, she was the only person ever to have received two Nobel Prizes.

Self-Assessment Questions

1. When Roentgen saw an X-ray image of his hand, the bones were darker than the glowing paper because the X-rays were
   a. absorbed more by bone than by flesh
   b. radiation that is less energetic than visible light
   c. made up of fast-moving atoms
   d. a type of radioactivity
2. Radioactivity arises from elements that
   a. absorb radio waves and release stronger radiation
   b. are unstable and emit radiation
   c. give off X-rays
   d. undergo fission (splitting) of their atoms when they absorb energy

Answers: 1, a; 2, b

3.3 Three Types of Radioactivity

Learning Objective › Distinguish the three main kinds of radioactivity: alpha, beta, and gamma.

Scientists soon showed that three types of radiation emanated from various radioactive elements. Ernest Rutherford (1871–1937), a New Zealander who pursued his career in Canada and Great Britain, chose the names *alpha*, *beta*, and *gamma* for

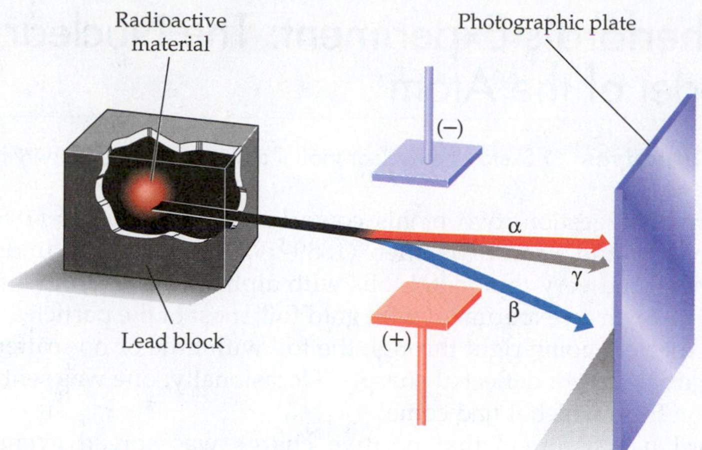

◀ **Figure 3.5** Behavior of a beam of radioactivity in an electric field.

Q: *Why are alpha rays deflected upward in this figure? Why are beta rays deflected downward?*

the three types of radioactivity. When passed through a strong magnetic or electric field, the alpha type was deflected in a manner indicating that it consisted of a beam of positive particles (Figure 3.5). Later experiments showed that an **alpha particle** has a mass four times that of a hydrogen atom and a charge twice the magnitude of, but opposite in sign to, that of an electron. An alpha particle is in fact identical to the nucleus (Section 3.4) of a helium atom and is often symbolized by He^{2+}.

The beta radiation was shown to be made up of negatively charged particles identical to those of cathode rays. Therefore, a **beta particle** is an electron, although it has much more energy than an electron in an atom. **Gamma rays** are not deflected by a magnetic field. They are a form of electromagnetic radiation, much like the X-rays used in medical work but even more energetic and more penetrating. The three types of radioactivity are summarized in Table 3.1.

The discoveries of the late nineteenth century paved the way for an entirely new picture of the atom, which developed rapidly during the early years of the twentieth century.

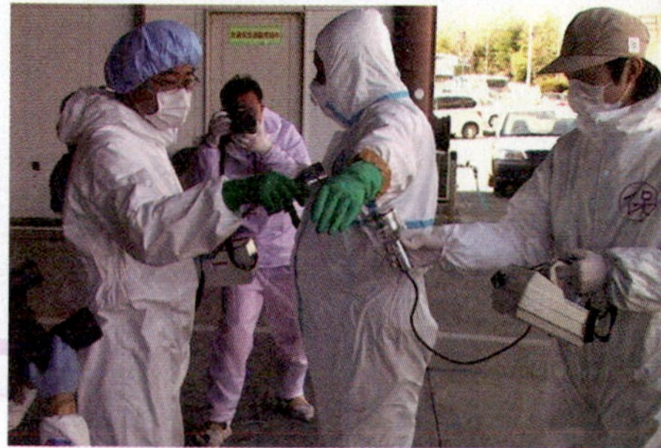

▲ **It DOES Matter!**

It is important to distinguish between the *rays* given off by a radioactive element and the radioactive element itself. Like light, alpha, beta, and gamma rays can be absorbed by materials and do not generally cause problems thereafter. A potato that has absorbed gamma rays is not harmful to eat. The serious problem from nuclear disasters, such as the Fukushima disaster of March 2011, arises because radioactive atoms escape from the reactor. Those atoms can lodge on or be absorbed by materials and give off damaging alpha, beta, or gamma rays when those materials are used. These workers from the Fukushima plant are being checked for radioactive particles on their clothing. This topic is covered in more detail in Chapter 11.

Table 3.1 Types of Radioactivity

Name	Greek Letter	Mass (u)	Charge
Alpha	α	4	2+
Beta	β	$\frac{1}{1837}$	1−
Gamma	γ	0	0

Self-Assessment Questions

1. The mass of an alpha particle is about
   a. four times that of a hydrogen atom
   b. the same as that of an electron
   c. the same as that of a hydrogen atom
   d. the same as that of a beta particle
2. Compared to the charge on an electron (designated 1−), the charge on an alpha particle is about
   a. 4− b. 1− c. 1+ d. 2+ e. 4+
3. A beta particle is a(n)
   a. boron atom b. electron c. helium nucleus d. proton
4. The mass of a gamma ray is
   a. −1 u b. 0 u c. 1 u d. 4 u

Answers: 1, a; 2, d; 3, b; 4, b

3.4 Rutherford's Experiment: The Nuclear Model of the Atom

Learning Objectives › Sketch the nuclear model of the atom, and identify its parts.

At Rutherford's suggestion, two of his coworkers—Hans Geiger (1882–1945), a German physicist, and Ernest Marsden (1889–1970), an English undergraduate student—bombarded very thin metal foils with alpha particles from a radioactive source (Figure 3.6). In an experiment with gold foil, most of the particles behaved as Rutherford expected, going right through the foil with little or no scattering. However, a few particles were deflected sharply. Occasionally, one was sent right back in the direction from which it had come!

Rutherford had assumed that positive charge was spread evenly over all the space occupied by the atom, but obviously it was not. To explain the results, Rutherford concluded that all the positive charge and nearly all the mass of an atom are concentrated at the center of the atom in a tiny core called the **nucleus**.

When an alpha particle, which is positively charged, directly approached the positively charged nucleus, it was strongly repelled and therefore sharply deflected (Figure 3.7). Because only a few alpha particles were deflected, Rutherford concluded that the nucleus must occupy only a tiny fraction of the volume of an atom. Most of the alpha particles passed right through because most of an atom is empty space. The space outside the nucleus isn't completely empty, however. It contains

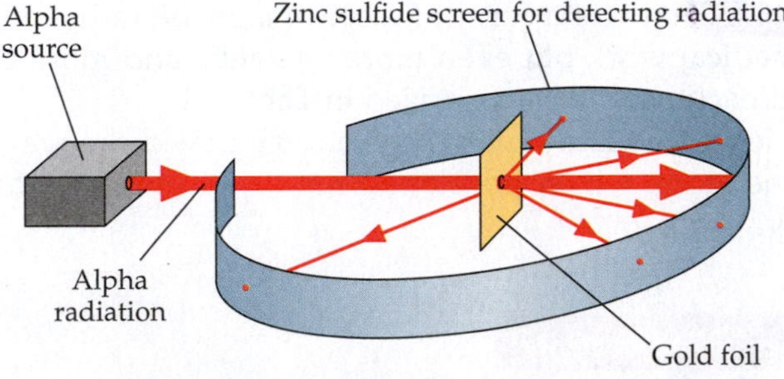

▶ **Figure 3.6** Rutherford's gold-foil experiment. Most alpha particles passed right through the gold foil, but now and then a particle was deflected.

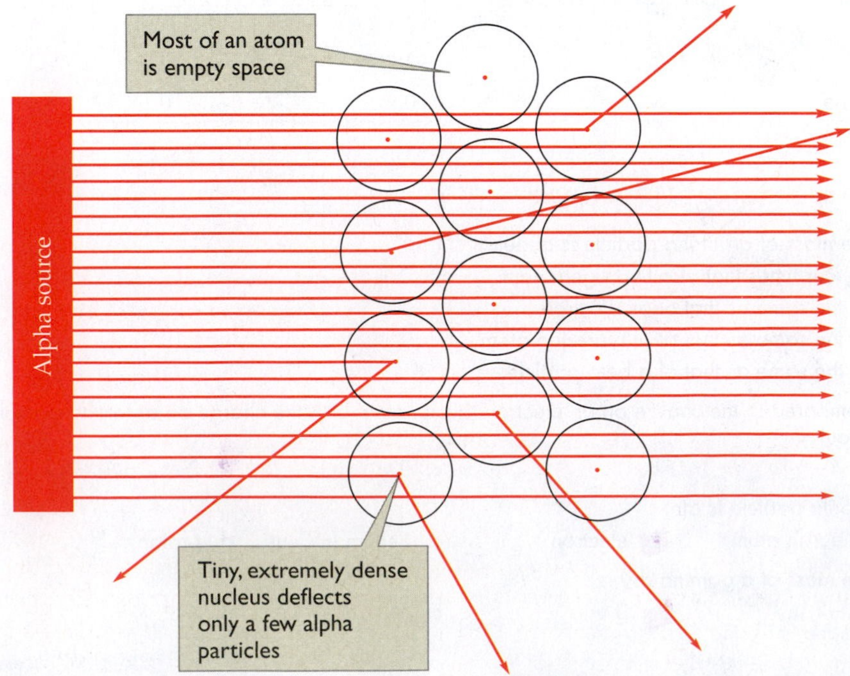

▶ **Figure 3.7** Model explaining the results of Rutherford's gold-foil experiment. Most of the alpha particles pass right through the foil because the gold atoms are mainly empty space. But some alpha particles are deflected as they pass close to a dense, positively charged atomic nucleus. Once in a while, an alpha particle encounters an atomic nucleus head-on and is knocked back in the direction from which it came.

the negatively charged electrons. Rutherford concluded that the electrons had so little mass that they were no match for the alpha particle "bullets." It would be analogous to a mouse trying to stop a charging hippopotamus.

Rutherford's nuclear theory of the atom, set forth in 1911, was revolutionary. He postulated that all the positive charge and nearly all the mass of an atom are concentrated in a tiny, tiny nucleus. The negatively charged electrons have almost no mass, yet they occupy nearly all the volume of an atom. To picture Rutherford's model, visualize a sphere as big as the largest covered football stadium. The nucleus at the middle of the sphere is as small as a pea but weighs several million tons. A few flies flitting here and there throughout the sphere represent the electrons.

Self-Assessment Questions

1. The most persuasive evidence from Rutherford's gold-foil experiment was that
   a. all the alpha particles were deflected a bit
   b. most of the alpha particles went right through the foil, but a tiny fraction were reflected right back toward the source
   c. some gold atoms were converted to lead atoms
   d. some gold atoms were split
2. Rutherford's gold-foil experiment showed that
   a. gold atoms consisted of protons in a "pudding" of electrons
   b. the nucleus was huge and positively charged
   c. the nucleus was tiny and positively charged
   d. some gold atoms were shattered by alpha particles
3. From his gold-foil experiment, Rutherford concluded that atoms consist mainly of
   a. electrons
   b. empty space
   c. neutrons
   d. protons
4. The positively charged part of the atom is its
   a. cation
   b. nucleus
   c. outer electrons
   d. widespread cloud of electrons

Answers: 1, b; 2, c; 3, b; 4, b

3.5 The Atomic Nucleus

Learning Objectives › List the particles that make up the nucleus of an atom, and give their relative masses and electric charges. › Identify elements and isotopes from their nuclear particles.

In 1914, Rutherford suggested that the smallest positive particle (the one formed when there is hydrogen gas in Goldstein's apparatus—see Section 3.1) is the unit of positive charge in the nucleus. This particle, called a **proton**, has a charge equal in magnitude to that of the electron and has nearly the same mass as a hydrogen atom. Rutherford's suggestion was that protons constitute the positively charged matter in all atoms. The nucleus of a hydrogen atom consists of one proton, and the nuclei of larger atoms contain greater numbers of protons.

But most atomic nuclei are heavier than is indicated by the number of positive charges (number of protons). For example, the helium nucleus has a charge of 2+ (and therefore two protons, according to Rutherford's theory), but its mass is *four* times that of hydrogen. This excess mass puzzled scientists at first. Then, in 1932, English physicist James Chadwick (1891–1974) discovered a particle with about the same mass as a proton but with no electrical charge. It was called a **neutron**, and its existence explains the unexpectedly high mass of the helium nucleus. Whereas the

Table 3.2 Subatomic Particles

Particle	Symbol	Mass (u)	Charge	Location in Atom
Proton	p^+	1	1+	Nucleus
Neutron	n	1	0	Nucleus
Electron	e^-	$\frac{1}{1837}$	1−	Outside nucleus

hydrogen nucleus contains only one proton of mass 1 u, the helium nucleus contains not only two protons (2 u) but also two neutrons (2 u), giving it a total mass of 4 u.

With the discovery of the neutron, the list of "building blocks" we will need for "constructing" atoms is complete. The properties of these particles are summarized in Table 3.2. (There are dozens of other subatomic particles, but most exist only momentarily and are not important to our discussion.)

Atomic Number

The number of protons in the nucleus of an atom of any element is the **atomic number (*Z*)** of that element. This number determines the kind of atom—that is, the identity of the element—and it is found on any periodic table or list of the elements. Dalton thought that the mass of an atom determines the element. We now know it is not the mass but the number of protons that determines the identity of an element. For example, every atom with 26 protons is an atom of iron (Fe), whose atomic number $Z = 26$. Any atom with 50 protons is an atom of tin (Sn), which has $Z = 50$. In a neutral atom (one with no electrical charge), the positive charge of the protons is exactly neutralized by the negative charge of the electrons. The attractive forces between the unlike charges help hold the atom together.

A proton and a neutron have almost the same mass, 1.0073 u and 1.0087 u, respectively. This difference is so small that it usually can be ignored. Thus, for many purposes, we can assume that the masses of the proton and the neutron are the same, 1 u. The proton has a charge equal in magnitude but opposite in sign to that of an electron. This charge on a proton is written as 1+. The electron has a charge of 1− and a mass of 0.00055 u. The electrons in an atom contribute so little to its total mass that their mass is usually disregarded (treated as if it were 0).

Isotopes

We can now more precisely define *isotopes*, a term we mentioned in Section 2.3. Atoms of a given element can have different numbers of neutrons in their nuclei. For example, most hydrogen atoms have a nucleus consisting of a single proton and no neutrons. However, about 1 hydrogen atom in 6700 has a neutron as well as a proton in its nucleus. This heavier hydrogen atom is called *deuterium*. A third, rare isotope of hydrogen is *tritium*, which has two neutrons and one proton in the nucleus. Whether it has one neutron, two neutrons, or none, any atom with $Z = 1$—that is, with one proton—is a hydrogen atom. Atoms that have this sort of relationship—having the same number of protons but different numbers of neutrons—are called **isotopes** (Figure 3.8).

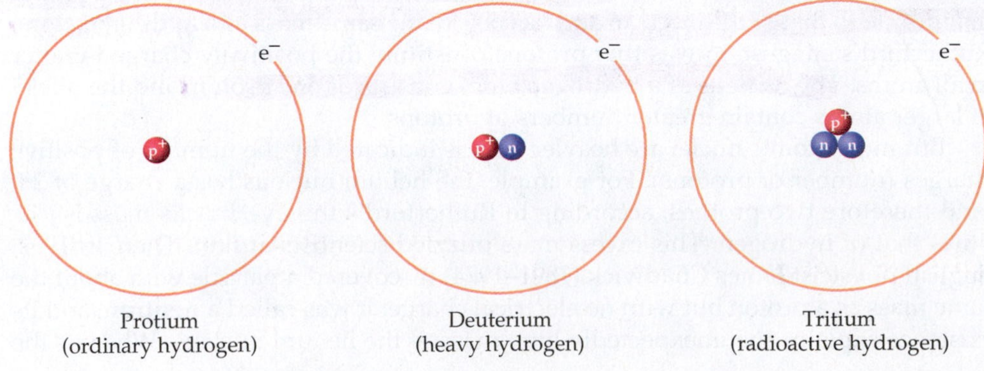

▶ **Figure 3.8** The three isotopes of hydrogen. Each has one proton and one electron, but they differ in the number of neutrons in the nucleus.

Q: *What is the atomic number and mass number of each of the isotopes? What is the mass of each, in atomic mass units, to the nearest whole number?*

Most, but not all, elements exist in nature in isotopic forms. For example, tin is present in nature in 10 different isotopic forms. It also has 15 radioactive isotopes that do not occur in nature. Aluminum, on the other hand, has only one naturally occurring isotope.

Isotopes usually have little or no effect on ordinary chemical reactions. For example, all three hydrogen isotopes react with oxygen to form water. Because these isotopes differ in mass, compounds formed with them have different physical properties, but such differences are usually slight. For example, water in which both hydrogen atoms are deuterium is called *heavy water*, often represented as D_2O. Heavy water boils at 101.4 °C (instead of 100 °C) and freezes at 3.8 °C (instead of 0 °C). In nuclear reactions, however, isotopes are of the utmost importance, as we shall see in Chapter 11.

Symbols for Isotopes

Collectively, the two main nuclear particles, protons and neutrons, are called **nucleons**. Isotopes are represented by symbols with subscripts and superscripts.

$$^{A}_{Z}\mathrm{X}$$

In this general symbol, *Z* is the nuclear charge (atomic number, or number of protons), and *A* is the **mass number**, or the **nucleon number** because it is the number of nucleons. (*Nucleon number* is the term recommended by the International Union of Pure and Applied Chemistry.) As an example, the isotope with the symbol

$$^{35}_{17}\mathrm{Cl}$$

has 17 protons and 35 nucleons. The number of neutrons is therefore 35 − 17 = 18.

Isotopes often are named by adding the mass number as a suffix to the name of the element. The three hydrogen isotopes are represented as

$$^{1}_{1}\mathrm{H} \quad ^{2}_{1}\mathrm{H} \quad ^{3}_{1}\mathrm{H}$$

and named hydrogen-1, hydrogen-2, and hydrogen-3.

Example 3.1 Number of Neutrons

How many neutrons are there in the $^{235}_{92}\mathrm{U}$ nucleus?

Solution

We simply subtract the atomic number *Z* (number of protons) from the mass number *A* (number of protons plus number of neutrons).

$$A - Z = \text{number of neutrons}$$

$$235 - 92 = 143$$

There are 143 neutrons in the $^{235}_{92}\mathrm{U}$ nucleus.

■ EXERCISE 3.1A

How many neutrons are there in the $^{60}_{27}\mathrm{Co}$ nucleus?

■ EXERCISE 3.1B

An iodine isotope has 78 neutrons in its nucleus. What is the mass number and the name of the isotope?

CONCEPTUAL Example 3.2 Isotopes

Refer to the following isotope symbols, in which the letter X replaces each element symbol. **(a)** Which represent isotopes of the same element? **(b)** Which have the same mass number? **(c)** Which have the same number of neutrons?

$$^{16}_{8}\mathrm{X} \quad ^{16}_{7}\mathrm{X} \quad ^{14}_{7}\mathrm{X} \quad ^{14}_{6}\mathrm{X} \quad ^{12}_{6}\mathrm{X}$$

Solution

a. Isotopes of the same element have the same atomic number (subscript). Therefore, $^{16}_{7}X$ and $^{14}_{7}X$ are isotopes of nitrogen (N), and $^{14}_{6}X$ and $^{12}_{6}X$ are isotopes of carbon (C).

b. The mass number is the superscript, so $^{16}_{8}X$ and $^{16}_{7}X$ have the same mass number. The first is an isotope of oxygen, and the second an isotope of nitrogen. $^{14}_{7}X$ and $^{14}_{6}X$ also have the same mass number. The first is an isotope of nitrogen, and the second an isotope of carbon.

c. To determine the number of neutrons, we subtract the atomic number from the mass number. We find that $^{16}_{8}X$ and $^{14}_{6}X$ each have eight neutrons ($16 - 8 = 8$ and $14 - 6 = 8$, respectively).

■ EXERCISE 3.2A

Which of the following represent isotopes of the same element?

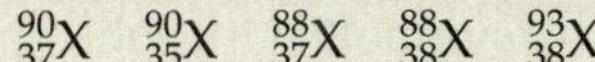

$^{90}_{37}X$ $^{90}_{35}X$ $^{88}_{37}X$ $^{88}_{38}X$ $^{93}_{38}X$

■ EXERCISE 3.2B

How many different elements are represented in Exercise 3.2A?

Self-Assessment Questions

1. The three basic components of an atom are
a. protium, deuterium, and tritium
b. protons, neutrinos, and ions
c. protons, neutrons, and electrons
d. protons, neutrons, and ions

2. The identity of an element is determined by its
a. atomic mass
b. number of atoms
c. number of electrons
d. number of protons

3. How many electrons are required to equal the mass of one proton?
a. 1 **b.** 18 **c.** about 1800 **d.** 1×10^{27}

4. Which particles have approximately the same mass?
a. electrons and neutrons
b. electrons and protons
c. electrons, neutrons, and protons
d. neutrons and protons

5. A change in the number of protons of an atom produces a(n)
a. compound
b. atom of a different element
c. ion
d. different isotope of the same element

6. The number of protons plus neutrons in an atom is its
a. atomic mass **b.** atomic number **c.** isotope number **d.** nucleon number

7. How many protons (p) and how many neutrons (n) are there in a $^{15}_{7}N$ nucleus?
a. 7 p, 7 n **b.** 7 p, 8 n **c.** 7 p, 15 n **d.** 8 p, 8 n

8. A neutral atom has 5 electrons and 6 neutrons. Its atomic number is
a. 1 **b.** 5 **c.** 6 **d.** 11

9. The symbol for the isotope potassium-40 is
a. $^{21}_{19}K$ **b.** $^{39}_{19}K$ **c.** $^{40}_{19}K$ **d.** $^{19}_{40}K$

Answers: 1, c; 2, d; 3, c; 4, d; 5, b; 6, d; 7, b; 8, b; 9, c

3.6 Electron Arrangement: The Bohr Model

Learning Objectives › Define *quantum*. › Arrange the electrons in a given atom in energy levels (shells).

Let's turn our attention once more to electrons. Rutherford demonstrated that atoms have a tiny, positively charged nucleus with electrons outside it. Evidence soon accumulated that the electrons were not randomly distributed but were arranged in an ordered fashion. We will examine that evidence soon. But first, let's take a side trip into some colorful chemistry and physics to provide a background for our study of the arrangement of electrons in atoms.

▲ The brilliant colors of a fireworks display come from compounds added to the fireworks. Strontium compounds produce red, copper compounds produce blue or violet, and barium compounds produce green.

Fireworks and Flame Tests

Chemists of the eighteenth and nineteenth centuries developed flame tests that used the colors of flames to identify several elements (Figure 3.9). Sodium salts produce a persistent yellow flame, potassium salts a fleeting lavender flame, and lithium salts a brilliant red flame. It was not until the structure of atoms was better understood, however, that scientists could explain why each element emits a distinctive color of light.

Fireworks originated earlier than flame tests, in ancient China. The brilliant colors of aerial displays still mark our celebrations of patriotic holidays. The colors of fireworks are attributable to specific elements. Brilliant reds are produced by strontium compounds, whereas barium compounds are used to produce green, sodium compounds yield yellow, and copper salts produce blue or violet. However, the colors of fireworks and flame tests are not as simple as they seem to the unaided eye.

4. Most lightbulbs produce white light. Why does a neon light appear orange? When a solid is heated, it goes through a stage of red heat, then yellow, and finally white light is emitted, which consists of all wavelengths. When a gas such as neon is heated, we get a line spectrum (Figure 3.11), which gives a specific color to the light.

Continuous and Line Spectra

When white light from an incandescent lamp is passed through a prism, it produces a continuous spectrum, or rainbow of colors (Figure 3.10). A similar phenomenon occurs when sunlight passes through raindrops. The different colors of light correspond to different wavelengths. Blue light has shorter wavelengths than red light, but there is no sharp transition in moving from one color to the next. All wavelengths are present in a continuous spectrum (Figure 3.11, top). White light is simply a combination of all the various colors.

If the light from a colored flame test or a gas-discharge tube containing a particular element is passed through a prism, only narrow colored lines are observed (Figure 3.11). Each line corresponds to light of a particular wavelength. The pattern of lines emitted by an element is called its *line spectrum*. The line spectrum of an element is characteristic of that element and can be used to identify it. Not all the lines in the spectrum of an atom are visible; some are infrared or ultraviolet radiation.

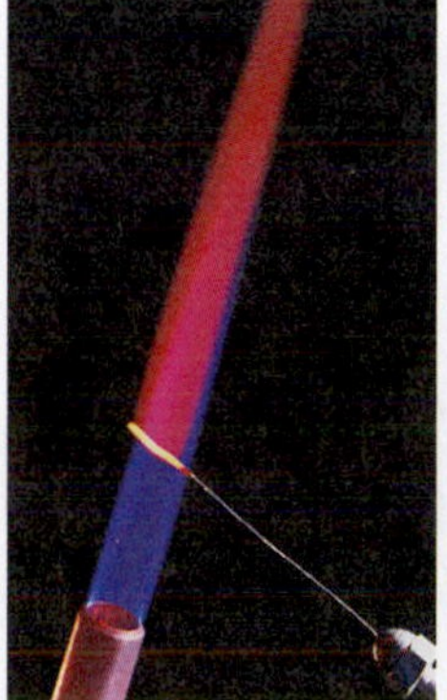

Lithium, Li

Sodium, Na

Potassium, K

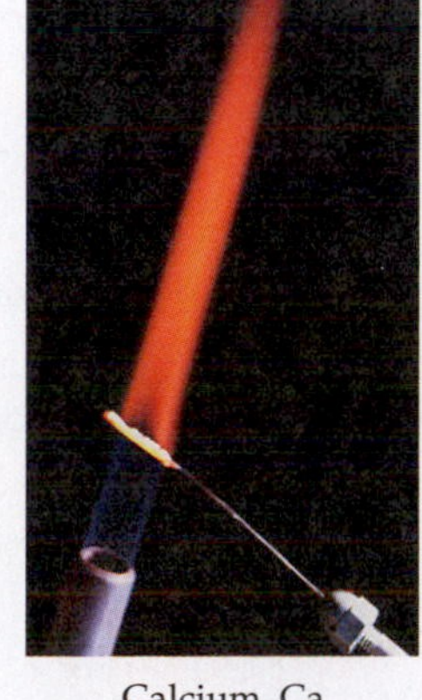

Calcium, Ca

Strontium, Sr

▲ **Figure 3.9** Certain chemical elements can be identified by the characteristic colors their compounds impart to flames. Five examples are shown here.

▲ **Figure 3.10** A glass prism separates white light into a continuous spectrum, or rainbow, of colors just as sunlight passing through raindrops causes a rainbow in the sky.

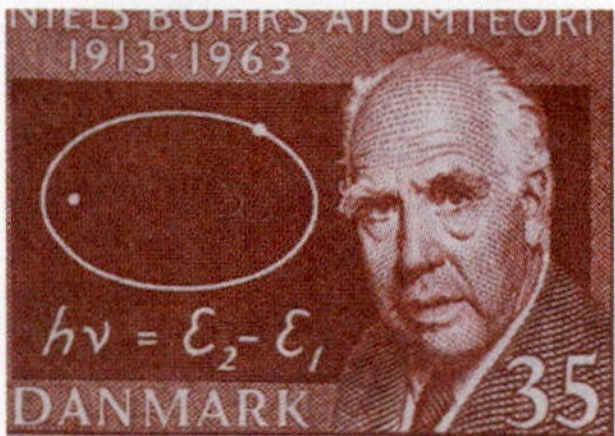

▲ Danish physicist Niels Bohr received the 1922 Nobel Prize in Physics for his planetary model of the atom with its quantized electron energy levels. Element 107 is named bohrium (Bh) in his honor.

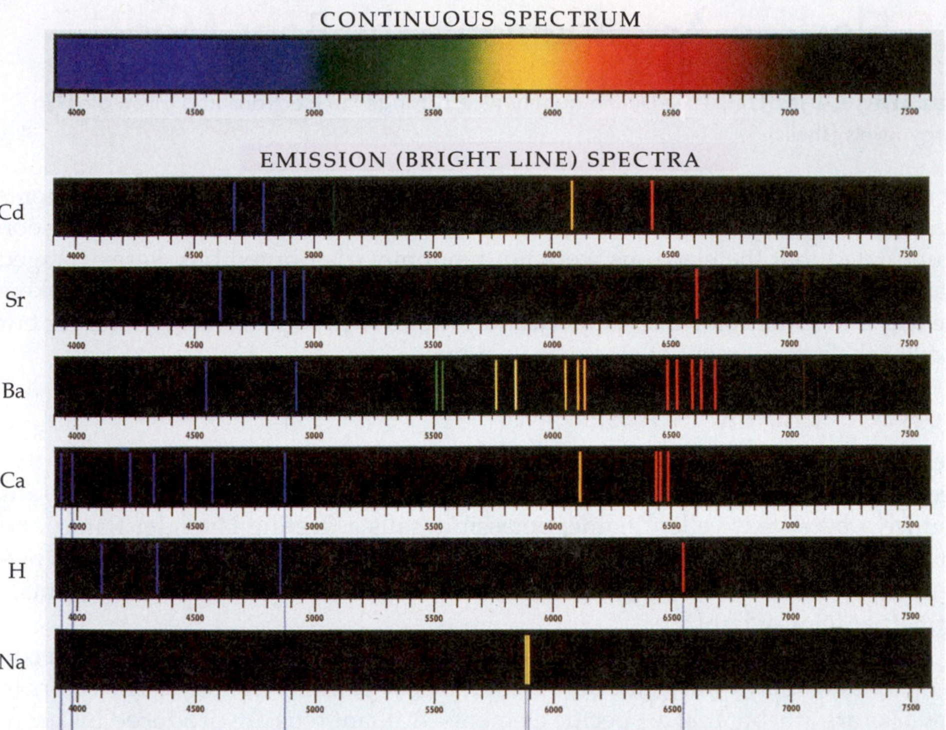

▲ **Figure 3.11** Line spectra of selected elements. Some of the components of the light emitted by excited atoms appear as colored lines. A continuous spectrum is shown at the top for comparison. The numbers are wavelengths of light given in Angstrom units (1 Å = 10^{-10} m). Each element has its own characteristic line spectrum that differs from all others and can be used to identify the element.

5. What does the word *quantum* actually mean? Just as an atom is the smallest unit of an element, a quantum is the smallest unit of energy. There are different sizes of quanta, but energy is produced or consumed in discrete rather than continuous units. "Quantum leap" comes from the idea suggested by Figure 3.12, where an electron can "leap" from one energy level to another.

The visible line spectrum of hydrogen is fairly simple, consisting of four lines in that portion of the electromagnetic spectrum. To explain the hydrogen spectrum, Danish physicist Niels Bohr (1885–1962) worked out a model for the electron arrangement of the hydrogen atom.

Bohr's Explanation of Line Spectra

Niels Bohr presented his explanation of line spectra in 1913. He suggested that electrons cannot have just any amount of energy but can have only certain specified amounts; that is, the energy of an electron is *quantized*. A **quantum** (plural: *quanta*) is a tiny unit of energy, whose value depends on the frequency of the radiation. A specified energy value for an electron is called its **energy level**.

By absorbing a quantum of energy (for example, when atoms of the element are heated), an electron is elevated to a higher energy level (Figure 3.12). By giving up

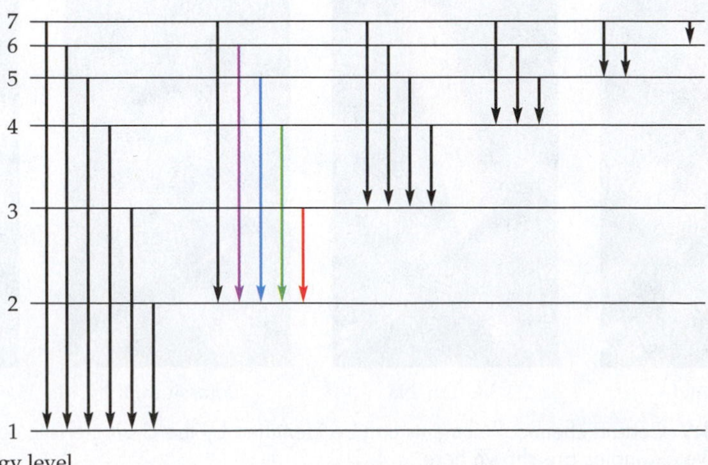

▶ **Figure 3.12** Possible electron shifts between energy levels in atoms to produce the lines found in spectra. Not all of the lines are in the visible portion of the spectrum. The four colored arrows correspond to the four colored lines in the hydrogen spectrum seen in Figure 3.11.

Q: *Which transition involves the greater change in energy, a drop from energy level 6 to energy level 2, or a drop from energy level 7 to energy level 6? What color of light is absorbed when an electron in a hydrogen atom is boosted from energy level 2 to energy level 3?*

a quantum of energy, the electron can return to a lower energy level. The energy released shows up as a line spectrum. Each line has a specific wavelength corresponding to a quantum of energy. An electron moves practically instantaneously from one energy level to another, and there are no intermediate stages.

Consider the analogy of a person on a ladder. A person can stand on the first rung, the second rung, the third rung, and so on, but is unable to stand between rungs. As the person goes from one rung to another, the potential energy (energy due to position) changes by definite amounts. As an electron moves from one energy level to another, its total energy (both potential and kinetic) also changes by definite amounts, or quanta.

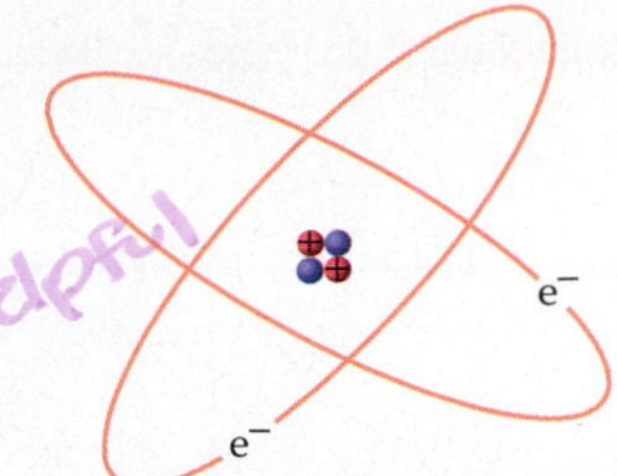

▲ **Figure 3.13** The nuclear atom, as envisioned by Bohr. Most of its mass is in an extremely small nucleus. Bohr thought that electrons orbited about the nucleus in the same way that planets orbit the sun.

Bohr based his model of the atom on the laws of planetary motion that had been set down by the German astronomer Johannes Kepler (1571–1630) three centuries before. Bohr imagined the electrons to be orbiting about the nucleus much as planets orbit the sun (Figure 3.13). Different energy levels were pictured as different orbits. The modern picture of the atom is different, as we will see in the next section.

Ground States and Excited States

The electron in a hydrogen atom is usually in the first, or lowest, energy level. Electrons tend to stay in their lowest possible energy levels (those nearest the nucleus). Atoms with their electrons thus situated are said to be in their **ground state**. When a flame or other source supplies energy to an atom (of hydrogen, for example) and an electron jumps from the lowest possible level to a higher level, the atom is said to be in an **excited state**. An atom in an excited state eventually emits a quantum of energy—often a *photon*, or "particle," of light—as the electron jumps back down to one of the lower levels and ultimately reaches the ground state.

Bohr's theory was spectacularly successful in explaining the line spectrum of hydrogen. It established the important idea of energy levels in atoms. Bohr was awarded the Nobel Prize in Physics in 1922 for this work.

Atoms larger than hydrogen have more than one electron, and Bohr was also able to deduce that a given energy level of an atom could contain at most only a certain number of electrons. The maximum number of electrons that can be in a given level is indicated by the formula

$$\text{Maximum number of electrons} = 2n^2$$

where n is the energy level being considered. For the first energy level ($n = 1$), the maximum number of electrons is $2 \times 1^2 = 2 \times 1 = 2$. For the second energy level ($n = 2$), the maximum number is $2 \times 2^2 = 2 \times 4 = 8$. For the third level, the maximum number is $2 \times 3^2 = 2 \times 9 = 18$.

The various energy levels are often called **shells**. The first energy level ($n = 1$) is the first shell, the second energy level ($n = 2$) is the second shell, and so on.

Example 3.3 Electron-Shell Capacity

What is the maximum number of electrons in the fifth shell (fifth energy level)?

Solution

The maximum number of electrons in a given shell is given by $2n^2$. For the fifth level, $n = 5$, and so we have

$$2 \times 5^2 = 2 \times 25 = 50 \text{ electrons}$$

■ EXERCISE 3.3A

What is the maximum number of electrons in the fourth shell (fourth energy level)?

■ EXERCISE 3.3B

What is the lowest energy level that can hold 18 electrons?

Building Atoms: Main Shells

Imagine building up atoms by adding one electron to the proper shell as *each* proton is added to the nucleus, keeping in mind that electrons will go to the lowest energy level (shell) available. For hydrogen, with a nucleus containing only one proton (Z = 1), the single electron goes into the first shell. For helium, with a nucleus having two protons (Z = 2), both electrons go into the first shell. According to Bohr, two electrons is the maximum population of the first shell, and that level is filled in the helium atom. (We can ignore the neutrons in the nucleus; they are not involved in this process.)

With lithium (Z = 3), two electrons go into the first shell, and the third must go into the second shell. This process of adding electrons is continued until the second shell is filled with eight electrons, as in a neon atom (Z = 10), which has two of its 10 electrons in the first shell and the remaining eight in the second shell.

A sodium atom (Z = 11) has 11 electrons. Two are in the first shell, the second shell is filled with eight electrons, and the remaining electron is in the third shell. We can represent the **electron configuration** (or arrangement) of the first 11 elements as follows:

Element	1st shell	2nd shell	3rd shell
H	1		
He	2		
Li	2	1	
⋮	⋮	⋮	
Ne	2	8	
Na	2	8	1

Sometimes the main-shell electron configuration is abbreviated by writing the symbol for the element followed by the numbers of electrons in each shell, separated by commas, starting with the lowest energy level. Following the color scheme from the preceding table, the main-shell configuration for sodium is simply

Na 2, 8, 1

We can continue to add electrons to the third shell until we get to argon. The main-shell configuration for argon is

Ar 2, 8, 8

After argon, the notation for electron configurations is enhanced with more detail. This notation is discussed in greater detail in Section 3.8. Meanwhile, Example 3.4 shows how to determine a few main-shell configurations.

Example 3.4 Main-Shell Electron Configurations

What is the main-shell electron configuration for fluorine?

Solution

Fluorine has the symbol F (Z = 9). It has nine electrons. Two of these electrons go into the first shell, and the remaining seven go into the second shell.

F 2, 7

■ EXERCISE 3.4

Write the main-shell electron configurations for (a) beryllium and (b) magnesium. These elements are in the same column of the periodic table. What do you notice about the number of electrons in their outermost shells?

Self-Assessment Questions

1. When electrified in a gas-discharge tube, different elements emit light that forms narrow lines that are
   a. characteristic of each particular element
   b. the same as those of the hydrogen spectrum
   c. the same for all elements but with differing colors
   d. the same for all elements but with differing intensities
2. When an electron in an atom goes from a higher energy level to a lower one, the electron
   a. absorbs energy
   b. changes its volume
   c. changes its charge
   d. releases energy
3. An atom in an excited state is one with an electron that has
   a. moved to a higher energy level
   b. been removed
   c. bonded to another atom to make a molecule
   d. combined with a proton to make a neutron
4. The maximum number of electrons in the first shell of an atom is
   a. 2 b. 6 c. 8 d. unlimited
5. The maximum number of electrons in the third shell of an atom is
   a. 6 b. 8 c. 18 d. 32
6. The main-shell electron configuration of aluminum is
   a. 2, 8, 1 b. 2, 8, 3 c. 2, 8, 13 d. 2, 8, 8, 8, 1
7. The main-shell electron configuration of sulfur is
   a. 2, 8, 4 b. 2, 8, 6 c. 2, 8, 8, 8, 6 d. 2, 8, 18, 4

Answers: 1, a; 2, d; 3, a; 4, a; 5, c; 6, b; 7, b

3.7 Electron Arrangement: The Quantum Model

Learning Objectives › Relate the idea of a quantum of energy to an orbital. › Write an electron configuration (in subshell notation) for a given atom.

Bohr's simple planetary model of the atom has been replaced for many purposes by more sophisticated models in which electrons are treated as *both* particles and waves. The electrons have characteristic wavelengths and their locations are indicated as probabilities. The theory that the electron should have wavelike properties was first suggested in 1924 by Louis de Broglie (1892–1987), a young French physicist. Although it was hard to accept because of Thomson's evidence that electrons are particles, de Broglie's theory was experimentally verified within a few years.

Erwin Schrödinger (1887–1961), an Austrian physicist, used highly mathematical *quantum mechanics* in the 1920s to develop equations that describe the properties of electrons in atoms. Fortunately, we can make use of some of Schrödinger's results without understanding his elaborate equations. The solutions to these equations express the probability of finding an electron in a given volume of space. These variously shaped volumes of space, called **orbitals**, replace the planetary orbits of the Bohr model.

Suppose you had a camera that could photograph electrons and you left the shutter open while an electron zipped about the nucleus. The developed picture would give a record of where the electron had been. (Doing the same thing with an electric fan would give a blurred image of the rapidly moving blades, an image resembling a disk.) The electrons in the first shell would appear as a fuzzy ball (often referred to as a *charge cloud* or an *electron cloud* [Figure 3.14]).

An *s* orbital

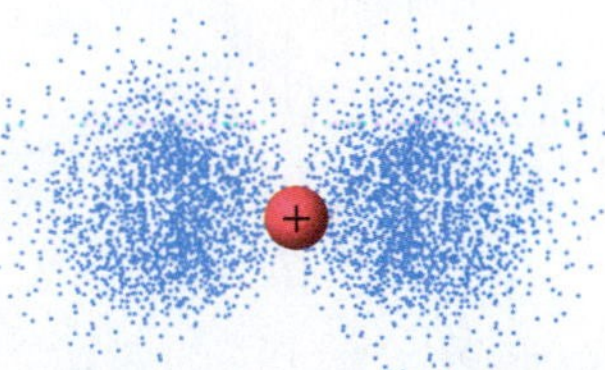

A *p* orbital

▲ **Figure 3.14** The modern charge-cloud representation of an atomic orbital is more accurate than the Bohr model (Figure 3.13). An electron cloud is the "fuzzy" region around an atomic nucleus where an electron is likely to be. The type of orbital determines the general shape of the cloud, as seen here.

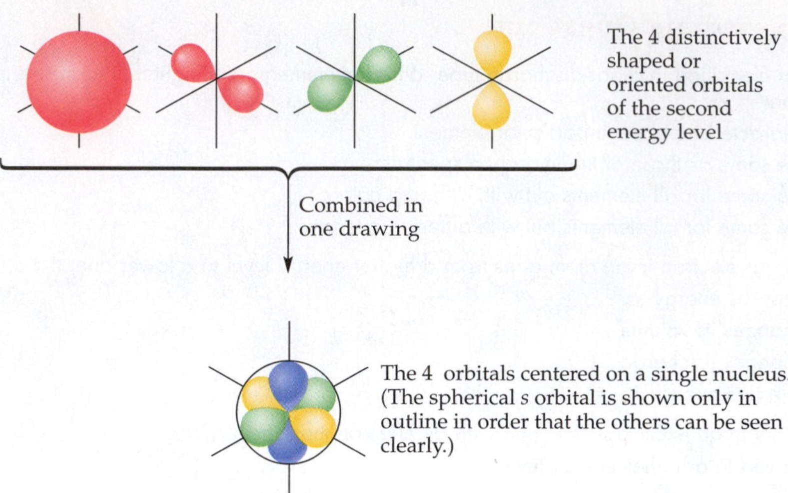

The 4 distinctively shaped or oriented orbitals of the second energy level
Combined in one drawing
The 4 orbitals centered on a single nucleus. (The spherical *s* orbital is shown only in outline in order that the others can be seen clearly.)

▶ **Figure 3.15** Electron orbitals of the second main shell. In these drawings, the nucleus of the atom is located at the intersection of the axes. The eight electrons that would be placed in the second shell of Bohr's model are distributed among these four orbitals in the current model of the atom, with two electrons per orbital.

Building Atoms by Orbital Filling

Schrödinger concluded that each electron orbital could contain a maximum of two electrons and that some shells could contain more than one orbital. The first shell contains a single spherical orbital called 1*s*. The second shell contains four orbitals: 2*s* is spherical, and the other three orbitals, called 2*p*, are dumbbell-shaped (Figure 3.15). Orbitals in the same shell that have the same letter designation make up a **subshell (sublevel)**. The second shell has two subshells, the 2*s* subshell with only one orbital and the 2*p* subshell with three orbitals. The third shell contains nine orbitals distributed among three subshells: a spherical 3*s* orbital in the 3*s* subshell, three dumbbell-shaped 3*p* orbitals in the 3*p* subshell, and five 3*d* orbitals with more complicated shapes in the 3*d* subshell.

In building up the electron configurations of atoms of the various elements, the lower sublevels (subshells) are filled first.

Hydrogen (Z = 1) has only one electron in the *s* orbital of the first shell. The electron configuration is

$$\text{H} \quad 1s^1$$

Helium (Z = 2) has two electrons and its electron configuration is

$$\text{He} \quad 1s^2$$

Lithium (Z = 3) has three electrons—two in the first shell and one in the *s* orbital of the second shell:

$$\text{Li} \quad 1s^2 2s^1$$

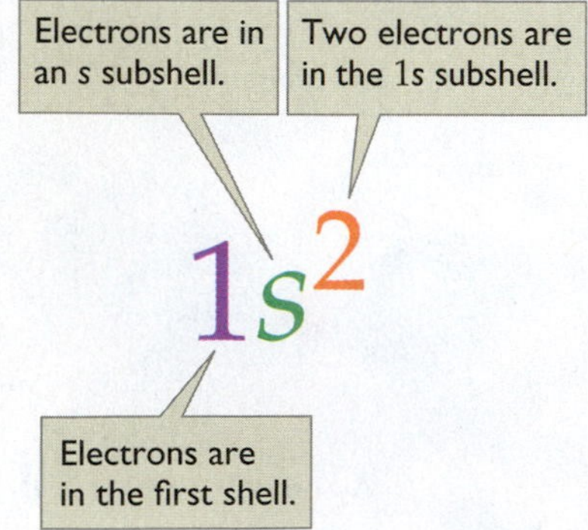

Skipping to nitrogen (Z = 7), the seven electrons are arranged as follows:

$$\text{N} \quad 1s^2 2s^2 2p^3$$

Let's review what this notation means:

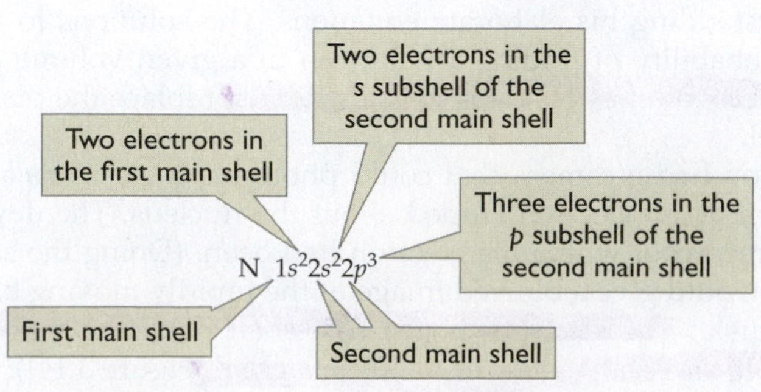

For argon ($Z = 18$), with its 18 electrons, the configuration is

$$\text{Ar} \quad 1s^22s^22p^63s^23p^6$$

Note that the highest occupied subshell, $3p$, is filled. However, the order of subshell filling for elements with Z greater than 18 is not intuitively obvious. In potassium ($Z = 19$), for example, the $4s$ subshell fills before the $3d$ subshell. The order in which the various subshells are filled is shown in Figure 3.16, and Table 3.3 gives the electron configurations for the first 20 elements. The electrons in the outermost main shell, called *valence electrons* (Section 3.8), are shown in color.

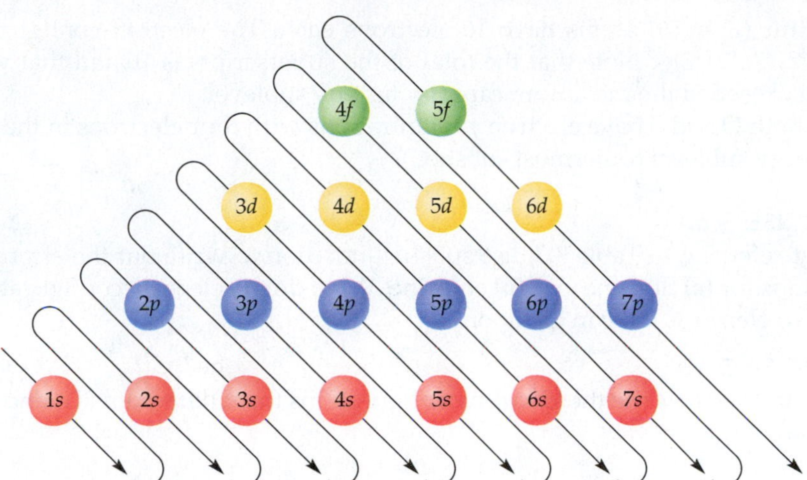

◀ **Figure 3.16** An order-of-filling chart for determining the electron configurations of atoms.

Table 3.3 Electron Configurations for Atoms of the First 20 Elements

Name	Atomic Number	Electron Configuration
Hydrogen	1	$1s^1$
Helium	2	$1s^2$
Lithium	3	$1s^22s^1$
Beryllium	4	$1s^22s^2$
Boron	5	$1s^22s^22p^1$
Carbon	6	$1s^22s^22p^2$
Nitrogen	7	$1s^22s^22p^3$
Oxygen	8	$1s^22s^22p^4$
Fluorine	9	$1s^22s^22p^5$
Neon	10	$1s^22s^22p^6$
Sodium	11	$1s^22s^22p^63s^1$
Magnesium	12	$1s^22s^22p^63s^2$
Aluminum	13	$1s^22s^22p^63s^23p^1$
Silicon	14	$1s^22s^22p^63s^23p^2$
Phosphorus	15	$1s^22s^22p^63s^23p^3$
Sulfur	16	$1s^22s^22p^63s^23p^4$
Chlorine	17	$1s^22s^22p^63s^23p^5$
Argon	18	$1s^22s^22p^63s^23p^6$
Potassium	19	$1s^22s^22p^63s^23p^64s^1$
Calcium	20	$1s^22s^22p^63s^23p^64s^2$

Example 3.5 Subshell Notation

Without referring to Table 3.3, use subshell notation to write the electron configurations for **(a)** oxygen and **(b)** sulfur. What do the electron configurations of these two elements have in common?

Solution

a. Oxygen (Z = 8) has eight electrons. We place them in subshells, starting with the lowest energy level. Two go into the 1*s* orbital and two into the 2*s* orbital. That leaves four electrons to be placed in the 2*p* subshell. The electron configuration is $1s^2 2s^2 2p^4$.

b. Sulfur (Z = 16) atoms have 16 electrons each. The electron configuration is $1s^2 2s^2 2p^6 3s^2 3p^4$. Note that the total of the superscripts is 16 and that we have not exceeded the maximum capacity for any sublevel.

Both O and S have electron configurations with four electrons in the highest energy sublevel (outermost subshell).

■ EXERCISE 3.5A

Without referring to Table 3.3, use subshell notation to write out the electron configurations for **(a)** fluorine and **(b)** chlorine. What do the electron configurations for these two elements have in common?

■ EXERCISE 3.5B

Use Figure 3.16 to write the electron configurations for **(a)** titanium (Ti) and **(b)** gallium (Ga).

Self-Assessment Questions

1. The shape of a 1*s* orbital is
- **a.** circular
- **b.** a dumbbell
- **c.** spherical
- **d.** variable

2. The maximum number of electrons in an atomic orbital
- **a.** depends on the main shell
- **b.** depends on the subshell
- **c.** is always 2
- **d.** is always 8

3. Which of the following subshells has the highest energy?
a. 2*p* **b.** 2*s* **c.** 3*p* **d.** 3*s*

4. What is the lowest-numbered main shell to have *d* orbitals?
a. 1 **b.** 2 **c.** 3 **d.** 4

5. Which of the following atoms has a half-filled subshell in the ground state?
- **a.** beryllium
- **b.** neon
- **c.** nitrogen
- **d.** oxygen

6. Which subshell has a total of three orbitals?
a. *d* **b.** *f* **c.** *p* **d.** *s*

7. In what main shell is a 3*d* subshell located?
a. 1 **b.** 3 **c.** 5 **d.** none

8. The electron capacity of the 4*p* subshell is
a. 3 **b.** 4 **c.** 6 **d.** 10

Answers: 1, c; 2, c; 3, c; 4, c; 5, c; 6, c; 7, b; 8, c

3.8 Electron Configurations and the Periodic Table

Learning Objective › Describe how an element's electron configuration relates to its location in the periodic table.

In general, the properties of elements can be correlated with their electron configurations. (We will explore bond formation using electron configurations in Chapter 4.) Because the number of electrons equals the number of protons, the periodic table tells us about electron configuration as well as atomic number.

The modern periodic table (inside front cover) has horizontal rows and vertical columns.

- Each vertical column is a **group**, or *family*. Elements in a group have similar chemical properties.
- A horizontal row of the periodic table is called a **period**. The properties of elements change in a recurring manner across a period.

In the United States, the groups are often indicated by a numeral followed by the letter A or B.

- An element in an A group is a **main group element**.
- An element in a B group is a **transition element**.

The International Union of Pure and Applied Chemistry (IUPAC) recommends numbering the groups from 1 to 18. Both systems are indicated on the periodic table on the inside front cover, but this book uses the traditional U.S. system.

Family Features: Outer Electron Configurations

The period in which an element appears in the periodic table tells us how many main shells an atom of that element has. Phosphorus, for example, is in the third period, and so the phosphorus atom has three main shells. The U.S. group number (for main group elements) tells us how many electrons are in the outermost shell. An electron in the outermost shell of an atom is called a **valence electron**. From the fact that phosphorus is in group 5A, we can deduce that it has five valence electrons. Two of these are in an *s* orbital, and the other three are in *p* orbitals. We can indicate the outer electron configuration of the phosphorus atom as

$$\mathrm{P} \quad 3s^2 3p^3$$

The valence electrons determine most of the chemistry of an atom. Since all the elements in the same group of the periodic table have the same number of valence electrons, they should have similar chemistry, and they do. Figure 3.17 relates the subshell configurations to the groups in the periodic table.

Family Groups

Elements within a group have similar properties. All the elements in group 1A have one valence electron, and all except hydrogen are very reactive metals (hydrogen is a nonmetal). All group 1A elements have the outer electron configuration ns^1, where n denotes the number of the outermost main shell.

The metals in group 1A are called **alkali metals**. They react vigorously with water, producing hydrogen gas. There are noticeable trends in properties within this family. For example, lithium is the hardest metal in the group. Sodium is softer than lithium; potassium is softer still; and so on down the group. Lithium is also the least reactive toward water. Sodium, potassium, rubidium, and cesium are progressively more reactive. Francium is highly radioactive and extremely rare. Few of its properties have been measured.

6. What is periodic about the periodic table? Figure 3.17 shows why there are periodic, or recurring, trends in the periodic table. Elements in the same column have similar electron configurations and often have similar chemical and physical characteristics as well.

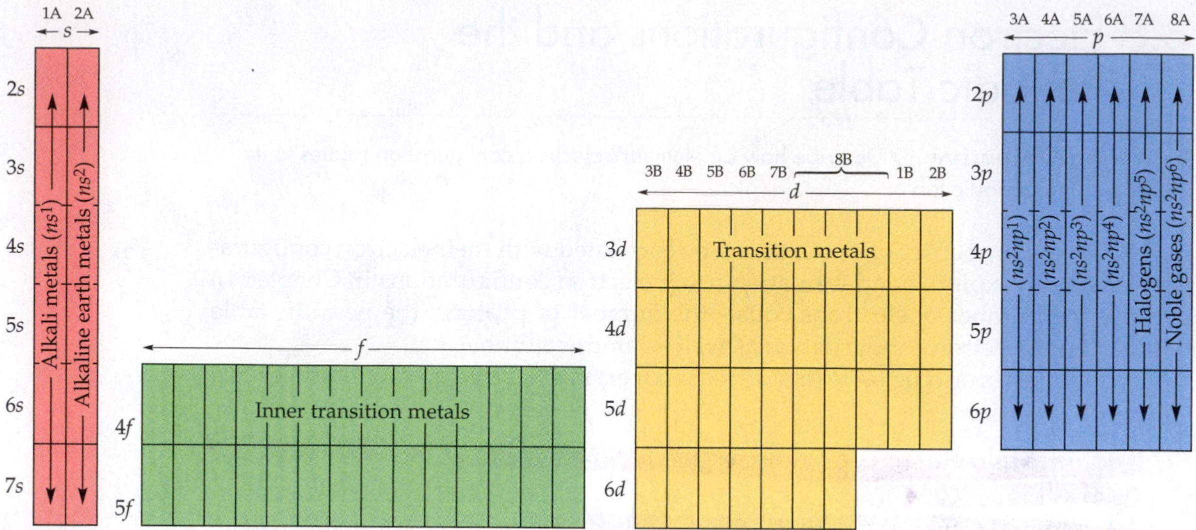

▲ **Figure 3.17** Valence-shell electron configurations and the periodic table.

▲ (Above) Lithium, an alkali metal, reacts with water to form hydrogen gas. (Below) Potassium, another alkali metal, undergoes the same reaction but much more vigorously.

Hydrogen is the odd one in group 1A. It is not an alkali metal but rather a typical nonmetal. Based on its properties, hydrogen probably should be put in a group of its own.

Group 2A elements are known as **alkaline earth metals.** The metals in this group have the outer electron configuration ns^2. Most are fairly soft and moderately reactive with water. Beryllium is the odd member of the group in that it is rather hard and does not react with water. As in other families, there are trends in properties within the group. For example, magnesium, calcium, strontium, barium, and radium are progressively more reactive toward water.

Group 7A elements, often called **halogens,** also consist of reactive elements. All have seven valence electrons with the configuration ns^2np^5. Halogens react vigorously with alkali metals to form crystalline solids (this is discussed further in Chapter 4). There are trends in the halogen family as you move down the group. Fluorine is most reactive toward alkali metals, chlorine is the next most reactive, and so on. Fluorine and chlorine are gases at room temperature, bromine is a liquid, and iodine is a solid. (Astatine, like francium, is highly radioactive and extremely rare; few of its properties have been determined.)

Members of group 8A, to the far right on the periodic table, have a complete set of valence electrons and therefore undergo few, if any, chemical reactions. They are called **noble gases**, for their lack of chemical reactivity.

Example 3.6 Valence-Shell Electron Configurations

Use subshell notation to write the electron configurations for the outermost main shell of **(a)** strontium (Sr) and **(b)** arsenic (As).

Solution

a. Strontium is in group 2A and thus has two valence electrons in an *s* subshell. Because strontium is in the fifth period of the periodic table, its outer main shell is $n = 5$. Its outer electron configuration is therefore $5s^2$.

b. Arsenic is in group 5A and the fourth period. Its five outer (valence) electrons are in the $n = 4$ shell, and the configuration is $4s^24p^3$.

■ EXERCISE 3.6A

Use subshell notation to write the configurations for the outermost main shell of **(a)** rubidium (Rb), **(b)** selenium (Se), and **(c)** germanium (Ge).

■ EXERCISE 3.6B

The valence electrons in aluminum have the configuration $3s^2 3p^1$. In the periodic table, gallium is directly below aluminum, and indium is directly below gallium. Use only this information to write the configurations for the valence electrons in **(a)** gallium and **(b)** indium.

Metals and Nonmetals

Elements in the periodic table are divided into two classes by a heavy, stepped line (see inside front cover). Those to the left of the line are *metals.* A **metal** has a characteristic luster (shininess) and generally is a good conductor of heat and electricity. Except for mercury, which is a liquid, all metals are solids at room temperature. Metals generally are *malleable*; that is, they can be hammered into thin sheets. Most also are *ductile,* which means that they can be drawn into wires.

Elements to the right of the stepped line are *nonmetals.* A **nonmetal** lacks metallic properties. Several nonmetals are gases (oxygen, nitrogen, fluorine, and chlorine). Others are solids (e.g., carbon, sulfur, phosphorus, and iodine). Bromine is the only nonmetal that is a liquid at room temperature.

Some of the elements bordering the stepped line are called *semimetals*, or *metalloids*, and these have intermediate properties that may resemble those of both metals and nonmetals. There is a lack of agreement on just which elements fit in this category.

▲ (Top) Metals such as gold are easily shaped, and they conduct heat and electricity well. (Bottom) Nonmetals such as sulfur are usually brittle, melt at low temperatures, and often are good insulators.

Which Model to Use

For some purposes in this text, we use only main-shell configurations of atoms to picture the distribution of electrons in atoms. At other times, the electron clouds of the quantum mechanical model are more useful. Even Dalton's model sometimes proves to be the best way to describe certain phenomena (the behavior of gases, for example). The choice of model is always based on which one is most helpful in understanding a particular concept. This, after all, is the purpose of scientific models.

Self-Assessment Questions

1. Which pair of elements has the most similar chemical properties?
   a. Ca and Cd **b.** Cl and Br **c.** P and S **d.** Sb and Sc
2. Elements within a period of the periodic table have the same number of
   a. electrons in the outermost shell
   b. neutrons in the nucleus
   c. occupied main shells
   d. protons in the nucleus
3. The valence-shell electron configuration of the halogens is
   a. ns^1 **b.** ns^2np^3 **c.** ns^2np^5 **d.** ns^2np^6
4. The alkali metals are members of group
   a. 1A **b.** 2A **c.** 7A **d.** 8A
5. What is the total number of valence electrons in an atom of bromine?
   a. 5 **b.** 7 **c.** 17 **d.** 35
6. Which of the following sets of elements exhibits the most similar chemical properties?
   a. Al, Sc, Si **b.** Hg, Br, Se **c.** Li, Na, K **d.** N, O, F
7. In the ground state, atoms of a fourth period element must have
   a. a 3*f* sublevel
   b. electrons in the fourth shell
   c. four valence electrons
   d. properties similar to those of other elements in the fourth period

Answers: 1, b; 2, c; 3, c; 4, a; 5, b; 6, c; 7, b

GREEN CHEMISTRY

Principles 1, 6, 7, 9

Scott Cummings, *Kenyon College*

Clean Energy from Solar Fuels

Imagine a world powered by a clean fuel which is manufactured using sunlight and water, and produces no carbon dioxide emissions when used. This has been the dream of chemists around the world, who have been working for many years to develop a "solar fuel" that might someday replace some of the fossil fuels that are so important to us—oil, coal, and natural gas.

Sunlight is a free and abundant power source. More solar energy reaches Earth's surface in one hour than all of the fossil fuel energy that human beings use in one year. The goal for chemists is to develop efficient methods to capture just a tiny part of this sunlight and convert it into a useful form such as electricity. For now, this is accomplished using solar panels constructed from photovoltaic cells, devices usually made of silicon. But sunshine is intermittent; we need to convert radiant solar energy into chemical energy—a storable fuel. One idea for a solar fuel is hydrogen. Learning how to utilize sunlight to make hydrogen is one of the grand challenges of chemistry.

A full hydrogen energy cycle uses solar energy to split water (H_2O) into hydrogen (H_2) and oxygen (O_2) and then uses the hydrogen as a clean fuel to produce either heat (when burned) or electricity (using a fuel cell). Splitting water requires energy input to break the bonds that hold together the O and H atoms in water molecules. One of the simplest ways to do this is by electrolysis (Section 3.1), which requires electrical energy. If the electricity is produced using a solar panel, then the hydrogen formed is a solar fuel. This approach is currently quite expensive, and much research in chemistry is aimed at discovering new and inexpensive photovoltaic materials—including plastics—from which to construct solar panels. Chemists also seek electrodes and other components that can be made from abundant elements instead of the precious metal platinum (Pt) that is typically used.

For a different approach to hydrogen production, chemists are turning to green plants for inspiration. Plants use photosynthesis to take energy from the sun and store it in the chemical bonds of compounds known as *carbohydrates* (Section 8.10). This chemical process is essential to sustain life on the planet and depends on the ability to split water molecules with sunlight. Chemists are hoping to unlock the secrets of the leaf to develop "artificial photosynthesis" and use solar energy to produce hydrogen fuel from water.

PHOTOSYNTHESIS

carbon dioxide + water → carbohydrate + oxygen

ARTIFICIAL PHOTOSYNTHESIS

water → hydrogen + oxygen

Two ways to make solar fuels. Green plants use photosynthesis to produce carbohydrate fuels. Chemists are trying to produce hydrogen fuel. Both reactions use water and solar energy.

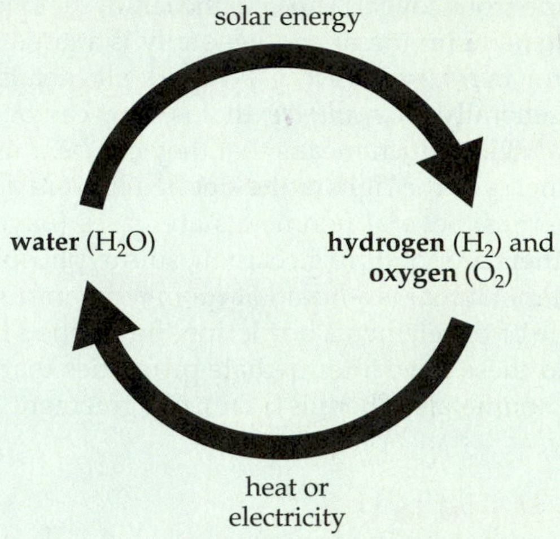

Clean energy cycle. Solar energy is used to produce hydrogen and oxygen from water (top). Hydrogen fuel reacts with oxygen to produce water and releases energy as either heat or electricity.

In natural photosynthesis, plants employ many different molecules to capture and convert solar energy. Chlorophyll molecules absorb part of the solar spectrum, giving a leaf its green color. To mimic this process, chemists are designing colorful synthetic dyes to capture photons from the sun. When a dye absorbs light, one of its electrons is excited, which generates an excited-state molecule. But rather than emitting the energy back as a photon (Section 3.6), the energy can be harnessed to split water. Plants also employ a cluster of manganese, calcium, and oxygen atoms to crack apart water molecules and produce oxygen. Chemists have been active in trying to mimic this reaction as well, using compounds made in the laboratory.

Solar fuels such as hydrogen embody several green chemistry principles. Hydrogen fuel is only as green as the method used to make it. If produced using sunlight as the energy source and water as the chemical feedstock, though, the fuel can be clean and renewable (Principle 7). Unlike fossil fuels, hydrogen is a carbon-free fuel that, when produced from sunlight, prevents carbon dioxide emissions (Principle 1). A solar-hydrogen system relies on compounds that increase efficiency and facilitate both the water-splitting chemistry and the use of hydrogen (Principle 9). If these materials are earth-abundant and do not cause harm to the environment, this process closes the clean-fuel cycle.

CRITICAL THINKING  EXERCISES

Apply knowledge that you have gained in this chapter and one or more of the FLaReS principles (Chapter 1) to evaluate the following statements or claims.

3.1 Suppose you read in the newspaper that a chemist in South America claims to have discovered a new element with an atomic mass of 34. Extremely rare, it was found in a sample taken from the Andes Mountains. Unfortunately, the chemist has used all of the sample in his analyses.

3.2 Some aboriginal tribes have rain-making ceremonies in which they toss pebbles of gypsum up into the air. (Gypsum is the material used to make plaster of Paris by heating the rock to remove some of its water.) Sometimes it does rain several days after these rain-making ceremonies.

3.3 Some scientists have recently suggested that bacteria from California's Mono Lake may be able to use arsenic (As) in place of phosphorus (P) in their proteins and DNA.

SUMMARY

Section 3.1—Davy, Faraday, and others showed that matter is electrical in nature. They were able to decompose compounds into elements by **electrolysis** or passing electricity through molten salts. **Electrodes** are carbon rods or metal strips that carry electricity into the **electrolyte**, the solution or compound that conducts electricity. The electrolyte contains **ions**—charged atoms or groups of atoms. The **anode** is the positive electrode, and **anions** (negatively charged ions) move toward it. The **cathode** is the negative electrode, and **cations** (positively charged ions) move toward it. Experiments with **cathode rays** in gas-discharge tubes showed that matter contained negatively charged particles, which were called **electrons**. Thomson determined the mass-to-charge ratio for the electron. Goldstein's experiment showed that matter also contained positively charged particles. Millikan's oil-drop experiment measured the charge on the electron, so its mass could then be calculated.

Section 3.2—In his studies of cathode rays, Roentgen accidentally discovered **X-rays**, a highly penetrating form of radiation now used in medical diagnosis. Becquerel accidentally discovered another type of radiation that comes from certain unstable elements. Marie Curie named this new discovery **radioactivity** and studied it extensively.

Section 3.3—Radioactivity was soon classified as three different types of radiation: **Alpha particles** have four times the mass of a hydrogen atom and a positive charge twice that of an electron. **Beta particles** are energetic electrons. **Gamma rays** are a form of energy like X-rays but more penetrating.

Section 3.4—Rutherford's experiments with alpha particles and gold foil showed that most of the alpha particles emitted toward the foil passed through it. A few were deflected or, occasionally, bounced back almost directly toward the source. This indicated that all the positive charge and most of the mass of an atom must be in a tiny core, which Rutherford called the **nucleus**.

Section 3.5—Rutherford called the smallest unit of positive charge the **proton**; it has about the mass of a hydrogen atom and a charge equal in size but opposite in sign to the electron. In 1932, Chadwick discovered the **neutron**, a nuclear particle as massive as a proton but with no charge. The number of protons in an atom is the **atomic number** (Z). Atoms of the same element have the same number of protons but may have different numbers of neutrons; such atoms are called **isotopes**. Different isotopes of an element are nearly identical chemically. Protons and neutrons collectively are called **nucleons**, and the number of nucleons is called the **mass number** or **nucleon number**. The difference between the mass number and the atomic number is the number of neutrons. The general symbol for an isotope of element X is written $^{A}_{Z}\text{X}$, where A is the mass number and Z is the atomic number.

Section 3.6—Light from the sun or from an incandescent lamp produces a continuous spectrum, containing all colors. Light from a gas-discharge tube produces a line spectrum, containing only certain colors. Bohr explained line spectra by proposing that an electron in an atom resides only at certain discrete **energy levels**, which differ from one another by a **quantum**, or discrete unit of energy. An atom drops to the lowest energy state, or **ground state**, after being in a higher energy state, or **excited state**. The energy emitted when electrons move to lower energy levels manifests as a line spectrum characteristic of the particular element, with the lines corresponding to specific wavelengths (colors) of light. Bohr also deduced that the energy levels of an atom could hold at most $2n^2$ electrons, where n is the number of the energy level, or **shell**. A description of the shells occupied by the electrons of an atom is one way of giving the atom's **electron configuration**, or arrangement of electrons.

Section 3.7—de Broglie theorized that electrons have wave properties. Schrödinger developed equations that described each electron's location in terms of an **orbital**, a volume of space that the electron usually occupies. Each orbital holds at most two electrons. Orbitals in the same shell and with the same energy make up a **subshell**, or sublevel, each of which is designated by a letter. An *s* orbital is spherical and a *p* orbital is dumbbell-shaped. The *d* and *f* orbitals have more complex shapes. The first main shell can hold only one *s* orbital; the second can hold one *s* and three *p* orbitals; and the third can hold one *s*, three *p*, and five *d* orbitals. In writing an electron configuration using subshell notation, we give the shell number and subshell letter, followed by a superscript indicating the number of electrons in that subshell. The order of the shells and subshells can be remembered with a chart or by looking at the periodic table.

Section 3.8—Elements in the periodic table are arranged vertically in **groups** and horizontally in **periods**. Electrons in the outermost shell of an atom, called **valence electrons**, determine the reactivity of that atom. Elements in a group usually have the same number of valence electrons and similarities in properties. We designate groups by a number and the letter A or B. The A-group elements are **main group elements**. The B-group elements are **transition elements**. Group 1A elements are the **alkali metals**. Except for hydrogen, they are all soft, low-melting, highly reactive metals. Group 2A consists of the **alkaline earth metals**, fairly soft and reactive metals. Group 7A elements, the **halogens**, are reactive nonmetals. Group 8A elements, the **noble gases**, react very little or not at all. A stepped line divides the periodic table into **metals**, which conduct electricity and heat and are shiny, malleable, and ductile, and **nonmetals**, which tend to lack the properties of metals. Some elements bordering the stepped line, called *metalloids*, have properties intermediate between those of metals and nonmetals.

Green chemistry Hydrogen is a promising clean fuel because it can be manufactured using sunlight and water and using it does not produce carbon dioxide as waste. Using a solar cell, energy from sunlight can be converted into electricity, which can then be used to split water into hydrogen and oxygen; this splitting of water can also be accomplished by a process that mimics photosynthesis. The hydrogen can be burned to produce heat or used in a fuel cell to produce electricity.

Learning Objectives

› Explain the electrical properties of an atom. (3.1)	Problems 16, 23, 24
› Describe how the properties of electricity explain the structure of atoms. (3.1)	Problems 13, 14, 19, 20
› Describe the experiments that led to the discovery of X-rays and an explanation of radioactivity. (3.2)	Problem 2
› Distinguish the three main kinds of radioactivity: alpha, beta, and gamma. (3.3)	Problem 3
› Sketch the nuclear model of the atom, and identify its parts. (3.4)	Problem 6
› List the particles that make up the nucleus of an atom, and give their relative masses and electric charges. (3.5)	Problems 7–9
› Identify elements and isotopes from their nuclear particles. (3.5)	Problems 8, 9, 15–18
› Define *quantum*. (3.6)	Problem 10
› Arrange the electrons in a given atom in energy levels (shells). (3.6)	Problems 33, 38–40
› Relate the idea of a quantum of energy to an orbital. (3.7)	Problem 11
› Write an electron configuration (in subshell notation) for a given atom. (3.7)	Problems 19–32, 37
› Describe how an element's electron configuration relates to its location in the periodic table. (3.8)	Problems 34 and 35
› Distinguish the conversion of solar energy into electrical energy in a solar cell from the conversion of solar energy into the chemical-bond energy of a solar fuel.	Problems 42–44
› Explain why splitting water into the elements hydrogen and oxygen requires an energy input and producing water by the reaction of hydrogen and oxygen releases energy.	Problem 43

REVIEW QUESTIONS

1. What did each of the following scientists contribute to our knowledge of the atom?
   a. William Crookes
   b. Eugen Goldstein
   c. Michael Faraday
   d. J. J. Thomson
2. What is radioactivity? How did the discovery of radioactivity contradict Dalton's atomic theory?
3. How are X-rays and gamma rays similar? How are they different?
4. Define or identify each of the following.
   a. deuterium
   b. tritium
   c. photon
5. The following table describes four atoms.

	Atom A	Atom B	Atom C	Atom D
Number of protons	17	18	18	17
Number of neutrons	18	17	18	17
Number of electrons	17	18	18	17

Are atoms A and B isotopes? A and C? A and D? B and C?

6. Compare Dalton's model of the atom with the nuclear model of the atom.
7. Which two atoms in Question 5 have about the same mass?
8. What are the symbol, name, and atomic number of the element with $Z = 76$? You may use the periodic table and a table of atomic masses.
9. What are the symbol, name, and atomic number of the element that has 21 protons in the nuclei of its atoms?
10. Explain what is meant by the term *quantum*.
11. Which atom absorbs more energy, one in which an electron moves from the second shell to the third shell or an otherwise identical atom in which an electron moves from the first to the third shell?
12. How did Bohr refine the model of the atom?
13. Use the periodic table to determine the number of protons in an atom of each of the following elements.
 a. lithium **b.** magnesium
 c. chlorine **d.** fluorine
 e. aluminum **f.** phosphorus
14. How many electrons are there in each neutral atom of the elements listed in Question 13?

PROBLEMS

Nuclear Symbols and Isotopes

15. Give the symbol and name for **(a)** an isotope with a mass number of 42 and an atomic number of 20 and **(b)** an isotope with 28 neutrons and 23 protons.
16. Fill in the table:

Element	Mass Number	Number of Protons	Number of Neutrons
Nickel	60		
	108	46	
		7	7
Iodine			74

17. How many different elements are listed here?
 $^{23}_{11}X$ $^{22}_{10}X$ $^{11}_{5}X$ $^{24}_{11}X$ $^{25}_{12}X$
18. How many different isotopes of silver are listed here? (The X does not necessarily represent any specific element.)
 $^{108}_{47}X$ $^{108}_{48}X$ $^{110}_{47}X$ $^{109}_{46}X$ $^{107}_{47}X$

Subshell Notation for Electron Configurations

19. Without referring to the periodic table, give the atomic numbers of the elements with the following electron configurations.
 a. $1s^2\,2s^2\,2p^3$
 b. $1s^2\,2s^2\,2p^6\,3s^2\,3p^1$
 c. $1s^2\,2s^2\,2p^6\,3s^2\,3p^6\,4s^1$
20. Without referring to the periodic table, give the atomic numbers of the elements with the following electron configurations.
 a. $1s^2\,2s^2\,2p^6\,3s^2\,3p^3$
 b. $1s^2\,2s^2\,2p^4$
 c. $1s^2\,2s^2\,2p^6\,3s^1$
21. Indicate whether each electron configuration represents an atom in the ground state or in a possible excited state or is incorrect. In each case, explain why.
 a. $1s^12s^1$ **b.** $1s^22s^22p^7$
 c. $1s^22p^2$ **d.** $1s^22s^22p^2$
22. Indicate whether each electron configuration represents an atom in the ground state or in a possible excited state or is incorrect. In each case, explain why.
 a. $1s^22s^23s^2$
 b. $1s^22s^22p^23s^1$
 c. $1s^22s^22p^62d^5$
 d. $1s^22s^42p^2$
23. Suppose that one electron is added to the outermost shell of a fluorine atom. What element's electron configuration would the atom then have?
24. Suppose that each of the following changes is made. Give the symbol for the element whose electron configuration matches the result.
 a. Two electrons are added to an oxygen atom.
 b. Two electrons are removed from a calcium atom.
 c. Three electrons are removed from an aluminum atom.
25. Referring only to the periodic table, tell how the electron configurations of silicon (Si) and germanium (Ge) are similar. How are they different?
26. Referring only to the periodic table, tell how the electron configurations of fluorine (F) and chlorine (Cl) are similar. How are they different? How do you expect the electron configurations of bromine (Br) and iodine (I) to be similar to those of fluorine and chlorine?
27. Refer to the periodic table to identify each element as a metal or a nonmetal.
 a. manganese
 b. strontium
 c. cesium
 d. argon

Use the following list of elements to answer Problems 28–32:
Mg, Cs, Ne, P, Kr, K, Ra, N, Fe, Ca, Mo

28. Which element(s) is (are) alkali metals?
29. Which element(s) is (are) noble gases?
30. Which element(s) is (are) transition metals?
31. How many of the elements are nonmetals?
32. All elements with more than 83 protons are *radioactive*, as we shall see in Chapter 11. Are any of the elements in the list above necessarily radioactive? If so, which one(s)?

ADDITIONAL PROBLEMS

33. An atom of an element has two electrons in the first shell, eight electrons in the second shell, and five electrons in the third shell. From this information, give the element's **(a)** atomic number, **(b)** name, **(c)** total number of electrons in each of its atoms, **(d)** total number of *s* electrons, and **(e)** total number of *d* electrons.

34. Refer to Problem 24. Explain how you can answer the three parts of that problem just by looking at a periodic table, and without writing electron structures.

35. Without referring to any tables in the text, mark an appropriate location for each of the following in the blank periodic table provided: **(a)** the fourth period noble gas, **(b)** the third period alkali metal, **(c)** the fourth period halogen, and **(d)** a metal in the fourth period and in group 3B.

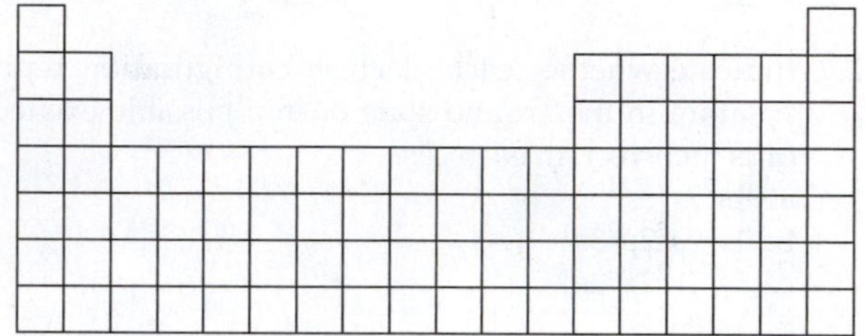

36. Look again at Figure 3.11. A patient is found to be suffering from heavy-metal poisoning. An emission spectrum is obtained from a sample of the patient's blood, by spraying a solution of the blood into a flame. The brightest emission lines are found at 5520, 5580, 5890, and 5900 Å. What two elements are likely to be present? Which one is more likely to be the culprit?

37. Refer to Figure 3.16 and write the electron configurations of **(a)** iron (Fe), **(b)** tin (Sn), and **(c)** lead (Pb).

38. Atoms of two adjacent elements in the third period are in the ground state. An atom of element A has only *s* electrons in its valence shell. An atom of element B has at least one *p* electron in its valence shell. Identify elements A and B.

39. Atoms of two adjacent elements in the fifth period are in the ground state. An atom of element L has only *s* electrons in its valence shell. An atom of element M has at least one *d* electron in an unfilled shell. Identify elements L and M.

40. Atoms of two elements, one above the other in the same group, are in the ground state. An atom of element Q has two *s* electrons in its outer shell and no *d* electrons. An atom of element R has *d* electrons in its configuration. Identify elements Q and R.

41. Which of the following is true of the water-splitting reaction on page 84?
a. It produces energy, for example, electricity or heat.
b. It requires an energy input, for example, electricity or sunlight.
c. It produces twice as much oxygen as hydrogen.
d. It occurs inside a fuel cell.

42. What is produced when solar energy is converted into chemical-bond energy in the water-splitting reaction?
a. hydrogen and nitrogen
b. oxygen and carbon
c. hydrogen and oxygen
d. oxygen and calcium

43. Which of the following is *not* a benefit of using a solar fuel such as hydrogen?
a. A solar fuel can store the energy of sunlight, which is intermittent.
b. A solar fuel can replace some fossil fuels.
c. Using a solar fuel such as hydrogen produces no carbon dioxide emissions.
d. Electrodes used in electrolysis rely on platinum metal.

44. Isotopes played an important role in one of the most important experiments investigating photosynthesis, the chemical reaction that converts water (H_2O) and carbon dioxide (CO_2) into glucose ($C_6H_{12}O_6$) and oxygen (O_2). For most of the early twentieth century, scientists thought that the oxygen produced by photosynthetic plants and algae came from carbon dioxide they absorbed. To investigate this question, in the early 1940s, chemists at Stanford University used an isotope of oxygen to study the mechanism of the photosynthetic reaction. The researchers fed photosynthesizing algae with water enriched with oxygen-18 and discovered that the oxygen produced was enriched with oxygen-18. Did this result support or refute the hypothesis that the O_2 produced by photosynthesis comes from CO_2?

COLLABORATIVE GROUP PROJECTS

Prepare a PowerPoint, poster, or other presentation (as directed by your instructor) to share with the class.

1. Prepare a brief biographical report on one of the following.
a. Humphry Davy
b. William Crookes
c. Wilhelm Roentgen
d. Marie Curie
e. Robert Millikan
f. Niels Bohr
g. Alessandro Volta
h. Ernest Rutherford
i. Michael Faraday
j. J. J. Thomson

2. Draw a grid containing 16 squares, in two rows of 8, representing the 16 elements in the periodic table from lithium to argon. For each of the elements, give **(a)** the main-shell electron configuration and **(b)** the subshell notation for the electron configuration.

3. Prepare a brief report on one of the **(a)** alkali metals, **(b)** alkaline earth metals, **(c)** halogens, or **(d)** noble gases. List sources and commercial uses.

4. Many different forms of the periodic table have been generated. Prepare a brief report showing at least three different versions of the periodic table, and comment on their utility.

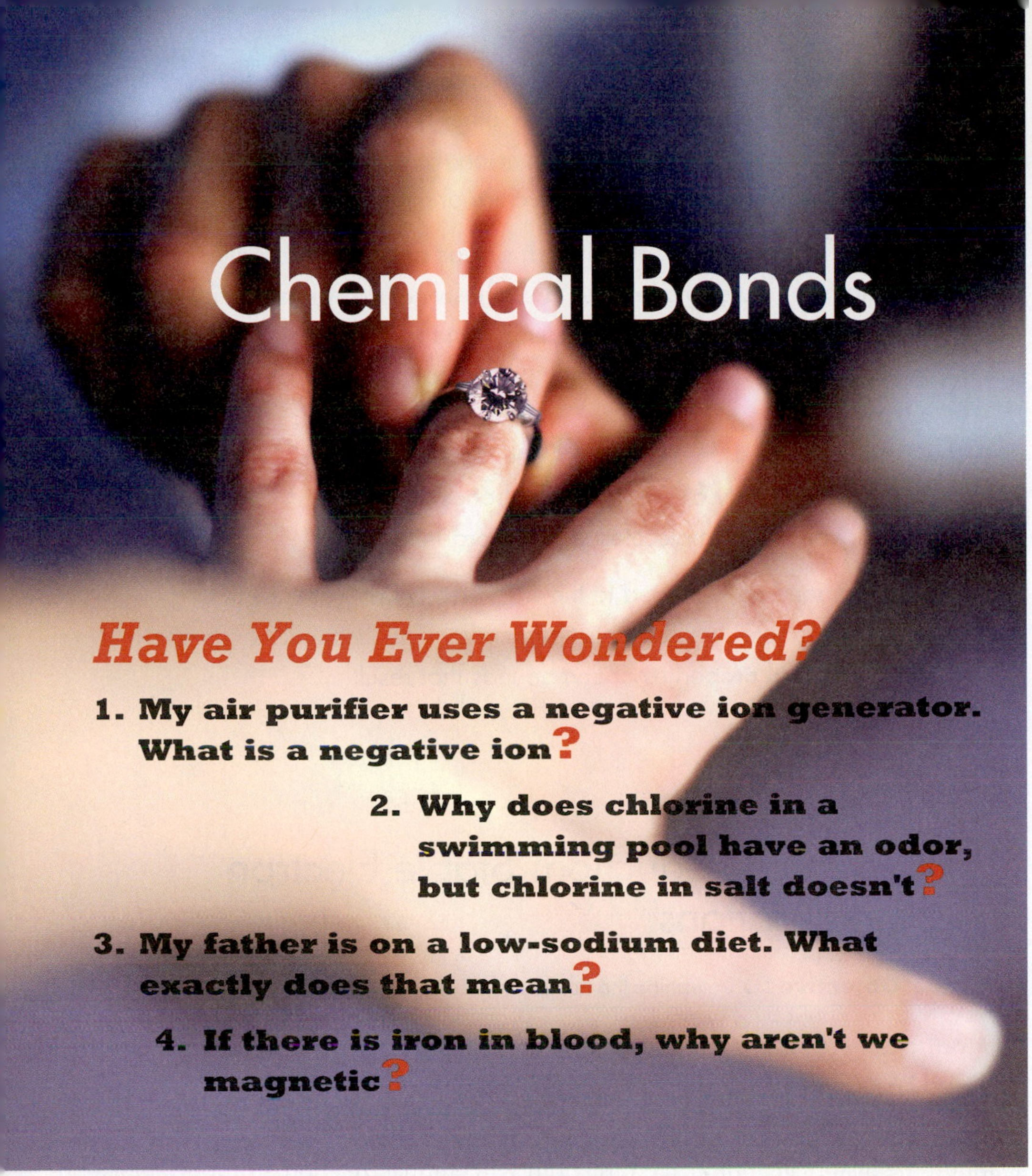

Chemical Bonds

Have You Ever Wondered?

1. **My air purifier uses a negative ion generator. What is a negative ion?**
2. **Why does chlorine in a swimming pool have an odor, but chlorine in salt doesn't?**
3. **My father is on a low-sodium diet. What exactly does that mean?**
4. **If there is iron in blood, why aren't we magnetic?**

Learning Objectives

- Determine the number of electrons in an ion. (4.1)
- Write the Lewis symbol for an atom or ion. (4.2)
- Distinguish between an ion and an atom. (4.3)
- Describe the nature of the attraction that leads to formation of an ionic bond. (4.3)
- Write symbols for common ions, and determine their charges. (4.4)
- Describe the relationship between the octet rule and the charge on an ion. (4.4)
- Name and write formulas for binary ionic compounds. (4.5)
- Explain the difference between a covalent bond and an ionic bond. (4.6)
- Name and write formulas for covalent compounds. (4.6)
- Classify a covalent bond as polar or nonpolar. (4.7)
- Use electronegativities of elements to determine bond polarity. (4.7)
- Predict the number of bonds formed by common nonmetals (the HONC rules). (4.8)
- Recognize common polyatomic ions and be able to use them in naming and writing formulas for compounds. (4.9)
- Write Lewis formulas for simple molecules and polyatomic ions. (4.10)
- Identify free radicals. (4.10)
- Predict the shapes of simple molecules from their Lewis formulas. (4.11)
- Classify a simple molecule as polar or nonpolar from its shape and the polarity of its bonds. (4.12)
- Explain how shape and composition change the properties of molecules.
- Describe the concept of molecular recognition.
- Explain the green chemistry advantages of using production methods based on molecular recognition.

The Ties that Bind

The element carbon is commonly found as soft, black soot formed by incomplete combustion. By heating that soot under tremendous pressure, we can make the hardest material known—diamond. We have not changed the carbon in soot to a different element in this process ... so why is diamond so different from soot? The answer lies in the bonds that hold the carbon atoms together. We have learned a bit about the structure of the atom. Now we are ready to consider chemical bonds, the ties that bind atoms together.

Chemical bonds are the forces that hold atoms together in molecules and hold ions together in ionic crystals. The vast number and incredible

Atoms combine by forming chemical bonds. These bonds determine, to a great extent, the properties of the substance. Here we see carbon in the form of diamonds, which can form from carbon in the form of graphite (pencil lead) or soot. The only difference between the forms of carbon are the bonds between the carbon atoms. The arrangement and number of these bonds in diamond make it by far the hardest natural material in the world. In this chapter, we will look at the different kinds of bonding that can occur.

variety of chemical compounds—tens of millions are known—result from the fact that atoms can form bonds with many other types of atoms. In addition, chemical bonds determine the three-dimensional shapes of molecules. Some important consequences of chemical structure and bonding include

- Whether a substance is a solid, liquid, or gas at room temperature
- The strengths of materials (as well as adhesives that hold materials together) used for building bridges, houses, and many other structures
- Whether a liquid is light and volatile (like gasoline) or heavy and viscous (like corn syrup)
- The taste, odor, and drug activity of chemical compounds
- The structural integrity of skin, muscles, bones, and teeth
- The toxicity of certain molecules to living organisms

Chemical bonding is related to the arrangement of electrons in compounds. In this chapter, we look at different types of chemical bonds and some of the unusual properties of compounds that result.

4.1 The Art of Deduction: Stable Electron Configurations

Learning Objective › Determine the number of electrons in an ion.

In our discussion of the atom and its structure (Chapters 2 and 3), we followed the historical development of some of the more important atomic concepts. We could continue to look at chemistry in this manner, but that would require several volumes of print—and perhaps more of your time than you care to spend. We won't abandon the historical approach entirely but will emphasize another important aspect of scientific endeavor: deduction.

The art of deduction works something like this.

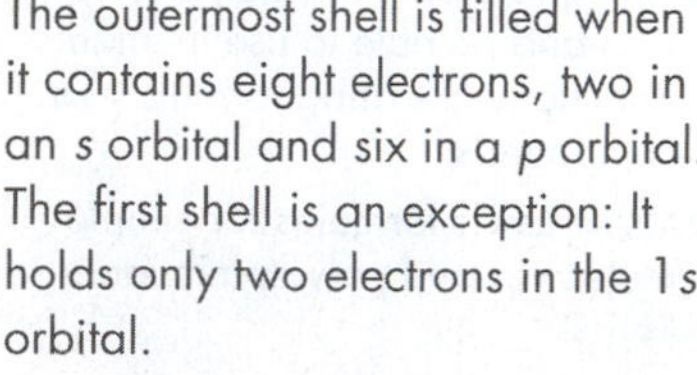
The outermost shell is filled when it contains eight electrons, two in an *s* orbital and six in a *p* orbital. The first shell is an exception: It holds only two electrons in the 1*s* orbital.

- **Fact:** Noble gases, such as helium, neon, and argon, are inert; they undergo few, if any, chemical reactions.
- **Theory:** The inertness of noble gases results from their electron configurations. Each (except helium) has an octet of electrons in its outermost shell.
- **Deduction:** Other elements that can alter their electron configurations to become like those of noble gases would become less reactive by doing so.

We can use an example to illustrate this deductive argument. Sodium has 11 electrons, one of which is in the third shell. Recall that electrons in the outermost shell are called **valence electrons,** while those in all the other shells are lumped together as **core electrons**. If the sodium atom got rid of its valence electron, its remaining core electrons would have the same electron configuration as an atom of the noble gas neon. Using main-shell configurations (Chapter 3), we can represent this as

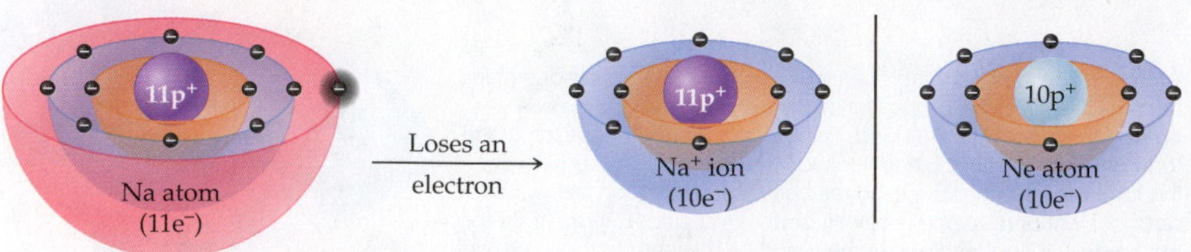

Similarly, if a chlorine atom gained an electron, it would have the same electron configuration as argon.

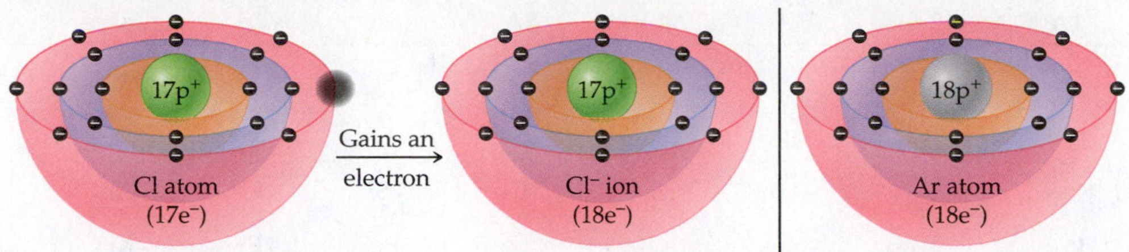

The sodium atom, having lost an electron, becomes positively charged. It has 11 protons (11+) and only 10 electrons (10−). It is symbolized by Na^+ and is called a *sodium ion*. The chlorine atom, having gained an electron, becomes negatively charged. It has 17 protons (17+) and 18 electrons (18−). It is symbolized by Cl^- and is called a *chloride ion*. Note that a positive charge, as in Na^+, indicates that one electron has been lost. Similarly, a negative charge, as in Cl^-, indicates that one electron has been gained.

It is important to note that even though Cl^- and Ar are **isoelectronic** (have the same electron configuration), they are *different* chemical species. In the same way, a sodium atom does not *become* an atom of neon when it loses an electron; the sodium ion is simply isoelectronic with neon.

1. My air purifier uses a negative ion generator. What is a negative ion? A negative ion is an atom or a group of atoms with one or more extra electrons. In a negative ion generator, a high voltage produces negative ions.

Self-Assessment Questions

1. Which group of elements in the periodic table is characterized by an especially stable electron arrangement?
   a. 2A **b.** 2B **c.** 8A **d.** 8B
2. The structural difference between a sodium atom and a sodium ion is that the sodium ion has one
   a. less proton than the sodium atom
   b. less electron than the sodium atom
   c. more proton and one less electron than the sodium atom
   d. more proton than the sodium atom
3. Which of the following are isoelectronic?
   a. K^+ and Ar **b.** Mg^{2+} and Ar **c.** Ne and Cl^- **d.** Xe and Kr
4. The anion Cl^- is isoelectronic with the cation
   a. Ca^{2+} **b.** Li^+ **c.** Mg^{2+} **d.** Na^+

Answers: 1, c; 2, b; 3, a; 4, a

4.2 Lewis (Electron-Dot) Symbols

Learning Objective › Write the Lewis symbol for an atom or ion.

In forming ions, the cores of sodium atoms and chlorine atoms do not change. It is convenient therefore to let the element symbol represent the *core* of the atom (nucleus plus inner electrons). The valence electrons are then represented by dots. The equations of the preceding section then can be written as follows:

$$\text{Na}\cdot \rightarrow \text{Na}^+ + 1\,e^-$$

and

$$\cdot\ddot{\underset{\cdot\cdot}{\text{Cl}}}: \; + \; 1\,e^- \longrightarrow :\ddot{\underset{\cdot\cdot}{\text{Cl}}}:^-$$

In these representations, the element symbol represents the core, and dots stand for valence electrons. These electron-dot symbols are usually called **Lewis symbols**.

▲ Electron-dot symbols are called *Lewis symbols* after G. N. Lewis, the famous American chemist (1875–1946) who invented them. Lewis also made important contributions to our understanding of thermodynamics, acids and bases, and spectroscopy.

Table 4.1 Lewis Symbols for Selected Main Group Elements

Group 1A	Group 2A	Group 3A	Group 4A	Group 5A	Group 6A	Group 7A	Noble Gases
H·							He:
Li·	·Be·	·Ḃ·	·Ċ· (4 dots)	:Ṅ·	:Ö·	:F̤̈·	:N̤̈e:
Na·	·Mg·	·Ȧl·	·Ṡi· (4 dots)	:Ṗ·	:S̈·	:C̤̈l·	:Ä̤r:
K·	·Ca·				:S̈e·	:B̤̈r·	:K̤̈r:
Rb·	·Sr·				:T̈e·	:Ï̤·	:Ẍ̤e:
Cs·	·Ba·						

Lewis Symbols and the Periodic Table

It is especially easy to write Lewis symbols for most of the main group elements. The number of valence electrons for most of these elements is equal to the group number (Table 4.1). Because of their more complicated electron configurations, elements in the central part of the periodic table (the transition metals) cannot easily be represented by electron-dot symbols.

In writing a Lewis symbol, only the *number* of dots is important. The dots need not be drawn in any specific positions, except that there should be no more than two dots on any given side of the chemical symbol (right, left, top, or bottom).

Example 4.1 Writing Lewis Symbols

Without referring to Table 4.1, write Lewis symbols for magnesium, oxygen, and phosphorus. You may use the periodic table.

Solution

Magnesium is in group 2A, oxygen is in group 6A, and phosphorus is in group 5A. The Lewis symbols, therefore, have two, six, and five dots, respectively. They are

·Mg· :Ọ̇: :Ṗ·

■ EXERCISE 4.1

Without referring to Table 4.1, write Lewis symbols for each of the following elements. You may use the periodic table.

a. Ar **b.** Ca **c.** F **d.** N **e.** K **f.** S

Self-Assessment Questions

1. How many dots surround Be in the Lewis symbol for beryllium?
   a. 2 **b.** 4 **c.** 5 **d.** 9
2. How many dots surround F in the Lewis symbol for fluorine?
   a. 1 **b.** 5 **c.** 7 **d.** 9
3. Which of the following Lewis symbols is *incorrect*?
   a. ·Ċ̣· **b.** :C̤̈l· **c.** Li: **d.** :Ṅ·
4. Which of the following Lewis symbols is *incorrect*?
   a. ·Ȧs· **b.** :Ö· **c.** Rb· **d.** ·Ṩi·

Answers: 1, a; 2, c; 3, c; 4, a

4.3 The Reaction of Sodium and Chlorine

Learning Objectives › Distinguish between an ion and an atom. › Describe the nature of the attraction that leads to formation of an ionic bond.

Sodium (Na) is a highly reactive metal. It is soft enough to be cut with a knife. When freshly cut, it is bright and silvery, but it dulls rapidly because it reacts with oxygen in the air. In fact, it reacts so readily in air that it is usually stored under oil or

(a)

(b)

(c)

◀ **Figure 4.1** (a) Sodium, a soft, silvery metal, and chlorine, a greenish gas (b). The two react violently, to form sodium chloride (ordinary table salt), a white crystalline solid (c).

Q: *What kinds of particles, ions or molecules, make up sodium chloride?*

kerosene. Sodium reacts violently with water, too, becoming so hot that it melts. A small piece forms a spherical bead after melting and races around on the surface of the water as it reacts.

Chlorine (Cl_2) is a greenish-yellow gas. It is familiar as a disinfectant for drinking water and swimming pools. (The actual substance added is often a compound that reacts with water to form chlorine.) Chlorine is extremely irritating to the eyes and nose. In fact, it was used as a poison gas in World War I.

If a piece of sodium is dropped into a flask containing chlorine gas, a violent reaction ensues, producing sodium chloride, beautiful white crystals that you might sprinkle on your food at the dinner table. These white crystals are ordinary table salt. Sodium chloride has very few properties in common with either sodium or chlorine (Figure 4.1).

Chlorine gas is composed of Cl_2 molecules, not separate Cl atoms. Each atom of the chlorine molecule takes an electron from a sodium atom. Two sodium ions and two chloride ions are formed.

$Cl_2 + 2\,Na \rightarrow 2\,Cl^- + 2\,Na^+$

The Reaction of Sodium and Chlorine: Theory

A sodium atom achieves a filled valence shell by losing one electron. A chlorine atom achieves a filled valence shell by adding one electron. What happens when sodium atoms come into contact with chlorine atoms? The obvious: A chlorine atom takes an electron from a sodium atom.

2. Why does chlorine in a swimming pool have an odor, but chlorine in salt doesn't? Chlorine used in swimming pools is often the element, Cl_2, while the chlorine in salt exists as chlor*ide* ions, Cl^-. An element is chemically quite different from its ions.

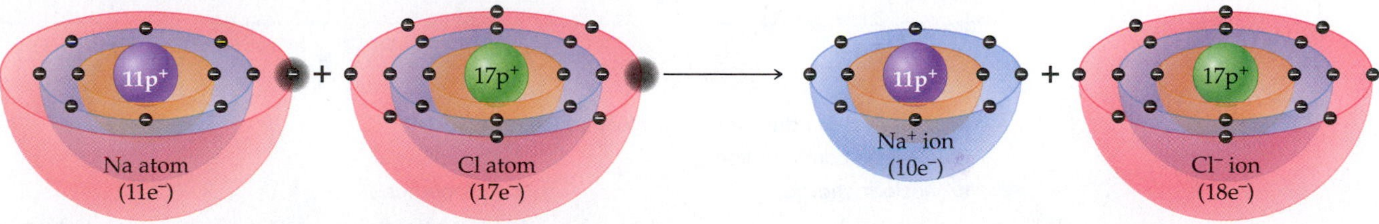

With Lewis symbols, this reaction is written as

$$\text{Na}\cdot + :\ddot{\underset{..}{\text{Cl}}}\cdot \longrightarrow \text{Na}^+ + :\ddot{\underset{..}{\text{Cl}}}:^-$$

Ionic Bonds

The Na^+ and Cl^- ions formed from sodium and chlorine atoms have opposite charges and are strongly attracted to one another. These ions arrange themselves in an orderly fashion. Each sodium ion attracts (and is attracted to) six chloride ions (above and below, front and back, left and right), as shown in Figure 4.2a. The arrangement is repeated many times in all directions (Figure 4.2b). The result is a **crystal** of sodium chloride. The orderly microscopic arrangement of the ions is reflected in the macroscopic shape, a cube, of a salt crystal (Figure 4.2c). Even the tiniest grain of salt has billions and billions of each type of ion. The forces holding the crystal together—the attractive forces between positive and negative ions—are called **ionic bonds**.

3. My father is on a low-sodium diet. What exactly does that mean? It means that he must restrict his intake of sodium *ions*. For many people, too many sodium ions in the body can increase blood pressure.

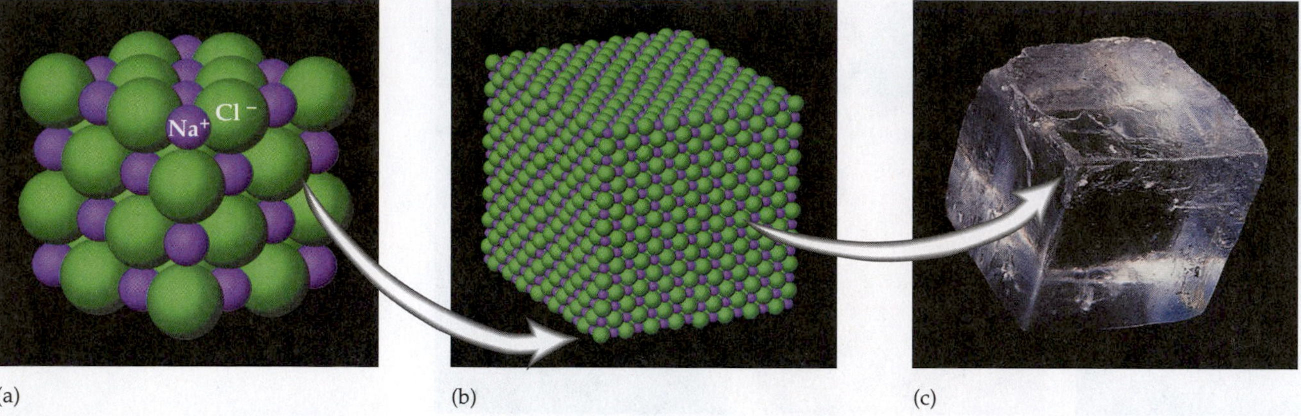

▲ **Figure 4.2** Molecular and macroscopic views of a sodium chloride crystal. (a) Each Na^+ ion (small purple spheres) is surrounded by six Cl^- ions (large green spheres), and each Cl^- ion by six Na^+ ions. (b) This arrangement repeats itself many, many times. (c) The highly ordered pattern of alternating Na^+ and Cl^- ions is observed in the macroscopic world as a crystal of sodium chloride.

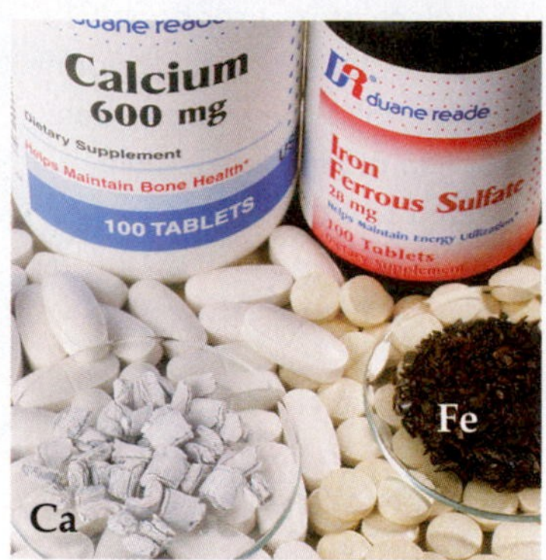

▲ **Figure 4.3** Forms of iron and calcium that are useful to the human body are the ions (usually Fe^{2+} and Ca^{2+}) in ionic compounds such as $FeSO_4$ and $CaCO_3$. The elemental forms (Fe and Ca) are chemically very different from the forms found in ionic compounds.

Atoms and Ions: Distinctively Different

Ions are emphatically different from the atoms from which they are made, much as a whole peach (an atom) and a peach pit (a positive ion) are different from one another. The names and symbols of an atom and its ion may look a lot alike, but the actual entities are very different (Figure 4.3). Unfortunately, the situation is confusing because people talk about needing iron to perk up "tired blood" and calcium for healthy teeth and bones. What they really need is iron(II) *ions* (Fe^{2+}) and calcium *ions* (Ca^{2+}). You wouldn't think of eating iron nails to get iron (although some enriched cereals do indeed have powdered iron added; the iron metal is readily converted to Fe^{2+} ions in the stomach). Nor would you eat highly reactive calcium metal.

Similarly, if you are warned to reduce your sodium intake, your doctor is not concerned that you are eating too much sodium metal—that would be exceedingly unpleasant—but that your intake of Na^+ *ions*—usually as sodium chloride—may be too high. Although the names are similar, the atom and the ion are quite different chemically. It is important to make careful distinctions and use precise terminology, as we shall do here.

Self-Assessment Questions

1. A potassium ion and an argon atom have the same
   a. electron configuration **b.** net charge
   c. nuclear charge **d.** properties
2. How many dots are shown on the Lewis symbol for chloride ion, and what is the ion's charge?
   a. five dots, no charge **b.** six dots, + charge
   c. seven dots, − charge **d.** eight dots, − charge
3. The bonding between K^+ ions and F^- ions in potassium fluoride is
   a. covalent **b.** ionic **c.** nonpolar **d.** polar

Answers: 1, a; 2, d; 3, b

4.4 Using Lewis Symbols for Ionic Compounds

Learning Objectives › Write symbols for common ions and determine their charges. › Describe the relationship between the octet rule and the charge on an ion.

Potassium, a metal in the same family as sodium and therefore similar to sodium in properties, also reacts with chlorine. The reaction yields potassium chloride (KCl).

$$K\cdot + \cdot\ddot{\underset{..}{Cl}}: \longrightarrow K^+ + :\ddot{\underset{..}{Cl}}:^-$$

Potassium also reacts with bromine, a reddish-brown liquid in the same family as chlorine and therefore similar to chlorine in properties. The product, potassium bromide (KBr), is a stable, white, crystalline solid.

$$\text{K}\cdot + \cdot\ddot{\underset{\cdot\cdot}{\text{Br}}}\!: \longrightarrow \text{K}^+ + :\!\ddot{\underset{\cdot\cdot}{\text{Br}}}\!:^-$$

Example 4.2 Electron Transfer to Form Ions

Use Lewis symbols to show the transfer of electrons from sodium atoms to bromine atoms to form ions with noble gas configurations.

Solution

Sodium has one valence electron, and bromine has seven. Transfer of the single valence electron from sodium to bromine leaves each with a noble gas configuration.

$$\text{Na}\cdot + \cdot\ddot{\underset{\cdot\cdot}{\text{Br}}}\!: \longrightarrow \text{Na}^+ + :\!\ddot{\underset{\cdot\cdot}{\text{Br}}}\!:^-$$

■ EXERCISE 4.2A

Use Lewis symbols to show the transfer of electrons from lithium atoms to fluorine atoms to form ions with noble gas configurations.

■ EXERCISE 4.2B

Use Lewis symbols to show the transfer of electrons from rubidium atoms to iodine atoms to form ions with noble gas configurations.

Magnesium, a group 2A metal, is harder and less reactive than sodium. Magnesium reacts with oxygen, a group 6A element that is a colorless gas, to form a stable, white, crystalline solid called magnesium oxide (MgO).

$$\cdot\text{Mg}\cdot + \cdot\ddot{\underset{\cdot\cdot}{\text{O}}}\!: \longrightarrow \text{Mg}^{2+} + :\!\ddot{\underset{\cdot\cdot}{\text{O}}}\!:^{2-}$$

When an Mg atom becomes an Mg^{2+} ion, its second shell becomes its outermost shell. The Mg^{2+} ion is isoelectronic with the Ne atom and has the same stable main-shell electron configuration: 2 8.

Magnesium must give up two electrons and oxygen must gain two electrons for each to have the same configuration as the noble gas neon.

An atom such as oxygen, which needs two electrons to achieve a noble gas configuration, may react with potassium atoms, which have only one electron each to give. In this case, two atoms of potassium are needed for each oxygen atom. The product is potassium oxide (K_2O).

$$\begin{matrix}\text{K}\cdot \\ \text{K}\cdot\end{matrix} + \cdot\ddot{\underset{\cdot}{\text{O}}}\!: \longrightarrow \begin{matrix}\text{K}^+ \\ \text{K}^+\end{matrix} + :\!\ddot{\underset{\cdot\cdot}{\text{O}}}\!:^{2-}$$

Through this reaction, each potassium atom achieves the argon configuration. As before, oxygen ends up with the neon configuration.

Example 4.3 Electron Transfer to Form Ions

Use Lewis symbols to show the transfer of electrons from magnesium atoms to nitrogen atoms to form ions with noble gas configurations.

Solution

$$\begin{matrix}\cdot\text{Mg}\cdot \\ \cdot\text{Mg}\cdot \\ \cdot\text{Mg}\cdot\end{matrix} + \begin{matrix}\cdot\ddot{\text{N}}\cdot \\ \cdot\ddot{\text{N}}\cdot\end{matrix} \longrightarrow \begin{matrix}\text{Mg}^{2+} \\ \text{Mg}^{2+} \\ \text{Mg}^{2+}\end{matrix} + \begin{matrix}:\!\ddot{\underset{\cdot\cdot}{\text{N}}}\!:^{3-} \\ :\!\ddot{\underset{\cdot\cdot}{\text{N}}}\!:^{3-}\end{matrix}$$

▲ It DOES Matter!
Loss of electrons is known as *oxidation*, and gain of electrons is called *reduction*. Oxidation by oxygen gas is both useful and destructive. Oxygen gas oxidizes fuels to produce energy, but it also oxidizes iron metal into familiar orange or red rust (Fe_2O_3), which causes billions of dollars of damage each year. We explore the concepts of oxidation and reduction in greater detail in Chapter 8.

Each of the three magnesium atoms gives up two electrons (a total of six), and each of the two nitrogen atoms acquires three electrons (a total of six). Notice that the total positive and negative charges on the products are equal (6+ and 6−). Magnesium reacts with nitrogen to yield magnesium nitride (Mg_3N_2).

■ EXERCISE 4.3
Use Lewis symbols to show the transfer of electrons from aluminum atoms to oxygen atoms to form ions with noble gas configurations.

Generally speaking, metallic elements in groups 1A and 2A (those from the left side of the periodic table) react with nonmetallic elements in groups 6A and 7A (those from the right side) to form ionic compounds. These products are stable crystalline solids.

The Octet Rule

Each atom of a metal tends to give up the electrons in its outer shell, and each atom of a nonmetal tends to take on enough electrons to complete its valence shell. The resulting ions have noble gas configurations. A set of eight valence electrons—an *octet*—is characteristic of all noble gases except helium. When atoms react with each other, they often tend to attain this stable noble-gas electron configuration. Thus, they are said to follow the **octet rule**, or the "rule of eight." (In the case of helium, a maximum of two electrons can occupy its single electron shell, and so hydrogen follows the "rule of two.")

In following the octet rule, atoms of group 1A metals give up one electron to form 1+ ions, those of group 2A metals give up two electrons to form 2+ ions, and those of group 3A metals give up three electrons to form 3+ ions. Group 7A nonmetal atoms take on one electron to form 1− ions, and group 6A atoms tend to pick up two electrons to form 2− ions. Atoms of B group metals can give up various numbers of electrons to form positive ions with various charges. These periodic relationships are summarized in Figure 4.4.

Table 4.2 lists symbols and names for some ions formed when atoms gain or lose electrons. (The ion names are explained in the next section.) You can calculate the charge on the negative ions in the table by subtracting 8 from the group number. For example, the charge on the oxide ion (oxygen is in group 6A) is $6 - 8 = -2$. The nitride ion (nitrogen is in group 5A) has a charge of $5 - 8 = -3$.

Example 4.4 Determining Formulas by Electron Transfer

What is the formula of the compound formed by the reaction of sodium and sulfur?

Solution
Sodium is in group 1A; the sodium atom has one valence electron. Sulfur is in group 6A; the sulfur atom has six valence electrons.

$$Na\cdot \quad \cdot\ddot{\underset{..}{S}}\cdot$$

1A	2A	3B	4B	5B	6B	7B	8B			1B	2B	3A	4A	5A	6A	7A	Noble gases
Li^+														N^{3-}	O^{2-}	F^-	
Na^+	Mg^{2+}											Al^{3+}		P^{3-}	S^{2-}	Cl^-	
K^+	Ca^{2+}						Fe^{2+} Fe^{3+}			Cu^+ Cu^{2+}	Zn^{2+}					Br^-	
Rb^+	Sr^{2+}									Ag^+						I^-	
Cs^+	Ba^{2+}																

▶ Figure 4.4 Periodic relationships of some simple ions. Many of the transition elements (B groups) can form different ions with different charges.

Q: *Can you write a formula for the simple ion formed from selenium (Se)? For the simple ion formed from indium (In)?*

Table 4.2 Symbols and Names for Some Simple (Monatomic) Ions

Group	Element	Name of Ion	Symbol for Ion
1A	Hydrogen	Hydrogen ion	H^+
	Lithium	Lithium ion	Li^+
	Sodium	Sodium ion	Na^+
	Potassium	Potassium ion	K^+
2A	Magnesium	Magnesium ion	Mg^{2+}
	Calcium	Calcium ion	Ca^{2+}
3A	Aluminum	Aluminum ion	Al^{3+}
5A	Nitrogen	Nitride ion	N^{3-}
6A	Oxygen	Oxide ion	O^{2-}
	Sulfur	Sulfide ion	S^{2-}
7A	Fluorine	Fluoride ion	F^-
	Chlorine	Chloride ion	Cl^-
	Bromine	Bromide ion	Br^-
	Iodine	Iodide ion	I^-
1B	Copper	Copper(I) ion (cuprous ion)	Cu^+
		Copper(II) ion (cupric ion)	Cu^{2+}
	Silver	Silver ion	Ag^+
2B	Zinc	Zinc ion	Zn^{2+}
8B	Iron	Iron(II) ion (ferrous ion)	Fe^{2+}
		Iron(III) ion (ferric ion)	Fe^{3+}

4. If there is iron in blood, why aren't we magnetic? Iron metal is magnetic, but compounds—such as the hemoglobin in blood—that have iron usually have iron(II) ions or iron(III) ions. The ions differ chemically and physically from the metal and are not magnetic.

Sulfur needs two electrons to gain an argon configuration, but sodium has only one to give. The sulfur atom therefore must react with two sodium atoms.

$$\begin{matrix} Na\cdot \\ Na\cdot \end{matrix} + \cdot\ddot{\underset{\cdot\cdot}{S}}\cdot \longrightarrow \begin{matrix} Na^+ \\ Na^+ \end{matrix} + :\ddot{\underset{\cdot\cdot}{S}}:^{2-}$$

The formula of the compound, called sodium sulfide, is Na_2S.

■ EXERCISE 4.4A

What are the formulas of the compounds formed by the reaction of **(a)** calcium with fluorine and **(b)** lithium with oxygen?

■ EXERCISE 4.4B

Use Figure 4.4 to predict the formulas of the two compounds that can be formed from iron (Fe) and chlorine.

Self-Assessment Questions

1. Which of the following pairs of elements would be most likely to form an ionic compound?
   a. Ca and Mg **b.** Cd and Ca **c.** K and S **d.** Ne and Na
2. Sulfur forms a simple (monatomic) ion with a charge of
   a. 6− **b.** 2− **c.** 2+ **d.** 6+
3. Magnesium forms a simple (monatomic) ion with a charge of
   a. 2− **b.** 2+ **c.** 4+ **d.** 8+
4. Mg and N react to form Mg_3N_2, an ionic compound. How many electrons are there in the valence shell of the N^{3-} ion?
   a. 2 **b.** 6 **c.** 8 **d.** 18

5. The formula of the ionic compound formed by lithium and oxygen is
   a. LiO b. Li_2O c. LiO_2 d. Li_2O_3
6. The formula of the ionic compound formed by magnesium and bromine is
   a. MgBr b. Mg_2Br c. $MgBr_2$ d. Mg_2Br_3
7. Only one of the following ions is likely to be formed in an ordinary chemical reaction; it is
   a. Ar^{3-} b. Br^- c. K^{2+} d. S^-

Answers: 1, c; 2, b; 3, b; 4, c; 5, b; 6, c; 7, b

4.5 Formulas and Names of Binary Ionic Compounds

Learning Objective › Name and write formulas for binary ionic compounds.

Names of simple positive ions (*cations*) are derived from those of their parent elements by the addition of the word *ion*. A sodium atom, on losing an electron, becomes a *sodium ion* (Na^+). A magnesium atom (Mg), on losing two electrons, becomes a *magnesium ion* (Mg^{2+}). When a metal forms more than one ion, the charges on the different ions are denoted by Roman numerals in parentheses. For example, Fe^{2+} is iron(II) ion and Fe^{3+} is iron(III) ion.

Names of simple negative ions (*anions*) are derived from those of their parent elements by changing the usual ending to *-ide* and adding the word *ion*. A chlor*ine* atom, on gaining an electron, becomes a chlor*ide ion* (Cl^-). A sulf*ur* atom gains two electrons, becoming a sulf*ide ion* (S^{2-}).

Simple ions of opposite charge can be combined to form **binary** (two-element) **ionic compounds**. To get the correct formula for a binary ionic compound, write each ion with its charge (positive ion to the left), then transpose the charge numbers (but not the plus and minus signs) and write them as subscripts. The process is best learned by practice, which is provided in the following examples and exercises and in the problems at the end of the chapter.

Example 4.5 Determining Formulas from Ionic Charges

Write the formulas for **(a)** calcium chloride and **(b)** aluminum oxide.

Solution

a. First, we write the symbols for the ions. (We write the charge on chloride ion explicitly as "1−" to illustrate the method. You may omit the "1" when you are comfortable with the process.)

$$Ca^{2+}\ Cl^{1-}$$

We cross over the charge numbers (without the charges) as subscripts.

Then we write the formula. The formula for calcium chloride is

Ca_1Cl_2 or (dropping the "1") simply $CaCl_2$

b. We write the symbols for the ions.

$$Al^{3+}\ O^{2-}$$

We cross over the charge numbers as subscripts.

We write the formula for aluminum oxide as

$$Al_2O_3$$

■ EXERCISE 4.5

Write the formulas for **(a)** potassium oxide, **(b)** calcium nitride, and **(c)** calcium sulfide.

The method just described, called the *crossover method,* works because it is based on the transfer of electrons and the conservation of charge. Two Al atoms lose three electrons each (a total of six electrons lost), and three O atoms gain two electrons each (a total of six electrons gained). The electrons lost must equal the electrons gained. Similarly, two Al^{3+} ions have six positive charges (three each), and three O^{2-} ions have six negative charges (two each). The net charge on Al_2O_3 is zero, just as it should be.

Now you are able to translate chemical words, such as aluminum oxide, into a chemical formula, Al_2O_3. You also can translate in the other direction, as shown in Example 4.6.

A Compound by Any Other Name ...

As you read labels on foodstuffs and pharmaceuticals, you will see some names that are beginning to sound familiar, and some that are confusing or mysterious. For example, why do we have two names for Fe^{2+}? Some names are historical: Iron, copper, gold, silver, and other elements have been known for thousands of years. In naming compounds of these elements, the ending *-ous* came to be used for the ion of smaller charge, and the ending *-ic* for the ion of larger charge. The modern system uses Roman numerals to indicate ionic charge. Although the new system is more logical and easier to apply, the old names persist, especially in everyday life and in some of the biomedical sciences.

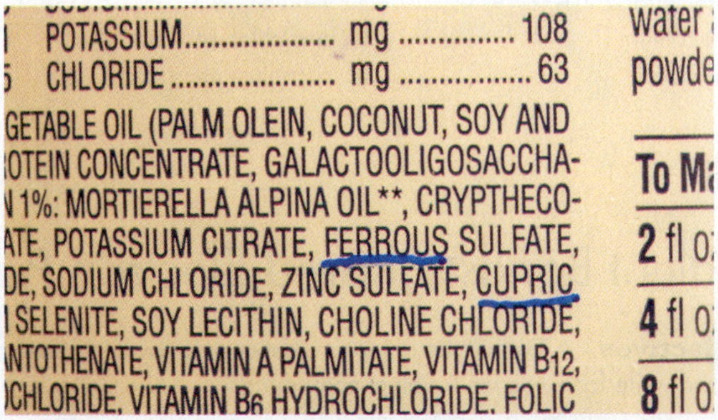

▲ Labels for dietary supplements often use older, Latin-derived names.

Example 4.6 Naming Ionic Compounds

What are the names of **(a)** MgS and **(b)** $FeCl_3$?

Solution

a. From Table 4.2, we can determine that MgS is made up of Mg^{2+} (magnesium ion) and S^{2-} (sulfide ion). The name is simply magnesium sulfide.

b. From Table 4.2, we can determine that the ions in $FeCl_3$ are

$$Fe^{3+} \quad Cl^{-}$$

How do we know the iron ion in $FeCl_3$ is Fe^{3+} and not Fe^{2+}? Because there are three Cl^- ions, each with a 1− charge, the single Fe ion must have a 3+ charge since the compound, $FeCl_3$, is neutral. The names of these ions are iron(III) ion (or ferric ion) and chloride ion. Therefore, the compound is iron(III) chloride (or, by the older system, ferric chloride).

■ EXERCISE 4.6

What are the names of **(a)** CaF_2 and **(b)** $CuBr_2$?

Self-Assessment Questions

1. The formula for the binary ionic compound of barium and sulfur is
a. BaS **b.** Ba_2S **c.** BaS_2 **d.** Ba_2S_3

2. Which of the following formulas is incorrect?
a. AlF_3 **b.** K_2S **c.** MgF **d.** NaI

3. Which of the following formulas is incorrect?
a. $AlCl_3$ **b.** Al_3P_2 **c.** CaS **d.** Cs_2S

4. The correct name for KCl is
a. krypton chloride **b.** krypton chlorine
c. potassium chloride **d.** potassium chlorine

5. The correct name for Al_2S_3 is
a. aluminum sulfide **b.** aluminum trisulfide
c. antimony sulfide **d.** antimony trisulfide

6. The correct name for LiI is
a. indium lithide **b.** iodine lithide
c. lithium indide **d.** lithium iodide

7. The correct name for $ZnCl_2$ is
a. dichlorozirconium **b.** zinc chloride
c. zinc dichloride **d.** zirconium chloride

Answers: 1, a; 2, c; 3, b; 4, c; 5, a; 6, d; 7, b

4.6 Covalent Bonds: Shared Electron Pairs

Learning Objectives › Explain the difference between a covalent bond and an ionic bond. › Name and write formulas for covalent compounds.

We might expect a hydrogen atom, with its one electron, to acquire another electron and achieve the configuration of the noble gas helium. In fact, hydrogen atoms do just that in the presence of atoms of a reactive metal such as lithium—that is, a metal that readily gives up an electron.

$$Li\cdot + H\cdot \longrightarrow Li^{+} + H{:}^{-}$$

But what if there are no other kinds of atoms around, only hydrogen? One hydrogen atom can't gain an electron from another, for all hydrogen atoms have an equal attraction for electrons. Two hydrogen atoms can compromise, however, by *sharing a pair* of electrons.

$$H\cdot + \cdot H \longrightarrow H{:}H$$

By sharing electrons, the two hydrogen atoms form a hydrogen molecule. The bond formed when atoms share electrons is called a **covalent bond**. If one pair of electrons is shared, the bond is a **single bond**.

H:H
↑ covalent bond (shared pair of electrons)

Let's consider chlorine next. A chlorine atom readily takes an extra electron from anything willing to give one up. But again, what if the only things around are other chlorine atoms? Chlorine atoms can also attain a more stable arrangement by sharing a pair of electrons.

$$:\ddot{\underset{..}{Cl}}\cdot + \cdot\ddot{\underset{..}{Cl}}: \longrightarrow :\ddot{\underset{..}{Cl}}:\ddot{\underset{..}{Cl}}:$$

The shared pair of electrons in the chlorine molecule is another example of a covalent bond; they are called a **bonding pair**. The electrons that stay on one atom and are not shared are called *nonbonding pairs*, or **lone pairs**.

$$:\ddot{\underset{..}{Cl}}:\ddot{\underset{..}{Cl}}:$$

For simplicity, the hydrogen molecule is often represented as H_2, and the chlorine molecule as Cl_2. In each case, the covalent bond between the atoms is understood. Sometimes the covalent bond is indicated by a dash: H—H and Cl—Cl. Lone pairs of electrons often are not shown. Each chlorine atom in a chlorine molecule has eight electrons around it, an arrangement like that of the noble gas argon. Thus, the atoms involved in a covalent bond follow the octet rule by sharing electrons, just as those linked by an ionic bond follow it by giving up or accepting electrons.

Multiple Bonds

In some molecules, atoms must share more than one pair of electrons to follow the octet rule. In carbon dioxide (CO_2), for example, the carbon atom shares *two* pairs of electrons with each of the two oxygen atoms.

$$:\ddot{O}::C::\ddot{O}:$$

Note that each atom has an octet of electrons around it as a result of this sharing. We say that the atoms are joined by a **double bond**, a covalent linkage in which two atoms share two pairs of electrons. A double bond is indicated by a double dash between atoms (O=C=O).

Two atoms also can share three pairs of electrons. In the nitrogen (N_2) molecule, for example, each nitrogen atom shares three pairs of electrons with the other.

$$:N:::N:$$

The atoms are joined by a **triple bond**, a covalent linkage in which two atoms share three pairs of electrons (N≡N). Note that each of the nitrogen atoms has an octet of electrons around it.

Covalent bonds are usually represented as dashes. The three kinds of covalent bonds are simply written as follows:

H—Cl O=C=O N≡N

Names of Covalent Compounds

Covalent, or *molecular*, compounds are those in which electrons are shared, not transferred. Such compounds generally have molecules that consist of two or more nonmetals. Many covalent compounds have common and widely used names. Examples are water (H_2O), ammonia (NH_3), and methane (CH_4).

For most other covalent compounds, the naming process is more systematic. The prefixes *mono-*, *di-*, *tri-*, and so on are used to indicate the number of atoms of each element in the molecule. A list of these prefixes for up to 10 atoms is given in Table 4.3. For example, the compound N_2O_4 is called *dinitrogen tetroxide*. (The ending vowel is often dropped from *tetra-* and other prefixes when they precede another vowel.) We often leave off the prefix *mono-* (NO is nitrogen oxide) but include it when we need to distinguish between two compounds of the same pair of elements (CO is carbon monoxide; CO_2 is carbon dioxide).

Table 4.3 Prefixes That Indicate the Number of Atoms of an Element in a Covalent Compound

Prefix	Number of Atoms
Mono-	1
Di-	2
Tri-	3
Tetra-	4
Penta-	5
Hexa-	6
Hepta-	7
Octa-	8
Nona-	9
Deca-	10

Example 4.7 Naming Covalent Compounds

What are the names of **(a)** SCl_2 and **(b)** P_4S_3?

Solution

a. With one sulfur atom and two chlorine atoms, SCl_2 is sulfur dichloride.

b. With four phosphorus atoms and three sulfur atoms, P_4S_3 is tetraphosphorus trisulfide.

■ EXERCISE 4.7

What are the names of **(a)** BrF_3, **(b)** BrF_5, **(c)** N_2O, and **(d)** N_2O_5?

You can have fun with chemical names. Some compounds have strange—even funny—common names. Curious? Curium(III) chloride ($CmCl_3$) is curous chloride. Nickel(II) curate ($NiCmO_3$) is nickelous curate. Titanium(IV) chloride ($TiCl_4$) is titanic chloride. Some ions of uranium, such as UO_2^{2-}, UO_3^{2-}, $U_2O_7^{2-}$, are uranates. The hydrides of group 4 elements include methane (CH_4), silane (SiH_4), and germane (GeH_4). Is GeH_4 relevant?

Example 4.8 Formulas of Covalent Compounds

Write the formula for tetraphosphorus hexoxide.

Solution

The prefix *tetra-* indicates four phosphorus atoms, and *hex-* specifies six oxygen atoms. The formula is P_4O_6.

■ EXERCISE 4.8

Write the formulas for **(a)** phosphorus trichloride, **(b)** dichlorine heptoxide, **(c)** nitrogen triiodide, and **(d)** disulfur dichloride.

Self-Assessment Questions

1. A bond formed when two atoms share a pair of electrons is
a. covalent **b.** ionic **c.** nonpolar **d.** polar

2. The bond in Br_2 is
a. double covalent **b.** ionic
c. single covalent **d.** triple covalent

3. The bond in N_2 is
a. double covalent **b.** ionic
c. single covalent **d.** triple covalent

4. The formula for phosphorus trichloride is
a. KCl_3 **b.** K_3Cl **c.** PCl_3 **d.** P_3Cl

5. The formula for disulfur difluoride is
a. SF_2 **b.** S_2F_2 **c.** SFe_2 **d.** S_2Fl_2

6. The correct name for N_2S_4 is
a. dinitrogen disulfide **b.** dinitrogen tetrasulfide
c. tetrasulfodinitrogen **d.** tetrasulfur dinitride

7. The correct name for I_2O_5 is
a. diiodine pentoxide **b.** diiodopentoxide
c. iridium pentoxide **d.** pentaoxodiiodine

Answers: 1, a; 2, c; 3, d; 4, c; 5, b; 6, b; 7, a

4.7 Unequal Sharing: Polar Covalent Bonds

Learning Objectives › Classify a covalent bond as polar or nonpolar. › Use electronegativities of elements to determine bond polarity.

So far, we have seen that atoms combine in two different ways. Atoms that are quite different in electron configuration (from opposite sides of the periodic table) react by the complete transfer of one or more electrons from one atom to another to form an ionic bond. Some identical nonmetal atoms (such as two chlorine atoms or two hydrogen atoms) combine by sharing a pair of electrons to form a covalent bond. Now let's consider bond formation between atoms that are different, but not different enough to form ionic bonds.

Hydrogen Chloride

Hydrogen and chlorine react to form a colorless gas called *hydrogen chloride*. This reaction may be represented as

$$\text{H}\cdot + \cdot\ddot{\underset{\cdot\cdot}{\text{Cl}}}\text{:} \longrightarrow \text{H:}\ddot{\underset{\cdot\cdot}{\text{Cl}}}\text{:}$$

Ignoring the lone pairs of electrons and using a dash to represent the covalent bond, we can write the hydrogen chloride molecule as H—Cl. Both hydrogen and chlorine need an electron to achieve a noble gas configuration—a helium configuration for hydrogen and an argon configuration for chlorine. They achieve these configurations by sharing a pair of electrons to form a covalent bond.

Example 4.9 Covalent Bonds from Lewis Symbols

Use Lewis symbols to show the formation of a covalent bond **(a)** between two fluorine atoms and **(b)** between a fluorine atom and a hydrogen atom.

Solution

$$\text{:}\ddot{\underset{\cdot\cdot}{\text{F}}}\cdot + \cdot\ddot{\underset{\cdot\cdot}{\text{F}}}\text{:} \longrightarrow \text{:}\ddot{\underset{\cdot\cdot}{\text{F}}}\text{:}\ddot{\underset{\cdot\cdot}{\text{F}}}\text{:} \text{ — bonding pair}$$

$$\text{H}\cdot + \cdot\ddot{\underset{\cdot\cdot}{\text{F}}}\text{:} \longrightarrow \text{H:}\ddot{\underset{\cdot\cdot}{\text{F}}}\text{:} \text{ — bonding pair}$$

■ EXERCISE 4.9

Use Lewis symbols to show the formation of a covalent bond between **(a)** two bromine atoms, **(b)** a hydrogen atom and a bromine atom, and **(c)** an iodine atom and a chlorine atom.

You might reasonably ask why a hydrogen molecule and a chlorine molecule react at all. Have we not just learned that these molecules form because the result is a stable arrangement of electrons? Yes, indeed, that is the case. But there is stable, and there is *more* stable. The chlorine molecule represents a more stable arrangement than two separate chlorine atoms. However, given the opportunity, a chlorine atom selectively forms a bond with a hydrogen atom rather than with another chlorine atom.

For convenience and simplicity, the reaction of hydrogen (molecule) and chlorine (molecule) to form hydrogen chloride is often represented as

$$H_2 + Cl_2 \longrightarrow 2\,HCl$$

The bonds between the atoms and the lone pairs on the chlorine atoms are not shown explicitly, but remember that they are there.

Each molecule of hydrogen chloride consists of one atom of hydrogen and one atom of chlorine. These unlike atoms share a pair of electrons. *Share*, however, does not necessarily mean "share equally." Chlorine atoms have a greater attraction for a shared pair of electrons than hydrogen atoms do. Chlorine is said to be more *electronegative* than hydrogen.

Electronegativity

The **electronegativity** of an element is a measure of the attraction of an atom of that element *in a molecule* for a pair of shared electrons. The atoms to the right in the periodic table are, in general, more electronegative than those to the left. The ones on the right are precisely the atoms that, in forming ions, tend to gain electrons and form negative ions. The ones on the left—metals—tend to give up electrons and become positive ions. Within a column, electronegativity tends to be higher at the top and lower at the bottom of the column.

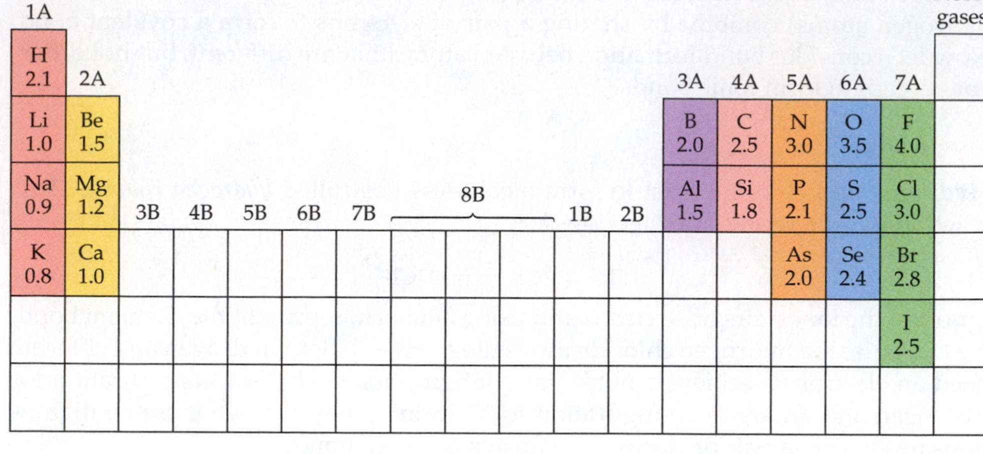

▶ **Figure 4.5** Pauling electronegativity values for several common elements.

Q: *Can you estimate a value for the electronegativity of germanium (Ge)? For the electronegativity of rubidium (Rb)?*

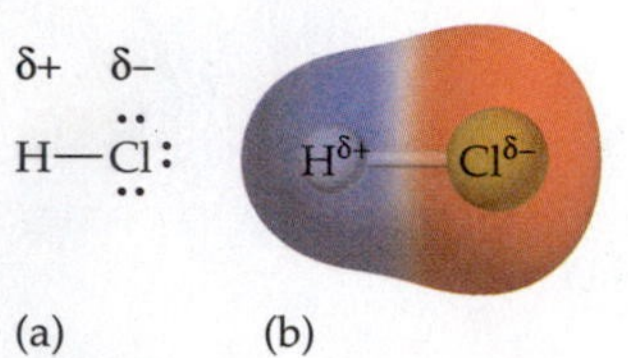

▲ **Figure 4.6** Representation of the polar hydrogen chloride molecule. (a) The electron-dot formula, with the symbols δ+ and δ− indicating the partial positive and partial negative charge, respectively. (b) An *electrostatic potential diagram* depicting the unequal distribution of electron density in the hydrogen chloride molecule.

▲ Chlorine hogs the electron blanket, leaving hydrogen partially, but positively, exposed.

The more electronegative an atom is, the greater its tendency to pull the electrons in the bond toward its end of the bond when it is involved in covalent bonding. The American chemist Linus Pauling (1901–1994) devised a scale of relative electronegativity values by assigning fluorine, the most electronegative element, a value of 4.0. Figure 4.5 displays the electronegativity values for some of the common elements that we will encounter in this text.

Chlorine (3.0) is more electronegative than hydrogen (2.1). In the hydrogen chloride molecule, the shared electrons are held more tightly by the chlorine atom. Thus, the chlorine end of the molecule is more negative than the hydrogen end. When the electrons in a covalent bond are not equally shared, the bond is said to be *polar*. The bond in a hydrogen chloride molecule is described as a **polar covalent bond**, whereas the bond in a hydrogen molecule or a chlorine molecule is a **nonpolar covalent bond**. A polar covalent bond is not an ionic bond. In an ionic bond, one atom completely loses an electron. In a polar covalent bond, the atom at the positive end of the bond (hydrogen in HCl) still has a fractional share in the bonding pair of electrons (Figure 4.6). To distinguish this kind of bond from an ionic bond or a nonpolar covalent bond, the following notation is used:

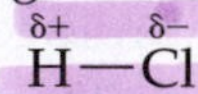

$$\overset{\delta+}{\mathrm{H}}-\overset{\delta-}{\mathrm{Cl}}$$

The line between the atoms represents the covalent bond, a pair of shared electrons. The δ+ and δ− (read "delta plus" and "delta minus") signify which end of the bond is partially positive and which is partially negative. (The word *partially* is used to distinguish these charges from the full charges on ions.)

We can use the electronegativity values for the two atoms joined by a bond to predict the type of bonding. When the electronegativity difference is zero or very small (<0.5), the bond is *nonpolar covalent*, with nearly equal sharing of the electrons. When the electronegativity difference is large (>2.0), complete electron transfer occurs and an *ionic* bond is formed, as in the case of sodium and chlorine. When the electronegativity difference is between 0.5 and 2.0, a *polar covalent* bond is formed.

Example 4.10 Using Electronegativities to Classify Bonds

Use data from Figure 4.5 to classify the bond between each of the following pairs of atoms as nonpolar covalent, polar covalent, or ionic:

a. H, H **b.** O, H **c.** C, H

Solution

a. Two H atoms have exactly the same electronegativity. The electronegativity difference is 0. The bond is nonpolar covalent.

b. The electronegativity difference is $3.5 - 2.1 = 1.4$. The bond is polar covalent.

c. The electronegativity difference is $2.5 - 2.1 = 0.4$. The bond is nonpolar covalent.

■ EXERCISE 4.10A

Use data from Figure 4.5 to classify the bond between each of the following pairs of atoms as nonpolar covalent, polar covalent, or ionic:

a. H, Br **b.** Na, O **c.** C, C

■ EXERCISE 4.10B

Use the periodic table to classify the following bonds as nonpolar covalent or polar covalent:

a. C—N **b.** C—O **c.** C=C

Self-Assessment Questions

1. When HCl is formed,
- **a.** a Cl atom gives one valence electron to an H atom
- **b.** an H atom gives one valence electron to a Cl atom
- **c.** a pair of valence electrons is shared, one each from the H atom and the Cl atom
- **d.** a pair of valence electrons is shared, none from the H atom and two from the Cl atom

2. Which of the following bonds is least polar?

a. C—Br **b.** C—Cl **c.** C—F **d.** H—H

3. Which of the following bonds is most polar?

a. C—C **b.** C—F **c.** C—O **d.** F—F

4. In a polar covalent bond, the atom with greater electronegativity bears a

a. full negative charge **b.** full positive charge
c. partial negative charge **d.** partial positive charge

5. For an ionic bond to exist between two atoms, their difference in electronegativity should be

a. between 0 and 0.5 **b.** between 0.5 and 2.0
c. greater than 2.0 **d.** zero

Answers: 1, c; 2, d; 3, b; 4, c; 5, c

4.8 Polyatomic Molecules: Water, Ammonia, and Methane

Learning Objective › Predict the number of bonds formed by common nonmetals (the HONC rules).

To obtain an octet of electrons, an oxygen atom must share electrons with *two* hydrogen atoms, a nitrogen atom must share electrons with *three* hydrogen atoms, and a carbon atom must share electrons with *four* hydrogen atoms. In general, nonmetals tend to form a number of covalent bonds that is equal to eight minus the group number. Oxygen, which is in group 6A, forms $8 - 6 = 2$ covalent bonds in most molecules. Nitrogen, in group 5A, forms $8 - 5 = 3$ covalent bonds in most molecules. Carbon, in group 4A, forms $8 - 4 = 4$ covalent bonds in most molecules, including those of the great host of organic compounds (Chapter 9). The following simple guidelines—sometimes called the HONC rules—will enable you to write formulas for many molecules.

- Hydrogen forms 1 bond.
- Oxygen forms 2 bonds.
- Nitrogen forms 3 bonds.
- Carbon forms 4 bonds.

Water

Water is one of the most familiar chemical substances. The electrolysis experiment of Nicholson and Carlisle (Chapter 2) and the fact that both hydrogen and oxygen are diatomic (two-atom) gases indicate that the molecular formula for water is H_2O. To attain an octet, oxygen shares two pairs of electrons. Because a hydrogen atom shares only one pair of electrons, however, an oxygen atom must bond with two hydrogen atoms, forming a *polyatomic* molecule—a molecule containing more than two atoms.

$$\cdot\ddot{\underset{\cdot}{O}}: + 2\,H\cdot \longrightarrow H:\ddot{\underset{\cdot\cdot}{O}}: \text{ or } H{-}O$$
$$\qquad\qquad\qquad\qquad H \qquad\qquad\quad\ | $$
$$\qquad\qquad\qquad\qquad\qquad\qquad\qquad H$$

This arrangement completes the valence shell octet of the oxygen atom, giving it the neon configuration. It also completes the outer shell of each hydrogen atom, giving each of these atoms the helium configuration. Oxygen has a higher electronegativity than does hydrogen, so the H—O bonds formed are *polar covalent*.

Ammonia

A nitrogen atom has five electrons in its valence shell. It can attain the neon configuration by sharing three pairs of electrons with *three* hydrogen atoms. The result is the compound ammonia.

$$\cdot\ddot{\underset{\cdot}{N}}\cdot + 3\,H\cdot \longrightarrow H:\ddot{\underset{\cdot\cdot}{N}}:H \text{ or } H{-}N{-}H$$
$$\qquad\qquad\qquad\qquad H \qquad\qquad\quad | $$
$$\qquad\qquad\qquad\qquad\qquad\qquad\qquad H$$

In ammonia, the bond arrangement is that of a tripod (see Figure 4.10) with a hydrogen atom at the end of each leg and the nitrogen atom with its unshared pair of electrons at the top. (We will see why it has this shape in Section 4.11.) The electronegativity of N is 3.0, and that of H is 2.1, so all three N—H bonds are *polar covalent*.

Methane

A carbon atom has four electrons in its valence shell. It can achieve the neon configuration by sharing pairs of electrons with four hydrogen atoms, forming the compound methane.

$$\qquad\qquad\qquad\quad H \qquad\qquad\qquad H$$
$$\qquad\qquad\qquad\quad \cdot\cdot \qquad\qquad\qquad\ | $$
$$\cdot\dot{\underset{\cdot}{C}}\cdot + 4\,H\cdot \longrightarrow H:\underset{\cdot\cdot}{\overset{\cdot\cdot}{C}}:H \text{ or } H{-}C{-}H$$
$$\qquad\qquad\qquad\quad H \qquad\qquad\qquad\ | $$
$$\qquad\qquad\qquad\qquad\qquad\qquad\quad H$$

The methane molecule, as shown above, appears to be planar but actually is not—as we shall see in Section 4.11. The electronegativity difference between H and C is so small that the C—H bonds are considered nonpolar.

Self-Assessment Questions

1. When two H atoms each share an electron with an O atom to form H_2O, the bonding is
   a. diatomic
   b. ionic
   c. nonpolar covalent
   d. polar covalent
2. How many electrons are in the valence shell of the N atom in an ammonia molecule?
   a. 2
   b. 5
   c. 6
   d. 8
3. To gain an octet of electrons in forming methane, a carbon atom must share an electron with each of
   a. 2 H atoms
   b. 4 H atoms
   c. 6 H atoms
   d. 8 H atoms

Answers: 1, d; 2, d; 3, b

4.9 Polyatomic Ions

Learning Objective › Recognize common polyatomic ions and be able to use them in naming and writing formulas for ionic compounds.

Many compounds contain both ionic and covalent bonds. Sodium hydroxide, commonly known as lye, consists of sodium ions (Na^+) and hydroxide ions (OH^-). The hydroxide ion contains an oxygen atom covalently bonded to a hydrogen atom,

Table 4.4 Some Common Polyatomic Ions

Charge	Name	Formula
1+	Ammonium ion	NH_4^+
	Hydronium ion	H_3O^+
1−	Hydrogen carbonate (bicarbonate) ion	HCO_3^-
	Hydrogen sulfate (bisulfate) ion	HSO_4^-
	Acetate ion	$CH_3CO_2^-$ (or $C_2H_3O_2^-$)
	Nitrite ion	NO_2^-
	Nitrate ion	NO_3^-
	Cyanide ion	CN^-
	Hydroxide ion	OH^-
	Dihydrogen phosphate ion	$H_2PO_4^-$
	Permanganate ion	MnO_4^-
2−	Carbonate ion	CO_3^{2-}
	Sulfate ion	SO_4^{2-}
	Chromate ion	CrO_4^{2-}
	Hydrogen (monohydrogen) phosphate ion	HPO_4^{2-}
	Oxalate ion	$C_2O_4^{2-}$
	Dichromate ion	$Cr_2O_7^{2-}$
3−	Phosphate ion	PO_4^{3-}

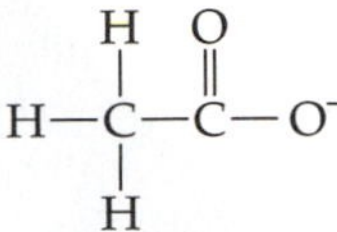

Acetate ion

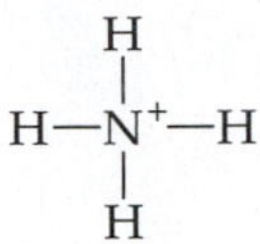

Ammonium ion

H—O—C(=O)—O⁻

Hydrogen carbonate ion (bicarbonate ion)

⁻O—C(=O)—O⁻ O=N—O⁻

Carbonate ion Nitrite ion

plus an "extra" electron. That extra electron gives hydroxide ion a negative charge and gives the O and the H atom each a filled shell.

$$e^- + \cdot\ddot{\underset{\cdot\cdot}{O}}\cdot + \cdot H \longrightarrow :\ddot{\underset{\cdot\cdot}{O}}:H^-$$

The formula for sodium hydroxide is NaOH. For each sodium ion, there is one hydroxide ion.

There are many groups of atoms that (like hydroxide ion) remain together through most chemical reactions. **Polyatomic ions** are charged particles containing two or more covalently bonded atoms. A list of common polyatomic ions is given in Table 4.4. You can use these ions, in combination with the simple ions in Table 4.2, to determine formulas for many ionic compounds.

Example 4.11 Formulas with Polyatomic Ions

What is the formula for ammonium sulfide?

Solution

Ammonium ion is found in Table 4.4. Sulfide ion is a sulfur atom (group 6A) with two additional electrons. The ions are

$$NH_4^+ \ S^{2-}$$

Crossing over gives

$$NH_4^{(1)+} \quad S^{(2)-}$$

The formula for ammonium sulfide is $(NH_4)_2S$. (Note the parentheses.)

■ EXERCISE 4.11A

What are the formulas for **(a)** calcium acetate, **(b)** potassium oxide, and **(c)** aluminum sulfate?

■ EXERCISE 4.11B

How many **(a)** sulfur atoms are in the formula for aluminum sulfate, how many and **(b)** how many carbon atoms are in the formula for calcium acetate?

Example 4.12 Naming Compounds with Polyatomic Ions

What are the names of **(a)** NaCN and **(b)** $Fe(OH)_2$?

Solution

As with compounds containing only monatomic ions, we name the cation and then the anion.

a. The cation is sodium ion, and the anion is cyanide ion (Table 4.4). The compound is sodium cyanide.

b. The cation is an iron ion, and the anion is hydroxide ion (Table 4.4). There are two hydroxide ions, each with a charge of 1−, so the iron ion must be a 2+ ion [iron(II)]. The compound is iron(II) hydroxide.

■ EXERCISE 4.12A

What are the names of **(a)** $CaCO_3$, **(b)** $Mg_3(PO_4)_2$, and **(c)** K_2CrO_4?

■ EXERCISE 4.12B

What are the names of **(a)** $(NH_4)_2SO_4$, **(b)** KH_2PO_4, and **(c)** $CuCr_2O_7$?

Self-Assessment Questions

1. Which of the following compounds incorporates a polyatomic ion?
a. CO_2 **b.** $C_6H_{12}O_6$ **c.** K_2SO_3 **d.** $SrBr_2$

2. The formula for ammonium phosphate is
a. NH_4PO_3 **b.** $NH_4(PO_4)_2$ **c.** $(NH_4)_2PO_4$ **d.** $(NH_4)_3PO_4$

3. The formula for sodium hydrogen carbonate is
a. $NaHCO_3$ **b.** Na_2HCO_3 **c.** NaH_2CO_3 **d.** $NaHCO_4$

4. The formula for copper(I) hydrogen sulfate is
a. $CuHSO_4$ **b.** Cu_2HSO_3 **c.** Cu_2HSO_4 **d.** $Cu(HSO_4)_2$

5. The formula for calcium nitrate is
a. $CaNO_3$ **b.** Ca_2NO_3 **c.** $Ca(NO_3)_2$ **d.** $CaNO_4$

6. The correct name for NH_4HCO_3 is
a. ammonium acetate **b.** ammonium carbonate
c. ammonium hydrogen carbonate **d.** ammonium cyanide

Answers: 1, c; 2, d; 3, a; 4, a; 5, c; 6, c

4.10 Rules for Writing Lewis Formulas

Learning Objectives › Write Lewis formulas for simple molecules and polyatomic ions. › Identify free radicals.

As we have seen, electrons are transferred or shared in ways that leave most atoms with octets of electrons in their outermost shells. This section describes how to write **Lewis formulas** for molecules and polyatomic ions. To write a Lewis formula, we first put the atoms of the molecule or ion in their proper places, and then we place all the valence electrons so that each atom has a filled shell.

The *skeletal structure* of a molecule tells us the order in which the atoms are attached to one another. Drawing a skeletal structure takes some practice. However, if there is no experimental evidence, the following guidelines help us to devise likely skeletal structures:

- Hydrogen atoms form only single bonds. They are always at the end of a sequence of atoms. Hydrogen is often bonded to carbon, nitrogen, or oxygen.
- Oxygen tends to have two bonds, nitrogen usually has three bonds, and carbon has four bonds.
- Polyatomic molecules and ions often consist of a central atom surrounded by atoms of higher electronegativity. (Hydrogen is an exception; it is always on the outside, even when bonded to a more electronegative element.) The central atom of a polyatomic molecule or ion is often the *least* electronegative atom.

After choosing a skeletal structure for a polyatomic molecule or ion, we can use the following steps to write the Lewis formula:

1. Determine the total number of valence electrons. This total is the sum of the valence electrons for all the atoms in the molecule or ion. You must also account for the charge(s) on a polyatomic ion. For a polyatomic anion, *add* to its total number of valence electrons the number of negative charges. For a polyatomic cation, *subtract* the number of positive charges.

   Examples:

   N_2O_4 has $(2 \times 5) + (4 \times 6) = 34$ valence electrons.

   NO_3^- has $[(1 \times 5) + (3 \times 6)] + 1 = 24$ valence electrons.

   NH_4^+ has $[(1 \times 5) + (4 \times 1)] - 1 = 8$ valence electrons.

2. Write a reasonable skeletal structure and connect bonded pairs of atoms by a dash (one shared electron pair).
3. Place electrons in pairs around outer atoms so that each (except hydrogen) has an octet.
4. Subtract the number of electrons assigned so far (both in bonds and as lone pairs) from the total calculated in step 1. Any electrons that remain are assigned in pairs to the central atom(s).
5. If a central atom has fewer than eight electrons after step 4, one or more multiple bonds are likely. Move one or more lone pairs from an outer atom to the space between the atoms to form a double or triple bond. A deficiency of two electrons suggests a double bond, and a shortage of four electrons indicates a triple bond or two double bonds to the central atom.

Example 4.13 Writing Lewis Formulas

Write Lewis formulas for **(a)** methanol (CH_3OH), **(b)** the BF_4^- ion, and **(c)** carbon dioxide (CO_2).

Solution

a. We start by following the preceding rules:
   1. The total number of valence electrons is $4 + (4 \times 1) + 6 = 14$.
   2. The skeletal structure must have all the H atoms on the outside. That means the C and O atoms must be bonded to each other. A reasonable skeletal structure is

```
     H
     |
  H—C—O—H
     |
     H
```

   3. Now, we count five bonds with two electrons each, making a total of ten electrons. Thus, four of the 14 valence electrons are left to be assigned. They are placed (as two lone pairs) on the oxygen atom.

```
     H
     |   ..
  H—C—O—H
     |   ..
     H
```

   (The remaining steps are not necessary. Both carbon and oxygen now have octets of electrons.)

b. Again, we start by applying the preceding rules:

1. There are 3 + (4 × 7) + 1 = 32 valence electrons.
2. The skeletal structure is

```
      F
      |
  F — B — F
      |
      F
```

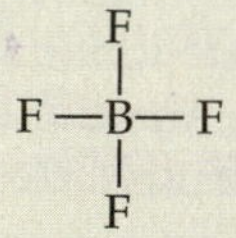

3. Placing three lone pairs on each fluorine atom gives

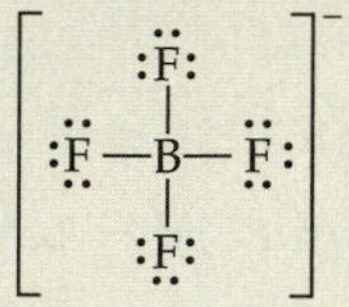

```
 ┌      ..      ┐ -
 |     :F:      |
 |  ..  |   ..  |
 | :F — B — F:  |
 |  ..  |   ..  |
 |     :F:      |
 └      ..      ┘
```

4. We have assigned 32 electrons. None remains to be assigned. Brackets and a negative sign are added to show that this is the structure for an anion, not a molecule. The charge is written outside the brackets to indicate the charge is on the ion as a whole, not necessarily on any particular atom.

c. Again, we start by applying the rules:

1. There are 4 + (2 × 6) = 16 valence electrons.
2. The skeletal structure is O—C—O.
3. We place three lone pairs on each oxygen atom.

```
 ..       ..
:O — C — O:
 ..       ..
```

4. We have assigned 16 electrons. None remains to be placed.
5. The central carbon atom has only four electrons. It needs to have two double bonds in order to achieve an octet. We move a lone pair from each oxygen atom to the space between the atoms to form a double bond on each side of the carbon atom.

```
 ..     ..
:O=C=O:
```

■ EXERCISE 4.13A

Write Lewis formulas for **(a)** oxygen difluoride, OF_2, and **(b)** methyl chloride, CH_3Cl.

■ EXERCISE 4.13B

Write Lewis formulas for **(a)** the azide ion, N_3^-, and **(b)** the nitryl fluoride molecule, NO_2F (O—N—O—F skeleton).

The rules we have used here lead to the results for selected elements that are summarized in Table 4.5. Figure 4.7 relates the number of covalent bonds that a particular element forms to its position on the periodic table.

Odd-Electron Molecules: Free Radicals

There are some classes of molecules in which atoms do not conform to the octet rule. *Free radicals* are one such class. (See Problems 51 and 52 for two other types.) Molecules with odd numbers of valence electrons obviously cannot satisfy the octet rule. Examples of such molecules are nitrogen monoxide (NO, also called nitric oxide), with 5 + 6 = 11 valence electrons; nitrogen dioxide (NO_2), with 17 valence electrons; and chlorine dioxide (ClO_2), which has 19 valence electrons.

An atom or molecule with unpaired electrons is called a **free radical**. Most free radicals are highly reactive and exist for only a very brief time before reacting with another species. Every atom or molecule with an odd number of electrons must have one unpaired electron. Filled shells and subshells contain all paired electrons, with two electrons in each orbital (Section 3.7). Therefore, we need only consider valence electrons to determine whether an atom or molecule is a free radical. Lewis

Table 4.5 Number of Bonds Formed by Selected Elements

Lewis Symbol	Bond Picture	Number of Bonds	Representative Molecules	Ball-and-Stick Models
H·	H—	1	H—H H—Cl	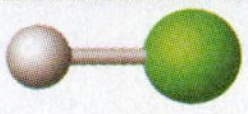 HCl
He:		0	He	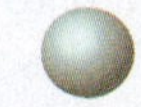 He
·C·	—C—	4	CH_4 HC(=O)F	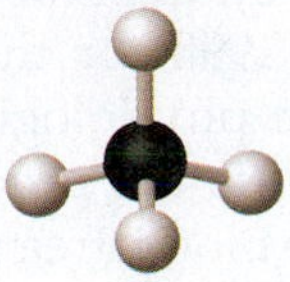 CH_4
·N·	—N—	3	NH_3 H—C(=N—O—H)—H	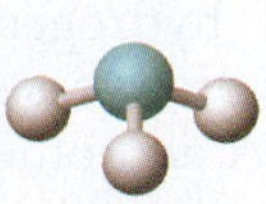 NH_3
·O:	—O	2	H—O—H H—C(=O)—H	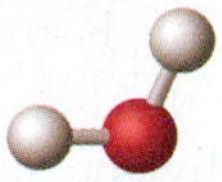 H_2O
·F:	—F	1	H—F F—F	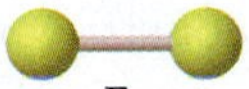 F_2
·Cl:	—Cl	1	Cl—Cl CH_3Cl	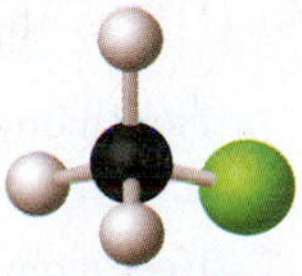 CH_3Cl

1A 2A 3B 4B 5B 6B 7B 8B 1B 2B 3A 4A 5A 6A 7A Noble gases

–Be–, B, C, N, O, F, Si, P, S, Cl, Br, I, –Hg–

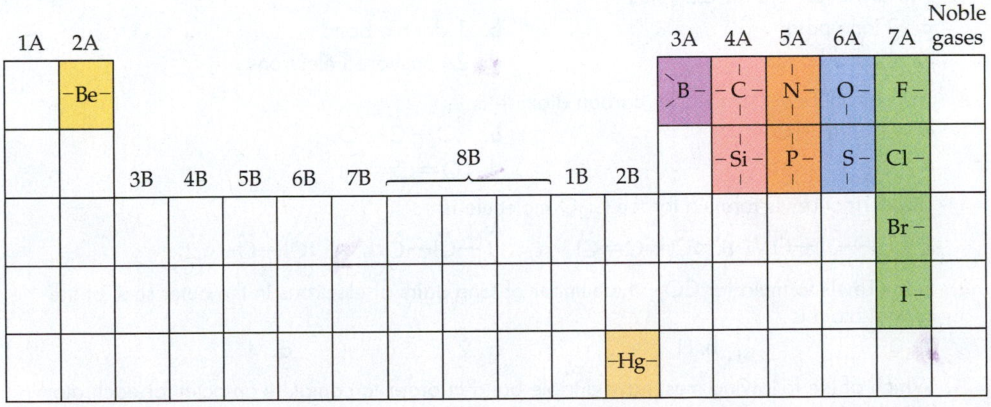

◀ **Figure 4.7** Covalent bonding of representative elements on the periodic table.

Q: *What is the relationship between an atom's position on the periodic table and the number of covalent bonds it tends to form? Why are the group 1A and most of the group 2A elements omitted from the table?*

formulas of NO, NO_2, and ClO_2 each have one atom with an unpaired electron. An atom having an unpaired electron cannot have an octet of electrons in its outer shell.

:N::Ö: :Ö:N::Ö: :Ö:Cl:Ö:

Nitrogen oxides are major components of smog (Chapter 13). Chlorine atoms from the breakdown of chlorofluorocarbons in the stratosphere lead to depletion of the ozone layer (Chapter 13). Some free radicals are quite stable, however, and have important functions in the body as well as in industrial processes (see the box on page 112).

Useful Applications of Free Radicals

The very reactive nature of free radicals does not preclude their importance and use in a variety of natural and industrial applications.

- Nitric oxide (NO) has been shown to be a signaling molecule in the human cardiovascular system. American scientists Robert F. Furchgott, Louis J. Ignarro, and Ferid Murad won the Nobel Prize in Physiology or Medicine in 1998 for that discovery. Interestingly, one of the physiological effects of sildenafil citrate (Viagra®) is the production of small quantities of NO in the bloodstream.
- Hydroxyl radicals (·OH) are produced in the body in the process of oxidation of foods and by radiation. The decomposition of hydrogen peroxide (HOOH) and other peroxides produces ·OH. These radicals inflict havoc on DNA and other essential substances and they have been implicated in the formation of cancerous cells due to their rapid reaction with DNA. Hydroxyl radicals are also play a role in air pollution (Chapter 13).
- Many plastics, including polyethylene and polyvinyl chloride (PVC), are made using free radicals to initiate the reactions. Liquid polyester resin is used to repair automobiles and to construct small boats and surfboards. The resin is converted to hard plastic by the addition of a free-radical catalyst called *methyl ethyl ketone peroxide*.
- The free radical chlorine dioxide (ClO_2) is widely used to bleach paper and other products, including flour. Unbleached flour (left) is a pale cream color; bleached flour (right) is whiter and is considered more attractive to consumers.

▲ Chlorine dioxide (ClO_2) is used to bleach flour. Unbleached flour (left) and bleached flour (right).

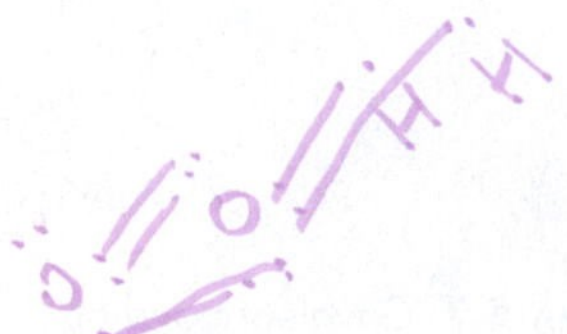

Self-Assessment Questions

1. How many lone pairs of electrons are there in the Lewis formula of CF_4?
   a. 4 b. 12 c. 14 d. 16
2. How many unshared electrons are there in the Lewis formula of H_2O_2?
   a. 3 b. 8 c. 14 d. 18
3. The Lewis formula for CCl_4 has
   a. 0 lone pairs b. 1 double bond
   c. 4 ionic bonds d. 24 unshared electrons
4. The correct Lewis formula for carbon dioxide is
   a. O—C—O b. :O—C—O:
   c. :Ö—C—Ö: (each O with three lone pairs) d. :Ö=C=Ö:
5. The correct Lewis formula for the Cl_2O molecule is
   a. :C̤̈l—C̤̈l—Ö: b. :C̤̈l=O=C̤̈l c. :Ö—C̤̈l—Ö: d. :C̤̈l—Ö—C̤̈l:
6. In the Lewis formula for CO_2, the number of lone pairs of electrons in the outer shell of the central atom is
   a. 0 b. 1 c. 2 d. 4
7. Which of the following must have a triple bond in order to complete an octet for each atom in its Lewis formula?
   a. F_2 b. HCN c. HI d. O_2
8. The Lewis formula for the SO_3^{2-} ion that follows the octet rule is
   a. $[$:Ö—S—Ö: with :Ö: below S$]^{2-}$ (no lone pair on S) b. $[$:Ö—S=O: with :Ö: below S$]^{2-}$ c. $[$:O=S=O: with :Ö: below S$]^{2-}$ d. $[$:Ö—S̈—Ö: with :Ö: below S$]^{2-}$

Answers: 1. b; 2. b; 3. d; 4. d; 5. d; 6. a; 7. b; 8. d

4.11 Molecular Shapes: The VSEPR Theory

Learning Objective › Predict the shapes of simple molecules from their Lewis formulas.

We have represented molecules in two dimensions on paper, but molecules have three-dimensional shapes that are important in determining their properties. For example, the shapes of the molecules that make up gasoline determine its octane rating (Chapter 15), and drug molecules must have the right atoms in the right places to be effective (Chapter 18). We can use Lewis formulas as part of the process of predicting molecular shapes. Figure 4.8 shows the shapes that we consider in this book.

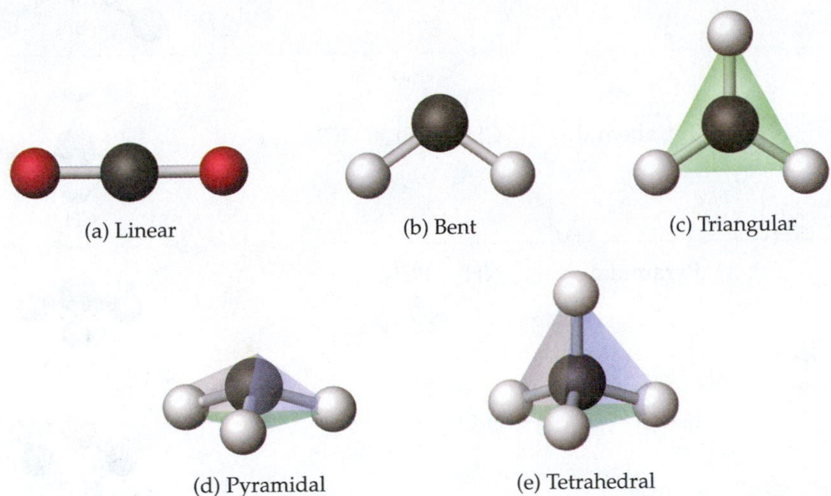

▲ **Figure 4.8** Shapes of molecules. In a *linear* molecule (a), all the atoms are along a line; the bond angle is 180°. A *bent* molecule (b) has an angle less than 180°. Connecting the three outer atoms of a *triangular* molecule (c) with imaginary lines produces a triangle with an atom at the center. Imaginary lines connecting all four atoms of a *pyramidal* molecule (d) form a three-sided pyramid. Connecting the four outer atoms of a *tetrahedral* molecule (e) with imaginary lines produces a tetrahedron (a four-sided figure in which each side is a triangle) with an atom at the center.

We use the **valence shell electron pair repulsion (VSEPR) theory** to predict the arrangement of atoms about a central atom in a molecule. The basis of the VSEPR theory is that electron pairs arrange themselves about a central atom in a way that minimizes repulsions between these like-charged particles. This means that electron pairs (both lone pairs and shared pairs in bonds) will be as far apart as possible. In applying the VSEPR theory to predict molecular shapes, we will use the term *electron set* to refer to either a lone pair on a central atom or a bond—single, double, or triple—between the central atom and another atom. Table 4.6 presents the geometric shapes associated with the arrangement of two, three, or four electron sets about a central atom.

- When *two* electron sets are as far apart as possible, they are on opposite sides of the central atom at an angle of 180°.
- *Three* electron sets assume a triangular arrangement about the central atom, forming angles of separation of 120°.
- *Four* electron sets form a tetrahedral array around the central atom, giving a separation of about 109.5°.

We can determine the shapes of many molecules (and polyatomic ions) by following this simple procedure:

1. Draw a Lewis formula in which a shared electron pair (bonding pair) is indicated by a line. Use dots to show any unshared pairs (lone pairs) of electrons.

Table 4.6 Bonding and the Shapes of Molecules

Number of Bonded Atoms	Number of Lone Pairs	Number of Electron Sets	Molecular Shape	Examples of Molecules	Ball-and-Stick Models
2	0	2	Linear	$BeCl_2$ $HgCl_2$ CO_2 HCN	$BeCl_2$
3	0	3	Triangular	BF_3 $AlBr_3$ CH_2O	BF_3
4	0	4	Tetrahedral	CH_4 CBr_4 $SiCl_4$	CH_4
3	1	4	Pyramidal	NH_3 PCl_3	NH_3
2	2	4	Bent	H_2O H_2S SCl_2	H_2O
2	1	3	Bent	SO_2 O_3	SO_2

2. To determine shape, count the number of electron sets around the *central* atom. Recall that a multiple bond counts only as one electron set. Examples are

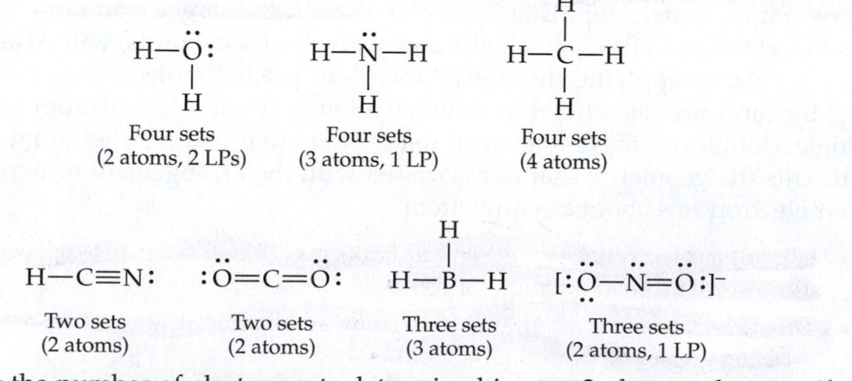

3. Using the number of electron sets determined in step 2, draw a shape *as if* all the sets were bonding pairs and place these electron sets as far apart as possible (Table 4.6).
4. If there are *no* lone pairs, the shape from step 3 is the shape of the molecule. If there *are* lone pairs, remove them, leaving the bonding pairs exactly as they were. (This may seem strange, but it stems from the fact that *all* the sets determine the geometry, but only the arrangement of bonded atoms is considered in the shape of the molecule.)

Example 4.14 Shapes of Molecules

What are the shapes of **(a)** the H_2CO molecule and **(b)** the SCl_2 molecule?

Solution

a. We follow the preceding rules, starting with the Lewis formula.

1. The Lewis formula for H_2CO is

```
  H
  |    ..
  C == O
  |    ..
  H
```

2. There are three sets of electrons: two C—H single bonds and one C=O double bond.

3. A triangular arrangement puts the three electron sets as far apart as possible.

```
H    120°
  \     ..
   C == O:
  /
H
```

4. All the electron sets are bonding pairs; the molecular shape is triangular, the same as the arrangement of the electron sets.

b. Again, we follow the rules, starting with the Lewis formula.

1. The Lewis formula for SCl_2 is

```
 ..   ..
:S — Cl:
 |    ..
:Cl:
 ..
```

2. There are four sets of electrons on the sulfur atom.

3. A tetrahedral arrangement around the central atom puts the four sets of electrons as far apart as possible.

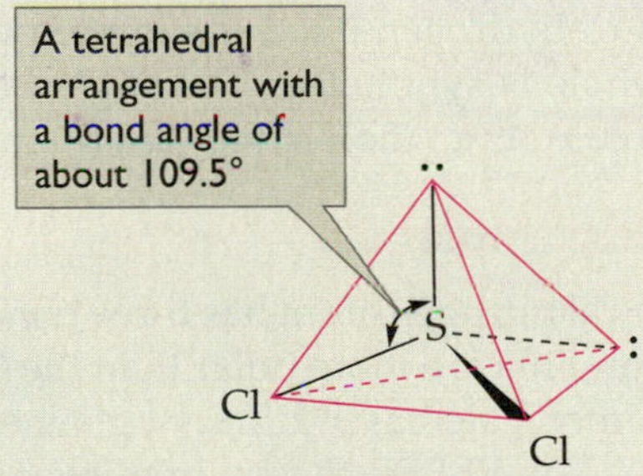

4. Two of the electron sets are bonding pairs and two are lone pairs. Ignore the lone pairs. The molecular shape is *bent*, with a bond angle of about 109.5°.

■ EXERCISE 4.14A

What are the shapes of **(a)** the PH_3 molecule and **(b)** the nitrate ion (NO_3^-)?

■ EXERCISE 4.14B

What are the shapes of **(a)** the carbonate ion (CO_3^{2-}) and **(b)** the hydrogen peroxide (H_2O_2) molecule?

Self-Assessment Questions

Match the formula in the left column with the molecular shape in the right column.

1. CS_2	**a.** bent
2. H_2S	**b.** linear
3. PF_3	**c.** pyramidal
4. SiF_4	**d.** tetrahedral

Answers: 1, b; 2, a; 3, c; 4, d

4.12 Shapes and Properties: Polar and Nonpolar Molecules

Learning Objective › Classify a simple molecule as polar or nonpolar from its shape and the polarity of its bonds.

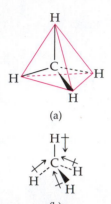

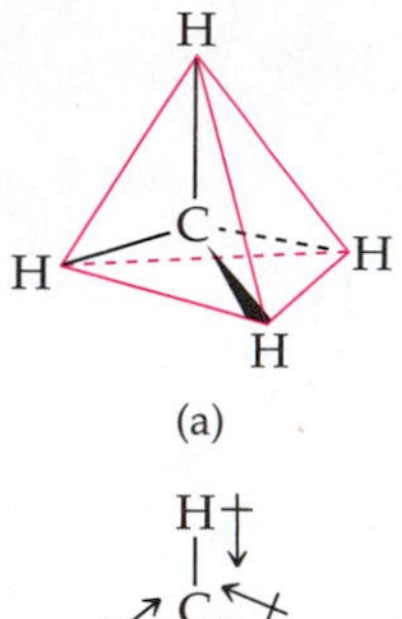

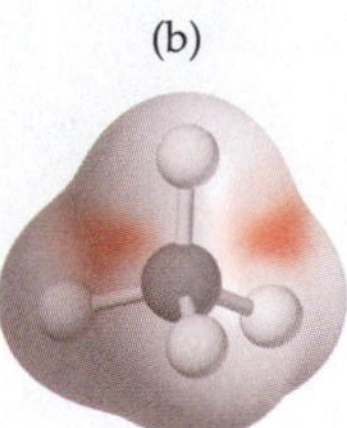

▲ **Figure 4.9** The methane molecule. In (a), black lines indicate covalent bonds; the red lines outline a tetrahedron; and all bond angles are 109.5°. The slightly polar C—H bonds cancel each other (b), resulting in a nonpolar, tetrahedral molecule (c).

Q: *How does the electrostatic potential diagram in (c) look different from the one in Figure 4.6?*

Section 4.7 discussed polar and nonpolar bonds. A diatomic molecule is nonpolar if its bond is nonpolar, as in H_2 or Cl_2, and polar if its bond is polar, as in HCl. Recall from Section 4.7 that the partial charges in a polar bond are indicated by δ+ and δ−. In the case of a **dipole**, a molecule with a positive end and a negative end, the polarity is commonly indicated with an arrow with a plus sign at the tail end (↦). The plus sign indicates the part of the molecule with a partial positive charge, and the head of the arrow signifies the end of the molecule with a partial negative charge.

$$\underbrace{\mathrm{H{-}H} \quad \text{and} \quad \mathrm{Cl{-}Cl}}_{\text{Nonpolar}} \qquad \underbrace{\overset{\delta+}{\mathrm{H}}{-}\overset{\delta-}{\mathrm{Cl}} \quad \text{or} \quad \overset{\longmapsto}{\mathrm{H{-}Cl}}}_{\text{Polar}}$$

For a molecule with three or more atoms, we must consider the polarity of the individual bonds as well as the overall geometry of the molecule to determine whether the molecule as a whole is polar. A **polar molecule** has separate centers of positive and negative charge, just as a magnet has north and south poles. Many properties of compounds—such as melting point, boiling point, and solubility—depend on the polarity of their molecules.

Methane: A Tetrahedral Molecule

There are four electron sets around the central carbon atom in methane, CH_4. Using the VSEPR theory, we would expect a tetrahedral arrangement and bond angles of 109.5° (Figure 4.9a). The actual bond angles are 109.5°, as predicted by the theory. All four electron sets are shared with hydrogen atoms and, therefore, occupy identical volumes. Each carbon-to-hydrogen bond is slightly polar (Figure 4.9b), but the methane molecule as a whole is symmetric. The slight bond polarities cancel out, leaving the methane molecule, as a whole, nonpolar (Figure 4.9c).

Ammonia: A Pyramidal Molecule

In ammonia, NH_3, the central nitrogen atom has three bonds and a lone pair around it. The N—H bonds of ammonia are more polar than the C—H bonds of methane. More important, the NH_3 molecule has a different geometry as a result of the lone pair on the nitrogen atom. The VSEPR theory predicts a tetrahedral arrangement of the four sets of electrons, giving bond angles of 109.5° (Figure 4.10a). However, the lone pair of electrons occupies a greater volume than a bonding pair, pushing the bonding pairs slightly closer together and resulting in actual bond angles of about 107°. The pyramidal geometry can be envisioned as a tripod with a hydrogen atom at the end of each leg and the nitrogen atom with its lone pair sitting at the top. Each nitrogen-to-hydrogen bond is somewhat polar (Figure 4.10b). The asymmetric structure makes the ammonia molecule polar, with a partial negative charge on the nitrogen atom and partial positive charges on the three hydrogen atoms (Figure 4.10c).

Water: A Bent Molecule

The O—H bonds in water are even more polar than the N—H bonds in ammonia because oxygen is more electronegative than nitrogen. (Recall that electronegativity increases from left to right in the periodic table.) Just because a molecule contains polar bonds, however, does not mean that the molecule as a whole is polar. If the atoms in the water molecule were in a straight line (that is, in a linear arrangement, as in CO_2), the two polar bonds would cancel one another and the molecule would be nonpolar.

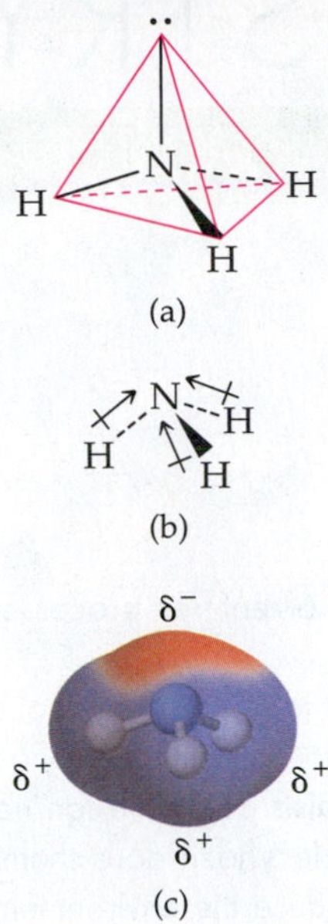

▲ **Figure 4.10** The ammonia molecule. In (a), black lines indicate covalent bonds. The red lines outline a tetrahedron. The polar N—H bonds do not cancel each other completely in (b), resulting in a polar, pyramidal molecule (c).

Q: *How does the electrostatic potential diagram in Figure 4.10 (c) resemble the one in Figure 4.6?*

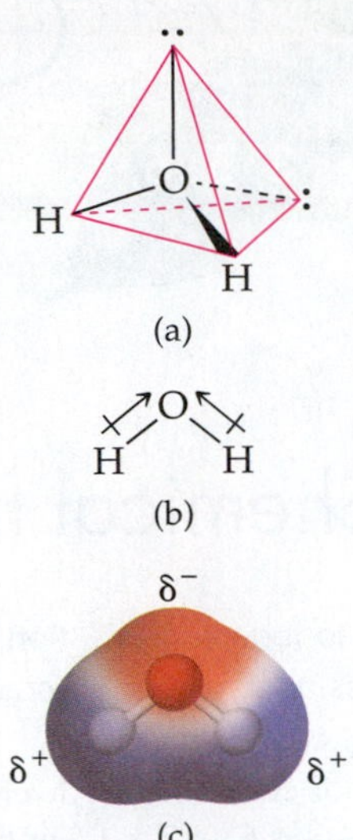

▲ **Figure 4.11** The water molecule. In (a), black lines indicate covalent bonds, and the red lines outline a tetrahedron. The polar O—H bonds do not cancel each other in (b), resulting in a polar, bent molecule (c).

In its physical and chemical properties, however, water acts like a polar molecule. Molecules such as water and ammonia, in which the polar bonds do not cancel out, act as dipoles. Such molecules have a positive end and a negative end.

We can understand the dipole in the water molecule by using the VSEPR theory. The two bonds and two lone pairs should form a tetrahedral arrangement of electron sets (Figure 4.11a). Ignoring the lone pairs, the molecular shape has the atoms in a bent arrangement, with a bond angle of about 104.5° (instead of 109.5°). As with ammonia, the actual angle is slightly smaller than the predicted angle because of the greater volume of space occupied by the two lone pairs compared to the bonding pairs. The larger space occupied by the lone pairs reduces the space in which the bonding pairs reside, pushing them closer together. The two polar O—H bonds do not cancel each other (Figure 4.11b), making the bent water molecule polar (Figure 4.11c).

Self-Assessment Questions

1. Which of the following molecules is polar?
a. Br_2 **b.** CH_4 **c.** CO_2 **d.** NH_3

2. Which of the following molecules is polar?
a. C_2H_2 (linear) **b.** Cl_2 **c.** CCl_4 **d.** PF_3

3. Which of the following molecules is polar?
a. CF_4 **b.** C_2H_4 (planar) **c.** NF_3 **d.** O_2

4. Which of the following molecules has polar bonds but is not polar?
a. CCl_4 **b.** Cl_2 **c.** NCl_3 **d.** OF_2

Answers: 1, d; 2, d; 3, c; 4, a

GREEN CHEMISTRY

Principles 3, 5, 6, 8

John C. Warner, *Warner Babcock Institute for Green Chemistry*

Amy S. Cannon, *Beyond Benign*

Green Chemistry and Chemical Bonds

You learned in this chapter that atoms bond together to form compounds and these new compounds have properties that differ greatly from the component elements. In molecular compounds (molecules), atoms join by forming covalent bonds that cause the molecules to adopt specific geometric shapes (Sections 4.6, 4.7, 4.12). Each atom is held in a specific position relative to other atoms in the molecule. In ionic compounds, atoms are held together through ionic bonds (Section 4.3).

Molecular shape and composition of compounds control reactivity and interactions with other substances. As a chemist manipulates the geometry and composition of molecules, the properties can change drastically. A wonderful example of how shape impacts the design of molecules is seen in medicine. Within our bodies, biological molecules have particular shapes that are recognized by enzymes and other receptors, in the same way that a key matches a lock (Chapter 16). The molecule and the receptor fit together to form complexes through *noncovalent forces* (intermolecular forces, Section 6.3).

Medicinal chemists design new medicines and drug molecules (Chapter 18) so that they will resemble biological molecules and bind to enzymes or receptors in our body. But these molecule-receptor complexes must behave differently from the biological molecule. The binding triggers a response in our bodies and helps us to heal. Medicinal chemists use the shapes of molecules and forces between them to create new life-saving or life-changing medicines. Interaction between molecules caused by the geometric orientations of their atoms is called **molecular recognition**. The 1987 Nobel Prize in Chemistry was awarded to Donald J. Cram, Jean-Marie Lehn, and Charles J. Pedersen for pioneering work in this area. Scientists are now learning to use molecular recognition to control molecular properties and create not only new medicines but also new materials.

What does this have to do with green chemistry? The processes that chemists rely on to make materials often use large amounts of energy or highly reactive and toxic chemicals. New production methods that take advantage of molecular recognition typically use lower energy, solvent-free processes that do not require harsh conditions.

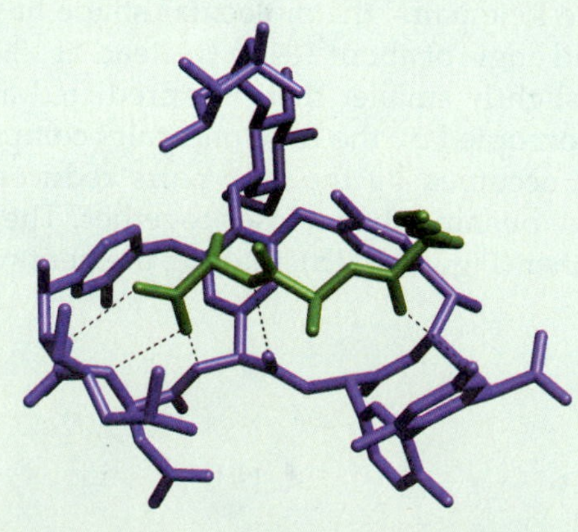

The antibiotic *vancomysin* carries out its function using molecular recognition. Vancomysin undergoes strong, selective hydrogen bonding with *peptides* (small protein chains) of bacteria, preventing formation of the cell wall.

This way of making materials takes advantage of several of the twelve principles of green chemistry. Principles 3, 5, 6, and 8 focus on the choices we make as chemists as we design new molecules and materials. For example, using less hazardous chemicals to make new medicines means we can reduce the environmental impact of the manufacturing process for these compounds. Doing so ensures that they can change the lives of sick patients as well as provide safer workplaces for the workers making the new medicines.

Typical reactions carried out in laboratories use solvents that dissolve the molecules (solutes) (Section 5.5) and allow them to react to form new molecules. Many solvents can be hazardous to human health and the environment. Processes for making new noncovalent complexes that rely on molecular recognition often do not require solvents. This drastically reduces the environmental impact of these processes.

Many traditional processes require high temperatures, which translates to high energy use. Noncovalent complexes created through molecular recognition function in much the same way as molecules interact within our bodies at moderate temperatures. Therefore, these new approaches use very little energy, which benefits the environment and reduces the manufacturing cost. Also, many processes that generate new molecules and materials are quite complex. By understanding how molecules interact by shape and noncovalent forces, we can reduce the complexity in these processes and avoid the generation of waste and the reliance on hazardous materials.

By understanding molecular shape, the nature of chemical bonds, and how molecules interact with other molecules through noncovalent forces, chemists are able to design new medicines, molecules, and materials that benefit society and, at the same time, have minimal impact on the environment and human health. Green chemistry allows chemists to use these skills combined with new innovative techniques to design chemicals that do not harm our environment in the process.

A Chemical Vocabulary

Learning chemical symbolism is much like learning a foreign language. Once you have learned the basic "vocabulary," the rest is a lot easier. At first, the task is complicated because different chemical species or definitions sound a lot alike (sodium atoms versus sodium ions). Another complication is that we have several different ways to represent the *same* chemical species (Figure 4.12).

Ammonia ⟶ NH_3 ⟶ H—N̈—H (with H below N) ⟶ [molecular model: N, H, H, H]

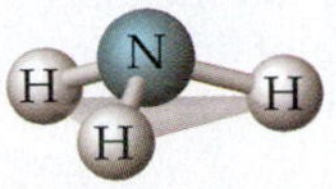

Name | Chemical formula | Lewis formula | Molecular geometry

▲ **Figure 4.12** Several representations of the ammonia molecule.

In Chapter 1, we introduced symbols for the chemical elements. Chapter 3 discussed the structure of the nucleus and the symbolism for distinguishing different isotopes. This chapter covered chemical names and chemical formulas. Now you also know how to write Lewis symbols and formulas using dots to represent valence electrons and you can predict the shapes of thousands of different molecules with the VSEPR theory. In the next chapter, you will add the mathematics of chemistry to your toolbox.

CRITICAL THINKING  EXERCISES

Apply knowledge that you have gained in this chapter and one or more of the FLaReS principles (Chapter 1) to evaluate the following statements or claims.

4.1 Some people believe that crystals have special powers. Crystal therapists claim that they can use quartz crystals to restore balance and harmony to a person's spiritual energy.

4.2 A "fuel-enhancer" device is being sold by an entrepreneur. The device contains a powerful magnet and is placed on the fuel line of an automobile. The inventor claims that the device "separates the positive and negative charges in the hydrocarbon fuel molecules, increasing their polarity and allowing them to react more readily with oxygen."

4.3 Sodium chloride (NaCl) is a metal–nonmetal compound held together by ionic bonds. A scientist has studied mercury(II) chloride ($HgCl_2$) and says that its atoms are held together by covalent bonds. The scientist says that since a solution of this substance in water does not conduct an electric current, it does not contain an appreciable amount of ions.

4.4 Another scientist, noting that the noble gas xenon does not contain any ions, states that xenon atoms must be held together by covalent bonds.

4.5 A web page claims, "Fifty years ago, the hydrogen bond angle in water was 108° and you rarely heard of anyone with cancer. Today, it's only 104° and, as a result, cancer is an epidemic!"

SUMMARY

Section 4.1—Outermost shell electrons are called **valence electrons**; those in all other shells are **core electrons**. The noble gases are inert because they (except He) have an octet of valence electrons. Atoms of other elements become more stable by gaining or losing electrons to attain an electron configuration that makes them **isoelectronic** with (having the same electron configuration as) a noble gas.

Section 4.2—The number of valence electrons for most main group elements is the same as the group number. Electron-dot symbols, or **Lewis symbols**, use dots singly or in pairs to represent valence electrons of an atom or ion.

Section 4.3—The element sodium reacts violently with elemental chlorine to give sodium chloride, or table salt. In this reaction, an electron is transferred from a sodium atom to a chlorine atom, forming ions.

The ions formed have opposite charges and are strongly attracted to one another; this attraction results in an **ionic bond**. The positive and negative ions arrange themselves in a regular array, forming a **crystal** of sodium chloride. The ions of an element have very different properties from the atoms of that element.

Section 4.4—Metal atoms tend to give up their valence electrons to become positively changed ions, and nonmetal atoms tend to accept (8 − group number) electrons to become negatively changed ions. In either case, the ions formed (except hydrogen ions and lithium ions) tend to have eight valence electrons. The formation of ions is thus said to follow the **octet rule**. The symbol for an ion is the element symbol with a superscript that indicates the number and type (+ or −) of charge. Some elements, especially the transition metals, can form ions of different charges. The formula of an ionic compound always has the same number of positive charges as negative charges.

Section 4.5—A **binary ionic compound** contains two different elements; it has a cation of a metal and an anion of a nonmetal. The formula of a binary ionic compound represents the numbers and types of ions in the compound. The formula is found by crossing over the charge numbers of the ions (without the plus and minus signs).

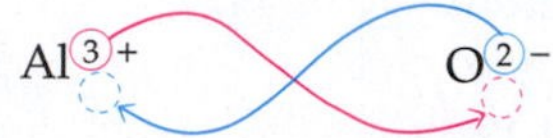

Binary ionic compounds are named by naming the cation first, and then putting an *-ide* ending on the stem of the anion name. Examples are calcium chloride, potassium oxide, aluminum nitride, and so on. Differently charged cations of a metal are named with Roman numerals to indicate the charge: Fe^{2+} is iron(II) ion and Fe^{3+} is iron(III) ion.

Section 4.6—Nonmetal atoms can bond by sharing one or more pairs of electrons, forming a **covalent bond**. A **single bond** is one pair of shared electrons; a **double bond** is two pairs; and a **triple bond** is three pairs. Shared pairs of electrons are called **bonding pairs**, and unshared pairs are called nonbonding pairs, or **lone pairs**. Most binary covalent compounds are named by naming the first element in the formula, followed by the stem of the second element with an *-ide* ending. Prefixes such as *mono-*, *di-*, *tri-*, and so on, are used to indicate the number of atoms of each element.

Section 4.7—Bonding pairs are shared equally when the two atoms are the same but may be unequally shared when the atoms are different. The **electronegativity** of an element is the attraction of an atom in a molecule for a bonding pair. Electronegativity generally increases toward the right and up on the periodic table, so fluorine is the most electronegative element. When electrons of a covalent bond are shared unequally, the more electronegative atom takes on a partial negative charge (δ−), the other atom takes on a partial positive charge (δ+), and the bond is said to be a **polar covalent bond**. The greater the difference in electronegativity, the more polar is the bond. A bonding pair shared equally is a **nonpolar covalent bond**.

Section 4.8—Carbon tends to form four covalent bonds, nitrogen three, and oxygen two; hydrogen can form only one bond. A water molecule has two bonding pairs (O—H bonds) and two lone pairs, an ammonia molecule has three bonding pairs (N—H bonds) and one lone pair, and a methane molecule has four bonding pairs (C—H bonds).

Section 4.9—A **polyatomic ion** is a charged particle containing two or more covalently bonded atoms. Compounds containing polyatomic ions are named, and their formulas written, in the same fashion as compounds containing monatomic ions, except that parentheses are placed around the formula for a polyatomic ion if there is more than one of it in the compound. Names of polyatomic ions often end in *-ate* or *-ite*.

Section 4.10—A **Lewis formula** shows the arrangement of atoms, bonds, and lone pairs in a molecule or polyatomic ion. To draw a Lewis formula, we (a) count the valence electrons; (b) draw a reasonable skeletal structure, showing the arrangement of atoms; (c) connect bonded atoms with a dash (one electron pair); (d) place electron pairs around outer atoms to give each an octet; and (e) place remaining electrons in pairs on the central atom. A multiple bond is included if there are not enough electrons to give each atom (except hydrogen) an octet. There are exceptions to the octet rule. Atoms and molecules with unpaired electrons are called **free radicals**. They are highly reactive and short-lived. Examples of free radicals are NO and ClO_2.

Section 4.11—The shape of a molecule can be predicted with the **VSEPR theory**, which assumes that sets of electrons (either lone pairs or electrons in a bond) around a central atom will get as far away from each other as possible. Two sets of electrons are 180° apart, three sets are about 120° apart, and four sets are about 109° apart. Once these angles have been established, we determine the shape of the molecule by examining only the bonded atoms. Simple molecules have shapes described as linear, bent, triangular, pyramidal, or tetrahedral.

Section 4.12—Like a polar bond, a **polar molecule** has separation between its centers of positive charge and negative charge. A molecule with nonpolar bonds is nonpolar. A molecule with polar bonds is nonpolar if its shape causes the polar bonds to cancel one another. If the polar bonds do not cancel, the molecule is polar or is said to be a **dipole**. The water molecule has polar O—H bonds and is bent, so it is polar.

Green chemistry Chemists manipulate the geometry and composition of molecules to change the properties of both molecules and materials. Typical methods for making these molecules and materials use highly reactive and toxic chemicals and high-energy processes. Greener approaches that take advantage of molecular recognition can instead use low energy, solvent-free processes that do not require harsh conditions.

Learning Objectives

› Determine the number of electrons in an ion. (4.1)	Problems 1–4
› Write the Lewis symbol for an atom or ion. (4.2)	Problems 7, 8
› Distinguish between an ion and an atom. (4.3)	Problems 1, 2, 59
› Describe the nature of the attraction that leads to formation of an ionic bond. (4.3)	Problems 41, 42
› Write symbols for common ions, and determine their charges. (4.4)	Problems 3, 11–16

› Describe the relationship between the octet rule and the charge on an ion. (4.4)	Problem 4
› Name and write formulas for binary ionic compounds. (4.5)	Problems 9, 10, 17–20, 55, 67
› Explain the difference between a covalent bond and an ionic bond. (4.6)	Problems 23–28, 41, 42
› Name and write formulas for covalent compounds. (4.6)	Problems 23–30
› Classify a covalent bond as polar or nonpolar. (4.7)	Problems 35–42
› Use electronegativities of elements to determine bond polarity. (4.7)	Problem 57
› Predict the number of bonds formed by common nonmetals (the HONC rules). (4.8)	Problems 5, 6
› Recognize common polyatomic ions and be able to use them in naming and writing formulas for compounds. (4.9)	Problems 21, 22, 65
› Write Lewis formulas for simple molecules and polyatomic ions. (4.10)	Problems 31–34, 56, 66
› Identify free radicals. (4.10)	Problems 49, 50
› Predict the shapes of simple molecules from their Lewis formulas. (4.11)	Problems 43–44
› Classify a simple molecule as polar or nonpolar from its shape and the polarity of its bonds. (4.12)	Problems 45–48
› Explain how shape and composition change the properties of molecules.	Problem 68
› Describe the concept of molecular recognition.	Problems 68, 69
› Explain the green chemistry advantages of using production methods based on molecular recognition.	Problems 70, 71

REVIEW QUESTIONS

1. How does sodium metal differ from sodium ions (in sodium chloride, for example) in properties?
2. What are the structural differences among chlorine atoms, chlorine molecules, and chloride ions? How do their properties differ?
3. What are the charges on simple ions formed from atoms of the following?
   a. group 1A elements
   b. group 6A elements
   c. group 5A elements
   d. group 2A elements
4. In what group of the periodic table would elements that form ions with the following charges likely be found?
   a. 2− b. 3+
   c. 1+ d. 2+
5. How many covalent bonds do each of the following usually form? You may refer to the periodic table.
   a. H b. Cl
   c. S d. F
   e. N f. P
6. Of the elements H, O, N, and C, which one(s) can readily form triple bonds?

PROBLEMS

Lewis Symbols for Elements

7. Write Lewis symbols for each of the following elements. You may use the periodic table.
   a. calcium b. sulfur
   c. silicon
8. Write Lewis symbols for each of the following elements. You may use the periodic table.
   a. phosphorus b. fluorine
   c. boron

Lewis Formulas for Ionic Compounds

9. Write Lewis formulas for each of the following.
   a. sodium iodide b. potassium sulfide
   c. calcium chloride d. aluminum fluoride
10. Write Lewis formulas for each of the following.
   a. lithium bromide
   b. strontium sulfide
   c. sodium nitride
   d. aluminum oxide

Names and Symbols for Simple Ions

11. Without referring to Table 4.2, supply a symbol given the name or a name given the symbol for each of the following ions:
   a. magnesium ion b. Na^+
   c. oxide ion d. Cl^-
   e. zinc ion f. Cu^+

12. Without referring to Table 4.2, supply a symbol given the name or a name given the symbol for each of the following ions:
   a. sulfide ion   b. K^+
   c. Br^- d. fluoride ion
   e. Ca^{2+} f. iron(III) ion
13. Refer to page 98; then use that information to name the following ions:
   a. Cr^{2+} b. Cr^{3+}
   c. Cr^{6+}
14. Refer to page 98; then use that information to name the following ions.
   a. Mo^{4+} b. Mo^{6+}
15. Refer to page 98; then write symbols for:
   a. vanadium(II) ion
   b. titanium(II) ion
   c. titanium(IV) ion
16. Refer to page 98; then write symbols for:
   a. manganese(II) ion
   b. manganese(III) ion
   c. manganese(VII) ion

Names and Formulas for Binary Ionic Compounds

17. Write a formula to match the name or a name to match the formula of the following binary ionic compounds:
   a. sodium iodide   b. KCl
   c. copper(I) oxide   d. MgF_2
   e. iron(II) bromide   f. $FeBr_3$
18. Write a formula to match the name or a name to match the formula of the following binary ionic compounds:
   a. LiF   b. calcium chloride
   c. MgS   d. silver iodide
   e. CuO   f. copper(I) sulfide
19. There are two common binary ionic compounds formed from chromium and oxygen. One of them contains chromium(III) ions; the other contains chromium(VI) ions. Write the formulas for the two compounds, and name them.
20. One of two binary ionic compounds is often added to toothpaste. One of these compounds contains sodium and fluorine; the other contains tin(II) ions and fluorine. Write the formulas for these two compounds, and name them.

Names and Formulas for Ionic Compounds with Polyatomic Ions

21. Supply a formula to match the name or a name to match the formula for the following:
   a. potassium hydroxide   b. $MgCO_3$
   c. iron(III) cyanide   d. iron(II) oxalate
   e. $CuSO_4$ f. $Na_2Cr_2O_7$
22. Supply a formula to match the name or a name to match the formula for the following:
   a. $AgNO_2$ b. lithium chromate
   c. $(NH_4)_2SO_3$
   d. magnesium hydrogen carbonate
   e. copper(I) phosphate
   f. $Al(MnO_4)_3$

Molecules: Covalent Bonds

23. Use Lewis symbols to show the sharing of electrons between a hydrogen atom and a fluorine atom.
24. Use Lewis symbols to show the sharing of electrons between two bromine atoms to form a bromine (Br_2) molecule. Label all electron pairs as bonding pairs (BPs) or lone pairs (LPs).
25. Use Lewis symbols to show the sharing of electrons between a phosphorus atom and hydrogen atoms to form a molecule in which phosphorus has an octet of electrons.
26. Use Lewis symbols to show the sharing of electrons between a silicon atom and hydrogen atoms to form a molecule in which silicon has an octet of electrons.
27. Use Lewis symbols to show the sharing of electrons between a carbon atom and chlorine atoms to form a molecule in which each atom has an octet of electrons.
28. Use Lewis symbols to show the sharing of electrons between a nitrogen atom and fluorine atoms to form a molecule in which each atom has an octet of electrons.

Names and Formulas for Covalent Compounds

29. Supply a formula for the name or a name for the formula for the following covalent compounds:
   a. dinitrogen tetroxide
   b. bromine trichloride
   c. OF_2
   d. nitrogen triiodide
   e. CBr_4
   f. N_2S_4
30. Supply a formula for the name or a name for the formula for the following covalent compounds:
   a. carbon disulfide   b. chlorine trifluoride
   c. PF_5 d. CI_4
   e. tricarbon dioxide   f. P_4S_3

Lewis Formulas for Molecules and Polyatomic Ions

31. Write Lewis formulas that follow the octet rule for the following covalent molecules:
   a. SiH_4 b. N_2F_4
   c. CH_5N d. H_2CO
   e. NOH_3 f. H_3PO_3
32. Write Lewis formulas that follow the octet rule for the following covalent molecules:
   a. NH_2Cl b. C_2H_4
   c. H_2SO_4 d. C_2N_2
   e. $COCl_2$ f. SCl_2
33. Write Lewis formulas that follow the octet rule for the following ions:
   a. ClO^- b. $HPO_4{}^{2-}$
   c. $BrO_3{}^-$
34. Write Lewis formulas that follow the octet rule for the following ions:
   a. CN^- b. $ClO_2{}^-$
   c. $HSO_4{}^-$

Electronegativity: Polar Covalent Bonds

35. Classify the following covalent bonds as polar or nonpolar.
   a. H—O   b. N—F
   c. Cl—B
36. Classify the following covalent bonds as polar or nonpolar.
   a. H—N   b. O—Be
   c. P—F
37. Use the symbol ↔ to indicate the direction of the dipole in each polar bond in Problem 35.

38. Use the symbol $\mapsto$ to indicate the direction of the dipole in each polar bond in Problem 36.

39. Use the symbols δ+ and δ− to indicate partial charges, if any, on the following bonds.
a. Si—O   b. F—F
c. F—N

40. Use the symbols δ+ and δ− to indicate partial charges, if any, on the following bonds.
a. O—H   b. C—F
c. C=C

Classifying Bonds

41. Classify the bonds in the following as ionic or covalent. For bonds that are covalent, indicate whether they are polar or nonpolar.
a. K_2O b. BrCl
c. MgF_2 d. I_2

42. Classify the bonds in the following as ionic or covalent. For bonds that are covalent, indicate whether they are polar or nonpolar.
a. Na_2O b. $CaCl_2$
c. NBr_3 d. CS_2

VSEPR Theory: The Shapes of Molecules

43. Use the VSEPR theory to predict the shape of each of the following molecules:
a. silane (SiH_4)
b. hydrogen selenide (H_2Se)
c. phosphine (PH_3)
d. silicon tetrafluoride (SiF_4)
e. oxygen difluoride (OF_2)
f. formaldehyde (H_2CO)

44. Use VSEPR theory to predict the shape of each of the following molecules:
a. chloroform ($CHCl_3$)
b. boron trichloride (BCl_3)
c. carbon tetrafluoride (CF_4)
d. sulfur difluoride (SF_2)
e. nitrogen triiodide (NI_3)
f. dichlorodifluoromethane (CCl_2F_2)

Polar and Nonpolar Molecules

45. The molecule BeF_2 is linear. Is it polar or nonpolar? Explain.

46. The molecule SF_2 is bent. Is it polar or nonpolar? Explain.

47. Look again at the molecules in Problem 43. For each one, are the bonds polar? What are the approximate bond angles? Is the molecule as a whole polar?

48. Look again at the molecules in Problem 44. For each one, are the bonds polar? What are the approximate bond angles? Is the molecule as a whole polar?

Molecules That Are Exceptions to the Octet Rule

49. Which of the following species (atoms or molecules) are free radicals?
a. Br   b. F_2
c. CCl_3

50. Which of the following species (atoms or molecules) are free radicals?
a. S   b. NO_2
c. N_2O_4

51. Free radicals are one class of molecules in which atoms do not conform to the octet rule. Another exception involves atoms with fewer than eight electrons, as seen in elements of group 3 and in beryllium. In some covalent molecules, these atoms can have six or four electrons, respectively. Write Lewis structures for the following covalent molecules:
a. $AlBr_3$ b. BeH_2
c. BH_3

52. Exceptions to the octet rule include molecules that have atoms with more than eight valence electrons, most typically 10 or 12. Atoms heavier than Si can expand their valence shell, meaning that they can accommodate the "extra" electrons in unoccupied, higher-energy orbitals. Draw Lewis structures for the following molecules or ions:
a. XeF_4 b. I_3^-
c. SF_4 d. KrF_2

ADDITIONAL PROBLEMS

53. Why does neon tend not to form chemical bonds?

54. Draw an electrostatic potential diagram of the H_2S molecule. Use the symbols δ+ and δ− to indicate the polarity of the molecule.

55. The gas phosphine (PH_3) is used as a fumigant to protect stored grain and other durable produce from pests. Phosphine is generated where it is to be used by adding water to aluminum phosphide or magnesium phosphide. Give formulas for these two phosphides.

56. There are two different covalent molecules with the formula C_2H_6O. Write Lewis formulas for the two molecules.

57. Solutions of iodine chloride (ICl) are used as disinfectants. Is the compound ICl ionic, polar covalent, or nonpolar covalent?

58. Consider the hypothetical elements X, Y, and Z, which have the following Lewis symbols:

:Ẍ·   :Ÿ·   :Ż·

a. To which group in the periodic table would each element belong?
b. Write the Lewis formula for the simplest compound each would form with hydrogen.
c. Write Lewis formulas for the ions that would be formed when X reacted with sodium and when Y reacted with sodium.

59. Potassium is a soft, silvery metal that reacts violently with water and ignites spontaneously in air. Your doctor recommends that you take a potassium supplement. Would you take potassium metal? If not, what would you take?

60. What is wrong with the phrase "just a few molecules of potassium iodide"?

61. Use subshell notation to write an electron configuration for the most stable simple ion formed by each of the following elements.
a. Ca b. Rb
c. S d. I
e. N f. Se

62. Why is Na^+ smaller than Na? Why is Cl^- larger than Cl?

63. The halogens (F, Cl, Br, and I) tend to form only one single bond in binary molecules. Explain.

64. A science magazine for the general public contains this statement: "Some of these hydrocarbons are very light, like methane gas—just a single carbon molecule attached to three hydrogen molecules." Evaluate the statement, and correct any inaccuracies.

65. Sodium tungstate is Na_2WO_4. What is the formula for aluminum tungstate?

66. Scientists estimate that the atmosphere of Titan (a moon of Saturn) consists of about 98.4% nitrogen and 1.6% methane. They have also found traces of organic molecules with the molecular formulas C_2H_4, C_3H_4, C_4H_2, HCN, HC_3N, and C_2N_2. Write possible Lewis formulas for each of these molecules.

67. What is the formula for the compound formed by the imaginary ions Q^{2+} and ZX_4^{3-}?

68. Give two design criteria that chemists use to design new medicines.

69. What is the term for the science that explains how molecules interact through geometric orientation of atoms?

70. Give three ways that molecular recognition approaches can support greener methods for making molecules and materials.

71. How can an understanding of enzymes and biological receptors guide medicinal chemists?

COLLABORATIVE GROUP PROJECTS

Prepare a PowerPoint, poster, or other presentation (as directed by your instructor) for presentation to the class. Projects 1 and 2 are best done by a group of four students.

1. Make a form like that in Problem 3, page 40, but replace the column headings "Word" and "Definition" with "Name" and "Lewis Formula." Student 1 should write the name from the list below in the first column of the form and its Lewis formula in the second column. Proceed as in Problem 3, page 40, ending by comparing the name in the last column with that in the first column. Discuss any differences in the two names. If the name in the last column differs from that in the first column, determine what went wrong in the process.
a. bromide ion
b. calcium fluoride
c. phosphorus trifluoride
d. carbon disulfide

2. Make a form like that in Problem 3, page 40, using the column headings "Name" and "Structure." Then student 1 should write a name from the list below in the first column of the form and its structure in the second column. Proceed as in Problem 3, page 40, ending by comparing the name in the last column with that in the first column. Discuss any differences in the two names. If the name in the last column differs from that in the first column, determine what went wrong in the process.
a. ammonium nitrate b. potassium phosphate
c. lithium carbonate d. copper(I) chloride

3. Starting with 20 balloons, blown up to about the same size and tied, tie two balloons together. Next, tie three balloons together. Repeat this with four, five, and six balloons. (*Suggestion*: Three sets of two balloons can be twisted together to form a six-balloon set, and so on.) Show how these balloon sets can be used to illustrate the VSEPR theory.

4. Prepare a brief biographical report on one of the following:
a. Gilbert N. Lewis b. Linus Pauling

5. There are several different definitions and scales for electronegativity. Search for information on these, and write a brief compare-and-contrast essay about two of them.

Chemical Accounting

Have You Ever Wondered?

1. How can a car make more pollution than the gasoline it uses?

2. What's the difference between 14K gold and 18K gold?

3. Does 2% milk have just 2% of the calories of whole milk?

4. What does a cholesterol level of 200 mean?

Learning Objectives

- Identify balanced and unbalanced chemical equations, and balance equations by inspection. (5.1)
- Determine volumes of gases that react, using a balanced equation for a reaction. (5.2)
- Calculate the formula mass, molecular mass, or molar mass of a substance. (5.3)
- Convert from mass to moles and from moles to mass of a substance. (5.4)
- Calculate the mass or number of moles of a reactant or product from the mass or number of moles of another reactant or product. (5.4)
- Calculate the concentration (molarity, percent by volume, or percent by mass) of a solute in a solution. (5.5)
- Calculate the amount of solute or solution given the concentration and the other amount. (5.5)
- Explain how the concept of atom economy can be applied to pollution prevention and environmental protection.
- Calculate the atom economy for chemical reactions.

Mass and Volume Relationships

We can look at or represent chemical phenomena on three levels:

1. Macro and tangible: for example, a sample of yellow powder or a blue solution in a beaker.
2. Particle (atom, molecule, or ion) and invisible: for example, a sulfur atom, a carbon dioxide molecule, or a chloride ion.
3. Symbolic and mathematical: for example, S, CO_2, Cl, or $d = m/V$.

Macro-level representations of chemicals are familiar from everyday life. It is easy to visualize salt crystals in a shaker, gold in jewelry, baking soda in a box, aspirin in tablets, and many other common substances, because they are tangible. We can see them and touch them.

Everything that burns fuel requires oxygen, and the human body is no exception. At the top of Mt. Everest, there is not enough oxygen in the air to keep people alive, so climbers making the ascent must bring oxygen with them. But how much oxygen should each climber bring? A knowledge of chemistry allows this question to be answered, thus promoting the safety of the climbers and the success of their venture.

The other representations were introduced in earlier chapters. You may have recognized the mathematical equation for density from Chapter 1. We employed symbols when discussing atoms in Chapters 2 and 3 and formulas in our discussion of molecules and ions in Chapter 4. In this chapter, we consider symbolic and mathematical descriptions of chemical changes.

Much chemistry can be discussed and understood with little or no mathematics, but the quantitative aspects can shed a great deal of light on properties of matter. In this chapter, we will consider some of the basic calculations used in chemistry and related fields such as biology and medicine. Chemists use many kinds of mathematics, from simple arithmetic to sophisticated calculus and complicated computer algorithms, but our calculations here will require at most a bit of algebra.

5.1 Chemical Sentences: Equations

Learning Objective › Identify balanced and unbalanced chemical equations, and balance equations by inspection.

Chemistry is a study of matter and the changes it undergoes and of the energy that brings about these changes or is released when these changes happen. The symbols and formulas we have used to represent elements and compounds make up the letters (symbols) and words (formulas) of our chemical language. Using them, we can write sentences (chemical equations). A **chemical equation** uses symbols and formulas to represent the elements and compounds involved in the change.

At the macro level, we can describe a chemical reaction in words. For example,

Carbon reacts with oxygen to form carbon dioxide.

We can describe the same reaction symbolically.

$$C + O_2 \longrightarrow CO_2$$

The plus sign (+) indicates that carbon and oxygen are added together or combined in some way. The arrow ($\longrightarrow$) is read "yield(s)" or "react(s) to produce." Substances on the left of the arrow (C and O_2 in this case) are **reactants**, or *starting materials*. Those on the right (here, CO_2) are the **products** of the reaction. Reactants and products need not be written in any particular order in a chemical equation, except that all reactants must be to the left of the arrow and all products to the right. In other words, we could also write the preceding equation as

$$O_2 + C \longrightarrow CO_2$$

At the atomic or molecular level, the equation means that one carbon (C) atom reacts with one oxygen (O_2) molecule to produce one carbon dioxide (CO_2) molecule.

Sometimes, we indicate the physical states of the reactants and products by writing the initial letter of the state immediately following the formula: (g) indicates a gaseous substance, (l) a liquid, and (s) a solid. The label (aq) indicates that the substance is in an aqueous (water) solution. Using state labels, the above equation becomes

$$C(s) + O_2(g) \longrightarrow CO_2(g)$$

Balancing Chemical Equations

We can represent the reaction of carbon and oxygen to form carbon dioxide quite simply, but many other chemical reactions require more thought. For example, hydrogen reacts with oxygen to form water. Using formulas, we can represent this reaction as

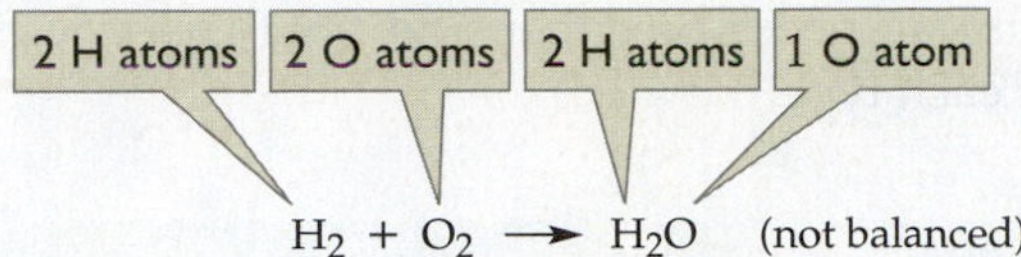

However, this representation shows two oxygen atoms in the reactants (as O_2), but only one in the product (in H_2O). Because matter is neither created nor destroyed in a chemical reaction (the law of conservation of mass, Section 2.2), the equation must be *balanced* to represent the chemical reaction correctly. That means the same number of each type of atom must appear on both sides of the arrow. To balance the oxygen atoms, we need only place the coefficient 2 in front of the formula for water.

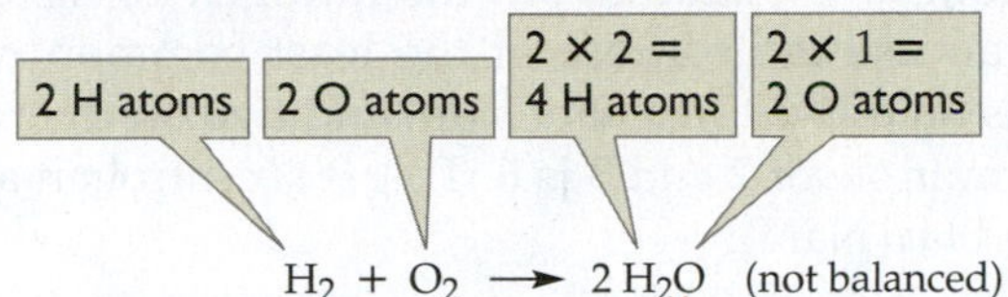

This coefficient means that two molecules of water are produced. As is the case with a subscript 1, a coefficient of 1 is understood when there is no number in front of a formula. *Everything* in a formula is multiplied by the coefficient. In the preceding equation, adding the coefficient 2 before H_2O not only increases the number of oxygen atoms on the product side to two but also increases the number of hydrogen atoms to four.

But the equation is still not balanced. As we took care of the oxygen, we unbalanced the hydrogen. To balance the hydrogen, we place a coefficient 2 in front of H_2.

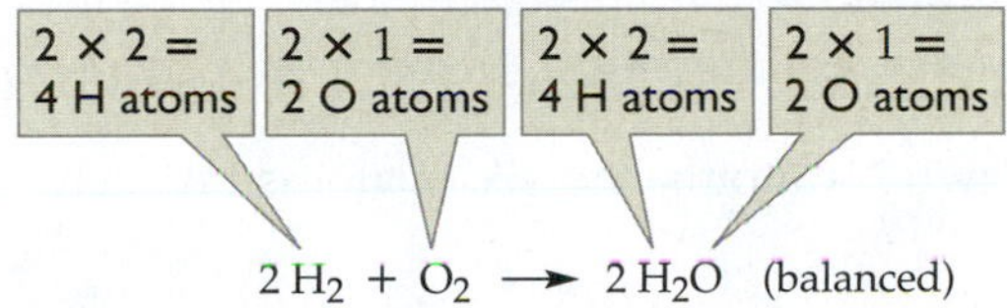

Now there are four hydrogen atoms and two oxygen atoms on each side of the equation. Atoms are conserved: The equation is balanced (Figure 5.1), and the law of conservation of mass is obeyed. Figure 5.2 illustrates two common pitfalls in the process of balancing equations, as well as the correct method. Remember not to

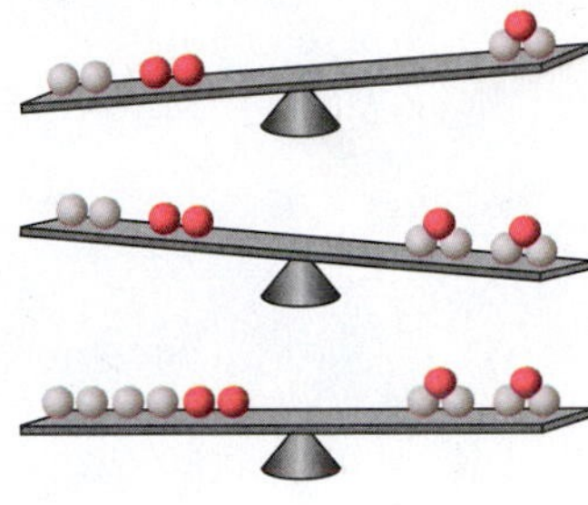

▲ **Figure 5.1** To balance the equation for the reaction of hydrogen and oxygen to form water, the same number of each kind of atom must appear on each side (atoms are conserved). When the equation is balanced, there are four H atoms and two O atoms on each side.

Q: *Why can't you balance the equation by removing one of the oxygen atoms from the left side of the top balance?*

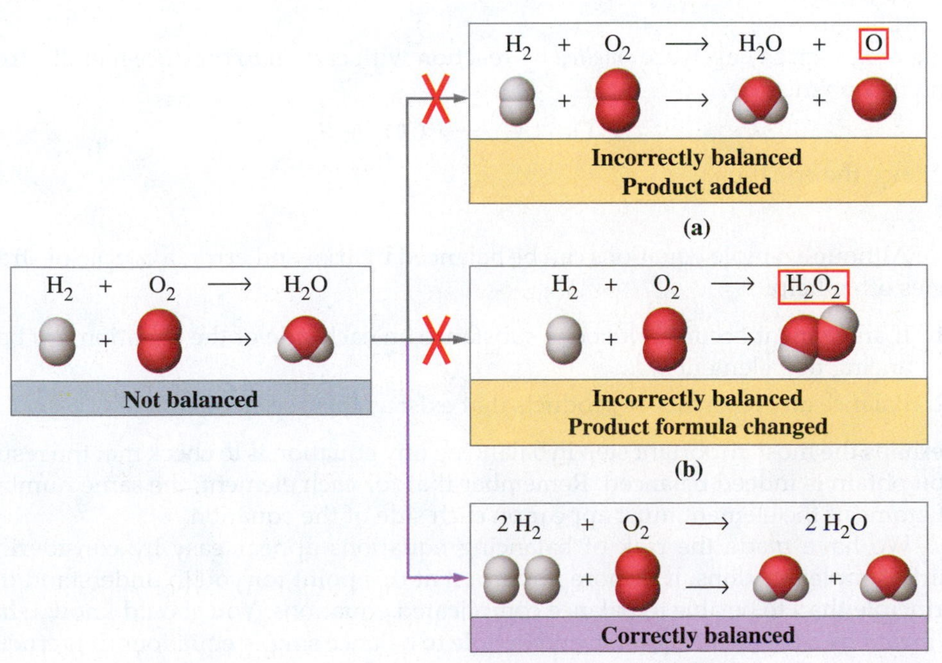

◀ **Figure 5.2** Balancing the equation for the reaction between hydrogen and oxygen to form water. (a) Incorrect. There is no atomic oxygen (O) as a product. Other products cannot be introduced simply to balance an equation. (b) Incorrect. The product of the reaction is water (H_2O), not hydrogen peroxide (H_2O_2). A formula can't be changed simply to balance an equation. (c) Correct. An equation can be balanced only by using the correct formulas and adjusting the coefficients.

add to or change chemical species on either side, but to use coefficients to equate the numbers of atoms of each type.

Example 5.1 Balancing Equations

Balance the following chemical equation, which represents the reaction that occurs when an airbag in a car deploys.

$$NaN_3 \longrightarrow Na + N_2$$

Solution

The sodium (Na) atoms are balanced, but the nitrogen atoms are not. To balance this equation, we can use the concept of the least common multiple. There are three nitrogen atoms on the left (reactant side) and two on the right (product side). The least common multiple of 2 and 3 is 6. To get *six* nitrogen atoms on each side, we need *three* N_2 and *two* NaN_3:

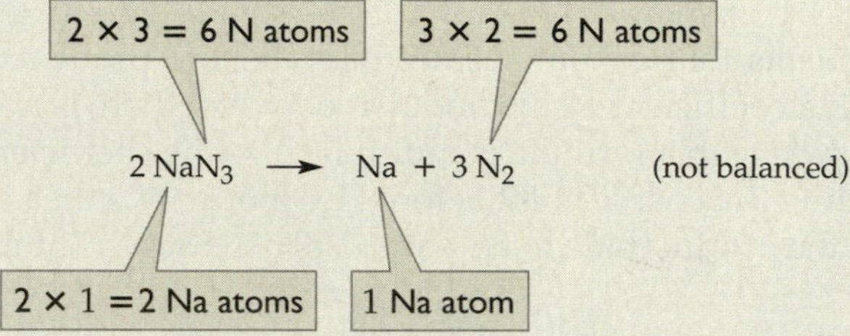

We now have *two* sodium atoms on the left. We can get two on the right by placing the coefficient 2 in front of Na.

$$2\,NaN_3 \longrightarrow 2\,Na + 3\,N_2 \quad \text{(balanced)}$$

Checking, we count two Na atoms and six N atoms on each side. The equation is balanced.

■ EXERCISE 5.1A

The reaction between hydrogen and nitrogen to give ammonia, called the *Haber process,* is typically the first step in the industrial production of nitrogen fertilizers.

$$H_2 + N_2 \longrightarrow NH_3$$

Balance the equation.

■ EXERCISE 5.1B

Iron ores such as Fe_2O_3 are *smelted* by reaction with carbon to produce metallic iron and carbon dioxide.

$$Fe_2O_3 + C \longrightarrow CO_2 + Fe$$

Balance the equation.

Although simple equations can be balanced by trial and error, a couple of strategies often help:

1. If an element occurs in just one substance on each side of the equation, try balancing that element *first*.
2. Balance any reactants or products that exist as the free element *last*.

Perhaps the most important step in balancing any equation is to check that the result you obtain is indeed balanced. Remember that for each element, the same number of atoms of the element must appear on each side of the equation.

We have made the task of balancing equations appear easy by considering fairly simple reactions. It is more important at this point for you to understand the principle than to be able to balance complicated equations. You should know what is meant by a balanced equation and be able to balance simple equations. It is crucial that you understand the information that is contained in balanced equations.

Self-Assessment Questions

1. Which of the following equations are balanced? (You need not balance the equations. Just determine whether they are balanced as written.)
   I. $Ca + 2\ H_2O \longrightarrow Ca(OH)_2 + H_2$
   II. $4\ LiH + AlCl_3 \longrightarrow 2\ LiAlH_4 + 2\ LiCl$
   III. $2\ LiOH + CO_2 \longrightarrow Li_2CO_3 + H_2O$
   IV. $2\ Sn + 2\ H_2SO_4 \longrightarrow 2\ SnSO_4 + SO_2 + 2\ H_2O$
   a. I and II **b.** I and III **c.** II and III **d.** II and IV
2. Consider the equation for the reaction of phosphine with oxygen to form tetraphosphorus decoxide and water:
   $$PH_3 + O_2 \longrightarrow P_4O_{10} + H_2O \quad \text{(not balanced)}$$
   When the equation is balanced, how many molecules of water are produced for each molecule of P_4O_{10} formed?
   a. 1 **b.** 4 **c.** 6 **d.** 12

Items 3–5 refer to the following equation for the reaction of calcium hydroxide [$Ca(OH)_2$] with phosphoric acid (H_3PO_4).

$$Ca(OH)_2 + H_3PO_4 \longrightarrow H_2O + Ca_3(PO_4)_2 \quad \text{(not balanced)}$$

3. When the equation is balanced, how many H_2O molecules will be produced for each H_3PO_4 molecule that reacts?
   a. 1 **b.** 2 **c.** 3 **d.** 6
4. When the equation is balanced, how many H_3PO_4 molecules must react to produce one $Ca_3(PO_4)_2$ formula unit?
   a. 1 **b.** 2 **c.** 3 **d.** 6
5. When the equation is balanced, how many $Ca(OH)_2$ formula units are needed to react with six H_3PO_4 molecules?
   a. 1 **b.** 1.5 **c.** 6 **d.** 9

Answers: 1, b; 2, c; 3, c; 4, b; 5, d

Just as a molecule is the smallest unit of a molecular compound, a *formula unit* is the smallest unit of an ionic compound.

5.2 Volume Relationships in Chemical Equations

Learning Objective › Determine volumes of gases that react, using a balanced equation for a reaction.

So far we have looked at chemical reactions in terms of individual atoms and molecules. In the real world, however, chemists work with quantities of matter that contain billions of billions of atoms. John Dalton postulated that atoms of different elements have different masses. Therefore, equal masses of different elements must contain different numbers of atoms. By analogy, a kilogram of golf balls contains a smaller number of balls than a kilogram of Ping-Pong balls, because a golf ball is heavier than a Ping-Pong ball. One could determine the number of balls in each case simply by counting them. For atoms, however, counting is not so straightforward. The smallest visible particle of matter contains more atoms than could be counted in ten lifetimes! Even so, we can determine the number of atoms in a substance, as you will learn in this chapter.

Studies of gases in the eighteenth century advanced our understanding of how to account for atoms involved in chemical reactions. The interesting nature and behavior of gases are explored in Chapter 6; here we focus on some historical experiments with gases that revealed how chemical equations can be balanced. Experiments with gases led French scientist Joseph Louis Gay-Lussac (1778–1850) to an approach to quantifying atoms. In 1808, he announced the results of some chemical reactions that he had carried out with gases and summarized these experiments in a new law. The **law of combining volumes** states that when all measurements are made at the same temperature and pressure, the volumes of gaseous reactants and products are in small whole-number ratios. One such experiment is illustrated in

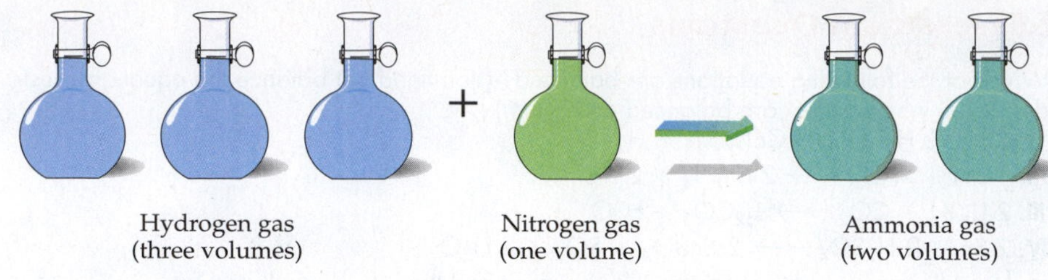

▶ **Figure 5.3** Gay-Lussac's law of combining volumes. Three volumes of hydrogen gas react with one volume of nitrogen gas to yield two volumes of ammonia gas, when measured at the same temperature and pressure.

Q: *Can you sketch a similar figure for the reaction* $2\ SO_2(g) + O_2(g) \longrightarrow 2\ SO_3(g)$*?*

Figure 5.3. When hydrogen reacts with nitrogen to form ammonia, three volumes of hydrogen combine with one volume of nitrogen to yield two volumes of ammonia. The small whole-number ratio is 3:1:2.

Gay-Lussac thought there must be some relationship between the numbers of molecules and the volumes of gaseous reactants and products. But it was Amedeo Avogadro who first explained the law of combining volumes in 1811. **Avogadro's hypothesis**, based on a shrewd interpretation of experimental facts, was that equal volumes of all gases, when measured at the same temperature and pressure, contain the same number of molecules (Figure 5.4).

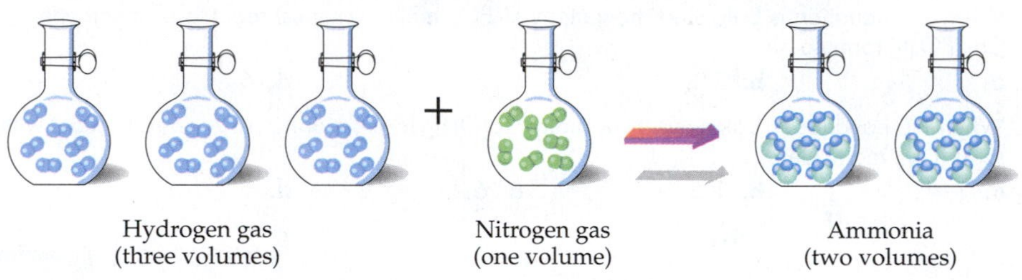

▶ **Figure 5.4** Avogadro's explanation of Gay-Lussac's law of combining volumes. Equal volumes of all the gases contain the same number of molecules.

Q: *Can you sketch a similar figure for the reaction* $2\ NO(g) + O_2(g) \longrightarrow 2\ NO_2(g)$*?*

▲ Amedeo Avogadro (1776–1856) and his hypothesis. The quotation reads, "Equal volumes of all gases at the same temperature and pressure contain the same number of molecules."

The equation for the combination of hydrogen and nitrogen to form ammonia is

$$3\ H_2(g) + N_2(g) \longrightarrow 2\ NH_3(g)$$

Note that the coefficients of the molecules correlate with the combining ratio of the gas volumes, 3:1:2 (Figure 5.3). The equation says that three H_2 molecules react with one N_2 molecule to produce two NH_3 molecules. The balanced equation provides the combining ratios. If you had 3 million H_2 molecules, you would need 1 million N_2 molecules to produce 2 million NH_3 molecules. According to the equation, three volumes of hydrogen react with one volume of nitrogen to produce two volumes of ammonia because each volume of hydrogen contains the same number of molecules as that same volume of nitrogen.

Example 5.2 Volume Relationships of Gases

What volume of oxygen is required to burn 0.556 L of propane in the following combustion reaction, assuming that both gases are measured at the same temperature and pressure?

$$C_3H_8(g) + 5\ O_2(g) \longrightarrow 3\ CO_2(g) + 4\ H_2O(g)$$

Solution

The coefficients in the equation indicate that each volume of $C_3H_8(g)$ requires five volumes of O_2 gas. Thus, we use $5\ L\ O_2(g)/1\ L\ C_3H_8(g)$ as a conversion factor to find the volume of oxygen required. (Conversion factors are explained in Section A.3 of the Appendix.)

$$?\ L\ O_2(g) = 0.556\ \cancel{L\ C_3H_8(g)} \times \frac{5\ L\ O_2(g)}{1\ \cancel{L\ C_3H_8(g)}} = 2.78\ L\ O_2(g)$$

■ EXERCISE 5.2A

Using the equation in Example 5.2, calculate the volume of $CO_2(g)$ produced when 0.492 L of propane is burned if the two gases are compared at the same temperature and pressure.

■ EXERCISE 5.2B

If 10.0 L each of propane and oxygen are combined at the same temperature and pressure, which gas will be left over after reaction? What volume of that gas will remain?

Self-Assessment Questions

1. In the reaction $2\ H_2(g) + O_2(g) \longrightarrow 2\ H_2O(g)$, with all substances at the same temperature and pressure, the ratio of volumes, for H_2, O_2, and H_2O, respectively, is
   a. 1:0:1 **b.** 2:0:2 **c.** 1:1:1 **d.** 2:1:2
2. How many CO_2 molecules are produced in the following reaction if 50 O_2 molecules react?

$$2\ C_8H_{18}(l) + 25\ O_2(g) \longrightarrow 16\ CO_2(g) + 18\ H_2O(l)$$

   a. 25 molecules **b.** 50 molecules **c.** 32 molecules **d.** 16 molecules
3. In the reaction $N_2(g) + 3\ H_2(g) \longrightarrow 2\ NH_3(g)$, with all substances at the same temperature and pressure, what volume of ammonia is produced when 4.50 L of nitrogen reacts with excess hydrogen?
   a. 3.00 L **b.** 4.50 L **c.** 6.75 L **d.** 9.00 L

Answers: 1, d; 2, c; 3, d

5.3 Avogadro's Number and the Mole

Learning Objectives › Calculate the formula mass, molecular mass, or molar mass of a substance.

Avogadro's hypothesis, which has been verified many times and in several ways over the years, states that equal volumes of gases at the same temperature and pressure contain equal numbers of molecules. This means that if we weigh equal volumes of different gases, the gases won't weigh the same. The ratio of their masses should be the same as the mass ratio of the molecules themselves.

Avogadro's Number: 6.02×10^{23}

Avogadro had no way of knowing how many molecules were in a given volume of gas. Scientists since his time have determined the number of atoms in various weighed samples of substances. Atoms are so incredibly small that these numbers are extremely large, even for tiny samples. Recall that the mass of a carbon-12 atom is exactly 12 atomic mass units (u) (Section 2.4, page 51) because the carbon-12 atom sets the standard for atomic mass. The number of carbon-12 atoms in a 12-g sample of carbon-12 is called **Avogadro's number** and has been determined experimentally to be 6.0221367×10^{23}. We usually round this number to three significant figures: 6.02×10^{23}.

The Mole: "A Dozen Eggs and a Mole of Sugar, Please"

We buy socks by the pair (2 socks), eggs by the dozen (12 eggs), and pencils by the gross (144 pencils). A dozen is the same number whether we are counting eggs or oranges. But a dozen eggs and a dozen oranges do not weigh the same. If an orange weighs five times as much as an egg, a dozen oranges will weigh five times as much as a dozen eggs.

▶ How big is Avogadro's number?

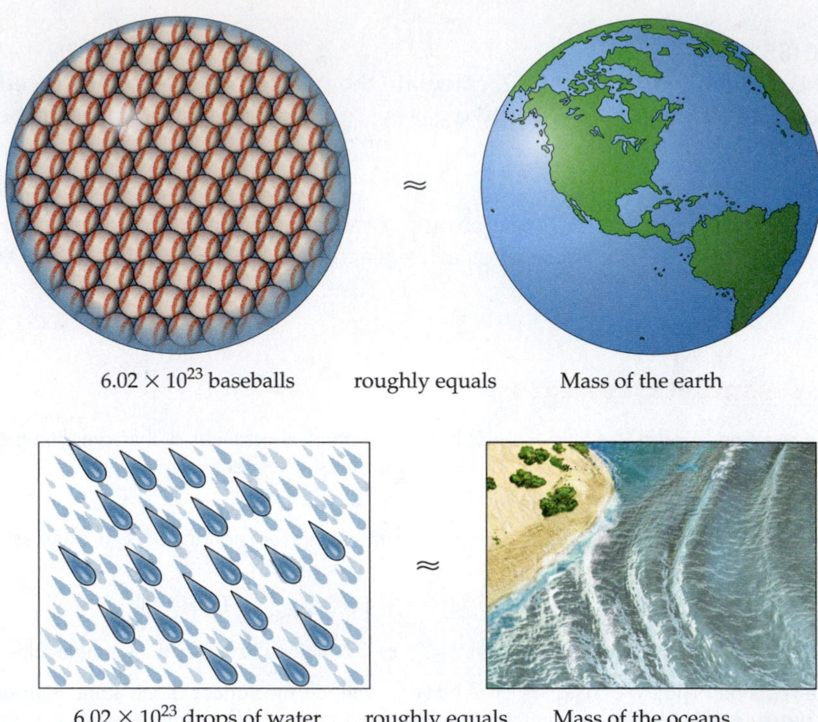

6.02×10^{23} baseballs roughly equals Mass of the earth

6.02×10^{23} drops of water roughly equals Mass of the oceans

Chemists count atoms and molecules by the *mole*. A single carbon atom is much too small to see or weigh, but a mole of carbon atoms fills a tablespoon and weighs 12 g. A mole of carbon and a mole of titanium each contain the same number of atoms. But a titanium atom has a mass four times that of a carbon atom, so a mole of titanium has a mass four times that of a mole of carbon.

A **mole (mol)** is an amount of substance that contains the same number of elementary units as there are atoms in exactly 12 g of carbon-12. That number is 6.02×10^{23}, Avogadro's number. The elementary units may be atoms (such as S or Ca), molecules (such as O_2 or CO_2), ions (such as K^+ or SO_4^{2-}), or any other kind of formula unit. A mole of NaCl, for example, contains 6.02×10^{23} NaCl formula units, which means that it contains 6.02×10^{23} Na^+ ions and 6.02×10^{23} Cl^- ions.

Formula Masses

Each element has a characteristic atomic mass. Because chemical compounds are made up of two or more elements, the masses of compounds are combinations of atomic masses. For any substance, the **formula mass** is the sum of the masses of the atoms represented in the formula. If the formula represents a molecule, the term *molecular mass* is often used. For example, because the formula CO_2 specifies one carbon atom and two oxygen atoms per molecule of carbon dioxide, the formula (or molecular) mass of carbon dioxide (CO_2) is the atomic mass of carbon plus twice the atomic mass of oxygen.

$$\begin{aligned}\text{Formula mass } CO_2 &= 1 \times \text{atomic mass of C} + 2 \times \text{atomic mass of O}\\ &= 1 \times 12.0\text{ u} + 2 \times 16.0\text{ u} = 44.0\text{ u}\end{aligned}$$

Example 5.3 Calculating Molecular Masses

Calculate **(a)** the molecular mass of nitrogen dioxide (NO_2), an amber-colored gas that is a constituent of smog, and **(b)** the formula mass of ammonium sulfate [$(NH_4)_2SO_4$], a fertilizer commonly used by home gardeners.

Solution

a. We start with the molecular formula: NO_2. Then, to determine the molecular mass, we simply add the atomic mass of nitrogen to twice the atomic mass of oxygen.

$$1 \times \text{atomic mass of N} = 1 \times 14.0\ \text{u} = 14.0\ \text{u}$$
$$2 \times \text{atomic mass of O} = 2 \times 16.0\ \text{u} = \underline{32.0\ \text{u}}$$
$$\text{Formula mass of } NO_2 = 46.0\ \text{u}$$

b. The formula $(NH_4)_2SO_4$ signifies two nitrogen atoms, eight hydrogen atoms, one sulfur atom, and four oxygen atoms. Combining the atomic masses, we have

$$(2 \times 14.0\ \text{u}) + (8 \times 1.01\ \text{u}) + (1 \times 32.0\ \text{u}) + (4 \times 16.0\ \text{u}) = 132.1\ \text{u}$$

■ EXERCISE 5.3

Calculate the formula mass of **(a)** sodium azide (NaN_3), used in automobile airbags, **(b)** phosphoric acid (H_3PO_4), used to flavor some cola drinks, **(c)** *para*-dichlorobenzene ($C_6H_4Cl_2$), used as a moth repellent, and **(d)** calcium dihydrogen phosphate $[Ca(H_2PO_4)_2]$, used as a mineral supplement in foods.

Percent Composition of a Compound from Formula Masses

A formula represents not only an atom ratio, but also a mass ratio. For example, the mass of 1.00 mol CO_2 is 44.0 g, of which 12.0 g is carbon and 32.0 g is oxygen. The composition of CO_2 can be expressed as percents by mass of carbon and of oxygen:

$$\%\ \text{by mass C} = \frac{\text{mass C}}{\text{mass } CO_2} \times 100\% = \frac{12.0\ \text{g}}{44.0\ \text{g}} \times 100\% = 27.3\%$$

Because oxygen is the only other element in CO_2, its percent by mass is $100\% - 27.3\% = 72.7\%$ oxygen.

The idea of percent composition by mass is useful in several applications. Dietary sodium limits are usually indicated in milligrams of Na^+. We consume Na^+ mainly as sodium chloride. The American Heart Association (AHA) recommends a maximum intake of 2400 mg Na^+ per day. Example 5.4 shows how we can relate this amount to the NaCl in one teaspoon of table salt.

Example 5.4 Calculating Percent Composition from a Formula

What mass of Na^+ is present in one teaspoon (6.0 g) of NaCl? How does this compare to the maximum intake of 2400 mg Na^+ per day recommended by the AHA?

Solution

A mole of sodium chloride has one mole (23.0 g) Na^+ and one mole (35.5 g) Cl^-. The percent by mass of Na^+ is

$$\%\ \text{by mass Na} = \frac{\text{mass Na}}{\text{mass NaCl}} \times 100\% = \frac{23.0\ \text{g}}{58.5\ \text{g}} \times 100\% = 39.3\%$$

So in 100 g of NaCl there are 39.3 g of Na^+. One teaspoon (6.0 g) of NaCl has

$$6.0\ \text{g NaCl} \times \frac{39.3\ \text{g } Na^+}{100\ \text{g NaCl}} = 2.4\ \text{g } Na^+$$

That is 2400 mg Na^+, the maximum recommended for one day's intake.

■ EXERCISE 5.4

Calculate the percent by mass of nitrogen in **(a)** KNO_3 and **(b)** $(NH_4)_2S$.

Many environmental pollutants are reported as elements even when the actual pollutant is a compound or a mixture of compounds. For example, nitrates (NO_3^-) in groundwater (Chapter 14) are reported as parts per million nitrogen, and carbon dioxide emissions (Chapter 13) often are reported as tons of carbon. The idea of percent by mass is useful in understanding these reported quantities.

Self-Assessment Questions

1. How many carbon-12 atoms are there in exactly 12 g of carbon-12?
   a. 1 **b.** 12 **c.** 144 **d.** 6.02×10^{23}
2. The mass of 1 mol of carbon-12 atoms is
   a. 12 g **b.** 12.011 g **c.** 12 u **d.** 12.011 u
3. Which of the following has the smallest molecular mass?
   a. CH_4 **b.** HF **c.** H_2O **d.** NH_3
4. How many moles of sulfur atoms are in 1 mol $Fe_2(SO_4)_3$?
   a. 1 mol **b.** 3 mol **c.** 15 mol **d.** 17 mol
5. How many moles of hydrogen atoms are present in 2.00 mol of ammonia (NH_3)?
   a. 2.00 mol **b.** 3.00 mol **c.** 6.00 mol **d.** 8.00 mol
6. Sodium chloride, by mass, is
   a. about 40% Na^+ and 60% Cl^- **b.** 50% Na^+ and 50% Cl^-
   c. about 60% Na^+ and 40% Cl^- **d.** 23.0% Na^+ and 35.5% Cl^-

Answers: 1, d; 2, a; 3, a; 4, b; 5, c; 6, a

5.4 Molar Mass: Mole-to-Mass and Mass-to-Mole Conversions

Learning Objectives › Convert from mass to moles and from moles to mass of a substance. › Calculate the mass or number of moles of a reactant or product from the mass or number of moles of another reactant or product.

The **molar mass** of a substance is just what the name implies: the mass of one mole of that substance. The molar mass is numerically equal to the atomic mass, molecular mass, or formula mass, but it is expressed in the unit *grams per mole* (g/mol). The atomic mass of sodium is 23.0 u, so its molar mass is 23.0 g/mol. The molecular mass of carbon dioxide is 44.0 u; its molar mass is 44.0 g/mol. The formula mass of ammonium sulfate is 132.1 u; its molar mass is 132.1 g/mol. We can use these facts, together with the definition of the mole, to write the following relationships.

$$1 \text{ mol Na} = 23.0 \text{ g Na}$$
$$1 \text{ mol } CO_2 = 44.0 \text{ g } CO_2$$
$$1 \text{ mol } (NH_4)_2SO_4 = 132.1 \text{ g } (NH_4)_2SO_4$$

These relationships supply the conversion factors we need to convert between mass in grams and amount in moles, as illustrated in the following examples.

Example 5.5 Conversions Involving Moles and Mass

a. What mass in grams of N_2 is 0.400 moles N_2? **(b)** Calculate the number of moles of Na in a 62.5 g sample of sodium metal.

Solution

a. The molecular mass of N_2 is $2 \times 14.0 \text{ u} = 28.0 \text{ u}$. The molar mass of N_2 is therefore 28.0 g/mol. Using this molar mass as a conversion factor (red), we have

$$? \text{ g } N_2 = 0.400 \cancel{\text{mol } N_2} \times \frac{28.0 \text{ g } N_2}{1 \cancel{\text{mol } N_2}} = 11.2 \text{ g } N_2$$

b. The molar mass of Na is 23.0 g/mol. To convert from mass to moles, we must use the *inverse* of the molar mass as a conversion factor (1 mol Na/23.0 g Na) to cancel units of mass. When we start with grams, we must have grams in the denominator of our conversion factor (red).

$$? \text{ mol Na} = 62.5 \cancel{\text{g Na}} \times \frac{1 \text{ mol Na}}{23.0 \cancel{\text{g Na}}} = 2.72 \text{ mol Na}$$

■ EXERCISE 5.5A

Calculate the mass, in grams, of **(a)** 0.0728 mol silicon, **(b)** 55.5 mol H_2O, and **(c)** 0.0728 mol $Ca(H_2PO_4)_2$.

■ EXERCISE 5.5B

Calculate the amount, in moles, of **(a)** 3.71 g Fe, **(b)** 165 g C_4H_{10}, and **(c)** 0.100 g $Mg(NO_3)_2$.

Figure 5.5 shows one-mole samples of several different substances. Each container holds Avogadro's number of formula units of the substance. That is, there are just as many sugar molecules in the largest dish as there are helium atoms in the balloon.

◀ **Figure 5.5** One mole of each of several familiar substances. From left to right on the table are sugar, salt, carbon, and copper. Behind them, the balloon contains helium. Each container holds Avogadro's number of elementary units of the substance. There are 6.02×10^{23} molecules of sugar ($C_{12}H_{22}O_{11}$), 6.02×10^{23} formula units of NaCl, 6.02×10^{23} atoms of carbon, 6.02×10^{23} atoms of copper, and 6.02×10^{23} atoms of helium in the respective samples.

Q: *How many Na^+ ions and how many Cl^- ions are there in the dish of salt? If the balloon was filled with oxygen gas (O_2), how many oxygen atoms would it contain?*

Mole and Mass Relationships in Chemical Equations

Chemists, other scientists, and engineers are often confronted with questions such as "How much iron can be obtained from 1.0 ton of Fe_2O_3?" or "How much carbon dioxide is produced by burning 1000 g of propane?" There is no simple way to calculate the mass of one substance directly from the mass of another in the same reaction. Because chemical reactions involve atoms and molecules, quantities in reactions are calculated in moles of atoms, ions, or molecules. To do such calculations, it is necessary to convert grams of a substance to moles, as we did in Example 5.5. We also must write balanced equations to determine molar ratios.

Recall that chemical equations provide not only ratios of atoms and molecules but also mole ratios. For example, the equation

$$C + O_2 \longrightarrow CO_2$$

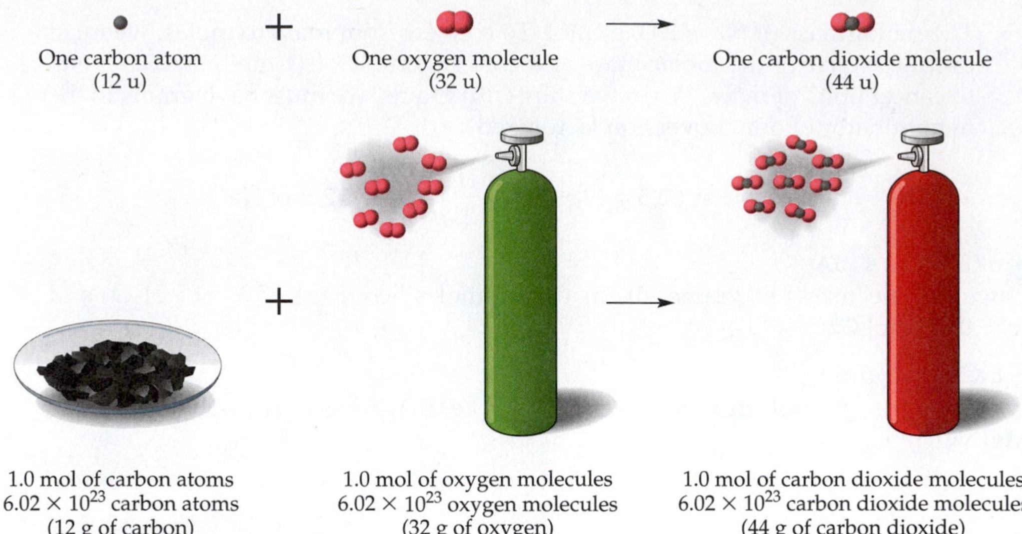

▲ **Figure 5.6** We cannot weigh single atoms or molecules, but we can weigh equal numbers of these tiny particles.

▲ **It DOES Matter!**
If there is not enough oxygen gas to react completely with burning carbon, some of the carbon will be incompletely oxidized and deadly carbon monoxide will form. Most of the 65 deaths in the Midwestern ice storm in January–February 2009 were the result of burning fuels (charcoal, kerosene, or gasoline, in an electricity generator) indoors without adequate oxygen.

tells us that one C atom reacts with one O_2 molecule (two atoms) to form one CO_2 molecule (one C atom and two O atoms). The equation also means that 1 mol (6.02×10^{23}atoms) of carbon reacts with 1 mol (6.02×10^{23} molecules) of oxygen to yield 1 mol (6.02×10^{23}molecules) of carbon dioxide. Because the molar mass in grams of a substance is numerically equal to the formula mass of the substance in atomic mass units, the equation also tells us (indirectly) that 12.0 g (1 mol) C reacts with 32.0 g (1 mol) O_2 to yield 44.0 g (1 mol) CO_2 (Figure 5.6).

The important thing is to maintain the *ratio* of masses. For example, in the preceding reaction, the mass ratio of oxygen to carbon is 32.0:12.0, or 8.0:3.0. Thus, 8.0 g O and 3.0 g C will produce 11.0 g CO_2. In fact, to calculate the amount of oxygen needed to react with a given amount of carbon, we need only multiply the amount of carbon by the factor 32.0:12.0. The following examples illustrate these relationships.

CONCEPTUAL Example 5.6 Molecular, Molar, and Mass Relationships

Nitrogen monoxide (nitric oxide), an air pollutant discharged by internal combustion engines, combines with oxygen to form nitrogen dioxide, a yellowish-brown gas that irritates our respiratory systems and eyes. The equation for this reaction is

$$2\,NO + O_2 \longrightarrow 2\,NO_2$$

State the molecular, molar, and mass relationships indicated by this equation.

Solution

The molecular and molar relationships can be obtained directly from the equation; no calculation is necessary. The mass relationship requires a little calculation.

Molecular: Two molecules of NO react with one molecule of O_2 to form two molecules of NO_2.

Molar: 2 mol NO reacts with 1 mol O_2 to form 2 mol NO_2.

Mass: 60.0 g NO (2 mol NO × 30.0 g/mol) reacts with 32.0 g (1 mol O_2 × 32.0 g/mol) O_2 to form 92.0 g (2 mol NO_2 × 46.0 g/mol) NO_2.

■ EXERCISE 5.6

Hydrogen sulfide, a gas that smells like rotten eggs, burns in air to produce sulfur dioxide and water according to the equation

$$2\,H_2S + 3\,O_2 \longrightarrow 2\,SO_2 + 2\,H_2O$$

State the molecular, molar, and mass relationships indicated by this equation.

Molar Relationships in Chemical Equations

The quantitative relationship between reactants and products in a chemical reaction is called **stoichiometry**. The ratio of moles of reactants and products is given by the coefficients in a balanced chemical equation. Consider the combustion of propane, the main component of bottled gas.

$$C_3H_8 + 5\,O_2 \longrightarrow 3\,CO_2 + 4\,H_2O$$

The coefficients in the balanced equation allow us to make statements such as

- 1 mol C_3H_8 reacts with 5 mol O_2.
- 3 mol CO_2 is produced for every 1 mol C_3H_8 that reacts.
- 4 mol H_2O is produced for every 3 mol CO_2 produced.

We can turn these statements into conversion factors known as stoichiometric factors. A **stoichiometric factor** relates the amounts, in *moles*, of any two substances involved in a chemical reaction. Note that we can set up stoichiometric factors for any two substances involved in a reaction. Also note that stoichiometric factors, because they come from the balanced equation for a reaction, involve small whole numbers. In the examples that follow, stoichiometric factors are shown in color.

Example 5.7 Molar Relationships

When 0.105 mol of propane is burned in a plentiful supply of oxygen, how many moles of oxygen are consumed?

$$C_3H_8 + 5\,O_2 \longrightarrow 3\,CO_2 + 4\,H_2O$$

Solution

The equation tells us that 5 mol O_2 is required to burn 1 mol C_3H_8. From this relationship, we can construct conversion factors to relate moles of oxygen to moles of propane. The possible conversion factors are

$$\frac{1\text{ mol }C_3H_8}{5\text{ mol }O_2} \quad \text{and} \quad \frac{5\text{ mol }O_2}{1\text{ mol }C_3H_8}$$

Which one do we use? Only if we multiply the given quantity (0.105 mol C_3H_8) by the factor on the *right* will the answer be expressed in the units requested (moles of oxygen).

$$?\text{ mol }O_2 = 0.105\text{ }\cancel{\text{mol }C_3H_8} \times \frac{5\text{ mol }O_2}{1\text{ }\cancel{\text{mol }C_3H_8}} = 0.525\text{ mol }O_2$$

■ EXERCISE 5.7A

Consider the combustion (burning) of propane presented in Example 5.7. **(a)** How many moles of CO_2 are formed when 0.529 mol C_3H_8 is burned? **(b)** How many moles of CO_2 are produced when 1.010 mol O_2 is consumed?

■ EXERCISE 5.7B

For the combustion of propane in Example 5.7, suppose that 50.0 mol O_2 and 25.0 mol propane are combined. After reaction, which reactant will be used up, and how many moles of the other reactant will be left over? (*Hint:* Calculate the number of moles of propane that will react with the oxygen given. Is there enough propane?)

Mass Relationships in Chemical Equations

A chemical equation defines the stoichiometric relationship in terms of moles, but problems are seldom presented in terms of moles. Typically, you are given the mass (grams) of one substance and asked to calculate the mass of another substance that will react or can be produced. Such calculations involve several steps:

1. Write a balanced chemical equation for the reaction.
2. Determine the molar masses of the substances involved in the calculation.
3. Write down the given quantity and use the molar mass to convert this quantity to moles.
4. Use coefficients (stoichiometric relationship) from the balanced chemical equation to convert moles of the given substance to moles of the desired substance.
5. Use the molar mass to convert moles of the desired substance to grams of the desired substance.

If we know the quantity of any substance in an equation, we can determine the quantities of all the other substances. The conversion process is diagrammed in Figure 5.7. It is best learned by studying examples and working exercises.

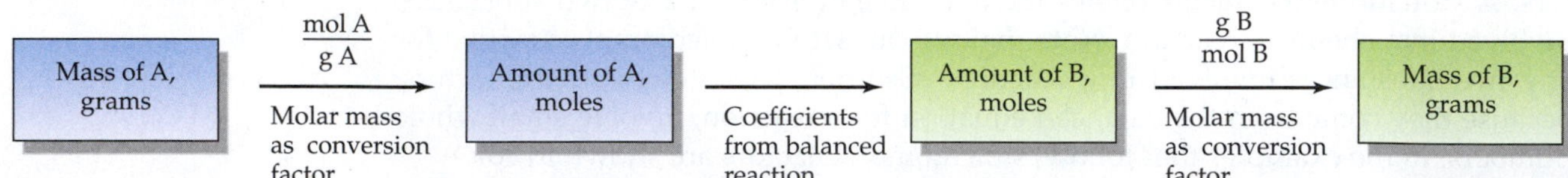

▲ **Figure 5.7** We can use a chemical equation to relate the numbers of *moles* of any two substances represented in the equation. These substances may be a reactant and a product, two reactants, or two products. We cannot directly relate the mass of one substance to the mass of another substance involved in the same reaction. To obtain *mass* relationships, we must convert the mass of each substance to moles, relate moles of one substance to moles of the other through a stoichiometric factor, and then convert moles of the second substance to its mass.

Example 5.8 Mass Relationships

Calculate the mass of oxygen needed to react with 10.0 g of carbon in the reaction that forms carbon dioxide.

Solution

Step 1: The balanced equation is

$$C + O_2 \longrightarrow CO_2$$

Step 2: The molar masses are 12.0 g/mol for C and $2 \times 16.0 = 32.0$ g/mol for O_2.

Step 3: We convert the given mass of carbon to an amount in moles.

$$? \text{ mol C} = 10.0 \cancel{\text{g C}} \times \frac{1 \text{ mol C}}{12.0 \cancel{\text{g C}}} = 0.833 \text{ mol C}$$

Step 4: We use coefficients from the balanced equation to establish the stoichiometric factor (red) that relates the amount of oxygen to that of carbon.

$$0.833 \cancel{\text{mol C}} \times \frac{1 \text{ mol } O_2}{1 \cancel{\text{mol C}}} = 0.833 \text{ mol } O_2$$

Step 5: We convert from moles of oxygen to grams of oxygen.

$$0.833 \cancel{\text{mol } O_2} \times \frac{32.0 \text{ g } O_2}{1 \cancel{\text{mol } O_2}} = 26.7 \text{ g } O_2$$

We can also combine the five steps into a single setup. Note that the units in the denominators of the conversion factors are chosen so that each cancels the unit in the numerator of the preceding term.

We start here | This converts g C to mol C | This relates mol C to mol O_2 | This converts mol O_2 to g O_2 | The answer: the number and the unit

$$10.0 \cancel{\text{g C}} \times \frac{1 \cancel{\text{mol C}}}{12.0 \cancel{\text{g C}}} \times \frac{1 \cancel{\text{mol } O_2}}{1 \cancel{\text{mol C}}} \times \frac{32.0 \text{ g } O_2}{1 \cancel{\text{mol } O_2}} = 26.6 \text{ g } O_2$$

(The answers are slightly different due to rounding in the intermediate steps.)

■ EXERCISE 5.8A

Calculate the mass of oxygen (O_2) needed to react with 0.334 g nitrogen (N_2) in the reaction that forms nitrogen dioxide.

■ EXERCISE 5.8B

Calculate the mass of carbon dioxide formed by burning 775 g each of **(a)** methane (CH_4) and **(b)** butane (C_4H_{10}) in oxygen gas. (*Hint:* The reaction in Example 5.7 may help in balancing the equations.)

1. How can a car make more pollution than the gasoline it uses? A mole of carbon (12 g) combines with oxygen from the atmosphere to form a mole of carbon dioxide (44 g). Gasoline is mostly carbon by weight, so the mass of carbon dioxide formed is greater than the mass of gasoline burned. Carbon dioxide is a major greenhouse gas (Chapter 13).

Self-Assessment Questions

1. The mass of 4.75 mol H_2SO_4 is
   - **a.** 314 g
   - **b.** 456 g
   - **c.** 466 g
   - **d.** 564 g
2. For which of the following would a 10.0-g sample contain the most moles?
   - **a.** Cu
   - **b.** Fe
   - **c.** Si
   - **d.** S
3. How many moles of CO_2 are there in 1 lb (453.6 g) CO_2?
   - **a.** 0.0969 mol
   - **b.** 9.20 mol
   - **c.** 10.3 mol
   - **d.** 14.2 mol
4. How many moles of benzene (C_6H_6) are there in a 7.81-g sample of benzene?
   - **a.** 0.100 mol
   - **b.** 1.00 mol
   - **c.** 7.81 mol
   - **d.** 610 mol

Items 5–7 refer to the equation $2\ H_2 + O_2 \longrightarrow 2\ H_2O$.

5. At the molar level, the equation means that
   - **a.** 2 mol H reacts with 1 mol O to form 2 mol H_2O
   - **b.** 4 mol H reacts with 2 mol O to form 4 mol H_2O
   - **c.** 2 mol H_2 reacts with 1 mol O_2 to form 2 mol H_2O
   - **d.** 2 mol O_2 reacts with 1 mol H_2 to form 2 mol H_2O
6. How many moles of water can be formed from 0.500 mol H_2?
   - **a.** 0.500 mol
   - **b.** 1.00 mol
   - **c.** 2.00 mol
   - **d.** 4.00 mol
7. How many moles of oxygen (O_2) are required to form 0.222 mol H_2O?
   - **a.** 0.111 mol
   - **b.** 0.222 mol
   - **c.** 0.444 mol
   - **d.** 1.00 mol

Answers: 1, c; 2, c; 3, c; 4, a; 5, c; 6, a; 7, a

GREEN CHEMISTRY

Principles 1, 2

Margaret Kerr, *Worcester State University*

Atom Economy

Imagine yourself in the future. Your job is related to environmental protection, which requires that you provide information to practicing chemists as they design new processes and reactions. Waste management is one of your top concerns. Although waste typically has been addressed after the production of desired commodities, you realize that a greener approach enables minimizing the waste from the start. What tools would you use in this job? What topics are important? How can chemists provide new products while protecting the environment?

Intrinsic in greener approaches to waste management is the concept of *atom economy*, a calculation of the number of atoms conserved in the desired product rather than in waste. In 1998, Barry Trost (Stanford University) won a Presidential Green Chemistry Challenge Award for his work in developing this concept. By calculating the number of atoms that will not become part of the desired product and, therefore, will enter the waste stream, chemists can precisely determine the minimum amount of waste that will be produced by chemicals used in a reaction before even running the reaction.

You have learned how to write and balance chemical equations (Section 5.1) and you also can calculate molar mass, convert from mass to moles, and determine the amount of product formed from given amounts of reactants (Sections 5.3, 5.4). Other ways of calculating the efficiency of a reaction has traditionally been expressed using *theoretical yield*, *experimental yield*, and *percent yield*. The theoretical yield is the maximum amount of desired product that can be produced by the amounts of reactants used. Under laboratory conditions, the theoretical yield of a reaction is not usually obtained. The actual amount of desired product collected is called the experimental yield. Chemists often express their experimental results in percent yield, which is simply the experimental yield divided by the theoretical yield, then multiplied by 100.

$$\%\text{ yield} = \frac{\text{experimental yield}}{\text{theoretical yield}} \times 100\%$$

A report of a 100% yield for a reaction seems good, but the percent yield considers only the desired product. Any other substance formed (for instance, a byproduct) is not counted in the percent yield. Byproducts often become part of the chemical waste stream. Some reactions actually produce more byproducts than desired products.

Atom economy is a better way to measure reaction efficiency. Percent atom economy (% A.E.) measures the proportion of the atoms in the reaction mixture that actually become part of the desired product. Reactant atoms that do not appear in the product are considered waste. The % A.E. is given by the following relationship:

$$\%\text{ A.E.} = \frac{\text{molar mass of desired product}}{\text{molar masses of all reactants}} \times 100\%$$

A reaction can have a poor atom economy even when the percent yield is near 100%.

Consider the following two ways to make ethyl bromide (C_2H_5Br), a compound used as a solvent, an anesthetic, a refrigerant, and a fumigant. First, ethyl bromide can be made using ethanol (C_2H_5OH) and phosphorus tribromide (PBr_3).

$$3\ C_2H_5OH + PBr_3 \rightarrow 3\ C_2H_5Br + H_3PO_3$$

In this reaction, a Br atom substitutes for the OH group of the alcohol. In reactions like this one, generally only one product is desired and all other products are not utilized. The wasted atoms in the preceding equation are shown in red.

We can calculate the atom economy for this reaction.

$$\%\text{ A.E.} = \frac{3 \times \text{molar mass } C_2H_5Br}{3 \times \text{molar mass } C_2H_5OH + \text{molar mass } PBr_3} \times 100\%$$

$$= \frac{3 \times 108.97\text{ g/mol}}{(3 \times 46.07\text{ g/mol}) + 270.69\text{ g/mol}} \times 100\% = 79.9\%$$

These substitution reactions never have 100% atom economy because there is always a byproduct. This results in some atoms going into the waste stream.

Ethyl bromide can also be made using ethylene (C_2H_4) and hydrogen bromide:

$$C_2H_4 + HBr \rightarrow C_2H_5Br$$

In this reaction, all of the atoms in both reactants appear in the desired product C_2H_5Br and none go into the waste stream. The percent atom economy is 100%.

$$\%\text{ A.E.} = \frac{\text{molar mass } C_2H_5Br}{\text{molar mass } C_2H_4 + \text{molar mass HBr}} \times 100\%$$

$$= \frac{108.97\text{g/mol}}{28.05\text{g/mol} + 80.91\text{g/mol}} \times 100\% = 100\%$$

Because the concept of atom economy offers a way to predict waste, it can lead to innovative design processes that eliminate or minimize waste. By focusing on waste from the beginning of the reaction, we reduce or eliminate cleanup at the end.

5.5 Solutions

Learning Objectives › Calculate the concentration (molarity, percent by volume, or percent by mass) of a solute in a solution. › Calculate the amount of solute or solution given the concentration and the other amount.

Many chemical reactions take place in solutions. A **solution** is a homogeneous mixture of two or more substances. The substance being dissolved is the *solute*, and the substance doing the dissolving is the *solvent*. The solvent is usually present in greater quantity than the solute. There are many solvents: Kerosene dissolves grease; ethanol dissolves many drugs; isopentyl acetate, a component of banana oil, is a solvent for model airplane glue.

Water is no doubt the most familiar solvent, dissolving as it does many common substances such as sugar, salt, and ethanol. We focus our discussion here on **aqueous solutions**, those in which water is the solvent, and we take a more quantitative look at the relationship between solute and solvent.

Solution Concentrations

We say that some substances, such as sugar and salt, are *soluble* in water. Of course, there is a limit to the quantity of sugar or salt that we can dissolve in a given volume of water. Yet we still find it convenient to say that they are soluble in water because an appreciable quantity dissolves. Other substances, such as an iron nail or sand (silicon dioxide), we consider to be *insoluble* because their solubility in water is near zero. Such terms as *soluble* and *insoluble* are useful, but they are imprecise and must be used with care.

Two other roughly estimated but sometimes useful terms are *dilute* and *concentrated*. A **dilute solution** is one that contains a little bit of solute in lots of solvent. For example, a pinch of sugar in a cup of tea makes a dilute, faintly sweet, sugar solution. A **concentrated solution** is one with a relatively large amount of solute dissolved in a relatively small amount of solvent. Pancake syrup, with lots of sugar solute in a relatively small amount of water, is a concentrated, and very sweet, solution.

Scientific work generally requires more precise concentration units than "a pinch of sugar in a cup of tea." Further, quantitative work often requires the *mole* unit because substances enter into chemical reactions according to *molar* ratios.

▲ **It DOES Matter!**
The ethanol content of a beverage is almost always expressed by *volume* (see Example 5.13A). This may be done partly as a marketing ploy. Ethanol is about 20% less dense than water, so a beverage that is labeled "12% alcohol by volume" is only about 10% ethanol by weight. The higher percent by volume may make purchasers think they are getting "more for the money."

Molarity

A concentration unit that chemists often use is *molarity*. For reactions involving solutions, the amount of solute is usually measured in moles and the quantity of solution in liters or milliliters. The **molarity (M)** is the amount of solute, in moles, per liter of solution.

$$\text{Molarity (M)} = \frac{\text{moles of solute}}{\text{liters of solution}}$$

Example 5.9 Solution Concentration: Molarity and Moles

Calculate the molarity of a solution made by dissolving 3.50 mol NaCl in enough water to produce 2.00 L of solution.

Solution

$$\text{Molarity (M)} = \frac{\text{moles of solute}}{\text{liters of solution}} = \frac{3.50 \text{ mol NaCl}}{2.00 \text{ L solution}} = 1.75 \text{ M NaCl}$$

We read 1.75 M NaCl as "1.75 molar sodium chloride."

■ EXERCISE 5.9A

Calculate the molarity of a solution that has 0.0500 mol NH_3 in 5.75 L of solution.

■ EXERCISE 5.9B

Calculate the molarity of a solution made by dissolving 0.750 mol H_3PO_4 in enough water to produce 775 mL of solution.

Usually, when preparing a solution, we must *weigh* the solute. Balances do not display units of moles, so we usually work with a given mass and divide by the molar mass of the substance, as illustrated in Example 5.10.

Example 5.10 Solution Concentration: Molarity and Mass

What is the molarity of a solution in which 333 g potassium hydrogen carbonate is dissolved in enough water to make 10.0 L of solution?

Solution

First, we must convert grams of $KHCO_3$ to moles of $KHCO_3$.

$$333\ \text{g KHCO}_3 \times \frac{1\ \text{mol KHCO}_3}{100.1\ \text{g KHCO}_3} = 3.33\ \text{mol KHCO}_3$$

Next, we use this value as the numerator in the defining equation for molarity. The solution volume, 10.0 L, is the denominator.

$$\text{Molarity} = \frac{3.33\ \text{mol KHCO}_3}{10.0\ \text{L solution}} = 0.333\ \text{M KHCO}_3$$

■ EXERCISE 5.10A

Calculate the molarity of **(a)** 18.0 g H_2SO_4 in 2.00 L of solution and **(b)** 3.00 g KI in 2.39 L of solution.

■ EXERCISE 5.10B

Calculate the molarity of 0.206 g HF in 752 mL of solution (HF is used for etching glass).

Often, we need to know the *mass* of solute required to prepare a given volume of a solution of a particular molarity. In such calculations, we can use molarity as a conversion factor between moles of solute and liters of solution. For instance, in Example 5.11, the expression "0.15 M NaCl" means 0.15 mol NaCl per liter of solution, expressed as the conversion factor

$$\frac{0.15\ \text{mol NaCl}}{1\ \text{L solution}}$$

Example 5.11 Solution Preparation: Molarity

What mass in grams of NaCl is required to prepare 0.500 L of typical over-the-counter saline solution (about 0.15 M NaCl)?

Solution

First, we use the molarity as a conversion factor to calculate moles of NaCl.

$$0.500\ \text{L solution} \times \frac{0.15\ \text{mol NaCl}}{1\ \text{L solution}} = 0.075\ \text{mol NaCl}$$

Then, we use the molar mass to calculate grams of NaCl.

$$0.75 \text{ mol NaCl} \times \frac{58.5 \text{ g NaCl}}{1 \text{ mol NaCl}} = 44 \text{ g NaCl}$$

■ EXERCISE 5.11

What mass in grams of potassium hydroxide is required to prepare **(a)** 2.00 L of 6.00 M KOH and **(b)** 100.0 mL of 1.00 M KOH?

Quite often, solutions of known molarity are available commercially. For example, concentrated hydrochloric acid is 12 M. How would you determine the *volume* of this solution that contains a certain number of moles of solute? We can again rearrange the definition of molarity to obtain the volume.

$$\text{Liters of solution} = \frac{\text{moles of solute}}{\text{molarity}}$$

2. What's the difference between 14K gold and 18K gold? A karat (K) is a traditional way of expressing the concentration of gold. A 14K gold necklace contains 14 g of gold per 24 g of the necklace (58% gold by mass). An 18K gold ring contains 18 g of gold per 24 g of the ring (75% gold by mass). So what do you suppose is the percent by mass of gold in 24K gold?

Example 5.12 Moles from Molarity and Volume

Concentrated hydrochloric acid is 12.0 M HCl. What volume in milliliters of this solution contains 0.425 mol HCl?

Solution

$$\text{Liters of HCl solution} = \frac{\text{moles of solute}}{\text{molarity}} = \frac{0.425 \text{ mol HCl}}{12.0 \text{ M HCl}}$$

$$= \frac{0.425 \text{ mol HCl}}{12.0 \text{ mol HCl/L}} = 0.0354 \text{ L}$$

In this case, 0.0354 L (35.4 mL) of the solution contains 0.425 mol of the solute. Remember that molarity is moles per liter of *solution*, not per liter of solvent.

■ EXERCISE 5.12A

What volume in milliliters of 15.0 M aqueous ammonia (NH_3) solution contains 0.445 mol NH_3?

■ EXERCISE 5.12B

What mass in grams of HNO_3 is in 500 mL of acid rain that has a concentration of 2.00×10^{-5} M HNO_3?

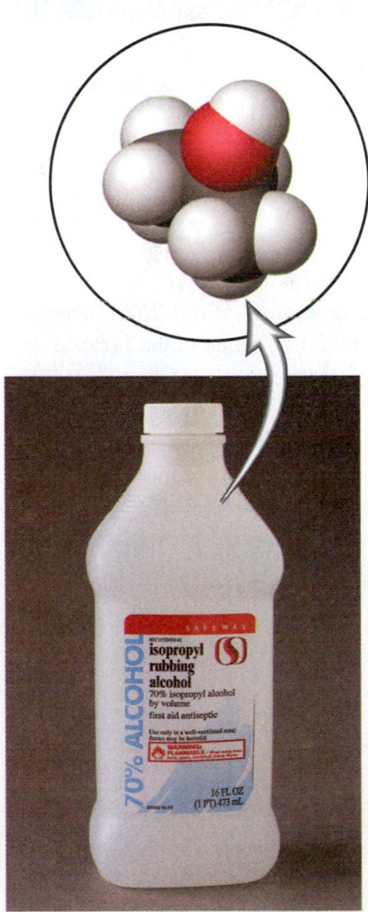

▲ Rubbing alcohol is a water–isopropyl alcohol solution that is 70% isopropyl alcohol [$(CH_3)_2CHOH$] by volume.

Percent Concentrations

For many practical applications, including those in medicine and pharmacy, solution concentrations are often expressed in percentages. There are different ways to express percentages, depending on whether mass or volume is being measured. If both solute and solvent are liquids, **percent by volume** is often used because liquid volumes are easily measured.

$$\text{Percent by volume} = \frac{\text{volume of solute}}{\text{volume of solution}} \times 100\%$$

In calculating percent by volume, we can measure the solute and solution in any unit of volume as long as we use the same unit for both. For example, we can measure both volumes in milliliters or in gallons. Ethanol (CH_3CH_2OH) for medicinal

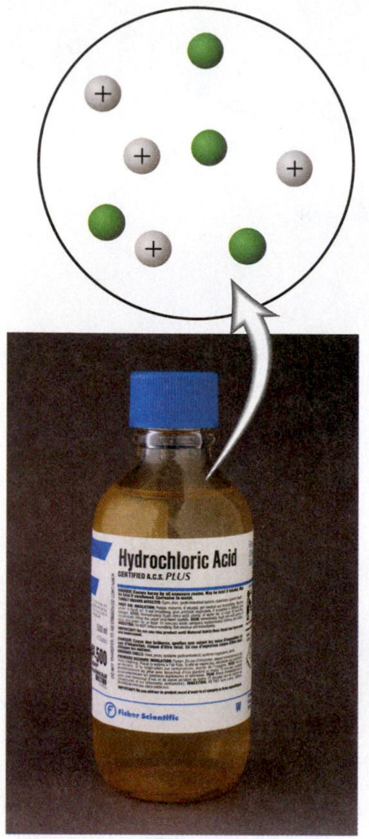

▲"Reagent grade" concentrated hydrochloric acid is a 38% by mass solution of HCl in water.

3. Does 2% milk have just 2% of the calories of whole milk? No. Whole milk contains at least 3.25% butterfat by mass. Some of the butterfat is removed to make 2% milk, which is 2% butterfat by mass. Actually, 2% milk has about 75% of the calories of whole milk.

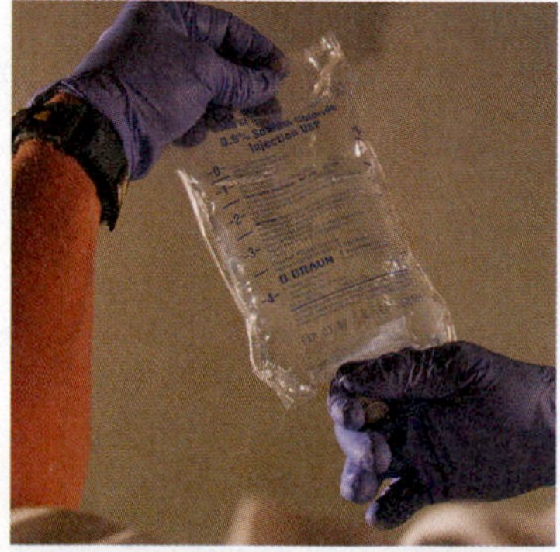

▲ **It Does Matter!** An isotonic, or "normal," intravenous solution must have the proper concentration of solute to avoid damage to blood cells.

purposes is 95% by volume. That is, it consists of 95 mL CH_3CH_2OH per 100 mL of aqueous solution.

Example 5.13 Percent by Volume

Two-stroke engines use a mixture of 120 mL of oil dissolved in enough gasoline to make 4.0 L of fuel. What is the percent by volume of oil in this mixture?

Solution

$$\text{Percent by volume} = \frac{120 \text{ mL oil}}{4000 \text{ mL solution}} \times 100\% = 3.0\%$$

■ EXERCISE 5.13A

What is the volume percent of ethanol in a solution of 625 mL of an ethanol–water solution that contains 58.0 mL of water?

■ EXERCISE 5.13B

Determine the volume percent of toluene ($C_6H_5CH_3$) in a solution made by mixing 40.0 mL of toluene with 75.0 mL of benzene (C_6H_6). Assume that the volumes are additive.

Many commercial solutions are labeled with the concentration in **percent by mass**. For example, sulfuric acid is sold in several concentrations: 35.7% H_2SO_4 for use in storage batteries, 77.7% H_2SO_4 for the manufacture of phosphate fertilizers, and 93.2% H_2SO_4 for pickling steel. Each of these percentages is by mass: 35.7 g of H_2SO_4 per 100 g of sulfuric acid solution, and so on.

$$\text{Percent by mass} = \frac{\text{mass of solute}}{\text{mass of solution}} \times 100\%$$

As with percent by volume, we can express the masses of solute and solution in any mass unit, as long as we use the same unit for both.

Example 5.14 Percent by Mass

What is the percent by mass of NaCl if 25.5 g of it is dissolved in 425 g (425 mL) of water?

Solution

We use these values in the above percent-by-mass equation:

$$\text{Percent by mass} = \frac{25.5 \text{ g NaCl}}{(25.5 + 425) \text{ g solution}} \times 100\% = 5.66\% \text{ NaCl}$$

■ EXERCISE 5.14A

Hydrogen peroxide solution for home use is 3.0% by mass of H_2O_2 in water. What is the percent by mass of a solution of 9.40 g H_2O_2 dissolved in 335 g (335 mL) of water?

■ EXERCISE 5.14B

Sodium hydroxide (NaOH, lye) is used to make soap and is quite soluble in water. What is the percent by mass of NaOH in a solution that contains 1.00 kg NaOH in 950 mL water?

Example 5.15 Solution Preparation: Percent by Mass

Describe how to make 430 g of an aqueous solution that is 4.85% by mass $NaNO_3$.

Solution

We begin by rearranging the equation for percent by mass to solve for mass of solute.

$$\text{Mass of solute} = \frac{\text{percent by mass} \times \text{mass of solution}}{100\%}$$

Substituting, we have

$$\frac{4.85\% \times 430\text{ g}}{100\%} = 20.9\text{ g}$$

We would weigh out 20.9 g $NaNO_3$ and add enough water to make 430 g of solution.

■ EXERCISE 5.15A

Describe how you would prepare 125 g of an aqueous solution that is 4.50% glucose by mass.

■ EXERCISE 5.15B

Describe how you would prepare 1750 g of *isotonic saline*, a commonly used intravenous (IV) solution that is 0.89% sodium chloride by mass.

Note that for percent concentrations, the mass or volume of the solute needed doesn't depend on what the solute is. A 10% by mass solution of NaOH contains 10 g NaOH per 100 g of solution. Similarly, 10% HCl and 10% $(NH_4)_2SO_4$ and 10% $C_{110}H_{190}N_3O_2Br$ each contain 10 g of the specified solute per 100 g of solution. For *molar* solutions, however, the mass of solute in a solution of specified molarity is different for different solutes. A liter of 0.10 M solution requires 4.0 g (0.10 mol) NaOH, 3.7 g (0.10 mol) HCl, 13.2 g (0.10 mol) $(NH_4)_2SO_4$, or 166 g (0.10 mol) $C_{110}H_{190}N_3O_2Br$.

4. What does a cholesterol level of 200 mean? Concentrations of solutes in body fluids are often too low to be expressed conveniently as percentages. A common unit is milligrams (of solute) per deciliter of blood (or other fluid). A cholesterol level of 200 means 200 mg of cholesterol per dL (100 mL) of blood.

Self-Assessment Questions

1. In a solution of 85.0 g water and 5.0 g sucrose ($C_{12}H_{22}O_{11}$), the
   a. solute is sucrose and the solution is the solvent
   b. solute is sucrose and the solvent is water
   c. solute is water and sucrose is the solvent
   d. water and sucrose are both solutes
2. What is the molarity of a sodium hydroxide solution having 0.500 mol NaOH in 250 mL of solution?
   a. 0.00200 M b. 0.200 M c. 2.00 M d. 8.00 M
3. How many moles of sugar are required to make 4.00 L of 0.600 M sugar solution?
   a. 1.20 mol b. 2.40 mol c. 24.0 mol d. 6.67 mol
4. What mass of NaCl in grams is needed to prepare 2.500 L of a 0.800 M NaCl solution?
   a. 2.00 g b. 4.00 g c. 58.5 g d. 117 g
5. What volume of 6.00 M HCl solution contains 1.50 mol HCl?
   a. 250 mL b. 300 mL c. 900 mL d. 9.00 L
6. What is the percent by volume of ethanol in a solution made by adding 50.0 mL of pure ethanol to enough water to make 250 mL of solution?
   a. 16.7% b. 20.0% c. 25.0% d. 80.0%
7. A solution contains 15.0 g sucrose and 60.0 g of water. What is the percent by mass of sucrose in the solution?
   a. 15.0% b. 20.0% c. 25.0% d. 80.0%
8. What volume of water should be added to 23.4 g NaCl to make 100.0 mL of 4.00 M NaCl solution?
   a. 76.6 mL b. 96.0 mL
   c. 100.0 mL d. enough to make 100.0 mL of solution

Answers: 1, b; 2, c; 3, b; 4, d; 5, a; 6, b; 7, b; 8, d

CRITICAL THINKING EXERCISES

Apply knowledge that you have gained in this chapter and one or more of the FLaReS principles (Chapter 1) to evaluate the following statements or claims.

5.1 Suppose that someone has published a paper claiming to have established a new value for Avogadro's number. The author says that he has made some very careful laboratory measurements and his calculations indicate that the true value for Avogadro's number is 3.01875×10^{23}. Is this claim credible in your opinion? What questions would you ask the author about his claim?

5.2 A chemistry teacher asked her students, "What is the mass, in grams, of a mole of bromine?" One student answered 80; another said 160; and several others gave answers of 79, 81, 158, and 162. The teacher stated that all of these answers were correct. Do you believe her statement?

5.3 A website on fireworks provides directions for preparing potassium nitrate, KNO_3 (molar mass = 101 g/mol), using potassium carbonate (138 g/mol) and ammonium nitrate (80 g/mol), according to the following equation:

$$K_2CO_3 + 2\,NH_4NO_3 \longrightarrow 2\,KNO_3 + CO_2 + H_2O + NH_3$$

The directions state: "Mix one kilogram of potassium carbonate with two kilograms of ammonium nitrate. The carbon dioxide and ammonia come off as gases, and the water can be evaporated, leaving two kilograms of pure potassium nitrate." Use information from this chapter to evaluate this statement.

5.4 A battery manufacturer claims that lithium batteries deliver the same power as batteries using nickel, zinc, or lead, but the lithium batteries are much lighter because lithium has a lower atomic mass than does nickel, zinc, or lead.

5.5 After working Problem 66 of Additional Problems, evaluate the claim that homeopathy is a valid alternative medical treatment.

SUMMARY

Section 5.1—A **chemical equation** is shorthand for a chemical change, using symbols and formulas instead of words: for example, $C + O_2 \longrightarrow CO_2$. Substances to the left of the arrow are starting materials, or **reactants**; those to the right of the arrow are **products**, or what the reaction produces. Physical states may be indicated with (s), (l), or (g). Because matter is conserved, a chemical equation must be balanced. It must have the same numbers and types of atoms on each side. Equations are balanced by placing coefficients in front of the formula for each reactant or product; we do *not* balance an equation by changing the formulas of reactants or products. The balanced equation $2\,NaN_3 \longrightarrow 2\,Na + 3\,N_2$ means that two formula units of NaN_3 react to give two atoms of Na and three molecules of N_2.

Section 5.2—Gay-Lussac's experiments led him to the **law of combining volumes**: At a given temperature and pressure, the volumes of gaseous reactants and products are in a small whole-number ratio (such as 1:1, 2:1, 4:3). **Avogadro's hypothesis** explained this law by stating that equal volumes of all gases contain the same number of molecules at fixed temperature and pressure.

Section 5.3—**Avogadro's number** is defined as the number of ^{12}C atoms in exactly 12 grams of ^{12}C, that is, 6.02×10^{23} atoms. A **mole (mol)** is the amount of a substance that contains Avogadro's number of elementary units—atoms, molecules, or formula units, depending on the substance. The **formula mass** is the sum of masses of the atoms represented in the formula of a substance. If the formula represents a molecule, the term *molecular mass* often is used. A formula represents a mass ratio as well as an atom ratio, and the composition by mass of a compound may be calculated from the formula.

Section 5.4—The **molar mass** is the mass of one mole of a substance. Molar mass has the same number as formula mass, molecular mass, or atomic mass but is expressed in units of grams per mole (g/mol). Molar mass is used to convert from grams to moles of a substance, and vice versa. A balanced equation can be read in terms of atoms and molecules or in terms of moles. **Stoichiometry**, or mass relationships in chemical reactions, can be found by using **stoichiometric factors**, which relate moles of one substance to moles of another. Stoichiometric factors can be obtained without calculation, directly from the balanced equation. To evaluate mass relationships in chemical reactions, molar masses and stoichiometric factors are both used as conversion factors.

Section 5.5—A **solution** is a homogeneous mixture of two or more substances, often consisting of a solute dissolved in a solvent. A substance is soluble in a solvent if some appreciable quantity of the substance dissolves in the solvent. Any substance that does not dissolve significantly in a solvent is insoluble in that solvent. An **aqueous solution**, indicated by the label (aq), has water as the solvent. The concentration of a solution can be expressed in many ways. A **concentrated solution** has a relatively large amount of solute compared to solvent, and a **dilute solution** has only a little solute in a large amount of solvent. One quantitative unit of concentration is **molarity (M)**, moles of solute dissolved per liter of solution.

$$\text{Molarity (M)} = \frac{\text{moles of solute}}{\text{liters of solution}}$$

There are several ways to express concentration using percentages. Two important ones are **percent by volume** and **percent by mass**.

$$\text{Percent by volume} = \frac{\text{volume of solute}}{\text{volume of solution}} \times 100\%$$

$$\text{Percent by mass} = \frac{\text{mass of solute}}{\text{mass of solution}} \times 100\%$$

For each concentration unit, if we know two of the three terms in the equation, we can solve for the third.

Green chemistry Atom economy is an important component of green chemistry and waste prevention. By strategically designing reactions to maximize the number of atoms utilized, a chemist has the ability to reduce waste production.

Learning Objectives

› Identify balanced and unbalanced chemical equations, and balance equations by inspection. (5.1)	Problems 4, 11–16, 51–53, 62
› Determine volumes of gases that react, using a balanced equation for a reaction. (5.2)	Problems 2, 3, 17–22, 55
› Calculate the formula mass, molecular mass, or molar mass of a substance. (5.3)	Problems 27–34
› Convert from mass to moles and from moles to mass of a substance. (5.4)	Problem 71
› Calculate the mass or number of moles of a reactant or product from the mass or number of moles of another reactant or product. (5.4)	Problems 35–38, 54, 56–58, 62, 69
› Calculate the concentration (molarity, percent by volume, or percent by mass) of a solute in a solution. (5.5)	Problems 39–50, 60, 61
› Calculate the amount of solute or solution given the concentration and the other amount. (5.5)	Problems 59, 64, 65
› Explain how the concept of atom economy can be applied to pollution prevention and environmental protection.	Problems 73, 74
› Calculate the atom economy for chemical reactions.	Problems 72–76

REVIEW QUESTIONS

1. Define or illustrate each of the following.
   a. formula unit **b.** formula mass
   c. mole **d.** Avogadro's number
   e. molar mass **f.** molar volume (of a gas)
2. Explain the difference between the atomic mass of chlorine and the formula mass of chlorine gas.
3. What is Avogadro's hypothesis? How does it explain Gay-Lussac's law of combining volumes?
4. Referring to the law of conservation of mass, explain why we must work with balanced chemical equations.
5. Define or explain and illustrate the following terms.
   a. solution **b.** solvent
   c. solute **d.** aqueous solution
6. Define or explain and illustrate the following terms.
   a. concentrated solution **b.** dilute solution
   c. soluble **d.** insoluble

PROBLEMS

Interpreting Formulas

7. How many oxygen atoms does each of the following contain?
   a. $Al(H_2PO_4)_3$ **b.** $HOC_6H_4COOCH_3$
   c. $(BiO)_2SO_4$
8. How many carbon atoms does each of the following contain?
   a. $Fe_2(CO_3)_3$ **b.** $Al(CH_3COO)_3$
   c. $(CH_3)CCH(CH_3)_2$
9. How many atoms of each element (N, P, H, and O) does the notation $3\ (NH_4)_2HPO_4$ indicate?
10. How many atoms of each element (Fe, C, H, and O) does the notation $4\ Fe(HOOCCH_2COO)_3$ indicate?

Interpreting Chemical Equations

11. Consider the following equation. **(a)** Explain its meaning at the molecular level. **(b)** Interpret it in terms of moles. **(c)** State the mass relationships conveyed by the equation.
$$2\,H_2O_2 \longrightarrow 2\,H_2O + O_2$$
12. Express each chemical equation in terms of moles.
   a. $2\,Ca + O_2 \longrightarrow 2\,CaO$
   b. $CH_4 + 2\,O_2 \longrightarrow CO_2 + 2\,H_2O$

Balancing Chemical Equations

13. Balance the following equations.
    a. $Mg + O_2 \longrightarrow MgO$
    b. $C_3H_8 + O_2 \longrightarrow CO_2 + H_2O$
    c. $H_2 + Ta_2O_3 \longrightarrow Ta + H_2O$
14. Balance the following equations.
    a. $K + O_2 \longrightarrow K_2O_2$
    b. $FeCl_2 + Na_2SiO_3 \longrightarrow NaCl + FeSiO_3$
    c. $F_2 + AlCl_3 \longrightarrow AlF_3 + Cl_2$
15. Write balanced equations for the following processes.
    a. Nitrogen gas and oxygen gas react to form nitrogen oxide (NO).
    b. Ozone (O_3) decomposes into oxygen gas.
    c. Uranium(IV) oxide reacts with hydrogen fluoride (HF) to form uranium(IV) fluoride and water.
16. Write balanced equations for the following processes.
    a. Iron metal reacts with oxygen gas to form rust [iron(III) oxide].
    b. Calcium carbonate (the active ingredient in many antacids) reacts with stomach acid (HCl) to form calcium chloride, water, and carbon dioxide.
    c. Heptane (C_7H_{16}) burns in oxygen gas to form carbon dioxide and water.

Volume Relationships in Chemical Equations

17. Make a sketch similar to Figure 5.3 to show the reaction of hydrogen gas with oxygen gas to form steam [$H_2O(g)$] at 100 °C.
18. Make a sketch similar to Figure 5.3 to show that when hydrogen reacts with oxygen to form steam at 100 °C, each volume of gas—hydrogen, oxygen, or steam—contains the same number of molecules.
19. Consider the following equation, which represents the combustion (burning) of hexane (C_6H_{14}).

$$2\,C_6H_{14}(g) + 19\,O_2(g) \longrightarrow 12\,CO_2(g) + 14\,H_2O(g)$$

    a. What volume, in liters, of $CO_2(g)$ is formed when 20.6 L of $C_6H_{14}(g)$ is burned? Assume that both gases are measured under the same conditions.
    b. What volume, in milliliters, of $C_6H_{14}(g)$ has to burn to react with 29.0 mL $O_2(g)$? Assume that both gases are measured under the same conditions.
20. Consider the following equation, which represents the combustion of ammonia.

$$4\,NH_3(g) + 3\,O_2(g) \longrightarrow 2\,N_2(g) + 6\,H_2O(g)$$

    a. What volume, in liters, of $N_2(g)$ is formed when 125 L of $NH_3(g)$ is burned? Assume that both gases are measured under the same conditions.
    b. What volume, in liters, of $O_2(g)$ is required to form 36 L of $H_2O(g)$? Assume that both gases are measured under the same conditions.
21. Using the equation in Problem 19, determine the ratio of volume of $CO_2(g)$ formed to volume of $C_6H_{14}(g)$ that reacts, assuming that both gases are measured under the same conditions.
22. Using the equation in Problem 20, determine the ratio of volume of $H_2O(g)$ formed to volume of $NH_3(g)$ that reacts, assuming that both gases are measured under the same conditions.

Avogadro's Number

23. How many **(a)** sulfur *molecules* and how many **(b)** sulfur *atoms* are there in 1.00 mol S_8?
24. How many **(a)** magnesium ions and how many **(b)** nitride ions are there in 1.00 mol Mg_3N_2?
25. Choose one of the following to complete this statement correctly: One *mole* of bromine (Br_2) gas ________.
    a. has a mass of 79.9 g
    b. contains 6.02×10^{23} Br atoms
    c. contains 12.04×10^{23} Br atoms
    d. has a mass of 6.02×10^{23} g
26. **(a)** How many barium ions and how many nitrate ions are there in 1.00 mol $Ba(NO_3)_2$? **(b)** How many nitrogen atoms and how many oxygen atoms are there in 1.00 mol $Ba(NO_3)_2$?

Formula Masses and Molar Masses

You may round atomic masses to one decimal place.

27. Calculate the molar mass of each of the following compounds.
    a. $AgNO_3$
    b. $Mg(ClO)_2$
    c. $Zn(IO_4)_2$
    d. $CH_3(CH_2)_3COF$
28. Calculate the molar mass of each of the following compounds.
    a. Bi_2O_3
    b. $FeSO_4$
    c. $Ca(CH_3COO)_2$
    d. $(NH_4)_2Cr_2O_7$
29. Calculate the mass, in grams, of each of the following.
    a. 7.57 mol $BaSO_4$
    b. 0.0472 mol $CuCl_2$
    c. 0.250 mol $C_{12}H_{22}O_{11}$
30. Calculate the mass, in grams, of each of the following.
    a. 4.61 mol PCl_3
    b. 6.15 mol Cr_2O_3
    c. 0.158 mol IF_5
31. Calculate the amount, in moles, of each of the following.
    a. 6.63 g Sb_2S_3
    b. 19.1 g MoO_3
    c. 434 g $AlPO_4$
32. Calculate the amount, in moles, of each of the following.
    a. 16.3 g SF_6
    b. 25.4 g $Pb(C_2H_3O_2)_2$
    c. 15.6 g $CoCl_3$
33. Calculate the percent by mass of N in **(a)** $NaNO_3$ and **(b)** NH_4Cl.
34. Calculate the percent by mass of C, H, and O in glucose ($C_6H_{12}O_6$).

Mole and Mass Relationships in Chemical Equations

35. Consider the reaction for the combustion of butane (C_4H_{10}), a component of liquefied petroleum (LP) gas.

$$2\,C_4H_{10}(g) + 13\,O_2(g) \longrightarrow 8\,CO_2(g) + 10\,H_2O(g)$$

    a. How many moles of CO_2 are produced when 8.12 mol of butane are burned?
    b. How many moles of oxygen are required to burn 3.13 mol of butane?
36. Consider the reaction for the combustion of octane (C_8H_{18}).

$$2\,C_8H_{18} + 25\,O_2 \longrightarrow 16\,CO_2 + 18\,H_2O$$

    a. How many moles of H_2O are produced when 0.281 mol of octane is burned?
    b. How many moles of CO_2 are produced when 8.12 mol of oxygen reacts with octane?

37. What mass in grams **(a)** of ammonia can be made from 440 g H_2 and **(b)** of hydrogen is needed to react completely with 892 g N_2?

$$N_2 + H_2 \longrightarrow NH_3 \quad \text{(not balanced)}$$

38. Toluene (C_7H_8) and nitric acid (HNO_3) are used in the production of trinitrotoluene (TNT, $C_7H_5N_3O_6$), an explosive.

$$C_7H_8 + HNO_3 \longrightarrow C_7H_5N_3O_6 + H_2O \quad \text{(not balanced)}$$

What mass in grams **(a)** of nitric acid is required to react with 454 g C_7H_8 and **(b)** of TNT can be made from 829 g C_7H_8?

Molarity of Solutions

39. Calculate the molarity of each of the following solutions.
   a. 23.4 mol HCl in 10.0 L of solution
   b. 0.0875 mol Li_2CO_3 in 632 mL of solution

40. Calculate the molarity of each of the following solutions.
   a. 8.82 mol H_2SO_4 in 7.50 L of solution
   b. 1.22 mol C_2H_5OH in 96.3 mL of solution

41. What mass in grams of solute is needed to prepare **(a)** 3.50 L of 0.500 M NaOH and **(b)** 65.0 mL of 1.45 M $C_6H_{12}O_6$?

42. What mass in grams of solute is needed to prepare **(a)** 0.250 L of 0.167 M $K_2Cr_2O_7$ and **(b)** 625 mL of 0.0200 M $KMnO_4$?

43. What volume in liters of **(a)** 6.00 M NaOH contains 2.50 mol NaOH and **(b)** 0.0500 M KH_2AsO_4 contains 8.10 g KH_2AsO_4?

44. What volume in liters of **(a)** 0.250 M NaOH contains 1.05 mol NaOH and **(b)** 4.25 M $H_2C_2O_4$ contains 0.225 g $H_2C_2O_4$?

Percent Concentrations of Solutions

45. What is the percent by volume concentration of **(a)** 58.0 mL of water in 625 mL of an acetic acid–water solution and **(b)** 79.1 mL of methanol in 755 mL of a methanol–water solution?

46. What is the percent by volume concentration of **(a)** 35.0 mL of water in 725 mL of an ethanol–water solution and **(b)** 78.9 mL of acetone in 1550 mL of an acetone–water solution?

47. Describe how you would prepare 3375 g of an aqueous solution that is 8.2% NaCl by mass.

48. Describe how you would prepare 2.44 kg of an aqueous solution that is 16.3% KOH by mass.

49. Describe how you would prepare 2.00 L of an aqueous solution that is 2.00% acetic acid by volume.

50. Describe how you would prepare 500.0 mL of an aqueous solution that is 30.0% isopropyl alcohol by volume.

ADDITIONAL PROBLEMS

51. Both magnesium and aluminum react with hydrogen ions in aqueous solution to produce hydrogen. Why is it that only one of the following equations correctly describes the reaction?

$$Mg(s) + 2\,H^+(aq) \longrightarrow Mg^{2+}(aq) + H_2(g)$$
$$Al(s) + 2\,H^+(aq) \longrightarrow Al^{3+}(aq) + H_2(g)$$

52. Which of the following correctly represents the decomposition of potassium chlorate to produce potassium chloride and oxygen gas?
   a. $KClO_3(s) \longrightarrow KClO_3(s) + O_2(g) + O(g)$
   b. $2\,KClO_3(s) \longrightarrow 2\,KCl(s) + 3\,O_2(g)$
   c. $KClO_3(s) \longrightarrow KClO(s) + O_2(g)$
   d. $KClO_3(s) \longrightarrow KCl(s) + O_3(g)$

53. Write a balanced chemical equation to represent **(a)** the decomposition, by heating, of solid mercury(II) nitrate to produce pure liquid mercury, nitrogen dioxide gas, and oxygen gas, and **(b)** the reaction of aqueous sodium carbonate with aqueous hydrochloric acid (hydrogen chloride) to produce water, carbon dioxide gas, and aqueous sodium chloride.

54. Joseph Priestley discovered oxygen in 1774 by heating "red calx of mercury" [mercury(II) oxide]. The calx decomposed to its elements. The equation is

$$HgO \longrightarrow Hg + O_2 \quad \text{(not balanced)}$$

What mass of oxygen is produced by the decomposition of 1.08 g HgO?

55. Consider 1.00 mol $H_2(g)$, 2.00 mol He(g), and 0.50 mol $C_2H_2(g)$ at the same temperature and pressure. **(a)** Do the three samples have the same number of atoms? **(b)** Which sample has the greatest mass?

56. What mass in grams of the magnetic oxide of iron (Fe_3O_4) can be made from 24.0 g of pure iron and an excess of oxygen? The equation is

$$Fe + O_2 \longrightarrow Fe_3O_4 \quad \text{(not balanced)}$$

57. When heated above ~900 °C, limestone (calcium carbonate) decomposes to quicklime (calcium oxide), which is used to make cement, and carbon dioxide. What mass in grams of quicklime can be produced from 4.72×10^9 g of limestone?

58. Ammonia reacts with oxygen to produce nitric acid (HNO_3) and water. What mass of nitric acid, in grams, can be made from 971 g of ammonia?

59. Hydrogen peroxide solution sold in drugstores is 3.0% H_2O_2 by mass dissolved in water. How many moles of H_2O_2 are in a typical 16-fl. oz. bottle of this solution? (1 fl. oz. = 29.6 mL; density = 1.00 g/mL)

60. What is the mass percent of **(a)** NaOH in a solution of 4.12 g NaOH in 100.0 g of water and **(b)** ethanol in a solution of 5.00 mL of ethanol (density = 0.789 g/mL) in 50.0 g of water?

61. What is the volume percent of **(a)** ethanol in 625 mL of an ethanol–water solution that contains 58.0 mL of water and **(b)** acetone in 1.25 L of an acetone–water solution that contains 10.00 mL of acetone?

62. Laughing gas (dinitrogen monoxide, N_2O, also called nitrous oxide) can be made by very carefully heating ammonium nitrate. The other product is water.
   a. Write a balanced equation for the process.
   b. Draw the Lewis structure for N_2O.
   c. What mass in grams of N_2O can be made from 48.0 g of ammonium nitrate?

63. In Table 1.6 we listed some multiplicative prefixes used with SI base units. In the 1990s, some new prefixes were recommended:

   zetta- (Z, 10^{21}) *yotta-* (Y, 10^{24})
   zepto- (z, 10^{-21}) *yocto-* (y, 10^{-24})

   a. What is the mass of 1.00 ymol of uranium in yoctograms?
   b. How many atoms are in 1.00 zmol of uranium?

64. What volume of 0.0859 M oxalic acid contains 31.7 g of oxalic acid ($H_2C_2O_4$)?

65. In tests for intoxication, blood alcohol levels are expressed as percents by volume. A blood alcohol level of 0.080% by volume means 0.080 mL of ethanol per 100 mL of blood and is considered proof of intoxication. If a person's total blood volume is 5.0 L, what volume of alcohol in the blood gives a blood alcohol level of 0.165% by volume?

66. Homeopathic remedies are prepared using a process of dilution, starting with a substance that causes symptoms of the illness being treated. Some homeopaths use a scale (X) in which the substance is diluted by a factor of ten at each stage. For example, for a 6X remedy, the original substance is diluted tenfold six times, for a total dilution of 10^6. (Many homeopathic remedies are diluted far more than six times.)
   a. If the original substance is in the form of a 1.00 M solution, what would be the yoctomolar concentration of a 24X remedy? (Few starting solutions are 1 M; most are far less concentrated.)
   b. How many molecules of the original substance remain in 1.00 L of a 24X remedy?

67. Evaluate this statement: "One cup of water has more molecules than there are cups of water in all of Earth's oceans" (1 cup = 236 mL = 236 cm^3). For the volume of the oceans, see Problem 25, page 36.

68. If a Neanderthal excreted 500 mL of urine into the ocean 50,000 years ago, how many molecules in 500 mL of water you drink today are from that urine? Refer to Problem 67, and assume complete mixing of the waters of Earth over 50,000 years.

69. A truck carrying about 31,000 kg of sulfuric acid (H_2SO_4) is involved in an accident, spilling the acid. What mass of sodium bicarbonate ($NaHCO_3$) is needed to react with and neutralize the sulfuric acid? The products of the reaction are sodium sulfate (Na_2SO_4), water, and carbon dioxide.

70. Referring to Problem 69, determine the mass of sodium carbonate (Na_2CO_3) needed to neutralize the acid. (The products of the reaction are the same.)

71. How many moles of H_2O are in 1.00 L of water? (d = 1.00 g/mL)

72. Consider the following equation for the reaction of sodium azide that forms nitrogen gas in airbags. **(a)** What is the atom economy for the production of N_2? **(b)** What is the mass in grams of N_2 that is formed if 2.52 g of NaN_3 are reacted?

$$2\,NaN_3 \longrightarrow 2\,Na + 3\,N_2$$

73. Ethanol (C_2H_5OH) is a very important chemical. In addition to being widely used as an industrial solvent, a gasoline additive, and an alternative fuel, it is well-known as the alcohol in alcoholic beverages. A common name for ethanol is *grain alcohol* because it is formed by the fermentation of glucose ($C_6H_{12}O_6$) and other sugars in grains such as corn, wheat, and barley:

$$C_6H_{12}O_6 \longrightarrow C_2H_5OH + CO_2$$

The previous reaction has been carried out for many centuries and is one of the oldest manufacturing processes. In a more recent development, ethanol can be prepared by reacting ethylene (found in petroleum) with water:

$$C_2H_4 + H_2O \longrightarrow C_2H_5OH$$

   a. Write the *balanced* equation for each of the two reactions above.
   b. Calculate the %A.E. (for the product ethanol) for each of the two reactions.
   c. Explain how you can determine which reaction has the higher atom economy *without* doing the calculation in part (b) above.
   d. Is either method sustainable? Which one? Justify your answer.
   e. Given the results from parts (b) and (d) above, select one of the two methods as the best candidate overall for preparing ethanol. Justify your selection.

74. Formation of butene (C_4H_8) can be accomplished in several different ways. Two are shown below.

Reaction A:

$$C_4H_9Br + NaOH \longrightarrow C_4H_8 + H_2O + NaBr$$

Reaction B:

$$C_4H_6 + H_2 \longrightarrow C_4H_8$$

Which reaction has a higher atom economy?

75. Consider the following equation for the formation of carbon dioxide (CO_2), a known greenhouse gas, from the combustion of hydrocarbons.

$$C_5H_{12} + O_2 \longrightarrow CO_2 + H_2O \text{ (not balanced)}$$

   a. What is the percent atom economy based on carbon dioxide as the target product?
   b. How many grams of CO_2 form if 10.0 g C_5H_{12} is burned?
   c. What is the percent yield of the reaction if 25.4 g CO_2 are formed at the end of the reaction? (Hint: Use the information in the Atom Economy essay for this calculation.)

76. Balance each reaction and calculate the percent atom economy based on the underlined molecule as your desired product.
   a. $CuCl_2(aq) + Na_2CO_3(aq) \longrightarrow \underline{CuCO_3(s)} + NaCl(aq)$
   b. $NH_3(g) + O_2(g) \longrightarrow \underline{NO(g)} + H_2O(g)$
   c. $KMnO_4(aq) + KOH(aq) + KI(aq) \longrightarrow \underline{K_2MnO_4(aq)} + KIO_3(aq) + H_2O(l)$

 COLLABORATIVE GROUP PROJECTS

Prepare a PowerPoint, poster, or other presentation (as directed by your instructor) to share with the class.

1. Prepare a brief biographical report on Amedeo Avogadro.
2. In the view of many scientists, hydrogen holds great promise as a source of clean energy. A 2008 report by the U.S. National Research Council suggested that a government subsidy of roughly $4 billion per year through 2023 could make hydrogen cars competitive with petroleum-powered vehicles. Search the web to explore the proposals for using hydrogen as a fuel. Write a brief summary of what you find, and use an appropriate balanced equation to explain why hydrogen is considered a clean, renewable source. More discussion of hydrogen as a fuel is found in Chapter 15.

6 Gases, Liquids, Solids . . . and Intermolecular Forces

Learning Objectives

- Explain how the different properties of solids, liquids, and gases are related to the motion and spacing of atoms, molecules, or ions. (6.1)
- Identify some differences between ionic and molecular substances, and explain why these differences exist. (6.2)
- Classify forces between molecules as dipole–dipole forces, dispersion forces, or hydrogen bonds. (6.3)
- Explain why nonpolar solutes tend to dissolve in nonpolar solvents and polar and ionic solutes tend to dissolve in polar solvents. (6.4)
- List the five basic concepts of the kinetic–molecular theory of gases. (6.5)
- State the three simple gas laws, by name and mathematically. (6.6)
- Use any gas law to find the value of one variable if the other values are given. (6.6)
- State the ideal gas law, and use it to calculate one of the quantities if the others are given. (6.7)
- Describe how Green Chemistry Principle 3 must be considered in designing chemical reactions and processes.
- Identify the properties that make supercritical fluids applicable in greener chemical processes.

Have You Ever Wondered?

1. **Why does Silly Putty® have such strange properties?**
2. **What does "10W40" on a bottle of motor oil mean?**
3. **What is it that keeps oil and water from mixing?**
4. **Why doesn't creamy Italian dressing separate like ordinary Italian dressing does?**
5. **How cold can it possibly get, and how hot can it possibly get?**
6. **Why are we supposed to measure bicycle tire pressure when tires are cold?**

We introduced the three states of matter—gas, liquid, and solid—in Chapter 1. Water is the most familiar substance that we experience in all three states: as Earth's most common liquid, as a solid (ice), and as a gas (steam). Many other substances can exist in the three states, depending on conditions. An understanding of those conditions is important for our understanding of matter. The state that a substance exhibits depends on the physical properties of that substance, on the pressure, and especially on the temperature. When it is very cold, water exists as solid ice. When it is warmer, water is a liquid. At still higher temperatures, water boils and becomes steam.

Water is an unusual substance in a number of ways. It is the only common substance that exists in all three states—solid ice, liquid water, and gaseous steam—in Earth's biosphere. A small amount of solid water (left) can cool a relatively large amount of liquid water very quickly. Liquid water (center) is also a good cooling agent, and it dissolves many substances both ionic and covalent. Interestingly, the visible cloud often referred to as steam (top) is actually many microscopic droplets of liquid water; steam is an invisible gas. The properties mentioned here are largely due to the *intermolecular forces* that exist in water. We will learn about those forces in this chapter.

Chapter 4 described the forces called *chemical bonds* that bind atoms together within molecules. Chemical bonds are *intra*molecular forces that determine such molecular properties as geometry and polarity. Forces *between* molecules—*inter*molecular forces—determine the macroscopic physical properties of liquids and solids. Intermolecular forces are also related to the kinds of bonds found in substances. Figure 6.1 compares intermolecular and intramolecular forces. If there were no intermolecular attractive forces, there would be no liquids or solids—everything would be in a gaseous state.

The shape, size, and polarity of molecules determine how they interact with each other. The physical state of a material depends on the strength of the intermolecular forces that hold the molecules or ions together, relative to the thermal energy (temperature) that acts to separate them.

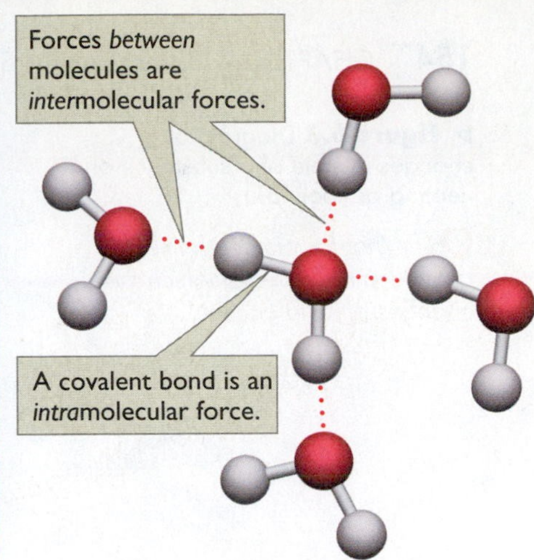
Forces *between* molecules are *inter*molecular forces.
A covalent bond is an *intra*molecular force.

▲ **Figure 6.1** Intramolecular and intermolecular forces. The gray "sticks" represent covalent bonds in water molecules—*intra*molecular forces, or pairs of shared electrons. The dotted red lines represent forces between water molecules—*inter*molecular forces.

6.1 Solids, Liquids, and Gases

Learning Objective › Explain how the different properties of solids, liquids, and gases are related to the motion and spacing of atoms, molecules, or ions.

Most solids are highly ordered assemblies of atoms, molecules, or ions in close contact with one another, as suggested by Figure 6.2(a). This makes it difficult to compress solids. The motion of these particles is primarily vibration. Table salt (sodium chloride) is a typical crystalline solid. In this solid, ionic bonds hold the Na^+ and Cl^- ions in position and maintain the orderly arrangement (look again at Figure 4.2).

In liquids, the particles are still in close contact, but they are randomly arranged and are freer to move about [Figure 6.2(b)]. Like solids, liquids are difficult to compress, but they are able to flow and to conform to the shape of their container. To get a better image of a liquid at the molecular level, think of a box of marbles being shaken continuously. The marbles move back and forth, rolling over one another. The particles of a liquid (like the marbles) are not held in place as rigidly as the particles in a solid are. Even so, there must be some force attracting the particles in a liquid to one another. Otherwise, they would not stay close to one another.

In gases, the particles are separated by relatively great distances and are moving quite rapidly in random directions [Figure 6.2(c)]. In this state, the atoms or molecules have no interactions with one another. We will look more closely at gases in Section 6.5.

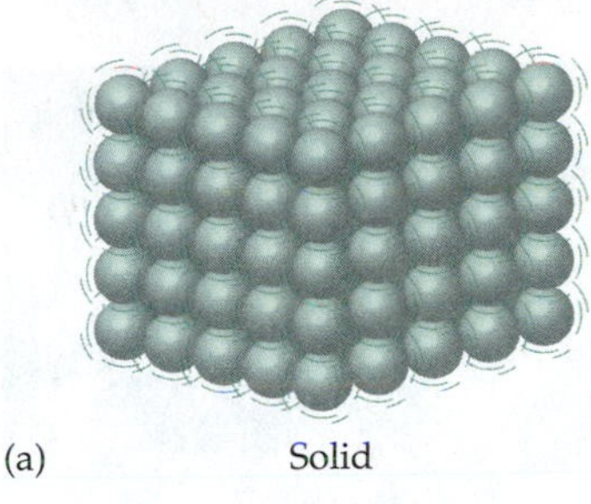

(a) Solid

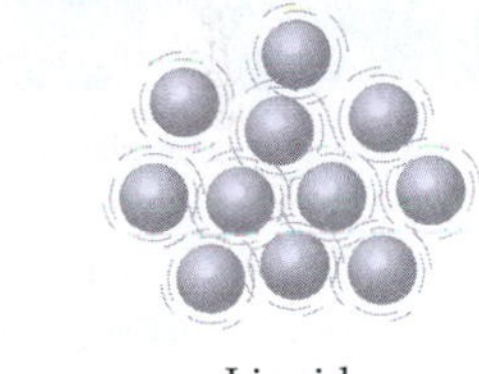

(b) Liquid

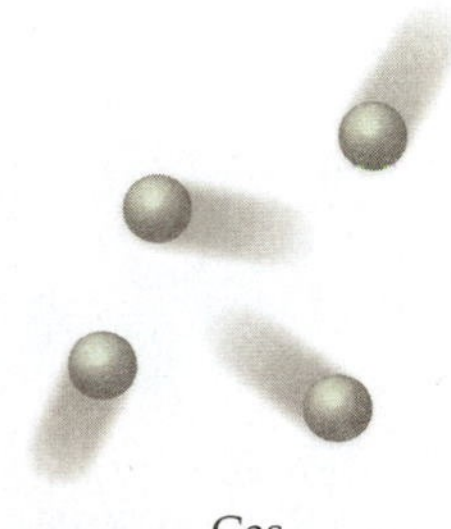

(c) Gas

▲ **Figure 6.2** Three states of matter. (a) Most solids have molecules (or atoms) that vibrate around fixed positions. (b) In liquids, the molecules are still close together but are free to move about like people in a crowded room. (c) Molecules of gases are widely spaced and move freely and randomly.

▲ Most solids are made up of highly ordered particles. Glass is an exception. The particles that make up glass (Chapter 12) are randomly arrayed.

1. Why does Silly Putty® have such strange properties? Although it appears to be a solid, Silly Putty® is actually a liquid—a very thick, slow-flowing (viscous) liquid.

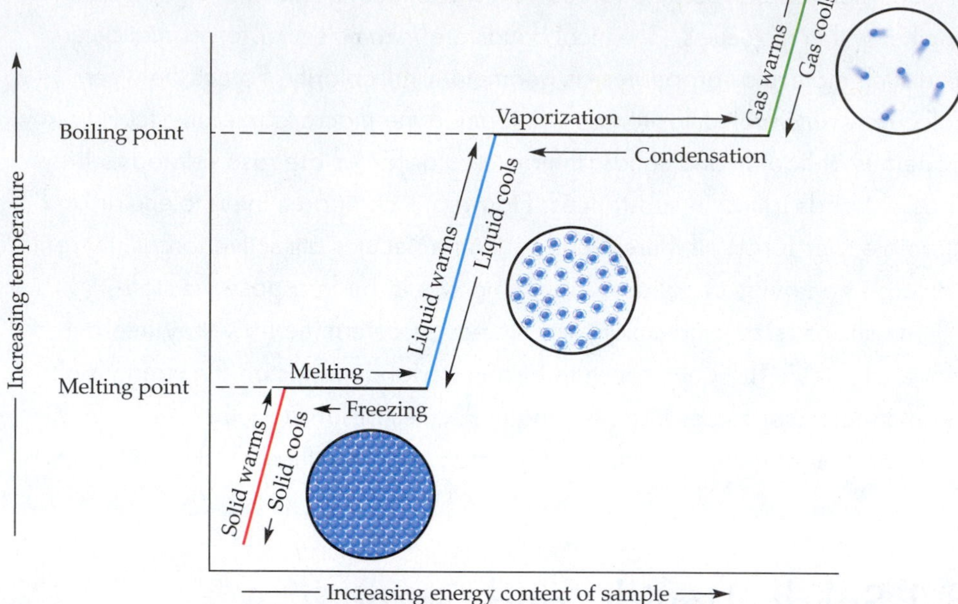

▶ **Figure 6.3** Diagram of changes in state of a substance on heating or cooling.

Q: *What factors determine the actual temperatures at which the changes of state occur?*

▲ The reverse of sublimation is *deposition*, a process that occurs on cold mornings. Water vapor deposits directly onto the grass as solid frost.

Most solids can be changed to liquids; that is, they can be *melted*. When a solid is heated, the thermal energy is absorbed by the particles of the solid. The energy causes the particles to vibrate more vigorously until, finally, the forces holding the particles in their regular arrangement are overcome. The solid becomes a liquid. The temperature at which this happens is the **melting point** of the solid. A high melting point indicates that the forces holding a solid together are very strong.

A liquid can change to a gas in a process called **vaporization**. Again, all that is needed to achieve this change is enough heat. Energy is absorbed by the liquid particles, which move faster and faster as a result. Finally, this increasingly violent motion overcomes the attractive forces holding the liquid particles close to one another and the particles fly apart. The liquid becomes a gas. The temperature at which this happens is the **boiling point** of the liquid.

Removing energy from the gas and slowing down the particles can reverse the sequence of changes. A gas changes to a liquid in a process called **condensation**; a liquid changes to a solid in a process called *freezing*. Figure 6.3 presents a diagram of the changes in state that occur as energy is added to or removed from a sample. Some substances go directly from the solid state to the gaseous state, a process called **sublimation**. For example, ice cubes left in a freezer for a long time shrink, and solid mothballs slowly disappear in a drawer or closet. In each case, the solid undergoes sublimation.

Self-Assessment Questions

1. Molecules are farthest apart in a(n)
   a. covalent solid **b.** gas **c.** ionic solid **d.** liquid
2. Liquids are
   a. difficult to compress and have no definite shape
   b. difficult to compress and have no definite volume
   c. easy to compress and have a definite shape
   d. easy to compress and have no definite volume
3. When a liquid changes into a gas, the process is called
   a. condensation **b.** fusion **c.** gasification **d.** vaporization
4. When a liquid changes into a solid, the process is called
   a. condensation **b.** freezing **c.** fusion **d.** melting
5. When a solid changes directly into a gas, the process is called
   a. evaporation **b.** fusion **c.** sublimation **d.** vaporization

Answers: 1, b; 2, a; 3, d; 4, b; 5, c

GREEN CHEMISTRY

Principles 3, 5

Doug Raynie, *South Dakota State University*

Supercritical Fluids

Many chemical reactions take place in solution (Section 5.5), and most chemical processes involve a separation of components at some stage. Water is an excellent solvent for many substances, but some substances do not dissolve in water under ordinary conditions. Chemists have traditionally used organic solvents such as benzene (C_6H_6), a cancer-causing aromatic hydrocarbon (Section 9.2), and methylene chloride (CH_2Cl_2), a toxic chlorinated hydrocarbon (Section 9.3), to dissolve nonpolar and slightly polar substances. Wouldn't it be nice to have a nontoxic, benign solvent that could be recycled readily?

Let's look again at the states of matter and changes of state (Section 6.1), particularly the change from liquid to gas. Have you ever used a pressure cooker, or tried to cook food while backpacking in the mountains? If you have, you've probably noticed that boiling point changes with pressure. In a pressure cooker, the increase in pressure lets us cook at higher temperatures. In the mountains, where the air pressure is lower, water boils at a lower temperature, so it takes longer to prepare a meal. This behavior is shown in the following graph called a *phase diagram*:

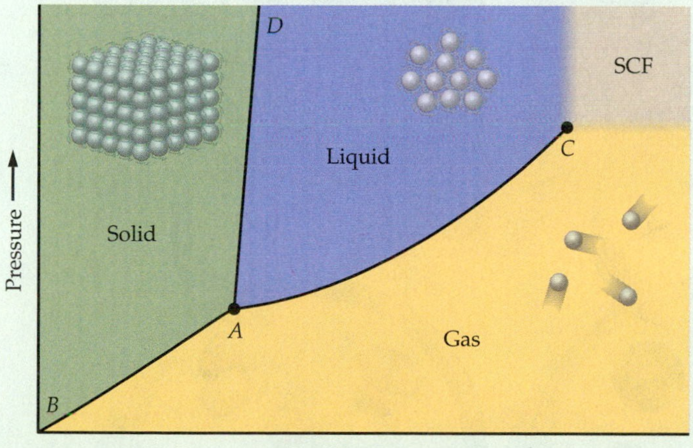

▲ A phase diagram shows the physical state of a material at given temperatures and pressures. As the temperature and pressure increase, the material shown in the graph changes from a solid to a liquid or gas. Above a certain temperature and pressure (the critical point *C*), the material is neither gas nor liquid but becomes a supercritical fluid.

The curve *AC* slopes upward, showing that the boiling point increases with increasing pressure. Notice that the line *AC* does not continue forever. Eventually, continued heating will take a substance to point *C*, called the *critical point*. Above the critical point, matter exists as neither a gas nor a liquid but as a kind of a hybrid called a **supercritical fluid**. We can think of supercritical fluids as having properties of both gases and liquids. Most importantly, they can dissolve things as liquids do, but they flow rapidly like gases. We can vary these properties to make the fluid more liquid-like or more gas-like by changing the temperature or pressure.

The most commonly used supercritical fluid is carbon dioxide ($scCO_2$), an inexpensive, convenient-to-use, nonflammable, and nontoxic substance. Carbon dioxide becomes a supercritical fluid at temperatures greater than 31 °C and pressures greater than 73 atm. As a solvent, carbon dioxide (nonpolar) is a complement to water (polar), giving us two environmentally friendly solvents with different properties and uses. Individually or combined, these supercritical fluids can dissolve a wide range of chemical compounds. Also, because they can flow like gases, supercritical fluids can often make processes occur more quickly.

Supercritical water and $scCO_2$ are "generally regarded as safe" by the U.S. Food and Drug Administration and are often used in the food industry. For example, coffee is sometimes decaffeinated using $scCO_2$ extraction. After the extraction, the $scCO_2$ is decompressed and returned to a gaseous state, leaving the caffeine behind. The gaseous CO_2 is cooled and compressed to return it to a liquid form to be used again. This process is much greener than the older one using toxic methylene chloride, a liquid that had to be removed from the coffee by distillation. In the green chemistry essay "Green Dry Cleaning" in Chapter 21, you will see that carbon dioxide can also be used to replace perchloroethylene (C_2Cl_4), another toxic chlorinated hydrocarbon long used in dry cleaning.

Flavors and fragrances are often isolated using $scCO_2$. In the cosmetics industry, oils such as palm oil or jojoba oil are isolated from their plant sources using $scCO_2$. Supercritical fluids are used to clean or degrease precision parts in electronic instruments. In more specialized cases, chemical reactions are carried out using supercritical fluid solvents. The main drawback to the use of supercritical fluids is that special equipment is needed to control the temperatures and high pressures required for these processes.

Nearly all chemical processes require the separation of one chemical from a mixture of others. Water and $scCO_2$ give us a pair of inexpensive and safe solvents that dissolve a wide range of chemical compounds—an excellent application of Green Chemistry Principle 5, which urges the use of safer reaction conditions and less toxic solvents.

▲ It DOES Matter!
A salt lamp has a lightbulb mounted in a large piece of sodium chloride. Some vendors claim that the heat from the lamp causes negative ions to be emitted from the salt. But ionic compounds like sodium chloride have extremely high melting and boiling points, far above the temperature of an ordinary lightbulb. No significant amount of ions can be produced from such a lamp, and there is no conclusive evidence that such ions would be beneficial anyway.

6.2 Comparing Ionic and Molecular Substances

Learning Objective › Identify some differences between ionic and molecular substances, and explain why these differences exist.

Recall that Figure 6.1 illustrates *intermolecular* forces. Ionic substances such as sodium chloride (recall Figure 4.2) are made of ions, not molecules, so "intermolecular forces" really doesn't apply to them. Nevertheless, there are attractive forces between ions, and we can compare them to the forces between molecules. First, let's consider some differences between ionic and molecular substances.

- Nearly all ionic compounds, such as NaCl, KBr, $CaCO_3$, and NH_4NO_3, are solids at room temperature. Some molecular substances are liquids or gases at room temperature, although many are solids. Ethane (CH_3CH_3), hydrogen sulfide (H_2S), and chlorine (Cl_2) are gases. Ethanol (CH_3CH_2OH), bromine (Br_2), and phosphorus trichloride (PCl_3) are liquids. Sulfur (S_8), glucose ($C_6H_{12}O_6$), and iodine (I_2) are solids.
- Ionic compounds generally have much higher melting points and boiling points than molecular compounds. High temperatures are necessary to overcome the strong ionic bonds (Section 4.3) in ionic compounds. Less energy is required to overcome the weak attractions between molecules (Section 6.3). For example, sodium chloride (NaCl) must be heated to 801 °C before it melts, but the molecular compound ethane (CH_3CH_3) melts at −184 °C.
- It generally takes ten to a hundred times as much energy to melt one mole of a typical ionic compound as it does to melt one mole of a typical molecular compound. To melt one mole of sodium chloride requires almost 30 kJ, while it takes only about 3 kJ to melt one mole of ethane.

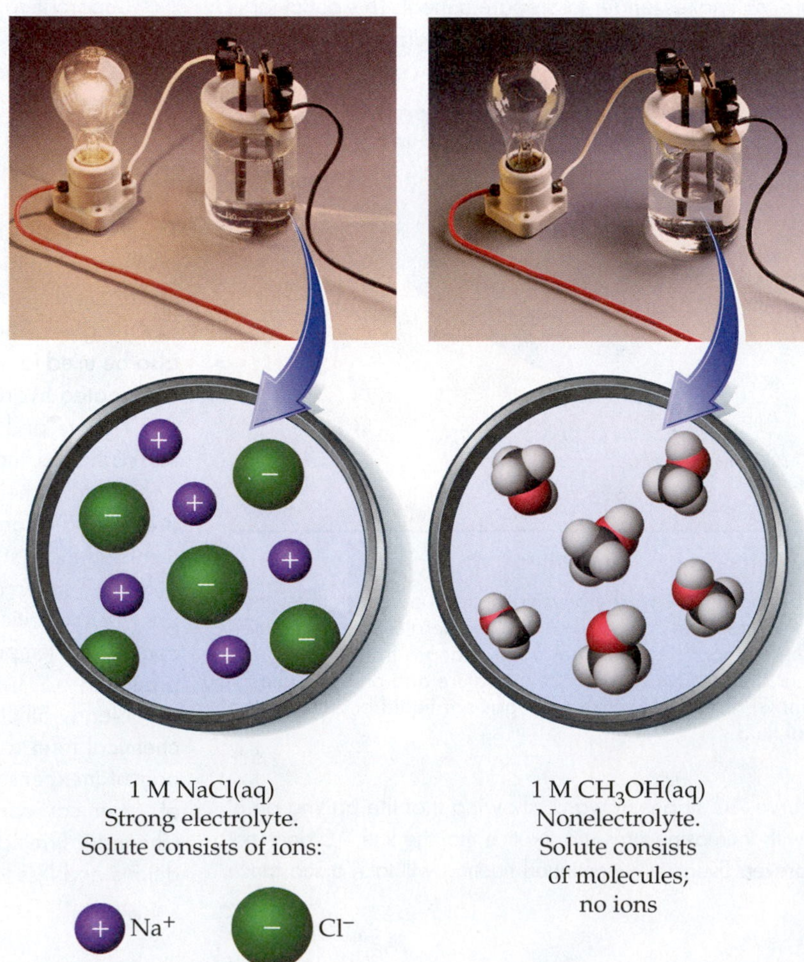

▶ Figure 6.4 (Left) The bulb lights because the solution of sodium chloride contains ions. The ions carry current, and the solution conducts electricity. (Right) A solution of methanol contains no ions and does not conduct electricity.

- Many familiar ionic compounds dissolve in water; those that do form solutions that conduct electricity. The dissociated ions carry the electric current through the solution. Most molecular compounds, even those that dissolve in water, do not dissociate into ions and thus do not form conducting solutions. A solution of sodium chloride conducts electricity, as seen in Figure 6.4, while a solution of methanol (CH_3OH) does not.
- As solids, most ionic compounds are crystalline, hard, and often quite brittle. Solid molecular compounds are usually much softer than ionic ones.

Next, we consider some other interactions that hold the particles of solids and liquids together.

Self-Assessment Questions

1. Which of the following is not composed of particles that exhibit intermolecular forces?
   a. Br_2 **b.** N_2 **c.** NaBr **d.** NBr_3
2. Which of the following solids is likely to require the greatest input of energy to melt?
   a. O_2 **b.** N_2O **c.** KBr **d.** Kr

Answers: 1, c; 2, c

6.3 Forces between Molecules

Learning Objective › Classify forces between molecules as dipole–dipole forces, dispersion forces, or hydrogen bonds.

As we have noted, many substances, such as water and carbon dioxide, do not consist of ions but instead are molecular compounds. Molecular compounds are characterized by covalent bonds—*intra*molecular forces. For example, in a hydrogen chloride molecule, a covalent bond holds the hydrogen and chlorine *atoms* together. But what makes one HCl molecule interact with another? In this section, we examine several types of *inter*molecular forces—forces *between* molecules.

Dipole–Dipole Forces

Recall that the hydrogen chloride molecule is a *dipole*: a molecule with a positive end and a negative end (see Figure 4.6, page 104). When oppositely charged ends of two dipoles are brought close enough together, they attract one another. In solid HCl, the molecules line up so that the positive end of one molecule attracts the negative end of neighboring molecules, as suggested by Figure 6.5(a). If we heat the solid sufficiently, the orderly arrangement is undone and the solid melts. In the liquid state, the oppositely charged dipoles in the liquid still attract one another, but more randomly, as shown in Figure 6.5(b). These **dipole–dipole forces** occur

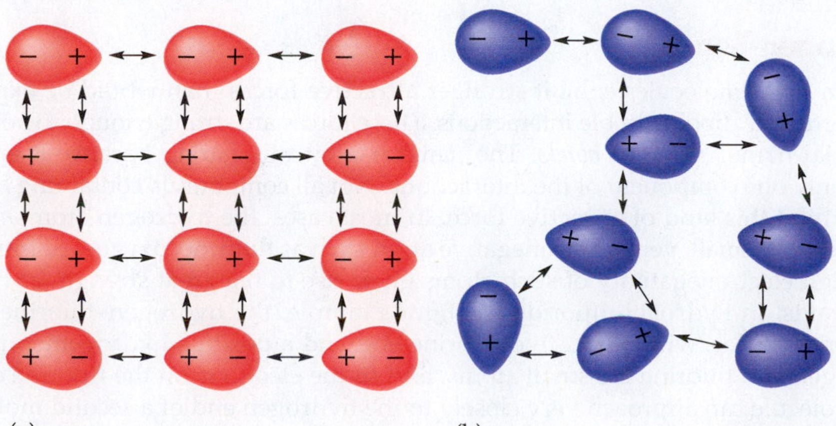

◀ **Figure 6.5** An idealized representation of dipole–dipole forces in (a) a solid and (b) a liquid. In a real liquid or solid, the interactions between particles are more complex.

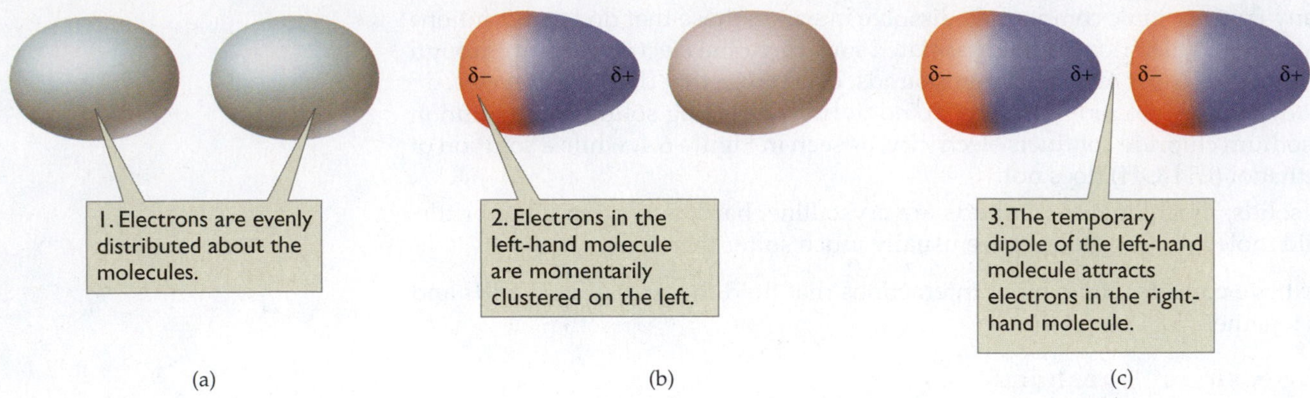

▲ **Figure 6.6** Mechanism underlying dispersion forces.

between any two polar molecules. Generally, these forces are much weaker than ionic bonds, but they are stronger than the forces between nonpolar molecules of comparable size. The more polar the molecules, the stronger are the dipole–dipole forces are.

Dispersion Forces

Dispersion forces are weak for small, nonpolar molecules such as H_2, N_2, and CH_4. For molecules of similar size and shape, intermolecular forces range in strength from dispersion forces (the weakest) to dipole–dipole forces to hydrogen bonds (the strongest).

It is easy enough to understand how ions or polar molecules maintain contact with one another. After all, opposite charges attract. But how can we explain the fact that *nonpolar* substances can exist in the liquid and solid states? Even hydrogen (H_2) can exist as a liquid or a solid if the temperature is low enough (its melting point is −259 °C). Some force must be holding nonpolar molecules close to one another in the liquid and solid states.

Figure 6.6(a) suggests that the electrons in a covalent bond are evenly distributed between the two atoms sharing the bond. Recall, however, that electrons are *not* stationary but move continuously. Within a covalent bond, electrons are moving around their respective nuclei. On *average*, the two electrons in a nonpolar bond are between and equidistant from the two nuclei. But, at any given instant, it is possible for the electrons in one molecule to be at one end of that molecule [Figure 6.6(b)], causing a temporary negative charge at that end. This causes electrons in an adjacent molecule to move toward the opposite end of that molecule, as in Figure 6.6(c). Thus, at this instant, an attractive force is created between the electron-rich end of one molecule and the electron-poor end of the next.

These momentary, usually weak, attractive forces between molecules are called **dispersion forces**. Because the electrons are in constant motion, dispersion forces can be thought of as dipole–dipole forces in which the dipoles are constantly shifting. To a large extent, dispersion forces determine the physical properties of nonpolar compounds. However, dispersion forces do exist between *any* two particles, whether polar, nonpolar, or ionic.

2. What does "10W40" on a bottle of motor oil mean? Oil must have the proper *viscosity* or thickness—which depends on the strength of its intermolecular forces—to lubricate an engine properly. High temperatures in the summer make the oil flow more easily, so a thicker oil (viscosity of 40) is needed. Lower temperatures require thinner oil (viscosity of 10). An oil labeled "10W40" has molecules with intermolecular forces that are about the same whether the oil is cold or hot, and such oil can be used in both summer and winter.

Hydrogen Bonds

Certain polar molecules exhibit stronger attractive forces than would be expected from ordinary dipole–dipole interactions. These forces are strong enough to be given a special name, *hydrogen bonds*. The name is a bit misleading because it emphasizes only one component of the interactions. Not all compounds containing hydrogen exhibit this kind of attractive force. In most cases, the hydrogen atom *must* be attached to a small, very electronegative atom such as fluorine, oxygen, or nitrogen. The high electronegativity of such atoms gives rise to the great strength of hydrogen bonds. In hydrogen fluoride (HF), for example, the hydrogen–fluorine bond is strongly polar, with a negative fluorine end and a positive hydrogen end. Both hydrogen and fluorine are small atoms, and so the electrons on the fluorine end of one molecule can approach very closely to the hydrogen end of a second molecule. This unusually strong interaction between molecules that contain hydrogen bound to a small electronegative atom is called a **hydrogen bond**. Hydrogen bonds are often explicitly represented by *dotted* lines (see Figure 6.7) to emphasize that their strength is much greater than that of other intermolecular forces.

Water has both an unusually high melting point (0 °C) and an unusually high boiling point (100 °C) for a compound with such small molecules. These abnormal values are attributed to the water molecules' ability to form hydrogen bonds. Remember, however, that during melting and boiling, only the hydrogen bonds *between water molecules* are overcome. The covalent bonds between the hydrogen atoms and the oxygen atom in each water molecule remain intact. No chemical change occurs when there is a change in state because covalent bonds are much stronger than hydrogen bonds.

The unique properties of water resulting from hydrogen bonding are discussed in Chapter 14. Hydrogen bonding also plays an important role in biological molecules. The three-dimensional structures of proteins and enzymes and the arrangement of DNA (Chapter 16) are dependent on the presence and strength of hydrogen bonds.

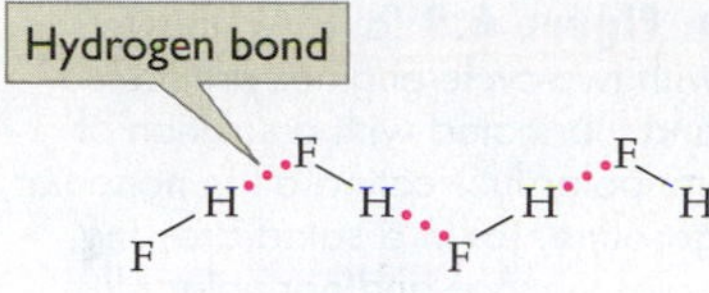

Hydrogen fluoride

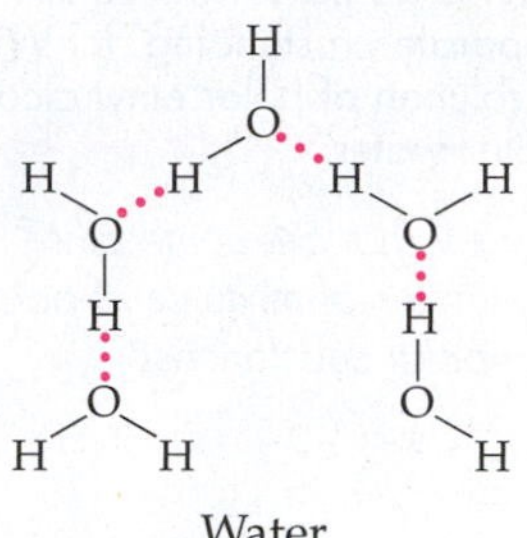

Water

▲ **Figure 6.7** Hydrogen bonding in hydrogen fluoride and in water. See also Figure 6.1.

Self-Assessment Questions

1. What intermolecular forces are most significant in accounting for the high boiling point of liquid water relative to other substances of similar molecular weight?
   a. dispersion forces **b.** dipolar attractions
   c. hydrogen bonds **d.** ionic bonds
2. Which one of the following interactions is the strongest?
   a. covalent bonds **b.** dipole–dipole forces **c.** dispersion forces **d.** hydrogen bonds
3. In ethanol (CH_3CH_2OH), the attractions between neighboring molecules are
   a. covalent bonds and dispersion forces only
   b. covalent bonds and hydrogen bonds only
   c. covalent bonds only
   d. hydrogen bonds and dispersion forces only
4. The molecules of liquid water in a beaker are held to each other by
   a. covalent bonds **b.** intramolecular forces
   c. intermolecular forces **d.** ionic bonds
5. Of CH_3OH, H_2, HF, and H_2O, which molecule(s) can form hydrogen bonds?
   a. H_2 only **b.** H_2O only
   c. CH_3OH, HF, and H_2O **d.** all four
6. Which one of the following molecules does *not* form hydrogen bonds?
   a. ammonia (NH_3) **b.** chloroform ($CHCl_3$)
   c. methyl alcohol (CH_3OH) **d.** ethylene glycol ($HOCH_2CH_2OH$)

Answers: 1, c; 2, a; 3, d; 4, c; 5, c; 6, b

6.4 Forces in Solutions

Learning Objective › Explain why nonpolar solutes tend to dissolve in nonpolar solvents and polar and ionic solutes tend to dissolve in polar solvents.

To complete our look at intermolecular forces, let's briefly examine the interactions that occur in solutions. A **solution** is an intimate, homogeneous mixture of two or more substances. Here *intimate* means that mixing occurs down to the level of individual ions and molecules, as suggested in Figure 6.8. For example, a sugar-in-water solution has separate sugar molecules randomly distributed among water molecules. *Homogeneous* means that all parts of the solution have the same distribution of components. A sugar solution is equally sweet at the top, bottom, and middle of the solution. The substance being dissolved, and usually present in a lesser amount, is called the **solute**. The substance doing the dissolving, and usually present in a greater amount, is the **solvent**. In a sugar-in-water solution, sugar is the solute and water is the solvent.

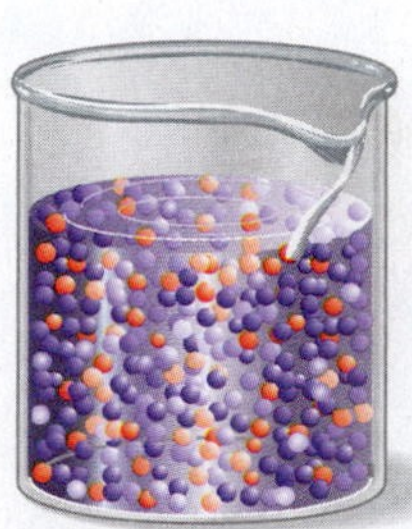

● = Solvent molecule
● = Solute molecule

▲ **Figure 6.8** In a solution, solute molecules (orange spheres) are randomly distributed among solvent molecules (purple spheres).

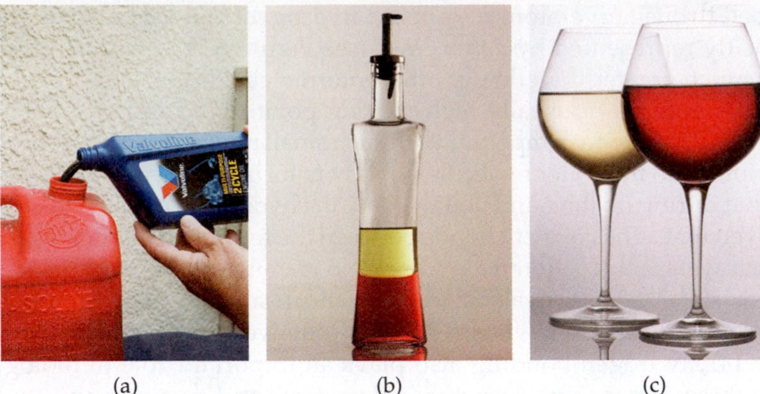

▶ **Figure 6.9** (a) Lawn mowers with two-cycle engines are fueled and lubricated with a solution of nonpolar lubricating oil in nonpolar gasoline. (b) In a salad dressing, polar vinegar and nonpolar olive oil are mixed. However, the two liquids do not form a solution and separate on standing. (c) Wine is a solution of polar ethyl alcohol in polar water.

Q: *What are some other examples of mixtures of polar and nonpolar substances?*

3. What is it that keeps oil and water from mixing? Oil molecules are nonpolar, and water molecules are very polar. The weak forces between oil and water molecule aren't strong enough to overcome the strong forces between the water molecules. Thus, oil and water don't mix.

4. Why doesn't creamy Italian dressing separate like ordinary Italian dressing does? Both kinds of dressings contain oil and vinegar. However, proteins (from egg yolk or other sources) are mixed into the creamy dressing. The protein molecules have both polar parts and nonpolar parts and keep tiny droplets of oil suspended in the vinegar.

Ordinarily, solutions form most readily when the substances involved have *similar* strengths of forces between their molecules (or atoms or ions). An old chemical adage is, "Like dissolves like." Nonpolar solutes dissolve best in nonpolar solvents. For example, oil and gasoline, both nonpolar, mix [Figure 6.9(a)], but oil and vinegar do not [Figure 6.9(b)]. Vinegar is mostly water, and the strong hydrogen bonds between water molecules do not allow nonpolar oil molecules (which have much weaker dispersion forces) to mix freely with them. On the other hand, both ethyl alcohol molecules and water molecules can form hydrogen bonds. Thus, ethyl alcohol readily dissolves in water [Figure 6.9(c)]. In general, a solute dissolves when attractive forces between it and the solvent overcome the attractive forces operating in the pure solute and in the pure solvent.

Why, then, does salt dissolve in water? Ionic solids are held together by strong ionic bonds. We have already seen that high temperatures are required to melt ionic solids and break these bonds. Yet if we simply place sodium chloride in water at room temperature, the salt dissolves. And when such a solid dissolves, its bonds *are* broken. The difference between the two processes is the difference between brute force and persuasion. In the melting process, we simply put in enough energy (as heat) to break the crystal down. In the dissolving process, we offer the ions an attractive alternative to their ionic interactions in the crystal.

When a salt crystal dissolves, water molecules first surround the crystal. The molecules that approach a negative ion align themselves so that the positive ends of their dipoles point toward the ion, as shown in Figure 6.10. The molecules that approach a positive ion align themselves so that the negative ends of their dipoles

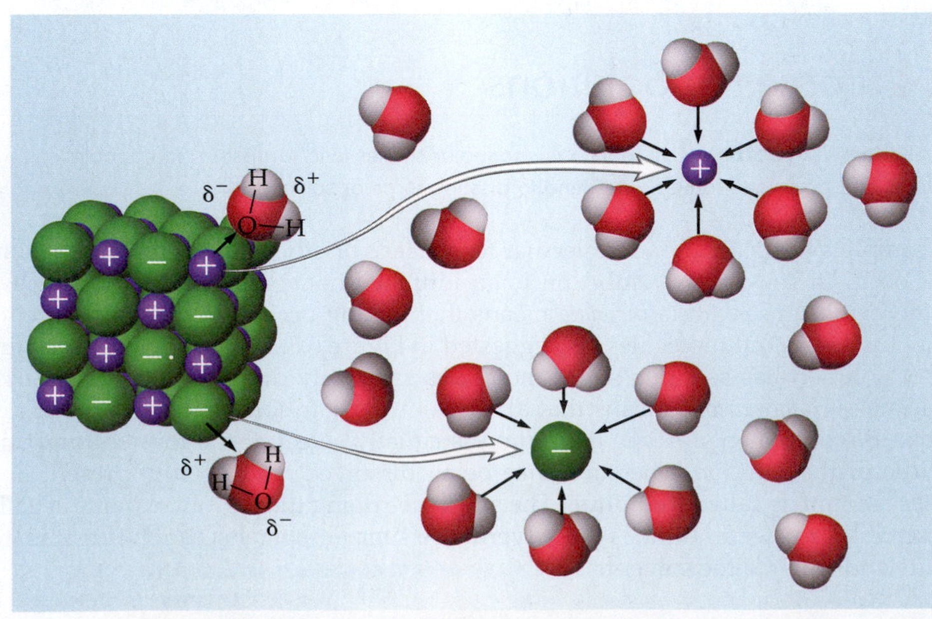

▶ **Figure 6.10** An ionic solid (sodium chloride) dissolving in a polar solvent (water). The hydrogen ends of the water molecules surround the negatively charged chloride ions, while the oxygen ends of the water molecules surround the positively charged sodium ions.

point toward the ion. Although the attraction between a dipole and an ion is not as strong as that between two ions, several water molecules surround each ion, and the many *ion–dipole* interactions overcome the ionic bonds.

In an ionic solid, the positive and negative ions are strongly bonded together in an orderly crystalline arrangement. In solution, cations and anions move about more or less independently, each surrounded by a cage of solvent molecules. Water—including the water in our bodies—is an excellent solvent for many ionic compounds. Water also dissolves many molecules that are polar covalent like itself. These solubility principles explain how nutrients reach the cells of our bodies (dissolved in blood, which is mostly water) and how many kinds of pollutants get into our water supplies.

Self-Assessment Questions

1. A solution is a mixture that is
   a. heterogeneous **b.** homogeneous **c.** homologous **d.** humectic
2. Which of the following pairs of substances is *least likely* to form a solution?
   a. an ionic compound in a nonpolar solvent
   b. an ionic compound in a polar solvent
   c. a nonpolar compound in a nonpolar solvent
   d. a polar compound in a polar solvent
3. A positive test for iodine is the purple color of a solution of I_2 in hexane (C_6H_{14}). What type of solute–solvent interaction is most important in a solution of nonpolar I_2 in nonpolar C_6H_{14}?
   a. dipole–dipole forces **b.** dispersion forces
   c. ion–dipole interactions **d.** hydrogen bonds
4. What type of solute–solvent interaction is most important in a solution of calcium chloride ($CaCl_2$) in water?
   a. dipole–dipole forces **b.** ion–dipole interactions
   c. ion–dispersion forces **d.** ion–hydrogen bonds
5. What type of solute–solvent interaction is most important in a solution of acetic acid (CH_3COOH) in water?
   a. dipole–dipole forces **b.** dipole–hydrogen bonds
   c. hydrogen bonds **d.** ion–hydrogen bonds
6. Which of the following solutes will dissolve in octane (C_8H_{18}), a component of gasoline?
   a. $CH_3(CH_2)_4CH_3$ **b.** $CaCl_2$
   c. KCl **d.** MgO

Answers: 1, b; 2, a; 3, b; 4, b; 5, c; 6, a

6.5 Gases: The Kinetic–Molecular Theory

Learning Objective › List the five basic concepts of the kinetic–molecular theory of gases.

At the macroscopic level, gases may seem more difficult to understand than liquids and solids—perhaps because most gases are invisible, while we can see and feel liquids and solids. However, at the microscopic level, gases are more readily treated mathematically. Gas molecules are so far apart that intermolecular forces can be ignored. In liquids and solids, the intermolecular forces are stronger, although they vary depending on the type of molecules and the distance between them. This variation complicates any theoretical treatment.

Experiments with gases were instrumental in developing the concepts of Avogadro's number and of molar ratios in reactions. Let's look at the behavior of gases more closely, using a model known as the **kinetic–molecular theory** (Figure 6.11). There are five basic concepts of this theory.

1. Particles of a gas (usually *molecules*, but *atoms* in the case of noble gases) are in rapid, constant motion and move in straight lines.
2. The particles of a gas are tiny compared with the distances between them.

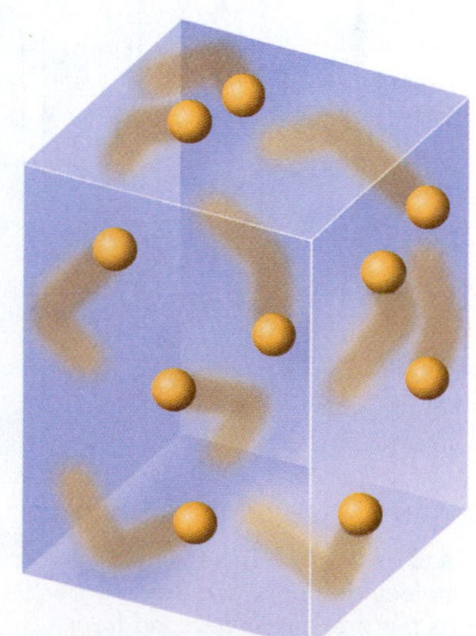

▲ **Figure 6.11** According to the kinetic–molecular theory, particles (molecules or atoms) of a gas are in constant, random motion. They move in straight lines and undergo collisions with each other and with the walls of the container.

3. Because the particles of a gas are so far apart, there is very little attraction between them.
4. Particles of a gas collide with one another. Energy is *conserved* in these collisions; energy lost by one particle is gained by the other.
5. Temperature is a measure of the average kinetic energy (energy of motion) of the gas particles.

Section 6.3 described how intermolecular forces hold molecules together in solids and liquids. In gases, the particles are separated by relatively great distances and are moving about randomly. Although these particles can collide, they seldom interact.

Self-Assessment Questions

1. Which of the following is *not* a concept of the kinetic–molecular theory of gases?
   - **a.** Particles of a gas are in constant chaotic motion.
   - **b.** The pressure and volume of a gas are inversely related.
   - **c.** Temperature is a measure of the average kinetic energy of the gas particles.
   - **d.** The particles are very small compared to the distances between them.
2. According to the kinetic–molecular theory of gases, a gas particle
   - **a.** will collide with another gas particle with no loss of kinetic energy for either
   - **b.** follows a well-defined pathway
   - **c.** is tiny compared to the volume occupied by the gas
   - **d.** repels another gas particle when the two come close together
3. In collisions between gas particles, the total energy
   - **a.** decreases slightly
   - **b.** decreases considerably
   - **c.** increases slightly
   - **d.** remains the same

Answers: 1, b; 2, c; 3, d

6.6 The Simple Gas Laws

Learning Objectives › State the three simple gas laws, by name and mathematically. › Use any gas law to find the value of one variable if the other values are given.

The behavior of gases can be described by mathematical relationships called *gas laws*. These equations use four variables to specify properties of a sample of gas: its amount in moles (n), its volume (V), its temperature (T), and its pressure (P). These variables are related through simple laws that show how one of the variables (for example, V) changes as a second variable (for example, P) changes and the other two (for example, n and T) remain constant.

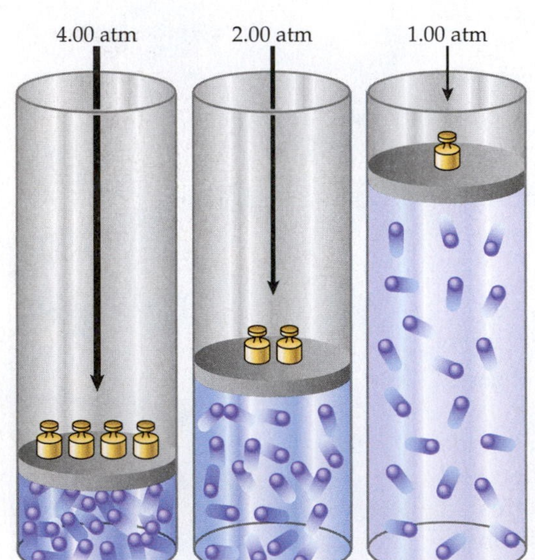

▲ **Figure 6.12** The kinetic–molecular theory and Boyle's law. As the pressure is reduced from 4.00 atm to 2.00 atm and then to 1.00 atm, the volume of the gas doubles and then doubles again.

Q: *What would happen to the volume of the gas if the pressure were changed to 0.500 atm?*

Boyle's Law: Pressure and Volume

The first gas law was discovered by Robert Boyle in 1662. It describes the relationship between the pressure and the volume of a gas. **Boyle's law** states that *for a given amount of gas at a constant temperature, the volume of the gas varies inversely with its pressure*. That is, when the pressure in a closed container of gas increases, the volume decreases; when the pressure decreases, the volume increases.

A bicycle pump illustrates Boyle's law. When you push down on the plunger, you decrease the volume of the air in the pump. The pressure of the air increases, and the higher-pressure air flows into the bicycle tire.

Think of gases as pictured by the kinetic–molecular theory. A gas exerts a particular pressure because its molecules bounce against the container walls with a certain frequency and speed. If the volume of the container is increased while the amount of gas remains fixed, the number of molecules per unit volume decreases (Figure 6.12). The frequency with which molecules strike a unit area of the container

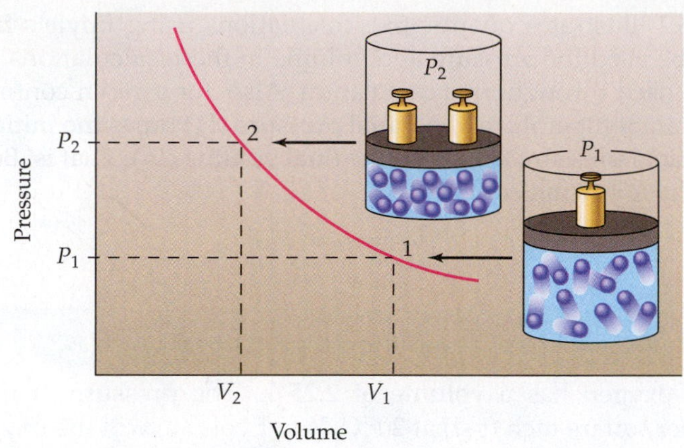

◀ **Figure 6.13** A graphic representation of Boyle's law. As the pressure is increased, the volume of a gas decreases. When the pressure is doubled ($P_2 = 2 \times P_1$), the volume of the gas decreases to one-half of its original value ($V_2 = \frac{1}{2} \times V_1$). The pressure–volume product is a constant ($PV = a$).

Q: *What would happen to the volume of the gas if the pressure were quadrupled?*

walls decreases, and the gas pressure decreases. Thus, as the volume of a gas is increased, its pressure decreases.

Mathematically, for a given amount of gas at a constant temperature, Boyle's law is written

$$V \propto \frac{1}{P}$$

where the symbol $\propto$ means "is proportional to." This relationship can be changed to an equation by inserting a proportionality constant, a.

$$V = \frac{a}{P}$$

Multiplying both sides of the equation by P, we get

$$PV = a \quad \text{(at constant temperature and amount of gas)}$$

Another way to state Boyle's law, then, is that for a given amount of gas at a constant temperature, the product of the pressure and the volume is a constant. This is an elegant and precise way of summarizing a lot of experimental data. If the product $P \times V$ is constant, then, when V increases, P must decrease, and vice versa. This relationship is illustrated in Figure 6.13 by a pressure–volume graph.

Boyle's law has a number of practical applications, which are perhaps best introduced through some examples. In Example 6.1, we see how to estimate an answer. Sometimes an estimate is all we need. Even when we need a quantitative answer, however, an estimate helps us determine whether or not the answer we get is reasonable.

Example 6.1 Boyle's Law: Pressure–Volume Relationships

A gas is enclosed in a cylinder fitted with a piston. The volume of the gas is 2.00 L at 0.524 atm. The piston is moved to increase the pressure to 5.15 atm. Which of the following is a reasonable value for the volume of the gas at the greater pressure?

0.20 L 0.40 L 1.00 L 16.0 L

Solution

The pressure increase from 0.524 atm to 5.15 atm is almost tenfold. The volume should drop to about one-tenth of the initial value. Thus, we estimate a volume of 0.20 L. (The calculated value is 0.203 L.)

■ EXERCISE 6.1

Argon gas is enclosed in a 10.2-L tank at 1208 mmHg (*mmHg* is a pressure unit: 760 mmHg = 1 atm). Which of the following is a reasonable value for the pressure when the argon is transferred to a 30.0-L tank?

300 mmHg 400 mmHg 3600 mmHg 12,000 mmHg

Example 6.2 illustrates quantitative calculations using Boyle's law. Note that any units can be used for pressure and volume in these calculations as long as the same units are used throughout a calculation. Also, for a given confined sample of a gas at a constant temperature, the initial pressure (P_1) times the initial volume (V_1) is equal to the final pressure (P_2) times the final volume (V_2). That is, Boyle's law can be written as the following equation.

$$P_1V_1 = a = P_2V_2$$

Example 6.2 Boyle's Law: Pressure–Volume Relationships

A cylinder of oxygen has a volume of 2.25 L. The pressure in the cylinder is 1470 pounds per square inch (psi) at 20 °C. What volume will the oxygen occupy at standard atmospheric pressure (14.7 psi), assuming no temperature change?

Solution

We find it helpful to first separate the initial and final conditions.

Initial	Final	Change
$P_1 = 1470$ psi	$P_2 = 14.7$ psi	↓
$V_1 = 2.25$ L	$V_2 = ?$	↑

The pressure goes down; therefore, the volume goes up.

Next, we solve the equation $P_1V_1 = P_2V_2$ for the desired volume or pressure. In this case, we solve for V_2. Finally, we substitute the given values for P_1, V_1, and P_2.

$$V_2 = \frac{P_1V_1}{P_2}$$

$$V_2 = \frac{1470 \cancel{\text{psi}} \times 2.25 \text{ L}}{14.7 \cancel{\text{psi}}} = 225 \text{ L}$$

Because the final pressure (14.7 psi) is *less than* the initial pressure (1470 psi), we expect the final volume (225 L) to be *larger than* the original volume (2.25 L), and we see that it is.

■ EXERCISE 6.2A

A sample of air occupies 73.3 mL at 98.7 atm and 0 °C. What volume will the air occupy at 4.02 atm and 0 °C?

■ EXERCISE 6.2B

A sample of helium occupies 535 mL at 988 mmHg and 25 °C. If the sample is transferred to a 1.05-L flask at 25 °C, what will the gas pressure in the flask be?

Charles's Law: Temperature and Volume

In 1787, the French physicist Jacques Charles (1746–1823), a pioneer hot-air balloonist, studied the relationship between volume and temperature of gases. He found that when a fixed mass of gas is cooled at constant pressure, its volume decreases. When the gas is heated, its volume increases. Temperature and volume vary directly; that is, they rise or fall together. But this relationship is a bit more complex. If a quantity of gas that occupies 1.00 L is heated from 100 °C to 200 °C at constant pressure, the volume does not double but increases only to about 1.27 L. The relationship between temperature and volume is not as simple as it may seem at first.

For most measurements and quantities, "zero" means "none." A measured pressure of 0 atm means no measureable pressure, and it is not possible to have a lower pressure than 0 atm. On the other hand, zero degrees Celsius (0 °C) merely signifies the freezing point of water. Temperatures below 0 °C are often encountered. Decreasing the temperature of 1 L of a gas from 20 °C to 0 °C does not cause the volume to decrease to zero. Instead, the volume decreases only to about 0.92 L.

5. How cold can it possibly get, and how hot can it possibly get? At 0 K (absolute zero, −273.15 °C), molecular motion would stop. Because molecules cannot move any slower than "standing still," no lower temperature is possible. Theoretically, atoms can move almost as fast as the speed of light, so there is also an upper temperature limit; that limit is so high, however, that temperature ceases to have meaning.

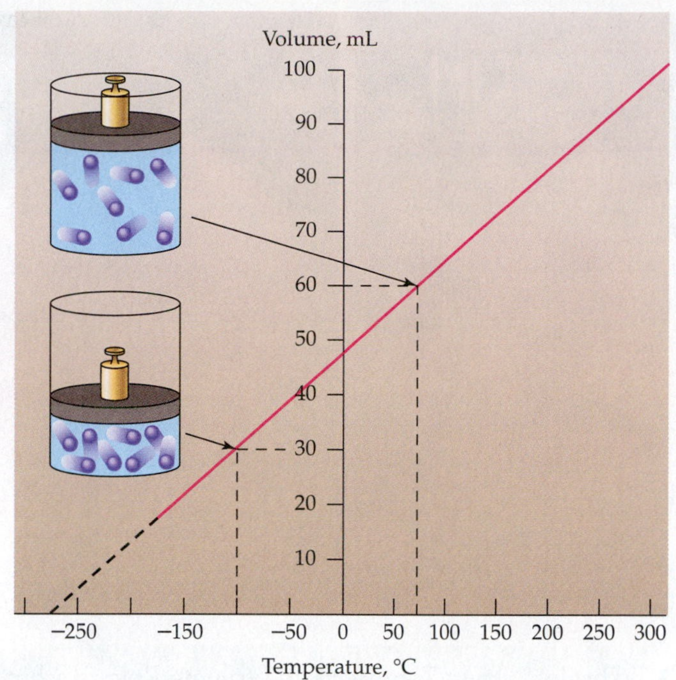

▲ **Figure 6.14** Charles's law relates gas volume to temperature at constant pressure. In the case shown, when the gas is at about 70 °C, its volume is 60 mL. As the temperature is lowered from about 70 °C to −100 °C, the volume drops to 30.0 mL. The volume continues to fall as the temperature is lowered. The extrapolated (dashed) line intersects the temperature axis (corresponding to a volume of zero) at about −273 °C.

Q: *What would be the approximate volume of the gas at a temperature of 150 °C?*

Charles noted that for each degree Celsius that the temperature rises, the volume of a gas increases by $\frac{1}{273}$ of its volume at 0 °C. A plot of volume against temperature is a straight line (Figure 6.14). We can extrapolate (extend) the line to the temperature at which the volume of the gas should become zero. This temperature is −273.15 °C. In 1848, William Thomson (Lord Kelvin) made this temperature the zero point on an absolute temperature scale now called the Kelvin scale. As noted in Chapter 1, the unit on this temperature scale is the kelvin (K).

A modern statement of **Charles's law** is that *the volume of a fixed amount of a gas at a constant pressure is directly proportional to its absolute temperature.* Mathematically, this relationship is expressed as

$$V = bT \quad \text{or} \quad \frac{V}{T} = b$$

where b is a proportionality constant. To keep V/T at a constant value, when the temperature increases, the volume must also increase. When the temperature decreases, the volume must decrease accordingly (Figure 6.15).

With a given sample of trapped gas at a constant pressure, the initial volume (V_1) divided by the initial absolute temperature (T_1) is equal to the final volume (V_2) divided by the final absolute temperature (T_2). We can therefore use the following equation to solve problems involving Charles's law.

$$\frac{V_1}{T_1} = \frac{V_2}{T_2}$$

The kinetic–molecular model readily explains the relationship between gas volume and temperature. When we heat a gas, the gas molecules absorb energy and move faster. These speedier molecules strike the walls of the container harder and more often. For the pressure to stay the same, the volume of the container must increase so that the increased molecular motion will be distributed over a greater space.

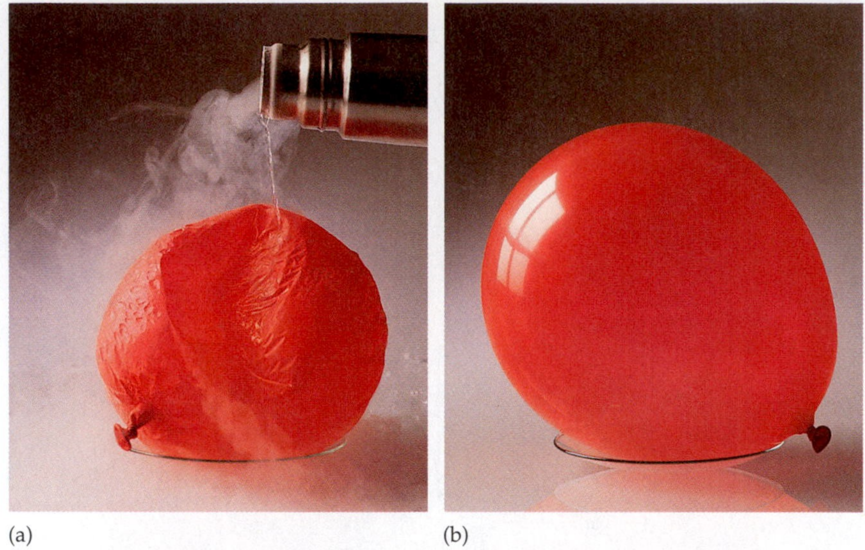
(a) (b)

▶ **Figure 6.15** A dramatic illustration of Charles's law. (a) Liquid nitrogen (boiling point, −196 °C) cools the balloon and its contents to a temperature far below room temperature. (b) As the balloon warms back to room temperature, the volume of air increases proportionately (about fourfold).

Example 6.3 Charles's Law: Temperature–Volume Relationship

In a room at 27 °C, a balloon has a volume of 2.00 L. What would its volume be **(a)** in a sauna, where the temperature is 47 °C, and **(b)** outdoors, where the temperature is −23 °C? Assume that there is no change in pressure in either case.

Solution

First, and most important, we convert all temperatures to the Kelvin scale:

$$T(\text{K}) = t\,(°\text{C}) + 273$$

The initial temperature (T_1) in each case is 27 + 273 = 300 K, and the final temperatures are **(a)** 47 + 273 = 320 K and **(b)** −23 + 273 = 250 K.

a. We start by separating the initial from the final condition.

Initial	Final	Change
$T_1 = 300$ K	$T_2 = 320$ K	⇑
$V_1 = 2.00$ L	$V_2 = ?$	⇑

Solving the equation

$$\frac{V_1}{T_1} = \frac{V_2}{T_2}$$

for V_2, we have

$$V_2 = \frac{V_1 T_2}{T_1}$$

Substituting the known values gives

$$V_2 = \frac{2.00\ \text{L} \times 320\ \cancel{\text{K}}}{300\ \cancel{\text{K}}} = 2.13\ \text{L}$$

As expected, because the temperature increases, the volume must also increase.

b. We have the same initial conditions as in **(a)** but different final conditions.

Initial	Final	Change
$T_1 = 300$ K	$T_2 = 250$ K	⇓
$V_1 = 2.00$ L	$V_2 = ?$	⇓

Again, using Charles's law, we solve the equation for V_2 and substitute the known quantities.

$$V_2 = \frac{V_1 T_2}{T_1}$$

$$V_2 = \frac{2.00\text{ L} \times 250\text{ K}}{300\text{ K}} = 1.67\text{ L}$$

As expected, the volume decreases because the temperature decreases.

■ EXERCISE 6.3A

A sample of ethane gas occupies a volume of 16.8 L at 25 °C. What volume will this sample occupy at 109 °C? (Assume no change in pressure.)

■ EXERCISE 6.3B

At what Celsius temperature will the initial volume of ethane in Exercise 6.3A occupy 0.750 L? (Assume no change in pressure.)

Molar Volume

As Section 5.2 described, Amedeo Avogadro proposed a hypothesis to explain the volume ratios in which gases combine during chemical reactions. His hypothesis states that equal numbers of molecules of different gases at the same temperature and pressure occupy equal volumes. Thus, Avogadro's hypothesis relates an amount of gas (numbers of molecules, or moles) to the gas volume when temperature and pressure remain constant. We call the simple gas law implied by this relationship **Avogadro's law**: *At a fixed temperature and pressure, the volume of a gas is directly proportional to the amount of gas (that is, to the number of moles of gas,* n, *or to the number of molecules of gas).* If we double the number of moles of gas at a fixed temperature and pressure, the volume of the gas doubles. Mathematically, we can state Avogadro's law as

$$V \propto n \quad \text{or} \quad V = cn \quad (\text{where } c \text{ is a constant})$$

A mole of gas contains Avogadro's number of molecules (or atoms if it is a noble gas). Furthermore, a gas sample consisting of Avogadro's number of molecules occupies the same volume (at a given temperature and pressure) regardless of the size or mass of the individual molecules. The volume occupied by 1 mole of gas is the **molar volume** of a gas.

Because the volume of a gas is altered by changes in temperature or pressure, a particular set of conditions has been chosen as the standard set for reference purposes. Standard pressure is 1 atmosphere (atm), which is the normal pressure of the air at sea level. Standard temperature is 0 °C, which is the freezing point of water. A mole of any gas at **standard temperature and pressure (STP)** occupies a volume of about 22.4 L, slightly more than a five-gallon water bottle (Figure 6.16). This is known as the *standard molar volume* of a gas. At a temperature of 0 °C and 1 atm pressure, a 22.4-L container holds one mole (28.0 g) of N_2, one mole (32.0 g) of O_2, one mole (44.0 g) of CO_2, and so on.

We can readily calculate the density (g/L) of a gas at STP. We begin with the molar mass of the gas (g/mol) and use the conversion factor 1 mol gas = 22.4 L. Because the conversion factor can be inverted, we can also use it to calculate molar mass from density.

▲ **Figure 6.16** An "empty" bottle from an office water cooler is not really empty. It holds five gallons of air, slightly less than 22.4 L— the volume of one mole of a gas at STP.

Q: *About how many C_2H_6 molecules would the bottle hold at STP?*

Example 6.4 Density of a Gas at STP

Calculate the density of **(a)** nitrogen gas and **(b)** methane (CH_4) gas, both at STP.

Solution

a. The molar mass of N_2 gas is 28.0 g/mol. We multiply by the conversion factor 1 mol N_2 = 22.4 L, arranged to cancel units of *moles*.

$$\frac{28.0\text{ g }N_2}{1\text{ }\cancel{\text{mol }N_2}} \times \frac{1\text{ }\cancel{\text{mol }N_2}}{22.4\text{ L }N_2} = 1.25\text{ g/L}$$

b. The molar mass of CH_4 gas is (1×12.0) g/mol + (4×1.01) g/mol = 16.0 g/mol. Again, we use the conversion factor 1 mol CH_4 = 22.4 L.

$$\frac{16.0\text{ g }CH_4}{1\text{ }\cancel{\text{mol }CH_4}} \times \frac{1\text{ }\cancel{\text{mol }CH_4}}{22.4\text{ L }CH_4} = 0.714\text{ g/L}$$

■ EXERCISE 6.4A

Calculate the density of xenon gas at STP.

■ EXERCISE 6.4B

Estimate the density of air at STP (assume that air is 78% N_2 and 22% O_2), and compare this value to the value you calculated for xenon in Exercise 6.4A.

Self-Assessment Questions

1. Gas pressure is caused by
- **a.** gas molecules colliding with each other
- **b.** gas molecules colliding with vessel walls
- **c.** gas molecules condensing to form a liquid
- **d.** measurement with a barometer

2. Boyle's law states that the pressure of a gas is inversely proportional to its
- **a.** amount
- **b.** mass
- **c.** temperature
- **d.** volume

3. A gas occupies 6.00 L at 2.00 atm pressure. At what pressure would the volume be 1.50 L if the temperature remains constant?
- **a.** 0.500 atm
- **b.** 8.00 atm
- **c.** 9.00 atm
- **d.** 12.00 atm

4. When the temperature is changed at constant pressure, the volume of a gas is halved. How is the final temperature related to the initial temperature?
- **a.** The Celsius temperature is doubled.
- **b.** The Celsius temperature is halved.
- **c.** The Kelvin temperature is doubled.
- **d.** The Kelvin temperature is halved.

5. One 1.00-L flask (Flask A) contains NO gas, and another 1.00-L flask (Flask B) contains NO_2 gas, both at STP. Flask A contains
- **a.** less mass and fewer particles than Flask B
- **b.** less mass but the same number of particles as Flask B
- **c.** less mass but more particles than Flask B
- **d.** more mass and more particles than Flask B

6. How many moles are there in 5.60 L of a gas at STP?
a. 0.250 mol **b.** 0.500 mol **c.** 4.00 mol **d.** 125 mol

Answers: 1, b; 2, d; 3, b; 4, d; 5, b; 6, a

6.7 The Ideal Gas Law

Learning Objective › State the ideal gas law, and use it to calculate one of the quantities if the others are given.

Boyle's law, Charles's law, and Avogadro's law are useful when two variables of four (P, V, n, and T) can be held constant. Often, however, both the temperature and the pressure change at the same time. In such cases, the simple gas laws can be incorporated into a single relationship called the **combined gas law**. Mathematically, this law is written as

$$\frac{PV}{T} = k \quad \text{or} \quad PV = kT$$

where k is a constant. For comparing the same sample of gas under two different sets of conditions, the combined gas law can be written as

$$\frac{P_1V_1}{T_1} = \frac{P_2V_2}{T_2}$$

Because the amount of gas, n, may change as well, incorporating this variable gives an expression called the **ideal gas law**, which involves all four variables.

$$\frac{PV}{nT} = R \quad \text{or} \quad PV = nRT$$

In this equation, R is a constant (called the *gas constant*), which can be calculated from the fact that 1 mole of gas occupies 22.4 L at 273 K (0 °C) and 1 atm (Section 6.6). If P is in atmospheres, V in liters, and T in kelvins, then R has a value of

$$0.0821 \, \frac{\text{L} \cdot \text{atm}}{\text{mol} \cdot \text{K}}$$

The ideal gas equation can be used to calculate the value of any of the four variables—P, V, n, or T—if the other three values are known.

6. Why is it recommended that bicycle tire pressure be measured when tires are cold? Tire pressure is measured when the tires are cold because a tire has nearly constant volume. According to the combined gas law, if the temperature increases (by friction from the road), the pressure increases, too. If the tire pressure were adjusted right after a long, hard bike ride, the tires might be soft and underpressurized the next morning.

Example 6.5 Combined Gas Law

A balloon used for underwater salvage is inflated to 50.0 L at a depth of 200 ft, where the pressure is 6.89 atm and the temperature is 3 °C. The balloon rises to the surface (22 °C and 0.988 atm). What is the new volume of the balloon?

Solution

We start by solving the combined gas law equation for V_2.

$$\frac{P_1V_1}{T_1} = \frac{P_2V_2}{T_2}$$

$$V_2 = \frac{P_1V_1T_2}{T_1P_2}$$

We have $T_1 = 3 + 273 = 276$ K, and $T_2 = 22.0 + 273 = 295$ K.

$$V_2 = \frac{6.89 \, \text{atm} \times 50.0 \, \text{L} \times 295 \, \text{K}}{276 \, \text{K} \times 0.988 \, \text{atm}} = 373 \, \text{L}$$

■ EXERCISE 6.5

What will be the final volume of a 425-mL sample of a gas initially at 22.0 °C and 760 mmHg pressure when the temperature is changed to 30.0 °C and the pressure to 360 mmHg?

Example 6.6 Ideal Gas Law

Use the ideal gas law to calculate (**a**) the volume occupied by 1.00 mol N_2 gas at 244 K and 1.00 atm pressure and (**b**) the pressure exerted by 0.500 mol O_2 gas in a 15.0-L container at 303 K.

Solution

a. We solve the ideal gas equation for V and substitute the known quantities.

$$V = \frac{nRT}{P}$$

$$V = \frac{1.00\ \cancel{\text{mol}}}{1.00\ \cancel{\text{atm}}} \times \frac{0.0821\ \text{L}\cdot\cancel{\text{atm}}}{\cancel{\text{mol}}\cdot\cancel{\text{K}}} \times 244\ \cancel{\text{K}} = 20.0\ \text{L}$$

b. Here we solve the ideal gas equation for P and substitute the known quantities.

$$P = \frac{nRT}{V}$$

$$P = \frac{0.500\ \cancel{\text{mol}}}{15.0\ \cancel{\text{L}}} \times \frac{0.0821\ \cancel{\text{L}}\cdot\text{atm}}{\cancel{\text{mol}}\cdot\cancel{\text{K}}} \times 303\ \cancel{\text{K}} = 0.829\ \text{atm}$$

■ EXERCISE 6.6A

Determine (**a**) the pressure exerted by 0.0450 mol O_2 gas in a 22.0-L container at 313 K and (**b**) the volume occupied by 0.400 mol N_2 gas at 298 K and 0.980 atm.

■ EXERCISE 6.6B

Determine the volume occupied by 132 g N_2 gas at 25 °C and 1.03 atm.

Self-Assessment Questions

1. In the ideal gas equation, $PV = nRT$, the variable n stands for
a. a constant
b. the number of atoms
c. the number of moles
d. the principal quantum number

2. At STP, 1.00 mole of an ideal gas occupies 22.4 L. What volume does 1.00 mole of an ideal gas occupy at 20 °C and 1.00 atm?
a. 20.9 L **b.** 22.4 L **c.** 24.0 L **d.** 448 L

3. The molar volume of an ideal gas at 2.00 atm and 546 K is
a. 5.60 L **b.** 22.4 L **c.** 44.8 L **d.** 89.6 L

Answers: 1, c; 2, c; 3, b

CRITICAL THINKING EXERCISES

Apply knowledge that you have gained in this chapter and one or more of the FLaReS principles (Chapter 1) to evaluate the following statements or claims.

6.1 Some tire stores claim that filling your car tires with pure, dry nitrogen is much better than using plain air. They make the following claims: (1) The pressure inside N_2-filled tires does not rise or fall with temperature changes. (2) Nitrogen leaks out of tires much more slowly than air because the N_2 molecules are bigger. (3) Nitrogen is not very reactive, and moisture and O_2 in air cause corrosion that shortens tire life by 25–30%.

6.2 A researcher claims to have discovered why the gecko can walk on walls and ceilings. His claim is that the lizard's feet have many microscopic hair-like protrusions that get close enough to the wall or ceiling surface to allow intermolecular forces to "take over" and hold the gecko to the surface.

6.3 A microbrewery claims to have prepared "hydrogen beer." This beer is reportedly "carbonated" with H_2 gas instead of CO_2 gas. A chemist at the brewery claims that the H_2 gas molecules engage in hydrogen bonding with the water molecules in the beer, so that more gas can dissolve in the beer.

6.4 A student in an advanced chemistry course has been assigned to determine the density of the vapor from an unknown liquid. She claims that the density is 0.053 g/L.

SUMMARY

Section 6.1—When a substance is melted or vaporized, the forces that hold its particles (molecules, atoms, or ions) close to one another are overcome. Several properties are related to the strengths of those forces. The **melting point** of a solid is the temperature at which the forces holding the particles together in a regular arrangement are overcome. The reverse of the melting process, a liquid changing to a solid, is called *freezing*. **Vaporization** is the conversion of a liquid to a gas; the reverse process is called **condensation**. The temperature at which a substance vaporizes is called its **boiling point**. Some substances undergo **sublimation**, a conversion directly from the solid to the gaseous state.

Section 6.2—Ionic solids have very strong forces holding the ions to one another, so most ionic compounds have higher melting points and higher boiling points than molecular compounds.

Section 6.3—**Dipole–dipole forces** are due to the attraction of the positive end of one dipole for the negative end of another dipole. Nonpolar molecules also have forces between them. These **dispersion forces** result from electron motions within molecules, which cause tiny, short-lived dipoles. Dispersion forces are generally weak. An especially strong type of dipolar force occurs when the positive end of a dipole is a hydrogen atom attached to F, O, or N and the negative end is the F, O, or N atom. Such a force is called a **hydrogen bond**.

Section 6.4—A **solution** is a homogeneous mixture of two (or more) substances. The substance that is dissolved is called the **solute**, and the dissolving substance is called the **solvent**. Nonpolar solutes dissolve in nonpolar solvents. Polar and ionic solutes dissolve in polar solvents.

Section 6.5—The behavior of gases is explained using **kinetic–molecular theory**, which describes gas particles: (1) They move rapidly and constantly and in straight lines; (2) they are far apart; (3) there is little attraction between them; (4) when they collide, energy is conserved; (5) temperature is a measure of their average kinetic energy.

Section 6.6—**Boyle's law** says that the volume of a fixed amount of a gas varies inversely with pressure at constant temperature, or $P_1V_1 = P_2V_2$. **Charles's law** says that the volume of a fixed amount of a gas varies directly with absolute (Kelvin) temperature, or $V_1/T_1 = V_2/T_2$. **Avogadro's law** states that at constant temperature and pressure the volume of a gas is directly proportional to the number of moles of gas, $V = cn$. The **molar volume** of any gas is the volume occupied by 1 mole of the gas. At 0 °C and 1 atm, known as **standard temperature and pressure (STP)**, the molar volume is 22.4 L for any gas. We can use that molar volume to convert from moles of gas to volume, and vice versa.

Section 6.7—The simple gas laws can be incorporated into a single relationship called the **combined gas law**. The **ideal gas law** shows the relationship among pressure (P), volume (V), number of moles (n), and absolute temperature (T): $PV = nRT$. When P is in atmospheres, V is in liters, n is moles of gas, and T is in kelvins, the value of the constant R is 0.0821 liter · atm/(mole · K).

Green chemistry While we are familiar with gases, liquids, and solids, a fourth phase of matter, **supercritical fluid**, exists at higher temperatures and pressures. Supercritical fluids have solubility properties similar to liquids, yet they flow like gases. The most common of these, $scCO_2$, is considered an environmentally friendly solvent and is replacing more toxic solvents in laboratories and industrial processes.

Learning Objectives

› Explain how the different properties of solids, liquids, and gases are related to the motion and spacing of atoms, molecules, or ions. (6.1)	Problems 1, 2, 4, 6
› Identify some differences between ionic and molecular substances, and explain why these differences exist. (6.2)	Problems 10–12
› Classify forces between molecules as dipole–dipole forces, dispersion forces, or hydrogen bonds. (6.3)	Problems 3, 7–10
› Explain why nonpolar solutes tend to dissolve in nonpolar solvents and polar and ionic solutes tend to dissolve in polar solvents. (6.4)	Problems 11, 12
› List the five basic concepts of the kinetic–molecular theory of gases. (6.5)	Problem 38
› State the three simple gas laws, by name and mathematically. (6.6)	Problem 38
› Use any gas law to find the value of one variable if the other values are given. (6.6)	Problems 5, 13–26
› State the ideal gas law, and use it to calculate one of the quantities if the others are given. (6.7)	Problems 27–34
› Describe how Green Chemistry Principle 3 must be considered in designing chemical reactions and processes.	Problems 49–51
› Identify the properties that make supercritical fluids applicable in greener chemical processes.	Problems 49, 50

REVIEW QUESTIONS

1. In what ways are liquids and solids similar? In what ways are they different?
2. Define each of the following terms.
   a. melting   b. vaporization
   c. condensation   d. freezing
3. List four types of interactions between the particles of a substance in the liquid and solid states. Give an example of each type.
4. In which process is energy absorbed by the substance undergoing the change of state?
   a. melting or freezing
   b. condensation or vaporization
5. In the combined gas law, is the volume of a gas directly proportional or inversely proportional to the pressure? Is the volume directly or inversely proportional to the absolute temperature?
6. Label each arrow with the correct term from Question 2 that identifies the process.

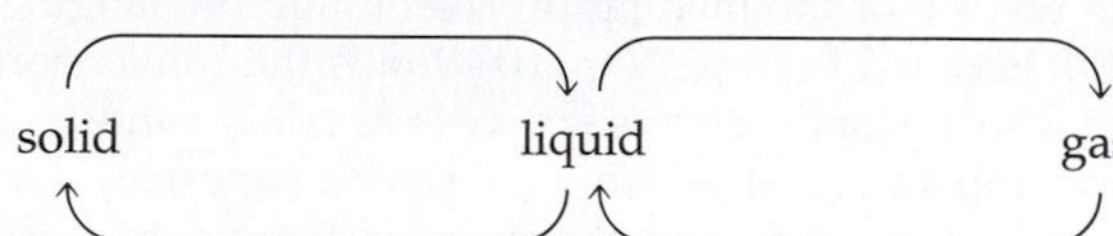

PROBLEMS

Intermolecular Forces

7. For which of the following would hydrogen bonding be an important intermolecular force?

```
a.  H—S          b.      H
       |                 |
       H            H—C—N—H
                      |  |
                      H  H

c.     H         d.      H
       |                 |
    H—C—F           H—C—O
       |                 |  |
       H                 H  H

e.  H  H
    |  |
 H—C—C—H
    |  |
    H  H
```

8. In which of the following are dispersion forces the only type of intermolecular force: N_2, NH_3, NCl_3?
9. In which of the following substances are dipole–dipole forces an important intermolecular force: Br_2, HBr, NaBr?
10. Which of the following have ionic bonds: N_2, NBr_3, NaBr?
11. Hexane (C_6H_{14}) is a nonpolar solvent. Would you expect KNO_3 to dissolve in hexane? Explain.
12. Which of the following would you expect to dissolve in water and which in carbon tetrachloride (CCl_4)?
    a. NaCl   b. C_5H_{12}
    c. C_8H_{18} d. Li_2CO_3

Boyle's Law

13. A sample of helium occupies 1820 mL at 719 mmHg. Assume that the temperature is held constant and determine **(a)** the volume of the helium at 752 mmHg and **(b)** the pressure, in mmHg, if the volume is changed to 345 mL.
14. A decompression chamber used by deep-sea divers has a volume of 10.1 m^3 and operates at an internal pressure of 4.25 atm. What volume, in cubic meters, would the air in the chamber occupy if it were at 1.00 atm pressure, assuming no temperature change?
15. Oxygen used in respiratory therapy is stored at room temperature under a pressure of 150 atm in a gas cylinder with a volume of 60.0 L.
    a. What volume would the oxygen occupy at 0.925 atm? Assume no temperature change.
    b. If the oxygen flow to the patient is adjusted to 6.00 L/min at room temperature and 0.925 atm, how long will the tank of gas last?
16. The pressure within a 4.50-L balloon is 1.10 atm. If the volume of the balloon increases to 9.95 L, what will the final pressure within the balloon be if the temperature does not change?

Charles's Law

17. A balloon is filled with helium. Its volume is 5.90 L at 26 °C. What will its volume be at 78 °C, assuming no pressure change?
18. A gas at a temperature of 100 °C occupies a volume of 154 mL. What will the volume be at 10 °C, assuming no change in pressure?
19. A sample of gas at STP is to be heated at constant pressure until its volume triples. What will the final gas temperature be?
20. A 567-mL sample of a gas at 305 °C and 1.20 atm is cooled at constant pressure until its volume becomes 425 mL. What is the final gas temperature?

Molar Volume and Gas Densities

21. What is the volume of each of the following samples of gas at STP?
    a. 1.00 mol Kr   b. 1.75 mol H_2
    c. 0.225 mol C_2H_4

22. What is the mass in grams of one molar volume of each of the gases in Problem 21?

23. Calculate the density, in grams per liter, of radon (Rn) gas at STP.

24. Calculate the density, in grams per liter, of carbon dioxide (CO_2) gas at STP.

25. Calculate the molar mass of **(a)** a gas that has a density of 2.12 g/L at STP and **(b)** an unknown liquid, whose vapor has a density of 2.97 g/L at STP.

26. Calculate the molar mass of **(a)** a gas that has a density of 1.98 g/L at STP and **(b)** an unknown liquid for which 3.33 L of its vapor at STP weighs 10.88 g.

The Ideal Gas Law

27. Will the volume of a fixed amount of a gas increase, decrease, or remain unchanged with
    a. an increase in pressure at constant temperature?
    b. a decrease in temperature at constant pressure?
    c. a decrease in pressure coupled with an increase in temperature?

28. Will the pressure of a fixed amount of a gas increase, decrease, or remain unchanged with
    a. an increase in temperature at constant volume?
    b. a decrease in volume at constant temperature?
    c. an increase in temperature coupled with a decrease in volume?

29. According to the kinetic–molecular theory, **(a)** what change in temperature occurs if the particles of a gas begin to move more slowly, on average, and **(b)** what change in pressure occurs when the particles of a gas strike the walls of the container less often?

30. For each of the following, indicate whether a given gas will have the same or different densities in the two containers. If the densities are different, in which container is the density greater?
    a. Containers A and B have the same volume and are at the same temperature, but the gas in A is at a higher pressure.
    b. Containers A and B are at the same pressure and temperature, but the volume of A is greater than that of B.
    c. Containers A and B are at the same pressure and volume, but the gas in A is at a higher temperature.

31. Calculate **(a)** the volume, in liters, of 0.00600 mol of a gas at 31 °C and 0.870 atm and **(b)** the pressure, in atmospheres, of 0.0108 mol $CH_4(g)$ in a 0.265-L flask at 37 °C.

32. Calculate (a) the volume, in liters, of 1.12 mol $H_2S(g)$ at 62 °C and 1.38 atm and (b) the pressure, in atmospheres, of 4.64 mol CO(g) in a 3.96-L tank at 29 °C.

33. How many moles of Kr(g) are there in 0.555 L of the gas at 0.918 atm and 25 °C?

34. How many grams of CO(g) are there in 74.5 mL of the gas at 0.933 atm and 30 °C?

ADDITIONAL PROBLEMS

35. What mass of He(g) will occupy the same volume at STP as 0.75 mol H_2 at STP? (Hint: It is not necessary to find the volume of the H_2 at STP.)

36. How many liters of hydrogen gas (at STP) are produced from the electrolysis of 1.00 L $H_2O(l)$? (Hint: 1.00 L H_2O weighs 1.00 kg.)

37. Which of the following will *not* result in an increase in the volume of a gas?
    a. an increase in temperature
    b. an increase in pressure
    c. a decrease in temperature
    d. a threefold increase in pressure together with a twofold reduction in Kelvin temperature

38. What are the five basic postulates of kinetic-molecular theory? Which postulate best explains why a gas can be compressed?

39. Which of the following gases has the greatest density at STP? Explain how this question may be answered *without* calculating the densities.
    a. BF_3 b. SO_3
    c. OF_2 d. PF_3

40. Choose the answer that correctly completes the statement: At 0 °C and 0.500 atm, 4.48 L $NH_3(g)$ **(a)** contains 0.20 mol NH_3; **(b)** has a mass of 3.40 g; **(c)** contains 6.02×10^{22} molecules; **(d)** contains 0.40 mol NH_3

41. Look again at Figure 6.15. If the balloon has a volume of a 1.50 L at 20 °C, what will its final volume be in part (a), assuming that the air in the balloon reaches the temperature of the liquid nitrogen? You may ignore the stretching forces in the rubber.

42. Butane (C_4H_{10}), a gas at room temperature, is compressed to a liquid and used as a fuel in cigarette lighters and camping stoves. If the 5.00 mL of liquid butane ($d = 0.601$ g/mL at 20 °C) in a lighter vaporizes, about what volume will the gas occupy at STP?

43. Three 2.00-L flasks, labeled X, Y, and Z, each at 758 mmHg and 21 °C, contain neon (Flask X), argon (Flask Y), and krypton (Flask Z). **(a)** Which flask holds the most atoms of gas? **(b)** In which flask does the gas have the greatest density? **(c)** If Flask X is heated and Flask Y is cooled, which of the flasks will have the highest pressure? **(d)** If the temperature of Flask X is lowered and that of Flask Z is raised, which of the three flasks will contain the largest number of moles of gas?

44. A 14.4-g sample of an unknown gas has a volume of 8.00 L at 760 mmHg and 25 °C. What is the molar mass of the gas?

45. Another simple gas law, sometimes called *Amontons's law*, states that pressure of a fixed amount of gas in a constant volume is proportional to its Kelvin temperature. Use this relationship to answer the following question. If a

basketball is inflated to an internal pressure of 1.32 atm at 25 °C and then taken outside, where the temperature is 10 °C, what will be the final pressure in the ball?

46. What is the volume **(a)** in cubic meters and **(b)** in liters of a room that is 4.6 m × 4.9 m × 3 m? **(c)** What mass in kg of $CO_2(g)$ at STP will the room hold?

47. A gas at 750 mmHg and 27 °C has a density of 2.32 g/L. Which of the following could it be: CO_2, Kr, H_2S, or C_4H_{10}?

48. The density (mass per unit volume) of air in the atmosphere is proportional to the atmospheric pressure. At sea level, mean atmospheric pressure is 760 mmHg. Boyle's law, which relates the pressure of a given amount of gas to its volume, indicates that density decreases with altitude in the atmosphere. As altitude increases, there is less mass of air above a given point; thus, less pressure is exerted. About half the mass of the atmosphere lies below an altitude of about 5.5 km, about 95% of the mass lies below 25 km, and 99% below 30 km. What is the approximate pressure at an altitude of **(a)** 5.5 km, **(b)** 25 km, and **(c)** 30 km?

49. Which of the following properties must be considered when selecting a solvent for a chemical process?
    a. Solute and solvent polarity
    b. Ease of isolation of solute
    c. Flammability
    d. Toxicity
    e. All of the above

50. Many of the Presidential Green Chemistry Challenge Awards have involved the use of liquid or supercritical carbon dioxide. What properties of $scCO_2$ support its use in greener chemical processing?

51. Give two examples of solvents previously used in industrial processes that have been replaced by $scCO_2$.

52. In addition to Green Chemistry Principles 3 and 5, how else might the use of an environmentally friendly solvent like $scCO_2$ impact green chemistry?

COLLABORATIVE GROUP PROJECTS

Prepare a PowerPoint, poster, or other presentation (as directed by your instructor) to share with the class.

1. Look ahead to Table 9.3 (page 234) and consider this series of compounds: methane (CH_4), ethane (CH_3CH_3), propane ($CH_3CH_2CH_3$), butane ($CH_3CH_2CH_2CH_3$), and pentane ($CH_3CH_2CH_2CH_2CH_3$). For each compound: **(a)** Indicate whether its molecules are polar or nonpolar. **(b)** Indicate the predominant type of intermolecular forces in the liquid state. **(c)** Calculate the molar mass. **(d)** Convert each boiling point from Celsius degrees to kelvins. **(e)** Plot a graph of boiling point (in K) versus molar mass. **(f)** Is there any discernable relationship between molar mass and boiling point?

2. Consider this series of compounds: methane (CH_4), fluoromethane (CH_3F), chloromethane (CH_3Cl), bromomethane (CH_3Br), and iodomethane (CH_3I). Repeat parts **(a)** through **(e)** of Project 1 for these compounds. Boiling points may be found in a printed reference work, such as the *CRC Handbook* or *Merck Index*, or on a Web site such as that of the National Institute for Standards and Technology (NIST). Is there any discernable relationship between molar mass and boiling point? How does the graph for these compounds differ from that in Project 1? Suggest a reason for the difference.

3. Most ionic compounds are solids, but *ionic liquids* have recently been made and have found many uses. Search the Web for information on ionic liquids. In particular, find out why they are liquids rather than solids, and report on some of their current and potential applications.

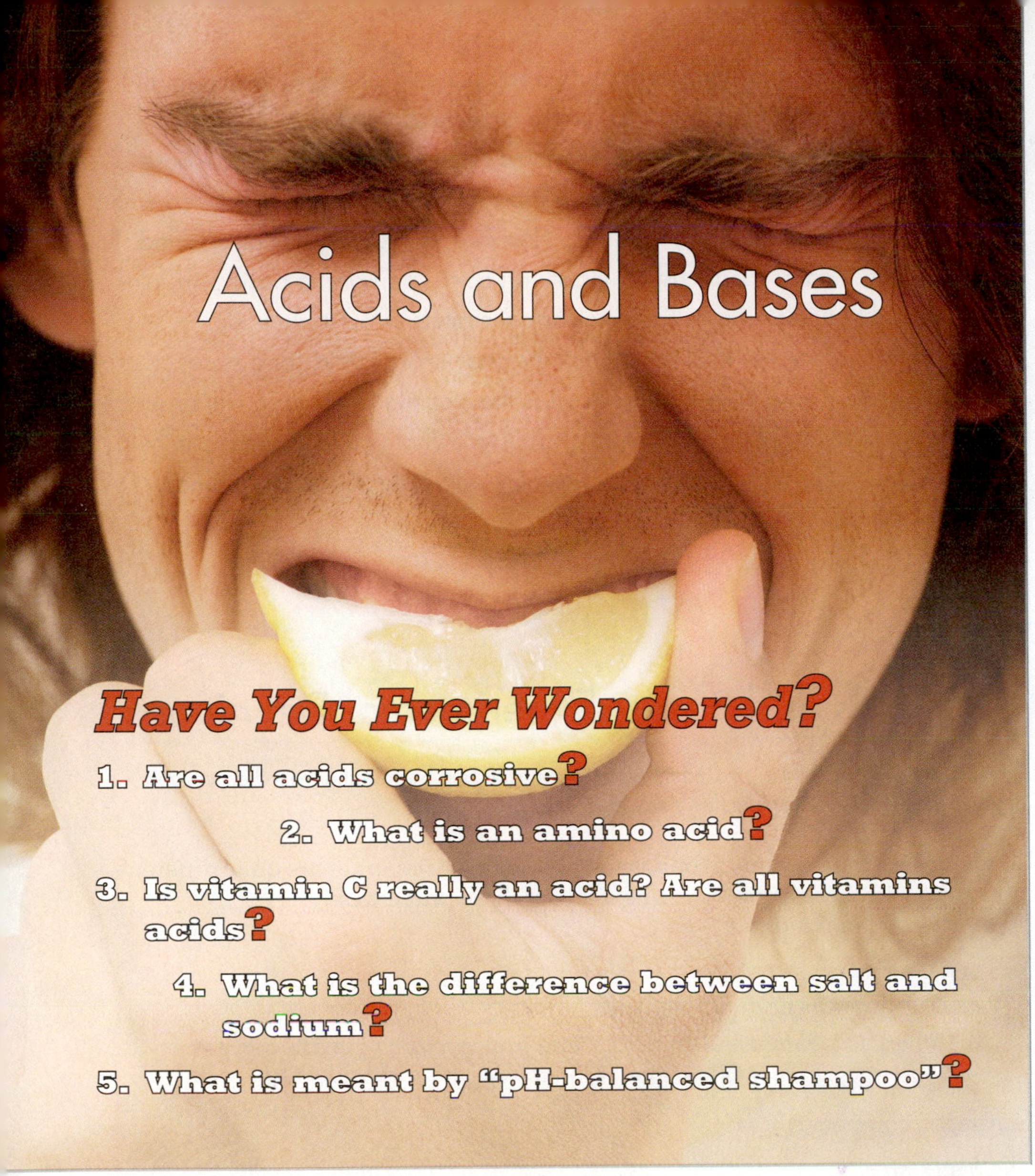

Acids and Bases

Have You Ever Wondered?

1. Are all acids corrosive?
2. What is an amino acid?
3. Is vitamin C really an acid? Are all vitamins acids?
4. What is the difference between salt and sodium?
5. What is meant by "pH-balanced shampoo"?

Learning Objectives

- Distinguish between acids and bases using their chemical and physical properties. (7.1)
- Explain how an acid–base indicator works. (7.1)
- Identify Arrhenius and Brønsted–Lowry acids and bases. (7.2)
- Write a balanced equation for a neutralization or an ionization. (7.2)
- Identify acidic and basic anhydrides, and write equations showing their reactions with water. (7.3)
- Define and identify strong and weak acids and bases. (7.4)
- Identify the reactants and predict the products in a neutralization reaction. (7.5)
- Describe the relationship between the pH of a solution and its acidity or basicity. (7.6)
- Find the molar concentration of hydrogen ion, $[H^+]$, from a pH value or the pH value from $[H^+]$. (7.6)
- Write the formula for the conjugate base of an acid or for the conjugate acid of a base. (7.7)
- Describe the action of a buffer. (7.7)
- Describe everyday uses of acids and bases and how they affect daily life. (7.8)
- Write equations for the production of soap and of biofuel.
- Describe ways by which acids and bases can contribute to greener production of consumer products.

Please pass the protons Have you ever tasted a lemon or a grapefruit? Or felt a burning sensation on your arm after using a cleaning solution containing ammonia? These are but two examples of acids (citric acid in lemons and grapefruit) and bases (ammonia in cleaning solutions) we encounter in our daily lives. Other familiar acids are vinegar (acetic acid), vitamin C (ascorbic acid), and battery acid (sulfuric acid). Some familiar bases are drain cleaner (sodium hydroxide), baking soda (sodium bicarbonate), and antacids.

From "acid indigestion" to "acid rain," the word *acid* appears frequently in the news and in advertisements. Air and water pollution often involve acids

The chemical substances we call acids and bases are all around us. Acids are used in steel production and metal plating, as well as in chemical analysis. Acids are even found in the food we eat. Pancakes and muffins rise because of acids and bases in the ingredients, and the tart taste of fruit comes from the different acids in its flesh. Although the items described and shown here are dramatically different, the acids in them have something in common. All of them can provide hydrogen (hydronium) ions.

and bases. Acid rain, for example, is a serious environmental problem. In arid areas, alkaline (basic) water is sometimes undrinkable.

Did you know that our senses recognize four tastes related to acid–base chemistry? Acids taste sour, bases taste bitter, and the compounds formed when acids react with bases (salts) taste salty. The sweet taste is more complicated. To taste sweet, a compound must have both an acidic part and a basic part, plus just the right geometry to fit the sweet-taste receptors of our taste buds.

In this chapter, we discuss some of the chemistry of acids and bases. You use them every day. Your body processes them continuously. You will probably hear and read about them as long as you live. What you learn here can help you gain a better understanding of these important classes of compounds.

⚠ SAFETY ALERT: Although all acids taste sour and all bases taste bitter, a taste test is not the best general-purpose way to determine whether a substance is an acid or a base. Some acids and bases are poisonous, and some are quite corrosive unless greatly diluted. NEVER TASTE LABORATORY CHEMICALS. Too many of them are toxic, and others might be contaminated.

▲ Many skin-peel preparations used by cosmetologists contain alpha-hydroxy acids such as glycolic acid or lactic acid.

7.1 Acids and Bases: Experimental Definitions

Learning Objectives › Distinguish between acids and bases using their chemical and physical properties. › Explain how an acid–base indicator works.

Acids and bases are chemical opposites, and so their properties are quite different—often opposite. Let's begin by listing a few of these properties.
An *acid* is a compound that

- tastes sour.
- causes litmus indicator dye to turn red.
- dissolves active metals such as zinc and iron, producing hydrogen gas.
- reacts with bases to form water and ionic compounds called *salts*.

A *base* is a compound that

- tastes bitter.
- causes litmus indicator dye to turn blue.
- feels slippery on the skin.
- reacts with acids to form water and salts.

1. Are all acids corrosive? It is clear from Table 7.1 that *acid* does not necessarily mean "corrosive." Many acids are harmless enough to be included in foods we eat, and some are necessary to life.

We can identify foods that are acidic by their sour taste. Vinegar and lemon juice are examples. Vinegar is a solution of acetic acid (about 5%) in water. Lemons, limes, and other citrus fruits contain citric acid. Lactic acid gives yogurt its tart taste, and phosphoric acid is often added to carbonated drinks to impart tartness. The bitter taste of tonic water, on the other hand, comes in part from quinine, a base. Figure 7.1 shows some common acids and bases.

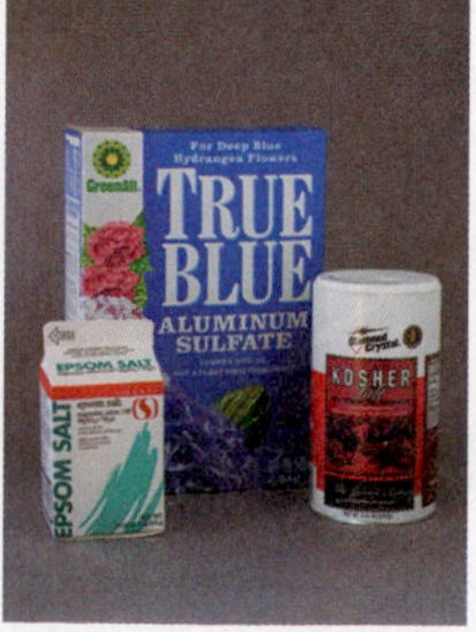

▶ **Figure 7.1** Some common acids (left), bases (center), and salts (right). Acids, bases, and salts are components of many familiar consumer products.

Q: *How would each of the three classes of compounds affect the indicator dye litmus? (See Figure 7.2.)*

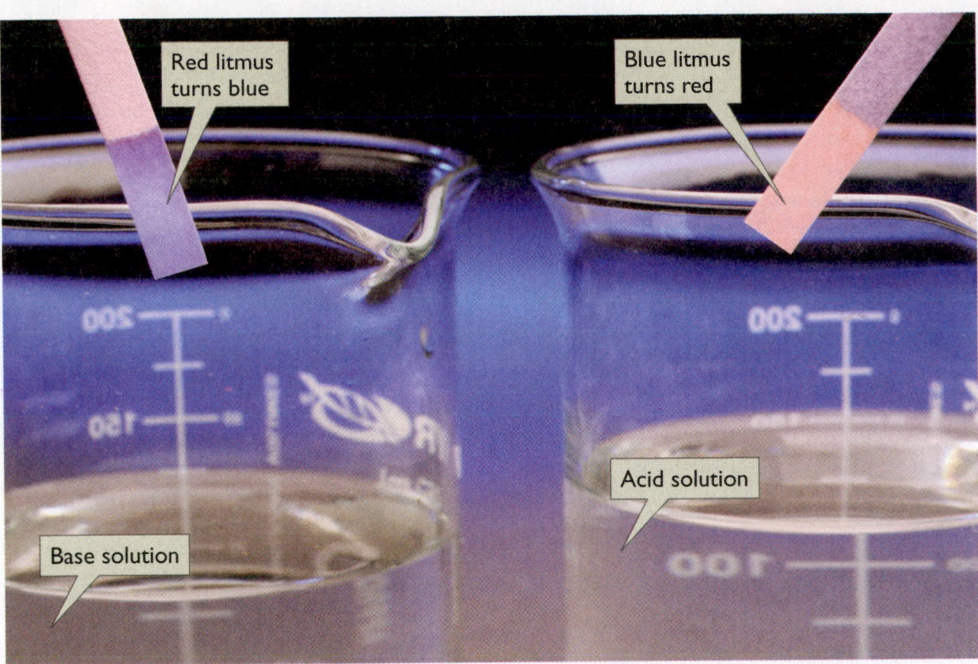

▲ **Figure 7.2** Strips of paper impregnated with litmus dye (extracted from a fungus) are often used to distinguish between acids and bases. The sample on the left turns litmus blue and is therefore basic. The sample on the right turns litmus red and is acidic.

▲ **It DOES Matter!**
Hydrangea is one of many types of flowers that may show different colors depending on the acidity of the soil in which it is grown. Some varieties are blue (top) when planted in slightly acidic soil and pink (bottom) when planted in more basic soil.

A litmus test is a common way to identify a substance as an acid or a base. Litmus (Figure 7.2) is an **acid–base indicator**, one of many such compounds. If you dip a strip of neutral (violet-colored) litmus paper into an unknown solution and the strip turns pink, the solution is acidic. If it turns blue, the solution is basic. If the strip does not turn pink or blue, the solution is neither acidic nor basic. Many substances, such as those that give the colors to grape juice, red cabbage, blueberries, and many flower petals, are acid–base indicators.

▲ You can make your own indicator dye. Chop about 2 cups of red cabbage. Cover with boiling water. Stir. After about 10 min, filter out the solids with a coffee filter. Use about 50 mL of the liquid to test various household chemicals (vinegar, baking soda, ammonia, and so on) for pH. The indicator changes from red at about pH 2 to purple at pH 4, violet at pH 6, blue at pH 8, blue-green at pH 10, and greenish-yellow at pH 12. Other plant materials that contain indicators include blackberries, black raspberries, red radish peels, red rose petals, and turmeric.

Self-Assessment Questions

1. Which of the following is *not* a property of acids?
- **a.** feel slippery on the skin
- **b.** react with Zn to form hydrogen gas
- **c.** taste sour
- **d.** turn litmus red

2. Which of the following is *not* a property of bases?
- **a.** feel slippery on the skin
- **b.** react with salts to form acids
- **c.** taste bitter
- **d.** turn litmus blue

3. In general, when an acid and a base are mixed,
- **a.** a new acid and a salt are formed
- **b.** a new base and a salt are formed
- **c.** no reaction occurs
- **d.** a salt and water are formed

4. A common substance that contains lactic acid is
- **a.** salad oil
- **b.** soap
- **c.** vinegar
- **d.** yogurt

5. The sour taste of grapefruit is due to
- **a.** acetic acid
- **b.** ammonia
- **c.** carbonic acid
- **d.** citric acid

Answers: 1, a; 2, b; 3, d; 4, d; 5, d

▲ Swedish chemist Svante Arrhenius (1859–1927) proposed the theory that acids, bases, and salts in water are composed of ions. He also was the first to relate carbon dioxide in the atmosphere to the greenhouse effect (Chapter 13).

7.2 Acids, Bases, and Salts

Learning Objectives › Identify Arrhenius and Brønsted–Lowry acids and bases. › Write a balanced equation for a neutralization or an ionization.

Acids and bases have certain characteristic properties. But why do they have these properties? We use several different theories to explain these properties.

The Arrhenius Theory

Svante Arrhenius developed the first successful theory of acids and bases in 1887. According to Arrhenius's concept, an **acid** is a molecular substance that breaks up in aqueous solution into hydrogen ions (H^+) and anions. (Because a hydrogen ion is a hydrogen atom from which the sole electron has been removed, H^+ ions are also called *protons*.) The acid is said to *ionize*. For example, nitric acid ionizes in water.

$$HNO_3(aq) \longrightarrow H^+(aq) + NO_3^-(aq)$$

In water, then, the properties of acids are those of the H^+ ion. It is the hydrogen ion that turns litmus red, tastes sour, and reacts with active metals and bases. Table 7.1 lists some common acids. Notice that each formula contains one or more hydrogen atoms. Chemists often indicate an acid by writing the formula with the H atom(s) first. HCl, H_2SO_4, and HNO_3 are acids; NH_3 and CH_4 are not. The formula $HC_2H_3O_2$ (acetic acid) indicates that one H atom ionizes when this compound is in aqueous solution, and three do not.

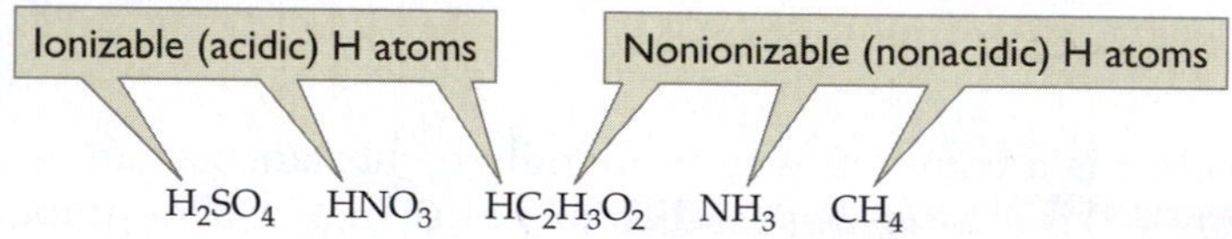

An Arrhenius **base** is defined as a substance that releases hydroxide ions (OH^-) in aqueous solution. Some bases are ionic solids that contain OH^-, such as sodium hydroxide (NaOH) and calcium hydroxide [$Ca(OH)_2$]. These compounds simply release hydroxide ions into the solution when the solid is dissolved in water:

$$NaOH(s) \xrightarrow{H_2O} Na^+(aq) + OH^-(aq)$$

We write H_2O over the arrow to indicate that it is a solvent, not a reactant.

Other bases are molecular substances such as ammonia that ionize to produce OH^- when placed in water (see page 181).

Experimental evidence indicates that the properties of bases in water are due to OH^-. Table 7.2 lists some common bases. Most of these are ionic compounds containing positively changed metal ions, such as Na^+ or Ca^{2+}, and negatively charged hydroxide ions. When these compounds dissolve in water, they all provide OH^- ions, and thus they are all bases. The properties of bases are those of hydroxide ions, just as the properties of acids are those of hydrogen ions.

Table 7.1 Some Common Acids

Name	Formula	Acid Strength	Common Uses/Notes
Sulfuric acid	H_2SO_4	Strong	Battery acid; ore processing, fertilizer manufacturing, oil refining
Hydrochloric acid	HCl	Strong	Cleaning of metals and bricks, removing scale from boilers
Phosphoric acid	H_3PO_4	Moderate	Used in colas and rust removers
Lactic acid	$CH_3CHOHCOOH$	Weak	Yogurt; acidulant (food additive to increase tartness), lotion additive
Acetic acid	CH_3COOH	Weak	Vinegar; acidulant
Boric acid	H_3BO_3	Very weak	Antiseptic eyewash, roach poison
Hydrocyanic acid	HCN	Very weak	Plastics manufacture; extremely toxic

Table 7.2 Some Common Bases

Name	Formula	Classification	Common Uses/Notes
Sodium hydroxide	$NaOH$	Strong	Acid neutralization; soap making
Potassium hydroxide	KOH	Strong	Making liquid soaps and biodiesel fuels
Lithium hydroxide	$LiOH$	Strong	Alkaline storage batteries
Calcium hydroxide	$Ca(OH)_2$	Strong[a]	Plaster, cement; soil neutralizer
Magnesium hydroxide	$Mg(OH)_2$	Strong[a]	Antacid, laxative
Ammonia	NH_3	Weak	Fertilizer, household cleansers

[a]Although these bases are classified as strong, they are not very soluble in water. Calcium hydroxide is only slightly soluble, and magnesium hydroxide is practically insoluble.

Arrhenius further proposed that the essential reaction between an acid and a base, **neutralization**, is the combination of H^+ and OH^- to form water. The cation that was originally associated with the OH^- combines with the anion that was associated with the H^+ to form an ionic compound, a **salt**.

$$\text{An acid} + \text{a base} \longrightarrow \text{a salt} + \text{water}$$

CONCEPTUAL Example 7.1 Ionization of Acids and Bases

Write equations showing **(a)** the ionization of nitric acid (HNO_3) in water and **(b)** the ionization of solid potassium hydroxide (KOH) in water.

Solution

a. An HNO_3 molecule ionizes to form a hydrogen ion and a nitrate ion. Because this reaction occurs in water, we can use the label "(aq)" to indicate that the substances involved are in aqueous solution.

$$HNO_3(aq) \longrightarrow H^+(aq) + NO_3^-(aq)$$

b. Potassium hydroxide (KOH), an ionic solid, simply dissolves in the water, forming separate $K^+(aq)$ and $OH^-(aq)$ ions.

$$KOH(s) \xrightarrow{H_2O} K^+(aq) + OH^-(aq)$$

■ EXERCISE 7.1A

Write equations showing **(a)** the ionization of HBr (hydrobromic acid) in water and **(b)** the ionization of solid calcium hydroxide in water.

■ EXERCISE 7.1B

Historically, formulas for carboxylic acids (compounds containing a —COOH group; see Chapter 9) are often written with the ionizable hydrogen *last*. For example, instead of writing the formula for acetic acid as $HC_2H_3O_2$, it can be written as CH_3COOH. Write an equation showing the ionization of CH_3COOH in water.

2. What is an amino acid? An amino acid is a molecule that contains both −COOH, which is acidic, and —NH_2 (an *amino group*; see Sections 9.8 and 9.9), which is basic. Amino acids undergo acid-base reactions with one another and link together to form the proteins in living tissue.

Limitations of the Arrhenius Theory

The Arrhenius theory is limited in several ways.

- A simple free proton does not exist in water solution. The H^+ ion has such a high positive charge density that it is immediately attracted to a lone pair of electrons on an O atom of an H_2O molecule, forming a *hydronium ion*, H_3O^+.

$$\underset{\text{Water}}{H\!:\!\ddot{\underset{\cdot\cdot}{O}}\!:\atop H} + H^+ \longrightarrow \underset{\text{Hydronium ion}}{\left[H\!:\!\ddot{\underset{\cdot\cdot}{O}}\!:\!H \atop H\right]^+}$$

- It does not explain the basicity of ammonia and related compounds. Ammonia seems out of place in Table 7.2 because it contains no hydroxide ions.
- It applies only to reactions in aqueous solution.

As with many scientific theories, a better one based on newer data has supplanted Arrhenius's theory.

The Brønsted–Lowry Acid–Base Theory

The shortcomings of the Arrhenius theory were largely overcome by a theory proposed in 1923, by J. N. Brønsted in Denmark and T. M. Lowry in Great Britain, who were working independently. In the Brønsted–Lowry theory,

- an acid is a *proton donor*, and
- a base is a *proton acceptor*.

The theory portrays the ionization of hydrogen chloride in this way:

$$HCl(aq) + H_2O \longrightarrow H_3O^+(aq) + Cl^-(aq)$$

Here, water is a reactant. The acid molecules donate hydrogen ions (protons) to the water molecules, so the acid (HCl) acts as a proton donor.

$$\text{H}:\ddot{\underset{..}{\text{Cl}}}: \ + \ \text{H}:\ddot{\underset{..}{\text{O}}}:\text{H} \longrightarrow \left[\text{H}:\ddot{\underset{..}{\text{O}}}:\text{H}_2\right]^+ \ + \ :\ddot{\underset{..}{\text{Cl}}}:^-$$

Acid (proton donor) — Hydrochloric acid

In water, an H^+ ion is associated with several H_2O molecules—for example, four H_2O molecules in the ion $H(H_2O)_4{}^+$, or $H_9O_4{}^+$. For most purposes, we simply use H^+ and ignore the associated water molecules. However, keep in mind that the notation H^+ is a simplification of the real situation: Protons in water actually exist associated with water molecules.

The HCl molecule donates a proton to a water molecule, producing a hydronium ion and a chloride ion and forming a solution called *hydrochloric acid*. Other acids react similarly; they donate hydrogen ions to water molecules to produce hydronium ions. If we let HA represent any acid, the reaction is written as

$$HA(aq) + H_2O \longrightarrow H_3O^+(aq) + A^-(aq)$$

Even when the solvent is something other than water, the acid acts as a proton donor, transferring H^+ ions to the solvent molecules.

CONCEPTUAL Example 7.2 Brønsted–Lowry Acids

Write an equation showing the reaction with water of HNO_3 as a Brønsted–Lowry acid. What is the role of water in the reaction?

Solution

As a Brønsted–Lowry acid, HNO_3 donates a proton to a water molecule, forming a hydronium ion and a nitrate ion.

$$HNO_3(aq) + H_2O \longrightarrow H_3O^+(aq) + NO_3{}^-(aq)$$

The water molecule accepts a proton from HNO_3. Water is a Brønsted–Lowry base in this reaction.

■ EXERCISE 7.2A

Write an equation showing the reaction with water of HBr as a Brønsted–Lowry acid.

■ EXERCISE 7.2B

Write an equation showing the reaction of methanol (CH_3OH) with $HClO_4$ as a Brønsted–Lowry acid.

Where does the OH^- come from when bases such as ammonia (NH_3) are dissolved in water? The Arrhenius theory proved inadequate in answering this question, but the Brønsted–Lowry theory explains how ammonia acts as a base in water.

Ammonia is a gas at room temperature. When it is dissolved in water, some of the ammonia molecules react as shown by the following equation.

$$NH_3(aq) + H_2O \longrightarrow NH_4^+(aq) + OH^-(aq)$$

An ammonia molecule accepts a proton from a water molecule; NH_3 acts as a Brønsted–Lowry base. (Recall that the N atom of ammonia has a lone pair of electrons, which it can share with a proton.) The water molecule acts as a proton donor—an acid. The ammonia molecule accepts the proton and becomes an ammonium ion. When a proton leaves a water molecule, it leaves behind the electron pair that it shared with the O atom. The water molecule becomes a negatively charged hydroxide ion.

In general, then, *a base is a proton acceptor* (Figure 7.3). This definition includes not only hydroxide ions but also neutral molecules such as ammonia and *amines* (organic compounds such as CH_3NH_2 that are derived from ammonia). It also includes other negative ions such as the oxide (O^{2-}), carbonate (CO_3^{2-}), and bicarbonate (HCO_3^-) ions. The idea of an acid as a proton donor and a base as a proton acceptor greatly expands our concept of acids and bases.

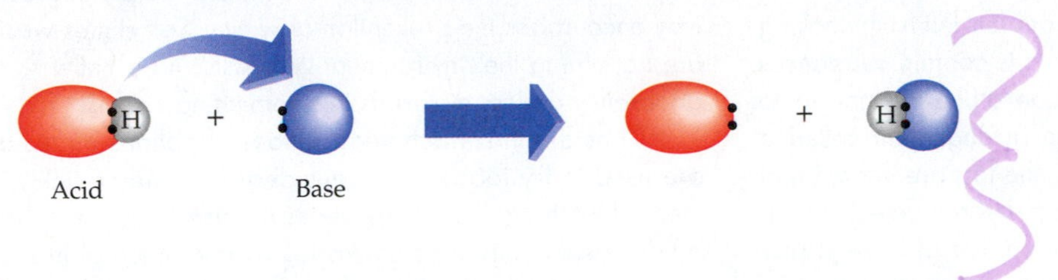

◀ **Figure 7.3** A Brønsted–Lowry acid is a proton donor. A base is a proton acceptor.

Q: *Can you write an equation in which the acid is represented as HA and the base as :B⁻?*

Salts

Salts, formed from the neutralization reactions of acids and bases, are ionic compounds composed of cations and anions. These ions can be simple ions, such as sodium ion (Na^+) and chloride ion (Cl^-), or polyatomic ions, such as ammonium ion (NH_4^+), sulfate ion (SO_4^{2-}), and acetate ion (CH_3COO^-). Sodium chloride, ordinary table salt, is probably the most familiar salt.

Salts that conduct electricity when dissolved in water are called *electrolytes*. Various electrolytes, in certain amounts, are critical for many bodily functions including nerve conduction, heartbeat, and fluid balance. Medical blood tests often check levels of Na^+, K^+, Cl^-, HCO_3^-, and other electrolyte ions (Chapter 19).

There are many common salts with familiar uses. Sodium chloride and calcium chloride are used to melt ice on roads and sidewalks in winter. Copper(II) sulfate is used to kill tree roots in sewage lines. We will encounter many other examples in later chapters as dietary minerals (Chapter 17), fertilizers (Chapter 20), and more. Table 7.3 lists some salts used in medicine.

Table 7.3 Some Salts with Present or Past Uses in Medicine

Name	Formula	Uses
Silver nitrate	$AgNO_3$	Germicide and antiseptic
Stannous fluoride [tin(II) fluoride]	SnF_2	Toothpaste additive to prevent dental cavities
Calcium sulfate (plaster of Paris)	$(CaSO_4)_2 \cdot H_2O$[a]	Plaster casts
Magnesium sulfate (Epsom salts)	$MgSO_4 \cdot 7H_2O$[a]	Laxative, foot baths
Potassium permanganate	$KMnO_4$	Cauterizing agent, antiseptic
Ferrous sulfate [iron(II) sulfate]	$FeSO_4$	Prescribed for iron deficiency (anemia)
Zinc sulfate	$ZnSO_4$	Skin treatment (eczema)
Barium sulfate	$BaSO_4$	Provides the contrast material in "barium cocktail" given for gastrointestinal X-rays
Mercurous chloride [mercury(I) chloride; calomel]	Hg_2Cl_2	Laxative; no longer used

[a] These compounds are hydrates, substances containing water molecules combined in a definite ratio as an integral part of the compound.

GREEN CHEMISTRY

Principles 1, 4, 7, 9, 10

Irv Levy, *Gordon College*

Sustainability: It's Basic (and Acidic)

Green chemistry is a part of sustainable chemistry. Sustainability, often defined as "meeting the needs of the present generation without compromising the ability of future generations to meet their needs," is much in the news these days. Green chemistry is one of the critical means of attaining sustainability. Understanding of acids and bases has led to greener, more sustainable methods for producing consumer products. Two important examples are soap and renewable biofuels.

Soap traditionally has been made from fats left from cooking meats and from vegetable oils. Fats and oils contain substances composed of three long chains of carbon atoms connected to a central set of three carbon atoms, an arrangement called a *triglyceride* (Chapter 16). To make soap, the fats are heated and mixed with lye solution (aqueous sodium hydroxide—a base). Each mole of triglyceride reacts with three moles of base to produce three moles of soap and one mole of the byproduct glycerol (also called glycerin). Soaps are salts (Section 7.2) of carboxylic acids that usually have a long chain of carbon atoms. An example of a typical soap is sodium palmitate. Its chemical formula is shown here.

$$CH_3(CH_2)_{14}COO^-Na^+$$

The byproduct glycerol has a number of uses, including as a moisturizing ingredient in soap. Chemists at Gordon College (Wenham, MA) found that adding glycerol to the fats and oils traditionally used in soap-making decreased the quantity of starting materials required for soap production. Much more glycerol byproduct is produced industrially than can be used by the soap industry, however, so the search continues for other green uses for glycerol.

The chemistry of biodiesel fuel production (also see Chapter 15) is much like that of soap-making. In both processes, bases are used and glycerol is formed. With the use of methanol (CH_3OH) in place of water and a catalytic amount of base, though, the triglycerides are converted to compounds called *esters* (Section 9.7). An example of a typical biodiesel molecule is shown here.

$$CH_3(CH_2)_{14}COOCH_3$$

Although the long chains of carbon atoms in biodiesel often are the same as in soap molecules, biodiesel molecules have a different group on one end of the chain. Compare these compounds to a typical diesel molecule from petroleum that does not contain any atoms other than carbon and hydrogen.

$$CH_3(CH_2)_{14}CH_3$$

What do soap, biodiesel, and glycerol have to do with sustainability and green chemistry? The first principle of green chemistry encourages the prevention of waste. Sometimes wastes also are harmful to the environment. Wouldn't it be better to redirect apparently useless materials into something useful?

Consider this: Each year billions of gallons of fats and oils are used to fry foods. Fryer oils degrade fairly quickly in commercial kitchens. For many years the used oils were carted off by disposal companies as waste. Today, much of that used oil is converted into biodiesel fuel, providing an alternative fuel that doesn't deplete fossil petroleum reserves. This approach satisfies the green chemistry principle of using renewable resources while providing new use for what was once considered waste. And it gets better! Petroleum diesel fuel is hazardous to humans and toxic to the environment. Biodiesel is much safer.

Acids also are involved in green processes such as cleaning. For example, polylactic acid (PLA) is a type of biodegradable and renewable plastic made from chemicals derived from corn (see green chemistry essay, Chapter 10). PLA plastic, made by companies such as NatureWorks, is found in many consumer materials, such as plastic cups. Research at Simmons College in Boston has led to a new way to convert used PLA cups into an antimicrobial cleaning solution containing lactic acid ($CH_3CHOHCOOH$). The shredded plastic is mixed with alcohol and base to break down the polymer to sodium lactate ($CH_3CHOHCOONa$). The basic sodium lactate solution is neutralized with acid to form the lactic acid cleaner, which is useful for wiping away soap scum.

In the quest for sustaisnability, acids and bases are an essential part of the toolbox that will continue to be used as chemists search for better ways to prevent waste and use renewable starting materials. You might argue that sustainability is basic—not to mention acidic.

▲ Biodiesel is made from waste fats and oils used in cooking. In the past, those wastes would require disposal; now, they are useful. Biodiesel is an excellent example of sustainable chemistry.

Self-Assessment Questions

For Questions 1–5, match each formula with the compound's application.

1. CH_3COOH	(a) battery acid
2. H_3BO_3	(b) soap making
3. HCl	(c) antiseptic eyewash
4. H_2SO_4	(d) remove boiler scale
5. $NaOH$	(e) vinegar

6. Which of the following equations best represents what happens when hydrogen bromide dissolves in water?

a. $2\ HBr \xrightarrow{H_2O} Br_2 + H_2$ **b.** $HBr(g) \xrightarrow{H_2O} H(aq) + Br(aq)$

c. $HBr \longrightarrow H^+(aq) + Br^-(aq)$ **d.** $HBr(g) + H_2O \longrightarrow Br^-(aq) + H_3O^+(aq)$

For Questions 7–10, match each term with the correct definition.

7. Arrhenius acid	(a) proton acceptor
8. Arrhenius base	(b) proton donor
9. Brønsted acid	(c) produces H^+ in water
10. Brønsted base	(d) produces OH^- in water

Answers: 1, e; 2, c; 3, d; 4, a; 5, b; 6, d; 7, c; 8, d; 9, b; 10, a

7.3 Acidic and Basic Anhydrides

Learning Objective › Identify acidic anhydrides and basic anhydrides, and write equations showing their reactions with water.

Certain metal and nonmetal oxides are well known for their ability to produce or to neutralize acids or bases. For example, nitrogen dioxide (NO_2) and sulfur dioxide (SO_2) are notorious for producing acid rain. Calcium oxide (quicklime, CaO) is widely used to neutralize acidic soils. In the Brønsted–Lowry view, many metal oxides act directly as bases because the oxide ion can accept a proton. These metal oxides also react with water to form metal hydroxides, compounds that are bases in the Arrhenius sense. And many nonmetal oxides react with water to form acids.

Nonmetal Oxides: Acidic Anhydrides

Many acids are made by reacting nonmetal oxides with water. For example, sulfur trioxide reacts with water to form sulfuric acid.

$$SO_3 + H_2O \longrightarrow H_2SO_4$$

Similarly, carbon dioxide reacts with water to form carbonic acid.

$$CO_2 + H_2O \longrightarrow H_2CO_3$$

In general, nonmetal oxides react with water to form acids.

$$\text{Nonmetal oxide} + H_2O \longrightarrow \text{acid}$$

Nonmetal oxides that act in this way are called **acidic anhydrides.** *Anhydride* means "without water." These reactions explain why rainwater is acidic (Section 7.8).

CONCEPTUAL Example 7.3 Acidic Anhydrides

Give the formula for the acid formed when sulfur dioxide reacts with water.

Solution

The formula for the acid, H_2SO_3, is obtained by adding the two H atoms and one O atom of water to SO_2. The equation for the reaction is simply

$$SO_2 + H_2O \longrightarrow H_2SO_3$$

▲ **It DOES Matter!**
Slaked lime is inexpensive, easily made from cheap raw materials, and low in toxicity. These properties make it the most widely used base for neutralizing acids. It is an ingredient in such diverse materials as bricklayer's mortar, plaster, glues, and even pickles and corn tortillas. The whitewash made famous in Mark Twain's *Adventures of Tom Sawyer* was a simple mixture of slaked lime and water.

■ EXERCISE 7.3A
Give the formula for the acid formed when selenium dioxide (SeO_2) reacts with water.

■ EXERCISE 7.3B
Give the formula for the acid formed when dinitrogen pentoxide (N_2O_5) reacts with water. (*Hint:* Two molecules of acid are formed.)

Metal Oxides: Basic Anhydrides

Just as acids can be made from nonmetal oxides, many common hydroxide bases can be made from metal oxides. For example, calcium oxide reacts with water to form calcium hydroxide ("slaked lime").

$$CaO + H_2O \longrightarrow Ca(OH)_2$$

Another example is the reaction of lithium oxide with water to form lithium hydroxide.

$$Li_2O + H_2O \longrightarrow 2\,LiOH$$

In general, metal oxides react with water to form bases (Figure 7.4). These metal oxides are called **basic anhydrides**.

$$\text{Metal oxide} + H_2O \longrightarrow \text{base}$$

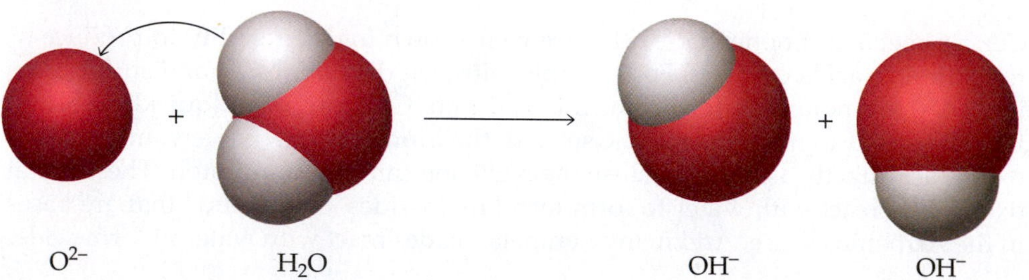

▲ **Figure 7.4** Metal oxides are basic because the oxide ion reacts with water to form two hydroxide ions.

Q: *Can you write an equation that shows how solid sodium oxide (Na_2O) reacts with water to form sodium hydroxide?*

CONCEPTUAL Example 7.4 Basic Anhydrides

Give the formula for the base formed by the addition of water to barium oxide (BaO).

Solution

Again, we add the atoms of a water molecule to BaO. Because a barium ion has a 2+ charge, the formula for the base has *two* hydroxide (1–) ions.

$$BaO + H_2O \longrightarrow Ba(OH)_2$$

■ EXERCISE 7.4A
Give the formula for the base formed by the addition of water to strontium oxide (SrO).

■ EXERCISE 7.4B
What base is formed by the addition of water to potassium oxide (K_2O)? (*Hint:* Two moles of base are formed for each mole of potassium oxide.)

Self-Assessment Questions

1. Selenic acid (H_2SeO_4) is an extremely corrosive acid that when heated is capable of dissolving gold. It is quite soluble in water. The anhydride of selenic acid is
   a. SeO
   b. SeO_2
   c. SeO_3
   d. SeO_4
2. Zinc hydroxide [$Zn(OH)_2$] is used as an absorbent in surgical dressings. The anhydride of zinc hydroxide is
   a. ZnO
   b. ZnOH
   c. ZnO_2
   d. Zn_2O_3

Answers: 1, c; 2, a

7.4 Strong and Weak Acids and Bases

Learning Objective › Define and identify strong and weak acids and bases.

When gaseous hydrogen chloride (HCl) reacts with water, it reacts completely to form hydronium ions and chloride ions.

$$HCl + H_2O \longrightarrow H_3O^+ + Cl^-$$

For many purposes, we simply write this reaction as the ionization of HCl and use (aq) to indicate a solution in water.

$$HCl(aq) \longrightarrow H^+(aq) + Cl^-(aq)$$

Most acids do not ionize completely, however. The poisonous gas hydrogen cyanide (HCN) also ionizes in water to produce hydrogen ions and cyanide ions. But HCN ionizes only to a slight extent. In a solution that has 1 mol of HCN in 1 L of water, only one HCN molecule in 40,000 ionizes to produce a hydrogen ion.

$$HCN(aq) \rightleftharpoons H^+(aq) + CN^-(aq)$$

We represent this slight ionization by using a double arrow. The opposite-pointing arrows indicate that the reaction is reversible; the ions can also combine to form HCN molecules. A short arrow points to the right and a longer arrow points to the left to indicate that most of the HCN remains intact as HCN molecules.

Clearly, acids can be classified according to their extent of ionization.

- An acid such as HCl that ionizes completely in (reacts completely with) water is called a **strong acid**.
- An acid such as HCN that ionizes only slightly in water is a **weak acid**.

There are only a few strong acids. The first two acids listed in Table 7.1 (sulfuric and hydrochloric) are the common ones. The other strong acids are nitric acid (HNO_3), hydrobromic acid (HBr), hydroiodic acid (HI), and perchloric acid ($HClO_4$). Most acids are weak acids.

Bases are also classified as strong or weak.

- A **strong base** is completely ionized in water.
- A **weak base** is only slightly ionized in water.

Perhaps the most familiar strong base is sodium hydroxide (NaOH), commonly called *lye*. It exists as sodium ions and hydroxide ions even in the solid state. Other strong bases include potassium hydroxide (KOH) and the hydroxides of all the other group 1A metals. Except for $Be(OH)_2$, the hydroxides of group 2A metals are also strong bases. However, $Ca(OH)_2$ is only slightly soluble in water, and $Mg(OH)_2$ is nearly insoluble. The concentration of hydroxide ions in a solution of $Ca(OH)_2$ or $Mg(OH)_2$ is, therefore, not very high.

The word *strong* does not refer to the *amount* of acid or base in a solution. As mentioned in Section 5.5, a solution that contains a relatively large amount of an acid or a base, whether strong or weak, as the solute in a given volume of solution is called a *concentrated* solution. A solution with only a little solute in that same volume of solution is a *dilute* solution.

3. Is vitamin C really an acid? Are all vitamins acids?

Yes, vitamin C is a complex organic compound known as *ascorbic acid*. Some, but not all, vitamins are acids (including folic acid and niacin). Like most acids, these vitamins are weak acids. Not only are they not corrosive but they are necessary to health.

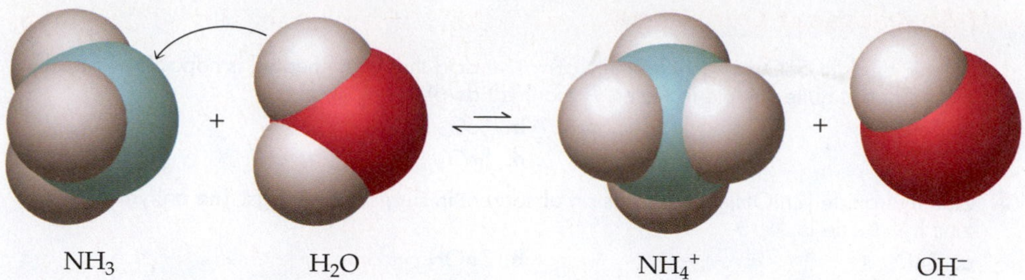

▲ **Figure 7.5** Ammonia is a base because it accepts a proton from water. A solution of ammonia in water contains ammonium ions and hydroxide ions. Only a small fraction of the ammonia molecules react, however; most remain unchanged. Ammonia is therefore a *weak* base.

Q: *Amines are related to ammonia; in an amine, one or more of the H atoms of NH_3 is replaced by a carbon-containing group. Amines react in the same way as ammonia does. Can you write an equation that shows how the amine CH_3NH_2 reacts with water? One product is hydroxide ion.*

The most familiar weak base is ammonia (NH_3). It reacts with water to a slight extent to produce ammonium ions (NH_4^+) and hydroxide ions (Figure 7.5).

$$NH_3 + H_2O \rightleftharpoons NH_4^+ + OH^-$$

In its reaction with HCl (page 180), water acts as a base (proton acceptor). In its reaction with NH_3, water acts as an acid (proton donor). A substance such as water that can either donate a proton or accept a proton is said to be *amphiprotic* (see also Additional Problem 65).

Self-Assessment Questions

For Questions 1–7, select the correct classification (more than one substance may fit into a given classification).

1. $Ca(OH)_2$
2. HCN
3. HF
4. HNO_3
5. H_3PO_4
6. KOH
7. NH_3

(a) strong acid
(b) strong base
(c) weak acid
(d) weak base

8. Acetic acid reacts with water to form
a. $CH_3COO^+ + H_2O$
b. $CH_3COOH + OH^-$
c. $CH_3COO^- + H_3O^-$
d. $CH_3COO^+ + OH^-$

9. Ammonia reacts with water to form
a. $NH_3 + H_2O$
b. $NH_4^+ + OH^-$
c. $NH_2^- + H_3O^+$
d. $NH_3 + OH^-$

Answers: 1, b; 2, c; 3, c; 4, a; 5, c; 6, b; 7, d; 8, c; 9, b

7.5 Neutralization

Learning Objective › Identify the reactants and predict the products in a neutralization reaction.

When an acid reacts with a base, the products are water and a salt. If a solution containing hydrogen ions (an acid) is mixed with another solution containing exactly the same amount of hydroxide ions (a base), the resulting solution does not change the color of litmus, dissolve zinc or iron, or feel slippery on the skin. It is no longer either acidic or basic. It is neutral. As was mentioned earlier, the reaction of an acid with a base is called *neutralization* (Figure 7.6).

$$H^+ + OH^- \longrightarrow H_2O$$

(a)

(b)

(c)

◀ **Figure 7.6** The amount of acid (or base) in a solution is determined by careful neutralization. Here a 5.00-mL sample of vinegar, some water, and a few drops of phenolphthalein (an acid–base indicator) are placed in a flask (a). A solution of 0.1000 M NaOH is added to the flask slowly from a buret (a device for precise measurement of volumes of solutions) (b). As long as the acid is in excess, the solution is colorless. When the acid has been neutralized and a tiny excess of base is present, the phenolphthalein indicator turns pink (c).

Q: *Can you write an equation for the reaction of acetic acid (CH_3COOH), the acid in vinegar, with aqueous NaOH?*

If sodium hydroxide is neutralized by hydrochloric acid, the products are water and sodium chloride (ordinary table salt)

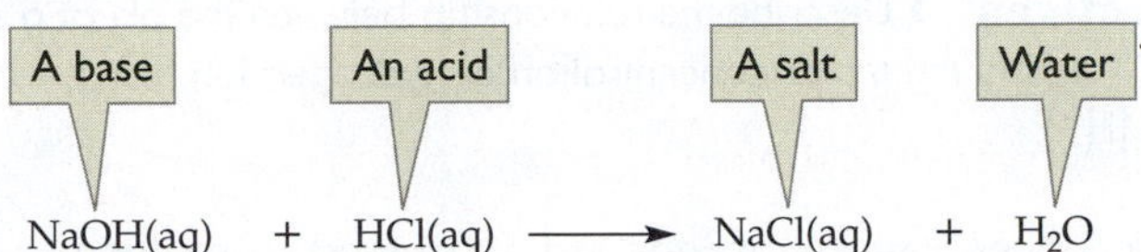

$$NaOH(aq) + HCl(aq) \longrightarrow NaCl(aq) + H_2O$$

Example 7.5 Neutralization Reactions

Potassium nitrate, a component of black powder gunpowder and some fertilizers, was obtained from the late Middle Ages through the nineteenth century by precipitation from urine. Commonly called *saltpeter*, it can be prepared by the reaction of nitric acid with potassium hydroxide. Write the equation for this neutralization reaction.

Solution

The OH^- from the base and the H^+ from the acid combine to form water. The cation of the base (K^+) and the anion of the acid (NO_3^-) form a solution of the salt (potassium nitrate, KNO_3).

$$KOH(aq) + HNO_3(aq) \longrightarrow KNO_3(aq) + H_2O(l)$$

■ EXERCISE 7.5A

Countertop spills of lye solutions (aqueous sodium hydroxide) can be neutralized with vinegar (aqueous acetic acid; see Table 7.1). Write the equation for the neutralization reaction.

■ EXERCISE 7.5B

A toilet-bowl cleaner contains hydrochloric acid. An emergency first-aid treatment for accidental ingestion is a teaspoon of milk of magnesia (magnesium hydroxide). Write the equation for the neutralization reaction between magnesium hydroxide and hydrochloric acid. (*Hint:* Be sure to write the correct formulas for the reactants and the salt before attempting to balance the equation.)

4. What is the difference between salt and sodium? A salt is any ionic compound formed by reacting an acid and a base. In everyday life, *salt* usually means table salt—sodium chloride (NaCl). Sodium is a highly reactive metal element. Sodium ions are essential for life, but you wouldn't want to eat pure sodium. It reacts violently with water.

Self-Assessment Questions

1. When equal amounts of acids and bases are mixed,
   a. the acid becomes stronger
   b. the base becomes stronger
   c. no reaction occurs
   d. they neutralize each other
2. What amount in moles of hydrochloric acid is needed to neutralize 1.5 mol of sodium hydroxide?
   a. 1 mol
   b. 1.5 mol
   c. 3.0 mol
   c. 4.5 mol

3. What amount in moles of hydrochloric acid is needed to neutralize 2.4 mol of calcium hydroxide?
   a. 1.2 mol b. 2.4 mol
   c. 3.0 mol d. 4.8 mol
4. What amount in moles of sodium hydroxide is needed to neutralize 1.5 mol of phosphoric acid?
   a. 0.5 mol b. 3.0 mol
   c. 4.5 mol d. 6.0 mol

Answers: 1. d; 2. b; 3. d; 4. c

Table 7.4 Relationship between pH and Concentration of H^+ Ion

Concentration of H^+(mol/L)	pH
1×10^{-0}	0
1×10^{-1}	1
1×10^{-2}	2
1×10^{-3}	3
1×10^{-4}	4
1×10^{-5}	5
1×10^{-6}	6
1×10^{-7}	7
1×10^{-8}	8
1×10^{-9}	9
1×10^{-10}	10
1×10^{-11}	11
1×10^{-12}	12
1×10^{-13}	13
1×10^{-14}	14

The relationship between pH and $[H^+]$ is perhaps easier to see when the equation is written in the following form. $[H^+] = 10^{-pH}$

7.6 The pH Scale

Learning Objectives › Describe the relationship between the pH of a solution and its acidity or basicity. › Find the molar concentration of hydrogen ion, $[H^+]$, from a pH value or the pH value from $[H^+]$.

In solutions, the concentrations of ions are expressed in moles per liter (molarity; see Section 5.5). Because hydrogen chloride is completely ionized in water, a 1 molar solution of hydrochloric acid (1 M HCl), for example, contains 1 mol H^+ ions per liter of solution. Likewise, 1 L of 3 M HCl contains 3 mol H^+ ions, and 0.500 L of 0.00100 M HCl contains 0.500 L × 0.00100 mol/L = 0.000500 mol H^+ ions.

We can describe the acidity of a particular solution in moles per liter: The hydrogen ion concentration of a 0.00100 M HCl solution is 1×10^{-3} mol/L. However, exponential notation isn't very convenient. More often, the acidity of this solution is reported simply as pH 3.

We usually use the **pH scale,** first proposed in 1909 by the Danish biochemist S. P. L. Sørensen, to describe the degree of acidity or basicity. Most solutions have a pH that lies in the range from 0 to 14. The neutral point on the scale is 7, with values below 7 indicating increasing acidity and those above 7 increasing basicity. Thus, pH 6 is slightly acidic, whereas pH 12 is strongly basic (Figure 7.7).

The numbers on the pH scale are directly related to the hydrogen ion concentration. We might expect pure water to be completely in the form of H_2O molecules, but it turns out that about 1 out of every 500 million water molecules splits into H^+ and OH^- ions. This gives a concentration of hydrogen ion and of hydroxide ion in pure water of 0.0000001 mol/L, or 1×10^{-7} M. Can you see why 7 is the pH of pure water? It is simply the power of 10 for the molar concentration of H^+, with the negative sign removed. (The H in pH stands for "hydrogen," and the p for "power.") Thus, pH is defined as the negative logarithm of the molar concentration of hydrogen ion (refer to Table 7.4):

$$\text{pH} = -\log[H^+]$$

The brackets around H^+ mean "molar concentration."

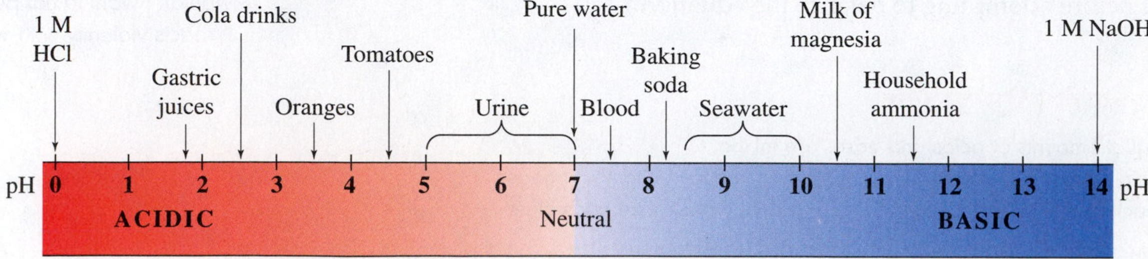

▲ **Figure 7.7** The pH scale. A change in pH of one unit means a tenfold change in the hydrogen ion concentration.

Q: *Are tomatoes more acidic or less acidic than oranges? About how many times more (or less) acidic?*

Table 7.5 Approximate pH Values of Some Common Solutions

Solution	pH
Hydrochloric acid (4%)	0
Gastric juice	1.6–1.8
Soft drink	2.0–4.0
Lemon juice	2.1
Vinegar (4%)	2.5
Urine	5.5–7.0
Rainwater[a]	5.6
Saliva	6.2–7.4
Milk	6.3–6.6
Pure water	7.0
Blood	7.4
Fresh egg white	7.6–8.0
Bile	7.8–8.6
Milk of magnesia	10.5
Washing soda	12.0
Sodium hydroxide (4%)	13.0

[a] Saturated with carbon dioxide from the atmosphere but unpolluted.

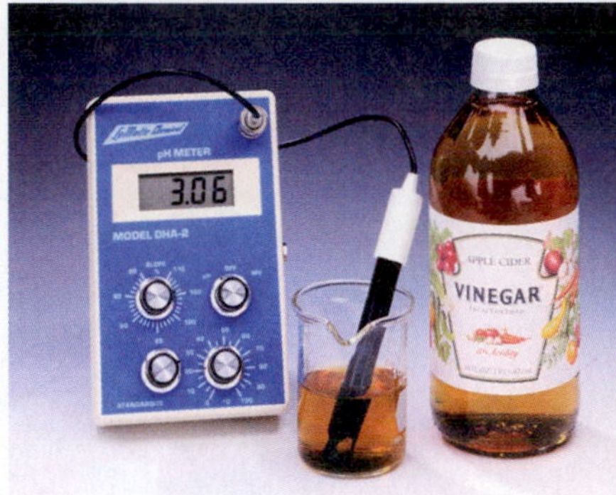

▲ A pH meter is a device for determining pH quickly and accurately.

Q: *Is the solution in the beaker more basic or less basic than household ammonia? (Refer to Figure 7.7.)*

Although pH is an acidity scale, note that its value goes down when acidity goes up. Not only is the relationship an inverse one, but it is also logarithmic. A decrease of 1 pH unit represents a tenfold increase in acidity, and when pH goes down by 2 units, acidity increases by a factor of 100. This relationship may seem strange at first, but once you understand the pH scale, you will appreciate its convenience.

Table 7.4 summarizes the relationship between hydrogen ion concentration and pH. A pH of 4 means a hydrogen ion concentration of 1×10^{-4} mol/L, or 0.0001 M. If the concentration of hydrogen ions is 0.01 M, or 1×10^{-2} M, the pH is 2. Typical pH values for various common solutions are listed in Table 7.5.

5. What is meant by "pH-balanced shampoo"? Shampoo on either end of the pH scale would damage hair (and probably skin as well!). Most shampoos are formulated to be neutral (pH 7) or slightly basic.

Example 7.6 pH from Hydrogen Ion Concentration

What is the pH of a solution that has a hydrogen ion concentration of 1×10^{-5} M?

Solution

The hydrogen ion concentration is 1×10^{-5} M. The exponent is -5; the pH is, therefore, the negative of this exponent: $-(-5)$ or 5.

■ EXERCISE 7.6A

What is the pH of a solution that has a hydrogen ion concentration of 1×10^{-9} M?

■ EXERCISE 7.6B

What is the pH of a solution that is 0.010 M HCl? (*Hint:* HCl is a strong acid.)

Example 7.7 Finding Hydrogen Ion Concentration from pH

What is the hydrogen ion concentration of a solution that has a pH of 4?

Solution

A pH value of 4 means that the exponent of 10 is -4. The hydrogen ion concentration is, therefore, 1×10^{-4} M.

■ EXERCISE 7.7A

What is the hydrogen ion concentration of a solution that has a pH of 2?

■ EXERCISE 7.7B

What is the hydrogen ion concentration of a HI solution that has a pH of 3? (*Hint:* HI is a strong acid.)

CONCEPTUAL Example 7.8 Estimating pH from Hydrogen Ion Concentration

Which of the following is a reasonable pH for a solution that is 8×10^{-4} M in H^+?

a. 2.9 **b.** 3.1 **c.** 4.2 **d.** 4.8

Solution

The $[H^+]$ is greater than 1×10^{-4} M, and so the pH must be less than 4. That rules out answers (c) and (d). The $[H^+]$ is less than 10×10^{-4} (or 1×10^{-3} M), and so the pH must be greater than 3. That rules out answer (a). The only reasonable answer is (b), a value between 3 and 4.

(With a scientific calculator, you can calculate the actual pH, usually with the following keystrokes: (8)(exp)(4)(±)(log) This gives a value of −3.1 for the log of 8×10^{-4}. Because pH is the *negative* log of the H^+ concentration, the pH value is 3.1.)

■ EXERCISE 7.8

Which of the following is a reasonable pH for a solution that is 2×10^{-10} M in H^+?

a. 2.0 **b.** 8.7 **c.** 9.7 **d.** 10.2

It's not obvious right away, but every aqueous solution contains *both* hydrogen ions and hydroxide ions. An acidic solution contains more H^+ ions than OH^- ions. For example, a solution with a pH of 4 is 1×10^{-4} M in H^+ ions but only 1×10^{-10} M in OH^- ions. On the other hand, a basic solution contains more OH^- ions than H^+ ions. A solution with a pH of 12 is 1×10^{-12} M in H^+ ions and 1×10^{-2} M in OH^- ions. And a neutral solution contains equal concentrations of H^+ ions and OH^- ions; both are 1×10^{-7} M.

CONCEPTUAL Example 7.9 Hydrogen and Hydroxide Ions in Acids and Bases

Classify the three aqueous solutions shown below as acidic, basic, or neutral. (Water molecules are not shown.)

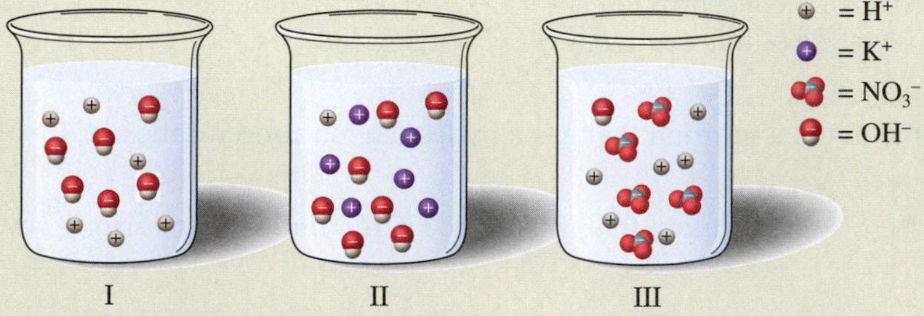

Solution

Beaker I contains equal numbers of OH^- ions and H^+ ions—six of each—so that solution is neutral. Beaker II contains more OH^- ions (seven) than H^+ ions (one), so its solution is basic. Beaker III contains six H^+ ions and one OH^- ion; the solution is acidic.

■ EXERCISE 7.9

What is the formula of the compound that was dissolved in Beaker III of Example 7.9? What is the formula of the compound that was dissolved in Beaker II?

Self-Assessment Questions

1. The hydrogen ion concentration, $[H^+]$, of a 0.0010 M HNO_3 solution is
   a. 1.0×10^{-4} M   b. 1.0×10^{-3} M
   c. 1.0×10^{-2} M   d. 10 M
2. What is the pH of a solution that has a hydrogen ion concentration of 1.0×10^{-11} M?
   a. 1.0   b. 3   c. 10   d. 11
3. Swimming pool water with a pH of 8 has a hydrogen ion concentration of
   a. 8.0 M   b. 8.0×10^{-8} M
   c. 1.0×10^{-8} M   d. 1.0×10^{8} M
4. The pH of pure water is
   a. 0   b. 1   c. 7   d. 10   e. 14
5. Which of the following is a reasonable pH for 0.15 M HCl?
   a. 0.15   b. 0.82   c. 8.24   d. 13.18
6. Which of the following is a reasonable pH for 0.15 M NaOH?
   a. 0.15   b. 0.82   c. 8.24   d. 13.18
7. Physiological pH (7.4) is the average pH of blood. Which of the following is a reasonable hydrogen ion concentration of a solution at physiological pH?
   a. −7.4 M   b. 0.6 M   c. 6×10^{-7} M
   d. 1×10^{-8} M   e. 4×10^{-8}

Answers: 1, b; 2, d; 3, c; 4, c; 5, b; 6, d; 7, e

7.7 Buffers and Conjugate Acid–Base Pairs

Learning Objectives › Write the formula for the conjugate base of an acid or for the conjugate acid of a base. › Describe the action of a buffer.

In the Brønsted–Lowry theory, a pair of compounds or ions that differ by one proton (H^+) is called a **conjugate acid–base pair.** HF and F^- are a conjugate acid-base pair, as are NH_3 and NH_4^+. When a base (for example, NH_3) accepts a proton, it becomes an acid because it now has a proton that it can donate. NH_4^+ is an acid; it can donate its "extra" proton. Similarly, when an acid (for example, HF) donates a proton, it becomes a base, because it can now accept a proton. F^- is a base; it can accept a proton.

CONCEPTUAL Example 7.10 Conjugate Acid–Base Pairs

What is the conjugate base **(a)** of HBr and **(b)** of HNO_3? What is the conjugate acid **(c)** of OH^- and **(d)** of HSO_4^-?

Solution

a. Removing a proton from HBr leaves Br^-; the conjugate base of HBr is Br^-.
b. Removing a proton from HNO_3 leaves NO_3^-; the conjugate base of HNO_3 is NO_3^-.
c. Adding a proton to OH^- gives H_2O; the conjugate acid of OH^- is H_2O.
d. Adding a proton to HSO_4^- gives H_2SO_4; the conjugate acid of HSO_4^- is H_2SO_4.

■ EXERCISE 7.10

What is the conjugate base **(a)** of HCN and **(b)** of H_3O^+? What is the conjugate acid **(c)** of SO_4^{2-} and **(d)** of HCO_3^-?

Buffer Solutions

A **buffer solution** maintains an almost constant pH when small amounts of a strong acid or a strong base are added to it. Buffer solutions have many important applications in industry, in the laboratory, and in living organisms because some chemical reactions consume acids, others produce acids, and many are catalyzed by acids[1]. A buffer solution consists of a weak acid and its conjugate base (for example, $HC_2H_3O_2$ and $C_2H_3O_2^-$) or a weak base and its conjugate acid (for example, NH_3 and NH_4^+).

Consider the equation for the ionization of acetic acid, in which the double arrow indicates the slight extent to which the acid ionizes.

$$HC_2H_3O_2(aq) \rightleftharpoons H^+(aq) + C_2H_3O_2^-(aq)$$

If we add sodium acetate to a solution of acetic acid, we are adding the conjugate base of acetic acid—that is, acetate ion—thus forming a buffer solution. If we add a little strong base to this solution, it will react with the weak acid.

$$OH^- + HC_2H_3O_2 \longrightarrow H_2O + C_2H_3O_2^-$$

Do you see that the solution no longer contains the strong base? Instead, it has a little more weak base and a little less weak acid than it did before the strong base was added. The pH remains very nearly constant. Likewise, if a little strong acid is added, it will react with the weak base.

$$H^+ + C_2H_3O_2^- \longrightarrow HC_2H_3O_2$$

The strong acid is consumed, a weak acid is formed, and the solution pH increases slightly. This behavior of buffered solutions contrasts sharply with that of unbuffered solutions, in which any added strong acid or base changes the pH greatly.

A dramatic and essential example of the action of buffers is found in our blood. Blood must maintain a pH very close to 7.4 or it cannot carry oxygen from the lungs to cells. The most important buffer for maintaining acid–base balance in the blood is the carbonic acid–bicarbonate ion (H_2CO_3/HCO_3^-) buffer.

Self-Assessment Questions

1. Which of the following pairs is a conjugate acid–base pair?
   a. CH_3COOH and OH^-
   b. HCN and CN^-
   c. HCN and OH^-
   d. HCl and OH^-
2. Which of the following is *not* a conjugate acid–base pair?
   a. CH_3COO^- and CH_3COOH
   b. F^- and HF
   c. H_2O and H_3O^+
   d. NH_3 and H_3O^+
3. A buffer solution is made from formic acid (HCOOH) and sodium formate (HCOONa). Added acid will react with
   a. $HCOO^-$
   b. HCOOH
   c. Na^+
   d. OH^-
4. Which of the following pairs could form a buffer?
   a. C_6H_5COOH and C_6H_5COONa
   b. HCl and NaCl
   c. HCl and NaOH
   d. NH_3 and NO_3^-

Answers: 1, b; 2, d; 3, a; 4, a

7.8 Acids and Bases in Industry and in Daily Life

Learning Objective › Describe everyday uses of acids and bases and how they affect daily life.

Acids and bases play an important role in our bodies, in medicine, in our homes, and in industry, they are useful products in many ways, As industrial by-products, they can damage the environment. Their use requires caution, and their misuse can be dangerous to human health.

[1]A *catalyst* is a substance or mixture that speeds up a reaction. Unlike a reactant, a catalyst can be recovered unchanged after the reaction is complete, and ordinarily it can be reused. For example, the breakdown of some flavoring components of fruits is catalyzed by acid, and the formation of biodiesel fuel from waste oil is catalyzed by a strong base such as sodium hydroxide.

Acid Rain

Carbon dioxide is the anhydride of carbonic acid (Section 7.3). Raindrops falling through the air absorb CO_2, which is converted to H_2CO_3 in the drops. Rainwater is thus a dilute solution of carbonic acid, a weak acid. Rain saturated with carbon dioxide has a pH of 5.6. In many areas of the world, particularly those downwind from industrial centers, rainwater is much more acidic, with a pH as low as 3 or less. Rain with a pH below 5.6 is called **acid rain**.

Acid rain is due to acidic pollutants in the air. As we shall see in Chapter 13, several air pollutants are acid anhydrides. These include sulfur dioxide (SO_2), mainly from the burning of high-sulfur coal in power plants and metal smelters, and nitrogen dioxide (NO_2) and nitric oxide (NO), from automobile exhaust fumes.

Some acid rain is due to natural pollutants, such as those resulting from volcanic eruptions and lightning. Volcanoes give off sulfur oxides and sulfuric acid, and lightning produces nitrogen oxides and nitric acid from nitrogen, oxygen, and water in the air.

Acid rain is an important environmental problem that involves both air pollution (Chapter 13) and water pollution (Chapter 14). It can have serious effects on plant and animal life.

Antacids: A Basic Remedy

The stomach secretes hydrochloric acid to aid in the digestion of food. Sometimes overindulgence or emotional stress leads to *hyperacidity* (too much acid is secreted). Hundreds of brands of antacids (Figure 7.8) are sold in the United States to treat this condition. Despite the many brand names, there are only a few different antacid ingredients, all of which are bases. Common ingredients are sodium bicarbonate, calcium carbonate, aluminum hydroxide, magnesium carbonate, and magnesium hydroxide. Even a single brand name often encompasses a variety of products. For example, there are more than a dozen varieties of Alka-Seltzer®.

Sodium bicarbonate ($NaHCO_3$), commonly called *baking soda*, was one of the first antacids and is still used occasionally. It is the principal antacid in most forms of Alka-Seltzer for heartburn relief. The bicarbonate ions react with the acid in the stomach to form carbonic acid, which then breaks down to carbon dioxide and water.

$$HCO_3^-(aq) + H^+(aq) \longrightarrow H_2CO_3(aq)$$

$$H_2CO_3(aq) \longrightarrow CO_2(g) + H_2O(l)$$

The $CO_2(g)$ is largely responsible for the burps that bicarbonate-containing antacids produce. Overuse of sodium bicarbonate can make the blood too alkaline,

You can make your own aspirin-free "Alka-Seltzer." Simply place half a teaspoon of baking soda in a glass of orange juice. (What is the acid and what is the base in this reaction?)

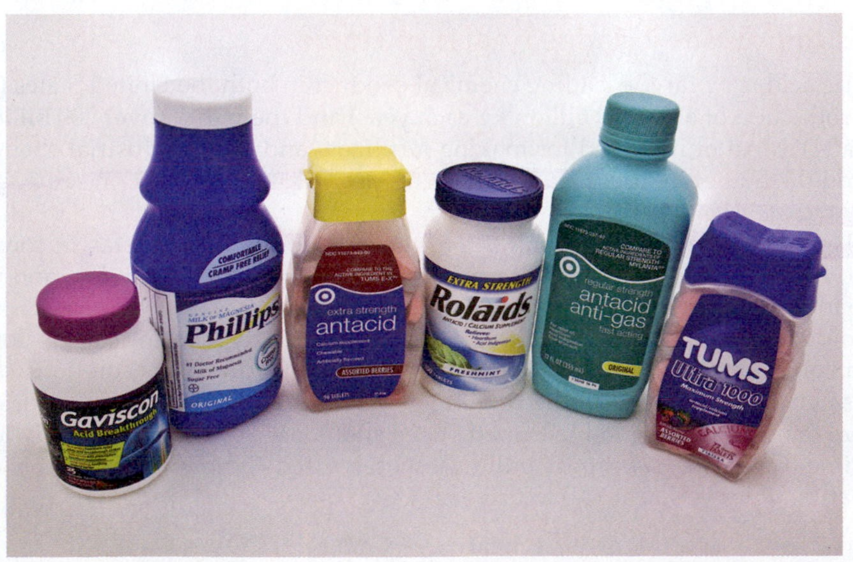

◀ **Figure 7.8** Claims that antacids are "fast acting" are almost meaningless because most common acid–base reactions are almost instantaneous. Some tablets may dissolve a little more slowly than others. You can speed their action by chewing them.

Why Doesn't Stomach Acid Dissolve the Stomach?

We know that strong acids are corrosive to skin. Look back at Table 7.1 and you will see that the gastric juice in your stomach is extremely acidic. Gastric juice is a solution containing about 0.5% hydrochloric acid. Why doesn't the acid in your stomach destroy your stomach lining? The cells that line the stomach are protected by a layer of mucus, a viscous solution of a sugar–protein complex called *mucin* and other substances in water. The mucus serves as a physical barrier, but its role is broader than that. The mucin acts like a sponge that soaks up bicarbonate ions from the cells lining the stomach and hydrochloric acid from within the stomach. The bicarbonate ions neutralize the acid within the mucus.

It used to be thought that stomach acid was the cause of ulcers, but it is now known that the acid plays only a minor role in ulcer formation. Research has shown that most ulcers develop as a result of infection with a bacterium called *Helicobacter pylori* (*H. pylori*) that damages the mucus, exposing cells in the stomach lining to the harsh stomach acid. Other agents, such as aspirin and alcohol, may be contributing factors to the development of ulcers. Treatment usually involves antibiotics that kill *H. pylori*.

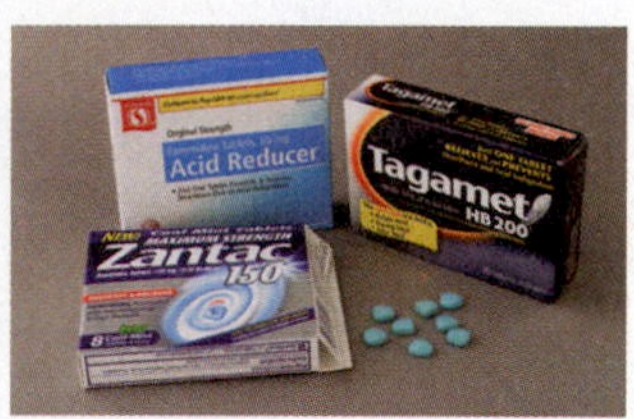

▲ Drugs such as ranitidine (Zantac™), famotidine (Pepcid AC™), cimetidine (Tagamet HB™), and omeprazole (Prilosec) are not antacids. Rather than neutralizing stomach acid, these drugs act on cells in the lining of the stomach, reducing the amount of acid that is produced.

a condition called **alkalosis**. Also, antacids that contain sodium ion are not recommended for people with hypertension (high blood pressure).

Calcium carbonate ($CaCO_3$) is safe in small amounts, but regular use can cause constipation. Also, taking large amounts of calcium carbonate can actually result in increased acid secretion after a few hours. Tums® and many store brands of antacids have calcium carbonate as the only active ingredient.

Aluminum hydroxide $[Al(OH)_3]$, like calcium carbonate, can cause constipation. There is also some concern that antacids containing aluminum ions can deplete the body of essential phosphate ions. Aluminum hydroxide is the active ingredient in Amphojel®.

A suspension of magnesium hydroxide $[Mg(OH)_2]$ in water is sold as *milk of magnesia*. Magnesium carbonate ($MgCO_3$) is also used as an antacid. These magnesium compounds act as antacids in small doses, but as laxatives in large doses.

Many antacid products have a mixture of antacids. Rolaids® and Mylanta® contain calcium carbonate and magnesium hydroxide. Maalox® liquid has aluminum hydroxide and magnesium hydroxide. These products balance the tendency of magnesium compounds to cause diarrhea with that of aluminum and calcium compounds to cause constipation.

Although antacids are generally safe for occasional use, they can interact with other medications. Anyone who has severe or repeated attacks of indigestion should consult a physician. Self-medication can sometimes be dangerous.

Acids and Bases in Industry and at Home

Sulfuric acid is by far the leading chemical product in both the United States (average production of about 40 billion kg each year) and the world (over 200 billion kg annually). Most of it is used for making fertilizers and other industrial chemicals. Around the home, we use sulfuric acid in automobile batteries and in some special kinds of drain cleaners.

Hydrochloric acid is used in industry to remove rust from metal, in construction to remove excess mortar from bricks and etch concrete for painting, and in the home to remove lime deposits from fixtures and toilet bowls. The product used in the home is often called *muriatic acid*, an old name for hydrochloric acid. Concentrated solutions (about 38% HCl) cause severe burns, but dilute solutions can be used safely in the home if handled carefully. Yearly production of hydrochloric acid is more than 4 billion kg in the United States and about 20 billion kg worldwide.

Lime (CaO) is the cheapest and most widely used commercial base. It is made by heating limestone ($CaCO_3$) to drive off CO_2.

$$CaCO_3(s) + \text{heat} \longrightarrow CaO(s) + CO_2(g)$$

Yearly production of calcium oxide is about 22 billion kg in the United States and about 280 billion kg worldwide. Adding water to lime forms calcium hydroxide [$Ca(OH)_2$], or slaked lime, which is generally safer to handle. Slaked lime is used in agriculture and to make mortar and cement.

Sodium hydroxide (NaOH, lye) is the strong base most often used in the home. It is employed in products such as Easy Off® for cleaning ovens, in products such as Drano® for unclogging drains, and to make both commercial and homemade soaps. Yearly U.S. production of sodium hydroxide is about 9 billion kg.

Ammonia (NH_3) is produced in huge volume, mainly for use as fertilizer. Yearly U.S. production is nearly 11 billion kg. Ammonia is used around the home in a variety of cleaning products (Chapter 21).

▲ It DOES Matter!
The proper pH is as important for plant growth as fertilizer is. Soil that is "sour," or too acidic, is "sweetened" by adding slaked lime (calcium hydroxide). A few plants, such as blueberries and citrus fruit, require acidic soil, and an acid such as vinegar may have to be periodically added to the soil they grow in.

Acids and Bases in Health and Disease

When they are misused, acids and bases can be damaging to human health. Concentrated strong acids and bases are corrosive poisons (Chapter 22) that can cause serious chemical burns. Once the chemical agents are removed, these injuries resemble burns caused by heat and are often treated in the same way. Besides being a strong acid, sulfuric acid is also a powerful dehydrating agent that can react with water in the cells.

Strong acids and bases, even in dilute solutions, break down, or *denature*, the protein molecules in living cells, much as cooking does. Generally, the fragments are not able to carry out the functions of the original proteins. If exposure to the acid or base is sustained, this fragmentation continues until the tissue has been completely destroyed.

Acids and bases affect human health in more subtle ways. A delicate balance between acids and bases must be maintained in the blood, other body fluids, and cells. If the acidity of the blood changes too much, the blood loses its capacity to carry oxygen. In living cells, proteins function properly only at an optimal pH. If the pH changes too much in either direction, the proteins can't carry out their functions. Fortunately, the body has a complex but efficient mechanism for maintaining a proper acid–base balance.

▲ Safety Alert
Concentrated acids and bases can cause severe burns and are especially damaging to the eyes. Use great care in working with them. Always follow directions carefully. Wear chemical-splash safety goggles to protect your eyes and clothing that will protect your skin and clothes.

Self-Assessment Questions

1. Which of the following is a common ingredient in antacids?
   a. $CaCO_3$
   b. $Ca(OH)_2$
   c. HCl
   d. KOH
2. When a person with excess stomach acid takes an antacid, the pH of the person's stomach changes
   a. from a low value to a value nearer 7
   b. from 7 to a much higher value
   c. from a low value to an even lower value
   d. from a high value to a lower value
3. The leading chemical product of U.S. industry is
   a. ammonia
   b. lime
   c. pesticides
   d. sulfuric acid
4. The acid used in automobile batteries is
   a. citric acid
   b. hydrochloric acid
   c. nitric acid
   d. sulfuric acid
5. The base often used in soap making is
   a. $Ca(OH)_2$
   b. $Mg(OH)_2$
   c. NaOH
   d. NH_3

Answers: 1, a; 2, a; 3, d; 4, d; 5, c

CRITICAL THINKING EXERCISES

Apply knowledge that you have gained in this chapter and one or more of the FLaReS principles (Chapter 1) to evaluate the following statements or claims.

7.1 A television advertisement claimed that the antacid Maalox neutralizes stomach acid faster and, therefore, relieves heartburn faster than Pepcid AC®, a drug that inhibits the release of stomach acid. To illustrate this claim, two flasks of acid were shown. In one, Maalox rapidly neutralized the acid. In the other, Pepcid AC did not neutralize the acid.

7.2 Some people claim that putting salt on grapefruit takes away a little of the acidity.

7.3 Testifying in a court case, a witness makes the following statement: "Although runoff from our plant did appear to contaminate a stream, the pH of the stream before the contamination was 6.4, and after contamination it was 5.4. So the stream is now only slightly more acidic than before."

7.4 A Jamaican fish recipe calls for adding the juice of several limes to the fish, but no heat is used to cook the fish. The directions state that the lime juice in effect "cooks" the fish.

7.5 An advertisement claims that vinegar in a glass-cleaning product will remove the spots left on glasses by tap water. The spots are largely calcium carbonate deposits.

SUMMARY

Section 7.1—Acids taste sour, turn litmus red, and react with active metals to form hydrogen. Bases taste bitter, turn litmus blue, and feel slippery to the skin. Acids and bases react to form salts and water. An **acid–base indicator** such as litmus has different colors in acid and in base and is used to determine whether solutions are acidic or basic.

Section 7.2—According to Arrhenius's definition, an *acid* produces hydrogen ions (H^+, also called protons) in aqueous solution, and a *base* produces hydroxide ions (OH^-). **Neutralization** is the combination of H^+ and OH^- to form water. The anion and cation that were associated with H^+ and OH^- ions combine to form an ionic **salt**. In the more general Brønsted–Lowry acid–base theory, an **acid** is a proton donor and a **base** is a proton acceptor. When a Brønsted–Lowry acid dissolves in water, the H_2O molecules pick up H^+ to form hydronium ions (H_3O^+). A Brønsted–Lowry base in water accepts a proton from a water molecule, forming OH^-.

Section 7.3—Some nonmetal oxides (such as CO_2 and SO_3) are **acidic anhydrides** in that they react with water to form acids. Some metal oxides (such as Li_2O and CaO) are **basic anhydrides**; they react with water to form bases.

Section 7.4—A **strong acid** is one that ionizes completely in water to form H^+ ions and anions. A **weak acid** ionizes only slightly in water; most of the acid exists as intact molecules. Common strong acids are sulfuric, hydrochloric, and nitric acids. Likewise, a **strong base** is completely ionized in water, and a **weak base** is only slightly ionized. Sodium hydroxide and potassium hydroxide are common strong bases.

Section 7.5—The reaction between an acid and a base is called *neutralization*. In aqueous solution, it is the combination of H^+ and OH^- that forms water. The other anions and cations form an ionic salt.

Section 7.6—The **pH** scale indicates the degree of acidity or basicity; pH is defined as $pH = -\log[H^+]$, where $[H^+]$ is the molar concentration of hydrogen ion. A pH of 7 ($[H^+] = 1 \times 10^{-7}$ M) is neutral; pH values lower than 7 represent increasing acidity, and pH values greater than 7 represent increasing basicity. A change in pH of one unit represents a tenfold change in $[H^+]$.

Section 7.7—A pair of compounds or ions that differ by one proton (H^+) is called a **conjugate acid–base pair**. A **buffer solution** is a mixture of a weak acid and its conjugate base or a weak base and its conjugate acid. A buffer maintains a nearly constant pH when a small amount of a strong acid or a strong base is added.

Section 7.8—An antacid is a base such as sodium bicarbonate, magnesium hydroxide, aluminum hydroxide, or calcium carbonate that is taken to relieve hyperacidity. Overuse of some antacids can make the blood too alkaline (basic), a condition called **alkalosis**. **Acid rain** is rain with a pH less than 5.6. The acidity is due to sulfur oxides and nitrogen oxides from natural sources as well as industrial air pollution and automobile exhaust fumes. Acid rain can have serious effects on plant and animal life. Sulfuric acid is the number one chemical produced in the United States and is used for making fertilizers and other industrial chemicals. Hydrochloric acid is used for rust removal and etching mortar and concrete. Lime (calcium oxide) is made from limestone and is the cheapest and most widely used base. It is an ingredient in plaster and cement and is used in agriculture. Sodium hydroxide is used to make many industrial products, as well as soap. Amm onia is a weak base produced mostly for use as fertilizer. Concentrated strong acids and bases are corrosive poisons that can cause serious burns. Living cells have an optimal pH that is necessary for the proper functioningof proteins.

Green chemistry Base is used to convert renewable fats and oils into products such as soaps and biofuels. Treatment with acid can decompose special plastics (such as polylactic acid, PLA) into a useful antimicrobial cleaner. Application of the Twelve Principles of Green Chemistry can guide us to find practical uses for materials that were once considered waste.

Learning Objectives

› Distinguish between acids and bases using their chemical and physical properties. (7.1)	Problems 1, 26, 27
› Explain how an acid–base indicator works. (7.1)	Problem 2
› Identify Arrhenius and Brønsted–Lowry acids and bases. (7.2)	Problems 4, 12–22, 59
› Write a balanced equation for a neutralization or an ionization. (7.2)	Problems 8, 39–46, 60, 67
› Identify acidic and basic anhydrides, and write equations showing their reactions with water. (7.3)	Problems 7, 29, 30
› Define and identify strong and weak acids and bases. (7.4)	Problems 5, 9, 10, 31–38, 61
› Identify the reactants and predict the products in a neutralization reaction. (7.5)	Problems 43–46
› Describe the relationship between the pH of a solution and its acidity or basicity. (7.6)	Problems 47–54
› Find the molar concentration of hydrogen ion, $[H^+]$, from a pH value or the pH value from $[H^+]$. (7.6)	Problems 49–54
› Write the formula for the conjugate base of an acid or for the conjugate acid of a base. (7.7)	Problems 55, 56
› Describe the action of a buffer. (7.7)	Problem 65
› Describe everyday uses of acids and bases and how they affect daily life. (7.8)	Problems 11, 57, 58
› Write equations for the production of soap and of biofuel.	Problem 73
› Describe ways by which acids and bases can contribute to greener production of consumer products.	Problems 71, 72, 74

REVIEW QUESTIONS

1. Define the following terms, and give an example of each.
   a. acid b. base c. salt
2. Describe the effect on litmus and the action on iron or zinc of a solution that has been neutralized.
3. List four general properties **(a)** of acidic solutions and **(b)** of basic solutions.
4. Can a substance be a Brønsted–Lowry acid if it does not contain H atoms? Are there any characteristic atoms that must be present in a Brønsted–Lowry base?
5. Both strong bases and weak bases have properties characteristic of hydroxide ions. How do strong bases and weak bases differ?
6. What is meant by a proton in acid–base chemistry? How does it differ from a nuclear proton (Chapter 3)?
7. What is an acidic anhydride? A basic anhydride?
8. Describe the neutralization of an acid or a base.
9. Magnesium hydroxide is completely ionic, even in the solid state, yet it can be taken internally as an antacid. Explain why taking it does not cause injury although taking sodium hydroxide would.
10. What are the effects of strong acids and strong bases on the skin?
11. What is alkalosis? What antacid ingredient might cause alkalosis if taken in excess?
12. According to the Arrhenius theory, all acids have one element in common. What is that element? Are all compounds containing that element acids? Explain.

PROBLEMS

Acids and Bases: The Arrhenius Theory

13. Write an equation that represents how perchloric acid ($HClO_4$) behaves as an Arrhenius acid.
14. Write an equation that represents how dihydrogen phosphate ion ($H_2PO_4^-$) behaves as an Arrhenius acid. (Be sure to include the correct charges for ions.)
15. Write an equation showing that rubidium hydroxide (RbOH) acts as an Arrhenius base in water.
16. Write an equation showing that calcium hydroxide acts as an Arrhenius base in water.

Acids and Bases: The Brønsted–Lowry Acid–Base Theory

17. Use the Brønsted–Lowry definitions to identify the first compound in each equation as an acid or a base. (*Hint:* What is produced by the reaction?)
    a. $(CH_3)_2NH + H_2O \longrightarrow (CH_3)_2NH_2^+ + OH^-$
    b. $C_6H_5NH_2 + H_2O \longrightarrow C_6H_5NH_3^+ + OH^-$
    c. $C_6H_5CH_2NH_2 + H_2O \longrightarrow C_6H_5CH_2NH_3^+ + OH^-$
18. Use the Brønsted–Lowry definitions to identify the first compound in each equation as an acid or a base.
    a. $CH_3NH_2 + H_2O \longrightarrow CH_3NH_3^+ + OH^-$
    b. $H_2O_2 + H_2O \longrightarrow H_3O^+ + HO_2^-$
    c. $NH_2Cl + H_2O \longrightarrow NH_3Cl^+ + OH^-$

19. Write the equation that shows hydrogen chloride gas reacting as a Brønsted–Lowry acid in water. What is the name of the acid formed?

20. Write the equation that shows hydrogen iodide gas reacting as a Brønsted–Lowry acid in water. Based on the answer to Problem 19, suggest a name for the acid formed.

21. Write the equation that shows how ammonia acts as a Brønsted–Lowry base in water.

22. Hydroxylamine ($HONH_2$) is not an Arrhenius base, even though it contains OH, but it *is* a Brønsted–Lowry base. Write an equation that shows how hydroxylamine acts as a Brønsted–Lowry base in water.

Acids and Bases: Names and Formulas

23. For the following acids and bases, supply a formula to match the name or a name to match the formula.
a. HCl **b.** strontium hydroxide
c. KOH **d.** boric acid

24. For the following acids and bases, supply a formula to match the name or a name to match the formula.
a. rubidium hydroxide **b.** $Al(OH)_3$
c. hydrocyanic acid **d.** HNO_3

25. Name the following, and classify each as an acid or a base.
a. H_3PO_4 **b.** CsOH **c.** H_2CO_3

26. Name the following, and classify each as an acid or a base.
a. $Mg(OH)_2$ **b.** NH_3 **c.** CH_3COOH

27. When an acid name ends in *-ic acid*, there is often a related acid whose name ends in *-ous acid*. The formula of the *-ous* acid has one less oxygen atom than that of the *-ic* acid. With this information, write formulas for **(a)** nitrous acid and **(b)** phosphorous acid.

28. Refer to Problem 27 and Table 7.1. Tellurium is chemically similar to sulfur. Use this information to write the formulas for **(a)** telluric acid and **(b)** tellurous acid.

Acidic and Basic Anhydrides

29. Give the formula for the compound formed when **(a)** sulfur trioxide reacts with water and **(b)** magnesium oxide reacts with water. In each case, is the product an acid or a base?

30. Give the formula for the compound formed when **(a)** potassium oxide reacts with water and **(b)** carbon dioxide reacts with water. In each case, is the product an acid or a base?

Strong and Weak Acids and Bases

31. When 1.0 mol of hydrogen iodide (HI) gas is dissolved in a liter of water, the resulting solution contains 1.0 mol of hydronium ions and 1.0 mol of iodide ions. Classify HI as a strong acid, a weak acid, a weak base, or a strong base.

32. Thallium hydroxide (TlOH) is a water-soluble ionic compound. Classify TlOH as a strong acid, a weak acid, a weak base, or a strong base.

33. Methylamine (CH_3NH_2) gas reacts slightly with water to form relatively few hydroxide ions and methylammonium ions ($CH_3NH_3^+$). Classify CH_3NH_2 as a strong acid, a weak acid, a weak base, or a strong base.

34. When 1 mol of hydrogen sulfide (H_2S) gas is dissolved in a liter of water, the resulting solution contains about 0.0004 mol of H^+ ions and about 3×10^{-11} mol of OH^- ions. Classify H_2S as a strong acid, a weak acid, a weak base, or a strong base.

35. Identify each of the following substances as a strong acid, a weak acid, a strong base, a weak base, or a salt.
a. LiOH **b.** HBr **c.** HNO_2 **d.** $CuSO_4$

36. Identify each of the following substances as a strong acid, a weak acid, a strong base, a weak base, or a salt.
a. K_3PO_4 **b.** $CaBr_2$
c. $Mg(OH)_2$ **d.** $BaCO_3$

37. Which of the following aqueous solutions has the highest concentration of H^+ ions? Which has the lowest?
a. 0.10 M HNO_3 **b.** 0.10 M NH_3
c. 0.10 M CH_3COOH

38. Consider 0.10 M solutions of acetic acid, ammonia, hydrochloric acid, and sodium hydroxide. Rank these solutions in order of increasing pH.

Ionization of Acids and Bases

39. Write equations showing the ionization of the following as Arrhenius acids or bases.
a. HNO_2
b. $Ba(OH)_2$
c. HBr

40. Write equations showing the ionization of the following as Arrhenius acids or bases.
a. HI **b.** LiOH **c.** $HClO_2$

41. Write equations showing the ionization of the following as Brønsted–Lowry acids in water.
a. HClO **b.** HNO_2 **c.** H_2S

42. Write equations showing the ionization of the following as Brønsted–Lowry acids in water.
a. HI **b.** $HClO_3$
c. $CFH_2CHOHCOOH$

Neutralization

43. Write equations for the reaction **(a)** of potassium hydroxide with hydrochloric acid and **(b)** of lithium hydroxide with nitric acid.

44. Write equations for the reaction **(a)** of 1 mol of calcium hydroxide with 2 mol of hydrochloric acid and **(b)** of 1 mol of sulfuric acid with 2 mol of potassium hydroxide.

45. Write the equation for the reaction of 1 mol of sulfurous acid (H_2SO_3) with 1 mol of magnesium hydroxide.

46. Write the equation for the reaction of 1 mol of phosphoric acid with 1 mol of aluminum hydroxide.

The pH Scale

47. Indicate whether each of the following pH values represents an acidic, basic, or neutral solution.
a. 4 **b.** 7 **c.** 3.5 **d.** 9

48. Lime juice is quite sour. Which of the following is a reasonable pH for lime juice?
a. 2 **b.** 6 **c.** 7.8 **d.** 12

49. What is the pH of a solution that has a hydrogen ion concentration of 1.0×10^{-5} M?

50. What is the pH of a solution that has a hydrogen ion concentration of 1.0×10^{-9} M?

51. What is the hydrogen ion concentration of a solution that has a pH of 3?

52. What is the hydrogen ion concentration of a solution that has a pH of 11?

53. Milk of magnesia has a hydrogen ion concentration between 1.0×10^{-10} M and 1.0×10^{-11} M. What two whole-number values is the pH of milk of magnesia between?

54. Oven cleaner has a pH between 13 and 14. What two whole-number values of x should be used in 1.0×10^{-x} M to express the range of hydrogen ion concentration?

Conjugate Acid–Base Pairs

55. In the following reaction in aqueous solution, identify **(a)** which of the reactants is the acid and which is the base, **(b)** the conjugate base of the acid, and **(c)** the conjugate acid of the base.

$$HNO_3\ (aq) + NH_3(aq) \longrightarrow NO_3^-\ (aq) + NH_4^+\ (aq)$$

56. In the following reaction in aqueous solution, identify **(a)** which of the reactants is the acid and which is the base, **(b)** the conjugate base of the acid, and **(c)** the conjugate acid of the base.

$$CH_3CH_2COOH + H_2O \longrightarrow CH_3CH_2COO^- + H_3O^+$$

Antacids

57. Mylanta liquid has 200 mg of $Al(OH)_3$ and 200 mg of $Mg(OH)_2$ per teaspoonful. Write the equation for the neutralization of stomach acid [represented as HCl(aq)] by each of these substances.

58. What is the Brønsted–Lowry base in each of the following compounds, which are ingredients in antacids?
   a. $NaHCO_3$
   b. $Mg(OH)_2$
   c. $MgCO_3$
   d. $CaCO_3$

ADDITIONAL PROBLEMS

59. According to the Arrhenius theory, is every compound that contains OH a base? Explain.

60. Lime deposits on brass faucets are mostly $CaCO_3$. The deposits can be removed by soaking the faucets in hydrochloric acid. Write an equation for the reaction that occurs.

61. The conjugate base of a very weak acid is a strong base, and the conjugate base of a strong acid is a weak base. **(a)** Is Cl^- ion a strong base or a weak base? **(b)** Is CN^- a strong base or a weak base?

62. Strontium iodide can be made by the reaction of solid strontium carbonate ($SrCO_3$) with an acid. Identify the acid, and write the balanced equation for the reaction.

63. The *pOH* is related to $[OH^-]$ just as pH is related to $[H^+]$. What is the pOH **(a)** of a solution that has a hydroxide ion concentration of 1.0×10^{-3} M? **(b)** Of a 0.01 M KOH solution?

64. Rank 0.1 M solutions of **(a)** acetic acid ($HC_2H_3O_2$), **(b)** ammonia (NH_3), **(c)** nitric acid (HNO_3), **(d)** sodium chloride (NaCl), and **(e)** sodium hydroxide (NaOH) from the highest pH to the lowest pH.

65. Human blood contains buffers that minimize changes in pH. One blood buffer is the hydrogen phosphate ion (HPO_4^{2-}). Like water, HPO_4^{2-} is amphiprotic. That is, it can act either as a Brønsted–Lowry acid or as a Brønsted–Lowry base. Write equations that illustrate the reaction with water of HPO_4^{2-} as an acid and as a base.

66. Three varieties of Tums have calcium carbonate as the only active ingredient: Regular Tums tablets have 500 mg; Tums E-X, 750 mg; and Tums ULTRA, 1000 mg. How many regular Tums would you have to take to get the same quantity of calcium carbonate as you would get with two Tums E-X? With two Tums ULTRA tablets?

67. The active ingredient in the antacid Basaljel is a gel of solid aluminum carbonate. Write the equation for the neutralization of aluminum carbonate by stomach acid (aqueous HCl).

68. Milk of magnesia has 400 mg of $Mg(OH)_2$ per teaspoon. Calculate the mass of stomach acid that can be neutralized by 1.00 teaspoon of milk of magnesia, assuming that the stomach acid is 0.50% HCl by mass.

69. When a well is drilled into rock that contains sulfide minerals, some of the minerals may dissolve in the well water, yielding "sulfur water" that smells like rotten eggs. The water from these wells feels slightly slippery, contains HS^- ions, and turns litmus paper blue. From this information, write an equation representing the reaction of HS^- ions with water.

70. Sulfuric acid is produced from elemental sulfur by a three-step process: (1) Sulfur is burned to produce sulfur dioxide. (2) Sulfur dioxide is oxidized to sulfur trioxide using oxygen and a vanadium (V) oxide catalyst. (3) Finally, the sulfur trioxide is reacted with water to produce 98% sulfuric acid. Write equations for the three reactions.

71. The pH of soap is sometimes adjusted by adding citric acid before the raw soap is formed into bars. Would citric acid increase or decrease the pH of the finished soap?

72. Write an equation to show soap [as $CH_3(CH_2)_{14}COO^-Na^+$] acting as a base with sulfuric acid.

73. Write an equation for the neutralization reaction of a fatty acid ($HC_{16}H_{31}O_2$) with potassium hydroxide (KOH) in water. Is the product of this reaction a fuel or a soap?

74. Most soaps have a bitter taste and a slippery feel. What does this hint indicate about the pH of most soaps?

COLLABORATIVE GROUP PROJECTS

Prepare a PowerPoint, poster, or other presentation (as directed by your instructor) to share with the class.

1. Prepare a brief report on one of the following acids or bases. List sources (including local sources for the acid or base, if available) and commercial uses.
   a. ammonia **b.** hydrochloric acid
   c. phosphoric acid **d.** nitric acid
   e. sodium hydroxide **f.** sulfuric acid
2. Examine the labels of at least five antacid preparations. Make a list of the ingredients in each. Look up the properties (medical use, side effects, toxicity, and so on) of each ingredient on the Web or in a reference book such as *The Merck Index*.
3. Examine the labels of at least five toilet-bowl cleaners and five drain cleaners. Make a list of the ingredients in each. Look up the formulas and properties of each ingredient on the Web or in a reference book such as *The Merck Index*. Which ingredients are acids? Which are bases?
4. A web page on making biodiesel claims that any water in the waste oil must be removed before starting the reaction.

Oxidation and Reduction

Have You Ever Wondered?

1. **Why do AA and D batteries have the same voltage?**
2. **Why does it hurt my teeth when I bite on aluminum foil?**
3. **Why does a battery go dead?**
4. **Why are some batteries rechargeable, but others aren't?**
5. **Why does steel rust, while aluminum doesn't?**
6. **Does hydrogen have a promising future as a fuel?**

Learning Objectives

- Identify an oxidation–reduction reaction. (8.1)
- Classify a particular change within a redox reaction as either oxidation or reduction. (8.1)
- Identify the oxidizing agent and the reducing agent in a redox reaction. (8.2)
- Balance redox equations. (8.3)
- Identify and write the half-reactions in an electrochemical cell. (8.3)
- Describe the reactions that occur when iron rusts. (8.4)
- Explain why an explosive reaction is so energetic. (8.4)
- Write equations for reactions in which oxygen is an oxidizing agent. (8.5)
- List some of the common oxidizing agents encountered in daily life. (8.5)
- Identify some common reducing agents. (8.6)
- Write the overall equations for the metabolism of glucose and for photosynthesis. (8.7)
- Distinguish between the objectives of chemists producing industrial chemicals and those of chemists producing specialty chemicals.
- Explain how green chemistry can be applied to the design of new catalysts.

Burn and Unburn From a simple campfire to the most advanced electric battery, from the trees in a rainforest that consume carbon dioxide and make oxygen to the people hurrying along a city street, we depend on an important group of reactions called *oxidation–reduction reactions*, or *redox reactions* (a shortening of *reduction–oxidation*). These reactions are extremely diverse: charcoal burns, iron rusts, bleach removes stains, the food we eat is converted to energy for our brain and muscles, and plants use the sun's energy to produce food.

We see the long-term product of automotive steel and our atmosphere above: rust. The orange color is from iron(III) oxide. Steel is mostly iron, and iron undergoes an undesirable oxidation-reduction (redox) reaction in the presence of air and water. That reaction costs almost $10 billion every year, as engineers and manufacturers look for ways to minimize or prevent that redox reaction. Other redox reactions are desirable, or even necessary, to life itself. In this chapter, we will examine the nature of redox reactions, and we will look at some of their applications in life and in modern technology.

Oxidation and reduction always occur together. They are opposite aspects of a single process, a redox reaction. You can't have one without the other (Figure 8.1). When one substance is oxidized, another is reduced. However, it is sometimes convenient to discuss only a part of the process—the oxidation part or the reduction part.

Reduced forms of matter—foods, coal, and gasoline—are high in energy. *Oxidized* forms—carbon dioxide and water—are low in energy. The energy in foods and fossil fuels is released when these materials are oxidized. In this chapter, we examine the processes of oxidation and reduction in some detail to better understand the chemical reactions that keep us alive and maintain our civilization.

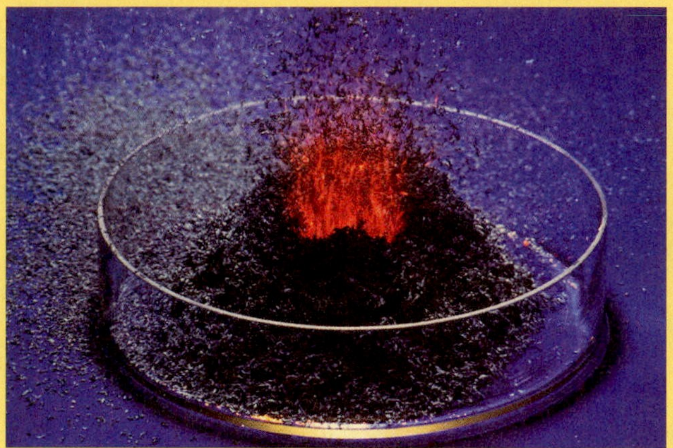

▲ **Figure 8.1** Oxidation and reduction always occur together. Pictured here on the left is a reaction called the ammonium dichromate volcano. In the reaction, the ammonium ion (NH_4^+) is oxidized and the dichromate ion ($Cr_2O_7^{2-}$) is reduced. Considerable heat and light are evolved. The equation for the reaction is

$$(NH_4)_2Cr_2O_7 \longrightarrow Cr_2O_3 + N_2 + 4\ H_2O$$

The water is driven off as vapor, and the nitrogen gas escapes, leaving pure Cr_2O_3 as the visible product (right).

8.1 Oxidation and Reduction: Three Views

Learning Objectives › Identify an oxidation–reduction reaction. › Classify a particular change within a redox reaction as either oxidation or reduction.

The term *oxidation* stems from the early recognition of oxygen's involvement in oxide formation; *reduction* originally meant removal of oxygen from an oxide. When oxygen combines with other elements or compounds, the process is called **oxidation**. The substances that combine with oxygen are said to have been *oxidized*. Originally, the term *oxidation* was limited to reactions involving combination with oxygen. As chemists came to realize that combination with chlorine (or bromine or another active nonmetal) was not all that different from combination with oxygen, they broadened the definition of oxidation to include reactions involving these other substances—as we shall shortly see.

Reduction is the opposite of oxidation. When hydrogen burns, it combines with oxygen to form water.

$$2\ H_2 + O_2 \longrightarrow 2\ H_2O$$

The hydrogen is oxidized in this reaction, but at the same time the oxygen is reduced. Whenever oxidation occurs, reduction must also occur. Oxidation and reduction always happen at the same time and in exactly equivalent amounts.

Because oxidation and reduction are chemical opposites and constant companions, their definitions are linked. We can view oxidation and reduction in at least three different ways (Figure 8.2).

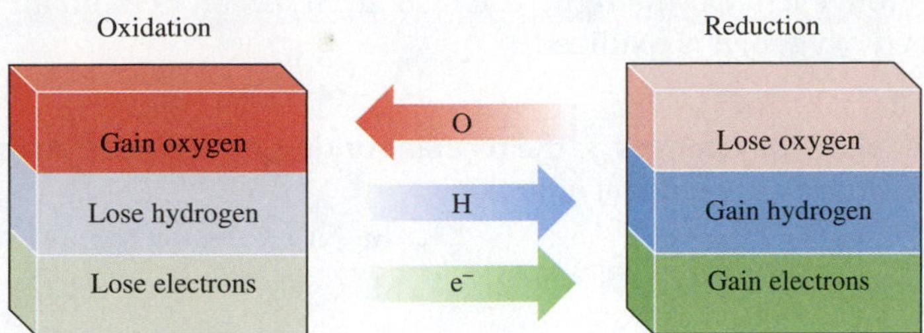

◀ **Figure 8.2** Three different views of oxidation and reduction.

1. *Oxidation* is a gain of oxygen atoms.
   Reduction is a loss of oxygen atoms.

At high temperatures (such as those in automobile engines), nitrogen, which is normally quite unreactive, combines with oxygen to form nitric oxide.

$$N_2 + O_2 \longrightarrow 2\ NO$$

Nitrogen gains oxygen atoms; there are no O atoms in the N_2 molecule and one O atom in each of the NO molecules. Therefore, nitrogen is oxidized.

Now consider what happens when methane is burned to form carbon dioxide and water. Both carbon and hydrogen gain oxygen atoms, and so both elements are oxidized.

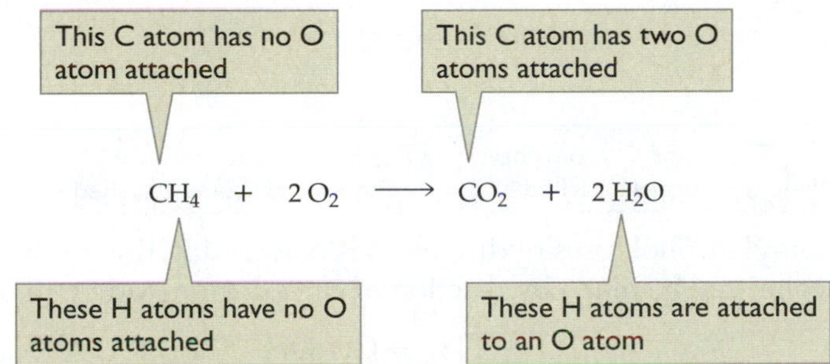

When lead dioxide is heated at high temperatures, it decomposes as follows:

$$2\ PbO_2 \longrightarrow 2\ PbO + O_2$$

This Pb atom has two O atoms attached

This Pb atom has only one O atom attached

The lead dioxide loses oxygen, so it is reduced.

CONCEPTUAL Example 8.1 Redox Processes—Gain or Loss of Oxygen Atoms

In each of the following changes, is the reactant undergoing oxidation or reduction? (These are not complete chemical equations.)

a. $Pb \longrightarrow PbO_2$ **b.** $SnO_2 \longrightarrow SnO$

c. $KClO_3 \longrightarrow KCl$ **d.** $Cu_2O \longrightarrow 2\ CuO$

Solution

a. Lead gains oxygen atoms (it has none on the left and two on the right); it is oxidized.

b. Tin loses an oxygen atom (it has two on the left and only one on the right); it is reduced.

c. There are three O atoms on the left and none on the right. The compound loses oxygen; it is reduced.

d. The two copper atoms on the left share a single oxygen atom, that is, half an oxygen atom each. On the right, each Cu atom has an O atom all its own. Cu has gained oxygen; it is oxidized.

■ EXERCISE 8.1

In each of the following changes, is the reactant undergoing oxidation or reduction? (These are not complete chemical equations.)

a. $3\ Fe \longrightarrow Fe_3O_4$ **b.** $NO \longrightarrow NO_2$

c. $CrO_3 \longrightarrow Cr_2O_3$ **d.** $C_3H_6O \longrightarrow C_3H_6O_2$

A second view of oxidation and reduction involves hydrogen atoms.

2. *Oxidation* is a loss of hydrogen atoms.

Reduction is a gain of hydrogen atoms.

Look once more at the burning of methane:

$$CH_4 + 2\ O_2 \longrightarrow CO_2 + 2\ H_2O$$

The oxygen gains hydrogen to form water, so the oxygen is reduced. Methane loses hydrogen and is oxidized. (We see that the carbon and hydrogens of CH_4 also gain oxygen, so our two views of oxidation and reduction are consistent with one another.)

Methyl alcohol (CH_3OH), when passed over hot copper gauze, forms formaldehyde and hydrogen gas.

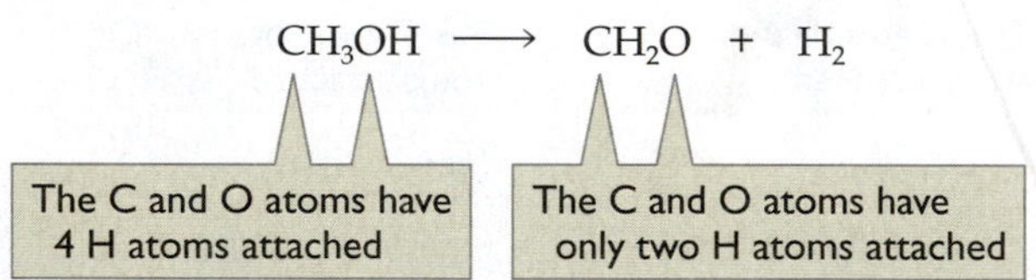
CH3OH ⟶ CH2O + H2
The C and O atoms have 4 H atoms attached
The C and O atoms have only two H atoms attached

Because the methyl alcohol loses hydrogen, it is oxidized in this reaction.

Methyl alcohol can be made by reaction of carbon monoxide with hydrogen.

$$CO + 2\ H_2 \rightarrow CH_3OH$$

Because the carbon monoxide gains hydrogen atoms, it is reduced.

Biochemists often find the gain or loss of hydrogen atoms a useful way to look at oxidation–reduction processes. For example, a substance called NAD^+ is changed to NADH in a variety of biochemical redox reactions. The actual molecules are rather complex, but we can write the equation for the oxidation of ethyl alcohol to acetaldehyde, one step in the metabolism of the alcohol, as follows.

$$CH_3CH_2OH + NAD^+ \longrightarrow CH_3CHO + NADH + H^+$$

We can see that ethyl alcohol is oxidized (loses hydrogen) and NAD^+ is reduced (gains hydrogen).

CONCEPTUAL Example 8.2 Redox Processes—Gain or Loss of Hydrogen Atoms

In each of the following changes, is the reactant undergoing oxidation or reduction? (These are not complete chemical equations.)

a. $C_2H_6O \longrightarrow C_2H_4O$ **b.** $C_2H_2 \longrightarrow C_2H_6$

Solution

a. There are six H atoms in the reactant on the left and only four in the product on the right. The reactant loses H atoms; it is oxidized.

b. There are two H atoms in the reactant on the left and six in the product on the right. The reactant gains H atoms; it is reduced.

■ EXERCISE 8.2

In each of the following changes, is the reactant undergoing oxidation or reduction? (These are not complete chemical equations.)

a. $C_3H_6O \longrightarrow C_3H_8O$ b. $C_3H_6 \longrightarrow C_3H_4$

A third view of oxidation and reduction involves gain or loss of electrons.

3. *Oxidation* is a loss of electrons.

Reduction is a gain of electrons.

When magnesium metal reacts with chlorine, magnesium ions and chloride ions are formed.

$$Mg + Cl_2 \longrightarrow Mg^{2+} + 2Cl^-$$

Because the magnesium atom loses electrons, it is oxidized, and because the chlorine atoms gain electrons, they are reduced.

It is easy to see that when magnesium atoms become Mg^{2+} ions, they lose electrons, and that when chlorine atoms become Cl^- ions, they must gain electrons. But which is oxidation and which is reduction? Perhaps Figure 8.3 can help. The charge on a simple ion is often referred to as its *oxidation number*. An increase in oxidation number (increase in positive charge) is oxidation; a decrease in oxidation number is reduction. The charge on an Mg atom is zero, therefore, conversion to Mg^{2+} is an increase in oxidation number (oxidation). For Cl atoms, the charge is also zero, and a change to Cl^- is a decrease in oxidation number (reduction).

This view of oxidation and reduction as a gain or loss of electrons is especially useful in electrochemistry (Section 8.3).

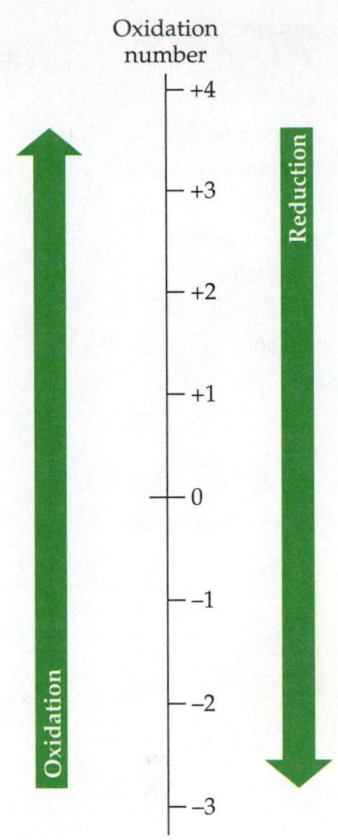

▲ **Figure 8.3** An increase in oxidation number means a loss of electrons and is therefore oxidation. A decrease in oxidation number means a gain of electrons and is therefore reduction.

Q: *Manganese's oxidation number changes from +4 in MnO_2 to +7 in MnO_4^-. Is it oxidized or reduced? Sulfur's oxidation number changes from 0 in S_8 to −2 in S^{2-}. Is it oxidized or reduced?*

CONCEPTUAL Example 8.3 Redox Processes—Gain or Loss of Electrons

In each of the following changes, is the reactant undergoing oxidation or reduction? (These are not complete chemical equations.)

a. $Zn \longrightarrow Zn^{2+}$ b. $Fe^{3+} \longrightarrow Fe^{2+}$

c. $S^{2-} \longrightarrow S$ d. $AgNO_3 \longrightarrow Ag$

Solution

a. In forming a 2+ ion, a Zn atom loses two electrons. Its oxidation number increases from 0 to +2. Zinc is oxidized.

b. To change from a 3+ ion to a 2+ ion, Fe gains an electron. Its oxidation number decreases from +3 to +2. The Fe^{3+} ion is reduced.

c. To change from a 2− ion to an atom with no charge, S loses two electrons. Its oxidation number increases. Sulfide ion is oxidized.

d. To answer this question, you must recognize that $AgNO_3$ is an ionic compound consisting of Ag^+ and NO_3^- ions. In changing from Ag^+ to Ag, silver gains an electron. Its oxidation number decreases. Silver ion is reduced.

■ EXERCISE 8.3

In each of the following changes, is the reactant undergoing oxidation or reduction? (These are not complete chemical equations.)

a. $Cr^{6+} \rightarrow Cr^{3+}$ b. $Sn^{2+} \longrightarrow Sn^{4+}$

c. $MnO_4^{2-} \longrightarrow MnO_4^-$ d. $Ti \rightarrow TiO_2$

Why do we have different ways to look at oxidation and reduction? Oxidation as a gain of oxygen is historical and specific, but the definition in terms of electrons applies more broadly. Which one should we use? Ordinarily, the definitions are consistent with one another, so we use the most convenient one. For the combustion (burning) of carbon,

$$C + O_2 \longrightarrow CO_2$$

Two mnemonics:

LEO the lion says GER.

Loss of
Electrons is
Oxidation.
Gain of
Electrons is
Reduction.

OIL RIG

Oxidation
Is
Loss of electrons.
Reduction
Is
Gain of electrons.

it is most convenient to see that carbon is oxidized by gaining oxygen atoms. Similarly, for the reaction

$$CH_2O + H_2 \longrightarrow CH_4O$$

it is easy to see that the reactant CH_2O gains hydrogen atoms and is thereby reduced. Finally, in the case of the reaction

$$3\ Sn^{2+} + 2\ Bi^{3+} \longrightarrow 3\ Sn^{4+} + 2\ Bi$$

it is clear that tin is oxidized because it loses electrons, increasing its oxidation number from +2 to +4. Similarly, we see that bismuth is reduced because it gains electrons, decreasing its oxidation number from +3 to 0.

Self-Assessment Questions

1. Which of the following is *not* one of the ways we can view oxidation?
a. electrons gained **b.** electrons lost
c. hydrogen atoms lost **d.** oxygen atoms gained

2. Which of the following partial equations represents an oxidation of nitrogen?
a. $NH_3 \rightarrow NH_4^+$ **b.** $N_2O_4 \rightarrow NI_3$ **c.** $NO_3^- \rightarrow NO$ **d.** $NO_2 \rightarrow N_2O_5$

3. When CrO_4^- reacts to form Cr^{3+}, the chromium in CrO_4^- is
a. reduced; it loses electrons
b. reduced; it loses oxygen
c. oxidized; its oxidation number increases
d. oxidized; it gains positive charge

4. Which of the following partial equations best represents a reduction of molybdenum?
a. $MoO_2 + H_2O \rightarrow H_2MoO_3$ **b.** $MoO_2 + 4\ H_2 \rightarrow Mo + 2\ H_2O$
c. $2\ MoO_2 + O_2 \rightarrow 2\ MoO_3$ **d.** $MoO_2 + 4\ H^+ \rightarrow Mo^{4+} + 2\ H_2O$

5. According to the following partial equation, Cl_2 is

$$3\ Cl_2 + 2\ Al \rightarrow 2\ AlCl_3$$

a. both oxidized and reduced **b.** neither oxidized nor reduced
c. oxidized, only **d.** reduced only

6. According to the following partial equation, manganese

$$Mn \rightarrow Mn^{2+} + 2\ e^-$$

a. gains electrons and is oxidized **b.** gains electrons and is reduced
c. loses electrons and is oxidized **d.** loses electrons and is reduced

7. When an element is oxidized, its oxidation number
a. decreases, as electrons are gained **b.** decreases, as electrons are lost
c. increases, as electrons are gained **d.** increases, as electrons are lost

Answers: 1, a; 2, d; 3, b; 4, b; 5, d; 6, c; 7, d

8.2 Oxidizing and Reducing Agents

Learning Objective › Identify the oxidizing agent and the reducing agent in a redox reaction.

Oxidation and reduction occur together. However, in looking at oxidation–reduction reactions, we often find it convenient to focus on the role played by a particular reactant. For example, in the reaction

$$CuO + H_2 \longrightarrow Cu + H_2O$$

we see that copper oxide is reduced and hydrogen is oxidized. We can conclude that if one substance is oxidized, the other must *cause* it to be oxidized. In the above reaction, CuO causes H_2 to be oxidized. Therefore, CuO is called the **oxidizing agent**. Conversely, H_2 causes CuO to be reduced, so H_2 is the **reducing agent**. Each oxidation–reduction reaction has an oxidizing agent and a reducing agent among the reactants. The reducing agent is the substance being oxidized; the oxidizing agent is the substance being reduced.

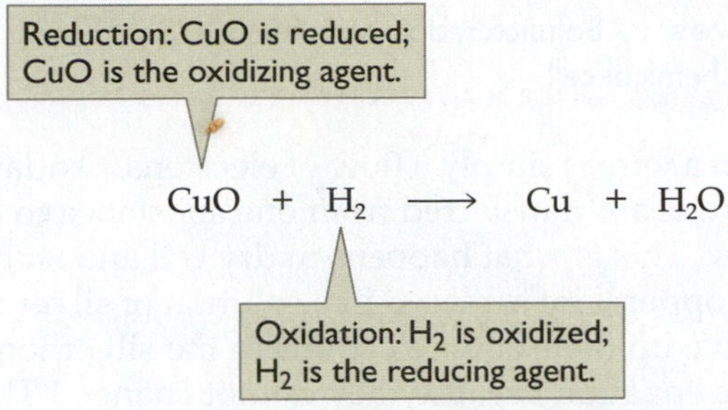

Reduction: CuO is reduced; CuO is the oxidizing agent.
$CuO + H_2 \longrightarrow Cu + H_2O$
Oxidation: H_2 is oxidized; H_2 is the reducing agent.

CONCEPTUAL Example 8.4 Oxidizing and Reducing Agents

Identify the oxidizing agents and reducing agents in the following reactions.

a. $2\,C + O_2 \longrightarrow 2\,CO$

b. $N_2 + 3\,H_2 \longrightarrow 2\,NH_3$

c. $SnO + H_2 \longrightarrow Sn + H_2O$

d. $Mg + Cl_2 \longrightarrow Mg^{2+} + 2Cl^-$

Solution

We can determine the answers by applying the three definitions of oxidation and reduction.

a. C gains oxygen and is oxidized, so it must be the reducing agent. O_2 is therefore the oxidizing agent.

b. N_2 gains hydrogen and is reduced, so it is the oxidizing agent. H_2 therefore is the reducing agent.

c. SnO loses oxygen and is reduced, so it is the oxidizing agent. H_2 is therefore the reducing agent.

d. Mg loses electrons and is oxidized, so it is the reducing agent. Cl_2 is therefore the oxidizing agent.

■ EXERCISE 8.4

Identify the oxidizing agents and reducing agents in the following reactions.

a. $Se + O_2 \longrightarrow SeO_2$

b. $2\,K + Br_2 \longrightarrow 2\,K^+ + 2\,Br^-$

c. $CH_3CN + 2\,H_2 \longrightarrow CH_3CH_2NH_2$

d. $V_2O_5 + 2\,H_2 \longrightarrow V_2O_3 + 2H_2O$

Self-Assessment Questions

1. A reducing agent

a. gains electrons **b.** gains protons **c.** loses electrons **d.** loses protons

2. Which substance is the oxidizing agent in the following reaction?

$$Cu(s) + 2\,Ag^+(aq) \rightarrow Cu^{2+}(aq) + 2\,Ag(s)$$

a. Ag **b.** Ag^+ **c.** Cu **d.** Cu^{2+}

3. In the following reaction, the reducing agent is

$$Al(s) + Cr^{3+}(aq) \rightarrow Al^{3+}(aq) + Cr(s)$$

a. Al(s) **b.** $Al^{3+}(aq)$ **c.** $Cr^{3+}(aq)$ **d.** Cr(s)

4. What is the oxidizing agent in the following reaction?

$$Zn(s) + 2\,Tl^+(aq) \rightarrow Zn^{2+}(aq) + 2\,Tl(s)$$

a. Tl(s) **b.** $Tl^+(aq)$ **c.** Zn(s) **d.** $Zn^{2+}(aq)$

5. What is the reducing agent in the following reaction?

$$12\,H^+(aq) + 2\,IO_3^-(aq) + 10\,Fe^{2+}(aq) \rightarrow 10\,Fe^{3+}(aq) + I_2(s) + 6\,H_2O(l)$$

a. $Fe^{2+}(aq)$ **b.** $H^+(aq)$ **c.** $I_2(s)$ **d.** $IO_3^-(aq)$

Answers: 1, c; 2, b; 3, a; 4, b; 5, a

8.3 Electrochemistry: Cells and Batteries

Learning Objectives › Balance redox equations. › Identify and write the half-reactions in an electrochemical cell.

We saw in Chapter 3 that electricity can produce chemical change, a process called *electrolysis*. For example, an electric current passed through molten sodium chloride produces sodium metal and chlorine gas. Here we focus on the reverse process, in which chemical change produces electricity.

An electric current in a wire is simply a flow of electrons. Oxidation–reduction reactions in which electrons are transferred from one substance to another can be used to produce electricity. This is what happens in dry cell and storage batteries.

When a coil of copper wire is placed in a solution of silver nitrate (Figure 8.4a), the copper atoms give up their outer electrons to the silver ions. (We can omit the nitrate ions from the equation because they do not change.) The copper metal dissolves, going into solution as copper(II) ions that color the solution blue. The silver ions come out of solution as beautiful needles of silver metal (Figure 8.4b). The copper is oxidized; the silver ions are reduced.

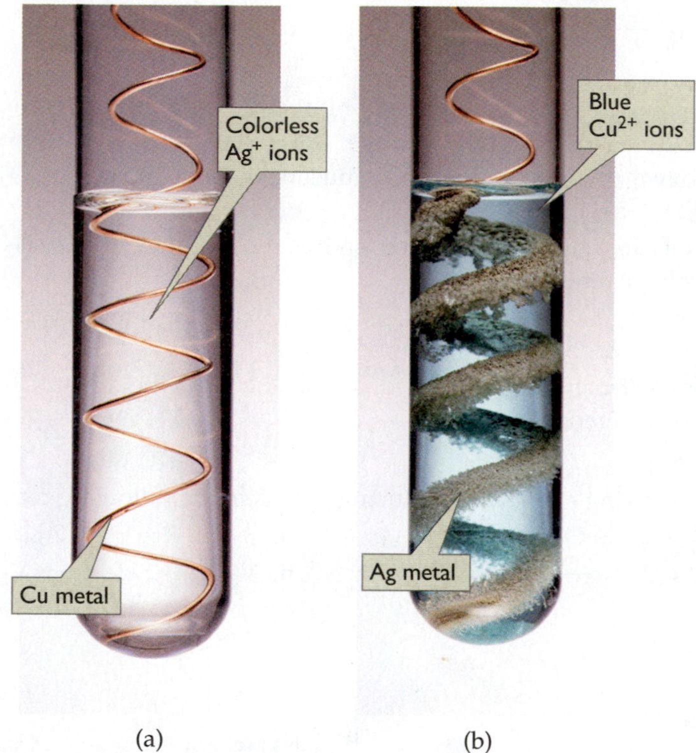

▶ **Figure 8.4** A coil of copper wire is immersed in a colorless solution of Ag^+ ions (a). As the reaction progresses, the more active copper displaces the less active silver from solution, producing needle-like crystals of silver metal (b) and a blue solution of Cu^{2+} ions. The equation for the reaction is $2Ag^+(aq) + Cu(s) \longrightarrow 2Ag(s) + Cu^{2+}(aq)$.

Because the reaction involves only the transfer of electrons, it can occur even when the silver ions are separated from the copper metal. If we place the reactants in separate compartments and connect them with a wire, the electrons will flow through the wire to get from the copper metal to the silver ions. This flow of electrons constitutes an electric current, and it can be used to run a motor or light a lamp.

In the **electrochemical cell** pictured in Figure 8.5, there are two separate compartments. One contains copper metal in a blue solution of copper(II) sulfate, and the other contains silver metal in a colorless solution of silver nitrate. Copper atoms give up electrons much more readily than silver atoms do, so electrons flow away from the copper compartment and toward the silver. The copper metal slowly dissolves as copper atoms give up electrons to form copper(II) ions. The electrons flow through the wire to the silver compartment, where silver ions pick them up to become silver atoms.

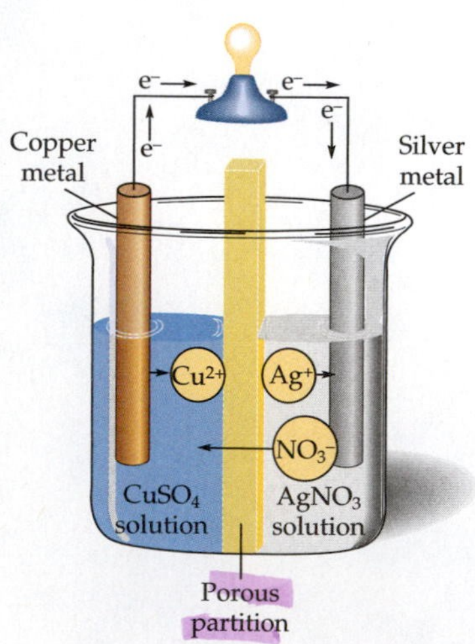

▲ **Figure 8.5** A simple electrochemical cell. The half-reactions are *Oxidation* (anode):

$$Cu(s) \longrightarrow Cu^{2+}(aq) + 2\,e^-$$

Reduction (cathode):

$$Ag^+(aq) + e^- \longrightarrow Ag(s)$$

Q: *To balance the equation for the overall reaction, you need to add a coefficient of 2 before Ag^+ and Ag(s). Why?*

As time goes by, the copper bar slowly disappears and the silver bar gets bigger. The blue solution becomes darker blue as Cu atoms are converted to Cu^{2+} ions. Those Cu^{2+} ions give the left compartment a positive charge, so (negative) nitrate ions move from the right compartment, through the porous partition, into the copper sulfate solution. (That is why the partition is porous. If the nitrate ions were unable to move through it, the cell would not work.) For each copper atom that gives up two electrons, two silver ions each pick up one electron, and two nitrate ions move from the right compartment to the left compartment.

The two pieces of metal where electrons are transferred are called **electrodes**. The electrode where oxidation occurs is called the **anode**. The one where reduction occurs is the **cathode**. In our example cell, copper gives up electrons, it is oxidized, and the copper bar is therefore the anode. Silver ions gain electrons and are reduced, so the silver bar is the cathode.

Electrochemical reactions are often represented as two *half-reactions*. The following representation shows the two half-reactions for the copper–silver cell and their addition to give the overall cell reaction.

$$\begin{array}{ll} \textit{Oxidation:} & Cu(s) \longrightarrow Cu^{2+}(aq) + 2\,e^- \\ \textit{Reduction:} & 2\,Ag^+(aq) + 2\,e^- \longrightarrow 2\,Ag(s) \\ \hline \textit{Overall reaction:} & Cu(s) + 2\,Ag^+(aq) \longrightarrow Cu^{2+}(aq) + 2\,Ag(s) \end{array}$$

Note that the electrons cancel when the two half-reactions are added.

1. Why do AA and D batteries have the same voltage? Cell voltage depends almost entirely on the overall cell reaction. Cells with the same cell reaction will have virtually the same voltage. However, a larger cell (D or flashlight battery) contains more reactants and will last longer in a particular device than would a smaller cell (AA or penlight battery).

2. Why does it hurt my teeth when I bite on aluminum foil? If you have an amalgam (metal) filling, aluminum touching the metal can cause a redox reaction in which the aluminum is oxidized. Only a small voltage is produced, but it can be enough to irritate the tooth's nerve causing a lot of discomfort!

CONCEPTUAL Example 8.5 Oxidation and Reduction Half-Reactions

Represent the following reaction as two half-reactions, and label them as an oxidation half-reaction and a reduction half-reaction.

$$Mg + Cl_2 \longrightarrow Mg^{2+} + 2\,Cl^-$$

Solution

Magnesium is oxidized from Mg to Mg^{2+}, a process that involves loss of two electrons from the Mg atom. The oxidation half-reaction is therefore

$$\textit{Oxidation:}\quad Mg \longrightarrow Mg^{2+} + 2\,e^-$$

The reduction half-reaction involves chlorine. Each of the two Cl atoms in the Cl_2 molecule must gain an electron to form a Cl^- ion. The reduction half-reaction is therefore

$$\textit{Reduction:}\quad Cl_2 + 2\,e^- \longrightarrow 2\,Cl^-$$

■ EXERCISE 8.5

Represent the following reaction as two half-reactions, and label them as an oxidation half-reaction and a reduction half-reaction.

$$2\,Co + 3\,S \rightarrow 2\,Co^{3+} + 3\,S^{2-}$$

Example 8.6 Balancing Redox Equations

Balance the following half-reactions, and combine them to give a balanced overall reaction.

$$\begin{array}{l} Sn^{2+} \longrightarrow Sn^{4+} \\ Bi^{3+} \longrightarrow Bi \end{array}$$

Solution

Atoms are balanced in both half-reactions, but electric charge is not. To balance charge in the first half-reaction, we add two electrons on the right side.

$$Sn^{2+} \longrightarrow Sn^{4+} + 2\,e^-$$

The second half-reaction requires three electrons on the left side.

$$Bi^{3+} + 3\,e^- \longrightarrow Bi$$

Before we can combine the two, however, we must set electron loss equal to electron gain. Electrons lost by the substance being oxidized must be gained by the substance being reduced. To make electron loss and gain equal, we multiply the first half-reaction by 3 and the second by 2.

$$3 \times (Sn^{2+} \longrightarrow Sn^{4+} + 2\,e^-) \quad = \quad 3\,Sn^{2+} \longrightarrow 3\,Sn^{4+} + 6\,e^-$$
$$2 \times (Bi^{3+} + 3\,e^- \longrightarrow Bi) \quad = \quad 2\,Bi^{3+} + 6\,e^- \longrightarrow 2\,Bi$$
$$3\,Sn^{2+} + 2\,Bi^{3+} \longrightarrow 3\,Sn^{4+} + 2\,Bi$$

Note that both atoms and charges balance in the overall reaction.

■ **EXERCISE 8.6A**

Balance the following half-reactions, and combine them to give a balanced overall reaction.

$$Fe \longrightarrow Fe^{3+}$$
$$Mg^{2+} \longrightarrow Mg$$

■ **EXERCISE 8.6B**

Balance the following half-reactions, and combine them to give a balanced overall reaction.

$$Pb \longrightarrow Pb^{2+}$$
$$Ag(NH_3)_2^{\ +} \longrightarrow Ag + 2\,NH_3$$

Photochromic Glass

Eyeglasses with photochromic lenses eliminate the need for sunglasses because the lenses darken when exposed to bright light. This response to light is the result of oxidation–reduction reactions. Ordinary glass is a complex matrix of silicates (Chapter 12) that is transparent to visible light. Photochromic lenses have silver chloride (AgCl) and copper(I) chloride (CuCl) crystals uniformly embedded in the glass. Silver chloride is susceptible to oxidation and reduction by light. First, the light displaces an electron from a chloride ion.

$$Cl^- \xrightarrow{\text{oxidation}} Cl + e^-$$

The electron then reduces a silver ion to a silver atom.

$$Ag^+ + e^- \xrightarrow{\text{reduction}} Ag$$

Clusters of silver atoms block the transmittance of light, causing the lenses to darken. This process occurs quite quickly. The degree of darkening depends on the intensity of the light.

To be useful in eyeglasses, the photochromic process must be reversible. The darkening process is reversed by the copper(I) chloride. When the lenses are removed from light, the chlorine atoms formed by the exposure to light are reduced by the copper(I) ions, which are oxidized to copper(II) ions.

$$Cl + Cu^+ \longrightarrow Cu^{2+} + Cl^-$$

The copper(II) ions then oxidize the silver atoms.

$$Cu^{2+} + Ag \longrightarrow Cu^+ + Ag^+$$

The net effect is that the silver and chlorine atoms are converted to their original oxidized and reduced states, and the lenses become transparent once more.

▲ Photochromic glass darkens in the presence of light.

Dry Cells

The familiar *dry cell* (Figure 8.6) is used in flashlights and some small portable devices. It has a cylindrical zinc case that acts as the anode. A carbon rod in the center of the cell is the cathode. The space between the cathode and the anode contains a moist paste of graphite powder (carbon), manganese dioxide (MnO_2), and ammonium chloride (NH_4Cl). The anode reaction is the oxidation of the zinc cylinder to zinc ions. The cathode reaction involves reduction of manganese dioxide. A simplified version of the overall reaction is

$$Zn + 2\,MnO_2 + H_2O \longrightarrow Zn^{2+} + Mn_2O_3 + 2\,OH^-$$

The ordinary dry cell has largely been replaced by the alkaline cell, which is similar but contains potassium hydroxide instead of ammonium chloride. Alkaline cells are more expensive than zinc–carbon dry cells, but they last longer—both in storage and in use.

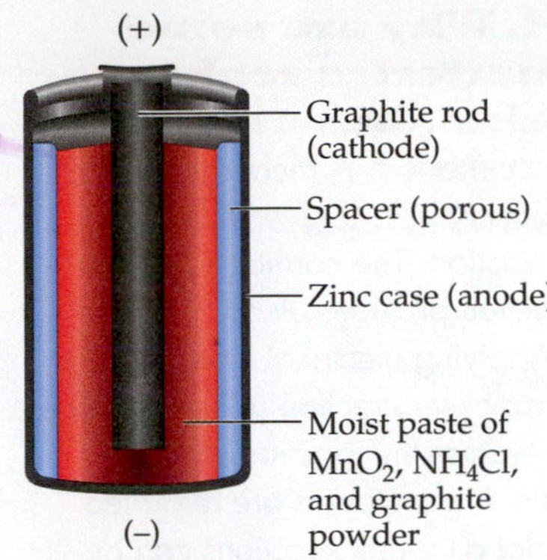

▲ **Figure 8.6** Cross section of a zinc–carbon cell. The half-reactions are

Oxidation (anode):

$$Zn(s) \longrightarrow Zn^{2+}(aq) + 2\,e^-$$

Reduction (cathode):

$$2MnO_2(s) + H_2O + 2\,e^- \longrightarrow Mn_2O_3(s) + 2\,OH^-(aq)$$

Lead Storage Batteries

Although we often refer to dry cells as batteries, a **battery** is actually a collection of electrochemical cells. The 12-volt (V) storage battery used in automobiles, for example, is a series of six 2-V cells. Each cell (Figure 8.7) contains a pair of electrodes, one lead and the other lead dioxide, in a chamber filled with sulfuric acid. Lead–acid batteries have been known for 150 years. They are used mainly in automobiles. Three hundred million of them are made per year.

An important feature of the lead storage battery is that it can be recharged. It discharges as it supplies electricity when the ignition is turned on to start a car or when the motor is off and the lights are on. It is recharged when the car is moving and an electric current created by the mechanical action of the car is supplied to the battery. The net reaction during discharge is

$$Pb + PbO_2 + 2\,H_2SO_4 \longrightarrow 2\,PbSO_4 + 2\,H_2O$$

The reaction during recharge is the reverse.

$$2\,PbSO_4 + 2\,H_2O \longrightarrow Pb + PbO_2 + 2\,H_2SO_4$$

Lead storage batteries are durable, but they are heavy, contain corrosive sulfuric acid, and lead is a toxic environmental problem.

▲ **It DOES Matter!**

Batteries labeled "Heavy Duty" or "Super" may be ordinary dry cells and may not have the longer shelf life and operating life of alkaline cells. Usually, alkaline cells are labeled as such and are only slightly higher in cost, making them a better buy.

3. Why does a battery go dead? When one or more of the reactants (zinc and MnO_2 in a dry cell) is essentially used up, the cell can no longer provide useful energy.

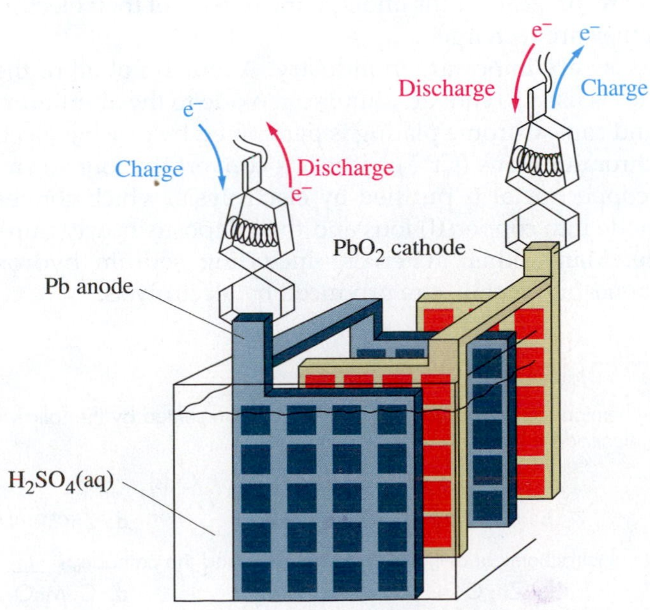

◄ **Figure 8.7** One cell of a lead-storage battery has two anode plates and two cathode plates. Six such cells make up the common 12-V car battery. The half-reactions are

Oxidation (anode):

$$Pb(s) + SO_4^{\,2-}(aq) \longrightarrow PbSO_4(s) + 2\,e^-$$

Reduction (cathode):

$$PbO_2(s) + 4\,H^+(aq) + SO_4^{\,2-}(aq) + 2\,e^- \longrightarrow PbSO_4(s) + 2\,H_2O$$

4. Why are some batteries rechargeable, but others aren't? A rechargeable battery uses a *reversible* redox reaction. The normal, forward reaction provides electrical energy. Applying electrical energy in the opposite direction using a charger reverses the reaction, and the starting materials are reformed. Not all redox reactions can be reversed in this manner.

Other Batteries

Much current battery technology involves the use of lithium, which has an extraordinarily low density and provides a higher voltage than other metals. Lithium cells make today's lightweight laptop computers possible. Lithium–SO_2 cells are used in submarines and rockets; lithium–iodine cells are used in pacemakers; and lithium–FeS_2 batteries are used in cameras, radios, and compact disc players.

Lithium cells provide so much energy and have such a compact volume that there have been incidents when the cells burst or even caught fire while being rapidly charged or discharged. Several manufacturers recalled millions of computer and telephone batteries between 2005 and 2011 because of the potential for such incidents.

The rechargeable NiCad cell (Cd anode, NiO cathode) has long been popular for portable radios and cordless tools. Its biggest competitor is the nickel–metal hydride cell, in which cadmium is replaced by a hydrogen-absorbing nickel alloy, such as $ZrNi_2$ or $LaNi_5$.

The button batteries used in hearing aids and hand calculators formerly contained mercury (zinc anode, HgO cathode), but these cells are gradually being phased out and replaced with zinc–air cells. Tiny silver oxide cells (zinc anode, Ag_2O cathode) are used mainly in watches and cameras.

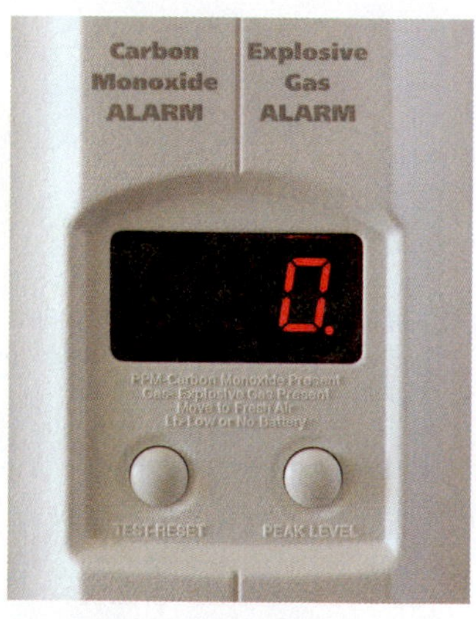

▲ Some carbon monoxide detectors use an electrochemical cell in which carbon monoxide is oxidized to carbon dioxide at the anode, and oxygen is consumed at the cathode. Sulfuric acid serves as the electrolyte. The cell produces current related to the CO concentration in the air, and the current triggers an alarm or produces a readout of the CO concentration.

Fuel Cells

An interesting kind of battery is the fuel cell. In a **fuel cell**, the oxidizing agent (usually oxygen) and the reducing agent are supplied continuously to the cell. Unlike other cells, a fuel cell does not "go dead" as long as the reactants are supplied. Moreover, when fossil fuels such as coal are burned to generate electricity, at most 35–40% of the energy from the combustion is actually harnessed. In a fuel cell, the fuel is oxidized and oxygen is reduced with 70–75% efficiency. As we shall see in Chapter 15, most present-day fuel cells use hydrogen as the fuel with platinum, nickel, or rhodium electrodes, in a solution of potassium hydroxide.

Electrolysis

Dry cells and fuel cells produce electricity from chemical reactions. Sometimes, we can reverse the process. In electrolysis (discussed briefly in Section 3.1), electricity supplied externally causes a chemical reaction to occur. The charging reaction of the lead storage cell shown in Figure 8.7 is one type of electrolysis. The car's alternator provides electric current, causing lead(II) sulfate to be converted back to lead metal and PbO_2. Other rechargeable cells undergo the reverse of their electricity-producing reaction when they are recharged.

Electrolysis is very important in industry. About 1% of all of the electricity in the United States is used to convert aluminum oxide to the aluminum metal we use for pots, foil, and cans. Chrome plating is performed by passing electricity through a solution of chromium ions (Cr^{6+}); electrons convert the ions to shiny chromium metal. Crude copper metal is purified by electrolysis, which converts the copper metal at the anode into copper(II) ions and then deposits nearly pure copper metal at the cathode. Many other materials—including sodium hydroxide, chlorine bleach, and magnesium metal—are produced by electrolysis.

Self-Assessment Questions

1. In the electrochemical cell whose overall reaction is represented by the following equation, the negative electrode is

$$Zn(s) + Cu^{2+}(aq) \rightarrow Zn^{2+}(aq) + Cu(s)$$

a. Cu(s) **b.** $Cu^{2+}(aq)$ **c.** Zn(s) **d.** $Zn^{2+}(aq)$

2. In one kind of electrochemical cell, the anode is ____ and the cathode is ____.

a. Zn, MnO_2 **b.** Zn, C **c.** C, Zn **d.** C, MnO_2

3. In an electrochemical cell composed of two half-cells, ions flow from one half-cell to another through
   a. electrodes
   b. an external conductor
   c. a porous partition
   d. a voltmeter
4. For the following reaction, the oxidation half-reaction is
   $$Mg + CuO \rightarrow MgO + Cu$$
   a. $Cu^{2+} + 2\,e^- \rightarrow CuO$
   b. $CuO \rightarrow Cu^{2+} + 2\,e^-$
   c. $Mg^{2+} + 2\,e^- \rightarrow MgO$
   d. $Mg \rightarrow Mg^{2+} + 2\,e^-$
5. In a lead storage battery, the product of both cathode and anode half-reactions is
   a. H_2SO_4
   b. Pb
   c. PbO_2
   d. $PbSO_4$
6. The fluid in the chamber of a lead storage battery is
   a. hydrochloric acid
   b. hydrofluoric acid
   c. methanol
   d. sulfuric acid
7. The overall electricity-producing reaction in the H_2/O_2 fuel cell is
   $$2\,H_2(g) + O_2(g) \rightarrow 2\,H_2O(g)$$
   The half-reaction at the cathode is
   a. $H_2 \rightarrow 2\,H^+ + 2\,e^-$
   b. $2\,H^+ + 2\,e^- \rightarrow H_2$
   c. $O_2(g) + 4\,H^+ + 4\,e^- \rightarrow 2\,H_2O$
   d. $2\,H_2O \rightarrow O_2(g) + 4\,H^+ + 4\,e^-$

Answers: 1, c; 2, b; 3, c; 4, d; 5, d; 6, d; 7, c

8.4 Corrosion and Explosion

Learning Objectives › Describe the reactions that occur when iron rusts. › Explain why an explosive reaction is so energetic.

You might think *corrosion* and *explosion* have little in common except that they rhyme. However, both processes involve redox reactions. Corrosion of metals is of great economic importance. In the United States alone, corrosion costs about $276 billion a year. Perhaps 20% of all the iron and steel produced in the United States each year goes to replace corroded items. Explosions can bring economic benefit when used in mining and road building. Or they can cause enormous loss in war and accidents.

The Rusting of Iron

In moist air, iron is oxidized, particularly at a nick or scratch.

$$Fe(s) \longrightarrow Fe^{2+}(aq) + 2\,e^-$$

As iron is oxidized, oxygen is reduced.

$$O_2(g) + 2\,H_2O(l) + 4\,e^- \longrightarrow 4\,OH^-(aq)$$

The net result, initially, is the formation of insoluble iron(II) hydroxide, which appears dark green or black.

$$2\,Fe(s) + O_2(g) + 2\,H_2O(l) \longrightarrow 2\,Fe(OH)_2(s)$$

This product is usually further oxidized to iron(III) hydroxide.

$$4\,Fe(OH)_2(s) + O_2(g) + 2\,H_2O(l) \longrightarrow 4\,Fe(OH)_3(s)$$

Iron(III) hydroxide $[Fe(OH)_3]$, sometimes written as $Fe_2O_3 \cdot 3\,H_2O$, is the familiar iron rust.

Oxidation and reduction often occur at separate points on the metal's surface. Electrons are transferred through the iron metal. The circuit is completed by an electrolyte in aqueous solution. In the Snow Belt, this solution is often the slush from road salt and melting snow. The metal is pitted in an anodic area, where iron is oxidized to Fe^{2+}. These ions migrate to the cathodic area, where they react with hydroxide ions formed by the reduction of oxygen.

$$Fe^{2+}(aq) + 2\,OH^-(aq) \longrightarrow Fe(OH)_2(s)$$

As noted previously, the iron(II) hydroxide is then oxidized to $Fe(OH)_3$, or rust. This process is diagrammed in Figure 8.8. Note that the anodic area is protected from oxygen by a water film, while the cathodic area is exposed to air.

▶ **Figure 8.8** The corrosion of iron requires water, oxygen, and an electrolyte.

Protection of Aluminum

Aluminum is more reactive than iron, yet corrosion is not a serious problem with aluminum. We use aluminum foil, we cook with aluminum pots, and we buy beverages in aluminum cans. Even after many years, they do not corrode. How is this possible?

The aluminum at the surface reacts with oxygen in the air to form a thin layer of oxide. Instead of being porous and flaky like iron oxide, however, aluminum oxide is hard and tough and adheres strongly to the surface of the metal, protecting if from further oxidation.

Nonetheless, corrosion can sometimes be a problem with aluminum. Certain substances, such as salt, can interfere with the protective oxide coating on aluminum, allowing the metal to oxidize. This problem has caused mag wheels on automobiles to crack, and some planes with aluminum landing gear have had wheels shear off.

5. Why does steel rust, while aluminum doesn't? Both steel (iron) and aluminum undergo oxidation. But the product from iron flakes off, exposing a fresh iron surface that will rust again. The aluminum oxide formed when aluminum "rusts" adheres strongly to the surface of the metal, protecting it from further oxidation.

Silver Tarnish

The tarnish on silver results from oxidation of the silver surface by hydrogen sulfide (H_2S) in the air or from food. It produces a film of black silver sulfide (Ag_2S) on the metal surface. You can use silver polish to remove the tarnish, but in doing so, you also lose part of the silver. An alternative method involves the use of aluminum metal.

$$3\,Ag^+(aq) + Al(s) \longrightarrow 3\,Ag(s) + Al^{3+}(aq)$$

This reaction also requires an electrolyte, and sodium bicarbonate ($NaHCO_3$) is usually used. The tarnished silver is placed in contact with aluminum metal (often in the form of foil) and covered with a hot solution of sodium bicarbonate. The silver ions are reduced to silver metal at the expense of the cheaper metal.

▲ Silver tarnish (Ag_2S) is readily removed from silver metal brought into contact with aluminum metal in a baking soda solution. Working in a sink, add about 1 cup of baking soda to 1 gal of hot water. Immerse a piece of aluminum and then the tarnished silver object so it touches the aluminum.

Q: *To what is the Ag_2S converted? To what is the Al converted?*

Explosive Reactions

Corrosive reactions are often quite slow. A chemical explosion (that is, not one based on nuclear fission or fusion) is usually an extremely rapid redox reaction, often accompanied by a considerable increase in volume. The redox reaction often involves a compound of nitrogen, such as nitroglycerin (the active ingredient in dynamite), ammonium nitrate (NH_4NO_3, a common fertilizer), or trinitrotoluene (TNT). These compounds can decompose readily, yielding nitrogen gas as one of the products.

Explosive mixtures are used for mining, earthmoving projects, and the demolition of buildings. *ANFO* (Ammonium Nitrate mixed with Fuel Oil) is an inexpensive and effective explosive, widely used for mining salt, coal, and other minerals. When ANFO explodes, ammonium ion is the reducing agent and nitrate ion is the oxidizing agent. The fuel oil provides additional oxidizable material. Using $C_{17}H_{36}$ as the formula for a typical molecule in fuel oil, we can write the equation for the explosive reaction.

$$52\ NH_4NO_3(s) + C_{17}H_{36}(l) \longrightarrow 52\ N_2(g) + 17\ CO_2(g) + 122\ H_2O(g)$$

Notice that the starting materials, 53 mol of a solid and a liquid, generate 191 mol of gaseous products. This reaction produces a huge volume increase, which becomes part of the explosive force.

Unfortunately, ANFO has also been used in terrorist attacks around the world. Ammonium nitrate is a widely used fertilizer, and fuel oil is used in many home furnaces. The fact that both these materials are readily accessible to potential terrorists is cause for some concern.

Self-Assessment Questions

1. What type of reaction is the corrosion of iron?
   a. acid–base **b.** addition
   c. oxidation–reduction **d.** neutralization
2. Corrosion of aluminum is not as big a problem as corrosion of iron because aluminum
   a. forms an oxide layer that adheres to the metal's surface
   b. is less reactive than Fe
   c. needs water to corrode
   d. has a higher oxidation number
3. Silver tarnish is mainly
   a. AgCl **b.** Ag_2O **c.** Ag_2S **d.** Fe_2O_3
4. In a typical explosive reaction, which of the following usually occurs?
   a. Gases are converted from one form to another.
   b. Liquids or solids are converted to aqueous solutions.
   c. Liquids or solids are converted to gases.
   d. Nitrogen nuclei are split.
5. Black powder is a mixture of charcoal (carbon), potassium nitrate, and sulfur. The oxidizing agent in black powder is
   a. charcoal **b.** nitroglycerin **c.** potassium nitrate **d.** sulfur

Answers: 1, c; 2, a; 3, c; 4, c; 5, c

8.5 Oxygen: An Abundant and Essential Oxidizing Agent

Learning Objectives › Write equations for reactions in which oxygen is an oxidizing agent. › List some of the common oxidizing agents encountered in daily life.

Oxygen itself is the most common oxidizing agent. Many other oxidizing agents—sometimes called *oxidants*—are important in the laboratory, in industry, and in the home. They are used as antiseptics, disinfectants, and bleaches and play a role in many chemical syntheses.

Oxygen: Occurrence and Properties

Certainly one of the most important elements on Earth, oxygen is one of about two dozen elements essential to life. Making up one-fifth of the air, it oxidizes the wood in our campfires and the gasoline in our automobiles. It even "burns" the food we eat to give us the energy to move and to think. It is found in most compounds that are important to living organisms. Foodstuffs—carbohydrates, fats, and proteins—all contain oxygen. The human body is approximately 65% water (by mass). Because water is 89% oxygen by mass and many other compounds in your body also contain oxygen, almost two-thirds of your body mass is oxygen.

The structure and chemistry of Earth are discussed in Chapter 12, of the atmosphere in Chapter 13, and of water in Chapter 14.

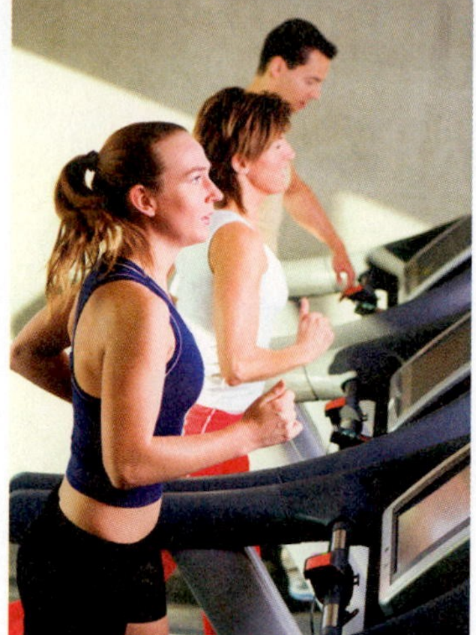

▲ **It DOES Matter!**
Physical activity under conditions in which plenty of oxygen is available to body tissues is called *aerobic* exercise. When the available oxygen is insufficient, the exercise is called *anaerobic*, and it often leads to weakness and pain resulting from "oxygen debt." (See Chapter 19.)

Oxygen comprises about half of the accessible portion of Earth by mass. It occurs in all three subdivisions of Earth's outermost structure. Oxygen occurs as O_2 molecules in the atmosphere (the gaseous mass surrounding Earth). In the hydrosphere (the oceans, seas, rivers, and lakes), oxygen is combined with hydrogen in water. In the lithosphere (the outer solid portion of the Earth's crust), oxygen is combined with silicon (sand is SiO_2), aluminum (in clays), and other elements.

The atmosphere is about 21% elemental oxygen (O_2) by volume. The rest is about 78% nitrogen (N_2) and 1% argon (Ar), both of which are quite unreactive. The free, uncombined oxygen in the air is taken into our lungs, passes into our bloodstreams, is carried to our body tissues, and reacts with the food we eat. This is the process that provides us with all our energy.

Fuels such as natural gas, gasoline, and coal also need oxygen to burn and release their stored energy. Oxidation, or combustion, of these fossil fuels currently supplies about 86% of the energy that turns the wheels of civilization.

Pure oxygen is obtained by liquefying air and then letting the nitrogen and argon boil off. Nitrogen boils at −196 °C, argon at −186 °C, and oxygen at −183 °C. About 20 billion kg of oxygen is produced annually in the United States, but most of it is used directly by industry, much of it in steel plants. About 1% is compressed into tanks for use in welding, hospital respirators, and other purposes.

Not everything that oxygen does is desirable. In addition to causing corrosion (Section 8.4), it promotes food spoilage and wood decay.

Oxygen: Reactions with Other Elements

Many oxidation reactions involving atmospheric oxygen are quite complicated, but we can gain some understanding by looking at some of the simpler ones. For example, as we have seen, oxygen combines with many metals to form metal oxides and with nonmetals to form nonmetal oxides.

Example 8.7 Writing Equations: Reaction of Oxygen with Other Elements

Magnesium combines readily with oxygen when ignited in air. Write the equation for this reaction.

Solution

Magnesium is a group 2A metal. Oxygen occurs as diatomic molecules (O_2). The two react to form MgO. The reaction is

$$Mg(s) + O_2(g) \longrightarrow MgO(s) \quad \text{(not balanced)}$$

To balance the equation, we need 2 MgO and 2 Mg.

$$2\,Mg(s) + O_2(g) \longrightarrow 2\,MgO(s)$$

■ EXERCISE 8.7

Write equations for the following reactions.

a. Zinc burns in air to form zinc oxide (ZnO).

b. Selenium (Se) burns in air to form selenium dioxide.

▲ Fuels burn more rapidly in pure oxygen than in air. Huge quantities of liquid oxygen are used to burn the fuels that blast rockets into orbit.

Oxygen: Reactions with Compounds

Oxygen reacts with many compounds, oxidizing one or more of the elements in the compound. As we have seen, combustion of a fuel is oxidation and produces oxides. There are many other examples. Hydrogen sulfide, a gaseous compound with a rotten-egg odor, burns to produce oxides of hydrogen (water) and of sulfur (sulfur dioxide).

$$2\,H_2S(g) + 3\,O_2(g) \longrightarrow 2\,H_2O(l) + 2\,SO_2(g)$$

Example 8.8 Writing Equations: Reaction of Oxygen with Compounds

Carbon disulfide, a highly flammable liquid, combines readily with oxygen, burning with a blue flame. What products are formed? Write the equation.

Solution

Carbon disulfide is CS_2. The products are oxides of carbon (carbon dioxide) and of sulfur (sulfur dioxide). The balanced equation is

$$CS_2(g) + 3\,O_2(g) \longrightarrow CO_2(g) + 2\,SO_2(g)$$

■ EXERCISE 8.8A

When heated in air, lead sulfide (PbS) combines with oxygen to form lead(II) oxide (PbO) and sulfur dioxide. Write a balanced equation for the reaction.

■ EXERCISE 8.8B

Write a balanced equation for the combustion (reaction with oxygen) of ethanol (C_2H_5OH).

Ozone: Another Form of Oxygen

In addition to diatomic O_2, oxygen also has a triatomic form (O_3) called *ozone*. Ozone is a powerful oxidizing agent and a harmful air pollutant. It can be extremely irritating to both plants and animals and is especially destructive to rubber. On the other hand, a layer of ozone in the upper stratosphere serves as a shield that protects life on Earth from ultraviolet radiation from the sun (Chapter 13). Ozone clearly illustrates that the same substance can be extremely beneficial or quite harmful, depending on the context.

Other Common Oxidizing Agents

Oxidizing agents used around the home include antiseptics, disinfectants, and bleaches. Many others are used in workplaces and in laboratories.

Disinfectants and antiseptics are alike in that both are materials used to destroy microorganisms (that is, they are germicidal), but antiseptics are applied mainly to living tissue and disinfectants to nonliving things. A good example of a disinfectant is chlorine, which is used to kill disease-causing microorganisms in drinking water and some swimming pools. The actual disinfecting agent is hypochlorous acid (HOCl), formed by the reaction of chlorine with water.

$$Cl_2(g) + H_2O(l) \longrightarrow HOCl(aq) + HCl(aq)$$

In recent years, concern has been raised over by-products that form when chlorine is used to disinfect water containing certain impurities. Although chlorine kills harmful microorganisms, it can also oxidize certain small molecules to form harmful by-products, such as chloroform.

Swimming pools are often chlorinated with calcium hypochlorite $[Ca(OCl)_2]$. Because calcium hypochlorite is alkaline, it also raises the pH of the water. (When a pool becomes too alkaline, the pH is lowered by adding hydrochloric acid. Swimming pools are usually maintained at pH 7.2–7.8.)

Hydrogen peroxide (H_2O_2) is a common oxidizing agent that has the advantage of being converted to water in most reactions. Pure hydrogen peroxide is a syrupy liquid. It is available (in laboratories) as a dangerous 30% solution that has powerful oxidizing power or as a 3% solution (sold in stores) for various uses around the home. When combined with a specially designed catalyst, hydrogen peroxide can be used to oxidize colored compounds and water impurities.

As a dilute aqueous solution, hydrogen peroxide is used to bleach hair (which gave rise to the phrase "peroxide blonde"). Dilute H_2O_2 is used medically to clean and deodorize wounds and ulcers.

Iodine is used as an antiseptic, either in an alcoholic solution (called *tincture of iodine*) or in Lugol's iodine solution (which contains no alcohol).

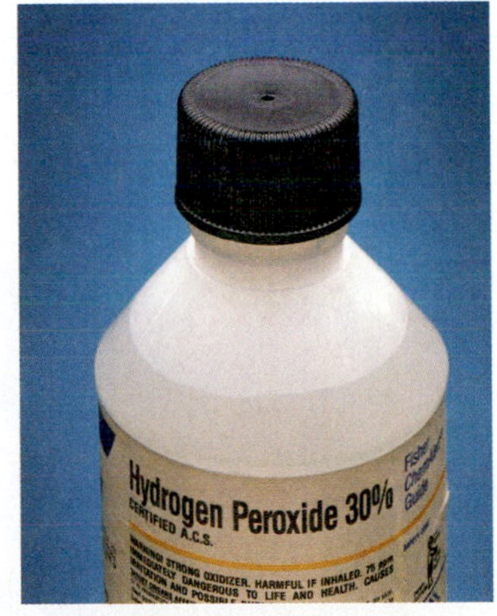

▲ Hydrogen peroxide is a powerful oxidizing agent. Dilute solutions are used as disinfectant and to bleach hair.

⚠ SAFETY ALERT

Strong oxidizing agents such as 30% aqueous hydrogen peroxide can cause severe burns. In general, strong oxidizing agents are corrosive, and many are highly toxic. They can also initiate a fire or increase the severity of a fire when brought into contact with combustible materials.

Solutions of potassium permanganate ($KMnO_4$), a common laboratory oxidizing agent, are good disinfectants. Such solutions are a deep purplish pink. Highly diluted solutions are pale pink (called "pinky water" in India) and are used in developing countries to disinfect foods. Their use is limited because the permanganate ion is reduced to brown manganese dioxide, leaving a brown stain on the treated substance.

An oxidizing agent sometimes used in the laboratory is potassium dichromate ($K_2Cr_2O_7$). It is an orange substance that turns green when it is reduced to chromium(III) compounds. One of the compounds that potassium dichromate oxidizes is ethyl alcohol. The early Breathalyzer test for intoxication made use of a dichromate solution. The exhaled breath of the person being tested was mixed with the acidic dichromate, and the degree of color change indicated the level of alcohol.

Ointments for treating acne often contain 5–10% benzoyl peroxide, a powerful antiseptic and also a skin irritant. It causes old skin to slough off and be replaced by new, fresher-looking skin. When used on areas exposed to sunlight, however, benzoyl peroxide may promote skin cancer.

Bleaches are oxidizing agents, too. A **bleach** removes unwanted color from fabrics or other material. Most bleaches work by oxidizing carbon-carbon double bonds in the colored substances to single bonds. This renders the stain colorless or nearly so. Almost any oxidizing agent could do the job, but some might be unsafe to use, or harmful to fabrics, or perhaps too expensive.

Bleaches (Chapter 21) are usually sodium hypochlorite (NaOCl) in aqueous solution (in laundry products such as Purex® and Clorox®), often called *chlorine bleaches*, or calcium hypochlorite $[Ca(OCl)_2]$, known as *bleaching powder*. The powder is usually preferred for large industrial operations, such as the whitening of paper or fabrics. Nonchlorine bleaches, often called *oxygen bleaches*, contain sodium percarbonate (a combination of Na_2CO_3 and H_2O_2) or sodium perborate (a combination of $NaBO_2$ and H_2O_2).

Stain removal is more complicated than bleaching. A few stain removers are oxidizing agents, but some are reducing agents, some are solvents or detergents, and some have quite different action. Stains often require rather specific stain removers.

▲ Pure water (left) has little effect on a dried tomato sauce stain. Sodium hypochlorite bleach (right) removes the stain by oxidizing the colored tomato pigments to colorless products.

Self-Assessment Questions

1. When CH_4 is burned in plentiful air, the products are
   a. $C + H_2$ **b.** $CH_2 + H_2O$ **c.** $CO_2 + H_2$ **d.** $CO_2 + H_2O$
2. When sulfur burns in plentiful air, the product is
   a. CO_2 **b.** H_2S **c.** H_2SO_4 **d.** SO_2
3. Which of the following is a common oxidizing agent?
   a. HCl **b.** H_2O_2 **c.** NaOH **d.** NaCl
4. Which of the following is a common oxidizing agent?
   a. Cl_2 **b.** H_2 **c.** HCl **d.** KOH
5. The main active ingredient in common household bleach, often called *chlorine bleach*, is
   a. HCl **b.** NaOCl **c.** NaOH **d.** NaCl
6. Bleach for hair usually contains
   a. ammonia **b.** hydrochloric acid
   c. hydrogen peroxide **d.** sodium hypochlorite
7. Many disinfectants are
   a. oxidizing agents **b.** reducing agents
   c. strong acids **d.** strong bases

Answers: 1, d; 2, d; 3, b; 4, a; 5, b; 6, c; 7, a

8.6 Some Common Reducing Agents

Learning Objective › Identify some common reducing agents.

In every reaction involving oxidation, the oxidizing agent is reduced, and the substance undergoing oxidation acts as a reducing agent. Let's now consider reactions in which the purpose of the reaction is reduction.

Metals

Most metals occur in nature as compounds. To prepare the free metals, the compounds must be reduced. Metals are often freed from their ores by using coal or *coke* (elemental carbon obtained by heating coal to drive off volatile matter). Tin(IV) oxide is one of the many ores that can be reduced with coal or coke.

$$SnO_2(s) + C(s) \longrightarrow Sn(s) + CO_2(g)$$

Sometimes a metal can be obtained by heating its ore with a more active metal. Chromium oxide, for example, can be reduced by heating it with aluminum.

$$Cr_2O_3(s) + 2\,Al(s) \longrightarrow Al_2O_3(s) + 2\,Cr(s)$$

▲ **It DOES Matter!**
In making a black-and-white photograph, silver bromide in the film is exposed to light. The silver ions so exposed can then be reduced to black silver metal, forming a photographic negative.

Antioxidants

In food chemistry, certain reducing agents are called **antioxidants**. Ascorbic acid (vitamin C) can prevent the browning of fruit (such as sliced apples or pears) by inhibiting air oxidation. Vitamin C is water soluble, but tocopherol (vitamin E) and beta-carotene (a precursor of vitamin A) are fat-soluble antioxidants. All these vitamins are believed to retard various oxidation reactions that are potentially damaging to vital components of living cells (Chapter 17).

Hydrogen as a Reducing Agent

Hydrogen is an excellent reducing agent that can free many metals from their ores, but it is generally used to produce more expensive metals, such as tungsten (W).

$$WO_3(s) + 3\,H_2(g) \longrightarrow W(s) + 3\,H_2O(l)$$

Hydrogen can be used to reduce many kinds of chemical compounds. Ethylene, for example, can be reduced to ethane.

$$C_2H_4(g) + H_2(g) \longrightarrow C_2H_6(g)$$

The reaction requires a **catalyst**, a substance that increases the rate of a chemical reaction without itself being used up. (Catalysts lower the *activation energy*—the minimum energy needed to get a reaction started; they are further explored in Chapter 15.) Nickel is the catalyst used in this case.

A nickel catalyst is used in converting unsaturated fats to saturated fats (Chapter 17). Unsaturated fats ordinarily react very slowly with hydrogen, but in the presence of nickel metal, the reaction proceeds readily. The nickel increases the rate of the reaction, but it does not increase the amount of product formed.

Hydrogen also reduces nitrogen, from air, in the industrial production of ammonia.

$$N_2(g) + 3\,H_2(g) \longrightarrow 2\,NH_3(g)$$

Ammonia is the source of most nitrogen fertilizers in modern agriculture. The reaction that produces ammonia employs an iron catalyst.

A stream of pure hydrogen burns quietly in air with an almost colorless flame, but when a mixture of hydrogen and oxygen is ignited by a spark or a flame, an explosion results. The product in both cases is water.

$$2\,H_2(g) + O_2(g) \longrightarrow 2\,H_2O(l)$$

Certain metals, including platinum and palladium, have an unusual affinity for hydrogen. They absorb large volumes of the gas. Palladium can absorb up to 900 times its own volume of hydrogen. It is interesting to note that hydrogen and oxygen can be mixed at room temperature with no perceptible reaction. If a piece of platinum gauze is added to the mixture, however, the gases react violently. The platinum acts as a catalyst. The heat from the initial reaction heats up the platinum, making it glow; it then ignites the hydrogen–oxygen mixture, causing an explosion.

Nickel, platinum, and palladium are often used as catalysts for reactions involving hydrogen. These metals have the greatest catalytic activity when they are finely divided and have lots of active surface area. Hydrogen adsorbed on the surface of these metals is more reactive than ordinary hydrogen gas.

Catalysts are an important area of research in green chemistry. Chemists are able to develop more energy-efficient and sustainable processes by designing catalysts that enable chemical reactions to occur at lower temperatures or pressures.

GREEN CHEMISTRY

Principle 1, 2, 3, 4, 6, 8, 9

Colin P. Horwitz, *GreenOx Catalysts, Inc.*

Green Oxidation Catalysts

A catalyst provides a pathway for chemicals (reactants) to combine in a more effective manner than is possible without it. Catalysis is also central to green chemistry (Green Chemistry Principle 9). Catalysts increase efficiency and efficacy of chemical and energy resources and reduce reaction time, which also lead to cost savings.

Catalysts are widely used in oxidation reactions, especially those reactions that produce industrial and specialty chemicals. Industrial chemicals are produced on a scale of millions of tons per year and generally cost less than \$0.50/lb. They are often building blocks for more sophisticated chemicals. On the other hand, specialty chemicals are produced on a smaller scale. They generally are more complex than industrial chemicals and have higher value in the marketplace.

There is great reliance on catalysts in the production of industrial chemicals because they must be made cheaply. For example, to produce terephthalic acid, *p*-xylene is oxidized with oxygen using a Co/Mn/Br catalyst. The terephthalic acid can then be converted to polyethylene terephthalate (PET), the major component of soft-drink bottles.

Another example is the oxidation of propylene to propylene oxide. Attempts to make this process greener began in the early 1990s and included using hydrogen peroxide, H_2O_2, as the oxidizing agent (Section 8.5). A titanium silicalite, TS-1, was the catalyst. Green benefits of this catalyst include the fact that Ti is both earth-abundant and nontoxic (see the Green Chemistry essay in Chapter 2). This research resulted in the HPPO process, which uses hydrogen peroxide and propylene oxide and is much greener than currently used methods. The propylene is oxidized under mild reaction conditions in aqueous methanol, and high selectivity for product over byproducts is reported. The methanol also is recycled. This process received a 2010 Presidential Green Chemistry Challenge Award and is being commercialized by a BASF–Dow Chemical Company partnership.

The complexity of specialty chemicals makes their synthesis challenging. Many reactions are based on oxidation, and a need for efficient routes has led to the development of an array of catalytic and noncatalytic methods. These approaches have often relied on chemical reagents that lead to the desired product but are environmentally harmful. A classic example of a noncatalytic method is the dichromate oxidation of an alcohol to an aldehyde.

$$3\ C_2H_6O + Cr_2O_7^{2-} + 8\ H^+ \rightarrow 3\ C_2H_4O + 2\ Cr^{3+} + 7\ H_2O$$

In this reaction, Cr^{6+} in the dichromate ion, $Cr_2O_7^{2-}$, is reduced to Cr^{3+}, and the alcohol is oxidized to an aldehyde. Although the product is formed, Cr^{6+} is a likely carcinogen, the noncatalytic reaction produces lots of waste, and the atom economy (see the Green Chemistry essay in Chapter 5) is poor.

There are many opportunities to employ green chemistry through the development of catalysts that make oxidations like the example above unnecessary. Many oxidation catalysts rely on transition metals (Section 3.8) attached to organic molecules. Catalyst design can be difficult because the organic part can become a target for oxidation during reactions. When this happens, complex protection schemes for the organic portion or high quantities of catalyst are required.

Professor Terry Collins at Carnegie Mellon University took a unique design approach in which weak links in the organic framework were replaced with more robust ones. An earth-abundant and nontoxic element, iron, was chosen as the metal, and the organic portions were designed to bind strongly to iron. The organic parts also contain biochemically common elements, C, H, N, and O. The resulting catalysts are soluble in water and can survive thousands of catalytic cycles. Also, the greener oxidant hydrogen peroxide, H_2O_2, can be used, which leads to oxidation products with low or no toxicity. The design process has yielded an expanding family of iron-based TAML® catalysts that can rapidly oxidize and thus destroy pollutants in water. This work garnered Collins a 1997 Presidential Green Chemistry Challenge Award.

Recent work with the TAML® catalysts has shown that they are effective at levels as low as a single part per million, are efficient users of H_2O_2, function in water over a wide pH range, and offer an alternative to other processes that also use H_2O_2 but much less efficiently. In some applications, the temperature of the reaction can be lowered, which saves energy, and the amounts of chemicals can be decreased because of the efficiency of the TAML® catalyst.

Using a catalyst can also allow a reaction to occur using milder reactants, such as oxygen or hydrogen peroxide instead of chlorine for oxidizing stains on clothes or destroying harmful microorganisms in drinking water.

A Closer Look at Hydrogen

Hydrogen is an especially vital element because it and oxygen are the components of water. By mass, hydrogen makes up only about 0.9% of the Earth's crust and oceans. However, because it has such a low atomic mass, it ranks third in abundance by number of atoms. A random sample of 10,000 atoms from this portion of Earth would have 1510 hydrogen atoms.

Hydrogen ranks low in abundance by mass on Earth. If we look beyond our home planet, however, hydrogen becomes much more significant. The sun, for example, is made up largely of hydrogen. The planet Jupiter is also mainly hydrogen. In fact, the universe is about 72% by mass H, 26% He, and 1% O.

Unlike oxygen, hydrogen is rarely found as a free, uncombined element on Earth. Most of it is combined with oxygen in water. Some is combined with carbon in petroleum and natural gas, which are mixtures of hydrocarbons. Nearly all compounds derived from plants and animals contain hydrogen.

Because hydrogen has the lowest atomic number ($Z = 1$) and the smallest atoms of any element, it is first in the periodic table. However, it is difficult to know exactly where to place it. Hydrogen is usually shown as the first member of group 1A because it has the same valence electronic structure (ns^1) as alkali metals. Like the atoms of elements in group 1A, a hydrogen atom can lose an electron to form a 1+ ion; but, unlike the other group 1A elements, hydrogen is not a metal. Like the atoms of group 7A elements, a hydrogen atom can pick up an electron to become a 1− ion; but, unlike the other group 7A elements, hydrogen is not a halogen. We place hydrogen in group 1A in the periodic table on the inside front cover, but you should keep in mind that it is a unique element, and is in a class by itself.

Small amounts of elemental hydrogen can be made for laboratory use by reacting zinc with hydrochloric acid (Figure 8.9).

$$Zn(s) + 2\,HCl(aq) \longrightarrow ZnCl_2(aq) + H_2(g)$$

◀ **Figure 8.9** Hydrogen gas can be prepared in the laboratory by the reaction of zinc metal with hydrochloric acid.

Commercial quantities of hydrogen are obtained as by-products of petroleum refining or from the reaction of natural gas with steam. About 8 billion kg of hydrogen is produced each year in the United States. At present, hydrogen is used mainly to make ammonia and methanol. Its possible use as a fuel in the future is discussed in Chapter 15.

Hydrogen is a colorless, odorless gas and the lightest of all substances. Its density is only one-fourteenth that of air, and for this reason it was once used in lighter-than-air craft (Figure 8.10). Unfortunately, hydrogen can be ignited by a spark, as occurred in 1937 when the German airship *Hindenburg* was destroyed in a disastrous fire and explosion while landing in Lakehurst, New Jersey. The use of hydrogen in airships was discontinued after that, and the industry never recovered. Today, the few airships that are still in service are filled with nonflammable helium, but they are used mainly in advertising.

▲ **Figure 8.10** Hydrogen is the most buoyant gas, but it is highly flammable. The disastrous fire that destroyed the hydrogen-filled German airship *Hindenburg* led to the replacement of hydrogen by nonflammable helium, which buoys the Goodyear blimp.

Q: *What is the equation for the reaction pictured on the left? Would a similar reaction occur if lightning struck the Goodyear blimp? Explain.*

6. Does hydrogen have a promising future as a fuel? Gram for gram, hydrogen provides more energy than any other chemical fuel. Also, when hydrogen is oxidized by oxygen, the product is ordinary water. Unfortunately, it takes more energy to produce hydrogen than we get from burning the hydrogen. Until we can use renewable energy to generate hydrogen, its future as a fuel will remain in question.

Self-Assessment Questions

1. Which of the following is a common reducing agent?
   a. Cl_2 **b.** F_2 **c.** H_2 **d.** I_2
2. Which of the following is a common reducing agent?
   a. C **b.** Cl_2 **c.** F_2 **d.** I_2
3. All the following metals are used as catalysts for reactions involving hydrogen gas *except*
   a. aluminum **b.** nickel **c.** palladium **d.** platinum
4. A catalyst changes the rate of a chemical reaction by
   a. changing the products of the reaction
   b. changing the reactants involved in the reaction
   c. increasing the frequency of molecular collisions
   d. lowering the activation energy
5. By number of atoms, what is the rank of hydrogen in abundance in the accessible portion of Earth?
   a. first **b.** second **c.** tenth **d.** third
6. Hydrogen gas can be produced by reacting an active metal such as zinc with
   a. an acid **b.** ammonia
   c. an oxidizing agent **d.** a reducing agent
7. Although helium gas is twice as dense as hydrogen gas, modern blimps are filled with helium because hydrogen is
   a. highly flammable **b.** more expensive
   c. rarer **d.** toxic

Answers: 1, c; 2, a; 3, a; 4, d; 5, d; 6, a; 7, a

8.7 Oxidation, Reduction, and Living Things

Learning Objective › Write the overall equations for the metabolism of glucose and for photosynthesis.

Perhaps the most important oxidation–reduction processes are the ones that maintain life on this planet. We obtain energy for all our physical and mental activities by metabolizing food in a process called *cellular respiration.* The process has many steps, but eventually the food we eat is converted mainly into carbon dioxide, water, and energy.

Bread and many of the other foods we eat are largely made up of carbohydrates, composed of carbon, hydrogen, and oxygen (Chapter 17). If we represent carbohydrates with the simple example of glucose ($C_6H_{12}O_6$), we can write the overall equation for their metabolism as follows.

$$C_6H_{12}O_6 + 6\ O_2 \longrightarrow 6\ CO_2 + 6\ H_2O + \text{energy}$$

This process occurs constantly in animals, including humans. The carbohydrate is oxidized in the process.

Meanwhile, plants need carbon dioxide, water, and energy from the sun to produce carbohydrates. The process by which plants synthesize carbohydrates is called **photosynthesis** (Figure 8.11). The overall chemical equation is

$$6\ CO_2 + 6\ H_2O + \text{energy} \longrightarrow C_6H_{12}O_6 + 6\ O_2$$

◀ **Figure 8.11** Photosynthesis occurs in green plants. The chlorophyll pigments that catalyze the photosynthesis process give the green color to much of the land area of Earth.

Notice that this process in plant cells is exactly the reverse of the process going on inside animals. In food metabolism in animals, we focus on an oxidation process. In photosynthesis, we focus on a reduction process.

The carbohydrates produced by photosynthesis are the ultimate source of all our food because fish, fowl, and other animals either eat plants or eat other animals that eat plants. Note that the photosynthesis process not only makes carbohydrates but also yields free elementary oxygen (O_2). In other words, photosynthesis does not just provide the food we eat, it also provides the oxygen we breathe.

There are many oxidation reactions that occur in nature (with oxygen being reduced in the process). The net photosynthesis reaction is unique in that it is a natural reduction of carbon dioxide (with oxygen being oxidized). Many processes in nature use oxygen. Photosynthesis is the only natural process that produces it.

Self-Assessment Questions

1. The main process by which animals obtain energy from food is
   a. acidification
   b. cellular respiration
   c. photosynthesis
   d. reduction of CO_2
2. The only natural process that produces O_2 is
   a. acidification of carbonates
   b. photosynthesis
   c. oxidation of CO_2
   d. reduction of metal oxide

Answers: 1, b; 2, b

CRITICAL THINKING  EXERCISES

Apply knowledge that you have gained in this chapter and one or more of the FLaReS principles (Chapter 1) to evaluate the following statements or claims.

8.1 Over the years, some people have claimed that someone has invented an automobile engine that burns water instead of gasoline. They say that we have not heard about it because the oil companies have bought the rights to the engine from the inventor so that they can keep it from the public and people will continue to burn gasoline in their cars.

8.2 In January 2011, Italian scientists claimed to have constructed an apparatus to produce energy. The apparatus uses hydrogen and nickel and is supposed to give several hundred times as much energy as would be obtained by merely burning the hydrogen.

8.3 A Web site claims that electricity can remove rust. The procedure is described as follows: Connect a wire to the object to be derusted, and immerse in a bath of sodium carbonate (washing soda) solution. Immerse a second wire in the bath. Connect the wires to a battery so that the object to be derusted is the cathode. The site claims that hydrogen gas is produced at the cathode and oxygen at the anode. The hydrogen then changes the rust back to iron metal.

8.4 A friend claims that an automobile can be kept free of rust simply by connecting the negative pole of the car's battery to the car's body. He reasons that this action makes the car the cathode, and oxidation does not occur at the cathode. He claims that for years he has kept his car from rusting by doing this.

8.5 A salesman claims that your tap water is contaminated. As evidence, he connects a battery to a pair of "special electrodes" and dips the electrodes in a glass of your tap water. Within a few minutes, white and brown "gunk" appears in the water. The salesman sells a special purifying filter that he claims will remove the contaminants and leave the water pure and clear.

SUMMARY

Section 8.1—Oxidation and reduction are processes that occur together. They may be defined in three ways. **Oxidation** occurs when a substance gains oxygen atoms or loses hydrogen atoms or loses electrons. **Reduction** is the opposite of oxidation; it occurs when a substance loses oxygen atoms or gains hydrogen atoms or gains electrons. We usually use the definition that is most convenient for the situation.

Section 8.2—In an oxidation–reduction (or redox) reaction, the substance that causes oxidation is the **oxidizing agent**. The substance that causes reduction is the **reducing agent**. In a redox reaction, the oxidizing agent is reduced, and the reducing agent is oxidized.

Section 8.3—A redox reaction involves a transfer of electrons. That transfer can be made to take place in an **electrochemical cell**, which has two solid **electrodes** where the electrons are transferred. The electrode where oxidation occurs is the **anode**, and the one where reduction occurs is the **cathode**. Electrons are transferred from anode to cathode through a wire; their flow is an electric current. When the oxidation half-reaction is added to the reduction half-reaction, the electrons in the half-reactions cancel and we get the overall cell reaction. Knowing this, we can balance many redox reactions.

A dry cell (flashlight battery) has a zinc case and a central carbon rod and contains a paste of manganese dioxide with graphite powder and ammonium chloride. Alkaline cells are similar but contain potassium hydroxide instead of ammonium chloride. A **battery** is a series of connected cells. An automobile's lead storage battery contains six cells. Each cell contains lead and lead dioxide electrodes in sulfuric acid, and the battery can be recharged. A **fuel cell** generates electricity by oxidizing a fuel in a cell to which the fuel and oxygen are supplied continuously.

Section 8.4—Corrosion of metals is ordinarily an undesirable redox reaction. When iron corrodes, the iron is first oxidized to Fe^{2+} ions, and oxygen gas is reduced to hydroxide ions. The $Fe(OH)_2$ that forms is further oxidized to $Fe(OH)_3$, or rust. Oxidation and reduction often occur in separate places on the metal surface, and an electrolyte (such as salt) on the surface can intensify the corrosion reaction. Aluminum corrodes, but the oxide layer is tough and adherent and protects the underlying metal. Silver corrodes in the presence of sulfur compounds, forming black silver sulfide, which can be removed electrochemically. An explosive reaction is a redox reaction that occurs rapidly and with a considerable increase in volume (due to the formation of gases).

Section 8.5—Oxygen is an oxidizing agent that is essential to life. It makes up about one-fifth of the air and about two-thirds of our body mass. Our food is "burned" in oxygen as we breathe, and fuels such as coal react with oxygen when they burn and release most of the energy used in civilization. Pure oxygen is obtained from liquefied air, and most of it is used in industry. Oxygen reacts with metals and nonmetals to form oxides. It reacts with many compounds to form oxides of the elements in the compound. Ozone, O_3, is a form of oxygen that is an air pollutant in the lower atmosphere but provides a shield from ultraviolet radiation in the upper atmosphere. Other oxidizing agents include hydrogen peroxide, potassium dichromate, benzoyl peroxide, and chlorine. A **bleach** is an oxidizing agent that removes unwanted color from fabric or other material.

Section 8.6—Most metals are reducing agents. An **antioxidant** is a reducing agent that retards damaging oxidation reactions in living cells. Vitamins C and E and beta-carotene are antioxidants. Common reducing agents include carbon, hydrogen, and active metals. Carbon in the form of coal or coke is often used as a reducing agent to obtain metals from their oxides. Active metals such as aluminum are also used for this purpose. Hydrogen can free many metals from their ores. Some reactions of hydrogen require a **catalyst**, which speeds up a reaction without itself being used up. Formation of ammonia from hydrogen and nitrogen uses a catalyst.

Hydrogen is a vital element because it is a component of water and of living tissue. Because it has the lowest atomic number and the smallest atoms, its behavior is unique among the elements. Hydrogen is produced in petroleum refining or from the reaction of natural gas with steam; it is used to make ammonia and methanol. Hydrogen was once used for lighter-than-air craft but its flammability caused it to be replaced by helium.

Section 8.7—Oxidation of carbohydrates and other substances in foods produces the energy humans and other animals need to survive. The reduction of carbon dioxide in **photosynthesis** is the most important reduction process on Earth. We could not exist without it. Photosynthesis provides the food we eat and the oxygen we breathe.

Green chemistry When a chemist needs to use an oxidation reaction to produce a chemical, it is important to find a catalyst that makes the reaction proceed efficiently so that energy and chemical resources are used wisely. To further the principles of green chemistry, the catalyst should be composed of nontoxic and earth-abundant elements.

Learning Objectives

› Identify an oxidation–reduction reaction. (8.1)	Problems 13–16
› Classify a particular change within a redox reaction as either oxidation or reduction. (8.1)	Problems 1, 4, 13, 14, 41–43, 47, 50, 54
› Identify the oxidizing agent and the reducing agent in a redox reaction. (8.2)	Problems 17–22, 27–36, 39, 48, 49
› Balance redox equations. (8.3)	Problems 25, 26, 51
› Identify and write the half-reactions in an electrochemical cell. (8.3)	Problems 2, 3, 5–8, 15, 16, 23, 24
› Describe the reactions that occur when iron rusts. (8.4)	Problem 9
› Explain why an explosive reaction is so energetic. (8.4)	
› Write equations for reactions in which oxygen is an oxidizing agent. (8.5)	Problems 37, 38
› List some of the common oxidizing agents encountered in daily life. (8.5)	Problems 10, 11
› Identify some common reducing agents. (8.6)	Problems 29–36
› Write the overall equations for the metabolism of glucose and for photosynthesis. (8.7)	Problems 12, 46, 53
› Distinguish between the objectives of chemists producing industrial chemicals and those of chemists producing specialty chemicals.	Problem 55
› Explain how green chemistry can be applied to the design of new catalysts.	Problems 56–58

REVIEW QUESTIONS

1. What happens to the oxidation number of one of its elements when a compound is oxidized? When it is reduced?
2. What is an electrochemical cell? A battery?
3. What is the purpose of a porous partition between the two electrode compartments in an electrochemical cell?
4. What is a half-reaction? How are half-reactions combined to give an overall cell reaction?
5. From what material is the case of a zinc–carbon dry cell made? What purpose does this material serve? What happens to it as the cell discharges?
6. How does an alkaline cell differ from a zinc–carbon dry cell?
7. What happens when a lead storage battery is charged?
8. Describe what happens when a lead storage battery discharges.
9. Describe what happens when iron corrodes. How does road salt intensify this process?
10. Describe how a bleaching agent, such as hypochlorite (ClO^-), works.
11. How does silver tarnish? How can the tarnish be removed without the loss of silver?
12. Relate the chemistry of photosynthesis to the chemical process that provides energy for your heartbeat.

PROBLEMS

Recognizing Oxidation and Reduction

13. Indicate whether the reactant in each of the following partial equations is being oxidized or reduced. Explain.
a. $Fe \rightarrow Fe^{3+}$
b. $H_2O \rightarrow O_2$
c. $Sr \rightarrow Sr^{2+}$
d. $P_4 \rightarrow 4\,P^{3-}$
e. $CH_4O \rightarrow CH_2O$

14. In which of the following changes is the reactant undergoing oxidation? Explain.
a. $C_2H_4 \rightarrow C_2H_6$
b. $CrO_3 \rightarrow Cr$
c. $Fe^{3+} \longrightarrow Fe^{2+}$
d. $C_{27}H_{33}N_9O_{15}P_2 \longrightarrow C_{27}H_{35}N_9O_{15}P_2$
e. $2\,Cl^- \rightarrow Cl_2$

15. Write a balanced oxidation half-reaction similar to $Na \longrightarrow Na^+ + e^-$ for each of the following metals.
a. Ca
b. Al
c. Cu (two different equations)

16. Write a balanced reduction half-reaction similar to $Cl_2 + 2\,e^- \longrightarrow 2\,Cl^-$ for each of the following nonmetals.
a. I_2
b. N_2
c. S_8

Oxidizing Agents and Reducing Agents

17. Identify the oxidizing agent and the reducing agent in each reaction.
a. $3\,C + Fe_2O_3 \longrightarrow 3\,CO + 2\,Fe$
b. $P_4 + 5\,O_2 \longrightarrow P_4O_{10}$
c. $C + H_2O \longrightarrow CO + H_2$
d. $H_2SO_4 + Zn \longrightarrow ZnSO_4 + H_2$

18. Identify the oxidizing agent and the reducing agent in each reaction.
a. $CuS + H_2 \longrightarrow Cu + H_2S$
b. $4\,K + CCl_4 \longrightarrow C + 4\,KCl$
c. $C_3H_4 + 2\,H_2 \longrightarrow C_3H_8$
d. $Fe^{3+} + Ce^{3+} \longrightarrow Fe^{2+} + Ce^{4+}$

19. Look again at Figure 8.4. What is the reducing agent?

20. What is the oxidizing agent in Figure 8.4?

21. Look again at Figure 8.6. Identify the oxidizing and reducing agents.

22. Look again at Figure 8.7. **(a)** Is SO_4^{2-} the oxidizing agent, the reducing agent, both, or neither? **(b)** When the cell is being charged, the discharge half-reactions are reversed. During charging, is Pb^{2+} being oxidized, reduced, both, or neither?

Half-Reactions

23. Separate the following redox reactions into half-reactions, and label each half-reaction as oxidation or reduction.
a. $Fe(s) + 2\,H^+(aq) \longrightarrow Fe^{2+}(aq) + H_2(g)$
b. $2\,Al(s) + 3\,Cr^{2+}(aq) \longrightarrow 3\,Cr(s) + 2\,Al^{3+}(aq)$

24. Separate the following redox reactions into half-reactions, and label each half-reaction as oxidation or reduction.
a. $2\,Al(s) + 6\,H^+(aq) \longrightarrow 2\,Al^{3+}(aq) + 3\,H_2(g)$
b. $2\,Cu^+(aq) + Mg(s) \longrightarrow Mg^{2+}(aq) + 2\,Cu(s)$

25. Label each of the following half-reactions as oxidation or reduction, and then combine them to obtain a balanced overall redox reaction.
a. $2\,H_2O_2 \longrightarrow 2\,O_2 + 4\,H^+ + 4\,e^-$ and $Fe^{3+} + e^- \longrightarrow Fe^{2+}$
b. $WO_3 + 6\,H^+ + 6\,e^- \longrightarrow W + 3\,H_2O$ and $C_2H_6O \longrightarrow C_2H_4O + 2\,H^+ + 2\,e^-$

26. Label each of the following half-reactions as oxidation or reduction, and then combine them to obtain a balanced overall redox reaction.
a. $2\,I^- \longrightarrow I_2 + 2\,e^-$ and $Cl_2 + 2\,e^- \longrightarrow 2\,Cl^-$
b. $HNO_3 + H^+ + e^- \longrightarrow NO_2 + H_2O$ and $SO_2 + 2\,H_2O \longrightarrow H_2SO_4 + 2\,H^+ + 2\,e^-$

Oxidation and Reduction: Chemical Reactions

27. In the following reactions, which substance is oxidized? Which is the oxidizing agent?
a. $2\,HNO_3 + SO_2 \longrightarrow H_2SO_4 + 2\,NO_2$
b. $2\,CrO_3 + 6\,HI \longrightarrow Cr_2O_3 + 3\,I_2 + 3\,H_2O$

28. In the following reactions, which element is oxidized and which is reduced?
a. $CH_3CHO + H_2O_2 \rightarrow CH_3COOH + H_2O$
b. $5\,C_2H_6O + 4\,MnO_4^- + 12\,H^+ \longrightarrow 5\,C_2H_4O_2 + 4\,Mn^{2+} + 11\,H_2O$

29. Ethylene (C_2H_4) reacts with hydrogen to form ethane (C_2H_6). Is the ethylene oxidized or reduced? Explain.

30. Unsaturated vegetable oils react with hydrogen to form saturated fats. A typical reaction is

$$C_{57}H_{104}O_6 + 3\,H_2 \longrightarrow C_{57}H_{110}O_6$$

Is the unsaturated oil oxidized or reduced? Explain.

31. Tantalum, a metal used in electronic devices such as cellular phones and computers, can be manufactured by the reaction of its oxide with molten sodium metal.

$$Ta_2O_5 + 10\,Na \rightarrow 2\,Ta + 5\,Na_2O$$

Which substance is reduced? Which is the reducing agent?

32. To test for iodide ions (for example, in iodized salt), a solution is treated with chlorine to liberate iodine.

$$2\,I^- + Cl_2 \longrightarrow I_2 + 2\,Cl^-$$

Which substance is oxidized? Which is reduced?

33. In the Fukushima nuclear reactor that failed in March 2011, zirconium metal reacted with steam to produce hydrogen gas.

$$Zr + 2\,H_2O \longrightarrow ZrO_2 + 2\,H_2$$

What substance was oxidized in the reaction? What was the oxidizing agent?

34. Unripe grapes are exceptionally sour because of a high concentration of tartaric acid ($C_4H_6O_6$). As the grapes

ripen, this compound is converted to glucose ($C_6H_{12}O_6$). Is the tartaric acid oxidized or reduced?

35. Vitamin C (ascorbic acid) is thought to protect our stomachs from the carcinogenic effect of nitrite ions (NO_2^-) by converting the ions to nitric oxide (NO). Is the nitrite ion oxidized or reduced? Is ascorbic acid an oxidizing agent or a reducing agent?

36. In the reaction in Problem 35, ascorbic acid ($C_6H_8O_6$) is converted to dehydroascorbic acid ($C_6H_6O_6$). Is ascorbic acid oxidized or reduced in this reaction?

Combination with Oxygen

37. Write formula(s) for the product(s) formed when each of the following substances reacts with oxygen (O_2).
   a. S
   b. CH_3OH
   c. C_3H_6O

38 Write formula(s) for the product(s) formed when each of the following substances reacts with oxygen (O_2). (There may be more than one correct answer.)
   a. N_2
   b. CS_2
   c. C_5H_{12}

Additional Problems

39. The dye indigo (used to color blue jeans) is formed by exposure of indoxyl to air.

$$\underset{\text{Indoxyl}}{2\,C_8H_7ON} + O_2 \longrightarrow \underset{\text{Indigo}}{C_{16}H_{10}N_2O_2} + 2\,H_2O$$

What substance is oxidized? What is the oxidizing agent?

40. Why do some mechanics lightly coat their tools with grease or oil before storing them?

41. When an aluminum wire is placed in a blue solution of copper(II) chloride, the blue solution turns colorless and reddish-brown copper metal comes out of solution. Write an equation for the reaction. (Chloride ion is not involved in the reaction.)

42. Researchers led by Elisabeth Bouwman, a chemist at Leiden University in the Netherlands, discovered a copper-based catalyst that can convert CO_2 from the air to oxalate ion ($C_2O_4^{2-}$). Write the equation for the half-reaction. Is the CO_2 oxidized or reduced?

43. When exposed to air containing hydrogen sulfide, lead-based paints turn black because the Pb^{2+} ions react with the H_2S to form black lead sulfide (PbS). This has caused the darkening of old oil-based paintings. Hydrogen peroxide lightens the paints by oxidizing the black sulfide (S^{2-}) to white sulfates (SO_4^{2-}). **(a)** Write the equation for the darkening reaction. **(b)** Write the equation for this reaction that lightens the paints.

44. The oxidizing agent our bodies use to obtain energy from food is oxygen (from the air). If you breathe 15 times a minute (at rest), taking in and exhaling 0.5 L of air with each breath, what volume of air do you breathe each day? Air is 21% oxygen by volume. What volume of oxygen do you breathe each day?

45. To oxidize 1.0 kg of fat, our bodies require about 2000 L of oxygen. A healthy diet contains not more than about 80 g of fat per day. What volume (at STP) of oxygen is required to oxidize that fat?

46. The photosynthesis reaction (page 223) can be expressed as the net result of two processes, one of which requires light and is called the *light reaction*. This reaction may be written as

$$12\,H_2O \xrightarrow{\text{light}} 6\,O_2 + 24\,H^+ + 24\,e^-$$

   a. Is the light reaction an oxidation or reduction?
   b. Write the equation for the other half-reaction, called the *dark reaction*, for photosynthesis.

47. Indicate whether the first-named substance in each change undergoes an oxidation, a reduction, or neither. Explain your reasoning.
   a. A violet solution of vanadium(II) ions, V^{2+}(aq), is converted to a green solution of V^{3+}(aq).
   b. Nitrogen dioxide converts to dinitrogen tetroxide when cooled.
   c. Carbon monoxide reacts with hydrogen to form methanol.

48. As a rule, metallic elements act as reducing agents, not as oxidizing agents. Explain. (*Hint:* Consider the charges on metal ions.) Do nonmetals act only as oxidizing agents and not as reducing agents? Explain your answer.

49. If a stream of hydrogen gas is ignited in air, the flame can be immersed in a jar of chlorine gas and it will still burn. Write the balanced equation for the reaction that occurs in the jar. What is the oxidizing agent in the reaction?

50. Consider the following reaction of calcium hydride (CaH_2) with molten sodium metal. Identify the species being oxidized and the species being reduced according to **(a)** the second definition shown in Figure 8.2 and **(b)** the third definition in Figure 8.2. What difficulty arises?

$$CaH_2(s) + 2\,Na(l) \longrightarrow 2\,NaH(s) + Ca(l)$$

51. Aluminum metal can react with water, but the oxide coating normally found on the metal prevents that reaction. In 2007, a Purdue University researcher found that adding gallium to aluminum prevented the formation of the oxide coating, allowing the aluminum to react with water to form hydrogen gas. This process might lead to a compact source of hydrogen gas for fuel. Write a balanced equation for the reaction of aluminum with water (aluminum hydroxide is the other product), and identify the oxidizing and reducing agents in the reaction.

52. Refer to Problem 51. Aluminum has a density of 2.70 g/cm^3. What volume in cubic centimeters of aluminum metal would be needed to produce 2.0×10^4 L of hydrogen gas at STP? How many times smaller is this volume of aluminum than is the volume of hydrogen gas? (Recall that at STP, 1 mol of gas occupies 22.4 L.)

53. Consider the oxidation of ethanol (CH_3CH_2OH) to acetaldehyde (CH_3CHO) by NAD^+ (page 204). **(a)** Write half-reactions for the process. **(b)** NADH is a biochemical reducing agent, in the reverse of the oxidation reaction. Write half-reactions for the reduction of pyruvic acid ($CH_3COCOOH$) to lactic acid ($CH_3CHOHCOOH$) by NADH, and then combine these two half-reactions to get the equation for the overall reaction.

54. Following are some organic chemistry processes. Classify each as an oxidation or a reduction. R represents a hydrocarbon group, and does not change in the process.
   a. RCH_3 (alkane) → RCH_2OH (alcohol)
   b. RCHO (aldehyde) → RCH_2OH (alcohol)
   c. RCHO (aldehyde) → RCOOH (carboxylic acid)
   d. RCOOH (carboxylic acid) → RCHO (aldehyde)
   e. RCH_2OH (alcohol) → RCHO (aldehyde)

55. Which of the following describe industrial chemicals, and which describe specialty chemicals?
   a. made on a large scale
   b. complex molecules
   c. high-value chemicals
   d. building blocks for other chemicals

56. A green catalyst is one that
   a. contains earth-abundant elements
   b. makes reagents react more efficiently
   c. decreases the cost of producing a chemical
   d. does all of the above

57. Give one reason why it can be difficult to design a long-lived oxidation catalyst.

58. Identify the oxidizing agent and the substance that is oxidized in the following reaction.

$$3\,C_2H_6O + Cr_2O_7^{2-} + 8\,H^+ \longrightarrow 3\,C_2H_4O + 2\,Cr^{3+} + 7\,H_2O$$

COLLABORATIVE GROUP PROJECTS

Prepare a PowerPoint, poster, or other presentation (as directed by your instructor) to share with the class.

1. Prepare a brief report on one of the following types of electrochemical cells or batteries. If possible, give the half-reactions, the overall reaction, and typical uses.
   a. lithium–SO_2 cell
   b. lithium–iodine cell
   c. lithium–FeS_2 battery
   d. Ni–Cad cell
   e. silver oxide cell
   f. nickel–metal hydride cell

2. Prepare a brief report on one of the following methods of protecting steel from corrosion. Identify the chemical reactions involved in the process, and tell how the process is related to oxidation and reduction.
   a. galvanization
   b. coating with tin
   c. cathodic protection

3. Batteries contain toxic substances and should be recycled rather than thrown in the trash. Prepare a brief report on battery recycling. Are there facilities in your area for recycling batteries?

4. Military personnel, outdoor recreation enthusiasts such as wilderness campers and trekkers, and others often have to drink water from untreated streams or lakes. People who temporarily lack safe drinking water after a natural disaster also need a way to purify water. A variety of water purification tablets are available to treat contaminated water. Research several such tablets, and list their ingredients.

5. Visit one or more Web sites about fuel cells. Write the reactions that occur in the different types of fuel cells in development. Prepare a brief report on one of the following topics:
   a. a cost–benefit analysis of using fuel cells in automobiles versus using gasoline, electricity from batteries, or natural gas
   b. safety considerations about the hydrogen–oxygen fuel cell
   c. political–economic factors that may be hindering or promoting fuel cell research

9 Organic Chemistry

Have You Ever Wondered?

1. **Does organic food have anything to do with organic chemistry?**
2. **What is the "petroleum distillate" that I see listed on some product labels?**
3. **If a compound has *benzene* in its name, is the compound a carcinogen?**
4. **Why do some mouthwashes taste "medicine-y"?**
5. **Why does fresh fruit smell so good and rotting fruit so bad?**
6. **Why do dead animals smell so bad?**

Learning Objectives

- Define *hydrocarbon*, and recognize structural features of alkanes, alkenes, and alkynes. (9.1)
- Identify hydrocarbon molecules as alkanes, alkenes, or alkynes, and name them. (9.1)
- Define *aromatic compound*, and recognize the structural feature such compounds share. (9.2)
- Name simple aromatic hydrocarbons. (9.2)
- Name a halogenated hydrocarbon given its formula, and write the formula for such a compound given its name. (9.3)
- Classify an organic compound according to its functional group(s), and explain why the concept of a functional group is useful in the study of organic chemistry. (9.4)
- Recognize and write the formulas of simple alkyl groups. (9.4)
- Recognize the general structure for an alcohol, a phenol, and an ether. (9.5)
- Name simple alcohols, phenols, and ethers. (9.5)
- Name simple aldehydes and ketones, and list their important properties. (9.6)
- Name simple carboxylic acids and esters, and list their important properties. (9.7)
- Name and write the formulas of simple amines and amides. (9.8)
- Recognize a structure as that of a heterocyclic compound. (9.8)
- Identify greener solvents that can replace those from nonrenewable fossil fuels, methods for incorporating renewable resources into organic synthesis, and efficient energy sources for enhancing chemical reactions.

The Infinite Variety of Carbon Compounds

The definition of organic chemistry has changed over the years. The changes exemplify the dynamic character of science and exemplify how scientific concepts change in response to experimental evidence. Until the nineteenth century, chemists believed that *organic* chemicals originated only in tissues of living *organisms* and required a "vital force" for their production. All chemicals not manufactured by living tissue were regarded

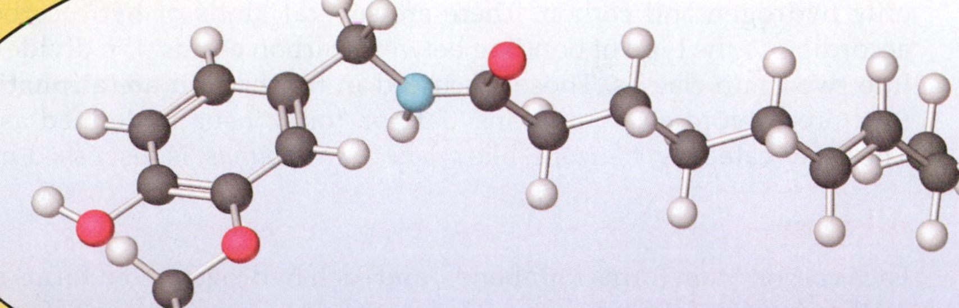

The compound capsaicin, a molecular model of which is shown here, is the principal compound responsible for the "hotness" of chili peppers. Capsaicin is organic in the original sense because it is obtained from a plant. It is also organic in the modern sense in that it is a compound containing carbon. Numerous organic chemicals are obtained from plants and animals, but many of the millions of organic compounds known today are synthetic. See Problem 51, page 264.

1. Does organic food have anything to do with organic chemistry? The word *organic* has several different meanings. Organic fertilizer is organic in the original sense; it is derived from living organisms. Organic foods are those grown without synthetic pesticides or fertilizers. Organic chemistry is simply the chemistry of carbon-containing compounds.

In addition to carbon, almost all organic compounds also contain hydrogen, many contain oxygen and/or nitrogen, and quite a few contain sulfur or halogens. Nearly all the common elements are found in at least a few organic compounds.

as *inorganic*. Some chemists even believed that organic and inorganic chemicals followed different laws. This all changed in 1828, when Friedrich Wöhler synthesized the organic compound urea (found in urine) from ammonium cyanate, an inorganic compound. This important event led other chemists to attempt synthesis of organic chemicals from inorganic ones and changed the very definition of organic chemicals.

Organic chemistry is now defined as the chemistry of carbon-containing compounds. Most of these compounds do come from living things or from things that were once living, but some do not. Perhaps the most remarkable thing about organic compounds is their sheer number. Of the tens of millions of known chemical compounds, more than 95% are compounds of carbon.

One reason for the huge number of organic compounds is the carbon atom itself. Carbon is unique in that its atoms bond readily to each other and form long chains. (Silicon and a few other elements can form chains, but only short ones.) Carbon chains can also have branches or form rings of various sizes. When we consider that carbon atoms also bond strongly to other elements, particularly nonmetals such as hydrogen, oxygen, and nitrogen, and that these atoms can be arranged in many different ways, it soon becomes obvious why there are so many organic compounds.

In addition to the millions of carbon compounds already known, new ones are being discovered every day. Carbon can form an almost infinite number of molecules of various shapes, sizes, and compositions. We use thousands of carbon compounds every day without even realizing it because they are silently carrying out important chemical reactions within our bodies. Many of these carbon compounds are so vital that we cannot live without them.

9.1 Aliphatic Hydrocarbons

Learning Objectives › Define *hydrocarbon*, and recognize structural features of alkanes, alkenes, and alkynes. › Identify hydrocarbon molecules as alkanes, alkenes, or alkynes, and name them.

The simplest organic compounds are hydrocarbons. A **hydrocarbon** contains only hydrogen and carbon. There are several kinds of hydrocarbons, classified according to the type of bonding between carbon atoms. We divide hydrocarbons into two main classes. Those discussed in this section are **aliphatic compounds** (the Greek word *aleiphar* means "fat" or "oil"), usually defined as nonaromatic. The other category, benzene-like *aromatic compounds*, is discussed in Section 9.2.

Alkanes

Each carbon atom forms four bonds, and each hydrogen atom forms only one bond, so the simplest hydrocarbon molecule possible is methane, CH_4. Methane is the main component of natural gas. It has the structure

```
    H
    |
H—C—H
    |
    H
```

(a)

(b)

◀ **Figure 9.1** Ball-and-stick (a) and space-filling (b) models of methane (left) and ethane (right).

Methane is the first member of a group of related compounds called **alkanes**, hydrocarbons that contain only single bonds. Alkanes can have from one to several hundred or more carbon atoms. The next member of the series is ethane,

$$\begin{array}{ccccccc} & & H & & H & & \\ & & | & & | & & \\ H & - & C & - & C & - & H \\ & & | & & | & & \\ & & H & & H & & \end{array}$$

Ethane is a minor constituent of natural gas. It is seldom encountered as a pure compound in everyday life, but many common compounds are derived from it.

We saw in Chapter 4 that the methane molecule is tetrahedral, in accord with the VSEPR theory. In fact, the tetrahedral shape results whenever a carbon atom is connected to four other atoms, whether they are hydrogen, carbon, or other elements. Figure 9.1 shows models of methane and ethane. The ball-and-stick models show the bond angles best, but the space-filling models more accurately reflect the shapes of the molecules. Ordinarily, we use simple structural formulas such as the one shown previously for ethane because they are much easier to draw. A **structural formula** shows which atoms are bonded to each other, but it does not attempt to show the actual shape of the molecule.

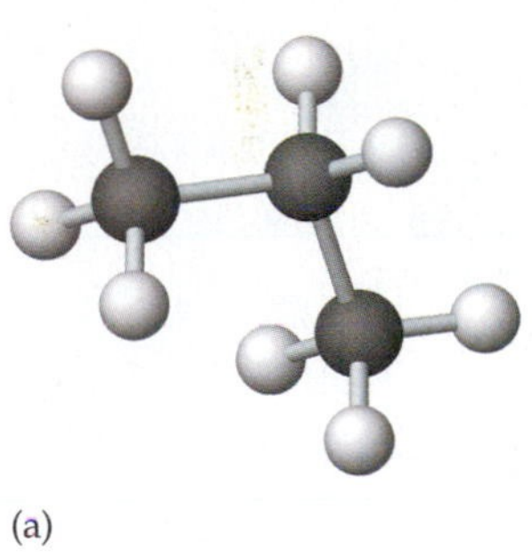

(a)

(b)

▲ **Figure 9.2** Ball-and-stick (a) and space-filling (b) models of propane.

Alkanes are often called **saturated hydrocarbons** because each carbon atom is *saturated* with hydrogen atoms; that is, each carbon is bonded to the maximum number of hydrogen atoms. In constructing a formula, we connect the carbon atoms to each other through single bonds; then we add enough hydrogen atoms to give each carbon atom four bonds. All alkanes have two more than twice as many hydrogen atoms as carbon atoms. That is, alkanes can be represented by a general formula C_nH_{2n+2}, in which n is the number of carbon atoms.

The three-carbon alkane is propane. Models of propane are shown in Figure 9.2. To draw its structural formula, we place three carbon atoms in a row.

$$C-C-C$$

Then we add enough hydrogen atoms (eight in this case) to give each carbon atom a total of four bonds. Therefore, the structural formula of propane is

$$\begin{array}{ccccccccc} & & H & & H & & H & & \\ & & | & & | & & | & & \\ H & - & C & - & C & - & C & - & H \\ & & | & & | & & | & & \\ & & H & & H & & H & & \end{array}$$

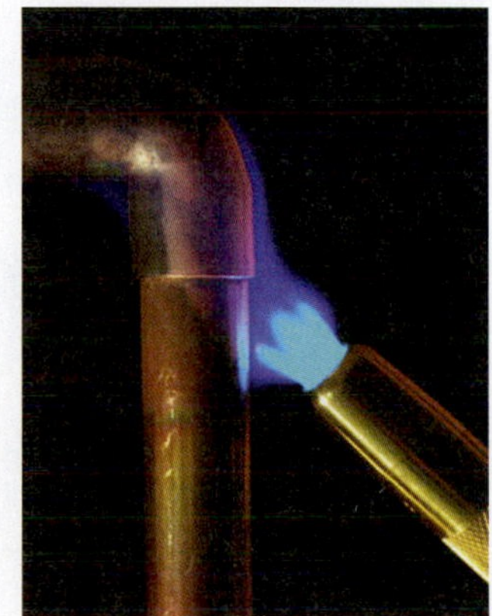

▲ A propane torch. Propane burns in air with a hot flame.

Condensed Structural Formulas

The complete structural formulas that we have used so far show all the carbon and hydrogen atoms and how they are attached to one another. But these formulas take up a lot of space, and they can be a bit of trouble to draw. For these reasons, chemists usually prefer to use **condensed structural formulas**. These formulas show how

Table 9.1 Stems for Organic Molecule Names

Stem	Number of Carbon Atoms
Meth-	1
Eth-	2
Prop-	3
But-	4
Pent-	5
Hex-	6
Hept-	7
Oct-	8
Non-	9
Dec-	10

many hydrogen atoms are attached to each carbon atom without showing the bond to each hydrogen atom. For example, the condensed structural formulas for ethane and propane are written $CH_3—CH_3$ and $CH_3—CH_2—CH_3$, respectively. These formulas can be simplified even further by omitting some (or all) of the remaining bond lines, resulting in CH_3CH_3 and $CH_3CH_2CH_3$.

Homologous Series

Note that methane, ethane, and propane form a pattern. We can build alkanes of any length simply by joining carbon atoms together in long chains and adding enough hydrogen atoms to give each carbon atom four bonds. Even the naming of these compounds follows a pattern (Table 9.1), with a stem name indicating the number of carbon atoms. For compounds of five carbon atoms or more, each stem is derived from the Greek or Latin name for the number. The compound names end in *-ane*, signifying that the compounds are *alkanes*. Table 9.2 gives condensed structural formulas and names for the continuous-chain (straight-chain, or unbranched) alkanes with up to ten carbon atoms.

Notice that the molecular formula for each alkane in Table 9.2 differs from the one preceding it by precisely one carbon atom and two hydrogen atoms—that is, by a CH_2 unit. Such a series of compounds has properties that vary in a regular and predictable manner. This principle, called *homology*, gives order to organic chemistry in much the same way that the periodic table gives organization to the chemistry of the elements. Instead of studying the chemistry of a bewildering array of individual carbon compounds, organic chemists study a few members—called *homologs*—of a **homologous series**, from which they can deduce the properties of other compounds in the series.

We need not stop at ten carbon atoms as Table 9.2 does. Hundreds, thousands, even millions of carbon atoms can be linked together. We can make an infinite number of alkanes simply by lengthening the chain. But lengthening the chain is not the only option. Beginning with alkanes having four carbon atoms, chain branching is also possible.

Isomerism

When we extend the carbon chain to four atoms and add enough hydrogen atoms to give each carbon atom four bonds, we get $CH_3CH_2CH_2CH_3$. This formula represents butane, a compound that boils at about 0 °C. A second compound, which has a boiling point of −12 °C, has the same molecular formula, C_4H_{10}, as butane. The structure of this compound, however, is not the same as that of butane. Instead of having four carbon atoms connected in a continuous chain, this compound has a continuous chain of only three carbon atoms. The fourth carbon is branched off the

Table 9.2 The First Ten Continuous-Chain Alkanes

Name	Molecular Formula	Condensed Structural Formula	Number of Possible Isomers
Methane	CH_4	CH_4	—
Ethane	C_2H_6	CH_3CH_3	—
Propane	C_3H_8	$CH_3CH_2CH_3$	—
Butane	C_4H_{10}	$CH_3CH_2CH_2CH_3$	2
Pentane	C_5H_{12}	$CH_3CH_2CH_2CH_2CH_3$	3
Hexane	C_6H_{14}	$CH_3CH_2CH_2CH_2CH_2CH_3$	5
Heptane	C_7H_{16}	$CH_3CH_2CH_2CH_2CH_2CH_2CH_3$	9
Octane	C_8H_{18}	$CH_3CH_2CH_2CH_2CH_2CH_2CH_2CH_3$	18
Nonane	C_9H_{20}	$CH_3CH_2CH_2CH_2CH_2CH_2CH_2CH_2CH_3$	35
Decane	$C_{10}H_{22}$	$CH_3CH_2CH_2CH_2CH_2CH_2CH_2CH_2CH_2CH_3$	75

middle carbon of the three-carbon chain. To show the two structures more clearly, let's use complete structural formulas, showing all the bonds to hydrogen atoms.

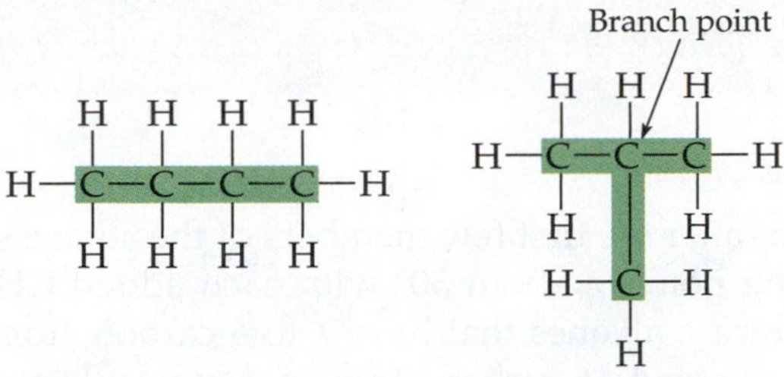

Compounds that have the same molecular formula but different structural formulas are called **isomers**. Because it is an isomer of butane, the branched four-carbon alkane is sometimes called *isobutane*. Condensed structural formulas for the two isomeric butanes are written as follows.

$$\underset{\text{Butane}}{CH_3CH_2CH_2CH_3} \qquad \underset{\text{Isobutane}}{\begin{array}{c}CH_3CHCH_3\\ \vert \\ CH_3\end{array}}$$

Figure 9.3 shows ball-and-stick models of the two compounds.

The number of isomers increases rapidly with the number of carbon atoms (Table 9.2). There are three pentanes, five hexanes, nine heptanes, and so on. Isomerism is common in carbon compounds and provides another reason for the existence of millions of organic compounds.

Propane and the butanes are familiar fuels. Although they are gases at ordinary temperatures and under normal atmospheric pressure, they are liquefied under pressure and are usually supplied in tanks as liquefied petroleum gas (LPG). Gasoline is a mixture of hydrocarbons, mostly alkanes, with 5–12 carbon atoms.

Not all the possible isomers of the larger molecules have been isolated. Indeed, the task rapidly becomes more and more prohibitive going up the series. There are, for example, 4,111,846,763 possible isomers with the molecular formula $C_{30}H_{62}$.

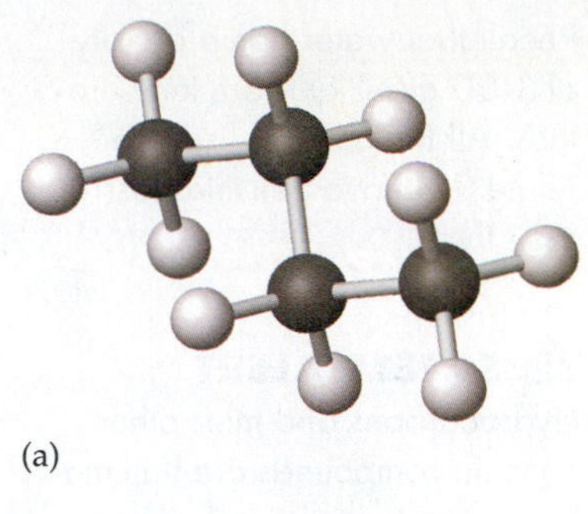

(a)

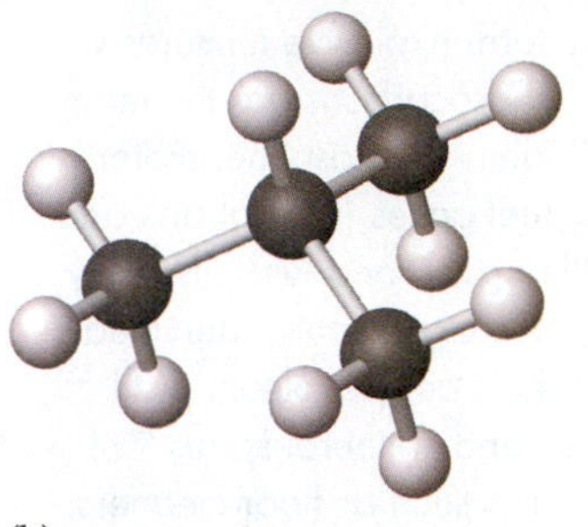

(b)

▲ **Figure 9.3** Ball-and-stick models of (a) butane and (b) isobutane.

Example 9.1 Hydrocarbon Formulas

Without referring to Table 9.2, write the molecular formula, the complete structural formula, and the condensed structural formula for heptane.

Solution

The stem *hept-* means seven carbon atoms, and the ending *-ane* indicates an alkane. For the complete structural formula, we write a string of seven carbon atoms.

C—C—C—C—C—C—C

Then we attach enough hydrogen atoms to the carbon atoms to give each carbon four bonds. This requires three hydrogens on each end carbon and two hydrogens on each of the other carbons.

```
   H  H  H  H  H  H  H
   |  |  |  |  |  |  |
H—C—C—C—C—C—C—C—H
   |  |  |  |  |  |  |
   H  H  H  H  H  H  H
```

For the condensed form, we simply write each set of hydrogen atoms following the carbon atom to which they are bonded.

$$CH_3CH_2CH_2CH_2CH_2CH_2CH_3$$

For the molecular formula, we can simply count the carbon and hydrogen atoms to arrive at C_7H_{16}. Alternatively, we could use the general formula C_nH_{2n+2}, with $n = 7$, to get C_7H_{16}.

▲ Gasoline is a mixture containing dozens of hydrocarbons, many of which are alkanes.

2. What is the "petroleum distillate" that I see listed on some product labels? Petroleum distillates are various components of crude oil, most of which are hydrocarbons. Paint thinner, lighter fluid, paraffin wax, petroleum jelly, and asphalt are all petroleum distillates.

Recall that water has a density of 1.00 g/mL at room temperature. All the alkanes listed in Table 9.3 have densities less than that.

⚠ **SAFETY ALERT**
Hydrocarbons and most other organic compounds are flammable or combustible. Volatile ones may form explosive mixtures with air. Hydrocarbons are the main ingredients in gasoline, motor oils, fuel gases (natural gas and bottled gas), and fuel oils. They are also ingredients, identified on labels as "petroleum distillates" and "mineral spirits," of products such as floor cleaners, furniture polishes, paint thinners, wood stains and varnishes, and car waxes and polishes. Some products also contain flammable alcohols, esters, and ketones. Products containing flammable substances can be dangerous but may be used safely with proper precautions. Use only as directed and keep all such products away from open flames.

■ EXERCISE 9.1
Write the molecular, complete structural, and condensed structural formulas for **(a)** hexane and **(b)** octane.

Properties of Alkanes

Note in Table 9.3 that after the first few members of the alkane series, the rest show an increase in boiling point of about 30° with each added CH_2 group. Note also that at room temperature alkanes that have 1 to 4 carbon atoms per molecule are gases, those with 5 to about 16 carbon atoms per molecule are liquids, and those with more than 16 carbon atoms per molecule are solids. The densities of liquid and solid alkanes are less than that of water. Alkanes are nonpolar molecules and are insoluble in water; thus, they float on top of water. They dissolve many organic substances of low polarity—such as fats, oils, and waxes.

Alkanes undergo few chemical reactions, but one important chemical property is that they burn, producing a lot of heat. Alkanes have many uses, but they mainly serve as fuels.

The effects of alkanes on the human body vary. Methane appears to be physiologically inert. We probably could breathe a mixture of 80% methane and 20% oxygen without ill effect. This mixture would be flammable, however, and no fire or spark of any kind could be permitted in such an atmosphere. Breathing an atmosphere of pure methane (the "gas" of a gas-operated stove) can lead to death—not because of the presence of methane but because of the absence of oxygen, a condition called *asphyxia*.

Light liquid alkanes such as those in gasoline will dissolve and wash away body oils when spilled on the skin. Repeated contact may cause dermatitis. (Other components of gasoline are less innocuous.) If swallowed, most alkanes do little harm in the stomach; in fact, mineral oil is a mixture of long-chain liquid alkanes that has been used for many years as a laxative.

Heavier liquid alkanes act as emollients (skin softeners). Petroleum jelly (Vaseline™ is one brand) is a semisolid mixture of hydrocarbons that can be applied as an emollient or simply as a protective film. (Skin lotions and creams are discussed in Chapter 21.) However, in the lungs, alkanes cause chemical pneumonia by dissolving fatlike molecules from the cell membranes in the alveoli, allowing the lungs to fill with fluid.

Table 9.3 Physical Properties, Uses and Occurrences of Selected Alkanes

Name	Molecular Formula	Melting Point (°C)	Boiling Point (°C)	Density[a] at 20 °C (g/mL)	Use/Occurrence
Methane	CH_4	−183	−162	(Gas)	Natural gas (main component); fuel
Ethane	C_2H_6	−172	−89	(Gas)	Natural gas (minor component); plastics
Propane	C_3H_8	−188	−42	(Gas)	LPG (bottled gas); plastics
Butane	C_4H_{10}	−138	0	(Gas)	LPG; lighter fuel
Pentane	C_5H_{12}	−130	36	0.626	Gasoline component
Hexane	C_6H_{14}	−95	69	0.659	Gasoline component; extraction solvent for food oils
Heptane	C_7H_{16}	−91	98	0.684	Gasoline component
Octane	C_8H_{18}	−57	126	0.703	Gasoline component
Decane	$C_{10}H_{22}$	−30	174	0.730	Gasoline component
Dodecane	$C_{12}H_{26}$	−10	216	0.749	Gasoline component
Tetradecane	$C_{14}H_{30}$	6	254	0.763	Diesel fuel component
Hexadecane	$C_{16}H_{34}$	18	280	0.775	Diesel fuel component
Octadecane	$C_{18}H_{38}$	28	316	(Solid)	Paraffin wax component
Eicosane	$C_{20}H_{42}$	37	343	(Solid)	Paraffin wax and asphalt component

[a]Densities of the gaseous alkanes vary with pressure. Densities of the solids are not available.

Cyclic Hydrocarbons: Rings and Things

The hydrocarbons we have encountered so far (alkanes) have open-ended chains of carbon atoms. Carbon atoms can also connect to form closed rings. The simplest possible ring-containing hydrocarbon, or **cyclic hydrocarbon**, has the molecular formula C_3H_6 and is called *cyclopropane* (Figure 9.4).

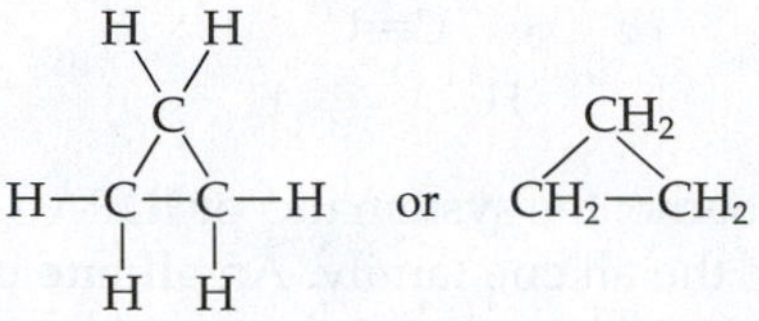

```
     H  H
      \/
      C                  CH2
     / \                /   \
H—C—C—H      or    CH2—CH2
  |    |
  H    H
```

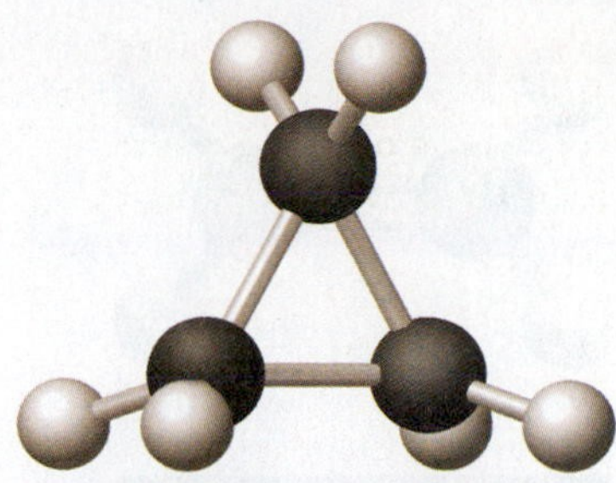

▲ **Figure 9.4** Ball-and-stick model of cyclopropane. Cyclopropane is a potent, quick-acting anesthetic with few undesirable side effects. It is no longer used in surgery, however, because it forms an explosive mixture with air at nearly all concentrations.

Names of *cycloalkanes* (cyclic hydrocarbons containing only single bonds) are formed by adding the prefix *cyclo-* to the name of the open-chain compound with the same number of carbon atoms as are in the cycloalkane's ring.

Chemists often use geometric shapes to represent cyclic compounds (Figure 9.5). For example, a triangle is used to represent the cyclopropane ring, and a hexagon represents cyclohexane. Each corner of such a shape represents a carbon atom with its associated hydrogen atoms.

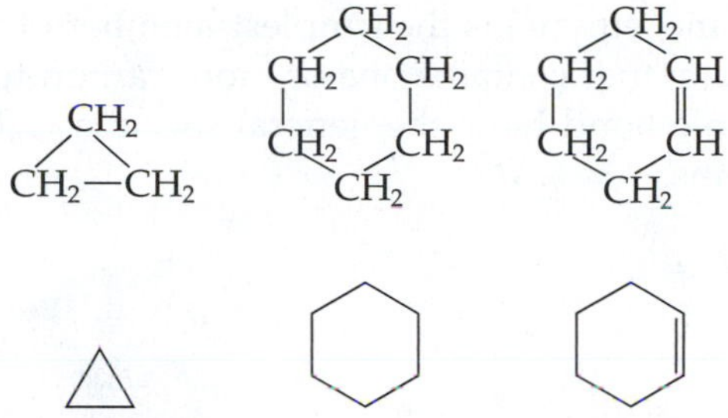

```
                       CH2               CH2
                    /      \          /      \
                 CH2       CH2     CH2        CH
     CH2          |         |       |         ||
    /   \        CH2       CH2     CH2        CH
CH2—CH2             \      /          \      /
                       CH2               CH2
```

Cyclopropane   Cyclohexane   Cyclohexene

◀ **Figure 9.5** Structural formulas and symbolic representations of some cyclic hydrocarbons.

Example 9.2 Structural Formulas of Cyclic Hydrocarbons

Write the structural formula for cyclobutane. What geometric figure is used to represent cyclobutane?

Solution

Cyclobutane has four carbon atoms arranged in a ring.

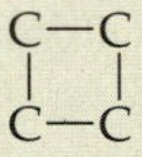

```
C—C
|  |
C—C
```

Each carbon atom needs two hydrogen atoms to complete its set of four bonds.

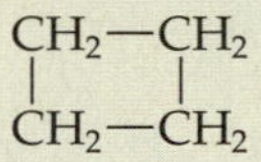

```
CH2—CH2
 |     |
CH2—CH2
```

Cyclobutane can also be represented by a square.

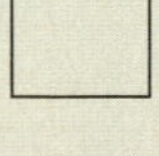

■ EXERCISE 9.2A

Write the structural formula for cyclopentane and the geometric shape used to represent it.

■ EXERCISE 9.2B

What is the general formula for a cycloalkane?

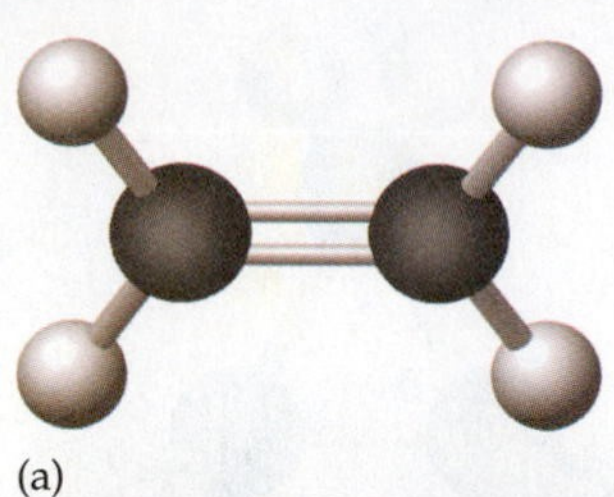

▲ **Figure 9.6** Ball-and-stick (a) and space-filling (b) models of ethylene.

Unsaturated Hydrocarbons: Alkenes and Alkynes

Two carbon atoms can share more than one pair of electrons. In ethylene (C_2H_4), the two carbon atoms share two pairs of electrons and are therefore joined by a double bond (Figure 9.6).

$$\begin{matrix} H & & H \\ & \ddot{C}::\ddot{C} & \\ H & & H \end{matrix} \quad \text{or} \quad \begin{matrix} H & & H \\ & C=C & \\ H & & H \end{matrix} \quad \text{or} \quad CH_2=CH_2$$

(Ethylene is the common name; the systematic, or IUPAC, name is *ethene*.) Ethylene is the simplest member of the alkene family. An **alkene** is a hydrocarbon that contains one or more carbon-to-carbon double bonds. Alkenes with one double bond have the general formula C_nH_{2n}, where n is the number of carbon atoms.

Ethylene is the most important organic chemical commercially. Annual U.S. production is over 20 billion kg. More than half goes into the manufacture of polyethylene, one of the most familiar plastics. Another 15% or so is converted to ethylene glycol, the major component of many formulations of antifreeze used in automobile radiators.

In acetylene (C_2H_2), the two carbon atoms share three pairs of electrons. The carbon atoms are joined by a triple bond (Figure 9.7).

$$H:C:::C:H \quad \text{or} \quad H—C{\equiv}C—H$$

Acetylene (IUPAC name, ethyne) is the simplest member of the alkyne family. An **alkyne** is a hydrocarbon that contains one or more carbon-to-carbon triple bonds. Alkynes with one triple bond have the general formula C_nH_{2n-2}, where n is the number of carbon atoms.

▶ **Figure 9.7** Ball-and-stick (a) and space-filling (b) models of acetylene.

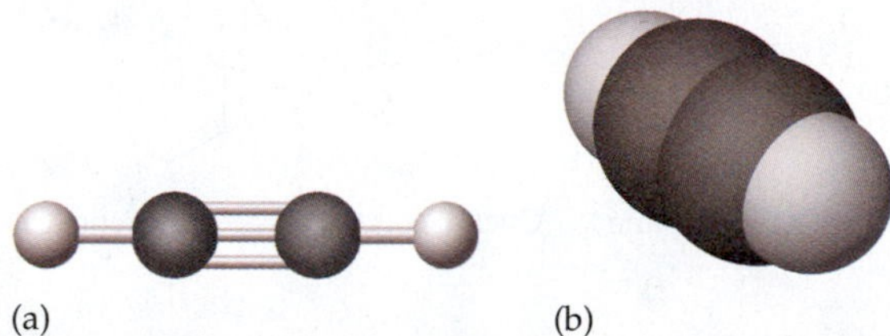

Acetylene is used in oxyacetylene torches for cutting and welding metals. Such torches can produce very high temperatures. Acetylene is also converted to a variety of other chemical products.

Collectively, alkenes and alkynes are called *unsaturated hydrocarbons*. Recall that a *saturated hydrocarbon* (alkane) has the maximum number of hydrogen atoms attached to each carbon atom; it has no double or triple bonds. An **unsaturated hydrocarbon** can have more hydrogen atoms added to it.

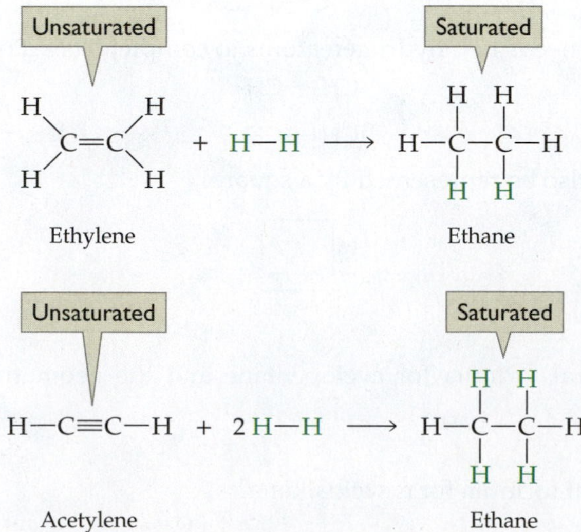

Example 9.3 Molecular Formulas of Unsaturated Hydrocarbons

What is the molecular formula for 1-hexene? (The "1-" is a part of a systematic name that indicates the location of the double bond, which in this case connects the first carbon atom of the chain to the second.)

Solution

The stem *hex-* indicates six carbon atoms, the ending *-ene* tells us that the compound is an alkene. Using the general formula C_nH_{2n} for an alkene, with $n = 6$, we see that an alkene with six carbon atoms has the molecular formula C_6H_{14}.

■ EXERCISE 9.3

What are the molecular formulas for **(a)** 2-hexene and **(b)** 3-heptyne?

▲ It DOES Matter!

Fats are probably the best-known examples of compounds that can be saturated or unsaturated. In saturated fats, all the carbon-carbon bonds are single bonds. These fats are found mostly in milk, meats, and eggs, and their consumption tends to increase low-density lipoproteins ("bad" cholesterol) in the human bloodstream. Most plant oils are unsaturated fats, with one or more carbon-carbon double bonds. Consumption of unsaturated fats tends to increase high-density lipoproteins ("good" cholesterol) in the blood.

Properties of Alkenes and Alkynes

The physical properties of alkenes and alkynes are much like those of the corresponding alkanes. Unsaturated hydrocarbons with 2 to 4 carbon atoms per molecule are gases at room temperature, those with 5 to 18 carbon atoms are liquids, and most of those with more than 18 carbon atoms are solids. Like alkanes, alkenes and alkynes are insoluble in, and float on, water.

Like alkanes, both alkenes and alkynes burn. However, these unsaturated hydrocarbons undergo many more chemical reactions than alkanes do. An alkene or alkyne can undergo an **addition reaction** to the double or triple bond, in which all the atoms of the reactants are incorporated into a single product. In the preceding reactions, ethylene (C_2H_4) adds hydrogen (H_2) to form ethane (C_2H_6), and acetylene (C_2H_2) adds two moles of hydrogen (2 H_2) to form ethane. Chlorine, bromine, water, and many other kinds of small molecules also add to double and triple bonds.

One of the most unusual features of alkene (and alkyne) molecules is that they can add *to each other* to form large molecules called *polymers*. These interesting molecules are discussed in Chapter 10.

An unsaturated hydrocarbon tends to burn with a smoky flame, especially if the oxygen supply is limited. Saturated hydrocarbons usually burn with a clean yellow flame. Burning of natural gas, propane, and butane is almost soot-free, but paint thinner, gasoline, and kerosene (all containing unsaturated hydrocarbons) burn with sooty flames.

Self-Assessment Questions

1. Which of the following is *not* a reason for the great number of carbon compounds?
   a. Carbon atoms can form chains.
   b. Carbon compounds are easily oxidized.
   c. Carbon atoms can form rings.
   d. The same carbon atoms can be arranged different ways.
2. A saturated hydrocarbon is one that
   a. contains only carbon-carbon single bonds
   b. has the maximum number of carbon atoms
   c. has a vapor pressure equal to atmospheric pressure
   d. is solid at room temperature
3. Successive members of the alkane series differ from the preceding member by one additional
   a. C atom and one H atom **b.** C atom and two H atoms
   c. C atom and three H atoms **d.** H atom and two C atoms
4. Isomers are compounds whose molecules have the same
   a. numbers of C atoms but different numbers of H atoms
   b. numbers of H atoms but different numbers of C atoms
   c. numbers and kinds of atoms but different structures
   d. kinds of atoms but different numbers of these atoms
5. As the molecular mass of the members of the alkane series increases, their boiling points
   a. decrease **b.** increase **c.** remain the same **d.** vary randomly
6. A cyclic compound with 6 C atoms and 12 H atoms is
   a. cyclobutane **b.** cycloheptane **c.** cyclohexane **d.** cyclosexane

7. The family of hydrocarbons whose molecules have a triple bond between carbon atoms is the
   a. alkanes b. alkenes c. alkynes d. aromatic hydrocarbons
8. Addition reactions occur with alkenes but not with alkanes because alkenes have
   a. double bonds b. a greater molecular mass
   c. more C atoms per molecule d. a tetrahedral arrangement of bonds
9. The following equation is an example of what kind of reaction?

$$C_2H_4 + H_2 \longrightarrow C_2H_6$$

   a. addition b. neutralization c. oxidation d. ionization

Answers: 1. b; 2. a; 3. b; 4. c; 5. b; 6. c; 7. c; 8. a; 9. a

9.2 Aromatic Compounds: Benzene and its Relatives

Learning Objectives › Define *aromatic* compound, and recognize the structural feature such compounds share. › Name simple aromatic hydrocarbons.

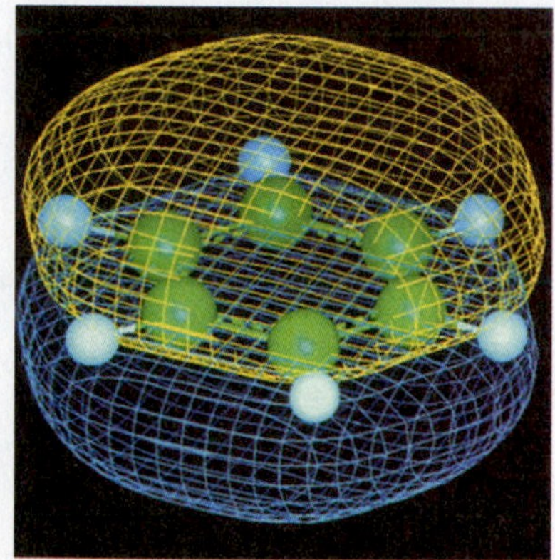

▲ **Figure 9.8** A computer-generated model of the benzene molecule. The six unassigned electrons occupy the yellow and blue areas above and below the plane of the ring of carbon atoms.

An important and interesting hydrocarbon is benzene. Discovered by Michael Faraday in 1825, benzene has the molecular formula C_6H_6. The structure of benzene puzzled chemists for decades. The formula seems to indicate an unsaturated compound, but benzene does not react as if it contains any double or triple bonds. It does not readily undergo addition reactions the way unsaturated compounds usually do.

Finally, in 1865, August Kekulé proposed a structure with a ring of six carbon atoms, each attached to one hydrogen atom.

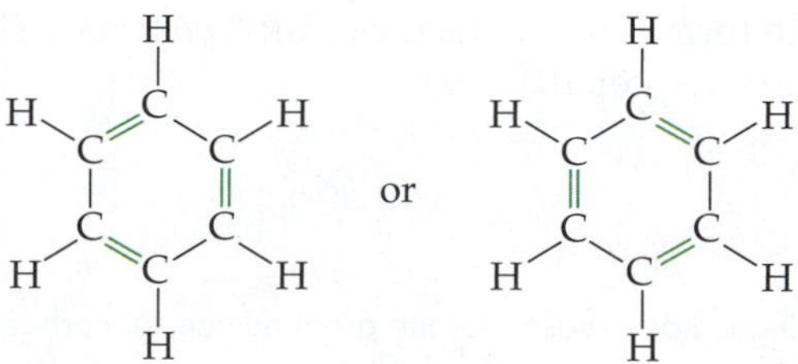

The two structures shown appear to contain double bonds, but in fact they do not. Both structures represent the same molecule, and the actual structure of this molecule is a *hybrid* of these two structures. The benzene molecule actually has six identical carbon-to-carbon bonds that are neither single bonds nor double bonds but something in between. In other words, the three pairs of electrons that would form the three double bonds are not tied down in one location but are spread around the ring (Figure 9.8). Today, we usually represent the benzene ring with a circle inside a hexagon.

A circle inside a ring indicates that a compound is aromatic. It does not always mean six electrons. The structural formula for naphthalene (Figure 9.9), for example, has a circle in each ring, indicating that it is an aromatic hydrocarbon. The total number of unassigned electrons, however, is only ten. Some chemists still prefer to represent naphthalene (and other aromatic compounds) with alternating double and single bonds.

The hexagon represents the ring of six carbon atoms, and the inscribed circle represents the six unassigned electrons. Because its ring of electrons resists being disrupted, the benzene molecule is exceptionally stable.

Benzene and similar compounds are called *aromatic hydrocarbons*, because quite a few of the first benzene-like substances to be discovered had strong aromas. Even though many compounds derived from benzene have turned out to be odorless, the name has stuck. Today, an **aromatic compound** is any compound that contains a benzene ring or has certain properties like those of benzene. All other compounds are said to be aliphatic (Section 9.1).

Structures of some common aromatic hydrocarbons are shown in Figure 9.9. Benzene, toluene, and the xylenes are all liquids that float on water. They are used mainly as solvents and fuels but are also used to make other benzene derivatives. Their vapors can act as narcotics when inhaled. Because benzene may cause leukemia after long exposure, its use has been restricted. Naphthalene is a volatile, white, crystalline solid used as an insecticide, especially as a moth repellant.

Monosubstituted benzenes—in which one hydrogen is replaced by another atom or group, called a **substituent**—are often represented in by condensed formulas—for example, toluene is $C_6H_5CH_3$ and ethylbenzene is $C_6H_5CH_2CH_3$. Similar designations are sometimes used for disubstituted aromatic rings, indicating the relative positions of substituents with numbers, as in 1,4-$C_6H_4(CH_3)_2$ for 1,4-dimethylbenzene.

3. If a compound has *benzene* in its name, is the compound a carcinogen? No. Aromatic compounds are often named as derivatives of benzene simply because their structures contain a benzene ring. In fact, many compounds that are useful or even necessary to life contain benzene rings, including penicillin, aspirin, and the amino acids phenylalanine and tryptophan.

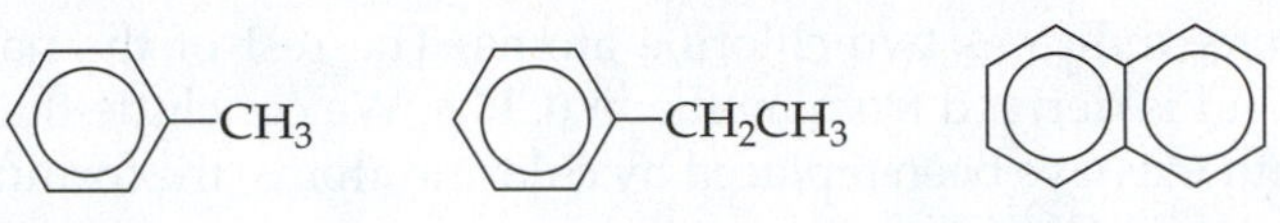

$-CH_3$ Toluene

$-CH_2CH_3$ Ethylbenzene

Naphthalene

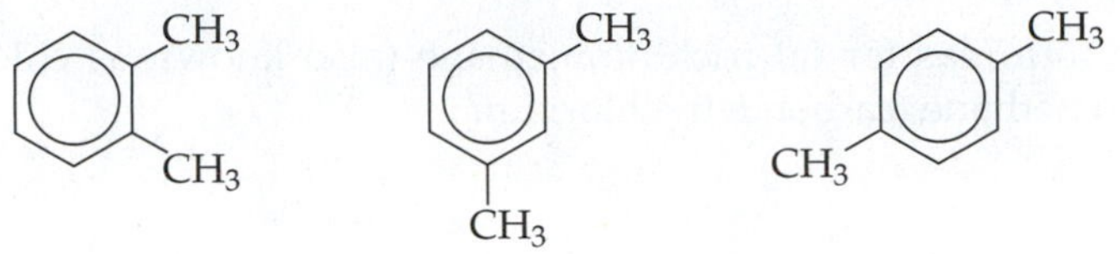

CH_3 CH_3 *ortho*-Xylene (1,2-Dimethylbenzene)

CH_3 CH_3 *meta*-Xylene (1,3-Dimethylbenzene)

CH_3 CH_3 *para*-Xylene (1,4-Dimethylbenzene)

◀ **Figure 9.9** Some aromatic hydrocarbons. Like benzene, toluene and the three xylenes are components of gasoline and also serve as solvents. All these compounds are intermediates in the synthesis of polymers (Chapter 10) and other organic chemicals.

Self-Assessment Questions

1. The molecular formula of benzene is
   a. C_4H_4 b. C_4H_{10} c. C_6H_6 d. C_6H_{10}
2. Which compound is an aromatic hydrocarbon?
   a. acetylene b. butadiene c. chlorobenzene d. cyclohexene
3. Which organic molecule is represented as a hybrid of two structures?
   a. benzene b. butadiene c. 1-butene d. propyne
4. Naphthalene is an
   a. alkane b. alkene c. alkyne d. aromatic hydrocarbon
5. The reactivity of the benzene ring reflects
   a. its aromatic odor
   b. the presence of carbon-carbon double bonds
   c. its saturated structure
   d. the spreading of six electrons over all six carbon atoms

Answers: 1, c; 2, c; 3, a; 4, d; 5, d

9.3 Chlorinated Hydrocarbons: Many Uses, Some Hazards

Learning Objective › Name a chlorinated hydrocarbon given its formula, and write the formula for such a compound given its name.

Many other organic compounds are derived from hydrocarbons by replacing one or more hydrogen atoms by another atom or group of atoms. For example, replacement of hydrogen atoms by chlorine atoms gives chlorinated hydrocarbons. When chlorine gas (Cl_2) is mixed with methane gas (CH_4) in the presence of ultraviolet (UV) light, a reaction takes place at a very rapid, even explosive, rate. The result is a mixture of products, some of which may be familiar to you (see Example 9.4 and Exercise 9.4). Several billion kilograms of chlorinated methanes are produced each year for use as solvents and as starting materials for other commercially valuable compounds. We can write an equation for the reaction in which one hydrogen atom of methane is replaced by a chlorine atom to give methyl chloride (chloromethane).

$$CH_4(g) + Cl_2(g) \longrightarrow CH_3Cl(g) + HCl(g)$$

Example 9.4 Formulas of Chlorinated Hydrocarbons

What is the formula for dichloromethane (also known as methylene chloride)?

Solution

The prefix *dichloro-* indicates two chlorine atoms. The rest of the name indicates that the compound is derived from methane (CH_4). We conclude that two hydrogen atoms of methane have been replaced by chlorine atoms; the formula for dichloromethane is therefore CH_2Cl_2.

■ EXERCISE 9.4

What are the formulas for **(a)** trichloromethane (also known as chloroform) and **(b)** tetrachloromethane (carbon tetrachloride)?

Methyl chloride is used mainly in making silicone polymers (Chapter 10). Methylene chloride (dichloromethane) is a solvent used, for example, as a paint remover. Chloroform (trichloromethane), also a solvent, was once used as an anesthetic, but such use is now considered dangerous. The dosage required for effective anesthesia is too close to a lethal dose. Carbon tetrachloride (tetrachloromethane) has been used as a dry-cleaning solvent and in fire extinguishers, but it is no longer recommended for either use. Exposure to carbon tetrachloride or most other chlorinated hydrocarbons can cause severe damage to the liver. The use of a carbon tetrachloride fire extinguisher in conjunction with water to put out a fire can be deadly. Carbon tetrachloride reacts with water at elevated temperatures to form phosgene ($COCl_2$), an extremely poisonous gas that was used against troops during World War I.

A number of chlorinated hydrocarbons are of considerable interest. Vinyl chloride ($CH_2{=}CHCl$) is the starting material for manufacture of polyvinylchloride (Chapter 10).

Many chlorinated hydrocarbons have similar properties. Most are only slightly polar and do not dissolve in (highly polar) water. Instead, they dissolve (and dissolve in) fats, oils, greases, and other substances of low polarity. This is why certain chlorinated hydrocarbons make good degreasing and dry-cleaning solvents; they remove grease and oily stains from fabrics. This is also why DDT and PCBs cause problems for fish and birds and perhaps for people; these toxic substances are concentrated in fatty animal tissues rather than being easily excreted in (aqueous) urine. DDT (dichlorodiphenyltrichloroethane) and other chlorinated hydrocarbon insecticides are discussed in Chapter 20. In Chapter 10, we will discuss polychlorinated biphenyls (PCBs).

Chlorofluorocarbons and Fluorocarbons

Compounds containing carbon and both fluorine and chlorine are called *chlorofluorocarbons (CFCs)*. CFCs have been used as the dispersing gases in aerosol cans, for making foamed plastics, and as refrigerants. Three common CFCs are best known by their industrial code designations:

$CFCl_3$	CF_2Cl_2	CF_2ClCF_2Cl
CFC 11	CFC 12	CFC 114

At room temperature, CFCs are gases or liquids with low boiling points. They are insoluble in water and inert toward most other substances. These properties make them ideal propellants in aerosol cans for deodorant, hair spray, and food products. CFCs are being phased out because their inertness allows them to persist in the environment and diffuse into the stratosphere, where they participate in chemical reactions that lead to depletion of the ozone layer that protects Earth from harmful UV radiation. We will look at this problem and some attempts to solve it in Chapter 13.

Fluorinated compounds have found some interesting uses. Some have been used as blood extenders. Oxygen is quite soluble in certain *perfluorocarbons*. (The prefix *per-* means that all hydrogen atoms have been replaced, in this case, by fluorine atoms.) These compounds can therefore serve as temporary substitutes for hemoglobin, the oxygen-carrying protein in blood. Perfluoro compounds have been used to treat premature babies, whose lungs are often underdeveloped.

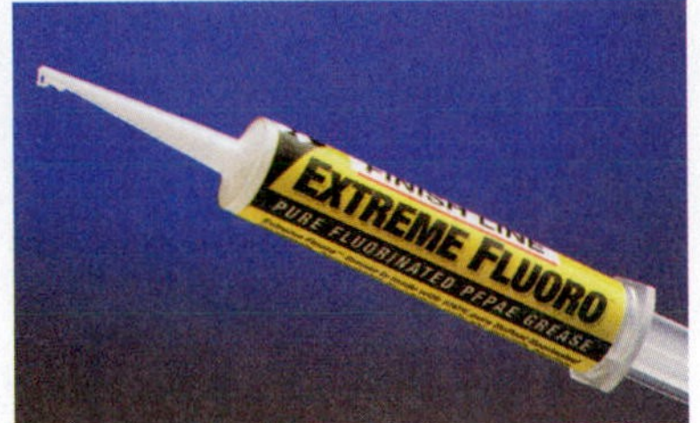

▲ Perfluorinated lubricants are used where highly corrosive or reactive conditions would cause most hydrocarbon greases to burst into flame.

Polytetrafluoroethylene (PTFE, or Teflon®, discussed in Chapter 10) is a perfluorinated polymer. It has many interesting applications because of its resistance to corrosive chemicals and to high temperatures. It is especially noted for its unusual nonstick properties.

Self-Assessment Questions

1. The compound CH_3Cl is named
   a. chloroform
   b. methyl chloride
   c. methylene chloride
   d. methyl formate
2. The compound CF_2Cl_2 is
   a. a chlorofluorocarbon
   b. chloroform
   c. methyl chloride
   d. methylene chloride
3. Which of the following is an isomer of 2-chloropropane ($CH_3CHClCH_3$)?
   a. butane **b.** 2-chlorobutane
   c. 1-chloropropane **d.** propane

Answers: 1, b; 2, a; 3, c

9.4 The Functional Group

Learning Objectives › Classify an organic compound according to its functional group(s), and explain why the concept of a functional group is useful in the study of organic chemistry. › Recognize and write the formulas of simple alkyl groups.

Many organic compounds contain oxygen as well as carbon and hydrogen. This section introduces several important families of oxygen-containing organic compounds. First, however, we need to cover a fundamental concept of organic chemistry.

Double and triple carbon–carbon bonds and halogen substituents are examples of **functional groups**, atoms or groups of atoms that give a family of organic compounds its characteristic chemical and physical properties. Table 9.4 lists a number of common functional groups found in organic molecules. Each of these groups is the basis for its own homologous series.

In many simple molecules, a functional group is attached as a substituent to a hydrocarbon stem called an *alkyl group*. An **alkyl group** is derived from an alkane by removing a hydrogen atom. The methyl group ($CH_3—$), for example,

Table 9.4 Selected Organic Functional Groups

Name of Class	Functional Group[a]	General Formula of Class
Alkane	None	R—H
Alkene	$-\overset{\vert}{C}=\overset{\vert}{C}-$	$R_2C=CR_2$
Alkyne	$-C\equiv C-$	$RC\equiv CR$
Alcohol	$-\overset{\vert}{\underset{\vert}{C}}-OH$	R—OH
Ether	$-\overset{\vert}{\underset{\vert}{C}}-O-\overset{\vert}{\underset{\vert}{C}}-$	R—O—R′
Aldehyde	$-\overset{O}{\overset{\Vert}{C}}-H$	$R-\overset{O}{\overset{\Vert}{C}}-H$
Ketone	$-\overset{O}{\overset{\Vert}{C}}-$	$R-\overset{O}{\overset{\Vert}{C}}-R'$
Carboxylic acid	$-\overset{O}{\overset{\Vert}{C}}-OH$	$R-\overset{O}{\overset{\Vert}{C}}-O-H$
Ester	$-\overset{O}{\overset{\Vert}{C}}-O-\overset{\vert}{\underset{\vert}{C}}-$	$R-\overset{O}{\overset{\Vert}{C}}-O-R'$
Amine	$-\overset{\vert}{\underset{\vert}{C}}-\underset{\vert}{N}-$	$R-\overset{H}{\overset{\vert}{N}}-H$ $R-\overset{H}{\overset{\vert}{N}}-R'$ $R-\overset{R'}{\overset{\vert}{N}}-R''$
Amide	$-\overset{O}{\overset{\Vert}{C}}-\underset{\vert}{N}-$	$R-\overset{O}{\overset{\Vert}{C}}-\underset{H}{\underset{\vert}{N}}-H$ $R-\overset{O}{\overset{\Vert}{C}}-\underset{H}{\underset{\vert}{N}}-R'$ $R-\overset{O}{\overset{\Vert}{C}}-\underset{R''}{\underset{\vert}{N}}-R'$

[a] Neutral functional groups are shown in green, acidic groups in red, and basic groups in blue.

is derived from methane (CH_4), and the ethyl group ($CH_3CH_2—$) from ethane (CH_3CH_3). Propane yields two different alkyl groups, depending on whether the hydrogen atom is removed from an end or from the middle carbon atom; see Table 9.5. Table 9.5 also lists the four alkyl groups derived from the two butanes.

Often the letter R is used to stand for an alkyl group in general. Thus, ROH is a general formula for an alcohol, and RCl represents any alkyl chloride.

Table 9.5 Common Alkyl Groups

	Name	Structural Formula	Condensed Structural Formula
Derived from Propane	Propyl	H H H H—C—C—C— H H H	$CH_3CH_2CH_2$—
	Isopropyl	H H H H—C—C—C—H H H (bond from middle C)	CH_3CHCH_3 (bond from middle C)
Derived from Butane	Butyl	H H H H H—C—C—C—C— H H H H	$CH_3CH_2CH_2CH_2$—
	Secondary butyl (*sec*-butyl)	H H H H H—C—C—C—C—H H H H (bond from second C)	$CH_3CHCH_2CH_3$ (bond from second C)
Derived from Isobutane	Isobutyl	H H—C—H H H H—C—C—C— H H H	CH_3 CH_3CHCH_2—
	Tertiary butyl (*tert*-butyl)	H H—C—H H H H—C—C—C—H H H (bond from central C)	CH_3 CH_3—C—CH_3 (bond from central C)

Self-Assessment Questions

1. A specific arrangement of atoms that gives characteristic properties to an organic molecule is called a(n)
   - **a.** alkyl group
   - **b.** carbonyl group
   - **c.** functional group
   - **d.** hydroxyl group
2. The formula $CH_3CH_2CH_2$— represents
   - **a.** an alkyl group
   - **b.** a functional group
   - **c.** propane
   - **d.** propylene
3. How many carbon atoms are there in a butyl group?
   - **a.** 2
   - **b.** 3
   - **c.** 4
   - **d.** 6
4. The formula $CH_3CH_2CH_2CH_2$— represents a(n)
   - **a.** butyl group
   - **b.** isobutyl group
   - **c.** isopropyl group
   - **d.** propyl group

Answers: 1, c; 2, a; 3, c; 4, a

9.5 Alcohols, Phenols, and Ethers

Learning Objectives › Recognize the general structure for an alcohol, a phenol, and an ether. › Name simple alcohols, phenols, and ethers.

When a hydroxyl group (—OH) is substituted for any hydrogen atom in an alkane (R—H), the molecule becomes an **alcohol** (ROH). Like many organic compounds, alcohols can be called by their common names or by the systematic names of IUPAC. The IUPAC names for alcohols are based on those of alkanes, with the ending changed from *-e* to *-ol*. Methanol, ethanol, and 1-propanol are the first three members of the homologous series of straight-chain alcohols.

A number designates the carbon to which the —OH group is attached when more than one location is possible. For example, the 1 in 1-propanol indicates that —OH is attached to an end carbon atom of the three-carbon chain; the isomeric compound, 2-propanol, has the —OH group on the second (middle) carbon atom of the chain.

$CH_3—OH$	$CH_3CH_2—OH$	$CH_3CH_2CH_2—OH$	CH_3CHCH_3 (with OH on the middle C)
Methanol	Ethanol	1–Propanol	2–Propanol

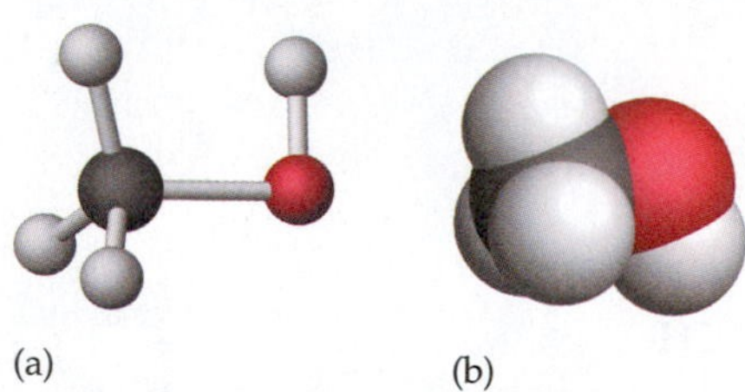

(a) (b)

▲ **Figure 9.10** Ball-and-stick (a) and space-filling (b) models of methanol.

Common names for these alcohols are methyl alcohol, ethyl alcohol, and propyl alcohol. The IUPAC names are the ones used in most scientific literature.

Methyl Alcohol (Methanol)

The simplest alcohol is *methanol*, or *methyl alcohol* (Figure 9.10). Methanol is sometimes called *wood alcohol* because it was once made from wood. The modern industrial process makes methanol from carbon monoxide and hydrogen at high temperature and pressure in the presence of a catalyst.

$$CO(g) + 2\,H_2(g) \longrightarrow CH_3OH(l)$$

Methanol is important as a solvent and as a chemical intermediate. It is also a gasoline additive and a potential replacement for gasoline in automobiles.

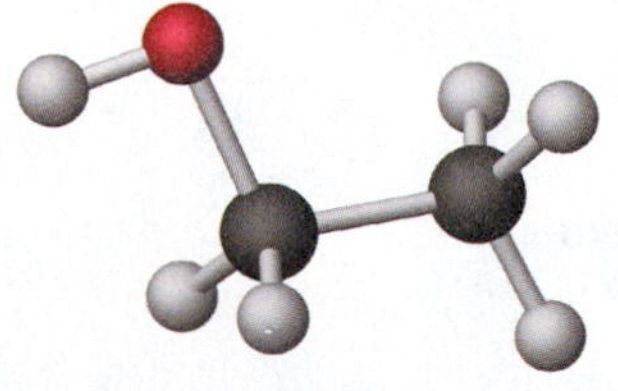

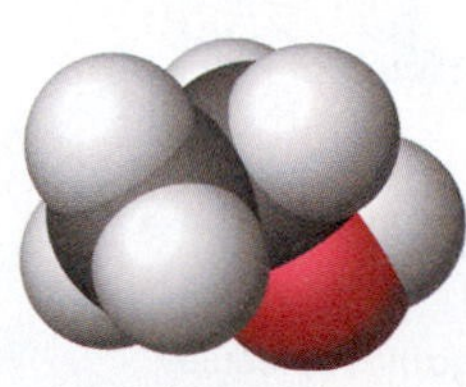

(a) (b)

▲ **Figure 9.11** Ball-and-stick (a) and space-filling (b) models of ethanol.

Ethyl Alcohol (Ethanol)

The next member of the homologous series of alcohols is *ethyl alcohol* (CH_3CH_2OH), also called ethanol or *grain alcohol* (Figure 9.11). Ethanol is made by fermentation of grain (or other starchy or sugary materials). If the sugar is glucose, the reaction is

$$C_6H_{12}O_6(aq) \xrightarrow{\text{yeast}} 2\,CH_3CH_2OH(aq) + 2\,CO_2(g)$$

Ethanol for beverages and for automotive fuel is made in this way. Ethanol for industrial use is made by reacting ethylene with water.

$$CH_2{=}CH_2(g) + H_2O(l) \xrightarrow{H^+} CH_3CH_2OH(l)$$

This industrial alcohol is identical to that made by fermentation and is generally cheaper, but by law, it cannot be used in alcoholic beverages. Because it carries no excise tax, the law requires that noxious substances be added to this alcohol to prevent people from drinking it. The resulting *denatured alcohol* is not fit to drink. This is the kind of alcohol commonly found on the shelves in chemical laboratories.

Is it poisonous? That seems to be a simple question, but it is a difficult one to answer. Toxicity depends on the nature of the substance, the amount, and the route by which it is taken into the body. Toxicity is discussed in detail in Chapter 22.

Table 9.6 Approximate Relationship among Drinks Consumed, Blood-Alcohol Level, and Behavior[a]

Number of Drinks[b]	Blood-Alcohol Level (percent by volume)	Behavior[c]
2	0.05	Mild sedation; tranquility
4	0.10	Lack of coordination
6	0.15	Obvious intoxication
10	0.30	Unconsciousness
20	0.50	Possible death

[a]Data are for a 70-kg (154-lb) moderate drinker.

[b]Rapidly consumed 30-mL (1-oz) shots of 90-proof whiskey, 360-mL (12-oz) bottles of beer, or 150-mL (5-oz) glasses of wine.

[c]An inexperienced drinker would be affected more strongly, or more quickly, than someone who is ordinarily a moderate drinker. Conversely, an experienced heavy drinker would be affected less.

The *proof* of an alcoholic beverage is twice the percentage of alcohol by volume. The term originated in a seventeenth-century English method for testing whiskey to ensure that a dealer was not increasing profits by adding water to the booze. A qualitative test was to pour some of the whiskey on gunpowder and ignite it. Ignition of the gunpowder after the alcohol had burned away was considered "proof" that the whiskey did not contain too much water.

Gasoline in many parts of the United States contains up to 10% ethanol that is produced by fermentation. Because the United States has a large corn (maize) surplus, there is a generous government subsidy for gasoline producers who use ethanol made this way. As a result, many factories now make ethanol by fermentation of corn.

Toxicity of Alcohols

Although ethanol is an ingredient in wine, beer, and other alcoholic beverages, alcohols in general are rather toxic. Methanol, for example, is oxidized in the body to formaldehyde (HCHO). Drinking as little as 1 oz (about 30 mL or 2 tablespoonfuls) can cause blindness and even death. Several poisonings each year result when people mistake methanol for the less toxic ethanol.

Ethanol is not as poisonous as methanol, but it is still toxic. About 50,000 cases of ethanol poisoning are reported each year in the United States, and dozens of people die of acute ethanol poisoning.

Generally, ethanol acts as a mild depressant; it slows down both physical and mental activity. Table 9.6 lists the effects of various doses. Although ethanol generally is a depressant, small amounts of it seem to act as a stimulant, perhaps by relaxing tensions and relieving inhibitions.

Ingesting too much ethanol over a long period of time can alter brain-cell function, cause nerve damage, and shorten life span by contributing to diseases of the liver, cardiovascular system, and practically every other organ of the body. In addition, about half of fatal automobile accidents involve at least one drinking driver. Babies born to alcoholic mothers often are small, deformed, and mentally retarded. Some investigators believe that this *fetal alcohol syndrome* can occur even if mothers drink only moderately. Ethanol, by far the most abused drug in the United States, is discussed more fully in Chapter 18.

▲ Warning labels on alcoholic beverages alert consumers to the hazards of consumption.

Rubbing alcohol is a 70% solution of isopropyl alcohol. Because isopropyl alcohol is also more toxic than ethanol, it is not surprising that people become ill, and sometimes die, after drinking rubbing alcohol.

Multifunctional Alcohols

Several alcohols have more than one hydroxyl group. Examples are ethylene glycol, propylene glycol, and glycerol.

```
   H  H            H  H  H             H  H  H
   |  |            |  |  |             |  |  |
H—C—C—H        H—C—C—C—H         H—C—C—C—H
   |  |            |  |  |             |  |  |
  OH OH            H OH OH            OH OH OH
```

Ethylene glycol — Propylene glycol — Glycerol

Ethylene glycol is the main ingredient in many permanent antifreeze mixtures. Its high boiling point keeps it from boiling away in automobile radiators. Ethylene glycol is a syrupy liquid with a sweet taste, but it is quite toxic. It is oxidized in the liver to oxalic acid.

$$\underset{\text{Ethylene glycol}}{\overset{\text{OH}\quad\text{OH}}{CH_2{-}CH_2}} \xrightarrow{\text{liver enzymes}} \underset{\text{Oxalic acid (toxic)}}{HO{-}\overset{O}{\overset{\|}{C}}{-}\overset{O}{\overset{\|}{C}}{-}OH}$$

Oxalic acid forms crystals of its calcium salt, calcium oxalate (CaC_2O_4), which can damage the kidneys, leading to kidney failure and death. Propylene glycol, a high-boiling substance that is not poisonous, is now marketed as a safer permanent antifreeze.

Glycerol (or glycerin) is a sweet, syrupy liquid that is a by-product from fats during soap manufacture (Chapter 21). It is used in lotions to keep the skin soft and as a food additive to keep cakes moist. Its reaction with nitric acid makes nitroglycerin, the explosive material in dynamite. Nitroglycerin is also important as a vasodilator, a medication taken by heart patients to relieve angina pain.

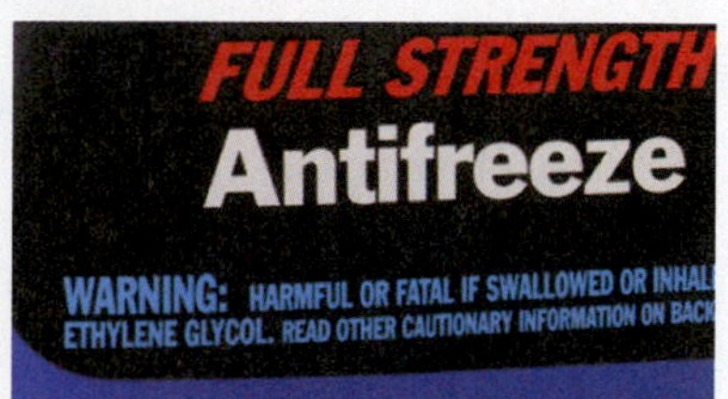

▲ It DOES Matter! Antifreeze containing ethylene glycol should always be drained into a container and disposed of properly. Pets have been known to die from licking the sweet, but toxic, ethylene glycol mixture from a driveway or open container.

Example 9.5 Structural Formulas of Alcohols

Write the structural formula for *tert*-butyl alcohol, sometimes used as an octane booster in gasoline.

Solution

An alcohol consists of an alkyl group joined to a hydroxyl group. From Table 9.5, we see that the *tert*-butyl group is

$$CH_3{-}\overset{\overset{CH_3}{|}}{\underset{\underset{CH_3}{|}}{C}}{-}$$

Connecting this group to an OH group gives *tert*-butyl alcohol.

$$CH_3{-}\overset{\overset{CH_3}{|}}{\underset{\underset{CH_3}{|}}{C}}{-}OH$$

■ EXERCISE 9.5

Write the structural formulas for **(a)** butyl alcohol and **(b)** *sec*-butyl alcohol.

4. Why do some mouthwashes taste "medicine-y"? Some mouthwashes and sore-throat remedies contain certain phenols, which often have what might be termed a "hospital" odor and a medicinal taste.

Phenols

When a hydroxyl group is attached to a benzene ring, the compound is called a **phenol**. Although a phenol may appear to be an alcohol, it is not. The benzene ring greatly alters the properties of the hydroxyl group. Unlike alcohols, phenol is a weak acid (sometimes called *carbolic acid*), and it is quite poisonous compared to most simple alcohols.

$$C_6H_5{-}OH$$

Phenol

Phenol was the first antiseptic used in an operating room—by Joseph Lister in 1867. Up until that time, surgery was not antiseptic, and many patients died from infections following surgical operations. Although phenol has a strong germicidal action, it is far from an ideal antiseptic because it causes severe skin burns and kills healthy cells along with harmful microorganisms.

Phenol is still sometimes employed as a disinfectant for floors and furniture, but other phenolic compounds are now used as antiseptics. Hexylresorcinol, for example, is a more powerful germicide than phenol, and it is less damaging to the skin and has fewer other side effects.

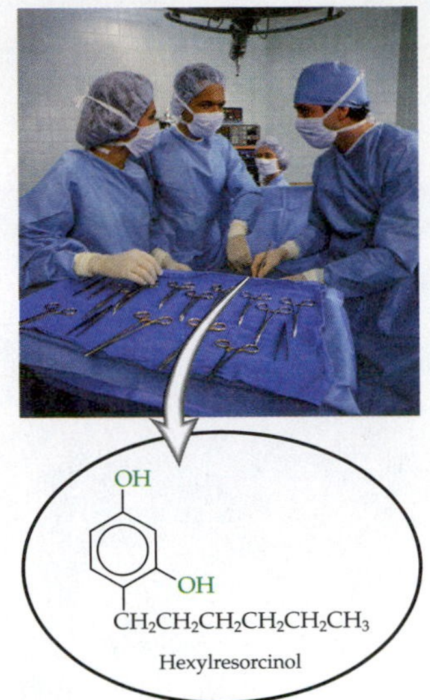

▲ Phenolic compounds help to ensure antiseptic conditions in hospital operating rooms.

Ethers

Compounds with two alkyl or aromatic groups attached to the same oxygen atom are called **ethers**. The general formula is ROR (or ROR′ because the alkyl groups need not be alike). The best-known ether is *diethyl ether* ($CH_3CH_2OCH_2CH_3$), often called simply *ether*.

Diethyl ether was once used as an anesthetic but is now used mainly as a solvent. It dissolves many organic substances that are insoluble in water. It boils at 36 °C, which means that it evaporates readily, making it easy to recover dissolved materials. Although diethyl ether has little chemical reactivity, it is highly flammable. Great care must be taken to avoid sparks or flames when it is in use.

Diethyl ether was introduced in 1842 as a general anesthetic for surgery and was once the most widely used anesthetic. It is rarely used for humans today because it has undesirable side effects, such as postanesthetic nausea and vomiting. We will discuss modern anesthesia in Chapter 18.

Another problem with ethers is that they can react slowly with oxygen to form unstable peroxides, which may decompose explosively. Beware of previously opened containers of ether, especially old ones.

The ether produced in the largest amount commercially is a cyclic compound called *ethylene oxide*. Its two carbon atoms and one oxygen atom form a three-membered ring. Ethylene oxide is a toxic gas, used mainly to make ethylene glycol.

$$\underset{\text{Ethylene oxide}}{H_2C{-}CH_2\ (\text{ring via }O)} + \underset{\text{Water}}{H_2O} \xrightarrow{H^+} \underset{\text{Ethylene glycol}}{\underset{OH\quad\ OH}{CH_2{-}CH_2}}$$

Ethylene oxide is also used to sterilize medical instruments and as an intermediate in the synthesis of some detergents (Chapter 21). Most of the ethylene glycol produced is used in making polyester fibers (Chapter 10) and antifreeze.

Like cyclic hydrocarbons, cyclic ethers can be represented by geometric shapes. Each corner of such a shape (except the O) stands for a C atom with enough H atoms attached to give the carbon four bonds. For example, ethylene oxide is represented as

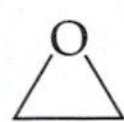

CONCEPTUAL Example 9.6 Identifying Functional Groups

Classify each of the following as an alcohol, an ether, or a phenol.

(a) HO–C_6H_4–Cl (para-chlorophenol ring structure)

(b) $CH_3CH_2OCH_3$

(c) $CH_3CHCH_2CH_3$ with OH on the second carbon

(d) C_6H_5–CH_2OH

(e) five-membered ring containing O

Solution

a. The OH functional group, is attached directly to the benzene ring; the compound is a phenol.
b. The O atom is between two alkyl groups; the compound is an ether.

c. The OH group is attached to an alkyl group; the compound is an alcohol.
d. The compound is an alcohol; the OH is not attached directly to the benzene ring.
e. The compound is an ether; the O atom is between two C atoms.

■ EXERCISE 9.6

Classify each of the following as an alcohol, an ether, or a phenol.

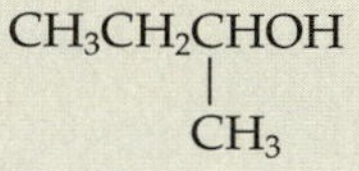

(a) CH_3CH_2CHOH with CH_3 on the CHOH carbon

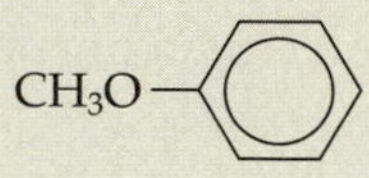

(b) CH_3O— attached to a benzene ring

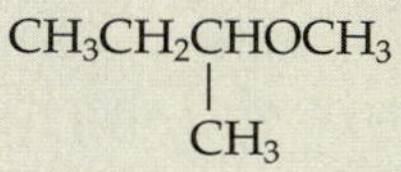

(c) $CH_3CH_2CHOCH_3$ with CH_3 on the CH carbon

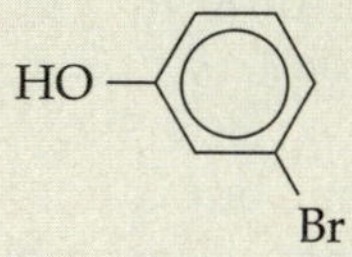

(d) HO— attached to a benzene ring with Br

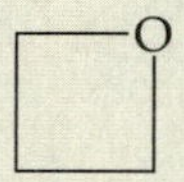

(e) four-membered ring containing O

Example 9.7 Formulas for Ethers

What is the formula for isopropyl methyl ether?

Solution

Isopropyl methyl ether has an oxygen atom joined to an isopropyl group (three carbons joined to oxygen by the middle carbon) and a methyl group. The formula is

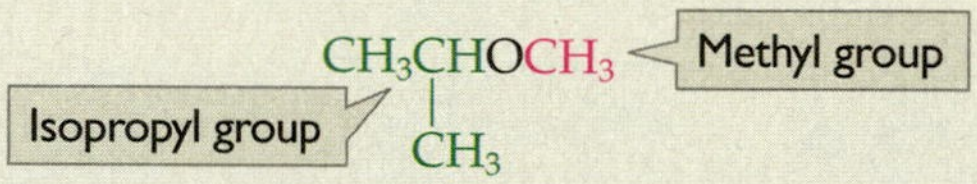

CH_3CHOCH_3 with CH_3 on the CH carbon

Methyl group
Isopropyl group

■ EXERCISE 9.7

Write formulas for **(a)** methyl propyl ether and **(b)** ethyl *tert*-butyl ether.

Self-Assessment Questions

1. Which of the following formulas represents an alcohol?
a. $CH_3CHOHCH_2CH_3$ **b.** CH_3COCH_3
c. CdOH **d.** CH_3CHO

2. Which of the following alcohols has molecules with more than one hydroxyl group?
a. 2-butanol **b.** glycerol **c.** 4-octanol **d.** 3-pentanol

3. The formula for ethylene glycol is
a. CH_3CH_2OH **b.** $CH_3CH(OH)_2$
c. $C_3H_5(OH)_3$ **d.** $HOCH_2CH_2OH$

4. A structural formula that has a hydroxyl (OH) group attached to a benzene ring represents a(n)
a. alcohol **b.** ether **c.** hexanol **d.** phenol

5. An important use of phenols is as
a. anesthetics **b.** antiseptics **c.** flavors **d.** solvents

6. The general formula R—O—R′ represents a(n)
a. ester **b.** ether **c.** ketone **d.** phenol

7. The formula $CH_3CH_2OCH_2CH_3$ represents
a. 2-butanol **b.** 2-butanone **c.** butyraldehyde **d.** diethyl ether

8. The formula for butyl ethyl ether is
a. $CH_3CH_2OCH_2CH_3$ **b.** $CH_3OCH_2CH_2CH_3$
c. $CH_3CH_2CH_2OCH_2CH_3$ **d.** $CH_3CH_2OCH_2CH_2CH_2CH_3$

9. The compound $CH_3CHOHCH_2CH_3$ is an isomer of
   a. $CH_3COCH_2CH_2CH_3$
   b. $CH_3CH_2OCH_2CH_3$
   c. $CH_3COOCH_2CH_3$
   d. $CH_3CH_2CH_2COOH$

Answers: 1. a; 2. b; 3. d; 4. d; 5. b; 6. b; 7. d; 8. d; 9. b

9.6 Aldehydes and Ketones

Learning Objective › Name simple aldehydes and ketones, and list their important properties.

Two families of organic compounds that share the same functional group are **aldehydes** and **ketones**. Both types of compounds contain the **carbonyl group** (C═O), but aldehydes have at least one hydrogen atom attached to the carbonyl carbon, whereas ketones have two other carbon atoms joined to the carbonyl carbon.

$-\overset{\overset{\large O}{\|\|}}{C}-$	$R-\overset{\overset{\large O}{\|\|}}{C}-H$	$R-\overset{\overset{\large O}{\|\|}}{C}-R'$
A carbonyl group	An aldehyde	A ketone

To simplify typing, these structures are often written on one line with the C═O bond omitted.

—C(═O)— or —CO—	R—CH(═O) or R—CHO	R—C(═O)—R′ or R—CO—R′
A carbonyl group	An aldehyde	A ketone

Models of three familiar carbonyl compounds are shown in Figure 9.12.

Some Common Aldehydes

The simplest aldehyde is *formaldehyde* (HCHO). It is a gas at room temperature but is readily soluble in water. As a 40% solution called *formalin*, it is used as a preservative for biological specimens and in embalming fluid. Systematic names for aldehydes are based on those of alkanes, with the ending changed from *-e* to *-al*. Thus, by the IUPAC system, formaldehyde is named methanal. IUPAC names are seldom used for simple aldehydes because of possible confusion with the corresponding alcohols. For example, "methanal" is easily confused with "methanol," when spoken or (especially) when handwritten.

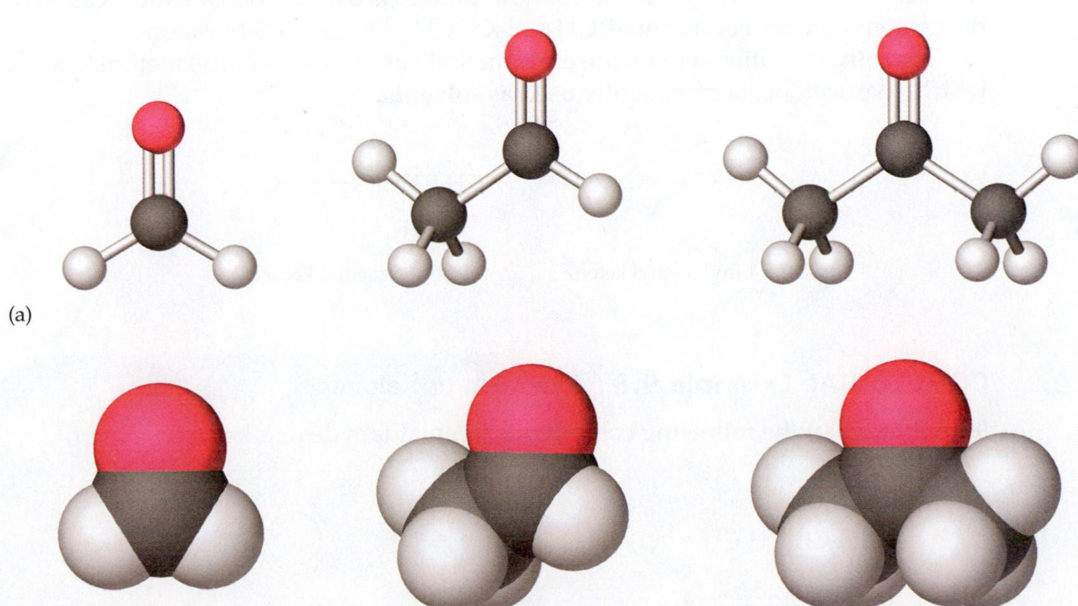

◀ **Figure 9.12** Ball-and-stick (a) and space-filling (b) models of formaldehyde (left), acetaldehyde (center), and acetone (right).

Formaldehyde is used in making certain plastics (Chapter 10). It also is used to disinfect homes, ships, and warehouses. Commercially, formaldehyde is made by the oxidation of methanol. The same net reaction occurs in the human body when methanol is ingested and accounts for the high toxicity of that alcohol.

Organic chemists often write equations that show only the organic reactants and products. Inorganic substances are omitted for the sake of simplicity.

$$\underset{\text{Methanol}}{CH_3OH} \xrightarrow{\text{oxidation}} \underset{\text{Formaldehyde}}{H{-}\overset{\overset{\displaystyle O}{\|}}{C}{-}H}$$

The next member of the homologous series of aldehydes is acetaldehyde (ethanal), formed by the oxidation of ethanol.

$$\underset{\text{Ethanol}}{CH_3CH_2OH} \xrightarrow{\text{oxidation}} \underset{\text{Acetaldehyde}}{CH_3{-}\overset{\overset{\displaystyle O}{\|}}{C}{-}H}$$

The next two members of the aldehyde series are propionaldehyde (propanal) and butyraldehyde (butanal). Both have strong, unpleasant odors. Benzaldehyde has an aldehyde group attached to a benzene ring. Also called (synthetic) oil of almond, benzaldehyde is used in perfumery, and is the flavor ingredient in maraschino cherries.

$$\underset{\text{Propionaldehyde}}{CH_3CH_2{-}\overset{\overset{\displaystyle O}{\|}}{C}{-}H} \qquad \underset{\text{Butyraldehyde}}{CH_3CH_2CH_2{-}\overset{\overset{\displaystyle O}{\|}}{C}{-}H} \qquad \underset{\text{Benzaldehyde}}{C_6H_5{-}\overset{\overset{\displaystyle O}{\|}}{C}{-}H}$$

Some Common Ketones

The simplest ketone is *acetone*, made by the oxidation of isopropyl alcohol.

$$\underset{\text{Isopropyl alcohol}}{CH_3{-}\overset{\overset{\displaystyle OH}{|}}{CH}{-}CH_3} \xrightarrow{\text{oxidation}} \underset{\text{Acetone}}{CH_3{-}\overset{\overset{\displaystyle O}{\|}}{C}{-}CH_3}$$

Acetone is a common solvent for such organic materials as fats, rubbers, plastics, and varnishes. It is also used in paint and varnish removers and is a major ingredient in some fingernail polish removers. By the IUPAC system, acetone is named propanone. The systematic names for ketones are based on those of alkanes, with the ending changed from *-e* to *-one*. When necessary, a number is used to indicate the location of the carbonyl group. For example, $CH_3CH_2COCH_2CH_2CH_3$ is 3-hexanone.

Two other familiar ketones are ethyl methyl ketone and isobutyl methyl ketone, which, like acetone, are frequently used as solvents.

$$\underset{\text{Ethyl methyl ketone}}{CH_3CH_2{-}\overset{\overset{\displaystyle O}{\|}}{C}{-}CH_3} \qquad \underset{\text{Isobutyl methyl ketone}}{CH_3\underset{\underset{\displaystyle CH_3}{|}}{C}HCH_2{-}\overset{\overset{\displaystyle O}{\|}}{C}{-}CH_3}$$

CONCEPTUAL Example 9.8 Aldehyde or Ketone?

Identify each of the following compounds as an aldehyde or a ketone.

$$\underset{\text{(a)}}{CH_3CH_2CH_2CH_2{-}\overset{\overset{\displaystyle O}{\|}}{C}{-}H} \qquad \underset{\text{(b)}}{C_6H_{10}{=}O} \qquad \underset{\text{(c)}}{C_6H_5{-}\overset{\overset{\displaystyle O}{\|}}{C}{-}CH_3}$$

A ketone is a carbon chain
With a carbonyl inside.
If the carbonyl is on the end,
Then it's an aldehyde.

Solution

a. A hydrogen atom is attached to the carbonyl carbon atom; the compound is an aldehyde.

b. The carbonyl group is between two other (ring) carbon atoms; the compound is a ketone.

c. The compound is a ketone. (Remember that the corner of the hexagon stands for a carbon atom.)

■ EXERCISE 9.8

Identify each of the following compounds as an aldehyde or a ketone.

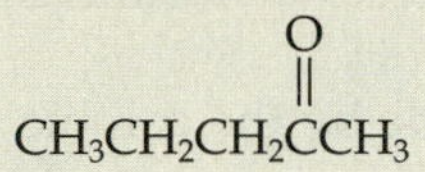

$CH_3CH_2CH_2\overset{\overset{\displaystyle O}{\|}}{C}CH_3$ (a)

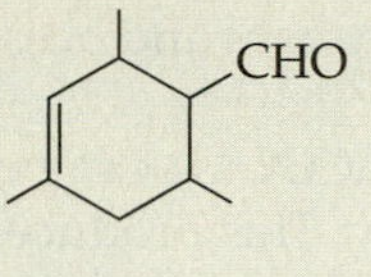

CHO (b)

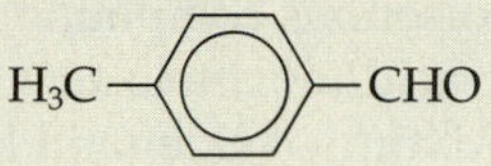

H_3C—⬡—CHO (c)

Self-Assessment Questions

1. The aldehyde functional group has a carbonyl group attached to
a. an H atom **b.** an N atom **c.** an OH group **d.** two other C atoms

2. The ketone functional group has a carbonyl group attached to
a. an OH group **b.** an OR group
c. two other C atoms **d.** two OR groups

3. The general formula R—CO—R′ represents a(n)
a. ester **b.** ether **c.** ketone **d.** phenol

4. A name for $CH_3COCH_2CH_3$ is
a. 2-butanal **b.** ethyl methyl ether
c. ethyl methyl ketone **d.** 2-propanone

5. A name for $CH_3CH_2CH_2CHO$ is
a. 1-butanone **b.** butyraldehyde **c.** propanone **d.** propylaldehyde

6. Which alcohol is oxidized to produce formaldehyde?
a. CH_3OH **b.** CH_3CH_2OH
c. $CH_3CH_2CH_2OH$ **d.** $CH_3CHOHCH_3$

7. Which alcohol is oxidized to produce acetone?
a. CH_3OH **b.** CH_3CH_2OH
c. $CH_3CH_2CH_2OH$ **d.** $CH_3CHOHCH_3$

Answers: 1, a; 2, c; 3, c; 4, c; 5, b; 6, a; 7, d

9.7 Carboxylic Acids and Esters

Learning Objective › Name simple carboxylic acids and esters, and list their important properties.

Carboxylic Acids

The functional group of organic acids is called the **carboxyl group**, and the acids are called **carboxylic acids**.

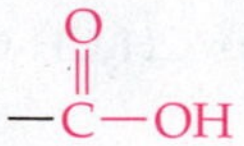

$$-\overset{\overset{\displaystyle O}{\|}}{C}-OH \qquad R-\overset{\overset{\displaystyle O}{\|}}{C}-OH$$

A carboxyl group 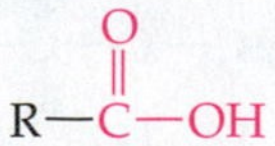 A carboxylic acid

As with aldehydes and ketones, these formulas are often written on one line:

$$—C(=O)OH \text{ or } —COOH \qquad R—C(=O)OH \text{ or } R—COOH$$

A carboxyl group A carboxylic acid

The simplest carboxylic acid is formic acid (HCOOH). The systematic (IUPAC) names for carboxylic acids are based on those of alkanes, with the ending changed from *-e* to *-oic acid*. For example, the IUPAC name for formic acid is methanoic acid, and $CH_3CH_2CH_2CH_2COOH$ is pentanoic acid.

Formic acid was first obtained by the destructive distillation of ants (the Latin word *formica* means "ant"). It smarts when an ant bites because the ant injects formic acid into the skin. The stings of wasps and bees also contain formic acid (as well as other poisonous compounds).

▲ Acetic acid is a familiar weak acid in chemistry laboratories. It is also the principal active ingredient in vinegar.

Acetic acid (ethanoic acid, CH_3COOH) can be made by the aerobic fermentation of a mixture of cider and honey. This produces a solution (vinegar) containing about 4–10% acetic acid plus a number of other compounds that add flavor. Acetic acid is probably the most familiar weak acid used in academic and industrial chemistry laboratories.

The third member of the homologous series of acids, propionic acid (propanoic acid, CH_3CH_2COOH), is seldom encountered in everyday life. The fourth member is more familiar, at least by its odor. If you've ever smelled rancid butter, you know the odor of butyric acid (butanoic acid, $CH_3CH_2CH_2COOH$). It is one of the most foul-smelling substances imaginable. Butyric acid can be isolated from butterfat or synthesized in the laboratory. It is one of the ingredients of body odor, and extremely small quantities of this acid and other chemicals enable bloodhounds to track lost people and fugitives.

The acid with a carboxyl group attached directly to a benzene ring is called *benzoic acid*.

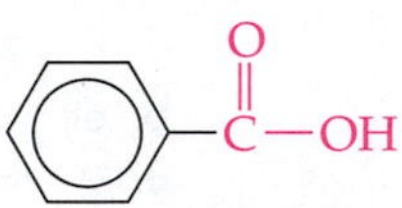

Benzoic acid

Carboxylic acid salts—calcium propionate, sodium benzoate, and others—are widely used as food additives to prevent mold (Chapter 17).

Example 9.9 Structural Formulas of Oxygen-Containing Organic Compounds

Write the structural formula for each of the following compounds.

a. propionaldehyde **b.** ethanoic acid **c.** ethyl methyl ketone

Solution

a. Propionaldehyde has three carbon atoms with an aldehyde function.

$$C—C—\overset{\overset{\large O}{\|}}{C}—H$$

Adding the proper number of hydrogen atoms to the other two carbon atoms gives the structure

$$H—\underset{\underset{\large H}{|}}{\overset{\overset{\large H}{|}}{C}}—\underset{\underset{\large H}{|}}{\overset{\overset{\large H}{|}}{C}}—\overset{\overset{\large O}{\|}}{C}—H \quad \text{or} \quad CH_3CH_2CHO$$

b. Ethanoic acid has two carbon atoms with a carboxylic acid function.

$$\mathrm{H{-}\overset{\overset{\large H}{|}}{\underset{\underset{\large H}{|}}{C}}{-}\overset{\overset{\large O}{\|}}{C}{-}OH} \quad \text{or} \quad \mathrm{CH_3COOH}$$

c. Ethyl methyl ketone has a ketone function between an ethyl and a methyl group.

$$\mathrm{H{-}\overset{\overset{\large H}{|}}{\underset{\underset{\large H}{|}}{C}}{-}\overset{\overset{\large H}{|}}{\underset{\underset{\large H}{|}}{C}}{-}\overset{\overset{\large O}{\|}}{C}{-}\overset{\overset{\large H}{|}}{\underset{\underset{\large H}{|}}{C}}{-}H} \quad \text{or} \quad \mathrm{CH_3CH_2COCH_3}$$

■ EXERCISE 9.9

Write the structural formula for each of the following compounds.

a. butyric acid	**b.** acetaldehyde	**c.** diethyl ketone
d. 3-octanone	**e.** heptanal	**f.** hexanoic acid

Esters: The Sweet Smell of RCOOR′

Esters are derived from carboxylic acids and alcohols or phenols. The general reaction involves splitting out a molecule of water.

$$\underset{\text{An acid}}{\mathrm{R{-}\overset{\overset{\large O}{\|}}{C}{-}OH}} + \underset{\text{An alcohol}}{\mathrm{R'OH}} \overset{H^+}{\rightleftharpoons} \underset{\text{An ester}}{\mathrm{R{-}\overset{\overset{\large O}{\|}}{C}{-}OR'}} + \mathrm{HOH}$$

The name of an ester ends in *-ate* and is formed by naming the part from the alcohol first and the part from the carboxylic acid last. For example, the ester derived from butyric acid and methyl alcohol is methyl butyrate.

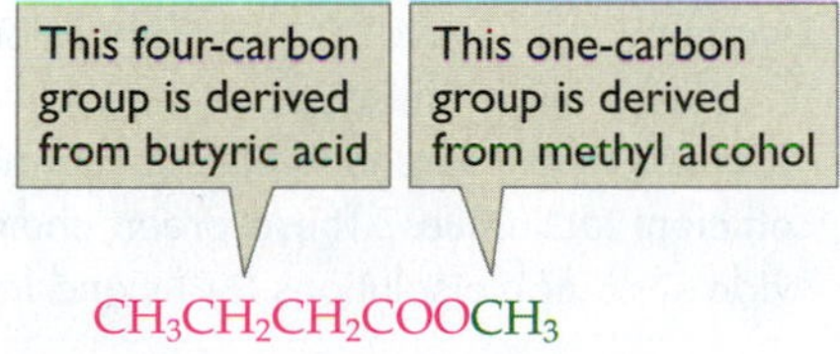
This four-carbon group is derived from butyric acid
This one-carbon group is derived from methyl alcohol

$\mathrm{CH_3CH_2CH_2COOCH_3}$

Although carboxylic acids often have strongly unpleasant odors, the esters derived from them are usually quite fragrant, especially when dilute. Many esters have fruity odors and tastes. Some examples are given in Table 9.7. Esters are widely used as flavorings in cakes, candies, and other foods and as ingredients in perfumes.

5. Why does fresh fruit smell so good and rotting fruit so bad? Esters are often the main components of fruity flavors. When fruit is broken down by bacteria, the esters are often broken down into their corresponding alcohols and (unpleasant!) carboxylic acids.

Table 9.7 Ester Flavors and Fragrances

Ester	Formula	Flavor/Fragrance
Methyl butyrate	$\mathrm{CH_3CH_2CH_2COOCH_3}$	Apple
Ethyl butyrate	$\mathrm{CH_3CH_2CH_2COOCH_2CH_3}$	Pineapple
Propyl acetate	$\mathrm{CH_3COOCH_2CH_2CH_3}$	Pear
Pentyl acetate	$\mathrm{CH_3COOCH_2CH_2CH_2CH_2CH_3}$	Banana
Pentyl butyrate	$\mathrm{CH_3CH_2CH_2COOCH_2CH_2CH_2CH_2CH_3}$	Apricot
Octyl acetate	$\mathrm{CH_3COOCH_2CH_2CH_2CH_2CH_2CH_2CH_2CH_3}$	Orange
Methyl benzoate	$\mathrm{C_6H_5COOCH_3}$	Ripe kiwifruit
Ethyl formate	$\mathrm{HCOOCH_2CH_3}$	Rum
Methyl salicylate	$o\text{-}\mathrm{HOC_6H_4COOCH_3}$	Wintergreen
Benzyl acetate	$\mathrm{CH_3COOCH_2C_6H_5}$	Jasmine

GREEN CHEMISTRY

Principles 1, 3, 5, 6, 7

Thomas E. Goodwin, *Hendrix College*

The Art of Organic Synthesis: Green Chemists Find a Better Way

At one time or another, most of us have taken medicines purchased over the counter or obtained by prescription. Many of these are synthetic drugs prepared by an organic chemist at a pharmaceutical company or in a research lab at a college or university, not compounds that occur in nature. These drugs are synthesized via chemical transformations that make more complicated organic compounds from simpler ones. (You will learn more about drugs in Chapter 18.)

Chemical reactions generally proceed faster when collision probabilities for reacting molecules are high, as they are in heated, homogeneous solutions. In the past, many reactions were carried out in nonrenewable, petroleum-based solvents such as hydrocarbons, chlorinated hydrocarbons, esters, ketones, and ethers (Sections 9.1, 9.3, and 9.5–9.7). These solvents are often flammable, toxic, or both and present serious disposal problems. Using the Twelve Principles of Green Chemistry (inside front cover), chemists are now replacing these solvents with greener alternatives—or using no solvent at all. They also are seeking to improve the efficiency of reactions by reducing energy, time, and chemical quantities.

An increasing number of chemical reactions are run successfully in the absence of a solvent but more often in solvents from renewable resources in place of petrochemicals (Principle 5). Aqueous media have become popular because water is an ideal green solvent: cheap, abundant, and safe.

Unfortunately, many organic compounds have little solubility in water. Solutions normally form readily when intermolecular forces in the solvent and solute are of similar strength (Section 6.4). Most organic compounds have relatively weak dispersion and dipole–dipole intermolecular forces, whereas water molecules are held together by a strong network of hydrogen bonds. Therefore, water molecules tend to stay associated with one another rather than exchanging some of their hydrogen bonds for weaker attractions to the nonpolar organic solutes.

Homogeneity is not always required, however. K. B. Sharpless (2001 Nobel Laureate) and his colleagues developed procedures in which the reactants are simply floated on water. In these "on water" reactions, rapid stirring produces suspensions of reactants with large surface contact areas that enhance reaction rates. Green benefits include reduced use of organic solvents, faster reaction times, and simplified isolation of hydrophobic products.

Green organic chemistry is also demonstrated in the Pfizer pharmaceutical company's improved route to the antidepressant sertraline (Zoloft®) (Section 18.7). Four solvents (toluene, tetrahydrofuran, dichloromethane, and hexane) were replaced with ethanol (Section 9.5). In addition, overall solvent use was reduced from 60,000 gallons to 6,000 gallons per ton of sertraline. Pfizer received a Presidential Green Chemistry Challenge Award in 2002 for its improvements.

Another green organic synthesis was developed by Dow Chemical Company to prepare the high-volume commercial chemical epichlorohydrin. Although the compound itself is hazardous, its value in the production of epoxies, paints, and resins has led to a green chemistry focus on improving its synthesis. The traditional synthesis used a petrochemical reactant and only incorporated one-fourth of the Cl atoms used. The Dow process utilizes glycerol, a by-product from the production of biodiesel (see green chemistry essay, Chapter 7), to produce epichlorohydrin under solventless reaction conditions. This process prevents the generation of waste and turns a waste material into a valuable product.

Green chemistry can also use microwaves to speed up reactions and reduce energy consumption. Microwaves are a form of electromagnetic radiation (Section 3.2) and are more energetic than radio waves but less energetic than X-rays (essay Section 11.1). In kitchen microwave ovens, the targets for microwave energy are the water, sugar, and fat molecules in food. Although home microwave ovens must not be used to carry out chemical reactions due to potential dangers, specially designed microwave ovens are available for laboratory use.

Organic chemists today are actively designing ways to use greener solvents, renewable starting materials, and more energy-efficient techniques. These green chemistry innovations will provide sustainable solutions for us and for future generations.

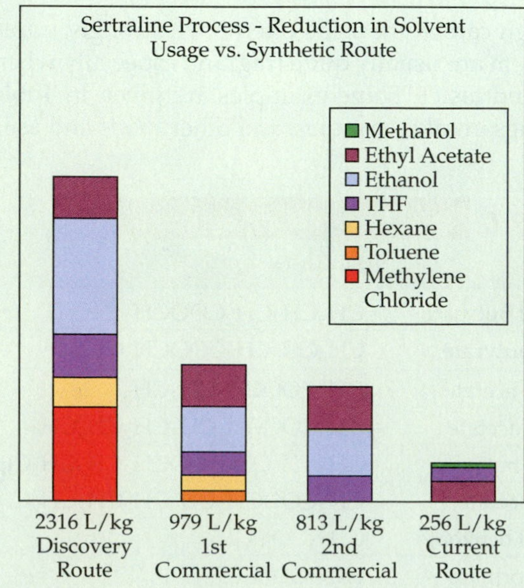

▲ Proper application of green chemistry principles in the synthesis of Sertraline reduced the amount of solvents used by almost 90 percent!

Salicylates: Pain Relievers Based on Salicylic Acid

Salicylic acid is both a carboxylic acid and a phenol. We can use it to illustrate some of the reactions of these two families of compounds.

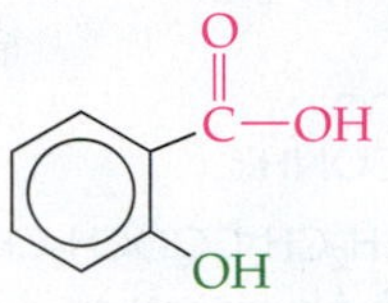

Salicylic acid

Since ancient times, various peoples around the world have used willow bark to treat fevers. Edward Stone, an English clergyman, reported to the Royal Society in 1763 that an extract of willow bark was useful in reducing fever.

Salicylic acid was first isolated from willow bark in 1838. It was first prepared synthetically in 1860 and soon was used in medicine as an *antipyretic* (fever reducer) and as an *analgesic* (pain reliever). However, it is sour and irritating when taken orally. Chemists sought to use chemical reactions to modify its structure so that these undesirable properties would be reduced while retaining or even enhancing its desirable properties. These reactions are summarized in Figure 9.13. The first such modification was simply to neutralize the acid (Reaction 1 in Figure 9.13). The resulting salt, sodium salicylate, was first used in 1875. It was less unpleasant to swallow than the acid but was still highly irritating to the stomach.

By 1886, chemists had produced another derivative (Reaction 2), the phenyl ester of salicylic acid, called *phenyl salicylate*, or *salol*. Salol was less unpleasant to swallow, and it passed largely unchanged through the stomach. In the small intestine, salol was converted to the desired salicylic acid, but phenol was formed as a by-product. A large dose could produce phenol poisoning.

Acetylsalicylic acid, an ester formed when the phenol group of salicylic acid reacts with acetic acid, was first produced in 1853. It is usually made by reacting salicylic acid with acetic anhydride, the acid anhydride of acetic acid (Reaction 3). The German Bayer Company introduced acetylsalicylic acid as a medicine in 1899 under the trade name Aspirin. It soon became the best-selling drug in the world.

Another derivative, methyl salicylate, is made by reacting the carboxyl group of salicylic acid with methanol, producing a different ester (Reaction 4). Methyl salicylate, called *oil of wintergreen*, is used as a flavoring agent and in rub-on analgesics. When applied to the skin, it causes a mild warming sensation, providing some relief for sore muscles.

Aspirin and its use as a drug are discussed in more detail in Chapter 18.

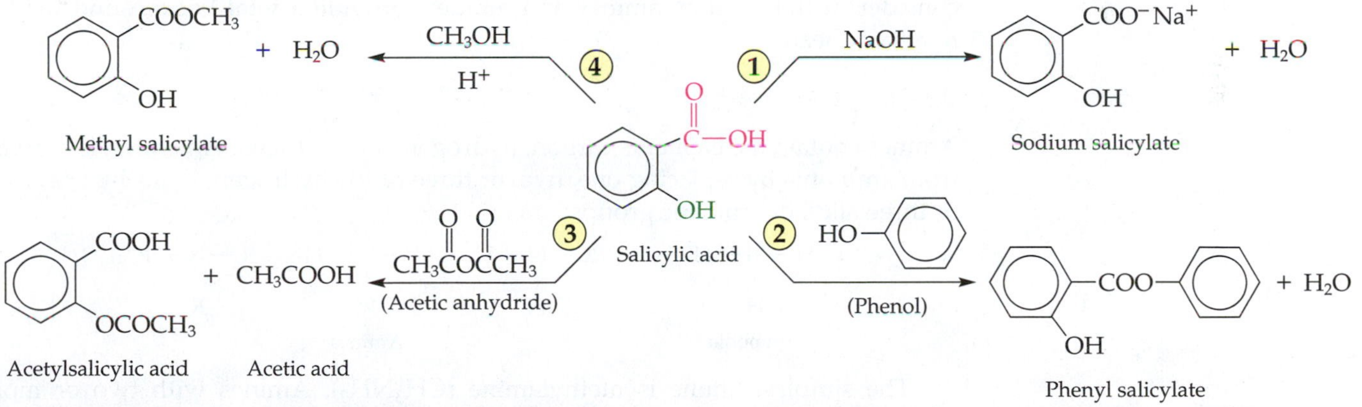

Methyl salicylate + H_2O ← (CH_3OH, H^+) ④ Salicylic acid ① (NaOH) → Sodium salicylate (COO^-Na^+) + H_2O

Acetylsalicylic acid ($COOH$, $OCOCH_3$) + CH_3COOH (Acetic acid) ← ③ CH_3COCCH_3 (Acetic anhydride) Salicylic acid ② HO–C₆H₅ (Phenol) → Phenyl salicylate + H_2O

▲ **Figure 9.13** Some reactions of salicylic acid. In Reactions 1, 2, and 4, salicylic acid reacts as a carboxylic acid; the reactions occur at the carboxyl group. In Reaction 3, salicylic acid reacts as a phenol; the reaction takes place at the hydroxyl group.

Q: *Can you identify and name the functional groups present in (a) salicylic acid, (b) methyl salicylate, (c) acetylsalicylic acid, and (d) phenyl salicylate?*

Self-Assessment Questions

1. Which of the following formulas represents a carboxylic acid?
   a. $CH_3CH_2CH_2OH$ **b.** CH_3CH_2COOH
   c. CH_3COOCH_3 **d.** $CH_3CH_2CH_2CHO$
2. Which of the following is the formula for butanoic acid?
   a. CH_3CH_2COOH **b.** $CH_3CH_2CH_2CH_2OH$
   c. $CH_3CH_2CH_2CHO$ **d.** $CH_3CH_2CH_2COOH$

3. The carboxylic acid that has a —COOH group attached to a benzene ring is
   a. benzoic acid b. benzylic acid
   c. phenol d. phenolic acid
4. Alcohols can be oxidized with hot copper oxide to form carboxylic acids. If the alcohol is ethanol, the carboxylic acid will be
   a. CH_3COOH b. CH_3CH_2OH
   c. $CH_3CH_2CH_2OH$ d. CH_3CH_2COOH
5. The general formula for an ester is
   a. ROR′ b. RCOR′
   c. RCOOR′ d. RCONHR′
6. A name for the compound with the formula $CH_3CH_2CH_2COOCH_2CH_3$ is
   a. ethyl propanoate b. ethyl butanoate
   c. methyl pentanoate d. propyl propanoate
7. A name for the compound with the formula $CH_3CH_2COOCH_3$ is
   a. ethyl acetate b. ethyl propanoate
   c. methyl pentanoate d. methyl propanoate

Answers: 1. b; 2. d; 3. a; 4. a; 5. c; 6. b; 7. d

9.8 Nitrogen-Containing Compounds: Amines and Amides

Learning Objectives › Name and write formulas for simple amines and amides.
› Recognize a structure as that of a heterocyclic compound.

Many organic substances of interest to us in the chapters that follow contain nitrogen, which is the fourth most common element in organic compounds after carbon, hydrogen, and oxygen. The two nitrogen-containing functional groups that we consider in this section, amines and amides, provide a vital background for the material ahead.

Amines

Amines contain the elements carbon, hydrogen, and nitrogen. An **amine** is derived from ammonia by replacing one, two, or three of the hydrogen atoms by one, two, or three alkyl or aromatic groups:

```
H—N—H        R—N—H      R—N—H      R—N—R″
   |            |          |          |
   H            H          R′         R′
Ammonia                 Amines
```

The simplest amine is methylamine (CH_3NH_2). Amines with two or more carbon atoms can be isomers: Both ethylamine ($CH_3CH_2NH_2$) and dimethylamine (CH_3NHCH_3) have the molecular formula C_2H_7N. With three carbon atoms, there are several possibilities, including trimethylamine $[(CH_3)_3N]$.

CONCEPTUAL Example 9.10 Amine Isomers: Structures and Names

Write structural formulas and names for the other three-carbon amines.

Solution

Three carbon atoms can be in one alkyl group, and there are two such propyl groups.

```
CH3CH2CH2NH2      CH3CHCH3
                     |
                    NH2
Propylamine       Isopropylamine
```

Three carbon atoms can also be split into one methyl group and one ethyl group.

$CH_3CH_2NHCH_3$

Ethylmethylamine

■ EXERCISE 9.10

Write structural formulas for the following amines.

a. butylamine
b. diethylamine
c. methylpropylamine
d. isopropylmethylamine

6. Why do dead animals smell so bad? Most amines have unpleasant odors, and many of the compounds formed when animal matter breaks down—such as putrescine and cadaverine—are amines.

The amine with an $—NH_2$ group (called an **amino group**) attached directly to a benzene ring has the special name *aniline*. Like many other aromatic amines, aniline is used in making dyes. Aromatic amines tend to be toxic, and some are strongly carcinogenic.

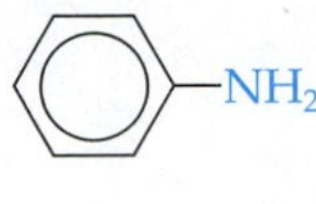

Aniline

Simple amines are similar to ammonia in odor, basicity, and other properties. The larger and aromatic amines are more interesting. Figure 9.14 shows a variety of these.

$C_6H_5—CH_2—CH(CH_3)—NH_2$

Amphetamine

$H_2NCH_2CH_2CH_2CH_2CH_2CH_2NH_2$

1,6-Hexanediamine

$H_2NCH_2CH_2CH_2CH_2CH_2NH_2$

Cadaverine

Pyridoxamine (pyridine ring bearing HO, CH_2NH_2, CH_2OH, H_3C substituents and ring N)

◀ **Figure 9.14** Some amines of interest. Amphetamine is a stimulant drug (Chapter 18). Cadaverine has the odor of decaying flesh. 1,6-Hexanediamine is used in the synthesis of nylon (Chapter 10). Pyridoxamine is a B vitamin (Chapter 17).

Q: *1,6-Hexanediamine is the IUPAC name for a compound also known by the common name hexamethylenediamine. Cadaverine is a common name. What is the IUPAC name for cadaverine?*

Among the most important kinds of organic molecules are *amino acids*. As the name implies, these compounds have both amine and carboxylic acid functional groups. Amino acids are the building blocks of proteins. The simplest amino acid, H_2NCH_2COOH, is glycine. Amino acids and proteins are considered in detail in Chapter 15.

Amides

Another important nitrogen-containing functional group is the **amide group**, which contains a nitrogen atom attached directly to a carbonyl group.

$—C(=O)—N<$ (Amide group)

$R—C(=O)—NH_2$ $\quad$ $R—C(=O)—NHR'$ $\quad$ $R—C(=O)—NR'R''$ (Amides)

Like those of other compounds that have C=O groups, the formulas of amides are often written on one line.

$RCONH_2 \quad RCONHR' \quad RCONR'R''$

Note that urea (H_2NCONH_2), the compound that helped change the understanding of organic chemistry (page 230), is an amide.

Complex amides are of much greater interest than the simple ones considered here. Your body contains many kinds of proteins, all held together by amide linkages (Chapter 15). Nylon, silk, and wool molecules also contain hundreds of amide functional groups.

Names for simple amides are derived from those of the corresponding carboxylic acids. For example, $HCONH_2$ is formamide (IUPAC name, methanamide), and CH_3CONH_2 is acetamide (IUPAC name, ethanamide). Alternatively, we can also view amide names as based on those of alkanes, with the ending changed from *-e* to *-amide*. For example, $CH_3CH_2CH_2CH_2CONH_2$ is pentanamide.

CONCEPTUAL Example 9.11 Amine or Amide?

Which of the following compounds are amides and which are amines? Identify the functional groups.

a. $CH_3CH_2CH_2NH_2$ **b.** CH_3CONH_2
c. $CH_3CH_2NHCH_3$ **d.** $CH_3COCH_2CH_2NH_2$

Solution

a. An amine: NH_2 is an amine group; there is no C=O group.
b. An amide: $CONH_2$ is the amide functional group.
c. An amine: NH is an amine functional group.
d. An amine: NH_2 is an amine functional group; there is a C=O group, but the NH_2 is not attached to it.

■ EXERCISE 9.11

Which of the following compounds are amides and which are amines? Identify the functional groups.

a. CH_3NHCH_3 **b.** $CH_3CONHCH_3$
c. $CH_3CH_2N(CH_3)_2$ **d.** $CH_3NHCH_2CONH_2$

Heterocyclic Compounds: Alkaloids and Others

Cyclic hydrocarbons feature rings of carbon atoms. Now let's look at some compounds that have atoms other than carbon within the ring. These **heterocyclic compounds** usually have one or more nitrogen, oxygen, or sulfur atoms.

CONCEPTUAL Example 9.12 Heterocyclic Compounds

Which of the following structures represent heterocyclic compounds?

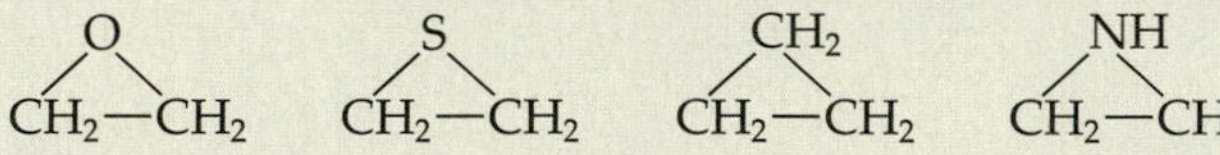 O	S	CH_2	NH
CH_2—CH_2	CH_2—CH_2	CH_2—CH_2	CH_2—CH_2
(a)	(b)	(c)	(d)

Solution

Compounds a, b, and d have an oxygen, a sulfur, and a nitrogen atom, respectively, in a ring structure; these are heterocyclic compounds.

■ EXERCISE 9.12

Which of the following structures represent heterocyclic compounds?

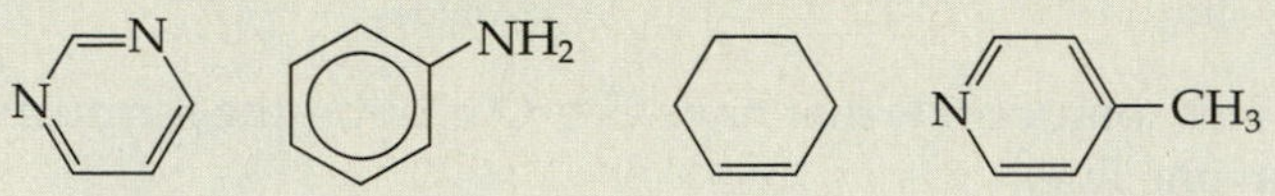 N, N	NH_2		N, CH_3
(a)	(b)	(c)	(d)

Many amines, particularly heterocyclic ones, occur naturally in plants. Like other amines, these compounds are basic. They are called **alkaloids**, which means "like alkalis." Among the familiar alkaloids are morphine, caffeine, nicotine, and cocaine. The actions of these compounds as drugs are considered in Chapter 18.

Other important heterocyclic amines are pyrimidine, which has two nitrogen atoms in a six-membered ring, and purine, which has four nitrogen atoms in two rings that share a common side. Compounds related to pyrimidine and purine are constituents of nucleic acids (Chapter 16).

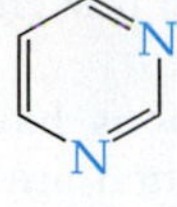

Pyrimidine

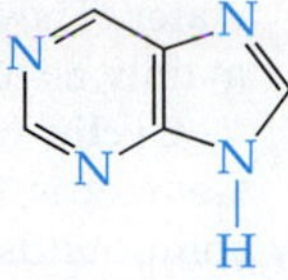

Purine

Self-Assessment Questions

1. A name for $CH_3CH_2CH_2CH_2NH_2$ is
   a. butanamide b. butylamine c. propanamide d. propylamide
2. A name for $CH_3CH_2NHCH_3$ is
   a. butylamine b. ethylmethylamine c. propanamide d. propylamine
3. A name for CH_3CONH_2 is
   a. acetamide b. ethylamine c. propanamide d. propylamine
4. The amide functional group has a carbonyl group attached to
   a. an H atom. b. an N atom c. an OH group d. two other C atoms
5. A cyclic organic compound that contains at least one atom that is not a carbon atom is called a(n)
   a. aromatic compound b. cyclic amide
   c. heterocyclic compound d. saturated compound
6. A basic organic heterocyclic compound that contains at least one nitrogen atom and is found in plants is called a(n)
   a. alkaloid b. amide c. cyclic ester d. phenol

Answers: 1, b; 2, b; 3, a; 4, b; 5, c; 6, a

CRITICAL THINKING EXERCISES

Apply knowledge that you have gained in this chapter and one or more of the FLaReS principles (Chapter 1) to evaluate the following statements or claims.

9.1 A television advertisement claims that gasoline with added ethanol burns more cleanly than gasoline without added ethanol.

9.2 A news feature states that scientists have found that the odor of a certain ester improves workplace performance.

9.3 An environmental activist states that all toxic chemicals should be banned from the home.

9.4 An advertisement claims that calcium carbonate from oyster shells is superior to other forms of calcium carbonate because it contains a life force.

9.5 A Web page claims that acetylsalicylic acid (aspirin), polyester plastics, and polystyrene plastics are all carcinogens (cancer-causing agents). The reason given is that all three contain benzene rings in their structures, and benzene is a carcinogen.

9.6 A television program suggests that life on a distant planet could be based on silicon instead of carbon, because silicon (like carbon) tends to form four bonds. The narrator of the program proposes that long protein molecules and DNA molecules could be based on silicon chains.

SUMMARY

Section 9.1—**Organic chemistry** is the chemistry of carbon-containing compounds. More than 95% of all known compounds contain carbon. Carbon is unique in its ability to form long chains, rings, and branches. **Hydrocarbons** contain only carbon and hydrogen. One main class of hydrocarbons is **aliphatic compounds**. **Alkanes** are hydrocarbons that contain only single bonds; they have names ending in *-ane*. Alkanes are **saturated hydrocarbons** because each of their carbon atoms is bonded to the maximum number of hydrogen atoms. A **structural formula** shows which atoms are bonded to one another. A **condensed structural formula** omits the C—H bond lines and is easier to write. A larger straight-chain alkane can be generated by inserting a CH_2 unit into a given straight-chain alkane. A **homologous series** of such compounds has properties that vary in a regular and predictable manner. A member of a homologous series is called a *homolog*.

Alkanes with more than three carbon atoms have **isomers**, compounds with the same molecular formula but different structures. Alkanes are nonpolar and insoluble in water. They undergo few chemical reactions and are used mainly as fuels.

Cyclic hydrocarbons have one or more closed rings. Geometric figures often are used to represent such cyclic compounds: for example, a triangle for cyclopropane and a hexagon for cyclohexane.

An **alkene** is a hydrocarbon with at least one carbon-carbon double bond. Ethylene ($CH_2{=}CH_2$) is the simplest alkene and the most important one commercially. It is used to make polyethylene plastic and ethylene glycol. An **alkyne** is a hydrocarbon with at least one carbon-to-carbon triple bond. Acetylene ($HC{\equiv}CH$), the simplest alkyne, is used in welding torches and as a starting material for other chemical products. Alkenes and alkynes are **unsaturated hydrocarbons**, to which more hydrogen atoms can be added. They undergo **addition reactions** in which hydrogen or another small molecule adds to the double or triple bond. They can also add to one another to form polymers.

Section 9.2—Benzene (C_6H_6) can be drawn as though it has three double bonds, but its ring of carbon atoms has six pairs of bonding electrons between the carbon atoms, plus six unassigned electrons spread over the ring. Benzene and similar compounds with this type of stable ring structure are called **aromatic compounds**. Substituted benzenes have one or more H atoms replaced by another atom or group called a **substituent**. Aromatic hydrocarbons are used as solvents and fuels and to make other aromatic compounds.

Section 9.3—Chlorinated hydrocarbons are derived from hydrocarbons by replacing one or more hydrogen atoms with chlorine atom(s). Chlorofluorocarbons (CFCs) contain both chlorine and fluorine. They are used as aerosol propellants and as refrigerants, but their use has been restricted because of their role in the depletion of the ozone layer. Perfluorinated compounds, in which all hydrogens have been replaced with fluorine, have important uses in plastics manufacture and in medicine.

Section 9.4—A **functional group** is an atom or group of atoms that confers characteristic properties to a family of organic compounds. Compounds with the same functional group undergo similar reactions and have similar properties. A functional group is often attached to an **alkyl group** ($R{-}$), an alkane with a hydrogen atom removed.

Section 9.5—A hydroxyl group ($-OH$) joined to an alkyl group produces an **alcohol** (ROH). Methanol (CH_3OH), ethanol (CH_3CH_2OH), and 2-propanol [$(CH_3)_2CHOH$] are well-known and widely used alcohols. Alcohols with more than one —OH group include ethylene glycol, used in antifreeze, and glycerol, used in skin lotions and as a food additive. A **phenol** is a compound with an —OH group attached to a benzene ring. Phenols are slightly acidic, and some are used as antiseptics.

An **ether** has two alkyl or aromatic groups attached to the same oxygen atom (ROR′). Ethers are used as solvents, and they can react slowly with oxygen to form explosive peroxides. Diethyl ether ($CH_3CH_2OCH_2CH_3$) is a commonly used solvent. Ethylene oxide is a cyclic ether used to make ethylene glycol and to sterilize instruments.

Section 9.6—An **aldehyde** contains a **carbonyl group** ($C{=}O$) with a hydrogen atom attached to the carbonyl carbon. A **ketone** has two carbon atoms attached to the carbonyl carbon. Formaldehyde is used in making plastics and as a preservative and a disinfectant. Benzaldehyde is a flavoring ingredient. Acetone, the simplest ketone, is a widely used solvent.

Section 9.7—A **carboxylic acid** has a **carboxyl group** ($-COOH$) as its functional group. Formic acid (HCOOH) is the acid in ant, bee, and wasp stings. Acetic acid (CH_3COOH) is the acid in vinegar. Butyric acid is the substance that gives rancid butter its odor. Carboxylic acid salts are used as food additives to prevent mold.

The structure of an **ester** (RCOOR′) is similar to that of a carboxylic acid, with an alkyl group replacing the hydrogen atom of the carboxyl group. Esters are made by reaction of a carboxylic acid with an alcohol or phenol. They often have fruity or flowery odors and are used as flavorings and in perfumes.

Section 9.8—An **amine** is an organic derivative of ammonia in which one or more hydrogen atoms are replaced by alkyl or aromatic groups. Many amines consist of an alkyl group joined to an **amino group** ($-NH_2$). Like ammonia, amines are basic and often have strong odors. Amino acids, the building blocks of proteins, contain both amine and carboxylic acid functional groups. An **amide group** consists of a carbonyl group whose carbon atom is attached to a nitrogen atom. Proteins, nylon, silk, and wool contain amide groups.

A **heterocyclic compound** has one or more rings containing one or more nitrogen, sulfur, or oxygen atoms. **Alkaloids** are (usually heterocyclic) amines that occur naturally in plants and include morphine, caffeine, nicotine, and cocaine. Heterocyclic structures are constituents of DNA and RNA.

Green chemistry Organic chemistry plays an important role in enhancing the quality of human life, such as in the preparation of new life-saving drugs. Organic chemists are designing ways to use greener solvents, renewable starting materials, and more energy-efficient techniques.

Learning Objectives

› Define *hydrocarbon*, and recognize structural features of alkanes, alkenes, and alkynes.	Problems 17, 18, 20, 21, 53, 54
› Identify hydrocarbon molecules as alkanes, alkenes, or alkynes, and name them.	Problems 2, 17–26, 45, 46
› Define *aromatic compound*, and recognize the structural feature such compounds share.	Problems 5, 6
› Name simple aromatic hydrocarbons.	Problem 22
› Name a halogenated hydrocarbon given its formula, and write the formula for such a compound given its name.	Problem 52
› Classify an organic compound according to its functional group(s), and explain why the concept of a functional group is useful in the study of organic chemistry.	Problems 47–51, 62

› Recognize and write the formulas of simple alkyl groups.	Problems 25, 26
› Recognize the general structure for an alcohol, a phenol, and an ether.	Problems 30, 48, 56, 61, 63
› Name simple alcohols, phenols, and ethers.	Problems 9, 27–32
› Name simple aldehydes and ketones, and list their important properties.	Problems 33, 34
› Name simple carboxylic acids and esters, and list their important properties.	Problems 12, 35–38
› Name and write the formulas of simple amines and amides.	Problems 39, 40
› Recognize a structure as that of a heterocyclic compound.	Problems 49, 50
› Identify greener solvents that can replace those from nonrenewable fossil fuels, methods for incorporating renewable resources into organic synthesis, and efficient energy sources for enhancing chemical reactions.	Problems 66–71

REVIEW QUESTIONS

1. List three characteristics of the carbon atom that make possible the existence of millions of organic compounds.
2. Define or give an example for each of the following terms.
   a. hydrocarbon b. alkyne
   c. alkane d. alkene
3. What are isomers? How can you tell whether or not two compounds are isomers?
4. What is an unsaturated hydrocarbon? Give examples of two types of unsaturated hydrocarbons.
5. What is the meaning of the circle inside the hexagon in the modern representation of the structure of benzene?
6. What is an aromatic hydrocarbon? How can you recognize an aromatic compound from its structure?
7. Which alkanes are gases at room temperature? Which are liquids? Which are solids? State your answers in terms of the number of carbon atoms per molecule.
8. Compare the densities of liquid alkanes with that of water. If you added hexane to water in a beaker, what would you expect to observe?
9. What are the systematic names for the alcohols known by the following familiar names?
   a. grain alcohol b. rubbing alcohol
   c. wood alcohol
10. What are some of the long-term effects of excessive ethanol consumption?
11. State an important historical use of diethyl ether. What is its main use today?
12. How do carboxylic acids and esters differ in odor? In chemical structure?
13. For what family is each of the following the general formula?
    a. ROH b. RCOR′ c. RCOOR′
    d. ROR′ e. RCOOH f. RCHO
14. What is an alkaloid? Name three common alkaloids.

PROBLEMS

Organic and Inorganic Compounds

15. Which of the following compounds are organic?
    a. $CH_3CH_2SCH_2CH_3$ b. $F_3CCH_2CH_3$
    c. $HONH_2$ d. H_2SiCl_2
16. Which of the following compounds are organic?
    a. $C_8H_{18}O$ b. H_2CS
    c. OsO_4 d. $Co(NH_3)_6Cl_2$

Names and Formulas of Hydrocarbons

17. How many carbon atoms are there in a molecule of each of the following?
    a. hexane b. decane
    c. cyclopentane d. 2-pentene
18. How many carbon atoms are there in a molecule of each of the following?
    a. ethane b. 1-butyne
    c. propene d. cyclooctane
19. The general formula for an alkane is given on page 231. Give the molecular formulas for the alkanes with **(a)** 9 carbon atoms and **(b)** 13 carbon atoms.
20. A particular alkyne has one triple bond and five carbon atoms. How many hydrogen atoms does it have?
21. Name the following hydrocarbons.
    a. $CH_3CH_2CH_2CH_3$ b. $H_2C{=}CH_2$
    c. $HC{\equiv}CH$
22. Name the following hydrocarbons.

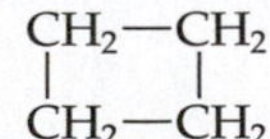

a.

b.

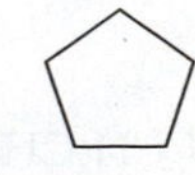

c.

23. Write the molecular formulas and condensed structural formulas for **(a)** pentane and **(b)** nonane.
24. Write the structural formulas for the four-carbon alkanes (C_4H_{10}). Identify butane and isobutane.

25. Name the following alkyl groups.
a. CH_3-
b. CH_3CH_2CH- with CH_3 attached below the CH

26. Name the following alkyl groups.
a. CH_3-CH- with CH_3 attached below the CH
b. CH_3-C- with CH_3 attached above and CH_3 attached below the C

Names and Formulas: Alcohols and Phenols

27. Give a structure to match the name or a name to match the structure for each of the following compounds.
a. CH_3OH
b. $CH_3CH_2CH_2OH$
c. ethanol
d. 1-heptanol

28. Give a structure to match the name or a name to match the structure for each of the following compounds.
a. $CH_3CH_2CHCH_3$ with OH attached below the CH
b. $CH_3CH_2CH_2CH_2CH_2CH_2OH$
c. *sec*-butyl alcohol
d. isobutyl alcohol

29. Phenols and other aromatic compounds are often named by numbering the carbon atoms of the benzene ring, starting with the carbon atom bounded to the major functional group. (In a phenol, this group is the —OH group.) To illustrate, the structure in Exercise 9.6d (page 248) is named 3-bromophenol. With this information, write the structures for **(a)** 2-methylphenol and **(b)** 4-iodophenol.

30. How do phenols differ from alcohols? How are they similar?

Names and Formulas: Ethers

31. Write the structure for each of the following.
a. dipropyl ether
b. butyl ethyl ether

32. Write the structure for **(a)** methyl propyl ether, an anesthetic known as Neothyl, and **(b)** dimethyl ether, used as a compressed gas to "freeze" warts from the skin. What alcohol is an isomer of dimethyl ether?

Names and Formulas: Aldehydes and Ketones

33. Give a structure to match the name or a name to match the formula of each of the following compounds.
a. acetone
b. formaldehyde
c. $CH_3CH_2CH_2C(=O)-H$
d. $CH_3CH_2-C(=O)-CH_2CH_2CH_2CH_3$

34. Give a structure to match the name or a name to match the formula of each of the following compounds.
a. ethyl methyl ketone
b. propionaldehyde
c. $CH_3CH_2-C(=O)-CH_2CH_3$
d. $C_6H_5-C(=O)-H$ (benzene ring bonded to C(=O)—H)

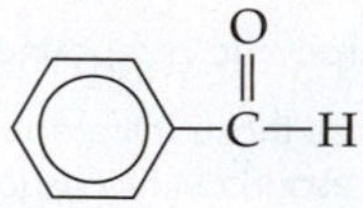

Names and Formulas: Carboxylic Acids

35. Give a structure to match the name or a name to match the structure for each of the following compounds.
a. CH_3COOH
b. $CH_3CH_2CH_2CH_2COOH$
c. formic acid
d. octanoic acid

36. Give a structure to match the name or a name to match the structure for each of the following compounds.
a. CH_3CH_2COOH
b. $CH_3CH_2CH_2CH_2CH_2COOH$
c. butanoic acid
d. chloroacetic acid [*Hint*: To what atom must the chlorine atom (chloro group) be attached?]

Names and Formulas: Esters

37. Give a structure to match the name or a name to match the structure for each of the following.
a. ethyl acetate
b. methyl butyrate
c. $CH_3CH_2C(=O)OCH_2CH_3$

38. Give a structure to match the name or a name to match the structure for each of the following.
a. ethyl butyrate
b. methyl acetate
c. $H-C(=O)-OCH_2CH_2CH_2CH_3$

Names and Formulas: Nitrogen-Containing Compounds

39. Give a structural formula to match the name or a name to match the structure for each of the following.
a. methylamine
b. ethylmethylamine
c. $CH_3CH_2CH_2NH_2$
d. $CH_3CH_2NHCH_3$

40. Give a structural formula to match the name or a name to match the structure for each of the following.
a. ethylamine
b. isopropylamine
c. $CH_3CH_2NHCH_2CH_3$
d. $C_6H_5-NH_2$ (benzene ring bonded to NH_2)

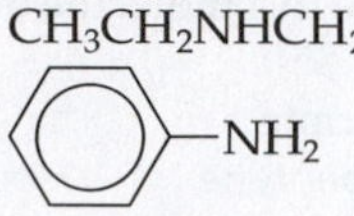

Isomers and Homologs

41. Indicate whether the structures in each pair represent the same compound or isomers.

a. 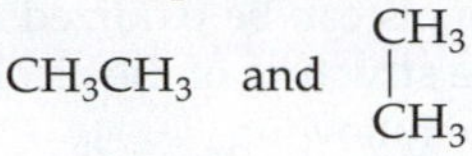 CH_3CH_3 and $\begin{matrix} CH_3 \\ | \\ CH_3 \end{matrix}$

b. 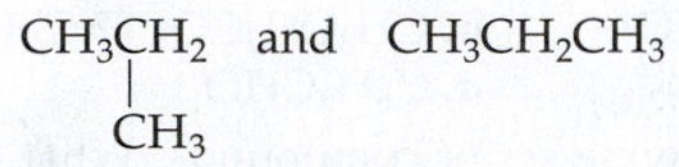 $\begin{matrix} CH_3CH_2 \\ | \\ CH_3 \end{matrix}$ and $CH_3CH_2CH_3$

c. 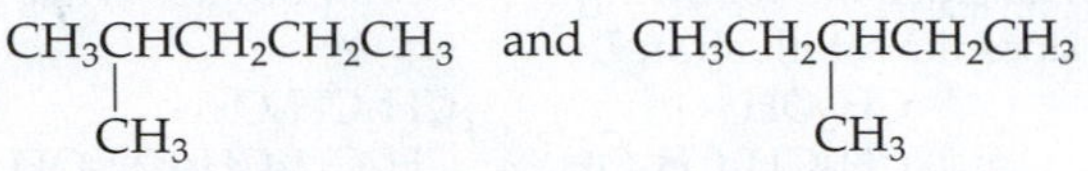 $\begin{matrix} CH_3CHCH_2CH_2CH_3 \\ | \\ CH_3 \end{matrix}$ and $\begin{matrix} CH_3CH_2CHCH_2CH_3 \\ | \\ CH_3 \end{matrix}$

42. Indicate whether the structures in each pair represent the same compound or isomers.

a. 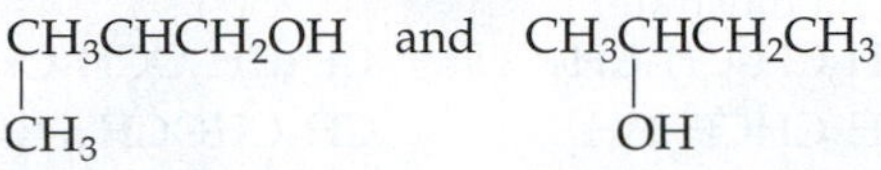 $\begin{matrix} CH_3CHCH_2OH \\ | \\ CH_3 \end{matrix}$ and $\begin{matrix} CH_3CHCH_2CH_3 \\ | \\ OH \end{matrix}$

b. 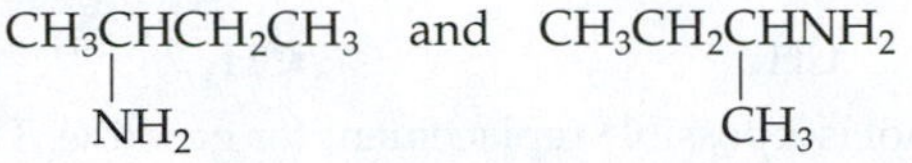 $\begin{matrix} CH_3CHCH_2CH_3 \\ | \\ NH_2 \end{matrix}$ and $\begin{matrix} CH_3CH_2CHNH_2 \\ | \\ CH_3 \end{matrix}$

43. Classify the following pairs as homologs, the same compound, isomers, or none of these.

a. $CH_3CH_2CH_3$ and $CH_3CH_2CH_2CH_3$

b. 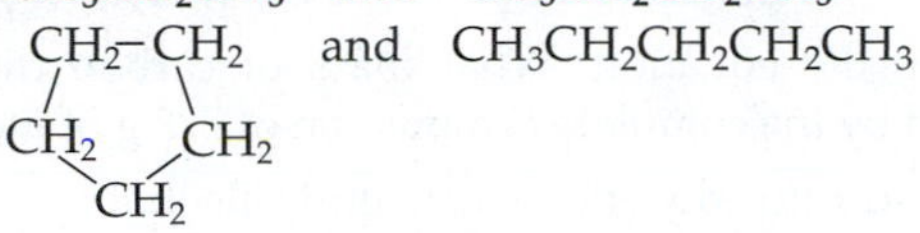 $\begin{matrix} CH_2-CH_2 \\ / \quad \backslash \\ CH_2 \quad CH_2 \\ \backslash \; / \\ CH_2 \end{matrix}$ and $CH_3CH_2CH_2CH_2CH_3$

44. Classify the following pairs as homologs, the same compound, isomers, or none of these.

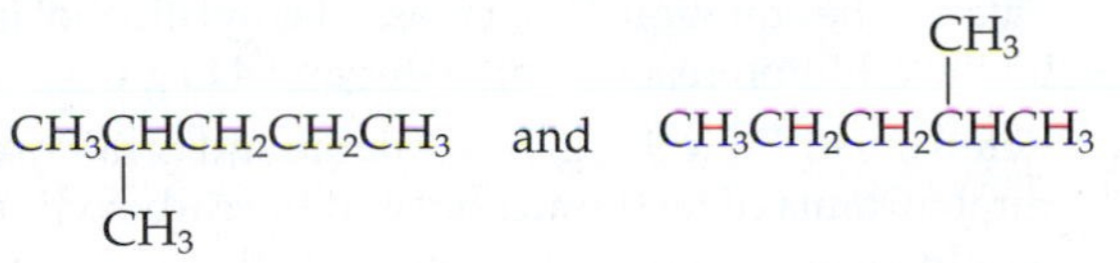

a. $\begin{matrix} CH_3CHCH_2CH_2CH_3 \\ | \\ CH_3 \end{matrix}$ and $\begin{matrix} CH_3 \\ | \\ CH_3CH_2CH_2CHCH_3 \end{matrix}$

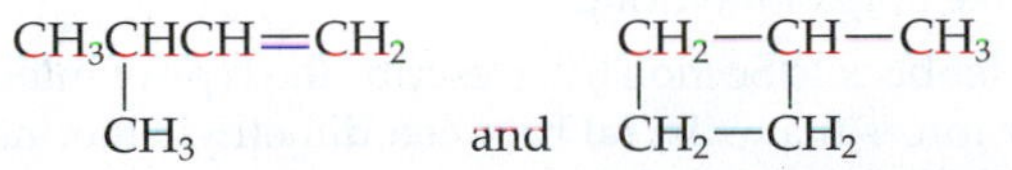

b. $\begin{matrix} CH_3CHCH=CH_2 \\ | \\ CH_3 \end{matrix}$ and $\begin{matrix} CH_2-CH-CH_3 \\ | \quad\quad | \\ CH_2-CH_2 \end{matrix}$

Classification of Hydrocarbons

45. Indicate whether each of the following compounds is saturated or unsaturated. Classify each as an alkane, alkene, or alkyne.

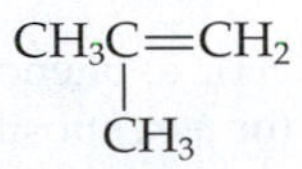

a. $\begin{matrix} CH_3C=CH_2 \\ | \\ CH_3 \end{matrix}$

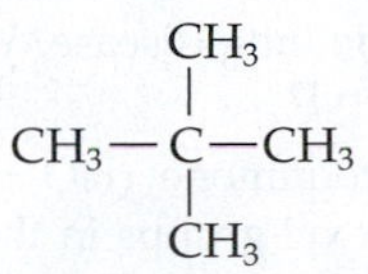

b. $\begin{matrix} CH_3 \\ | \\ CH_3-C-CH_3 \\ | \\ CH_3 \end{matrix}$

46. Indicate whether each of the following compounds is saturated or unsaturated. Classify each as an alkane, alkene, or alkyne.

a. $CH_3-C{\equiv}C-CH_3$

b. 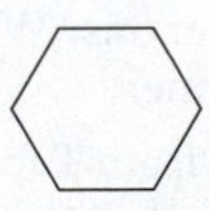

Functional Groups

47. Classify each of the following as an alcohol, amine, amide, ketone, aldehyde, ester, carboxylic acid, or ether. Identify the functional group in each.

a. 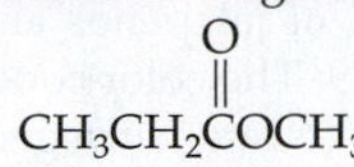 $\begin{matrix} O \\ \| \\ CH_3CH_2COCH_3 \end{matrix}$

b. 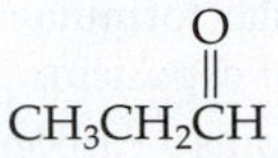 $\begin{matrix} O \\ \| \\ CH_3CH_2CH \end{matrix}$

c. $CH_3CH_2CH_2NH_2$

d. $CH_3CH_2OCH_3$

e. 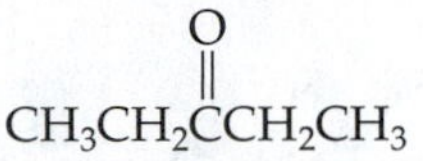 $\begin{matrix} O \\ \| \\ CH_3CH_2CCH_2CH_3 \end{matrix}$

f. 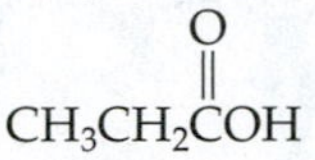 $\begin{matrix} O \\ \| \\ CH_3CH_2COH \end{matrix}$

48. Classify each of the following as an alcohol, amine, amide, ketone, aldehyde, ester, carboxylic acid, or ether. Identify the functional group in each.

a. $HCOOH$
b. $CH_3CH_2COOCH_3$
c. $CH_3CH_2CH_2CH_2OH$
d. $CH_3CH_2CONHCH_2CH_2CH_3$
e. $CH_3CH_2CH_2COOH$
f. $HCOOCH_2CH_2CH_3$

49. Which of the following represents a heterocyclic compound? Classify each compound as an amine, ether, or cycloalkane.

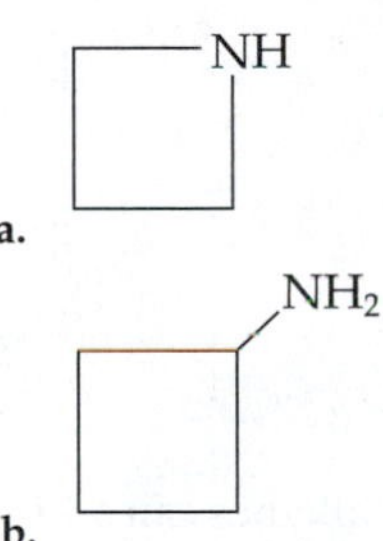

50. Which of the following represents a heterocyclic compound? Classify each compound as an amine, ether, or cycloalkane.

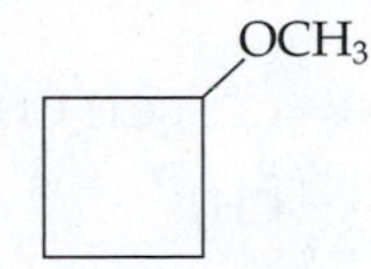

a.

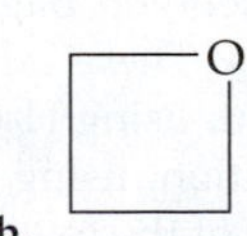

b.

ADDITIONAL PROBLEMS

51. A molecular model of capsaicin, the compound primarily responsible for the "hotness" of jalapenos and other hot peppers, is shown on page 229. The color code for the atoms is carbon (black), hydrogen (white), nitrogen (blue), and oxygen (red). What is the molecular formula of capsaicin? Name three functional groups of capsaicin.

52. Noting the following color code for atoms—carbon (black), hydrogen (white), oxygen (red), nitrogen (blue), and chlorine (green)—write the structural and molecular formulas for the compounds whose models are shown here.

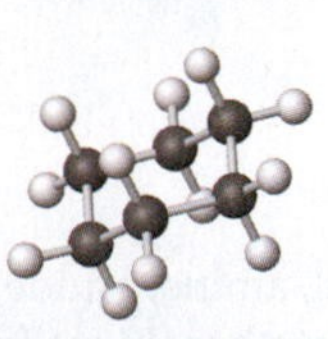

a.

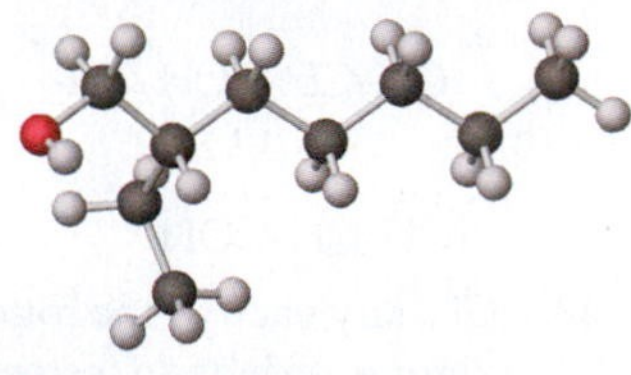

b.

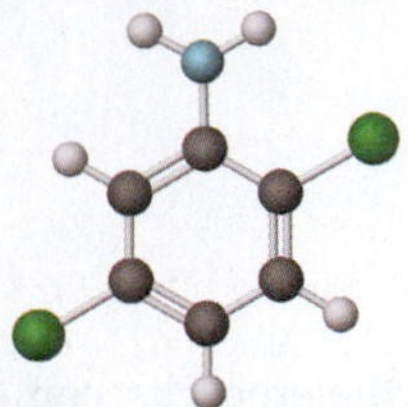

c.

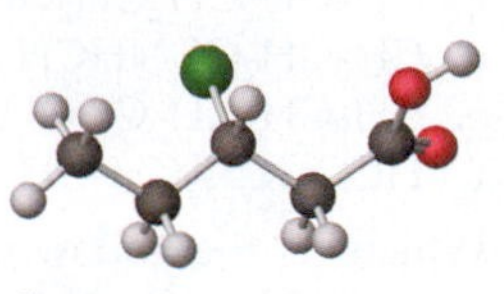

d.

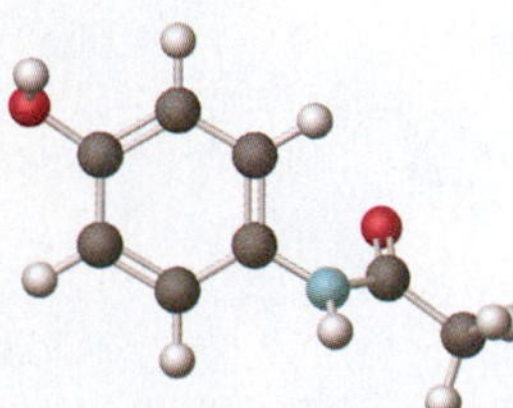

e.

53. As noted on page 236, alkenes and alkynes can add hydrogen to form alkanes. These addition reactions, called *hydrogenations*, are carried out using H_2 gas and a catalyst such as nickel or platinum. Write equations, using condensed structural formulas, for the complete hydrogenation of each of the following.

a. $CH_3CH_2C{\equiv}CCH_3$

b. $CH_3CH{=}\underset{\displaystyle CH_3}{\underset{|}{C}}CH_2CH_2CH_2CH_3$

54. As exemplified by the reaction of ethylene on page 244, alkenes can add water to form alcohols. These addition reactions, called *hydrations*, are carried out using H_2O and an acid (H^+) as catalyst. Write an equation, using structural formulas, for the hydration of each of the following.

a. (cyclohexene) b. $CH_3CH{=}CHCH_3$

55. As shown on page 250, alcohols can be oxidized to aldehydes and ketones. Write the structure of the alcohol that can be oxidized to each of the following.

a. $CH_3CH_2CH_2CHO$ b. $CH_3CH_2COCH_2CH_3$
c. $CH_3COCH(CH_3)_2$ d. C_6H_5CHO

56. Consider the following set of compounds. What concept does the set illustrate?

CH_3OH CH_3CH_2OH
$CH_3CH_2CH_2OH$ $CH_3CH_2CH_2CH_2OH$

57. Consider the following set of compounds. What concept does the set illustrate?

$CH_3CH_2CH_2CH_2OH$ $CH_3CH_2OCH_2CH_3$
$CH_3\underset{\displaystyle CH_3}{\underset{|}{C}H}CH_2OH$ $CH_3\underset{\displaystyle CH_3}{\underset{|}{C}H}OCH_3$

58. Methanol is a possible replacement for gasoline. The complete combustion of methanol forms carbon dioxide and water.

$$CH_3OH + O_2 \longrightarrow CO_2 + H_2O$$

Balance the equation. What mass of carbon dioxide is formed by the complete combustion of 775 g of methanol?

59. Water adds to ethylene to form ethyl alcohol.

$$CH_2{=}CH_2 + H_2O \xrightarrow{H^+} CH_3CH_2OH$$

Balance the equation. What mass of ethyl alcohol is formed by the addition reaction of water and 445 g of ethylene?

60. Referring to Table 9.7, give the name and condensed structural formula of **(a)** the alcohol and the carboxylic acid that would be needed to make pineapple flavoring and **(b)** the alcohol and the carboxylic acid that would be needed to make apricot flavoring.

61. Refer back to Section 6.3. Describe the type of intermolecular forces that exist **(a)** between dimethyl ether molecules and **(b)** between ethanol molecules. Use this information to explain why ethanol is a liquid at room temperature but dimethyl ether is a gas.

62. Diacetyl ($CH_3COCOCH_3$) is an additive used to impart buttery flavor to popcorn. Popcorn-factory workers exposed to high levels of diacetyl may develop a characteristic lung disease. What functional group is present in diacetyl?

63. Hydroquinone ($HO{-}C_6H_4{-}OH$), a phenol with two hydroxyl groups in the 1 and 4 (or *para*) positions on the ring, is commonly used as a developer in black and white photography. **(a)** Write the structural formula for hydroquinone. (*Hint*: See Figure 9.9.) **(b)** In the developing process, hydroquinone is oxidized to *para*-benzoquinone ($C_6H_4O_2$), a compound that is not aromatic and has two ketone functions. Write the structural formula for *para*-benzoquinone.

64. Using data from Table 9.3, a printed reference such as the *CRC Handbook* or the *Merck Index*, or an online source such as the Web site of the National Institutes for Standards and

Technology (NIST), state which of each pair of isomers boils at a lower temperature.

a. hexane or 2,3-dimethylbutane
b. pentane or neopentane (2,2-dimethylpropane)
c. heptane or 2,4-dimethylpentane
d. octane or 2,2,4-trimethylpentane

Use this information to form a generalization about the boiling points of branched-chain versus straight-chain alkanes.

65. Use the ideal gas law to determine the densities in grams per milliliter of the first four alkanes in Table 9.3 at 1.00 atm and 20.0 °C. (*Hint*: Begin with one mole of each gas.) Suggest a more appropriate unit for expressing these densities.

66. Give three reasons why water is often considered to be a green solvent for organic synthesis.

67. Which of the following is a potential drawback to using water as a solvent for organic synthesis?
a. Water is derived from fossil fuels.
b. Many organic molecules have limited solubility in water.
c. The intermolecular forces in water are similar to those in most organic solvents.
d. Reaction rates are always slower in water.

68. In an "on water" reaction:
a. Reactants are floated on water.
b. Rapid stirring leads to large surface contact areas.
c. Reactions often occur faster than if the reactants were dissolved in an organic solvent.
d. Insoluble products can be separated easily.
e. All of the above are true.

69. Identify two aspects of the new synthesis of sertraline that make it greener than the traditional process.

70. Give two examples of ways in which the improved synthesis of epichlorohydrin is more environmentally benign.

71. What advantage does microwave heating provide in carrying out chemical reactions? Why does it have this advantage?

COLLABORATIVE GROUP PROJECTS

Prepare a PowerPoint, poster, or other presentation (as directed by your instructor) to share with the class.

1. The theory that organic chemistry was the chemistry of living organisms, which was overturned by Wöhler's discovery in 1828, was known as *vitalism*. Search the Internet for information about this theory. What was the effect of this philosophy on areas outside chemistry?

2. Many organic molecules contain more than one functional group. Look up the structural formula for each of the following in this text (use the index), by searching online, or in a reference work such as the *Merck Index*. Identify and name the functional groups in each.
a. butesin b. estrone c. tyrosine
d. morphine e. eugenol f. methyl anthranilate

3. Prepare a brief report on one of the alcohols with three or more carbon atoms per molecule. List sources and commercial uses.

4. Prepare a brief report on one of the carboxylic acids with three or more carbon atoms per molecule. List sources and commercial uses.

5. Consider the series of compounds methane (CH_4), chloromethane (CH_3Cl), dichloromethane (CH_2Cl_2), trichloromethane ($CHCl_3$), and tetrachloromethane (CCl_4). Repeat parts (a) through (e) of Problem 49 (Chapter 6) for these compounds. Boiling points may be found in a printed reference such as the *CRC Handbook* or the *Merck Index* or on a Web site such as that of the National Institutes for Standards and Technology (NIST). Use intermolecular forces to explain any deviation in the relationship between molar mass and boiling point.

6. Referring to the graph from Problem 49 (Chapter 6), use the molar mass to estimate boiling points for (a) acetic acid (CH_3COOH), (b) acetone (CH_3COCH_3), (c) ethanol (CH_3CH_2OH), (d) hexane ($CH_3CH_2CH_2CH_2CH_2CH_3$), and (e) methyl acetate (CH_3COOCH_3). Compare the values obtained from the graph with the actual boiling points. Is molar mass alone a good predictor of boiling point? Explain.

10 Polymers

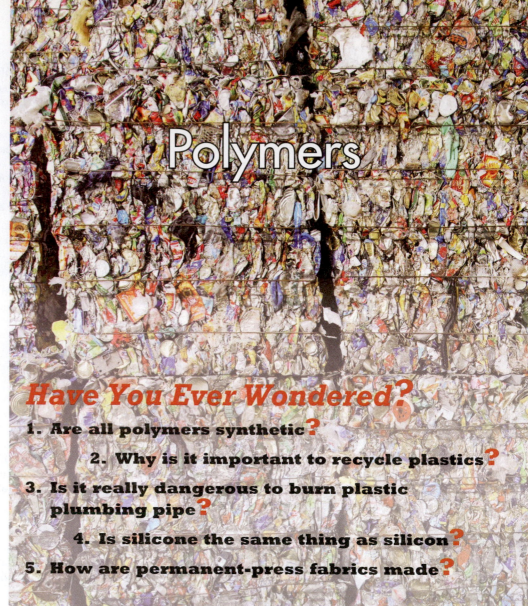

Learning Objectives

- Define *polymer* and *monomer*. (10.1)
- List several natural polymers including a chemically modified one. (10.1)
- Describe the structure and properties of the two main types of polyethylene. (10.2)
- Use the terms *thermoplastic* and *thermosetting* to explain how polymer structure determines properties. (10.2)
- Identify the monomer(s) of an addition polymer, and write the structural formula for a polymer from its monomer structure(s). (10.3)
- Define *cross-linking*, and explain how it changes the properties of a polymer. (10.4)
- Differentiate between addition and condensation polymerization. (10.5)
- Write the structures of the monomers that form polyesters and polyamides. (10.5)
- Understand the concept of the glass transition temperature. (10.6)
- Explain how crystallinity affects the physical properties of polymers. (10.6)
- Describe the environmental problems associated with plastics and plasticizers. (10.7)
- Name two types of sustainable, non-petroleum-derived polymers and give their sources. (10.7)
- Describe plastic recycling, biodegradation, and production from renewable resources.

Have You Ever Wondered?

1. Are all polymers synthetic?
2. Why is it important to recycle plastics?
3. Is it really dangerous to burn plastic plumbing pipe?
4. Is silicone the same thing as silicon?
5. How are permanent-press fabrics made?

Giants Among Molecules

Look around you. Polymers are everywhere. Carpets, curtains, upholstery, towels, sheets, floor tile, books, furniture, most toys and containers (not to mention such things as telephones, toothbrushes, and piano keys), and even your clothes are made of polymers. Your car's dashboard, seats, tires, steering wheel, floor mats, and many parts that you cannot see are made of polymers. Much of the food you eat contains polymers, and many vital molecules in your body are polymers. You couldn't live without them. Some of the polymers that permeate our lives come from nature, but many are synthetic, made in chemical plants in an attempt to improve on nature in some way.

Plastics—synthetic polymers—are used in most consumer items, including bottles, telephones, calculators, computers, cooking utensils, wire insulation, sunglasses, pens, and most types of packaging. The source of most of these polymers is crude oil, of which there is a limited supply. This means that it is important to recycle these polymers when possible. The bales of plastics shown above are ready to go to the recycling center, where they may be used directly to make toys, pipes, or building materials. Or the recycled material may be converted to shreds or beads of plastic (left) that can be used by molding machines. In this chapter, we examine how polymers are made, review their useful properties, and explain why they have those properties.

10.1 Polymerization: Making Big Ones Out of Little Ones

Learning Objectives › Define *polymer* and *monomer*. › List several natural polymers including a chemically modified one.

Polymers are composed of *macromolecules* (from the Greek *makros*, meaning "large" or "long"). Macromolecules are not actually very large (in fact, most such "giant" molecules are invisible to the human eye), but compared to other molecules, they are enormous.

A **polymer** (from the Greek *poly*, meaning "many," and *meros*, meaning "part") is made from much smaller molecules called *monomers* (from the Greek *monos*, meaning "one"). Hundreds, even thousands, of monomer units combine to make one polymer molecule. A **monomer** is a small-molecule building block from which a polymer is made. The process by which monomers are converted to polymers is called *polymerization*. A polymer is as different from its monomer as a long strand of spaghetti is from tiny specks of flour. For example, polyethylene, the familiar waxy material used to make plastic bags, is made from the monomer ethylene, a gas.

▲ Cotton is nearly pure cellulose, a natural polymer of the simple sugar glucose.

1. Are all polymers synthetic? The total weight of natural polymers on Earth's surface far exceeds the weight of synthetic polymers. Starches, proteins, cellulose, latex, DNA, and RNA all are natural polymers.

Natural Polymers

Polymers have served humanity for centuries in the starches and proteins in our food, in the wood we use for shelter, and in the wool, cotton, and silk we make into clothing. Starch is a polymer made up of glucose ($C_6H_{12}O_6$, a simple sugar) units. Cotton is made of cellulose, also a glucose polymer; and wood is largely cellulose as well. Proteins are polymers made up of amino acid monomers. Wool and silk are two of the thousands of different kinds of proteins found in nature.

Living things could not exist without polymers. Each plant and animal requires many different specific types of polymers. Probably the most amazing natural polymers are nucleic acids, which carry the coded genetic information that makes each individual unique. The polymers found in nature are discussed in Chapter 15. In this chapter, we focus mainly on macromolecules made in the laboratory.

Celluloid: Billiard Balls and Collars

The oldest attempt to improve on natural polymers involved chemical modification of a common macromolecule. The semisynthetic material **celluloid**, as its name implies, was derived from natural cellulose (from cotton and wood, for example). When cellulose is treated with nitric acid, a derivative called *cellulose nitrate* is formed.

In response to a contest to find a substitute for ivory to use in billiard balls, American inventor John Wesley Hyatt (1837–1920) found a way to soften cellulose nitrate by treating it with ethyl alcohol and camphor. The softened material could be molded into smooth, hard balls. Thus, Hyatt brought the game of billiards within the economic reach of more people—and saved a number of elephants.

Celluloid was also used in movie film and for stiff shirt collars (which didn't require laundering and repeated starching). Because of its dangerous flammability (cellulose nitrate is also used as smokeless gunpowder), celluloid was removed from the market when safer substitutes became available. Today, movie film is made mainly from polyethylene terephthalate, a polyester (Section 10.5). And high, stiff collars on men's shirts are out of fashion.

It didn't take long for the chemical industry to recognize the potential of synthetics. Scientists found ways to make macromolecules from small molecules rather than simply modifying large ones. The first such truly synthetic polymers were phenol–formaldehyde resins (such as Bakelite), first made in 1909. These complex polymers are discussed in Section 10.5. We'll look at some simpler ones next.

A century ago, celluloid was widely used as a substitute for more expensive substances such as ivory, amber, and tortoiseshell. The movie industry was once known as the "celluloid industry." The 1988 Oscar-winning Italian movie *Cinema Paradiso* shows the evolution of film technology and includes a tragic scene in which the heat from a bulb in the movie projector ignites a fire in a film that failed to wind properly through the machine.

Self-Assessment Questions

1. A long-chain protein molecule is an example of a(n)
   a. fat **b.** isomer **c.** monomer **d.** polymer
2. Which is *not* a polymer?
   a. cellulose **b.** glucose **c.** silk **d.** wool
3. The first semisynthetic polymer was actually made from a natural polymer. It was
   a. Bakelite, based on bacon grease
   b. celluloid, based on cellulose from cotton
   c. polypropylene, based on isopropyl alcohol
   d. polypantene, based on human hair
4. The first truly synthetic polymer was
   a. Bakelite, made from phenol and formaldehyde
   b. cellulose, made from glucose
   c. polyethylene, made from ethanol
   d. rubber, made from isoprene

Answers: 1, d; 2, b; 3, b; 4, a

10.2 Polyethylene: From the Battle of Britain to Bread Bags

Learning Objectives › Describe the structure and properties of the two main types of polyethylene. › Use the terms *thermoplastic* and *thermosetting* to explain how polymer structure determines properties.

The prevalent plastic *polyethylene* is the simplest and least expensive synthetic polymer. It is familiar to us in the form of plastic bags used for packaging fruit and vegetables, garment bags for dry-cleaned clothing, garbage-can liners, and many other items. Polyethylene is made from ethylene ($CH_2{=}CH_2$), an unsaturated hydrocarbon (Chapter 9). Ethylene is produced in large quantities from the cracking of petroleum, a process by which large hydrocarbon molecules are broken down into simpler hydrocarbons.

With pressure and heat and in the presence of a catalyst, ethylene monomers join together in long chains.

The ellipses (···) and tildes (~) serve as *et ceteras;* they indicate, respectively, that the number of monomers is greater than the four shown and that the polymer structure extends for many more units in each direction.

$$\cdots+\begin{matrix}\mathrm{H}&&\mathrm{H}\\|&&|\\\mathrm{C}&=&\mathrm{C}\\|&&|\\\mathrm{H}&&\mathrm{H}\end{matrix}+\begin{matrix}\mathrm{H}&&\mathrm{H}\\|&&|\\\mathrm{C}&=&\mathrm{C}\\|&&|\\\mathrm{H}&&\mathrm{H}\end{matrix}+\begin{matrix}\mathrm{H}&&\mathrm{H}\\|&&|\\\mathrm{C}&=&\mathrm{C}\\|&&|\\\mathrm{H}&&\mathrm{H}\end{matrix}+\begin{matrix}\mathrm{H}&&\mathrm{H}\\|&&|\\\mathrm{C}&=&\mathrm{C}\\|&&|\\\mathrm{H}&&\mathrm{H}\end{matrix}+\cdots\longrightarrow\sim\begin{matrix}\mathrm{H}&&\mathrm{H}&&\mathrm{H}&&\mathrm{H}&&\mathrm{H}&&\mathrm{H}&&\mathrm{H}&&\mathrm{H}\\|&&|&&|&&|&&|&&|&&|&&|\\\mathrm{C}&-&\mathrm{C}&-&\mathrm{C}&-&\mathrm{C}&-&\mathrm{C}&-&\mathrm{C}&-&\mathrm{C}&-&\mathrm{C}\\|&&|&&|&&|&&|&&|&&|&&|\\\mathrm{H}&&\mathrm{H}&&\mathrm{H}&&\mathrm{H}&&\mathrm{H}&&\mathrm{H}&&\mathrm{H}&&\mathrm{H}\end{matrix}\sim$$

Using condensed formulas, this becomes

$$\cdots + CH_2{=}CH_2 + CH_2{=}CH_2 + CH_2{=}CH_2 + CH_2{=}CH_2 + \cdots \longrightarrow \sim CH_2CH_2CH_2CH_2CH_2CH_2CH_2CH_2\sim$$

Such equations can be tedious to draw, so we often use abbreviated forms like these:

$$n\,\begin{matrix}\mathrm{H}&&\mathrm{H}\\|&&|\\\mathrm{C}&=&\mathrm{C}\\|&&|\\\mathrm{H}&&\mathrm{H}\end{matrix}\longrightarrow\left[\begin{matrix}&\mathrm{H}&&\mathrm{H}&\\&|&&|&\\-&\mathrm{C}&-&\mathrm{C}&-\\&|&&|&\\&\mathrm{H}&&\mathrm{H}&\end{matrix}\right]_n \quad\text{or}\quad n\,CH_2{=}CH_2 \longrightarrow \left[CH_2CH_2\right]_n$$

The molecular fragment within square brackets is called the *repeat unit* of the polymer. In the formula for the polymeric product, the repeat unit is placed within brackets with bonds extending to both sides. The subscript *n* indicates that this unit is repeated many times (*n* in the equation above) in the full polymer structure.

The simplicity of the abbreviated formulas facilitates certain comparisons between the monomer and the polymer. Note that the monomer ethylene contains a double bond and polyethylene does not. The double bond of the reactant consists of two shared pairs of electrons. One of these pairs is used to connect one monomer unit to the next in the polymer (indicated by the lines sticking out to the sides in the repeat unit). This leaves only a single pair of electrons—a single bond—between the two carbon atoms of the repeat unit. Note also that each repeat unit in the polymer has the same composition (C_2H_4) as the monomer.

Molecular models provide three-dimensional representations. Figure 10.1 presents models of a tiny part of a very long polyethylene molecule, whose number of carbon atoms can vary from a few hundred to several thousand.

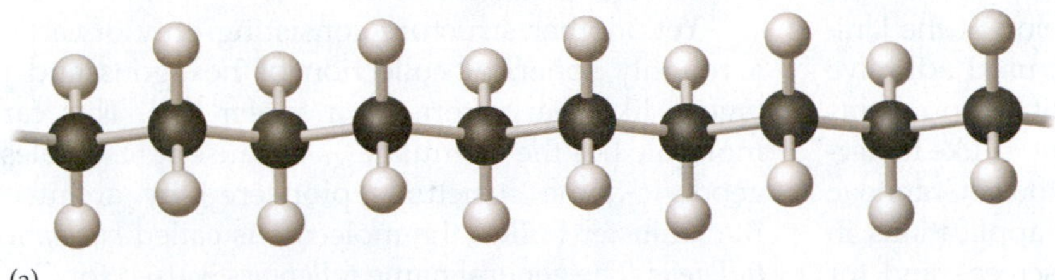

(a)

(b)

◀ **Figure 10.1** Ball-and-stick (a) and space-filling (b) models of a short segment of a polyethylene molecule.

2. Why is it important to recycle plastics?
Polyethylene and most other polymers are made of petroleum. Since our supply of petroleum is limited, we can make the best use of that resource by reusing those polymers. Most plastic items are imprinted with a code number so that they can be sorted for recycling.

Polyethylene was invented shortly before the start of World War II. It proved to be tough and flexible, excellent as an electric insulator, and able to withstand both high and low temperatures. Before long, it was used for insulating cables in radar equipment, a top-secret invention that helped British pilots detect enemy aircraft before the aircraft could be spotted visually. Without polyethylene, the British could not have had effective radar, and without radar, the Battle of Britain might have been lost. The invention of this simple plastic helped change the course of history.

Types of Polyethylene

Today, there are three main kinds of polyethylene. *High-density polyethylene* (*HDPE*) has mostly linear molecules that pack closely together and can assume a fairly well-ordered, crystalline structure. HDPEs therefore are rather rigid and have good tensile strength. As the name implies, the densities of HDPEs (0.94–0.96 g/cm^3) are high compared to those of other polyethylenes. HDPEs are used for such items as threaded bottle caps, toys, bottles, and milk jugs.

Low-density polyethylene (*LDPE*), on the other hand, has many side chains branching off the polymer molecules. The branches prevent the molecules from packing closely together and assuming a crystalline structure. LDPEs are waxy,

The Many Forms of Carbon

In many of the smaller molecules that we studied in Chapter 9 and the macromolecules that we encounter here, carbon atoms are bonded to other atoms, especially hydrogen. Carbon atoms alone can form a variety of interesting structures, however, some of which have been known since ancient times. Diamond is pure crystalline carbon, in which each atom is bonded to four other atoms. In graphite, the black material of pencil lead, each carbon atom is bonded to three others. But the most intriguing forms of carbon were discovered only in the last few decades.

Andre Geim and Konstantin Novoselov of the University of Manchester, United Kingdom, used adhesive tape to lift one-atom-thick planar sheets of carbon atoms from graphite. The material, called *graphene*, is like molecular-scale chicken wire made of carbon atoms. Graphene has properties that make it suitable for applications in electronics, sensing devices, and touch screens and for fundamental studies of electron flow in two-dimensional materials. Geim and Novoselov were awarded the 2010 Nobel Prize in Physics for their work on graphene.

Graphite is composed of many stacked graphene layers. A stack of three million graphene sheets would be only a millimeter thick. Graphene can also be thought of as an extremely large aromatic molecule, a system of fused benzene rings.

Many other structures are formed exclusively of carbon atoms. The tube-shaped carbon molecule called a *nanotube* can be visualized as a sheet of graphene rolled into a hollow cylinder. Nanotubes have unusual mechanical and electrical properties. They are good conductors of heat, and they are among the strongest and stiffest materials known.

Yet another structure consisting only of carbon is a roughly spherical collection of hexagons and pentagons like the pattern on a soccer ball. This carbon molecule has the formula C_{60}. Because it resembles the geodesic-dome structures pioneered by architect R. Buckminster Fuller, the molecule is called *buckminsterfullerene*. The general name *fullerenes* is used for C_{60} and similar molecules with formulas such as C_{70}, C_{74}, and C_{82}, which are often colloquially referred to as "buckyballs." These materials have enormous potential in basic studies as well as in applied research.

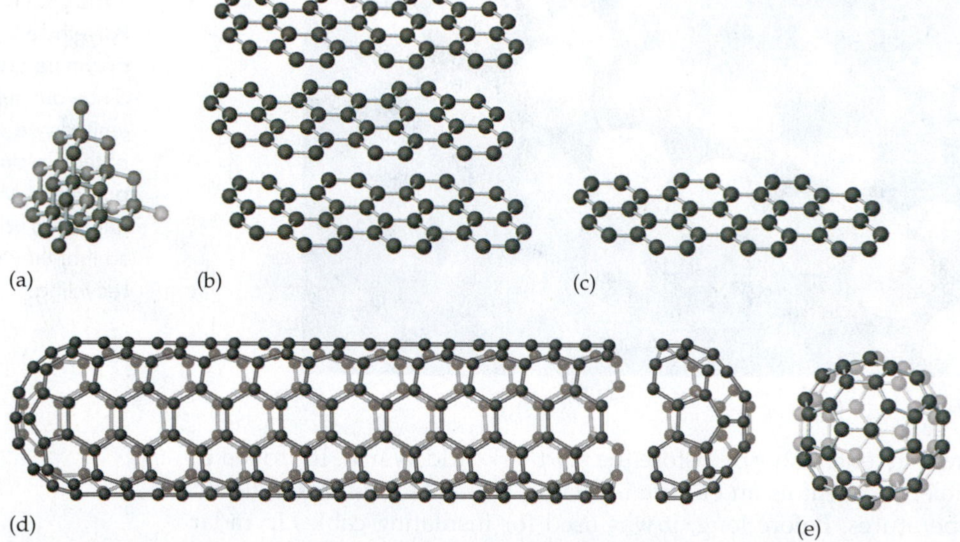

▲ Different forms of carbon have dramatically different properties. (a) Diamond is hard and transparent. (b) Graphite is soft, gray, and conducts electricity. (c) Graphene is a single layer of graphite. (d) Rolling a sheet of graphene into a cylinder makes a carbon nanotube, the strongest material known. (e) Buckminsterfullerene, a C_{60} molecule, resembles a soccer ball.

Scientists estimate that plastic bags and other plastic trash thrown into the ocean kill as many as a million sea creatures each year.

bendable plastics that have lower densities (0.91–0.94 g/cm^3) and are lower melting than high-density polyethylenes. Objects made of HDPE hold their shape in boiling water, whereas those made of LDPE are severely deformed (Figure 10.2). LDPEs are used to make plastic bags, plastic film, squeeze bottles, electric wire insulation, and many common household products for which flexibility is important.

The third type of polyethylene, called *linear low-density polyethylene* (LLDPE), is actually a **copolymer**, a polymer formed from two (or more) different monomers. LLDPEs are made by polymerizing ethylene with a branched-chain alkene such as 4-methyl-1-pentene.

$$n\,CH_2{=}CH_2 + m\,\underset{\underset{CH_3-CH-CH_3}{|}}{\underset{CH_2}{\underset{|}{CH_2{=}CH}}} \longrightarrow -\!\!\left[CH_2-CH_2\right]_n\!\!-\left[\underset{\underset{CH_3-CH-CH_3}{|}}{\underset{CH_2}{\underset{|}{CH_2-CH}}}\right]_m$$

Ethylene 4-Methyl-1-pentene An LLDPE

LLDPEs are used to make such things as plastic films for use as landfill liners, trash cans, tubing, and automotive parts.

▲ **It DOES Matter!**

Polyethylene with a molecular mass from two to six million, called *ultra-high-molecular-weight polyethylene (UHMWPE)*, is used to make fibers 10 times stronger than steel and around 40% stronger than Kevlar (see Problem 30 on page 292) for use in body armor. Most modern skis are coated with UHMWPE on the bottom surface.

Thermoplastic and Thermosetting Polymers

Polyethylene is one of a variety of thermoplastic polymers. Because its molecules can slide past one another when heat and pressure are applied, a **thermoplastic polymer** can be softened and then reshaped. It can be repeatedly melted down and remolded. Total annual production of thermoplastic polymers in the United States is about 40 billion kg, of which 17 billion kg is polyethylene.

Not all polymers can be readily melted. About 12% of U.S. production of polymers consists of *thermosetting polymers*, which harden permanently when formed. They cannot be softened by heat and remolded. Instead, strong heating causes them to discolor and decompose. The permanent hardness of thermosetting plastics is due to cross-linking (side-to-side connection) of the polymer chains, which we'll discuss later in this chapter.

About 180 billion kg of various plastics and 22 billion kg of rubber are manufactured globally each year.

Self-Assessment Questions

1. When addition polymers form, the monomer units are joined by
   a. delocalized electrons that flow along the polymer chain
   b. dispersion forces
   c. double bonds
   d. new bonds formed by electrons from the double bonds in the monomers
2. Compared to HDPE, LDPE has a lower melting point because it
   a. is made from less polar monomers
   b. is composed of molecules with a much lower molecular mass
   c. has fewer cross-links
   d. has more branches in its molecules, preventing them from packing closely
3. Which of the following is *not* made of polyethylene?
   a. electric wire insulation
   b. foamed coffee cups
   c. plastic grocery bags
   d. squeeze bottles
4. A copolymer is made
   a. by blending two simple polymers
   b. from cobalt and an alkene
   c. from two identical monomers
   d. from two different monomers
5. A polymer that cannot be melted and reshaped is said to be
   a. highly crystalline
   b. rubbery
   c. thermoplastic
   d. thermosetting

Answers: 1, d; 2, d; 3, b; 4, d; 5, d

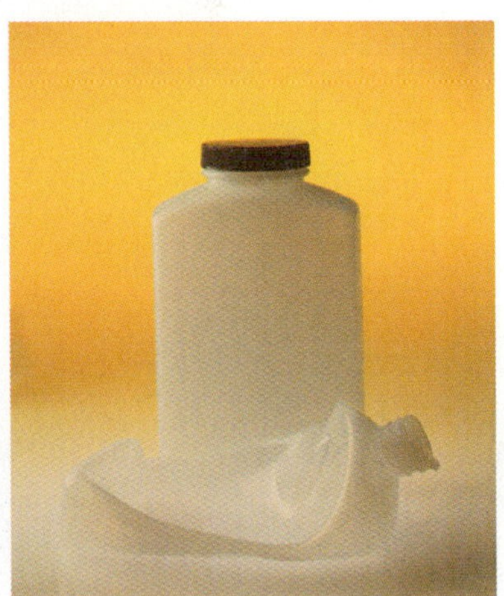

▲ **Figure 10.2** Two bottles, both made of polyethylene, were heated in the same oven for the same length of time.

Q: *Which of these bottles is made of HDPE and which of LDPE? Explain.*

10.3 Addition Polymerization: One + One + One + · · · Gives One!

Learning Objectives › Identify the monomer(s) of an addition polymer, and write the structural formula for a polymer from its monomer structure(s).

There are two general types of polymerization reactions: addition polymerization and condensation polymerization. In **addition polymerization** (also called *chain-reaction polymerization*), the monomer molecules add to one another in such a way that the polymeric product contains all the atoms of the starting monomers. The polymerization of ethylene to form polyethylene is an example. In polyethylene, as we noted in Section 10.2, the two carbon atoms and the four hydrogen atoms of each monomer molecule are incorporated into the polymer structure. In *condensation polymerization* (Section 10.5), some part of each monomer molecule is not incorporated in the final polymer.

Polypropylene

Most of the many familiar addition polymers are made from derivatives of ethylene in which one or more of the hydrogen atoms are replaced by another atom or group. Replacing one of the hydrogen atoms with a methyl group gives the monomer propylene (propene). Polypropylene molecules look much like polyethylene's molecules, except that there is a methyl group ($—CH_3$) attached to every other carbon atom.

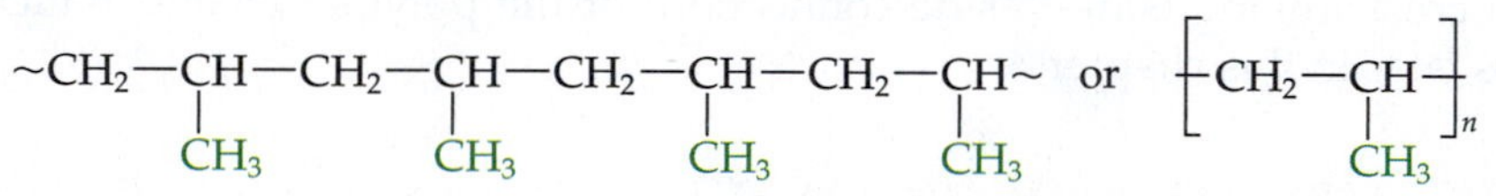

$$\sim CH_2-\underset{\large CH_3}{\underset{|}{CH}}-CH_2-\underset{\large CH_3}{\underset{|}{CH}}-CH_2-\underset{\large CH_3}{\underset{|}{CH}}-CH_2-\underset{\large CH_3}{\underset{|}{CH}}\sim \quad \text{or} \quad \left[CH_2-\underset{\large CH_3}{\underset{|}{CH}}\right]_n$$

Polypropylene

The chain of carbon atoms is called the polymer *backbone*. Groups attached to the backbone, such as the CH_3 groups of polypropylene, are called *pendant groups*.

Polypropylene is a tough plastic material that resists moisture, oils, and solvents. It is molded into hard-shell luggage, battery cases, and various kinds of appliance parts. It is also used to make packaging material, fibers for textiles such as upholstery fabrics and carpets, and ropes that float. Because of polypropylene's high melting point (121 °C), objects made of it can be sterilized with steam.

Polystyrene

Replacing one of the hydrogen atoms in ethylene with a benzene ring gives a monomer called *styrene*, which has the formula $C_6H_5CH{=}CH_2$, where C_6H_5 represents the benzene ring. Polymerization of styrene produces polystyrene, which has benzene rings as pendant groups.

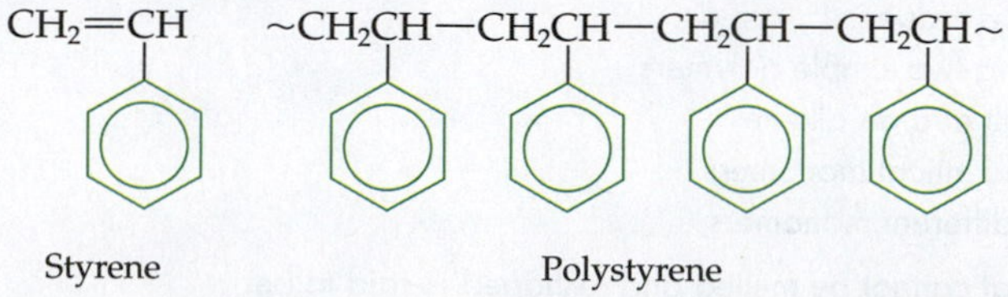

$$CH_2{=}\underset{C_6H_5}{\underset{|}{CH}} \qquad \sim CH_2\underset{C_6H_5}{\underset{|}{CH}}-CH_2\underset{C_6H_5}{\underset{|}{CH}}-CH_2\underset{C_6H_5}{\underset{|}{CH}}-CH_2\underset{C_6H_5}{\underset{|}{CH}}\sim$$

Styrene Polystyrene

Americans throw away about 25 billion coffee cups made of polystyrene foam each year.

Polystyrene is the plastic used to make transparent disposable drinking cups. With color and filler added, it is the material of thousands of inexpensive toys and household items. When a gas is blown into polystyrene liquid, it foams and hardens into the familiar material (called Styrofoam®) of ice chests and disposable coffee cups. The polymer can easily be formed into shapes as packing material for shipping instruments and appliances, and it is widely used for home insulation.

▲ Styrofoam insulation saves energy by reducing the transfer of heat from the warm interior of a house to the outside in winter and from the hot outside to the cooled interior in summer.

Vinyl Polymers

Would you like a tough synthetic material that looks like leather at a fraction of the cost? Perhaps a clear, rigid material from which unbreakable bottles could be made? Do you need an attractive, long-lasting floor covering? Or lightweight, rustproof, easy-to-connect plumbing? Polyvinyl chloride (PVC) has all these properties—and more.

Replacing one of the hydrogen atoms of ethylene with a chlorine atom gives vinyl chloride ($CH_2{=}CHCl$), a compound that is a gas at room temperature. Polymerization of vinyl chloride yields the tough thermoplastic material PVC. A segment of the PVC molecule is shown below.

$$\sim CH_2\underset{\displaystyle Cl}{\underset{|}{C}}H-CH_2\underset{\displaystyle Cl}{\underset{|}{C}}H-CH_2\underset{\displaystyle Cl}{\underset{|}{C}}H-CH_2\underset{\displaystyle Cl}{\underset{|}{C}}H\sim$$

Polyvinyl chloride (PVC)

PVC is readily formed into various shapes. The clear, transparent polymer is used in plastic wrap and clear plastic bottles. Adding color and other ingredients to a vinyl plastic yields artificial leather. Most floor tile and shower curtains are made from vinyl plastics, which are also widely used to simulate wood in home siding panels and window frames. About 40% of the PVC produced is molded into pipes.

◀ Some furniture, window sashes, house trim, and waterproof clothing are made from PVC. PVC can also be coated onto copper wire for insulation, made into colorful resilient flooring, or formed into many other familiar consumer products.

Vinyl chloride, the monomer from which vinyl plastics are made, is a carcinogen. Several people who worked closely with this gas later developed a kind of cancer called *angiosarcoma*. (Carcinogens are discussed in Chapter 22.)

3. Is it really dangerous to burn plastic plumbing pipe? Most plastic plumbing pipe is made of PVC. When PVC is burned, its carcinogenic monomer, vinyl chloride, can be released. PVC may be safely burned in specially constructed incinerators that reach temperatures that decompose the monomer.

PTFE: The Nonstick Coating

In 1938, young Roy Plunkett, a chemist at DuPont, was working with the gas tetrafluoroethylene ($CF_2{=}CF_2$). He opened the valve on a tank of the gas—and nothing came out. Rather than discarding the tank, he decided to investigate. The tank was found to be filled with a waxy, white solid. He attempted to analyze the solid but ran into a problem: It simply wouldn't dissolve, even in hot concentrated acids. Plunkett had discovered polytetrafluoroethylene (PTFE), the polymer of tetrafluoroethylene, best known by its trade name, Teflon®.

$$\sim CF_2-CF_2-CF_2-CF_2-CF_2-CF_2-CF_2-CF_2\sim$$

Teflon

Because its C—F bonds are exceptionally strong and resistant to heat and chemicals, PTFE is a tough, unreactive, nonflammable material. It is used to make electric insulation, bearings, and gaskets, as well as to coat surfaces of cookware to eliminate sticking of food.

▲ Frying pans, baking pans, and other cookware often take advantage of the inert, non-stick nature of PTFE.

CONCEPTUAL Example 10.1 Repeat Units in Polymers

What is the repeat unit in polyvinylidene chloride? A segment of the polymer is represented as

$$\begin{array}{ccccccccccccc} & \text{H} & & \text{Cl} & & \text{H} & & \text{Cl} & & \text{H} & & \text{Cl} & \\ & | & & | & & | & & | & & | & & | & \\ \sim & \text{C} & - & \text{C} & - & \text{C} & - & \text{C} & - & \text{C} & - & \text{C} & \sim \\ & | & & | & & | & & | & & | & & | & \\ & \text{H} & & \text{Cl} & & \text{H} & & \text{Cl} & & \text{H} & & \text{Cl} & \end{array}$$

Solution

Inspection of the segment above reveals that it consists of three repeat units, each with two carbon atoms, two hydrogen atoms, and two chlorine atoms. Placing a double bond between the carbon atoms of one unit, we get

$$\begin{array}{ccc} \text{H} & & \text{Cl} \\ | & & | \\ \text{C} & = & \text{C} \\ | & & | \\ \text{H} & & \text{Cl} \end{array}$$

Joining hundreds of these units would yield a molecule of the polymer.

■ EXERCISE 10.1

What is the repeat unit in polyacrylonitrile? A segment of the polymer is represented as

$$\sim CH_2\underset{\overset{|}{CN}}{CH}CH_2\underset{\overset{|}{CN}}{CH}CH_2\underset{\overset{|}{CN}}{CH}CH_2\underset{\overset{|}{CN}}{CH}CH_2\underset{\overset{|}{CN}}{CH}CH_2\underset{\overset{|}{CN}}{CH}\sim$$

▲ Granular polymeric resins are the basic stock for many molded plastic goods.

Example 10.2 Structure of Polymers

Write the structure of the polymer made from vinyl fluoride ($CH_2{=}CHF$). Show at least four repeat units.

Solution

The carbon atoms bond to form a chain with only single bonds between carbon atoms. The fluorine atom is a pendant group on the chain. (Two of the electrons in the double bond of the monomer form the bond joining units.) The polymer is

$$\sim CH_2\underset{\overset{|}{F}}{CH}CH_2\underset{\overset{|}{F}}{CH}CH_2\underset{\overset{|}{F}}{CH}CH_2\underset{\overset{|}{F}}{CH}\sim$$

■ EXERCISE 10.2

Write the structures of the polymers made from **(a)** methyl vinyl ketone ($CH_2{=}CHCOCH_3$) and **(b)** vinyl acetate ($CH_2{=}CHOCOCH_3$). Show at least four repeat units of each polymer.

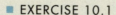

▲ Large plastic items with thin walls, such as the polyethylene terephthalate containers shown here, are often blow-molded. Blow molding is very similar to blowing a soap bubble, except that the bubble is blown inside a mold.

Processing Polymers

In everyday life, many polymers are called plastics. In chemistry, a *plastic* material is one that can be made to flow under heat and pressure. The material can then be shaped in a mold or in other ways. Plastic products are often made from granular polymeric material. In *compression molding*, heat and pressure are applied directly to such grains in the mold cavity. In *transfer molding*, the polymer is softened by heating before being poured into molds to harden.

There also are several methods of molding molten polymers. In *injection molding,* the plastic is melted in a heating chamber and then forced by a plunger into cold molds to set. In *extrusion molding,* the melted polymer is extruded through a die in continuous form to be cut into lengths or coiled. Bottles and similar hollow objects often are *blow-molded;* a "bubble" of molten polymer is blown up like a balloon inside a hollow mold.

Table 10.1 lists some of the more important addition polymers, along with a few of their uses.

Table 10.1 Some Addition Polymers

Monomer	Polymer	Polymer Name	Some Uses
$CH_2{=}CH_2$	$\left[-CH_2-CH_2-\right]_n$	Polyethylene	Bags, bottles, toys, electrical insulation
$CH_2{=}CH-CH_3$	$\left[-CH_2-CH(CH_3)-\right]_n$	Polypropylene	Carpeting, bottles, luggage
$CH_2{=}CH-C_6H_5$	$\left[-CH_2-CH(C_6H_5)-\right]_n$	Polystyrene	Simulated wood furniture, insulation, cups, toys, packing materials
$CH_2{=}CH-Cl$	$\left[-CH_2-CH(Cl)-\right]_n$	Polyvinyl chloride (PVC)	Food wrap, simulated leather, plumbing, garden hoses, floor tile
$CH_2{=}CCl_2$	$\left[-CH_2-CCl_2-\right]_n$	Polyvinylidene chloride (Saran®)	Food wrap, seat covers
$CF_2{=}CF_2$	$\left[-CF_2-CF_2-\right]_n$	Polytetrafluoroethylene (Teflon)	Nonstick coating for cooking utensils, electrical insulation
$CH_2{=}CH-C{\equiv}N$	$\left[-CH_2-CH(CN)-\right]_n$	Polyacrylonitrile (Acrilan, Creslan, Dynel)	Yarns, wigs, paints
$CH_2{=}CH-OCOCH_3$	$\left[-CH_2-CH(O-C(=O)-CH_3)-\right]_n$	Polyvinyl acetate	Adhesives, textile coatings, chewing gum resin, paints
$CH_2{=}C(CH_3)COOCH_3$	$\left[-CH_2-C(CH_3)(C(=O)-O-CH_3)-\right]_n$	Polymethyl methacrylate (Lucite, Plexiglas)	Glass substitute, bowling balls

Conducting Polymers: Polyacetylene

Acetylene (H—C≡C—H) has a triple bond rather than a double bond, but it can still undergo addition polymerization, forming polyacetylene (Figure 10.3). Notice that, unlike polyethylene, which has a carbon chain containing only single bonds, every other carbon to carbon bond in polyacetylene is a double bond.

~CH=CH—CH=CH—CH=CH—CH=CH—CH=CH—CH=CH~

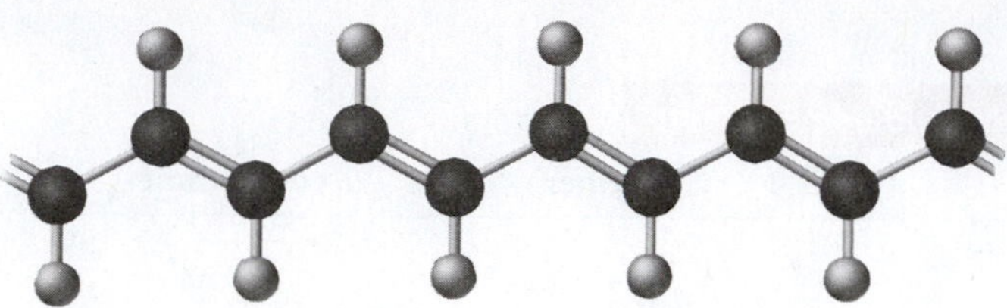

Figure 10.3 A ball-and-stick model of polyacetylene.

Q: *Write an equation for the formation of polyacetylene similar to that for polyethylene on page 268, in which the repeat polymer unit is placed within brackets.*

The alternating double and single bonds form a *conjugated* system. Such a system makes it easy for electrons to travel along the chain, so polyacetylene is able to conduct electricity. Most other plastics are electrical insulators. Polyacetylene and similar conjugated polymers can be used as lightweight substitutes for metal. In fact, the plastic even has a silvery luster like metal.

Polyacetylene, the first conducting polymer, was discovered in 1970. Since then, a number of other polymers that conduct electricity have been made.

▲ Conducting polymers have conjugated systems, as seen in Figure 10.3, and they are used to make electronic sensors, such as the ones shown here. The conductivity of the polymer is affected by impurities on the surface. The change in conductivity varies with the concentration of that impurity.

Self-Assessment Questions

1. Starting materials for many polymers are
   a. alkanes **b.** alkenes **c.** carboxylic acids **d.** esters **e.** ethers
2. The monomer styrene ($C_6H_5CH{=}CH_2$, where C_6H_5 represents a benzene ring) forms a polymer that has chains with repeating
   a. eight-carbon units in the backbone
   b. six-carbon units in the backbone and two-carbon groups as pendants
   c. CH_2CH units in the backbone and C_6H_5 groups as pendants
   d. $CH_2{=}CH$ units in the backbone and C_6H_5 groups as pendants
3. Which of the following could *not* serve as the monomer to make an addition polymer?
   a. $C_2H_2F_2$ **b.** C_2F_4 **c.** C_2H_5Cl **d.** $C_2H_3C_6H_5$
4. A buckyball is a
   a. large carbon molecule (C_{60})
   b. carbon nanotube wound up like a ball of string
   c. long polymer molecule wound up like a ball of string
   d. circular ring of carbon atoms

Answers: 1, b; 2, c; 3, c; 4, a

10.4 Rubber and Other Elastomers

Learning Objectives › Define *cross-linking*, and explain how it changes the properties of a polymer.

Although rubber is a natural polymer, it was the basis for much of the development of the synthetic polymer industry. During World War II, Japanese occupation of Southeast Asia cut off most of the Allies' supply of natural rubber. The search for synthetic substitutes resulted in much more than just a replacement for natural rubber. The plastics industry, to a large extent, developed out of the search for synthetic rubber.

Natural rubber can be broken down into a simple hydrocarbon called *isoprene*. Isoprene is a volatile liquid, whereas rubber is a semisolid, elastic material. Chemists can make polyisoprene, a substance identical to natural rubber, except that the isoprene comes from petroleum refineries rather than from the cells of rubber trees.

$$n\,\mathrm{CH_2{=}\underset{\displaystyle CH_3}{\underset{|}{C}}{-}CH{=}CH_2} \longrightarrow \mathrm{\left[CH_2{-}\underset{\displaystyle CH_3}{\underset{|}{C}}{=}CH{-}CH_2\right]_n}$$

Isoprene — Polyisoprene (rubber)

Chemists have also developed several synthetic rubbers and devised ways to modify these polymers to change their properties.

Vulcanization: Cross-Linking

The long-chain molecules that make up rubber are coiled and twisted and intertwined with one another. When rubber is stretched, its coiled molecules are straightened. Natural rubber is soft and tacky when hot. It can be made harder by reaction with sulfur. In this process, called **vulcanization**, sulfur atoms *cross-link* the hydrocarbon chains side-to-side (Figure 10.4). Charles Goodyear discovered vulcanization and was issued U.S. Patent 3633 in 1844 for the process.

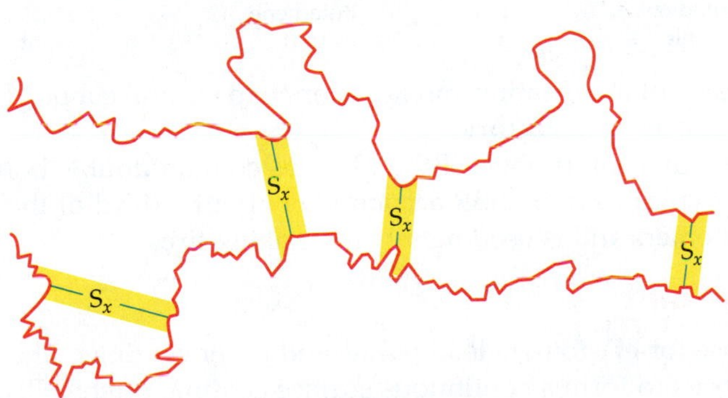

◀ **Figure 10.4** Vulcanized rubber has long hydrocarbon chains (represented here by red lines) cross-linked by short chains of sulfur atoms. The subscript *x* indicates a small, indefinite number of S atoms, usually not more than four.

Its cross-linked structure makes vulcanized rubber a harder, stronger substance that is suitable for automobile tires. Surprisingly, cross-linking also improves the elasticity of rubber. With just the right degree of cross-linking, the individual chains are still free to uncoil and stretch somewhat. When stretched vulcanized rubber is released, the cross-links pull the chains back to their original arrangement (Figure 10.5). Rubber bands owe their snap to this sort of molecular structure. Materials that can be extended and will return to their original size are called **elastomers**.

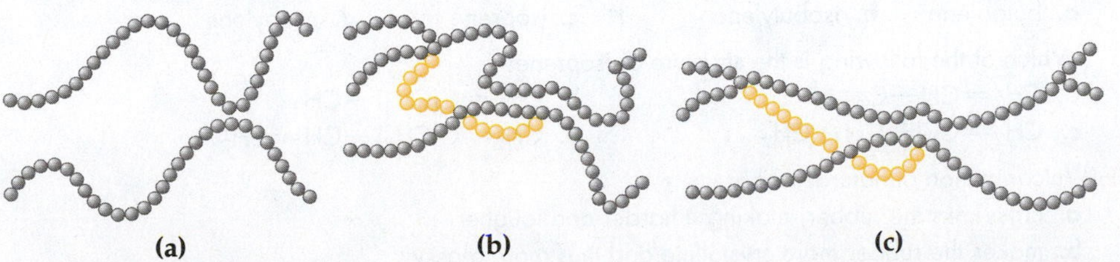

● = Carbon

● = Sulfur

▲ **Figure 10.5** Vulcanization of rubber cross-links the hydrocarbon chains. (a) In unvulcanized rubber, the chains slip past one another when the rubber is stretched. (b) Vulcanization involves the addition of sulfur cross-links between the chains. (c) When vulcanized rubber is stretched, the sulfur cross-links prevent the chains from slipping past one another. Vulcanized rubber is stronger than unvulcanized rubber.

Synthetic Rubber

Natural rubber is a polymer of isoprene, and some synthetic elastomers are closely related to natural rubber. For example, polybutadiene is made from the monomer butadiene ($CH_2{=}CH{-}CH{=}CH_2$), which differs from isoprene only in that it lacks a methyl group on the second carbon atom. Polybutadiene is made rather easily from this monomer.

$$n\,CH_2{=}CH{-}CH{=}CH_2 \longrightarrow \left[CH_2{-}CH{=}CH{-}CH_2 \right]_n$$

However, this polymer has only fair tensile strength and poor resistance to gasoline and oils. These properties limit its value for automobile tires, the main use of elastomers.

Another synthetic elastomer, polychloroprene (Neoprene), is made from a monomer similar to isoprene, but with a chlorine in place of the methyl group on isoprene.

$$n\,CH_2{=}\underset{\displaystyle Cl}{\underset{|}{C}}{-}CH{=}CH_2 \longrightarrow \left[CH_2{-}\underset{\displaystyle Cl}{\underset{|}{C}}{=}CH{-}CH_2 \right]_n$$

Neoprene is more resistant to oil and gasoline than other elastomers are. It is used to make gasoline pump hoses and similar items used at automobile service stations.

Styrene–butadiene rubber (SBR) is a copolymer of styrene (about 25%) and butadiene (about 75%). A segment of an SBR molecule might look something like this.

$$\sim CH_2CH{=}CHCH_2{-}\underset{\displaystyle C_6H_5}{\underset{|}{CH_2CH}}{-}CH_2CH{=}CHCH_2{-}CH_2CH{=}CHCH_2\sim$$

Butadiene unit   Styrene unit   Butadiene unit   Butadiene unit

SBR is more resistant to oxidation and abrasion than natural rubber, but its mechanical properties are less satisfactory.

Like those of natural rubber, SBR molecules contain double bonds and can be cross-linked by vulcanization. SBR accounts for about a third of the total U.S. production of elastomers and is used mainly for making tires.

▲ **It DOES Matter!**
A polymer related to SBR is poly(styrene-butadiene-styrene), or SBS. Called a *block copolymer*, SBS has molecules made up of three segments: one end is a chain of polystyrene repeat units; the middle is a long chain of polybutadiene repeat units; and the other end is another chain of polystyrene repeat units. SBS is a hard rubber used in items where durability is important, such as shoe soles and tire treads.

Polymers in Paints

A surprising use for elastomers is in paints and other coatings. The substance in a paint that hardens to form a continuous surface coating, often called the *binder*, or resin, is a polymer, usually an elastomer. Paint made with elastomers is resistant to cracking. Various kinds of polymers can be used as binders, depending on the specific qualities desired in the paint. Latex paints, which have polymer particles dispersed in water, and thus avoiding the use of organic solvents, are most common. Brushes and rollers are easily cleaned in soap and water. This replacement of the hazardous organic solvents historically used in paints with water is a good example of green chemistry.

▲ Synthetic polymers serve as binders in paints. Pigments provide color and opacity to the paint. Titanium dioxide (TiO_2), a white solid, is the most widely used pigment.

Self-Assessment Questions

1. Natural rubber is a polymer of
   a. butadiene b. isobutylene c. isoprene d. propylene
2. Which of the following is the structure of isoprene?
   a. $CH_2{=}CH{-}C{\equiv}N$ b. $CH_2{=}C(CH_3){-}CH_3$
   c. $CH_2{=}CCl{-}CH{-}CH_2$ d. $CH_2{=}C(CH_3){-}CH{=}CH_2$
3. Vulcanization of natural rubber
   a. cross-links the rubber, making it harder and tougher
   b. makes the rubber more crystalline and thus more glassy
   c. makes the rubber totally amorphous
   d. makes the rubber tacky, forming rubber cement
4. Charles Goodyear discovered that natural rubber could be cross-linked by heating it with
   a. a binder b. carbon c. isoprene d. sulfur

5. Styrene–butadiene rubber is an example of a
   a. copolymer b. natural elastomer
   c. natural cross-linked polymer d. polyamide
6. Polymers, usually elastomers, are used in paints as the
   a. binder b. initiator c. pigment d. solvent

Answers: 1, c; 2, d; 3, a; 4, d; 5, a; 6, a

10.5 Condensation Polymers

Learning Objectives › Differentiate between addition and condensation polymerization. › Write the structures of the monomers that form polyesters and polyamides.

The polymers considered so far are all addition polymers. All the atoms of the monomer molecules are incorporated into the polymer molecules. In a *condensation polymer*, part of the monomer molecule is not incorporated in the final polymer. During **condensation polymerization**, also called *step-reaction polymerization*, a small molecule, usually water but sometimes methanol, ammonia or HCl, is formed as a by-product.

Nylon and Other Polyamides

As an example, let's consider the formation of nylon. The monomer in one type of nylon, called *nylon 6*, is a six-carbon carboxylic acid with an amino group on the sixth carbon atom: 6-aminohexanoic acid ($HOOCCH_2CH_2CH_2CH_2CH_2NH_2$). (There are several different nylons, each prepared from a different monomer or set of monomers, but all share certain common structural features.)

In the polymerization reaction, a carboxyl group of one monomer molecule forms an amide bond with the amine group of another.

$$n\,HO{-}\overset{\overset{\displaystyle O}{\|}}{C}CH_2(CH_2)_3CH_2\overset{\overset{\displaystyle H}{|}}{N}{-}H + n\,HO{-}\overset{\overset{\displaystyle O}{\|}}{C}CH_2(CH_2)_3CH_2\overset{\overset{\displaystyle H}{|}}{N}{-}H \longrightarrow$$

$$\sim\overset{\overset{\displaystyle O}{\|}}{C}CH_2(CH_2)_3CH_2\overset{\overset{\displaystyle H}{|}}{N}{-}\overset{\overset{\displaystyle O}{\|}}{C}CH_2(CH_2)_3\overset{\overset{\displaystyle H}{|}}{N}\sim + 2n\,H_2O$$

Amide linkage

Water molecules are formed as a by-product. This formation of a nonpolymeric by-product distinguishes condensation polymerization from addition polymerization. Note that the formula of a repeat unit of a condensation polymer is not the same as that of the monomer.

Because the linkages holding the polymer together are amide bonds, nylon 6 is a **polyamide**. Another nylon is made by the condensation of two different monomers: 1,6-hexanediamine ($H_2NCH_2CH_2CH_2CH_2CH_2CH_2NH_2$) and adipic acid ($HOOCCH_2CH_2CH_2CH_2COOH$). Each monomer has six carbon atoms; the polymer is called *nylon 66*.

$$\underset{\text{1,6-Hexanediamine}}{n\,H{-}\overset{\overset{\displaystyle H}{|}}{N}CH_2CH_2CH_2CH_2CH_2CH_2\overset{\overset{\displaystyle H}{|}}{N}{-}H} + \underset{\text{Adipic acid}}{n\,HO{-}\overset{\overset{\displaystyle O}{\|}}{C}(CH_2)_4\overset{\overset{\displaystyle O}{\|}}{C}{-}OH} \longrightarrow$$

$$\left[\overset{\overset{\displaystyle H}{|}}{N}CH_2CH_2CH_2CH_2CH_2CH_2\overset{\overset{\displaystyle H}{|}}{N}{-}\overset{\overset{\displaystyle O}{\|}}{C}CH_2CH_2CH_2CH_2\overset{\overset{\displaystyle O}{\|}}{C}\right]_n + 2n\,H_2O$$

Amide linkage

This was the original nylon polymer discovered in 1937 by DuPont chemist Wallace Carothers. Note that one monomer has two amino groups and the other has two carboxyl groups, but the product is still a polyamide, quite similar to nylon 6. Silk and wool, which are protein fibers, are natural polyamides.

Although nylon can be molded into various shapes, most nylon is made into fibers. Some is spun into fine thread to be woven into silklike fabrics, and some is made into yarn that is much like wool. Carpeting, which was once made primarily from wool, is now made largely from nylon.

Polyethylene Terephthalate and Other Polyesters

A **polyester** is a condensation polymer made from molecules with alcohol and carboxylic acid functional groups. The most common polyester is made from ethylene glycol and terephthalic acid. It is called *polyethylene terephthalate (PET).*

$$n\,HO{-}CH_2CH_2{-}OH \;+\; n\,HO{-}\overset{O}{\overset{\|}{C}}{-}C_6H_4{-}\overset{O}{\overset{\|}{C}}{-}OH \longrightarrow$$

Ethylene glycol — Terephthalic acid

Ester linkage

$$\left[O{-}CH_2CH_2{-}O{-}\overset{O}{\overset{\|}{C}}{-}C_6H_4{-}\overset{O}{\overset{\|}{C}}\right]_n \;+\; 2n\,H_2O$$

Polyethylene terephthalate

The hydroxyl groups in ethylene glycol react with the carboxylic acid groups in terephthalic acid to produce long chains held together by many ester linkages.

PET can be molded into bottles for beverages and other liquids. It can also be formed into a film, which is used to laminate documents and to make tough packaging tape. Polyester finishes are used on premium wood products such as guitars, pianos, and the interiors of vehicles and boats. Polyester fibers are strong, quick-drying, and resistant to mildew, wrinkling, stretching, and shrinking. They are used in home furnishings such as carpets, curtains, sheets and pillow cases, and upholstery. Because polyester fibers do not absorb water, they are ideal for outdoor clothing to be worn in wet and damp environments and for insulation in boots and sleeping bags. For other clothing, they are often blended with cotton for a more natural feel. A familiar use of polyester film (Mylar®) is in the shiny balloons that are filled with helium to celebrate special occasions.

Phenol–Formaldehyde and Related Resins

Let's go back to Bakelite, the original synthetic polymer. Bakelite, a phenol–formaldehyde resin, was first synthesized by Leo Baekeland, who received U.S. Patent 942,699 for the process in 1909. Phenolic resins are no longer important as industrial polymers, but they are used as a substitute for porcelain and in board and tabletop game pieces such as billiard balls, dominoes, and checkers.

Phenol–formaldehyde resins are formed in a condensation reaction that also yields water molecules, the hydrogen atoms coming from the benzene ring of phenol and the oxygen atoms from the aldehyde. The reaction proceeds stepwise, with formaldehyde first adding to the 2 or 4 position of the phenol molecule.

$$2\,C_6H_5OH \;+\; 2\,H{-}\overset{O}{\overset{\|}{C}}{-}H \longrightarrow \text{2-}(CH_2OH)C_6H_4OH \;+\; \text{4-}(CH_2OH)C_6H_4OH$$

Phenol — Formaldehyde

The substituted phenol molecules then link up as water molecules are formed. (Remember that there are hydrogen atoms at all the unsubstituted corners of a benzene ring.) The hookup of molecules continues until an extensive network is achieved.

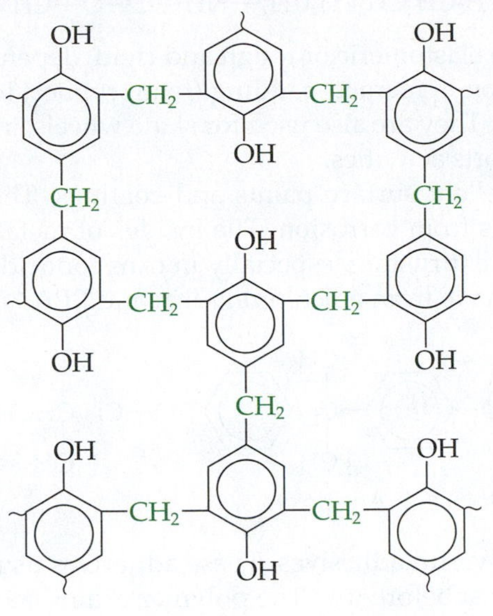

OH OH
—CH_2— —CH_2—
OH
CH_2 CH_2
OH
—CH_2— —CH_2—
OH OH
CH_2
OH OH
—CH_2— —CH_2—
OH

Phenol–formaldehyde resin

Water is driven off by heat as the polymer sets. The structure of the polymer is extremely complex, a three-dimensional network somewhat like the framework of a giant building. Note that the phenolic rings are joined together by CH_2 units from the formaldehyde. These network polymers are **thermosetting resins**; they cannot be melted and remolded. Instead, they decompose when heated to high temperatures.

Formaldehyde is also condensed with urea [$H_2N(C{=}O)NH_2$] to make urea–formaldehyde resins and with melamine to form melamine–formaldehyde resins. (Melamine is formed by condensation of three molecules of urea.)

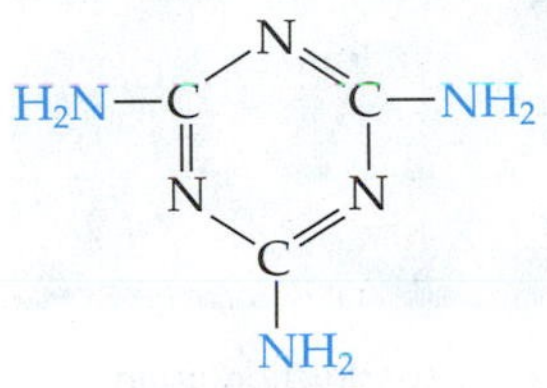

$H_2N—C$ (ring: N, C, N, C, N) $C—NH_2$, NH_2

Melamine

These resins, like phenolic resins, are thermosetting. The polymers are complex three-dimensional networks formed by the condensation reaction of formaldehyde ($H_2C{=}O$) molecules and amino ($—NH_2$) groups. Urea–formaldehyde resins are used to bind wood chips together in panels of particle board. Melamine–formaldehyde resins are used in plastic (Melmac) dinnerware and laminate countertops.

Other Condensation Polymers

There are many other kinds of condensation polymers, but we will look at only a few.

Polycarbonates are "clear as glass" polymers tough enough to be used in bulletproof windows. They are also used in protective helmets, safety glasses, clear plastic water bottles, baby bottles, and even dental crowns. One polycarbonate is made from bisphenol-A (BPA) and phosgene ($COCl_2$).

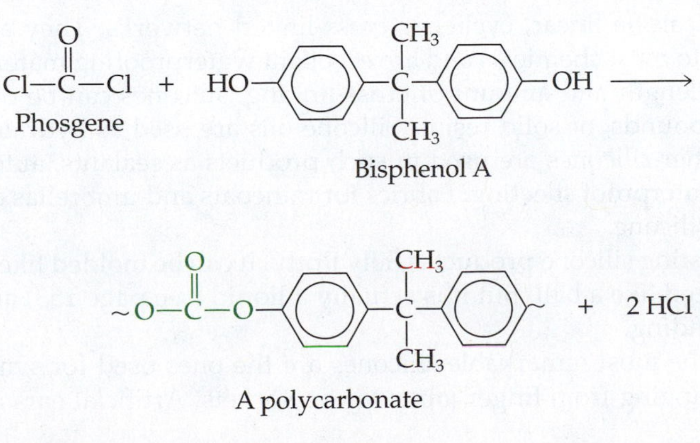

$$Cl—\overset{O}{\overset{\|}{C}}—Cl + HO—C_6H_4—\underset{CH_3}{\overset{CH_3}{C}}—C_6H_4—OH \longrightarrow$$

Phosgene   Bisphenol A

$$\sim O—\overset{O}{\overset{\|}{C}}—O—C_6H_4—\underset{CH_3}{\overset{CH_3}{C}}—C_6H_4\sim + 2\,HCl$$

A polycarbonate

▲ **It DOES Matter!**
Bisphenol-A (BPA) is an endocrine disruptor in laboratory animals; that is, it can act like a hormone. A tiny amount of BPA leaches out of polycarbonate bottles, especially when they are heated. Concern over long-term, low-dose exposure to BPA led Canada to ban BPA in baby bottles in 2008. Threats of legislation in the United States and elsewhere caused manufacturers of polycarbonate bottles to switch to BPA-free bottles.

▲ Composite construction using carbon fiber and epoxies makes bicycle frames incredibly strong and light (about 1 kg!). The direction of the carbon fiber allows the maker to tailor the material for maximum strength where needed.

Polyurethanes are similar to nylon polymers in structure. The repeat unit in one common polyurethane is

$$\sim\overset{\overset{\displaystyle O}{\|}}{C}-NH-CH_2CH_2CH_2CH_2CH_2CH_2-NH-\overset{\overset{\displaystyle O}{\|}}{C}-O-CH_2CH_2CH_2CH_2-O\sim$$

Polyurethanes may be elastomeric or tough and rigid, depending on the monomers used. They are common in foamed padding (foam rubber) in cushions, mattresses, and padded furniture. They are also used for skate wheels, in running shoes, and in protective gear for sports activities.

Epoxies make excellent surface paints and coatings. They are used to protect steel pipes and fittings from corrosion. The insides of metal cans are often coated with an epoxy to prevent rusting, especially in cans for acidic foods like tomatoes. A common epoxy is made from epichlorohydrin and BPA.

$$\sim O-C_6H_4-C(CH_3)_2-C_6H_4-O-CH_2\underset{\underset{\displaystyle OH}{|}}{C}HCH_2\sim$$

An epoxy

Epoxies also make powerful adhesives. These adhesives usually have two components that are mixed just before use. The polymer chains become cross-linked, and the bonding is extremely strong.

Composite Materials

Composite materials are made up of high-strength fibers (of glass, graphite, synthetic polymers, or ceramics) held together by a polymeric matrix, usually a thermosetting condensation polymer. The fiber reinforcement provides the support, and the surrounding plastic keeps the fibers from breaking.

Among the most commonly used composite materials are polyester resins reinforced with glass fibers. These are widely used in boat hulls, molded chairs, automobile panels, and sports gear such as tennis rackets. Some composite materials have the strength and rigidity of steel but with a fraction of the weight of steel.

Silicones

Silicon is in the same group (4A) as carbon and, like carbon, is tetravalent and able to form chains. However, carbon can form chains consisting only of carbon atoms (as in polyethylene), whereas the chains of silicone polymers have alternating silicon and oxygen atoms.

Not all polymers are based on chains of carbon atoms. A good example of a different type of polymer is **silicone** (polysiloxane), whose chains have a series of alternating silicon and oxygen atoms.

$$\sim SiR_2-O-SiR_2-O-SiR_2-O-SiR_2-O-SiR_2-O-SiR_2-O-SiR_2\sim$$

(In simple silicones, R represents a hydrocarbon group, such as methyl, ethyl, or butyl.)

Silicones can be linear, cyclic, or cross-linked networks. They are heat-stable and resistant to most chemicals and are excellent waterproofing materials. Depending on chain length and amount of cross-linking, silicones can be oils or greases, rubbery compounds, or solid resins. Silicone oils are used as hydraulic fluids and lubricants; other silicones are used in such products as sealants, auto polish, shoe polish, and waterproof sheeting. Fabrics for raincoats and umbrellas are frequently treated with silicone.

An interesting silicone product is Silly Putty. It can be molded like clay or rolled up and bounced like a ball. But it is actually a liquid (see page 153) and flows very slowly on standing.

4. Is silicon the same thing as silicone? Although the names are very similar, the materials are quite different. *Silicon* is a hard, brittle element. A *silicone* is a polymer that contains silicon as well as carbon, hydrogen, and oxygen. Most silicones are flexible.

Perhaps the most remarkable silicones are the ones used for synthetic human body parts, ranging from finger joints to eye sockets. Artificial ears and noses are also made from silicone polymers. These can even be specially colored to match the surrounding skin.

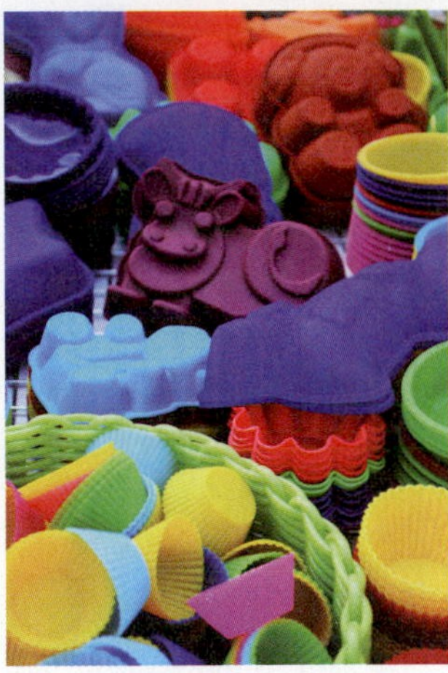

▲ Cookware made of silicone is colorful, flexible, and nonstick.

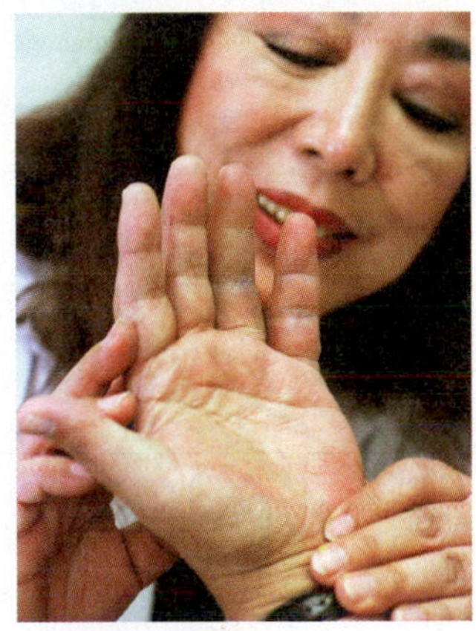

▲ Silicone is an excellent material for some replacement body parts. It is very flexible and chemically inert; the body does not often reject silicone.

Example 10.3 Condensed Structural Formulas for Polymers

Write the condensed structural formula for the polymer formed from dimethylsilanol, $(CH_3)_2Si(OH)_2$.

Solution

Let's start by writing the structural formula of the monomer.

$$\begin{array}{c} CH_3 \\ | \\ HO-Si-OH \\ | \\ CH_3 \end{array}$$

Because there are no double bonds in this molecule, we do not expect it to undergo addition polymerization. Rather, we expect a condensation reaction, in which an OH group of one molecule and an H atom of another combine to form a molecule of water. Moreover, because there are two OH groups per molecule, each monomer can form bonds with two others, on both sides. This is a key requirement for polymerization. We can represent the reaction as follows.

$$\begin{array}{c} CH_3 \\ | \\ HO-Si-OH \\ | \\ CH_3 \end{array} + \begin{array}{c} CH_3 \\ | \\ HO-Si-OH \\ | \\ CH_3 \end{array} + \begin{array}{c} CH_3 \\ | \\ HO-Si-OH \\ | \\ CH_3 \end{array} + \cdots \longrightarrow \left[\begin{array}{c} CH_3 \\ | \\ -Si-O- \\ | \\ CH_3 \end{array}\right]_n + n\,H_2O$$

■ EXERCISE 10.3

a. Write the structural formula for the polymer formed from glycolic acid (hydroxyacetic acid, $HOCH_2COOH$), showing at least four repeat units.

b. Write a condensed structural formula in which the repeat unit in part (a) is shown in brackets.

Self-Assessment Questions

1. In a condensation polymerization, the two products formed are a polymer and (usually)
   a. an acid
   b. a base
   c. carbon dioxide
   d. water
2. Which of the following pairs of molecules can form a polyester?
   a. $HOCH_2CH_2OH$ and $HOCH_2CH_2CH_2CH_2OH$
   b. $H_2NCH_2CH_2CH_2CH_2CH_2NH_2$ and $HOOCCH_2CH_2CH_2CH_2COOH$
   c. $H_2NCH_2CH_2CH_2CH_2CH_2NH_2$ and $HOCH_2CH_2CH_2CH_2CH_2OH$
   d. $HOOCCH_2CH_2CH_2CH_2COOH$ and $HOCH_2CH_2CH_2CH_2OH$
3. Which of the following molecules can serve as the sole monomer for a polyamide?
   a. $H_2NCH_2CH_2CH_2CH_2OH$
   b. $H_2NCH_2CH_2CH_2CH_2NH_2$
   c. $HOOCCH_2CH_2CH_2CH_2CH_2NH_2$
   d. $HOOCCH_2CH_2CH_2CONH_2$
4. Thermosetting polymers
   a. are easily recycled
   b. are always addition polymers
   c. cannot be melted and remolded
   d. usually melt at a lower temperature than do thermoplastic polymers
5. The backbone of a silicone polymer chain is composed of the repeating unit
   a. ~OCH_2CH_2OSi~
   b. ~OCH_2CH_2Si~
   c. ~SiO~
   d. ~OSiSi~

Answers: 1, d; 2, d; 3, c; 4, c; 5, c

10.6 Properties of Polymers

Learning Objectives › Understand the concept of the glass transition temperature. › Explain how crystallinity affects the physical properties of polymers.

Polymers differ from substances consisting of small molecules in three main ways. First, the long chains can be entangled with one another, much like the strands in a dish of spaghetti. It is difficult to untangle the polymer molecules, especially at low temperatures. This property lends strength to many plastics, elastomers, and other materials.

Second, although intermolecular forces affect polymers just as they do small molecules, these forces are greatly multiplied for large molecules. The larger the molecules are, the greater the intermolecular forces between them. Even when ordinarily weak dispersion forces are the only intermolecular forces present, they can strongly bind polymer chains. This property, too, provides strength in polymeric materials. For example, polyethylene is nonpolar, with only dispersion forces between its molecules. As noted on page 271, though, ultra-high-molecular-weight polyethylene forms fibers so strong they can be used in bullet-proof vests.

Third, large polymer molecules move more slowly than small molecules do. A group of small molecules (monomers) can move around more rapidly and more randomly when independent than they can when joined together in a long chain (polymer). The slower molecular speed makes a polymeric material different from one made of small molecules. For example, a polymer dissolved in a solvent will form a solution that is a lot more viscous than the pure solvent.

Crystalline and Amorphous Polymers

Some polymers are highly crystalline; their molecules line up neatly to form long fibers of great strength. Other polymers are largely amorphous, composed of randomly oriented molecules that get tangled up with one another (Figure 10.6). Crystalline polymers tend to make good synthetic fibers, while amorphous polymers are often elastomers.

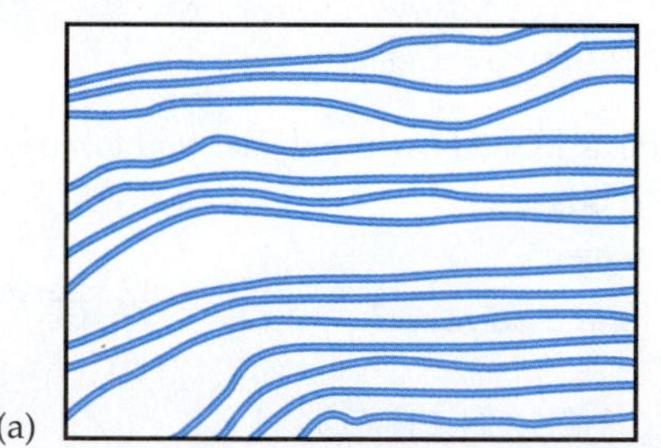

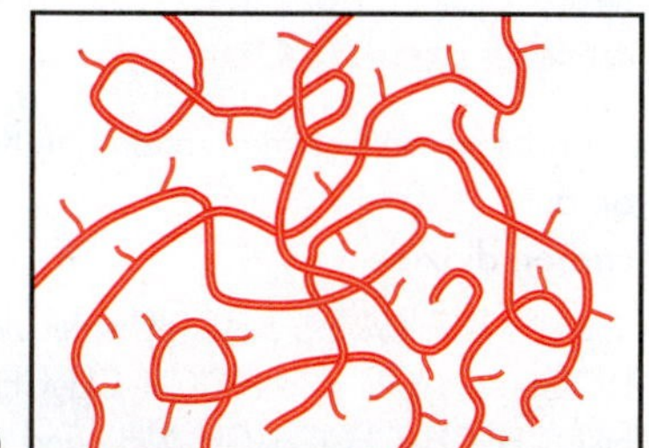

▶ **Figure 10.6** Organization of polymer molecules. (a) Crystalline arrangement. (b) Amorphous arrangement.

Sometimes, the same polymer is crystalline in one region and amorphous in another. For example, scientists designed spandex fibers (used in stretch fabrics [Lycra] in ski pants, exercise clothing, and swimsuits) to combine the tensile strength of crystalline fibers with the elasticity of amorphous rubber. Two molecular structures are combined in one polymer chain, with crystalline blocks alternating with amorphous blocks. The amorphous blocks are soft and rubbery, while the crystalline parts are quite rigid. The resulting polymer exhibits both sets of properties—flexibility and rigidity.

We can apply the glass transition temperature in everyday life. For example, we can remove chewing gum from clothing by applying ice to lower the temperature of the polyvinyl acetate resin that gives the gum its "chewiness" below its T_g. The cold, brittle resin then crumbles readily and can be removed.

The Glass Transition Temperature

An important property of most thermoplastic polymers is the **glass transition temperature** (T_g). Above this temperature, the polymer is rubbery and tough. Below it, the polymer is like glass: hard, stiff, and brittle. Each polymer has a characteristic T_g.

We want automobile tires to be tough and elastic, so we make them from polymers with low T_g values. On the other hand, we want plastic substitutes for glass to be glassy. Therefore, these polymers have T_g values well above room temperature.

Fiber Formation

Not all synthetic polymers can be formed into useful fibers, but those that can often yield fibers with properties superior to those of natural fibers. More than half of the 60 billion kg of textile fibers produced each year in the United States are synthetic.

Silk fabrics are beautiful and have a luxurious "feel," but nylon fabrics are also attractive and feel much like silk. Moreover, nylon fabrics wear longer, are easier to care for, and are less expensive than silk.

Polyesters such as PET can substitute for either cotton or silk, but they outperform the natural fibers in many ways. Polyesters are not subject to mildew as cotton is, and many polyester fabrics do not need ironing. Fabrics in which polyester fibers are blended with 35–50% cotton combine the comfort of cotton with the no-iron easy care of polyester.

Acrylic fibers, made from polyacrylonitrile, can be spun into yarns that look like wool. Acrylic sweaters have the beauty and warmth of wool, but they do not shrink in hot water, are not attacked by moths, and do not cause the allergic skin reaction wool causes in some people.

Exceedingly fine fibers—called *microfibers* because they measure less than 10 μm in diameter, half as thick as a silk fibers—can be made from almost any fiber-forming polymer, but most are made of polyesters or polyamides or a combination of the two. Varying the size, shape, and composition of the fibers results in products that are water repellent (for apparel) or absorbent (for a mop). Microfibers can be shaped for efficient trapping of dust or for wicking away liquids. These fibers already have many uses and are likely to have many more.

5. How are permanent-press fabrics made? Cotton is largely cellulose, which can engage in hydrogen bonding among its molecules. Moisture causes random hydrogen bonding in cotton fabric, which causes wrinkles. The earliest permanent-press fabrics were designed to allow less hydrogen bonding than in cotton. Newer permanent-press clothing takes advantage of the fabric's low T_g to minimize wrinkles after drying.

▲ Formation of fibers by extrusion through a spinneret. A melted polymer is forced through the tiny holes to make fibers that solidify as they cool.

Self-Assessment Questions

1. The glass transition temperature of a polymer is the temperature
   a. above which the polymer becomes highly crystalline
   b. at which the polymer changes to a thermosetting material
   c. at which the polymer melts to a clear liquid
   d. below which the polymer becomes glassy and brittle
2. Crystalline polymers are
   a. elastic b. flexible c. highly cross-linked d. used in fibers

Answers: 1, d; 2, d

10.7 Plastics and the Environment

Learning Objectives › Describe the environmental problems associated with plastics and plasticizers. › Name two types of sustainable, non-petroleum-derived polymers and give their sources.

An advantage of many plastics is that they are durable and resistant to environmental conditions. Perhaps some of them are too resistant: They last almost forever. Once plastic objects are dumped, they do not go away. You see them littering our parks, our sidewalks, and our highways, and if you should go out into the middle of the ocean, you would see them there, too. Many small fish have been found dead with their digestive tracts clogged by bits of plastic foam ingested with their food.

Plastics make up about 12% by mass of solid waste in the United States, but about 25% by volume. Their bulk creates a problem because 55% of all solid waste

Americans use about 60 million plastic bottles each day, with only about 12% being recycled. Recycling one plastic bottle conserves enough energy to burn a 60-W lightbulb for six hours. Recycling plastics reduces our dependency on oil and decreases CO_2 emissions due to the use of fossil fuels.

goes into landfills, and it is increasingly difficult to find suitable landfill space. (Solid wastes are discussed in more detail in Chapter 12.)

Another way to dispose of discarded plastics is to burn them. Most plastics have a high fuel value. For example, a pound of polyethylene has about the same energy content as a pound of fuel oil. Some communities generate electricity with the heat from garbage incinerators. Some utility companies burn powdered coal mixed with a small proportion of ground-up rubber tires, thereby not only obtaining extra energy from the tires but also helping to solve the problem of tire disposal.

On the other hand, the burning of plastics and rubber can create new problems. For example, PVC produces toxic hydrogen chloride and vinyl chloride gases when it burns, and burning automobile tires give off soot and a stinking smoke. Incinerators are corroded by acidic fumes and clogged by materials that are not readily burned.

▲ Recycled plastic can be used for many things. The Adirondack chair and the cafe chair are colorful and strong and made from recycled milk jugs.

Degradable Plastics

About half of the waste plastic generated in the United States is from packaging. One approach to the problem of disposal of plastics is to make plastic packages that are biodegradable or photodegradable (broken down in the presence of bacteria or light). Of course, such packages must remain intact and not start to decompose while still being used. And many people still seem reluctant to pay extra for garbage bags that are designed to fall apart. Recently, though, there has been an increase in degradable, more environmentally friendly plastic items, including plastic tableware, cups, bottles, and delicatessen food containers.

Recycling

Recycling is perhaps the best way to handle waste plastics. The plastics must be collected, sorted, chopped, melted, and then remolded. Collection works well when there is strong community cooperation. The separation step is simplified by code numbers stamped on plastic containers. Once the plastics have been separated, they can be chopped into flakes, melted, and remolded or spun into fibers.

Only two kinds of plastics are recycled on a large scale, PET (28% recycled) and HDPE (29%). PET bottles can be made into fibers, mainly for carpets, and HDPE containers can be remolded into detergent bottles. Recycling is green because it keeps plastics out of landfills, and it increases sustainability by lessening the use of petroleum-derived monomers or hazardous chemicals. We have a long way to go: in 2009, only about 7% of the 27 billion kg per year of plastic wastes in the United States are recycled.

Plastics and Fire Hazards

The accidental ignition of fabrics, synthetic or other, has caused untold human misery. The U.S. Department of Health and Human Services estimates that fires involving flammable fabrics kill several thousand people annually and injure between 150,000 and 200,000.

Research has led to a variety of flame-retardant fabrics. Many incorporate chlorine and bromine atoms within the polymeric fibers. In particular, federal regulations require that children's sleepwear be made of such flame-retardant materials.

Another synthetic fabric, meta-aramid, or Nomex (from DuPont), has such high heat resistance that it is used for protective clothing for firefighters and race-car drivers. The fibers don't ignite or melt when exposed to flames or high heat. Nomex is also used in electric insulation and for machine parts exposed to high heat.

Burning plastics often produce toxic gases. Hydrogen cyanide is formed in large quantities when polyacrylonitrile and other nitrogen-containing polymers burn. Lethal amounts of cyanide found in the bodies of victims of plane crashes have been traced to burned plastics. Firefighters often refuse to enter burning buildings without gas masks for fear of being overcome by fumes from burning plastics. Smoldering fires also produce lethal quantities of carbon monoxide. To make plastics safer, green chemists are making new kinds of polymers that don't burn or that don't generate toxic chemicals when burned.

GREEN CHEMISTRY

Principles 1, 7, 10

Jennifer L. Young, *ACS Green Chemistry Institute®*

Greener Polymers

Many products that we use today are made of plastic. Therefore, it is important to apply the twelve principles of green chemistry to plastics and polymers. You might ask, how can plastics be made sustainably using green chemistry? Two areas where greener processes have had large impacts are the recycling and biodegradation of plastics (Section 10.7, Principle 10) and the production of plastics from renewable resources (Principle 7).

You probably use polyethylene bags (Section 10.2), polystyrene cups (Section 10.3), polyethylene terephthalate (PET) soft drink bottles (Section 10.5), nylon clothing and carpeting (Section 10.5), and styrene–butadiene rubber tires (Section 10.4). These polymers and most others on the market are made from nonrenewable resources and do not biodegrade. After use, the polymers often are discarded into the environment or buried in landfills.

There are other, greener options for plastic materials. Many polymers that you use every day are recyclable. Recycling decreases the amount of plastic that ends up in landfills and also reduces the amount of new plastic that must be made from fossil fuels.

To make recycling easier, most plastic objects are stamped with a triangular recycle symbol and a number code. These numbers, called *resin identification codes*, identify types of plastics as follows: #1, polyethylene terephthalate (PET or PETE); #2, high-density polyethylene (HDPE); #3, polyvinyl chloride (PVC or V); #4, low-density polyethylene (LDPE); #5, polypropylene (PP); #6, polystyrene (PS); and #7, all other kinds of polymers.

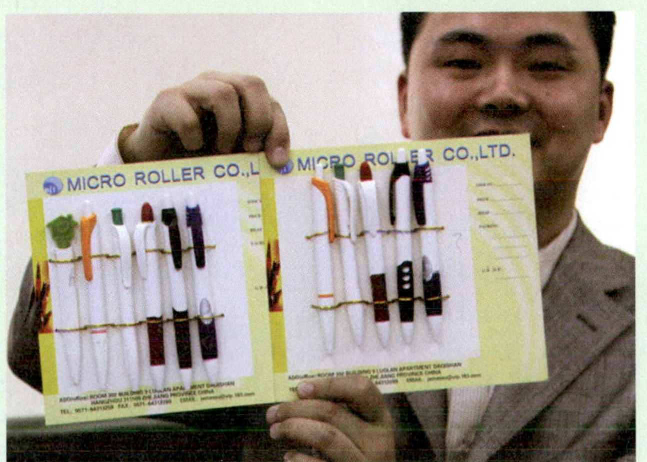

▲ Although they may appear to be like any other pens at first glance, these pens from Micro Roller are made from corn and straw. The pens are over 70% degradable within a relatively short period of time.

PET (#1) and HDPE (#2) are the most commonly recycled plastics. Other types may also be accepted for recycling in some locales. In the recycling process, the plastics are separated by resin identification code. The plastic is then chopped up, softened by raising the temperature above the polymer's glass transition temperature (Section 10.6), molded into a new shape, and cooled back to room temperature to harden. Because the process uses heat to recycle the polymer, only thermoplastics (not thermosetting polymers; Section 10.2) can be recycled in this way.

Typically, recycled plastic is used to make different objects than the things recycled because the polymer's properties are changed. For example, park benches and plastic outdoor decking material are made from recycled plastic bottles. Just because a polymer falls into the "other" category (#7) does not mean that the polymer cannot be recycled. For instance, nylon-based carpet is commonly recycled.

Some polymers, including PET, can be depolymerized. Chemical reactions can reverse the polymerization and break the polymer into the original monomer units. The monomer can then be polymerized again to make polymer that is as pure as the original material. Since the new polymer has the same properties as the original polymer, it can be used to make the same objects. Some companies that make these types of plastics will accept their plastic products for recycling, then depolymerize and reuse the monomers.

Some types of plastics can be degraded into carbon dioxide and water. Over some period of time, these polymers will biodegrade under the right conditions of temperature and moisture or in the presence of microorganisms. This means biodegradable plastics generally do not degrade readily when thrown at the side of the road or when dumped into trash that ends up in a landfill. Official bodies apply different definitions for biodegradability. For instance, the USA ASTM D6400 Standard requires 60% conversion into carbon dioxide in 180 days, and the European Standard EN13432 requires 90% conversion over the same span of time.

New kinds of polymers are being made from renewable resources, such as corn, soy, grass, and other types of biomass. One example is polylactic acid (PLA), made from corn. PLA is used to make plastic bottles, salad containers, coffee mugs, and even fibers for clothing. PLA can be depolymerized to monomers and can also degrade by composting. Cargill Dow LLC (now NatureWorks LLC) received a Presidential Green Chemistry Challenge Award for developing PLA from renewable resources. Polyhydroxyalkanoates (PHAs) are made from plant sugars and oils, are biodegradable, and can even be made using bacteria. Metabolix, Inc. was awarded a Presidential Green Chemistry Challenge Award for producing PHAs with microorganisms. For many plastics, the most sustainable approach is using renewable resources—especially nonfood crops—as the source of the monomer.

Plasticizers and Pollution

Chemicals used in plastics manufacture can also present problems. Plasticizers are an important example. Some plastics, particularly vinyl polymers, are hard and brittle and thus difficult to process. A **plasticizer** can make such a plastic more flexible and less brittle by lowering its glass transition temperature. Unplasticized PVC is rigid and is used for water pipes. Thin sheets of pure PVC crack and break easily, but plasticizers make them soft and pliable. Plastic raincoats, garden hoses, and seat covers for automobiles can be made from plasticized PVC. Plasticizers are liquids of low volatility, but they are generally lost by diffusion and evaporation as a plastic article ages. The plastic becomes brittle and then cracks and breaks.

Once used widely as plasticizers but now banned, polychlorinated biphenyls (PCBs) are derived from biphenyl ($C_{12}H_{10}$), a hydrocarbon that has two benzene rings joined at a corner. In PCBs, some of the hydrogen atoms of biphenyl are replaced with chlorine atoms (Figure 10.7). Note that PCBs are structurally similar to the insecticide DDT.

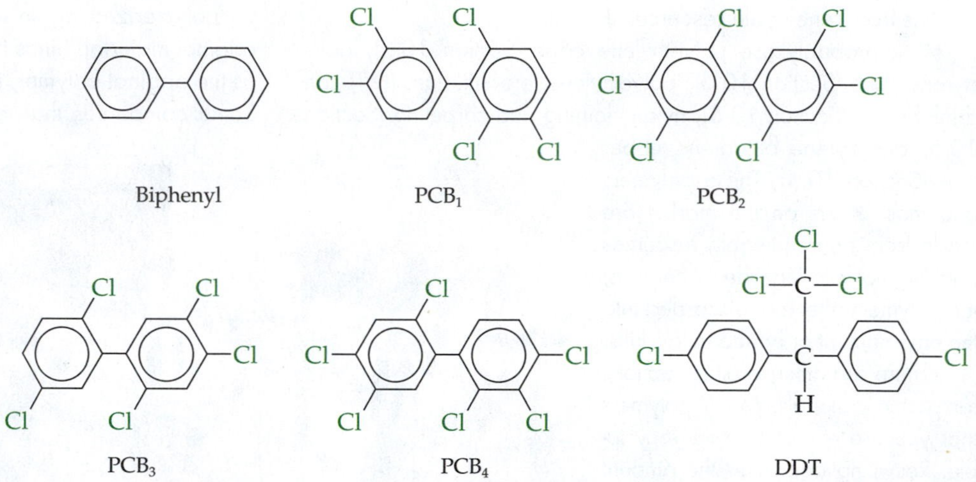

▶ **Figure 10.7** Biphenyl and some of the PCBs derived from it (only a few of the hundreds of possible PCBs). DDT is also shown for comparison.

Biphenyl

PCB_1

PCB_2

PCB_3

PCB_4

DDT

PCBs were also widely used as insulating materials in electric transformers because their stability and low polarity gave them high electrical resistance and the ability to absorb heat. The same properties that made PCBs so desirable as industrial chemicals cause them to be an environmental hazard. They degrade slowly in nature, and their solubility in nonpolar media—animal fat as well as vinyl plastics—leads to their becoming concentrated in the food chain, PCB residues have been found in fish, birds, water, and sediments. The physiological effect of PCBs is similar to that of DDT. Monsanto Corporation, the only company in the United States that produced PCBs, discontinued production in 1977, but the compounds still remain in the environment.

Today, the most widely used plasticizers for vinyl plastics are phthalate esters, a group of diesters derived from phthalic acid (1,2-benzenedicarboxylic acid). Phthalate plasticizers (Figure 10.8) have low acute toxicity and, although some studies have suggested possible harm to young children, the FDA has recognized these plasticizers as being generally safe. They pose little threat to the environment because they degrade fairly rapidly. Another approach of green chemists is to make plastics that have the right amount of flexibility and thus do not require any plasticizers when they are manufactured.

Plastics and the Future

Widely used today, synthetic polymers are the materials of the future. New kinds and new uses will be discovered. We already have polymers that conduct electricity, amazing adhesives, and synthetic materials that are stronger than steel but much lighter in weight. Plastics present problems, but they have become such an important part of our daily lives that we would find it difficult to live without them.

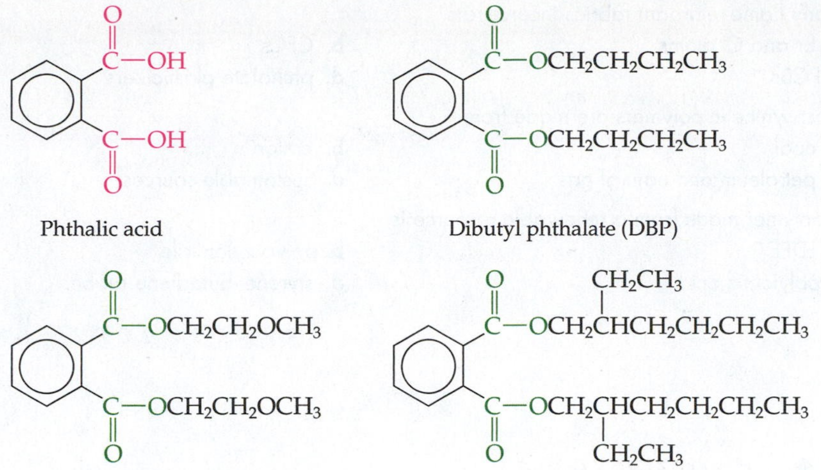

Phthalic acid

Dibutyl phthalate (DBP)

Dimethoxyethyl phthalate (DMEP)

Dioctyl phthalate (DOP)

◀ **Figure 10.8** Phthalic acid and some esters derived from it. Dioctyl phthalate is also called di-2-ethylhexyl phthalate.

In medicine, body replacement parts made from polymers have become common. There are about 200,000 total hip replacements in the United States each year. Artificial lungs and artificial hearts are available, but they are enormously expensive and used for the most part only during recovery from injury or illness or until donor organs are available for transplantation. The cost of these replacements is likely to drop, and their efficacy will probably improve, in the future.

PVC water pipes, siding, and window frames, plastic foam insulation, and polymeric surface coatings are used in home construction today. Some homes also contain lumber and wall panels of artificial wood, made from recycled plastics.

Synthetic polymers are used extensively in airplane interiors, and the bodies and wings of some planes are made of lightweight composite materials. Many automobiles have bodies made from plastic composites. Electrically conducting polymers will aid in making lightweight batteries for electric automobiles. The electronics industry will use increasing amounts of electrically conducting thermoplastics in miniaturized circuits.

But here is something to think about: Most synthetic polymers are made from petroleum or natural gas. Both of these natural resources are nonrenewable, and our supplies are limited. We are likely to run out of petroleum during this century. You might suppose that we would be actively conserving this valuable resource, but unfortunately this is not the case. We are taking petroleum out of the ground at a rapid rate, converting most of it to gasoline and other fuels, and then simply burning it. There are other sources of energy, but is there anything that can replace petroleum as the raw material for making plastics? Yes! Several new types of plastics, such as polylactic acid and polyhydroxybutyrates, are made from renewable resources such as corn, soybeans, and sugarcane. Polymers are an active area of green chemistry research.

Self-Assessment Questions

1. In general, the best way to dispose of plastics is
- **a.** composting **b.** incineration
- **c.** in landfills **d.** recycling

2. Many plastics are fire hazards because they burn and produce
- **a.** CFCs **b.** nitrogen oxides
- **c.** solid wastes **d.** toxic gases

3. A plasticizer acts by
- **a.** initiating addition polymerization **b.** lowering the glass transition temperature
- **c.** participating in condensation polymerization **d.** wetting polymer powders

4. Many flame-retardant fabrics incorporate
   a. Br and Cl atoms
   b. CFCs
   c. PCBs
   d. phthalate plasticizers
5. Most synthetic polymers are made from
   a. coal
   b. cotton
   c. petroleum and natural gas
   d. sustainable sources
6. A polymer made from a renewable resource is
   a. LDPE
   b. polyacrylonitrile
   c. polylactic acid
   d. styrene–butadiene rubber

Answers: 1, d; 2, d; 3, b; 4, a; 5, c; 6, c

CRITICAL THINKING  EXERCISES

Apply knowledge that you have gained in this chapter and one or more of the FLaReS principles (Chapter 1) to evaluate the following statements or claims.

10.1 An environmental activist states that all synthetic plastics should be banned and replaced by those derived from natural materials.

10.2 A news report states that incinerators that burn plastics are a major source of chlorine-containing toxic compounds called *dioxins* (Chapter 20).

10.3 Vinyl chloride is a carcinogen. Some people warn that children will get cancer from playing with toys made of PVC.

10.4 The Plastics Division of the American Chemistry Council says that, in comparison to paper bags, "plastic bags are . . . an environmentally responsible choice."

SUMMARY

Section 10.1—A **polymer** is a giant molecule made from smaller molecules. The small molecules that are the building blocks used to make polymers are called **monomers**. There are many natural polymers, including starch, cellulose, nucleic acids, and proteins.

Celluloid was the first semisynthetic polymer, made from natural cellulose treated with nitric acid.

Section 10.2—The simplest, least expensive, and highest-volume synthetic polymer is polyethylene, made from the monomer ethylene. High-density polyethylene molecules can pack closely together to yield a rigid, strong structure. Low-density polyethylene molecules have many side chains, resulting in more flexible plastics. Linear low-density polyethylene is a **copolymer**, formed from two (or more) different monomers.

Polyethylene is one of many **thermoplastic polymers** that can be softened and reshaped with heat and pressure. *Thermosetting* polymers decompose, rather than soften, when heated. They cannot be reshaped.

Section 10.3—In **addition polymerization**, the monomer molecules add to one another; the polymer contains all the atoms of the monomers. Addition polymers, such as polyethylene, polypropylene, polystyrene, and PVC, are made from monomers containing carbon-to-carbon double bonds. Polypropylene is tough and resists moisture, oils, and solvents. Polystyrene is used mainly to make Styrofoam. PVC or polyvinyl chloride is used for plumbing, artificial leather, and flexible tubing. PTFE, or Teflon, is chemically inert and nonflammable; it is widely used in nonstick coatings. Thermoplastic polymers can be molded in many different ways.

Section 10.4—Natural rubber is an **elastomer**, a material that returns to its original shape after being stretched. The monomer of natural rubber, isoprene, can be made artificially and polymerized. Polyisoprene is soft and tacky when hot. In a process called **vulcanization**, polyisoprene is reacted with sulfur. The sulfur atoms cross-link the hydrocarbon chains, making the rubber harder, stronger, and more elastic.

Other elastomers that are similar in structure to polyisoprene include polybutadiene, polychloroprene, and styrene–butadiene rubber (SBR). All of these have molecules that can coil and uncoil. Elastomers are used as binders in paints.

Section 10.5—In **condensation polymerization**, parts of the monomer molecules are not incorporated in the product. Small molecules such as water are formed as by-products. Nylon is a condensation polymer that is a **polyamide**, with amide [—(CO)NH—] linkages joining the monomers.

A **polyester** is a condensation polymer made from monomers with alcohol and carboxylic acid functional groups. Polyethylene terephthalate (PET) is the most common polyester.

Various **thermosetting resins** can be prepared by condensing formaldehyde with urea, melamine, or phenol. Other condensation polymers include polycarbonates (bulletproof windows), polyurethanes (foam rubber), and epoxies (coatings and adhesives). Combining a polymer with high-strength fibers gives a composite material that exploits the best properties of both materials. **Silicones**, which have chains consisting of silicon and oxygen atoms instead of carbon atoms, have varied structures and many uses.

Section 10.6—Properties of polymers differ greatly from those of their monomers. A polymer's strength arises partly because the molecules entangle with one another and partly because the large molecules have strong dispersion forces. Polymers may be crystalline or amorphous. Above the **glass transition temperature (T_g)** a polymer is rubbery and tough; below it, the polymer is brittle. Strong synthetic fibers are made from crystalline polymers because their long molecules align neatly with one another.

Section 10.7—The durability of plastics means that they make up a large fraction of the content of landfills. Proper incineration is one way of disposing of discarded plastics, but it can produce toxic gases. Some polymers are engineered to be degradable. Recycling of plastics requires that they be collected and sorted according to the code numbers. Recycled plastics are being used more and more. Flame-retardant fabrics for clothing are made of polymers that often incorporate chlorine or bromine atoms.

The chemicals used in manufacturing plastics, especially plasticizers, can present problems. A **plasticizer** makes a polymer more flexible. Polychlorinated biphenyls (PCBs) were once used as plasticizers but are now banned. Phthalate esters are the most widely used plasticizers today.

Synthetic polymers will be used even more in the future. However, most synthetic polymers come from petroleum, a limited and nonrenewable resource. This is another important reason for recycling plastics.

Green chemistry Many products we use today are made of plastic. Green chemistry applies to the recycling and biodegradation of plastics and to the production of plastics from renewable resources.

Learning Objectives

› Define *polymer* and *monomer*.	Problems 3, 5, 7
› List several natural polymers including a chemically modified one.	Problems 9, 43, 55
› Describe the structure and properties of the two main types of polyethylene.	Problems 13, 14
› Use the terms *thermoplastic* and *thermosetting* to explain how polymer structure determines properties.	Problem 8
› Identify the monomer(s) of an addition polymer, and write the structural formula for a polymer from its monomer structure(s).	Problems 15–20 , 21, 37–39, 41–45, 52, 53
› Define *cross-linking*, and explain how it changes the properties of a polymer.	Problem 22
› Differentiate between addition and condensation polymerization.	Problems 3, 35, 36
› Write the structures of the monomers that form polyesters and polyamides.	Problem 46
› Understand the concept of the glass transition temperature.	Problems 33, 40
› Explain how crystallinity affects the physical properties of polymers.	Problems 13, 14, 33, 34
› Describe the environmental problems associated with plastics and plasticizers.	Problems 11, 12
› Name two types of sustainable, non-petroleum-derived polymers and give their sources.	Problems 54, 55, 57
› Describe plastic recycling, biodegradation, and production from renewable resources.	Problems 55–58

REVIEW QUESTIONS

1. How does the structure of PVC differ from that of polyethylene? List several uses of PVC.
2. Define the following terms.
   a. macromolecule b. elastomer
   c. copolymer d. plasticizer
3. What is addition polymerization? What structural feature usually characterizes molecules used as monomers in addition polymerization?
4. What is Teflon? What special property does it have? What are some of its uses?
5. From what monomer are disposable foamed plastic coffee cups made?
6. What plastic is used to make **(a)** gallon milk jugs and **(b)** 2-L soft drink bottles?
7. What is Bakelite? From what monomers is it made?
8. What is a thermosetting polymer? Give an example.
9. Which type of fibers, natural or synthetic, is used most in the United States? Why?
10. What are PCBs? Why are they no longer used as plasticizers?
11. What steps must be taken to recycle plastics?
12. What problems arise when plastics are **(a)** discarded into the environment, **(b)** disposed of in landfills, and **(c)** disposed of by incineration?

PROBLEMS

Polyethylene

13. Describe the structure of low-density polyethylene (LDPE). How does this structure explain the properties of this polymer?

14. Describe the structure of high-density polyethylene (HDPE). How does this structure explain the properties of this polymer?

Addition Polymerization

15. Write the structure of the monomer from which each of the following polymers is made.
    a. polyethylene
    b. polyacrylonitrile

16. Write the structure of the monomer from which each of the following polymers is made.
    a. polypropylene
    b. polytetrafluoroethylene

17. Write the structure of a chain segment that is at least eight carbon atoms long for the polymer made from each of the following.
    a. polyvinyl chloride
    b. vinylidene fluoride ($H_2C{=}CF_2$)

18. Write the structure of a chain segment that is at least four repeat units long for the polymer formed from each of the following monomers.
    a. styrene
    b. methyl methacrylate

$$\begin{array}{c} CH_3 \\ | \\ CH_2{=}CCOOCH_3 \end{array}$$

19. Write the structure of the polymer made from each of the following. Show at least four repeat units.
    a. 1-pentene ($CH_2{=}CHCH_2CH_2CH_3$)
    b. methyl cyanoacrylate

$$\begin{array}{c} C{\equiv}N \\ | \\ CH_2{=}CCOOCH_3 \end{array}$$

20. Write the structure of the polymer made from each of the following. Show at least four repeat units.
    a. vinyl acetate [$H_2C{=}CH{-}O(C{=}O)CH_3$]
    b. methyl acrylate [$H_2C{=}CH{-}(C{=}O)OCH_3$]

Rubber and Other Elastomers

21. Draw the structure of the monomer from which polybutadiene is made.

22. Describe the process of vulcanization. How does vulcanization change the properties of rubber?

23. Explain why rubber is elastic, while many other polymers are rigid.

24. How does polybutadiene differ from natural rubber in properties? In structure?

25. How is SBR made? From what monomer(s) is it made?

26. Name three synthetic elastomers and the monomer(s) from which they are made.

Condensation Polymers

27. Nylon 88 is made from the monomers $H_2N(CH_2)_8NH_2$ and $HOOC(CH_2)_6COOH$. Draw the structure of nylon 88, showing at least two repeat units from each monomer.

28. Kodel is a polyester fiber. The monomers used to make it are terephthalic acid (page 280) and 1,4-cyclohexanedimethanol (shown below). Write a condensed structural formula for the repeat unit of Kodel molecule.

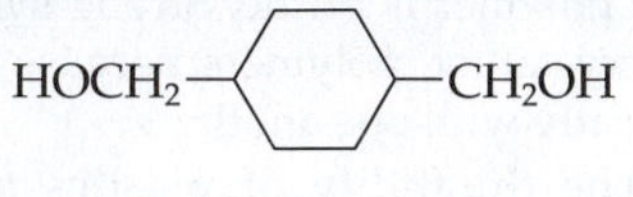

$HOCH_2$—(cyclohexane ring)—CH_2OH

1,4-Cyclohexanedimethanol

29. Draw the structure of a polymer made from glycolic acid (hydroxyacetic acid, $HOCH_2COOH$). Show at least four repeat units. (*Hint:* Compare with nylon 6 in Section 10.5.)

30. Kevlar, a polyamide used to make bulletproof vests, is made from terephthalic acid (page 280) and *para*-phenylenediamine (shown below). Write a condensed structural formula for the repeat unit of the Kevlar molecule.

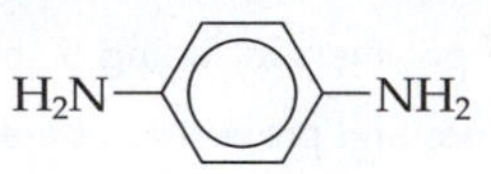

H_2N—(benzene ring)—NH_2

para-Phenylenediamine

Properties of Polymers

31. What three factors give polymers properties that are different from those of materials made up of small molecules?

32. What does the word *plastic* mean **(a)** in everyday life and **(b)** in chemistry?

33. What is the glass transition temperature (T_g) of a polymer? For what uses do we want polymers with a low T_g? With a high T_g?

34. How do plasticizers make polymers less brittle?

Additional Problems

35. In the following equation, identify the parts labeled a, b, and c as monomer, polymer, and repeat unit. What type of polymerization (addition or condensation) is represented?

$$n\,\overbrace{CH_2{=}CHF}^{a} \longrightarrow$$

$$\underbrace{\sim CH_2{-}CHF{-}\overbrace{CH_2{-}CHF}^{b}{-}CH_2{-}CHF{-}CH_2{-}CHF\sim}_{c}$$

36. Is nylon 88 (Problem 27) an addition polymer or a condensation polymer? Explain.

37. One type of Saran has the structure shown below. Write the structures of the two monomers from which it is made.

$$\sim CH_2CCl_2{-}CH_2CHCl{-}CH_2CCl_2{-}CH_2CHCl\sim$$

38. From what monomers could the following copolymer, called poly(styrene-co-acrylonitrile) (SAN), be made?

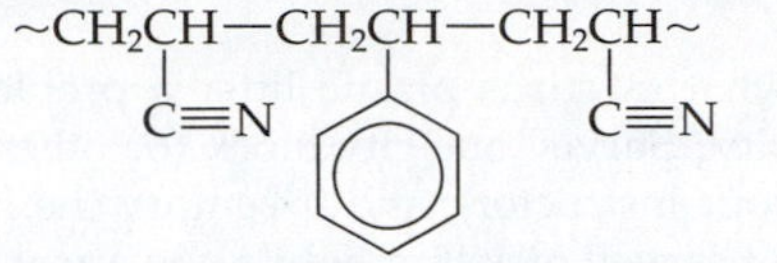

$$\sim CH_2CH{-}CH_2CH{-}CH_2CH\sim$$
(with $C{\equiv}N$ on the first and third CH, and a benzene ring on the middle CH)

39. Cyanoacrylates, such as those made from methyl cyanoacrylate (Problem 19b), are used in instant-setting "superglues." However, poly(methyl cyanoacrylate) can irritate tissues. Cyanoacrylates with longer alkyl ester groups are less harsh and can be used in surgery in place of sutures. A good example is poly(octyl cyanoacrylate). Write a polymerization reaction for the formation of poly(octyl cyanoacrylate) from octyl cyanoacrylate, using a condensed structural formula to show the repeat unit of the polymer.

40. Polyethylene terephthalate has a high T_g. How can its T_g be lowered so that a manufacturer can permanently crease a pair of polyethylene terephthalate slacks?

41. Isobutylene $[CH_2{=}C(CH_3)_2]$ polymerizes to form polyisobutylene, a sticky polymer used as an adhesive. Draw the structure of polyisobutylene. Show at least four repeat units.

42. Copolymerization of isoprene and isobutylene (Problem 41) forms butyl rubber. Write the structure of butyl rubber. Show at least three isobutylene repeat units and one isoprene repeat unit.

43. The bacteria *Alcaligenes eutrophus* produce a polymer called polyhydroxybutyrate whose structure is shown below. Write the structure of the hydroxy acid from which this polymer is made.

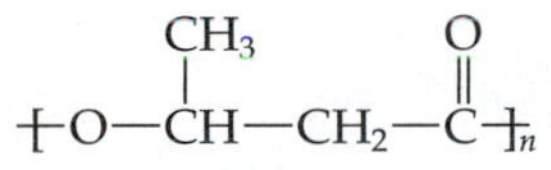

$$\left[O{-}\underset{CH_3}{\underset{|}{CH}}{-}CH_2{-}\overset{O}{\overset{\|}{C}} \right]_n$$

44. DSM Engineering Plastics makes two specialty polymers: Stanyl® nylon 46 and polytetramethylene terephthalamide (PA_4T). (A methylene group is CH_2; tetramethylene consists of four methylene groups: $CH_2CH_2CH_2CH_2$.) Both polymers are made using 1,4-diaminobutane as the diamine. **(a)** What diacid is used for each? Write a condensed structural formula showing the repeat unit of **(b)** Stanyl® nylon 46 and **(c)** PA_4T.

45. A student writes the formula for polypropylene as shown below. Identify the error(s) in the formula.

$$\left[CH_2{-}CH{-}CH_3 \right]_n$$

46. Based on the condensed structural formula of the repeat unit of poly(ethylene naphthalate) (PEN) shown below, **(a)** write the structure(s) of the monomer(s) and **(b)** state whether the polymer is a polyester or a polyamide.

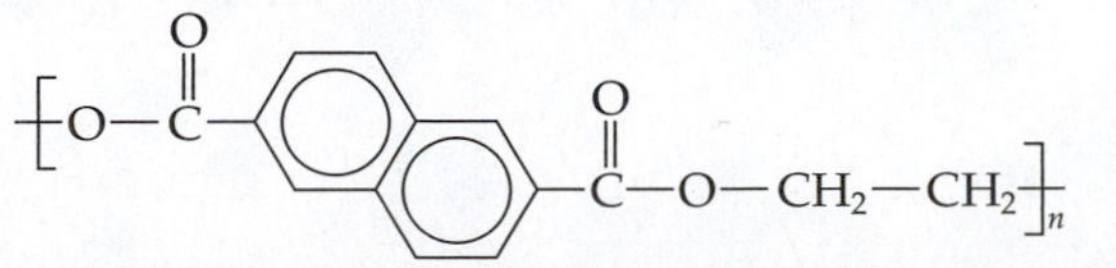

$$\left[O{-}\overset{O}{\overset{\|}{C}}{-}C_{10}H_6{-}\overset{O}{\overset{\|}{C}}{-}O{-}CH_2{-}CH_2 \right]_n$$
(the $C_{10}H_6$ unit is drawn as a naphthalene ring system)

47. A rubber ball dropped from 100 cm will bounce back up to about 60 cm. Balls made from polybutadiene, called SuperBalls, bounce back up to about 85 cm. Golf balls, made from cross-linked polybutadiene, bounce back up to 89 cm. What type of polymer are all three balls made of? Which kind of ball exhibits the property of this type of polymer to the greatest degree?

48. Draw a structure of a likely product if 1,3-propanediol ($HOCH_2CH_2CH_2OH$) is substituted for ethylene glycol in the reaction with terephthalic acid (page 280).

49. A student is asked to synthesize a polyester from terephthalic acid (page 280) and 1,4-butanediol ($HOCH_2CH_2CH_2CH_2OH$). By mistake, the student uses 1-butanol rather than 1,4-butanediol. What is the likely result of this substitution?

50. A student is asked to synthesize a polyester from terephthalic acid and 1,4-butanediol ($HOCH_2CH_2CH_2CH_2OH$). By mistake, the student uses isophthalic acid (shown below) rather than terephthalic acid (page 280). What is the likely result of this substitution?

(benzene ring with COOH groups in the 1 and 3 positions)

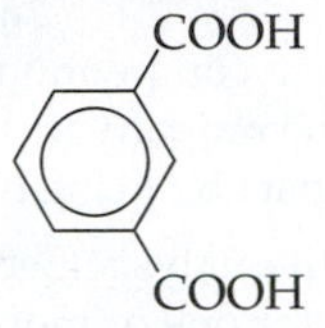

51. Draw the structure of the silicone polymer formed from the compound shown below, showing four repeating units.

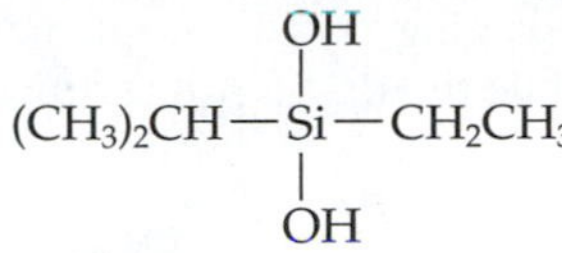

$$(CH_3)_2CH{-}\underset{OH}{\underset{|}{\overset{OH}{\overset{|}{Si}}}}{-}CH_2CH_3$$

52. The two alkenes shown below are different compounds, but when each undergoes addition polymerization, the same polymer is formed. Explain.

$$CH_3{-}\underset{Cl}{\underset{|}{C}}{=}\underset{Br}{\underset{|}{C}}{-}CH_2CH_3 \qquad CH_3{-}\underset{Cl}{\underset{|}{C}}{=}\underset{CH_2CH_3}{\underset{|}{C}}{-}Br$$

53. The structures of epoxies contain heterocyclic rings, similar to those shown in Example 9.12. Some heterocyclic rings are polymerized by breaking one of the bonds between a carbon atom and the oxygen, nitrogen, or sulfur atom and then undergoing an addition reaction. Draw the structures of the polymers that could result from polymerization of the molecules in parts (a) and (b) of Example 9.12. Show four repeat units for each polymer.

54. Each *amino acid* shown in Table 15.3 (page 417) has an amino group ($—NH_3^+$) and a carboxylic acid group ($—COO^-$). (In each case, a proton has been donated from the carboxylic group to the amino group.) Proteins are polymers of amino acids. Draw the structure of the protein formed by polymerization of glycine, showing four repeat units.

55. Which polymer can be made from renewable resources such as corn?

a. polystyrene (PS)
b. polylactic acid (PLA)
c. polyethylene terephthalate (PET)
d. polyvinyl chloride (PVC)

56. Will a biodegradable polymer degrade in a landfill?

57. Which two polymers are most commonly recycled?

a. polystyrene (PS) and polyvinyl chloride (PVC)
b. low-density polyethylene (LDPE) and polypropylene (PP)
c. polyethylene terephthalate (PET) and high-density polyethylene (HDPE)
d. polylactic acid (PLA) and polyhydroxyalkanoate (PHA)

58. Which type of polymer can be recycled using heat?

COLLABORATIVE GROUP PROJECTS

Prepare a PowerPoint, poster, or other presentation (as directed by your instructor) to share with the class.

1. Prepare a brief report on possible sources of plastics when Earth's supplies of coal and petroleum become scarce.
2. Prepare a brief report on biobased polymers such as bioHDPE, nylon 11 (polyundecylamide), biobased PET, and biobased polytrimethylene terephthalate (PTT). Identify the natural source from which each is derived, and describe intermediate steps from source to final product.
3. Evaluate fully the competition between Pepsi and Coca-Cola as to which company is doing more to reduce its environmental impact by using biobased plastic bottles.
4. Do a risk–benefit analysis (Section 1.4) of the use of synthetic polymers for one or more of the following.
   a. grocery bags **b.** building materials
   c. clothing **d.** carpets
   e. food packaging **f.** picnic coolers
   g. automobile tires **h.** artificial hip sockets
5. To what extent is plastic litter a problem in your community? Survey one city block (or other area as directed by your instructor), and inventory the litter found. (You might as well pick it up while you are at it.) What proportion of the litter is plastics? What proportion of it is fast-food containers? To what extent are plastics recycled in your community? What factors limit further recycling?
6. Prepare a brief report on one of the following polymers. List sources and commercial uses.
   a. polybutadiene **b.** ethylene–propylene rubber
   c. polyurethanes **d.** epoxy resins
7. Do some research on Kevlar, which is used in body armor. Report on its other uses, and explain why it is so strong. Describe the Kevlar Survivors' Club, jointly sponsored by the International Chiefs of Police and DuPont.
8. Compare the treatment of the topic of the environmental impact of plastics and other polymers at several Web sites, such as those of the American Plastics Council, an industry group, and an environmental group such as Greenpeace or the Sierra Club.

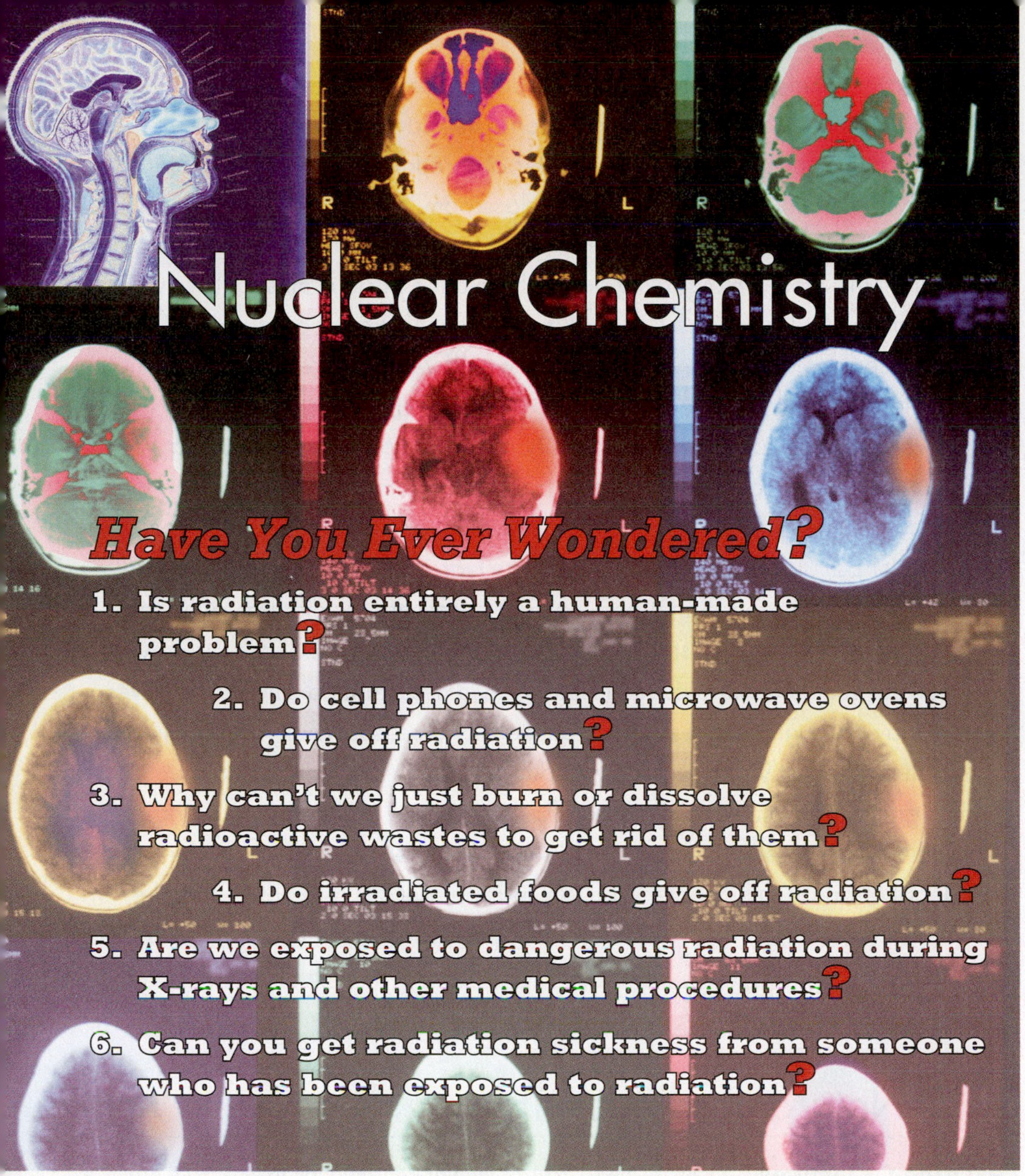

Nuclear Chemistry

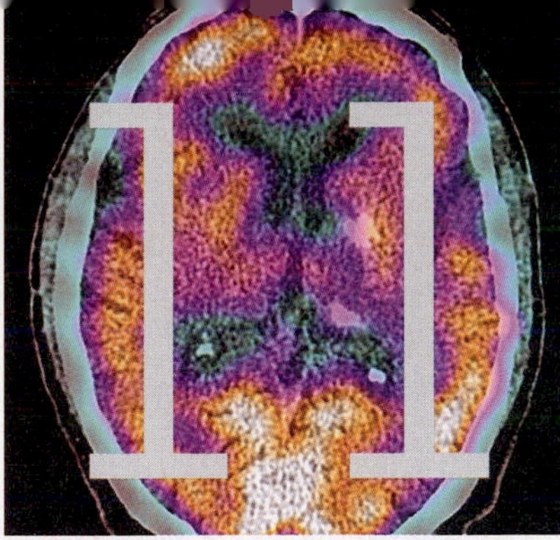

Have You Ever Wondered?

1. Is radiation entirely a human-made problem?
2. Do cell phones and microwave ovens give off radiation?
3. Why can't we just burn or dissolve radioactive wastes to get rid of them?
4. Do irradiated foods give off radiation?
5. Are we exposed to dangerous radiation during X-rays and other medical procedures?
6. Can you get radiation sickness from someone who has been exposed to radiation?

Learning Objectives

- Identify the sources of the natural radiation to which we are exposed. (11.1)
- List the sources and dangers of ionizing radiation. (11.1)
- Balance nuclear equations. (11.2)
- Identify the products formed by various decay processes. (11.2)
- Solve simple half-life problems. (11.3)
- Use the concept of half-life to solve simple radioisotopic dating problems. (11.3)
- Write a nuclear equation for a transmutation, and identify the product element formed. (11.4)
- List some applications of radioisotopes. (11.5)
- Describe the nature of materials needed to block alpha, beta, and gamma radiation (11.6)
- Explain where nuclear energy comes from. (11.7)
- Describe the difference between fission and fusion. (11.7)
- Describe how uranium and plutonium bombs are made. (11.8)
- Identify the most hazardous fallout isotopes, and explain why they are particularly dangerous. (11.8)
- List some uses of nuclear energy. (11.9)
- Identify green chemistry principles that can help solve existing problems in nuclear chemistry.
- Explain how molecules used in nuclear waste processing can be designed to be safer, and give examples of such molecules.

The heart of matter

Many people associate the term *nuclear energy* with fearsome images of a mighty force: giant mushroom clouds from nuclear explosions that devastated cities, and nuclear power plant accidents at Three Mile Island, Pennsylvania, in 1979, Chernobyl, Ukraine, in 1986, and Fukushima, Japan, in 2011 (discussed in Chapter 15). But some amazing stories can also be told about life-giving applications of nuclear energy.

The discussion of atomic structure in Chapter 3 focused mainly on the electrons, because the electrons are the particles that determine an element's chemistry. In this chapter, we take a closer look at that tiny speck in the center of the atom—the atomic nucleus.

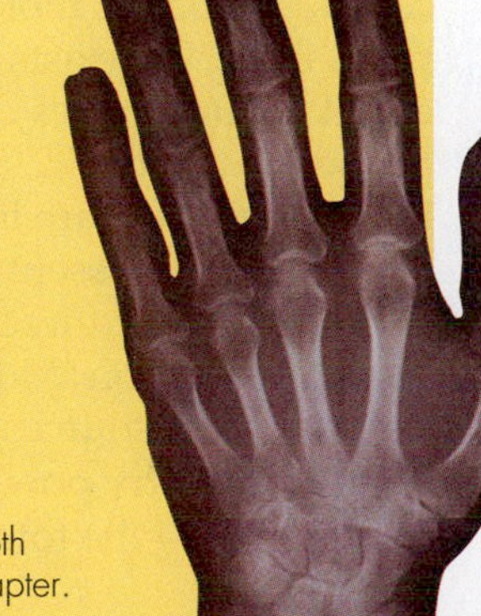

The photos show images from MRI (magnetic resonance imaging), PET (positron emission tomography), and x-rays for examining bones and internal organs. All of these diagnostic techniques use radiation or a radioactive isotope. With these techniques, we can examine tissues and diagnose diseases that were previously possible only by biopsy or exploratory surgery. The nuclear age has produced both serious problems and tremendous advantages, which will be examined in this chapter.

An atom is incomprehensibly small, but the infinitesimal size of the atomic nucleus is almost beyond our imagination. The diameter of an atom is roughly 100,000 times greater than the diameter of its nucleus. If an atom could be magnified until it was as large as your classroom, the nucleus would be about as big as the period at the end of this sentence. Yet this tiny nucleus contains almost all the atom's mass. How dense the atomic nucleus must be! A cubic centimeter of water weighs 1 g, and a cubic centimeter of gold about 19 g. A cubic centimeter of pure atomic nuclei would weigh more than 100 million metric tons!

Even more amazing than the density of the nucleus is the enormous amount of energy contained within it. Some atomic nuclei undergo reactions that can fuel the most powerful bombs ever built or provide electricity for millions of people. Our sun is one huge nuclear power plant, supplying the energy that warms our planet and the light necessary for plant growth. The twinkling light from every star we see in the night sky is produced by powerful nuclear reactions. Radioactive isotopes are used in medicine to save lives every day, through diagnosis and treatment of diseases. Many applications of nuclear chemistry in science and industry have improved the human condition significantly. Nuclear reactions allow us to date archaeological and geological finds, to assess the quality of industrial materials, and to be alerted to deadly fires. In this chapter, you will learn about the destructive and the healing power of that infinitesimally small and wonderfully dense heart of every atom—the nucleus.

11.1 Natural Radioactivity

Learning Objectives › Identify the sources of the natural radiation to which we are exposed. › List the sources and dangers of ionizing radiation.

Recall from Chapter 3 that most elements occur in nature in several isotopic forms, whose nuclei differ in their number of neutrons. Many of these nuclei are unstable and undergo **radioactive decay**. The nuclei that undergo such decay are called **radioisotopes**, and the process produces one or more types of radiation.

Background Radiation

Humans have always been exposed to radiation. Even as you read this sentence, you are being bombarded by *cosmic rays,* which originate from the sun and outer space. Other radiation reaches us from natural radioactive isotopes in air, water, soil, and rocks. We cannot escape radiation, because it is part of many natural processes, including those in our bodies. A naturally occurring radioactive isotope of potassium, ^{40}K, exists in all our cells and in many foods. The average person absorbs about 4000 particles of radiation each second from ^{40}K and another 1200 particles per second from ^{14}C. (This may sound like a lot, but recall how small atoms are and how many there are in even a tiny sample of matter.)

This ever-present natural radiation is called **background radiation**. Figure 11.1 shows that over three-fourths of the average radiation exposure comes from background radiation. Most of the remainder comes from medical irradiation such as X-rays. Other sources, such as fallout from testing of nuclear bombs, releases from nuclear industry power plants, and occupational exposure, account for only a minute fraction of the total average exposure.

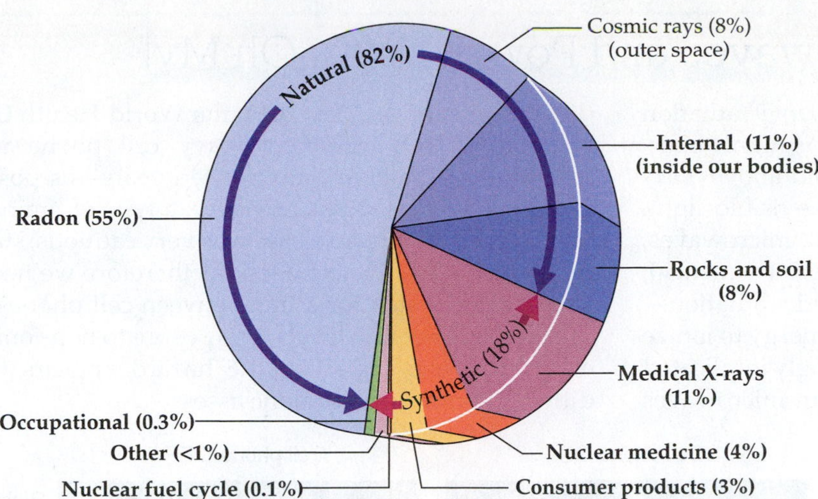

◀ **Figure 11.1** Most of the radiation to which we are exposed comes from natural sources (blue shades). About 18% of this radiation comes from human activities (other colors).

Q: *What natural source of ionizing radiation contributes most to our exposure? What source provides the largest proportion of our exposure due to human activities?*

Harmful effects arise from the interaction of radiation with living tissue. Radiation with enough energy to knock electrons from atoms and molecules, converting them into ions (electrically charged atoms or groups of atoms), is called **ionizing radiation**. Nuclear radiation and X-rays are examples. Because radiation is invisible and because it has such great potential for harm, we are very much concerned with our exposure to it. However, it is worth noting that the total amount of background radiation the average person is exposed to is less than 0.5% of the amount that can cause symptoms of radiation sickness.

1. Is radiation entirely a human-made problem?

Figure 11.1 shows that the majority of the ionizing radiation to which we are exposed is from natural sources.

Radiation Damage to Cells

Radiation-caused chemical changes in living cells can be highly disruptive. Ionizing radiation can devastate living cells by interfering with their normal chemical processes. Molecules can be splintered into reactive fragments called *free radicals* (Section 4.10), which can disrupt vital cellular processes. White blood cells, the body's first line of defense against bacterial infection, are particularly vulnerable. High levels of radiation also affect bone marrow, causing a drop in the production of red blood cells, which results in anemia. Radiation has also been shown to induce leukemia, a disease of the blood-forming organs.

Ionizing radiation also can cause changes in the molecules of heredity (DNA) in reproductive cells. Such changes can show up as mutations in the offspring of exposed parents. Little is known of the effects of such exposure on humans. However, many of the mutations that occurred during the evolution of present species may have been caused by background radiation.

Because of these potentially devastating effects on living things, knowledge of radiation, radioactive decay, and nuclear chemistry in general is crucial. Next, we will see how to write balanced nuclear equations and how to identify the various types of radiation that are emitted.

In 1993, a Ukrainian Academy of Science study group led by Vladimir Chernousenko investigated the aftereffects of the Chernobyl nuclear accident. Chernousenko claimed that 15,000 of those who helped clean up the accident site have died and that another 250,000 have become invalids. He also said that 200,000 children have experienced radiation-induced illnesses and that half of the children in Ukraine and Belarus have symptoms.

Self-Assessment Questions

1. What percentage of background radiation comes from natural sources?
   a. 5% **b.** 18% **c.** 45% **d.** 82%
2. The largest artificial source of background radiation is
   a. accidents at nuclear power plants **b.** consumer products
   c. fallout from tests of nuclear bombs **d.** medical X-rays
3. The largest source of natural background radiation is
   a. cosmic rays **b.** isotopes in the body
   c. radon **d.** isotopes in rocks and soil

Answers: 1, d; 2, d; 3, c

Cell Phones and Microwaves and Power Lines, Oh My!

There are many types of radiation. *Ionizing* radiation that comes from decaying atomic nuclei is highly energetic and can damage tissue, as discussed above. *Electromagnetic* radiation has many forms—visible light, radio waves, television broadcast waves, microwaves, ultraviolet light, military ULF (ultra-low-frequency), and others. A few types of electromagnetic radiation—X-rays and gamma rays—have enough energy to ionize tissue, and ultraviolet light has been strongly implicated in *melanoma* (skin cancer). But what about microwaves and radio waves, which don't have nearly as much energy? Although very large amounts of microwaves can cause burns (by heating), there is no conclusive evidence that low levels of microwaves pose significant threat to human health. A 2006 study involving almost half a million Danish citizens failed to show a relationship between cell phone use and cancer, though some scientists consider this study inconclusive. However, higher levels of radio frequencies over long periods of time *may* be a different matter. In May 2011, the World Health Organization (WHO) classified heavy cell phone use—30 minutes of talking daily for ten years—as possible posing an increased risk of *glioma*, a type of brain cancer. The WHO's press release was very cautious, stating that "there could be some risk … therefore we need to keep a close watch for a link between cell phones and cancer risk." For low levels of exposure to non-ionizing electromagnetic radiation, the hazard appears to be difficult to measure, let alone assess.

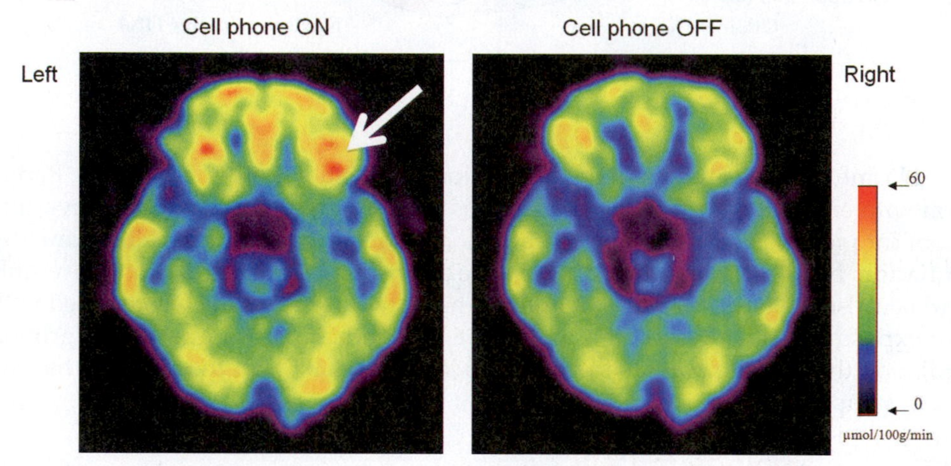

▲ A brain scan shows slight differences when a cell phone held to the ear is on (left) and off (right).

2. Do cell phones and microwave ovens give off radiation? Cell phones and microwave ovens *do* give off radiation, but it is not ionizing radiation and thus does not cause cell damage.

11.2 Nuclear Equations

Learning Objectives › Balance nuclear equations. › Identify the products formed by various decay processes.

Writing balanced equations for nuclear processes is relatively simple. Nuclear equations differ in two ways from the chemical equations discussed in Chapter 5. First, while chemical equations must have the same elements on both sides of the arrow, nuclear equations rarely do. Second, while we balance atoms in ordinary chemical equations, we balance the *nucleons* (protons and neutrons) in nuclear equations. What this really means is that we must balance the atomic numbers (number of protons) and nucleon numbers (number of nucleons) of the starting materials and products. For this reason, we must always specify the *isotope* of each element appearing in a nuclear equation. We use nuclear symbols (Section 3.5) when writing nuclear equations because they make the equations easier to balance.

In one example of a nuclear reaction, radon-222 atoms break down spontaneously in a process called **alpha decay**, giving off alpha (α) particles, as shown in Figure 11.2(a). Because alpha particles are identical to helium nuclei, this reaction can be summarized by the equation

Mass number of starting material = 222

Mass numbers of products = 4 + 218 = 222

$$^{222}_{86}\text{Rn} \longrightarrow {}^{4}_{2}\text{He} + {}^{218}_{84}\text{Po}$$

Atomic number of starting material = 86

Atomic numbers of products = 2 + 84 = 86

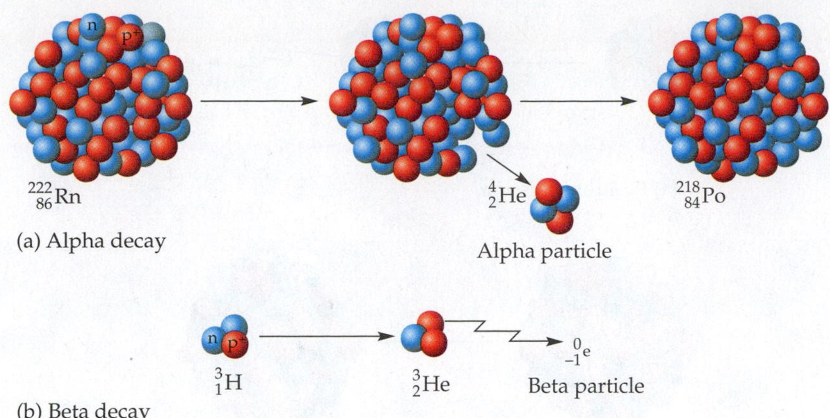

◀ **Figure 11.2** Nuclear emission of (a) an alpha particle and (b) a beta particle.

Q: *What changes occur in a nucleus when it emits an alpha particle? A beta particle?*

We use the symbol $^{4}_{2}He$ (rather than α) for the alpha particle because it allows us to check the balancing of mass and atomic numbers more readily. The atomic number, $Z = 84$, identifies the element produced as polonium (Po). In nuclear chemistry, the mass number, A, equates with the number of nucleons in the starting material. The number of nucleons in the starting material must equal the total number of the nucleons in the products. The same is true for the atomic numbers.

The heaviest isotope of hydrogen, hydrogen-3, often called *tritium*, decomposes by a process called **beta decay** (Figure 11.2b). Because a beta (β) particle is identical to an electron, this process can be written as

Mass number of starting material = 3

Mass numbers of products = 0 + 3 = 3

$$^{3}_{1}H \longrightarrow {}^{0}_{-1}e \quad 1 \quad {}^{3}_{2}He$$

Atomic number of starting material = 1

Atomic numbers of products = (−1) + 2 = 1

The atomic number, $Z = 2$, identifies the product isotope as helium.

Beta decay is a little more complicated than indicated by the preceding reaction. In beta decay, a neutron within the nucleus is converted into a proton (which remains in the nucleus) and an electron (which is ejected).

$$^{1}_{0}n \longrightarrow {}^{1}_{1}p + {}^{0}_{-1}e$$

With beta decay, the atomic number increases, but the number of nucleons remains the same.

A third kind of radiation may be emitted in a nuclear reaction: gamma (γ) rays. **Gamma decay** is different from alpha and beta decay in that gamma radiation has no charge and no mass. Neither the nucleon number nor the atomic number of the emitting atom is changed; the nucleus simply become less energetic. Table 11.1 compares the properties of alpha, beta, and gamma radiation. Note that the penetrating power of gamma rays is extremely high. While a few millimeters of aluminum will stop most β particles, several centimeters of lead are needed to stop γ rays.

Table 11.1 Common Types of Radiation in Nuclear Reactions

Radiation	Mass (u)	Charge	Identity	Velocity[a]	Penetrating Power
Alpha (α)	4	2+	He^{2+}	$0.1c$	Very low
Beta (β)	0.00055	1−	e^-	$<0.9c$	Moderate
Gamma (γ)	0	0	High-energy photon	c	Extremely high

[a] c is the speed of light.

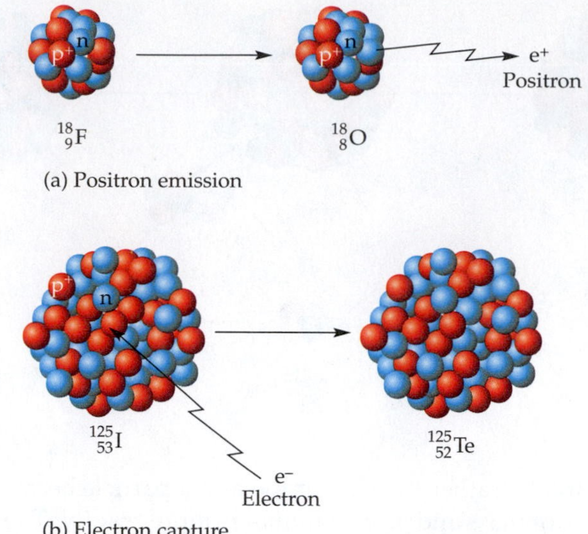

Figure 11.3 Nuclear change accompanying (a) positron emission and (b) electron capture.

Q: *What changes occur in a nucleus when it emits a positron? When it undergoes electron capture?*

Two other types of radioactive decay are *positron emission* and *electron capture*. These two processes have the same effect on the atomic nucleus, but they occur by different pathways. Both result in a decrease of one in atomic number with no change in nucleon number (Figure 11.3).

The **positron** (β^+) is a particle equal in mass but opposite in charge to the electron. It is represented as $^{0}_{+1}e$. Fluorine-18 decays by positron emission.

$$^{18}_{9}F \longrightarrow {}^{0}_{+1}e + {}^{18}_{8}O$$

We can envision positron emission as the change of a proton in the nucleus into a neutron and a positron.

$$^{1}_{1}p \longrightarrow {}^{1}_{0}n + {}^{0}_{+1}e$$

After the positron is emitted, the original nucleus has one less proton and one more neutron than it had before. The nucleon number of the product nucleus is the same, but its atomic number has been reduced by one. The emitted positron quickly encounters an electron (there are many electrons in all kinds of matter), and both particles are changing into energy—in this case, two gamma rays.

$$^{0}_{+1}e + {}^{0}_{-1}e \longrightarrow 2\,^{0}_{0}\gamma$$

Electron capture (EC) is a process in which a nucleus absorbs an electron from an inner electron shell, usually the first or second. When an electron from a higher shell drops to the level vacated by the captured electron, an X-ray is released. Once inside the nucleus, the captured electron combines with a proton to form a neutron.

$$^{1}_{1}p + {}^{0}_{-1}e \longrightarrow {}^{1}_{0}n$$

Iodine-125, used in medicine to diagnose pancreatic function and intestinal fat absorption, decays by electron capture.

$$^{125}_{53}I + {}^{0}_{-1}e \longrightarrow {}^{125}_{52}Te$$

Note that, unlike alpha, beta, gamma, or positron emission, electron capture has the electron as a reactant (on the left side) and not a product. Conversion of a proton to a neutron (by the absorbed electron) yields a nucleus with the atomic number lowered by 1 but unchanged in atomic mass. Emission of a positron and absorption of an electron have the same effect on an atomic nucleus (lowering the atomic number by 1), except that positron emission is accompanied by gamma radiation and electron capture by X-radiation. Positron-emitting isotopes and those that undergo electron capture have important medical applications (Section 11.5).

The five types of radioactive decay are summarized in Table 11.2.

Table 11.2 Radioactive Decay and Nuclear Change

Type of Decay	Decay Particle	Particle Mass (u)	Particle Charge	Change in Nucleon Number	Change in Atomic Number
Alpha decay	α	4	2+	Decreases by 4	Decreases by 2
Beta decay	β	0	1−	No change	Increases by 1
Gamma radiation	γ	0	0	No change	No change
Positron emission	β^+	0	1+	No change	Decreases by 1
Electron capture (EC)	e^- absorbed	0	1−	No change	Decreases by 1

Example 11.1 Balancing Nuclear Equations

Write balanced nuclear equations for the following processes. In each case, identify the product element formed.

a. Plutonium-239 emits an alpha particle when it decays.
b. Protactinium-234 undergoes beta decay.
c. Carbon-11 emits a positron when it decays.
d. Carbon-11 undergoes electron capture.

Solution

a. We start by writing the symbol for plutonium-239 and a partial equation showing that one of the products is an alpha particle (helium nucleus).

$$^{239}_{94}\text{Pu} \longrightarrow {}^{4}_{2}\text{He} + ?$$

For this equation to balance, the other product must have $A = 239 - 4 = 235$ and $Z = 94 - 2 = 92$. The atomic number 92 identifies the element as uranium (U).

$$^{239}_{94}\text{Pu} \longrightarrow {}^{4}_{2}\text{He} + {}^{235}_{92}\text{U}$$

b. We write the symbol for protactinium-234 and a partial equation showing that one of the products is a beta particle (electron).

$$^{234}_{91}\text{Pa} \longrightarrow {}^{0}_{-1}\text{e} + ?$$

The other product must have a nucleon number of 234 and $Z = 92$ to balance the equation. The atomic number identifies this product as another isotope of uranium.

$$^{234}_{91}\text{Pa} \longrightarrow {}^{0}_{-1}\text{e} + {}^{234}_{92}\text{U}$$

c. We write the symbol for carbon-11 and a partial equation showing that one of the products is a positron.

$$^{11}_{6}\text{C} \longrightarrow {}^{0}_{+1}\text{e} + ?$$

To balance the equation, a particle with $A = 11 - 0 = 11$ and $Z = 6 - 1 = 5$ (boron) is required.

$$^{11}_{6}\text{C} \longrightarrow {}^{0}_{+1}\text{e} + {}^{11}_{5}\text{B}$$

d. We write the symbol for carbon-11 and a partial equation showing it capturing an electron.

$$^{11}_{6}\text{C} + {}^{0}_{-1}\text{e} \longrightarrow ?$$

To balance the equation, the product must have $A = 11 + 0 = 11$ and $Z = 6 + (-1) = 5$ (boron).

$$^{11}_{6}\text{C} + {}^{0}_{-1}\text{e} \longrightarrow {}^{11}_{5}\text{B}$$

As we noted previously, positron emission and electron capture result in identical changes in atomic number and, therefore, affect a given nucleus in the same way, as parts **(c)** and **(d)** illustrate for carbon-11. Also note that carbon-11 (and certain other nuclei) can undergo more than one type of radioactive decay.

EXERCISE 11.1

Write balanced nuclear equations for the following processes. In each case, identify the product element formed.

a. Uranium-235 decays by alpha emission.
b. Lead-210 undergoes beta decay.
c. Fluorine-18 decays by positron emission.
d. Oxygen-13 undergoes electron capture.

We noted earlier that nuclear *equations* differ in two ways from ordinary chemical equations. Nuclear *reactions* also exhibit many differences from chemical reactions. Some important ones are summarized in Table 11.3. Some nuclear reactions also involve processes other than the five simple ones we have discussed here. Regardless, all nuclear equations must be balanced according to nucleon (mass) numbers and atomic numbers. When an unknown particle has an atomic number that does not correspond to an atom, that particle may be a subatomic particle. A list of nuclear symbols for subatomic particles is given in Table 11.4.

Table 11.3 Some Differences Between Chemical Reactions and Nuclear Reactions

Chemical Reactions	Nuclear Reactions
Atoms retain their identity.	Atoms usually change their identity—from one element to another.
Reactions involve only electrons and usually only outermost electrons.	Reactions involve mainly protons and neutrons. It does not matter what the valence electrons do.
Reaction rates can be increased by raising the temperature.	Reaction rates are unaffected by changes in temperature.
The energy absorbed or given off in reactions is comparatively small.	Reactions sometimes involve enormous changes in energy.
Mass is conserved. The mass of products equals the mass of starting materials.	Huge changes in energy are accompanied by measurable changes in mass ($E = mc^2$).

Table 11.4 Symbols for Subatomic Particles

Particle	Symbol	Nuclear Symbol
Proton	p	${}^{1}_{1}\mathrm{p}$ or ${}^{1}_{1}\mathrm{H}$
Neutron	n	${}^{1}_{0}\mathrm{n}$
Electron	e^- or β	${}^{0}_{-1}\mathrm{e}$ or ${}^{0}_{-1}\beta$
Positron	e^+ or β^+	${}^{0}_{+1}\mathrm{e}$ or ${}^{0}_{+1}\beta$
Alpha particle	α	${}^{4}_{2}\mathrm{He}$ or ${}^{4}_{2}\alpha$
Beta particle	β or β^-	${}^{0}_{-1}\mathrm{e}$ or ${}^{0}_{-1}\beta$
Gamma ray	γ	${}^{0}_{0}\gamma$

Self-Assessment Questions

Identify items 1–4 as one of the following.

a. alpha particle **b.** beta particle **c.** nucleon number **d.** radioactivity

1. an electron
2. atomic mass of 4 u
3. emission of particles and energy from a nucleus
4. number of protons and neutrons in an atom

5. What are the mass and the charge, respectively, of gamma radiation?
a. 0, − 1 **b.** 0, 0 **c.** 0, +1 **d.** 4, +2

6. What particle is needed to complete the following nuclear equation?

$$^{9}_{4}\text{Be} + ? \longrightarrow {}^{12}_{6}\text{C} + {}^{1}_{0}\text{n}$$

a. alpha particle **b.** beta particle **c.** neutron **d.** proton

Answers: 1, b; 2, a; 3, d; 4, c; 5, b; 6, a

11.3 Half-Life and Radioisotopic Dating

Learning Objectives › Solve simple half-life problems. › Use the concept of half-life to solve simple radioisotope dating problems.

Thus far, we have discussed radioactivity as applied to single atoms. In the laboratory, we generally deal with great numbers of atoms—numbers far larger than the number of all the people on Earth. If we could see the nucleus of an individual atom, we could tell whether or not it would undergo radioactive decay by noting its composition. Certain combinations of protons and neutrons are unstable. However, we could not determine *when* the atom would undergo a change. Radioactivity is a random process, generally independent of outside influences.

Half-Life

With large numbers of atoms, the process of radioactive decay becomes more predictable. We can measure the *half-life*, a property characteristic of each radioisotope. The **half-life** of a radioactive isotope is the time it takes for one-half of the original number of atoms to undergo radioactive decay.

Suppose, for example, we had 16.00 mg of the radioactive isotope iodine-131. The half-life of iodine-131 is 8.0 days. This means that in 8.0 days, half the iodine-131, or 8.00 mg, will have decayed, and there will be 8.00 mg left. In another 8.0 days, half of the remaining 8.00 mg will have decayed. After two half-lives, or 16.0 days, then, one-quarter of the original iodine-131, or 4.00 mg, will remain. Note that two half-lives, do not make a whole. The concept of half-life is illustrated by the graph in Figure 11.4. Half-lives of radio isotopes can differ enormously. The half-life of tellurium-128 is 8×10^{24} y, while that of beryllium-13 is 2.7×10^{-21} s.

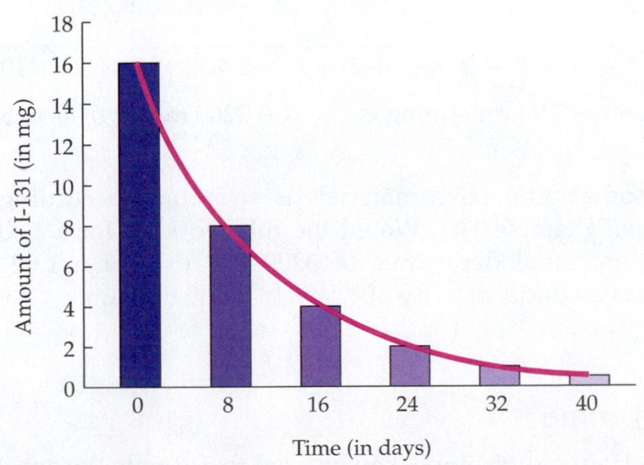

◀ **Figure 11.4** The radioactive decay of iodine-131, which has a half-life of 8 days.

Q: *How much of a 32-mg sample of iodine-131 remains after five half-lives have passed?*

The rate of decay is inversely related to half-life. An isotope with a long half-life decays slowly; an isotope with a short half-life decays at a high rate. We measure the rate of decay, also referred to as the isotope's **activity**, in disintegrations per second, a unit called a **becquerel (Bq)**.

We cannot say when *all* the atoms of a radioisotope will have decayed. For most samples, we can assume that the activity is essentially gone after about ten half-lives (when the activity is $\frac{1}{2^{10}} = \frac{1}{1024}$ of the original value). That is, about a thousandth of the original activity remains.

3. Why can't we just burn or dissolve radioactive wastes to get rid of them?
The half-life of a radioisotope is a nuclear property that isn't changed by chemical reactions. For example, if we burn radioactive carbon, we get radioactive carbon dioxide as the product. Dissolving radioactive plutonium in nitric acid produces radioactive plutonium nitrate. An isotope will be radioactive for a length of time determined by its half-life—and we can't change the half-life.

We can calculate the fraction of the original isotope that remains after a given number of half-lives from the relationship

$$\text{Fraction remaining} = \frac{1}{2^n}$$

where n is the number of half-lives.

Example 11.2 Half-Lives

A 4.00-mg sample of cobalt-60, half-life 5.271 y, is to be used for radiation treatment. How much cobalt-60 remains after 15.813 years (three half-lives)?

Solution

The fraction remaining after three half-lives is

$$\frac{1}{2^n} = \frac{1}{2^3} = \frac{1}{2 \times 2 \times 2} = \frac{1}{8}$$

The amount of cobalt-60 remaining is $\frac{1}{8} \times 4.00 \text{ mg} = 0.50 \text{ mg}$.

■ EXERCISE 11.2A

The half-life of phosphorus-32 is 14.3 days. What percentage of a sample of phosphorus-32 remains after four half-lives?

■ EXERCISE 11.2B

On April 4, 2011, a small fish caught about 50 mi south of the Fukushima nuclear complex had an activity of 4000 Bq of iodine-131 per kilogram. The half-life of iodine-131 is 8.0 d. What was the activity of the isotope **(a)** on April 28, 2011 (three half-lives later)? **(b)** On June 23, 2011 (ten half-lives later)?

CONCEPTUAL Example 11.3 Time and Radioactive Decay

We cannot determine how long it will take for *all* of a radioactive isotope to decay. For many isotopes, it is assumed that the activity is near zero after about ten half-lives. What mass of a 0.0260-mg sample of mercury-190, half-life 20 min, remains after ten half-lives?

Solution

The fraction remaining after ten half-lives is found in the usual manner.

$$\frac{1}{2^n} = \frac{1}{2^{10}} = \frac{1}{2 \times 2 \times 2 \times 2 \times 2 \times 2 \times 2 \times 2 \times 2 \times 2} = \frac{1}{1024}$$

The amount of mercury-190 remaining is $\frac{1}{1024} \times 0.0260 \text{ mg} = 0.000025 \text{ mg}$.

■ EXERCISE 11.3

The disposal of some radioactive materials is scheduled according to the rule stated in Conceptual Example 11.3. Would the rule work **(a)** for a 1.00-g sample of rubidium-87 with an initial decay rate of 3200 Bq? **(b)** For a 1.00-g sample of cobalt-60, which has an initial activity of 4.1×10^{13} Bq? Explain.

Radioisotopic Dating

The half-lives of certain radioisotopes can be used to estimate the ages of rocks and archaeological artifacts. Uranium-238 decays with a half-life of 4.5 billion years. The initial products of this decay are also radioactive, and they and subsequent products continue to decay until lead-206 is formed. By measuring the relative amounts of uranium-238 and lead-206, chemists can estimate the age of a rock. Some of the older rocks on Earth have been found to be 3.0–4.5 billion years old. Moon rocks

Why Are Isotopes Stable—or Unstable?

Most isotopes are radioactive, but some are stable. What factors tend to make an atomic nucleus stable? Stable isotopes tend to have:

1. *Even* numbers of either protons or neutrons or (especially) both. Of the 264 stable isotopes, 157 have *even* numbers of both protons and neutrons, and only four have odd numbers of both protons and neutrons. Elements with even *Z* have more stable isotopes than do those with odd *Z*.
2. So-called *magic numbers* of either protons or neutrons. (Magic numbers are 2, 8, 20, 50, 82, and 126.)
3. An atomic number of 83 or less. All isotopes with $Z > 83$ are radioactive.
4. Fewer, or the same number of, protons as neutrons in the nucleus, and a ratio of neutrons to protons close to 1 if the atomic number is 20 or below. As atomic number gets larger, the stable n/p ratio also increases, up to about 1.5. There is a zone of stability within which the n/p ratio should lie for an atom with a given atomic number.

and meteorites have been dated at a maximum age of about 4.5 billion years. Thus, the age of Earth (and the solar system itself) is generally estimated to be about 4.5 billion years.

The dating of artifacts derived from plants or animals usually involves radioactive carbon-14. Of the carbon on Earth, about 99% is carbon-12 and 1% is carbon-13, and both of these isotopes are stable. However, in the upper atmosphere, carbon-14 is formed by the bombardment of ordinary nitrogen by neutrons from cosmic rays.

$$^{14}_{7}\text{N} + ^{1}_{0}\text{n} \longrightarrow ^{14}_{6}\text{C} + ^{1}_{1}\text{H}$$

This process results in a tiny but steady concentration of carbon-14 in the CO_2 molecules of Earth's atmosphere. Plants use CO_2, and animals consume plants and other animals; thus, living things constantly incorporate this isotope into their cells. When organisms die, the incorporation of carbon-14 ceases, and the isotope begins to decay—with a half-life of 5730 years—back to nitrogen-14. We can measure the carbon-14 activity remaining in an artifact of plant or animal origin to determine its age, using the technique called **carbon-14 dating**. For instance, a sample that has half the carbon-14 activity of new plant material is 5730 years old; it has been dead for one half-life. Similarly, an artifact with a fourth of the carbon-14 activity of new plant material is 11,460 years old; it has been dead for two half-lives.

We have assumed that the formation of the carbon-14 isotope has been constant over the years, but this is not quite the case. For the last 7000 years or so, carbon-14 dates do correlate with those obtained from the annual growth rings of trees and with documents of known age. Calibration curves have been constructed from which accurate dates can be determined. Generally, carbon-14 is reasonably accurate for dating objects from about 100 to 50,000 years old. Newer objects may not yet have seen measurable decay of carbon-14. Objects older than 50,000 years have too little of the isotope left for accurate measurement.

Charcoal from the fires of ancient peoples, dated by determining the carbon-14 activity, is used to estimate the age of other artifacts found at the same archaeological sites. For example, carbon dating was used to confirm that ancient Hebrew writing found on a stone tablet unearthed in Israel dates from the ninth century B.C.E.

Tritium, the radioactive isotope of hydrogen, can also be used for dating materials. Its half-life of 12.26 years makes it useful for dating items up to about 100 years old. An interesting application of tritium dating is the dating of brandies. These alcoholic beverages are quite expensive when aged from 10 to 50 years. Tritium dating can be used to check the veracity of advertising claims about the ages of the most expensive kinds.

Many other isotopes are useful for estimating the ages of objects and materials. Several of the more important ones are listed in Table 11.5.

The Shroud of Turin

The Shroud of Turin is a very old piece of linen cloth, about 4 m long, bearing a faint human likeness. From about C.E. 1350 onward, it had been alleged to be part of the burial shroud of Jesus. However, carbon-14 dating studies in 1988 by three different laboratories indicated that the flax used to make the cloth was not grown until sometime between C.E. 1260 and 1390; therefore, the cloth could not possibly have existed at the time of Jesus. Unlike the Dead Sea Scrolls, which were shown by carbon-14 dating to be authentic records from a civilization that existed about 2000 years ago, the Shroud of Turin has been shown to be less than 800 years old. It is generally thought to be a work of art produced around that time.

Table 11.5 Several Isotopes Used in Radioactive Dating

Isotope	Half-Life (years)	Useful Range	Dating Applications
Carbon-14	5730	100 to 50,000 years	Charcoal, organic material
Hydrogen-3 (tritium)	12.26	1 to 100 years	Aged wines and brandies
Lead-210	22	1 to 75 years	Skeletal remains
Potassium-40	1.25×10^9	10,000 years to the oldest Earth samples	Rocks, Earth's crust, the moon's crust
Rhenium-187	4.3×10^{10}	4×10^7 years to the oldest samples in the universe	Meteorites
Uranium-238	4.51×10^9	10^7 years to the oldest Earth samples	Rocks, the Earth's crust

Example 11.4 Radioisotopic Dating

An old wooden implement shows carbon-14 activity that is one-eighth that of new wood. How old is the artifact? The half-life of carbon-14 is 5730 y.

Solution

Using the relationship

$$\text{Fraction remaining} = \frac{1}{2^n}$$

we see that one-eighth is $\frac{1}{2^n}$, where $n = 3$; that is, the fraction $\frac{1}{8}$ is $\frac{1}{2^3}$. The carbon-14 has gone through three half-lives. The wood is therefore about $3 \times 5730 = 17{,}190$ y old.

■ EXERCISE 11.4

Calculate the approximate age of each of the following. (a) Human remains have been preserved for centuries in the bogs of Northern Europe. How old is a bog body that has carbon-14 activity one-fourth that of living tissue? The half-life of carbon-14 is 5730 y. (b) How old is a bottle of brandy that has a tritium activity one-sixteenth that of new brandy? The half-life of tritium (hydrogen-3) is 12.26 years.

Self-Assessment Questions

1. A patient is given a 48-mg dose of technetium-99m (half-life 6.0 h) to treat a brain cancer. How much of it will remain in his body after 36 h?
   a. 0.75 mg b. 1.5 mg c. 3.0 mg d. 12 mg
2. What is the half-life of silver-112 if a 10.0-g sample decays to 2.5 g in 12.4 h?
   a. 1.6 h b. 3.1 h c. 6.2 h d. 12.4 h
3. Of a 64.0-g sample of strontium-90 (half-life 28.5 y) produced by a nuclear explosion, what mass in grams would remain unchanged after 285 y?
   a. 0.000 g b. 0.000625 g c. 0.00625 g d. 0.0625 g

4. Lead-210 (half-life 22.26 y) can be used to date skeletal remains. About how old is a bone that has an activity of 2.0 Bq if new bone has an activity of 16 Bq?
   a. 7.4 y b. 44.5 y c. 67 y d. 89 y

5. About how old is a piece of wood from an aboriginal burial site that has a carbon-14 (half-life 5730 y) activity of 3.9 counts/min per gram of carbon? Assume that the carbon-14 activity of the wood was 15.6 counts per minute per gram of carbon at the time of the burial.
   a. 2865 y b. 11,460 y c. 17,190 y d. 22,920 y

Answers: 1, a; 2, c; 3, d; 4, c; 5, b

Isotopic Signatures

For most chemical reactions, isotopes are unimportant. However, differences in isotopes can be quite important to some investigations. Isotopes' variance in mass affects their rates of reaction, with lighter isotopes generally moving a bit faster than heavier ones. This difference can lead to a measurable characteristic called an *isotopic signature* in an investigated material. For example, the ratio of carbon-13 to carbon-12 in materials formed by photosynthesis is less than that isotopic ratio in inorganic carbonates.

The ratio of oxygen-18 to oxygen-16 depends on the extent of evaporation that water has undergone because water molecules with oxygen-18 atoms are heavier and thus vaporize less readily than do water molecules with oxygen-16 atoms. This difference is less pronounced at higher temperatures. As oxygen is incorporated into the calcium carbonate shells of aquatic organisms, the isotopic ratio in the shells shifts. Fossilized shells thus provide a chronological record of the temperature of the water in which the organisms lived. The oxygen isotope ratio in the atmosphere varies with the season and with geographic location. This variation allows scientists to determine the location in which a material originated.

The ratio of nitrogen-14 to nitrogen-15 is different for herbivores and carnivores, because organisms higher in the food chain tend to concentrate the nitrogen-15 isotope in their tissues. Such variations enable scientists to determine much about the diet of people from ages past.

11.4 Artificial Transmutation

Learning Objective › Write a nuclear equation for a transmutation, and identify the product element formed.

During the Middle Ages, alchemists tried to turn base metals, such as lead, into gold. However, they were trying to do it chemically and were therefore doomed to failure because chemical reactions involve only atoms' outer electrons. **Transmutation** (changing one element into another) requires altering the *nucleus*.

Thus far, we have considered only natural forms of radioactivity. Nuclear reactions can also be brought about by bombardment of stable nuclei with alpha particles, neutrons, or other subatomic particles. These particles, given sufficient energy, can penetrate a stable nucleus and result in some kind of radioactive emission. Just as in natural radioactive processes, one element is changed into another. Because the change would not have occurred naturally, the process is called *artificial transmutation*.

In 1919, a few years after his famous gold-foil experiment (Section 3.4), Ernest Rutherford reported on the bombardment of a variety of light elements with alpha particles. One such experiment, in which he bombarded nitrogen, resulted in the production of protons, as shown in this balanced nuclear equation.

$$^{14}_{7}\text{N} + ^{4}_{2}\text{He} \longrightarrow ^{17}_{8}\text{O} + ^{1}_{1}\text{H}$$

(The hydrogen nucleus is simply a proton, which can be represented by the symbol $^{1}_{1}\text{H}$.) This provided the first empirical verification of the existence of protons in atomic nuclei, which Rutherford had first postulated in 1914.

Recall that Eugen Goldstein had produced protons in his gas-discharge tube experiments in 1886 (Section 3-1). The significance of Rutherford's experiment lay in the fact that he obtained protons from the *nucleus* of an atom other than hydrogen, thus establishing that protons are constituents of nuclei. Rutherford's experiment was the first induced nuclear reaction and the first example of artificial transmutation. In producing protons, he also changed nitrogen into oxygen.

▲ Ernest Rutherford (1871–1937) carried out the first nuclear bombardment experiment. Element 104 was named rutherfordium (Rf) in his honor.

Example 11.5 Artificial Transmutation Equations

When potassium-39 is bombarded with neutrons, chlorine-36 is produced. What other particle is emitted?

$$^{39}_{19}\text{K} + ^{1}_{0}\text{n} \longrightarrow ^{36}_{17}\text{Cl} + ?$$

Solution

To determine the particle, we need a balanced nuclear equation. To balance the equation, the unknown particle must have $A = 4$ and $Z = 2$—it is an alpha particle.

$$^{39}_{19}\text{K} + ^{1}_{0}\text{n} \longrightarrow ^{36}_{17}\text{Cl} + ^{4}_{2}\text{He}$$

■ EXERCISE 11.5A

Technetium-97 is produced by bombarding molybdenum-96 with a deuteron (a hydrogen-2 nucleus). What other particle is emitted?

$$^{96}_{42}\text{Mo} + ^{2}_{1}\text{H} \longrightarrow ^{97}_{43}\text{Tc} + ?$$

■ EXERCISE 11.5B

A team of scientists wants to form uranium-235 by bombarding a nucleus of another element with an alpha particle. They expect a neutron to be produced along with the uranium-235 nucleus. What nucleus must be bombarded with the alpha particle?

Self-Assessment Questions

1. What isotope is formed in the following artificial transmutation?

$$^{14}_{7}\text{N} + ^{1}_{0}\text{n} \longrightarrow ^{1}_{1}\text{H} + ?$$

a. carbon-12 b. carbon-14 c. nitrogen-15 d. oxygen-15

2. What isotope is formed in the following artificial transmutation?

$$^{9}_{4}\text{Be} + ^{1}_{1}\text{H} \longrightarrow ^{4}_{2}\text{He} + ?$$

a. boron-9 b. boron-10 c. lithium-6 d. lithium-7

3. What isotope is formed in the following artificial transmutation?

$$^{239}_{94}\text{Pu} + ^{4}_{2}\text{He} \longrightarrow ^{1}_{0}\text{n} + ?$$

a. americium-242 b. berkelium-242 c. curium-242 d. curium-243

Answers: 1, b; 2, c; 3, c

11.5 Uses of Radioisotopes

Learning Objective › List some applications of radioisotopes.

Most of the 3000 known radioisotopes are produced by artificial transmutation of stable isotopes. The value of both naturally occurring and artificial radioisotopes goes far beyond their contributions to our knowledge of chemistry.

Radioisotopes in Industry and Agriculture

Scientists in a wide variety of fields use radioisotopes as **tracers** in physical, chemical, and biological systems. Isotopes of a given element, whether radioactive or not, behave nearly identically in chemical and physical processes. Because radioactive isotopes are easily detected through their decay products, it is relatively easy to trace their movement, even through a complicated system. For example, tracing radioisotopes allows as to do the following:

- **Detect leaks in underground pipes.** Suppose there is a leak in a pipe that is buried beneath a concrete floor. We could locate the leak by digging up extensive areas of the floor, or we could add a small amount of radioactive material to liquid poured into the drain and trace the flow of the liquid with a Geiger counter (an instrument that detects radioactivity). Once we located the leak, only a small area of the floor would have to be dug up to repair it. A compound containing a short-lived isotope (for example, $^{131}_{53}I$, half-life 8.04 days) is usually employed for this purpose.

- **Measure thickness of sheet metal during production.** Radiation from a beta emitter is allowed to pass through sheet metal on the production line. The amount of radiation that passes through a sheet is related to its thickness.
- **Determine frictional wear in piston rings.** The ring is subjected to neutron bombardment, which converts some of the carbon in the steel to carbon-14. Wear in the piston ring is assessed by the rate at which the carbon-14 appears in the engine oil.
- **Determine the uptake of phosphorus and its distribution in plants.** This can be done by incorporating phosphorus-32, a β^- emitter with a half-life of 14.3 d, into phosphate fertilizers fed to plants.

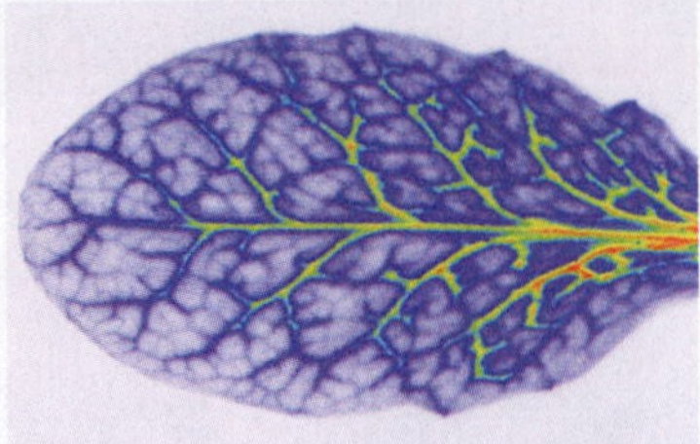

▲ Scientists can trace the uptake of phosphorus by a green plant by adding a compound containing some phosphorus-32 to the applied fertilizer. When the plant is later placed on photographic film, radiation from the phosphorus isotopes exposes the film, much as light does. This type of exposure, called a *radiograph*, shows the distribution of phosphorus in the plant.

Radioisotopes are also used to study the effectiveness of weed killers, compare the nutritional value of various feeds, determine optimal methods for insect control, and monitor the fate and persistence of pesticides in soil and groundwater.

One of the most successful applications of radioisotopes in agriculture involves inducing heritable genetic alterations known as *mutations*. Exposing seeds or other parts of plants to neutrons or gamma rays increases the likelihood of genetic mutations. At first glance, this technique may not seem very promising. However, genetic variability is vital, not only to improve varieties but also to protect species from extinction. Some hybrid plants, such as seedless watermelons and bananas, are sterile. The lack of genetic variability among these plants may place the entire population at risk.

Radioisotopes are also used to irradiate foodstuffs as a method of preservation (Figure 11.5). The radiation destroys microorganisms and enzymes that cause foods to spoil. Irradiated food shows little change in taste or appearance. Some people are concerned about possible harmful effects of chemical substances produced by the radiation, but there has been no good evidence of harm to laboratory animals fed irradiated food or any known adverse effects in humans living in countries where food irradiation has been used for years. No residual radiation remains in a food after irradiation because gamma rays do not have nearly enough energy to change nuclei.

4. Do irradiated foods give off radiation? Irradiated foods have absorbed energy in the form of gamma rays. But the foods are *not* radioactive.

Radioisotopes in Medicine

Nuclear medicine involves two distinct uses of radioisotopes: therapeutic and diagnostic. In a therapeutic application, an attempt is made to treat or cure disease with radiation. The diagnostic use of radioisotopes is aimed at obtaining information about the state of a patient's health.

◀ **Figure 11.5** Exposure to gamma radiation delays the decay of strawberries. Those on the right were irradiated; the ones on the left were not.

Q: *Are the strawberries on the right radioactive?*

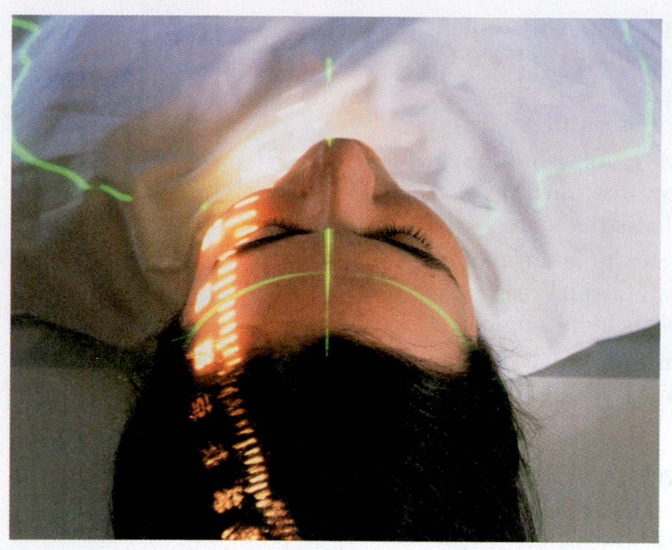

▲ **It DOES Matter!**
The difference between a radioactive isotope and the alpha, beta, gamma, or positron radiation that it produces is very important and often misunderstood. A radioisotope such as iodine-131 or radon-222, when absorbed by the human body, can cause great harm because the radiation continues to be released as the isotope decays. However, matter exposed to ionizing radiation simply absorbs that energy, causing a chemical change. A patient undergoing gamma-radiation treatment does *not* become radioactive.

Table 11.6 lists some radioisotopes in common use in medicine. The list is necessarily incomplete, but it should give you an idea of their importance. The claim that nuclear medicine has saved many more lives than nuclear bombs have taken is not an idle one.

Cancer is not one disease but many. Some forms are particularly susceptible to radiation therapy. The aim of **radiation therapy** is to destroy cancerous cells before too much damage is done to healthy tissue. Radiation is most lethal to rapidly reproducing cells, and rapid reproduction is the characteristic of cancer cells that allows radiation therapy to be successful. Radiation is carefully aimed at cancerous tissue while minimizing the exposure of normal cells. If the cancer cells are killed by the destructive effects of the radiation, the malignancy is halted.

Patients undergoing radiation therapy often get sick from the treatment. Nausea and vomiting are the usual early symptoms of radiation sickness. Radiation therapy can also interfere with the replenishment of white blood cells and thus increase patients' susceptibility to infection.

Radioisotopes used for diagnostic purposes provide information about the functioning of some part of the body or about the type or extent of an illness. For example, radioactive iodine-131 is used to determine the size, shape, and activity of the thyroid gland, as well as to treat cancers in this gland and to control its hyperactivity. Small doses are used for diagnostic purposes, and large doses for treatment of thyroid cancer. After the patient drinks a solution of potassium iodide incorporating iodine-131, the iodide ions become concentrated in the thyroid. A detector showing the differential uptake of the isotope is used in diagnosis. The resulting

5. Are we exposed to dangerous radiation during X-rays and other medical procedures? A number of medical procedures do use ionizing radiation or radioisotopes, but the amount of radiation is kept to a minimum. The hazard of the ionizing radiation is ordinarily much less than the risk due to a lack of diagnosis or treatment!

Table 11.6 Some Radioisotopes and Their Medical Applications

Isotope	Name	Half-Life[a]	Use
^{11}C	Carbon-11	20.39 min	Brain scans
^{51}Cr	Chromium-51	27.8 d	Blood volume determination
^{57}Co	Cobalt-57	270 d	Measuring vitamin B_{12} uptake
^{60}Co	Cobalt-60	5.271 y	Radiation cancer therapy
^{153}Gd	Gadolinium-153	242 d	Determining bone density
^{67}Ga	Gallium-67	78.1 h	Scan for lung tumors
^{131}I	Iodine-131	8.040 d	Thyroid diagnoses and therapy
^{192}Ir	Iridium-192	74 d	Breast cancer therapy
^{59}Fe	Iron-59	44.496 d	Detection of anemia
^{32}P	Phosphorus-32	14.3 d	Detection of skin cancer or eye tumors
^{238}Pu	Plutonium-238	86 y	Provision of power in pacemakers
^{226}Ra	Radium-226	1600 y	Radiation therapy for cancer
^{75}Se	Selenium-75	120 d	Pancreas scans
^{24}Na	Sodium-24	14.659 h	Locating obstructions in blood flow
^{99m}Tc	Technetium-99m	6.0 h	Imaging of brain, liver, bone marrow, kidney, lung, or heart
^{201}Tl	Thallium-201	73 h	Detecting heart problems during treadmill stress test
^{3}H	Tritium	12.26 y	Determining total body water
^{133}Xe	Xenon-133	5.27 d	Lung imaging

[a] Abbreviations: y, years; d, days; h, hours; min, minutes.

photoscan can pinpoint the location of tumors or other abnormalities in the thyroid. In cancer treatment, radiation from therapeutic (large) doses of iodine-131 kills the thyroid cells in which the radioisotope has concentrated.

The radioisotope gadolinium-153 is used to determine bone mineralization. Its widespread use is an indication of the large number of people, mostly women, who suffer from osteoporosis (reduction in the quantity of bone) as they grow older. Gadolinium-153 gives off two types of radiation: gamma rays and X-rays. A scanning device compares these types of radiation after they pass through bone. Bone density is then determined from the difference in absorption of the rays.

Technetium-99m is used in a variety of diagnostic tests (Figure 11.6). The *m* stands for *metastable*, which means that this isotope gives up some energy when it changes to a more stable version of technetium-99 (which has the same atomic number and same atomic mass). The energy it gives up is in the form of a gamma ray.

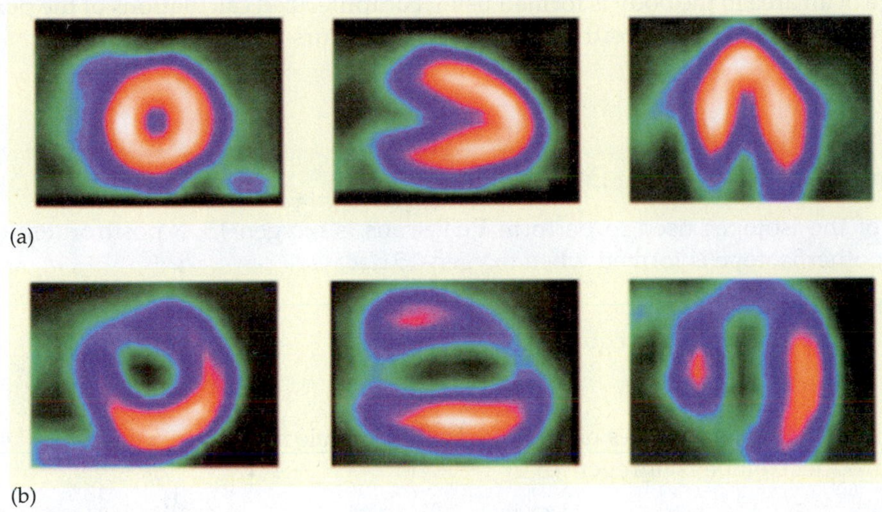

◀ **Figure 11.6** Gamma-ray imaging using technetium-99m. Directional slices through (a) a healthy human heart and (b) a diseased heart. The lighter regions of the images indicate regions receiving adequate blood flow.

$$^{99m}_{43}\text{Tc} \longrightarrow {}^{99}_{43}\text{Tc} + \gamma$$

Note that the decay of technetium-99m produces no alpha or beta particles that could cause unnecessary damage to the body. Technetium-99m also has a short half-life (6.0 h), which means that the radioactivity does not linger very long in the body after the scan has been completed. With so short a half-life, use of the isotope must be carefully planned. In fact, technetium-99m is not what is purchased by medical labs. Technetium-99m is formed by the decay of molybdenum-99.

$$^{99}_{42}\text{Mo} \longrightarrow {}^{99m}_{43}\text{Tc} + {}^{0}_{-1}\text{e} + \gamma$$

A container of this molybdenum isotope is obtained, and the decay product, technetium-99m, is "milked" from the container as needed.

Using modern computer technology, *positron emission tomography (PET)* can measure dynamic processes occurring in the body, such as blood flow or the rate at which oxygen or glucose is being metabolized. For example, PET scans have shown that the brain of a schizophrenic metabolizes only about one-fifth as much glucose as a normal brain. These scans can also reveal metabolic changes that occur in the brain during tactile learning (learning by the sense of touch). PET scans can also pinpoint the area of brain damage that triggers severe epileptic seizures.

Compounds incorporating a positron-emitting isotope, such as carbon-11 or oxygen-15, are inhaled or injected before the scan. Before the emitted positron can travel very far in the body, it encounters an electron (numerous in any ordinary matter), and two gamma rays are produced, exiting from the body in exactly opposite directions.

$$^{11}_{6}\text{C} \longrightarrow {}^{11}_{5}\text{B} + {}^{0}_{+1}\text{e}$$

$$^{0}_{+1}\text{e} + {}^{0}_{-1}\text{e} \longrightarrow 2\gamma$$

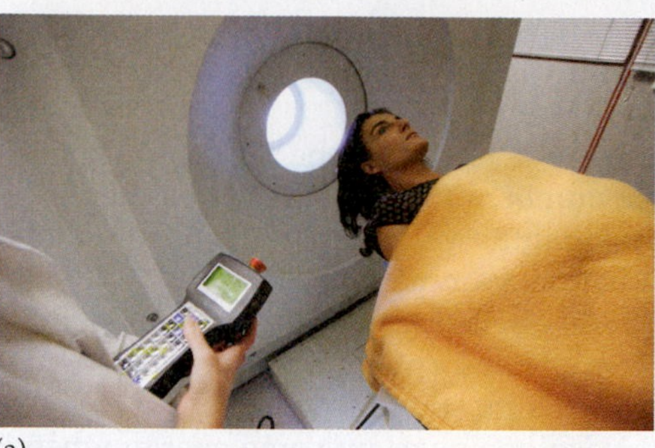
(a)

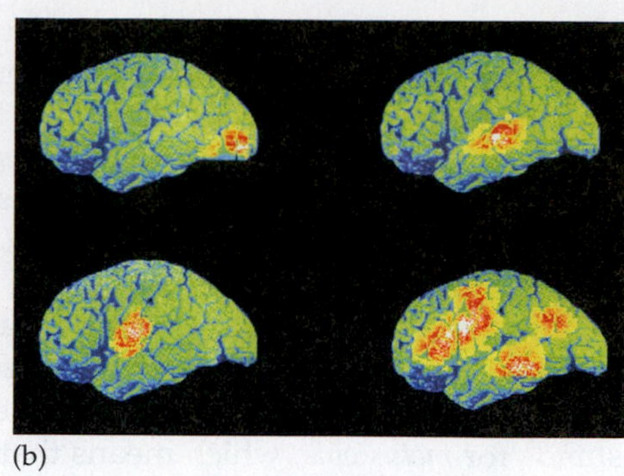
(b)

▶ **Figure 11.7** Modern computer technology used for medical diagnosis. (a) Patient undergoing positron emission tomography (PET), a technique that uses radioisotopes to scan internal organs. (b) Images created by PET scanning, showing parts of the brain involved in different functions.

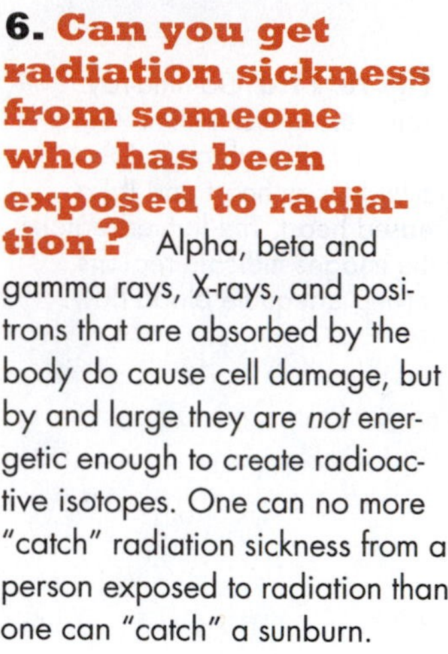

6. Can you get radiation sickness from someone who has been exposed to radiation? Alpha, beta and gamma rays, X-rays, and positrons that are absorbed by the body do cause cell damage, but by and large they are *not* energetic enough to create radioactive isotopes. One can no more "catch" radiation sickness from a person exposed to radiation than one can "catch" a sunburn.

Detectors, positioned on opposite sides of the patient, record the gamma rays. An image of an area in the body is formed using computerized calculations of the points at which annihilation of positrons and electrons occurs (Figure 11.7).

Example 11.6 Positron Emission Equations

One of the isotopes used to perform PET scans is oxygen-15, a positron emitter. What other isotope is formed when oxygen-15 decays?

Solution

First, we write the nuclear equation

$$^{15}_{8}\text{O} \longrightarrow \,^{0}_{+1}\text{e} + ?$$

The nucleon number, *A*, does not change, but the atomic number, *Z*, does: 8 − 1 = 7. The product isotope is nitrogen-15.

$$^{15}_{8}\text{O} \longrightarrow \,^{0}_{+1}\text{e} + \,^{15}_{7}\text{N}$$

■ EXERCISE 11.6

Phosphorus-30 is a positron-emitting radioisotope suitable for doing PET scans. What other isotope is formed when phosphorus-30 decays?

Self-Assessment Questions

1. Iodine-131 is sometimes used for detecting leaks in underground pipes because
   - **a.** it has a short half-life
   - **b.** it is highly penetrating
   - **c.** it is nontoxic
   - **d.** its radiation is harmless
2. What is used to irradiate foodstuffs to extend shelf life?
   - **a.** alpha particles
   - **b.** beta particles
   - **c.** gamma rays
   - **d.** microwaves

For items 3–7, match each radioisotope with a major use.

3. cobalt-60	(a) bone density
4. gadolinium-153	(b) brain images
5. iodine-131	(c) heart problems
6. technetium-99m	(d) radiation therapy
7. thallium-201	(e) thyroid disorders

8. What form of radiation is detected in PET scans?
   - **a.** beta
   - **b.** gamma
   - **c.** positron
   - **d.** X-rays

Answers: 1, a; 2, c; 3, d; 4, a; 5, e; 6, b; 7, c; 8, c

11.6 Penetrating Power of Radiation

Learning Objective › Describe the nature of materials needed to block alpha, beta, and gamma radiation.

The danger of radiation to living organisms comes from its potential for damaging cells and tissues. The ability to inflict injury relates to the penetrating power of the radiation. The two aspects of nuclear medicine just discussed (therapeutic and diagnostic) are also dependent on the penetrating power of various types of radiation.

All other things being equal, the more massive the particle, the less its penetrating power. *Alpha particles*, which are helium nuclei with a mass of 4 u, are the least penetrating of the three main types of radiation. *Beta particles*, which are identical to the almost massless electrons, are somewhat more penetrating. *Gamma rays*, like X-rays, have no mass; they are considerably more penetrating than the other two types.

But all other things are not always equal. The faster a particle moves or the more energetic the radiation is, the more penetrating power it has.

It may seem contrary to common sense that the biggest particles make the least headway. But keep in mind that penetrating power reflects the ability of radiation to make its way through a sample of matter. It is as if you were trying to roll some rocks through a field of boulders. The alpha particle acts as if it were a boulder itself. Because of its size, it cannot get very far before it bumps into and is stopped by other boulders. The beta particle acts as if it were a small stone. It can sneak between and perhaps ricochet off boulders until it makes its way farther into the field. The gamma ray can be compared with a grain of sand that can get through the smallest openings.

The danger of a specific type of radiation to human tissue depends on the location of the radiation's source as well as on its penetrating power. If the radioactive substance is outside the body, alpha particles are the least dangerous; they have low penetrating power and are stopped by the outer layer of skin. Beta particles are also usually stopped before they reach vital organs. Gamma rays readily pass through tissues, and so an external gamma source can be quite dangerous. People working with radioactive materials can protect themselves through one or both of the following actions:

- Move away from the source. The intensity of radiation decreases with distance from the source.
- Use shielding. A sheet of paper can stop most alpha particles, and a block of wood or a thin sheet of aluminum can stop most beta particles, but it takes a meter of concrete or several centimeters of lead to stop most gamma rays (Figure 11.8).

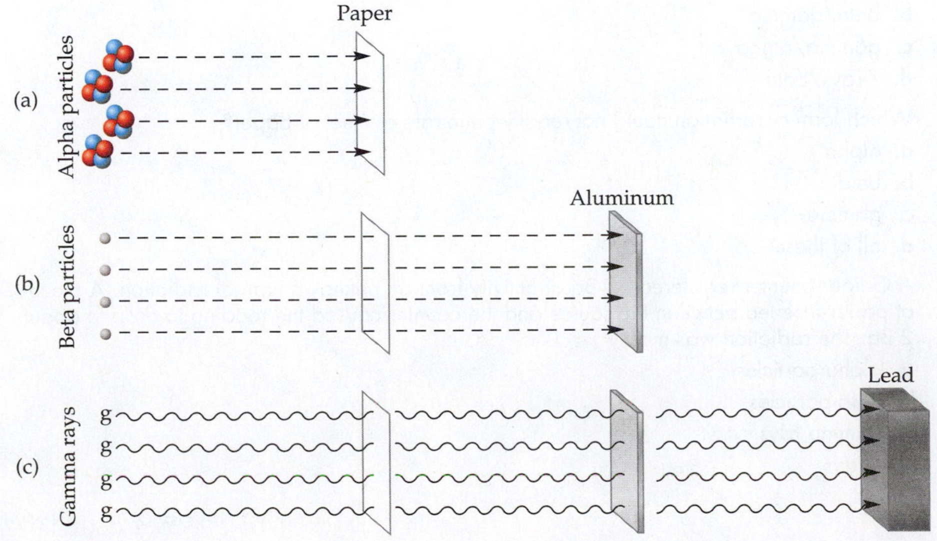

◄ **Figure 11.8** The relative penetrating power of alpha, beta, and gamma radiation. Alpha particles are stopped by a sheet of paper (a). Beta particles will not penetrate a sheet of aluminum (b). It takes several centimeters of lead to block gamma rays (c).

When the radioactive source is *inside* the body, as in the case of many medical applications, the situation is reversed. The nonpenetrating alpha particles can do great damage. All such particles are trapped within the body, which must then absorb all the energy the particles release. Alpha particles inflict all their damage in a tiny area because they do not travel far. Therefore, getting an alpha-emitting therapeutic radioisotope close to the targeted cells is vital.

Beta particles distribute their damage over a somewhat larger area because they travel farther. Tissue may recover from limited damage spread over a large area; it is less likely to survive concentrated damage.

Many diagnostic applications rely on the highly penetrating power of gamma rays. In most cases, the radiation created inside the body must be detected by instruments outside the body, so a minimum of absorption is desirable.

CONCEPTUAL Example 11.7 Radiation Hazard

Most modern smoke detectors contain a tiny amount of americium-241, a solid element that is an alpha emitter. The americium is in a chamber that includes thin aluminum shielding, and the device is usually mounted on a ceiling. Rate the radiation hazard of this device in normal use as (a) high, (b) moderate, or (c) very low. Explain your choice.

Solution

Alpha particles have very little penetrating ability—they are stopped by a sheet of paper or a layer of skin. The emitted alpha particles cannot exit the detector's chamber, because even thin metal is more than sufficient to absorb them. Even if alpha particles could escape, they would likely be stopped by the air after a short distance or by the dead cells of your skin. Therefore, the radiation hazard is rated (c)—very low.

■ EXERCISE 11.7

Radon-222 is a gas that can diffuse from the ground into homes. Like americium-241, it is an alpha emitter. Is the radiation hazard from radon-222 likely to be higher or lower than that from a smoke detector? Explain.

Self-Assessment Questions

1. Which of the following pairs represent the *most* and *least* (most/least) penetrating types of radiation?
   - **a.** alpha/gamma
   - **b.** beta/gamma
   - **c.** gamma/alpha
   - **d.** X-rays/beta
2. Which form of radiation could not readily penetrate a sheet of paper?
   - **a.** alpha
   - **b.** beta
   - **c.** gamma
   - **d.** all of these
3. A Geiger counter registered 50 Bq of activity from an unknown type of radiation. A piece of paper inserted between the source and the counter caused the reading to drop to about 2 Bq. The radiation was mostly
   - **a.** alpha particles
   - **b.** beta particles
   - **c.** gamma rays
   - **d.** X-rays

Answers: 1, c; 2, a; 3, a

11.7 Energy from the Nucleus

Learning Objectives › Explain where nuclear energy comes from. › Describe the difference between fission and fusion.

We have seen that radioactivity—quiet and invisible—can be beneficial or dangerous. A much more dramatic—and equally paradoxical—aspect of nuclear chemistry is the release of nuclear energy by either *fission* (splitting of heavy nuclei into smaller nuclei) or *fusion* (combining of light nuclei to form heavier ones).

▲ Albert Einstein (1879–1955). Element 99 was named einsteinium (Es) in his honor.

Einstein and the Equivalence of Mass and Energy

The potential power in the nucleus was established by Albert Einstein, a famous and most unusual scientist. Whereas most scientists work with glassware and instruments in laboratories, Einstein worked with a pencil and a notepad. By 1905, at the age of 26, he had already worked out his special theory of relativity and developed his famous **mass–energy equation**, in which mass (m) is multiplied by the square of the speed of light (c).

$$E = mc^2$$

The equation suggests that mass and energy are equivalent—just two different aspects of the same thing—and that a little bit of mass can yield enormous energy. The atomic bombs that destroyed Hiroshima and Nagasaki (Section 11.8) in World War II converted less than an ounce of matter into energy.

A chemical reaction that gives off heat must lose mass in the process, but the change in mass is far too small to measure. Reaction energy must be enormous—at the level of the energy given off by nuclear explosions—for the mass loss to be measurable. (If every atom in a 1-kg lump of coal became energy, it could produce 25 billion kWh of electricity—enough to keep a 100-W lightbulb going for 29 million years. Burning 1 kg of coal in a conventional power plant produces only enough energy to keep the bulb shining for 67 hours.)

Binding Energy

Nuclear fission releases the tremendous amounts of energy produced by atomic bombs and in nuclear power plants. Where does all this energy come from? It is locked inside the atomic nucleus. When protons and neutrons combine to form atomic nuclei, a small amount of mass is converted to energy. This is the **binding energy** that holds the nucleons together in the nucleus. For example, the helium nucleus contains two protons and two neutrons. The masses of these four particles add up to 2×1.0073 u $+ 2 \times 1.0087$ u $= 4.0320$ u (Figure 11.9). However, the actual mass of the helium nucleus is only 4.0015 u, and the missing mass—called the *mass defect*—amounts to 0.0305 u. Using Einstein's equation $E = mc^2$, we can calculate (see Problem 55) a value of 28.3 million electron volts (28 MeV; 1 MeV $= 1.6022 \times 10^{-13}$ J) for the binding energy of the helium nucleus. This is the amount of energy it would take to separate one helium nucleus into two protons and two neutrons.

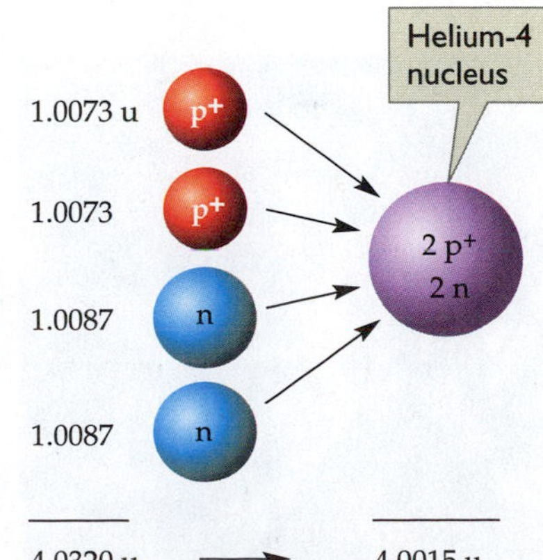

▲ **Figure 11.9** Nuclear binding energy in ^4_2He. The mass of a helium-4 nucleus is 4.0015 u, which is 0.0305 u less than the masses of two protons and two neutrons. The missing mass is equivalent to the binding energy of the helium-4 nucleus.

When the binding energy per nucleon is calculated for all the elements and plotted against nucleon number, a graph such as that in Figure 11.10 is obtained. The elements with the highest binding energies per nucleon have the most stable nuclei. They include iron and elements with nucleon members close to that of iron. When uranium atoms undergo nuclear fission, they split into atoms with higher binding energies. In other words, the fission reaction converts large atoms into smaller ones with greater nuclear stability.

We can also see from Figure 11.10 that even more energy can be obtained by combining small atoms, such as hydrogen or deuterium, to form larger atoms with more stable nuclei. This kind of reaction is called **nuclear fusion**. It is what happens when a hydrogen bomb explodes, and it is also the source of the sun's energy.

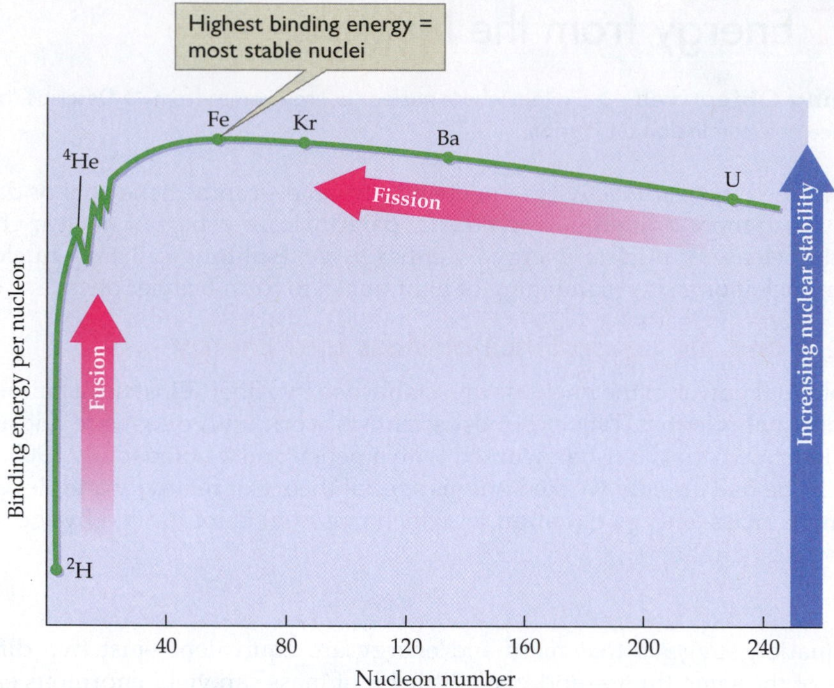

▶ **Figure 11.10** Nuclear stability is greatest for iron and elements near iron in the periodic table. Fission of very large nuclei or fusion of very small ones results in greater nuclear stability.

Q: *Which process, fission of uranium nuclei or fusion of hydrogen nuclei, releases more energy?*

▲ Enrico Fermi (1901–1954). Element 100 was named fermium (Fm) in his honor.

▲ Lise Meitner (1878–1968). Element 109 was named meitnerium (Mt) in her honor.

Nuclear Fission

In 1934, the Italian scientists Enrico Fermi and Emilio Segrè (1905–1989) bombarded uranium atoms with neutrons. They were trying to make elements with higher atomic numbers than uranium, which then had the highest known atomic number. To their surprise, they found four radioactive species among the products. One was presumably element 93, formed by the initial conversion of uranium-238 to uranium-239, which then underwent beta decay.

$$^{238}_{92}U + ^{1}_{0}n \longrightarrow ^{239}_{92}U$$

$$^{239}_{92}U \longrightarrow ^{239}_{93}Np + ^{0}_{-1}e$$

They were unable to explain the remaining radioactivity.

When repeating the Fermi–Segrè experiment in 1938, German chemists Otto Hahn (1879–1968) and Fritz Strassman (1902–1980) were perplexed to find isotopes of barium among the many reaction products. Hahn wrote to Lise Meitner, his former longtime colleague, to ask what she thought about these strange results.

Lise Meitner was an Austrian physicist who had worked with Hahn in Berlin. Because she was Jewish, she fled to Sweden when the Nazis took over Austria in 1938. On hearing about Hahn's work, she noted that barium atoms were only about half the size of uranium atoms. Was it possible that the uranium nuclei might be splitting into fragments? She made some calculations that convinced her that the uranium nuclei had indeed been split apart. Her nephew, Otto Frisch (1904–1979), was visiting for the winter holidays, and they discussed this discovery with great excitement. It was Frisch who later coined the term **nuclear fission** (Figure 11.11).

Frisch was working with Niels Bohr at the University of Copenhagen, and when he returned to Denmark, he took the news of the fission reaction to Bohr, who happened to be going to the United States to attend a physics conference. The discussions in the corridors about this new reaction would be the most important talks to take place at that meeting.

Meanwhile, Enrico Fermi had just received the 1938 Nobel Prize in physics. Because Fermi's wife, Laura, was Jewish, and the fascist Italian dictator Mussolini was an ally of Hitler, Fermi accepted the award in Stockholm and then immediately fled with Laura and their children to the United States. Thus, by 1939, the United States had received news about the German discovery of nuclear fission and had also acquired from Italy one of the world's foremost nuclear scientists.

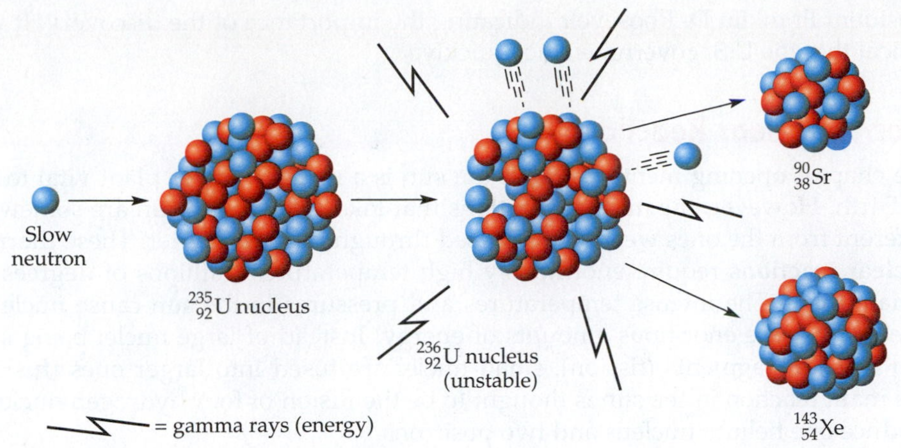

◀ **Figure 11.11** One possible way a uranium nucleus can undergo fission. The neutrons produced by the fission reactions can split other uranium nuclei, thus sustaining a chain reaction.

Q: *If each of the neutrons emitted by the ^{236}U nucleus caused another ^{235}U nucleus to split in the way shown here, how many more neutrons would be released?*

Nuclear Chain Reaction

Leo Szilard (1898–1964) was one of the first scientists to realize that nuclear fission could occur as a chain reaction. Szilard had been born in Hungary and educated in Germany, but he came to the United States in 1937 as one of the many Jewish refugees. He saw that neutrons released in the fission of one atom could trigger the fission of other uranium atoms, thus setting off a **chain reaction** (Figure 11.12). Because massive amounts of energy could be obtained from the fission of uranium, he saw that the chain reaction might be used in a bomb with tremendous explosive force.

Aware of the destructive forces that could be produced and concerned that Germany might develop such a bomb, Szilard prevailed on Einstein to sign a letter to

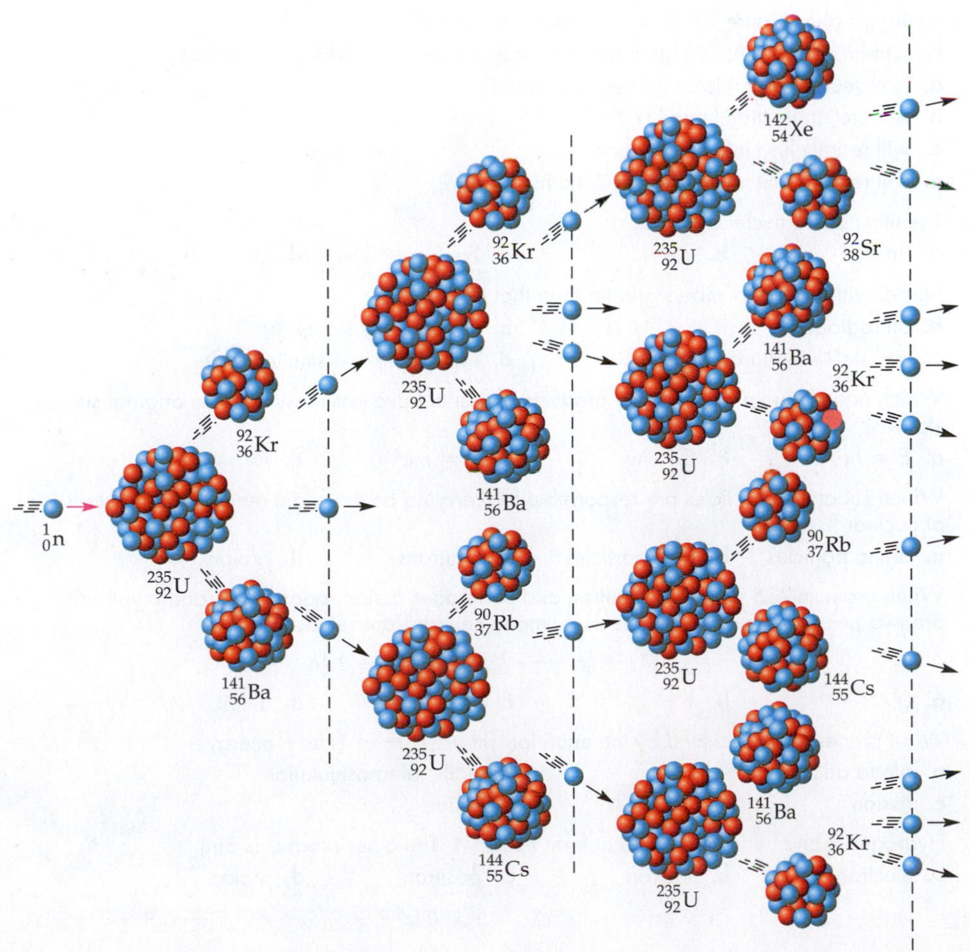

◀ **Figure 11.12** Schematic representation of a nuclear chain reaction. Neutrons released in the fission of one uranium-235 nucleus can strike other uranium-235 nuclei, causing them to split and release more neutrons as well as a variety of other nuclei. For simplicity, some fission fragments are not shown.

President Franklin D. Roosevelt indicating the importance of the discovery. It was critical that the U.S. government act quickly.

Thermonuclear Reactions

The chapter opening mentioned that the sun is a nuclear power plant vital to life on Earth. However, the nuclear reactions that take place in the sun are somewhat different from the ones we have discussed throughout this chapter. These **thermonuclear reactions** require enormously high temperatures (millions of degrees) to initiate them. The intense temperatures and pressures in the sun cause nuclei to fuse and release enormous amounts of energy. Instead of large nuclei being split into smaller fragments (fission), small nuclei are fused into larger ones (fusion). The main reaction in the sun is thought to be the fusion of four hydrogen nuclei to produce one helium nucleus and two positrons.

$$4\,{}^{1}_{1}\text{H} \longrightarrow {}^{4}_{2}\text{He} + 2\,{}^{\;\,0}_{+1}\text{e}$$

Fusion of 1 g of hydrogen releases an amount of energy equivalent to the burning of nearly 20 tons of coal. Every second, the sun fuses 600 tons of hydrogen, producing millions of times more energy than has been produced on Earth in the entire history of humankind. Much current research is aimed at reproducing such a reaction in the laboratory, by using ultrapowerful magnets to contain the intense heat required for ignition. Fusion technology is discussed further in Chapter 14. To date, however, fusion reactions on Earth have been limited to the uncontrolled reactions in explosion tests of hydrogen (thermonuclear) bombs and to small amounts of energy produced by very expensive experimental fusion reactors.

Self-Assessment Questions

Look at the graph in Figure 11.10 to answer questions 1–3.

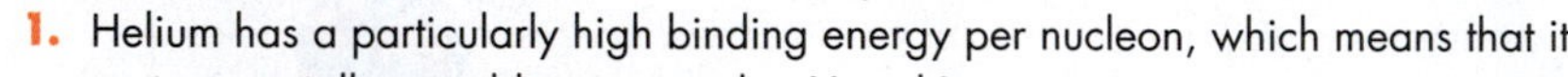

1. Helium has a particularly high binding energy per nucleon, which means that it
   - **a.** is especially unstable compared to H and Li
   - **b.** is more stable than H and Li
   - **c.** will readily fuse into larger nuclei
   - **d.** will readily split into hydrogen-2 atoms
2. The most stable nuclei are those of
   a. Ba **b.** He **c.** Fe **d.** U
3. Nuclei with nuclear numbers greater than that of iron are
   - **a.** all radioactive
   - **b.** increasingly stable
   - **c.** less stable than iron
   - **d.** easily split into smaller nuclei
4. Which equation explains why the products of fission have less mass than the original substances?
   a. $E = h\nu/\lambda$ **b.** $E = h\nu$ **c.** $E = mc^2$ **d.** $PV = nRT$
5. Which subatomic particles are responsible for carrying on the chain reactions characteristic of nuclear fission?
   a. alpha particles **b.** beta particles **c.** neutrons **d.** protons
6. When uranium-235 absorbs a neutron and undergoes fission, barium-142 and krypton-91 are two possible fission fragments. How many neutrons are released?
   $${}^{235}_{92}\text{U} + {}^{1}_{0}\text{n} \longrightarrow {}^{142}_{56}\text{Ba} + {}^{91}_{36}\text{Kr} + ?\,{}^{1}_{0}\text{n}$$
   a. 0 **b.** 1 **c.** 2 **d.** 3
7. What process is represented by the equation ${}^{2}_{1}\text{H} + {}^{2}_{1}\text{H} \longrightarrow {}^{4}_{2}\text{He}$ + energy?
   - **a.** alpha decay
   - **b.** artificial transmutation
   - **c.** fission
   - **d.** fusion
8. Hydrogen-2 and hydrogen-3 fuse to form helium-4. The other product is a(n)
   a. electron **b.** neutron **c.** positron **d.** proton

Answers: 1, b; 2, c; 3, c; 4, c; 5, c; 6, d; 7, d; 8, b

11.8 Nuclear Bombs

Learning Objectives › Describe how uranium and plutonium bombs are made.
› Identify the most hazardous fallout isotopes, and explain why they are particularly dangerous.

In 1939, President Roosevelt launched a highly secret research project for the study of atomic energy. Called the *Manhattan Project*, it eventually became a massive research effort involving more scientific brainpower than ever was or has been devoted to a single project. Amazingly, it was conducted under such extreme secrecy that even Vice President Harry Truman did not know of its existence until after Roosevelt's death.

The Manhattan Project included four separate research teams trying to learn how to

- sustain the nuclear-fission chain reaction,
- enrich uranium so that it contained about 90% of the fissionable isotope ^{235}U,
- make plutonium-239 (another fissionable isotope), and
- construct a bomb based on nuclear fission.

Sustainable Chain Reaction

By that time, it had been established that neutron bombardment could initiate the fission reaction, but many attributes of this reaction were unknown. Enrico Fermi and his group, working in a lab under the bleachers at Stagg Field on the campus of the University of Chicago, worked on the fission reaction itself and how to sustain it. They found that the neutrons used to trigger the reaction had to be slowed down to increase the probability that they would hit a uranium nucleus. Because graphite slows down neutrons, a large "pile" of graphite was built to house the reaction. Then the amount of uranium "fuel" was gradually increased. The major goal was to determine the **critical mass**—the amount of uranium-235 needed to sustain the fission reaction. There had to be enough fissionable nuclei in the "fuel" for the neutrons released in one fission process to have a good chance of being captured by another fissionable nucleus before escaping from the pile.

On December 2, 1942, Fermi and his group achieved the first sustained nuclear fission reaction. The critical mass of uranium (enriched to about 94% ^{235}U) for this reactor turned out to be about 16 kg.

Isotopic Enrichment

Natural uranium is 99.27% uranium-238, which does not undergo fission. Uranium-235, the fissionable isotope, makes up only 0.72% of natural uranium. Because making a bomb required *enriching* the uranium to about 90% uranium-235, it was necessary to find a way to separate the uranium isotopes. This was the job of the Manhattan Project research team in Oak Ridge, Tennessee.

Chemical separation was almost impossible; ^{235}U and ^{238}U are chemically almost identical. The separation method eventually used involved converting uranium to gaseous uranium hexafluoride, UF_6. Molecules of UF_6 containing uranium-235 are slightly lighter and therefore move slightly faster than molecules containing uranium-238. Uranium hexafluoride was allowed to pass through a series of thousands of pinholes, and the molecules containing uranium-235 gradually outdistanced the others. Enough enriched uranium-235 was finally obtained to make a small explosive device.

Synthesis of Plutonium

While the tedious work of separating uranium isotopes was underway at Oak Ridge, another research team, led by Glenn T. Seaborg, approached the problem of obtaining fissionable material by another route. Although uranium-238 would

▲ Glenn T. Seaborg (1912–1999). Element 106 was named seaborgium (Sg) in his honor. Seaborg is the only person to have had an element named for him while still alive. He is shown here pointing to his namesake element on the periodic table of elements.

not fission when bombarded by neutrons, it was found that this more common isotope of uranium *would* decay to form a new element, named neptunium (Np). This product quickly decayed to another new element, plutonium (Pu).

$$^{238}_{92}\text{U} + ^{1}_{0}\text{n} \longrightarrow ^{239}_{92}\text{U}$$

$$^{239}_{92}\text{U} \longrightarrow ^{0}_{-1}\text{e} + ^{239}_{93}\text{Np}$$

$$^{239}_{93}\text{Np} \longrightarrow ^{239}_{94}\text{Pu} + ^{0}_{-1}\text{e}$$

Plutonium-239 was found to be fissionable and thus was suitable material for the making of a bomb. A group of large reactors was built near Hanford, Washington, to produce plutonium.

Bomb Construction

The actual building of the nuclear bombs was carried out at Los Alamos, New Mexico, under the direction of J. Robert Oppenheimer (1904–1967). In a top-secret laboratory at a remote site, a group of scientists planned and then constructed what would become known as atomic bombs. Two different models were developed, one based on ^{235}U and the other on ^{239}Pu.

The critical mass of uranium-235 could not be exceeded prematurely, so it was important that no single piece of fissionable material in the bomb be that large. The bomb was designed to contain pieces of uranium of subcritical mass, plus a neutron source to initiate the fission reaction. Then, at the chosen time, all the pieces would be forced together using an ordinary high explosive, thus triggering a runaway nuclear chain reaction.

The synthesis of plutonium turned out to be easier than the isotopic separation, and by July 1945, enough fissionable material had been made for three bombs to be assembled—two using plutonium, and one using uranium. The first atomic bomb (one of the plutonium devices) was tested in the desert near Alamogordo, New Mexico, on July 16, 1945. The heat from the explosion vaporized the 30-m steel tower on which the bomb was placed and melted the sand for several hectares around the site. The light produced was the brightest anyone had ever seen.

Some of the scientists were so awed by the force of the blast that they argued against using the bombs on Japan. A few, led by Leo Szilard, suggested a demonstration of the bombs' power at an uninhabited site. But fear of a well-publicized "dud" and the desire to avoid millions of casualties in an invasion of Japan led President Harry Truman to order the dropping of the bombs on Japanese cities. The lone uranium bomb, called "Little Boy" (Figure 11.13), was dropped on Hiroshima on August 6, 1945, and caused over 100,000 casualties. Three days later, the other plutonium bomb, called "Fat Man," was dropped on Nagasaki with comparable results (Figure 11.14). World War II ended with the surrender of Japan on August 14, 1945.

Radioactive Fallout

When a nuclear explosion occurs in the open atmosphere, radioactive materials can rain down on parts of Earth thousands of miles away, days and weeks later in what is called **radioactive fallout**. The uranium atom can split in several different ways.

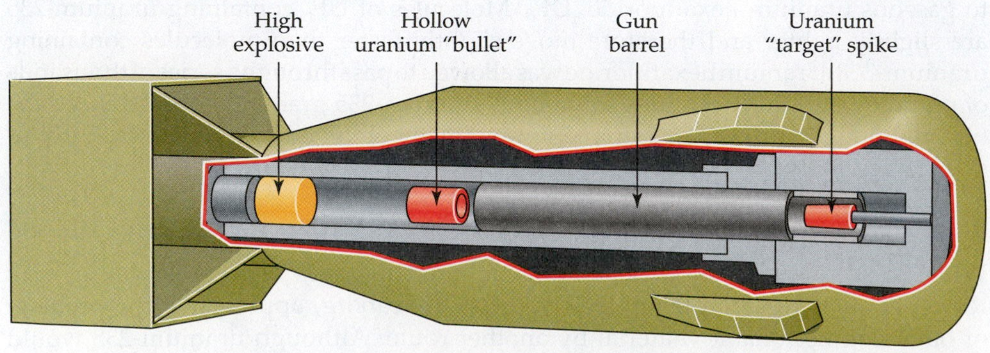

▶ **Figure 11.13** An internal schematic of the atomic bomb "Little Boy" dropped on Hiroshima. Each of the cylinders of uranium-235 had less than the critical mass. The high explosive shot the cylindrical "bullet" down the gun barrel and onto the target spike. The result was about two critical masses of uranium-235, and a nuclear explosion occurred about a millisecond later.

$$^{235}_{92}U + ^{1}_{0}n \longrightarrow ^{90}_{38}Sr + ^{143}_{54}Xe + 3\,^{1}_{0}n$$

$$\longrightarrow ^{102}_{39}Y + ^{131}_{53}I + 3\,^{1}_{0}n$$

$$\longrightarrow ^{95}_{37}Rb + ^{137}_{55}Cs + 4\,^{1}_{0}n$$

▲ **Figure 11.14** The mushroom cloud over Nagasaki, following the detonation of "Fat Man" on August 9, 1945.

The primary (first) fission products are radioactive. These decay to daughter isotopes, many of which are also radioactive. In all, over 200 different fission products are produced, with half-lives that vary from less than a second to more than a billion years. Also, the neutrons produced in the explosion act on molecules in the atmosphere to produce carbon-14, tritium, and other radioisotopes. Fallout is therefore exceedingly complex. We consider three of the more worrisome isotopes here.

Of all the isotopes, strontium-90 (half-life 28.5 y) presents the greatest hazard to people. Strontium-90 reaches us primarily through dairy products and vegetables. Because of its similarity to calcium (both are group 2A elements), strontium-90 is incorporated into bone. There it remains an internal source of radiation for many years.

Iodine-131 may present a greater threat immediately after a nuclear explosion or reactor meltdown. Its half-life is only 8 days, but it is produced in relatively large amounts. Iodine-131 is readily transferred up the food chain. In the human body, it is concentrated in the thyroid gland, and it is precisely this characteristic that makes a trace of iodine-131 so useful for diagnostic scanning. However, for a healthy individual, larger amounts of radioactive iodine offer only damaging side effects. To minimize the absorption of radioactive iodine, many people in the areas of Chernobyl and Fukushima were given large amounts of potassium iodide, which effectively diluted the amount of radioactive iodine absorbed by their thyroid glands.

Cesium-137 (half-life 30.2 y) is, like strontium-90, capable of long-term effects. Because of its similarity to potassium (both are group 1A elements), it is taken up by living organisms as part of body fluids. It can be obtained from sources in the environment and reconcentrated in living organisms.

By the late 1950s, radioactive isotopes from atmospheric testing of nuclear weapons were detected in the environment. Concern over radiation damage from nuclear fallout led to a movement to ban atmospheric testing. Many scientists were leaders in the movement. Linus Pauling, who won the Nobel Prize in Chemistry in 1954 for his bonding theories and for his work in determining the structure of proteins, was a particularly articulate advocate of banning atmospheric tests. In 1963, a nuclear test ban treaty was signed by the major nations—with the exception of France and the People's Republic of China, which continued aboveground tests. Since the signing of the treaty, other countries have joined the nuclear club. Pauling, who had endured being called a communist and a traitor because of his outspoken position, was awarded the Nobel Peace Prize in 1962.

Self-Assessment Questions

1. The isotope used in uranium fission reactions is
   a. uranium-232
   b. uranium-234
   c. uranium-235
   d. uranium-238
2. What fraction of natural uranium is the fissionable isotope?
   a. <1%
   b. 10%
   c. 50%
   d. >99%
3. Plutonium for fission reactions is
   a. made from uranium-238
   b. made from neptunium ores
   c. obtained from the dwarf planet Pluto
   d. obtained from plutonium ores

4. Strontium-90 substitutes for calcium in bones because Sr and Ca
   a. are in the same group of the periodic table
   b. are in the same period of the periodic table
   c. have identical electron configurations
   d. have identical half-lives
5. Which of the following radioisotopes in fallout is dangerous mainly because it becomes concentrated in the thyroid gland?
   a. cesium-137 b. iodine-131 c. strontium-90 d. radon-222

Answers: 1. c; 2. a; 3. a; 4. a; 5. b

11.9 Uses of Nuclear Energy

Learning Objective › List some uses of nuclear energy.

A significant portion of the electricity we use today is generated by nuclear power plants. In the United States, one-fifth of all the electricity produced comes from nuclear power plants. Europeans rely even more on nuclear energy. France, for example, obtains 80% of its electric power from nuclear plants, while Belgium, Spain, Switzerland, and Sweden generate about one-third of their power from nuclear reactors.

Ironically, the same nuclear chain reaction that occurred in the detonation of the bomb dropped on Hiroshima is used extensively today under the familiar concrete containment tower of a nuclear power plant. The key difference is that the power plant employs a *slow, controlled* release of energy from the nuclear chain reaction, rather than an explosion. The slowness of the process is due to the use of uranium fuel that is much less enriched (2.5–3.5% ^{235}U rather than the 90% enrichment of weapons-grade uranium).

One of the main problems with the production of nuclear power arises from the products of the nuclear reactions. As in nuclear fallout, most of the daughter nuclei produced by the fission of uranium-235 are also radioactive, some with very long half-lives. We will discuss the problems associated with nuclear waste further in Chapter 15. Perhaps a more serious problem is the potential transformation of spent nuclear fuel into weapons-grade material (see the box titled "Nuclear Proliferation and Dirty Bombs" on page 324).

▶ The core of a nuclear reactor contains hollow rods filled with uranium pellets. The heat generated by the fission reaction is used to boil water, which drives turbines to generate electricity in the same way as in coal-fired or gas-fired generating plant. Because the pellets are only about 3% uranium-235, a nuclear explosion cannot occur, though loss of coolant may lead to a reactor meltdown.

GREEN CHEMISTRY

Principles 1, 4, 6, 10, 12

Bevin W. Parks-Lee, *Industrial organic chemist*

Green Remediation of Nuclear Waste

You learned that a large amount of ^{239}Pu was manufactured in Hanford, Washington, for the Manhattan Project (Section 11.8). The plutonium was produced from uranium in a nuclear reactor much like the ones used to produce electricity today. After the uranium rods reacted long enough to produce usable amounts of plutonium, they were transferred from the reactor and prepared for reprocessing. The goal was to maximize the plutonium production. The waste, still highly radioactive, was stored in many million-gallon tanks. Some of these tanks have been in service for 70 years, and leaks have been detected. Green chemistry principles can guide the development of methods to handle this legacy waste responsibly.

The Manhattan Project generated more than 91 million gallons of extremely acidic radioactive waste left over from the recovery of Pu and U. The solutions, referred to as high-level liquid waste (HLLW), are radioactive because small amounts of U and Pu remain with many other radioactive *nuclides* (nuclei having specific mass numbers and atomic numbers) that were produced during the fission reactions, including Np, Am, and Nd (Sections 11.3 and 11.7). If this small amount of radioactive material (1–2% of the 91 million gallons) could be removed, the impact would be tremendous.

Spent fuel rods are made up of different metals that can be separated and reclaimed through reprocessing. The aim is to remove any remaining radioactive nuclides, but many steps are necessary to achieve this. To access the separate atoms and free them from the solid matrix, the fuel rods are dissolved in concentrated nitric acid. An oxidation-reduction reaction occurs between the acid and the metals (Sections 8.1 and 8.6). The protons from the acid are reduced to form hydrogen gas, and the metals are oxidized to produce cations. The radioactive metal cations remain in the acidic water. At this point, it is possible to selectively remove metals by using special organic solutions that bind specific nuclides.

Processes that reduce the amount of HLLW align with Green Chemistry Principles 1, 6, and 12. How can these principles be put into action? One way is to design remediation processes that target the radioactive parts of the waste. Specifically, isolating only the radioactive compounds that require treatment avoids the need to store millions of gallons of acidic solution. Also, since the half-lives of these nuclides are so long (Section 11.3), encasing the waste in glass (vitrification) has been proposed as a good storage approach. Decreasing the volume of waste, though, would minimize the use of vitrification, which is energy-intensive and expensive.

In reprocessing, specific molecules can be used to bind to the radioactive cations and to manipulate the properties (e.g., solubility) of the resulting metal compounds. The molecules react with the metals to make compounds soluble in organic solvents. This enables the radioactive materials to be removed from water and transferred into a small volume of organic solvent. If the molecules are selective for one metal over another, they will bind to and carry only that metal into the organic solvent. This reprocessing method offers the opportunity to separate and reclaim individual types of metals.

One type of organic molecule that can extract the radioactive nuclides is an *amide* (Section 9.8). Amides are easy to synthesize, and they are stable in the highly acidic and radioactive environment. A way to further reduce the volume of radioactive waste would be to burn off the organic components—the molecules bound to the metals and the solvent carrying them—leaving only solid metal waste. Amides (composed of only C, H, N, and O) will burn completely, making them a good fit with Green Chemistry Principle 10—designing for degradation. The simple amides tested first did not bind the metal ions as well as other types of molecules, which were harder to synthesize, degraded in the waste solutions, could not be incinerated, and tended to be toxic. Further research uncovered that molecules containing two amide groups bound the metal ions very well. This example shows the application of Green Chemistry Principle 4 through the design of a safer chemical.

Overall, green chemistry principles can be used to dramatically reduce amounts of radioactive waste and to reprocess the waste in ways that are safer for human health and the environment.

▲ Construction of the storage tanks of HLLW that are buried on completion.

Nuclear Proliferation and Dirty Bombs

As power is generated in nuclear plants, important changes occur in the fuel. Neutron bombardment converts ^{235}U to radioactive daughter products. Eventually, the concentration of ^{235}U becomes too low to sustain the nuclear chain reaction. The fuel rods must be replaced about every three years. The rods then become high-level nuclear waste.

As ^{235}U undergo fission, the nonfissionable (and very concentrated) ^{238}U nuclei absorb neutrons and are converted to ^{239}Pu, a transmutation described in Section 11.8). In time, some ^{240}Pu is also formed. However, if the fuel rods are removed after only about three months, the fissionable plutonium-239 can be easily separated from the other fission products by chemical means. Plutonium bombs require less sophisticated technology to produce than is needed to make nuclear weapons from uranium. Plutonium is thus of greater concern with respect to weapons proliferation, because operation of a nuclear plant can produce materials suitable for use in a bomb. North Korea has nuclear power plants and a plutonium separation facility capable of producing enough ^{239}Pu for several weapons each year (Figure 11.15). Iran also has a facility for enriching uranium, which could lead to the production of nuclear bombs. The activities of these and other developing countries raise the fear of a dangerous proliferation of nuclear weapons.

Another security concern is a "dirty bomb," a device that uses a conventional explosive, such as dynamite, to disperse radioactive material that might be stolen from a hospital or other facility that uses radioactive isotopes. In most cases, the conventional bomb would do more immediate harm than the radioactive substances. At the levels most likely to be used, the dirty bomb would not contain enough radioactive material to kill people or cause severe illness.

▲ **Figure 11.15** Satellite photograph of the plutonium processing plant at Yongbyon, North Korea.

The Nuclear Age

The splitting of the atom made the Chinese curse "May you live in interesting times" seem quite appropriate. The goal of the alchemists, to change one element into another, has been achieved through the application of scientific principles. New elements have been formed, and the periodic table has been extended well beyond

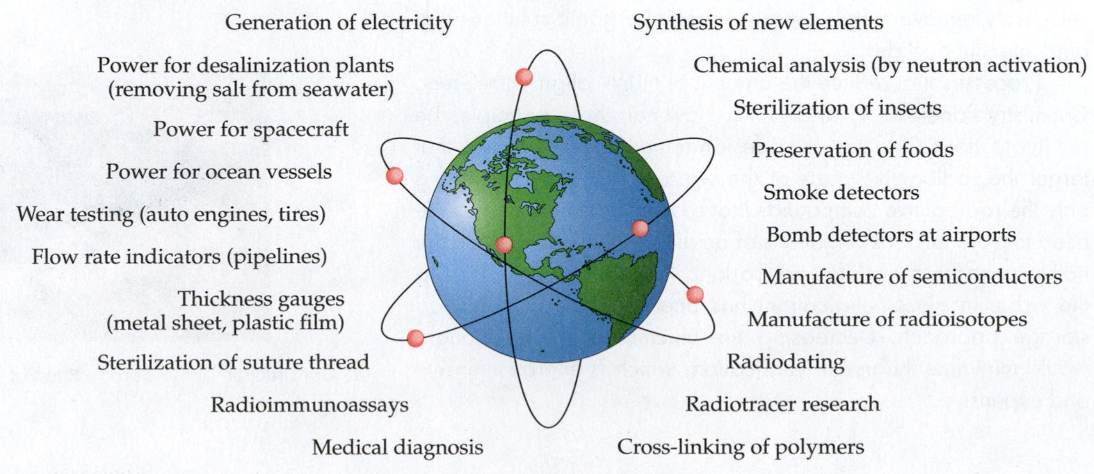

▲ **Figure 11.16** Some constructive uses of nuclear energy.

uranium (Z = 92). This modern alchemy produces plutonium by the ton; neptunium (Z = 93), americium (Z = 95), and curium (Z = 96) by the kilogram; and berkelium (Z = 97) and einsteinium (Z = 99) by the milligram.

As we have seen, radioactive isotopes have many uses, from killing tiny but deadly cancer cells and harmful microorganisms in food to serving as tracers in a variety of biological experiments and imaging technologies and generating fearsome weapons. Figure 11.16 displays a number of other constructive uses of nuclear energy. We live in an age in which the extraordinary forces present in the atom have been unleashed as a true double-edged sword. The threat of nuclear war—and nuclear terrorism—has been a constant specter for the last six decades, yet it is hard to believe that the world would be a better place if we had not discovered the secrets of the atomic nucleus.

CRITICAL THINKING  EXERCISES

Apply knowledge that you have gained in this chapter and one or more of the FLaReS principles (Chapter 1) to evaluate the following statements or claims.

11.1 Brazil nuts are known to absorb and concentrate the element barium. A nationally known laboratory announces that Brazil nuts contain tiny traces of radium.

11.2 For more than 600 years, it was alleged that the Shroud of Turin was the burial shroud of Jesus. In 1988, several laboratories carried out carbon-14 analyses indicating that the flax from which the shroud was made was grown between C.E. 1260 and 1390. Recently there have been claims that the 1988 analyses are unreliable because the shroud is contaminated with pollen from plants grown in the fourteenth century, and it is the age of this pollen that was actually measured in 1988. At least one of the scientists has offered to repeat the analysis on a very carefully cleaned sample of the cloth, but further access to the shroud has been refused.

11.3 A scientist reports that he has found an artifact that has been shown to be 80,000 years old by carbon-14 dating.

11.4 The americium in a smoke detector (see Conceptual Example 11.7) is encased in a chamber with aluminum shielding, about as thick as the wall of a soft-drink can. A woman who purchases a smoke detector mounts it at the highest point on the ceiling. She claims that this minimizes her exposure to the radiation.

11.5 A young girl refuses to visit her grandmother after the woman has undergone radiation therapy for breast cancer. The teenager is afraid that she will catch radiation sickness from her grandmother.

SUMMARY

Section 11.1—Some isotopes of elements have unstable nuclei, which undergo changes in nucleon number, atomic number, or energy; this process is called **radioactive decay**. The nuclei that undergo such changes are called **radioisotopes**. We are constantly exposed to naturally occurring radiation, called **background radiation**. Radiation that causes harm by dislodging electrons from living tissue and forming ions is called **ionizing radiation** and includes nuclear radiation and X-rays. Radiation can disrupt normal chemical processes in cells and can damage DNA, sometimes causing mutations.

Section 11.2—Nuclear equations are used to represent nuclear processes. These equations are balanced when the sum of nucleon numbers on each side is the same and the sum of atomic numbers on each side is the same. Four types of radioactive decay are **alpha** $\left({}^{4}_{2}\text{He}\right)$ **decay**, **beta** $\left({}^{\;0}_{-1}\text{e}\right)$ **decay, gamma** $\left({}^{0}_{0}\gamma\right)$ **decay**, and emission of a **positron** $\left({}^{\;0}_{+1}\text{e}\right)$. **Electron capture (EC)** is a fifth type of decay, in which a nucleus absorbs one of the atom's electrons. There are a number of important differences between nuclear reactions and chemical reactions.

Section 11.3—The rate of radioactive decay is measured in **becquerels (Bq)**.

$$1 \text{ becquerel (Bq)} = 1 \text{ disintegration/s}$$

The **half-life** of a radioactive isotope is the time it takes for half of a sample to undergo radioactive decay. The fraction of a radioisotope remaining after n half-lives is given by the expression

$$\text{Fraction remaining} = \frac{1}{2^n}$$

Half-lives of certain isotopes can be used to estimate the ages of various objects. **Carbon-14 dating** is the best-known of the radioisotopic dating techniques. Relying on carbon-14's half-life of 5730 years, this technique can be used to estimate the age of once-living items up to 50,000 years old. The decay of tritium can be used to date items up to 100 years old. Other isotopes can be used to date rocks, the Earth's crust, and meteorites.

Section 11.4—**Transmutation**, the conversion of one element into another, cannot be carried out by chemical means but can be accomplished by nuclear processes. Bombarding a stable nucleus with energetic particles can cause artificial transmutation. These processes can be represented with nuclear equations.

Section 11.5—Radioisotopes have many uses. A radioisotope and a stable isotope of an element behave nearly the same chemically, so radioisotopes can be used as **tracers** in physical and biological systems. A radioactive atom in a molecule labels it so that it can be followed by a radiation detector. Radioisotopes have many uses in agriculture, including the production of useful mutations. Radiation can be used to irradiate foodstuffs as a method of preservation. **Radiation therapy** to destroy cancer cells depends on the fact that radiation is more damaging to those rapidly reproducing cells than to healthy cells. Radioisotopes are used in the diagnosis of various disorders. Iodine-131 is used for thyroid diagnoses, gadolinium-153 for bone mineralization examinations, and technetium-99m for a variety of diagnostic tests. Positron emission tomography (PET) involves radioisotopes that emit positrons, which are then annihilated by electrons in the body, producing gamma rays that can be used to form an image.

Section 11.6—Different types of radiation have different penetrating abilities. *Alpha particles* (helium nuclei) are relatively slow and have low penetrating power. *Beta particles* (electrons) are much faster and more penetrating. *Gamma rays* (high-energy photons) travel at the speed of light and have great penetrating power. How hazardous radiation is depends on the location of the source; alpha particles from a source inside the body are highly damaging. Radiation hazard can be decreased by moving away from the source or by using shielding.

Section 11.7—Einstein's **mass–energy equation**, $E = mc^2$ shows that mass and energy are different aspects of the same thing. The total mass of the nucleons in a nucleus is greater than the actual mass of the nucleus. The missing mass, or the mass defect, is equivalent to the **binding energy** holding the nucleons together. Binding energy can be released either by breaking down heavy nuclei into smaller ones, a process called **nuclear fission**, or by joining small nuclei to form larger ones, called **nuclear fusion**.

Fermi and Segrè bombarded uranium atoms with neutrons and found radioactive species among the products, while Hahn and Strassman found light nuclei among the reaction products. Meitner, aided by Frisch, hypothesized that the uranium nuclei were undergoing fission. Szilard saw that neutrons released in the fission of one nucleus could trigger the fission of other nuclei, setting off a **chain reaction**.

Thermonuclear reactions (fusion reactions) combine small nuclei to form larger ones. Nuclear fusion produces even more energy than nuclear fission. Fusion is the basis of the hydrogen bomb and the source of the sun's energy. Much research is aimed at producing controlled fusion commercially.

Section 11.8—The nuclear fission reaction became the center of the Manhattan Project during World War II. Its goals were (1) to achieve sustained nuclear fission and determine the **critical mass**, or minimum amount, of fissionable material required; (2) to enrich the amount of fissionable uranium-235 in ordinary uranium; (3) to synthesize plutonium-239, which is also fissionable; and (4) to construct a nuclear fission bomb before the Germans were able to do so. World War II ended shortly after the dropping of atomic bombs on Hiroshima and Nagasaki.

In addition to the devastation at the site of a nuclear explosion, much radioactive debris, or **radioactive fallout,** is, produced. Strontium-90 and iodine-131 are particularly hazardous components of fallout. Partly because of fallout, a nuclear test ban treaty was signed by most of the major nations; only underground testing is not banned.

Section 11.9—Nuclear power plants use the same nuclear chain reaction as in atomic bombs, but the reaction is much slower and can be controlled because of the low concentration of fissionable material. Disposal of the products of nuclear fission in power plants is an important problem facing us, as is the potential conversion of nuclear fuel into weapons. The forces within the nucleus truly constitute a double-edged sword for civilization.

Green chemistry Radioactive waste must be handled responsibly, and green chemistry principles can guide the development of new methods. A greener approach is to selectively isolate and treat the small amounts of radioactive isotopes instead of the large volumes of liquid waste. This can now be accomplished using safer chemicals, thereby reducing the amount of hazardous waste and the need for expensive and energy-intensive processing or storage methods.

Learning Objectives

› Identify the sources of the natural radiation to which we are exposed.	Problems 15, 54
› List the sources and dangers of ionizing radiation.	Problem 15
› Balance nuclear equations.	Problems 19–25, 43
› Identify the products formed by various decay processes.	Problems 26–30, 47
› Solve simple half-life problems.	Problems 31–38, 51
› Use the concept of half-life to solve simple radioisotopic dating problems.	Problems 39–42
› Write a nuclear equation for a transmutation, and identify the product element formed.	Problems 45, 46, 58

› List some applications of radioisotopes.	Problems 39–42, 50
› Describe the nature of materials needed to block alpha, beta, and gamma radiation.	Problem 13
› Explain where nuclear energy comes from.	Problems 52, 55
› Describe the difference between fission and fusion.	Problem 17
› Describe how uranium and plutonium bombs are made.	Problem 18
› Identify the most hazardous fallout isotopes, and explain why they are particularly dangerous.	Problems 15, 52
› List some uses of nuclear energy.	Problems 31, 34, 39, 42, 44
› Identify green chemistry principles that can help solve existing problems in nuclear chemistry.	Problems 59, 62
› Explain how molecules used in nuclear waste processing can be designed to be safer, and give examples of such molecules.	Problems 60, 61

REVIEW QUESTIONS

1. Match each description with the type of change.
   (i) A new compound is formed. — **a.** nuclear
   (ii) A new element is formed. — **b.** chemical
   (iii) Size, shape, appearance, or volume is changed without changing the composition. — **c.** physical
2. Define or describe each of the following.
   a. half-life
   b. positron
   c. background radiation
   d. radioisotope
3. Write the nuclear symbols for protium, deuterium, and tritium (which are hydrogen-1, hydrogen-2, and hydrogen-3, respectively).
4. Why are isotopes important in nuclear reactions but not in most chemical reactions?
5. Write the nuclear symbols for the following isotopes. You may refer to the periodic table.
   a. cobalt-60
   b. iodine-127
   c. sodium-22
   d. calcium-42
6. Indicate the number of protons and the number of neutrons in atoms of the following isotopes.
   a. $^{65}_{30}\text{Zn}$ **b.** $^{236}_{93}\text{Np}$
   c. $^{101}_{43}\text{Tc}$ **d.** $^{81m}_{36}\text{Kr}$
7. Which of the following pairs represent isotopes? (X is a general symbol for an element.)
   a. $^{70}_{32}\text{X}$ and $^{70}_{32}\text{X}$
   b. $^{57}_{22}\text{X}$ and $^{52}_{22}\text{X}$
   c. $^{176}_{74}\text{X}$ and $^{167}_{74}\text{X}$
   d. $^{8}_{4}\text{X}$ and $^{16}_{8}\text{X}$
8. In which of the following atoms are there more protons than neutrons?
   a. ^{17}F **b.** ^{58}Ni **c.** ^{16}O **d.** ^{197}Au
9. The longest-lived isotope of einsteinium (Es) has a mass (nucleon) number of 254. How many neutrons are in the nucleus of an atom of this isotope?
10. The longest-lived isotope of polonium (Po) has 125 neutrons. What is a mass (nucleon) number of this isotope?
11. What changes occur in the nucleon number and the atomic number of a nucleus during emission of each of the following?
    a. alpha particle
    b. gamma ray
    c. proton
12. What changes occur in the nucleon number and atomic number of a nucleus during emission of each of the following?
    a. beta particle
    b. neutron
    c. positron
13. **(a)** From which type of radiation would a pair of gloves be sufficient to shield the hands: heavy alpha particles or massless gamma rays? **(b)** From which type of radiation would heavy lead shielding be necessary to protect a worker: alpha, beta, or gamma?
14. What are some of the characteristics that make technetium-99m such a useful radioisotope for diagnostic purposes?
15. Plutonium is especially hazardous when inhaled or ingested because it emits alpha particles. Why do alpha particles cause more damage to tissue than beta particles when their source is inside the body?
16. List two ways in which workers exposed to radioactive materials can protect themselves from radiation hazard.
17. Compare nuclear fission and nuclear fusion. Why is energy liberated in each case?
18. The compounds $^{235}UF_6$ and $^{238}UF_6$ are nearly chemically identical. How are they separated?

PROBLEMS

Nuclear Equations

19. Write a balanced equation for emission of **(a)** an alpha particle by californium-250, **(b)** a beta particle by bismuth-210, and **(c)** a positron by iodine-117.

20. Write a balanced equation for **(a)** alpha decay of gold-173, **(b)** beta decay of iodine-138, and **(c)** capture of an electron by cadmium-104.

21. Complete the following equations.
   a. ${}^{179}_{79}\text{Au} \longrightarrow {}^{175}_{77}\text{Ir} + ?$
   b. ${}^{12}_{6}\text{C} + {}^{2}_{1}\text{H} \longrightarrow {}^{13}_{6}\text{C} + ?$
   c. ${}^{154}_{62}\text{Sm} + {}^{1}_{0}\text{n} \longrightarrow ? + 2\,{}^{1}_{0}\text{n}$

22. Complete the following equations.
   a. ${}^{10}_{5}\text{B} + {}^{1}_{0}\text{n} \longrightarrow ? + {}^{4}_{2}\text{He}$
   b. ${}^{23}_{10}\text{Ne} \longrightarrow {}^{23}_{11}\text{Na} + ?$
   c. ${}^{121}_{51}\text{Sb} + ? \longrightarrow {}^{121}_{52}\text{Te} + {}^{1}_{0}\text{n}$

23. Radiological laboratories often have a container of molybdenum-99, which decays to form technetium-99m. What other particle is formed? Complete the equation.

$${}^{99}_{42}\text{Mo} \longrightarrow {}^{99\text{m}}_{43}\text{Tc} + ?$$

24. Complete the equation for the decay of technetium-99m to technetium-99.

$${}^{99\text{m}}_{43}\text{Tc} \longrightarrow {}^{99}_{43}\text{Tc} + ?$$

25. When a magnesium-24 nucleus is bombarded with a neutron, a proton is ejected. What element is formed? (*Hint:* Write a balanced nuclear equation.)

26. A radioisotope decays to give an alpha particle and a protactinium-233 nucleus. What was the original nucleus?

27. A radioactive isotope decays to give an alpha particle and a bismuth-211 nucleus. What was the original nucleus?

28. When silver-107 is bombarded with a neutron, a different isotope of silver forms and then undergoes beta decay. What is the final product? (*Hint:* Write two separate nuclear equations.)

29. A nucleus of astatine-210 decays by beta emission, forming nucleus A. Nucleus A also decays by beta emission to nucleus B. Write the nuclear symbol for B.

30. A proposed method of making fissionable nuclear fuel is to bombard the relatively abundant isotope thorium-232 with a neutron. The product X of this bombardment decays quickly by beta emission to nucleus Y, and nucleus Y decays quickly to fissionable nucleus Z. Write the nuclear symbol for Z.

Half-Life

31. Gallium-67 is used in nuclear medicine (Table 11.6). After treatment, a patient's blood shows an activity of 20,000 counts per minute (counts/min). How long will it be before the activity decreases to about 5000 counts/min?

32. How long will it take for a 12.0-g sample of iodine-131 to decay to leave a total of 1.5 g of the isotope? The half-life of iodine-131 is 8.07 days.

33. A lab worker reports an activity of 80,000 counts/s for a sample of magnesium-21, whose half-life is 122 ms. Exactly 5.00 min later, another worker records an activity of 10 counts/min on the same sample. What best accounts for this difference? Magnesium-21
   a. gives off only neutrinos
   b. has a very short half-life, so almost every radioactive atom in the sample has decayed
   c. is an alpha emitter
   d. is a gamma emitter

34. A patient is injected with a radiopharmaceutical labeled with technetium-99m, half-life of 6.0 h, in preparation for a gamma ray scan to evaluate kidney function. If the original activity of the sample was 48 μCi, what activity (in μCi) remains **(a)** after 24 h and **(b)** after 48 h?

35. Krypton-81m is used for lung ventilation studies. Its half-life is 13 s. How long does it take the activity of this isotope to reach one-quarter of its original value?

36. Radium-223 has a half-life of 11.4 days. Approximately how long would it take for the activity of a sample of ${}^{223}\text{Ra}$ to decrease to 1% of its initial value?

37. In an experiment with dysprosium-197, half-life of 8.1 h, an activity of 500 counts/min was recorded at 4:00 p.m. on a Friday. What was the approximate activity of this sample at 8:30 a.m. the following Monday morning, when the experiment was resumed?

38. In determining the half-life of sulfur-35, students collected the following data, with the time in days and the activity in counts/s.

Time	Activity	Time	Activity
0	1000	80	525
20	851	100	446
40	725	120	380
60	616	140	323

Without doing detailed calculations, estimate a value for the half-life.

Radioisotopic Dating

39. Living matter has a carbon-14 activity of about 16 counts/min per gram of carbon. What is the age of an artifact for which the carbon-14 activity is 8 counts/min per gram of carbon?

40. A piece of wood from an Egyptian tomb has a carbon-14 activity of 980 counts/h. A piece of new wood of the same size shows 3920 counts/h. What is the age of the wood from the tomb?

41. The ratio of carbon-14 to carbon-12 in a piece of charcoal from an archaeological excavation is found to be one-half the ratio in a sample of modern wood. Approximately how old is the charcoal? How old would it be if the isotopic ratio were 25% of that in a sample of modern wood?

42. You are offered a great price on a case of brandy supposedly bottled during the lifetime of Napoleon (1769–1821). Before buying it, you insist on testing a sample of the brandy and find that its tritium content is 12.5% of that of newly produced brandy. How long ago was the brandy bottled? Is it likely to be authentic Napoleon-era brandy?

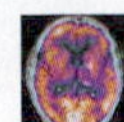

ADDITIONAL PROBLEMS

43. Write balanced nuclear equations for **(a)** the bombardment of $^{121}_{51}Sb$ by alpha particles to produce $^{124}_{53}I$, followed by **(b)** the radioactive decay of $^{124}_{53}I$ by positron emission.

44. A typical smoke detector contains about 0.25 mg of americium-241. The activity of 1 g of ^{241}Am is 1.26×10^{11} Bq. What is the activity of the americium-241 in the smoke detector?

45. In 2010, Russian and American scientists produced a few atoms of element 117 by shooting an intense beam of ions of the rare isotope calcium-48 at a target of berkelium-247. Two isotopes of element 117 were formed, one having 176 neutrons and the other 177 neutrons. Write two separate nuclear equations for the formation of the two isotopes. How many neutrons were released in each process?

46. Meitnerium undergoes alpha decay to form element 107, which in turn also emits an alpha particle. What are the atomic number and nucleon number of the isotope formed by these two steps? Write balanced nuclear equations for the two reactions.

47. Radium-223 nuclei usually decay by alpha emission. Once in every billion decays, a radium-223 nucleus emits a carbon-14 nucleus. Write a balanced nuclear equation for each type of emission.

48. A particular uranium alloy has a density of 18.75 g/cm^3. What volume is occupied by a critical mass of 49 kg of this alloy? The critical mass can be decreased to 16 kg if the alloy is surrounded by a layer of natural uranium (which acts as a neutron reflector). What is the volume of the smaller mass? Compare your answers to the approximate volumes of a baseball, a volleyball, and a basketball.

49. Plutonium has a density of 19.1 g/cm^3. What volume is occupied by a mass of 16.3 kg of plutonium? If a neutron-reflecting coating (made of beryllium) is used, the critical mass can be lowered to 2.5 kg. Compare the size of this mass to the volume of a baseball, a volleyball, and a basketball.

50. There are several technological applications for the transuranium elements ($Z > 92$). An important one is in smoke detectors, which can use the decay of a tiny amount of americium-241 to neptunium-237. What subatomic particle is emitted from that decay process?

51. The radioisotopic dating problems in this chapter are deceptively easy because they involve only integral numbers of half-lives. Calculations involving other than integral half-life values require a bit more complicated math. However, carbon-14 dating calculators that make the task quite easy can be accessed on the Web. Use one of those calculators to find **(a)** the age of a scrap of paper taken from the Dead Sea Scrolls that has a $^{14}C/^{12}C$ ratio that is 79.5% of that in living plants and **(b)** the age of a piece of charcoal from a Neanderthal site that has a $^{14}C/^{12}C$ ratio that is 17.5% of that in living plants.

52. In the first step of the chain reaction of a nuclear explosion, a ^{235}U nucleus absorbs a neutron. The resulting ^{236}U nucleus is unstable and can fission into ^{92}Kr and ^{141}Ba nuclei as shown in the figure. What are the other products of this reaction? After assessing this reaction, explain how the chain reaction can continue.

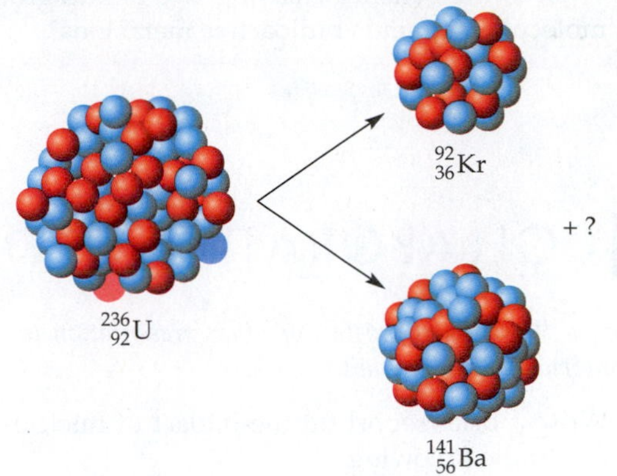

53. In 1932, James Chadwick discovered a new subatomic particle when he bombarded beryllium-9 with alpha particles. One of the products was carbon-12. What particle did Chadwick discover?

54. Several different radioisotopes can be used much like carbon-14 for determining the age of rocks and other matter. In the geosciences, the age of rocks may be determined using potassium-40, which decays to argon-40 with a half-life of 1.2 billion years. **(a)** Some rocks brought back from the moon were dated as being 3.6 billion years old. What percentage of the potassium-40 has decayed after that time? **(b)** Give a reason why uranium-238 (half-life of 4.6 billion years) is more useful for confirming this age than is carbon-14.

55. Einstein's mass–energy equation is $E = mc^2$, where mass is in kilograms and the speed of light is 3.00×10^8 m/s. The unit of energy is the joule (4.184 J = 1 cal; 1000 cal = 1 kcal).
   a. Calculate the energy released, in calories and kilocalories, when 1 g of matter is converted to energy.
   b. A bowl of cornflakes supplies 110 kcal (110 food calories). How many bowls of cornflakes would supply the same amount of energy as you calculated for 1 g of matter in part (a)?

56. Radioactive copper ($^{64}_{29}Cu$, half-life 12.7 h) is found in quantities exceeding the pollution standard in the sediments of a reservoir during a routine check on Monday, when 56 ppm/m^3 was measured. The standard allows up to 14 ppm/m^3. About when will the level of copper-64 return to 14 ppm/m^3?

57. An unidentified corpse was discovered on April 21 at 7:00 a.m. The pathologist discovered that there were 1.24×10^{17} atoms of $^{32}_{15}P$ remaining in the victim's bones and placed the time of death sometime on March 15. The half-life of $^{32}_{15}P$ is 14.28 days. How much $^{32}_{15}P$ was present in the bones at the time of death?

58. Scientists have tried to make element 120. Three different combinations of projectile and target were used to try to produce the nucleus $^{302}_{120}X$: **(a)** nickel-64 and uranium-238, **(b)** iron-58 and plutonium-244, and **(c)** chromium-54 and curium-248. However, after 120 days, no sign of element 120 was found. Write nuclear equations for the three expected reactions.

59. True or False? Green chemistry principles can be applied only as a process is being developed.

60. List four elements of which a compound that can be completely incinerated may be composed.

61. What is the benefit of having two amide groups on one molecule that binds radioactive metal ions?

62. Vitrification is an expensive and energy-intensive method involving encasing waste in glass. What portion of HLLW is radioactive, and why is that important with respect to vitrification?

COLLABORATIVE GROUP PROJECTS

Prepare a PowerPoint, poster, or other presentation (as directed by your instructor) to share with the class.

1. Write a brief report on the impact of nuclear science on one of the following.
   a. war and peace
   b. industrial progress
   c. medicine
   d. agriculture
   e. human, animal, and plant genetics
2. Write an essay on radioisotopic dating using one or more of the isotopes in Table 11.5 other than carbon-14 or tritium.
3. Write a brief biography of one of the following scientists.
   a. Otto Hahn
   b. Enrico Fermi
   c. Glenn T. Seaborg
   d. J. Robert Oppenheimer
   e. Lise Meitner
   f. Albert Einstein
4. The positron is a particle of antimatter. Search the Web for information about antimatter, and the positron in particular.
5. Find a Web site that is strongly in favor of nuclear power plants and one that is strongly opposed. Note the sites' sponsors, and analyze their viewpoints. Try to find a Web site with a balanced viewpoint.
6. In July 1999, researchers at Lawrence Berkeley Laboratory reported the creation of the heaviest element to date, element 118. Two years later, that report was found to be fraudulent. Report on the scientific ethical questions raised by this episode.
7. Find the location of the nuclear power plant closest to where you live. Try to determine risks and benefits of the plant. To how many houses does it provide power? What are the environmental impacts of the plant under normal operating conditions?
8. Assemble two teams of two to four people each to debate the following resolution: The dropping of the atomic bombs on Hiroshima and Nagasaki was justified. Decide beforehand which team will take the affirmative and which the negative. Each team member is to give a three- to six-minute speech followed by a cross-examination by the opposing team members. Have the rest of the class judge the debate and give written or oral comments.

Chemistry of Earth

Have You Ever Wondered?

1. How do we know what substances are common on other planets?
2. Why is asbestos dangerous?
3. Can you get lead poisoning from pottery?
4. If atoms are conserved, why do we need to recycle aluminum and iron?
5. Why do scrap metals bring such high prices?

Learning Objectives

- Name the regions of Earth's crust, and give the approximate composition of each. (12.1)
- List the most abundant elements in Earth's crust. (12.1)
- Describe the arrangement of silicate tetrahedra in common silicate minerals. (12.2)
- Describe how glass differs in structure from other silicates. (12.2)
- List the most important metals with their principal ores, and explain how they are extracted. (12.3)
- Describe some of the environmental costs associated with metal production. (12.3)
- List the main components of solid waste. (12.4)
- Name and describe the three Rs of garbage. (12.4)
- Identify the green chemistry principles that can guide the determination of which metal, Fe or Al, is greener.
- Describe how recycling supports sustainable use of natural resources.

Metals and Minerals

This wondrous world of ours is a fertile sphere blanketed in air, with about three-fourths of its surface covered by water. Although Spaceship Earth is about 40,000 km in circumference, with a surface area of 500 million km^2, it is but a tiny, blue-green jewel in the vastness of space.

Human astronauts have walked on the barren surface of Earth's airless moon. Unmanned craft have explored the desolate surface of Mars, the crushing pressure and hellish heat beneath the hurricane clouds of sulfuric acid on Venus, and the liquid hydrocarbon seas and water-ice rocks of Saturn's moon Titan. Probes have also given us close-up portraits of dry, pockmarked Mercury and of Jupiter and Saturn with their horrendous lightning storms and their turbulent atmospheres of hydrogen and helium.

Every area of earth is awash with minerals, many of which are useful to mankind. As the name implies, the otherwise barren Bonneville Salt Flats contain large amounts of sodium chloride, widely used in both industry and the home. Most sodium chloride is obtained from salt lakes and from the oceans. The water is evaporated, and the solids are heaped in piles as seen at right. After drying, purifying, and packaging, the product finds its way into our kitchens as table salt. Many other minerals make longer journeys to their final destination. We will examine some of them in this chapter.

Earth is but a small island in the inhospitable immensity of space, a tiny oasis perhaps uniquely suited to the life that inhabits it.

From earliest times, people have used Earth's resources. Primitive people used ordinary stones for hunting and as tools. Modern people mine ores and coal and drill for oil and gas. Spaceship Earth carries 7 billion passengers, and their numbers are increasing rapidly. What kinds of materials do we have aboard this spaceship? Are they sufficient for this enormous load of passengers? Let's begin by looking at the composition of Earth.

1. How do we know what substances are common on other planets? Recall Figures 3.9 and 3.11. We can view the spectra of celestial objects to identify the elements and compounds that are present. We can even get an idea of the relative amounts of those elements and compounds, from the brightness of the light.

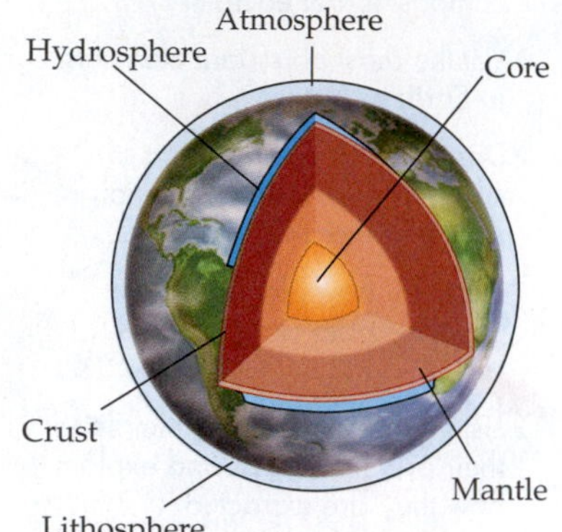

▲ **Figure 12.1** Diagram showing the structural regions of Earth (not to scale).

Q: *Earth is roughly 12,000 km in diameter, and the crust averages 35 km thick. Why is the crust not shown to scale?*

12.1 Spaceship Earth: The Materials Manifest

Learning Objectives › Name the regions of Earth's crust, and give the approximate composition of each. › List the most abundant elements in Earth's crust.

Earth is divided into three main regions: the core, the mantle, and the crust (Figure 12.1). The *core* is thought to consist largely of iron with some nickel. Because the core and the mantle are not accessible and do not seem likely to become so, we can't consider them as sources of materials. And we can't look to the moon, Mars, or asteroids as sources; access to any extraterrestrial resources is decades, if not centuries, in the future.

The *crust* is the outer solid shell of Earth, often called the *lithosphere*. The watery part, made up of the oceans, seas, lakes, rivers, and so on, is the *hydrosphere*. The *atmosphere* is the air that surrounds the planet. We discuss the atmosphere in Chapter 13 and the hydrosphere in Chapter 14. In this chapter, we focus on the lithosphere, which is about 35 km thick under the continents and about 10 km thick under the oceans. Through extensive sampling of the atmosphere, hydrosphere, and lithosphere, scientists have been able to estimate the elemental composition of the outer portion of Earth. An average randomized sample has the composition summarized in Table 12.1, which features the nine most abundant elements.

Table 12.1 Elemental Composition of the Earth's Surface

Element	Atom Percent	Percent by Mass
Oxygen	53.3	49.5
Silicon	15.9	25.7
Hydrogen	15.1	0.9
Aluminum	4.8	7.5
Sodium	1.8	2.6
Iron	1.5	4.7
Calcium	1.5	3.4
Magnesium	1.4	1.9
Potassium	1.0	2.4
All others	3.7	1.4
Total	100.0	100.0

More than half the atoms in the sample are O atoms, which occur in the atmosphere as molecular oxygen (O_2), in the hydrosphere in combination with hydrogen as water, and in the lithosphere in combination with silicon (pure sand is largely SiO_2) and various other elements. Silicon is the second most abundant element in the sample, and hydrogen is third, with most of the H atoms combined with oxygen in water. Because hydrogen is the lightest element, it makes up only 0.9% of Earth's crust by mass. Just three elements—oxygen, silicon, and hydrogen—make up 84.3% of the atoms in the sample, and the top nine elements account for 96.3% of the atoms, leaving only 3.7% of the atoms representing all the other elements. However, these minor constituents include some elements very important to life, such as carbon, nitrogen, and phosphorus.

▲ **It DOES Matter!** One of the more common rocks on Earth is limestone, which is calcium carbonate ($CaCO_3$). In nature, calcium carbonate is found in many different physical forms, including marble, seashells, eggshells, coral, pearls, and chalk. Striking examples of limestone formations are the stalagmites and stalactites in caves, such as those seen here from the Carlsbad Caverns National Park.

The Lithosphere: Organic and Inorganic

The lithosphere is mainly rocks and minerals. Prominent among these are

- *silicate minerals* (compounds of metals with silicon and oxygen),
- *carbonate minerals* (metals combined with carbon and oxygen),
- *oxide minerals* (metals combined with oxygen only), and
- *sulfide minerals* (metals combined with sulfur only).

Thousands of these mineral compounds make up the *inorganic* portion of the solid crust. We discuss some silicate minerals in Section 12.2. Some typical nonsilicate minerals are listed in Table 12.2.

Table 12.2 Some Nonsilicate Minerals of Economic Importance

Mineral Type	Name	Chemical Formula	Source and/or Use
Oxide	Hematite	Fe_2O_3	Ore of iron; pigment
	Magnetite	Fe_3O_4	Ore of iron
	Corundum	Al_2O_3	Gemstone; abrasive
Sulfide	Galena	PbS	Ore of lead
	Chalcopyrite	$CuFeS_2$	Ore of copper
Carbonate	Calcite	$CaCO_3$	Cement; lime

Although much, much smaller in quantity, the *organic* portion of Earth's outer layers includes all living creatures, their waste and decomposition products, and fossilized materials (such as coal, natural gas, petroleum, and oil shale) that once were living organisms. This organic material always contains carbon, nearly always hydrogen, and often oxygen, nitrogen, and other elements.

Meeting Our Needs: From Sticks to Bricks

People have long modified nature's materials to help satisfy their needs and wants, but for centuries, technological developments were based largely on trial and error. By developing an understanding of the structures of materials, modern science has greatly increased the human ability to modify natural materials.

Early people obtained food by hunting and gathering. After the agricultural revolution (about 10,000 years ago), people no longer were forced to search for food. Domesticated animals and plants supplied their needs for food and clothing. A reasonably assured food supply enabled them to live in villages and created a demand for more sophisticated building materials. People learned to convert natural materials into products with superior properties. For example, adobe bricks, which serve well in arid areas, could be made simply by drying a mixture of clay and straw in the sun.

Fire was one of the earliest agents of chemical change. When people learned to control fire, they learned that cooking improved the flavor and digestibility of meat and grains. People learned that heating adobe bricks made stronger ceramic bricks. Similarly, firing clay at high temperatures produced ceramic pots, making cooking and storage of food much easier. As they became able to produce higher temperatures, people learned to make glass and to extract metals from ores. They made tools from bronze, and later from iron.

Self-Assessment Questions

1. The regions of the Earth, listed in order from the center outward, are
   a. core, crust, mantle, hydrosphere
   b. core, mantle, crust
   c. core, crust, mantle, hydrosphere
   d. mantle, crust, core
2. Earth's core is composed mainly of
   a. lead
   b. iron
   c. radioactive elements
   d. sulfur
3. Three elements account for more than 80% of the Earth's crust by atom percent. In decreasing order of abundance, they are
   a. H, O, Si
   b. H, Si, O
   c. O, H, Si
   d. O, Si, H

Answers: 1, b; 2, b; 3, d

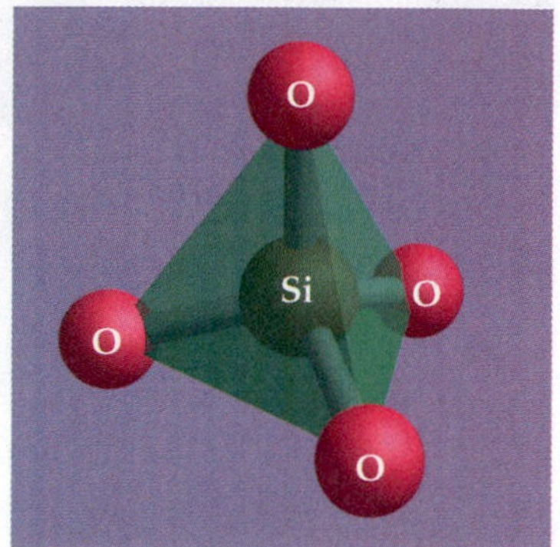

▲ **Figure 12.2** The silicate tetrahedron has a silicon atom at the center and an oxygen atom at each of the four corners. The shaded area (green) shows how the SiO_4 tetrahedron is typically represented in a mineral structure.

12.2 Silicates and the Shapes of Things

Learning Objectives › Describe the arrangement of silicate tetrahedra in common silicate minerals. › Describe how glass differs in structure from other silicates.

We will consider only a few representative minerals of the thousands that occur in the lithosphere. First, let's look at some silicates. The basic unit of silicate structure is the SiO_4 tetrahedron (Figure 12.2). As noted in Table 12.3, these tetrahedra can exist singly as silicate anions or can be joined in a variety of ways.

Table 12.3 Silicate Tetrahedra in Some Minerals

Mineral(s)	SiO_4 Arrangement	Formula	Uses
Zirconium silicate	Simple anion (SiO_4^{4-})	$ZrSiO_4$	Ceramics; gemstones (zircon)
Spodumene	Long chains	$LiAl(SiO_3)_2$	Source of lithium and its compounds
Chrysotile asbestos	Double chains	$Mg_3(Si_2O_5)(OH)_4$	Fireproofing (now banned)
Muscovite mica	Sheets	$KAl_2(AlSi_3O_{10})(OH)_4$	Insulation; lustrous paints; packing (vermiculite)
Quartz	Three-dimensional array	SiO_2	Making glass (sand); gemstones (amethyst, agate, citrine)

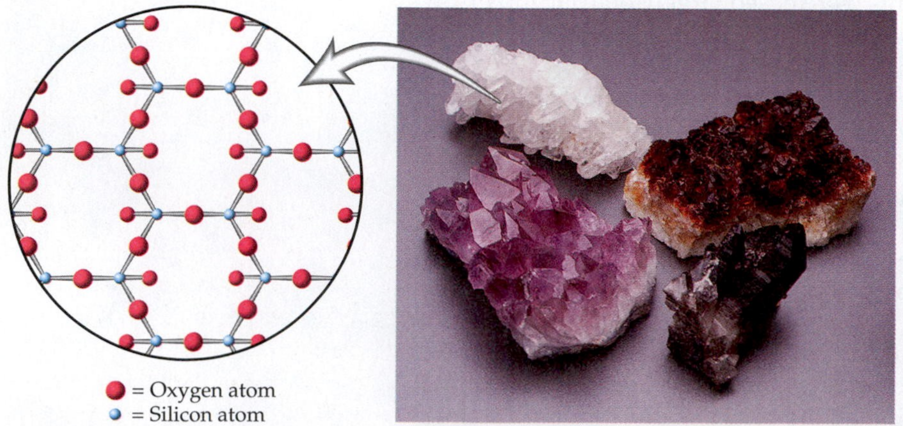

▲ **Figure 12.3** The collection of quartz crystals (above) includes (counterclockwise from upper right) citrine (yellowish quartz), colorless quartz, amethyst (purple quartz), and smoky quartz. The chemical structure of quartz (left) shows that each silicon atom is bonded to four oxygen atoms and each oxygen atom is bonded to two silicon atoms.

▲ Clothing made of asbestos fibers, shown in this photo of firefighters practicing with spraying equipment, was once widely used to protect workers from high temperatures and hot materials. For this purpose, asbestos has been replaced by synthetic polymers such as Nomex (Chapter 10).

Quartz is pure silicon dioxide, SiO_2. The ratio of silicon to oxygen atoms is 1:2. However, because each silicon atom is surrounded by *four* oxygen atoms, the basic unit of quartz is the SiO_4 tetrahedron. These tetrahedra are arranged in a complex three-dimensional structure. Crystals of pure quartz (rock crystal) are colorless, but impurities produce a variety of quartz crystals sometimes used as gems (Figure 12.3).

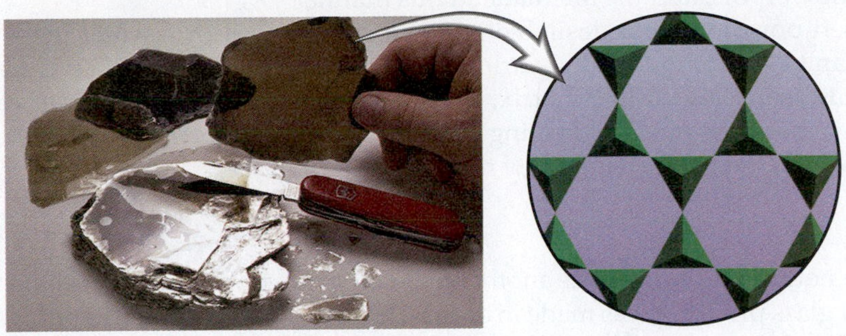

◀ **Figure 12.4** A sample of mica, showing cleavage into thin, transparent sheets. The chemical structure of mica shows sheets of SiO_4 tetrahedra. The sheets are linked by bonds between O atoms and cations, mainly Al^{3+} (not shown). Mica is used as transparent "window" material in industrial furnaces.

2. Why is asbestos dangerous? Asbestos fibers are extremely tiny and have very sharp edges. When inhaled, they are not easily expelled from the lungs and can cause long-term damage. A 2008 report suggests that carbon nanotubes may cause similar problems if inhaled.

Micas are composed of SiO_4 tetrahedra arranged in two-dimensional sheetlike arrays. Micas are easily cleaved into thin, transparent sheets (Figure 12.4). Micas are used as insulators for electronics and in high-temperature furnaces.

Asbestos is a generic term for a variety of fibrous silicates. Perhaps the best known of these is *chrysotile*, a magnesium silicate (Figure 12.5). Chrysotile has double chains of SiO_4 tetrahedra. The oxygen atoms that have only one covalent bond also bear a negative charge. Magnesium ions (Mg^{2+}) balance these negative charges.

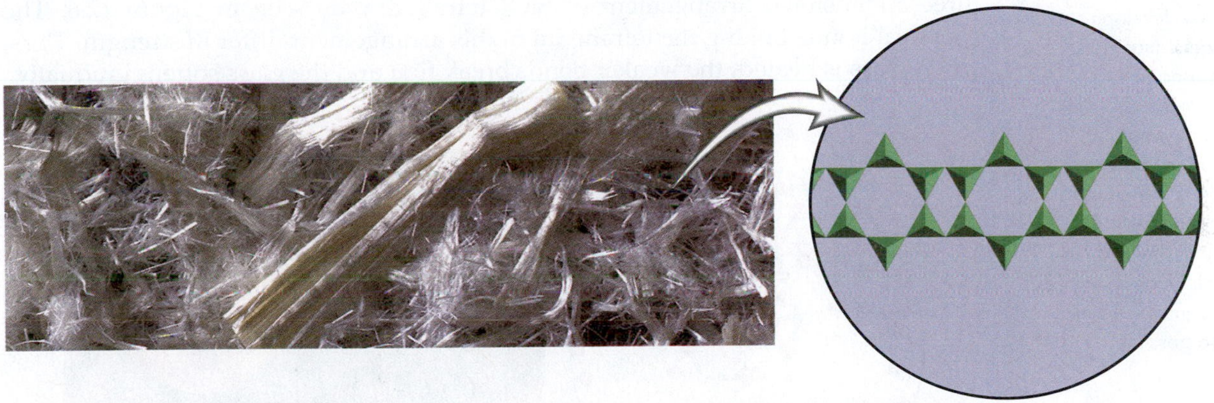

▲ **Figure 12.5** A sample of chrysotile, a type of asbestos. The chemical structure of chrysotile shows double chains of SiO_4 tetrahedra. The two chains are joined to each other through O atoms. The double chains in turn are linked by bonds between O atoms and cations, mainly Mg^{2+} (not shown).

Asbestos: Benefits and Risks

Asbestos is an excellent fireproof thermal insulator. It was once used widely to insulate furnaces, heating ducts, and steam pipes.

The health hazards to those who work with asbestos are well known. Inhalation of fibers 5–50 μm long over a period of 10–20 years can cause *asbestosis* and may lead to lung cancer or *mesothelioma*, a rare and incurable cancer of the linings of body cavities.

Long-term occupational exposure to asbestos increases the risk of lung cancer by a factor of two. Cigarette smoking causes a tenfold increase in the risk of lung cancer. We might expect asbestos workers who smoke to have a risk of developing lung cancer that is 20 times that of nonsmokers who do not work with asbestos, but instead their risk is increased by a factor of 90. Cigarette smoke and asbestos fibers act in such a way that each increases the effect of the other. Such a reinforcing interaction is called a **synergistic effect**.

3. Can you get lead poisoning from pottery? Some types of clay contain lead compounds. If a piece of pottery made from lead-containing clay is not thoroughly glazed to make it nonporous, the lead compounds can leach into food or drink contained in the piece. Happily, pottery made in the United States is not permitted to contain toxic levels of lead.

▲ **It DOES Matter!**
Research has led to the development of amazing new ceramic materials. Ceramics have been used to make rocket nose cones, heat-resistant tiles on the Space Shuttle, automobile engines, jet engine turbine blades, and memory elements in computers. *Superconducting ceramics* exhibit virtually no resistance to the flow of electricity; they make high-speed magnetically levitated (maglev) trains like that shown above possible.

Modified Silicates: Ceramics

Early people learned to modify natural materials such as sand, clay, and limestone, mainly by mixing and heating, to make much more useful products. Clays are complex materials, but they are basically aluminum silicates. Mixed with water, clays can be molded into any shape. Firing leaves a hard, durable (but porous) product. Bricks, flowerpots, and tile are made in this manner.

When porosity is not desirable—as in a cooking pot or a water jug—the clay object can be glazed by adding various salts to the surface. Heat then converts the entire surface to a glasslike matrix. Bricks and pottery are examples of **ceramics**, inorganic materials made by heating clay or other mineral matter to a high temperature at which the particles partially melt and fuse together.

Glass

Glass, a noncrystalline solid, is another technological development of ancient times. The first glass probably was made in ancient Egypt or Mesopotamia about 5000 years ago by heating a mixture of sand, "soda" (sodium carbonate, Na_2CO_3), and limestone (calcium carbonate, $CaCO_3$). As the mixture melts, it becomes a homogeneous liquid. When this liquid cools, it becomes hard and transparent.

Crystalline materials have a regular, repeated arrangement of atoms, ions, or molecules. The forces among these particles are the same throughout the material. When heated, crystalline materials melt over an extremely narrow temperature range. For example, sodium hydroxide, an ionic crystal, melts at 318 °C, and crystalline aspirin, a molecular substance, melts at 135 °C. Glasses behave differently; when heated, a glass gradually softens. While soft, it can be blown, rolled, pressed, or molded into almost any shape. The properties of glass result from an irregular three-dimensional arrangement of SiO_4 tetrahedra, as seen in Figure 12.6. The chemical bonds linking the tetrahedra in this arrangement differ in strength. Thus, when glass is heated, the weaker bonds break first and the glass softens gradually.

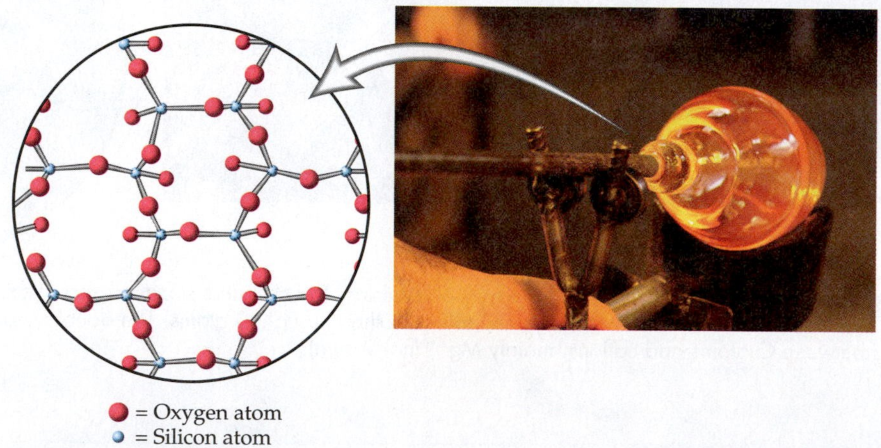

▲ **Figure 12.6** Heat-softened glass can be shaped by blowing or molding. Compare the irregular arrangement of atoms in glass to the regular arrangement of those in quartz (Figure 12.3).

The basic ingredients in glass can be mixed in different proportions. Ordinary window and container glass has a typical composition of about 75% SiO_2, 15% Na_2O, and 10% CaO. Oxides of various metals can be substituted for some or all of the sand, soda, or limestone. Thus, many special types of glass can be made. Some examples are given in Table 12.4.

Manufacture of ordinary glass uses no vital raw materials, but the furnaces used to melt and shape the glass expend energy. Glass is easily recycled. It can be melted and formed into new objects, using considerably less energy than manufacturing new glass.

Table 12.4 Compositions and Properties of Various Glasses

Type	Special Ingredient(s)	Special Properties and/or Uses
Soda–lime glass	Sodium and calcium silicates	Ordinary glass for windows, bottles, other housewares
Borosilicate glass	Boron oxide (instead of lime)	Heat-resistant, for laboratory ware and ovenware
Lead glass	Lead oxide (instead of lime)	Highly refractive (bends light); optical glass, art glass, table crystal
Colored glass	Selenium compounds	Red (ruby glass)
	Cobalt compounds	Blue (cobalt glass)
	Chromium compounds	Green
	Manganese compounds	Violet
	Carbon and iron oxide	Brown (amber glass)
Photochromic glass	Silver chloride or bromide	Darkens when exposed to light, for sunglasses, hospital windows

Cement and Concrete

Cement is a complex mixture of calcium and aluminum silicates. The raw materials for the production of cement are limestone and clay. The materials are finely ground, mixed, and roasted at about 1500 °C in a rotary kiln heated by burning natural gas or powdered coal. The finished product is mixed with sand, gravel, and water to form *concrete*.

Our understanding of the complex chemistry of cement is still imperfect. Nevertheless, extensive research has made various special cements available, including a fast-setting cement whose high strength is quickly established, a white cement, a waterproof cement, and a cement that sets at high temperatures.

Concrete is used widely in construction because it is inexpensive, strong, chemically inert, durable, and tolerant of a wide range of temperatures. However, its production involves extensive mining; entire mountains are torn down to extract limestone rocks. The rotary kiln consumes fossil fuels. Particulate matter from the crushing operations and smoke and sulfur dioxide from the burning of fossil fuels make air pollution by cement plants especially serious. On the positive side, the high temperatures of the rotary kiln can be used to destroy tires and toxic organic wastes. For disposal, concrete can be broken up and used as rock fill.

▲ **It DOES Matter!**

Optical fibers are hair-thin threads of glass, which carry messages as intermittent bursts of light. Sounds are translated into electric signals, which are converted into pulses of laser light that are transmitted by the glass fibers. At the end of the line, the light pulses are converted back to sound waves. A bundle of optical fibers can carry several hundred times as many messages as a copper cable of the same size, and these fiber bundles have replaced many old telephone lines and computer cables. They are also used in medicine in devices that provide visual access inside the body and that guide surgical instruments.

Self-Assessment Questions

1. All silicate minerals contain silicon and
   a. carbon b. hydrogen c. iron d. oxygen
2. The mineral composed of pure silicon dioxide (SiO_2) is
   a. asbestos b. calcite c. quartz d. zircon
3. The silicate tetrahedron consists of one ________ atom at the center and ________ atoms at the corners.
   a. O; 4 Si
   b. O; 2 Si and 2 Al
   c. Si; 4 O
   d. Si; 2 O and 2 Al

For items 4–7, match each substance with the correct structure.

4. asbestos (a) double chains
5. mica (b) sheets
6. quartz (c) simple anions
7. zircon (d) three-dimensional array
8. In causing cancer, asbestos acts synergistically with
   a. aerogels b. cigarette smoke c. glass fibers d. lead
9. One type of material that is hard and durable but brittle is a
   a. ceramic b. metal c. polymer d. semiconductor

▲ Portland cement is made by roasting a mixture of limestone, clay, and sand. This cement is the "glue" that holds concrete together. Over 3 billion tons of Portland cement were produced worldwide in 2008.

10. The main ingredients of ordinary glass are
    a. boron oxide, sand, and limestone
    b. clay and limestone
    c. coke, sand, and limestone
    d. sand, sodium carbonate, and limestone
11. The main ingredients of ordinary cement are
    a. clay and limestone
    b. coke, sand, and limestone
    c. sand and limestone
    d. sand, sodium carbonate, and limestone

Answers: 1, d; 2, c; 3, c; 4, a; 5, b; 6, d; 7, c; 8, b; 9, a; 10, d; 11, a

12.3 Metals and Ores

Learning Objectives › List the most important metals with their principal ores, and explain how they are extracted. › Describe some of the environmental costs associated with metal production.

▲ Soaring prices for scrap metal, largely due to increased demand in China and India, have led to thefts of copper and aluminum from construction sites, empty houses, and other places. Thieves have taken aluminum siding from houses, bleachers from athletic fields, and car wheel rims. Several deaths have resulted from attempts to remove copper wire from live electrical equipment.

Human progress through the ages is often described in terms of the materials used for making tools. We speak of the Stone Age, the Bronze Age, and the Iron Age. Ancient peoples knew about gold and silver because these metals are often found in the *native*, or uncombined, state in nature; however, they are too soft to use as tools. Metal tools were not possible until artisans learned to extract certain metals from ores by smelting.

Copper and Bronze

Copper is sometimes found in the native state, and it was probably also the first metal to be freed from its ore by early smelting techniques. Ancient records from the Middle East show that copper was known as far back as 10,000 years ago. The metal was probably isolated by heating copper sulfide (Cu_2S) ore.

$$Cu_2S(s) + O_2(g) \longrightarrow 2\,Cu(s) + SO_2(g)$$

Copper, an excellent electrical conductor, is used primarily for electric wiring and also for plumbing pipes.

More important than copper in early times was **bronze**, a copper alloy containing about 10% tin. An **alloy** is a mixture of two or more elements, at least one of which is a metal. Bronze is harder than copper, and it could therefore be made into many useful tools. In some societies, bronze remained the most widely used metal for about 2000 years.

Iron and Steel

The technology for production of iron and steel lagged far behind that for copper and bronze for two reasons. Iron reacts so readily with oxygen and sulfur that it is not found uncombined in nature, and it melts at a much higher temperature (1536 °C) than does copper (1084 °C) or bronze (600–950 °C). To produce iron from ore, carbon (coke) is employed as the reducing agent (Chapter 8). First, carbon is converted to carbon monoxide.

$$2\,C(s) + O_2(g) \longrightarrow 2\,CO(g)$$

Then, the carbon monoxide reduces the iron oxide in the ore to iron metal.

$$Fe_2O_3(s) + 3\,CO(g) \longrightarrow 2\,Fe(l) + 3\,CO_2(g)$$

Table 12.5 Some Alloys of Iron

Material	Alloying Elements	Properties
Cast iron (pig iron)	2–4% C	Strong, rigid, brittle
Wrought iron	Very low C	Tough, malleable, ductile, easily welded
Stainless steel	12–30% Cr; some Ni	Corrosion resistance
Manganese steel	13% Mn; some C	Hardness; wear resistance
Nickel steel	0.5–6.0% Ni; some C	Strength
Molybdenum steel	10–15% Mo; some C	Wear resistance
Tungsten steel	1–20% W; some C	Strength at high temperatures

The method used to produce aluminum today was discovered independently in 1886 by two college students, Charles Martin Hall in the United States and Paul Héroult in France. Both men were born in 1863, and both died in 1914 at the age of 51. Before the Hall-Héroult method was developed, aluminum was considered a precious metal. The French emperor Napoleon III reportedly reserved his aluminum utensils for his most honored guests; others had to make do with gold.

Iron can be made from its ore in a huge chimneylike vessel called a *blast furnace* (Figure 12.7). The raw materials fed into the furnace are iron ore, coke, and limestone. The coke (which is mainly carbon) is made by heating coal in the absence of air to drive off coal oil and tar. The limestone is added to combine with silicate impurities to form a molten **slag** that floats on top of the iron and is drawn off. Molten iron is drawn off at the bottom of the furnace. The product of the blast furnace, called *cast iron (or pig iron)*, has a moderate melting point and is easily shaped using molds.

Because cast iron is brittle and has many impurities, most iron from blast furnaces is *made* into **steel**, an alloy of iron with carbon and other metals. The properties of steel can be varied over a wide range by adjusting the amount of carbon in it. Other metals give the steel special properties such as hardness, toughness, or corrosion resistance (Table 12.5).

Because it is abundant and forms so many different alloys, iron is the most useful of the metals, accounting for about 95% of all metal production worldwide.

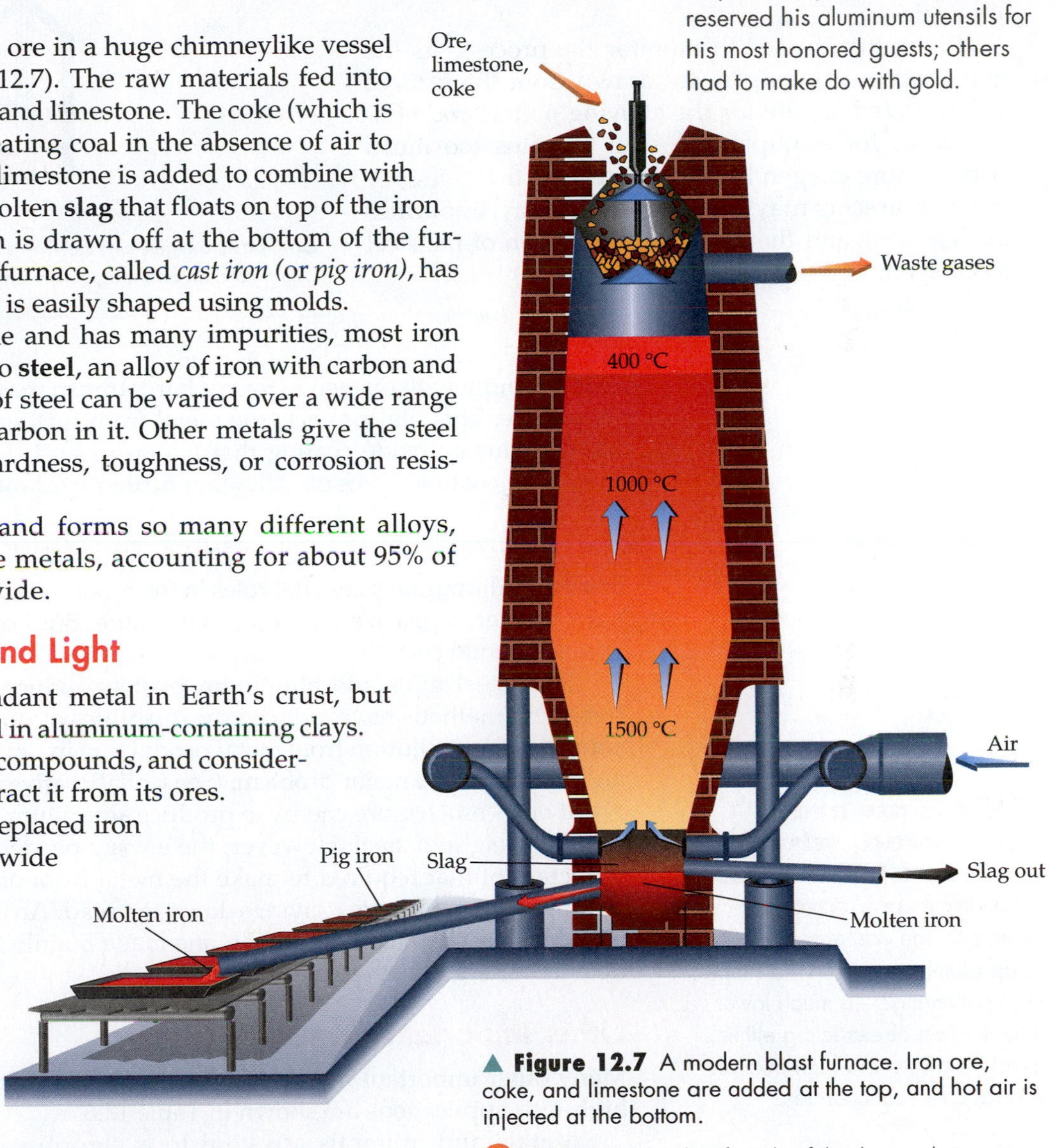

▲ **Figure 12.7** A modern blast furnace. Iron ore, coke, and limestone are added at the top, and hot air is injected at the bottom.

Q: *What is the role of each of the three substances added at the top of the furnace?*

Aluminum: Abundant and Light

Aluminum is the most abundant metal in Earth's crust, but much of it is thinly distributed in aluminum-containing clays. The metal is tightly bound in compounds, and considerable energy is required to extract it from its ores. Nevertheless, aluminum has replaced iron for many purposes. Worldwide production of aluminum is second to that of iron, at more than 32 billion kg per year. (Iron production is about 1400 billion kg annually.) The main ore of aluminum is *bauxite* impure aluminum oxide. The Al_2O_3 is extracted from the impurities with a strong base, and then the melted oxide is reduced by passing electricity through it.

$$2\,Al_2O_3 \xrightarrow{\text{electricity}} 4\,Al + 3\,O_2$$

It takes 2 metric tons (t) of aluminum oxide and 17,000 kilowatt hours (kWh) of electricity to produce 1 t of aluminum.

Aluminum is light and strong. An aluminum object weighs only one-third as much as a steel object the same size. Although it is considerably more reactive than iron, aluminum corrodes much more slowly. Freshly prepared aluminum metal

Modern Steelmaking

Most steel producers now use the *basic oxygen process*, in which pure oxygen is blown into a molten mix of blast-furnace iron and scrap iron. Powdered limestone is added just above the molten iron, and O_2 gas at about 10 atm pressure is also injected there. Metallic impurities in the pig iron are converted to oxides, which react with SiO_2 to form a slag that floats above the liquid iron and is poured off. Then any desired alloying elements are added, often by adding scrap steel of a particular composition.

Chemistry is used to monitor the process. As the melt progresses, samples are drawn from the furnace and analyzed on site for the alloying metals and nonmetals. If, for example, the steel contains too much carbon, more oxygen is used to burn off the excess, or low-carbon scrap may be added. In this way, impurities are removed, and the desired composition of the steel is achieved.

In the United States today, almost all automobiles are recycled, and about half of all steel comes from "minimills," which make steel from scrap iron instead of ore.

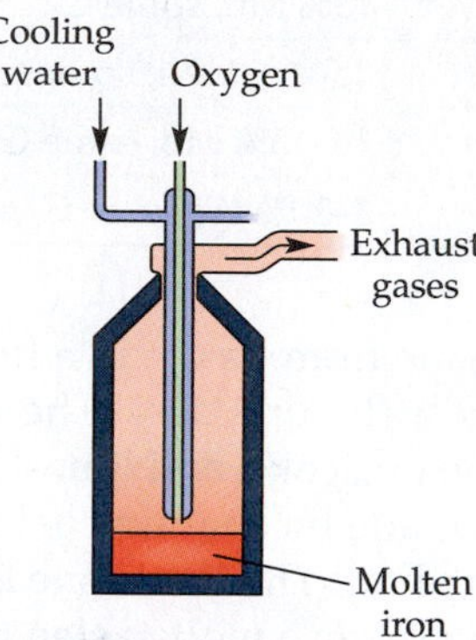

▲ A basic oxygen furnace. The steel vessel is lined with dolomite, a mixed calcium and magnesium carbonate ($CaCO_3 \cdot MgCO_3$).

reacts rapidly with oxygen to form a hard, transparent film of aluminum oxide over its surface. This film protects the metal from further oxidation. Iron, on the other hand, forms an oxide coating that is porous and flaky. Instead of protecting the metal, the coating flakes off, allowing further oxidation.

The Environmental Costs of Iron and Aluminum

Steel and aluminum play vital roles in the modern industrial world, and it would be hard to overemphasize their economic value. But both are produced at significant environmental cost.

Both steel mills and aluminum plants produce considerable waste. Modern treatment methods have reduced the quantities of pollutants released in developed countries, but pollution from metal production in developing nations such as China and India is still a major problem. (See Collaborative Group Project 4.)

It takes much more energy to produce aluminum than it does to produce a comparable weight of steel. However, the energy needed to recycle aluminum is only a fraction of that required to make the metal from ore. Further, the low density of aluminum means energy savings down the road. An automobile made largely from aluminum is so much lighter than one made mainly from steel that it takes a good deal less energy to operate it.

4. If atoms are conserved, why do we need to recycle aluminum and iron? The cost of melting scrap aluminum or iron—a simple physical change—is much lower than the cost of extracting either metal from its ore, which involves several chemical changes.

Other Important Metals

Many other important metals are essential to modern technology. Some that have high-tech applications are shown in Table 12.6.

Metals and minerals are vital to a vigorous economy, but no industrial nation is 100% self-sufficient in all the vital metals and minerals. The United States has depleted most of its high-grade ores and is now dependent on imports of many essential minerals, as shown in Table 12.6. Note especially the lanthanide elements, commonly called *rare earths*, over which China has a virtual monopoly.

How can we ever run short of a metal? Aren't atoms conserved? Yes, there is as much iron on Earth as there was 100 years ago, but in using it, we scatter the metal throughout the environment. Gathering used metal objects to make new objects requires energy, just as obtaining metals from low-grade ores requires more energy than extracting them from high-grade ores.

Table 12.6 Technologically Important Metals

Metal	Source(s)	Typical Use(s)	Annual World Production (t)
Indium	China, Canada	Transparent, conducting coatings on LCD displays and photovoltaic cells	625
Lithium	Chile, Argentina	Batteries for tools, laptops, digital cameras, and cell phones	30,200
Palladium	Russia	Catalytic converters, energy-storing capacitors in electronic devices	225
Platinum	South Africa, Russia	Catalytic converters, computer hard drives, glass for LCD displays, fuel cells	220
Rare earths (lanthanides)	China	Electronics, energy-efficient technologies	117,000
Europium		Red phosphor in CRT displays	
Cerium		Commercial catalysts, glass polishing, self-cleaning ovens	
Neodymium		Ingredient in super magnets and lasers	
Yttrium	China	Fluorescent lightbulbs, ceramics, lasers	500
Tantalum	Democratic Republic of the Congo	Electronic capacitors in computers, digital cameras, and cell phones	900

Self-Assessment Questions

1. The metal most likely to be found in its native state is
   a. aluminum **b.** copper **c.** iron **d.** sodium
2. When copper is produced from Cu_2S, the by-product is
   a. CuO **b.** CO_2 **c.** S **d.** SO_2
3. Bronze is an alloy of Cu and
   a. Fe **b.** Pb **c.** Sn **d.** Zn
4. The raw materials for the blast furnace production of iron are iron ore,
   a. coke and limestone
   b. coke, sand, and limestone
   c. coke and sandstone
   d. sand, sodium carbonate, and limestone
5. Aluminum is obtained by reducing its ore using
   a. carbon
   b. electrolysis
   c. magnesium
   d. scrap iron
6. Bauxite is impure
   a. Al_2O_3
   b. Cu_2S
   c. Fe_2O_3
   d. gold

Answers: 1, b; 2, d; 3, c; 4, a; 5, b; 6, a

▲ When the Europeans first came to North America, native copper (shown here) was readily available and was used by Native Americans. In the United States today, ore with less than 0.5% copper is mined.

12.4 Earth's Dwindling Resources

Learning Objectives › List the main components of solid waste. › Name and describe the three Rs of garbage.

For decades, international politics has created threats of shortages and high prices for various commodities, including metals and minerals. The United States has exhausted its high-grade ores of metals such as copper and iron. Australia has vast deposits of high-grade iron ore, but importing this ore is costly. Miners once found nuggets of pure gold and silver, but the "glory holes" of western North America are long gone. Now we mine ores with a fraction of an ounce of gold per ton of ore (see Figure 12.8). There remain very few high-grade deposits of any metal ores that are readily accessible to the industrialized nations.

What's wrong with low-grade ores? Because more material must be mined to obtain the same final amount of metal, there is more environmental disruption (see Figure 12.8), and more energy is required to concentrate the ores. Both environmental cleanup and energy cost money. Consider an analogy. A bag of popcorn is useful. You can pop it and eat it. The same popcorn, scattered all over your room, would be less useful. Of course, you could gather it all up and then pop it, but that would take a lot of energy—perhaps more energy than you would care to expend and perhaps more energy than you would get from eating the corn after popping it.

▶ **Figure 12.8** Miners must move 30 tons of rock to recover 1 oz of gold for a necklace. The crushed rock is leached with cyanide solution to dissolve the gold. The waste cyanide solution is stored in large containment ponds like the one shown here, which is part of a gold mining operation in Khakassia, Russia.

We also must import quite a few metals because their ores are not found in the United States. For example, we get tin from Bolivia, chromium from Kazakhstan and South Africa, rare earth elements from China, and platinum from South Africa and Russia. But the metal reserves in other countries are being depleted, too.

▲ Where will we get metals in the future? The sea is one possible source. Nodules rich in manganese cover vast areas of the ocean floor. These nodules also contain copper, nickel, and cobalt. Questions about who owns them and how they can be mined without major environmental disruption remain to be resolved.

Land Pollution: Solid Wastes

Productivity and creativity have enabled people in industrialized nations to possess a seemingly endless variety of consumer goods in enormous quantities. These goods are often packaged in paper or plastic. Their wrappers litter the environment and fill our disposal sites. As the goods break, wear out, or merely become obsolete, they add to our disposal problem. The approximate composition of municipal solid wastes (MSWs)—commonly known as trash or garbage—in the United States is given in Figure 12.9.

MSWs are handled in three principal ways. According to the U.S. Environmental Protection Agency (EPA), in 2010 in the United States, 33.8% of MSW was recovered and recycled or composted, 11.9% was burned at combustion facilities, and 54.3% was disposed of in *sanitary landfills*.

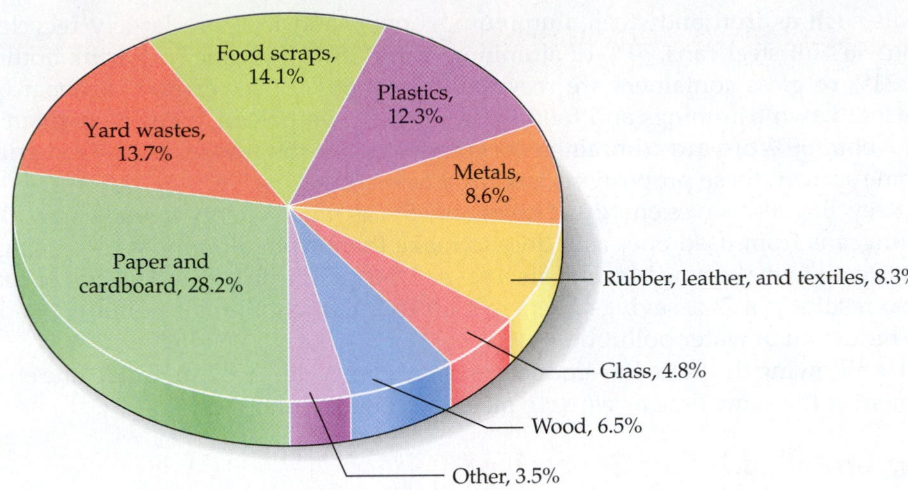

◀ **Figure 12.9** This pie chart shows the percentages of the various materials in municipal solid wastes. Municipal wastes in the United States are largely paper, cardboard, and yard wastes. Paper and cardboard can be recycled. Yard wastes and food wastes can be composted.

Q: *If paper, cardboard, yard wastes, and food wastes were recycled or composted, by about what percentage would municipal solid wastes decrease?*

When disposed of in a sanitary landfill, solid wastes are piled into a trench, compacted, and covered over. However, some landfills leak and contribute to groundwater contamination. Furthermore, materials in landfills decompose slowly. Newspapers are still readable after being entombed for 20 years. Without water and oxygen, microorganisms are unable to carry out the normal decay processes.

Disposal of solid wastes by *incineration*, when carried out in properly designed incinerators, produces minimal air pollution. However, many incinerators are old or poorly designed, and they generate much smoke and odor. Building new incinerators tends to be unpopular with local citizens.

Research in solid waste disposal has led to new processes. Wastes can be converted to gaseous or liquid fuels. However, these processes are too expensive to have much of an impact on MSW disposal.

Some cities not only burn their combustible solid wastes but also use the heat from the incinerators to warm buildings, to generate power, or both. A pound of polyethylene produces about 20,000 British thermal units (Btus) of energy, about the same as a pound of no. 2 fuel oil.

The Three Rs of Garbage: Reduce, Reuse, Recycle

Not all ways to deal with our garbage are equally desirable. The best approach to the solid waste problem is to *reduce* the amount of throwaway materials produced. This decreases the volume of materials produced and sold, saves resources and energy, and minimizes the disposal problem.

The next best approach is the *reuse* of materials. When possible, items should be made durable enough to withstand repeated use, rather than designed for a single use and disposal. Consider the grocery bag. At stores, we are often asked, "Paper or plastic?" Most studies show that the environmental impact of a plastic bag is somewhat less than that of a paper bag. Nonetheless, paper should be a better choice for several reasons.

- Plastic bags can be recycled, but only about 7% are. Most of the 500 billion to 1 trillion bags used worldwide each year end up in landfills. Many of the rest become litter, hanging from fences and trees, clogging storm drains, and harming wildlife, especially sea creatures that mistake floating bags for food.
- Plastic bags are made from petroleum, a nonrenewable resource, consuming large amounts of oil that could be used for fuel or heating. Paper is made from trees, a renewable resource. However, replacing billions of plastic bags with paper would require an enormous number of trees.
- Paper bags are less of a litter problem because they break down relatively quickly in the environment. Plastic bags last for years; the bags buried in landfills may be there for centuries.

So, which should we use, paper or plastic? Neither! The better answer is reusable shopping bags made of cloth that are not discarded after a single use. All factors must be examined when determining the best overall solution to a solid waste problem.

The third way to reduce the volume of wastes is to *recycle* them. Recycling requires energy and inevitably results in some loss of material, but it saves materials.

5. Why do scrap metals bring high prices? One factor that contributes to the value of scrap metal is the cost of energy needed to extract a metal from its ore. The greater the cost of energy, the more it costs to convert ore to metal. Because scrap metal does not require as much energy to be converted back to useful metal, its value is relatively high.

According to the Steel Recycling Institute, about 5740 kJ of energy is conserved for each pound of steel recycled. That is enough energy to light a 60-watt (W) bulb for more than 26 h.

Metals such as iron and steel, aluminum, copper, and lead are largely recycled. About 66% of steel cans, 51% of aluminum cans, 28% of plastic soft drink bottles, and 31% of glass containers are recycled. About 60% of paper and cardboard is recycled. Lawn trimmings and food wastes can be composted, converting them to soil. About 60% of yard trimmings are composted. In the future, as raw materials become scarcer, these proportions are likely to increase.

Recycling also saves energy. It takes only 5% as much energy to make new aluminum cans from used ones as it does to make them from aluminum ore. Using a ton of scrap to make new iron and steel saves 1.5 tons of iron ore and 0.3 ton of coal. It also results in a 74% savings in energy, an 86% reduction in air pollution, and a 76% reduction in water pollution.

By following the three Rs—reduce, reuse, and recycle—we can protect the environment at the same time as we save materials, energy, and money.

How Crowded Is Our Spaceship?

Each day, people die and others are born, but the number born is about 200,000 more than the number who die. Every five days, the world population goes up by a million people, and it reached 7 billion in 2011.

Figure 12.10 is a graphic picture of population growth. For tens of thousands of years, the human population was never more than a few hundred million. It did not reach the 1 billion mark until about 1800, after which the rate of growth skyrocketed. World population quadrupled during the twentieth century, with growth peaking in the 1960s at about 2.2% a year. The rate of growth in 2011 was 1.09% per year. The Population Division of the United Nations Department of Economic and Social Affairs estimates a world population of 8 billion by 2025 and 9 billion by 2045.

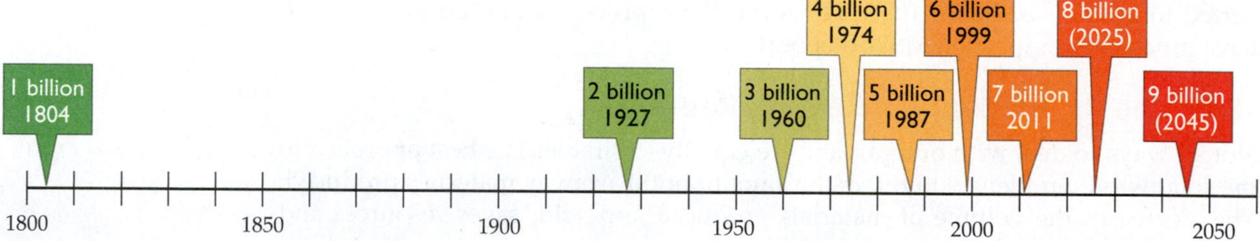

▲ **Figure 12.10** Two thousand years ago, Earth's population was about 300 million—about the same as the population of the United States today. Population changed little over the next thousand years and is estimated to have been only 310 million at the end of the first millennium. It reached 1 billion about 1804. This graph shows the intervals in which an additional billion people were added to Earth's population, with projections to 2045. (*Source:* United Nations, *World Population Prospects: The 2010 Revision*. New York: 2010.)

How many people can Spaceship Earth accommodate? Many believe that we have already gone beyond the optimal population for this planet. They predict increasing conflicts over resources and increasing pollution of the environment.

Why did Earth's population start increasing so rapidly after centuries of little change? Population growth depends on both the birth rate and the death rate. If they are equal, population growth is zero. After thousands of years of nearly equal rates, scientific progress in the nineteenth century led to a decline in the death rate in developed countries. Yet the birth rate changed little, and the population grew rapidly. These changes reached the less developed countries in the 1950s, when the death rate fell dramatically but the birth rate remained high—creating a population explosion.

Population and the food supply are discussed in Chapter 20.

Population growth has slowed considerably in recent years, especially in developed countries. Scientific progress continues to cause a decline in death rates, but birth rates have also declined, especially in Europe and East Asia. The decrease in birth rates in the less developed countries has come more slowly. With more people comes more waste to be processed. We must continue to develop technologies and methods to deal with our ever-increasing wastes.

GREEN CHEMISTRY

Principles 2, 3, 6, 7

Denyce K. Wicht, *Suffolk University*

We're Going to Need a Bigger Earth ...

One of the most famous lines in the movie *Jaws* is "You're gonna need a bigger boat." The police chief, the marine scientist, and the seasoned fisherman see the size of the great white shark that has been tormenting the people and realize that their boat is ill-equipped for the hunt. The phrase is now used when a situation seems increasingly more daunting and complex as facts emerge.

We have a challenge like the one faced in *Jaws*. Using natural resources in a sustainable manner can seem daunting. By forming testable hypotheses and designing and performing experiments (Section 1.3), scientists have estimated the elemental composition of the Earth's surface. The eight most abundant elements are O, Si, H, Al, Na, Fe, Ca, and Mg (Section 12.1). As you learned in Chapter 2, matter is neither created nor destroyed during a chemical change. Therefore, our challenge is to use the Earth's elements to meet our needs without jeopardizing the availability of natural resources for future generations. The principles of green chemistry, specifically Principles 2, 3 and 6, address these challenges.

In this chapter, you learned about the chemical processes used to produce the metals iron and aluminum. Let's see how green chemistry can be applied in analyzing the environmental costs of these two resources.

Green chemistry promotes the consideration of multiple factors when analyzing and improving existing chemical processes. For example, consider two reactions that can be used to convert magnetite (Fe_3O_4) to Fe, the feedstock for making steel:

$$Fe_3O_4 + 4\,CO \rightarrow 3\,Fe + 4\,CO_2$$

$$Fe_3O_4 + 4\,H_2 \rightarrow 3\,Fe + 4\,H_2O$$

Remember that reactions can be compared in terms of their atom economy (% A.E., page 140). The atom economy (Principle 2) of the first reaction is 49%, while that of the second is 70%. Furthermore, both reactions produce by-products. Water is more benign (Principle 3) than CO_2, which contributes to climate change. Taking these factors into account, the second reaction seems more desirable. However, both processes are energy intensive. Green chemists realize that the energy requirements of chemical processes should be evaluated (Principle 6) when seeking the best approach.

The value that steel provides to an industrialized society is clear. Yet conversion of Fe_3O_4 to Fe takes a toll on the environment, even when the most energy-efficient method is used (Section 12.3). One way to minimize that harm is to replace steel with aluminum whenever possible. As noted in Section 12.3, aluminum is obtained from the reduction of purified bauxite (Al_2O_3) by electrolysis.

$$2\,Al_2O_3 \rightarrow 4\,Al + 3\,O_2$$

How is aluminum greener than steel? It takes more energy to produce aluminum than to produce the same weight of steel (Section 12.3). How then can using more aluminum reduce energy requirements (Principle 6)? Furthermore, the atom economy of the above reaction is 53%. Doesn't this mean that the iron-producing reaction with 70% A.E. is greener than the aluminum-producing reaction (Principle 2)?

Why would green chemists recommend replacing steel with aluminum? Because of recycling! Postconsumer recycling of aluminum cans saves 95% of the energy required to produce aluminum from bauxite ore. Recycling steel cans is somewhat less economical than aluminum recycling, but still results in a savings of up to 66% over producing steel from magnetite. Green Chemistry Principle 7 calls for the use of nondepleting raw materials. Reclaiming postconsumer materials supports this principle by reducing the demand for natural resources. As you can see, the principles of green chemistry guide scientists in discovering and inventing more sustainable chemical processes and materials.

The question of whether steel or aluminum is greener is one example of how to think about using resources. To understand the complex and long-term implications of our use of Earth's materials, we must critically consider *all* of those resources.

Most experts agree that we can no longer take from Earth at the rate we have in the past. Recycling efforts have increased significantly in the recent years, but *recycle* is only one of the three Rs of garbage. We also have to *reduce* consumption and find more ways to *reuse* the materials we have already extracted and modified. Green scientists are challenged by these complex problems and are engaged in working toward the goal of a better Earth.

▲ The bands in these formations contain different minerals. The red color is due to deposits rich in iron oxides.

Self-Assessment Questions

1. Which kind of material is the largest component of the garbage we put in landfills?
   a. food b. metals c. paper d. plastic
2. What percentage of the energy required to make new aluminum cans from aluminum ore is needed to make them by recycling used ones?
   a. 5% b. 10% c. 25% d. 50%
3. The three Rs of garbage are
   a. reduce, recycle, and redeploy
   b. reuse, redeploy, and recycle
   c. reuse, reprocess, and recycle
   d. reduce, reuse, and recycle

Answers: 1, c; 2, a; 3, d

CRITICAL THINKING  EXERCISES

Apply knowledge that you have gained in this chapter and one or more of the FLaReS principles (Chapter 1) to evaluate the following statements or claims.

12.1 An economist has said that we need not worry about running out of copper because it can be made from other metals.

12.2 A citizen testifies against establishing a landfill near his home, claiming that the landfill will leak substances into the groundwater and contaminate his well water.

12.3 A citizen lobbies against establishing an incinerator near her home, claiming that plastics burned in the incinerator will release hydrogen chloride into the air.

12.4 An environmental activist claims that we could recycle all goods, leaving no need for the use of raw materials to make new ones.

12.5 A concerned parent demands that all the insulation on the steam pipes in the schools in her district be removed and replaced with new insulation. Her contention is that the pipe insulation may contain asbestos and therefore may cause cancer in the students.

SUMMARY

Section 12.1—Earth is divided into the core, the mantle, and the crust. The core is thought to be mainly iron. The crust consists of the solid lithosphere, the liquid (water) hydrosphere, and the gaseous atmosphere. Nine elements make up 96% of the atoms in the crust. The lithosphere is made up largely of rocks and minerals, including silicates, carbonates, oxides, and sulfides. The organic part of the lithosphere consists of all things once and currently living. People have manipulated the lithosphere to meet their wants and needs for about 10,000 years.

Section 12.2—Silicates contain SiO_4 tetrahedra in various arrangements. **Quartz** is a crystalline silicate that consists of a three-dimensional network of these tetrahedra. Sand is mainly quartz. The **micas** consist of sheets of SiO_4 tetrahedra. **Asbestos** is a fibrous silicate mineral made of chains of SiO_4 tetrahedra. Asbestos exposure has a **synergistic effect** with smoking; that is, the two together produce a higher risk of lung cancer than their simple combination indicates. Ceramics, glass, and cement are modified silicates. **Ceramics** are made by heating clay and other minerals to fuse them. **Glass** is a noncrystalline solid having no fixed melting point. Most glass is made from sand, with additives to impart desired properties such as heat resistance, color, and light sensitivity. Glass does not degrade in the environment, but it is easy to recycle. **Cement** is a complex mixture of calcium and aluminum silicates made from limestone and clay. Cement is mixed with gravel, sand, and water, to make concrete or with certain additives to yield cements with special properties.

Section 12.3—Copper was one of the first metals to be obtained from its ore, but it is too soft to be used for tools. **Bronze** is an **alloy**—a mixture of a metal and one or more other elements. Bronze contains copper and tin. Bronze is harder than copper, and tools made of it were used for thousands of years. Iron-making technology was developed much later. Iron is produced in a blast furnace from iron ore, limestone, and coke. The limestone combines with impurities to produce **slag** that floats on top of the iron and is removed. Cast iron is brittle, so it is usually further processed, changing the iron to **steel**, an alloy of iron and carbon. Other elements can be added to steel to vary its properties. Aluminum is less dense than steel and does not rust. Aluminum is isolated from its ore, bauxite, by a reduction process that uses electricity.

Section 12.4—We face potential shortages of many metals and minerals because most of the high-grade ores have been used up. The United States now imports some metals and ores that it used to mine because of these shortages. It takes much less energy to recycle most metals than it does to produce them from ores. However, there are other possible sources of some metals.

The United States produces large amounts of waste, most of which is paper, cardboard, and yard waste. Municipal solid waste (MSW) used to be discarded in open dumps, but now it is either buried in sanitary landfills, burned, or otherwise processed. Some wastes can be converted to fuels. The three Rs of garbage are as follows: Reduce the amount of throwaway materials produced; reuse items when possible; recycle as much materials as possible. Steel, aluminum, plastic, and paper are easily recycled, and yard waste can be composted.

Although birth rates have declined somewhat, Spaceship Earth is crowded and is going to become more so in years to come. We must develop technologies and methods to deal with ever-increasing wastes.

Green chemistry Green chemistry provides a useful framework for evaluating the environmental impacts of processes such as converting magnetite (Fe_3O_4) and purified bauxite (Al_2O_3) into metals. Postconsumer recycling of metals can reduce our need to convert naturally occurring ores into their elemental forms.

Learning Objectives

Objective	Problems
› Name the regions of Earth's crust, and give the approximate composition of each.	Problems 11, 12, 14
› List the most abundant elements in Earth's crust.	Problems 13, 14
› Describe the arrangement of silicate tetrahedra in common silicate minerals.	Problems 17–20
› Describe how glass differs in structure from other silicates.	Problems 21–24
› List the most important metals with their principal ores, and explain how they are extracted.	Problems 27–29, 31–34
› Describe some of the environmental costs associated with metal production.	Problems 41, 44–46
› List the main components of solid waste.	Problems 51, 52
› Name and describe the three Rs of garbage.	Problem 54
› Identify the green chemistry principles that can guide the determination of which metal, Fe or Al, is greener.	Problems 55, 56
› Describe how recycling supports sustainable use of natural resources.	Problem 57

REVIEW QUESTIONS

1. What is a synergistic effect? Give an example.
2. What is concrete?
3. What environmental problems are associated with the manufacture of cement?
4. Why was copper one of the first metals used?
5. Why did the Bronze Age precede the Iron Age in most places?
6. What is steel? How does it differ from pure iron in composition and in properties?
7. Aluminum is the most abundant metal in Earth's crust, yet aluminum ores are not very plentiful. Explain.
8. List three methods of solid waste disposal. Give the advantages and disadvantages of each.
9. If matter is conserved, how can we ever run out of a metal?
10. Explain why metals can be recycled fairly easily. What factors limit the recycling of metals?

PROBLEMS

Composition of Earth

11. Define *lithosphere*, *hydrosphere*, and *atmosphere*.
12. Name four kinds of minerals found in Earth's crust, and give an example of each.
13. What are the third, fourth, and fifth most abundant elements by mass in earth's crust? Why are there differences between the percent by mass and the atom percent values?
14. What materials make up the organic portion of the lithosphere?
15. Referring to Table 12.2, write a balanced equation for the dissolving of galena in hydrochloric acid. The products are hydrogen sulfide gas and lead(II) chloride.
16. How did the discovery of how to control fire change the types of materials humans could use?

Silicate Minerals

17. What is the chemical composition of quartz? How are the basic structural units of quartz arranged?

18. In silica, four O atoms surround each Si atom, yet the formula for silica is SiO_2. Explain how this can be.

19. Why does mica occur in sheets? How are the basic structural units of mica arranged?

20. Why does asbestos occur as fibers? How are the basic structural units of chrysotile asbestos arranged?

Modified Silicates

21. What are the three main raw materials used for making glass?

22. How does glass differ from crystalline silicates in structure and in properties?

23. How is the basic recipe for glass modified to make glasses with special properties?

24. Recycling glass is not quite as economically feasible as recycling other materials such as metals. Suggest a reason for this.

25. What are the two basic raw materials required for making cement?

26. What is the difference between cement and concrete?

Metals and Ores

27. What are the main raw materials used in modern iron production?

28. Write the balanced equation for the reduction of magnetite (Fe_3O_4) by carbon to form iron metal and carbon dioxide.

29. By what kind of chemical process (see Chapter 8) is a metal obtained from its ore? Give an example.

30. By what chemical process does a metal corrode? Give an example.

31. What is the purpose of limestone in iron production?

32. What functions are served by a blast furnace in the metallurgy of iron?

33. What is cast iron? What are its main impurities?

34. Which metal is the most widely used? Why?

Oxidation and Reduction

For Problems 35–38, first write (if it is not given) or complete and balance the equation for the reaction. Next, answer the following. **(a)** *What substance is reduced?* **(b)** *What is the reducing agent?* **(c)** *What substance is oxidized?* **(d)** *What is the oxidizing agent? (These questions require some knowledge of material in Chapter 8.)*

35. Vanadium metal can be prepared by reacting vanadium (V) oxide with calcium; the other product is calcium oxide.

36. Erbium metal (Er) can be prepared by reacting erbium(III) fluoride with magnesium; the other product is magnesium fluoride.

37. The Toth Aluminum Company produces aluminum from kaolin. One step converts aluminum oxide to aluminum chloride by the following reaction.

$$? + C + Cl_2 \longrightarrow AlCl_3 + CO$$

38. Europium (Eu) is used in older television screens to give a red color. The metal can be prepared by electrolysis of molten europium(III) chloride; chlorine gas is a byproduct.

Mass Relationships

Problems 39 and 40 require some knowledge of material in Chapter 5.

39. Neodymium metal, a vital component of the magnets used in gasoline-electric hybrid automobiles, is prepared by reduction of neodymium(III) fluoride with calcium metal.

$$2\ NdF_3 + 3\ Ca \longrightarrow 2\ Nd + 3\ CaF_2$$

What mass of neodymium is obtained from 143 g of NdF_3?

40. Indium is a vital component of the electrically conducting transparent coatings on LCD screens. Indium metal can be prepared by electrolysis of salts such as indium(III) chloride. What mass in grams of indium(III) chloride is required to produce 33.2 g of indium?

$$2\ InCl_3 \longrightarrow 2\ In + 3\ Cl_2$$

ADDITIONAL PROBLEMS

41. An aluminum plant produces 72 million kg of aluminum per year. How much aluminum oxide is required? How much bauxite is required? (It takes 2.1 kg of crude bauxite to produce 1.0 kg of aluminum oxide.)

42. It takes 17 kWh of electricity to produce 1.0 kg of aluminum. How much electricity does the plant in Problem 41 use for aluminum production in 1 year?

43. All the gold ever mined through 2009 totals about 165,000 metric tons (t; 1 t = 1000 kg). If all this gold were formed into a cube, what would be the length in meters of one edge of the cube? The density of gold is 19.3 g/cm^3, and 1 troy oz = 31.1 g.

44. Unless carefully refined, zinc metal contains cadmium as an impurity. Explain why this is to be expected.

45. A blast furnace produces 1.0×10^7 kg of pig iron per day. Assuming that the pig iron is 95% Fe by mass, what mass (in kilograms) of iron ore is consumed in this furnace per day? Assume that the ore is 82% by mass hematite (Fe_2O_3).

46. The blast furnace described in Problem 45 produces 0.50 kg of slag per kilogram of pig iron. What is the minimum daily requirement of limestone for this furnace? Assume that the limestone is 91% $CaCO_3$, that the slag

is exclusively $CaSiO_3$, and that the limestone is the only source of calcium in the slag.

47. The amount of trash produced per person per day in the United States is about 4.5 lb. If the trash has an average density of 85 lb/ft^3, how many cubic feet of trash are produced each year by a small town of 14,000 people? If a sanitary landfill is constructed that is 100 ft wide by 100 ft long, how deep must it be to contain this trash?

48. The equation for the reaction by which a sodium cyanide solution dissolves gold from its ore is

$$4\,Au + 8\,NaCN + 2\,H_2O + O_2 \longrightarrow 4\,NaAu(CN)_2 + 4\,NaOH$$

What is the minimum mass of NaCN required to dissolve the 10 g of Au in a ton of gold ore?

49. Some companies make iron from iron ore in a single-step, continuous process called *direct reduction*. They avoid the high energy requirements of a blast furnace by using temperatures below the melting points of any of the raw materials. The ore is reduced by H_2 and CO, which in turn are made from natural gas. This method is used mainly in developing countries that do not already have large iron and steel industries in place. Write equations for the reduction of Fe_2O_3 **(a)** by H_2 and **(b)** by CO.

50. Why is coal heated in the absence of air to make coke? What would happen if the coal were heated in air? Write the equation.

51. Based on Figure 12.9, about what percentage of municipal waste might be burned as fuel?

52. Look again at Figure 12.9. If everyone recycled all paper and cardboard, composted yard waste and food scraps, and recycled all plastics and metals, how would the answer to Problem 47 change?

53. One pound of plastic bags is about 67 bags. **(a)** What is the mass in kilograms of 500 billion bags? An Australian study concluded that 8.7 plastic bags equal the fuel consumed by driving a car 1 km. How many kilometers could a car travel on the fuel equivalent of **(b)** 1 lb of bags and **(c)** 500 billion bags?

54. Compare the environmental effects **(a)** of use of cleaning cloths, mop heads, and sponges that can be cleaned and reused and use of similar disposable products and **(b)** of use of cloth diapers that need to be washed and use of disposable diapers.

55. Most iron metal (Fe) is produced from the ore hematite (Fe_2O_3) with carbon monoxide as the reducing agent.

$$Fe_2O_3 + 3\,CO \longrightarrow 2\,Fe + 3\,CO_2$$

(a) Calculate the percent atom economy of this reaction. **(b)** How does it compare to the percent atom economy for the production of Fe from magnetite?

56. Which of the following factors should be considered when determining whether aluminum or steel is a greener metal?
   a. energy requirements of production process
   b. percent atom economy
   c. impact of byproducts from production
   d. recyclability of the metal
   e. all of the above

57. Describe two ways that recycling of aluminum can help save the Earth's resources.

COLLABORATIVE GROUP PROJECTS

Prepare a PowerPoint, poster, or other presentation (as directed by your instructor) to share with the class.

1. Prepare a brief report on one of the metals listed in Table 12.6. List the main ores, and describe how the metal is obtained from one of those ores. Describe some of the uses of the metal, and explain how its properties make it suitable for those uses.

2. Prepare a brief report on recycling one of the following types of municipal solid waste. List the advantages of recycling, and identify problems involved in the process.
   a. glass
   b. plastics
   c. yard waste
   d. paper
   e. lead
   f. aluminum

3. Compare disposal in landfills, incineration, and recycling as methods of dealing with each of the types of municipal solid waste listed in Problem 56. List advantages and disadvantages of each method for each type of waste.

4. Search the Internet for material on recent mine waste disasters or long-term mine waste problems. Prepare a brief report on one of the events or situations.

5. Search the Internet to find the current estimated population of the United States and of the world. What is the current rate of population growth, as a percentage per year, in **(a)** France, **(b)** Bolivia, **(c)** Uganda, **(d)** United States, and **(e)** the world?

Air

Learning Objectives

- List and describe the layers of the atmosphere. (13.1)
- Give the proportions of N_2, O_2, Ar, and CO_2 in Earth's atmosphere. (13.1)
- Describe the nitrogen and oxygen cycles. (13.2)
- Describe the origin and effects of temperature inversions. (13.2)
- List some natural sources of air pollution. (13.3)
- List the main pollutants formed by burning coal, and describe some technologies used to clean up these pollutants. (13.3)
- List the main gases in automobile emissions, and describe how catalytic converters reduce these gaseous pollutants. (13.4)
- Explain how carbon monoxide acts as a poison. (13.4)
- Distinguish the origin of photochemical smog from the origin of sulfurous smog. (13.5)
- Describe the technologies used to alleviate photochemical smog. (13.5)
- Name the air pollutants that contribute to acid rain. (13.6)
- List the major industrial and consumer sources of acid-rain-producing pollutants. (13.6)
- List the main indoor air pollutants and their sources. (13.7)
- Explain where radon comes from and why it is hazardous. (13.7)
- Explain the link between CFCs and depletion of the ozone layer. (13.8)
- Describe the consequences of stratospheric ozone depletion. (13.8)
- List the important greenhouse gases, and describe the mechanism and significance of the greenhouse effect. (13.9)
- Describe some strategies for reducing the amount of CO_2 released into the atmosphere. (13.9)
- List the EPA's criteria pollutants and the major air pollutants that come mainly from automobiles and mostly from industry. (13.10)

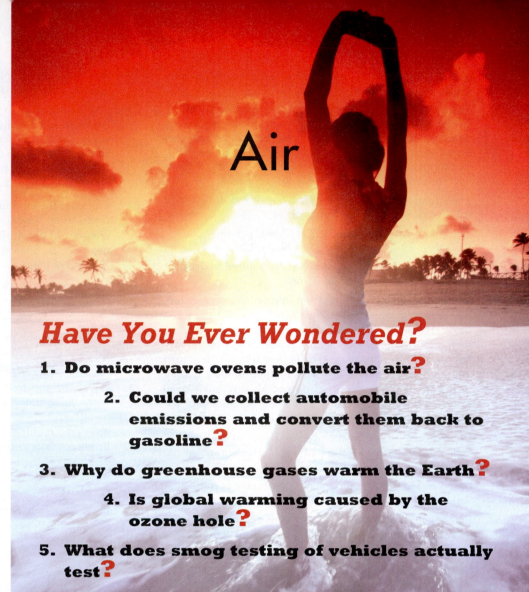

Have You Ever Wondered?

1. **Do microwave ovens pollute the air?**
2. **Could we collect automobile emissions and convert them back to gasoline?**
3. **Why do greenhouse gases warm the Earth?**
4. **Is global warming caused by the ozone hole?**
5. **What does smog testing of vehicles actually test?**

The Breath of Life

We could live about a month without food. We could live for several days without water. But without air we cannot live more than a few minutes. Under normal conditions, we cannot hold our breath for very long, even if we want to.

A person or a society may run short of food or fresh water, but we are not likely to run out of air. On the other hand, we *can* foul the air so badly that it becomes unfit or unhealthy to breathe. In some areas, the air is already so bad that people become sick from breathing it, and some even die. The World Health Organization (WHO) estimates that outdoor air pollution from vehicles and industrial emissions kills 2 million people a year worldwide.

We live at the bottom of an ocean—an ocean of air that is in many ways different from the more familiar oceans of water. The *atmosphere* is much deeper than the water oceans, rising more than 100 km above Earth's surface, and is about 1000 times less dense than water oceans. But there are similarities. The gaseous ocean is a mixture, containing nitrogen, oxygen, argon, carbon dioxide, and a number of trace gases. The atmosphere exerts pressure (Section 6.6), just as the liquid oceans do. And, unfortunately, the breath of life can be polluted by humans. In this chapter, we will learn about the types of air pollution, their causes, their effects, and how those pollutants and their effects can be minimized.

Another 1.6 million die from indoor air pollution, mainly caused by heating and cooking fuels. Most of the deaths occur in developing countries. This chapter first discusses the natural chemistry of the atmosphere and then presents some of the effects human intervention is having on the natural balance and some possible ways to reduce these effects.

Learning Objectives (cont'd)

› Identify that green chemistry assessment includes evaluation of the safety of substances as well as awareness of long-term effects.

› Explain how the green chemistry principles can be applied in the development of manufacturing processes.

13.1 Earth's Atmosphere: Divisions and Composition

Learning Objectives › List and describe the layers of the atmosphere. › Give the approximate proportions of N_2, O_2, Ar, and CO_2 in Earth's atmosphere.

We passengers on Spaceship Earth live under a thin blanket of air called the **atmosphere**. It is difficult to measure exactly how thick the atmosphere is, because it does not end abruptly but gradually gets thinner as it fades into space. We do know that 99% of the atmosphere lies within 30 km of Earth's surface. If Earth were the diameter of a large apple, the atmosphere would be thinner than the apple's skin.

The atmosphere is divided into four main layers (Figure 13.1). The temperature in each layer varies with altitude. The layer nearest Earth, the *troposphere*, harbors nearly all living things and nearly all human activity. Although other planets in our solar system have atmospheres, Earth's atmosphere is unique in its ability to support higher forms of life. Many people suppose that atmospheric temperature decreases as the altitude increases, but this is mainly true only for the troposphere and mesosphere. In the *stratosphere* and *thermosphere*, the temperature actually increases as you go higher.

The composition of dry air is summarized in Table 13.1. Moist air can contain up to about 4% water vapor. The atmosphere has a number of minor constituents, the most important of which is CO_2. The concentration of carbon dioxide in the atmosphere increased from about 280 parts per million (ppm) in the preindustrial world to 390 ppm in 2010, and it continues to rise at 2 ppm each year.

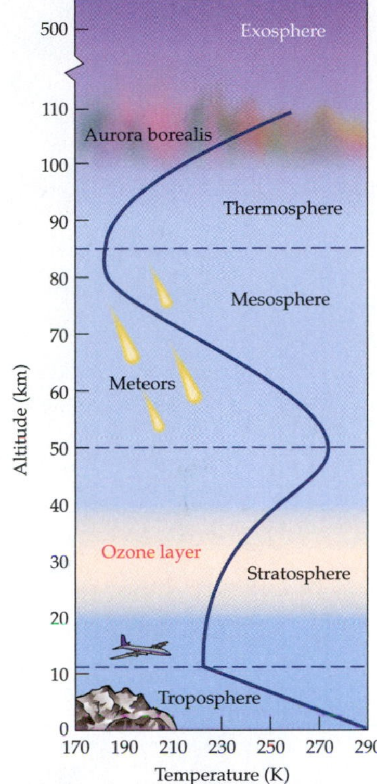

▲ **Figure 13.1** Approximate altitudes and temperature variations of the layers of the atmosphere. The height of the troposphere varies from about 8 km at the poles to 16 km at the equator.

Table 13.1 Approximate Composition of Clean Dry Air near Sea Level

Component	Percent by Volume
Nitrogen (N_2)	78.08
Oxygen (O_2)	20.94
Argon (Ar)	0.93
Carbon dioxide (CO_2)	0.039
Trace gases[a]	0.002

[a]Neon (Ne), helium (He), methane (CH_4), krypton (Kr), hydrogen (H_2), dinitrogen monoxide (N_2O), xenon (Xe), ozone (O_3), sulfur dioxide (SO_2), nitrogen dioxide (NO_2), ammonia (NH_3), carbon monoxide (CO), and iodine (I_2), plus some others.

▲ **It DOES Matter!**

Although the increase in atmospheric CO_2 over the last two centuries—from 0.028% to 0.039%—appears to be small, that increase represents a significant departure from previous conditions. The increased CO_2 comes from carbon (from fossil fuels) that has not been in the biosphere for tens of millions of years. The CO_2 that has been added to our atmosphere by burning fossil fuels is equivalent to the amount of carbon in 27 *trillion* people, or almost four thousand times the current population!

Self-Assessment Questions

1. Nearly all human activity occurs in the
   a. mesosphere b. stratosphere c. thermosphere d. troposphere
2. The ozone layer is found in the
   a. mesosphere b. stratosphere c. thermosphere d. troposphere
3. Earth's atmosphere
   a. blends into outer space
   b. ends abruptly at 30 km altitude
   c. ends abruptly at 50 km altitude
   d. ends abruptly at the exosphere

4. The approximate percentage of nitrogen in the atmosphere is
   a. 18% b. 28% c. 48% d. 78%
5. The three most abundant gases in dry air are nitrogen, oxygen, and
   a. argon b. carbon dioxide c. hydrogen d. ozone

Answers: 1, d; 2, b; 3, a; 4, d; 5, a

13.2 Chemistry of the Atmosphere

Learning Objectives › Describe the nitrogen and oxygen cycles. › Describe the origin and effects of temperature inversions.

Under ordinary conditions, nitrogen and oxygen gases coexist in the atmosphere as a simple mixture, with little or no reaction between them. Under certain circumstances, however, the two elements can combine, in a reaction essential to life itself.

Nitrogen makes up 78% of the atmosphere in the form of diatomic N_2 molecules. Nitrogen is essential to living things, but most animals and plants cannot assimilate N_2 directly. How then has nitrogen become a component of so many vital compounds, such as the proteins and nucleic acids of living organisms? The answer is that organisms first combine nitrogen with another element, a process called **nitrogen fixation**. This process does not occur readily because the nitrogen atoms in N_2 are held together by a strong triple bond ($N{\equiv}N$), which must be broken for fixation to take place.

The Nitrogen Cycle

Several natural phenomena convert nitrogen gas to more usable forms. Lightning fixes nitrogen by causing it to combine with oxygen, forming first nitrogen monoxide (NO), commonly called nitric oxide, and then nitrogen dioxide (NO_2).

$$N_2 + O_2 + \text{energy} \xrightarrow{\text{lightning}} 2\,NO$$
$$2\,NO + O_2 \longrightarrow 2\,NO_2$$

(These oxides of nitrogen, NO and NO_2, are collectively designated as NO_x.) Nitrogen dioxide reacts with water to form nitric acid (HNO_3).

$$3\,NO_2 + H_2O \longrightarrow 2\,HNO_3 + NO$$

Nitric acid in rainwater falls on Earth's surface, adding to the supply of available nitrates in the oceans and the soil.

Nitrogen is fixed industrially by combining nitrogen with hydrogen to form ammonia, a procedure called the *Haber–Bosch process* (descried in Chapter 20).

$$N_2 + 3\,H_2 \longrightarrow 2\,NH_3$$

This technology has greatly increased our food supply because the availability of fixed nitrogen is often the limiting factor in the production of food. Not all consequences of this intervention have been favorable, however. Excessive runoff of nitrogen fertilizer has led to serious water pollution problems in some areas (which we discuss in Chapter 14).

Most nitrogen fixation is performed by bacteria in the roots of legumes (peas, beans, clover, and the like). Certain types of bacteria reduce N_2 to ammonia (NH_3). Other bacteria oxidize ammonia to nitrites (NO_2^-), and still others oxidize nitrites to nitrates (NO_3^-). Plants are then able to take up the nitrates and ammonia from the soil. Animals in turn can get their required nitrogen compounds from the plants. The **nitrogen cycle** (Figure 13.2) is completed by the action of other types of microbes, which can use nitrate ions as their oxygen source for the decomposition of organic matter and release N_2 gas back to the atmosphere.

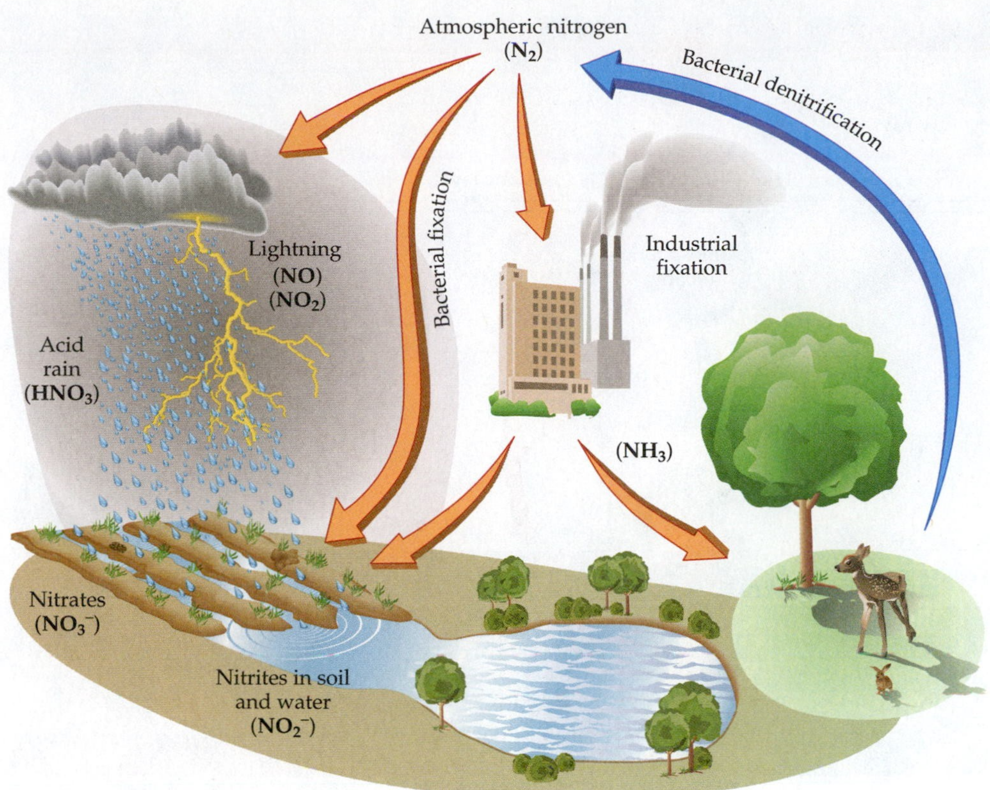

◀ **Figure 13.2** The nitrogen cycle. Atmospheric nitrogen is *fixed*, or converted to water-soluble forms, both naturally and industrially. Animal wastes and dead plants and animals are converted back to atmospheric nitrogen by certain bacteria.

The Oxygen Cycle

Oxygen makes up 21% of Earth's atmosphere. As with nitrogen, a balance is maintained between consumption and production of oxygen in the troposphere. Both plants and animals use oxygen in the metabolism of foods. The decay and combustion of plant and animal materials consume oxygen and produce carbon dioxide, as does the burning of fossil fuels like coal, natural gas, and oil. The rusting of metals and the weathering of rocks also consume oxygen. A simplified **oxygen cycle**, illustrated in Figure 13.3, shows the influence of green plants, including one-celled organisms (phytoplankton) in the sea, which consume carbon dioxide for photosynthesis and also replenish the oxygen supply.

$$6\,CO_2 + 6\,H_2O \longrightarrow C_6H_{12}O_6 + 6\,O_2$$

Another vital balancing act occurs in the stratosphere. There, oxygen is formed by the action of ultraviolet (UV) radiation on water molecules. Perhaps more important, some oxygen is converted to ozone (Section 13.8).

$$3\,O_2(g) + \text{energy (UV radiation)} \longrightarrow 2\,O_3(g)$$

This ozone absorbs high-energy UV radiation that might otherwise make higher forms of life on Earth impossible. We discuss the atmosphere in more detail in subsequent sections, paying particular attention to changes wrought by human activities.

Temperature Inversions

Normally, air is warmest near the ground and gets cooler at moderate altitudes. On clear nights, the ground cools rapidly, but the wind usually mixes the cooler air near the ground with the warmer air above it. Sometimes, the air is still, and the lower layer of cold air becomes trapped by the layer of warm air above it, a meteorological condition known as a **temperature inversion** (or *thermal inversion*). Pollutants in the cooler air are trapped near the ground, and the air can become quite seriously polluted in a short time (Figure 13.4).

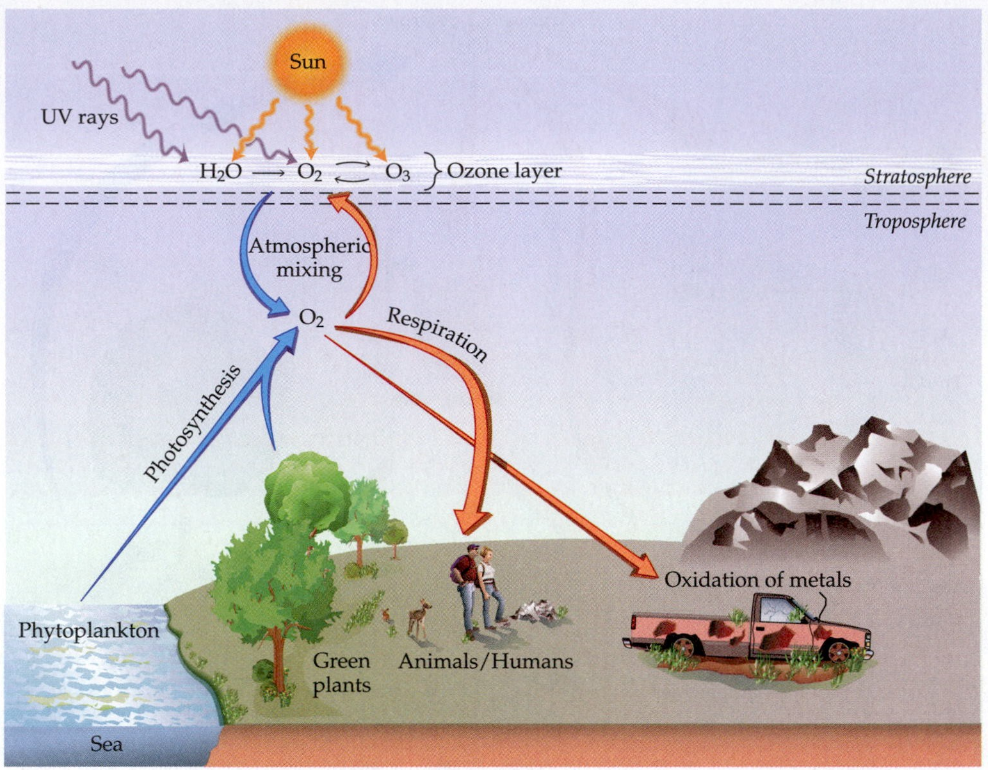

▶ **Figure 13.3** The oxygen cycle. Animals and people use oxygen gas and produce carbon dioxide. Plants, in turn, consume the carbon dioxide, converting it to oxygen gas and glucose for food. In the stratosphere, atmospheric oxygen is involved in ozone production.

A temperature inversion can also occur when a warm front collides with a cold front. The less dense warm air mass slides over the cold air mass, producing a condition of atmospheric stability. Because there is no vertical air movement, the air near the ground stagnates and air pollutants accumulate.

(a) Normal

(b) Temperature inversion

▶ **Figure 13.4** Ordinarily, the air gets colder as the altitude increases (a). During a temperature (thermal) inversion (b), a cooler layer near the surface lies beneath a warmer layer and usually becomes polluted quickly.

Self-Assessment Questions

1. Lightning can convert atmospheric N_2 to
   a. nitroglycerin **b.** ammonia **c.** nitrogen oxides **d.** proteins
2. Conversion of atmospheric N_2 to biologically useful forms is called nitrogen
   a. addition **b.** fixation **c.** reduction **d.** substitution
3. The starting materials in the industrial process for making ammonia are
   a. N_2 and H_2 **b.** N_2 and O_2 **c.** NO_3^- and H_2 **d.** NO_3^- and O_2
4. Which of the following processes removes carbon dioxide from the atmosphere?
   a. photosynthesis **b.** respiration
   c. temperature inversions **d.** volcanic eruptions

5. Which of the following processes consumes oxygen?
   a. breakdown of ozone
   b. corrosion of metals
   c. Haber–Bosch process
   d. photosynthesis
6. A temperature inversion is a meteorological condition that
   a. makes people put on thermal underwear
   b. commonly occurs over flat countryside
   c. concentrates air pollutants
   d. usually ends a bad air pollution episode

Answers: 1, c; 2, b; 3, a; 4, a; 5, b; 6, c

13.3 Pollution through the Ages

Learning Objectives › List some natural sources of air pollution. › List the main pollutants formed by burning coal, and describe some technologies used to clean up these pollutants.

Air pollution has always been with us. Wildfires, windblown dust, and volcanic eruptions added pollutants to the atmosphere long before humans existed. Volcanoes spew ash and poisonous gases into the atmosphere. The 1995 and subsequent eruptions of the Soufriere Hills volcano on Montserrat covered much of the Caribbean island with ash, destroying the capital city, Plymouth, and forcing the evacuation of two-thirds of the population. Kilauea volcano in Hawaii emits 1000–2000 t of sulfur dioxide per day, producing acid rain downwind that has helped create a barren region called the Kau Desert.

Dust storms, especially in arid regions, add massive amounts of particulate matter to the atmosphere. Dust from the Sahara Desert often reaches the Caribbean and South America. Dust and pollution from China blanket Japan and even reach western North America. Nature isn't always benign.

▲ **It DOES Matter!**
A vast plume of polluted air called the *atmospheric brown cloud (ABC)* drapes over South Asia and the Indian Ocean during the winter. It is so huge that it may cool the area as much as or more than the greenhouse gases warm it. The cloud is composed of soot and ash, sulfates, nitrates, and mineral dust. Burning of biomass in forest fires and cooking and heating are responsible for half or more of the pollution. Motor vehicles and factories also contribute.

The Air Our Ancestors Breathed

People have always altered their environment. The discovery of tools and the use of fire forever changed the balance between people and their environment. The problem of air pollution probably first occurred when fires were built in poorly ventilated caves or other dwellings. People cleared land, leading to larger dust storms. They built cities, and the soot from their hearths and the stench from their wastes filled the air. The Roman author Seneca wrote in C.E. 61 of the stink, soot, and "heavy air" of the imperial city. The first laws to regulate the burning of coal in cities in England were enacted in the thirteenth century. The Industrial Revolution brought even more air pollution, as coal was burned in large amounts to power factories. Soot, smoke, and sulfur dioxide filled the air. The good old days? Not in factory towns. But there were large rural areas that were less affected by air pollution.

Air pollution today is much more complex than that affecting our ancestors. When society changes its activities, the nature of its waste materials changes, including the ones it dumps into the atmosphere. The phenomenon is not new, but today's rapid rate of change is unprecedented. Our environment may not be able to absorb the changes.

Pollution Goes Global

Winds and precipitation purify the air, but we pour more pollutants into the atmosphere than it can readily handle. Air pollution knows no political boundaries. Pollution from Midwestern power plants leads to acid rain in the Northeast. Pollution originating in the United States contributes to acid rain in Canada. Contaminants

A Closed Ecosystem?

If you think for a moment about the oxygen and nitrogen cycles, you may realize that a *closed ecosystem* should be possible. In such a system, the plant and animal life would be balanced. The O_2 given off by the plants would sustain the animal life, and the CO_2 given off by the animals would keep the plants alive. Other animal wastes would supply the nitrogen needed by the plants, and the animals would consume some of the plants or one another for food. Trace elements would have to be present in sufficient quantity. Sunlight would provide the energy necessary to "run" the ecosystem. Nothing else goes in, and nothing comes out.

Earth is itself a closed ecosystem. The planet absorbs sunlight for energy, but little matter enters or leaves. But can such a system be constructed artificially?

▲ The Ecosphere® is a sealed, self-contained ecosystem in which plants and animals can live for a year or more, with sunlight as the only "input."

The answer is of interest in space exploration. A long space voyage would require huge amounts of resources to be carried along—at enormous expense. The required resources could be minimized by taking plants to provide oxygen and consume carbon dioxide and human wastes.

Tiny ecosystems are available commercially as desktop novelties. These systems have a limited lifetime of a few years. *Biosphere II* was a large-scale experiment involving humans and a semi-closed ecosystem. The experiment was cut short because of problems such as rising levels of nitrogen oxides, water pollution, and unforeseen low CO_2 levels. Although additional studies and experiments will be done, Earth remains the only successful long-term closed ecosystem.

from England and Germany pollute the snow in Norway. Satellites orbiting at 150 km and higher can trace plumes of pollution from China to North America. Within the United States, Los Angeles smog drifts to Colorado and beyond.

As the number of people increases, more of the world's population lives in cities. Especially in developing countries, industrialization takes precedence over the environment. Cities in China, Iran, Mexico, Indonesia, and many other countries have experienced frightening episodes of air pollution. Large metropolitan areas are troubled the most by air pollution, but rural areas are affected, too. Neighborhoods around smoky factories have seen evidence of increased rates of miscarriage and decreased wool quality in sheep, decreased egg production and high mortality in chickens, and increased feed and care requirements for cattle. Plants are stunted, deformed, and even killed.

1. Do microwave ovens pollute the air? Microwaves are a form of energy, like visible light, radio waves, and ultraviolet light from tanning beds. Although high levels of microwave radiation may be harmful, microwaves are not matter and are not pollutants.

What is a **pollutant**? It is too much of any substance in the wrong place or at the wrong time. A chemical may be a pollutant in one place and helpful in another. For example, ozone is a natural and important constituent of the stratosphere, where it shields Earth from life-destroying UV radiation. In the troposphere, however, ozone is a dangerous pollutant (Section 13.8).

Coal + Fire → Industrial (Sulfurous) Smog

The word *smog* is a contraction of the words *smoke* and *fog*. There are two basic types of smog (Table 13.2). Polluted air associated with industrial activities is often called **industrial smog**. It is characterized by the presence of smoke, fog, sulfur dioxide, and particulate matter such as ash and soot. The burning of coal, especially high-sulfur coal such as that found in the eastern United States, China, and Eastern Europe, causes most industrial smog. (Photochemical smog is discussed in Section 13.5.)

The chemistry of industrial smog is fairly simple. High-grade coal is a complex combination of organic materials and inorganic materials. The organic materials are mainly carbon and burn when the coal is combusted. The inorganic materials—

Air Pollution in China

As China becomes a major industrial power, its citizens pay a heavy price in terms of increased pollution. Three-fourths of China's commercial energy is generated from burning coal. The high sulfur content of the coal and the inadequate emission controls result in levels of sulfur dioxide and particulate matter (ash, soot, and dust) that are among the highest in the world. Over two-thirds of major Chinese cities have SO_2 or NO_x levels above the maximums identified by WHO guidelines. Many cities also exceed the WHO guidelines for particulate matter. Of 443 Chinese cities monitored, 189 suffered harm from acid rain. The World Bank predicts that, in the first two decades of the twenty-first century, about 590,000 people a year will die prematurely in China as a result of urban air pollution.

Private ownership of motor vehicles was almost unknown in China until the 1980s. Now, according to the Chinese Ministry of Communications, the number of cars on the roads is predicted to grow from 20 million in 2005 to 1 billion by 2050.

China cleaned up the air in Beijing for the 2008 Olympic Games and in Shanghai for the World Exposition in 2010. It is attacking the air-quality problem by closing heavily polluting factories in some larger metropolitan areas, investing in natural gas, and replacing raw coal with cleaner-burning briquettes for domestic cooking and heating. China is also emerging as a world leader in clean energy, producing compact fluorescent lightbulbs, solar water heaters, solar photovoltaic cells, and wind turbines.

▲ The polluted air of Beijing, China, shrouded the capital in a nasty haze on November 5, 2005. People were warned to stay indoors as the pollution index hit its highest level for the second day.

Table 13.2 Types of Smog

	Industrial Smog	Photochemical Smog
Alternative names	Winter smog, sulfurous smog, London smog	Summer smog, Los Angeles smog
Main initial components	SO_2, particulates	NO_x, hydrocarbons
Secondary components	SO_3, H_2SO_4	O_3, aldehydes, peroxyacetyl nitrate (PAN)
Main source(s)	Electric power plants, factories	Automobiles
Typical weather	Cold, damp, foggy	Warm, sunny, dry

▲ Burning of coal in electric power plants and other facilities is the main source of industrial smog, which is characterized by high levels of sulfur dioxide and particulate matter. Industrial smog can be reduced by the use of electrostatic precipitators, scrubbers, and other devices.

minerals—wind up as ash. Some coal can contain 10% sulfur or more. When burned, the carbon in coal is oxidized to carbon dioxide and heat is given off.

$$C(s) + O_2(g) \longrightarrow CO_2(g) + \text{heat}$$

Not all of the carbon is completely oxidized, however; some winds up as carbon monoxide.

$$2\,C(s) + O_2(g) \longrightarrow 2\,CO(g)$$

And some carbon, unburned, ends up as soot.

The sulfur in coal also burns, forming sulfur dioxide, a choking, acrid gas that gives rise to the term *sulfurous pollution*.

$$S(s) + O_2(g) \longrightarrow SO_2(g)$$

Sulfur dioxide is readily absorbed in the respiratory system. It is a powerful irritant, known to aggravate the symptoms of people who suffer from asthma, bronchitis, emphysema, and other lung diseases.

An Air Pollution Episode: London, England

Industrial smog was once so common a problem in London that it was called *London smog*. A notorious smog episode began in London on Thursday, December 4, 1952, when a cold air mass moved into the Thames River valley. A temperature inversion placed a blanket of warm air over the cold air. With nightfall, a dense fog and below-freezing temperatures caused Londoners to heap sulfur-rich coal into their stoves. These fires and coal-fired power plants poured SO_2 and soot into the air. The next day (Friday), schools closed and transportation was disrupted. People continued to burn coal because the temperature remained below freezing.

Saturday was a day of darkness. For 20 miles around London, no light came through the smog. A performance of the opera *La Traviata* had to be abandoned because smog obscured the stage. The air remained still and cold, and coal fires continued to burn throughout the weekend. On Monday, December 8, more than 100 people died of respiratory and related conditions. People tried to sleep sitting up in chairs to make it easier to breathe. The city's hospitals overflowed with patients with pneumonia and bronchitis.

By the time a breeze cleared the air on Tuesday, December 9, more than 4000 deaths had been attributed to the smog. Many other people became ill, and some of them died later. The total number of premature deaths before the death rate returned to normal the following summer is now estimated to be as high as 12,000. That is more people than were ever killed by any single tornado, mine disaster, shipwreck, or airplane crash. A second incident occurred in December 1991, in which 160 people died. Air pollution episodes may not be as dramatic as other disasters, but they can be just as deadly.

▲ The great London smog episode of 1952.

And things get worse. Some of the sulfur dioxide reacts further with oxygen in the air to form sulfur trioxide.

$$2\,SO_2(g) + O_2(g) \longrightarrow 2\,SO_3(g)$$

Collectively, the two oxides of sulfur are often designated as SO_x. Sulfur trioxide then reacts with water to form sulfuric acid.

$$SO_3(g) + H_2O(l) \longrightarrow H_2SO_4(l)$$

In air, this acid forms an *aerosol*, a dispersion of tiny particles (solid) or droplets (liquid) in a gas. Sulfuric acid is a strong acid, and this aerosol is even more irritating to the respiratory tract than sulfur dioxide.

Usually, industrial smog also has high levels of **particulate matter (PM)**, solid and liquid particles of greater than molecular size. The largest particles are often visible in the air as dust and smoke. PM consists mainly of soot and the mineral matter that occurs in coal.

Minerals do not burn, even in the roaring fire of a huge factory or power plant boiler. Some mineral matter is left behind as *bottom ash*, but much of it is carried aloft in the tremendous draft created by the fire. This *fly ash* settles over the surrounding area, covering everything with dust. It is also inhaled, contributing to respiratory problems in animals and humans.

▲ False-color scanning electron micrograph of PM from a coal-burning power plant.

Small particulates—less than 10 μm in diameter, called PM10—are believed to be especially harmful. They contribute to respiratory and heart disease. The U.S. Environmental Protection Agency (EPA) also monitors even finer particulates, called PM2.5. EPA studies indicate that tens of thousands of premature deaths a year are linked to PM and that 20,000 of them are due to PM2.5. Particulate concentrations have been lowered significantly since nationwide monitoring began in 1999. In 2010, three out of ten people in the United States lived in counties with particulate pollution levels above the EPA's standards for PM2.5, PM10, or both.

Health and Environmental Effects of Industrial Smog

Minute droplets of liquid sulfuric acid, as well as PM10 and smaller solids, are easily trapped in the lungs. Interaction can considerably magnify the harmful effects of pollutants. A certain level of sulfur dioxide, without the presence of PM, might be reasonably safe. A particular level of PM might be fairly harmless without sulfur dioxide around, but the effect of both together can be deadly. *Synergistic effects* such as this are quite common whenever chemicals act together. Two examples are the synergistic effects of asbestos and cigarette smoke (discussed in Chapter 12), and the synergistic effects of some drugs (discussed in Chapter 18).

When the pollutants in industrial smog come into contact with the alveoli of the lungs, the alveoli lose their resilience, making it difficult for them to expel carbon dioxide. Such lung damage contributes to pulmonary emphysema, a condition characterized by increasing shortness of breath.

Sulfuric acid and SO_x pollutants also damage plants. Leaves become bleached and splotchy when exposed to SO_x. The yield and quality of farm crops can be severely affected. These compounds are also major culprits in the production of acid rain.

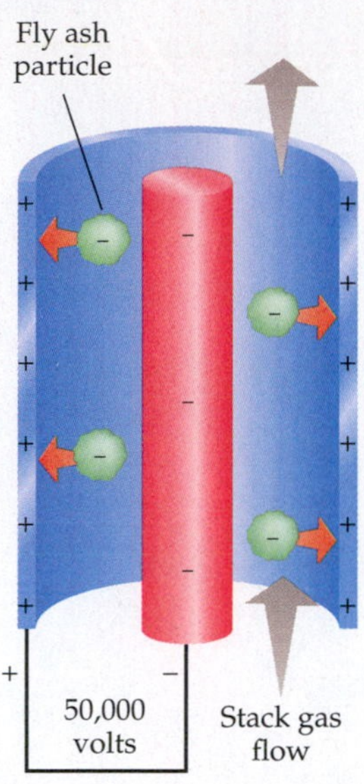

▲ **Figure 13.5** A cross section of a cylindrical electrostatic precipitator for removing particulate matter from smokestack gases. Electrons from the negatively charged discharge electrode (in the center) become attached to the particles of fly ash, giving them a negative charge. The charged particles are then attracted to and deposited on the outer, positively charged collector plate.

What to Do about Industrial Smog

Much effort is spent preventing and alleviating industrial smog. PM can be removed from smokestack gases by means of several devices.

- An **electrostatic precipitator** (Figure 13.5) induces electric charges on the particles, which are then attracted to oppositely charged plates and deposited.
- *Bag filtration* works much like the bag in a vacuum cleaner. Particle-laden gases pass through filters in a bag house. These filters can be cleaned by shaking and by periodically blowing air through them in the opposite direction.
- A *cyclone separator* causes the stack gases to spiral upward through it in a circular motion. The particles hit the outer walls, settle out, and are collected at the bottom.
- A **wet scrubber** removes PM by passing the stack gases through a fine mist of water. After use, the wastewater must be treated to remove the particulates, which adds to the cost of this method.

The choice of device depends on the type of coal being burned, the size of the plant, and other factors. All require energy—electrostatic precipitators use about 10% of the plant's output—and the collected ash has to be put somewhere. Some of the ash is used to make concrete, as a substitute for aggregate in road base, as a soil modifier, and for backfilling mines. The rest has to be stored. Most of it goes into ponds, and the rest into landfills.

Sulfur and SO_x are harder to get rid of than PM is. Sulfur can be removed by processing coal before burning, but both the flotation method and the gasification or liquefaction process (Chapter 15) are expensive. Another way to get rid of sulfur is to scrub sulfur dioxide out of stack gases after the coal has been burned.

The most common scrubber uses the limestone–dolomite process. Limestone ($CaCO_3$) and dolomite (a mixed calcium–magnesium carbonate) are pulverized and heated. Heat drives off carbon dioxide to form calcium oxide (lime), a basic oxide that reacts with sulfur dioxide to form solid calcium sulfite ($CaSO_3$).

$$CaCO_3(s) + \text{heat} \longrightarrow CaO(s) + CO_2(g)$$

$$CaO(s) + SO_2(g) \longrightarrow CaSO_3(s)$$

This by-product presents a sizable disposal problem. Removal of 1 t of sulfur dioxide produces almost 2 t of solids. Some modified scrubbers oxidize the calcium sulfite to calcium sulfate ($CaSO_4$).

$$2\,CaSO_3(s) + O_2(g) \longrightarrow 2\,CaSO_4(s)$$

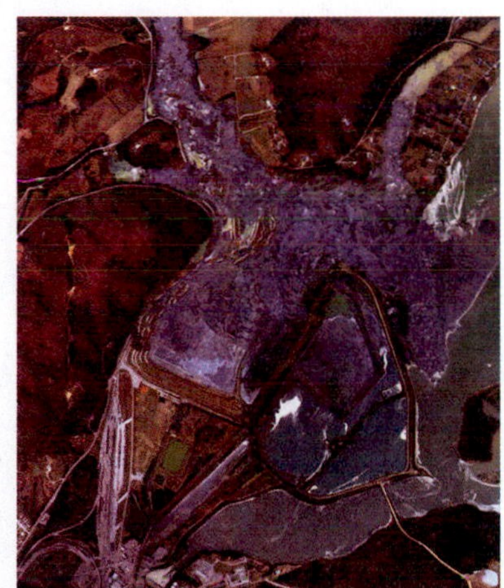

▲ Every industry produces some kind of waste that must be dealt with in some way. Once removed from the stack gases, fly ash may seem benign, but it is produced in enormous quantities that must be disposed of or stored. In 2008, in Kingston, Tennessee, a dike ruptured in a pond used to store ash slurry (fly ash plus water). Four million cubic meters of the slurry was released, covering 300 acres. It damaged homes, washed out a road, ruptured a gas line and a water main, blocked a rail line, and felled trees.

Calcium sulfate is much more useful than calcium sulfite; the sulfate is used to make commercial products such as plasterboard. In nature, calcium sulfate occurs as gypsum ($CaSO_4 \cdot 2H_2O$), which has the same composition as hardened plaster.

Self-Assessment Questions

1. The air in cities in thirteenth-century England
a. smelled of ale **b.** smelled of roses
c. was smoky from coal burning **d.** was pristine

2. Which of the following is *not* usually released from burning fossil fuels?
a. O_3 **b.** NO_x **c.** CO_2 **d.** SO_2

3. Carbon monoxide is formed as a product of
a. animal respiration
b. burning coal but not burning natural gas
c. combustion of fossil fuels with excess O_2
d. partial combustion of coal

4. The pollutant usually described by size rather than composition is
a. acid rain **b.** CFCs **c.** particulates **d.** photochemicals

5. Which of the following pairs of pollutant act synergistically in causing lung damage?
a. O_3 and soot **b.** O_3 and PM **c.** SO_2 and NO_x **d.** SO_2 and PM

6. A device that cleans stack gases by means of electric charges is called a(n)
a. catalytic converter **b.** electric generator
c. electrostatic precipitator **d.** particle accelerator

7. Which pollutant is removed from stack gases by scrubbers that use lime?
a. CO_2 **b.** CO **c.** NO_x **d.** SO_2

8. A common by-product of sulfur dioxide removal from stack gases is
a. CaO **b.** $CaSO_4$ **c.** $CaCO_3$ **d.** $CaCl_2$

Answers: 1, c; 2, b; 3, d; 4, c; 5, d; 6, c; 7, d; 8, b

13.4 Automobile Emissions

Learning Objectives › List the main gases in automobile emissions, and describe how catalytic converters reduce these gaseous pollutants. › Explain how carbon monoxide acts as a poison.

When a hydrocarbon burns in sufficient oxygen, the products are carbon dioxide and water. For example, consider the combustion of octane, one of the hundreds of hydrocarbons that make up the mixture we call gasoline:

$$2\,C_8H_{18}(l) + 25\,O_2(g) \longrightarrow 18\,H_2O(g) + 16\,CO_2(g)$$

Thus, the main components of automotive exhaust are water vapor, carbon dioxide, and unreacted nitrogen gas from the atmosphere. Water vapor and nitrogen are innocuous, but CO_2 contributes to global warming. Furthermore, the combustion process is never quite complete, and side reactions also occur. These factors give rise to smaller quantities of more harmful products.

- Carbon monoxide (CO) is a colorless, odorless, poisonous gas formed by incomplete combustion of fuels.
- Nitrogen oxides (NO_x) contribute to smog and acid rain and also cause irritation to human mucous membranes. Sunlight breaks down NO_2 to form NO and O atoms.
- Volatile organic compounds (VOCs) come mainly from unburned fuel or fuel that evaporates. They react with O atoms to form ground-level ozone (O_3), aldehydes (RCHO), and PAN ($RCOOONO_2$, page 362).

2. Could we collect automobile emissions and convert them back to gasoline? This *might* be possible, though it would be difficult. However, the energy required to convert the carbon dioxide and water vapor back to gasoline and oxygen would be *greater* than the energy that could be obtained from burning the gasoline we obtained!

Carbon Monoxide: The Quiet Killer

When insufficient oxygen is present during combustion, carbon monoxide (CO) is formed. In the United States, CO makes up more than 60% (by mass) of all air pollutants entering the atmosphere, with more than three-fourths of all CO emissions coming from transportation sources.

In urban areas, the proportion of CO pollution coming from motor vehicles can be 85–95%. Other sources of CO include industrial activities such as metal processing, residential wood burning, and natural sources such as forest fires. The EPA has set danger levels for CO at 9 ppm (average) over 8 h and 35 ppm (average) over 1 h. On city streets, these danger levels are exceeded much of the time. Even in off-street urban areas, levels often average 7–8 ppm. Such levels do not cause immediate death, but exposure over a long period can cause physical and mental impairment.

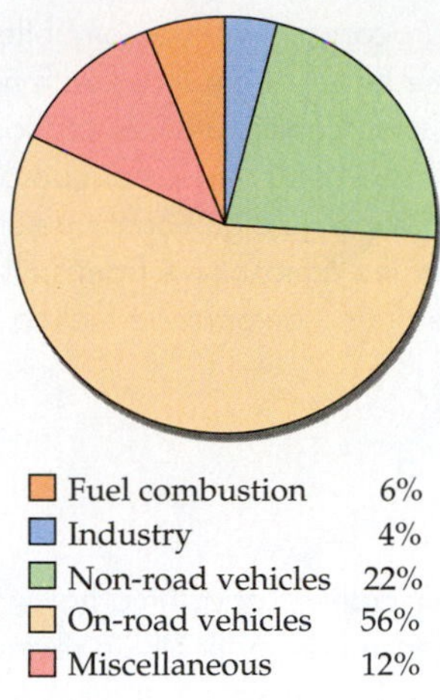

▲ Sources of carbon monoxide emissions in the United States.

We can't tell that carbon monoxide is present except by using CO detectors or test reagents. (Automobile exhaust gets its odor from unburned hydrocarbons, not carbon monoxide.) Drowsiness, usually the only early symptom, is not always unpleasant.

Carbon monoxide acts by tying up the hemoglobin in the blood. Normally, hemoglobin transports oxygen (Figure 13.6), but CO binds to hemoglobin much more strongly than oxygen does. The symptoms of carbon monoxide poisoning are therefore those of oxygen deprivation. All except the most severe cases of acute carbon monoxide poisoning are reversible, but prolonged hospital stays with oxygen therapy are sometimes necessary. Carbon monoxide poisoning is discussed further in Chapter 22.

Nitrogen Oxides: Some Chemistry of Amber Air

Nitrogen oxides are formed when N_2 reacts with O_2 at high temperatures. Because air contains both nitrogen and oxygen, NO_x can be formed during the combustion of any fuel regardless of whether nitrogen is present in the fuel. Automobile exhaust and power plants that burn fossil fuels are major sources of NO_x. The main product of the reaction of nitrogen and oxygen is nitrogen monoxide (NO, also called nitric oxide).

$$N_2(g) + O_2(g) \longrightarrow 2\,NO(g)$$

Nitric oxide is then oxidized by atmospheric oxygen to nitrogen dioxide, an amber-colored gas that causes eye irritation and creates a brownish haze.

$$2\,NO(g) + O_2(g) \longrightarrow 2\,NO_2(g)$$

The two nitrogen oxides play a vital but nasty role in atmospheric chemistry.

At present atmospheric levels, nitrogen oxides don't seem particularly dangerous in themselves. Nitric oxide at high concentrations reacts with hemoglobin. As in carbon monoxide poisoning, this leads to oxygen deprivation. Such high levels seldom, if ever, result from ordinary air pollution, but they might be reached in areas close to industrial sources.

The most serious environmental effect of nitrogen oxides is their role in smog formation. These gases also contribute to the fading and discoloration of fabrics and to acid rain when they form nitric acid (Section 13.6).

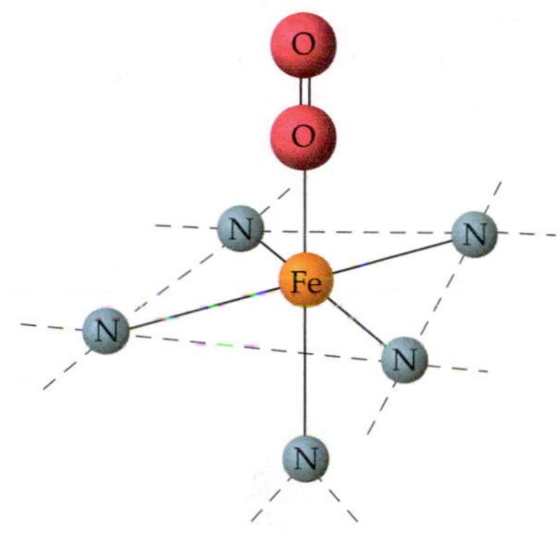

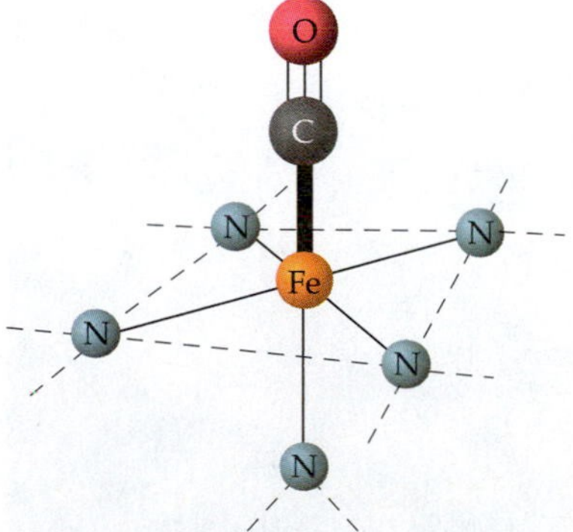

▲ **Figure 13.6** Schematic representations of a portion of the hemoglobin molecule (see Figure 16.15). Carbon monoxide bonds much more tightly than oxygen, as indicated by the heavier bond line.

Volatile Organic Compounds

Volatile organic compounds (VOCs) are organic substances that vaporize significantly at ordinary temperatures and pressures. They are major contributors to smog formation. There are many sources of VOCs, including trees, gasoline vapors, incomplete combustion of fuels, and consumer products such as paints and aerosol sprays. Many VOCs are hydrocarbons.

Hydrocarbons are released from a variety of natural sources, such as decay of plant matter in swamps. Only about 15% of all hydrocarbons found in the atmosphere are put there by people. In most urban areas, however, the processing and use of gasoline are the major sources of air-polluting hydrocarbons. Gasoline can evaporate anywhere it is used, contributing substantially to the total amount of hydrocarbons in urban air. This is why it is important to have a good seal on the cap

Hydrocarbons from automobiles come largely from those with no pollution control devices or those with devices that are not operating properly. Significant amounts enter the atmosphere from spillage during automobile fueling.

to your gas tank. The automobile's internal-combustion engine also contributes by exhausting unburned and partially burned hydrocarbons.

Hydrocarbons can act as pollutants even when they aren't burned. Certain hydrocarbons, particularly alkenes (Section 9.1), combine with oxygen atoms or ozone molecules to form aldehydes. Many aldehydes have foul, irritating odors. Another series of reactions involving hydrocarbons, oxygen, and nitrogen dioxide leads to the formation of peroxyacetyl nitrate (PAN).

$$CH_3\overset{\overset{\displaystyle O}{\|}}{C}{-}O{-}ONO_2$$

PAN

The incidence of asthma has increased dramatically in recent years. It is unlikely that air pollution is the direct cause of the increase. Rather, medical studies show that pollutants at moderate levels can exert a small but measurable effect on the lung function and level of symptoms of asthmatic individuals. It seems more likely that pollutants and allergens interact to enhance the severity of asthma attacks.

Ozone, aldehydes, and PAN are responsible for much of the destruction wrought by smog. They make breathing difficult and cause the eyes to smart and itch. People who already have respiratory ailments may be severely affected. The very young and the very old are particularly vulnerable.

Self-Assessment Questions

1. A colorless, odorless, and tasteless pollutant that is found at dangerous levels in many urban areas is
   a. CO b. CO_2 c. NO d. SO_2
2. Which of the following is *not* a problem caused by NO_x emissions?
   a. addiction b. formation of nitric acid, leading to acid rain
   c. formation of smog d. eye irritation
3. Many volatile organic compounds (VOCs) have molecules composed of
   a. C and H b. C and N c. N and H d. N and O
4. Volatile organic compounds (VOCs) come mainly from
   a. automobiles b. dry cleaning plants
   c. electric power plants d. natural sources
5. Alkenes react with oxygen atoms to form
   a. alcohols b. aldehydes c. alkanes d. ozone

Answers: 1, a; 2, a; 3, a; 4, d; 5, b

13.5 Photochemical Smog: Making Haze while the Sun Shines

Learning Objectives › Distinguish the origin of photochemical smog from the origin of sulfurous smog. › Describe the technologies used to alleviate photochemical smog.

▲ Photochemical smog results from the action of sunlight on nitrogen oxides emitted from automobiles and other high-temperature combustion sources. A brownish haze like that shown here over the Los Angeles harbor characterizes this type of smog.

Individually, hydrocarbons and nitrogen oxides are worrisome and have dramatic environmental impacts, including acid rain. Collectively, in the presence of sunlight, these pollutants can undergo a complex series of reactions that produce **photochemical smog**, visible as a brownish haze.

Unlike sulfurous smog, which accompanies cold, damp air, photochemical smog usually occurs during dry, sunny weather. The warm, sunny climate that has drawn so many people to the Los Angeles area is also the perfect setting for photochemical smog at any time of year. The principal culprits are unburned hydrocarbons and nitrogen oxides from automobiles.

The chemistry of photochemical smog is exceedingly complex (Figure 13.7). It starts when NO_2 absorbs a photon of sunlight and breaks apart to NO and O. The oxygen atoms are quite reactive. They readily combine with other components of automobile exhaust and the atmosphere to produce a variety of irritating and toxic chemicals, including ozone (O_3).

The development of air pollutants on a typical sunny summer day is shown in Figure 13.8. As traffic builds up in the early morning, NO enters the air in auto

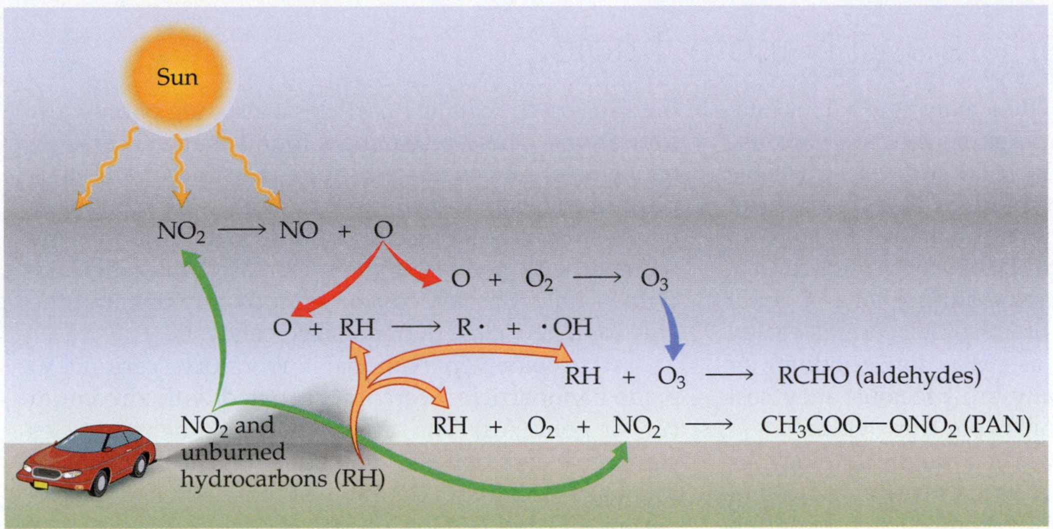

▲ **Figure 13.7** Some chemical processes involved in the formation of photochemical smog. Many other reactive intermediates have been omitted from this simplified scheme.

exhaust and begins to react with O_2 in the air to form NO_2. Hydrocarbons enter the air in exhaust as unburned components of fuel and from fueling leaks and spills. Sunlight splits the NO_2 into NO and O atoms. The O atoms react with O_2 to form O_3. Ozone levels continue to rise all day and then decrease after the sun sets because there are fewer reactant gases and no solar energy.

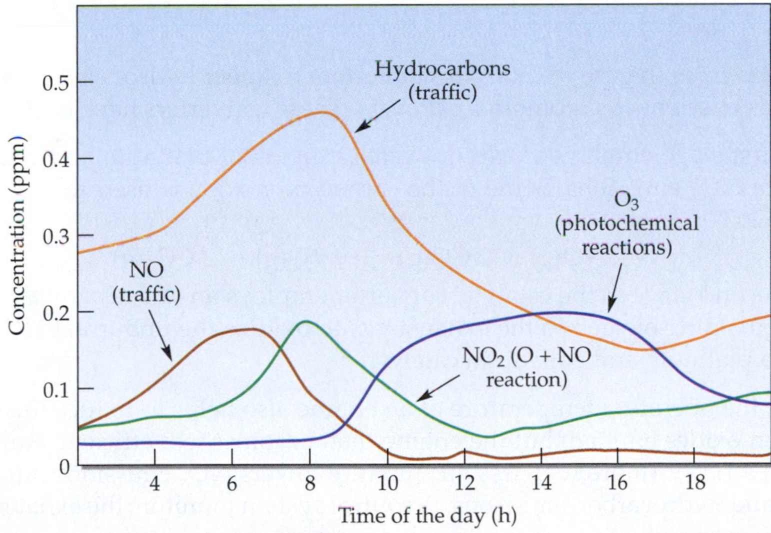

◀ **Figure 13.8** Concentrations of several urban air pollutants at different times during a typical sunny day. Hydrocarbons and NO are produced first. As they interact with sunlight, NO_2 and then ozone form.

Solutions to Photochemical Smog

Photochemical smog requires the action of sunlight on nitrogen oxides and hydrocarbons. Reducing the quantity of any of these would diminish the amount of smog. It isn't likely that we would want to reduce the amount of sunlight, so let's focus on the other two.

Hydrocarbons (commonly called HC in air pollution reports) have many important uses as solvents. If we could reduce the quantity of hydrocarbons entering the atmosphere, the amounts of aldehydes and PAN formed would also be reduced. Improved design of storage and dispensing systems has decreased HC emissions from gasoline stations. Modified gas tanks and crankcase ventilation systems have reduced evaporative emissions from automobiles. Most of the reduction, however,

Catalytic Converters and Nanotechnology

For maximum effectiveness, the catalysts inside a catalytic converter must have a large surface area because the reactions take place on the solid surface. To achieve this, the catalysts are thinly coated on a collection of small ceramic beads or a honeycomb matrix. One liter of ceramic pellets can have up to 500,000 m^3 of surface area. A honeycomb matrix can have a surface area of about 23,000 m^3. The surface area of either structure is coated with a precious metal such as palladium, rhodium, or platinum. (These metals really are precious; they cost hundreds or thousands of dollars per troy ounce.)

Catalytic converters have used nanotechnology for several decades. A converter uses only about 4–5 g of precious metal to coat the honeycomb structure or pellets. This technology exposes the exhaust stream of the vehicle to a catalyst area equal to that of several football fields.

Researchers continue to try to improve catalytic converters. They vary in particle size and composition and the support material (such as ceramic) on which the precious metals are deposited. For example, scientists at the University of California, Davis, are studying iridium (Ir) catalyst particles consisting of only just four atoms. These researchers found that the catalytic nanoclusters are chemically bonded to the ceramic support; previously, the support material was thought to be inert. By modifying the support material under the nanoparticles, the researchers increased the efficiency of the catalyst by a factor of ten, possibly opening the way for a new class of nano-sized catalysts.

At Brookhaven National Laboratory, cerium(IV) oxide nanoparticles were impregnated with zirconium (Zr) or gold (Au). The zirconium-doped nanoparticles store or release oxygen, depending on the engine conditions, thus making the catalyst more efficient in converting CO and NO to CO_2 and N_2.

Other experiments have shown that gold-doped nanoparticles act as active catalysts in helping CO combine with O_2 to make CO_2. Gold is not catalytic in its bulk form, but in the form of particles less than 6 nm in diameter, it is a very effective catalyst.

Nanoscale catalysts open the way for many innovations that will make various chemical processes more efficient and thus save resources.

has resulted from the use of **catalytic converters** to lower hydrocarbon and carbon monoxide emissions in automotive exhausts. These converters have two stages:

- The first stage employs a *reduction catalyst* made of platinum and rhodium to reduce NO_x emissions. Some of the carbon monoxide is used to reduce nitric oxide to N_2.

$$2\,NO(g) + 2\,CO(g) \longrightarrow N_2(g) + 2\,CO_2(g)$$

- The second stage in the catalytic converter employs an *oxidation catalyst*. It uses the remaining oxygen in the exhaust gas to oxidize the unburned HC and CO over a platinum and palladium catalyst.

Lowering the operating temperature of an engine also helps to reduce the quantity of nitrogen oxides emitted, but the engine then becomes less efficient. Running an engine on a richer (more fuel, less air) mixture lowers NO_x emissions but tends to raise CO and hydrocarbon emissions. A control system monitors the exhaust stream for optimum operation.

Catalytic converters convert more than 90% of HC, CO, and NO_x into less harmful CO_2, N_2 and water vapor. Over the past 30 years, their use has prevented more than 12 billion tons of harmful exhaust gases from entering Earth's atmosphere.

Many people now drive *hybrid vehicles* to save gasoline and to benefit the environment. A hybrid vehicle uses both an electric motor and a gasoline engine. The small gasoline engine drives the vehicle most of the time and recharges the batteries that run the electric motor. The electric motor provides additional power when it is needed (for example, when climbing a hill). Hybrid vehicles are much more efficient than conventional gasoline vehicles. Although these vehicles do provide a reduction in air pollution, a complete evaluation of their environmental impact has to include the production, replacement, and recycling of the batteries. Researchers are working to develop more compact, more efficient batteries that generate less pollution in manufacture.

There are a few electric-only vehicles in production. At present, their usefulness is somewhat limited. Electric vehicles have less range before recharging, take hours to recharge, and have poorer acceleration than gasoline-powered vehicles. To attain widespread use, electric cars need improved batteries to provide a longer range and faster recharging. More recharging stations and more power plants to provide the needed electricity will also be required.

Self-Assessment Questions

1. Nitrogen oxides and hydrocarbons combine in the presence of sunlight to cause
   a. acid rain **b.** global warming **c.** an ozone hole **d.** photochemical smog
2. An amber haze over a city indicates the presence of
   a. HNO_3 **b.** NO **c.** NO_2 **d.** O_3
3. Photochemical smog occurs mainly in
   a. cold, wet weather **b.** dry, sunny weather
   c. flat, dry areas **d.** snowy, mountainous areas
4. The main source of photochemical smog in most areas is
   a. automobiles **b.** electric power plants
   c. chemical factories **d.** solid waste burning
5. Removing NO_x from automobile exhaust requires a(n)
   a. bag filter **b.** electrostatic precipitator
   c. reduction catalyst **d.** wet scrubber

Answers: 1, d; 2, c; 3, b; 4, a; 5, c

13.6 Acid Rain: Air Pollution → Water Pollution

Learning Objectives › Name the air pollutants that create acid rain. › List the major industrial and consumer sources of acid-rain-producing pollutants.

We have seen how sulfur oxides are converted to sulfuric acid (Section 13.3) and nitrogen oxides to nitric acid (Section 13.2). These acids fall on Earth as acid rain or acid snow or are deposited from acid fog or adsorbed on particulates. **Acid rain** is defined as any form of precipitation having a pH less than 5.6. Rain with a pH as low as 2.1 and fog with a pH of 1.8 have been reported (Figure 13.9). These values are lower than the pH of vinegar or lemon juice.

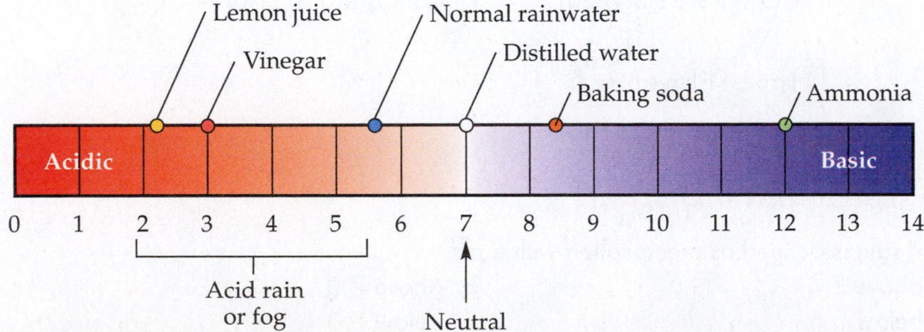

▲ **Figure 13.9** The pH of acid rain in relation to that of other familiar substances. Normal rainwater, if saturated with dissolved CO_2, has a pH of 5.6. During thunderstorms, the pH of rainwater can be much lower because of nitric acid formed by lightning. Recall (from Chapter 7) that a solution with a pH value one unit lower than that of another is ten times more acidic. A decrease in pH from 5.6 to 4.6, for example, means an increase in acidity by a factor of 10. Two pH units lower means 100 times more acidic, and three pH units lower means 1000 times more acidic.

▶ **Figure 13.10** Acid rain. The two main substances responsible for acid rain are sulfur dioxide (SO_2) from power plants and nitric oxide (NO) from power plants and automobiles. These oxides are converted to SO_3 and NO_2, which then react with water to form H_2SO_4 and HNO_3. The acids fall in rain, often hundreds of kilometers from their sources.

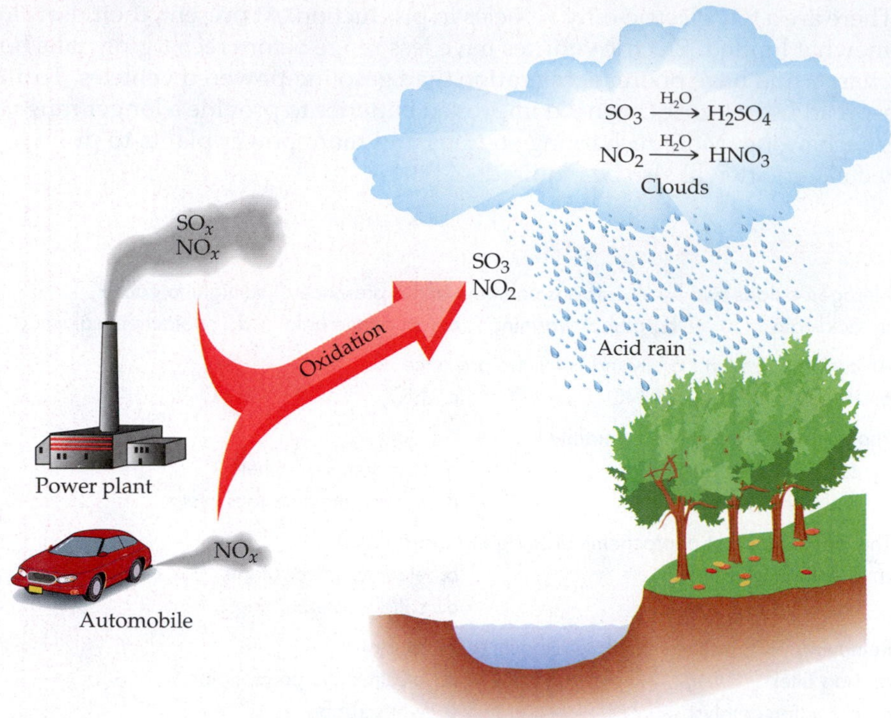

Acid rain is mainly due to sulfur oxides emitted from power plants and smelters and nitrogen oxides discharged from power plants and automobiles. These substances form acids that are often carried great distances before falling as rain or snow (Figure 13.10).

Acids corrode metals and can even erode stone buildings and statues. Sulfuric acid dissolves metals to form soluble salts and hydrogen gas.

$$Fe(s) + H_2SO_4(aq) \longrightarrow FeSO_4(aq) + H_2(g)$$

Iron (in steel) — A soluble salt

The reaction shown here is oversimplified. For example, in the presence of water and oxygen (air), the iron is converted to rust (Fe_2O_3). Marble or limestone buildings and statues disintegrate through a similar reaction with sulfuric acid that forms calcium sulfate, a slightly soluble, crumbly compound.

$$CaCO_3(s) + H_2SO_4(aq) \longrightarrow CaSO_4(aq) + H_2O + CO_2(g)$$

Marble or limestone

▲ Statues can be slowly eroded by the action of acid rain on marble (calcium carbonate).

The U.S. Environmental Protection Agency has a website with "Quick Finder" links that will lead you to more information on acid rain, air, Clean Air Act, climate change, ozone, radon, and more.

Self-Assessment Questions

1. Acid rain is defined as precipitation with a pH
- **a.** above 7.4
- **b.** above 7.0
- **c.** below 5.6
- **d.** below 7.0

2. Which of these reactions leads to acid rain?
- **a.** $C + O_2 \longrightarrow CO_2$
- **b.** $Cl_2 + H_2 \longrightarrow 2\ HCl$
- **c.** $N_2 + 3\ H_2 \longrightarrow 2\ NH_3$
- **d.** $S + O_2 \longrightarrow SO_2$

Answers: 1, c; 2, d

13.7 The Inside Story: Indoor Air Pollution

Learning Objectives › List the main indoor air pollutants and their sources. › Explain where radon comes from and why it is hazardous.

Indoor air pollution can pose a major health concern. It can be serious in the United States but is often much worse in developing countries where people use wood, charcoal, coal, or dried dung as fuel for heating and cooking.

EPA studies on human exposure to air pollutants indicate that indoor air levels of many pollutants may be 2–5 times higher, and on occasion more than 100 times higher, than outdoor levels. Near high-traffic areas, the air indoors has the same carbon monoxide level as the air outside. In some areas, office buildings, airport terminals, and apartments have indoor CO levels that exceed government safety standards. Woodstoves, gas stoves, cigarette smokers, and unvented gas and kerosene space heaters are also sources of CO indoors.

A kitchen with a gas range often has levels of nitrogen oxides above U.S. government standards. Freestanding kerosene stoves produce levels of NO_x up to 20 times greater than those permitted by federal regulations for outdoor air. (These regulations do not apply to indoor air.)

The box on page 357 noted the outdoor air pollution problems in China, but indoor air pollution in that country is actually much worse. According to the China Centre for Disease Control and Prevention, indoor pollution levels can be 5–10 times higher than those in the nation's very poor outdoor air. In China, formaldehyde, slowly released from building materials and new furniture, is perhaps the top indoor air pollutant, as a result of the ongoing building boom.

Wood Smoke

Many people like the smell of smoke from burning wood or leaves, but wood smoke is far from benign. Each kilogram of wood burned yields 80–370 g of carbon monoxide, 7–27 g of VOCs, 0.6–5.4 g of aldehydes, 1.8–2.4 g of acetic acid, and 7–30 g of particulates. The smoke also contains hydrocarbons, such as methane, benzene, and naphthalene, and carcinogenic polycyclic aromatic hydrocarbons (PAHs). The odor of wood smoke may evoke memories of autumns past or singing around a campfire, but inhaling the smoke can lead to asthma attacks and possible long-term harm to the lungs.

Cigarette Smoke

Another indoor polluter is tobacco smoke. Only about 15% of cigarette smoke is inhaled by the smoker; the rest remains in the air for others to breathe. More than 40 carcinogens have been identified among the 4000 or so chemical compounds found in cigarette smoke. The EPA classifies secondhand smoke as a Class A carcinogen, a substance known to cause cancer in humans.

The carcinogens (Chapter 22) in tobacco smoke are some of the same ones found in wood smoke. Tobacco smoke has PAHs, aromatic amines, nitrosamines, and radioactive polonium-210.

The health effects of smoking on the smoker (discussed in more detail in Chapter 19) are well known. Reports released by the Surgeon General of the United States have dealt with the effects of tobacco smoke as an air pollutant. Air quality in smoke-filled rooms is poor. Smoke from just one burning cigarette can raise the level of particulates above government standards. Even with good room ventilation, the level of carbon monoxide often equals or exceeds the legal limits for ambient air.

The risk to nonsmokers from cigarette smoke is also well established. Medical research has shown that nonsmokers who regularly breathe secondhand smoke suffer many of the same diseases as active smokers, including lung cancer and heart disease. Women who have never smoked but live with a smoker have a 91% greater risk of heart disease and twice the risk of dying from lung cancer. Women who are exposed to secondhand smoke during pregnancy have a higher rate of miscarriages and stillbirths. Their children have decreased lung function and a greater risk of sudden infant death syndrome (SIDS). Children exposed to secondhand smoke are more likely to experience middle ear and sinus infections. They also show an increased frequency of asthma, colds, bronchitis, pneumonia, and other lung diseases. These health problems and others have caused many states and municipalities to ban smoking in many public places.

Radon and Its Dirty Daughters

A most enigmatic indoor air pollutant is radon. A noble gas, radon is colorless, odorless, tasteless, and unreactive chemically. Radon is, however, radioactive. The decay products of the radon nucleus, called **daughter isotopes**, are the major problem. Radon-222 decays by alpha emission (Section 11.2) with a half-life of 3.8 days.

$$^{222}_{86}\text{Rn} \longrightarrow {}^{218}_{84}\text{Po} + {}^{4}_{2}\text{He}$$

When radon is inhaled, polonium-218 and other daughter isotopes, including lead-214 and bismuth-214, are trapped in the lungs, where their decay damages the tissues.

Radon is released naturally from soils and rocks, particularly granite and shale, and from minerals such as phosphate ores and pitchblende. The ultimate source is uranium atoms found in these materials. Radon is only one of several radioactive materials formed during the multistep decay of uranium. However, radon is unique in that it is a gas and escapes. The other decay products are solids and remain in the soil or rock.

Outdoors, radon dissipates and presents no problems. However, a house built on a solid concrete slab or over a basement can trap the gas inside. Radon levels build up, sometimes reaching several times the maximum safe level established by the EPA (0.15 Bq per liter of air). At five times this level, the hazard is thought to equal that of smoking two packs of cigarettes a day. Although the hazard has not been precisely determined, scientists at the National Cancer Institute estimate that radon may cause 20,000 lung cancer deaths a year. The "safe level" was set for people who work in uranium mines. These workers have high rates of lung cancer, but they also breathe radioactive dust and many smoke cigarettes. These risk factors may be synergistic and are difficult to evaluate separately.

Other Indoor Pollutants

Some people use kerosene heaters or unvented natural gas heaters to help reduce heating costs in the winter. Heating only the occupied areas of a home seems like a good idea. However, when such heaters are not properly adjusted, carbon monoxide can be generated. Carbon monoxide from gas stoves, gas furnaces, and gasoline generators or even from automobile exhaust in attached garages can also contribute to the high levels found in some houses. The EPA recommends a maximum level of 9 ppm CO over an eight-hour period. Carbon monoxide levels from a poorly adjusted gas heater can exceed 30 ppm—continuously. Commercial carbon monoxide detectors are readily available, reliable, and easy to install. Proper ventilation is key to preventing high levels of carbon monoxide.

Mold is an often-ignored pollutant in many homes. Leaky pipes or cool areas where water vapor condenses can lead to moisture problems, and mold will grow where there is moisture. Mold spores are a form of PM that can worsen asthma, bronchitis, and other lung diseases. Generally, mold is controlled by controlling moisture.

Electronic air cleaners are widely advertised. These seem a convenient solution to indoor air pollution: Just plug in a cleaner and let it remove all the bad pollutants. Unfortunately, some of these cleaners actually *produce* pollution. In particular, some of them generate ozone. As we shall see in the next section, ozone is quite reactive and can indeed reduce the levels of some pollutants by reacting with them. But, in doing so, it can generate other pollutants, such as formaldehyde. The EPA advises the public "to use proven methods of controlling indoor air pollution. These methods include eliminating or controlling pollutant sources, increasing outdoor air ventilation, and using proven methods of air cleaning."

GREEN CHEMISTRY

Principles 1, 4, 6, 12

Irv Levy, *Gordon College*

It's Not Easy Being Green

Global climate change and its impact on Earth are being discussed in classrooms, in the news, and in the political arena. Although there is controversy about whether climate change is caused by human activity, the air around us is on our minds more than usual.

If you have painted a room in your home, you've noticed the odor of solvents permeating the house. You may have opened a window to "air out" the room. After some fresh air, the room seems normal again . . . but is it? Although the unpleasant odor is no longer noticeable, you have only diluted the annoying VOCs (Section 13.4) by mixing them into the huge container of gases that is our atmosphere. Airing out foul or hazardous vapors moves the problem substances from a small space to a space so vast that we can easily forget that we released them into the air around us.

Many substances released into the environment are natural compounds that normally do not bother us. For example, the carbon dioxide that we exhale with every breath is essential to normal biological cycles. When we produce CO_2 quicker than the biosphere can absorb it, however, natural balances can be upset in alarming ways (Section 13.9). Other substances that we release did not exist on Earth before the twentieth century. Although humans may tolerate exposure to these compounds, some of them pose serious threats, including the possibility of reactions in the upper atmosphere that change the balances that have existed for millions of years (Sections 13.8 and 13.9).

The Twelve Principles of Green Chemistry suggest ways to reduce the impact of human activity on our atmosphere. One of the most obvious principles, preventing waste (Principle 1), suggests that not emitting chemicals into the atmosphere lessens the chance of harming it.

Sometimes, applying green chemistry is not as simple, and several principles may conflict. Consider the liquid crystal display (LCD) monitors that are in televisions and computer displays. LCD panels replaced cathode ray tube (CRT) displays that were shielded with lead. Lead is a toxic metal (green chemistry essay, Chapter 2) that must be used and disposed of carefully. Also, CRT displays use a lot of energy. Principles 4 and 6 suggest that LCD displays are greener than CRT displays because they are safer products with increased energy efficiency.

LCDs sound great, so where is the conflict? Use of LCDs becomes complicated because of the impact on the atmosphere during the manufacture of LCD panels. Producing LCDs also leads to unwanted materials that can harm the environment. One example is the use of nitrogen trifluoride (NF_3). About a decade ago, NF_3 was a relatively uncommon material, used only for special purposes like rocket fuel and lasers. Today, heavy demand by manufacturers of LCDs and solar panels has brought about dramatic increases in use of the gas. In 2008, about 4000 t of NF_3 were produced. In 2012, five times that amount (20,000 t) is expected to be produced. While not all of this gas is released to the atmosphere, estimates are that up to 16% of the NF_3 ends up in the air.

Scientists have reported that NF_3 contributes to global warming. As discussed in Section 13.9, the main contributor to global warming is CO_2, most of which is released into the atmosphere from the burning of fossil fuels. While the quantity of NF_3 released is much smaller than that of CO_2, studies show that NF_3 is about 17,000 times more efficient at trapping atmospheric heat than CO_2. It is a very good thing that NF_3 emissions are smaller than those of CO_2!

The risks that NF_3 presents to the environment have led to calls for restrictions in its use. Fluorine (F_2) has been suggested as an alternative to NF_3 because it works very well for processing the LCD panels and has no impact on global warming. Is that the greener solution? It might be, except that F_2 is highly toxic. Principle 12 reminds us to use inherently safer materials to avoid harmful accidents. There are serious safety concerns for those who could be exposed to large quantities of F_2.

Addressing global climate change and our effect on the Earth is clearly not as simple as we wish. Dealing with complex problems such as global warming requires cooperation from many people with differing perspectives. Guidance from the principles of green chemistry will catalyze successful collaborations to meet these, and other, challenges to sustainability.

▲ NF_3 is used in the cleaning process during the manufacture of LCD panels. Green chemists are investigating alternatives due to the potential impact of NF_3 on the environment.

Self-Assessment Questions

1. Gas ranges in kitchens are a source of the indoor air pollutant
   a. dioxins b. NO_x c. PAHs d. VOCs
2. Of the following indoor air pollutants, the most immediate threat is posed by
   a. carcinogens b. CO
   c. secondhand tobacco smoke d. radon
3. Radon in homes comes from
   a. gas cooking ranges b. fire alarms
   c. leaking heater exhausts d. soil and rocks
4. Which of the following is a radioactive radon daughter?
   a. cobalt-60 b. helium-4 c. polonium-218 d. uranium-238

Answers: 1, b; 2, b; 3, d; 4, c

13.8 Stratospheric Ozone: Earth's Vital Shield

Learning Objectives › Explain the link between CFCs and depletion of the ozone layer. › Describe the consequences of stratospheric ozone depletion.

The ordinary oxygen in the air we breathe is made up of O_2 molecules. As was noted earlier, ozone is a form of oxygen that consists of O_3 molecules. Ozone and oxygen are **allotropes**, different forms of the same element. As noted in Section 13.5, ozone is a constituent of photochemical smog. Inhaled ozone is highly toxic. However, ozone is also an important natural component of the stratosphere, where it shields Earth from life-destroying UV radiation.

Ozone is a good example of what a pollutant is: a chemical substance out of place in the environment. In the stratosphere, it helps make life possible. In the lower troposphere—the part we breathe—it makes life difficult.

Ozone as an Air Pollutant

▲ Ozone causes rubber to harden and crack. Tire manufacturers incorporate paraffin wax into the rubber to protect tires from ozone. The alkanes that make up the wax are among the few substances that are resistant to attack by ozone. As the wax wears off, more migrates to the surface to replace it.

Most U.S. urban areas have experienced ozone alerts. The American Lung Association estimates that one-third of the U.S. population lives in counties that exceed recommended concentrations of ozone.

Ozone is a powerful oxidizing agent and is highly reactive. This makes it a severe irritant to the respiratory system. Episodes of high ozone levels correlate with increased hospital admissions and emergency room visits for respiratory problems. At low levels, it causes eye irritation. Repeated exposure can make people more susceptible to respiratory infection, cause lung inflammation, aggravate asthma, decrease lung function, and increase chest pain and coughing.

Ozone is particularly damaging to children. The WHO estimates that 80% of all deaths attributed to air pollution occur among children.

Ozone causes economic damage beyond its adverse effect on health. It is a strong oxidizing agent that causes rubber to harden and crack, shortening the life of automobile tires and other rubber items. Ozone also causes extensive damage to crops, especially cotton, peanuts, and soybeans.

The Stratospheric Ozone Shield

In the mesosphere (Figure 13.1), some ordinary oxygen molecules are split into oxygen atoms by short-wavelength, high-energy UV radiation.

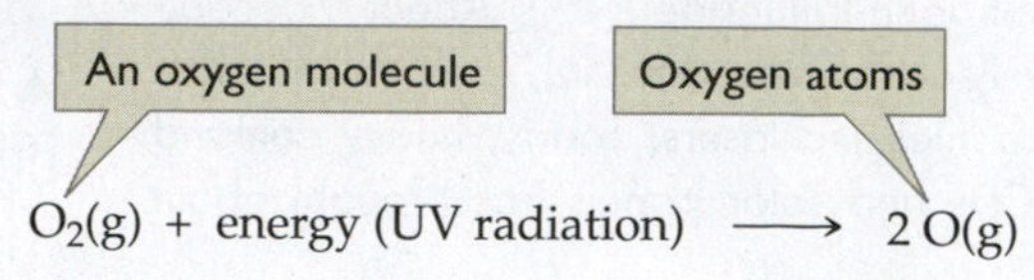

$$O_2(g) + \text{energy (UV radiation)} \longrightarrow 2\,O(g)$$

Some of these highly reactive atoms diffuse down to the stratosphere, where they react with O_2 molecules to form ozone molecules.

An oxygen molecule — An ozone molecule

$$O_2(g) + O(g) \longrightarrow O_3(g)$$

The ozone in turn absorbs longer-wavelength, but still lethal, UV radiation, thus shielding us from this harmful radiation. In absorbing it, the ozone molecules are converted back to oxygen molecules and oxygen atoms in a reversal of the previous reaction.

$$O_3(g) + \text{energy (UV radiation)} \longrightarrow O_2(g) + O(g)$$

Undisturbed, the concentration of ozone in the stratosphere remains fairly constant. Over 300 billion tons of ozone are destroyed and created every day by this cyclic process, in a layer of the stratosphere about 20 km thick. However, because of the reduced pressure and the low concentration of ozone in this layer, if it were compressed at normal sea level pressure, it would be only 3 mm thick! This delicate barrier protects all living things from harmful UV radiation. In recent decades, human activity has threatened to upset the balance and deplete some of the protective qualities of the ozone layer.

UV light is sometimes used to sterilize tools in hair salons and safety glasses in laboratories to prevent the transfer of infectious microorganisms from one person to another. We do not want the entire planet rendered sterile, however, for we are part of the life that would be harmed.

Chlorofluorocarbons and the Ozone Hole

The less ozone there is in the stratosphere, the more harmful UV radiation reaches Earth's surface. For humans, increased exposure to UV radiation can lead to skin cancer, cataracts, and impaired immune systems. The U.S. National Research Council predicts a 2–5% increase in skin cancer for each 1% depletion of the ozone layer. Even a 1% increase in UV radiation can lead to a 5% increase in melanoma, a deadly form of skin cancer. Increased UV also causes lower yields of many crops. Depletion of stratospheric ozone can also decrease the population of phytoplankton in the oceans, disrupting the web of sea life and the oxygen cycle (page 353).

The thickness of the ozone layer changes with latitude and also with the seasons. The cycling of ozone concentration is most prevalent over Antarctica, in part because the chemical reactions responsible for ozone destruction occur much more rapidly on the surfaces of ice crystals. During the Antarctic winter (June–August), more clouds containing ice crystals are formed and the levels of ozone decrease. In the early 1970s, serious concerns were raised because the ozone layer was not recovering properly during the warm months. In 1974, Mario Molina and F. Sherwood Rowland proposed a mechanism for the enhanced ozone depletion that implicated the presence of chlorofluorocarbons (CFCs) in the stratosphere. Their work was awarded the Nobel Prize in Chemistry in 1995.

▲ In 1986, Susan Solomon, a chemist at the Oceanic and Atmospheric Administration in Boulder, Colorado, proposed a mechanism for ozone depletion over the poles by CFCs. Later experiments confirmed her mechanism and led to an international ban on the use of CFCs. Solomon was awarded a 1999 National Medal of Science for her work.

CFCs were used as the dispersing gases in aerosol cans, as foaming agents for plastics, and as refrigerants. At room temperature, CFCs are either gases or liquids with low boiling points. They are almost completely insoluble in water and inert toward most other substances. These properties make them ideal for many uses. However, once CFCs are released into the atmosphere, their lack of reactivity allows them to persist and diffuse to the higher regions of the stratosphere. There, above the protective ozone layer, energetic UV radiation cleaves one of the C—Cl bonds and initiates a series of reactions.

$$CF_2Cl_2 + \text{energy (UV light)} \longrightarrow CF_2Cl\cdot + Cl\cdot$$
$$Cl\cdot + O_3 \longrightarrow ClO\cdot + O_2$$
$$\cdot ClO + O \longrightarrow Cl\cdot + O_2$$

Both products of the initial reaction are highly reactive free radicals (Section 4.10), species with an unpaired electron (indicated here by a dot). The chlorine atoms then react with ozone molecules to produce molecular oxygen. Note that the third reaction results in the formation of another chlorine atom, which can break down another molecule of ozone. The second and third steps are repeated many times. The decomposition of one CFC molecule in this *chain reaction* can result in the destruction of *thousands* of molecules of ozone.

International Cooperation

The United Nations has addressed the problem of ozone depletion through the 1987 Montreal Protocol, an international agreement enforcing the reduction and eventual elimination of the production and use of ozone-depleting substances. As a result, CFCs have been banned in the United States and many other countries, and the search for effective substitutes has been successful.

CFCs and other chlorine- and bromine-containing compounds that might diffuse into the stratosphere have been replaced for the most part by more benign substances. Hydrofluorocarbons (HFCs), such as CH_2FCF_3, and hydrochlorofluorocarbons (HCFCs), such as $CHCl_2CF_3$, are some of these alternatives. The C—H bonds in these compounds are more susceptible to reactive species such as hydroxyl radicals, so the molecules generally break down before reaching the stratosphere. For every solution, it seems there is a new problem; CFCs, HFCs, and HCFCs are all greenhouse gases (Section 13.9). Also, HFCs and HCFCs are more reactive than CFCs and can break down while in use, corroding components such as compressors and refrigeration coils.

The Montreal Protocol seems to be having the desired effects. The concentration of CFCs in the stratosphere has peaked. Chlorine concentrations leveled off in 1998 and will likely continue to decline slowly for decades. However, because the size of the ozone hole over Antarctica (Figure 13.11) varies from year to year with temperature and other meteorological factors, it may be several years before we can be sure that the problem is being solved.

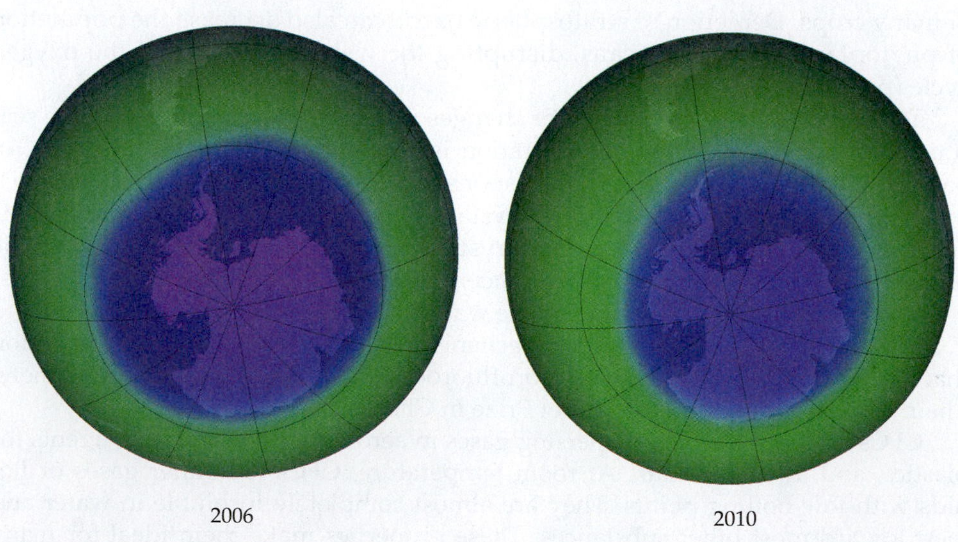

▶ **Figure 13.11** The ozone hole (purple) over Antarctica was at its largest in September 2006. Note the significant reduction in size as of September 2010.

Self-Assessment Questions

1. In the stratosphere, some O_2 is converted to
   a. acid rain b. ammonia c. ozone d. water
2. Ozone is an allotrope of
   a. carbon b. hydrogen c. nitrogen d. oxygen

3. The pollutant that is harmful at Earth's surface, yet protects life when in the stratosphere is
   a. carbon monoxide
   b. chlorine
   c. oxygen
   d. ozone
4. Automobiles emit
   a. CFCs that cause ozone depletion
   b. O_3 directly
   c. CO_2 which reacts with hydrocarbons in sunlight to produce ozone
   d. NO_x and VOCs that react in sunlight to produce ozone
5. In the mesosphere, oxygen atoms are produced by
   a. breakdown of O_3 molecules
   b. breakdown of H_2O molecules
   c. lightning
   d. splitting of O_2 molecules
6. Which portion of the Sun's radiation spectrum is absorbed by ozone?
   a. blue b. infrared c. violet d. ultraviolet
7. Chlorofluorocarbons harm the ozone layer by
   a. adding more ozone
   b. blocking UV radiation
   c. destroying oxygen
   d. destroying ozone

Answers: 1. c; 2. d; 3. d; 4. d; 5. d; 6. d; 7. d

13.9 Carbon Dioxide and Climate Change

Learning Objectives › List the important greenhouse gases, and describe the mechanism and significance of the greenhouse effect. › Describe some strategies for reducing the amount of CO_2 released into the atmosphere.

No matter how clean an engine or a factory is, if it burns coal or petroleum products, it produces carbon dioxide. The concentration of carbon dioxide in the atmosphere has increased nearly 40% since 1832, reaching 390 ppm in 2008. Since 2000, the concentration has increased at a rate of 2 ppm per year. Scientists attribute the increase to global industrialization and the burning of fossil fuels. Carbon dioxide is a natural component of the environment and is not considered toxic. The immediate effect of the carbon dioxide increase on us is slight, but what about its long-term effects?

The sun radiates many different types of radiation, of which visible, infrared, and ultraviolet are most prominent. About half of this energy is either reflected or absorbed by the atmosphere. The light that gets through (mostly visible) acts to heat the surface of Earth.

The three main constituents of the atmosphere—oxygen, nitrogen, and argon—are small, nonpolar molecules and do not absorb much infrared energy. However, carbon dioxide and some other gases produce a **greenhouse effect** (Figure 13.12). They let the sun's visible light pass through the atmosphere to warm the surface, but when the Earth radiates infrared energy back toward space, these greenhouse gases absorb and trap the energy. A similar thing happens in a car left in the sun with the windows closed. Visible light entering through the glass heats the interior, but the heat cannot efficiently escape back through the windows. The temperature inside the car can rise to be significantly higher than the outside temperature. Some greenhouse effect is necessary to life. Without an atmosphere, all of the radiated heat would be lost to outer space, and the Earth would be much colder than it is. In fact, based on the distance from the sun, it is estimated that the Earth's average temperature would be a cold −18 °C.

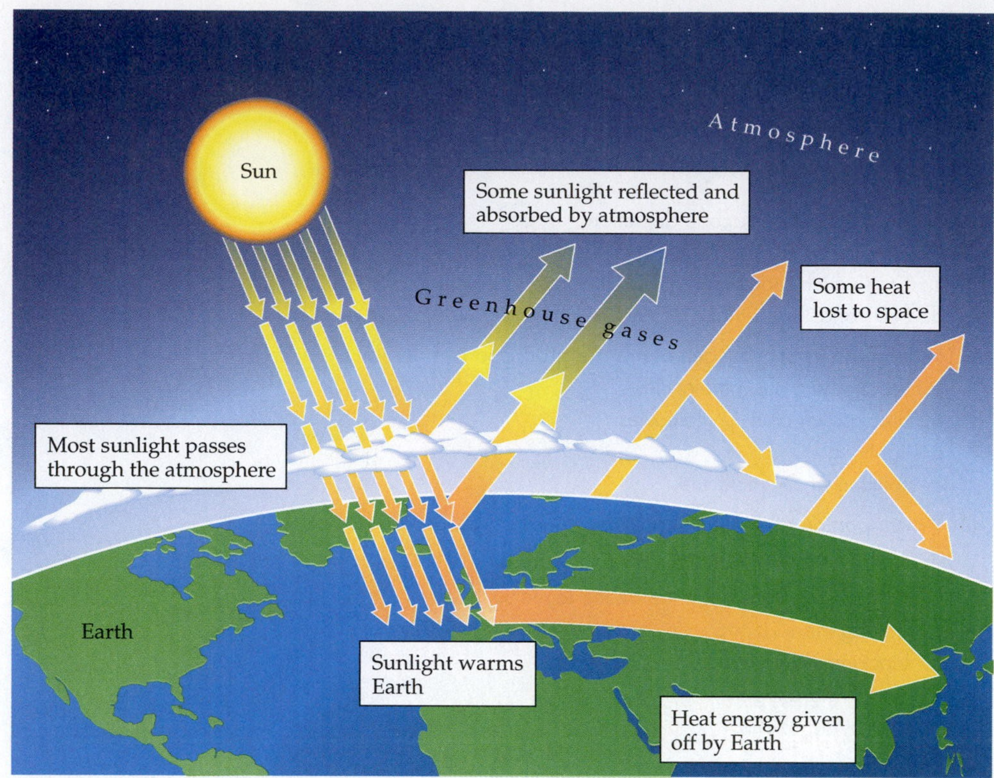

▶ **Figure 13.12** The greenhouse effect. Sunlight passing through the atmosphere is absorbed, warming Earth's surface. The warm surface re-emits energy as infrared radiation. Some of this radiation is absorbed by CO_2, H_2O, CH_4, and other gases and retained in the atmosphere as heat energy.

Example 13.1 CO_2 Stoichiometry

What mass of carbon dioxide (molar mass = 44.0 g/mol) is produced by burning 2670 g (1 gal) of gasoline? Gasoline may be represented by the formula C_8H_{18} (molar mass = 114.0 g/mol).

$$2\,C_8H_{18}(l) + 25\,O_2(g) \longrightarrow 18\,H_2O(g) + 16\,CO_2(g)$$

Solution

The problem gives us a mass of a reactant, and we are to find the mass of a product, so this is a stoichiometry problem (covered in Section 5.4).

We begin by converting the mass of the given substance, C_8H_{18}, to moles.

$$2670\text{ g } C_8H_{18} \times \frac{1\text{ mol } C_8H_{18}}{114.0\text{ g } C_8H_{18}} = 23.4\text{ mol } C_8H_{18}$$

Now we use a relationship from the balanced equation, that 2 mol of C_8H_{18} are equivalent to 16 mol of CO_2, to find the number of moles of CO_2 produced.

$$23.4\text{ mol } C_8H_{18} \times \frac{16\text{ mol } CO_2}{2\text{ mol } C_8H_{18}} = 187\text{ mol } CO_2$$

The final step is to use the molar mass of CO_2 to determine the mass of CO_2.

$$187\text{ mol } CO_2 \times \frac{44.0\text{ g } CO_2}{1\text{ mol } CO_2} = 8240\text{ g } CO_2$$

The mass of CO_2 is greater than the mass of gasoline consumed because the carbon of the gasoline combines with oxygen from the air.

■ EXERCISE 13.1A

Calculate the mass in grams of water vapor produced from burning 2670 g (1 gal) of gasoline.

■ EXERCISE 13.1B

Calculate the mass in kilograms of carbon dioxide produced by a class of 60 students in one week if each student uses 10 gal of gasoline in a week.

Greenhouse Gases and Global Warming

What many fear is an *enhanced* greenhouse effect caused by increased concentrations of carbon dioxide and other greenhouse gases in the atmosphere. This enhancement could lead to a rise in Earth's average temperature, an effect called **global warming** (Figure 13.13). Indeed, periods of high CO_2 concentration in Earth's past have correlated with increased global temperatures.

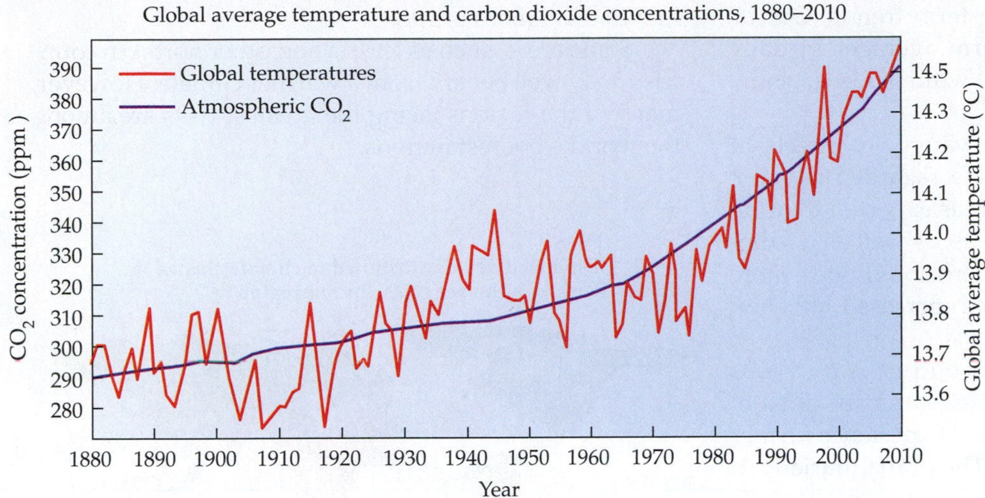

◀ **Figure 13.13** Carbon dioxide content of the atmosphere and surface temperature variations. The increase in carbon dioxide correlates with the beginning of the Industrial Revolution, around 1850.

Human activities add about 32 billion t of carbon dioxide to the atmosphere each year, of which 26 billion t comes from the burning of fossil fuels. About 55% of this CO_2 is removed, mostly by plants and soil (30%) and the oceans (24%), leaving a net addition to the atmosphere of 14 billion t CO_2 per year.

Methane also contributes to the greenhouse effect. The concentration of methane in the atmosphere increased from about 0.7 ppm in 1750 to about 1.75 ppm before stabilizing over the last few years. Most atmospheric methane comes from natural wetlands, in which methane-producing bacteria decompose organic material. Decomposition of organic materials in landfills is the largest human-related source of methane in the United States. Other sources include cattle and termites, which produce methane as part of microbial fermentation during their normal digestive processes. Researchers think that the stabilization of methane levels is due to reduction of the release of methane from natural gas pipelines and landfill sites and better management of rice paddies.

Molecules that are polar or are easily polarized (have moderate to strong dispersion forces) are very effective as greenhouse gases. Although present in much smaller amounts than carbon dioxide, trace gases such as methane, CFCs, and HCFCs are much more efficient at trapping heat. Methane is 20 times, CFCs 5000–14,000 times, and HCFCs 140–11,700 times as effective as carbon dioxide at holding heat in Earth's atmosphere. Water is only about one-tenth as efficient at trapping the heat, but when water is present in significant amounts, it has a noticeable effect. For instance, cloudy winter nights tend to be warmer than clear winter nights due to the presence of significant amounts of water in the clouds, which act to trap the heat close to the Earth's surface.

3. Why do greenhouse gases warm the Earth? Substances whose molecules are polar (recall Section 4.12) act as greenhouse gases because they strongly absorb infrared radiation (IR). Most of the radiation absorbed from the Sun is in the form of visible light, and most of the radiation emitted by the Earth is IR. The more polar the molecule, the more readily it can absorb IR and cause warming of the Earth.

Predictions and Consequences

A massive study by the United Nations' Intergovernmental Panel on Climate Change (*Fourth Assessment Report: Climate Change 2007*) provided a comprehensive review of past changes and predictions of future changes. The global average air temperature near the Earth's surface increased about 0.74 °C during the twentieth century.

Climate Change and Weather

We can look out the window and see weather, the conditions of the atmosphere over a short period of time. Weather forecasts are seldom accurate for more than a few days. Climate is an average of daily and seasonal weather events over a long period of time—decades or centuries. Even over a decade or so, short-term natural variability can mask long-term trends. *Climate change* means changes in long-term averages of daily weather—temperatures, rainfall, wind speeds, snow depths, and so on.

The IPCC panel predicted a variety of effects of global warming, some of which are regarded as more certain than others. Climate change is expected to bring more severe droughts to many areas, as well as harsher heat waves, stronger storms, more ferocious floods, more outbreaks of agricultural pests, and increased affliction by infectious diseases.

The potential impact on food output is a serious concern. Semiarid regions, where water is already scarce and cropland overused, could experience further devastation from climate change. The humanitarian crisis in the Darfur region of the Sudan is thought to be caused in part by the effect of global warming on crops and pastureland.

The rise in sea level can bring flooding that endangers low-lying islands and crowded river deltas such as those of Bangladesh and other southern Asian areas. In the United States, the Chesapeake Bay and the Gulf of Mexico coastal region are especially susceptible.

As carbon dioxide levels in the atmosphere increase, more CO_2 will dissolve in the oceans, making the seawater more acidic. This acidification will lead to the dissolving of the shells of marine animals that make these shells out of calcium carbonate. This effect could damage the coral reefs, which are vital to ocean ecosystems. Small floating animals that are a vital part of the oceanic food chain are also at risk as increased acidity weakens their shells and makes them more brittle.

Some areas, such as Russia and other northern countries, may well benefit from a warmer climate. However, many of the regions facing the greatest risks are among the world's poorest nations.

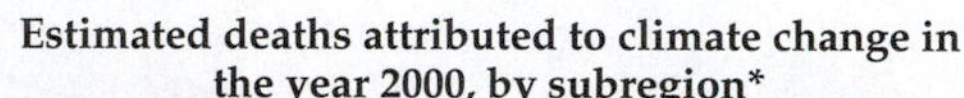

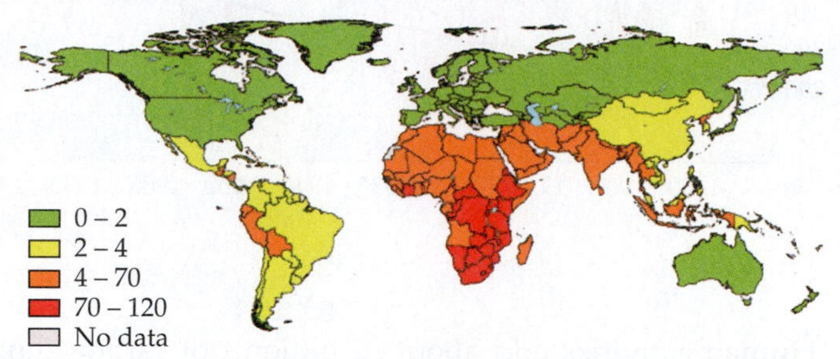

*Change in climate compared to baseline 1961–1990 climate

Data source:
McMichael, JJ, Campbell-Lendrum D, Kovats RS, et al. Global Climate. In comparative quantification of health risks: global and regional burden of disease due to selected major risk factors. M Ezzati, Lopez, AD, Rodgers A, Murray CJL. Geneva, World Health Organization, 2004.

▲ This map shows the areas where human health is most affected by global warming.

You can do your own sea rise experiment. To simulate melting of the floating Arctic ice cap, place some water and 2 ice cubes in a glass. Mark the water level. Has the level changed after the ice has melted? To simulate melting of the Antarctic or Greenland glaciers, place some rocks in a glass, and fill the glass with water to about a cm above the top of the rocks. Place two ice cubes on top of the rocks and mark the water level. Has the water level in the glass changed after the ice has melted?

The large number of interrelated natural variables (clouds, volcanoes, El Niño weather patterns, and so forth) as well as the varying estimates of future greenhouse gas emissions complicate predicting the magnitude of future warming, but the IPCC study predicts a further 1.1–6.4 °C increase by the year 2100. That temperature rise may not seem like much, but the ramifications of such warming can be severe. So far, predictions made by models have underestimated the actual changes, particularly at high latitudes. Losses from the ice sheets of Greenland and Antarctica have exceeded expectations. Satellite imagery in August 2007 showed the lowest extent of Arctic ice ever seen, and March 2011 was second lowest at the start of the summer season. If the overall trend continues, the Arctic Ocean may be ice-free in summers by 2030.

The polar ice caps need not melt completely for global warming to create problems. When water warms, it expands. The oceans have risen 222 mm since 1875, about 1.7 mm per year. Again, this rise may seem trivial, but even slight rises in ocean level increase tides and result in higher, more damaging storm surges. The IPCC report predicts a rise of 28–43 cm by 2100, but in recent years, ocean levels have been rising at a rate that would make them surpass the upper end of that range. Other studies predict rises of 100–150 cm by 2100. The IPCC shared the 2007 Nobel Peace Prize with Al Gore, former U.S. vice-president.

Mitigation of Global Warming

Scientists know in broad outline what we need to do to alleviate global warming: Technologically advanced countries must make quick and dramatic cuts in emissions. They also have to transfer technology to China, India, and the rest of the developing world so that those countries can continue to develop their economies without heavy use of coal-fired power plants. The problems involved in implementing these ideas are also well known: Can we make such rapid cuts? Are governments willing to tackle these issues?

We discuss a variety of alternatives to fossil fuels for energy production in Chapter 15. However, most scientists realize that no single alternative technology, such as solar power, nuclear power, biofuels, or wind power, will solve the problem of increasing CO_2 emissions. We will no doubt have to pursue several strategies.

More energy-efficient cars, appliances, and home heating and cooling systems will help somewhat, along with general energy conservation. Large-scale plans to capture CO_2 from smokestacks and sequester it underground are more costly and less certain. **Carbon sequestration** is the removal of CO_2 from the atmosphere by collecting and transporting of concentrated CO_2 from large emission sources, such as power plants and factories, and storing it in underground reservoirs. Sequestration also involves removal of CO_2 from the atmosphere by forestry and agricultural practices such as planting trees and stopping deforestation. All these alternatives are more difficult than simply burning coal or petroleum.

A few nations have moved forward in reducing or capping CO_2 emissions, but overall there has been little or no progress. China is building coal-fired power plants at a breakneck rate—in fact, in 2008, China surpassed the United States in CO_2 emissions. High oil prices have also led to the construction of new coal-fired plants in Italy.

4. Is global warming caused by the ozone hole? Only to a very small degree. The ozone hole does contribute to increased UV radiation reaching the Earth's surface. But the majority of global warming is the result of greenhouse gases absorbing IR radiation given off by the Earth. However, some gases, such as CFCs, do act as both ozone destroyers and greenhouse gases.

The WHO estimates that Earth's warming climate contributes to more than 150,000 deaths and 5 million illnesses each year and predicts that this toll could double by 2030. According to data published in the journal *Nature*, a warmer climate is driving up rates of malaria, malnutrition, and diarrhea.

Self-Assessment Questions

1. What type of radiation is trapped on Earth's surface by the greenhouse effect?
   a. gamma
   b. infrared
   c. ultraviolet
   d. visible
2. During the twentieth century, the global average air temperature near the Earth's surface increased about
   a. 0.5 °C
   b. 0.75 °C
   c. 1.25 °C
   d. 2.25 °C
3. The main cause of global warming is
   a. CO_2 from factories, power plants, and automobiles
   b. Earth's orbital eccentricities
   c. variations in the Sun's output
   d. water vapor
4. When CO_2 dissolves in the oceans, it
   a. decreases the acidity of the seawater
   b. forms an acid that dissolves shells of sea creatures
   c. is permanently removed from the atmosphere
   d. reacts with Ca^{2+} ions to form $CaCO_3$
5. To combat global warming, people should
   a. drain wetlands
   b. heat with charcoal
   c. pave dirt roads
   d. plant trees

Answers: 1, b; 2, b; 3, a; 4, b; 5, d

13.10 Who Pollutes? Who Pays?

Learning Objective › List the EPA's criteria pollutants and the major air pollutants that come mainly from automobiles and mostly from industry.

The EPA lists six *criteria pollutants*, so called because scientific criteria are employed to determine their health effects. Since the first Earth Day in 1970, nationwide emissions of the six criteria pollutants have declined dramatically (Table 13.3). These improvements in air quality have occurred even though the U.S. population increased by one-third and gross domestic product and vehicle miles traveled both tripled.

5. What does smog testing of vehicles actually test? Tests vary depending on the location, but almost always measure unburned hydrocarbons and carbon monoxide. Unburned hydrocarbons may come from the tailpipe or may arise from evaporation or leakage elsewhere in the fuel system. Some states and cities also test for nitrogen oxides or particulates.

Table 13.4 lists the main sources of seven major air pollutants along with their health and environmental effects. Note that motor vehicles are responsible for several of the major air pollutants; indeed, they are the source of nearly one-half (by mass) of all air pollutants. Our transportation system accounts for about 85% of urban carbon monoxide emissions, 40% of hydrocarbon emissions, and 40% of nitrogen oxide emissions. From the early twentieth century through the mid-1970s, cars were also a major source of lead in the air in the United States. The compound *tetraethyllead* was added to premium gasoline during those years. In 1976, the United States began phasing out the use of tetraethyllead in automobile fuels. Now the major sources of lead in the air are industrial processes and non-road equipment. Nonetheless, because most transportation in the United States is by private automobile, cars are a major source of air pollution.

On the other hand, most PM comes from power plants (about 40%) and industrial processes (about 45%). Similarly, more than 80% of sulfur oxide emissions come from power plants, with an additional 15% coming from other industries. Power plants alone contribute about 55% of nitrogen oxide emissions. Who uses electricity from power plants? We all do. A coal-fired plant must burn 275 kg of coal to light an ordinary 100-W bulb for one year.

Table 13.3 Ambient Air Quality Standards for Six Criteria Air Pollutants

Pollutant	Limit	Percent Change (1980–2009)
Carbon monoxide		−80
8-h average	9 ppm	
1-h average	35 ppm	
Nitrogen dioxide		−48
Annual average	0.053 ppm	
Ozone[a]		−30
8-h average	0.08 ppm	
1-h average	0.12 ppm	
Particulate matter		
PM10, 24-h average	150 μg/m^3	−38[b]
PM2.5, 24-h average	65 μg/m^3	−27
Sulfur dioxide		−76
Annual average	0.03 ppm	
24-h average	0.14 ppm	
3-h average	0.50 ppm	
Lead		−93
3-month average	1.5 μg/m^3	

[a]Formed from precursor volatile organic compounds (VOCs) and NO_x.
[b]This value is for 1990–2009.

Table 13.4 Seven Major Air Pollutants

Pollutant	Formula or Symbol	Major Sources	Health Effects	Environmental Effects
Carbon monoxide	CO	Motor vehicles	Interferes with oxygen transport; contributes to heart disease	Slight
Hydrocarbons	C_nH_m	Motor vehicles, industry, solvents	Narcotic at high concentrations; some aromatics are carcinogens	Precursors of aldehydes, PAN
Sulfur oxides	SO_x	Power plants, smelters	Irritate respiratory system; aggravate lung and heart diseases	Reduce crop yields; precursors of acid rain, SO_4^{2-} particulates
Nitrogen oxides	NO_x	Power plants, motor vehicles	Irritate respiratory system	Reduce crop yields; precursors of ozone and acid rain; produce brownish haze
Particulate matter	PM	Industry, power plants, dust from farms and construction sites, mold spores, pollen	Irritates respiratory system; synergistic with SO_2; contains adsorbed carcinogens and toxic metals	Impairs visibility
Ozone	O_3	Secondary pollutant from NO_2	Irritates respiratory system; aggravates lung and heart diseases	Reduces crop yields; kills trees (synergistic with SO_2); destroys rubber and paint
Lead	Pb	Motor vehicles, smelters	Toxic to nervous system and blood-forming system	Toxic to all living things

What is the worst pollutant? Carbon monoxide is produced in huge amounts and is quite toxic. However, it is deadly only in concentrations approaching 4000 ppm. Its contribution to cardiovascular disease, by increasing stress on the heart, is difficult to measure. The WHO rates sulfur oxides as the worst pollutants. They are powerful irritants, and, according to WHO, people with respiratory illnesses are more likely to die from exposure to SO_x than from exposure to any other kind of pollutant. Sulfur oxides and sulfuric acid formed from them have been linked to more than 50,000 deaths per year in the United States.

We all share the responsibility for pollution. In the words of Walt Kelly's comic-strip character Pogo, "We have met the enemy, and he is us." But we can all be part of the solution by conserving fuel and electricity. Many utility companies now offer suggestions for saving energy. Some even give free analyses of home energy use.

Paying the Price

Air pollution costs us tens of billions of dollars each year. It wrecks our health by causing or aggravating bronchitis, asthma, emphysema, and lung cancer. It destroys crops and sickens and kills livestock. It corrodes machines and blights buildings.

Elimination of air pollution will be neither cheap nor easy. It is especially difficult to remove the last fractions of pollutants. Cost curves are exponential, soaring toward infinity as pollutants approach zero. For example, if it costs $200 per car to reduce emissions by 50%, it usually costs about $400 to reduce them by 75%, $800 to reduce them by 87.5%, and so on. It would be extremely expensive to reduce emissions by 99%. We can have cleaner air, but how clean depends on how much we are willing to pay.

What would we gain by getting rid of air pollution? How much is it worth to see the clear blue sky or to see the stars at night? How much is it worth to breathe clean, fresh air?

Self-Assessment Questions

1. The U.S. agency responsible for gathering and analyzing air pollution data is
   a. EPA **b.** FAA
   c. FCC **d.** FDA
2. Air pollutants have decreased significantly since 1970 because there
   a. are fewer electric power plants
   b. are fewer people
   c. are more pollution controls
   d. is less driving
3. The largest source of carbon monoxide pollution is
   a. electric power plants
   b. industry
   c. motor vehicles
   d. smelters
4. Electric power plants are the largest source of
   a. CO pollution **b.** ozone
   c. SO_2 pollution **d.** VOCs
5. According to the World Health Organization, the worst pollutant in terms of health effects is
   a. CO **b.** ozone
   c. NO_x **d.** SO_2
6. The largest sources of NO_x pollution are
   a. electric power plants and motor vehicles
   b. electric power plants and industry
   c. industry and motor vehicles
   d. smelters and motor vehicles
7. The largest sources of particulate pollutants are
   a. electric power plants and motor vehicles
   b. electric power plants and industry
   c. industry and motor vehicles
   d. smelters and motor vehicles

Answers: 1, a; 2, c; 3, c; 4, c; 5, d; 6, a; 7, b

CRITICAL THINKING  EXERCISES

Apply knowledge that you have gained in this chapter and one or more of the FLaReS principles (Chapter 1) to evaluate the following statements or claims.

13.1 A councilman claims that the air pollution problem in the Los Angeles area could be solved by allowing only zero-emission vehicles to be sold and licensed there.

13.2 Ozone in aerosol cans was once used as a room deodorizer. An inventor proposes that such preparations be reintroduced because any ozone entering the environment would help to restore the protective ozone layer in the stratosphere.

13.3 Some people claim that aerosols will cool the planet, offsetting the enhanced greenhouse effect.

13.4 Some experts believe that global warming is mostly due to methane produced by such natural sources as plant decay in swamps and cattle flatulence. They say that industrial activities that produce carbon dioxide raise the standard of living and should be allowed to continue without interference because they are not the only sources of greenhouse gases.

13.5 An activist claims that if catalytic converters can remove 90% of pollutants from automobile exhaust, it would be easy to remove the other 10%.

13.6 A scientist claims that the increase in the atmosphere concentration of carbon dioxide from 0.02% to 0.04% is not important in terms of global warming. His reasoning is that water vapor makes up about 2–3% of the atmosphere and water vapor is only about one-tenth as effective as CO_2 as a greenhouse gas; thus, the 0.02% increase in CO_2 is equivalent to a trivial 0.2% increase in water vapor.

SUMMARY

Section 13.1—The thin blanket of air that is Earth's **atmosphere** is made up of layers: the troposphere (nearest Earth), the stratosphere (which includes the ozone layer), the mesosphere, and the thermosphere. Dry air is a mixture of about 78% nitrogen, 21% oxygen, and 1% argon by volume, plus small amounts of carbon dioxide and trace gases. Moist air can contain up to 4% water vapor.

Section 13.2—Animals and most plants cannot use atmospheric nitrogen unless it has undergone **nitrogen fixation** (combination with other elements). Nitrogen goes from the air into plants and animals and eventually back to the air via the **nitrogen cycle**. Oxygen from the air is involved in oxidation (of plant and animal materials) and is eventually returned to the air via the **oxygen cycle**. Oxygen is converted to ozone and then changed back to oxygen in the stratosphere. In this process, the ozone absorbs UV radiation that might otherwise make life on Earth impossible. A **temperature inversion** occurs when a layer of cooler air is trapped under a layer of warmer air. The cooler air can become quite polluted in a short time.

Section 13.3—A **pollutant** is a substance that is in the wrong place or time and causes problems. Air pollution has existed for millions of years. Natural air pollution includes dust storms, noxious gases from swamps, and ash and sulfur dioxide from erupting volcanoes. Today air pollution is more complex than in the past. Air pollution is a global problem because pollutants from one geographic area often migrate to another. The main air pollutants introduced by human activity are the smoke and gases produced by the burning of fuels and the fumes and particulates emitted by factories. **Industrial smog** is the kind of smog produced in cold, damp air by excessive burning of fossil fuels. It consists of a combination of smoke and fog with sulfur dioxide, sulfuric acid, and **particulate matter (PM)**, which consists of solid or liquid particles of greater than molecular size. Soot and fly ash from coal combustion are forms of PM. The pollutants that make up industrial smog can act synergistically to cause severe damage to living tissue. PM can be removed from smokestack gases using an **electrostatic precipitator**, which charges the particles, or with a **wet scrubber**, which passes the gases through water. Sulfur dioxide can be scrubbed from stack gasses using limestone to form calcium sulfite, which can then be oxidized to useful calcium sulfate.

Section 13.4—Complete combustion of gasoline produces carbon dioxide and water, but combustion is always incomplete. Carbon monoxide is one product of incomplete combustion, and three-fourths of the carbon monoxide produced results from transportation. Carbon monoxide is a poisonous gas that ties up hemoglobin in the blood so that it cannot transport oxygen to the cells. Nitrogen oxides are present in automobile exhaust gases and in emissions from power plants that burn fossil fuels. The greatest problem with nitrogen oxides is their contribution to smog. The amber color of nitrogen dioxide causes the brownish haze often seen over certain large cities. **Volatile organic compounds (VOCs)** are major contributors to smog. VOCs come from evaporation of gasoline, incomplete combustion of fuels, and some consumer products. Hydrocarbons can be pollutants in themselves and can react to form other pollutants such as aldehydes and peroxyacetyl nitrate (PAN), both of which are very irritating to tissues.

Section 13.5—**Photochemical smog** results when hydrocarbons and nitrogen oxides are exposed to bright sunlight. A complex series of reactions produce a variety of pollutants, including ozone. **Catalytic converters** in automobiles act to reduce photochemical smog by oxidizing unburned hydrocarbons and decreasing the emission of nitrogen oxides. Hybrid vehicles are more efficient than conventional vehicles and emit fewer pollutants.

Section 13.6—Nitrogen oxides (mainly from automobiles and power plants) and sulfur oxides (mainly from power plants) can dissolve in atmospheric moisture, forming **acid rain**. Acid rain often falls far from the original sources of the acids, and it can corrode metals and erode marble or limestone buildings and statues.

Section 13.7—Indoor pollution can be as bad as, or worse than, outdoor pollution. Cigarette smoke can raise both levels of PM and carbon monoxide above the allowed EPA safety standards. Because of the effects of secondhand smoke, most cities and states restrict tobacco smoking in public places. The radioactive gas radon can accumulate indoors in some cases, and inhaled radon produces **daughter isotopes** that are also radioactive and can accumulate in the lungs. Inhaled radon can produce a significant risk of lung cancer.

Section 13.8—Ozone, an **allotrope** of oxygen, is a harmful air pollutant in the troposphere but forms a protective layer in the stratosphere that shields Earth against UV radiation from the sun. Chlorofluorocarbons (CFCs) have been linked to the hole in the ozone layer and are now widely banned. This ban may stop the expansion of the ozone hole.

Section 13.9—Carbon dioxide and other gases contribute to the **greenhouse effect**, which occurs when infrared radiation emitted from the Earth's surface cannot escape the atmosphere. The result is **global warming**, an increase in the Earth's average temperature, which is predicted to cause undesirable climate change.

Section 13.10—The EPA has listed six criteria pollutants, which have all been reduced in recent years. Motor vehicles are a prominent source of carbon monoxide, hydrocarbons, and nitrogen oxides, while most PM and sulfur oxides come from industrial processes. Carbon monoxide and sulfur oxides are the most problematic pollutants. We all share responsibility for pollution—and the responsibility for reducing it.

Green chemistry Sometimes using green chemistry is not simple, and several principles may conflict. For example, liquid crystal display (LCD) monitors replaced cathode ray tube (CRT) displays, thus eliminating use of the toxic metal lead and conserving energy. However, LCDs use nitrogen trifluoride (NF_3) that is 17,000 times as effective as carbon dioxide in trapping atmospheric heat. Fluorine has been suggested as an alternative to NF_3 for processing LCDs because it has no impact on global warming, but fluorine is toxic.

Learning Objectives

› List and describe the layers of the atmosphere.	Problems 11, 12, 14
› Give the approximate proportion of N_2, O_2, Ar, and CO_2 in Earth's atmosphere.	Problem 10
› Describe the nitrogen and oxygen cycles.	Problems 10, 13
› Describe the origin and effects of temperature inversions.	Problem 15
› List some natural sources of air pollution.	Problem 16
› List the main pollutants formed by burning coal, and describe some technologies used to clean up these pollutants.	Problem 18
› List the main gases in automobile emissions, and describe how catalytic converters reduce these gaseous pollutants.	Problems 26, 32
› Explain how carbon monoxide acts as a poison.	Problem 31
› Distinguish the origin of photochemical smog from the origin of sulfurous smog.	Problems 23, 24
› Describe the technologies used to alleviate photochemical smog.	Problem 26
› Name the air pollutants that contribute to acid rain.	Problems 37, 38
› List the major industrial and consumer sources of acid-rain-producing pollutants.	Problems 37, 40
› List the main indoor air pollutants and their sources.	Problems 41, 44, 46
› Explain where radon comes from and why it is hazardous.	Problems 43, 45
› Explain the link between CFCs and depletion of the ozone layer.	Problem 35
› Describe the consequences of stratospheric ozone depletion.	Problem 6
› List the important greenhouse gases, and describe the mechanism and significance of the greenhouse effect.	Problems 47, 53
› Describe some strategies for reducing the amount of CO_2 released into the atmosphere.	Problem 48
› List the EPA's criteria pollutants and the major air pollutants that come mainly from automobiles and mostly from industry.	Problem 56
› Identify that green chemistry assessment includes evaluation of the safety of substances as well as awareness of long-term effects.	Problems 59–61
› Explain how the green chemistry principles can be applied in the development of manufacturing processes.	Problem 62

REVIEW QUESTIONS

1. List two (former) uses of CFCs.
2. Name one replacement for CFCs. What problems are associated with the replacements?
3. What is bottom ash? What is fly ash? Give two uses for fly ash.
4. Describe how **(a)** a bag filter and **(b)** a cyclone separator remove particulates from stack gases.
5. What is a greenhouse gas? Give three examples.
6. What are the health effects of (a) ground level ozone as an air pollutant and (b) depletion of stratospheric ozone?
7. What is smog?
8. How are the hole in the ozone layer and the phenomenon of global warming related?

PROBLEMS

The Atmosphere: Composition and Cycles

9. What is nitrogen fixation? Why is it important?
10. What are the approximate proportions of the four main components of dry air?
11. Look again of Figure 13.1. The X-15 was an experimental aircraft tested from 1959 to 1968. One test flew to an altitude of 67 miles. What layer of the atmosphere did the X-15 reach?
12. Referring to Figure 13.1, consider a small airplane flying at an altitude of 12,000 feet. In what layer of the atmosphere is the plane flying?
13. Figure 13.3 shows oxidation of metals as one aspect of the oxygen cycle. Write the balanced equations for **(a)** the oxidation of iron metal by atmospheric oxygen to form iron(III) oxide and **(b)** the oxidation of chromium metal to form chromium(III) oxide.

14. Trace gases in the atmosphere tend to be concentrated at different levels according to molar mass, with the heavier gases closer to the surface and the lighter gases at higher altitudes. Refer to Figure 13.1 and Table 13.1, and answer the following. **(a)** Which of the trace gases listed in Table 13.1 are likely to be found at altitudes above about 40 km? **(b)** Which ones are likely to be found below about 20 km? **(c)** Which gas is most likely to be found in the troposphere? [*Hint*: Consider the location of the ozone layer to answer parts (a) and (b).]

Industrial Smog

15. What weather conditions are associated with industrial smog?
16. Name two elements that are reactants in the production of industrial smog.

For Problems 17–20, write the balanced equation for the reaction described.

17. Sulfur is oxidized to sulfur dioxide by atmospheric oxygen.
18. Sulfur dioxide is oxidized to sulfur trioxide by atmospheric oxygen.
19. Sulfur dioxide reacts with hydrogen sulfide to form elemental sulfur and water.
20. Calcium sulfite is oxidized to calcium sulfate by atmospheric oxygen.
21. Describe how a limestone scrubber removes sulfur dioxide from stack gases. Write the equation(s) for the chemical reaction(s) involved.
22. Suggest a reason for the fact that PM2.5 is more hazardous to health than PM10.

Photochemical Smog

23. Under what conditions do nitrogen and oxygen combine? Give the equation for the reaction.
24. What is the formula for the oxide of nitrogen that initiates the formation of photochemical smog?
25. What is PAN? From what is it formed? What are its health effects?
26. Describe two ways in which the level of nitrogen oxide emissions from an automobile can be reduced.
27. Which of the following could be sources of VOCs?
    a. leftover oil-based paint;
    b. a truckload of plastic milk jugs;
    c. a cracked pipeline carrying crude oil from Alaska
28. An electrostatic precipitator could be useful for reducing soot emitted from a shoe factory but not for reducing noxious vapors from adhesives used in that factory. Explain.

Carbon Monoxide

29. Which of the following is a free radical: CO, SO_2, O_3, NO?
30. A fellow student claims that carbon monoxide has an odor and is colored, because he can easily see and smell automobile exhaust, especially in the winter. How might you correct his misconception?
31. How can exposure to carbon monoxide contribute to heart disease?
32. Write the equation for the reaction by which carbon monoxide reduces nitric oxide to nitrogen gas.

The Ozone Layer

33. Oxygen and ozone are the same element in two different forms. What term describes this phenomenon?
34. Seawater contains roughly 30 g of dissolved sodium chloride per liter. Suggest a reason why seawater is not a potent source of ozone-depleting chlorine atoms.
35. What environmental problem arises from the use of CFC substitutes?
36. How are free radicals related to the ozone layer?

Acid Rain

37. What two acids are mainly responsible for acid rain?
38. Write the equations for the reaction of each acid in Problem 37 with marble.
39. Write the equation for the reaction of nitric acid (from acid rain) with iron to form iron(III) nitrate and a gaseous product.
40. Acid rain can be formed by the reaction of water with sulfur dioxide to form *sulfurous* acid. Write the equation for this reaction.

Indoor Air Pollution

41. Name an indoor air pollutant that is also an outdoor pollutant. What is the major source of that pollutant in each environment?
42. List three risks associated with secondhand cigarette smoke.
43. Explain why a house built over a crawl space is likely to have less of a radon problem than a house built on a concrete slab.
44. How does better insulation of buildings make indoor air pollution worse?
45. What is the physical state of radon, and why does its physical state make it especially hazardous?
46. What kind of particulate matter is often found inside homes?

Carbon Dioxide and Climate

47. What is the greenhouse effect?
48. How can global warming be alleviated?

ADDITIONAL PROBLEMS

49. Why is zero pollution not possible?

50. The atmosphere contains about 5.2×10^{15} t of air. What mass in metric tons of carbon dioxide is in the atmosphere if the concentration of CO_2 is 395 ppm?

51. A person who exercises vigorously several hours a day might take in about 22 m^3 of air per day. What mass in milligrams of particulates would the person inhale in a day if the particulate level averages 312 $\mu g/m^3$?

52. A tree 33 m tall and 0.55 m in diameter at its base produces about 84,000 L of oxygen per year. How many people, breathing as described in Problem 51, would five such trees supply with oxygen?

53. Water vapor is a greenhouse gas that is present in significant concentrations in the Earth's atmosphere. Water is also a product of the combustion of fossil fuels. Why is there little concern about increasing atmospheric water vapor and its contribution to global warming?

54. Evaluate the claim, "There are more molecules in one breath of air than there are breaths in Earth's entire atmosphere." Use the following information. The total mass of the atmosphere is about 5.2×10^{21} g. The average molecular mass of air is about 29 u. An average breath has a volume of about 0.50 L and a density of about 1.3 g/L.

55. Evaluate the claim, "The breath that you just took contains at least one molecule of air that was in the last breath of the Buddha, Siddhartha Gautama, who died about 400 B.C.E." See Problem 54 and assume complete mixing of Earth's atmosphere over 2400 years.

56. What is a criteria pollutant? Which of the pollutants in Table 13.3 come mainly from automobiles and which come mostly from industry?

57. The reaction for formation of nitric acid is more complex than shown in Figure 13.10. In the first step, three molecules of nitrogen dioxide react with a water molecule to form nitric acid and nitrogen oxide. In the second step, the nitrogen oxide is oxidized by atmospheric oxygen to nitrogen dioxide, and then the cycle continues. Write balanced equations representing these two steps.

58. Although carbon dioxide is the actual greenhouse gas, emissions from the burning of fossil fuels are often reported as gigatons (Gt) of carbon. In 2007, the three largest emitters of carbon dioxide were China, the United States, and the European Union, with over 56% of the total emissions worldwide, with a combined mass of 4.51 Gt of carbon. To what mass in gigatons of CO_2 does this amount of carbon correspond?

59. If 1000 t of NF_3 is released into the air, what amount of CO_2 will its global warming effect match?

a. 17 million t **b.** 170,000 t **c.** 17,000 t **d.** 1700 t

60. If 16% of the 20,000 t of NF_3 produced globally in 2012 is released into the air, estimate the amount of NF_3 released.

a. 20,000 t **b.** 16,000 t **c.** 3200 t **d.** 320 t

61. If 16% of the 20,000 t of NF_3 produced globally in 2012 is released into the air, what amount of CO_2 will its global warming effect match?

62. Manufacturers provide hazard and risk data for the substances they sell. One common way to report this information is to provide hazard codes along with risk or safety phrases.

NF_3 has these risk phrases: R8; R20; R36/38
F_2 has risk phrases: R7; R8; R26; R35; R41

Which of these risk phrases indicates the most serious hazard?
(*Hint*: Do an Internet search for "chemical risk phrases.")

COLLABORATIVE GROUP PROJECTS

Prepare a PowerPoint, poster, or other presentation (as directed by your instructor) to share with the class.

1. What are the average and peak concentrations of each of the following in your community or in a nearby large city? How can you find out?

   a. carbon monoxide **b.** ozone **c.** nitrogen oxides
   d. sulfur dioxide **e.** particulate matter

2. The American Lung Association publishes a list of metropolitan areas with the worst ozone air pollution each year. Look up that list and others with other worst air problems. Find a list of areas with the best air quality.

3. The box on page 357 reports on air pollution in China. Prepare a similar short essay on India or another country as assigned by your instructor.

4. Using the Internet or reference books, compare the amount of sulfur dioxide produced by Mt. Kilauea in Hawaii with that from all U.S. industry. (Remember to use the same time span for both.)

5. Write a brief essay comparing the atmospheres of Venus and Mars to Earth's atmosphere and explaining the differences.

6. Air quality standards are maximum allowable amounts of various pollutants. The federal government and some state governments issue these standards. Using the Internet, find the current standards from by the EPA. Does your state issue such standards? (*Hint*: Try the EPA site and your own state's environmental protection site.)

7. Divide your class into several teams, each taking a different view of global warming. Possible positions are (1) we must act now, (2) we need more study before we act, (3) there is no global warming, and (4) human activity is a minor contributor to global warming. Research your position, and be prepared to state your case with data to support your arguments. Hold a debate with the other groups in your class, paying close attention to the information presented by the other groups. Are their arguments persuasive? Are their sources reliable? Are yours?

Water

Have You Ever Wondered?

1. Why isn't there a filter that removes all pollutants from water?
2. Why does only one-tenth of an iceberg show above the surface?
3. How did Earth get its water?
4. About how much water do we really use each day?
5. Is bottled water safer than tap water?
6. Is water that has been fortified with vitamins better for you?

Learning Objectives

- Relate water's unique properties to the polarity and the hydrogen bonding of its molecules. (14.1)
- Explain how water on the surface of Earth acts to moderate daily temperature variations. (14.1)
- Explain why humans can use less than 1% of all the water on Earth. (14.2)
- Describe how human activities affect water quality. (14.3)
- Give an example of a biological water contaminant. (14.3)
- List the major uses of water. (14.4)
- List some groundwater contaminants. (14.5)
- Identify the sources of nitrates in groundwater. (14.5)
- Describe how water is purified for drinking and other household uses. (14.6)
- Describe primary, secondary, and tertiary treatment of wastewater. (14.7)
- Describe the structures of zeolites and mesoporous materials.
- Explain how zeolites and mesoporous materials can be used to clean up contaminated water.

Rivers of Life, Seas of Sorrows

Earth is a water world. Most of its surface is covered with oceans and seas, lakes and rivers. People contain a lot of water, too. About two-thirds of our body weight is water, and water makes up 60–90% of a typical cell. The water in our blood is much like ocean water, containing a variety of dissolved ions. You might even say that we are walking sacks of seawater.

The presence of large quantities of water makes our planet unique in the solar system, the only planet capable of supporting higher forms of life. Water is the only substance on Earth that commonly exists in large amounts

Water is truly a unique substance. It is the most familiar substance that commonly exhibits all three physical states. The most common state, and the one that is most important to life, is the liquid state. Water is also known as the "universal solvent." This solvent power allows water to dissolve many of the substances plants and animals need for proper functioning. Unfortunately, the solvent power also makes water easy to contaminate and difficult to purify. In this chapter we will look at the nature of water, its many uses, and the methods currently used for purifying water.

in all three physical states. Go outside on a snowy day and you are likely to experience all three forms at once. Gaseous water vapor is invisible (and is all around us), but tiny droplets of liquid water form clouds. Solid water falls to the ground as snow and melts into puddles of liquid water.

The Ionian philosopher Thales (ca. sixth century B.C.E)—whom some consider the first scientist—held water in the highest regard, believing that it was the "primordial substance" from which all other things were made. Little wonder that a man from an island nation would think so. Water's unique nature makes it essential to life, and life as we know it is dependent on water. Our search for life on Mars is based to a large extent on evidence that the planet once had vast quantities of water and that relics of life from that time might still exist below the dry surface.

The properties that make water able to support life also make it easy to pollute and therefore potentially hazardous. Water, with its polar molecules, is a good solvent. Many substances are easily dispersed throughout the environment because they are soluble in water. Once dissolved, it is not easy to remove substances from water. Furthermore, many strains of bacteria and other microorganisms that are harmful to humans thrive in water.

We start this chapter by discussing some of the unusual properties of water. Then we look at water pollution and water treatment. We should neither underestimate the importance of clean drinking water nor take it for granted. We could live for several weeks without food, but without water, we would last a few days at most.

▲ Two photographs of a trench dug on Mars by the *Phoenix* lander, taken on June 15 and June 18, 2008. Chunks of matter in the shadowed part of the left-hand photo (see arrows) have disappeared in the right-hand photo. The chunks are thought to be ice that underwent sublimation (Section 6.1).

1. Why isn't there a filter that removes all pollutants from water? Some water pollutants are present at extremely low levels, and the removal techniques available to us just aren't precise enough to remove those pollutants. Also, water's polarity gives it a very strong attraction for many pollutants.

2. Why does only one-tenth of an iceberg show above the surface? Although ice is less dense ($d = 0.92\ g/cm^3$) than liquid water ($d = 1.00\ g/cm^3$), the density difference is rather small. A floating object displaces its mass of water, which means that a cubic meter (1000 L) of ice will have about 920 L of its volume below the water. Only 80 L will show above the water. Ice floats a little higher in seawater, because salty water is slightly denser than fresh water.

14.1 Water: Some Unique Properties

Learning Objectives › Relate water's unique properties to the polarity and the hydrogen bonding of its molecules. › Explain how water on the surface of Earth acts to moderate daily temperature variations.

Although water is quite familiar, it is a most unusual compound. It is the only common liquid on the surface of our planet. For most substances, the solid form is denser than the liquid. However, the solid form of water (ice) is less dense than the liquid. This means water expands when it freezes. The consequences of this unusual characteristic are essential for life on Earth. Ice forms on the surfaces of lakes and insulates the lower layers of water; this phenomenon allows fish and other aquatic organisms to survive winter in the temperate zones. If ice were denser than liquid water, it would sink to the bottom as it formed, and even the deeper lakes of the northern United States would freeze solid in winter.

The same property—that ice is less dense than liquid water—has dangerous consequences for living cells. When living tissues freeze, ice crystals are formed, and the expansion ruptures and kills cells. The slower the cooling, the larger the crystals of ice and the more damage there is to the cell. Frozen-food manufacturers make "flash-frozen" products by freezing foods so rapidly that the ice crystals are kept very small and thus do minimal damage to the cellular structure of the food.

Water also is denser than most other familiar liquids. As a consequence, liquids less dense than water and insoluble in water float on its surface. The massive oil spill that occurs when a tanker ruptures or an offshore well gets out of control is a fairly common problem. The oil floating on the surface of the water washes onto beaches, where it is unsightly and damaging to the environment. If water were less dense than oil, the problem would certainly be different, although not necessarily less serious.

Another unusual property of water is its high specific heat. Different substances have different capacities for storing energy absorbed as heat. **Specific heat** is the quantity of heat required to raise the temperature of 1 g of a substance by 1 °C. Table 14.1 gives the specific heats of several familiar substances in calories per gram per degree (cal/g °C) and in the SI units of joules per gram per kelvin (J/g K).

▲ Crude oil coats the surface in the Gulf of Mexico after the *Deepwater Horizon* oil rig sank following an explosion. The leak was a mile below the surface, making it difficult to estimate the size of the spill. One liter of oil can create a slick with an area of 2.5 hectares (6.3 acres). This and similar spills provide a reminder that hydrocarbons and water don't mix.

Table 14.1 Specific Heats of Some Familiar Substances at 25 °C

Substance	Specific Heat	
	(cal/g °C)	(J/g K)
Aluminum (Al)	0.216	0.902
Copper (Cu)	0.0920	0.385
Ethanol (CH_3CH_2OH)	0.588	2.46
Iron (Fe)	0.107	0.449
Lead (Pb)	0.0306	0.128
Silver (Ag)	0.0562	0.235
Sulfur (S)	0.169	0.706
Water	1.00[a]	4.180

[a]Note that in cal/g °C, the specific heat of water is 1.00. As the metric system was established, the properties of water were often taken as the standard.

Note that it takes almost ten times as much heat to raise the temperature of 1 g of water 1 °C as to raise the temperature of 1 g of iron by the same amount. Imagine heating two iron kettles on the stove, one empty and one filled with water. It takes much longer (and much more energy) to heat the water-filled kettle.

Conversely, to cause even a small drop in water temperature, a relatively large quantity of heat must be removed. Because water stores heat so well, the water-filled kettle mentioned earlier will stay hot a lot longer than the empty kettle when the stove is turned off. The vast amounts of water on the surface of Earth thus act as a giant heat reservoir to moderate daily temperature variations. The extreme temperature changes on the surface of the waterless moon, ranging from 100 °C at noon to −173 °C at night, dramatically illustrate this important property of water.

Water also is unique in having a high **heat of vaporization**; that is, a large amount of heat is required to evaporate a small amount of water. This fact is of enormous importance to us because large amounts of body heat can be dissipated by the evaporation of small amounts of water (perspiration) from the skin. Water's heat of vaporization also accounts in part for the climate-modifying property of lakes and oceans. A large portion of the heat that would otherwise raise the temperature of the air and land instead vaporizes water from the surface of lakes or seas. Thus, in summer, it is cooler near a large body of water than in interior land areas.

All these fascinating properties of water depend on the unique structure of the highly polar water molecule (Section 4.12). In the liquid state, the molecules are tumbling over one another but remain associated through strong hydrogen bonds. The tumbling becomes more and more violent as the temperature increases, until the boiling point is reached. At this point, a large fraction of the molecules have enough energy to break all of the hydrogen bonds linking them to surrounding molecules, and they fly out of the liquid into the gas phase.

Conversely, when water freezes, its molecules take on a more ordered arrangement, forming four hydrogen bonds per molecule. Thus, solid ice contains large

(a)

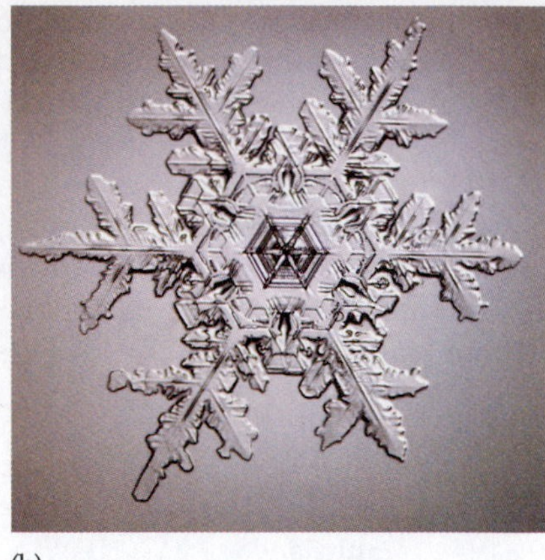

(b)

▶ **Figure 14.1** Hydrogen bonds in ice. (a) Oxygen atoms are stacked in layers of distorted hexagonal rings. Hydrogen atoms lie between pairs of oxygen atoms, closer to one (covalent bond) than to the other. The yellow dashed lines indicate hydrogen bonds. The structure has large "holes." (b) The hexagonal arrangement of water molecules in the crystal structure of ice is revealed at the macroscopic level in the hexagonal shapes of snowflakes.

hexagonal holes (Figure 14.1). This three-dimensional structure extends out for billions and billions of molecules. When the ice melts, the holes collapse, explaining why ice is less dense than liquid water.

Self-Assessment Questions

1. Which of the following is *not* a property of water?
   a. expands when it freezes
   b. has a low specific heat
   c. has a high heat of vaporization
   d. is a useful solvent for many substances
2. Water's unique properties arise because water molecules
   a. have hydrogen atoms that do not have a stable electron configuration
   b. associate through hydrogen bonds
   c. can form covalent bonds with ionic substances
   d. can form covalent bonds with nonpolar substances
3. In a collection of water molecules, hydrogen bonds form between
   a. an H atom in one H_2O molecule and the O atom in another H_2O molecule
   b. the O atoms in different H_2O molecules
   c. the two H atoms in a single H_2O molecule
   d. two H atoms in different H_2O molecules
4. Frozen water has an open structure with
   a. an amorphous molecular arrangement
   b. large hexagonal holes
   c. molecules that are in constant motion
   d. molecules that tend to repel each other

Answers: 1, b; 2, b; 3, a; 4, b

14.2 Water in Nature

Learning Objectives › Explain why humans can use less than 1% of all the water on Earth.

Three-fourths of the surface of Earth is covered with water, but nearly 98% of it is salty seawater—unfit for drinking and not suitable for most industrial purposes. Much of the fresh water is frozen in ice caps, leaving less than 1% of all Earth's water as available for human use. Of that, most is underground. Lakes and streams account for only 0.01% of the fresh water on the planet. Rain falls on Earth in enormous amounts, but most of it falls into the sea or on inaccessible land areas.

Because water is a polar solvent, it readily dissolves most ionic substances, which accounts for the saltiness of the oceans. Rainwater dissolves the ions of minerals, and these ions are carried by streams and rivers to the sea. There the heat of the sun evaporates part of the water, leaving the salts behind. Are the oceans growing saltier as the years go by? Apparently not. The rates of addition appear to be balanced by precipitation of minerals and absorption of ions onto clays.

Potable (suitable for drinking) water is generally readily available in the United States, but several cities are at risk of running out of fresh water: Los Angeles and the San Francisco Bay Area in California; Houston, San Antonio, and Fort Worth in Texas; Phoenix and Tucson in Arizona; Las Vegas, Nevada; Atlanta, Georgia; and Orlando, Florida.

In many nations around the world, the situation is much worse. About 875 million people have inadequate quantities of fresh water, and 2.7 billion people live without basic sanitation. About 3.6 million people—most of them children—die each year because they drink water contaminated with bacteria, viruses, or parasites. According to the Pacific Institute in Oakland, California, more than 76 million people will die from water-related diseases by 2020 unless major prevention efforts are undertaken. Water resources around the globe are threatened by pollution, misuse, and climate change.

3. How did Earth get its water? Scientists have put forth several hypotheses, but none have yet been fully accepted. One idea, long favored by many, was that water was carried to Earth by comets, many of which are little more than balls of ice. This hypothesis was recently disproved by isotope signatures (Section 11.3). Comet water has a deuterium-to-protium ratio ($^2H/^1H$) twice that of Earth's waters.

▲ An adequate supply of water is essential to life.

The Water Cycle and Natural Contaminants

Although the percentages of water apportioned to the oceans, the ice caps, and the freshwater rivers, lakes, and streams remain fairly constant, water is dynamically cycled among these various repositories (Figure 14.2). It constantly evaporates from both water and land surfaces, and water vapor condenses into clouds and returns to Earth as rain, sleet, and snow. This fresh water becomes part of the ice caps, runs off in streams and rivers, and fills both lakes and underground pools of water in rocks and sand called *aquifers*.

Gases

Rainwater is not pure H_2O. It picks up dust particles and dissolves some oxygen, nitrogen, and carbon dioxide as it falls through the atmosphere. The carbon dioxide makes natural rainwater slightly acidic because it reacts with water to form carbonic acid (H_2CO_3).

$$CO_2(g) + H_2O(l) \longrightarrow H_2CO_3(aq)$$

Lightning causes nitrogen, oxygen, and water vapor to combine to form nitric acid, which dissolves in rainwater as well.

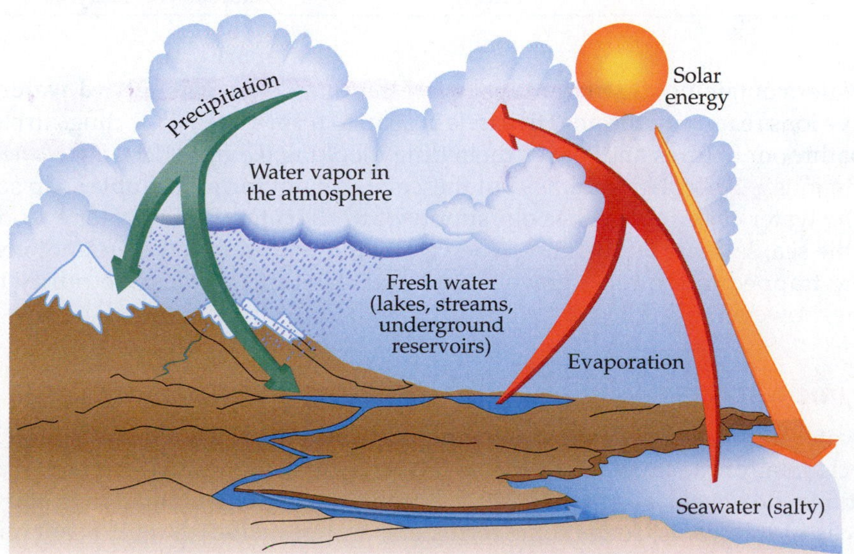

◀ **Figure 14.2** The water (hydrological) cycle. Powered by the sun (yellow arrow), evaporation of water from oceans, lakes, and land (red arrows) occurs. As moist air rises, it cools, and the water vapor condenses to form clouds. Water returns to the surface as precipitation (green arrows). Some of this water becomes groundwater and recharges aquifers. Some of it enters rivers and streams and is carried back to the oceans.

Groundwater also contains the naturally occurring gas radon (Section 13.7), a product of the decay of radioactive uranium and thorium. Although radon emits damaging ionizing radiation and produces a variety of hazardous daughter nuclei, it is only slightly soluble in water. Thus, the water used for showering, washing dishes, and cooking generally contributes only a small proportion (about 1–2%) of the total radon exposure indoors.

Dissolved Minerals

As water moves along or beneath the surface of Earth, it dissolves minerals from rocks and soil. Recall that minerals (salts) are ionic and that ions are either positively charged (cations) or negatively charged (anions). Table 14.2 lists the substances typically found in natural waters. The main cations in natural water, shown in red in Table 14.2, are ions of sodium, potassium, calcium, magnesium, and sometimes iron (as Fe^{2+} or Fe^{3+}). The anions (shown in blue) are usually sulfate, bicarbonate, and chloride ions.

Table 14.2 Some Substances Found in Natural Waters

Substance	Formula	Source
Carbon dioxide	CO_2	Atmosphere
Dust	—	Atmosphere
Nitrogen	N_2	Atmosphere
Oxygen	O_2	Atmosphere
Nitric acid	HNO_3	Atmosphere (thunderstorms)
Sand and soil particles	—	Soil and rocks
Sodium ions	Na^+	Soil and rocks
Potassium ions	K^+	Soil, rocks, and fertilizer
Calcium ions	Ca^{2+}	Limestone rocks
Magnesium ions	Mg^{2+}	Dolomite rocks
Iron(II) ions	Fe^{2+}	Soil and rocks
Chloride ions	Cl^-	Soil, rocks, and fertilizer
Sulfate ions	SO_4^{2-}	Soil, rocks, and fertilizer
Bicarbonate ions	HCO_3^-	Soil and rocks
Radon	Rn	Radioactive decay

Water containing calcium, magnesium, or iron salts is called **hard water**. The positive ions react with the negative ions in soap to form a scum that clings to clothes and bathroom fixtures and leaves them dingy looking (Chapter 21). *Soft water* may contain ions, such as Na^+ and K^+, but these ions do not form insoluble soap scum.

The water cycle replenishes our supply of fresh water. When water evaporates from the sea, salts are left behind. When water moves through the ground, impurities are trapped in the rock, gravel, sand, and clay. This capacity to purify is not infinite, however.

Organic Matter

Rainwater dissolves matter from decaying plants and animals. As part of the natural cycle in a forest, small quantities of this organic matter enrich the soil. In large quantities, however, it contaminates soil and water. Organic matter in the form of traces of lubricants, fuels, some fertilizers, and pesticides can also contaminate water. Bacteria, other microorganisms, and animal wastes are all potential contaminants of natural waters.

Some Biblical Chemistry

The biblical story of Moses illustrates that getting a dependable supply of fresh water has long been a problem. When Moses led the Israelites out of Egypt into the wilderness, he encountered a desert area where potable water was scarce. Many people know the biblical account of how Moses struck a rock to bring forth water. An incident at Marah, where the Israelites couldn't drink the water because it was bitter, is less well known. According to Exodus, God commanded Moses to throw a certain tree into the water to sweeten (neutralize) it.

Basic (alkaline) solutions are bitter. The pool at Marah was probably basic; such *alkaline* waters are common in desert areas. A possible chemical explanation has been given for Moses' purification of the brackish water. The tree was probably dead, its cellulose bleached by the desert sun, and its alcohol groups oxidized to carboxylic acid groups.

CH_2OH CH_2OH

Cellulose

↓

COOH COOH

Oxidized cellulose

These acidic groups could have neutralized the alkali in the water. (Tannins, found in plant material and composed of polyphenols and other acidic compounds, also may have contributed to the neutralization.) Moses didn't have to understand the science of water purification to apply appropriate technology.

Self-Assessment Questions

1. Energy to power the water cycle comes from
   a. electric power plants
   b. hurricanes
   c. the sun
   d. thunderstorms
2. Rainwater is naturally acidic because it contains dissolved
   a. CO_2
   b. N_2
   c. O_2
   d. SO_2
3. The main cations in water are
   a. Na^+, Al^{3+}, Ca^{2+}, and Mg^{2+}
   b. Na^+, K^+, Ca^{2+}, and Li^+
   c. Na^+, K^+, Ca^{2+}, and Mg^{2+}
   d. Ra^{2+}, Sr^{2+}, Ca^{2+}, and Mg^{2+}
4. Hard water may characterized by the presence of all of the following ions *except*
   a. Ca^{2+}
   b. Fe^{2+}
   c. K^+
   d. Mg^{2+}

Answers: 1, c; 2, a; 3, c; 4, c

14.3 Chemical and Biological Contamination

Learning Objectives › Describe how human activities affect water quality. › Give an example of a biological water contaminant.

Early people did little to pollute the water and the air, if only because their numbers were so few. Most pollutants at that time were natural: hard-water ions, alkaline contaminants, and animal wastes. The rise of agriculture and then cities brought together enough *Homo sapiens* to pollute the environment seriously. Even then, pollution was mostly local and largely biological. Human wastes were dumped on the ground or into the nearest stream. Disease organisms were transmitted through food, water, and direct contact.

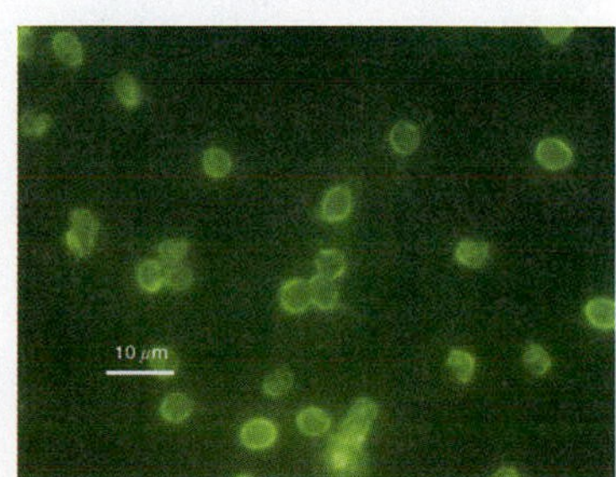

▲ *Cryptosporidium*, shown here in a fluorescent image, sickened 400,000 people and killed about 100 in the Milwaukee area in 1993. Since then, water utility companies have generally improved their treatment systems.

Waterborne Diseases

Contamination of water supplies by *pathogenic* (disease-causing) microorganisms from human wastes was a severe problem throughout the world until about 100 years ago. During the 1830s, severe epidemics of cholera swept the

▲ Contaminated beaches are closed to swimming and other recreational activities.

Western world. Typhoid fever and dysentery were common. In 1900, for example, there were more than 35,000 deaths from typhoid in the United States. Today, as a result of chemical treatment, municipal water supplies in developed nations are generally safe. However, waterborne diseases are still quite common in much of the developing world. For example, more than 5000 people died of cholera after an earthquake devastated Haiti in 2010. Dysentery is rampant much of the time in large parts of Asia, Africa, and Latin America. At any given time, about half the world's hospital beds are occupied by people who have waterborne diseases.

The threat of biological contamination has not been totally eliminated from developed nations. Millions of people in the United States are at risk because of bacterial contamination of drinking water. Ongoing threats include *Cryptosporidium* and *Giardia*, protozoans excreted in human and animal feces that resist standard chemical disinfection. Municipal water utilities are constantly improving their treatment systems to deal with biological contamination. Biological contamination also lessens the recreational value of water when it makes swimming, fishing, and other recreational activities hazardous.

Acid Waters

Acids formed from sulfur oxides (SO_x) and nitrogen oxides (NO_x) come down from the sky in acid rain, fog, and snow. These acids corrode metals, dissolve limestone and marble, and even ruin the finishes on our automobiles. Acids also flow into streams from abandoned mines.

▲ Acid water draining from an old mine.

Acid rain has been somewhat alleviated over the last few decades by the reduction of SO_x emissions (Section 13.6), but thousands of bodies of water in eastern North America remain acidified.

Acidic water is detrimental to life in lakes and streams. It has been linked to declining crop and forest yields. Acidic water probably affects living organisms in many ways. For example, aluminum ions, which are tightly bound in clays and other minerals, are released by acid. Aluminum ions have low toxicity for humans but they can be deadly to young fish. Many dying lakes have only old fish because none of the young survive. Ironically, lakes destroyed by excess acidity are often quite beautiful—clear and sparkling.

Acids are no threat to lakes and streams where limestone (calcium carbonate) is plentiful, because limestone can neutralize excess acid.

$$\underset{\text{Limestone}}{CaCO_3(s)} + \underset{\text{Acid}}{2\,H^+(aq)} \longrightarrow Ca^{2+}(aq) + CO_2(g) + H_2O$$

Where rock is mainly granite, however, no such neutralization occurs.

Sewage and Dying Lakes

Contamination by pathogenic microorganisms is not the only problem caused by the dumping of human sewage into our waterways. The breakdown of organic matter by bacteria depletes **dissolved oxygen (DO)** in the water and increases the plant nutrients in the water. A stream can handle a small amount of waste without difficulty, but when massive amounts of raw sewage are dumped into a waterway, undesirable changes occur.

▲ Sewage from homes and businesses depletes the dissolved oxygen in water.

Most organic material can be degraded (broken down) by microorganisms. Biodegradation can be either *aerobic* or *anaerobic*. **Aerobic oxidation** occurs in the presence of dissolved oxygen. A measure of the amount of oxygen needed for this degradation to occur is the **biochemical oxygen demand (BOD)**. The greater the quantity of degradable organic wastes, the higher the BOD. If the BOD in a lake or stream is high enough, dissolved oxygen is depleted and no life (other than odor-producing anaerobic microorganisms) can survive. Flowing streams can regenerate themselves. Those with rapids soon come alive again as the swirling water dissolves oxygen. Lakes with little or no flow can remain dead for years.

With adequate dissolved oxygen, aerobic bacteria (those that require oxygen) oxidize the organic matter to carbon dioxide, water, and a variety of inorganic ions (Table 14.3). The water is relatively clean, but the ions, particularly the nitrates and phosphates, may serve as nutrients for the growth of algae, which also cause problems. When the algae die, they become organic waste and increase the BOD of the water. This process is called **eutrophication.** The eutrophication of a lake is a natural process, but the action can be greatly accelerated by human wastes, phosphates from detergents, and the runoff of fertilizers from farms and lawns, which stimulates algal bloom and die-off. Streams and lakes die because nature cannot purify them nearly as quickly as we can pollute them.

Table 14.3 Some Substances Formed in Water by the Breakdown of Organic Matter

Substance	Formula
Aerobic conditions	
Carbon dioxide	CO_2
Nitrate ions	NO_3^-
Phosphate ions	PO_4^{3-}
Sulfate ions	SO_4^{2-}
Bicarbonate ions	HCO_3^-
Anaerobic conditions	
Methane	CH_4
Ammonia	NH_3
Amines	RNH_2
Hydrogen sulfide	H_2S
Methanethiol	CH_3SH

▲ The eutrophication of a lake is a natural process, but the process can be greatly accelerated by human wastes and the runoff from farms, lawns, and golf courses.

When too much organic matter—whether from sewage, dying algae, or other sources—depletes the dissolved oxygen in a body of water, **anaerobic decay** processes take over. Instead of oxidizing the organic matter, anaerobic bacteria reduce it. Methane (CH_4) is formed. Sulfur is converted to hydrogen sulfide (H_2S) and foul-smelling organic compounds. Nitrogen is reduced to ammonia and odorous amines (Section 9.8). The foul odors are a good indication that the water is overloaded with organic wastes. Only anaerobic microorganisms can survive in such water.

Dumping our sewage into waterways isn't the only way we can foul up their ecology. Fertilizer runoff from farm fields, golf courses, and lawns and seepage from feedlots all add inorganic nutrients to waterways, and an algal bloom can lead to oxygen depletion and death for the fish. Perhaps the most enigmatic influence of all has come from the introduction into the water cycle of substances from modern industrial and consumer society: pesticides, radioisotopes, detergents, drugs, toxic metals, and industrial chemicals.

The Industrial Revolution added a new dimension to water pollution problems. Factories were often built on the banks of streams, and wastes were dumped into the water to be carried away. The rise of modern agriculture led to increased contamination as fertilizers and pesticides found their way into waterways. Drilling for and transportation of petroleum has resulted in oil spills in oceans, estuaries, and rivers. Acids enter waterways from mines and factories and from acid precipitation. Household chemicals also contribute to water pollution when detergents, solvents, and other chemicals are dumped down drains.

The creation of new materials has wrought a variety of new ecological problems. Chemists and chemistry play a vital role in understanding pollution—how it occurs and how it can be mitigated. Monitoring by ever more sophisticated analytical methods and instruments has helped detect and define specific ecological problems. A stinking lake is obvious to everyone, but only by using advanced analytical techniques can scientists determine the level of dangerous, yet invisible, materials in the water we drink.

Self-Assessment Questions

1. It is estimated that half of the world's hospital beds are occupied by people with waterborne diseases. The main causes of these are
   a. microorganisms **b.** DDT and dioxins
   c. lead and mercury **d.** pesticides
2. Water in a lake made acidic by acid rain or mine drainage is often
   a. clear **b.** eutrophic
   c. rich in game fish **d.** rich in lime
3. Dissolved oxygen (DO) in water is important because a low DO level can affect
   a. light penetration
   b. phosphate concentration
   c. salt level (salinity)
   d. survival of aquatic animals
4. The biochemical oxygen demand (BOD) of a water sample indicates the
   a. dissolved oxygen level
   b. organic matter level
   c. phosphate level
   d. salt levels (salinity)
5. How are dissolved oxygen and BOD related?
   a. BOD has no impact on dissolved oxygen
   b. high BOD means a high level of dissolved oxygen
   c. high BOD reduces dissolved oxygen as the organic matter decays
   d. low BOD means a low level of dissolved oxygen
6. Anaerobic oxidation produces
   a. CO_2, H_2O, and inorganic ions
   b. CO, NH_3, and H_2O
   c. CH_4, NH_3, and H_2S
   d. sewage sludge
7. Excess nitrates or phosphates in a lake or river cause
   a. aerobic decay **b.** eutrophication
   c. an increase in game fish **d.** nitrogen fixation

Answers: 1, a; 2, a; 3, d; 4, b; 5, c; 6, c; 7, b

14.4 Water: Who Uses It and How Much?

Learning Objective › List the major uses of water.

The average American uses about 400 L of water a day. That amount does not include the water used to produce our food, clothes, and other items. For example, it takes several hundred kilograms of steel to produce a typical automobile. To make a metric ton (t) of steel requires about 100 t of water. About 4 t of water is lost through evaporation. The remainder is contaminated with acids, grease and oil, lime, and iron salts. This polluted water can be cleaned up, and most of it is recycled.

Given the environmental and economic costs of producing elastomers for tires, fabrics for upholstery, glass for windows, and so on, it is easy to see that the private automobile is an ecological problem even before it hits the road. And once on the road, it is a major contributor to air pollution (Chapter 13).

GREEN CHEMISTRY

Principles 1, 3, 6, 9

Randall Hicks, *Wheaton College (Norton, MA)*

Porous Materials in Water Remediation

Preventing waste is better than treating it, according to Green Chemistry Principle 1. However, there will always be water in need of remediation. As was pointed out in Section 14.2, very little of the world's water is available as fresh water, and many people do not have access to clean drinking water. Furthermore, industrialization has increased both use and contamination of our water supplies (Section 14.4). You have seen how wastewater must be treated before it can be returned to the environment (Section 14.7). Let's now examine some new materials that can be used to clean up and conserve water.

Zeolites are a class of solids that both occur naturally and can be synthesized. They exhibit different three-dimensional structures, but each has a well-defined network of pores and a large surface area (Figure 1). Zeolites found in nature are minerals that have a framework made from silicon, aluminum, and oxygen. Each of the Al and Si atoms is bonded to four O atoms that are shared by other Al and Si atoms. The open structure of zeolites allows them to be used in a variety of water-remediation applications.

In Chapters 3 and 4, you learned about valence electrons, positive ions (cations), and negative ion (anions). Al atoms have one less valence electron than Si atoms. The presence of an Al atom in a zeolite causes an excess of negative charge to build up, and another cation must be present to balance the charge. Sodium or potassium ions commonly meet this need, but any cation can do so. These charge-balancing cations are easily exchanged for other cations, making zeolites good materials for purifying water. For example, zeolites are used to replace calcium and magnesium cations with sodium and potassium cations, thereby "softening" the water. After exchanging all of their ions, zeolites can be regenerated simply by soaking them in a salt solution. The reusability of zeolites meets one of the goals of green chemistry.

Zeolites that have had their natural cations replaced by protons (H^+) can act as solid acid catalysts. Catalysts speed up reactions, are reusable, and need to be present in reactions only in small amounts (Section 8.8). Unlike many catalysts that are dissolved in reaction mixtures, zeolites are easily removed. Therefore, they do not become part of the waste generated in these processes. Instead, they reduce the amount of waste. Catalysts also allow many reactions to be performed under milder conditions, both in terms of reagents and temperature, consuming fewer resources and reducing waste, in accordance with Principles 1, 3, 6, and 9.

Zeolites are *microporous* (having pores less than 2 nm in diameter), which can limit their effectiveness in applications involving larger molecules. In the 1990s, researchers at Mobil (now ExxonMobil) solved this problem by synthesizing *mesoporous* (pore diameters between 2 nm and 50 nm) materials. Zeolite applications can now be extended to larger molecules. The surfaces of these materials can also be customized for specific applications, without fear of clogging the larger pores.

Consider the problem of removing toxic heavy metals from drinking water. The EPA has placed strict limits on the amounts of metals allowed in drinking water (Table 14.6). Sulfur binds well to these metals, as shown by the abundance of sulfide minerals in nature. To exploit this favorable interaction, sulfur-containing molecules can be anchored to the surfaces of mesoporous solids (Figure 2) to create a sponge that will bind and remove heavy metals from water. The large pores and surface areas of a mesoporous material allow a gram of it to extract hundreds of milligrams of heavy metal from water.

Water is one of Earth's greatest resources. Green chemistry approaches that reduce the use of water or provide greater access to clean water are important. Porous materials offer great promise in the design of green processes and in the meeting of many challenges in remediation of contaminated water.

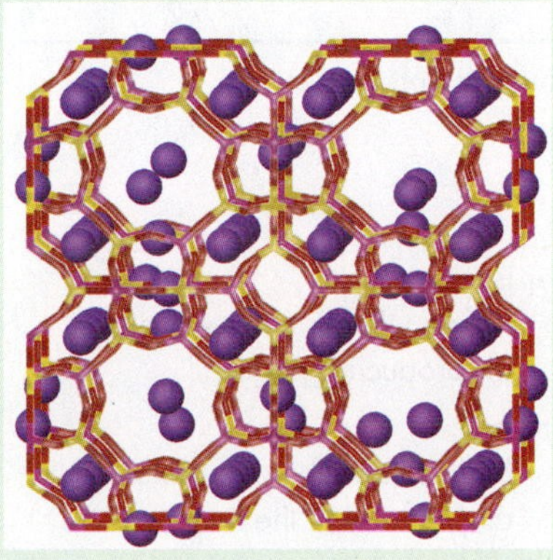

▲ Zeolite structure with cations inside the pores.

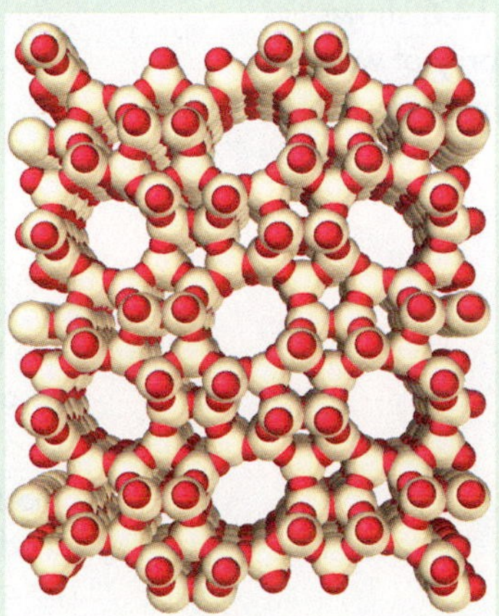

▲ Surface modified mesoporous materials structure.

▲ It DOES Matter!
Traditional paper production from virgin wood fibers uses enormous quantities of water. Worldwide water use for producing paper is about 315 billion kg each year, or about 100 lb of water for a single ream of paper. Wood is about half cellulose, but the cellulose fibers are held together by lignin, a resinous material that must be removed to make paper. According to the EPA, recycling can reduce water use in paper production by nearly 60% and energy consumption by 40%. The EPA also says that recycling causes 35% less water pollution and 74% less air pollution. An even more effective measure is to reduce paper use: Print only what you must!

Most other industries and activities also contribute to water pollution. About 70% of the world's freshwater supply is used in agriculture, almost all of it for irrigation.

Table 14.4 lists the quantities of water required for the production of a variety of industrial and consumer products. Much of this water is cleaned up and recycled, but the need for clean water is still enormous. Industries in the United States have substantially reduced their contribution to water pollution. Most are in compliance with the Water Pollution Control Act, which requires that they use the best practicable technology.

Table 14.4 Typical Quantities of Water Required[a] to Produce Various Materials

Industrial Products	Water Required[b] (t)	Consumer Products	Water Required (L)
Steel	100	Laptop computer	10,600
Paper	20	1 hamburger	2400
Copper	400	1 bowl rice	525
Rayon	800	1 kg bananas	860
Aluminum	1280	1 cup coffee	140
Synthetic rubber	2400	1 pair blue jeans	11,000

[a] Includes irrigation water, rainwater, water consumed directly, and water used in processing, cleaning, and waste disposal.
[b] Per metric ton of product.

How much water does one really need? Only about 1.5–2.0 L per day for drinking. Each day in the United States, every person uses about 7 L for drinking and cooking but directly uses a total of about 380 L. We use much more water *indirectly* in agriculture and industry (Table 14.5) to produce food and other materials; it takes 800 L of water to produce 1 kg of vegetables and 13,000 L of water to produce a steak. We also use water for recreation (for example, swimming, boating, and fishing). For most of these purposes, we need water that is free of bacteria, viruses, and parasitic organisms.

4. About how much water do we really use each day? Each person in the United States uses about 7 L per day for drinking and cooking, but we use directly a total of about 380 L per day (washing dishes, laundry, and cars and flushing toilets). However, Table 14.5 shows that the vast majority of water is used for energy production and agriculture.

Table 14.5 Use of Water in the United States

Use	Percentage of Total Usage
Coolant for electric power plants	48
Irrigation	34
Public water supplies	11
Industrial	5
Miscellaneous[a]	2

[a] Includes mining, livestock, aquaculture, and other uses.

Self-Assessment Questions

1. The human activity that uses the most water is
   - a. agriculture
   - b. manufacturing electronics
   - c. making rubber
   - d. producing paper
2. Most of the water used by the steel industry is
   - a. discharged untreated
   - b. lost through evaporation
   - c. recycled
   - d. included in the final product

Answers: 1, a; 2, c

14.5 Groundwater Contamination → Tainted Tap Water

Learning Objectives › List some groundwater contaminants. › Identify the sources of nitrates in groundwater.

About half of the people in the United States drink surface water (from streams and lakes). The other half get their drinking water from groundwater via wells or springs. In rural areas, 97% of people drink groundwater. Because rocks differ in porosity and permeability, water does not move within all rock in the same way. An aquifer forms when water-bearing rock readily transmits water to wells and springs. Wells are drilled into an aquifer, and water is pumped out. Precipitation recharges the aquifer. For many aquifers, the rate of pumping water out is much greater than the rate of recharge, and the water table drops. In most parts of the United States, the dropping water table requires that wells be drilled deeper and deeper.

Well water can be contaminated. Toxic chemicals have been found in the groundwater in some areas.

- Many wells throughout the United States are contaminated with the gasoline additive methyl *tert*-butyl ether (MTBE) (Section 15.6), making the water undrinkable by imparting an offensive taste and odor.
- Wells around the Rocky Mountain Arsenal, near Denver, are contaminated by wastes from the production of pesticides.
- Wells in many areas are contaminated with perfluorooctanoic acid [PFOA, $CF_3(CF_2)_6COOH$] and related compounds. PFOA is an industrial surfactant used for processing polytetrafluoroethylene (PTFE). These compounds persist in the environment where they accumulate in living organisms.
- Some community water supplies in New Jersey have been shut down because of contamination by industrial wastes.

Groundwater contamination is particularly alarming because, once contaminated, an underground aquifer may remain unusable for decades or longer. There is no easy way to remove the contaminants. Pumping out the water and purifying it could take years and cost billions of dollars. Let's examine a few important sources of groundwater contamination in a bit more detail.

Nitrates

In many agricultural areas, well water is contaminated with nitrate ions (NO_3^-). Excessive nitrates are especially dangerous to infants. In an infant's digestive tract, nitrate ion is reduced to nitrite ion. The result is *methemoglobinemia*, or blue baby syndrome. A baby who drinks nitrate-contaminated water turns blue and can die if not treated. In some farming areas, such as California's Imperial Valley, parents sometimes have to buy bottled water for their babies.

Nitrates in the groundwater (Figure 14.3) come from fertilizers used on farms and lawns, from the decomposition of organic wastes in sewage treatment, and from runoff from animal feedlots. They are highly soluble and thus difficult to remove from water, requiring expensive treatment.

▲ Half of Chinese cities have significantly polluted groundwater, and some cities are facing a water crisis. More than 400 Chinese cities are threatened with water shortages, with 136 of them experiencing severe shortages. Here, a water company worker takes a sample from the Songhua River in Songyuan, in China's northeastern Jilin Province.

Volatile Organic Chemicals

We mentioned volatile organic compounds (VOCs) as air pollutants (Section 13.4). VOCs are also water pollutants that add an undesirable odor to water. Many VOCs are suspected carcinogens. VOCs are used as solvents, cleaners, and fuels, and they are components of gasoline, spot removers, oil-based paints, inks, thinners, and some drain cleaners. Common VOCs are hydrocarbon solvents such as benzene (C_6H_6) and toluene ($C_6H_5{-}CH_3$) and chlorinated hydrocarbons such as carbon tetrachloride (CCl_4), chloroform ($CHCl_3$), and methylene chloride (CH_2Cl_2).

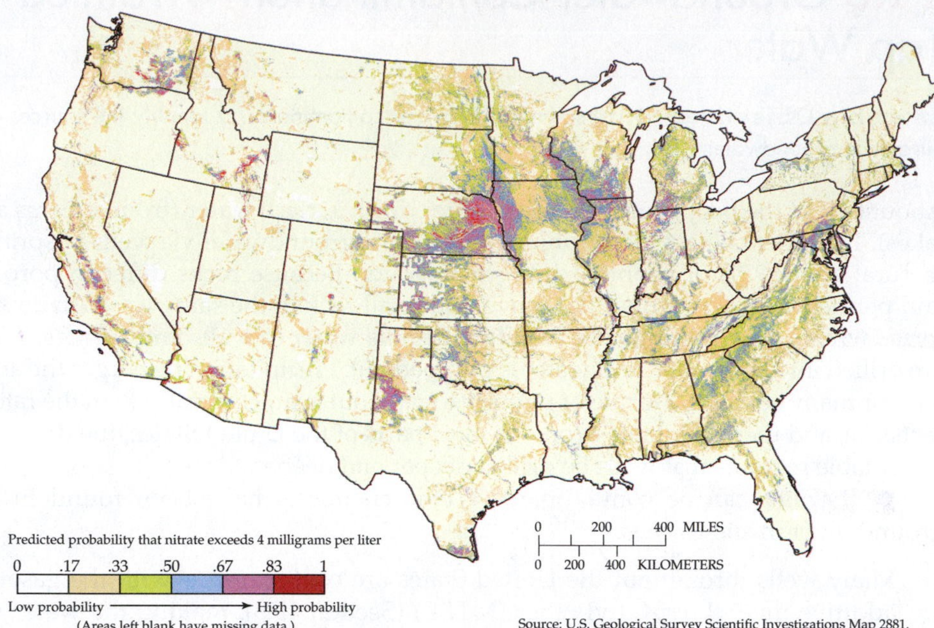

▶ **Figure 14.3** Areas of the contiguous United States where groundwater is likely to be contaminated by nitrates.

Q: *Why do you think that eastern Nebraska and western Iowa have high probabilities of nitrate contamination? Is your water supply threatened?*

Especially common is trichloroethylene ($CCl_2{=}CHCl$), widely used as a dry-cleaning solvent and as a degreasing compound. When spilled or discarded, VOCs enter the soil and eventually the groundwater.

Chemicals buried in dumps—often years ago, before there was much awareness of environmental problems—have infiltrated some groundwater supplies. Often, as at the Love Canal site in Niagara Falls, New York, people built schools and houses on or near old dump sites. (See Collaborative Group Project 8.) VOCs are generally only slightly soluble in water, with solubilities in the parts-per-million or parts-per-billion range. These trace amounts are found in groundwater. Many VOCs are characterized by a lack of reactivity. They react so slowly that they are likely to be around for a long time.

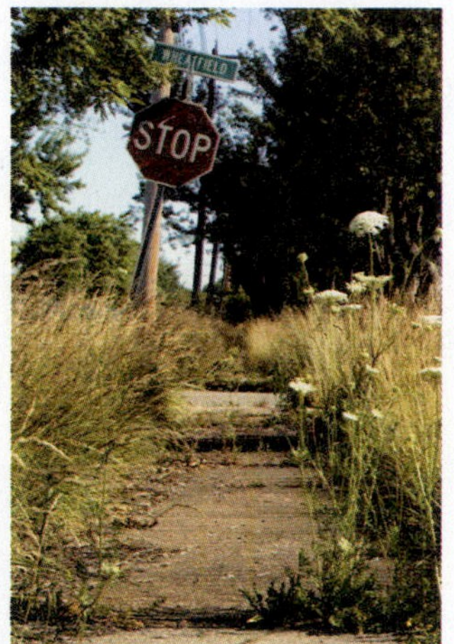

▲ **It DOES Matter!**
Homes and a school were built on the site of an old chemical dump in the Love Canal section of Niagara Falls, New York. A contaminated area around the old dump was fenced off to keep people out. Over 250 different industrial contaminants were found on the site. Cleanup was completed in the 1990s, and the evacuated neighborhood was repopulated and renamed Black Creek Village.

Leaking Underground Storage Tanks

A major source of groundwater contamination is underground storage tanks (USTs) that contain petroleum or hazardous chemicals. These buried steel tanks last an average of about 15 years before they rust through and begin to leak. In the 1980s, the EPA estimated that there were about 2.5 million such tanks. About 500,000 leaks from USTs have been detected, and 80% of those have been cleaned up. About 1,750,000 of all known tank sites have been cleaned up, and the frequency and severity of leaks from USTs have been reduced greatly. However, as of 2010, there were still 600,000 sites that had not been cleaned up.

Self-Assessment Questions

1. Which ion, from fertilizer runoff and wastewater discharges, can lead to methemoglobinemia in young children?
   a. Ca^{2+} b. K^+ c. NO_3^- d. PO_4^{3-}
2. Which of the following is a VOC that contaminates of groundwater?
   a. acetaldehyde from polluted air
   b. acetic acid from fermenting fruit
   c. PAN from polluted air
   d. toluene, a gasoline component

Answers: 1, c; 2, d

14.6 Making Water Fit to Drink

Learning Objective › Describe how water is purified for drinking and other household uses.

The per capita use of water in the United States is about 2.8 million L per year. This value includes water used for industrial, agricultural, and other purposes, and it is more than twice the per capita consumption in Europe. Although we often take drinking water for granted, significant energy and resources are spent every year to ensure the safety and quality of drinking water supplied by the 155,000 public water systems in the United States.

Safe Drinking Water Act

The U.S. Safe Drinking Water Act was passed in 1974 and amended in 1986 and 1996. The act gives the EPA power to set, monitor, and enforce national health-based standards for a variety of contaminants in municipal water supplies. As modern analytical techniques continue to improve, our ability to identify smaller and smaller concentrations of potentially harmful substances also improves. As a result, the number of regulated substances with *maximum contaminant levels (MCLs)* increased from 22 in 1976 to 90 in 2004. The 1996 amendments have MCLs for 7 types of bacteria or viruses, 7 disinfectants such as chlorine or disinfectant products such as bromate compounds, 16 inorganic compounds, 54 organic compounds, and 4 radioactive isotopes. Table 14.6 lists the MCLs for some of these contaminants.

Calculations of Parts per Million and Parts per Billion

We discussed solution concentrations in Section 5.5. For solutions that are extremely dilute, we often express concentrations in parts per million (ppm), parts per billion (ppb), or even parts per trillion (ppt). For example, in fluoridated drinking water, the fluoride ion concentration is maintained at about 1 ppm. A typical level of the contaminant chloroform ($CHCl_3$) in municipal drinking water taken from the lower Mississippi River is 8 ppb.

For aqueous solutions, ppm, ppb, and ppt are generally based on mass. Thus, 1 ppm of solute in a solution is the same as 1 g of solute per 1×10^6 g (1 million grams) of solution, and 1 ppb is 1 g of solute per 10^9 g (1 billion grams) of solution. In other words,

$$1\text{ ppm} = \frac{1\text{ g solute}}{10^6\text{ g solution}} \qquad 1\text{ ppb} = \frac{1\text{ g solute}}{10^9\text{ g solution}}$$

Calculations of these concentration levels are much like those for finding percents by mass (Section 5.4). Example 14.1 introduces a useful relationship for aqueous solutions.

Some Comparisons That Put the Figures in Perspective

1 PART PER MILLION (PPM) IS
- 1 inch in 16 miles
- 1 minute in 2 years
- 1 cent in $10,000

1 PART PER BILLION (PPB) IS
- 1 inch in 16,000 miles
- 1 second in 32 years
- 1 cent in $10 million

1 PART PER TRILLION (PPT) IS
- 1 inch in 16 million miles
- 1 second in 320 centuries
- 1 cent in $10 billion

Example 14.1 Contaminant Concentrations

According to standards, the EPA maximum allowable level of fluoride ion in drinking water is 4 mg F^- per liter. What is this level expressed in ppm?

Solution

The density of water, even if it contains traces of dissolved substances, is essentially 1.00 g/mL. One liter of water has a mass of 1000 g. So, we can express the allowable fluoride level as the ratio

$$\frac{4\text{ mg F}^-}{1000\text{ g water}}$$

To convert this fluoride level to ppm, we have to have the numerator and denominator in the same units. Using milligrams makes the denominator 1 million mg. The numerator then expresses the ppm of solute, that is, ppm F^-.

$$\frac{4\text{ mg F}^-}{1000\text{ }\cancel{\text{g water}}} \times \frac{1\text{ }\cancel{\text{g water}}}{1000\text{ mg water}} = \frac{4\text{ mg F}^-}{1{,}000{,}000\text{ mg water}} = 4\text{ ppm F}^-$$

■ EXERCISE 14.1A

What is the concentration in **(a)** ppb and **(b)** ppt that is equivalent to a maximum allowable level in water of 0.1 μg/L of the gasoline additive MTBE (methyl *tert*-butyl ether)?

■ EXERCISE 14.1B

What is the molarity of the MBTE solution in Exercise 14.1A?

Table 14.6 U.S. Environmental Protection Agency Drinking Water Standards for Selected Substances[a]

Substance	Maximum Contaminant Level (mg/L)
Primary standards: inorganic	
Arsenic	0.010
Barium	2
Copper	1.3
Cyanide ion	0.2
Fluoride ion	4.0
Lead	0.015
Nitrate ion	10[b]
Primary standards: organic	
Atrazine	0.003
Benzene	0.005
p-Dichlorobenzene	0.075
Dichloromethane	0.005
Heptachlor	0.0004
Lindane	0.0002
Toluene	1
Trichloroethylene	0.005
Secondary standards (nonenforceable)	
Chloride ion	250
Iron	0.3
Manganese	0.05
Silver	0.10
Sulfate ion	250
Total dissolved solids	500
Zinc	5

[a]A more extensive list and a more detailed explanation of the rules can be found on the EPA Web site.

[b]Measured as N. When measured as nitrate ion, the level is 45 mg/L.

But Not a Drop to Drink

Clean drinking water is scarce in Bangladesh and the Indian state of West Bengal, one of the poorest regions in the world. This area is also ravaged frequently by floods. The surface waters that supplied drinking water for most of the region until about 40 years ago were often contaminated by disease-causing microorganisms. During the 1970s, UNICEF and the World Bank provided funds for the construction of thousands of tubewells to provide a consistent supply of clean drinking water within 100 m of every family. The project halved the infant mortality rate during the 1980s.

Much to everyone's surprise, the wells brought a new risk: chronic arsenic poisoning. Arsenic occurs naturally in the mineral formations of the region, and it has contaminated the water collecting in many of the wells. Arsenic poisoning threatens over 100 million people in Bangladesh and West Bengal, perhaps as much as half the area's population. The initial stages of arsenic poisoning are characterized by skin pigmentation, warts, diarrhea, and ulcers. Arsenic also damages the lungs, kidneys, and other internal organs. In the most severe cases, arsenic poisoning causes liver and renal deficiencies or cancer that can lead to death. Deeper, more expensive wells that reach water below the arsenic-containing formations can alleviate the problem. A simple, inexpensive filter with layers of cast iron turnings, river sand, wood charcoal, and wet brick chips can remove most of the arsenic. However, nearly half of Bangladesh's people live on an income of less than a dollar per day, and even these cheap devices are beyond their reach. Regardless of the methods used, remediation could take decades and cost hundreds of millions of dollars.

▲ A village tubewell in Bangladesh.

Water Treatment

About two-thirds of the population of the United States gets its drinking water from treated surface water (lakes or reservoirs), while the other third uses groundwater supplies (wells and aquifers). Contamination can threaten either of these sources. Most cities in developed nations treat their water supply before it flows into homes (Figure 14.4).

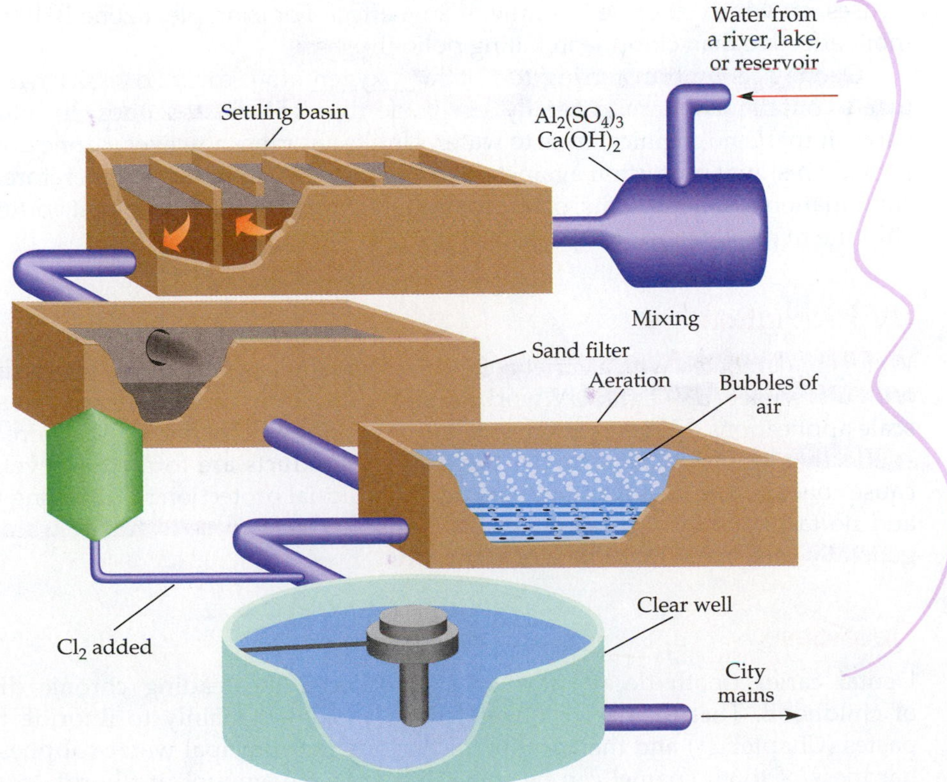

◀ **Figure 14.4** Diagram of a municipal water purification plant. The plant takes water from a river, lake, or waterway and removes suspended matter, kills microorganisms, and adds dissolved air before piping the water to consumers.

Q: *Why are aluminum sulfate and calcium hydroxide added before the water enters the settling basin?*

The water to be purified is usually placed in a settling basin where it is treated with slaked lime and a **flocculent** (a substance that causes particles to clump together), such as alum (aluminum sulfate). These materials react to form a gelatinous mass of aluminum hydroxide.

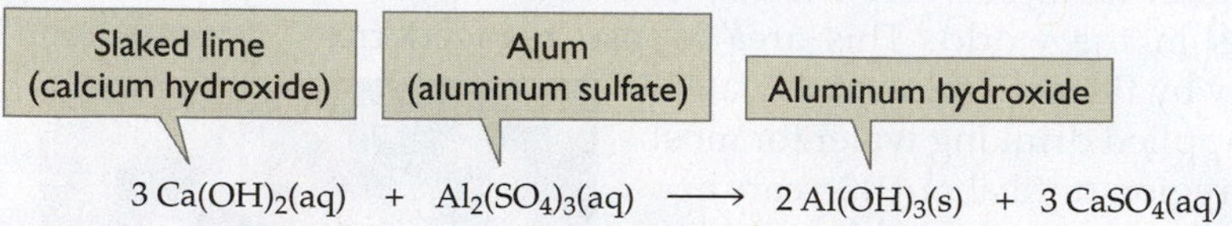

$$3\,Ca(OH)_2(aq) + Al_2(SO_4)_3(aq) \longrightarrow 2\,Al(OH)_3(s) + 3\,CaSO_4(aq)$$

The aluminum hydroxide carries down dirt particles and bacteria. The water is then filtered through sand and gravel, and sometimes through charcoal to remove colored and odorous compounds. The filtered water is usually further treated by *aeration*. It is sprayed into the air to remove odors and improve its taste. Water without dissolved air tastes flat.

Chemical Disinfection

In an emergency, small quantities of water that might be contaminated with bacteria or parasites can be purified. The water is first filtered through a clean cloth and allowed to settle for at least 30 min. It can then be purified by one of the following methods: (1) Heat the water to a full, rolling boil for at least 1 min; then let it cool. (2) Use commercial chlorine or iodine tablets, following the instructions on the package. (3) Pour the clear water into a clear plastic bottle and expose it to direct sunlight for at least 6 h.

In the final step of water treatment, chlorine is added to kill any remaining bacteria. In some communities that use river water, a lot of chlorine is needed to kill all the bacteria, and you can taste the chlorine in the water. Some people question the use of chlorine because it converts dissolved organic compounds into chlorinated hydrocarbons, including trihalomethanes such as chloroform ($CHCl_3$).

Analyses of the drinking water of several cities that take their water from rivers have found chlorinated hydrocarbons, including such known carcinogens as chloroform and carbon tetrachloride. The concentrations are in the parts-per-billion range, probably posing only a small threat, but worrisome nonetheless. (The presence of chlorinated hydrocarbons is not nearly so worrisome, however, as the waterborne diseases that prevail in much of the world where adequate water treatment is not available.)

Chlorination is not the only way to disinfect drinking water. Ozone (O_3) is used widely in Europe and increasingly in the United States. Ozone is more expensive than chlorine, but less of it is needed. An added advantage is that ozone kills viruses, on which chlorine has little, if any, effect. For example, ozone is 100 times more effective than chlorine in killing polioviruses.

Ozone acts by transferring its "extra" oxygen atom to the contaminant. Oxidized contaminants are generally less toxic than chlorinated ones. In addition, ozone imparts no chemical taste to water. Unlike chlorine, however, ozone does not provide residual protection against microorganisms. Some systems therefore use a combination of disinfectants: ozone for initial treatment and subsequent addition of chlorine to provide residual protection.

UV Irradiation

Water contaminated with a variety of microorganisms can be purified by irradiation with ultraviolet (UV) light. UV works rapidly, and it can be cost effective in small-scale applications. No generation, storage, or handling of chemicals is required. UV is effective against *Cryptosporidium*, and no by-products are formed at levels that cause concern. The disadvantages include no residual protection for drinking water and no taste and odor control. UV has limited effectiveness in turbid water and generally costs more than chlorine treatment.

Fluorides

Dental caries (tooth decay) was once considered the leading chronic disease of childhood. That this is no longer true is attributed mainly to fluoride toothpastes (Chapter 21) and the addition of fluoride to municipal water supplies. The hardness of tooth enamel can be correlated with the amount of fluoride present.

Tooth enamel is a complex calcium phosphate called *hydroxyapatite*. Fluoride ions replace some of the hydroxide ions, forming a harder mineral called *fluorapatite*.

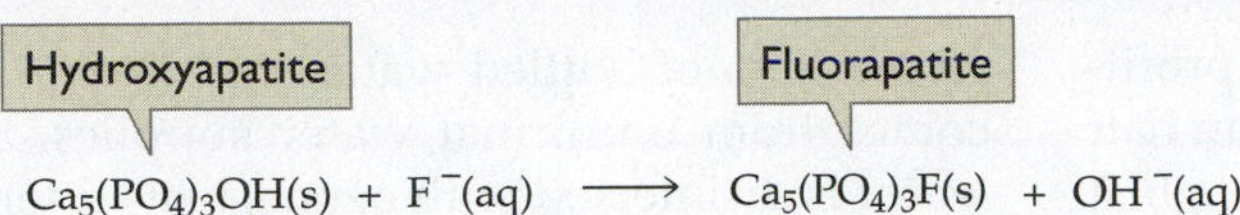

$$Ca_5(PO_4)_3OH(s) + F^-(aq) \longrightarrow Ca_5(PO_4)_3F(s) + OH^-(aq)$$

The fluoride concentration in the drinking water of many communities has been adjusted to 0.7–1.0 ppm (by mass) by adding fluoride, usually as H_2SiF_6 or Na_2SiF_6. Early studies showed reductions in the incidence of dental caries by 50–70%. More recent studies show a much smaller effect, perhaps because of the widespread use of fluoride toothpastes and the presence of fluoride in food products prepared with fluoridated water.

Some people object to water fluoridation. Fluoride salts are acute poisons in moderate to high concentrations. Indeed, sodium fluoride (NaF) is used as a poison for roaches and rats. Small amounts of fluoride ion, however, seem to contribute to our well-being through strengthening bones and teeth. There is some concern about the cumulative effects of consuming fluorides in drinking water, in the diet, in toothpaste, and from other sources. Excessive fluoride consumption during early childhood can cause mottling of tooth enamel. The enamel becomes brittle in certain areas and gradually discolors. Fluorides in high doses also interfere with calcium metabolism, with kidney action, with thyroid function, and with the actions of other glands and organs. Although there is little or no evidence that optimal fluoridation causes problems such as these, the fluoridation of public water supplies will most likely remain a subject of controversy.

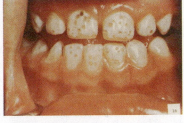

▲ Excessive fluoride consumption in early childhood can cause mottling of tooth enamel. The severe case shown here was caused by continuous consumption during childhood of water from a supply that had an excessive natural concentration of fluoride.

Self-Assessment Questions

1. About how many substances are regulated under EPA drinking water standards?
   a. 25 b. 45 c. 90 d. 180
2. A value of 3 ppm of dissolved oxygen means
   a. 3 mg O_2/L H_2O b. 3 mg O_2/mL H_2O
   c. 3 g O_2/mL H_2O d. 3 g O_2/L H_2O
3. In treatment of public water supplies, flocculation
   a. helps remove dirt and bacteria
   b. improves taste
   c. kills bacteria
   d. kills viruses
4. Public water supplies are aerated to
   a. improve the taste
   b. kill bacteria
   c. remove suspended matter
   d. remove trihalomethanes
5. Chlorine is added to public water supplies to
   a. improve the taste
   b. kill bacteria
   c. remove suspended matter
   d. remove trihalomethanes
6. What advantage does treatment of water with O_3 have over chlorination?
   a. O_3 is cheaper than Cl_2.
   b. O_3 provides residual protection; Cl_2 does not.
   c. Oxygenated by-products are generally less toxic than chlorinated by-products.
   d. Sedimentation is eliminated.
7. Fluoridation of drinking water strengthens tooth enamel by converting hydroxyapatite to
   a. $CaCO_3$ b. CaF_2
   c. fluorapatite d. fluorotartrate

Answers: 1, c; 2, a; 3, a; 4, a; 5, b; 6, c; 7, c

The Newest Soft Drink: Bottled Water

Bottled water is a fast-growing and extremely profitable segment of the beverage industry. More than half of all Americans drink bottled water, even though it costs 240–10,000 times as much per liter as tap water. Per capita consumption is 50 billion bottles per year in the United States and 200 billion bottles per year worldwide. This high level of consumption is based largely on the misconception that bottled water is safer or healthier than tap water.

The federal government considers bottled water a food, and therefore, it is regulated by the Food and Drug Administration (FDA) rather than the EPA. Although the FDA has adopted the EPA standards for tap water as the standards for bottled water, testing of bottled water is typically less rigorous than testing of municipal water.

Because municipal water supplies are usually chlorinated, tap water can have a chlorine taste. This taste might cause some to buy bottled water, but beware: About 25% of bottled water sold in the United States comes from municipal water supplies. Some bottled water is disinfected with ozone, just as some municipal water supplies are.

Just because water comes in a bottle with a glacier and a mountain spring on the label does not necessarily mean that it is "more pure." Mineral water in fact is likely to have *more dissolved ions* (typically Ca^{2+} and Mg^{2+}) than normal tap water. Fortunately, in the United States in general, both bottled water and tap water are quite safe. Yet some people will continue to buy bottled water for its convenience, taste, and assumed (but not actual) health benefits.

It takes about 1.5 million barrels of oil to make the polyethylene terephthalate (PET) water bottles that Americans use each year, enough to fuel 100,000 cars for a year. Only about 23% of those bottles are recycled. Add the fuel used for transporting bottled water to stores, and its environmental cost is even higher.

14.7 Wastewater Treatment

Learning Objective › Describe primary, secondary, and tertiary treatment of wastewater.

The wastes generated by nearly two-thirds of the U.S. population are gathered in sewer systems and carried to treatment plants by more than 50 billion L of water each day. The drinking water for two-thirds of the U.S. population comes from reservoirs, lakes, and rivers, and much of it has been used by other municipalities upstream. Cities have to treat the used water before discharging it back into the environment, but about 10% of it passes untreated into streams or the ocean. Treatment and purification of wastewater render it suitable for return to the water cycle.

Sewage Treatment Methods

For decades, most communities treated sewage simply by holding it in settling ponds for a while before discharging the effluent into a stream, lake, or ocean, a process now called **primary sewage treatment** (Figure 14.5). Primary treatment removes 40–60% of suspended solids as *sludge* and about 30% of organic matter. The effluent still has a BOD level two-thirds of the original level and nearly all its

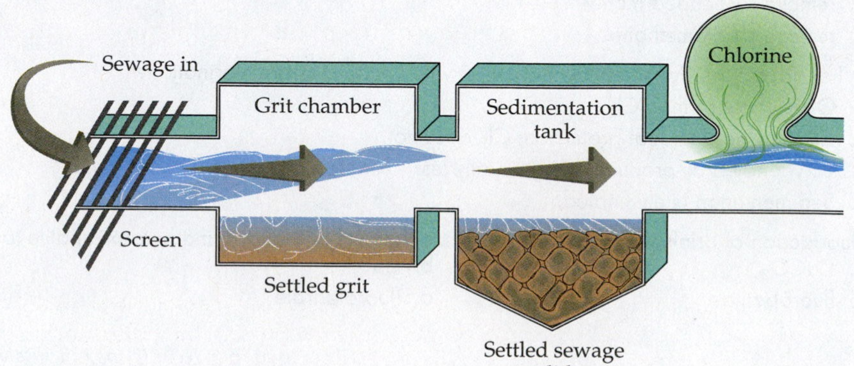

▶ **Figure 14.5** Diagram of a primary sewage treatment plant. Many years ago, sewage might be dumped into a river or stream without treatment. Today, wastewater is treated to some degree to minimize its effect on waterways.

Q: *Why isn't primary treatment alone sufficient for wastewater purification?*

nitrates and phosphates. All the dissolved oxygen in the pond may be used up, and anaerobic decomposition—with its resulting odors—takes over.

In **secondary sewage treatment**, the effluent from primary treatment is passed through sand and gravel filters. There is some aeration in this step, and aerobic bacteria convert much of the organic matter to inorganic materials. In the **activated sludge method** (Figure 14.6), a combination of primary and secondary treatment methods, the sewage is placed in tanks and aerated with large blowers. This causes the formation of large, porous clumps called *flocs*, which filter and absorb contaminants. Aerobic bacteria further convert the organic material to sludge. Part of the sludge is recycled to keep the process going, but huge quantities must be removed for disposal. This sludge is stored on land (where it requires large areas), dumped at sea (where it pollutes the ocean), or burned in incinerators (which requires energy—such as natural gas—and can contribute to air pollution). Some of the sludge is used as fertilizer.

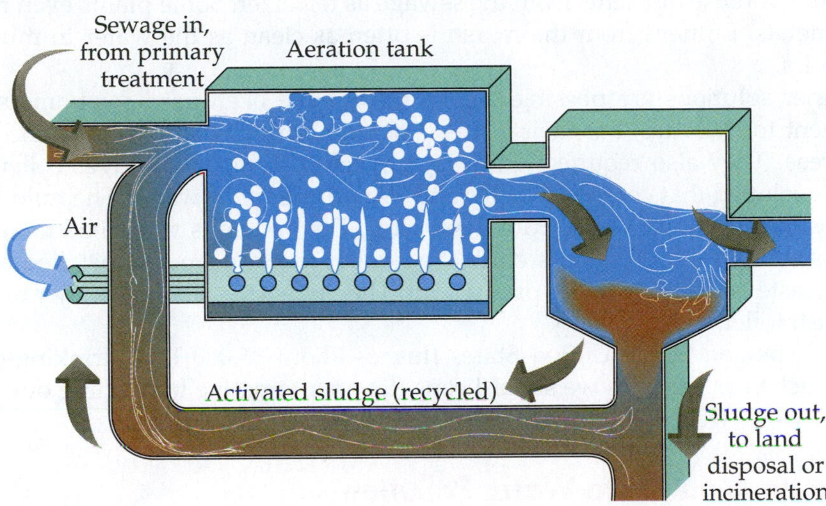

◀ **Figure 14.6** Diagram of a secondary sewage treatment plant that uses the activated sludge method.

Q: *After organic matter is converted to sludge, why is some of the sludge recycled to the aeration tank?*

Secondary treatment of wastewater lowers the BOD by about 90% but often does not adequately reduce nitrates and phosphates. To an increasing extent, federal mandates require **advanced treatment** (sometimes called *tertiary treatment*). Several advanced processes are in use, and most are quite costly.

- In **charcoal filtration**, charcoal adsorbs certain organic molecules, including trihalomethanes such as chloroform ($CHCl_3$), that are difficult to remove by any other method. The organic molecules are adsorbed on the surface of the charcoal and thus removed from the water. After a period of time, the charcoal becomes saturated and is no longer effective. It can be regenerated by heating it to drive off the adsorbed substances.
- In **reverse osmosis**, pressure forces the wastewater through a semipermeable membrane, leaving contaminants behind.
- **Phytoremediation** involves passage of the effluent into large natural or constructed lagoons for storage, allowing plants such as reeds to remove metals and other contaminants.

Finding the money to finance adequate sewage treatment will be a major political problem for years to come.

The effluent from sewage plants is usually treated with chlorine to kill any remaining pathogenic microorganisms before it is returned to a waterway. Chlorination has been quite effective in preventing the spread of waterborne infectious diseases such as typhoid fever. Further, some chlorine remains in the water, providing residual protection against pathogenic bacteria. However, chlorination is not effective against some viruses such as those that cause hepatitis.

5. Is bottled water safer than tap water? As noted in the text, bottled water is often just tap water that has been put into plastic bottles! It has never been demonstrated to be healthier or safer than tap water, nor has it been shown to be more hazardous to health than tap water. Bottled water is largely just a convenience.

Water Pollution and the Future

For most of human history, our body wastes were an integral part of Earth's natural recycling system. The wastes provided food for microorganisms that degraded them, returning nutrients to soil and water. But with the growth of cities, human waste became disconnected from the cycle. We now dump our wastes in waterways, fouling the water and wasting nutrients that could fertilize the land.

Many communities dry and sterilize sludge and then transport it to farmlands for return of nutrients to the soil. Others pump wet, suspended sludge directly to the fields. The water in the mixture irrigates the crops, and the sludge provides nutrients and humus. One concern is that the sludge is often contaminated with toxic metals that could be taken up by plants and eventually end up in our food.

A few communities treat their sewage by first holding it in sedimentation tanks, where the solids settle out as a sludge that is removed and processed for use as fertilizer. The effluent is then diverted into a marshy area where the marsh plants filter the water and use nutrients from the sewage as fertilizer. Some plants even remove toxic metals. Effluent from the marsh is often as clean as the water in municipal reservoirs.

Other solutions are possible. Septic tanks have been used for home sewage treatment for decades, but their use is generally limited to rural and some suburban areas. They also require significant upkeep to remain effective. Toilets have been developed that compost wastes and use no energy or water. The mild heat of composting drives off water from the wastes. The system is ventilated to keep the process aerobic, and no odors enter the house from a properly installed system. Dried waste is removed about once a year. The initial cost is much higher than that of a flush toilet.

Each person in the United States flushes about 35,000 L of drinking-quality water each year. Perhaps we should consider an alternative to flushing our wastes into the water we drink.

We're the Solution to Water Pollution

6. Is water that has been fortified with vitamins better for you? For the average person, water that has been fortified with vitamins, minerals, amino acids, herbal extracts, or other additives is unlikely to have any advantage over plain tap water. Most such additives in bottled water are there for marketing purposes and do not provide any significant health benefit.

We generally take our drinking water for granted. Perhaps we shouldn't. There are between 4000 and 40,000 cases of waterborne illnesses in the United States each year. Twenty million people have no running water at all, and many more obtain water from suspect sources: 10% of public water supplies do not meet one or more of the EPA standards. Another 30 million tap individual wells or springs whose water is often of unknown quality. Much remains to be done before we can all be assured of safe drinking water.

The Clean Water Act has drastically reduced water pollution from industrial sources. However, complete elimination of pollution is not possible—to use water is to pollute it. All of us can do our share by conserving water and by minimizing our use of products that require vast amounts of water to make. As our population grows, it will cost a lot just to maintain present water quality. To clean up our water, and then keep it clean, will cost more. However, the costs of unclean water are even higher—discomfort, loss of recreation, illness, and even death.

Self-Assessment Questions

1. At what stage in sewage treatment do bacteria consume dissolved organic matter?
   a. aeration
   b. primary
   c. secondary
   d. screening and sand removal
2. Trihalomethanes such as chloroform are formed when chlorine reacts with
   a. bacteria
   b. dissolved organic compounds
   c. ethanol
   d. phenols
3. Trihalomethanes such as chloroform can be removed from water by
   a. charcoal filtration
   b. chlorination
   c. flocculation
   d. sand filtration

4. Reverse osmosis is a way to purify water by using pressure to force the water through a
   a. charcoal filter b. sand filter
   c. semipermeable membrane d. trickling filter
5. A wastewater treatment plant treats 500,000 gal of sewage per day, using 16 lb of chlorine per day. Assume that 1 gal of sewage weighs about 8 lb. The chlorine concentration, in parts per million, of the wastewater is about
   a. 1 ppm b. 4 ppm c. 8 ppm d. 16 ppm

Answers: 1, c; 2, b; 3, a; 4, c; 5, b

CRITICAL THINKING  EXERCISES

Apply knowledge that you have gained in this chapter and one or more of the FLaReS principles (Chapter 1) to evaluate the following statements or claims.

14.1 An activist group claims that all chlorine compounds should be banned because they are toxic.

14.2 A mother discovers that tests have found 1.0 ppb of trichloroethylene in the well water her family uses for drinking, bathing, cooking, and so on. The family has used the well for 2 years. The mother decides that the whole family should be tested for cancer.

14.3 A group of citizens wants to ban fluoridation of a community water supply because fluorides are toxic.

14.4 A company claims that its "super-oxygenated water can boost athletic performance." (Note that, under pressure, the water could contain at most 0.3 g O_2/L H_2O, the amount in a 1-L breath.)

14.5 A company claims that its "oxygenated and structured water has smaller molecules that penetrate more quickly into the cells, and therefore hydrate your body faster and more efficiently."

SUMMARY

Section 14.1—Water has unusual properties: It is the only common liquid on Earth; its solid form is less dense than the liquid; and it is more dense than most other common liquids. **Specific heat** is the heat needed to raise the temperature of 1 g of a substance by 1 °C; for water, it is quite high: 1 cal/g °C. Water also has a high **heat of vaporization**, the amount of heat required to vaporize a fixed amount of water. These properties arise because of strong hydrogen bonding between water molecules.

Section 14.2—Water covers three-fourths of Earth's surface, but only about 1% of it is available as fresh water for human use. Water dissolves many ionic substances, which is why the oceans are salty. Potable water is readily available in most parts of the United States, but many other countries do not have enough fresh water. In the water (hydrological) cycle, water evaporates from oceans and lakes, condenses into clouds, and returns to Earth as rain or snow. During this cycle, it can be contaminated by various chemicals and microorganisms from both natural sources and human activities. **Hard water** is formed when minerals (salts of calcium, magnesium, and/or iron) dissolve in groundwater.

Section 14.3—Waterborne diseases such as cholera, typhoid fever, and dysentery were a severe problem until about 100 years ago and are still common in many parts of the world. Acid rain created by the release of sulfur oxides and nitrogen oxides when coal and other fuels are burned has caused acidification of thousands of bodies of water in North America. Besides corrosive effects, acid rain is detrimental to both plant and animal life. When sewage is dumped into waterways, the organic matter is biodegraded by microorganisms. **Aerobic oxidation** occurs in the presence of **dissolved oxygen**, and the **biochemical oxygen demand (BOD)** is a measure of the amount of oxygen needed. Sewage increases the BOD. If the BOD is high enough, only **anaerobic decay**, or decay in the absence of oxygen, can occur. High levels of nitrates and phosphates can accelerate **eutrophication**, in which algae grow and die, thereby increasing the BOD of the water. Other new substances introduced into the water cycle may cause new problems.

Section 14.4—Producing industrial and consumer products uses a great deal of water, which is polluted in the process and must be cleaned up and recycled. We need only about 1.5–2.0 L of water per day for drinking, but in the United States, each person directly uses a total of about 380 L per day.

Section 14.5—About half of the U.S. population drinks surface water and half drinks groundwater; use of groundwater is especially common in rural areas. The aquifers into which wells are drilled are being consumed faster than they are being recharged by precipitation, and deeper wells are now required in many places. Well water may be contaminated with various chemicals, including nitrates and VOCs.

Section 14.6—The U.S. Safe Water Drinking Act sets and enforces standards for water quality. In many cases, concentrations of contaminants must be expressed in tiny units such as parts per million (ppm) or parts per billion (ppb).

Treatment of water to make it safe to drink usually includes settling, treatment with a **flocculent** (to cause particles to clump together and settle out), filtration, aeration, and chemical disinfection with chlorine or ozone. Fluorides may also be added to prevent tooth decay.

Section 14.7—Treatment of wastewater (used water) begins with **primary sewage treatment**, allowing the wastes to settle and removing sludge before discharging the water into the environment. In **secondary sewage treatment**, the effluent is filtered through sand and gravel. The **activated sludge method**, in which the sewage is aerated and the sludge is removed, may be used instead. **Advanced treatment** (tertiary treatment) may involve **charcoal filtration** to adsorb organic compounds, **reverse osmosis** to remove contaminants by forcing the wastewater through a semipermeable membrane, or **phytoremediation**, to allow plants to remove metals and other contaminants by storing the wastewater in lagoons. These advanced processes are expensive.

Alternative methods for sewage treatment are being investigated. Maintaining water quality is expensive and will become more so, but not maintaining it will cost much more in terms of our health and comfort.

Green chemistry With their large pore volumes and surface areas, zeolites and related mesoporous materials can be used to clean contaminated waters. Zeolites can be used in applications that require replacement of ions, while mesoporous materials can be tailored to remove toxic heavy metals from water.

Learning Objectives

› Relate water's unique properties to the polarity and the hydrogen bonding of its molecules.	Problems 1, 2, 9, 13–15
› Explain how water on the surface of Earth acts to moderate daily temperature variations.	Problems 10–12, 14
› Explain why humans can use less than 1% of all the water on Earth.	Problems 16–20
› Describe how human activities affect water quality.	Problems 3–8, 18, 21–26
› Give an example of a biological water contaminant.	Problems 3, 4
› Know the major uses of water.	Problems 26, 44, 51
› List some groundwater contaminants.	Problems 5–8, 18, 30
› Identify the sources of nitrates in groundwater.	Problem 30
› Describe how water is purified for drinking and other household uses.	Problems 27, 29
› Describe primary, secondary, and tertiary treatment of wastewater.	Problems 31–35, 38, 43
› Describe the structures of zeolites and mesoporous materials.	Problems 53–55, 57
› Explain how zeolites and mesoporous materials can be used to clean up contaminated water.	Problems 53, 56

REVIEW QUESTIONS

1. A tanker filled with light crude oil sinks and breaks open. Will the oil dissolve in the water? Will it float or sink?
2. Why should foods be frozen swiftly rather than slowly?
3. What are pathogenic microorganisms?
4. List some waterborne diseases. Why are these diseases no longer common in developed countries?
5. List some ways in which groundwater is contaminated.
6. What problems do leaking underground storage tanks cause?
7. Why do chlorinated hydrocarbons remain in groundwater for such a long time?
8. List some common industrial contaminants of groundwater.

PROBLEMS

Properties of Water

9. Why is ice less dense than liquid water? What consequences does this property have for life in northern lakes?
10. Define *specific heat*. Why is the high specific heat of water important to Earth?

For Problems 11 and 12, you may wish to consult the Appendix, part A.5, "Calculations Involving Temperature and Heat."

11. Refer to Table 14.1. How much heat, in calories, does it take to warm 875 g of water from 3.0 °C to 37.0 °C?
12. How much heat, in calories, does it take to warm 875 g of iron from 3.0 °C to 37.0 °C? How does this compare to the

heat required to warm an equal quantity of water to the same extent? (See Problem 11.)

13. Why is the high heat of vaporization of water important to our bodily functions?

14. Why is it cooler near a lake than inland during the summer?

15. Why does your skin feel cool when you step out of a swimming pool into a breeze?

16. Why are oceans salty? Are they getting saltier?

Natural Waters

17. What impurities are present in rainwater?

18. What are the products of the breakdown of organic matter by anaerobic decay?

19. Water containing more than 3.0 grains of dissolved solids per gallon is considered to be hard [1 grain (gr) = 64.8 mg]. What is this "hardness limit" in milligrams of dissolved solids per liter?

20. Refer to Problem 19. A kettle contains 18 gal of tap water, which is allowed to evaporate. The solid material left behind has a mass of 1.7 g. Is the tap water considered to be hard?

Acidic Waters

21. List two ways in which lakes and streams become acidified.

22. List several ways in which the acidity of rain can be reduced.

23. Acidic water that is neutralized by natural rock often becomes hard water. Explain.

24. Water from a pond is found to have high levels of ammonia and methane and relatively low levels of carbon dioxide and nitrate ions. What kind of decay has probably occurred in this pond?

25. Why is acidic water especially harmful to fish?

26. How much water does a person need per day for drinking? How much water does the average person in the United States use indirectly?

Municipal Water Supplies

27. What is the optimal level of fluoride in drinking water?

28. What are some health effects of too much fluoride in the diet?

29. Can water be disinfected without adding chemicals? Explain.

30. What is methemoglobinemia? How is it caused?

Wastewater Treatment

31. Describe primary sewage treatment. What impurities does it remove?

32. Describe secondary sewage treatment. What impurities does it remove?

33. What substances remain in wastewater after effective secondary treatment?

34. Describe the activated sludge method of sewage treatment.

35. Identify each of the following as a primary, secondary, or tertiary method of wastewater treatment.
   a. charcoal filtration **b.** settling pond
   c. trickling filters

36. What are the advantages and disadvantages of spreading sewage sludge on farmland?

Chemical Equations

37. Write the balanced equation for the neutralization of acid rain (assume HNO_3 is dissolved in water) by limestone (calcium carbonate).

38. Write the balanced equation for the reaction of slaked lime (calcium hydroxide) with alum (aluminum sulfate) to form aluminum hydroxide used in wastewater treatment.

Parts per Million and Parts per Billion

39. Express each aqueous concentration in the unit indicated.
   a. 11 μg of benzene per liter of water, as ppb of benzene
   b. 0.014% $BaCO_3$, by mass, as ppm $BaCO_3$

40. Express each aqueous concentration in the unit indicated.
   a. 25 μg of trichloroethylene in 9.5 L of water, as ppb of trichloroethylene
   b. 38 g Cl_2 in 1.00×10^4 L of water, as ppm Cl_2

41. A 2.0-L sample of drinking water is found to contain 18 μg of copper and 16 mg of nitrate ion. Do either of these concentrations exceed the standards in Table 14.6?

42. A 0.50-L sample of drinking water is found to contain 4.0 μg of toluene. Does this exceed the standard in Table 14.6?

Additional Problems

43. What types of substances are most effectively removed by each of the following methods of water purification? Of the substances $CHCl_3$, NaCl, phosphate ion, and sand, which one(s) is effectively removed from water by each?
   a. charcoal filtration **b.** distillation
   c. filtration

44. Describe a modern alternative to the flush toilet.

45. Which takes more energy per gram: melting ice (solid at 0 °C to liquid at 0 °C) or boiling water (liquid at 100 °C to gas at 100 °C)? Explain briefly.

46. Express each aqueous concentration in the unit indicated.
   a. 2.4 ppm F^-, as molarity of fluoride ion
   b. 45 ppm NO_3^-, as molarity of nitrate ion
   c. Why do some scientists prefer to express concentrations of water contaminants in the units ppm and ppb rather than molarity?

47. Wastewater disinfected with chlorine must be dechlorinated before it is returned to sensitive bodies of water. The dechlorinating agent is often sulfur dioxide. The reaction is

$$Cl_2 + SO_2 + 2\,H_2O \longrightarrow 2\,Cl^- + SO_4^{2-} + 4\,H^+$$

Is the chlorine oxidized or reduced? Identify the oxidizing agent and reducing agent in the reaction.

48. Look back at the molecular formulas for volatile organic compounds (VOCs) on page 397. Write structural formulas for the following compounds.
   a. benzene **b.** toluene
   c. chloroform **d.** methylene chloride
   e. trichloroethylene

49. Radioactive aluminum-26 is used to study the release of aluminum ions by acidic waters. When it decays, the isotope is transmuted into magnesium-26. What kind of particle is emitted in this decay process?

50. The text indicates that radioactive radon gas is slightly soluble in water. What are the intermolecular forces responsible for the solubility?

51. A typical gas-fired home water heater holds 50 gal of water and has the thermostat set to 60 °C.
   a. If the inlet water supply is at 12 °C, how much heat, in kilocalories, is needed to bring the contents of the water heater to the set temperature? (1 gal = 3.8 L)
   b. Burning 1.00 mol of methane (CH_4), the major component of natural gas, produces 890 kJ of energy. What mass (in grams) of methane must be burned to produce the amount of heat determined in part (a)?
   c. What volume in cubic feet (at STP) of methane does the mass from part (b) correspond to? (1 ft^3 = 28.3 L)
   d. A *therm* of natural gas is about 100 ft^3 and costs about $1.50 (average U.S. price in 2011). Use the results from parts (a)–(c) to calculate how much it costs to take a 15-minute shower at a usage rate of 2.5 gal of hot water per minute.

52. How much calcium nitrate has to be added to 1000 L of solution to provide 180 ppm Ca^{2+} if the water supply contains 40 ppm Ca^{2+}? How much NO_3^-, in ppm, does this quantity of calcium nitrate add to the solution?

53. Which of the following ions cannot be exchanged by zeolites?
   a. Ca^{2+} b. Mg^{2+} c. PO_4^{3-} d. K^+

54. Which elements typically make up zeolite frameworks?

55. The chemical formula of a zeolite can be expressed as (__$AlSi_3O_8$), where the blank (__) represents the charge-balancing cation. Which one of the following satisfies the charge balance in the formula?
   a. one sodium atom
   b. two sodium atoms
   c. one calcium atom
   d. two calcium atoms

56. You have 2000 L of water contaminated by arsenic at a concentration of 50 ppb. (a) What mass, in grams, of a mesoporous material that can bind to heavy metal ions would be needed to reduce the concentration to 5 ppb (that is, below EPA limits)? Assume that the mesoporous material has a binding capacity of 500 mg As/g. (b) Find the mass of the mesoporous material that would be needed to completely remove arsenic from Mono Lake (in California), which has an estimated arsenic concentration of 15,000 ppb and a total volume of 3.2×10^{12} L.

57. What pore sizes are specified by the terms *microporous* and *mesoporous*? What size of pores do you think is specified by the term *macroporous*?

58. Why is it preferable to design a heavy metal sponge for extracting mercury, as described in the green chemistry essay, using a mesoporous material instead of a zeolite? Compare the physical dimensions of the two materials, assuming that the maximum diameter of the zeolite is 2 nm, the diameter of the mesoporous material is 5 nm, the length of the sulfur-containing organic molecule is 0.9 nm, and the diameter of a mercury atom is 0.35 nm.

COLLABORATIVE GROUP PROJECTS

Prepare a PowerPoint, poster, or other presentation (as directed by your instructor) to share with the class.

1. Consult online or print references, and prepare a report on the desalination of seawater by one of the following methods.
   a. distillation b. freezing
   c. electrodialysis d. reverse osmosis
   e. ion exchange

2. What sort of wastewater treatment is used in your community? Is it adequate?

3. Where does your drinking water come from? What steps are used in purifying it?

4. Call your local water utility's office or consult its Web site and obtain a chemical analysis of your drinking water. What substances are monitored? Are any of these substances considered problems? (If you use water from a private well, has the water been analyzed? If so, what were the results?)

5. The Web site of the EPA's Office of Wastewater Management (OWM) has a menu of numerous water-related topics. Choose one, and write a few paragraphs about that aspect of wastewater management.

6. Poll your class on consumption of bottled water. About how many bottles do they drink each year? Why do your classmates use it? Are there concerns regarding its purity?

7. Using the OWM site or your state's environmental Web site, see what you can learn about the water quality where you live.

8. The EPA's Web site identifies Superfund sites with a National Priorities List and a list by regions. These sites are uncontrolled or abandoned places where hazardous waste is located. If not cleaned up, these wastes can affect nearby people and ecosystems. Prepare a report on a site in your region, listing, if possible, the toxic materials involved.

9. Using the Web site of the Natural Resources Defense Council (NRDC) or another environmental group, investigate pollution from urban stormwater runoff, which some say rivals sewage plants and factories as a source of water contamination. Write a brief report on your findings.

Energy

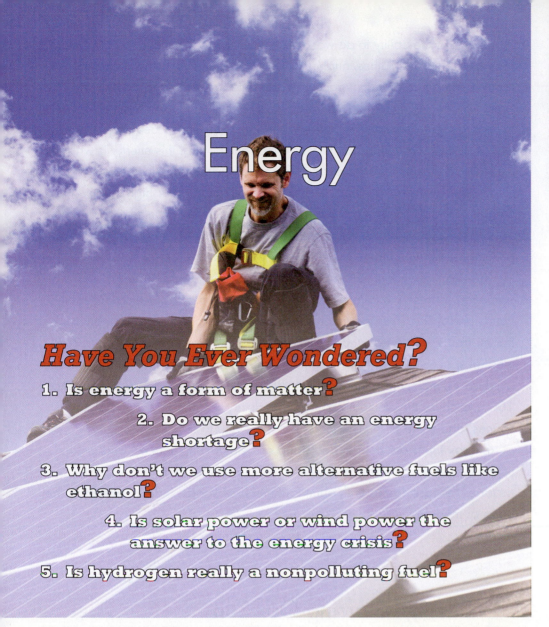

Have You Ever Wondered?

1. Is energy a form of matter?
2. Do we really have an energy shortage?
3. Why don't we use more alternative fuels like ethanol?
4. Is solar power or wind power the answer to the energy crisis?
5. Is hydrogen really a nonpolluting fuel?

Learning Objectives

- Perform power and energy calculations. (15.1)
- Classify chemical reactions and physical processes as exothermic or endothermic. (15.2)
- List factors that affect the rates of chemical reactions. (15.2)
- State the first and second laws of thermodynamics, and discuss their implications for energy production and use. (15.3)
- List the common fossil fuels, and describe how modern society is based on their use. (15.4)
- List advantages and disadvantages of coal as a fuel. (15.5)
- List the characteristics of natural gas and petroleum. (15.6)
- List advantages and disadvantages of natural gas and petroleum as fuels. (15.6)
- Explain why gaseous and liquid fuels are more convenient to use than solid fuels. (15.7)
- List advantages and disadvantages of nuclear energy. (15.8)
- Describe how a nuclear power plant generates electricity. (15.8)
- List important characteristics of renewable energy sources. (15.9)
- List advantages and disadvantages of various kinds of renewable energy. (15.9)
- Explain how applying the green chemistry principles can help identify improved methods for energy generation.
- Identify waste products from some current energy-generation processes.

A Fuel's Paradise

We were tempted to call this chapter "Fire" in order to have the titles of Chapters 12, 13, 14, and 15 be "Earth," "Air," "Water," and "Fire"—the four elements of the ancient Greeks.

Actually, "Fire" could be an appropriate title for this chapter. We obtain most of our energy by burning fuels, which certainly involves fire. Many sources of energy do not involve burning anything, however, and we will depend more heavily on these other sources as our reserves of fossil fuels are depleted.

Nearly all Earth's energy comes indirectly from the Sun, a nuclear fusion reactor about 150 million km away. The wind that drives windmills is a result of solar heating. Biofuels such as biodiesel and biomass come from plants, which use sunlight as their source of energy. Even fossil fuels are derived from the sun. An increasingly popular method of directly harnessing solar energy is the use of solar cells that convert sunlight to electricity. Today it is possible to buy enough solar cells to run an entire house, at fairly reasonable prices. In this chapter, we will look at the general nature and properties of energy and at various ways of generating energy or converting it from one form to another. Only tiny fractions of the energy we use come from Earth's internal heat, visible in geysers and tapped as geothermal energy, and from the Moon-powered tides.

1. Is energy a form of matter?

Energy is not matter. Unlike matter, energy has no mass and does not occupy volume. Energy is the *ability* of matter to do work. For example, thermal energy is the energy of molecules in motion. The moving molecules can do work.

Energy is the ability to do work (see Chapter 1). Everything we consume or use—our food and clothes, our homes and their contents, our cars and roads—requires energy to produce, package, distribute, operate, and discard. The United States, with less than 5% of the world's population, uses one-fifth of all the energy generated on the planet. Abundant energy provides people in the United States with a high standard of living. But much of this energy is wasted. Australia, Switzerland, France, and the Scandinavian countries achieve higher standards of living with lower per capita use of energy. Our high energy consumption has enormous costs: to our health, to the environment, and to our national security. It affects our foreign debt and the stability of other countries. It pollutes the air we breathe and the water we drink.

Industry uses about 30% of all energy produced in the United States. This energy is used to convert raw materials to the many products our society needs and wants. Transportation uses about 29%, to power automobiles, trucks, trains, airplanes, and buses. Private homes use about 22%, and commercial spaces use about 19%. Utilities use about 38% of the nation's energy production, mainly to generate electricity. (These figures add up to more than 100% because the electricity is used in industry, homes, and commercial spaces, and some of it is therefore counted twice.)

Energy lights our homes, heats and cools our living spaces, and makes us the most mobile society in the history of the human race. It powers the factories that provide us with abundant material goods. Indeed, energy is the basis of modern civilization.

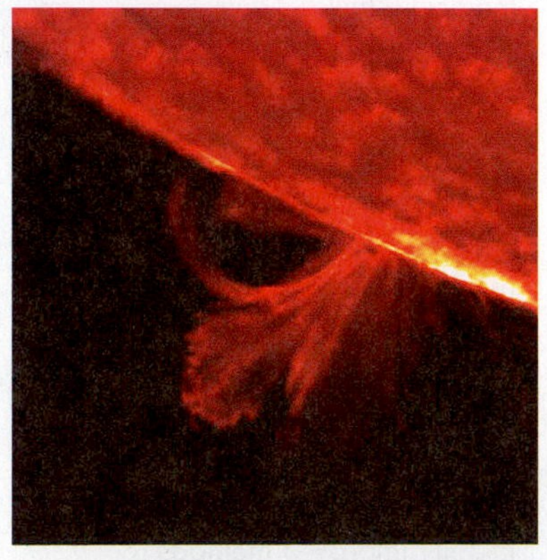

▲ Each second, the Sun fuses more than 600 million t of hydrogen into about 1 million t of helium and converts 4000 kg of hydrogen to energy in the form of gamma rays. Within the sun, the energy is absorbed and re-emitted at ever longer wavelengths, reaching the surface mainly as visible light. The Sun has enough hydrogen to last another 5 billion years. The solar flare shown here is over twenty times larger than Earth.

15.1 Energy: Starring Our Sun

Learning Objectives › Perform power and energy calculations.

All living things on Earth— including us—depend on nuclear energy for survival. Most of the energy available to us on this planet comes from the giant nuclear reactor we call the Sun. Although the Sun is about 150 million km away, it has supplied Earth with most of its energy for billions of years, and is likely to continue to do so for billions more (Table 15.1).

The SI unit of energy is the joule (J). A *watt* (W), the SI unit of power, is 1 joule per second (J/s).

$$1\,\text{W} = 1\frac{\text{J}}{\text{s}}$$

A unit of more convenient size is the kilowatt: 1 kW = 1000 W. To express energy consumption, the watt is combined with a unit of time. For example, electricity usage is usually measured (and billed for) in terms of the *kilowatt hour (kWh)*, the quantity of energy used by a 1-kW device in 1 h. There are 3600 seconds in an hour, so 1 kWh = 3600 kJ. Power is the *rate* at which energy is used (just as speed is the *rate* at which distance is covered).

Recall (Chapter 11) that the Sun is a nuclear fusion reactor that steadily converts hydrogen to helium. The Sun has a power output of 4×10^{26} W. Earth receives only about 1 part in 50 *billion* of this energy. Even so, this tiny fraction is equivalent to over 100 million nuclear power plants. In three days, Earth receives energy from the Sun equivalent to all our fossil fuel reserves!

Table 15.1 Earth's Energy Ledger (Estimated)

Item	Energy (TW)[a]	Approximate Percent
Energy in		
Solar radiation	174,000	99.97%
Internal heat	46	0.025%
Tides	3	0.002
Waste heat[b]	13	0.007
Energy out		
Direct reflection	52,000	30
Direct heating[c]	81,000	47
Water cycle[c]	40,000	23
Winds[c]	370	0.2
Photosynthesis[c]	40	0.02

[a]TW (terawatt) = 10^{12} W.
[b]From fossil fuel use.
[c]This energy is eventually returned to space by means of long-wave radiation (heat).

▲ **It DOES Matter!**
Consumers often have misconceptions about energy usage in the home. Appliances that generate or transfer heat usually consume a lot of energy. The two major energy "sinks" in most homes are the heating and cooling system and the water heater. Refrigerators, stoves, toasters, and similar appliances are also energy hogs. Lighting is often responsible for a surprisingly small fraction of the monthly energy bill. An ordinary toaster oven heating a slice of pizza for 10 minutes consumes as much energy as a 20-W fluorescent lightbulb uses in 10 hours.

Example 15.1 Power and Energy Conversion

How much electrical energy, in joules, is consumed by a 75-W bulb burning for 1.0 h?

Solution
One watt is 1 J/s, so we know that 75 W = 75 J/s. The bulb burns for 1 h so

$$1\ \cancel{h} \times \frac{60\ \cancel{min}}{1\ \cancel{h}} \times \frac{60\ s}{1\ \cancel{min}} = 3600\ s$$

$$3600\ \cancel{s} \times \frac{75\ J}{1\ \cancel{s}} = 270{,}000\ J$$

■ EXERCISE 15.1A
How much electrical energy, in joules, does a 650-W microwave oven consume in heating a cup of coffee for 1.0 min?

■ EXERCISE 15.1B
In January 2011, the average cost of residential electricity in the United States was 10.99¢/kWh. A typical desktop computer uses about 150 W. How much does it cost to run such a computer for 3.75 h at that rate?

Kinetic and Potential Energy

Energy exists in two main forms. Energy due to position or arrangement is called **potential energy**. The water at the top of a dam has potential energy due to gravitational attraction. When the water is allowed to flow through a turbine to a lower level, the potential energy is converted to **kinetic energy** (energy of motion). As the water falls, it moves faster. Its kinetic energy increases as its potential energy decreases. The turbine can convert part of the kinetic energy of the water into electrical energy. The electricity thus produced can be carried by wires to homes and factories, where it can be converted to light energy, to heat, or to mechanical energy. Table 15.2 gives examples of kinetic and potential energy.

Table 15.2 Some Examples of Potential and Kinetic Energy

Potential Energy	
Energy stored by position	Water at the top of a waterfall (hydroelectric power; Section 15.9) A hammer poised to drive a nail A rock teetering at the edge of a cliff A swimmer ready to dive
Energy stored in chemical bonds	Fuels (coal, gasoline, natural gas; Sections 15.5–15.7) Foods (carbohydrates, fats, proteins; Chapter 17) Explosives (nitroglycerin, TNT)
Energy stored in atomic nuclei	Nuclear energy (power plants, bombs; Section 15.8)
Kinetic Energy	
Energy of any moving object	A rolling freight train A spinning water turbine (hydroelectric power; Section 15.9) A rolling bowling ball A moving molecule A sailboat skimming across a lake A volleyball being spiked

Energy and the Life-Support System

The *biosphere* is the thin (about 15 km thick) film of air, water, and soil in which all life exists. Only a small fraction of the energy the biosphere receives is used to support life. About 30% of the incident solar radiation is immediately reflected back into space as ultraviolet and visible light. Nearly half is converted to heat, making our planet a warm and habitable place. About 23% of solar radiation powers the water cycle (Section 14.2), evaporating water from land and seas. The radiant energy of the Sun is converted to the potential energy of water vapor, water droplets, and ice crystals in the atmosphere. This potential energy is converted to the kinetic energy of falling rain and snow and of flowing rivers.

A tiny but most important fraction—less than 0.02%—of solar energy is absorbed by green plants, which use it to power **photosynthesis**. In the presence of chlorophyll and a series of enzymes, the energy converts carbon dioxide and water to glucose, a simple sugar rich in energy.

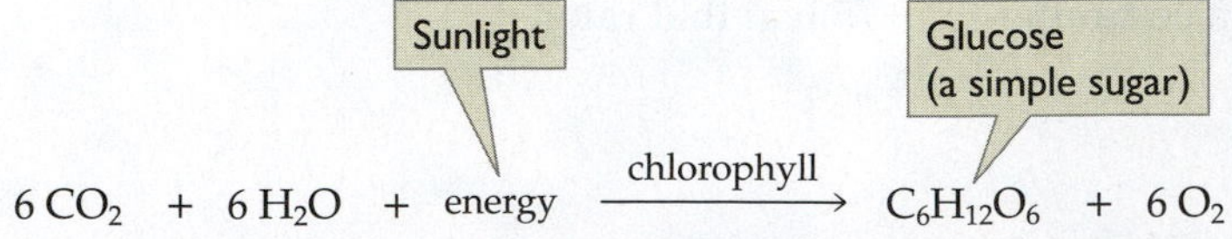

$$6\,CO_2 + 6\,H_2O + \text{energy} \xrightarrow{\text{chlorophyll}} C_6H_{12}O_6 + 6\,O_2$$

Photosynthesis also replenishes oxygen in the atmosphere. Glucose can be stored, or it can be converted to more complex foods and structural materials. All animals depend on the stored energy of green plants for survival.

Self-Assessment Questions

1. The ability or capacity to do work is
   a. force **b.** energy **c.** power **d.** pressure
2. What sector of the U.S. economy uses the largest fraction of the nation's energy?
   a. residential **b.** commercial **c.** industrial **d.** transportation
3. About how much of the world's energy is used by the United States?
   a. 3% **b.** 5% **c.** 10% **d.** 20%

4. An apple hanging on a branch above Isaac Newton's head has
   a. force energy b. kinetic energy c. potential energy d. rotational energy
5. The largest portion of Earth's incident solar radiation
   a. powers the water cycle b. is converted to heat
   c. powers photosynthesis d. is reflected back to space
6. About what percentage of Earth's incident solar radiation is used in photosynthesis?
   a. 0.02% b. 2% c. 5% d. 10%

Answers: 1, b; 2, c; 3, d; 4, c; 5, d; 6, a

15.2 Energy and Chemical Reactions

Learning Objectives › Classify chemical reactions and physical processes as exothermic or endothermic. › List factors that affect the rates of chemical reactions.

A study of chemistry is incomplete without a discussion of energy. Two areas of chemistry that focus on energy are *kinetics* and *thermodynamics*. Chemical kinetics describes the rate at which a chemical reaction occurs. That rate depends on several factors, including temperature, concentrations of reactants, and presence of catalysts.

Reactions generally proceed faster at higher temperatures. For example, at room temperature, coal (carbon) reacts so slowly with oxygen (from the air) that the change is imperceptible. However, if coal is heated to several hundred degrees, it reacts rapidly. The heat evolved in the reaction keeps the coal burning smoothly. We use the kinetic–molecular theory (Section 6.5) to explain this phenomenon. At high temperatures, molecules move faster and collide more frequently, increasing the chance that they will react. The increase in temperature also supplies more energy to break chemical bonds—a condition necessary for most reactions.

The concentrations of reactants affect the rate of most reactions, because when we crowd more molecules into a given volume of space, the molecules collide more often. More collisions each second means more reactions each second. For example, if you light a wood splint and then blow out the flame, the splint continues to glow as the wood reacts slowly with oxygen in the air. If the glowing splint is placed in pure oxygen—five times more concentrated than O_2 in air—the splint bursts into flame because of the increase in reaction rate.

Catalysts also affect the rates of chemical reactions. A carefully selected catalyst can increase the rate of a reaction that otherwise would be so slow as to be impractical. For example, the platinum in your automobile's catalytic converter causes carbon monoxide (CO) to react more rapidly with atmospheric oxygen. This means that less unreacted CO is emitted into our atmosphere. Catalysts are of great importance in the chemical industry and in biology.

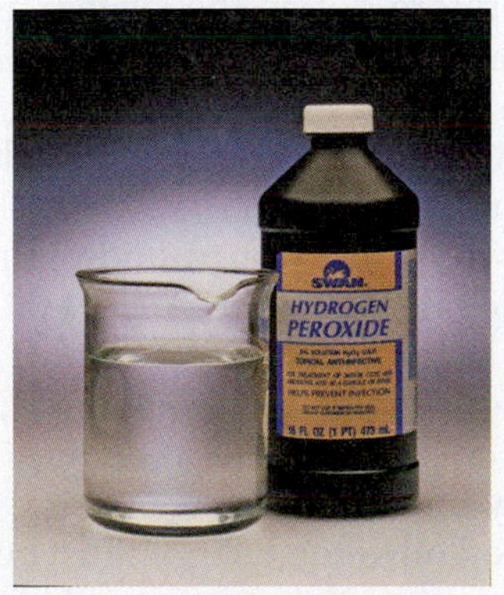

(a)

(b)

▲ The action of a catalyst is illustrated. Hydrogen peroxide decomposes slowly to water and oxygen (a). When platinum metal is inserted into a solution of hydrogen peroxide (b), the reaction proceeds rapidly. The heat released during the process produces steam, and the solution froths as oxygen gas is evolved.

▲ **It DOES Matter!**
We use the effect of temperature on chemical reactions in our daily lives. For example, we refrigerate milk or freeze vegetables to retard the chemical reactions that lead to spoilage. When we want to stir-fry faster, we turn up the temperature.

▲ When liquid oxygen—much more concentrated than oxygen gas—is poured on a lit cigarette, the cigarette sparks, bursts into flame, and quickly disintegrates.

Catalysts are vital in living organisms. Biological catalysts, called *enzymes*, mediate nearly all the chemical reactions that take place in living systems (Chapter 16).

Energy Changes and Chemical Reactions: Thermochemistry

The study of energy changes that occur during chemical reactions (and physical processes) is called **thermochemistry**. These energy changes are quantitatively related to the *amounts* of chemicals involved. For example, burning 1.00 mol (16.0 g) of methane to form carbon dioxide and water releases 803 kJ (192 kcal) of energy as heat. We can consider the amount of heat evolved as a *product* of the reaction.

To convert between the SI unit of energy, the joule (J), and the commonly used unit, the calorie (cal), we can use the equality 1 cal = 4.184 J.

$$CH_4(g) + 2\,O_2(g) \longrightarrow CO_2(g) + 2\,H_2O(g) + 803\text{ kJ}$$

Burning 2.00 mol (32.0 g) of methane produces twice as much heat, 1606 kJ.

Example 15.2 Energies of Chemical Reactions

Burning 1.00 mol of propane releases 2201 kJ of energy.

$$C_3H_8(g) + 5\,O_2(g) \longrightarrow 3\,CO_2(g) + 4\,H_2O(g) + 2201\text{ kJ}$$

How much energy in kilojoules is released when 15.0 mol of propane is burned?

Solution

We start with 15.0 mol C_3H_8 and use the balanced equation to form a conversion factor, just as we did with chemical conversions in Chapter 5.

$$15.0\text{ }\cancel{\text{mol } C_3H_8} \times \frac{2201\text{ kJ}}{1\text{ }\cancel{\text{mol } C_3H_8}} = 33{,}000\text{ kJ}$$

■ EXERCISE 15.2A

The reaction of nitrogen and oxygen to form nitrogen monoxide requires an input of energy.

$$N_2(g) + O_2(g) + 18.07\text{ kJ} \longrightarrow 2\,NO(g)$$

How much energy in kilojoules is absorbed when 10.1 mol N_2 reacts with O_2 to form NO?

■ EXERCISE 15.2B

In photosynthesis, carbon dioxide and water are converted to glucose in a reaction that requires an input of 2700 kJ of energy to produce 1.00 mol of glucose. How much energy, in kilojoules, is required to make 1.00 kg of glucose?

We usually discuss energy changes in terms of an object or region losing energy and another object or region gaining it. When we warm our cold hands over a campfire, the burning wood gives off energy (as heat) and our hands gain energy, raising their temperature. In science, however, we need to describe the two "somethings" that exchange energy more precisely. We therefore define the **system** as the part of the universe under consideration. A real or imaginary boundary separates the system from the rest of the universe. The **surroundings** are everything else—the rest of the universe in theory, but we usually limit the surroundings to those parts of the universe that exchange energy or matter or both with the system. For example, if the system is a block of frozen spinach in a dish, the surroundings are the air around the block and dish, the counter on which it sits, and the rest of the kitchen.

Chemical reactions (or physical processes) that result in the release of heat from the system to the surroundings are **exothermic**. The burning of methane, gasoline, and coal (Figure 15.1) are all exothermic reactions. In each case, chemical energy is converted to heat energy, which is absorbed by the surroundings.

In other reactions, such as the decomposition of water, energy must be supplied to the reactants from the surroundings. We can write the amount of heat required for this process as a reactant in the chemical equation:

$$2\,H_2O(g) + 573\text{ kJ} \longrightarrow 2\,H_2(g) + O_2(g)$$

◀ **Figure 15.1** Coal burns in a highly exothermic reaction. The heat released can convert water to steam that can turn a turbine to generate electricity.

▲ **Figure 15.2** A striking endothermic reaction occurs when barium hydroxide octahydrate reacts with ammonium thiocyanate to produce barium thiocyanate, ammonia gas, and water.

$$\text{Heat} + Ba(OH)_2 \cdot 8\,H_2O(s) + 2\,NH_4SCN(s) \longrightarrow Ba(SCN)_2(s) + 2\,NH_3(g) + 10\,H_2O(l)$$

Here the reaction is carried out in a flask placed on a wet block of wood. The temperature drops well below the freezing point of water, freezing the flask to the block.

In a reaction like this, which is **endothermic**, energy is absorbed as heat (Figure 15.2). It takes 573 kJ of energy to decompose 36.0 g (2.00 mol) of water into hydrogen and oxygen. Note that exactly the same amount of energy is released when enough hydrogen is burned to form 36.0 g of water.

$$2\,H_2(g) + O_2(g) \longrightarrow 2\,H_2O(g) + 573\text{ kJ}$$

Physical processes can also be either exothermic or endothermic. Table 15.3 lists several examples of physical and chemical processes and classifies them as exothermic or endothermic.

An endothermic reaction you can do: Dissolve about 15 g of citric acid ($H_3C_6H_5O_7$) in enough water to make about 25 mL of solution. Measure the initial temperature. Stir in 15 g of sodium bicarbonate (baking soda). Note the change in temperature. The reaction mixture can be discarded in the sink. No toxic substances are involved.

Table 15.3 Some Exothermic and Endothermic Processes

Exothermic Processes	Endothermic Processes
Freezing of water	Melting of ice
Condensation of water vapor	Evaporation of water
Metabolism in animals	Photosynthesis in plants
Forming chemical bonds	Breaking chemical bonds
Discharging a battery	Charging a battery
Explosion of dynamite	Evaporation of a chlorofluorocarbon

Example 15.3 Energy Changes in Chemical Reactions

How much energy, in kilojoules, is released when 225 g of propane (see Example 15.2) is burned?

Solution

The formula mass of propane, with 3 C atoms and 8 H atoms, is

$$(3 \times 12.0\text{ u}) + (8 \times 1.0) = 36.0\text{ u} + 8.0\text{ u} = 44.0\text{ u}$$

The molar mass is therefore 44.0 g. Next, we use the molar mass to convert grams of propane to moles of propane.

$$225\text{ g }\cancel{C_3H_8} \times \frac{1\text{ mol }C_3H_8}{44.0\text{ g }\cancel{C_3H_8}} = 5.11\text{ mol }C_3H_8$$

Now, proceeding as in Example 15.2,

$$5.11\ \cancel{\text{mol } C_3H_8} \times \frac{2201\ \text{kJ}}{1\ \cancel{\text{mol } C_3H_8}} = 11{,}200\ \text{kJ}$$

■ EXERCISE 15.3A

How much energy, in kilojoules, is released when 44.2 g of methane is burned?

$$CH_4(g) + 2\,O_2(g) \longrightarrow CO_2(g) + 2\,H_2O(g) + 803\ \text{kJ}$$

■ EXERCISE 15.3B

How much energy, in kilocalories, is absorbed when 0.528 g N_2 is converted to NO (see Exercise 15.2A)?

Self-Assessment Questions

1. The rate of a chemical reaction usually decreases when
   - **a.** a catalyst is added
   - **b.** a chemist is watching
   - **c.** the concentration of one of the reactants is decreased
   - **d.** the temperature is increased
2. Which of the following physical changes is exothermic?
   - **a.** $H_2O(s) \longrightarrow H_2O(l)$
   - **b.** $H_2O(g) \longrightarrow H_2O(l)$
   - **c.** $H_2O(s) \longrightarrow H_2O(g)$
   - **d.** $H_2O(l) \longrightarrow H_2O(g)$
3. How much heat is absorbed in the complete reaction of 0.10 mol SiO_2 with excess carbon, according to the following equation?

   $$SiO_2(g) + 3\,C(s) + 624.7\ \text{kJ} \longrightarrow SiC(s) + 2\,CO(g)$$

   - **a.** 20.8 kJ
   - **b.** 62.47 kJ
   - **c.** 208 kJ
   - **d.** 1870 kJ
4. When solid NaOH is dissolved in water, the water gets hotter, indicating that this dissolving is an
   - **a.** endothermic process because it absorbs heat
   - **b.** endothermic process because it releases heat
   - **c.** exothermic process because it absorbs heat
   - **d.** exothermic process because it releases heat

Answers: 1, c; 2, b; 3, b; 4, d

15.3 The Laws of Thermodynamics

Learning Objective › State the first and second laws of thermodynamics, and discuss their implications for energy production and use.

We will take a look at our present energy sources and our future energy prospects shortly. To do so scientifically, we first examine some natural laws. Recall that natural laws merely summarize the results of many experiments. We won't recount all those experiments here. We will merely state the laws and some of their consequences.

Energy and the Laws of Thermodynamics

The **first law of thermodynamics** states that energy can be neither created nor destroyed. The first law of thermodynamics (*thermo* refers to heat; *dynamics* refers to motion) grew out of a variety of experiments conducted during the early nineteenth century. By 1840, it was clear that energy can be changed from one form to another, but it is neither created nor destroyed. This law (also called the **law of conservation**

of energy) has been restated in several ways, including "You can't get something for nothing" and "There is no such thing as a free lunch." Energy cannot be made from nothing, which means that a machine cannot be made that produces more energy than it takes in. Nor does energy just disappear, although it may change to a different form.

From the first law alone, we might conclude that we can't possibly run out of energy because energy is conserved. This is true enough, but it doesn't mean that we don't have problems. There is another long-armed law from which we cannot escape.

Energy and the Second Law: You CAN'T Break Even

Despite innumerable attempts (and even the granting of several patents), no one has ever built a successful perpetual-motion machine. You can't make a machine that runs indefinitely without consuming energy. Even if an engine isn't doing any work, it loses energy (as heat) because of the friction of its moving parts. In fact, in any real engine, it impossible to get as much useful energy out as you put in. In other words, you can't break even.

If energy is neither created nor destroyed, why do we always need more? Won't the energy we have now last forever? The answer lies in these facts:

- Energy can be changed from one form to another.
- Not all forms are equally useful.
- More useful forms of energy are constantly being degraded into less useful forms.

Energy "flows downhill." Mechanical energy is eventually changed into heat energy. Heat always flows from a hot object to a cooler one (Figure 15.3). The reverse does not occur spontaneously. There is a tendency toward an even distribution of energy.

Observations of heat flow led to formulation of the **second law of thermodynamics**, which can be stated: The energy available for work in the universe is continually decreasing. The second law also can be stated: Energy does not flow spontaneously from a cold object to a hot one. (A *spontaneous* process is one that can proceed in a specified direction without being forced by an external source of energy.)

It is true that we can make energy flow from a cold region to a hot one—refrigerators and freezers do so—but we cannot do so without an input of energy and without producing changes elsewhere. We can reverse a spontaneous process

◀ **Figure 15.3** Energy always flows spontaneously from a hot object to a cold one, never the reverse. It flows from a hot fire to the cooler marshmallow. (A spontaneous event is one that occurs without outside influence.)

▲ **It DOES Matter!**
The tendency of energy to disperse helps to explain why it is relatively easy to pollute air or water and hard to clean up such pollution. For example, it would take little energy to dump a ton of a chlorofluorocarbon (CFC) into the air. The rapidly moving CFC molecules would quickly disperse among the nitrogen, oxygen, and other molecules in the air. Once the CFC molecules were scattered, the entire atmosphere would have to be processed to separate them from the air. Cleaning up pollution is good, but prevention of pollution is a far better alternative.

only at a price. The price, in the case of a refrigerator, is the consumption of electricity; that is, you must use energy to cause energy flow from a cold space to a warmer one.

When we change energy from one form to another, we can't concentrate all the energy in a particular source to do the job we want it to do. For example, we use the energy in a fuel to push a piston in a car engine, or we use water rushing down from the top of a dam to run dynamos to generate electricity. In either case—indeed in all cases—some of the energy is converted to heat and thus not available to do *useful* work.

Entropy

Yet another way to look at the second law is in terms of *entropy*. Scientists use **entropy** as a measure of the dispersal of energy in a system. The more the energy is spread out, the higher the entropy of the system and the less likely it is that this energy can be harnessed to do useful work. Spontaneous processes tend toward greater entropy or are exothermic, or both. The total entropy always increases for an isolated system.

As was noted in Chapter 6, molecules move about constantly. Their motion in solids is limited to rapid but tiny back-and-forth movements much like vibrations about a nearly fixed point. The molecules in liquids move more freely but still over only short distances. Those in gases move still more freely and over much greater distances.

In Chapter 3, we saw that the energy of light occurs in little packets called *photons*. Similarly, the energy of molecular motion is described using a concept called *microstates*. If you could take a snapshot capturing the positions of all molecules in a sample of matter at a given instant, you would have captured an image of a microstate. The number of microstates in which a given sample of matter can exist differs depending upon whether it is in the solid, liquid, or gaseous state. The number of possible energy microstates will be lowest for a solid because the molecules in a solid are limited mainly to vibrational motion. Because molecules in the liquid state can move more freely, the number of possible energy microstates is much larger for liquids than for solids. When converted to a gas, the molecules can move still more freely and for much greater distances, so even more microstates are available to molecules in the gaseous state.

As any form of matter is heated, the energy in it is spread out among more accessible microstates (see Figure 15.4). Technically, entropy is the dispersal of

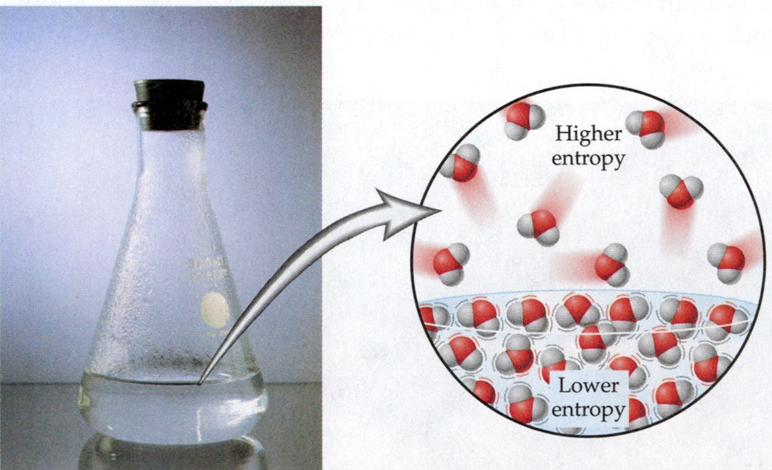

▲ **Figure 15.4** The photograph depicts the vaporization of water; a sample of liquid water [$H_2O(l)$] at room temperature spontaneously changes to $H_2O(g)$ through the process of evaporation. At the macroscopic level, nothing appears to be taking place. However, in the molecular view, we see that the molecules are in motion and are much more widely spaced in the gaseous state than in the liquid state. Vaporization is spontaneous because the gas has greater *entropy* than the liquid. Molecules in the gas can be "arranged" in many more ways in their spread-out spacing than can molecules of the liquid. We can make liquid water from water vapor but only by compressing the gas and/or lowering its temperature.

energy among these microstates. In practice, entropy is often thought of as being analogous to "molecular disorder." Of course, we can often reverse the tendency toward greater entropy—but only through an input of energy.

The energy to run an engine usually comes from the concentrated chemical energy inside molecules of oil or coal. In biochemistry, food molecules are the concentrated energy source. In either case, energy is spread out during the process. The spread-out energy in the product gases—CO_2 and H_2O, in each case—is less useful. A car won't run on exhaust gases, nor can organisms obtain energy for life processes from respiratory products.

Self-Assessment Questions

1. The first law of thermodynamics is also called the law of
   a. conservation of energy
   b. conservation of mass
   c. entropy
   d. perpetual motion
2. That energy always goes spontaneously from more useful forms to less useful forms is a statement of the
   a. first law of thermodynamics
   b. law of unintended consequences
   c. second law of thermodynamics
   d. standard law of energy conversion
3. According to the second law of thermodynamics, the
   a. entropy of a system always decreases
   b. entropy of a system always increases
   c. total entropy always decreases for an isolated system
   d. total entropy always increases for an isolated system
4. In the process represented by the equation $H_2O(l) \longrightarrow H_2O(g)$, the entropy
   a. decreases
   b. depends on the catalyst used
   c. increases
   d. remains the same

Answers: 1, a; 2, c; 3, d; 4, c

15.4 Power: People, Horses, and Fossils

Learning Objective › List the common fossil fuels, and describe how modern society is based on their use.

Early people obtained their energy (food and fuel) by collecting wild plants and hunting wild animals. They expended this energy in hunting and gathering. Domestication of horses and oxen increased the availability of energy only slightly. The raw materials used by these work animals were natural, replaceable plant materials.

A **fuel** is a substance that burns readily with the release of significant amounts of energy. Plant materials were also the first fuels. These combustible materials kept early fires burning. As late as 1760, wood was almost the only fuel in use. Wood, dried dung, and crop residues still remain the main sources of heat for about one-third of the world's people.

▲ Waterwheels at Hama, Syria, are 2000 years old. Some are more than 20 m high. Several are still used to lift water into aqueducts.

One of the first mechanical devices used to convert energy to useful work was the waterwheel. The Egyptians first used waterpower about 2000 years ago, mainly for grinding grain. Later on, waterpower was used for sawmills, textile mills, and other small factories. Windmills were introduced into Western Europe during the Middle Ages, mainly for pumping water and grinding grain. More recently, wind power has been used to generate electricity.

Windmills and waterwheels are fairly simple devices for converting the kinetic energy of blowing wind and flowing water to mechanical energy. They were sufficient to power the early part of the Industrial Revolution. The development of the steam engine allowed factories to be located away from waterways. Since 1850, turbines turned by water, steam, and gas, the internal-combustion engine, and a variety of other energy-conversion devices have boosted the energy available for society's use by an estimated factor of 10,000.

The Industrial Revolution was fueled, in effect, by fossils—the buried remains of living organisms. Combustion of this material initiated modern industrial civilization. Today, more than 85% of the energy used to support our way of life comes from **fossil fuels**—coal, petroleum, and natural gas that formed during Earth's Carboniferous period around 300 million years ago. In the following sections, we consider the origin and chemical nature of these fuels that release the energy captured by ancient plants from rays of sunlight.

Fuels are *reduced* forms of matter, and the burning process is an oxidation (Chapter 8). If an atom already has its maximum number of bonds to oxygen atoms (or to other electronegative atoms such as chlorine or bromine), the substance cannot serve as a fuel. Indeed, some such substances can be used to put out fires. Figure 15.5 shows some representative fuels and nonfuels.

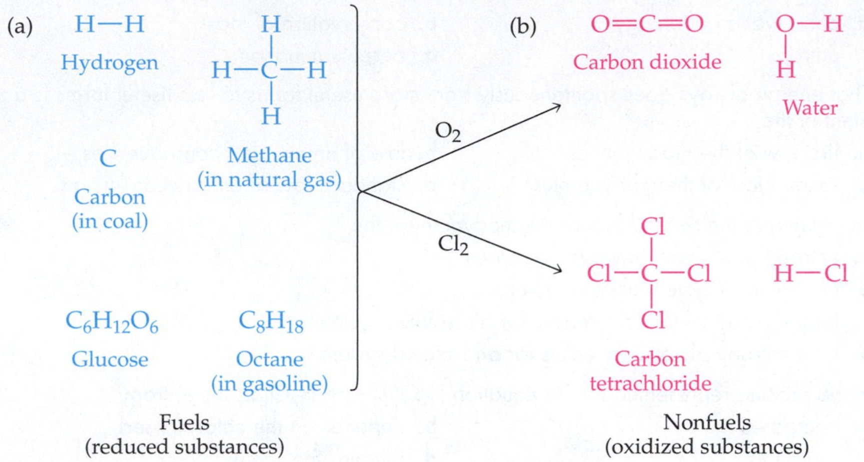

▶ **Figure 15.5** (a) Some fuels. Fuels are reduced forms of matter that release relatively large quantities of heat when burned. (b) Some nonfuels. These compounds are oxidized forms of matter.

Reserves and Consumption Rates of Fossil Fuels

2. Do we really have an energy shortage? There is no shortage of energy itself, but not all energy is equally useful to us. The supply of materials like fossil fuels that provide convenient, useful energy is dwindling.

Energy *production* refers to conversion of some form of energy into a more useful form. For example, production of petroleum means pumping, transporting, and refining it. Energy *consumption* involves using it in a way that changes it to a less useful form. In either case, energy is neither created nor destroyed.

Earth has a limited supply of fossil fuels. Estimated U.S. and world reserves and annual U.S. and world consumption are given in Table 15.4. Estimates of reserves vary greatly, depending on the assumptions made, and the numbers in the table imply far greater certainty than there is in reality. Even the most optimistic estimates, however, lead to the conclusion that these nonrenewable energy resources are being depleted rapidly. Indeed, in just a century, we will have used up more than half the fossil fuels that were formed over the ages. In only a few hundred more years, we will have removed from Earth and burned virtually all the remaining recoverable fossil fuels. Of all that ever existed, about 90% will have been used in a period of 300 years.

Within the lifetime of today's 18-year-olds, natural gas and petroleum will likely become so scarce and so expensive that they won't be used much as fuels. At the current rate of production, U.S. reserves of petroleum and natural gas will be substantially depleted sometime during this century. Coal reserves should last perhaps 300 years. However, the rate of use of all fossil fuels is increasing, especially in developing nations.

Presumably, fossil fuels are still being formed in nature, a process that is perhaps most evident in peat bogs. The rate of formation is extremely slow, estimated to be only one fifty-thousandth of the rate at which fuels are being used.

Table 15.4 Estimated U.S. and World Reserves of Economically Recoverable Fuels and Annual Consumption of Fossil Fuels[a]

	Reserves		Consumption	
Fuel	**United States**	**World**	**United States**	**World**
Coal	119,327	462,612	558	2,891
Petroleum	4,081	164,804	952	4,001
Natural gas	5,333	163,312	507	2,362
Total	128,741	790,728	2,017	9,254

Source: World Resources Institute, Washington, DC. The Web site (http://www.wri.org/) includes the assumptions made in making these estimates.

[a]Expressed in millions of metric tons of oil equivalents (Mtoe) for ready comparison of energy content. 1 metric ton oil equivalent (toe) = 7.8 barrels of oil = 1270 m^3 of natural gas = 2.3 metric ton (t) of coal.

Self-Assessment Questions

1. Coal, petroleum, and natural gas are called fossil fuels because they
   a. are burned to release energy
   b. are nonrenewable and will run out
   c. cause air pollution
   d. were formed over millennia from the remains of ancient plants and animals
2. Which of the following is *not* a fuel?
   a. C b. $CH_3CH_2CH_3$ c. CH_3CH_2OH d. CO_2
3. All fuels are
   a. carbon compounds b. hydrocarbons
   c. oxidized forms of matter d. reduced forms of matter

Answers: 1, d; 2, d; 3, d

15.5 Coal: The Carbon Rock of Ages

Learning Objectives › List advantages and disadvantages of coal as a fuel.

People probably have used small amounts of coal since prehistoric times. After the steam engine came into widespread use (by about 1850), the Industrial Revolution was powered largely by coal. By 1900, about 95% of the world's energy production came from the burning of coal. Today, coal supplies about 27% of worldwide energy production.

Coal is a complex combination of organic materials that burn and inorganic materials that produce ash. Its main element is carbon, but it also contains small percentages of other elements. The quality of coal is based on carbon content and those other elements. Complete combustion of carbon produces carbon dioxide.

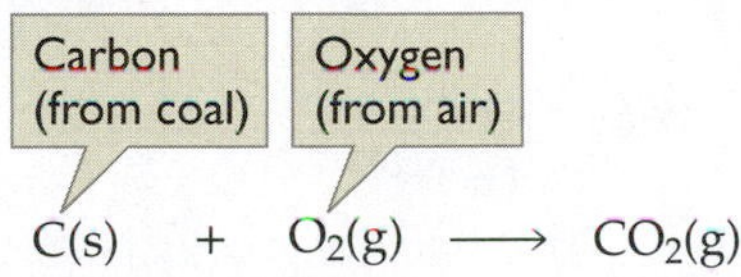

$$C(s) + O_2(g) \longrightarrow CO_2(g)$$

When combustion occurs in limited quantities of air, however, carbon monoxide and soot are formed.

$$2\,C(s) + O_2(g) \longrightarrow 2\,CO(g)$$

Soot is mostly unburned carbon.

Coal is ranked by carbon content, from low-grade peat and lignite to high-grade anthracite (Table 15.5). The energy obtained from coal is roughly proportional to

▲ Coal is a fossil fuel. Giant ferns, reeds, and grasses that grew during the Carboniferous period 300 million years ago were buried and then, through the ages, were converted to the coal we burn today.

Table 15.5 Approximate Composition (Percent by Mass) and Energy Content of Typical Grades of Coal (Dry Basis)

Grade of Coal	Carbon	Hydrogen	Oxygen	Nitrogen	Sulfur	Energy Content (MJ/kg)
Wood (for comparison)	50	6	43	1	0.05	—
Peat	60	6	33	2	0.26–0.48	14.7
Lignite (brown coal)	71	5	25	1	0.4	23
Bituminous (soft) coal	86–91	5	5–15	1	0.7–4.0	36
Anthracite (hard coal)	95	2–3	2–3	Trace	0.6–0.77	35.2

Source: Diessel, C. F. K. *Coal-Bearing Depositional Systems*. New York: Springer-Verlag, 1992.

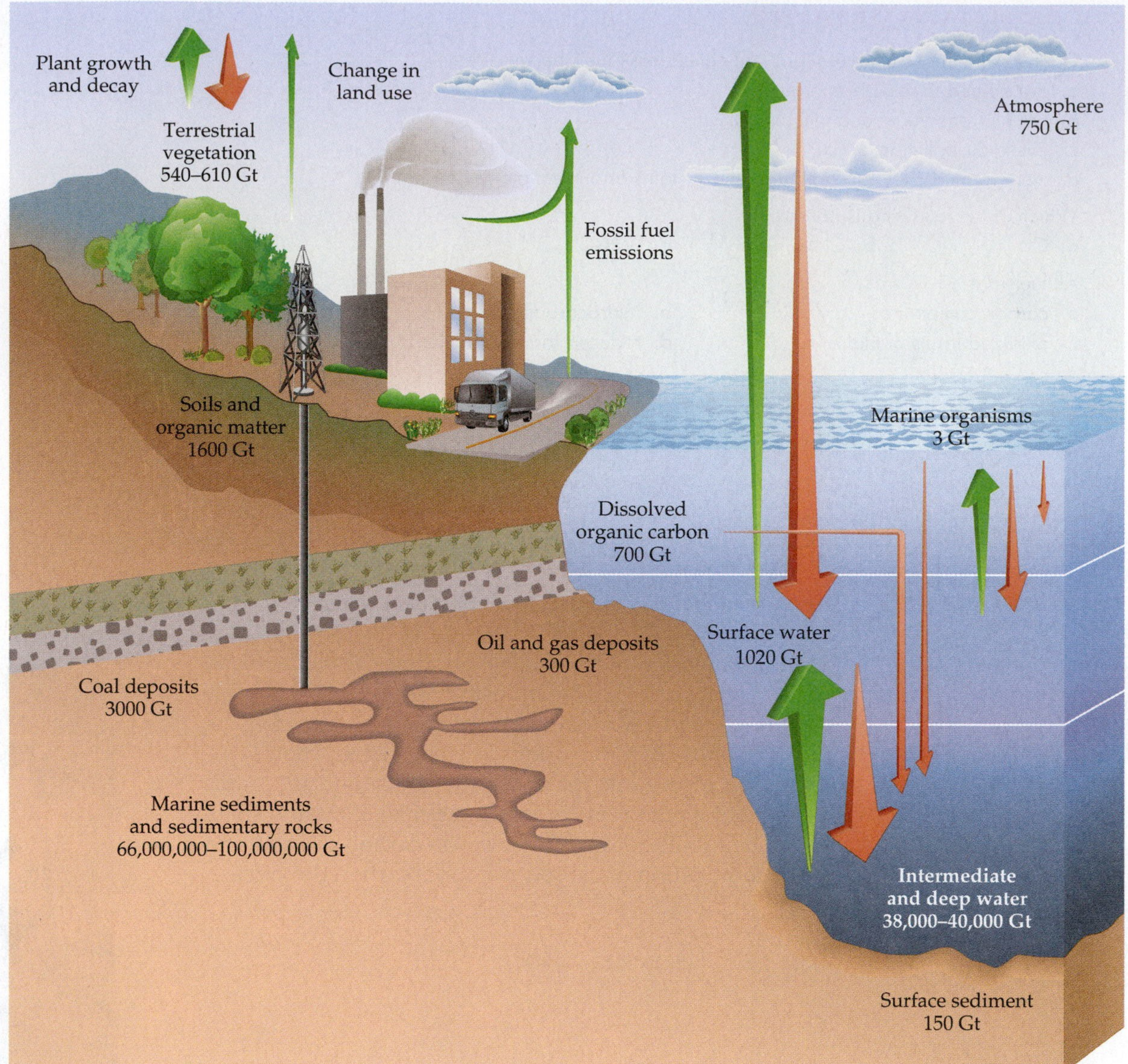

▲ **Figure 15.6** The carbon cycle. The numbers indicate the quantity of carbon, in gigatons ($1 Gt = 10^9$ t), in each location. The arrows indicate the general direction of travel of carbon during its cycle.

its carbon content. Soft (bituminous) coal is much more plentiful than hard coal (anthracite). Lignite and peat have become increasingly important as the supplies of higher grades of coal have been depleted.

Coal deposits that exist today are less than 600 million years old. For millions of years, Earth was much warmer than it is now, and plant life flourished. Most plants lived, died, and decayed—playing their normal role in the carbon cycle (Figure 15.6). But some plant material became buried under mud and water. There, in the absence of oxygen, it decayed only partially. The structural material of plants is largely cellulose $[(C_6H_{10}O_5)_n]$. Under increasing pressure, as the material was buried more deeply, the cellulose molecules broke down. Small molecules rich in hydrogen and oxygen escaped, leaving behind a material increasingly rich in carbon. Thus, peat is an immature coal, only partly converted, with plant stems and leaves clearly visible. Anthracite, on the other hand, has been almost completely carbonized.

Abundant but Inconvenient Fuel

Coal is by far the most plentiful fossil fuel. The United States has about a quarter of the world's reserves. Electric utilities in the United States burn 1.0 billion metric tons of coal each year, generating 3.78 trillion kWh of electricity (45% of the total).

Coal, a solid, is an inconvenient fuel to use and dangerous to obtain. Coal mining is one of the most dangerous occupations in the world, accounting for over

(a)

(b)

◀ Strip mining bares vast areas of vegetation. The exposed soil washes away, filling streams with mud and silt. U.S. laws now require the (expensive) restoration of most stripped areas. Unfortunately, much damage was done before these laws were passed, and many consider the present laws inadequate. These photographs show the site of a strip mine in Morgan County, Tennessee: (a) the abandoned mine in 1963 and (b) the area after it was reclaimed in a demonstration project in 1971.

100,000 deaths in the United States in the twentieth century alone. Strip mining, although efficient, can devastate large areas. Coal is hauled in trains, barges, and trucks. We continue to pay great costs to extract coal from the ground and to transport it to the power plants and factories where it is used.

Source of Pollution

Unlike natural gas and liquid petroleum, solid coal contains minerals that are left as ash when the coal is burned. As Chapter 13 noted, some minerals enter the air as particulate matter, constituting a major pollution problem.

Much of our remaining coal reserves are high in sulfur. When it burns, the stack gases must be scrubbed, or choking sulfur dioxide pours into the atmosphere. The SO_2 reacts with oxygen and moisture in the air to form sulfuric acid, which damages metal structures, marble buildings and statues, and human lungs. And coal is currently the largest single source of airborne mercury emissions in the United States.

▲ **It DOES Matter!**

Once removed from the flue gases, fly ash may seem benign, but it is produced in enormous quantities that must be disposed of or stored. A coal-burning plant in Kingston, Tennessee, stored ash as a slurry (a mixture of fly ash and water) in ponds. In 2008, an ash dike ruptured, releasing 4 million m^3 of coal fly-ash slurry, which covered 300 acres, damaging homes, washing out a road, rupturing a gas line and a water main, blocking a rail line, and felling trees.

Some coal is cleaned before it is burned. A flotation method makes use of the different densities of coal and its major impurities. Coal has a density of about 1.3 g/cm^3. Shale, a rock formed from hardened clay, has a density of about 2.5 g/cm^3. Pyrite (FeS_2), the major source of sulfur in coal, has a density of about 5.0 g/cm^3. A detergent solution of the proper density allows the coal to be floated off, leaving the heavier minerals behind. Coal can also be converted to more convenient gaseous and liquid fuels, again leaving the minerals behind. All these processes add to the cost of the coal.

Coal is more than just a fuel. When it is heated in the absence of air, volatile material is driven off, leaving behind a product—mostly carbon—called *coke*, which is used in the production of iron and steel. The more volatile material is condensed to liquid coal oil and a sticky mixture called *coal tar*, both of which are sources of organic chemicals for medical and industrial use.

The flotation method removes most inorganic sulfur compounds, such as pyrite, from coal. It does not remove sulfur atoms covalently bonded to the carbon atoms in the coal. This bound sulfur still contributes to pollution.

Self-Assessment Questions

1. Analysis of a solid fuel shows it to be 90% carbon. It is most likely
   a. anthracite coal **b.** bituminous coal
   c. peat **d.** wood
2. When coal is burned, the inorganic constituents end up as
   a. ash **b.** carbon monoxide
   c. flue gases **d.** organic matter
3. The most plentiful fossil fuel is
   a. coal **b.** natural gas **c.** petroleum **d.** propane
4. Which fossil fuel contributes the most to SO_x pollution?
   a. coal **b.** natural gas **c.** petroleum **d.** propane
5. On what physical property is the flotation method of coal cleaning based?
   a. density **b.** electrostatic precipitation
   c. melting point **d.** temperature

Answers: 1, b; 2, a; 3, a; 4, a; 5, a

15.6 Natural Gas and Petroleum

Learning Objectives › List the characteristics of natural gas and petroleum.
› List advantages and disadvantages of natural gas and petroleum as fuels.

Both natural gas and petroleum consist of hydrocarbons formed by the anaerobic decomposition of remains of living microorganisms. These remains settled to the bottom of the sea millions of years ago. The organic matter was buried under layers of mud and converted over the ages by high temperature and pressure to gaseous and liquid hydrocarbons.

Methane 82%
Pentanes
Butanes
Carbon dioxide
Propane
Nitrogen
Ethane

▲ Composition of typical natural gas. Natural gas is mostly methane, with small amounts of other hydrocarbons, nitrogen, and a few other gases.

Natural Gas

Natural gas, composed principally of methane, is the cleanest of the fossil fuels. Minor components of this gaseous fossil fuel vary greatly. In North America, a pipeline natural gas supply might contain about 82% methane, 6% ethane, 2% propane, and smaller amounts of butanes and pentanes.

Natural gas burns with a relatively clean flame, and the products are mainly carbon dioxide and water.

$$CH_4(g) + 2\,O_2(g) \longrightarrow CO_2(g) + 2\,H_2O(g) + \text{heat}$$

The gas, as it comes from the ground, often contains nitrogen (N_2), sulfur compounds, and other substances as impurities. As in any combustion in air, some nitrogen oxides are formed. When natural gas is burned in insufficient air, carbon monoxide and soot can be major products.

$$2\,CH_4(g) + 3\,O_2(g) \longrightarrow 2\,CO(g) + 4\,H_2O(g)$$

$$CH_4(g) + O_2(g) \longrightarrow C(s) + 2\,H_2O(g)$$

▲ Natural gas burns with a relatively clean flame.

Natural gas is trapped in geological formations capped by impermeable rock. It is removed through wells drilled into the gas-bearing formations. About 90% of today's natural gas in the United States is obtained by hydraulic fracturing, or fracking, of shale formations 5000 feet below ground. Fracking involves forcing chemically treated water under high pressure into the layers of rock. The fractured rock releases the gas. Fracking produces millions of gallons of wastewater that is often contaminated with chemicals. The process of fracking can also contaminate groundwater.

Most natural gas is used as fuel, supplying about 23% of worldwide energy consumption, but it is also an important raw material. In North America, a portion of the two- to four-carbon alkanes is separated from the rest of the natural gas. Ethane and propane are *cracked*—decomposed by heating with a catalyst—to form ethylene and propylene. These alkenes are intermediates in the synthesis of plastics (Chapter 10) and many other useful commodities. Natural gas is also the raw material from which methanol and many other organic compounds are made. Like other fossil fuels, its supply is limited (refer to Table 15.4).

Petroleum: Liquid Hydrocarbons

With the development of the internal combustion engine, petroleum became increasingly important and by 1950 had replaced coal as the principal fuel. **Petroleum** is an extremely complex liquid mixture of organic compounds—as many as 17,000 were separated from a sample of Brazilian crude oil. Most are hydrocarbons: alkanes, cycloalkanes, and aromatic compounds. As with natural gas, complete combustion of these substances yields mainly carbon dioxide and water. A representative reaction is that of an octane.

$$2\,C_8H_{18}(l) + 25\,O_2(g) \longrightarrow 16\,CO_2(g) + 18\,H_2O(g)$$

Combustion of petroleum in air also produces nitrogen oxides. Incomplete burning yields carbon monoxide and soot. Petroleum usually contains small amounts of sulfur compounds that produce sulfur dioxide when burned.

Petroleum is thought to be formed mainly from the fats of ocean-dwelling, microscopic animals because it is nearly always found in rocks of oceanic origin. Fats are made up mainly of compounds containing carbon, hydrogen, and a little oxygen (for example, $C_{57}H_{110}O_6$). Removal of some oxygen and slight rearrangement of the carbon and hydrogen atoms in these fats form typical petroleum hydrocarbon molecules.

Fuel oil, used for heating homes and to produce electricity, can be burned efficiently and thus contributes only moderately to air pollution. Gasoline, however, is the major fraction of petroleum and is used to power automobiles. Because internal combustion engines are both numerous and rather inefficient, the combustion of gasoline contributes greatly to air pollution (Chapter 13). Petroleum-derived fuels are generally dirtier than natural gas because they contain more impurities. However, both types of fuel are major sources of CO_2 emissions that are causing global climate change.

U.S. dependence on imported oil leads to economic and political problems. Political events in the oil-rich Middle East have caused huge oil price increases several times. Continued military involvement in Iraq, disastrous hurricanes in the Gulf of Mexico, and increased demand in developing countries, especially China, caused crude oil prices to hit record highs in 2008, with only small price drops afterward.

Air pollution isn't the only problem: Burning up our petroleum reserves will leave us without a ready source of many familiar materials. Most industrial organic chemicals come from petroleum (others are derived from coal and natural gas). These chemicals yield plastics, synthetic fibers, solvents, and many other consumer products.

Worldwide, petroleum still appears to be quite abundant (see Table 15.4). However, U.S. petroleum reserves have been declining since 1972. Further tapping of offshore deposits and deeper drilling would produce only a few years' supply and would require a great deal more energy (and money) than drilling on land.

The developed countries of North America, Western Europe, and Japan depend heavily on oil imports from politically unstable developing nations, making the industrial nations economically and politically vulnerable.

Obtaining and Refining Petroleum

Crude oil is liquid, a convenient form for transportation. Petroleum is pumped easily through pipelines or hauled across the oceans in giant tankers. Pumping petroleum from the ground requires little energy. As domestic supplies diminish, however, we will have to expend an increasing fraction of the energy content of petroleum to transport it to where it is needed. Also, as petroleum is pumped out of the ground, the remaining oil becomes increasingly difficult to extract. The oil that is left behind is more scattered, and more energy is required to collect it.

As it comes from the ground, crude oil is of limited use. To make it better suited to our needs, we separate it into fractions by boiling it in a distillation column (Figure 15.7). Petroleum deposits nearly always have associated natural gas, part or all of which also goes through a separation process. The lighter hydrocarbon molecules come off at the top of the column, and the heavier ones at the bottom (Table 15.6).

Table 15.6 Typical Petroleum Fractions

Fraction	Typical Size Range of Hydrocarbons	Approximate Range of Boiling Points (°C)	Typical Uses
Gas	CH_4 to C_4H_{10}	Less than 40	Fuel, starting materials for plastics
Gasoline	C_5H_{12} to $C_{12}H_{26}$	40–200	Fuel, solvents
Kerosene	$C_{12}H_{26}$ to $C_{16}H_{34}$	175–275	Diesel fuel, jet fuel, home heating, cracking to gasoline
Heating oil	$C_{15}H_{32}$ to $C_{18}H_{38}$	250–400	Industrial heating, cracking to gasoline
Lubricating oil	$C_{17}H_{36}$ and up	Above 300	Lubricants
Residue	$C_{20}H_{42}$ and up	Above 350 (some decomposition)	Paraffin, asphalt

Gasoline is usually the fraction of petroleum most in demand, and fractions that boil at higher temperatures are often converted to gasoline by cracking. This process, with $C_{14}H_{30}$ as an example, is illustrated in Figure 15.8. Cracking not only converts

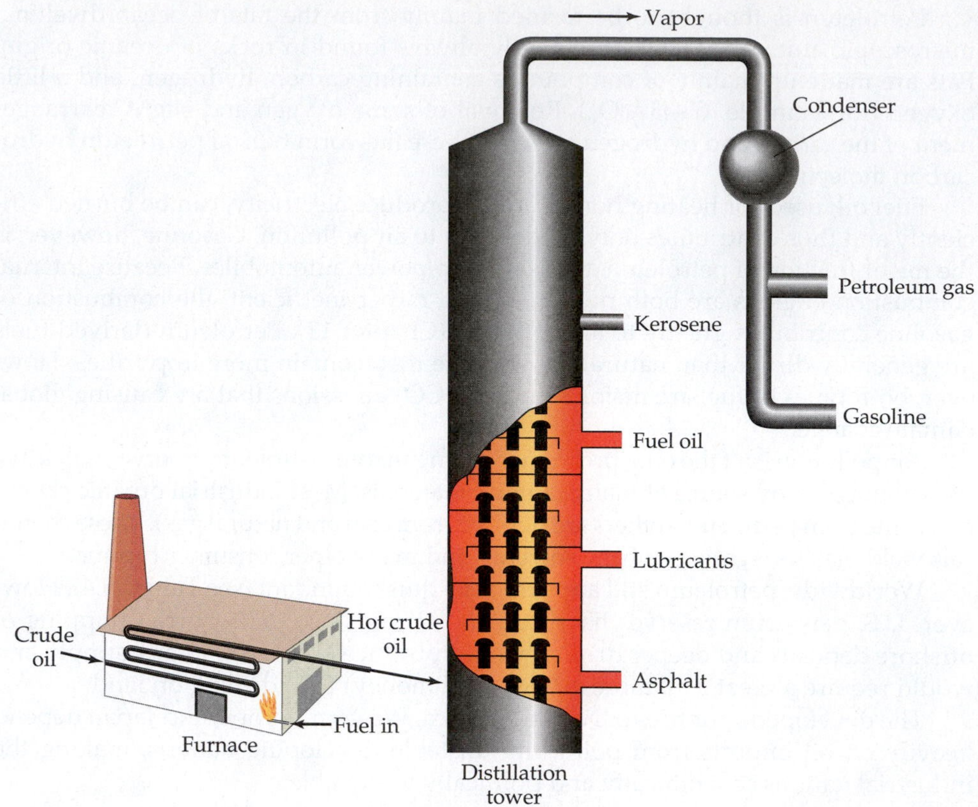

▶ **Figure 15.7** The fractional distillation of petroleum. Crude oil is vaporized, and the column separates the components according to their boiling points. The lower-boiling constituents reach the top of the column, and the higher-boiling components come off lower in the column. A nonvolatile residue collects at the bottom.

some of the large molecules to those in the gasoline range (C_5H_{12} through $C_{12}H_{26}$) but also produces a variety of useful by-products. The unsaturated hydrocarbons are starting materials for the manufacture of a host of petrochemicals.

▶ **Figure 15.8** Formulas of a few of the possible products formed when $C_{14}H_{30}$, a typical molecule in kerosene, is cracked. In practice, a wide variety of hydrocarbons (most of which have fewer than 15 carbon atoms), hydrogen gas, and char (mostly elemental carbon) are formed. Cyclic and branched-chain hydrocarbons are also produced.

$$CH_3CH_2CH_2CH_2CH_2CH_2CH_2CH_2CH_2CH_2CH_2CH_2CH_2CH_3 \xrightarrow[\text{catalyst}]{\text{heat}}$$

$$CH_3CH_2CH_2CH_2CH_2CH_2CH_2CH_2CH_2CH_2CH_2CH_3 + CH_2{=}CH_2$$

and

$$CH_3CH_2CH_2CH_2CH_2CH_2CH_2CH_2CH_2CH_2CH_3 + CH_3CH{=}CH_2$$

and

$$CH_3CH_2CH_2CH_2CH_2CH_2CH_2CH_3 + CH_3CH_2CH_2CH_2CH{=}CH_2$$

and so on

The cracking process illustrates the way chemists modify nature's materials to meet human needs and desires. Starting with petroleum or coal tar, chemists can create a dazzling array of substances with a wide variety of properties, including plastics, pesticides, herbicides, perfumes, preservatives, painkillers, antibiotics, stimulants, depressants, dyes, and detergents.

The ability to modify hydrocarbon molecules enables the petroleum industry to shift production to whatever fraction is desired. The industry can, on demand, increase the proportion of gasoline in summer, or of fuel oil in winter, from a given supply of petroleum. It can even make gasoline from coal. However, fossil fuels and other products from them are not sustainable. Scientists are seeking new sources of energy that do not depend on petroleum. Perhaps we can soon reduce this profligate waste of resources. Spaceship Earth has aboard it all the supplies it will have in the foreseeable future. We must use them wisely.

Gasoline

Gasoline, like the petroleum from which it is derived, is mainly a mixture of hydrocarbons. Commercial gasoline typically contains more than 150 different compounds, but up to 1000 have been identified in some blends. Among the hydrocarbons, a typical gasoline sample might have, by volume, 4–8% straight-chain alkanes, 25–40% branched-chain alkanes, 2–5% alkenes, 3–7% cycloalkanes, 1–4% cycloalkenes, and 20–50% aromatic hydrocarbons (0.5–2.5% benzene). Gasoline also contains a variety of additives, including antiknock agents, antioxidants, antirust agents, anti-icing agents, upper-cylinder lubricants, detergents, and dyes. Typical alkanes in gasoline range from C_5H_{12} to $C_{12}H_{26}$. There are also small amounts of some sulfur- and nitrogen-containing compounds.

The gasoline fraction of petroleum as it comes from a distillation column is called *straight-run gasoline*. It doesn't burn very well in modern high-compression automobile engines, but chemists are able to modify it to make it burn more smoothly.

The Octane Ratings of Gasolines

In an internal combustion engine, the gasoline–air mixture sometimes ignites before the spark plug "fires." This is called *knocking* and can damage the engine. Early on, scientists learned that some types of hydrocarbons, especially those with branched structures, burned more evenly and were less likely to cause knocking than others. An arbitrary performance standard, called the **octane rating**, was established in 1927. Isooctane was assigned an octane rating of 100. An unbranched-chain compound, heptane, was given an octane rating of 0. A gasoline rated 90 octane was one that performed the same as a mixture that was 90% isooctane and 10% heptane.

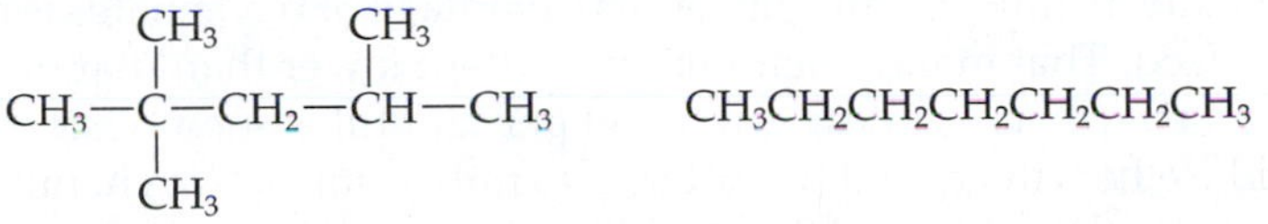

$$CH_3-C(CH_3)_2-CH_2-CH(CH_3)-CH_3 \qquad CH_3CH_2CH_2CH_2CH_2CH_2CH_3$$

Isooctane (Octane rating 100)   Heptane (Octane rating 0)

During the 1930s, chemists discovered that the octane rating of gasoline could be improved by heating it in the presence of a catalyst such as sulfuric acid (H_2SO_4) or aluminum chloride ($AlCl_3$). This *isomerizes* some of the unbranched molecules to highly branched molecules. For example, heptane molecules can be isomerized so that they have branched structures.

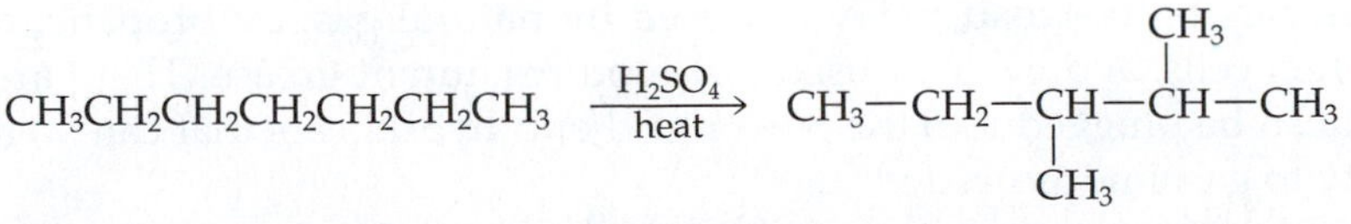

$$CH_3CH_2CH_2CH_2CH_2CH_2CH_3 \xrightarrow[\text{heat}]{H_2SO_4} CH_3-CH_2-CH(CH_3)-CH(CH_3)-CH_3$$

Unbranched, lower-octane fuel   Branched, higher-octane fuel

Chemists also can combine small hydrocarbon molecules (below the size range of gasoline) into larger ones more suitable for use as fuel. This process is called *alkylation*. In a typical alkylation reaction, shown below, isobutylene is reacted with propane.

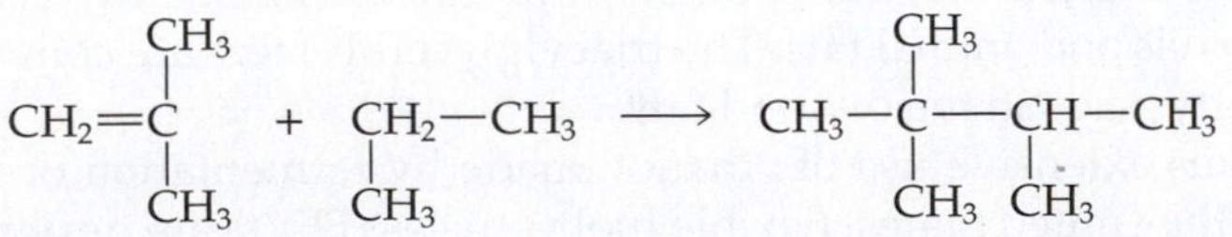

$$CH_2=C(CH_3)-CH_3 + CH_2(CH_3)-CH_3 \longrightarrow CH_3-C(CH_3)(CH_3)-CH(CH_3)-CH_3$$

Light molecules, unsuitable for automobile fuel   Heavier molecule, more suitable for automobiles

The product molecules are in the right size range for gasoline, and the highly branched molecules are high in octane number.

▲ Fuel with the octane booster tetraethyllead, called "ethyl gasoline," was available at many gas stations before the additive was phased out, beginning in the 1970s.

Certain additives substantially improve the antiknock quality of gasoline. Tetraethyllead $[Pb(CH_2CH_3)_4]$ was found to be especially effective. As little as 1 mL of tetraethyllead per liter of gasoline (1 part per 1000) increases the octane rating by 10 or more.

Lead fouls the catalytic converters used in modern automobiles. More important, lead is especially toxic to the brain. Even small amounts can lead to learning disabilities in children. In the United States, unleaded gasoline became available in 1974, and leaded gasoline has been phased out as automotive fuel.

Scientists have found other ways to get high octane ratings for unleaded fuels. For example, petroleum refineries use **catalytic reforming** to convert low-octane alkanes to high-octane aromatic compounds. Hexane (with an octane number of 25) is converted to benzene (octane number 106).

$$CH_3CH_2CH_2CH_2CH_2CH_3 \xrightarrow[\text{heat}]{\text{catalyst}} C_6H_6 + 4\,H_2$$

Hexane Octane 25 → Benzene Octane 106

Octane boosters that have replaced tetraethyllead include ethanol, methanol, *tert*-butyl alcohol, and methyl *tert*-butyl ether (MTBE). None of these is nearly as effective as tetraethyllead in boosting the octane rating. They must therefore be used in fairly large proportions. The EPA allows up to 15% ethanol in gasoline (E15 fuel) for cars built in 2001 or later.

Unlike gasoline, which is made up of hydrocarbons, the alcohols used as octane boosters all contain oxygen and therefore are sometimes called *oxygenates*. Not only do these additives improve the octane rating, but they also decrease the amount of carbon monoxide in auto exhaust gas. A disadvantage of oxygenates is that they are partially oxidized. That makes their energy content lower than that of pure hydrocarbon fuels, so the distance a car can travel per tankful is somewhat shorter.

MTBE, like ethers in general (Chapter 9), is rather unreactive chemically, but it is soluble in water to the extent of 4.8 g per 100 g of water. When gasoline spills or leaks from storage tanks, MTBE enters the groundwater, leading to widespread contamination. MTBE is listed as a hazardous substance under the federal Superfund Act and is considered a potential human carcinogen by the EPA. The exact threat to human health is far from clear, but use of MTBE in gasoline has been banned in many areas.

Alternative Fuels

An automobile engine can be made to run on nearly any liquid or gaseous fuel. There are cars on the road today powered by natural gas, by propane, by diesel fuel, by fuel cells, and even by used fast-food restaurant grease. There are electric cars that can be plugged into the power grid and hybrid cars that can switch from electricity to gasoline as needed.

Diesel fuel for automobiles overlaps the kerosene fraction of petroleum (refer to Table 15.6); it consists mainly of C_9 to C_{20} hydrocarbons with a boiling range of about 250–350 °C. Diesel fuel has a greater proportion of straight-chain alkanes than gasoline does. The standard for performance, called the *cetane number*, is based on hexadecane ($C_{16}H_{34}$), once known as cetane. A renewable fuel called *biodiesel* can be used in some unmodified diesel engines. Biodiesel is made by reacting ethanol with vegetable oils and animal fats. The triacylglycerol esters are converted to ethyl esters of the fatty acids in the oils and fats.

Brazil makes extensive use of ethanol, made by fermentation of sucrose from sugar cane. In the United States, flexible fuel vehicles (FFVs) are designed to run on E85 gasoline, a fuel that is 85% ethanol and 15% gasoline. Ethanol alone or blended with gasoline is not likely to be an answer to our energy problems. Most ethanol is made from corn, and widespread use would require conversion of huge tracts of farmland to corn production. And diversion of corn to ethanol production apparently leads to increased food prices.

Energy Return on Energy Invested

When evaluating an energy source, we need to consider the *energy return on energy invested* (EROEI) of exploiting the source. EROEIs are difficult to evaluate, and the results often have a high degree of uncertainty. However, these ratings can be quite important because if the EROEI of a source is 1 or less, it becomes an energy sink rather than a source.

In the early days of the petroleum industry, the EROEI for Texas crude oil may have been as much as 100:1; investing the equivalent of 1 barrel of oil could produce 100 barrels. The EROEI for oil from the Middle East is still about 10:1, and that of oil produced today in the United States is about 3:1. Oil from ever more remote places or ever deeper offshore wells will have ever lower EROEIs.

The EROEIs of alternative energy sources are often quite low. Canada has vast deposits of tar sands, but the EROEI is only about 1.5:1. Colorado has huge deposits of oil shale, but the EROEI is likely to be quite low.

The EROEI for ethanol is the subject of much debate, with proposed values ranging from a low of 0.78:1 to the highest estimate for ethanol from corn of 1.67:1. There are two reasons for the low EROEI for ethanol: Much energy is needed to distill or evaporate the ethanol after fermentation; and ethanol has a lower energy content than petroleum fuels.

The EROEI of wind energy in good locations is about 20:1, and that for silicon-based solar panels is about 12:1. Hydrogen has an EROEI of less than 1:1 because it can neither be extracted from the ground nor generated by a biosystem. Hydrogen can be generated by electricity or by heating steam to very high (2000 °C) temperatures. For now, those measures require more energy than the hydrogen produces when burned.

In addition to the EROEI, we have to consider the environmental consequences of exploiting an energy source. For example, getting oil from tar sands or oil shale is a messy process. Thus, our quest for plentiful energy will be costly and controversial.

Self-Assessment Questions

1. The main constituent in natural gas is
   a. CH_4 b. $CH_3CH_2CH_3$ c. C_6H_6 d. CH_3OH
2. Which of the fossil fuels is the cleanest and simplest in composition?
   a. coal b. it depends on the source
   c. petroleum d. natural gas
3. In the United States, oil production
   a. peaked in 1970 b. peaked in 1999
   c. peaked in 2010 d. will peak in 2030

Questions 4–7 refer to petroleum processing.

4. Cracking is used to
   a. convert heavier fractions to lighter ones
   b. improve the octane rating
   c. remove sulfur
   d. separate various fractions
5. An alkylation unit
   a. converts lighter fractions to heavier ones
   b. improves the asphalt yield
   c. removes sulfur
   d. separates various fractions
6. Isomerization is used to convert
   a. alcohols to ethers
   b. branched alkane molecules to straight-chain ones
   c. hexane to isooctane
   d. straight-chain molecules to branched ones
7. Catalytic reforming converts
   a. branched molecules to straight-chain ones
   b. branched molecules to aromatic ones
   c. straight-chain molecules to aromatic ones
   d. straight-chain molecules to branched ones

3. Why don't we use more alternative fuels like ethanol?

Use of alternative fuels is increasing, but the cost (EROEI) of those fuels is very high compared to that of fossil fuels. Also, the current infrastructure is set up to use fossil fuels, and it would be very costly to build new infrastructure (such as hydrogen filling stations or ethanol pumps and tanks).

8. The octane rating for gasoline is a measure of the fuel's
   a. concentration of octane (C_8H_{18})
   b. energy content in kilocalories
   c. power rating
   d. tendency to cause knocking
9. E15 fuel is
   a. 15% ethanol, 85% gasoline
   b. 85% ethanol, 15% gasoline
   c. 15% isooctane
   d. 15% ether

Answers: 1, a; 2, d; 3, a; 4, a; 5, a; 6, d; 7, c; 8, d; 9, a

15.7 Convenient Energy

Learning Objective › Explain why gaseous and liquid fuels are more convenient to use than solid fuels.

The convenience of a fuel depends on its physical state: Gases and liquids are convenient, while solids are much less so. Perhaps the most convenient form of energy is electricity (Table 15.7). We can use electricity to provide light and hot water and to run motors of all sorts. We can use it to heat and cool our homes and workplaces. When looking at future energy sources, then, we look to a large degree at ways of generating electricity.

Table 15.7 Convenience of Fuels in Various Physical States

				In Use	
Physical State	**Extraction**	**Transportation to Cities**	**Distribution within a City**	**Convenience**	**Cleanliness**
Solids (coal, wood)	Shovels, borers, blasting	Trucks, trains, barges (slurry with water in pipe)	Trucks, buckets	Least	Dirtiest
Liquids (gasoline, fuel oil)	Pumps	Pipelines, tankers, barges, trucks	Trucks		
Gases (natural gas)	Pumps	Pipeline	Pipes		
Electricity[a] (electron flow)	—	Wires	Wires	Most	Cleanest

[a]Produced by burning any of the primary fuels and included for comparison.

Any fuel can be burned to boil water, and the steam produced can turn a turbine to generate electricity. Figure 15.9 shows a coal-fired steam power plant. At present, about 45% of U.S. electric energy comes from coal-burning plants (Figure 15.10). Such facilities are at best only about 40% efficient. Thus, about 60% of the energy of the fossil fuel is wasted as heat, though some power installations use this waste heat to warm buildings.

Coal Gasification and Liquefaction

Coal can be converted to gas or oil. When we run short of gas and petroleum, why not make them from coal? The technology has been around for years. Gasification and liquefaction do have some advantages: Gases and liquids are easy to transport, and the process of conversion leaves much of the sulfur and minerals behind, thus overcoming a serious disadvantage of coal as a fuel.

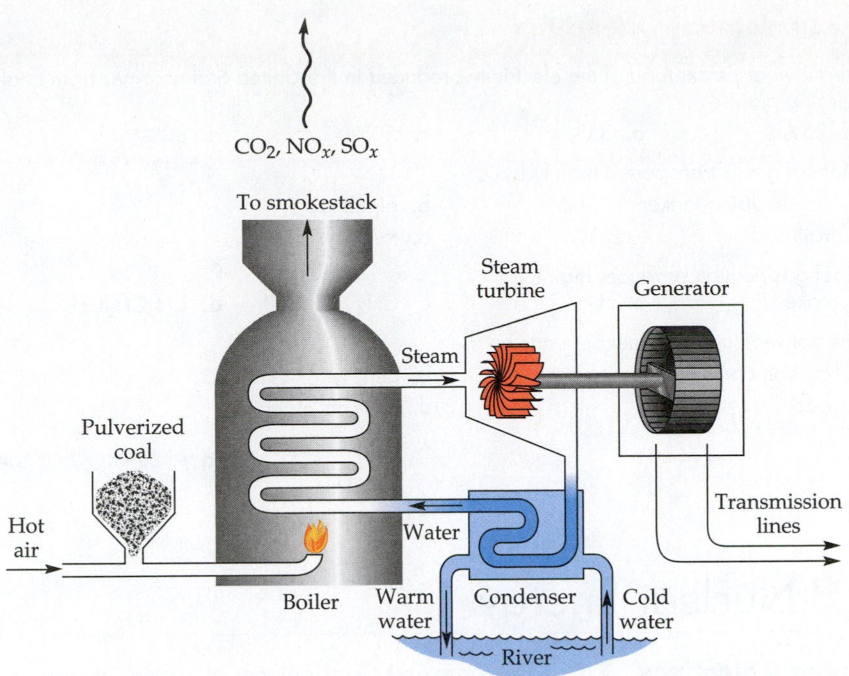

◀ **Figure 15.9** A diagram showing how a coal-burning power plant generates electricity.

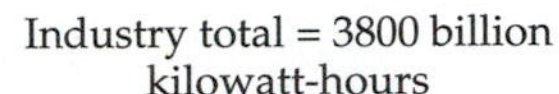

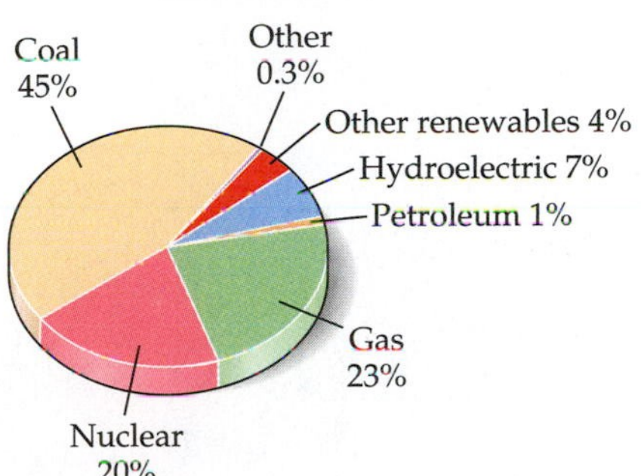

▲ **Figure 15.10** Percentages of electric power generation in the United States from various energy sources in 2009.

The basic process for converting coal to a synthetic gaseous fuel involves reduction of carbon by hydrogen. Passing steam over hot charcoal produces *synthesis gas*, a mixture of hydrogen and carbon monoxide.

$$C(s) + H_2O(g) \longrightarrow CO(g) + H_2$$

The hydrogen can be used to reduce the carbon in coal or other substances to form methane.

$$C(s) + 2\,H_2(g) \longrightarrow CH_4(g)$$

Coal can also be converted to methanol by way of synthesis gas. Part of the CO in synthesis gas is reacted with water to form more H_2.

$$CO(g) + H_2O(g) \longrightarrow CO_2(g) + H_2(g)$$

The remaining CO is combined with H_2 to form methanol.

$$CO(g) + 2\,H_2(g) \longrightarrow CH_3OH(l)$$

The methanol can be used directly as fuel or converted, in turn, to gasoline-like hydrocarbons that we represent as C_nH_m.

$$n\,CH_3OH(l) \longrightarrow C_nH_m(l) + x\,H_2O(l)$$

Each step requires an appropriate catalyst.

Both gasification and liquefaction of coal require a lot of energy: Up to one-third of the energy content of the coal is lost in the conversion. Liquid fuels from coal are high in unsaturated hydrocarbons and sulfur, nitrogen, and arsenic compounds, and their combustion products are high in particulate matter. Coal conversions also require large amounts of water, yet the large coal deposits that would be used are in arid regions. Furthermore, these processes are messy. Without stringent safeguards, conversion plants would seriously pollute both air and water.

Other processes that have been used to make liquid fuels from coal are the Bergius and Fischer–Tropsch methods. In the Bergius method, coal is reacted with hydrogen. In the Fischer–Tropsch method, coal is reacted with steam to make a mixture of carbon monoxide and hydrogen, which is then reacted over an iron catalyst to produce a mixture of hydrocarbons. Both processes were used in Germany during World War II. Since 1955, the Sasol company has used a variation of the Fischer–Tropsch method to provide a significant portion of liquid fuels for South Africa.

Self-Assessment Questions

1. About what percentage of the electricity produced in the United States comes from coal-burning plants?
   a. 25% b. 35% c. 50% d. 80%
2. Natural gas is transported mainly by
   a. ocean-going tanker
   b. pipelines
   c. railroad car
   d. truck
3. Coal gasification produces mainly
   a. coke b. H_2 c. CH_4 d. $CH_3CH_2CH_3$
4. The convenience of a fuel depends on its
   a. carbon content
   b. density
   c. odor
   d. physical state

Answers: 1, c; 2, b; 3, c; 4, d

15.8 Nuclear Energy

Learning Objectives › List advantages and disadvantages of nuclear energy. › Describe how a nuclear power plant generates electricity.

In Chapter 11, we explored nuclear reactions and noted that both nuclear fission and nuclear fusion can be used in bombs. So far, nuclear fusion reactions cannot be controlled for producing energy; they can be employed only in bombs. Nuclear fission reactions, however, can be controlled in a **nuclear reactor**. The energy released during fission can be used to generate steam, which can turn a turbine to generate electricity (Figure 15.11).

At the dawn of the nuclear age, some people envisioned nuclear power as likely to fulfill the biblical prophecy of a fiery end to our world. Others saw it as a source of unlimited energy. During the late 1940s, some claimed that electricity from nuclear power plants would become so cheap that it eventually would not have to be metered. Nuclear power has not yet brought either paradise or perdition, but it is highly controversial. Our great demand for energy indicates that the controversy will continue for years to come.

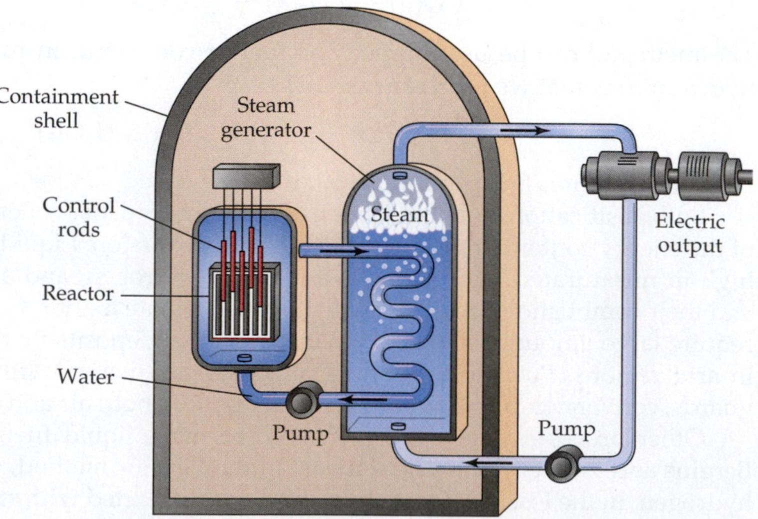

▲ **Figure 15.11** A diagram showing how a nuclear power plant generates electricity. Fission of uranium heats the water in the reactor, which generates steam that drives the turbines, producing electricity. Control rods absorb neutrons to slow the fission reaction as needed. Nuclear reactors are housed in containment buildings made of steel and reinforced concrete, designed to withstand nuclear accidents and prevent the release of radioactive substances into the environment.

Table 15.8 Electricity Generation Using Nuclear Power Plants (Selected Countries)

Country	Total Electricity from Nuclear Power (%)	Number of Operating Nuclear Power Plants	Number of Nuclear Power Plants Under Construction
China	2	14	27
France	74	58	1
Germany	28	17	0
India	3	20	5
Japan	29	50	2
Russian Federation	17	32	11
Sweden	38	10	0
Ukraine	48	15	2
United States	20	104	1
Other countries	—	120	15
World total	14	440	64

Source: International Atomic Energy Agency, *PRIS Database*. Vienna: 2010.

At present, about 20% of U.S. electricity comes from nuclear power plants. The eastern seaboard and upper midwestern states, many of which have minimal fossil fuel reserves, are heavily dependent on nuclear power for electricity.

The United States could do as other nations do and rely more on nuclear power (Table 15.8), but the public is quite fearful of nuclear power plants. This apprehension was exacerbated in 2011 by the accident at Fukushima, Japan. The United States has 104 operating nuclear reactors, but only one new plant has been ordered since 1978. It takes about 10 years to build a nuclear power plant. There will have to be a dramatic change in public attitude if nuclear power is to play a big role in our energy future.

Nuclear Power Plants

There are several types of nuclear power plants, but we won't discuss the different designs. The one illustrated in Figure 15.11 is a pressurized water reactor. Earlier models were mainly boiling water reactors, in which the steam from the reactor was used to power the turbine directly.

Nuclear power plants use the same fission reactions employed in nuclear bombs, but nuclear power plants cannot blow up like bombs. The uranium used in power plants is enriched to only 3–4% uranium-235. A bomb requires about 90% uranium-235.

In a nuclear power plant, a *moderator* is used to slow down the neutrons produced by the fission reaction so that they can be absorbed by uranium-235 atoms. Ordinary water serves as the moderator in 75% of reactors worldwide, graphite is used in 20% of reactors, and heavy water (^2H_2O or D_2O) in 5% of reactors. The fission reaction is controlled by the insertion of boron steel or cadmium *control rods*. Boron and cadmium absorb neutrons readily, preventing them from participating in the chain reaction. These rods are installed when the reactor is built. Removing them partway starts the chain reaction; pushing them in all the way stops the reaction.

The Nuclear Advantage: Minimal Air Pollution

The main advantage of nuclear power plants over those that burn fossil fuels is in what they do not do. Unlike fossil-fuel-burning power plants, nuclear power plants produce no carbon dioxide to add to the greenhouse effect, and they add no sulfur oxides, nitrogen oxides, soot, or fly ash to the atmosphere. They contribute almost nothing to global warming, air pollution, or acid rain. They reduce our dependence on foreign oil and lower our trade deficit. If the 104 nuclear plants in the United States were replaced by coal-burning plants, airborne pollutants would increase by 18,000 tons per day!

Problems with Nuclear Power

Nuclear power plants have some disadvantages. Elaborate and expensive safety precautions must be taken to protect plant workers and the inhabitants of surrounding areas from radiation. The reactor must be heavily shielded and housed inside a containment building of metal and reinforced concrete. Because loss of coolant water can result in a meltdown of the reactor core, backup emergency cooling systems are required.

Most of the nuclear waste currently awaiting disposal is from nuclear weapons production. High-level waste from nuclear power plant operation in the United States totals roughly 3000 tons per year. (Compare this to the coal ash produced in the U.S.: over 100 million tons per year!)

Despite what proponents call utmost precautions, some opponents of nuclear power still fear a runaway nuclear reaction in which a containment building is breached and massive amounts of radioactivity escape into the environment. The chance of such an accident is very small, but one did happen at Fukushima, Japan, when a tsunami caused by an earthquake hit the plant. Thousands of people were killed by the tsunami, and large areas were rendered uninhabitable by released radiation, perhaps for centuries. The benefit of nuclear power—abundant electric energy—is clear, but the small probability of a serious accident causes scientists and others to endlessly debate its desirability.

Another problem is that the fission products are highly radioactive and must be isolated from the environment for centuries. Again, scientists disagree about the feasibility of disposal of nuclear waste. Proponents of nuclear power say that such wastes can be safely stored in old salt mines or other geologic formations. Opponents fear that the wastes may rise from their "graves" and eventually contaminate the groundwater. It is impossible to do a million-year experiment in a few years to determine who is right. Federal funding for an underground repository at Yucca Mountain, Nevada, was terminated in 2011 after spending billions of dollars. This leaves the United States with no long-term storage site for high-level radioactive waste. These wastes are currently stored at 126 sites around the country.

▲ Mildly radioactive tailings are a by-product of the processing of uranium ores.

Mining and processing of uranium ore produce wastes called *tailings*. Over 200 million tons of tailings now afflict ten western states. These tailings are mildly radioactive, giving off radon gas and gamma radiation. Dust from the mounds of tailings is dispersed to surrounding areas.

Any power plant has another problem, thermal pollution, that is unavoidable. As the energy from any material is converted to heat to generate electricity, some of the energy is released into the environment as waste heat. Nuclear power plants generate more thermal pollution than plants that burn fossil fuels, but this difference is perhaps not as important as the other problems we have mentioned.

Nuclear Accidents

In 1979, a loss-of-coolant accident at the Three Mile Island nuclear power plant near Harrisburg, Pennsylvania, released a tiny amount of radioactivity into the environment. Although no one was killed or seriously injured, the accident heightened public fear of nuclear power.

A 1986 accident at Chernobyl, Ukraine, was much more frightening. There, a reactor core meltdown killed several people outright. Others died from radiation sickness in the following weeks and months, and 135,000 people were evacuated. The Ukraine Radiological Institute estimates that the accident caused more than 2500 deaths overall. A large area will remain contaminated for decades. Radioactive fallout spread across much of Europe. The thyroid cancer rate among Ukrainians increased tenfold, and the overall risk of cancer rose because of exposure to radiation. At Three Mile Island, a containment building kept nearly all the radioactive material inside. The Chernobyl plant had no such protective structure.

The earthquake and tsunami at Fukushima, Japan in 2011 destroyed the external power supply, leading to partial core meltdowns in three reactors, with widespread release of radiation. The Fukushima accident is rated as the second worst in history, after Chernobyl. Thousands were killed by the tsunami, but so far only a few by radiation.

There is considerable controversy over most aspects of nuclear power. Although scientists may be able to agree on the results of laboratory experiments, they don't always agree on what is best for society.

▲ A tsunami in March 2011 caused a meltdown and release of radiation at this nuclear power plant in Fukushima, Japan. It is already classified as the second worst nuclear accident (after Chernobyl), and there are concerns about fish and other products in the vicinity being used for food or shipped to other countries.

Breeder Reactors: Making More Fuel Than They Burn

The supply of the fissionable uranium-235 isotope is limited, as it makes up less than 1% of naturally occurring uranium. Separation of uranium-235 leaves behind large quantities of uranium-238, which is not fissionable. However, uranium-238 can be converted to fissionable plutonium-239 by bombardment with neutrons. Unstable uranium-239 is formed initially, but it rapidly decays to neptunium-239, which then decays to plutonium.

$$^{238}_{92}\text{U} + ^{1}_{0}\text{n} \longrightarrow ^{239}_{92}\text{U} \longrightarrow ^{239}_{93}\text{Np} + ^{0}_{-1}\text{e}$$

$$^{239}_{93}\text{Np} \longrightarrow ^{239}_{94}\text{Pu} + ^{0}_{-1}\text{e}$$

If a reactor is built with a core of fissionable plutonium surrounded by uranium-238, neutrons from the fission of plutonium convert the uranium-238 shield to more plutonium. In this way, the reactor, called a **breeder reactor**, produces more fuel than it consumes. There is enough uranium-238 to last a few centuries, so one of the disadvantages of nuclear plants could be overcome by the use of breeder reactors.

A 20-year study of 70,000 nuclear shipyard workers found that they had 24% *lower* mortality than nonnuclear workers in the general population. Those with the highest chronic radiation exposure had the *lowest* mortality from all causes—including cancer. Could it be that small doses of radiation are beneficial?

Breeder reactors have some problems of their own, however. Plutonium is fairly low melting (640 °C), and a plant is therefore limited to fairly cool, inefficient operation. Failure of the cooling system could cause the reactor's core to melt. Water is not adequate as a coolant, so molten sodium metal is used in the primary loop. These reactors are often called *liquid-metal fast breeder reactors*. If an accident occurred in such a breeder, the sodium could react violently with both the water and the air.

Plutonium is highly toxic and has a half-life of about 24,000 years. It emits alpha particles, making it especially dangerous if ingested. An estimated 1 μg in the lungs of a human is enough to induce lung cancer. Yet another problem is that plutonium is chemically different from uranium-238. That makes it much easier than uranium-235 to separate from uranium-238, for use in illicit nuclear weapons.

Thorium-232 is especially attractive for use in breeder reactors because it is quite abundant. There is about as much thorium in the Earth's crust as there is lead.

Another breeder reaction converts thorium-232 into fissionable uranium-233.

$$^{232}_{90}\text{Th} + ^{1}_{0}\text{n} \longrightarrow ^{233}_{90}\text{Th} \longrightarrow ^{233}_{91}\text{Pa} + ^{0}_{-1}\text{e}$$

$$^{233}_{91}\text{Pa} \longrightarrow ^{233}_{92}\text{U} + ^{0}_{-1}\text{e}$$

Uranium-233 is like plutonium in that it emits damaging alpha particles, but it is thought to be rather difficult to make bombs from reactor-grade uranium-233.

Only 11 breeder reactors with a production capacity of more than 100 MW have ever been built, none in the United States. And only one commercial breeder reactor is still operating (in Russia) in 2010, and it has never been fueled with plutonium.

Nuclear Fusion: The Sun in a Magnetic Bottle

Chapter 11 discussed the thermonuclear reactions that power the Sun and that occur in the explosion of hydrogen bombs. Control of these fusion reactions to produce electricity would give us nearly unlimited power. To date, fusion reactions have been useful only for making bombs, but research on the control of nuclear fusion is progressing (Figure 15.12).

Controlled fusion would have several advantages over nuclear fission as an energy source. The main fuel, deuterium ($^{2}_{1}$H), is plentiful and is obtained from *fractional electrolysis* (splitting apart by means of electricity) of water. (Only 1 hydrogen atom in 6500 is a deuterium atom, but we have oceans of water to work with.) The problem of radioactive wastes would be minimized. The end product, helium, is stable and biologically inert. Escape of tritium ($^{3}_{1}$H), which undergoes beta decay

▶ **Figure 15.12** A promising fusion reaction is the deuterium–tritium reaction. A hydrogen-2 (deuterium) nucleus fuses with a hydrogen-3 (tritium) nucleus to form a helium-4 nucleus. A neutron is released, along with a considerable quantity of energy.

Hydrogen-2 (deuterium) + Hydrogen-3 (tritium) → Helium-4 (stable) + n + Energy

$$^{2}_{1}\text{H} + {}^{3}_{1}\text{H} \longrightarrow {}^{4}_{2}\text{He} + {}^{1}_{0}\text{n}$$

with a half-life of 12.3 years, might be a problem because this hydrogen isotope would be readily incorporated into organisms. Also, neutrons are emitted in most fusion reactions, and neutrons can convert stable isotopes into radioactive ones. Finally, we would still be concerned with thermal pollution—the unavoidable loss of part of the energy as heat.

Great technical difficulties have to be overcome before a controlled fusion reaction can be used to produce energy. A sustainable fusion reaction would require

- attainment of a critical ignition temperature between 100 million °C and 200 million °C,
- a confinement time of 1–2 s, and
- an ion density of between 2×10^{20} and 3×10^{20} ions per cubic meter.

In practice, the required conditions are measured by a combination of these three values.

No molecule could hold together at the fusion temperature. No material on Earth can withstand more than a few thousand degrees. Even atoms are unstable under these conditions. Atoms are stripped of their electrons, and the nuclei and free electrons form a mixture called a *plasma*. The plasma, made of charged particles (nuclei and electrons), can be contained by a strong magnetic field (Figure 15.13).

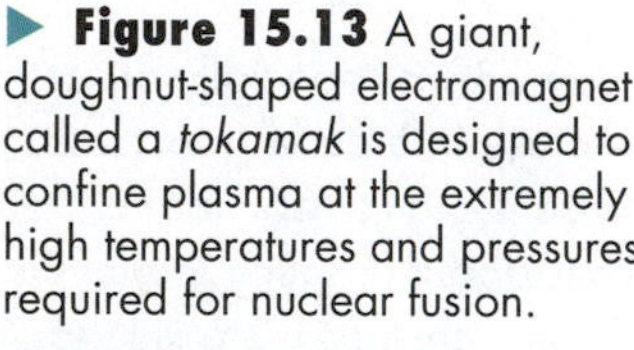

▶ **Figure 15.13** A giant, doughnut-shaped electromagnet called a *tokamak* is designed to confine plasma at the extremely high temperatures and pressures required for nuclear fusion.

Nuclear fusion may well be our best hope for producing relatively clean, abundant energy in the future, but much work remains to be done. Once controlled fusion is achieved in a laboratory, it will still be decades before it becomes a practical source of energy.

Self-Assessment Questions

1. In a nuclear fission reactor,
   a. carbon-14 decays to nitrogen-14
   b. hydrogen nuclei fuse to form helium
   c. uranium-235 absorbs a neutron and splits into two smaller nuclei
   d. uranium-238 decays to plutonium-238

2. The control rods in a nuclear reactor
   a. absorb neutrons, allowing them to initiate fission
   b. absorb neutrons, preventing them from causing fission
   c. slow the neutrons down so the moderator can stop them
   d. speed the neutrons up so they will initiate fission
3. What percentage of the electricity used in the United States is produced by nuclear power plants?
   a. 5% b. 10% c. 20% d. 50%
4. Nuclear reactors that produce more nuclear fuel than they consume
   a. are called breeder reactors b. are called fusion reactors
   c. are called transuranic reactors d. violate the law of conservation of energy
5. Approximately how many nuclear power plants are in operation in the United States?
   a. 50 b. 100 c. 200 d. 400
6. An advantage of nuclear power plants is that
   a. coal-burning plants have appalling safety records
   b. they produces no dangerous wastes
   c. they produces no greenhouse gases
   d. the reactor core cannot melt down
7. What is the missing product in the following nuclear reaction?

$$^{2}_{1}\text{H} + {}^{3}_{1}\text{H} \longrightarrow {}^{1}_{0}\text{n} + ?$$

   a. $^{3}_{1}\text{H}$ b. $^{3}_{2}\text{He}$ c. $^{4}_{2}\text{He}$ d. $^{5}_{2}\text{He}$
8. Fission, not fusion, is used in nuclear power plants because fusion
   a. uses expensive transuranium elements as fuel
   b. produces less heat than fission
   c. produces waste products that are radioactive for centuries
   d. requires temperatures of millions of degrees, making the reaction difficult to contain

Answers: 1, c; 2, b; 3, c; 4, a; 5, b; 6, c; 7, c; 8, d

15.9 Renewable Energy Sources

Learning Objectives › List important characteristics of renewable energy sources. › List advantages and disadvantages of various kinds of renewable energy.

Burning fossil fuels leads to air pollution and to the depletion of vital resources. Using nuclear power also presents problems. Nuclear fuel is not unlimited, and the problem of waste disposal remains unsolved. We are turning to renewable energy sources, which account for about 8–11% of the energy production in the United States. This section discusses these sustainable energy sources.

Section 15.1 noted that most of the energy available on Earth comes from the Sun. With all that energy from our celestial power plant, why are we currently dependent on fossil fuels or nuclear power? The answer lies in the fact that solar energy is thinly spread out and difficult to capture directly.

Solar Heating

Solar energy can be used directly for heating. As it arrives on the surface of Earth, 30% of solar energy is simply reflected back into space. About half is converted to heat. We can increase the efficiency of this conversion rather easily. A black surface absorbs heat better than a light-colored one. To make a simple solar collector, we only have to cover a black surface with a glass plate. The glass is transparent to the incoming solar radiation, but it partially prevents the heat from escaping back into space. The hot surface is used to heat water or other liquids, and the hot liquids are usually stored in an insulated reservoir.

Water heated this way can be used directly for bathing, dish washing, and laundry, or it can be used to heat a building. Air is passed around the warm reservoir,

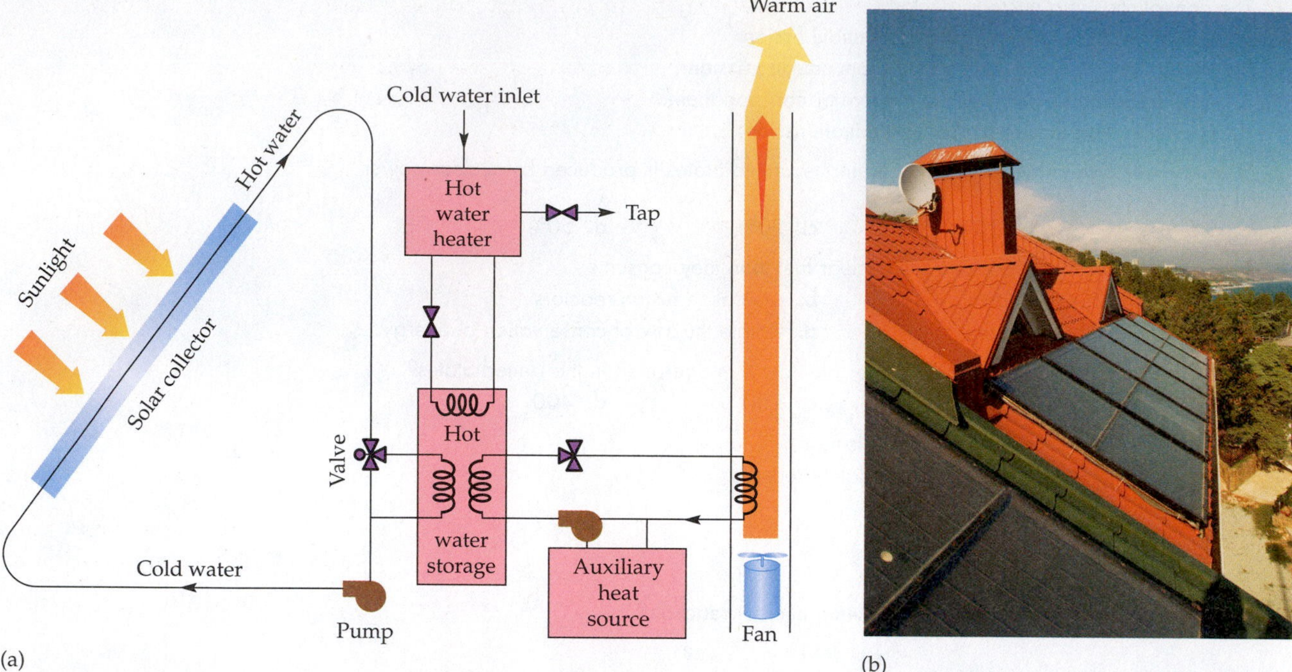

▲ **Figure 15.14** (a) Energy in sunlight is absorbed by solar collectors and used to heat water. The hot water can be used directly or circulated to partially heat a building. This diagram shows how a solar collector furnishes hot water and warm air for heating a building. (b) A variety of collectors can be used to absorb solar energy.

and the warmed air is then circulated through the building (Figure 15.14). Even in cold northern climates, solar collectors could meet about 50% of home heating requirements. These installations are expensive but can pay for themselves, through fuel savings, in a few years.

Solar Cells: Electricity from Sunlight

Sunlight also can be converted directly to electricity by devices called **photovoltaic cells**, or *solar cells*. These devices can be made from a variety of substances, but most are made from elemental silicon. In a crystal of pure silicon, each silicon atom has four valence electrons and is covalently bonded to four other silicon atoms (Figure 15.15). To make a solar cell, extremely pure silicon is "doped" with small amounts of specific impurities and formed into crystals.

▶ **Figure 15.15** Models of silicon crystals. Crystals doped with impurities such as arsenic and boron are more conductive than pure silicon and are used in solar cells.

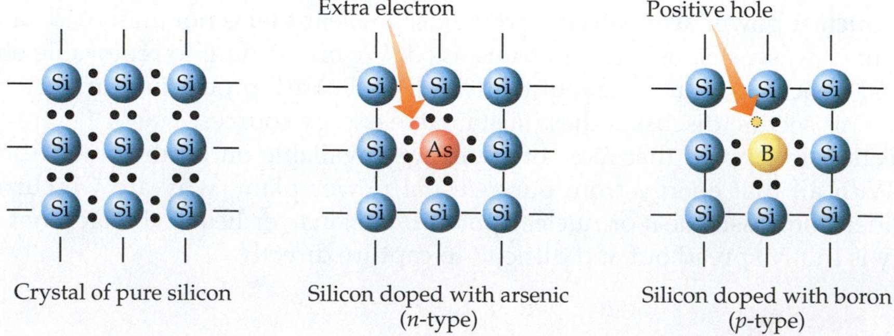

One type of silicon crystal has about 1 ppm of arsenic added. Arsenic atoms have five valence electrons, four of which are used to form bonds to silicon atoms. The fifth electron is relatively free to move around. Because this material has extra electrons, and electrons are negatively charged, it is called an *n-type* (negative) *semiconductor*. Adding about 1 ppm of boron to silicon forms a different type of material. Boron has three valence electrons, producing a shortage of one electron and leaving a *positive hole* in the crystal. This boron-doped silicon is called a *p-type semiconductor*.

Joining the two types of crystals (*n*-type and *p*-type) forms a photovoltaic cell (Figure 15.16). Electrons flow from the *n*-type region, which has a high concentration of them, to the p-type region. However, the holes near the junction are quickly filled by nearby mobile electrons, and the flow ceases.

When sunlight hits the photovoltaic cell, an electric current is generated. The energetic photons knock electrons out of the Si—Si bonds, creating more mobile electrons and more positive holes. Because of the barrier at the junction between the two semiconductors, electrons cannot move through the interface. When an external circuit connects the two crystals, electrons flow from the n-type region around the circuit to the p-type region and that current can be used directly.

An array of solar cells, combined to form a solar battery, can produce about 100 W/m^2 of surface. That is, it takes 1 m^2 of cells to power one 100-W lightbulb. Solar batteries have been used for years to power artificial Earth satellites. They are now widely used to power small devices such as electronic calculators. They are also used to provide electricity for weather instruments in remote areas.

Current solar cells are not very efficient, converting about 12–18% of incident sunlight into electricity, though experimental systems using mirrors have achieved efficiencies of more than 40%. Much of the sunlight striking them is reflected back into space or converted to heat. The generation of enough energy to meet a significant portion of our demands would require covering vast areas of desert land with solar cells. It would require about 20 km^2 (or 5000 acres) of cloud-free desert land to produce as much energy as one nuclear power plant. However, research has led to more efficient solar cells, and their cost is decreasing.

Using solar energy requires storing the energy for use at night and on cloudy days. The technology is now widely available for using solar energy for space heating and for providing hot water. Several companies sell home-sized solar electric systems that can be connected to the normal supply line and can reduce electric bills to nearly zero. However, these systems are quite expensive. Solar power currently provides less than 1% of U.S. energy needs. Though use of solar energy is increasing, widespread use is still some years away.

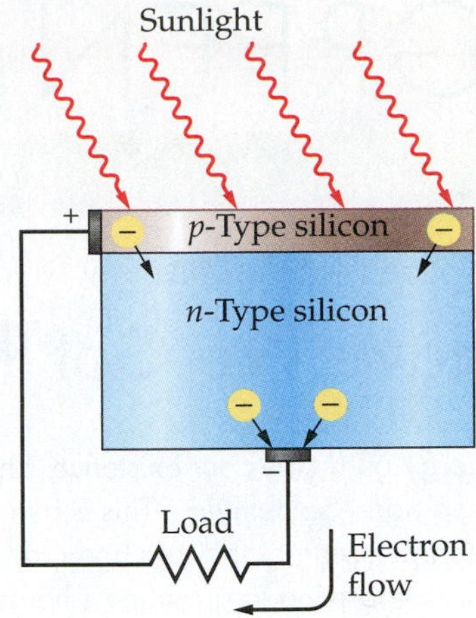

▲ **Figure 15.16** Schematic diagram of the operation of a solar cell. Electrons flow from the n-type region (lower layer) to the p-type region (upper layer) through the external circuit.

4. Is solar power or wind power the answer to the energy crisis? Both sources have made great progress but much work remains. Today's solar cells are far more expensive than fossil-fuel electricity and are too inefficient to provide a complete solution to our energy needs. Wind power is also expensive and has a high start-up cost. Neither source can directly power buses or cars.

Hemp, the fiber crop from which rope is made, is a good energy source. Its woody stalks are 77% cellulose, and hemp plants can produce 10 t of biomass per acre in just 4 months. The oil from hemp seeds can be used as diesel fuel. The problem is that hemp must be imported. It is illegal to raise hemp in the United States because the leaves and flowers of the female plant constitute the drug marijuana.

Biomass: Photosynthesis for Fuel

Why bother with solar collectors and photovoltaic cells to capture energy from the Sun when green plants do it every day? Indeed, dry plant material, called **biomass** when used as a fuel, burns quite well. It could be used to fuel a power plant for the generation of electricity. Biomass burns cleanly. The emissions are almost entirely water vapor and the carbon dioxide the plants took from the air in the first place. "Energy plantations" could grow plants for use as fuel. Biomass is a renewable resource whose production is powered by the Sun.

Unfortunately, there are several disadvantages to this energy source, too. Most available land is needed for the production of food. Even where productive land is available, plants have to be planted, harvested, and transported to the power plant. Often, the land is far from where the energy is needed. However, some hybrid species of trees grow quickly and densely, reducing the needed growing area. The overall efficiency of biomass as an energy source is even less than that of solar cells—only about 3% at best. Nevertheless, there is considerable research activity focused on biomass, because nature "constructs" plants much more easily and more quickly than we can construct industrial plants.

Also, we don't have to burn plant material directly.

- Starches and sugars from plants can be fermented to form ethanol. Wood can be distilled in the absence of air to produce methanol. Both alcohols are liquids and thus convenient to transport, and both are excellent fuels that burn quite cleanly.
- Bacterial breakdown of plant material produces methane. Under proper conditions, this process can be controlled to produce a clean-burning fuel similar to natural gas.
- Oils and fats can be converted to a fuel called *biodiesel*. The triacylglycerols are converted into the methyl esters of the constituent fatty acids. A typical biodiesel molecule from palm oil is methyl palmitate, $CH_3(CH_2)_{14}COOCH_3$. Biodiesel from waste, algae, or nonfood plants can have a reasonably high EROEI and can be profitable.

GREEN CHEMISTRY

Principles 1, 3, 4, 5, 6

Michael Heben, *University of Toledo*

Have We Got the Energy?

Energy permeates our existence. Energy is required anytime anything does "something." This is true whether we are considering a heart pumping blood in a body, an astronaut going to the Moon, a family driving to grandma's house, a plant fixing CO_2 to grow and produce food, an athlete playing sports, or a company making a chemical compound for industrial or pharmaceutical use.

Is there anything we do that does not require energy? No—and even thinking about the question can be exhausting—because thinking requires energy.

This chapter considers the sources of energy that are available to us. What we commonly consider to be energy sources, such as natural gas, coal, and oil, however, are not energy sources at all. Rather, these are fuels. They contain stored energy in carbon–carbon and carbon–hydrogen chemical bonds. These bonds react with oxygen during combustion, and the released heat can be used in homes or in industrial processes, to power an engine that does mechanical work, or to generate electricity.

The fossil fuels that we use today are the remains of ancient plant and animal matter. The energy source that produced the original organic matter via photosynthesis is our own star, the Sun (Section 15.1). Because the stored energy will be depleted in the not-too-distant future, it's good that we are working to use the energy from the Sun directly through technologies such as photovoltaic cells, wind power, and bioenergy. Consider this: If we covered an area comparable to a quarter of the area used for roads in the United States (around 9000 mi^2 or a little larger than the state of New Jersey) with 15% efficient solar panels, all of the country's electricity needs could be met.

Energy return on energy invested (EROEI) is a useful way to evaluate technology for fuel production (Section 15.6). The EROEI for fossil fuels has been dropping as easily tapped reserves have been depleted. Yet EROEI does not tell the whole story of a technology's impact because important aspects of its use are often ignored. A more complete analysis uses green chemistry principles and considers the impact of waste generation, toxic substances, renewable feedstocks, and overall energy efficiency. To generate energy efficiently, we need to minimize the inputs and maximize the energy output. Clearly, waste must be reduced, and other products are desired only if their formation and presence do not reduce or limit the primary goal—energy production.

An EROEI value measures only the energy inputs and outputs, and waste is not included. Combustion of oil, natural gas, and coal produces CO_2, which is the main contributor to the world's urgent climate-change problem. For technologies that have low EROEI values, CO_2 emissions are accelerated. For example, combustion of 100 units of a fuel obtained from a process with an EROEI of 2:1 would result in 43% more CO_2 emissions than combustion of 100 units of a fuel obtained from a process with an EROEI of 20:1.

An interesting case is the use of hydraulic fracturing (fracking) for production of natural gas (Section 15.6), in which high-pressure fluids are forced into fractures in rocks to remove the gas. Approximately 35,000 wells were fractured in 2010 in the United States, using about 100 billion gallons of water. Once considered an unconventional method, fracking now accounts for 50% of natural gas production in the United States. Hundreds of different chemicals, many of which are known carcinogens, are added to the fracture fluids. These and other species released by fracturing (including naturally occurring radioactive species) may reach aquifers or be diverted to municipal water-treatment facilities. Although EROEI values for fracking may not be terribly low, there are large amounts of waste that are not currently considered as part of the evaluation process. Also, besides the CO_2 emissions associated with combustion, considerable amounts of CH_4 leak into the atmosphere during natural gas production. Methane is 25 times more active as a greenhouse gas than CO_2.

The biggest hurdle to developing clean, renewable energy has to do with cost. If we do the accounting correctly and measure all inputs and outputs and impacts of a given process, the true costs to society will guide us in making good choices. New science and technology—and new mindsets—will be required. Perhaps you will want to help in this grand challenge.

▲ Biodiesel is another means of meeting our energy needs. It converts waste food oils and fats to fuel that can be used directly in many diesel-powered vehicles. However, it is not without its problems. Large quantities of corrosive sodium hydroxide or potassium hydroxide are used in this conversion.

All these conversions, however, result in the loss of a portion of the useful energy. The laws of thermodynamics tell us that we can get the most energy by burning the biomass directly rather than converting it to a more convenient liquid or gaseous fuel.

Biomass and biofuels currently provide about half of the renewable energy used in the United States, or about 5% of the country's overall energy needs. We could make greater use of these sources by converting appropriate materials to biodiesel, fermenting some agricultural wastes to ethanol, and fermenting human and animal wastes to produce methane. The technology for all these processes is available now and can be further improved.

▲ These willow trees are grown specifically as fuel. The biomass is harvested by cutting the trees near ground level, which stimulates regrowth. Willow is especially suitable for biomass because of its rapid growth.

Hydrogen: Light and Powerful

Natural gas is sent through pipes to wherever it is needed, and other fuel gases could be sent through the same pipes. One such gas is hydrogen.

When hydrogen burns, it produces water and gives off energy.

$$2\,H_2(g) + O_2(g) \longrightarrow 2\,H_2O(l) + 572\text{ kJ}$$

Gram for gram, hydrogen yields more energy than any other chemical fuel. It is also a clean fuel, yielding only water as a chemical product. Although hydrogen is the most abundant element in the universe, elemental hydrogen (H_2) is almost nonexistent on Earth. There is a lot of hydrogen on Earth, but it is tied up in chemical compounds, mainly water, and releasing it requires more energy than the hydrogen produces when it is burned. Hydrogen can be made from seawater, so the supply is almost inexhaustible, but the production process is costly.

Fuel Cells

A **fuel cell** is a device in which fuel is oxidized in an electrochemical cell (Section 8.3) so as to produce electricity directly. Fuel cells differ from the usual electrochemical cell in two ways:

- The fuel and oxygen are fed into the cell continuously. As long as fuel is supplied, current is generated.
- The electrodes are made of an inert material such as platinum that does not react during the process.

Most of today's fuel cells use hydrogen and oxygen (Figure 15.17). At the platinum anode, H_2 is oxidized to yield hydrogen ions and electrons.

$$2\,H_2(g) \longrightarrow 4\,H^+ + 4\,e^-$$

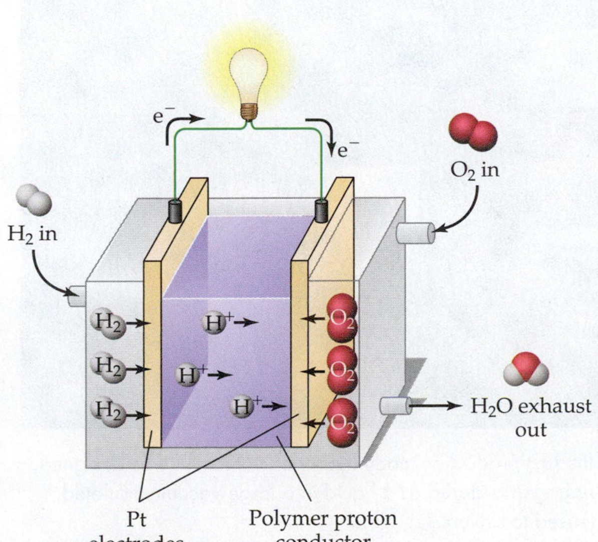

◀ **Figure 15.17** A hydrogen–oxygen fuel cell. The fuel cell continues to provide electricity as long as reactants are supplied.

Hydrogen in Your Future (Car)

Hydrogen can be used as a fuel for cars, either directly or in fuel cells. Among the advantages of hydrogen as a fuel are the following:

- The exhaust is almost entirely water vapor, which cuts down on urban air pollution and the production of the greenhouse gas CO_2.
- It can be produced from renewable sources.
- It could reduce U.S. reliance on foreign oil and the associated economic and political costs.

There are, however, significant obstacles to making the transition to hydrogen, so the roads will not be filled with hydrogen cars anytime soon. Among the problems are the following:

- Hydrogen is not a *source* of energy; there are no hydrogen "mines" or "reservoirs."
- The hydrogen-powered cars now available are expensive novelties, costing $100,000 or more.
- There is no widespread distribution system of hydrogen fueling stations.
- Hydrogen is a low-density gas that liquefies at −253 °C (20 K). Use of the gas requires large, heavy tanks. Liquid hydrogen must be maintained at a temperature only a few degrees above absolute zero. Therefore, storage, transportation, and dispensing of the fuel is problematic.

Some progress has been made, mostly with fleets of vehicles that operate in a limited area. Fuel-cell technology is becoming more efficient and costs are coming down, but there is still the problem of producing hydrogen gas economically. Hydrogen has to be made using another energy source: fossil fuels, nuclear power, or—preferably—some renewable source such as solar energy or wind power. Some experimental cells make hydrogen on-board from methanol or natural gas by a high-temperature process called *reforming*.

$$CH_4(g) + 2\,H_2O(g) \longrightarrow CO_2(g) + 4\,H_2(g)$$

The drawback is that reforming emits carbon dioxide, negating one of the reasons for using fuel cells in the first place.

Even liquid H_2, with a density of 0.07 g/cm^3, requires a large fuel tank, and the tank must be well insulated. It may be possible to store hydrogen in other ways: Scientists have found that various metals can absorb up to a thousand times their own volume of hydrogen gas. Special forms of carbon, such as ultrathin carbon nanotubes, may also hold large quantities of the gas.

The cost of establishing pipelines and filling stations to handle hydrogen will be immense. It takes many years for revolutionary technologies to come to the marketplace. The increased emphasis on research into hydrogen fuel cells appears to be a step in the right direction.

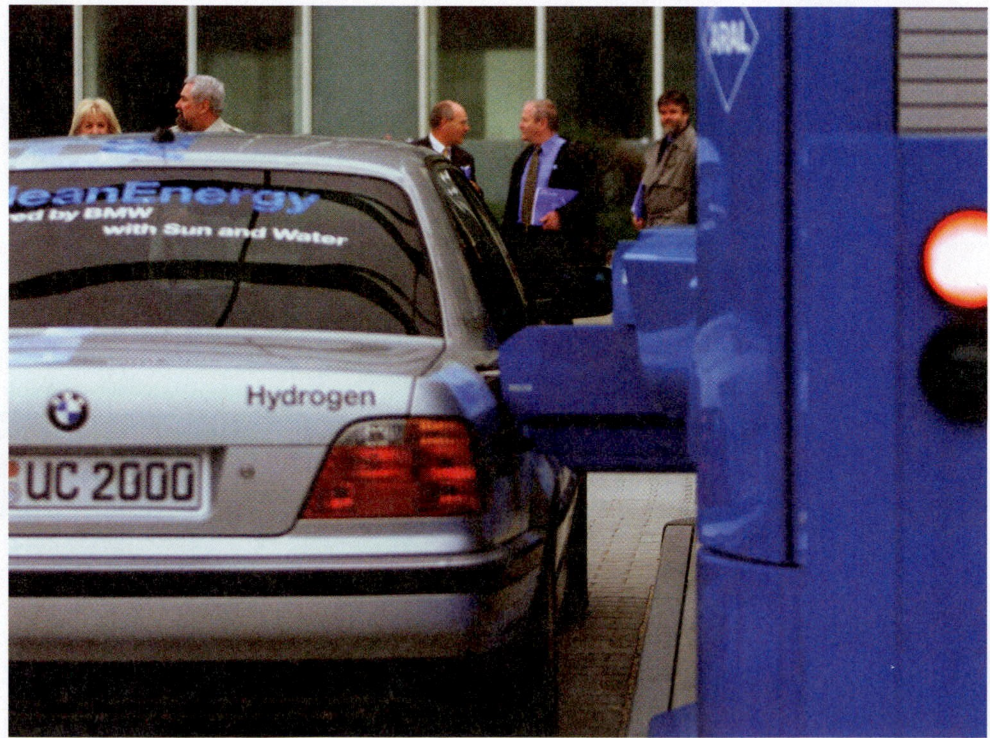

▲ The BMW Hydrogen-7 is claimed to be the first production-ready hydrogen vehicle. It was designed to run on either hydrogen or gasoline. The hydrogen is stored as a liquid in a large vacuum-insulated tank. In 2007, 100 of these vehicles were leased to drivers.

The electrons produced at the anode travel through the external circuit and arrive at the cathode, where they combine with the hydrogen ions and oxygen molecules to form water.

$$4\,e^- + O_2(g) + 4\,H^+ \longrightarrow 2\,H_2O(g)$$

The overall reaction (below) is identical to direct combustion of hydrogen, but not all the chemical energy is converted to heat. About 40–55% of the chemical energy is converted directly to electricity, making fuel cells much more efficient than internal combustion engines.

$$2\,H_2(g) + O_2(g) \longrightarrow 2\,H_2O(l)$$

Fuel cells are often used on spacecraft to produce electricity, mainly because they have a weight advantage over storage batteries—an important consideration when launching a spaceship—and the water produced can be used for drinking. Because they have no moving parts, fuel cells are usually tough and reliable.

On Earth, research is under way to reduce costs and design long-lasting cells. Perhaps fuel cells will someday provide electricity to meet peak needs in large power plants. Unlike huge boilers and nuclear reactors, they can be started and stopped simply by turning the fuel on or off.

Some people are afraid of using hydrogen as fuel for home heating because of the possibility of explosion, but natural gas leaks can also lead to serious explosions. Hydrogen escapes more readily than natural gas or gasoline because of its smaller molecular size, but it also dissipates more readily, rather than forming a flammable low-lying vapor as gasoline sometimes does.

5. Is hydrogen really a nonpolluting fuel? The only product from the combustion of hydrogen is water. However, an internal combustion engine runs at high temperatures and pressures. Under these conditions, some amount of nitrogen oxides, which are pollutants, forms. If hydrogen is used in a fuel cell instead of an internal combustion engine, pollution is negligible.

Other Renewable Energy Sources

Modern civilization requires tremendous amounts of energy and will require more and more in the coming years. We are depleting our reserves of fossil fuels, and many see significant disadvantages to nuclear power. Using the Sun's energy seems to be a good idea, but it would be difficult to meet all our needs with solar energy.

The Sun, by heating Earth, causes winds to blow and water to evaporate and rise into the air, later to fall as rain. The kinetic energy of blowing wind and flowing water can be used as sources of energy—as they have been for centuries.

Why not use wind power and waterpower to help solve the energy crisis? We do. Waterpower provides almost 7% of current electricity production in the United States, most of it in the mountainous west. In a modern hydroelectric plant, water is held behind huge dams. Some of it is released through penstocks against the blades of water turbines. The potential energy of the stored water is converted to the kinetic energy of flowing water. The moving water imparts mechanical energy to the turbine, which drives a generator that converts mechanical energy to electrical energy.

Hydroelectric plants are relatively clean, but most of the good dam sites in the United States are already in use. To obtain more hydroelectric energy, we would have to dam up scenic rivers and flood valuable cropland and recreational areas. Reservoirs silt up over the years, and sometimes dams break, causing catastrophic floods. Dams block the migration of fish upstream to spawning beds. Declining fish populations have led to closure of salmon fishing in waters off California and Oregon and removal of dams from a few rivers where salmon spawn.

Worldwide, hydroelectric plants provide about 20% of the electricity used, and more plants are being built in many developing countries. As a major example, China's huge Three Gorges project on the Yangtze River, completed in 2009, includes a 22,500-MW hydroelectric plant. It provides more than 10% of China's electricity. Unfortunately, the project displaced 1.3 million people and may cause significant environmental damage. Water quality in the Yangtze's tributaries is already deteriorating rapidly because the dammed river disperses pollutants less effectively and algae blooms flourish. The rising water caused extensive soil erosion, riverbank collapses, and landslides. Even renewable hydroelectric power has its problems.

▲ Hoover Dam, on the Colorado River, was completed in 1936. It generates 4 billion kWh a year—enough to supply 1.3 million people.

We could use more wind power. The kinetic energy of moving air is readily converted to mechanical energy to pump water, grind grain, or turn turbines and generate electricity. Wind power currently supplies only about 2% of U.S. energy production, but it is the fastest-growing energy source, increasing at an annual rate of 20–30%.

▶ Wind turbines, such as these in an off-coast wind farm, supply about 20% of Denmark's electricity. By the end of 2010, windmills with a generating capacity of almost 200,000 MW were operating worldwide, producing about 2.5% of the world's electricity.

Wind is clean, free, and abundant. However, it does not blow constantly, and some means of energy storage or an alternative source of energy is needed. Not all regions have enough wind to make wind power feasible. Some environmentalists oppose wind power because the rotating blades kill thousands of birds each year, but so do domestic cats and collisions with television and microwave towers. The amount of land required for windmills might become a problem if wind power were used widely, but the land under windmills could be used for farming or grazing.

How does chemistry relate to waterpower and wind power? Chemists produce new materials, such as metal alloys, reinforced plastics, and lubricants, that are vital to the construction and operation of dams, windmills, and turbines. Chemists also monitor water quality above and below dams and participate in other activities vital to protection of the environment around generating facilities.

Geothermal Energy

The interior of Earth is heated by immense gravitational forces and by natural radioactivity. This heat comes to the surface in some areas through geysers and volcanoes. **Geothermal energy** has long been used in Iceland, New Zealand, Japan, and Italy. It has some potential in the United States—it is being used now in California (Figure 15.18)—but in the near future this potential could be realized only in areas where steam or hot water is at or near the surface. One drawback of geothermal energy is that the wastewater is quite salty, and its disposal could be a problem.

(a)

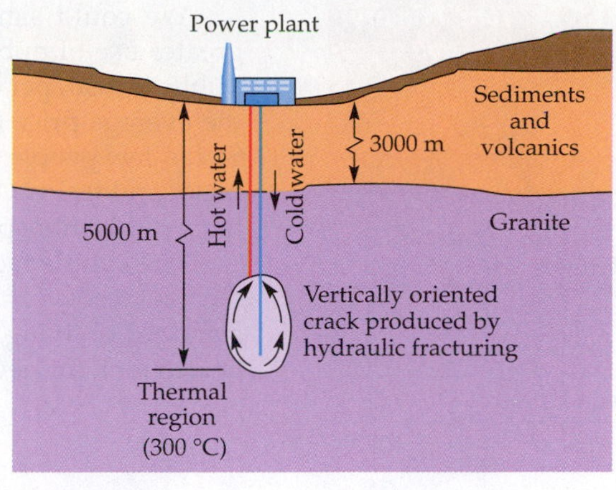

(b)

▲ **Figure 15.18** Geothermal energy contributes to energy supplies in some areas. (a) A geothermal field at Wairakei, New Zealand. (b) Energy is extracted from dry, hot rock 5 km below the surface by pumping water into the rock to be heated.

Oceans of Energy

The oceans that cover three-fourths of Earth's surface are an enormous reservoir of potential energy. The use of *ocean thermal energy* was first proposed in 1881 and was shown to be workable in the 1930s. The difference in temperature between the surface and the depths is 20 °C or more, enough to evaporate a liquid and use the vapor to drive a turbine. The liquid is then condensed by the cold from the ocean depths, and the cycle is repeated.

Other ways of using ocean energy have been tested. In some areas of the world, the daily rise and fall of the tide can be harnessed, in much the same way as the energy of a river is harnessed by a hydroelectric plant. At high tide, water fills a reservoir or bay. At low tide, the water escapes through a turbine to generate electricity. Even the energy of the waves crashing to shore can be used with the appropriate technology.

Energy: How Much Is Too Much?

Our energy future is quite uncertain. World petroleum production will peak soon—some claim this has already occurred. Developing nations will increasingly compete for fuels on the world market. Science and technology will have to be applied to provide an ever-growing supply of energy. The Energy Information Administration of the U.S. Department of Energy projected that world energy consumption will increase by 50% from 2007 to 2035, with much of the new demand from developing countries.

Each of the energy sources discussed in this chapter has advantages and disadvantages. How do we choose the best way to deal with energy problems? Wise choices require informed citizens who examine the process from beginning to end. We must realize what is involved in the construction of power plants, the production of fuels, and the ultimate use of energy in our homes and factories. We must recognize that energy is wasted (as heat) at every step in the process.

Will our profligate consumption of energy affect Earth's climate? Our activities have already modified the climate in and around metropolitan areas. The worldwide effects of our expanding energy consumption are harder to estimate.

What can we do as individuals? We can conserve. We can walk more and use cars less. We can reduce our wasteful use of electricity. We can buy more efficient appliances, and we can reduce our use of energy-intensive products (leaf blowers, lawn tractors, and larger automobiles).

Over the past three decades, we have made significant progress in energy conservation. Appliances are more energy efficient. New furnaces have efficiencies of 90–95%, as compared with the 60% efficiency of 20-year-old furnaces. New refrigerators and air conditioners use about 35% less energy than earlier models. Incandescent lamps are being replaced by compact fluorescent lamps, which are at least four times more energy efficient. Overall, U.S. industry has reduced its energy consumption per product by almost 30%.

Table 15.9 Total Primary Energy Consumption Per Capita, 2007 (in GJ)

Canada	469
United States	356
Russia	222
Japan	184
European Union	172
South Africa	109
Mexico	71
China	54
India	17
World	76

We could significantly reduce energy consumption in the United States by greater use of public transportation. In Europe, where there is much wider use of public transit, per capita energy use is considerably less (Table 15.9), partly because the average price for gasoline is usually more than twice that in the United States. So far, few people used to the convenience of personal cars seem eager to start using buses and trains. As the price of gasoline in the United States continues to rise, perhaps public transportation will seem more attractive.

The simple facts are that our population on Spaceship Earth is increasing and our fuel resources are decreasing. People in developing countries want to raise their standard of living, and that will require more energy. We need to conserve energy and to look for new energy sources.

Self-Assessment Questions

1. Which of the following is an *n*-type semiconductor?
a. arsenic doped with silicon
b. arsenic doped with germanium
c. silicon doped with arsenic
d. silicon doped with boron

2. *p*-Type semiconductors feature crystal sites with
a. photons
b. positrons
c. positive holes
d. protons

3. Which of the following is a renewable energy source?
a. biomass **b.** hydrogen
c. nuclear power **d.** tar sands

4. Biodiesel *cannot* be made from
a. corn starch **b.** olive oil
c. soybean oil **d.** waste cooking fat

5. The major product from burning hydrogen gas as a fuel is
a. CO_2 **b.** H_2 **c.** H_2O **d.** O_2

6. Which of the following fuels has the lowest EROEI?
a. biodiesel **b.** hydrogen
c. natural gas **d.** petroleum

7. Which of the following energy technologies does not use energy that originated in the Sun?
a. biomass **b.** hydroelectric **c.** nuclear **d.** wind

8. The fuel used by almost all current fuel cells is
a. electricity **b.** hydrogen **c.** natural gas **d.** propane

9. Fuel cells are
a. dependent on fuels from other sources
b. net sources of energy
c. producers of new fuels
d. renewable energy sources

10. The renewable energy source that provides the most electrical energy in the United States today is
a. geothermal **b.** hydroelectric **c.** solar **d.** wind

11. The energy that comes from the internal heat of the Earth is
a. bioenergy
b. geothermal energy
c. hydroelectricity
d. solar energy

Answers: 1, c; 2, c; 3, a; 4, a; 5, c; 6, b; 7, c; 8, b; 9, a; 10, b; 11, b

CRITICAL THINKING  EXERCISES

Apply knowledge that you have gained in this chapter and one or more of the FLaReS principles (Chapter 1) to evaluate the following statements or claims.

15.1 A futurist and inventor predicts that advances in nanotechnology will result in solar energy powering the world in just 16 years.

15.2 In 1996, Indian inventor Ramar Pillai claimed to have discovered a secret herbal formula that converted water to a hydrocarbon fuel.

15.3 An inventor claims to have discovered a catalyst that speeds the conversion of linear alkanes, such as hexane, to branched-chain isomers.

15.4 While watching TV during the summer, you hear someone proclaim that a way to cool your kitchen is to keep the refrigerator door open.

15.5 A fuel cell in every house can give each household energy independence.

15.6 I know the claim that modern electric automobiles are zero-emission vehicles is true because I found it on Wikipedia.

15.7 A company claims that it can use a metal such as magnesium as a fuel for automobiles. A coil of the metal would be fed into a chamber where it would react with superheated steam to produce hydrogen gas, which would power a fuel cell that would run the car.

SUMMARY

Section 15.1—**Energy** is the ability to do work. The United States has about 5% of the world's population but uses about one-fifth of all the energy generated. Most of the energy used on Earth comes from the Sun. The SI unit of energy is the joule (J), and the unit of power is the watt (W), which is 1 joule per second. Energy can be classified as **potential energy** (energy of position) or **kinetic energy** (energy of motion). In the process called **photosynthesis**, solar energy is absorbed by plants and used to produce glucose, and oxygen is generated.

Section 15.2—Rates of reactions are affected by temperature, by concentrations of the reactants, and by the presence of catalysts. The study of energy changes that occur during chemical reactions and physical processes is called **thermochemistry**. We define a **system** as the part of the universe under consideration. The **surroundings** are everything else. A chemical reaction or a physical process may be either **exothermic** (giving off energy) or **endothermic** (requiring energy). Reactions involving burning of fuels are all exothermic.

Section 15.3—The **first law of thermodynamics (law of conservation of energy)** says that energy can be neither created nor destroyed. The **second law of thermodynamics** states that in a spontaneous process, energy is degraded from more useful forms to less useful forms. **Entropy** is a measure of the dispersal of energy among the possible states of a system. There is a tendency for a system to increase in entropy.

Section 15.4—Ancient societies used human and animal power to do work. The main fuel was wood. A **fuel** is a substance that will burn readily with the release of significant energy. The first mechanical devices for doing work were the waterwheel and the windmill. Energy from water, steam, gas, the internal combustion engine, and other sources fueled the Industrial Revolution. **Fossil fuels** are natural fuels derived from once-living plants and animals. They include coal, petroleum, and natural gas.

Section 15.5—**Coal** is a solid fuel that is also a source of chemicals. The main element in coal is carbon. The quality of coal is determined mostly by its carbon and energy content, with anthracite being highest in rank and peat lowest. Coal is the most plentiful fossil fuel but is inconvenient to use and produces more pollution than other fuels.

Section 15.6—**Natural gas** is mainly methane and burns relatively cleanly. It is important both as a fuel and a raw material for synthesis of plastics and other products. **Petroleum**, or crude oil, is a thick liquid mixture of organic compounds, mainly hydrocarbons. Petroleum products can be burned fairly cleanly, but inefficient combustion produces pollution. Petroleum is refined by separating it, by distillation, into different fractions. **Gasoline** is the fraction consisting of hydrocarbons from about C_5 to C_{12}. Branched-chain hydrocarbons such as isooctane burn more smoothly than straight-chain hydrocarbons. The **octane rating** of gasoline compares its antiknock performance to that of pure isooctane. To raise the octane rating of gasoline, refineries use isomerization (to increase branching), **catalytic reforming** (to convert straight-chain hydrocarbons to aromatic hydrocarbons), and alkylation (to convert small hydrocarbons to larger branched molecules). Octane boosters such as methanol, ethanol, MTBE, and *tert*-butyl alcohol are added as well. Tetraethyllead was used to improve octane rating for more than 50 years but has been discontinued.

Section 15.7—Electricity is the most convenient form of energy. About half of the electricity in the United States is generated from coal-burning steam power plants. Coal can be converted to more convenient gaseous or liquid fuels, but at an energy cost.

Section 15.8—Nuclear fission reactions can be controlled in a **nuclear reactor**, which uses a low concentration (3–5%) of uranium-235. The reactions are controlled with rods of cadmium or boron steel. The energy released generates steam that turns a turbine to generate electricity. Approximately 20% of the United States' electricity comes from nuclear fission reactors. A nuclear power plant cannot explode like a nuclear bomb, it produces minimal air pollution, and its wastes are collected rather than dispersed. But elaborate safety precautions are needed to prevent escape of radioactive material, the needed fuel is limited in availability, and ultimate disposal of radioactive waste is an ongoing problem. A **breeder reactor** converts other isotopes to useful nuclear fuel and can make more fuel than it consumes. Nuclear fusion cannot yet be controlled, as there are great technical difficulties. Temperatures in the millions of degrees are needed to generate a **plasma** consisting of free electrons and nuclei, for controlled fusion. But fusion has very important potential advantages over most other energy sources.

Section 15.9—Solar energy is diffuse and difficult to collect. Simple solar collectors can produce hot water for heating. Solar cells, or **photovoltaic cells**, produce electricity directly from sunlight, using *n*-type and *p*-type semiconductors. The cells are becoming less expensive and more efficient, and photovoltaic systems require storage systems or connection to the local electricity grid. **Biomass** such as wood can be burned directly or converted to liquid or gaseous fuels, but it requires much land area to produce and has a very low overall efficiency. Hydrogen is an energy storage and transport method rather than an energy source. It burns cleanly but requires more energy to make than it produces. One advantage of hydrogen is that it can be used in **fuel cells**, which consume fuel and oxygen continuously to generate electricity efficiently. Other renewable energy sources include wind power and hydroelectric power, which can be harnessed only in certain locations. Both sources have high initial costs. Heat energy from the interior of Earth is **geothermal energy**. It can be used only in areas where steam or hot water is near the surface. We can also make use of the temperature difference between the ocean's surface and deep waters, tidal energy, and the energy of the waves. Renewable energy sources produced more than 10% of the electricity generated in the U.S. in 2010. Each energy source has advantages, limitations, and consequences. We can all conserve energy by using more efficient appliances and simply by using less energy.

Green chemistry Applying green chemistry principles and accounting for all inputs, outputs, and impacts are important for assessing the true value of technologies for energy generation and use.

Learning Objectives

› Perform power and energy calculations.	Problems 17–22, 69–72
› Classify chemical reactions and physical processes as exothermic or endothermic.	Problems 67, 68
› List factors that affect the rates of chemical reactions.	Problems 15, 16, 72
› State the first and second laws of thermodynamics, and discuss their implications for energy production and use.	Problems 23–28
› List the common fossil fuels, and describe how modern society is based on their use.	Problems 29, 30, 37–41
› List advantages and disadvantages of coal as a fuel.	Problem 29
› List the characteristics of natural gas and petroleum.	Problems 37, 39, 42, 78
› List advantages and disadvantages of natural gas and petroleum as fuels.	Problems 31–34, 38
› Explain why gaseous and liquid fuels are more convenient to use than solid fuels.	Problems 29, 30, 38
› List advantages and disadvantages of nuclear energy.	Problems 45–52
› Describe how a nuclear power plant generates electricity.	Problems 45–48, 55
› List important characteristics of renewable energy sources.	Problems 58, 62
› List advantages and disadvantages of various kinds of renewable energy.	Problems 59–61, 64
› Explain how applying the green chemistry principles can help identify improved methods for energy generation.	Problems 79–81
› Identify waste products from some current energy-generation processes.	Problem 79

REVIEW QUESTIONS

1. What kind of reaction powers the Sun?
2. What was the main fuel used in the United States before 1800?
3. What was the main fuel used in the United States from about 1850 to 1950? What has been the main fuel since 1950?
4. List some advantages and disadvantages of hydrogen as a fuel for vehicles.

Fuels and Combustion

5. Which of the following can serve as a fuel?
   a. fructose ($C_6H_{12}O_6$)
   b. propane (C_3H_8)
   c. hydrogen peroxide (H_2O_2)
6. Which of the following can serve as a fuel?
   a. hexafluoroethane (C_2F_6)
   b. stearic acid ($C_{18}H_{36}O_2$)
   c. tridecane ($C_{13}H_{28}$)
7. For each substance in Problem 5 that can serve as a fuel, write a balanced equation for its complete combustion in oxygen gas (O_2).
8. For each substance in Problem 6 that can serve as a fuel, write a balanced equation for its complete combustion in oxygen gas (O_2).
9. Write the equation for the complete combustion of coal, assuming that the coal is simply carbon.
10. Write the equation for the incomplete combustion of coal to form carbon monoxide, assuming that the coal is simply carbon.
11. Write the equation for the complete combustion of methane.
12. Write the equation for the incomplete combustion of methane to form carbon monoxide and water vapor.
13. Water gas is a mixture of H_2 and CO. Can water gas serve as a fuel? Explain.
14. Water gas (see Problem 13) can be made by reacting red hot charcoal with steam. Write the equation for this reaction.

Energy and Chemical Reactions

15. How does temperature affect the rate of a chemical reaction?
16. Why does wood burn more rapidly in pure oxygen than in air?
17. Burning 1.00 mol of methane releases 803 kJ of energy. How much energy is released by burning 24.5 mol of methane?

$$CH_4(g) + 2\,O_2(g) \longrightarrow CO_2(g) + 2\,H_2O(g) + 803\text{ kJ}$$

18. It takes 572 kJ of energy to decompose 2.00 mol of liquid water. How much energy does it take to decompose 55.5 mol of water?

$$2\,H_2O(l) + 572\text{ kJ} \longrightarrow 2\,H_2(g) + O_2(g)$$

19. When burned, 1.00 g of gasoline yields 1060 cal. What is this quantity in kilojoules?
20. How much heat, in kilojoules, is released when 4.301 g $H_2(g)$ reacts with $O_2(g)$ to form steam $[H_2O(g)]$ according to the following equation?

$$2\,H_2(g) + O_2(g) \longrightarrow 2\,H_2O(g) + 483.6\text{ kJ}$$

21. Refer to Problem 17, and determine how much energy, in kilojoules, must be supplied to convert 1.00 mol $CO_2(g)$ and 2.00 mol $H_2O(g)$ into $CH_4(g)$ and $O_2(g)$.
22. Refer to Problem 20, and determine how much energy, in kilojoules, must be supplied to convert 1 mol of water vapor into hydrogen gas and oxygen gas.

Energy and the Laws of Thermodynamics

23. State the first law of thermodynamics.
24. State the second law of thermodynamics in terms of energy flow and in terms of degradation of energy.
25. What is entropy? Does entropy increase or decrease when a fossil fuel is burned?
26. Energy is conserved. How can we ever run out of energy?
27. How does the statement "You can't get something for nothing" relate to the first law of thermodynamics?
28. How does the statement "You can't even break even" relate to the second law of thermodynamics?

Fossil Fuels

29. What are the advantages and disadvantages of coal as a fuel?
30. Why did the United States shift from coal to petroleum and natural gas when we have much larger reserves of coal than of the other two fuels?

Estimates in Problems 31–34 are from the U.S. Energy Information Administration.

31. The estimated proven world oil reserves in 2009 were 1342 billion barrels. The world annual rate of use was 31.1 billion barrels. How long will these reserves last if this rate of use continues? (The rate of use is actually likely to increase.)
32. The estimated proven U.S. oil reserves in 2009 were 21.3 billion barrels. **(a)** How long will these reserves last if there are no imports or exports and if the U.S. annual rate of use of 6.85 billion barrels continues? **(b)** Taking the mean projection for oil reserves in the Arctic National Wildlife Refuge—10.4 billion barrels—how long would exploiting that resource extend our reserves at the current U.S. annual rate of use?
33. The estimated world natural gas reserves in 2009 were 6254 trillion ft^3. The world annual rate of use was 103.8 trillion ft^3. How long will these reserves last if this rate of use continues?
34. The U.S. proven natural gas reserves in 2006 were 244 trillion ft^3. How long will these reserves last if there are no imports or exports and if the U.S. annual rate of use of 22.8 trillion ft^3 continues?

Natural Gas

35. Write a balanced equation for the combustion of ethane (C_2H_6, a component of natural gas) in oxygen gas to produce carbon dioxide and water vapor.
36. Write a balanced equation for the combustion of butane (C_4H_{10}, a minor component of natural gas) in oxygen gas to produce carbon dioxide and water vapor.

Petroleum

37. What is thought to be the origin of petroleum?
38. What are the advantages and disadvantages of petroleum as a source of fuels?
39. Use the term *molecular mass* to describe the difference between gasoline and kerosene.

40. How is crude petroleum modified to better meet our needs and wants? What are the advantages and disadvantages of tetraethyllead as an octane booster?

41. Consult Table 15.6, then suggest a reason why asphalt is so cheap that it is used to pave highways and driveways.

42. Which should have a higher octane rating: **(a)** octane ($CH_3CH_2CH_2CH_2CH_2CH_2CH_2CH_3$) or 2,3,3-trimethylpentane [$CH_3CH(CH_3)C(CH_3)_2CH_2CH_3$]? **(b)** benzene or hexane?

Nuclear Power

43. What proportion of U.S. electricity is generated by nuclear power plants?

44. What proportion of electricity in France is generated by nuclear power plants?

45. Can a nuclear power plant explode like a nuclear bomb? Explain.

46. Write nuclear equations showing how uranium-238 is converted to fissionable plutonium-239.

47. Can a nuclear bomb be made from reactor-grade uranium? Explain.

48. Can a nuclear bomb be made from reactor-grade plutonium?

49. How does a breeder reactor produce more fuel than it consumes? Does doing so violate the law of conservation of energy?

50. What are some of the disadvantages of breeder reactors?

51. List some possible advantages of a nuclear fusion reactor over a fission reactor. What is plasma?

52. List some possible problems with nuclear fusion reactors.

53. Write nuclear equations showing how thorium-232 is converted to fissionable uranium-233.

54. Write the nuclear equation that shows how deuterium and tritium fuse to form helium and a neutron.

55. The fission of 1 mol of uranium-235 can be represented by

$$^{235}_{92}U + ^{1}_{0}n \longrightarrow 2\,^{1}_{0}n + ^{139}_{54}Xe + ^{95}_{38}Sr + 1.8 \times 10^{10}\text{ kJ}$$

See the equation in Problem 11 for the combustion of methane. How many moles of methane must be burned to generate the energy produced by fission of 1.00 mol (235 g) of uranium-235? What is the mass of this amount of methane, in metric tons (1 t = 1000 kg)?

56. Coal is mostly carbon. Burning 1 mol (12.0 g) of carbon to form carbon dioxide releases 393 kJ of energy. Refer to Problem 55, and determine how many moles of carbon must be burned to generate the energy produced by fission of 1.00 mol (235 g) of uranium-235. What is the mass of this amount of carbon, in metric tons?

Renewable Energy Sources

57. What is a photovoltaic cell?

58. What are some problems associated with the use of solar energy?

59. The average power demand of an American household with nonelectric cooking is 1.2 kW. Solar cells can produce about 100 W/m^2. What area of solar cells is needed to meet this demand? What are the limits of this source of energy?

60. Large wind turbines can produce 1.5 MW of electrical power. How many of the homes described in Problem 59 could be powered by one big wind turbine? What are the limits of this source of energy?

61. What is biomass?

62. List some advantages and disadvantages of the use of biomass as a source of energy.

63. List two ways in which fuel cells differ from electrochemical cells.

64. List the advantages, disadvantages, and limitations of each of the following as an energy source.
a. wind power
b. geothermal power
c. biodiesel
d. hydroelectric power

Synthetic and Converted Fuels

65. Write the chemical equations for the basic processes by which coal (carbon) is converted to **(a)** methane and **(b)** carbon monoxide and hydrogen.

66. Write the chemical equations for **(a)** the conversion of carbon monoxide and hydrogen to methanol and **(b)** the reaction that occurs in a hydrogen–oxygen fuel cell.

ADDITIONAL PROBLEMS

67. A cold pack works by the dissolving of ammonium nitrate in water. Cold packs are carried by athletic trainers when transporting ice is not possible. Is this process endothermic or exothermic? Explain.

68. A hot pack hand warmer contains iron powder, water, salt, activated carbon, and vermiculite. It is activated by exposing the contents to air. Hot packs are used by hunters and other outdoor sportsmen and workers in places where access to heaters or fires is not possible. Is this process endothermic or exothermic? Explain.

69. The average human expends about 2100 kcal of energy per day. **(a)** What is this output in watts? **(b)** How does one human power compare to one horsepower? (See Problem 70.)

70. For a day of sustained work, an average workhorse expends about—you guessed it—one horsepower (hp). With the invention of the steam engine, inventors tried to standardize the unit to compare the output of steam engines to that of the horses the engines would replace. The modern value is about 1 hp = 745 W. A modern Formula One race car with a 2.4-L V8 engine can develop about 740 hp. What is its power output in kilowatts?

71. Both a banana and a hand grenade have about 170 kcal of energy. **(a)** What is the power output in watts of a banana if its energy is expended over 2.0 h by lying on a couch watching television? **(b)** What is the power output in watts of a hand grenade if its energy is expended in 0.0012 s? How do the banana and hand grenade compare in energy and in power?

72. Heats of combustion of several gaseous fuels, in kilojoules per mole, are given below. Which yields the most energy

(a) per kilogram and **(b)** per liter when the volume is measured under the same conditions of temperature and pressure?

Hydrogen (H_2), 286.6 kJ

Isobutane $[CH_3CH(CH_3)_2]$, 2868 kJ

Neopentane $[CH_3C(CH_3)_3]$, 3515 kJ

73. Name a natural process or processes by which carbon atoms are **(a)** removed from the atmosphere, **(b)** returned to the atmosphere, and **(c)** effectively withdrawn from the carbon cycle.

74. The United States leads the major developed countries in per capita emission of $CO_2(g)$ with a rate of 19.0 t per person per year (1 t = 1000 kg). What mass, in metric tons, of each of the following fuels would yield this quantity of CO_2?
    a. CH_4 **b.** C_8H_{18}
    c. coal that is 94.1% C by mass

75. A large coal-burning power plant burns 2500 tons of coal per day. The coal contains 0.65% S by mass. Assume that all the sulfur is converted to SO_2. What mass of SO_2 is formed? If a thermal inversion traps all this SO_2 in a volume of air that is 45 km by 60 km by 0.40 km, will the level of SO_2 in the air exceed the primary national air quality standard of 365 $\mu g\ SO_2/m^3$ air?

76. The contribution of the combustion of various fuels to the buildup of CO_2 in the atmosphere can be assessed in different ways. One way relates the mass of CO_2 formed to the mass of fuel burned; another relates the mass of CO_2 to the quantity of heat evolved in the combustion. Which of the three fuels, C(graphite), $CH_4(g)$, or $C_4H_{10}(g)$, produces the smallest mass of CO_2 **(a)** per gram of fuel and **(b)** per kilojoule of heat evolved? The heat released per mole of each substance is C(graphite), 393.5 kJ; $CH_4(g)$, 803 kJ; and $C_4H_{10}(g)$, 2877 kJ.

77. Estimates of recoverable energy are notoriously uncertain, but some scientists think that a total of only 9.92×10^6 terawatt-hours (TWh) of recoverable energy is stored in the Earth (in the form of oil, coal, natural gas, and uranium). Worldwide use is about 1.32×10^5 TWh per year. **(a)** If demand for energy remains the same as today, approximately how many years will it be before all the energy stored in the Earth is gone? **(b)** Per capita consumption in the United States (population of about 313,000,000) is about four times that of the rest of the world (population of about 7.0 billion). If all the countries throughout the world consumed energy at the same per capita rate as the United States, approximately how many years would it be before all the energy stored in the Earth is used up? **(c)** Evaluate your answers to parts (a) and (b).

78. Which of the following could be done to make hydraulic fracturing a greener process?
    a. Increase the use of water as a fracking fluid
    b. Use more chemical additives in the fracking fluid
    c. Capture or sequester CO_2 generated in the production and use of natural gas
    d. Monitor the amount of methane that escapes into the environment

79. When using the green chemistry principles to evaluate energy-generation processes, which of the following are considered?
    a. Energy invested and energy generated
    b. Feedstock source
    c. Waste products
    d. All of the above

80. When using EROEI to evaluate energy-generation processes, which of the following are considered?
    a. Energy invested and energy generated
    b. Feedstock source
    c. Waste products
    d. All of the above

COLLABORATIVE GROUP PROJECTS

Prepare a PowerPoint, poster, or other presentation (as directed by your instructor) to share with your class.

1. Which would you rather have in your neighborhood, a nuclear or a coal-burning power plant? Why? Explain.
2. What characteristics should an ideal energy source have? Which of these characteristics do the different sources of energy discussed in this chapter have?
3. Social-cost pricing takes into account all the costs of a product or activity that are not part of market costs. For example, one of the social costs of gasoline-based transportation is air pollution. Select three sources of energy, and list the possible social costs that should be considered.
4. Compare the quantity of electricity used for two appliances that are alike except for different efficiencies. Extend this comparison to CO_2 emissions from the appliances, assuming that the electricity is generated by burning coal.
5. Compare qualitatively the efficiency of heating a home with natural gas versus heating it with electricity produced from burning natural gas at a power plant.
6. Describe how each of the following types of nuclear reactors might serve as a future source of energy. Discuss possible advantages and disadvantages of each.
    a. a liquid fluoride–thorium reactor (LFTR)
    b. a very high temperature helium-cooled reactor
    c. a supercritical–water-cooled reactor
7. Which of the following is the best fuel for heating your home? What problems with supply, use, and waste products are involved in each case?
    a. natural gas **b.** electricity
    c. coal **d.** fuel oil
8. There was an accident at nuclear power plants at Fukushima, Japan, following an earthquake and tsunami on March 11, 2011. Using your favorite search engine, find out what happened and compare this accident with the ones at Chernobyl and Three Mile Island. How could these accidents have been avoided? Do these incidents prove that nuclear power plants should be phased out? Why or why not?
9. Use Internet sources to find directions and construct **(a)** a simple solar heater or **(b)** a solar oven.

Biochemistry

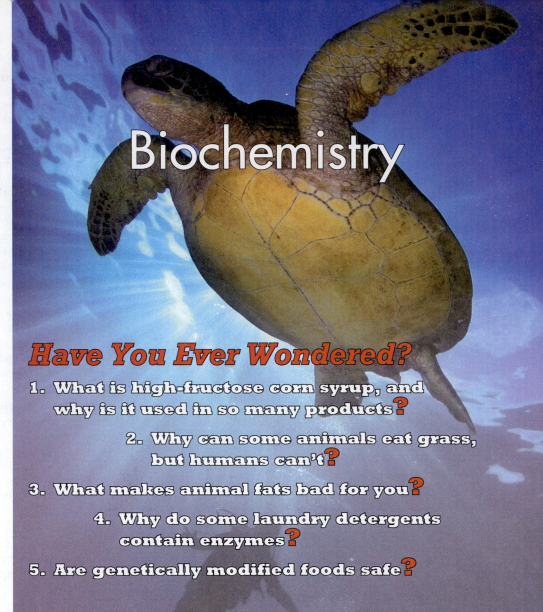

Learning Objectives

- List the major parts of a cell, and describe the function of each part. (16.1)
- Name the primary source of energy for plants and three classes of substances that are the sources of energy for animals. (16.1)
- Compare and contrast starch, glycogen, and cellulose. (16.2)
- Describe the fundamental structure of a fatty acid and of a fat. (16.3)
- Classify fats as saturated, monounsaturated, or polyunsaturated. (16.3)
- Draw the fundamental structure of an amino acid, and show how amino acids combine to make proteins. (16.4)
- Describe the four levels of protein structure, and give an example of each. (16.5)
- Describe how enzymes work as catalysts. (16.5)
- Name the two types of nucleic acids, and describe the function of each type. (16.6)
- Explain complementary base pairing, and describe how a copy of DNA is synthesized. (16.6)
- Explain how mRNA is synthesized from DNA and how a protein is synthesized from mRNA. (16.7)
- List important characteristics of the genetic code. (16.7)
- Describe recombinant DNA technology, and explain how it is used. (16.8)
- Name some advantages of using biochemistry to create useful molecules.
- Give examples of the use of biochemistry for energy production and other applications.

Have You Ever Wondered?

1. What is high-fructose corn syrup, and why is it used in so many products?
2. Why can some animals eat grass, but humans can't?
3. What makes animal fats bad for you?
4. Why do some laundry detergents contain enzymes?
5. Are genetically modified foods safe?

A Molecular View of Life

The human body is an incredible chemical factory, far more complex than any industrial plant. To stay in good condition and perform its varied tasks, it needs many specific chemical compounds—most of which it manufactures in an exquisitely organized network of chemical production lines.

Every minute of every day, thousands of chemical reactions take place within each of the 100 trillion tiny cells in your body. The study of these reactions and the chemicals they produce is called *biochemistry*.

Every form of life is chemical in nature. The substances and reactions that occur in living organisms are often more complex than the ones we have already studied. Nonetheless, basic chemical concepts such as acid-base reactions, intermolecular forces, and the reactivity of organic functional groups all apply to living organisms. In this chapter, we will examine acid-base reactions that govern the behavior of proteins in our bodies. We will look at intermolecular forces that influence the properties and behavior of DNA and RNA. And we will see that the functional groups on fats are the same as those on other organic compounds we have studied.

16.1 Energy and the Living Cell

Learning Objectives › List the major parts of a cell, and describe the function of each part. › Name the primary source of energy for plants and three classes of substances that are the sources of energy for animals.

Biochemistry is the chemistry of living things and life processes. The structural unit of all living things is the *cell*. Every cell is enclosed in a *cell membrane*, through which it gains nutrients and gets rid of wastes. Plant cells (Figure 16.1) also have walls made of cellulose. Animal cells (see Figure 16.2 on page 456) do not have cell walls. Cells have a variety of interior structures that serve a multiplicity of functions. We can consider only a few of them here.

The largest interior structure of a cell is usually the *nucleus*, which contains the material that controls heredity. Protein synthesis takes place in the *ribosomes*. The *mitochondria* are the cell's "batteries," where energy is produced. Plant cells (but not animal cells) also contain *chloroplasts*, in which energy from the Sun is converted to chemical energy, which is stored in the plant in the form of carbohydrates.

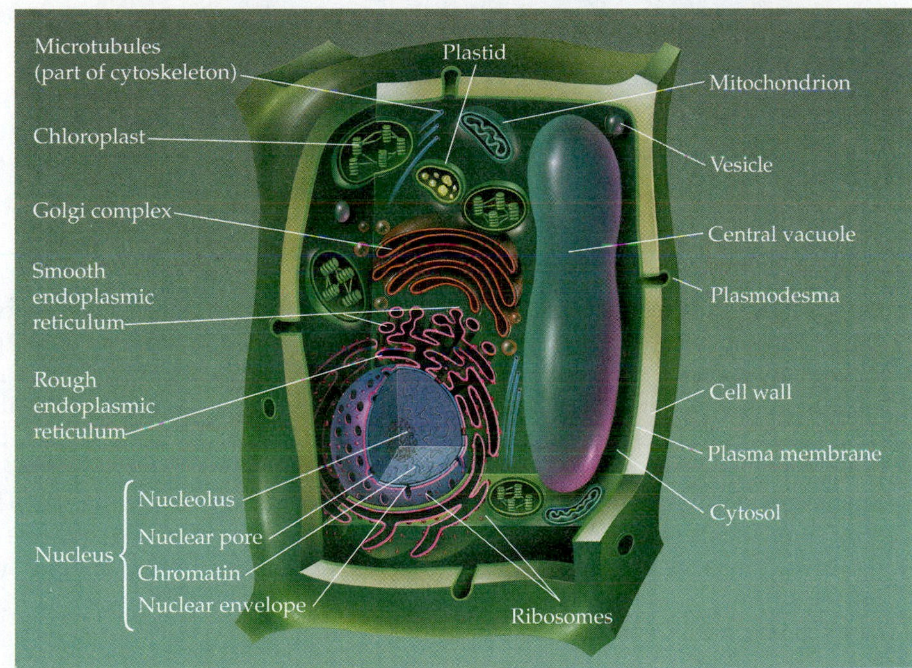

◀ **Figure 16.1** The general form of a plant cell. Not all the structures shown here occur in every type of plant cell.

Energy in Biological Systems

Life requires energy. Living cells are inherently unstable, and only a continued input of energy keeps them from falling apart. Living organisms are restricted to using certain forms of energy. Supplying a plant with heat energy by holding it in a flame will do little to prolong its life. On the other hand, a green plant is uniquely able to use sunlight, the richest source of energy on Earth. Chloroplasts in green plant cells capture the radiant energy of the Sun and convert it to chemical energy, which is then stored in carbohydrate molecules. The photosynthesis of glucose is represented by the equation

$$6\,CO_2 + 6\,H_2O \longrightarrow C_6H_{12}O_6 + 6\,O_2$$

Plant cells can also convert the carbohydrate molecules to fat molecules and, given the proper inorganic nutrients, to protein molecules.

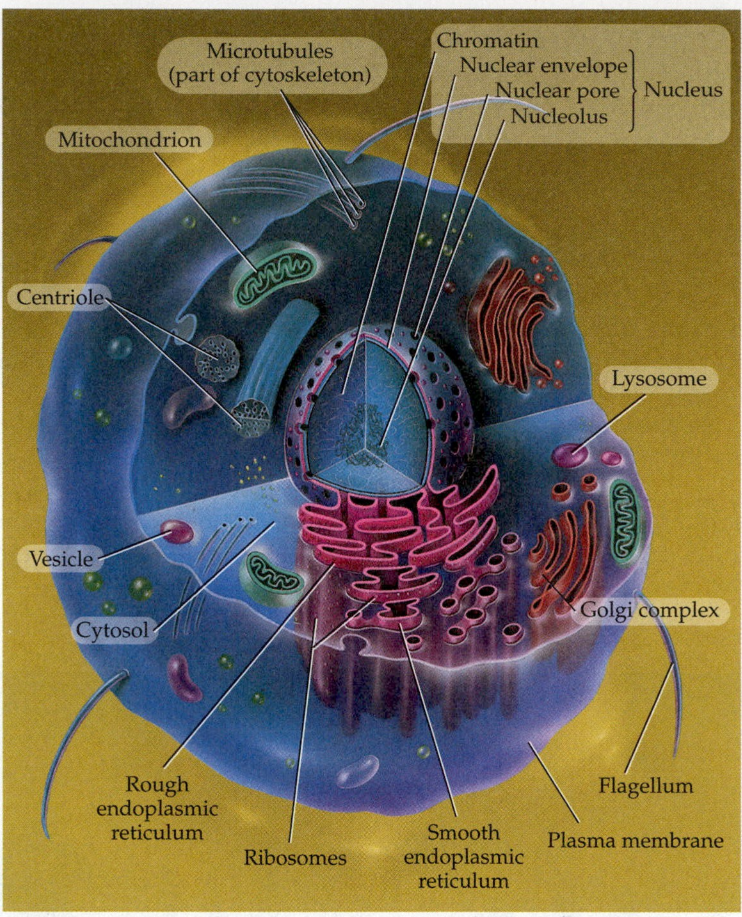

▶ **Figure 16.2** An animal cell. The entire range of structures shown here seldom occurs in a single cell, and only a few of them are discussed in this text. Each kind of plant or animal tissue has cells specific to the function of that tissue. Muscle cells differ from nerve cells, nerve cells differ from red blood cells, and so on.

Animals cannot directly use the energy of sunlight. They must get their energy by eating plants or by eating other animals that eat plants. Animals obtain energy from three major types of substances: carbohydrates, fats, and proteins.

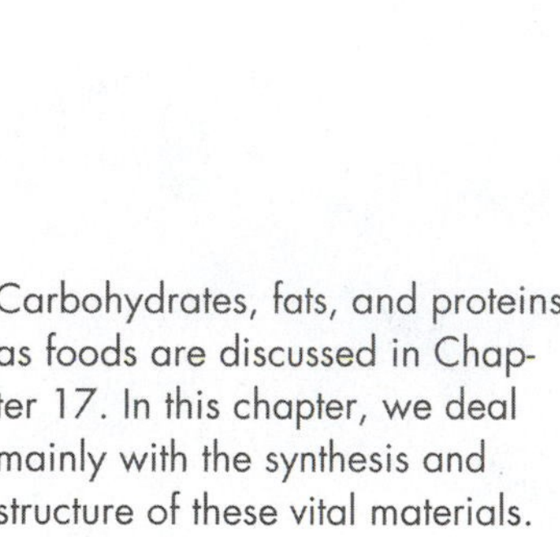

Carbohydrates, fats, and proteins as foods are discussed in Chapter 17. In this chapter, we deal mainly with the synthesis and structure of these vital materials.

Once digested and transported to a cell, a food molecule can be used as a building block to make new cell parts or to repair old ones, or it can be "burned" for energy. The entire series of coordinated chemical reactions that keep cells alive is called **metabolism**. In general, metabolic reactions are divided into two classes: The degrading of molecules to provide energy is called **catabolism**, and the process of building up, or synthesizing, the molecules of living systems is termed **anabolism**.

Self-Assessment Questions

1. The three major types of substances from which we obtain energy are
   a. amino acids, proteins, and carbohydrates
   b. burgers, pizza, and soft drinks
   c. carbohydrates, fats, and proteins
   d. proteins, nucleic acids, and oils
2. The process of degrading molecules to provide energy within a living cell is called
   a. anabolism
   b. catabolism
   c. depolymerization
   d. transcription
3. The overall set of chemical reactions that keep cells alive is called
   a. anabolism
   b. enzymology
   c. metabolism
   d. proteolysis

Answers: 1, c; 2, b; 3, c

16.2 Carbohydrates: A Storehouse of Energy

Learning Objectives › Compare and contrast starch, glycogen, and cellulose.

It is difficult to give a simple formal definition of *carbohydrates*. Chemically, **carbohydrates** are polyhydroxy aldehydes or ketones or compounds that can be hydrolyzed (split by water) to form such aldehydes and ketones. Composed of the elements carbon, hydrogen, and oxygen, carbohydrates include sugars, starches, and cellulose. Usually, the atoms of these elements are present in a ratio expressed by the formula $C_x(H_2O)_y$. Glucose, a simple sugar, has the formula $C_6H_{12}O_6$, which we can write as $C_6(H_2O)_6$. The term *carbohydrate* is derived from formulas written in this way, but keep in mind that carbohydrates are not actually hydrates of carbon.

Some Simple Sugars

Sugars are sweet-tasting carbohydrates. The simplest sugars are **monosaccharides**, carbohydrates that cannot be further hydrolyzed. Three familiar dietary monosaccharides are shown in Figure 16.3. They are *glucose* (also called *dextrose*), *galactose* (a component of lactose, the sugar in milk), and *fructose* (fruit sugar). Glucose and galactose are **aldoses**, monosaccharides with an aldehyde functional group (the functional groups were presented in Table 9.4). Fructose is a **ketose**, a monosaccharide with a ketone functional group. Pure fructose is about 25% sweeter than table sugar (sucrose, shown on page 458); glucose is about 25% less sweet than table sugar.

CONCEPTUAL Example 16.1 Classification of Monosaccharides

Shown below are structures of (left to right) erythrulose, used in some sunless tanning lotions; mannose, a sugar found in some fruits, including cranberries; and ribose, a component of ribonucleic acid (RNA; Section 16.7).

$$\begin{array}{c}
CH_2OH \\ | \\ C{=}O \\ | \\ HO{-}C{-}H \\ | \\ CH_2OH \\ \text{Erythrulose}
\end{array}
\qquad
\begin{array}{c}
CHO \\ | \\ HO{-}C{-}H \\ | \\ HO{-}C{-}H \\ | \\ H{-}C{-}OH \\ | \\ H{-}C{-}OH \\ | \\ CH_2OH \\ \text{Mannose}
\end{array}
\qquad
\begin{array}{c}
CHO \\ | \\ H{-}C{-}OH \\ | \\ H{-}C{-}OH \\ | \\ H{-}C{-}OH \\ | \\ CH_2OH \\ \text{Ribose}
\end{array}$$

Classify erythrulose and ribose as an aldose or a ketose.

Solution

Erythrulose is a ketose. The carbonyl (C=O) group is on the second C atom from the top; it is between two other C atoms, an arrangement that defines a ketone. Ribose is an aldose. The carbonyl group includes a chain-ending carbon atom, as in all aldehydes.

■ EXERCISE 16.1

How does the structure of mannose (shown above) differ from that of glucose?

The monosaccharides glucose, galactose, and fructose are represented in Figure 16.3 as open-chain compounds to show the aldehyde or ketone functional groups. However, these sugars exist in solution mainly as cyclic molecules (see Figure 16.4, page 458).

1. What is high-fructose corn syrup, and why is it used in so many products? High-fructose corn syrup (HFCS) has had some of its glucose enzymatically converted to fructose. This makes it significantly sweeter than ordinary corn syrup, because fructose is sweeter than glucose. HFCS is quite cheap in the United States. Unfortunately, like table sugar, it provides little more than empty calories.

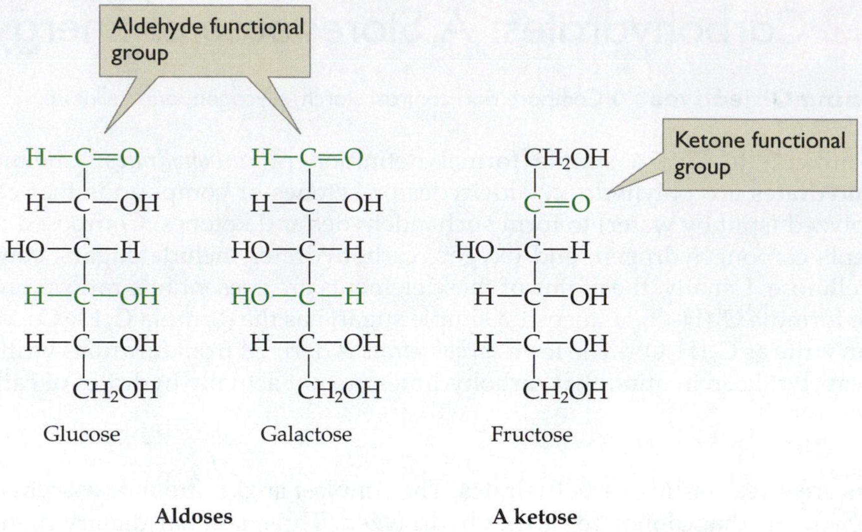

▶ **Figure 16.3** Three common monosaccharides. All have hydroxyl groups. Glucose and galactose have aldehyde functional groups, and fructose has a ketone group. Glucose and galactose differ only in the arrangement of the H and OH on the fourth carbon (green) from the top. Living cells use glucose as a source of energy. Fructose is fruit sugar, and galactose is a component of milk sugar.

Q: *What is the molecular formula of each of the three monosaccharides? How are the three compounds related?*

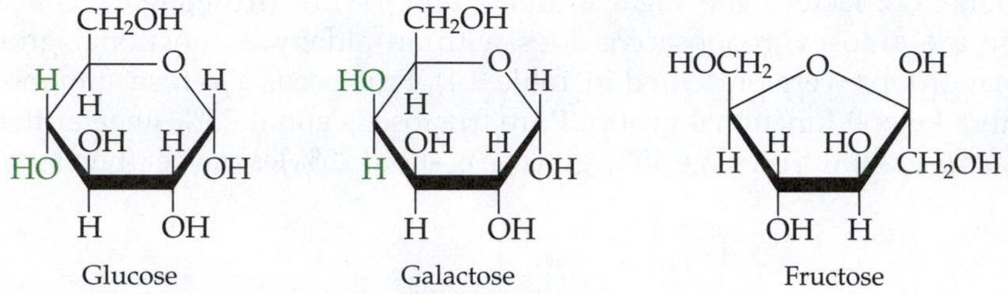

Aldehyde functional group

Ketone functional group

Glucose | Galactose | Fructose

Aldoses | **A ketose**

▶ **Figure 16.4** Cyclic structures for glucose, galactose, and fructose. A corner with no letter represents a carbon atom. Glucose and galactose differ only in the arrangement of the H and OH (green) on the fourth carbon. Some sugars exist in more than one cyclic form, but, for simplicity, only one form of each is shown here.

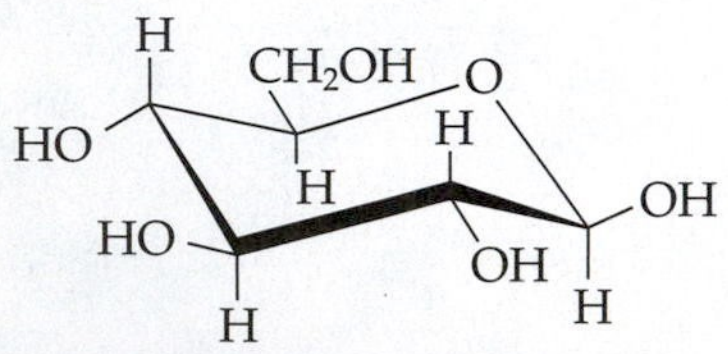

Glucose | Galactose | Fructose

▲ Although we have represented the cyclic monosaccharides as flat hexagons, they are actually three-dimensional. Most assume a conformation (shape) called a *chair conformation* because it somewhat resembles a reclining chair.

Sucrose and lactose are examples of **disaccharides**, carbohydrates whose molecules can be hydrolyzed to yield two monosaccharide units (Figure 16.5). Sucrose is split into glucose and fructose. Hydrolysis of lactose yields glucose and galactose.

$$\text{Sucrose} + H_2O \longrightarrow \text{Glucose} + \text{Fructose}$$

$$\text{Lactose} + H_2O \longrightarrow \text{Glucose} + \text{Galactose}$$

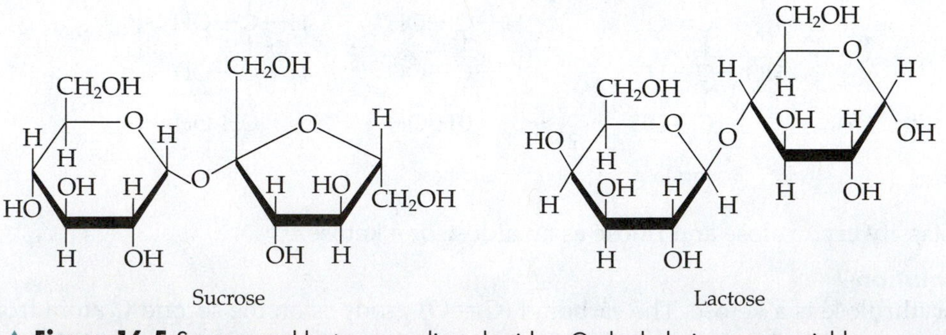

Sucrose | Lactose

▲ **Figure 16.5** Sucrose and lactose are disaccharides. On hydrolysis, sucrose yields glucose and fructose, whereas lactose yields glucose and galactose. Sucrose is cane or beet sugar, and lactose is milk sugar.

Q: *What is the molecular formula of each of these disaccharides? How are the two compounds related? Label the two monosaccharide units in each as fructose, galactose, or glucose.*

Polysaccharides: Starch and Cellulose

Polysaccharides are composed of large molecules that yield many monosaccharide units on hydrolysis. Polysaccharides include starches, which comprise the main energy-storage system of many plants, and cellulose, which is the structural material of plants. Figure 16.6 shows short segments of starch and cellulose molecules.

(a) Segment of a starch molecule

CH_2OH O HO HO O CH_2OH O HO HO O CH_2OH O HO HO O

α-linkage

α-linkage

(b) Segment of a cellulose molecule

β-linkage

β-linkage

CH_2OH O HO HO HO O O HO CH_2OH O CH_2OH O HO HO O

◀ **Figure 16.6** Both starch and cellulose are polymers of glucose. They differ in that the glucose units are joined by alpha linkages (blue) in starch and by beta linkages (red) in cellulose.

Q: *The formulas for most polymers can be written in condensed form (page 268). Write a condensed formula for starch. How would the condensed formula for cellulose differ from that of starch?*

Notice that both are polymers of glucose. Starch molecules generally have from 100 to about 6000 glucose units. Cellulose molecules are composed of 1800–3000 or more glucose units.

A crucial structural difference between starch and cellulose is the way the glucose units are hooked together. In starch, with the $-CH_2OH$ group at the top as a reference, the oxygen atom joining the glucose units is pointed *down*. This arrangement is called an *alpha linkage*. In cellulose, again with the $-CH_2OH$ group as the point of reference, the oxygen atom connecting the glucose units is pointed *up*, an arrangement called a *beta linkage*.

This subtle but important difference in linkage determines whether the material can be digested by humans (Chapter 17). The different linkages also result in different three-dimensional forms for cellulose and starch. For example, cellulose in the cell walls of plants is arranged in *fibrils*, bundles of parallel chains. As shown in Figure 16.7(a), these fibrils lie parallel to each other in each layer of the cell wall. In alternate layers, the fibrils are perpendicular, an arrangement that imparts great strength to the cell wall.

2. Why can some animals eat grass, but humans can't? Although both cellulose and starch are glucose polymers, humans do not have the enzyme to break the beta linkages in cellulose. The digestive systems of cows, horses, and deer contain bacteria that can break these linkages, allowing these ruminants to digest the cellulose in grass.

There are two kinds of starches found in plants. One, called *amylose*, has glucose units joined in a continuous chain like beads on a string. The other kind, *amylopectin*, has branched chains of glucose units. These starches are perhaps best represented schematically, as in Figure 16.8 on page 460, where each glucose unit is represented by filled circles.

(a)

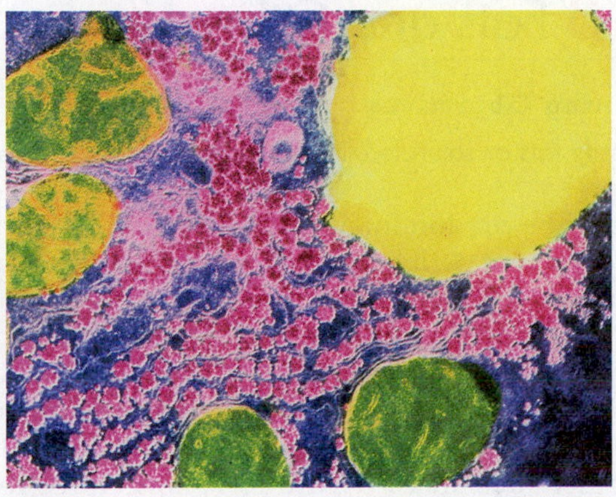
(b)

◀ **Figure 16.7** Cellulose molecules form fibers, whereas starch molecules (glycogen) form granules. Electron micrographs of (a) the cell wall of an alga, made up of successive layers of cellulose fibers in parallel arrangement, and (b) glycogen granules in a liver cell of a rat.

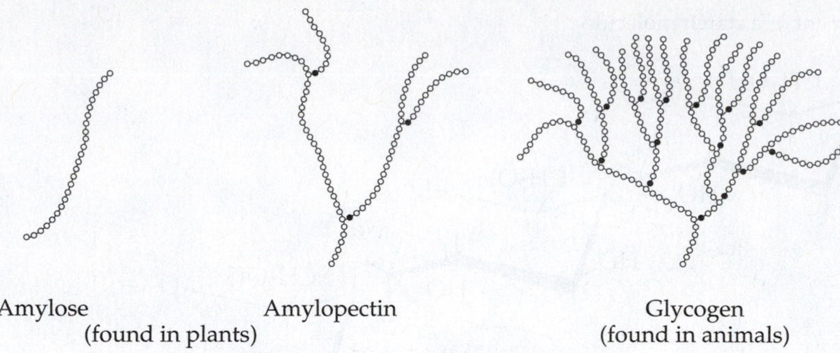

▶ **Figure 16.8** Schematic representations of amylose, amylopectin, and glycogen. Amylose is unbranched. Amylopectin has a branch approximately every 25 glucose units. Glycogen branches about every 10 glucose units.

When cornstarch is heated at about 400 °F for an hour, the starch polymers are broken down into shorter chains to form a product called *dextrin*, which has properties intermediate between those of sugars and starches. Mixed with water, dextrin makes a slightly thick, sticky mixture. Starch and dextrin adhesives account for about 58% of the U.S. packaging market.

Animal starch is called *glycogen*. Like amylopectin, it is composed of branched chains of glucose units. In contrast to cellulose, we see in Figure 16.7(b) that glycogen in muscle and liver tissue is arranged in granules, clusters of small particles. Plant starch, on the other hand, forms large granules. Granules of plant starch rupture in boiling water to form a paste, which gels when it cools. Potatoes and cereal grains form this type of starchy broth. All forms of starch are hydrolyzed to glucose during digestion.

Self-Assessment Questions

1. A monosaccharide with an aldehyde group is called
   a. an aldol **b.** an aldose **c.** aldicarb **d.** aldosterol
2. A ketose is a monosaccharide
   a. diet aid **b.** that forms polyhydroxy cellulose
   c. that causes ketosis **d.** with a ketone group
3. When most monosaccharides dissolve in water, they form
   a. branched polysaccharides **b.** disaccharides
   c. ring structures **d.** polysaccharides
4. The two monosaccharide units that make up a lactose molecule are
   a. both glucose **b.** fructose and galactose
   c. glucose and fructose **d.** glucose and galactose
5. Which of these polysaccharide molecules consists of branched chains of glucose units?
   a. amylose and amylopectin **b.** amylose and cellulose
   c. amylose and glycogen **d.** amylopectin and glycogen
6. Carbohydrates are stored in the liver and muscle tissue as
   a. amylose **b.** amylopectin **c.** cellulose **d.** glycogen

Answers: 1, b; 2, d; 3, c; 4, d; 5, d; 6, d

16.3 Fats and Other Lipids

Learning Objectives › Describe the fundamental structure of a fatty acid and of a fat. › Classify fats as saturated, monounsaturated, or polyunsaturated.

Fats are the predominant forms of a class of compounds called *lipids*. These substances are not defined by a functional group, as are most other families of organic compounds. Rather, lipids have common solubility properties. A **lipid** is a cellular component that is insoluble in water but soluble in organic solvents of low polarity, such as hexane, diethyl ether, and chloroform. In addition to fats, the lipid family includes **fatty acids** (long-chain carboxylic acids), steroids such as cholesterol and sex hormones (Chapter 18), fat-soluble vitamins (Chapter 17), and other substances. Figure 16.9 shows three representations of palmitic acid, a typical fatty acid.

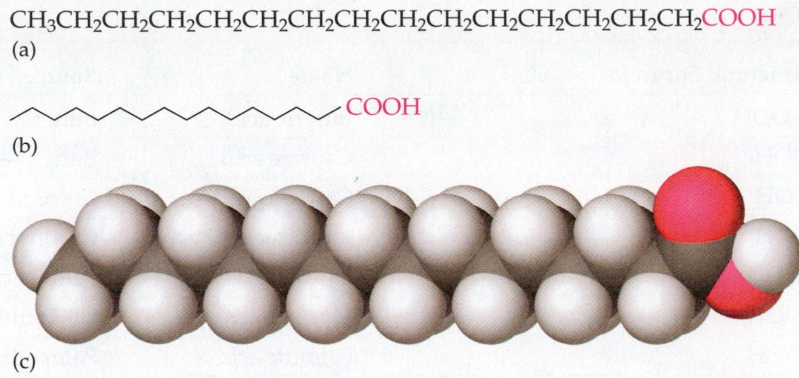

Figure 16.9 Three representations of palmitic acid: (a) Condensed structural formula. (b) Line-angle formula, in which the lines denote bonds and each intersection of lines or end of a line represents a carbon atom. (c) Space-filling model.

A **fat** is an ester of fatty acids and the trihydroxy alcohol glycerol (Figure 16.10). A fat has three fatty acid chains joined to glycerol through ester linkages (which is why fats are often called *triglycerides*, or triacylglycerols). Related compounds are also classified according to the number of fatty acid chains they contain: A *monoglyceride* has one fatty acid chain joined to glycerol, and a *diglyceride* has two.

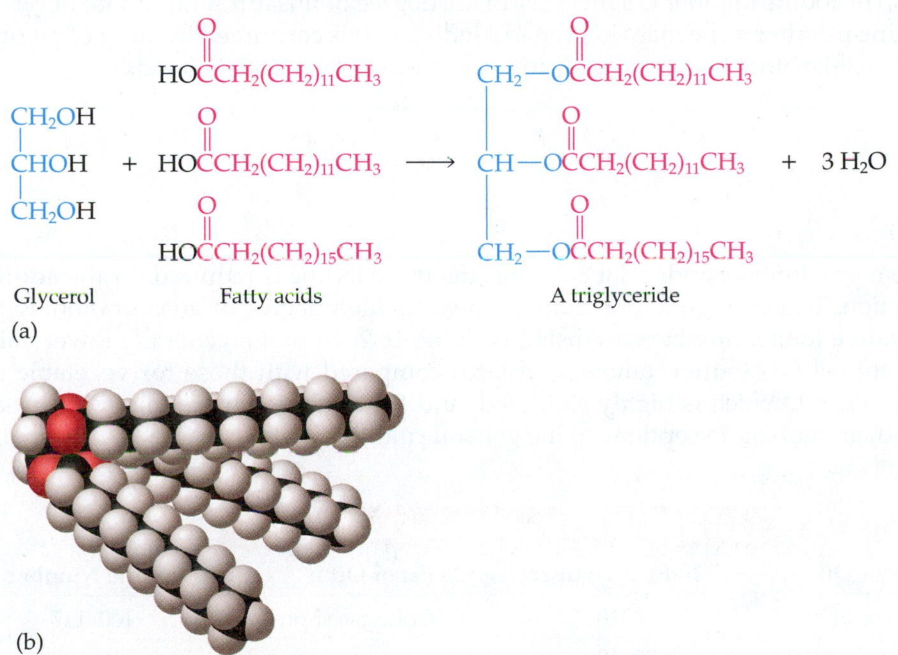

Figure 16.10 Triglycerides (triacylglycerols) are esters in which the trihydroxy (having three OH groups) alcohol glycerol is esterified with three fatty acid groups. (a) The equation for the formation of a triglyceride. (b) Space-filling model of a triglyceride.

Naturally occurring fatty acids nearly always have an even number of carbon atoms. Representative ones are listed in Table 16.1 on page 462. Animal fats are generally rich in saturated fatty acids (fatty acids with no carbon-to-carbon double bonds) and have a smaller proportion of unsaturated fatty acids. At room temperature, most animal fats are solids. Liquid fats, called *oils*, are obtained mainly from vegetable sources. Oils typically have a higher proportion of unsaturated fatty acid units than do fats. Fats and oils feel greasy. They are less dense than water and float on it.

Fats are often classified according to the degree of unsaturation of the fatty acids they incorporate. A *saturated fatty acid* contains no carbon-to-carbon double bonds, a *monounsaturated fatty acid* has one carbon-to-carbon double bond per molecule, and a *polyunsaturated fatty acid* has two or more carbon-to-carbon double bonds. A *saturated fat* contains a high proportion of saturated fatty acids; these fat molecules have relatively few carbon-to-carbon double bonds. A *polyunsaturated fat* (oil) incorporates mainly unsaturated fatty acids; these fat molecules have many double bonds.

Table 16.1 Some Fatty Acids in Natural Fats

Number of Carbon Atoms	Condensed Structural Formula	Name	Source
4	$CH_3CH_2CH_2COOH$	Butyric acid	Butter
6	$CH_3(CH_2)_4COOH$	Caproic acid	Butter
8	$CH_3(CH_2)_6COOH$	Caprylic acid	Coconut oil
10	$CH_3(CH_2)_8COOH$	Capric acid	Coconut oil
12	$CH_3(CH_2)_{10}COOH$	Lauric acid	Palm kernel oil
14	$CH_3(CH_2)_{12}COOH$	Myristic acid	Oil of nutmeg
16	$CH_3(CH_2)_{14}COOH$	Palmitic acid	Palm oil
18	$CH_3(CH_2)_{16}COOH$	Stearic acid	Beef tallow
18	$CH_3(CH_2)_7CH{=}CH(CH_2)_7COOH$	Oleic acid	Olive oil
18	$CH_3(CH_2)_4CH{=}CHCH_2CH{=}CH(CH_2)_7COOH$	Linoleic acid	Soybean oil
18	$CH_3CH_2(CH{=}CHCH_2)_3(CH_2)_6COOH$	Linolenic acid	Fish oils
20	$CH_3(CH_2)_4(CH{=}CHCH_2)_4CH_2CH_2COOH$	Arachidonic acid	Liver

3. What makes animal fats bad for you? The saturated fats found in most animal fats can pack closely together to form artery-clogging plaque, which contributes to heart disease. The structures of unsaturated fats do not stack neatly and do not form this plaque.

The iodine number is a measure of the degree of unsaturation of a fat or oil. The **iodine number** is the mass in grams of iodine that is consumed by 100 g of fat or oil. Iodine, like other halogens, adds to a carbon-to-carbon double bond.

$$>C{=}C< + I_2 \longrightarrow -\underset{I}{\overset{|}{C}}-\underset{I}{\overset{|}{C}}-$$

The more double bonds a fat contains, the more iodine is required for the addition reaction. Thus, a high iodine number means a high degree of unsaturation. Representative iodine numbers are listed in Table 16.2. Note the generally lower values for animal fats (butter, tallow, and lard) compared with those for vegetable oils. Coconut oil, which is highly saturated, and fish oils, which are relatively unsaturated, are notable exceptions to the general rule.

▲ Many salad dressings are made of an oil and vinegar. The one shown here has olive oil floating on balsamic vinegar, an aqueous solution of acetic acid.

Table 16.2 Typical Iodine Numbers for Some Fats and Oils[a]

Fat or Oil	Iodine Number	Fat or Oil	Iodine Number
Coconut oil	8–10	Cottonseed oil	100–117
Butter	25–40	Corn oil	115–130
Beef tallow	30–45	Fish oils	120–180
Palm oil	37–54	Canola oil	125–135
Lard	45–70	Soybean oil	125–140
Olive oil	75–95	Safflower oil	130–140
Peanut oil	85–100	Sunflower oil	130–145

[a]Oils shown in blue are from plant sources.

Self-Assessment Questions

1. Lipids are defined by their
   a. chemical reactivity
   b. functional group
   c. function in the body
   d. solubility properties

Questions 2–6 refer to the structures S, T, U, and V.

S: $CH_3(CH_2)_{10}COOH$ T: $CH_3(CH_2)_{16}COOH$

U: $CH_3(CH_2)_7CH{=}CH(CH_2)_7COOH$ V: $CH_3CH_2(CH{=}CHCH_2)_3(CH_2)_6COOH$

2. Which are saturated fatty acids?
   a. S and T b. S and U c. T and U d. U and V
3. Which is a monounsaturated fatty acid?
   a. S b. T c. U d. V
4. Which is a polyunsaturated fatty acid?
   a. S b. T c. U d. V
5. Saturated fats often have a high proportion of
   a. S and T b. S and U c. T and U d. U and V
6. Polyunsaturated fats (oils) often have a high proportion of
   a. S b. T c. U d. V
7. The iodine number of a fat or oil expresses its
   a. calories per gram
   b. degree of acidity
   c. degree of unsaturation
   d. digestibility
8. In general, animal fats differ from vegetable oils in that the fat molecules
   a. are higher in calories
   b. are shorter
   c. have fewer C=C bonds
   d. have more C=C bonds

Answers: 1, d; 2, a; 3, c; 4, d; 5, a; 6, d; 7, c; 8, c

16.4 Proteins: Polymers of Amino Acids

Learning Objective › Draw the fundamental structure of an amino acid, and show how amino acids combine to make proteins.

Proteins are vital components of all life. No living part of the human body—or of any other organism, for that matter—is completely without protein. There is protein in blood, muscles, brain, and even tooth enamel. The smallest cellular organisms—bacteria—contain protein. Viruses, so small that they make bacteria look like giants, are little more than proteins and nucleic acids, a combination that is the stuff of life itself.

Each type of cell makes its own kinds of proteins. Proteins serve as the structural materials of animals, much as cellulose does in plants. Muscle tissue is largely protein, and so are skin and hair. Silk, wool, nails, claws, feathers, horns, and hooves are proteins. All proteins contain the elements carbon, hydrogen, oxygen, and nitrogen, and most also contain sulfur. The structure of a short segment of a typical protein molecule is shown in Figure 16.11 on page 464.

Like starch and cellulose, *proteins* are polymers. They differ from other polymers that we have studied in that the monomer units are about 20 different amino acids (Table 16.3, page 465). The amino acids differ in their side chains (shown in green). An **amino acid** has two functional groups, an amino group ($-NH_2$) and a carboxyl group ($-COOH$), attached to the same carbon atom (called the *alpha carbon*).

$$H_2N-\underset{\displaystyle H}{\overset{\displaystyle R}{\underset{|}{\overset{|}{C}}}}-COOH$$

(a)

$$
\begin{array}{l}
\text{N—H} \\
\text{CH}_3\text{—CH} \\
\text{C=O} \\
\text{H—N} \\
\text{HC—CH}_2\text{CH}_2\text{COOH} \\
\text{O=C} \\
\text{N—H} \\
\text{HCH} \\
\text{C=O} \\
\text{H—N} \\
\text{HC—CH}_2\text{SH} \\
\text{O=C} \\
\text{N—H} \\
\text{CH}_3\text{—CH—CH} \\
\text{CH}_3 \quad \text{C=O} \\
\text{H—N} \\
\text{HC—CH}_2\text{CH}_2\text{CH}_2\text{CH}_2\text{NH}_2 \\
\text{O=C}
\end{array}
$$

(b)

▶ **Figure 16.11** Space-filling model (a) and structural formula (b) of a short segment of a protein molecule. In the structural formula, hydrocarbon side chains (green), an acidic side chain (red), a basic side chain (blue), and a sulfur-containing side chain (amber shading) are highlighted. The dashed lines crossing the formula indicate where two amino-acid units join (see Section 16.5).

Q: *The formulas for most polymers can be written in condensed form (page 268). Those for natural proteins cannot. Explain.*

In this formula, the R can be a hydrogen atom (as it is in glycine, the simplest amino acid) or any of the groups shown in green in Table 16.3. The formula shows the proper placement of the groups, but it is not really correct. Acids react with bases to form salts. The carboxyl group is acidic, and the amino group is basic. The two functional groups interact, the acid transferring a proton to the base. The resulting product is an inner salt, or **zwitterion**, a compound in which the negative charge and the positive charge are on different parts of the same molecule.

$$
\begin{array}{c}
\text{R} \\
| \\
\text{H}_3\text{N}^+\text{—C—COO}^- \\
| \\
\text{H}
\end{array}
$$

A zwitterion

Plants can synthesize proteins from carbon dioxide, water, and minerals such as nitrates (NO_3^-) and sulfates (SO_4^{2-}). Animals need to consume proteins in their foods. Humans can synthesize some of the amino acids in Table 16.3. Others must be part of the proteins consumed in a normal diet. The latter are called *essential amino acids*.

The Peptide Bond: Peptides and Proteins

The human body contains tens of thousands of different proteins. Each of us has a tailor-made set. Proteins are polyamides. The amide linkage is called a **peptide bond** (shaded part of the structure below) when it joins two amino-acid units.

$$
\begin{array}{c}
\text{R}_1 \quad\quad\quad \text{H} \quad \text{H} \\
\text{H}_2\text{N—C—C—N—C—COOH} \\
\text{H} \quad\; \text{O} \quad\quad\quad \text{R}_2
\end{array}
$$

Table 16.3 The 20 Amino Acids Specified by the Human Genetic Code

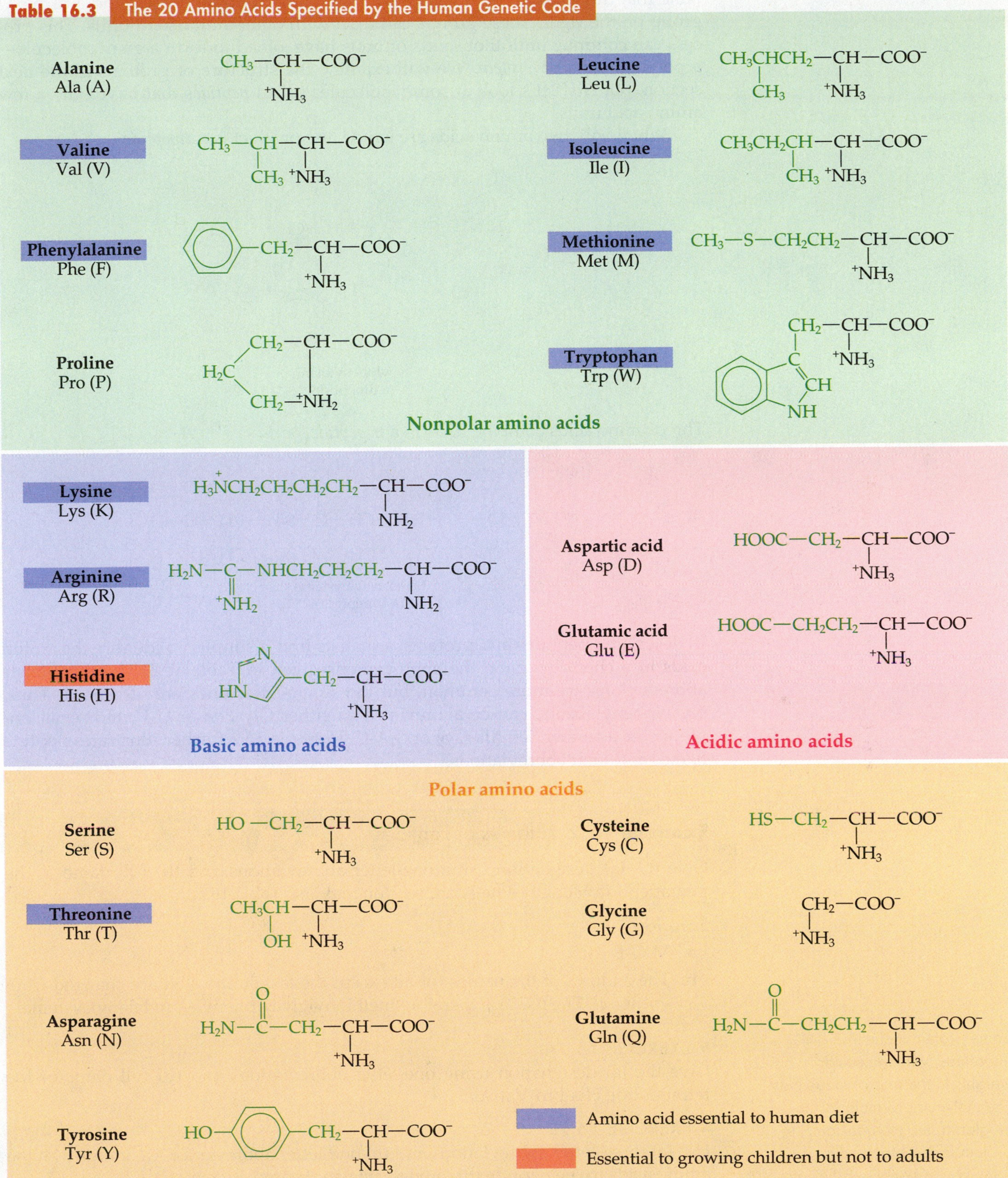

Alanine
Ala (A)
Leucine
Leu (L)
Valine
Val (V)
Isoleucine
Ile (I)
Phenylalanine
Phe (F)
Methionine
Met (M)
Proline
Pro (P)
Tryptophan
Trp (W)
Nonpolar amino acids
Lysine
Lys (K)
Arginine
Arg (R)
Histidine
His (H)
Basic amino acids
Aspartic acid
Asp (D)
Glutamic acid
Glu (E)
Acidic amino acids
Polar amino acids
Serine
Ser (S)
Cysteine
Cys (C)
Threonine
Thr (T)
Glycine
Gly (G)
Asparagine
Asn (N)
Glutamine
Gln (Q)
Tyrosine
Tyr (Y)
Amino acid essential to human diet
Essential to growing children but not to adults

Note that this molecule still has a reactive amino group on the left and a carboxyl group on the right. These groups can react with other amino-acid units. This process can continue until thousands of units have joined to form a giant molecule—a polymer called a *protein*. We will examine the structure of proteins in the next section, but first let's look at some molecules called *peptides* that have only a few amino-acid units.

When only two amino acids are joined, the product is a *dipeptide*.

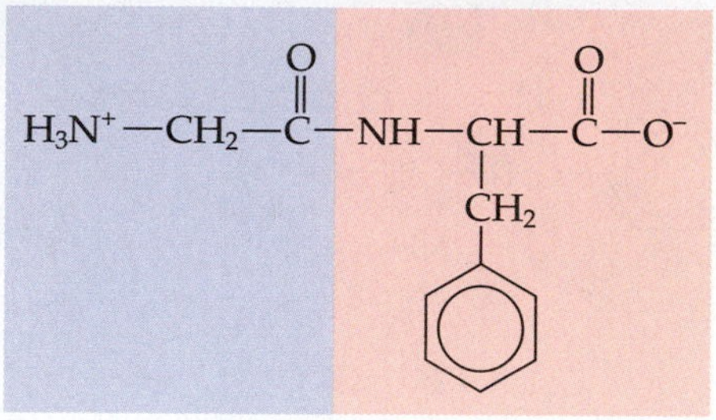

$$H_3N^+{-}CH_2{-}\overset{\overset{\displaystyle O}{\|}}{C}{-}NH{-}\underset{\underset{\displaystyle CH_2C_6H_5}{|}}{CH}{-}\overset{\overset{\displaystyle O}{\|}}{C}{-}O^-$$

Glycylphenylalanine
(a dipeptide)

Three amino acids combine to form a *tripeptide*.

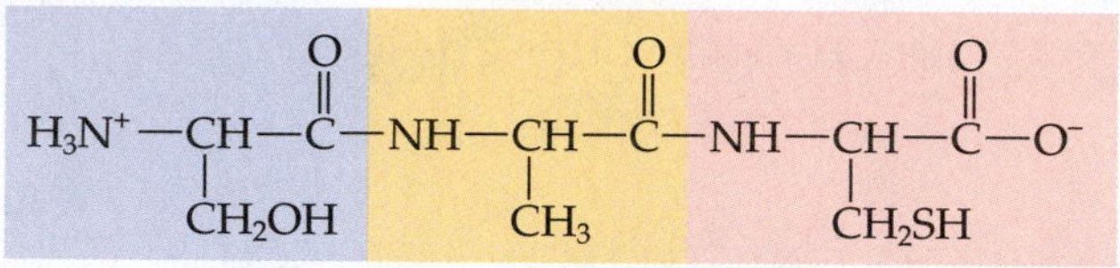

$$H_3N^+{-}\underset{\underset{\displaystyle CH_2OH}{|}}{CH}{-}\overset{\overset{\displaystyle O}{\|}}{C}{-}NH{-}\underset{\underset{\displaystyle CH_3}{|}}{CH}{-}\overset{\overset{\displaystyle O}{\|}}{C}{-}NH{-}\underset{\underset{\displaystyle CH_2SH}{|}}{CH}{-}\overset{\overset{\displaystyle O}{\|}}{C}{-}O^-$$

Serylalanylcysteine
(a tripeptide)

In describing peptides and proteins, scientists find it simpler to identify the amino acids in a chain by using the abbreviations given in Table 16.3. The three-letter abbreviations are more common, but the single-letter ones are also used. Thus, glycylphenylalanine can be abbreviated as either Gly-Phe or G-F, and serylalanylcysteine as either Ser-Ala-Cys or S-A-C. Example 16.2 further illustrates peptide names and their abbreviations.

Example 16.2 Names of Peptides

Give the **(a)** designation using one-letter abbreviations and **(b)** full name of the pentapeptide Met-Gly-Phe-Ala-Cys. You may use Table 16.3.

Solution

a. M-G-F-A-C

b. The endings of the names for all except the last amino acid are changed from *-ine* to *-yl*. The name is therefore methionylglycylphenylalanylalanylcysteine.

■ EXERCISE 16.2A

Give the **(a)** designation using one-letter abbreviations and **(b)** full name of the tetrapeptide His-Pro-Val-Ala.

■ EXERCISE 16.2B

Use **(a)** three-letter abbreviations and **(b)** one-letter abbreviations to identify all the amino acids in the peptide threonylglycylalanylalanylleucine.

A molecule with more than 10 amino-acid units is often simply called a **polypeptide**. When the molecular weight of a polypeptide exceeds about 10,000, it is called a **protein**. These distinctions are arbitrary and not always precisely applied.

Some protein molecules are enormous, with molecular weights in the tens of thousands. The molecular formula for hemoglobin, the oxygen-carrying protein in red blood cells, is $C_{3032}H_{4816}O_{780}N_{780}S_8Fe_4$, corresponding to a molar mass of 64,450 g/mol. Although they are huge compared with ordinary molecules, a billion average-sized protein molecules could still fit on the head of a pin.

GREEN CHEMISTRY

Principles 1, 2, 3, 4, 5, 6, 7, 8, 9, 10, 12

David A. Vosburg, *Harvey Mudd College*

Green Chemistry and Biochemistry

Chemistry has gone on constantly for millions of years in plants, animals, and bacteria. These living systems perform many chemical reactions, and plants have evolved to harness energy from the Sun using photosynthesis. Living things store energy in the form of carbohydrates (like glucose, sucrose, and cellulose, Section 16.2) and lipids (fats and oils, Section 16.3). These renewable feedstocks (Principle 7) hold great potential for supplying human energy needs in the future.

Chemists are devising ways of converting these natural energy reservoirs into substitutes for nonrenewable petroleum fuels, and biochemists are engineering existing biochemical pathways in various microorganisms to directly produce usable fuels. In 2009 and 2010, three Presidential Green Chemistry Challenge Awards were given for work in this area to Virent Energy Systems, James Liao, and LS9. Virent's process transforms plant carbohydrates into gasoline, which could reduce U.S. dependence on fossil fuels. Liao and coworkers (UCLA and Easel Biotechnologies) have engineered bacteria to turn carbohydrates and carbon dioxide into alcohols that can be used as fuels. The LS9 company developed microorganisms that directly produce hydrocarbon fuels. All of these achievements use the products or processes of biochemistry to address the energy needs of tomorrow.

Using biochemistry to make molecules has several distinct advantages over traditional chemical synthesis and invokes many of the green chemistry principles. The reactions normally occur in water, a ubiquitous, nontoxic, and nonflammable solvent (Principle 5). When reaction products are nonpolar, they can often be separated easily from the more polar water. In contrast to many current industrial reactions that are performed at very high temperatures and pressures, most biochemical reactions are extremely rapid and occur at mild temperatures and atmospheric pressure. These reactions reduce both energy costs and potential hazards (Principles 6 and 12). The atom economy of biochemical reactions is very high, as protecting groups and auxiliaries are not necessary (Principles 2 and 8), and toxic reagents and products can also be avoided in most cases (Principles 3 and 4). Biological reactions are frequently catalytic, using a single enzyme (Section 16.5) for thousands or millions of repeated reactions to selectively generate products with very little waste produced (Principles 1 and 9). Furthermore, the products formed (and the biological catalysts themselves) are generally biodegradable and innocuous (Principle 10). Also, when compounds are not themselves biodegradable, other biochemical pathways may be employed to degrade molecules that would otherwise persist in the environment. This bioremediation of environmental waste by cleaning up toxins and purifying water is a very important advantage of using biochemistry.

A common challenge associated with organic reactions is the production of specific isomers of molecules. Although these processes traditionally have relied on metal compounds as catalysts, new biochemical routes are increasingly preferred. For example, Merck and Codexis received a Presidential Green Chemistry Challenge Award in 2010 for their development of an enzyme catalyst for the production of the diabetes drug Januvia. As an example of the pace of innovation, the new method replaced a high-pressure reaction that used hydrogen gas and an expensive rhodium catalyst, a process that had been recognized with a Presidential Green Chemistry Challenge Award in 2006. The new biochemical pathway increases the yield of the drug and dramatically reduces the amount of waste produced. These innovations benefit the pharmaceutical companies, diabetics, the environment, and society at large.

The self-replicating nature of the cell and its DNA and the self-assembling (folding) properties of proteins (Section 16.5) make biological systems ideal candidates for the discovery and implementation of novel chemical processes. One of the greatest strengths of biochemical reactions is also the greatest challenge: specificity. Biological catalysts have evolved to have exquisite selectivity for their natural substrate(s), so adapting these catalysts to have more general function for a wider range of (potentially unnatural) substrates is difficult. Yet this is precisely what was done by Merck and Codexis for the synthesis of Januvia, so there is hope that similar approaches could lead to other successes.

▲ Genetic engineering of bacteria may transform natural energy sources into materials that will be energy-rich for human use. *Synechococcus elongatus*, shown here, may be particularly useful because of its small genome and its aptitude for photosynthesis.

The Sequence of Amino Acids

For peptides and proteins to function properly, it is not enough that they incorporate certain *amounts* of specific amino acids. The order, or *sequence*, in which the amino acids are connected, is also of critical importance. The sequence is written starting at the free amino group ($—NH_3^+$), called the *N-terminal* end, and continuing to the free carboxyl group ($—COO^-$), called the *C-terminal* end.

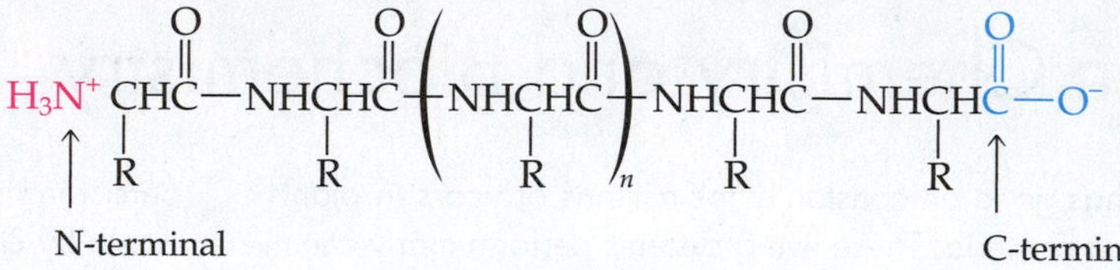

$$\underset{\uparrow\text{ N-terminal}}{H_3N^+}\,\underset{R}{CH}\overset{O}{\overset{\|}{C}}—NH\underset{R}{CH}\overset{O}{\overset{\|}{C}}\left(—NH\underset{R}{CH}\overset{O}{\overset{\|}{C}}—\right)_n NH\underset{R}{CH}\overset{O}{\overset{\|}{C}}—NH\underset{R}{CH}\overset{O}{\overset{\|}{C}}—O^- \;\; (\uparrow\text{ C-terminal})$$

N-terminal C-terminal

Glycylalanine (Gly-Ala) is therefore different from alanylglycine (Ala-Gly). Although the difference seems minor, the structures are different, and the two substances behave differently in the body.

$$H_3N^+\,CH_2CO—NH\underset{CH_3}{CH}COO^- \qquad H_3N^+\,\underset{CH_3}{CH}CO—NHCH_2COO^-$$

Glycylalanine Alanylglycine

As the length of a peptide chain increases, the number of possible sequential variations becomes enormous. Just as millions of different words can be made from the 26 letters of the English alphabet, millions of different proteins can be made from the 20 amino acids. And just as we can write gibberish with the English alphabet, nonfunctioning proteins can be formed by putting together the wrong sequence of amino acids.

Example 16.3 Numbers of Peptides

How many different tripeptides can be made from one unit each of the three amino acids methionine, valine, and phenylalanine? Write the sequences of these tripeptides, using the three-letter abbreviations in Table 16.3.

Solution

We write the various possibilities. Two begin with Met, two start with Val, and two with Phe:

Met-Val-Phe	Val-Met-Phe	Phe-Val-Met
Met-Phe-Val	Val-Phe-Met	Phe-Met-Val

There are six possible tripeptides.

■ EXERCISE 16.3A

How many different tripeptides can be made from two methionine units and one valine unit?

■ EXERCISE 16.3B

How many different tetrapeptides can be made from one unit each of the four amino acids methionine, valine, tyrosine, and phenylalanine?

Although the correct sequence is ordinarily of utmost importance, it is not always absolutely required. Just as you can sometimes make sense of incorrectly spelled English words, a protein with a small percentage of "incorrect" amino acids may function, but just not as well. And sometimes a seemingly minor difference can have a disastrous effect. Some people have hemoglobin with one incorrect amino-acid unit out of about 300. That "minor" error is responsible for sickle cell anemia, an inherited condition that often proves fatal.

Self-Assessment Questions

1. Proteins are polymers of
   a. amino acids
   b. fatty acids
   c. monoacylglycerides
   d. monosaccharides
2. The 20 amino acids that make up proteins differ mainly in their
   a. alpha carbon atoms
   b. amino groups
   c. carboxyl groups
   d. side chains
3. Which of the following is *not* an alpha amino acid?
   a. $CH_3C(CH_3)(NH_2)COOH$
   b. $(CH_3)_2CHCH(NH_2)COOH$
   c. H_2NCH_2COOH
   d. $H_2NCH_2CH_2CH_2COOH$
4. Which of the following is a zwitterion?
   a. $H_2NCH_2COO^-$
   b. $^-NHCH_2COO^-$
   c. $H_3N^+CH_2COOH$
   d. $^+H_3NCH_2COO^-$
5. In a dipeptide, two amino acids are joined through a(n)
   a. amide linkage
   b. dipolar interaction
   c. ionic bond
   d. hydrogen bond
6. The N-terminal amino acid and the C-terminal amino acid of the peptide Met-Ile-Val-Glu-Cys-Tyr-Gln-Trp-Asp are, respectively,
   a. Asp and Met
   b. Met and Asp
   c. Met and Ile
   d. Trp and Asp
7. How many different tripeptides can be formed from alanine, valine, and lysine, when each appears only once in each product?
   a. 1
   b. 3
   c. 6
   d. 9
8. The tripeptides represented as Ala-Val-Lys and Lys-Val-Ala are
   a. different only in name
   b. different in molar mass
   c. exactly the same
   d. two different peptides

Answers: 1, a; 2, d; 3, d; 4, d; 5, a; 6, b; 7, c; 8, d

16.5 Structure and Function of Proteins

Learning Objectives › Describe the four levels of protein structure, and give an example of each. › Describe how enzymes work as catalysts.

The structures of proteins have four organizational levels:

- **Primary structure.** Amino acids are linked by peptide bonds to form polypeptide chains. The primary structure of a protein molecule is simply the order of its amino acids. By convention, this order is written from the amino (N-terminal end) to the carboxyl (C-terminal end).
- **Secondary structure.** Polypeptide chains can fold into regular structures such as the alpha helix and the beta pleated sheet (described in this section).
- **Tertiary structure.** Protein folding creates spatial relationships between amino-acid units that are relatively far apart in the protein chain.
- **Quaternary structure.** Two or more polypeptide chains can assemble into multiunit structures.

To specify the primary structure, we write out the sequence of amino acids. For even a small protein molecule, this sequence can be quite long. For example, it takes about two pages, using the one-letter abbreviations, to give the sequence of the 1927 amino-acid units in lactase, the enzyme that catalyzes the hydrolysis of the disaccharide lactose into galactose and glucose. The primary structure of angiotensin II, a peptide that causes powerful constriction of blood vessels and is produced in the kidneys, is

Asp-Arg-Val-Tyr-Ile-His-Pro-Phe

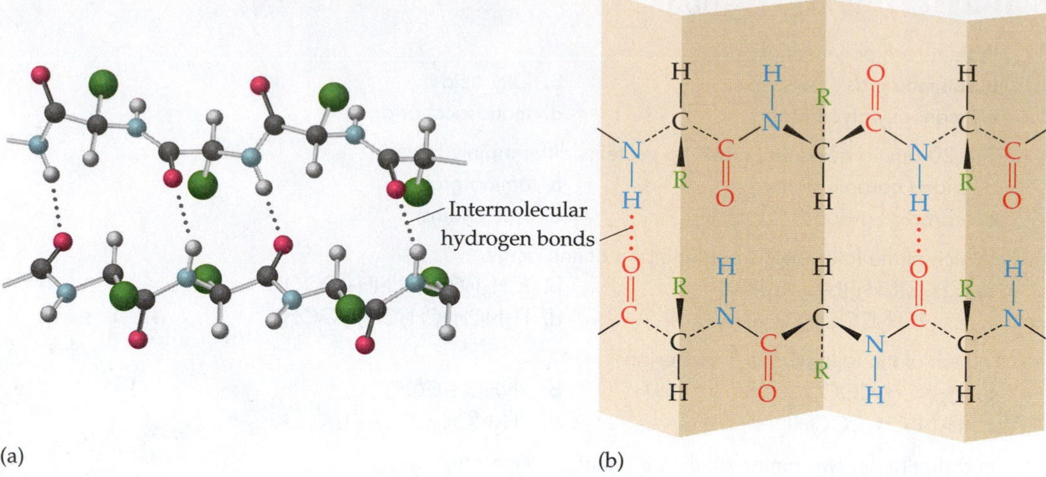

▶ **Figure 16.12** Beta pleated sheet structure consisting of protein chains. (a) Ball-and-stick model. (b) Model emphasizing the pleats. The side chains extend above or below the sheet and alternate along the chain. The protein chains are held together by interchain hydrogen bonds.

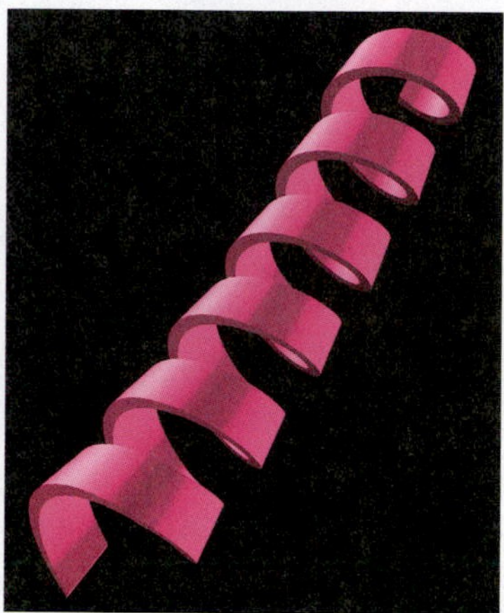

▲ The protein strands in an alpha helix are often represented as coiled ribbons.

This sequence specifies an octapeptide with aspartic acid at the N-terminal end, followed by arginine, valine, tyrosine, isoleucine, histidine, proline, and then phenylalanine at the C-terminal end.

The secondary structure of a protein refers to the arrangement of chains about an axis. The two main types of secondary structure are a *pleated sheet*, as in silk, and a *helix*, as in wool.

In the pleated-sheet conformation (Figure 16.12), protein chains are arranged in an extended zigzag arrangement, with hydrogen bonds holding adjacent chains together. The appearance gives this type of secondary structure its name, the **beta (β) pleated sheet**. This structure, with its multitude of hydrogen bonds, makes silk strong and flexible.

The protein molecules in wool, hair, and muscle contain large segments arranged in the form of a right-handed helix, or **alpha (α) helix** (Figure 16.13). Each turn of the helix requires 3.6 amino-acid units. The N—H group at one turn forms a hydrogen bond to a carbonyl (C═O) group at another turn. These helices wrap around one another in threes or sevens like strands of a rope. Unlike

▲ The protein strands in a pleated sheet are often represented as ribbons.

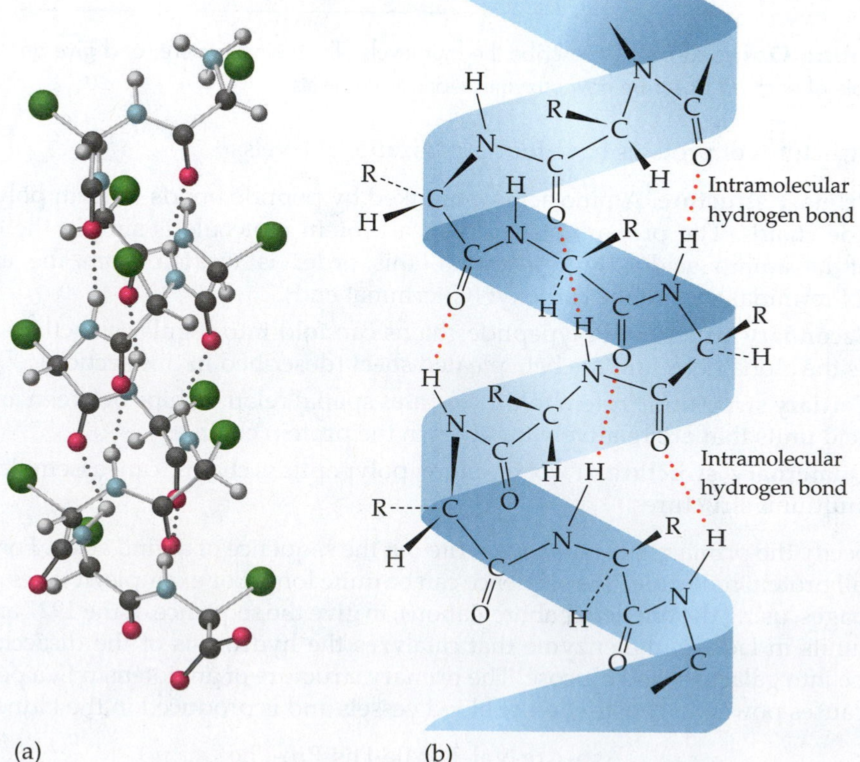

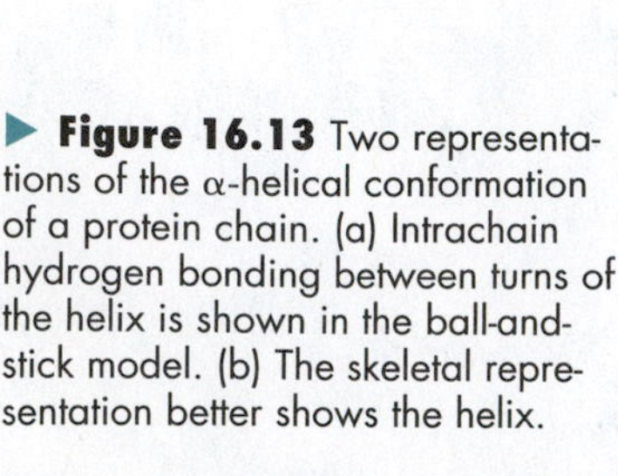

▶ **Figure 16.13** Two representations of the α-helical conformation of a protein chain. (a) Intrachain hydrogen bonding between turns of the helix is shown in the ball-and-stick model. (b) The skeletal representation better shows the helix.

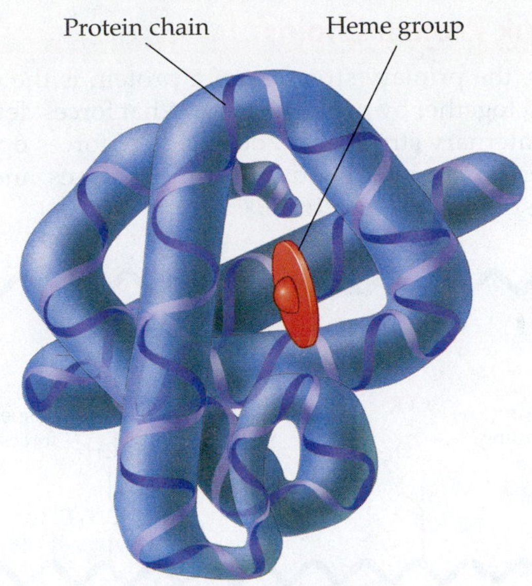

◀ **Figure 16.14** The tertiary structure of myoglobin. The protein chain is folded to form a globular structure, much as a string can be wound into a ball. The disk shape represents the heme group, which binds the oxygen carried by myoglobin (or hemoglobin).

silk, wool can be stretched, much like stretching a spring by pulling the coils apart.

The tertiary structure of a protein refers to folding that affects the spatial relationships between amino-acid units that are relatively far apart in the chain. An example is the protein chain in a **globular protein**. Figure 16.14 shows the tertiary structure of myoglobin, which is folded into a compact, spherical shape.

Quaternary structure exists only if there are two or more polypeptide chains, which can form an aggregate of subunits. Hemoglobin is the most familiar example. A single hemoglobin molecule contains four polypeptide units, and each unit is roughly comparable to a myoglobin molecule. The four units are arranged in a specific pattern (Figure 16.15). The quaternary structure of hemoglobin is this arrangement of the four units.

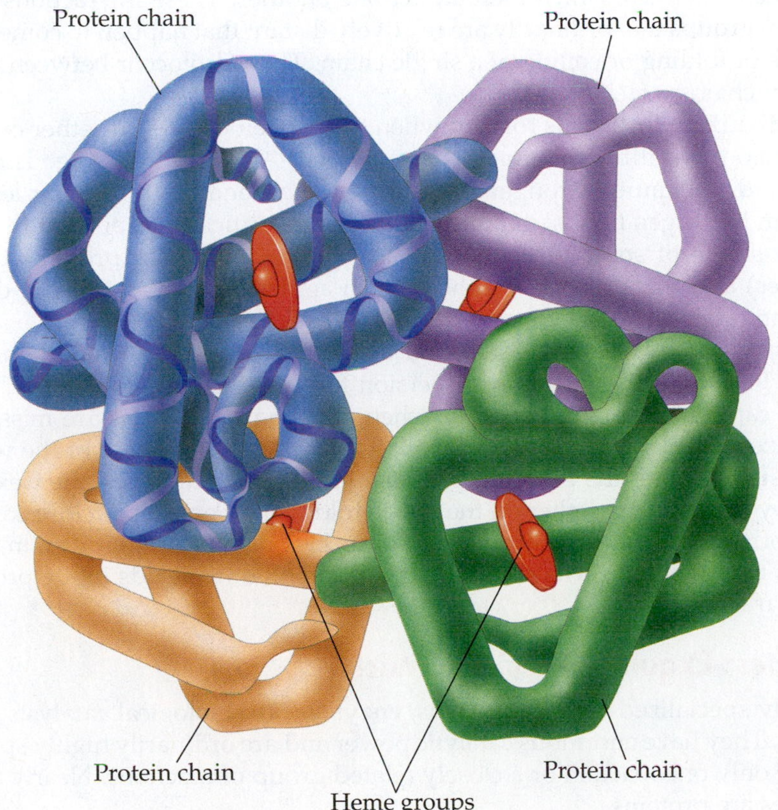

◀ **Figure 16.15** The quaternary structure of hemoglobin has four coiled protein chains, each analogous to myoglobin (Figure 16.14), grouped in a nearly tetrahedral arrangement.

Four Ways to Link Protein Chains

As we noted earlier, the primary structure of a protein is the order of the amino acids, which are held together by peptide bonds. What forces determine the secondary, tertiary, and quaternary structures? Four kinds of forces operate between protein chains: hydrogen bonds, ionic bonds, disulfide linkages, and dispersion forces. These forces are illustrated in Figure 16.16.

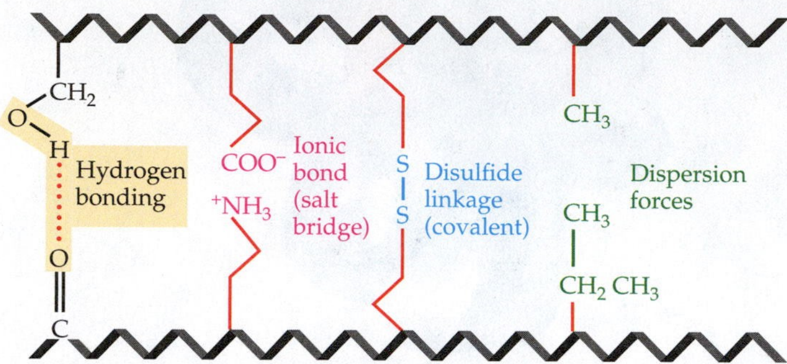

▶ **Figure 16.16** The tertiary structure of proteins is maintained by four different types of forces.

Hydrogen bonds and dispersion forces, introduced in Chapter 6 as intermolecular forces, can also be intramolecular, as occurs in proteins.

The most important hydrogen bonding in a protein involves an interaction between the atoms of one peptide bond and those of another. The amide hydrogen (N—H) of one peptide bond can form a hydrogen bond to a carbonyl (C=O) oxygen located (a) some distance away on the same chain, an arrangement that occurs in the secondary structure of wool (alpha helix), or (b) on an entirely different chain, as in the secondary structure of silk (beta pleated sheet). In either case, there is usually a pattern of such interactions. Because peptide bonds are regularly spaced along the chain, the hydrogen bonds also occur in a regular pattern, both intramolecularly (in wool) and intermolecularly (in silk). Other types of hydrogen bonding can occur (between side chains of amino acids, for example) but are less important.

Ionic bonds, sometimes called *salt bridges,* occur when an amino acid with a basic side chain is located near one with an acidic side chain. Proton transfer results in opposite charges, which then attract one another. These interactions can occur between groups that ordinarily are relatively distant that happen to come in contact because of folding or coiling of a single chain. They also occur between groups on adjacent chains.

A **disulfide linkage** is formed when two cysteine units (whether on the same chain or on two different chains) are oxidized. A disulfide linkage is a covalent bond, and thus much stronger than a hydrogen bond. Although far less numerous than hydrogen bonds, disulfide linkages are critically important in determining the shape of some proteins (for example, many of the proteins that act as enzymes) and the strength of others (such as the fibrous proteins in connective tissue and hair).

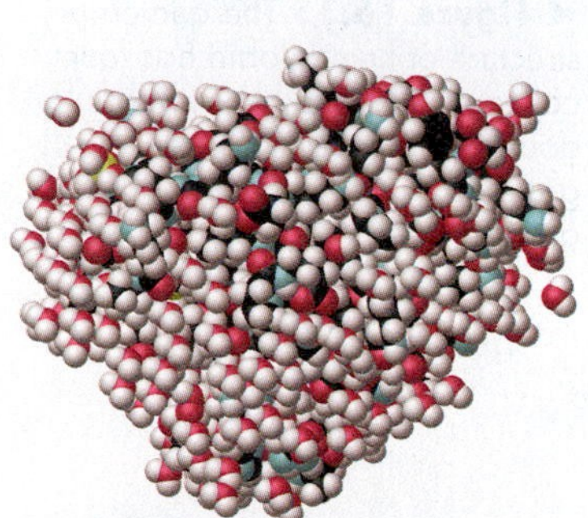

▲ **Figure 16.17** A protein chain often folds with its nonpolar groups on the inside, where they are held together by dispersion forces. The outside has polar groups, visible in this space-filling model of a myoglobin molecule as oxygen atoms (red) and nitrogen atoms (blue). The carbon atoms (black) are mainly on the inside.

Dispersion forces are the only kind of forces that exist between nonpolar side chains. Recall (Section 6.3) that dispersion forces are relatively weak. These interactions can be important, however, when other types of forces are missing or are minimized. Dispersion forces are increased by the cohesiveness of the water molecules surrounding the protein. Nonpolar side chains minimize their exposure to water by clustering together on the inside folds of the protein in close contact with one another (Figure 16.17). Dispersion forces become fairly significant in structures such as that of silk, in which a high proportion of amino acids in the protein have nonpolar side chains.

Enzymes: Exquisite Precision Machines

A highly specialized class of proteins, **enzymes**, are biological catalysts produced by cells. They have enormous catalytic power and are ordinarily highly specific, catalyzing only one reaction or a closely related group of reactions. Nearly all known enzymes are proteins.

Infectious Prions: Deadly Protein

In the early years of the twenty-first century, a malady called *mad cow disease* cast a shadow over the beef industry, causing concern over the safety of beef. Two cows in the United States were found to have the disease, properly called *bovine spongiform encephalopathy (BSE)*.

BSE is not a bacterial disease like anthrax or cholera, nor is it a viral disease like influenza and AIDS. Rather, BSE seems to be caused by an infectious *prion*, an abnormal form of a protein. Because they are simple proteins rather than living organisms, prions can remain unchanged when subjected to considerable heat, disinfectants, or antibiotics, conditions that are used to destroy bacteria and viruses.

Much of the fear over BSE is unfounded, because it is not contagious like bacterial and viral diseases. It is generally spread by consumption of contaminated feed. The U.S. Department of Agriculture has imposed restrictions on the materials that may be used in cattle feed, which have been quite effective. The incidence of prion-caused diseases is extremely low among people. The best-known example is *kuru*, or laughing sickness, which seems to arise from cannibalistic practices in certain societies. Nonetheless, the U.S. government continues to be vigilant in avoiding any potential spread of BSE because it is impossible to treat the disease once it is contracted.

Enzymes enable reactions to occur at much more rapid rates and lower temperatures than they otherwise would. They do this by changing the reaction path. The reacting substance, called the **substrate**, attaches to an area on the enzyme called the **active site**, to form an enzyme–substrate complex. Biochemists often use the model pictured in Figure 16.18, called the *induced-fit model*, to explain enzyme action. In this model, the shapes of the substrate and the active site are not perfectly complementary, but the active site adapts to fit the substrate, much as a glove molds to fit the hand that is inserted into it. The enzyme–substrate complex decomposes to form products, and the enzyme is regenerated. We can represent the process as follows.

$$\text{Enzyme} + \text{Substrate} \longrightarrow \text{Enzyme–substrate complex} \rightleftharpoons \text{Enzyme} + \text{Products}$$

An enzyme–substrate complex is also usually held together by electrical attraction. Certain charged groups on the enzyme complement certain charged or partially charged groups on the substrate. The formation of new bonds between enzyme and substrate weakens bonds within the substrate, and these weakened bonds can then be more easily broken to form products.

Portions of the enzyme molecule other than the active site may be involved in the catalytic process. Some interaction at a position remote from the active site can change the shape of the enzyme and thus change its effectiveness as a catalyst. In this way, it is possible to slow or stop the catalytic action. Figure 16.19 (page 474) illustrates a model for the inhibition of enzyme catalysis. An inhibitor molecule attaches to the enzyme at a position (called the *allosteric site*) away from the active site where the substrate is bound. The enzyme changes shape as it accommodates the inhibitor, and the substrate is no longer able to bind to the enzyme. This is one of the mechanisms by which cells "turn off" enzymes when their work is done.

Some enzymes consist entirely of protein chains. In others, another chemical component, called a **cofactor**, is necessary for proper function of the enzyme. This cofactor may be a metal ion such as zinc (Zn^{2+}), manganese (Mn^{2+}), magnesium (Mg^{2+}), iron(II) (Fe^{2+}), or copper(II) (Cu^{2+}). An organic cofactor is called a **coenzyme**. By definition, coenzymes are nonprotein. The pure protein part of an enzyme is called the **apoenzyme**. Both the coenzyme and the apoenzyme must be present for enzymatic activity to take place.

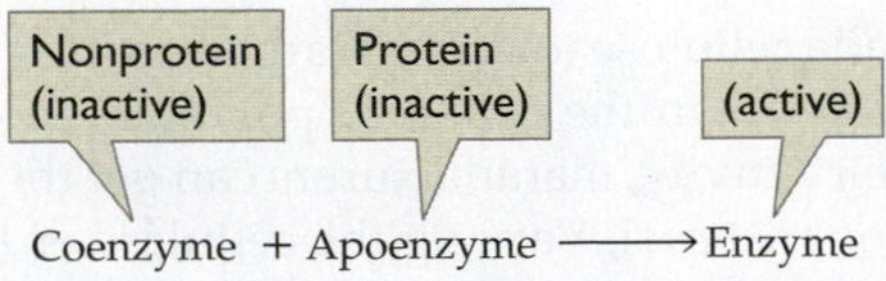

Many coenzymes are vitamins or are derived from vitamin molecules. Enzymes are essential to the function of every living cell.

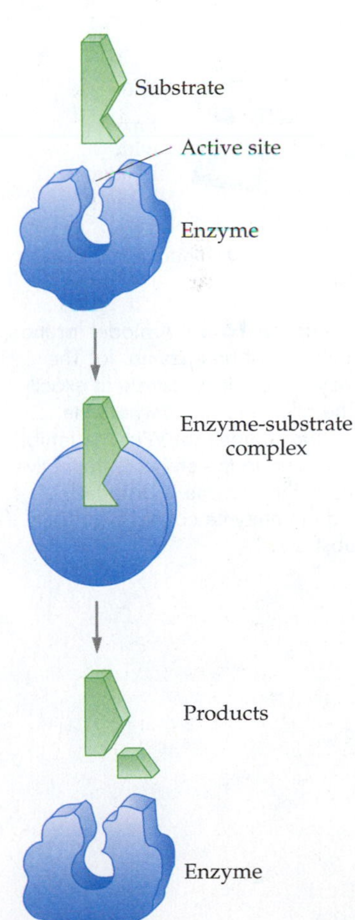

▲ **Figure 16.18** The induced-fit model of enzyme action. In this case, a single substrate molecule is broken into two product molecules.

Enzymes as Green Catalysts

Scientists are hard at work trying to find enzymes to carry out all kinds of chemical conversions. Enzymes are often more efficient than the usual chemical catalysts, and they are more specific in that they produce more of the desired product and fewer by-products that have to be disposed of. Further, processes involving enzymes do not require toxic solvents and thus produce less waste.

Companies have spent hundreds of millions of dollars studying the special characteristics of the enzymes inside *extremophiles*, microorganisms that live in harsh environments that would kill other creatures. Scientists hope to replace ordinary enzymes with enzymes from extremophiles. They are already finding uses for these enzymes in specialty chemicals and new drugs. Many industrial processes can only be carried out at high temperatures and pressures. Enzymes make it possible to carry out some of these processes at fairly low temperatures and atmospheric pressure, thus reducing the energy used and the need for expensive equipment.

Another area of enzyme use is in cleaning up pollution. For example, polychlorinated biphenyls (PCBs), notoriously persistent pollutants, are usually destroyed by incineration at 1200 °C. Microorganisms have been isolated that can degrade PCBs and thus have the potential to destroy these toxic pollutants. However, much research is still needed to make them cost-effective.

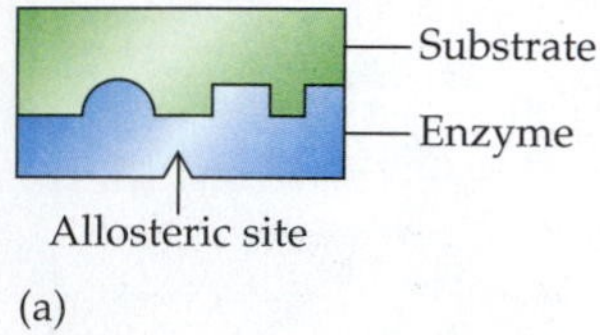

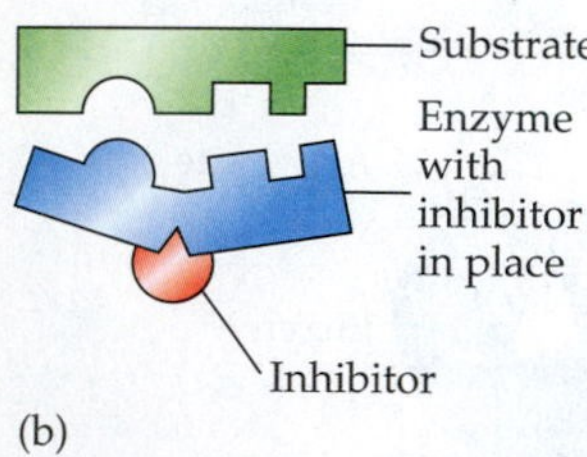

▲ **Figure 16.19** A model for the inhibition of an enzyme. (a) The enzyme and its substrate fit exactly. (The allosteric site is where the inhibitor binds.) (b) With the inhibitor bound to the enzyme, the active site of the enzyme is distorted, and the enzyme cannot bind to its substrate.

Applications of Enzymes

Enzymes find many uses in medicine, industry, and everyday life. One widespread use is in the test strips used by diabetics. Each strip contains *glucose oxidase*, an enzyme that catalyzes the oxidation of glucose at an electrode. The reaction generates an electrical current that is proportional to the amount of glucose in the blood that has reacted with the enzyme. The result is displayed directly on an external meter.

Clinical analysis for enzymes in body fluids or tissues is a common diagnostic technique in medicine. For example, enzymes normally found only in the liver may leak into the bloodstream from a diseased or damaged liver. The presence of these enzymes in blood confirms liver damage.

Enzymes are used to break up blood clots after a heart attack. If these medicines are given immediately after an attack, the patients' survival rate increases significantly. Other enzymes are used to do just the opposite: Blood-clotting factors are used to treat hemophilia, a disease in which the blood fails to clot normally.

Enzymes are widely used in a variety of industries, from baby foods to beer. Enzymes in intact microorganisms have long been used to make bread, beer, wine, yogurt, and cheese. Now the use of enzymes has been broadened to include such things as the following:

- Enzymes that act on proteins (called *proteases*) are used in the manufacture of baby foods to predigest complex proteins and make them easier for infants to digest.
- Enzymes that act on starches (*carbohydrases*) are used to convert corn starch to corn syrup (mainly glucose) for use as a sweetener.
- Enzymes called *isomerases* are used to convert the glucose in corn syrup into fructose, which is sweeter than glucose and can be used in smaller amounts to give the same sweetness. (Glucose and fructose are isomers, both having the molecular formula $C_6H_{12}O_6$.)
- Protease enzymes are used to make beer and fruit juices clear by breaking down the proteins that cause cloudiness.
- Enzymes that degrade cellulose (*cellulases*) are used in stonewashing blue jeans. These enzymes break down the cellulose polymers of cotton fibers. By carefully controlling their activity, manufacturers can get the desired effect without destroying the cotton material. Varying the cellulase enzymes creates different effects to make true "designer jeans."
- Proteases and carbohydrases are added to animal feed to make nutrients more easily absorbed and improve the animals' digestion.

Enzymes are important components in some detergents. Enzymes called *lipases* attack the fats and grease that make up many stains. Proteases attack the proteins in certain types of stains, such as those from blood, meat juice, and dairy products, breaking them down into smaller, water-soluble molecules. Total worldwide production of enzymes is worth more than $1 billion per year.

▲ It DOES Matter!

You can demonstrate protein hydrolysis. Mix a gelatin-dessert powder according to directions. Divide into two parts. Add fresh pineapple, kiwi, or papaya to one portion. Add cooked fruit or none at all to the other. The portion with the fresh fruit will not gel! These fruits contain a protease enzyme that breaks down proteins (gelatin is a protein). The enzyme is inactivated by cooking, so canned pineapple is perfectly fine in gelatin. (Why do you think cooking ham with pineapple tenderizes the ham, and eating too much raw pineapple can "burn" the lips?)

4. Why do some laundry detergents contain enzymes?

Enzymes in laundry detergents catalytically break down proteins that used to be difficult for detergents and bleaches to remove. Years ago, grass stains in children's clothing were almost impossible to remove, because the proteins of grass have a strong attraction for cotton and other cloth. Enzymes have alleviated that problem.

Self-Assessment Questions

1. Hydrogen bonds form between the N—H group of one amino acid and the C=O group of another, giving a protein molecule the form of an alpha helix or a beta pleated sheet. What level of protein structure do those forms represent?
   a. primary **b.** quaternary **c.** secondary **d.** tertiary
2. The folding of a protein chain into a globular form is an example of
   a. primary structure **b.** quaternary structure
   c. secondary structure **d.** tertiary structure
3. The arrangement of several protein subunits into a specific pattern, as in hemoglobin, is an example of
   a. primary structure **b.** quaternary structure
   c. secondary structure **d.** tertiary structure
4. The cross-links between cysteine units in protein chains of fibrous proteins such as those in hair are
   a. dispersion linkages **b.** disulfide linkages
   c. hydrogen bonds **d.** salt bridges
5. An acidic side chain of an amino-acid unit on a protein chain reacts with the basic side chain of an amino-acid unit on another chain or at some distance away on the same chain to form a
   a. dispersion linkage **b.** disulfide linkage
   c. hydrogen bond **d.** salt bridge
6. When nonpolar side chains of amino-acid units in a protein chain interact with other nonpolar side chains of amino-acid units on another chain or at some distance away on the same chain, the interactions are
   a. dispersion forces
   b. a disulfide linkage
   c. a hydrogen bond
   d. a salt bridge
7. The molecule on which an enzyme acts is called the enzyme's
   a. catalyst **b.** coenzyme **c.** cofactor **d.** substrate
8. According to the induced fit model of enzyme action, the
   a. action of an enzyme is enhanced by an inhibitor
   b. active site is the same as the allosteric site
   c. shapes of active sites are rigid and only fit substrates with exact complementary shapes
   d. shape of the active site can change somewhat to fit a substrate
9. An organic, nonprotein component of an enzyme molecule is called a(n)
   a. accessory enzyme
   b. allosteric group
   c. coenzyme
   d. stimulator
10. Enzyme cofactors are
    a. always ions such as Ca^{2+}, Mg^{2+}, and K^+
    b. always nonprotein organic molecules
    c. either ions such as Zn^{2+}, Mg^{2+}, and Mn^{2+} or nonprotein organic molecules
    d. small protein molecules
11. The pure protein part of an enzyme is called a(n)
    a. apoenzyme **b.** coenzyme
    c. holoenzyme **d.** ribozyme

Answers: 1, c; 2, d; 3, b; 4, b; 5, d; 6, a; 7, d; 8, d; 9, c; 10, c; 11, a

16.6 Nucleic Acids: Parts, Structure, and Function

Learning Objectives › Name the two types of nucleic acids, and describe the function of each type. › Explain complementary base pairing, and describe how a copy of DNA is synthesized.

Life on Earth has a fantastic range of forms, but all life arises from the same molecular ingredients: five nucleotides that serve as the building blocks for nucleic acids, and 20 amino acids (Section 16.4) that are the building blocks for proteins. These components limit the chemical reactions that can occur in cells and thus determine what Earth's living things are like.

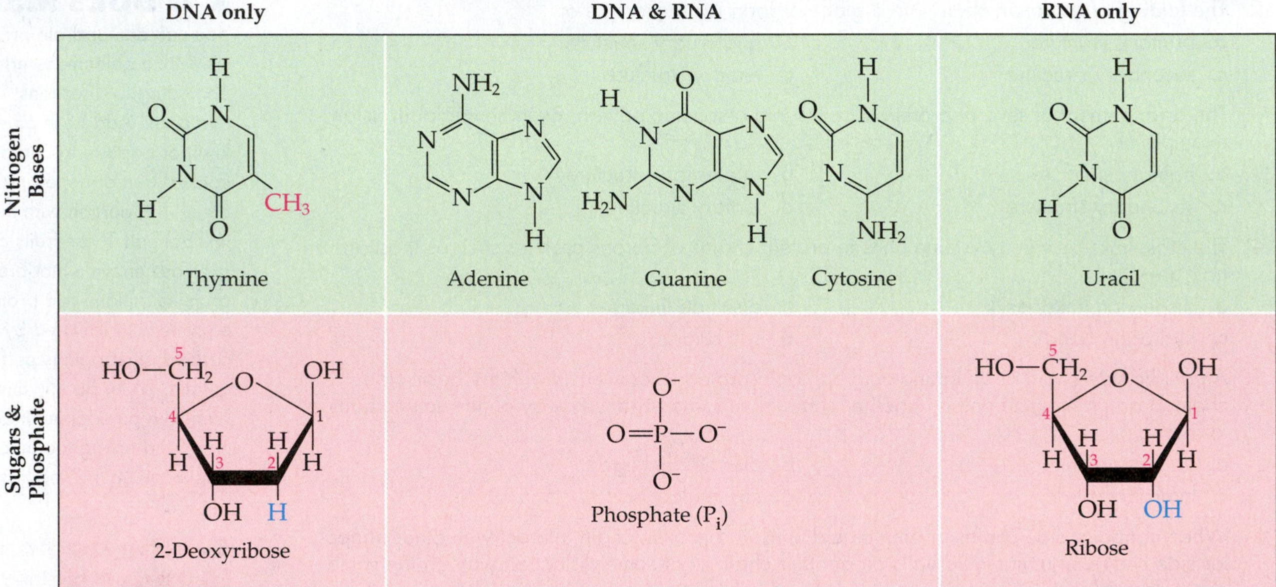

▲ **Figure 16.20** The components of nucleic acids. The sugars are 2-deoxyribose (in DNA) and ribose (in RNA). Note that deoxyribose differs from ribose in that it lacks an oxygen atom on the second carbon atom. *Deoxy* indicates that an oxygen atom is "missing." Phosphate units are often abbreviated as P_i ("inorganic phosphate"). Heterocyclic bases in nucleic acids are adenine, guanine, and cytosine in both DNA and RNA. Thymine occurs only in DNA, and uracil only in RNA. Note that thymine has a methyl group (red) that is lacking in uracil.

Nucleic acids serve as the information and control centers of the cell. There are two kinds of nucleic acids: *Deoxyribonucleic acid (DNA)* provides a mechanism for heredity and serves as the blueprint for all the proteins of an organism. *Ribonucleic acid (RNA)* carries out protein assembly. DNA is a coiled threadlike molecule found primarily in the cell nucleus. RNA is found in all parts of the cell, where different forms do different jobs. Both DNA and RNA are chains of repeating units called **nucleotides**. Each nucleotide in turn consists of three parts (Figure 16.20): a pentose (five-carbon sugar), a phosphate unit, and a heterocyclic amine (Section 9.8) base. The sugar is either ribose (in RNA) or deoxyribose (in DNA). Looking at the sugar in the nucleotide, note that the hydroxyl group on the first carbon atom is replaced by one of five bases. The bases with two fused rings, adenine and guanine, are classified as **purines**. The **pyrimidines**, cytosine, thymine, and uracil, have only one ring.

The hydroxyl group on the fifth carbon of the sugar unit is converted to a phosphate ester group. Adenosine monophosphate (AMP) is a representative nucleotide. In AMP, the base (blue) is adenine and the sugar (black) is ribose.

Phosphate ester linkage

Adenosine monophosphate

Nucleotides can be represented schematically as in the following, where P_i is biochemists' designation for "inorganic phosphate." A general representation is shown on the left, and a specific schematic for AMP on the right.

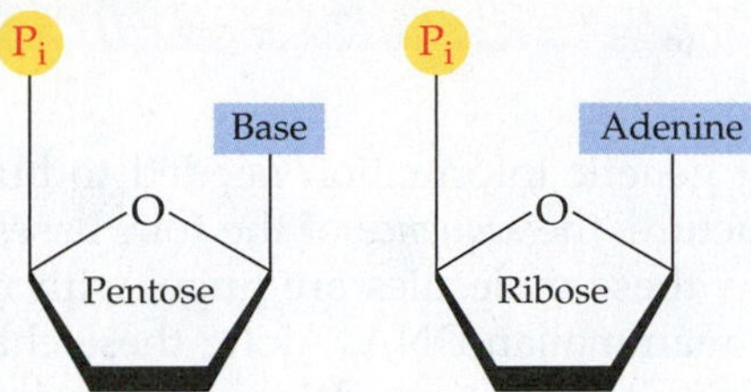

Nucleotides are joined to one another through the phosphate group to form nucleic acid chains. The phosphate unit on one nucleotide forms an ester linkage with the hydroxyl group on the third carbon atom of the sugar unit in a second nucleotide. This unit is in turn joined to another nucleotide, and the process is repeated to build up a long nucleic acid chain (Figure 16.21). The backbone of the chain consists of alternating phosphate and sugar units, and the heterocyclic bases are branches off this backbone.

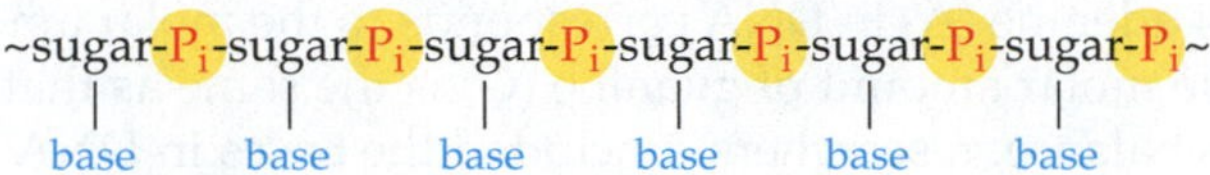

The numbers in Figure 16.21 refer to positions on the pentose sugar ring (look again at Figure 16.20). The 3′ end has a hydroxyl group and the 5′ end has a phosphate group. If the above diagram represents DNA, the sugar is deoxyribose and the bases are adenine, guanine, cytosine, and thymine. In RNA, the sugar is ribose and the bases are adenine, guanine, cytosine, and uracil.

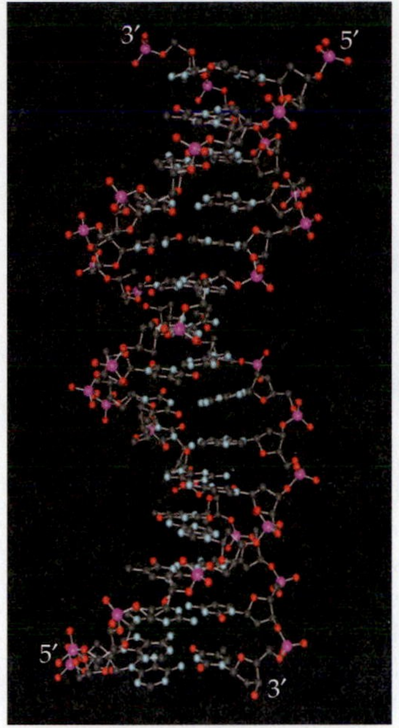

▲ **Figure 16.21** A DNA molecule. Each repeating unit is composed of a sugar, a phosphate unit, and a base. The sugar and phosphate units form backbones on the outside. The bases are attached to the sugar units. Pairs of bases make "steps" on the inside of the spiral staircase.

Example 16.4 Nucleotides

Consider the following nucleotide. Identify the sugar and the base. State whether it is found in DNA or RNA.

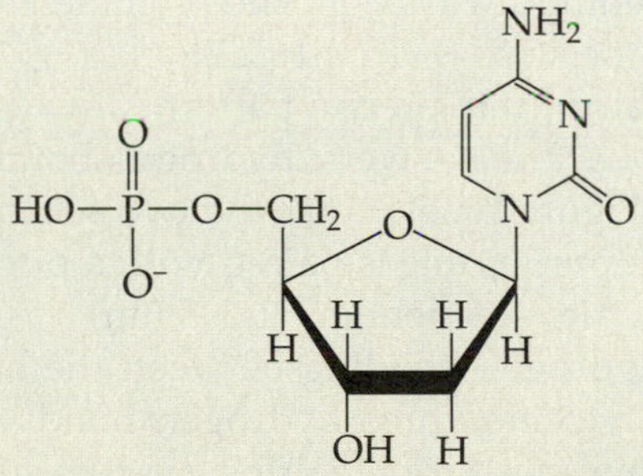

Solution

The sugar has two H atoms on the second C atom and therefore is deoxyribose, found in DNA. The base is a pyrimidine (one ring). The amino group ($—NH_2$) helps identify it as cytosine.

■ EXERCISE 16.4A

Consider the following nucleotide. Identify the sugar and the base. State whether it is found in DNA or RNA.

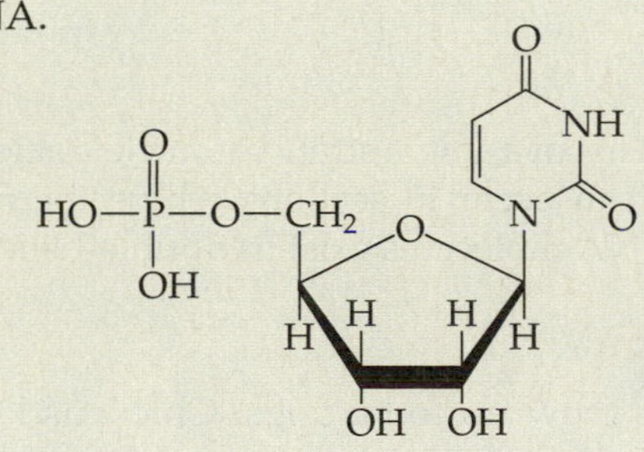

(continued)

▲ Francis H. C. Crick (1916–2004) (seated) and James D. Watson (b. 1928) used data obtained by British chemist Rosalind Franklin (1920–1958) to propose a double helix model of DNA in 1953. Franklin used a technique called X-ray diffraction, which showed DNA's helical structure. Without her permission, Franklin's colleague Maurice Wilkins shared her work with Watson and Crick. The data helped Watson and Crick decipher DNA's structure. Wilkins, Watson, and Crick were awarded the Nobel Prize for this discovery in 1962, a prize Franklin might have shared had she lived.

■ EXERCISE 16.4B

A nucleotide is composed of a phosphate unit, ribose, and thymine. Is it found in DNA, RNA, or neither? Explain.

The vast amount of genetic information needed to build living organisms is stored in a primary structure, the *sequence* of the four bases along the nucleic acid strand. Not surprisingly, these molecules are huge, with molecular masses ranging into the billions for mammalian DNA. Along these chains, the four bases can be arranged in almost infinite variations. We will examine this aspect of nucleic acid chemistry shortly, after considering another important feature of nucleic acid structure.

The Double Helix

The three-dimensional, or secondary, structure of DNA was the subject of an intensive research effort in the late 1940s and early 1950s. Experiments showed that the molar amount of adenine (A) in DNA corresponds to the molar amount of thymine (T). Similarly, the molar amount of guanine (G) is the same as that of cytosine (C). To maintain this balance, researchers concluded the bases in DNA must be paired, A to T and G to C. But how?

At the midpoint of the twentieth century, it was clear that whoever answered this question would win a Nobel Prize. Many illustrious scientists worked on the problem, but two who were relatively unknown announced in 1953 that they had worked out the structure of DNA. Using data that involved quite sophisticated chemistry, physics, and mathematics, and working with models not unlike a child's construction set, James D. Watson and Francis H. C. Crick determined that DNA must be composed of two helices wound about one another. The two strands are antiparallel; they run in opposite directions. The phosphate and sugar backbones of the polymer chains form the outside of the structure, which is rather like a spiral staircase. The heterocyclic amines are paired on the inside—with guanine always opposite cytosine and adenine always opposite thymine. In the spiral staircase analogy, these base pairs are the steps (Figure 16.22).

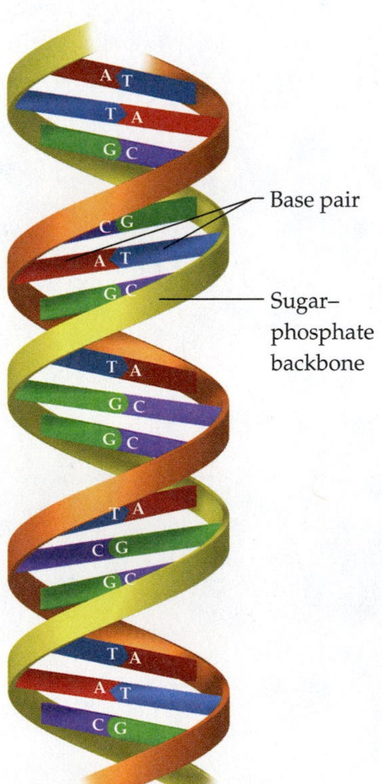

▲ **Figure 16.22** A model of a portion of a DNA double helix is shown in Figure 16.21. This schematic representation of the double helix shows the sugar–phosphate backbones as ribbons and the complementary base pairs as steps on the spiral staircase.

Why do the bases pair in this precise pattern, always A to T and T to A and always G to C and C to G? The answers: hydrogen bonding, and a truly elegant molecular arrangement. Figure 16.23 shows the two sets of base pairs. You should notice two things. First, a pyrimidine is paired with a purine in each case, and the long dimensions of both pairs are identical (1.085 nm).

Second, notice the hydrogen bonding between the bases in each pair. When guanine is paired with cytosine, three hydrogen bonds can be formed between the bases. No other pyrimidine–purine pairing permits such extensive interaction. Indeed, in the combinations shown in the figure, each pair of bases fits like a lock and a key.

Other scientists around the world quickly accepted the Watson–Crick structure because it answered so many crucial questions: how cells are able to divide and go on functioning, how genetic data are passed on to new generations, and even how proteins are built to required specifications. All of these processes depend on the base pairing.

Structure of RNA

Most RNA molecules consist of a single strand of nucleic acids. Some internal (intramolecular) base pairing can occur in sections where the molecule folds back on itself. Portions of some RNA molecules exist in double-helical form (Figure 16.24).

DNA: Self-Replication

Dogs have puppies that grow up to be dogs. Chickens lay eggs that hatch and grow up to be chickens. How is it that each species reproduces its own kind?

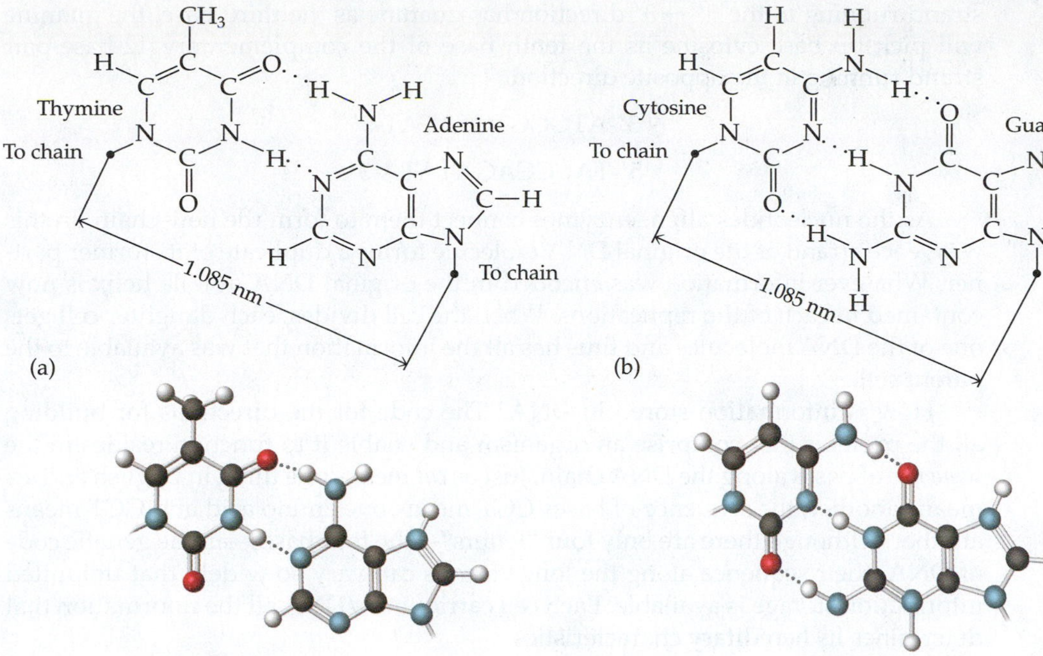

▲ **Figure 16.23** Pairing of the complementary bases thymine and adenine (a) and cytosine and guanine (b). The pairing involves hydrogen bonding.

How does a fertilized egg "know" that it should develop into a kangaroo and not a koala?

The physical basis of heredity has been known for a long time. Most higher organisms reproduce sexually. A sperm cell from the male unites with an egg cell from the female. The fertilized egg that results must carry all the information needed to make the various cells, tissues, and organs necessary for the functioning of a new individual. Further, if the species is to survive, information must be passed along in the germ cells—both sperm and egg—for the production of new individuals.

James D. Watson gave a personal account of the discovery of the structure of DNA in his book *The Double Helix* (New York: New American Library, 1968).

The hereditary material is found in the nuclei of all cells, concentrated in elongated, threadlike bodies called *chromosomes*. Chromosomes form compressed X-shaped structures when strands of DNA coil up tightly just before a cell divides. The number of chromosomes varies with the species. In sexual reproduction, chromosomes come in pairs, with one member of each pair provided by each parent. Each human inherits 23 pairs and so has 46 chromosomes in his or her body's cells. Thus, the entire complement of chromosomes is achieved only when the egg's 23 chromosomes combine with a like number from the sperm.

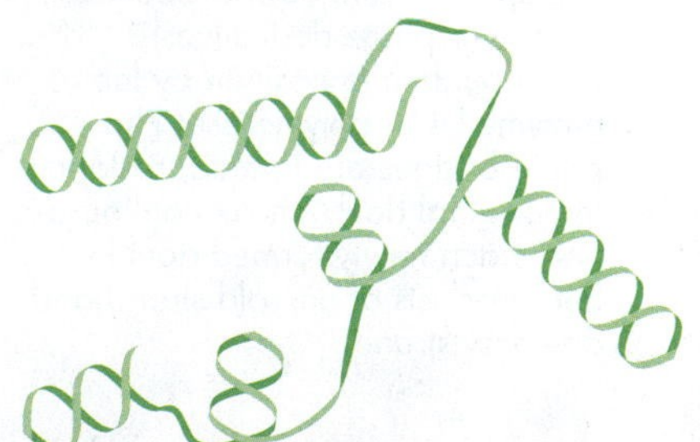

▲ **Figure 16.24** RNA occurs as single strands that can form double-helical portions through internal pairing of bases.

Chromosomes are made of DNA and proteins. Arranged along the chromosomes are the basic units of heredity, the genes. Structurally, a **gene** is a section of the DNA molecule, although some viral genes contain only RNA. Genes control the synthesis of proteins, which tell cells, organs, and organisms how to function in their surroundings. The environment helps determine which genes become active at a particular time. The complete set of genes of an organism is called its *genome*. When cell division occurs, each chromosome produces an exact duplicate of itself. Transmission of genetic information therefore requires the **replication** (copying or duplication) of DNA molecules.

The double helix provides a precise model for replication. If the two chains of the double helix are pulled apart, each chain can direct the synthesis of a new DNA chain using nucleotides from the cellular fluid surrounding the DNA. Each of the separating chains serves as a template, or pattern, for the formation of a new complementary chain. The two DNA strands are *antiparallel*. One chain runs in the direction labeled $3' \rightarrow 5'$, and the other runs in the appropriate direction labeled $5' \rightarrow 3'$. Synthesis begins with a base on a nucleotide pairing with its complementary base on the DNA strand—adenine with thymine and guanine with cytosine (Figure 16.25, page 480). Each base unit in the separated strand can only pick up a base unit identical to the one with which it was paired before. For example, if a 12-base-pair

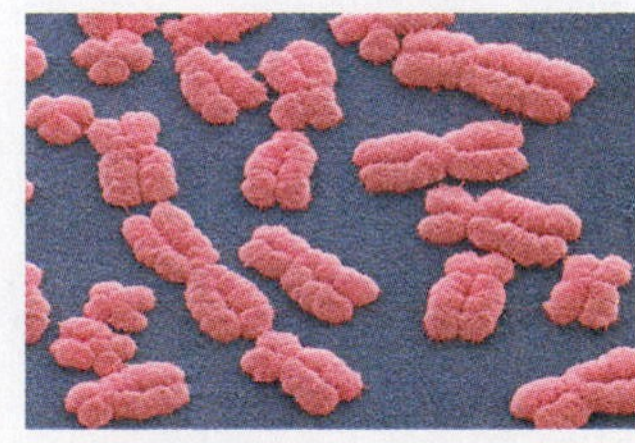

▲ Human chromosomes before cell division have a distinctive X-shape.

Genes have functional regions called *exons* interspersed with inactive portions called *introns*. During protein synthesis, introns are snipped out and not translated. Some genes, called *housekeeping genes*, are expressed in all cells at all times and are essential for the most basic cellular functions. Other genes are expressed only in specific types of cells or at certain stages of development. For example, the genes that encode brain nerve cells are expressed only in brain cells, not in the liver.

strand running in the $5' \rightarrow 3'$ direction has guanine as the third base, the guanine will pick up base cytosine as the tenth base of the complementary 12-base-pair strand running in the opposite direction.

3′-ATGGGTCTATAT-5′

5′-TACCCAGATATA-3′

As the nucleotides align, enzymes connect them to form the new chain. In this way, each strand of the original DNA molecule forms a duplicate of its former partner. Whatever information was encoded in the original DNA double helix is now contained in each of the replications. When the cell divides, each daughter cell gets one of the DNA molecules and thus has all the information that was available to the parent cell.

How is information stored in DNA? The code for the directions for building all the proteins that comprise an organism and enable it to function resides in the *sequence* of bases along the DNA chain. Just as *cat* means one thing in English and *act* means another, the sequence of bases CGT means one amino acid and GCT means another. Although there are only four "letters"—the four bases—in the genetic code of DNA, their sequence along the long strands can vary so widely that unlimited information storage is available. Each cell carries in its DNA all the information that determines its hereditary characteristics.

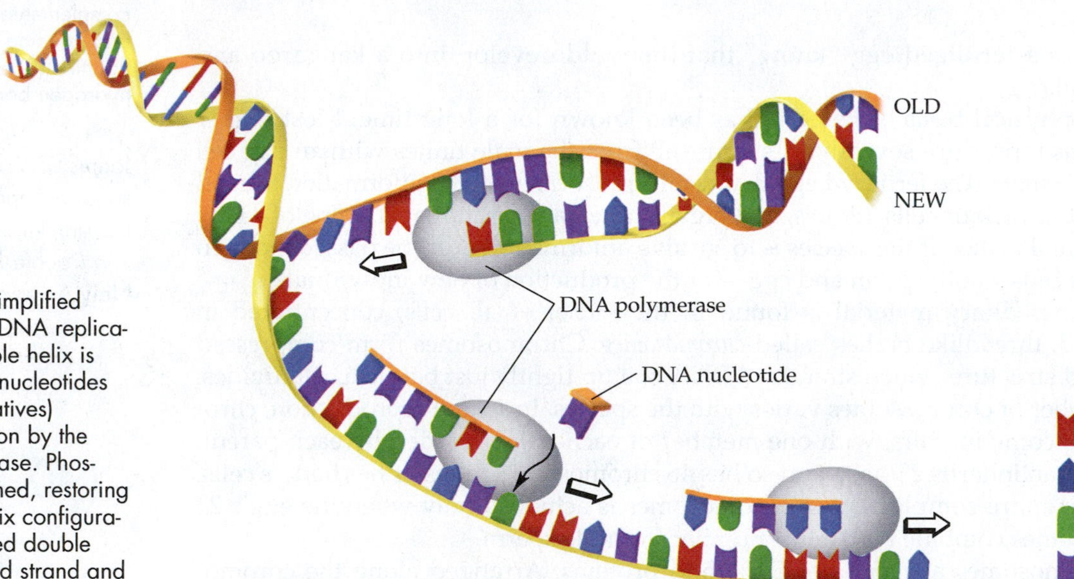

▶ **Figure 16.25** A simplified schematic diagram of DNA replication. The original double helix is "unzipped," and new nucleotides (as triphosphate derivatives) are brought into position by the enzyme DNA polymerase. Phosphate bridges are formed, restoring the original double-helix configuration. Each newly formed double helix consists of one old strand and one new strand.

Self-Assessment Questions

1. The monomer units of nucleic acids are
   a. amino acids
   b. monosaccharides
   c. nucleosomes
   d. nucleotides
2. A DNA nucleotide could contain
   a. A, P_i, and ribose
   b. G, P_i, and glucose
   c. T, P_i, and deoxyribose
   d. U, P_i, and deoxyribose
3. A possible base pair in DNA is
   a. A-G
   b. A-T
   c. A-U
   d. T-G
4. A possible base pair in RNA is
   a. A-G
   b. A-T
   c. A-U
   d. T-G
5. Nucleic acid base pairs are joined by
   a. amide bonds
   b. ester bonds
   c. glucosidic bonds
   d. hydrogen bonds

6. Replication of a DNA molecule involves breaking bonds between the
   a. base pairs b. pentose sugars
   c. phosphate units d. bases and pentoses
7. The first step of DNA replication involves
   a. bonding of free nucleotides in the correct sequence
   b. formation of a single-stranded RNA molecule
   c. linking of a phosphate group to an amino acid
   d. unzipping of the DNA molecule when the hydrogen bonds break
8. If an original DNA strand has the base sequence 3′-TAGC-5′, the complementary strand will have the base sequence
   a. 5′-ATCG-3′ b. 5′-GCAT-3′
   c. 5′-TACG-3′ d. 5′-UACG-3′
9. If a portion of a gene has the base sequence 3′-TCGAAT-5′, what base sequence appears in the complementary DNA strand when the gene is replicated?
   a. 5′-ACGTTA-3′ b. 5′-AGCTTA-3′
   c. 5′-TCGAAT-3′ d. 5′-UGCAAU-3′

Answers: 1, d; 2, c; 3, b; 4, c; 5, d; 6, a; 7, d; 8, a; 9, b

16.7 RNA: Protein Synthesis and the Genetic Code

Learning Objectives › Explain how mRNA is synthesized from DNA and how a protein is synthesized from mRNA. › List important characteristics of the genetic code.

DNA carries a message that must somehow be transmitted and then acted on in a cell. Because DNA does not leave the cell nucleus, its information, or "blueprint," must be transported by something else, and it is. In the first step, called **transcription**, a segment of DNA called the *template strand* transfers its information to a special RNA molecule called *messenger RNA* (*mRNA*). The base sequence of DNA specifies the base sequence of mRNA. Thymine in DNA calls for adenine in mRNA, cytosine specifies guanine, guanine calls for cytosine, and adenine requires uracil (Table 16.4). Remember that in RNA molecules, uracil appears in place of DNA's thymine. Notice the similarity in the structure of these two bases (revisit Figure 16.20). When transcription is completed, the RNA is released, and the DNA helix reforms.

Table 16.4 DNA Bases and Their Complementary RNA Bases

DNA Base	Complementary RNA Base
Adenine (A)	Uracil (U)
Thymine (T)	Adenine (A)
Cytosine (C)	Guanine (G)
Guanine (G)	Cytosine (C)

The next step in creating a protein involves deciphering the code copied by mRNA followed by **translation** of that code into a specific protein structure. The decoding occurs when the mRNA travels from the nucleus and attaches itself to a ribosome in the cytoplasm of the cell. Ribosomes are constructed of about 65% RNA and 35% proteins.

Another type of RNA molecule, called *transfer RNA* (*tRNA*), carries amino acids from the cell fluid to the ribosomes. A tRNA molecule has the looped structure shown in Figure 16.26. At the head of the molecule is a set of three base units, a *base triplet* called the *anticodon*, that pairs with a set of three complementary bases on mRNA, called the **codon**. The codon triplet determines which amino acid is carried

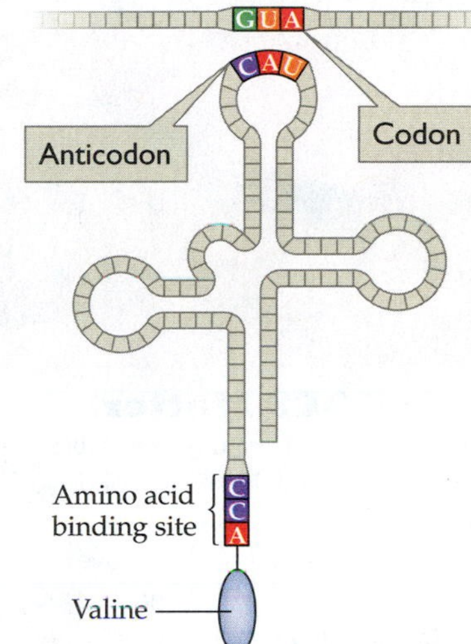

▲ **Figure 16.26** A transfer RNA (tRNA) molecule doubles back on itself, forming three loops with intermolecular hydrogen bonding between complementary bases. The anticodon triplet at the head of the molecule joins with a complementary codon triplet on mRNA. Here the base triplet CAU in the anticodon specifies the amino acid valine.

Why is a code that must specify 20 different amino acids based on a triplet of bases? Four "letters" can be arranged in $4 \times 4 \times 4 = 64$ possible three-letter "words." A "doublet" code of four letters would have only $4 \times 4 = 16$ different words, and a "quadruplet" code of four letters can be arranged in $4 \times 4 \times 4 \times 4 = 256$ different ways. A triplet code specifies 20 different amino acids with some redundancy, a doublet code is inadequate, and a quadruplet code would provide too much redundancy.

Errors can occur at each step in the replication–transcription–translation process. In replication alone, each time a human cell divides, 4 billion bases are copied to make a new strand of DNA, and there may be up to 2000 errors. Most such errors are corrected, and others are unimportant, but some have terrible consequences: genetic disease or even death may result.

at the tail of the tRNA. In Figure 16.26, for example, the codon GUA on the segment of mRNA pairs with the anticodon base triplet CAU on the tRNA molecule. All tRNA molecules with the base triplet CAU always carry the amino acid valine. Once the tRNA has paired with the base triplet of mRNA, it releases its amino acid and returns to the cell fluid to pick up another amino acid molecule.

Each of the 61 different tRNA molecules carries a specific amino acid into place on a growing peptide chain. The protein chain gradually built up in this way is released from the tRNA as it is formed. A complete dictionary of the genetic code has been compiled (Table 16.5). It shows which amino acids are specified by all the possible mRNA base triplets. There are 64 possible triplets and only 20 amino acids, so there is some redundancy in the code. Three amino acids (serine, arginine, and leucine) are each specified by six different codons. Two others (tryptophan and methionine) have only one codon each. Three base triplets on mRNA are "stop" signals that call for termination of the protein chain. The codon AUG signals "start" as well as specifying methionine in the chain. Figure 16.27 provides an overall summary of protein synthesis.

▲ It DOES Matter!

Blue eyes result from a genetic mutation that involved the change of a single base in the code, from A to G. This change is thought to have occurred between 6000 and 10,000 years ago; before that time, no humans had blue eyes. The mutation turned off a gene involved in the production of melanin, the pigment that gives color to hair, eyes, and skin. Only people who inherit this gene from both parents have blue eyes.

Table 16.5 The Genetic Code

FIRST BASE	SECOND BASE: U	SECOND BASE: C	SECOND BASE: A	SECOND BASE: G	THIRD BASE
U	UUU=Phe	UCU=Ser	UAU=Tyr	UGU=Cys	U
U	UUC=Phe	UCC=Ser	UAC=Tyr	UGC=Cys	C
U	UUA=Leu	UCA=Ser	UAA=Termination	UGA=Termination	A
U	UUG=Leu	UCG=Ser	UAG=Termination	UGG=Trp	G
C	CUU=Leu	CCU=Pro	CAU=His	CGU=Arg	U
C	CUC=Leu	CCC=Pro	CAC=His	CGC=Arg	C
C	CUA=Leu	CCA=Pro	CAA=Gln	CGA=Arg	A
C	CUG=Leu	CCG=Pro	CAG=Gln	CGG=Arg	G
A	AUU=Ile	ACU=Thr	AAU=Asn	AGU=Ser	U
A	AUC=Ile	ACC=Thr	AAC=Asn	AGC=Ser	C
A	AUA=Ile	ACA=Thr	AAA=Lys	AGA=Arg	A
A	AUG=Met	ACG=Thr	AAG=Lys	AGG=Arg	G
G	GUU=Val	GCU=Ala	GAU=Asp	GGU=Gly	U
G	GUC=Val	GCC=Ala	GAC=Asp	GGC=Gly	C
G	GUA=Val	GCA=Ala	GAA=Glu	GGA=Gly	A
G	GUG=Val	GCG=Ala	GAG=Glu	GGG=Gly	G

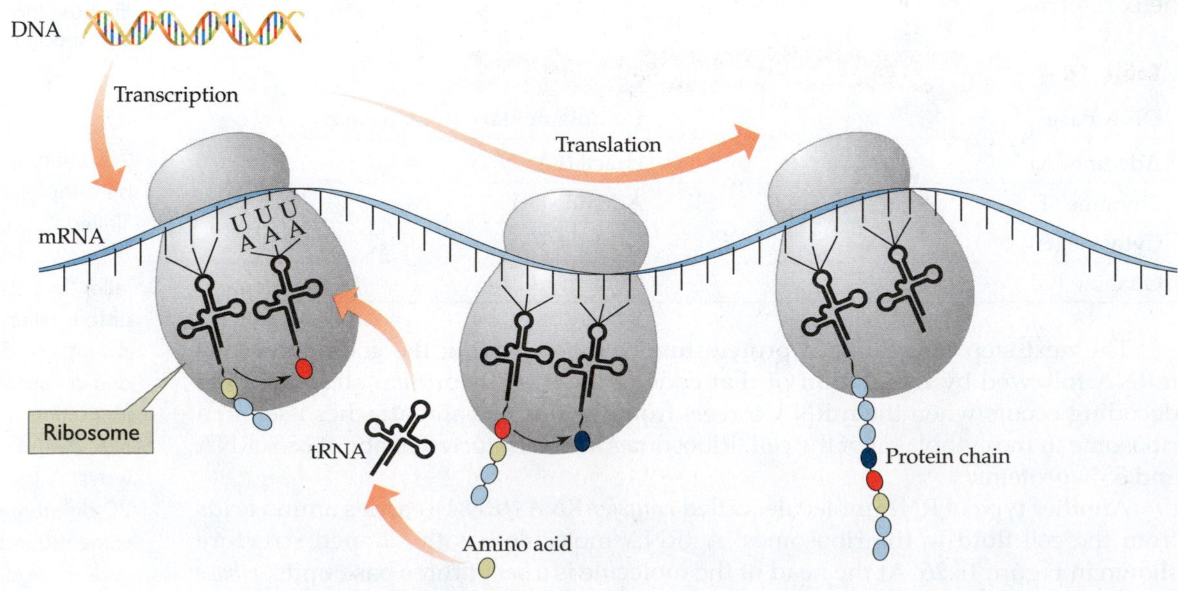

▲ Figure 16.27 Protein synthesis occurs by transcription from DNA to mRNA, translation by tRNA, and building of a protein.

Self-Assessment Questions

1. The synthesis of mRNA from a strand of DNA is called
   a. transaction **b.** transcription **c.** transition **d.** translation
2. The base sequence of a strand of mRNA that is transcribed from a segment of DNA that has the base sequence 5′-TACG-3′ is
   a. 3′-AUGC-5′ **b.** 3′-CGAU-5′ **c.** 3′-TAGC-5′ **d.** 3′-UAGC-5′
3. The anticodon base triplet is found on the
   a. original DNA **b.** ribosome **c.** mRNA **d.** tRNA
4. How many amino acids and how many codons are involved in the genetic code
   a. 20 amino acids, 20 codons **b.** 20 amino acids, 64 codons
   c. 64 amino acids, 20 codons **d.** 64 amino acids, 64 codons
5. Each amino acid except tryptophan and methionine is coded for by more than one codon, indicating that the genetic code has
   a. evolved **b.** redundancy
   c. sequence assurance **d.** translation equability
6. Refer to Table 16.5; the codon UUA
   a. codes for Leu and signals "start" **b.** codes for Leu and signals "stop"
   c. codes for Leu only **d.** signals "stop" only

Answers: 1, b; 2, a; 3, d; 4, b; 5, b; 6, c

16.8 The Human Genome

Learning Objective › Describe recombinant DNA technology, and explain how it is used.

In 1990, scientists set out to determine the sequence of all 3 billion base pairs in the human genome. The Human Genome Project was completed in 2003 at a cost of about $2.7 billion. We can now read the complete genetic blueprint for a human. This project has driven a worldwide revolution in biotechnology—and today a genome can be sequenced in a few days at a cost of a few hundred dollars.

Many human diseases have clear genetic components. Some are directly caused by one defective gene, and others arise through involvement of several genes. The Human Genome Project has already led to the discovery of 2000 or more genes related to disease, allowing the development of more than 2000 genetic tests for human disorders. These tests enable patients to learn their genetic risk for certain diseases and also help health-care professionals to diagnose these diseases.

A gene suspected of causing an inherited disease can be located on the human genome map in a few days, instead of the years it took before the genome sequence was known. Once the genes are identified, the ability to use this information to diagnose and cure genetic diseases will revolutionize medicine.

DNA is sequenced by using enzymes to cleave it into segments of a few to several hundred nucleotides each. These fragments differ in length from each other by a single base that is identified in a later step. The pieces are duplicated and amplified by a technique called the *polymerase chain reaction (PCR)*. PCR employs enzymes called *DNA polymerases* to amplify the small amount of DNA by making millions of copies of each fragment. This builds a minuscule sample into a far larger quantity, which is needed for DNA sequencing. An electric current is used to sort the DNA segments by length, and the base at the end of each fragment is identified. Computers are then used to compile the short sequences into longer segments that recreate the original sequence of bases for the short pieces generated in the first step.

Humans were long thought to have 80,000 or more active genes. When scientists completed the Human Genome Project in 2003, they had found only about 20,000 to 25,000 genes in the human genome.

DNA Profiling

About 99.9% of DNA sequences are the same in every human, yet the 0.1% difference is enough to distinguish one person from another (except for identical twins). DNA profiling does not require sequencing of an entire genome. Rather, it uses *short tandem repeats*, or *STRs*, at 13 particular locations on the human genome. An STR is typically from two to five base units long and is repeated several times. An example is ACGT-ACGT-ACGT. The number of such repeats at the key points differs from one person to another. This is the key to a DNA fingerprint. When all 13 points are considered, each person has a different profile.

DNA fingerprinting is used to screen newborn babies for inherited disorders such as cystic fibrosis, sickle cell anemia, Huntington's disease, hemophilia, and many others. Early detection of such disorders enables doctors and parents to choose and initiate proper treatment of the child.

Because children inherit half their DNA from each parent, DNA fingerprinting is also used to establish parentage when there is a question about paternity. The odds of identifying the father through DNA fingerprinting are at least 99.99%, and they are 100% for excluding a man as a possible father.

British scientist Alec Jeffreys invented DNA fingerprinting in 1985 and gave it its name. Like fingerprints, each person's DNA is unique. Any cells—skin, blood, semen, saliva, and so on—can supply the necessary DNA sample.

DNA fingerprinting was a major advance in criminal investigation, allowing thousands of criminal cases to be solved. DNA samples from evidence found at a crime scene are amplified by PCR and compared with DNA obtained from suspects and other people known to have been at the scene.

This technique has led to many criminal convictions, but perhaps more important, it can readily prove someone innocent. If the DNA does not match, the suspect could not have left the biological sample. Nearly 300 people have been shown to be innocent and freed, some after spending years in prison, including 17 who had been condemned to death. The technique is a major advance in the search for justice.

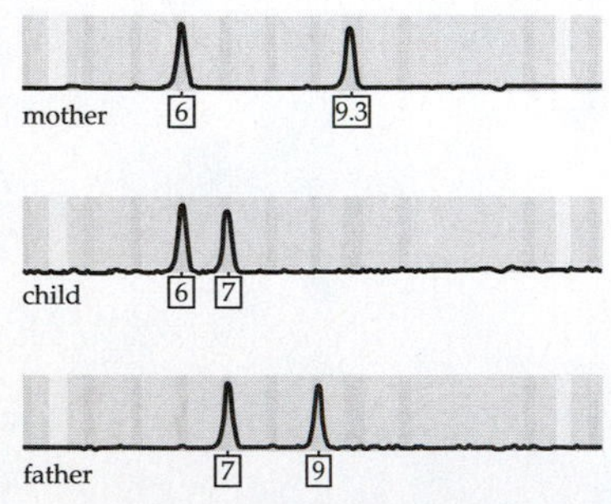

▲ This DNA test included samples from the mother (top), the child (middle), and the alleged father (bottom). The maternal marker 6 has been passed to the child. This means that marker 7 of the child must have come from the father, and the alleged father does indeed have a marker 7.

Recombinant DNA: Using Organisms as Chemical Factories

All living organisms (except some viruses) have DNA as their hereditary material. *Recombinant DNA* is DNA that has been created artificially. DNA from two different sources is incorporated into a single recombinant DNA molecule. The first step is to cut the DNA to extract a fragment of it, which scientists accomplish with an enzyme obtained from bacteria called an *endonuclease*. Endonuclease is a type of *restriction enzyme*, so called because its ability to cleave DNA is restricted to certain short sequences of DNA called *restriction sites*. This enzyme cuts two DNA molecules at the same site. There are three different methods by which recombinant DNA is made. We will consider just one of them here.

After scientists determine the base sequence of the gene that codes for a particular protein, they can isolate it and amplify it by PCR. The gene can then be spliced into a special kind of bacterial DNA called a *plasmid*. The recombined plasmid is then inserted into the host organism, the bacteria from which the plasmids came (Figure 16.28). Once inside the host bacteria, the plasmids replicate, making multiple exact copies of themselves, a process called *cloning*. As the engineered bacteria multiply, they become effective factories for producing the desired protein.

What kinds of proteins might scientists wish to produce using biotechnology? Insulin, a protein coded by DNA, is required for the proper use of glucose by cells. People with diabetes, an insulin-deficiency disease, formerly had to use insulin from pigs or cattle. Now human insulin is made using recombinant DNA technology. Scientists take the human gene for insulin production and paste it into the DNA of *Escherichia coli,* a bacterium commonly found in the human digestive tract. Expression factors, signals that provide instructions for transcription and translation of the gene by the cell, are also added. The bacterial cells multiply rapidly, making billions of copies of themselves, and each new *E. coli* cell carries in its DNA a replica of the gene for human insulin. The hope for the future is that a functioning gene for insulin can be incorporated directly into the cells of insulin-dependent diabetics.

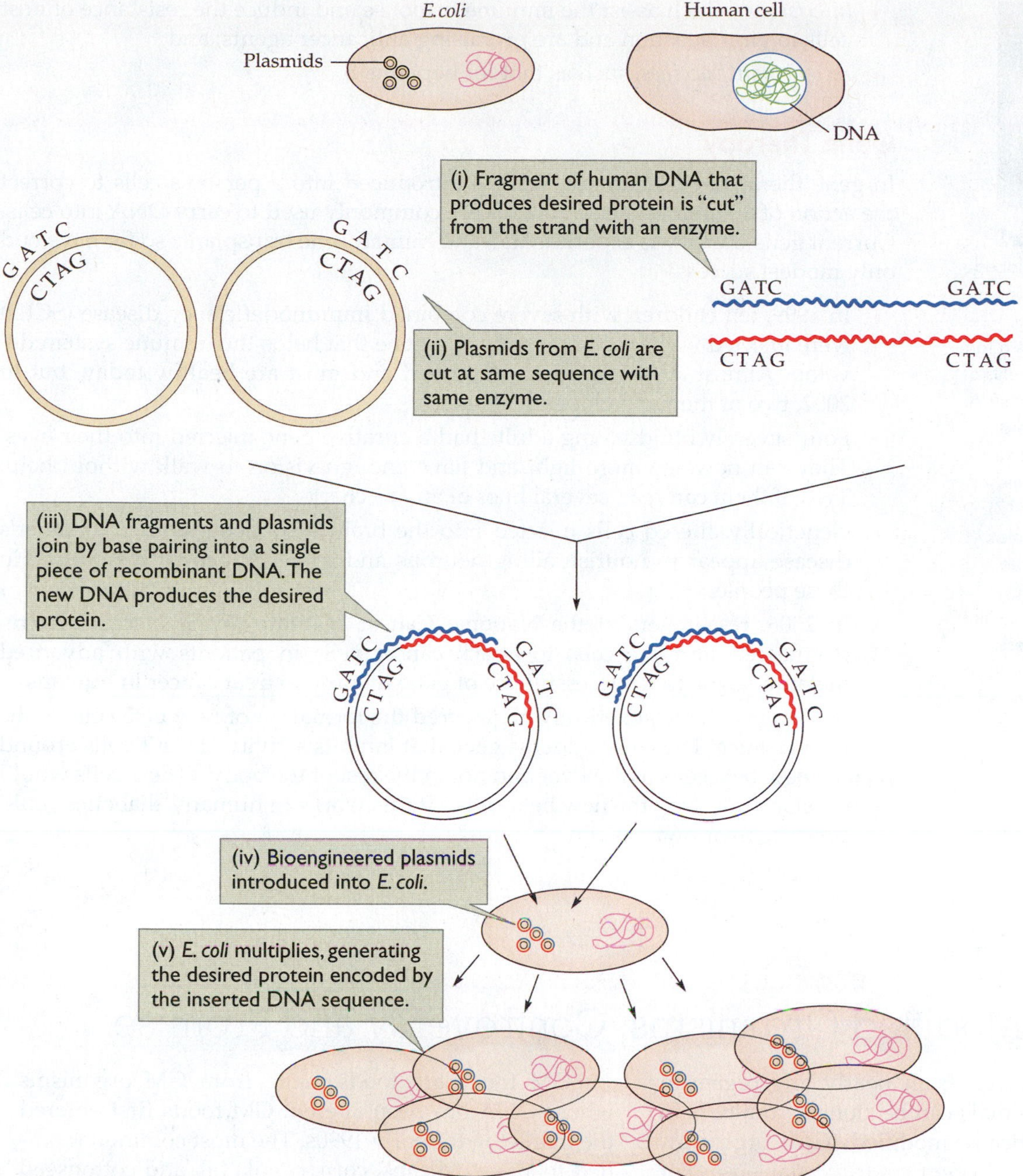

▲ **Figure 16.28** Recombinant DNA: cloning a human gene into a bacterial plasmid. The bacteria multiply and, in doing so, make multiple copies of the recombinant gene. The gene can be one that codes for insulin, human growth hormone, or another valuable protein. Potentially, a gene from any organism—microbe, plant, or animal—can be incorporated into any other organism.

In addition to insulin, many other valuable materials that are used in human therapy and are difficult to obtain in any other way can now be made using recombinant DNA technology. Some examples are

- *human growth hormone* (HGH), which replaced cadaver-harvested HGH for treating children who fail to grow properly;
- *erythropoietin* (EPO) for treating anemia resulting from chronic kidney disease and from treatment for cancer;
- *factor VIII* (formerly harvested from blood), a clotting agent for treating males with hemophilia;
- *tissue plasminogen activator* (TPA) for dissolving blood clots associated with diseases such as heart attack and stroke;

▲ **It DOES Matter!**
GM rice ("golden rice"), developed in 1999, has new genes implanted from daffodils and a bacterium. Golden rice was developed as a fortified food containing high amounts of β-carotene, a precursor of vitamin A. It was to be used in areas where children face a shortage of dietary vitamin A to help them overcome vitamin A deficiency (Chapter 17). An estimated 124 million people in Africa and Southeast Asia are affected by vitamin A deficiency, which has caused 1–2 million deaths and 500,000 cases of blindness. Opposition to and complex regulation of transgenic crops have prevented golden rice from being grown on farms; it is still in field trials.

- *interferons*, which assist the immune response and induce the resistance of host cells to viral infection and are promising anticancer agents; and
- *recombinant vaccines*, such as that for hepatitis B.

Gene Therapy

In gene therapy, a functioning gene is introduced into a person's cells to correct the action of a defective gene. Viruses are commonly used to carry DNA into cells. Current gene therapy is experimental, and human gene transplants so far have had only modest success.

- In 1999, ten children with severe combined immunodeficiency disease (SCID) were injected with working copies of a gene that helps the immune system develop. Almost all the children improved and most are healthy today, but in 2002, two of them developed leukemia.
- Four severely blind young adults had a curative gene injected into their eyes. They can now see more light and have enough vision to walk without help. Two of them can read several lines of an eye chart.
- Genetically altered cells injected into the brain of patients with Alzheimer's disease appear to nourish ailing neurons and may slow cognitive decline in these people.
- In 2006, researchers at the National Cancer Institute (NCI) successfully re-engineered immune cells to attack cancer cells in patients with advanced melanoma, the first successful use of gene therapy to treat cancer in humans.
- Researchers have genetically engineered the formation of new beta cells in the liver of mice. They also added a gene that inhibits activity of the T cells around the new beta cells in the liver and not in the rest of the body. (The T cells would otherwise destroy the new beta cells.) If this works in humans, diabetics could produce their own insulin.

Genetically Modified Organisms: Controversy and Promise

Genes can be transferred from nearly any organism to any other. New animals can be cloned from cells in adult animals. Genetically modified (GM) organisms are in widespread—and often controversial—use. For example, by 2010 in the United States, 93% of the soybeans, 93% of the cotton, and 86% of the maize (corn) planted were GM varieties.

- Genes for herbicide resistance are now incorporated into soybeans so that herbicide application will kill weeds without killing the soybean plants. People worry that these genes will escape into wild plants (weeds), making them resistant to herbicides.
- Genes from the bacteria *Bacillus thuringiensis* (Bt) are incorporated into corn and cotton plants. The genes cause the plants to produce a protein toxin that kills caterpillars that would otherwise feed on the plants. People worry that insects will quickly become resistant to the toxin and that butterflies and other desirable insects will also be killed by it.

GM foods are foods made from GM organisms whose DNA has been altered. GM foods first entered the market in the early 1990s. The most common modified foods—soybeans, corn, canola oil, and cottonseed oil—are derived from GM plants. People worry that GM foods will have proteins that will cause allergic reactions in some people. To protect against such developments, strict guidelines for recombinant DNA research have been instituted. Some people think that these are not strict enough.

Molecular genetics has already resulted in some impressive achievements. Its possibilities are mind-boggling—elimination of genetic defects, a cure for cancer, and who knows what else? Knowledge gives power, but it does not necessarily give wisdom. Who will decide what sort of creature the human species should be? The greatest problem we are likely to face in our use of bioengineering is choosing who is to play God with the new "secret of life."

Many problems remain, including getting the gene in the right place and targeting it so that it inserts itself only into the cells where it is needed. The stakes in gene therapy are huge. We all carry some defective genes. About one in ten people either has or will develop an inherited genetic disorder. Gene therapy could become an efficient way of curing many diseases.

5. Are genetically modified foods safe? There are potential problems with today's genetically modified foods, but in practice we have been using genetically modified foods for over a century—ever since Mendel discovered the concept of genetics. Most of today's foods are hybrids, the result of genetic modification by cross-breeding. Of course, sometimes a hybrid tomato isn't tasty or is too small. Likewise, some genetically modified plants aren't exactly what we'd like.

Self-Assessment Questions

1. Recombinant DNA cloning involves
   - **a.** combining DNA from two different organisms to make a single new organism
   - **b.** creating a genetically identical organism from a skin cell
   - **c.** isolation of a genetically pure colony of cells
   - **d.** splitting of a fertilized egg into two cells to generate identical twins
2. In producing recombinant DNA, the DNA from the two sources is cut with
   - **a.** DNA ligase
   - **b.** phages
   - **c.** restriction enzymes
   - **d.** vectors
3. Recombinant DNA is currently used in the biotechnology industry to
   - **a.** create new species of animals
   - **b.** eliminate all infectious diseases in domestic animals
   - **c.** increase the frequency of mutations
   - **d.** synthesize insulin, interferon, and human growth hormone
4. Some geneticists suggest transferring some genes that direct photosynthesis from an efficient crop plant to a less efficient one, thus producing a more productive plant variety. This project would most likely involve
   - **a.** genetic profiling
   - **b.** genetic engineering
   - **c.** genetic screening
   - **d.** transcription

Answers: 1, a; 2, c; 3, d; 4, b

CRITICAL THINKING  EXERCISES

Apply knowledge that you have gained in this chapter and one or more of the FLaReS principles (Chapter 1) to evaluate the following statements or claims.

16.1 The wrapper of an energy bar claims, in large print, "21,000 mg of amino acids in each bar!"

16.2 DNA is an essential component of every living cell. An advertisement claims that DNA is a useful diet supplement.

16.3 A restaurant menu states, "Other restaurants use saturated beef fat for frying. We use only pure vegetable oil to fry our fish and french fries, for healthier eating."

16.4 The label on a bag of sugar says, "NOW CERTIFIED CARBON FREE."

16.5 A dietician states that a recommendation of 60 g of protein per day for an adult is somewhat misleading. She claims that the right kinds of proteins, with the proper amino acids in them, must be consumed; otherwise, even a much larger amount of protein per day may be insufficient to maintain health.

16.6 A man convicted of rape claims that he is innocent because DNA fingerprinting of a semen sample taken from the rape victim showed that it contains DNA from another man.

SUMMARY

Section 16.1—**Biochemistry** is the chemistry of life processes. Life requires chemical energy. **Metabolism** is the set of chemical reactions that keep cells alive. Metabolism includes many processes of both **anabolism** (building up of molecules) and **catabolism** (breaking down of molecules). Substances that provide animals with energy are carbohydrates, fats, and proteins.

Section 16.2—A **carbohydrate** is a compound whose formula can be written as a hydrate of carbon. Sugars, starches, and cellulose are carbohydrates. The simplest sugars are **monosaccharides**, carbohydrates that cannot be further hydrolyzed. A monosaccharide is either an **aldose** (having an aldehyde functional group) or a **ketose** (having a ketone functional group). Glucose and fructose are monosaccharides. A **disaccharide** can be hydrolyzed to yield two monosaccharide units. Sucrose and lactose are disaccharides. **Polysaccharides** contain many monosaccharide units linked together. Starches and cellulose are polysaccharides. Starches are polymers of glucose units held together by alpha linkages; cellulose is a glucose polymer held together by beta linkages. There are two kinds of plant starches, amylose and amylopectin. Animal starch is called glycogen.

Section 16.3—A **lipid** is a cellular component that is insoluble in water and soluble in solvents of low polarity. Lipids include solid fats and liquid oils; both are triglycerides (esters of fatty acids with glycerol). Lipids also include steroids, hormones, and **fatty acids** (long-chain carboxylic acids). A **fat** is an ester of fatty acids and glycerol. Fats may be saturated (all carbon-to-carbon bonds in the fatty acid are single bonds), monounsaturated (one C=C), or polyunsaturated (more than one C=C). The **iodine number** of a fat or oil is the mass in grams of iodine that reacts with 100 g of the fat or oil. Oils tend to have higher iodine numbers than fats because there are more double bonds in oils.

Section 16.4—An **amino acid** contains an amino ($—NH_2$) group and a carboxyl (—COOH) group. An amino acid exists as a **zwitterion**, in which a proton from the carboxyl group has been transferred to the amino group. Proteins are polymers of amino acids, with 20 amino acids forming millions of different proteins. Plants can synthesize proteins from CO_2, water, and minerals, but animals require proteins in their diets.

The bond that joins two amino-acid units in a protein is called a **peptide bond**. Two amino acids form a dipeptide, three forms a tripeptide, and more than 10 forms a **polypeptide**. When the molecular weight of a polypeptide exceeds about 10,000, it is called a **protein**. The sequence of the amino acids in a protein is of great importance to its function. Three-letter or single-letter abbreviations are used to designate amino acids.

Section 16.5—Protein structure has four levels. The **primary structure** of a protein is simply the sequence of its amino acids. The **secondary structure** is the arrangement of polypeptide chains about an axis. Two such arrangements are the **beta pleated sheet**, in which the arrays of chains form zigzag sheets, and the **alpha helix**, in which protein chains coil around one another. The **tertiary structure** of a protein is its folding pattern; **globular proteins** such as myoglobin are folded into compact shapes. Some proteins have a **quaternary structure** consisting of an aggregate of subunits arranged in a specific pattern.

There are four types of forces that determine the secondary, tertiary, and quaternary structures of proteins: (a) hydrogen bonds; (b) ionic bonds formed between acidic and basic side chains; (c) **disulfide linkages**, which are S—S bonds formed between cysteine groups; and (d) dispersion forces arising between nonpolar side chains.

Enzymes are biological catalysts. In operation, the reacting substance, or **substrate**, attaches to the **active site** of the enzyme to form a complex, which then decomposes to the products. An enzyme is often made up of an **apoenzyme** (a protein) and a **cofactor** that is necessary for proper function and that may be a metal ion. An organic cofactor (such as a vitamin) is called a **coenzyme**.

Section 16.6—**Nucleic acids** are the information and control centers of a cell. DNA (deoxyribonucleic acid) and RNA (ribonucleic acid) are polymers of **nucleotides**. Each nucleotide contains a pentose sugar unit, a phosphate unit, and one of four amine bases. Bases with one ring are called **pyrimidines**, and those with two fused rings are **purines**. In DNA, the sugar is deoxyribose and the bases are adenine, thymine, guanine, and cytosine. In RNA, the sugar is ribose and the bases are the same as those in DNA, except that uracil replaces thymine. Nucleotides are joined through their phosphate groups to form nucleic acid chains. In DNA, the bases thymine and adenine are always paired, as are the bases cytosine and guanine. Pairing occurs via hydrogen bonding between the bases and gives rise to the double-helix structure of DNA. RNA consists of single strands of nucleic acids, some parts of which may hydrogen bond to form double helixes. Chromosomes are made of DNA and proteins. A **gene** is a section of DNA. Genetic information is stored in the base sequence; a three-base sequence code for a particular amino acid. Transmission of genetic information requires **replication**, or copying, of the DNA molecules. When the chains of DNA are pulled apart, each half can replicate using nucleotides in the cellular fluid. Each base unit picks up a unit identical to that with which it was paired before. Enzymes connect the paired nucleotides to form the new chain. When a cell divides, one DNA molecule goes to each daughter cell, providing all the necessary genetic information.

Section 16.7—In **transcription**, a segment of DNA transfers its information to messenger RNA (mRNA). The next step is the **translation** of the code into a specific protein structure. Transfer RNA (tRNA) delivers amino acids to the growing protein chain. Each base triplet on a tRNA pairs with a set of three complementary bases on mRNA, called the **codon**, which codes for a specific amino acid.

Section 16.8—Many diseases have genetic components. In genetic testing, DNA is cleaved and duplicated. The patterns of DNA fragments are examined and compared to those of individuals with genetic diseases, to identify and predict the occurrence of such diseases. A similar technique is used to compare DNA from different sources in DNA fingerprinting. In recombinant DNA technology, the base sequence for the gene that codes for a desired protein is determined and amplified; the gene is then spliced into a plasmid. The recombined plasmid is inserted into a host organism, which generates the protein as it reproduces. Gene therapy—replacement of defective genes—could be used to cure diseases. Genetic engineering holds great promise and carries with it great responsibility.

Green chemistry Biochemistry has important applications in renewable energy and offers several advantages over traditional chemical synthesis, including the use of water as the solvent and the low levels of waste and energy use. Drugs and fuels are examples of products that may be made using biochemical methods.

Learning Objectives

› List the major parts of a cell, and describe the function of each part.	Problem 2
› Name the primary source of energy for plants and three classes of substances that are the sources of energy for animals.	Problems 1, 4, 8
› Compare and contrast starch, glycogen, and cellulose.	Problems 19, 20
› Describe the fundamental structure of a fatty acid and of a fat.	Problems 31, 32, 35, 36
› Classify fats as saturated, monounsaturated, or polyunsaturated.	Problems 33, 34
› Draw the fundamental structure of an amino acid, and show how amino acids combine to make proteins.	Problems 39, 40, 42–48, 70
› Describe the four levels of protein structure, and give an example of each.	Problem 69
› Describe how enzymes work as catalysts.	Problem 50
› Name the two types of nucleic acids, and describe the function of each type.	Problems 51, 52
› Explain complementary base pairing, and describe how a copy of DNA is synthesized.	Problems 55, 56–58, 74
› Explain how mRNA is synthesized from DNA and how a protein is synthesized from mRNA.	Problems 59–68, 77
› List important characteristics of the genetic code.	Problems 14, 59
› Describe recombinant DNA technology, and explain how it is used.	Problem 15
› Name some advantages of using biochemistry to create useful molecules.	Problems 79, 82
› Give examples of the use of biochemistry for energy production and other applications.	Problems 80, 81

REVIEW QUESTIONS

1. What is the importance of photosynthesis to plants and animals?
2. Briefly identify and state a function of each of the following parts of a cell.
   a. cell membrane **b.** cell nucleus
   c. chloroplasts **d.** mitochondria
   e. ribosomes
3. In what parts of the body are proteins found? What tissues are largely proteins?
4. How does the elemental composition of proteins differ from those of carbohydrates and fats?
5. What is the chemical nature of proteins?
6. Amino-acid units in a protein are linked by peptide bonds. What is another name for this kind of bond?
7. What is the difference between a polypeptide and a protein?
8. What provides most of the energy for plants? Write the equation for the reaction that is driven by that energy.
9. What kind of intermolecular force is involved in base pairing?
10. Describe how replication and transcription are similar and how they differ.
11. How do DNA and RNA differ in structure?
12. What is the relationship among the cell parts called chromosomes, the units of heredity called genes, and the nucleic acid DNA?
13. What is the polymerase chain reaction (PCR)?
14. Explain what is meant by redundancy in the genetic code. Does redundancy exist for every amino acid?
15. List the steps in recombinant DNA technology.
16. How can a virus be used to replace a defective gene in a human being?

PROBLEMS

Carbohydrates

17. What is a monosaccharide? Name three common ones.
18. What is a disaccharide? Name three common ones.
19. What is glycogen? How does it differ from amylose? From amylopectin?
20. In what way are amylose and cellulose similar? What is the main structural difference between starch and cellulose?
21. Which of the following are monosaccharides?
    a. amylose **b.** cellulose
    c. mannose **d.** glucose

22. Which of the following are monosaccharides?
    a. sucrose b. galactose
    c. fructose d. lactose
23. Which of the carbohydrates in Problems 21 and 22 are disaccharides?
24. Which of the carbohydrates in Problems 21 and 22 are polysaccharides?
25. What are the hydrolysis products of each of the following?
    a. amylose b. glycogen
26. What are the hydrolysis products of each of the following?
    a. amylopectin b. cellulose
27. What functional groups are present in the formula for the open-chain form of fructose?
28. Write the formula for the open-chain form of glucose. What functional groups are present?
29. What functional groups are present in the formula for the open-chain form of galactose? How does the structure of galactose differ from that of glucose?
30. Mannose differs from glucose only in having the positions of the H and OH on the second carbon atom reversed. Write the formula for the open-chain form of mannose. What functional groups are present?

Lipids: Fats and Oils

31. How do fats and oils differ in structure? In properties?
32. Define *monoglyceride*, *diglyceride*, and *triglyceride*.
33. Which of the following fatty acids are saturated? Which are unsaturated?
    a. palmitic acid b. linoleic acid
    c. oleic acid d. stearic acid
34. Which of the fatty acids in Problem 33 are monounsaturated? Which are polyunsaturated?
35. How many carbon atoms are in a molecule of each of the following fatty acids?
    a. linoleic acid b. palmitic acid
    c. stearic acid
36. How many carbon atoms are in a molecule of each of the following fatty acids?
    a. linoleic acid b. oleic acid
    c. butyric acid
37. Which of the two foodstuffs shown below would you expect to have a higher iodine number? Explain your reasoning.

38. Which of the two fats shown below is likely to have a lower iodine number? Explain your reasoning.

Proteins

39. What functional groups does amino acid have? What is a zwitterion?
40. What is a dipeptide? A tripeptide? A polypeptide?
41. Of the amino acids glutamic acid, lysine, serine, leucine, and glycine, which are essential to the human diet?
42. Examine Table 16.3, and write the condensed structural formula for the part of each structure that is identical for 19 of the 20 amino acids. Which amino acid does not have this particular structural feature?
43. Write structural formulas for the following amino acids.
    a. alanine b. cysteine
44. Identify the following amino acids.

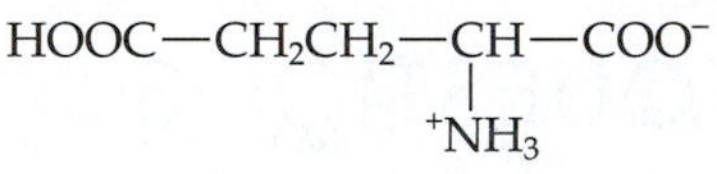

$$HOOC{-}CH_2CH_2{-}\underset{\displaystyle {}^{+}NH_3}{\underset{|}{CH}}{-}COO^-$$

(a)

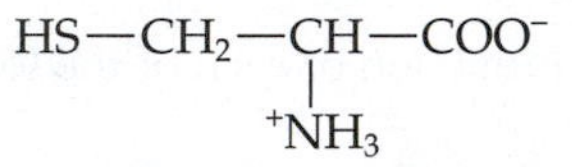

$$HS{-}CH_2{-}\underset{\displaystyle {}^{+}NH_3}{\underset{|}{CH}}{-}COO^-$$

(b)

45. Write structural formulas for the following dipeptides.
    a. glycylalanine b. alanylserine
46. Identify the following dipeptides.

$${}^{+}NH_3{-}\overset{\displaystyle OH{-}CH_2}{\overset{|}{CH}}{-}CONH{-}\overset{\displaystyle CH_2CH(CH_3)_2}{\overset{|}{CH}}{-}COO^-$$

(a)

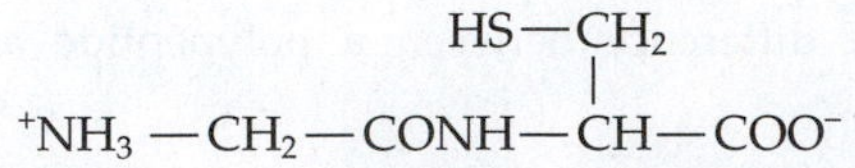

$${}^{+}NH_3{-}CH_2{-}CONH{-}\overset{\displaystyle HS{-}CH_2}{\overset{|}{CH}}{-}COO^-$$

(b)

47. The sweetener *aspartame* has the structure shown below, in which a CH_3O— group (at right) is attached to a dipeptide. Identify the dipeptide.

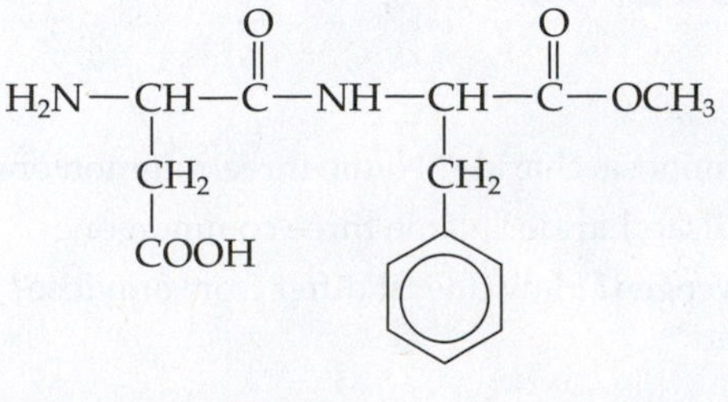

$$H_2N{-}\underset{\displaystyle \underset{|}{CH_2}\atop COOH}{\underset{|}{CH}}{-}\overset{\displaystyle O}{\overset{\|}{C}}{-}NH{-}\underset{\displaystyle \underset{|}{CH_2}\atop C_6H_5}{\underset{|}{CH}}{-}\overset{\displaystyle O}{\overset{\|}{C}}{-}OCH_3$$

48. Refer to Problem 47, and draw the structure of the other dipeptide that contains the same amino acids as aspartame.

49. List the four different forces that link protein chains.

50. Describe **(a)** the induced-fit model of enzyme action and **(b)** how an inhibitor deactivates an enzyme.

Nucleic Acids: Parts and Structure

51. Which of the following nucleotides can be found in DNA, which in RNA, and which in neither?

a. thymine | deoxyribose—P_i

b. adenine | ribose—P_i

c. cytosine | ribose—P_i

52. Which of the following nucleotides can be found in DNA, which in RNA, and which in neither?

a. uracil | ribose—P_i

b. adenine | deoxyribose—P_i

c. cytosine | deoxyribose—P_i

53. Identify the sugar and the base in the following nucleotide.

54. Identify the sugar and the base in the following nucleotide.

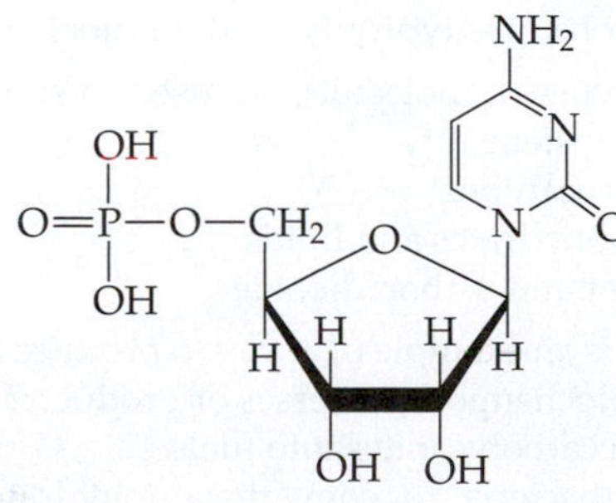

55. In DNA, which base would be paired with the base listed?

a. cytosine **b.** adenine
c. guanine **d.** thymine

56. In RNA, which base would be paired with the base listed?

a. adenine **b.** guanine
c. uracil **d.** cytosine

DNA: Self-Replication

57. In replication, a DNA molecule produces two daughter molecules. What is the fate of each strand of the original double helix?

58. DNA controls protein synthesis, yet most DNA resides within the cell nucleus and protein synthesis occurs outside the nucleus. How does DNA exercise its control?

RNA: Protein Synthesis and the Genetic Code

59. Which nucleic acid(s) is(are) involved in **(a)** the process referred to as transcription and **(b)** the process referred to as translation?

60. Explain the role of **(a)** mRNA and **(b)** tRNA in protein synthesis.

61. A portion of the code for a certain gene has the base sequence 5′-ATGAGCGACTTTGCGGGATTA-3′. What is the base sequence of the complementary strand of DNA?

62. What is the sequence of the mRNA that would be produced during transcription from the segment of DNA shown in Problem 61?

63. If the sequence of bases in an mRNA molecule is 3′-UCCGAU-5′, what was the sequence of the DNA template?

64. What anticodon on tRNA would pair with each of the following mRNA codons?

a. 5′-UUU-3′ **b.** 5′-CAU-3′
c. 5′-AGC-3′ **d.** 5′-CCG-3′

65. What codon on mRNA would pair with each of the following tRNA anticodons?

a. 5′-UUG-3′ **b.** 5′-GAA-3′
c. 5′-UCC-3′

66. What codon on mRNA would pair with each of the following tRNA anticodons?

a. UCC **b.** CAC
c. 5′-CAC-3′

67. Use Table 16.5 to identify the amino acids carried by each tRNA molecule in Problem 65.

68. Use Table 16.5 to determine the amino-acid sequence produced from the mRNA sequence 5′-AUGAGCGACUUUGCGGGAUUA-3′.

ADDITIONAL PROBLEMS

69. Human insulin molecules are made up of two chains with the following sequences.

Chain A: G-I-V-E-Q-C-C-T-S-I-C-S-L-Y-Q-L-E-N-Y-C-N

Chain B: F-V-N-Q-H-L-C-G-D-H-L-V-E-A-L-Y-L-V-C-G-E-R-G-F-F-Y-T-P-K-T

Chain A has a loop formed by a disulfide linkage between the sixth and eleventh amino acids (designated A-6 to A-11) and is joined to chain B by two disulfide linkages (A-7 to B-7 and A-20 to B-19). What level of protein structure is described by **(a)** the chain sequence of one-letter abbreviations and **(b)** the description of the loop and chain linkages?

70. Synthetic polymers can be formed from amino-acid units of a single kind. Write the formula for a segment of **(a)** polyglycine and **(b)** polyserine. Show at least four repeating units of each.

71. Identify the base in the structure in **(a)** Problem 53 and **(b)** Problem 54 as a purine or a pyrimidine.

72. Answer the following questions for the molecule shown.

a. Is the base a purine or a pyrimidine?
b. Would the compound be incorporated in DNA or in RNA?

73. Answer the questions posed in Problem 72 for the following compound.

74. Use Table 16.5 to determine the amino acid specified by the DNA triplet 5′-CTC-3′. What amino acid is specified if a mutation changes the DNA triplet to 5′-CTT-3′? To 5′-CTA-3′? to 5′-CAC-3′?

75. Many laundry detergents have enzymes to aid removal of stains of biological origin, such as those from food or blood. The enzyme subtilisin, produced by *Bacillus subtilis*, is one of these. The natural enzyme was not very effective because it was largely deactivated by the harsh detergent environment. A genetically modified form, in which the base sequence 5′-ACCAGCAUGGCG-3′ is replaced by 5′-ACCAGCGCGGCG-3′, is much more effective because it is more stable. What is the amino-acid sequence specified by the bases in this segment in **(a)** the original enzyme and **(b)** the genetically modified enzyme? You may consult Table 16.5.

76. In the novel *Jurassic Park* by Michael Crichton, the cloned dinosaurs were genetically engineered so as to be unable to survive outside the island park because they were unable to synthesize the amino acid lysine. This was supposed to make the dinosaurs dependent on their makers to feed them a source of lysine. Examine Table 16.3, and suggest a reason why this genetic engineering would not keep the dinosaurs from surviving elsewhere.

77. With what mRNA codon would the tRNA in the diagram form a codon–anticodon pair?

78. Write the abbreviated versions of the following structural formula using **(a)** the three-letter abbreviations and **(b)** the one-letter abbreviations.

$$H_3\overset{+}{N}-CH(CH_3)-\overset{O}{\overset{\|}{C}}-NH-CH(CH_2OH)-\overset{O}{\overset{\|}{C}}-NH-CH(CH_2SH)-\overset{O}{\overset{\|}{C}}-NH-CH(CH_2C_6H_5)-\overset{O}{\overset{\|}{C}}-NH-CH(H)-\overset{O}{\overset{\|}{C}}-NH-CH(H)-\overset{O}{\overset{\|}{C}}-O^-$$

79. What solvent is typically used for biochemical reactions?

80. What types of molecules are used to store energy in biological systems?
a. hydrocarbons
b. carbohydrates and lipids
c. water and carbon dioxide

81. Which is an example of a way to produce a renewable fuel using biochemical processes or products?
a. turn carbohydrates into fuels
b. use bacteria to convert carbohydrates or CO_2 into biofuels
c. engineer microbes to make gasoline
d. all of the above

82. Which of the following is NOT an advantage of using biochemical methods compared to traditional chemical synthesis?
a. Water is often used as a solvent.
b. Separation of products is difficult.
c. Reaction conditions are mild.
d. Reactions are usually catalytic.

COLLABORATIVE GROUP PROJECTS

Prepare a PowerPoint, poster, or other presentation (as directed by your instructor) to share with the class.

1. Prepare a brief report on (**a**) a carbohydrate such as fructose, glycogen, lactose, maltose, sucrose, or starch or (**b**) a lipid such as beef tallow, corn oil, lard, oleic acid, or palmitic acid. List principal sources and uses of the material.
2. Prepare a brief report on enzyme action, including a comparision of the induced-fit model of action with the older lock-and-key model.
3. Prepare a brief report on one of the following products of genetic engineering. List some advantages and disadvantages of the product.
   a. golden rice
   b. herbicide-resistant transgenic soybeans
   c. transgenic cotton that produces Bt toxin
   d. transgenic tobacco that produces human serum albumin
   e. transgenic tomatoes that have improved resistance to viruses
   f. transgenic *E. coli* that produce human interleukin-2, a protein that stimulates the production of T-lymphocytes that play a role in fighting selected cancers
4. Genetic testing carries both promise and peril, and its use is an important topic in bioethics today. After some online research, write a brief essay on one of the following—or on a similar question assigned by your instructor.
   a. In what cases might a person not want to be tested for a disease his or her parent had?
   b. When is genetic testing most valuable? What privacy issues must be addressed in this area?
   c. Does testing negative for the breast cancer genes mean that a woman doesn't have to have mammograms?

Food

Learning Objectives

- Identify dietary carbohydrates, and state their function. (17.1)
- Identify dietary lipids, and state their function. (17.2)
- List the essential amino acids, and explain why they are essential. (17.3)
- Describe some protein deficiency diseases and their causes. (17.3)
- Identify the vitamins and the bulk dietary minerals, and state their functions. (17.4)
- Describe the effects of starvation, fasting, and malnutrition. (17.5)
- List some common food additives and their purposes. (17.6)
- Identify and describe some of the main problems with harmful substances in our food. (17.7)
- Identify common molecules derived from food sources.
- Distinguish polar molecules from nonpolar molecules and predict which can be extracted with ethanol or supercritical carbon dioxide.
- Describe how green chemistry has made the extraction of natural products, bioactive food components, and essential oils from plants safer and less hazardous.

Have You Ever Wondered?

1. **The doctor said my father has high triglycerides. What are they?**
2. **Is high blood cholesterol mainly a problem for older people?**
3. **How much fat in the diet is "too much"?**
4. **Are large doses of vitamins beneficial?**
5. **Are some foods really "super foods" or "miracle foods"?**
6. **Should the government prohibit food additives?**

Molecular Gastronomy

FOOD! From holiday feasts to late-night snacks, many of life's joys involve food. Yet the prime purpose of food is not to give pleasure; it is to sustain life. Food supplies all the molecular building blocks from which our bodies are made and all the energy for our life activities. That energy comes ultimately from the Sun through photosynthesis.

In many places on Earth, some people never have enough food. According to *The Hunger Project*, about 1 billion people (one in seven) are always hungry. Poor nutrition contributes to the deaths of about 5 million children each year. The Hunger Project was started in 1977, when an estimated 15,000,000 people died of hunger each year. Now that estimate is 9,000,000 per year. Three-fourths are children under the age of five. Famine and wars make the news,

The food we eat supplies all the molecular building blocks from which our bodies are made and all the energy for our life activities. Those building blocks include carbohydrates, proteins, and fats. Carbohydrates supply most of our energy. Proteins are broken down into amino acids and reassembled into muscle, skin, hair, and other tissue. Fats, consumed in reasonable amounts, provide long-term storage of energy and some essential nutrients. But there is much more to a proper, healthy diet than an adequate supply of these three nutrients. In this chapter, we'll look at the properties of carbohydrates, proteins, fats, and other dietary essentials. That energy comes ultimately from the Sun through the remarkable process of photosynthesis.

but they cause just 10% of hunger deaths. Most result from chronic malnutrition. Worldwide, hunger and malnutrition are the greatest risk to health. And things may be getting worse. Increasing food prices have triggered food riots in several countries. Millions of additional people have fallen into poverty.

While millions starve, other locales have a surplus. Most of us in the Western world have an overabundance of food and often eat too much. Yet even in the United States, the U.S. Department of Agriculture estimates that 31 million people live in households that experience hunger or the risk of hunger. Nearly 9 million people, including more than 3.2 million children, experience hunger, frequently skipping meals or eating too little. These people often have lower-quality diets or must resort to seeking food from emergency sources.

Many of us also frequently eat the wrong kinds of food. Our diet, often too rich in saturated fats, sugar, and alcohol, has been linked in part to at least five of the ten leading causes of death in the United States: heart disease, cancer, stroke, diabetes, and kidney disease. The U.S. Centers for Disease Control and Prevention (CDC) found that 68% of the adults in the United States are overweight. According to the World Health Organization (WHO), 1.5 billion adults and 43 million children under the age of five worldwide are overweight. This excess weight contributes to poor health, increased risk of diabetes, heart attacks, strokes, and some forms of cancer. It also leads to increased susceptibility to other diseases.

The human body is a collection of chemicals. A chemical analysis of the human body would show that it is about two-thirds water. The body contains several minerals and thousands of other chemicals. Our foods are also made up of chemicals. They enable children to grow, provide people with energy, and supply the chemicals needed for the repair and replacement of body tissues.

In this chapter, we discuss food, what it's made of and the substances added to it—by accident or design. The three main classes of foods are carbohydrates, fats, and proteins. These, too, are chemicals. For proper nutrition, our diet should include balanced proportions of these three foodstuffs, plus water, vitamins, minerals, and fiber.

17.1 Carbohydrates in the Diet

Learning Objective › Identify dietary carbohydrates, and state their function.

Dietary carbohydrates include sugars and starches. Sugars are mainly monosaccharides and disaccharides; starches are polysaccharides.

Sugars have been used for ages to make food sweeter. Two monosaccharides, *glucose* (or *dextrose*) and *fructose* (fruit sugar), and the disaccharide *sucrose* are the most common dietary sugars (Figure 17.1, page 496). Common table sugar is sucrose, usually obtained from sugar cane or sugar beets. Glucose is the sugar used by the cells of our bodies for energy. Because it is the sugar that circulates in the bloodstream, it is often called **blood sugar**. Fructose is found in honey and in some fruits,

Some of the chemistry of carbohydrates is discussed in Section 16.2. The role of foods in health and fitness is discussed in Chapter 19.

▲ **Figure 17.1** The main sugars in our diet are sucrose (cane or beet sugar), glucose (corn syrup), and fructose (fruit sugar, often in the form of high-fructose corn syrup).

Q: *What is the molecular formula for glucose? For fructose? How are the two compounds related? How is sucrose related to glucose and fructose? (Hint: You may refer to Chapter 16, if necessary.)*

but much of it is made from glucose. Corn syrup, made from starch, is mainly glucose. *High-fructose corn syrup (HFCS)* is made by treating corn syrup with enzymes to convert much of the glucose to fructose. Fructose is sweeter than sucrose or glucose. Foods sweetened to the same degree with fructose have somewhat fewer calories than those sweetened with sucrose.

Since 1968, per capita consumption of sugars in the United States has skyrocketed from 11 kg/year to 71 kg/year, including 33 kg of HFCS. Most sugars are consumed in soft drinks, presweetened cereals, candy, and other highly processed foods with little or no nutritive value besides calories. The sugars in sweetened foods also contribute to tooth decay and obesity.

Digestion and Metabolism of Carbohydrates

Glucose and fructose are absorbed directly into the bloodstream from the digestive tract. Sucrose is hydrolyzed (split by water) during digestion to glucose and fructose.

$$\text{Sucrose} + H_2O \longrightarrow \text{Glucose} + \text{Fructose}$$

The disaccharide lactose occurs in milk. During digestion, it is hydrolyzed to two simpler sugars, glucose and galactose.

$$\text{Lactose} + H_2O \longrightarrow \text{Glucose} + \text{Galactose}$$

Nearly all human babies have the enzyme necessary to accomplish this breakdown, but many adults do not. People who lack the enzyme get digestive upsets from drinking milk, a condition called *lactose intolerance*. When milk is cooked or fermented, the lactose is at least partially hydrolyzed. People with lactose intolerance may be able to enjoy cheese, yogurt, or cooked foods containing milk with little or no discomfort. Lactose-free milk, made by treating milk with an enzyme that hydrolyzes lactose, is available in most grocery stores.

All monosaccharides are converted to glucose during metabolism. Some babies are born with *galactosemia*, a deficiency of the enzyme that catalyzes the conversion of galactose to glucose. For proper nutrition, they must be fed a synthetic formula (Figure 17.2) in place of milk.

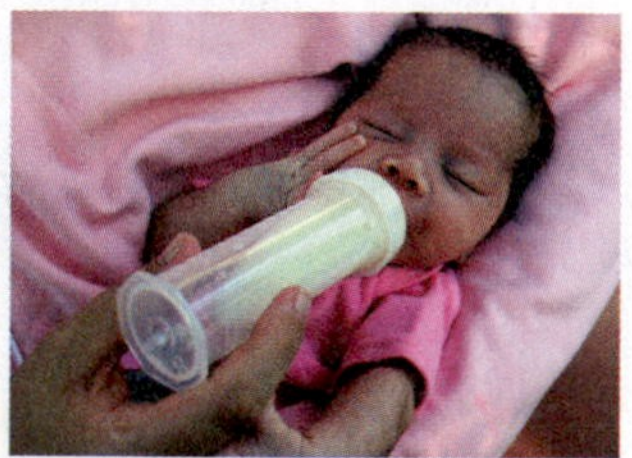

▲ **Figure 17.2** Infants born with galactosemia can thrive on a milk-free substitute formula.

Complex Carbohydrates: Starch and Cellulose

Starch and cellulose are both polymers of glucose, but the connecting links between the glucose units are different (Figure 16.6). Humans can digest starch, but not cellulose. **Starch**, a polymer of glucose in which the units are joined by alpha linkages, is an important part of any balanced diet (Figure 17.3). **Cellulose**, a glucose polymer with beta linkages, is an important component of dietary fiber.

▲ **Figure 17.3** Bread, flour, cereals, and pasta are rich in starches.

When digested, starch is hydrolyzed to glucose, as represented by the following equation:

$$\underset{\text{Starch}}{(C_6H_{10}O_5)_n} + n\,H_2O \xrightarrow{\text{Carbohydrates}} \underset{\text{Glucose}}{n\,C_6H_{12}O_6}$$

You can do your own carbohydrate digestion experiment. Chew an unsalted saltine cracker for several minutes, and you will notice a slight sweet taste. Your saliva contains enzymes that begin the digestion process. Explain the sweet taste.

The body then metabolizes the glucose, using it as a source of energy. Glucose is broken down in a complex set of more than 50 chemical reactions that produce carbon dioxide and water, with the release of energy.

$$C_6H_{12}O_6 + 6\,O_2 \longrightarrow 6\,CO_2 + 6\,H_2O + \text{Energy}$$

This net reaction is the reverse of photosynthesis. In this way, animals are able to make use of the energy from the Sun that was captured by plants using the process of photosynthesis.

Carbohydrates, which supply about 4 kcal of energy per gram, are our bodies' preferred fuels. When we eat more than our bodies can use, small amounts of carbohydrates can be stored in the liver and in muscle tissue as **glycogen** (animal starch), a highly branched polymer of α-glucose. Large excesses of carbohydrates are converted to fat for storage. Most health authorities recommend obtaining carbohydrates from a diet rich in whole grains, fruits, vegetables, and legumes (beans). We should minimize our intake of the simple sugars and refined starches found in many prepared foods.

Cellulose is the most abundant carbohydrate. It is present in all plants, forming their cell walls and other structural features. Wood is about 50% cellulose, and cotton is almost pure cellulose. Unlike starch, cellulose cannot be digested by humans and many other animals. We get no caloric value from dietary cellulose because its glucose units are joined by beta linkages, and most animals lack the enzymes needed to break this kind of bond. Certain bacteria that live in the gut of termites and in the digestive tract of grazing animals such as cows produce these enzymes, so that these animals can convert cellulose to glucose. Cellulose does, however, play an important role in human digestion, providing *dietary fiber* that absorbs water and helps move food through the digestive tract (Section 17.4).

▲ It DOES Matter!
With today's emphasis on low-carbohydrate foods, labels on some diet foods give the mass in grams of carbohydrate that can be readily digested. "Only 1 carb" means that a serving contains 1 g of readily digestible carbohydrate. It is important to read the labels of such foods carefully. They may contain a large amount of fat, including saturated fat. They may also contain relatively large amounts of additives (such as glycerin or xylitol) that are digested as carbohydrate—though much more slowly than sugars or even starches.

Self-Assessment Questions

1. About ________ people in the world are hungry today.
a. 1 in 4 **b.** 1 in 7
c. 1 in 12 **d.** 1 in 20

2. Digestion of lactose produces
a. galactose and fructose
b. galactose and glucose
c. glucose and fructose
d. only glucose

3. People who have lactose intolerance are deficient in the
a. enzyme that catalyzes the hydrolysis of lactose to galactose and glucose
b. enzyme that catalyzes the conversion of galactose to glucose
c. enzymes that catalyze the oxidation of lactose to CO_2 and H_2O
d. taste receptors for lactose, leaving a bitter taste

4. Galactosemia is an inherited disease that causes a baby to be deficient in the
a. enzyme that catalyzes the hydrolysis of lactose to galactose and glucose
b. enzyme that catalyzes the conversion of galactose to glucose
c. enzymes that catalyze the oxidation of galactose to CO_2 and H_2O
d. taste receptors for galactose, leaving a bitter taste

5. The monomer units of starch and cellulose, respectively, are
a. amino acids and glucose
b. α-glucose and β-glucose
c. β-glucose and α-glucose
d. glucose and fructose

6. Small quantities of carbohydrates can be stored in liver and muscle tissue as
a. amylose
b. cellulose
c. glucose
d. glycogen

7. Humans cannot digest cellulose because they lack enzymes for the hydrolysis of
a. α-amino acid linkages
b. α-glucose linkages
c. β-glucose linkages
d. sucrose

Answers: 1, b; 2, b; 3, a; 4, b; 5, b; 6, d; 7, c

17.2 Fats and Cholesterol

Learning Objective › Identify dietary lipids, and state their function.

Fats—esters of fatty acids and glycerol—are high-energy foods, yielding about 9 kcal of energy per gram. Some fats are "burned" as fuel for our activities. Others are used to build and maintain important constituents of our cells, such as cell membranes. The fat in our diet comes from many sources, some of which are shown in Figure 17.4.

1. The doctor said my father has high triglycerides. What are they? Triglycerides are a type of fat molecule found in the bloodstream. High triglycerides are often the result of a diet high in fats, and they contribute to heart disease.

Digestion and Metabolism of Fats

Dietary fats are mainly *triacylglycerols*, commonly called **triglycerides**. Fats are digested by enzymes called *lipases* and are ultimately broken down into fatty acids and glycerol (Figure 17.5). Some fat molecules are hydrolyzed to a monoglyceride (*monoacylglycerol*; glycerol combined with only one fatty acid) or a diglyceride (*diacylglycerol*; ester of two fatty acids and glycerol). Once absorbed, these products of

▲ **Figure 17.4** Cream, butter, margarine, cooking oils, and foods fried in fat are rich in fats. The average American diet contains too much fat. Americans get 37% of their calories from fat, while the recommendation of the FDA is 20–30% fat calories.

$$\begin{array}{l} CH_3(CH_2)_7CH{=}CH(CH_2)_7COOCH_2 \\ CH_3(CH_2)_7CH{=}CH(CH_2)_7COOCH \\ CH_3(CH_2)_{14}COOCH_2 \\ \text{Fat (triglyceride)} \end{array} \xrightarrow[\text{lipase}]{\text{water}} \begin{array}{c} 2\,CH_3(CH_2)_7CH{=}CH(CH_2)_7COOH \\ \text{Oleic acid} \\ + \\ CH_3(CH_2)_{14}COOH \\ \text{Palmitic acid} \end{array} + \begin{array}{l} HO{-}CH_2 \\ HO{-}CH \\ HO{-}CH_2 \\ \text{Glycerol} \end{array}$$

▲ **Figure 17.5** In the digestion of fats, a triglyceride is hydrolyzed to fatty acids and glycerol in a reaction catalyzed by the enzyme lipase.

Q: *What diglyceride is formed by removal of the palmitic acid part of the triglyceride? What monoglyceride is formed by removal of both oleic acid parts? (Hint: You may refer to Chapter 16, if necessary.)*

fat digestion are reassembled into triglycerides, which are attached to proteins for transportation through the bloodstream.

$$\begin{array}{l} HO{-}CH_2 \\ HO{-}CH \\ CH_3(CH_2)_{14}COOCH_2 \\ \text{A monoglyceride} \end{array} \qquad \begin{array}{l} CH_3(CH_2)_7CH{=}CH(CH_2)_7COOCH_2 \\ HO{-}CH \\ CH_3(CH_2)_{14}COOCH_2 \\ \text{A diglyceride} \end{array}$$

Fats are stored throughout the body, principally in **adipose tissue**, in locations called **fat depots**. Fat depots around vital organs, such as the heart, kidneys, and spleen, cushion and help prevent injury to these organs. Fat is also stored under the skin, where it helps to insulate against temperature changes.

When fat reserves are called on for energy, fat molecules are hydrolyzed back to glycerol and fatty acids. The glycerol can be burned for energy or converted to glucose. The fatty acids enter a process called the *fatty acid spiral* that removes carbon atoms two at a time. The two-carbon fragments can be used for energy or for the synthesis of new fatty acids.

Fats, Cholesterol, and Human Health

Dietary *saturated fats* and cholesterol have been implicated in *arteriosclerosis* ("hardening of the arteries"). Recall from Section 16.3 that saturated fats are those containing a large proportion of saturated fatty acids, such as palmitic and stearic acids. Incidence of cardiovascular disease is strongly correlated with diets rich in saturated fats. As the disease develops, deposits form on the inner walls of arteries. Eventually these deposits harden, and the vessels lose their elasticity (Figure 17.6). Blood clots tend to lodge in the narrowed arteries, leading to a heart attack (if the blocked artery is in heart muscle) or a stroke (if the blockage occurs in an artery that supplies the brain).

The plaque in clogged arteries is rich in cholesterol, a fatlike steroid alcohol found in animal tissues and various foods. Cholesterol is normally synthesized by the liver and is important as a constituent of cell membranes and a precursor to

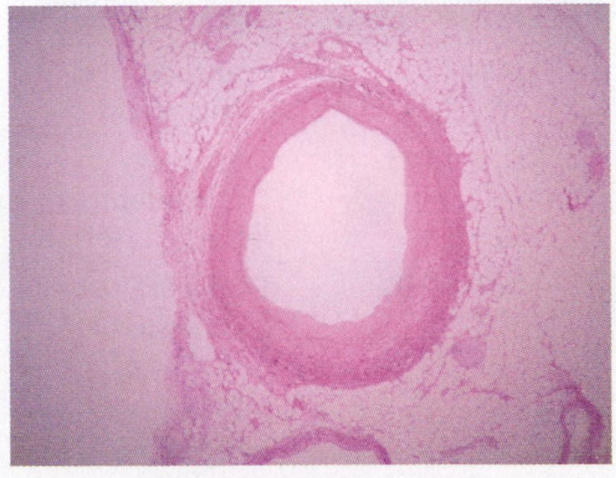

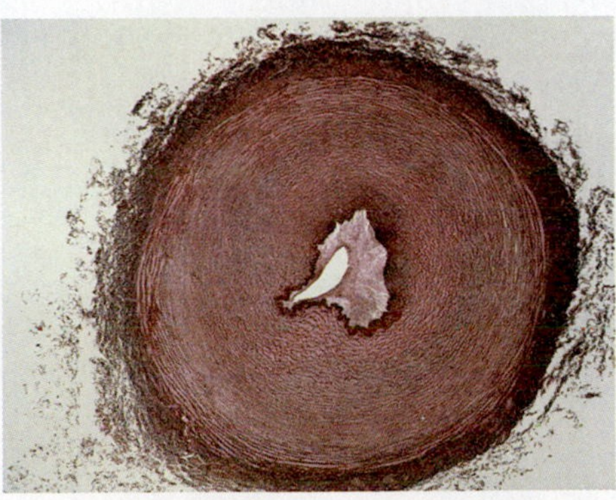

◀ **Figure 17.6** Photomicrographs of cross sections of a normal artery (left) and a "hardened" artery (right), which shows deposits of plaque that contain cholesterol.

Emulsions

When oil and water are vigorously shaken together, the oil is broken up into tiny, microscopic droplets and dispersed throughout the water, a mixture called an *emulsion*. Unless a third substance has been added, the emulsion usually breaks down rapidly, as the oil droplets recombine and float to the surface of the water.

Emulsions can be stabilized by adding a type of gum, a soap, or a protein that can form a protective coating around the oil droplets and prevent them from coming together. Lecithin in egg yolks keeps mayonnaise from separating, while casein in milk keeps fat droplets suspended. Compounds called *bile salts* keep tiny fat droplets suspended in aqueous media during human digestion. This greatly aids the digestive process. The tiny emulsified droplets provide a much greater surface area on which the water-soluble lipase enzymes can break down the triacylglycerides to glycerol and fatty acids.

▲ Many foods are emulsions. Milk is an emulsion of butterfat in water. The stabilizing agent is a protein called *casein*. Mayonnaise is an emulsion of vegetable oil in water, stabilized by egg yolk.

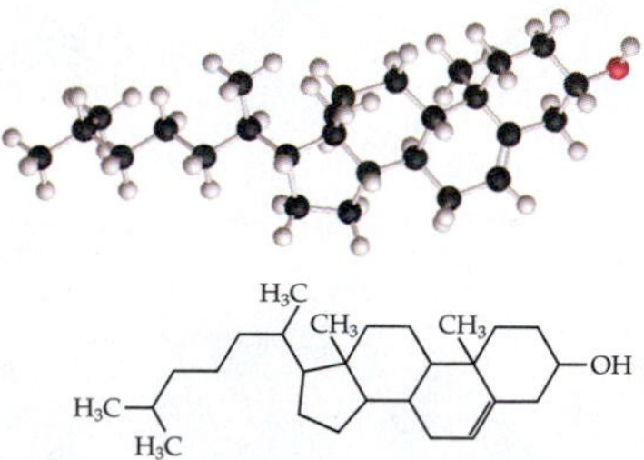

▲ Molecular model and structural formula of cholesterol.

steroid hormones. High blood levels of cholesterol, like those of triglycerides, correlate closely with the risk of cardiovascular disease. Like fats, cholesterol is insoluble in water, as we can determine from its molecular formula ($C_{27}H_{45}OH$) and structure (shown in the margin). Cholesterol is transported in blood by water-soluble proteins. The cholesterol–protein combination is an example of a **lipoprotein**, any of a group of proteins combined with a lipid, such as cholesterol or a triglyceride.

Lipoproteins are usually classified according to their density (Table 17.1). Very-low-density lipoproteins (VLDLs) serve mainly to transport triglycerides, whereas low-density lipoproteins (LDLs) are the main carriers of cholesterol. LDLs carry cholesterol to the cells for use, and these lipoproteins are the ones that deposit cholesterol in arteries, leading to cardiovascular disease. High-density lipoproteins (HDLs) also carry cholesterol, but they carry it to the liver for processing and excretion. Exercise is thought to increase the levels of HDLs, the lipoproteins sometimes called "good" cholesterol. High levels of LDLs, called "bad" cholesterol, increase the risk of heart attack and stroke. The American Heart Association recommends a maximum of 300 mg/day of cholesterol for the general population and 200 mg/day for people with heart disease or at risk for it.

2. Is high blood cholesterol mainly a problem for older people? The effects of high blood cholesterol are seen mainly in older people because the buildup of plaque in the blood vessels takes time. But those effects are often the result of years of an unhealthy diet and high levels of LDLs. To minimize the long-term effects of high cholesterol, you should consider early preventive measures. Reducing saturated fat in your diet is a good start.

Table 17.1 Lipoproteins in the Blood

Class	Abbreviation	Protein (%)	Density (g/mL)	Main Function
Very low density	VLDL	5	1.006–1.019	Transport triglycerides
Low density	LDL	25	1.019–1.063	Transport cholesterol to the cells for use
High density	HDL	50	1.063–1.210	Transport cholesterol to the liver for processing and excretion

Fats differ in their effect on blood cholesterol levels. Many nutritionists advise us to use olive oil and canola oil as our major sources of dietary lipids because they contain a high percentage of monounsaturated fatty acids, which have been shown to lower LDL cholesterol. There is also statistical evidence that fish oils can prevent heart disease. For example, Greenlanders who eat a lot of fish have a low risk of heart disease despite a diet that is high in total fat and cholesterol. The probable effective agents are polyunsaturated fatty acids such as eicosapentaenoic acid (EPA) and docosahexaenoic acid (DHA):

$$\underset{\text{EPA}}{CH_3(CH_2CH{=}CH)_5(CH_2)_3COOH} \qquad \underset{\text{DHA}}{CH_3(CH_2CH{=}CH)_6(CH_2)_2COOH}$$

These fatty acids are known as *omega-3 fatty acids* because they have a carbon-to-carbon double bond that begins at the *third* carbon from the end opposite the COOH group—the *omega* end. Studies have shown that adding omega-3 fatty acids to the diet leads to lower cholesterol and triglyceride levels in the blood.

Fats and oils containing carbon-to-carbon double bonds can undergo hydrogenation, addition of an H_2 molecule to each double bond. Hydrogenation of vegetable oils to produce semisolid fats is an important process in the food industry. The chemistry of this conversion process is identical to the hydrogenation reaction of alkenes described in Section 9.1.

$$\underset{\text{Oleic acid (monounsaturated)}}{CH_3(CH_2)_7CH{=}CH(CH_2)_7COOH} \xrightarrow[\text{Ni}]{H_2} \underset{\text{Stearic acid (saturated)}}{CH_3(CH_2)_7CH_2CH_2(CH_2)_7COOH}$$

By properly controlling the reaction conditions, inexpensive vegetable oils (cottonseed, corn, and soybean) can be partially hydrogenated to yield soft, spreadable fats suitable for use in margarine or fully hydrogenated to produce harder fats like shortening. The consumer would get much higher unsaturation by using the oils directly, but most people would rather spread margarine than pour oil on their toast.

Concern about the role of saturated fats in raising blood cholesterol and clogging arteries caused many consumers to switch from butter to margarine. However, some of the unsaturated fats that remain after partial hydrogenation of vegetable oils have structures similar to saturated fats. These unsaturated fats raise cholesterol levels and increase the risk of coronary heart disease.

Figure 17.7 presents molecular models of three types of fatty acids. Most naturally occurring unsaturated fatty acids have a *cis* arrangement about the double bond. For example, oleic acid has the structure given by Figure 17.7(c). Recall from Chapter 9 that a *cis* arrangement about double-bonded carbon atoms has both hydrogen atoms on the same side of the double bond. During hydrogenation, the

▲ **It DOES Matter!**
Half of the total fat, three-fourths of the saturated fat, and all the cholesterol in a typical human diet come from animal products such as meat, milk, cheese, and eggs. Advertising that a vegetable oil (for example) contains no cholesterol is silly. No vegetable product contains cholesterol.

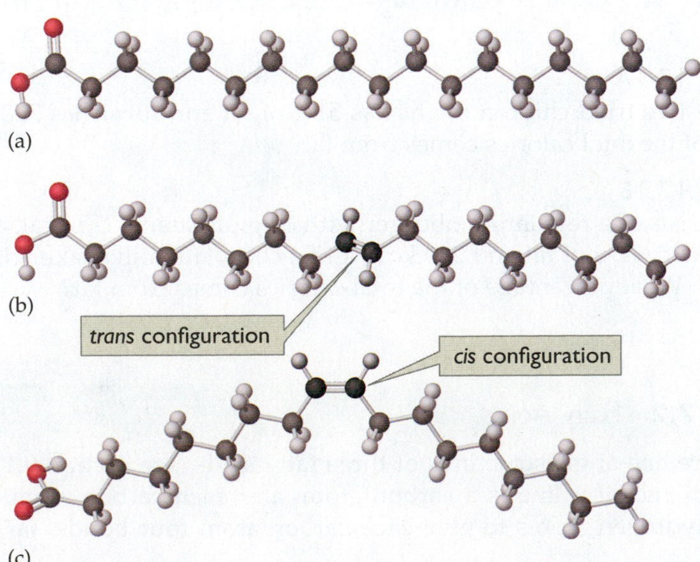

◄ **Figure 17.7** The structures of (a) stearic acid (a saturated fatty acid) and (b) the *trans* isomer of oleic acid (a *trans* unsaturated fatty acid) are similar in shape, and these acids behave similarly in the body; (c) oleic acid (a *cis* unsaturated fatty acid) has a very different shape.

arrangement in some of the molecules is changed so that the hydrogen atoms of the double-bonded carbon atoms are on opposite sides of the double bond, a *trans* arrangement, shown in Figure 17.7(b). If we draw a straight line passing through the double-bonded carbon atoms and if the hydrogen atoms on those carbon atoms are on the same side of the line, the molecule represents a *cis* fatty acid. If they are on opposite sides, it is a *trans* fatty acid.

Note in Figures 17.7(a) and 17.7(b) that both saturated fatty acids (such as stearic acid) and *trans* fatty acids are more or less straight and can stack neatly like logs. This maximizes the intermolecular attractive forces, making saturated and *trans* fatty acids more likely to be solids than *cis* fatty acids.

On the other hand, *cis* fatty acids [Figure 17.7(c)] have a bend in their structure, fixed in position by the double bond. They have weaker intermolecular forces and are more likely to be liquids. Because *trans* fatty acids also resemble saturated fatty acids in their tendency to raise blood levels of LDL cholesterol, the FDA requires manufacturers to provide the *trans* fat content of foods on labels.

Many Americans eat too much fat, especially saturated and *trans* fats. Health experts generally advise us to limit our overall intake of fats, and of saturated and *trans* fats in particular. Many health professionals recommend that fats should not exceed 30% of total calories, and no more than one-third of the fat should be saturated fat.

3. How much fat in the diet is "too much"? Not more than about 30% of total daily calories should come from fat, and not more than 10% should come from saturated fat. For a 2000-kcal daily allowance, this means less than 600 kcal from fat and less than 200 kcal from saturated fat.

Example 17.1 Nutrient Calculations

A single-serving pepperoni pan pizza has 38 g of fat and 780 total calories. (Recall that a food calorie is a kilocalorie.) Estimate the percentage of the total calories from fat. (Further calculations of this sort are found in Chapter 19.)

Solution

First, we calculate the calories from fat. Fat furnishes about 9 kcal/g, so 38 g of fat furnishes

$$38\ \cancel{\text{g fat}} \times \frac{9\ \text{kcal}}{1\ \cancel{\text{g fat}}} = 340\ \text{kcal}$$

Now, we divide the calories from fat by the total calories. Then multiply by 100% to get the percentage (parts per 100).

$$\text{Percentage of calories from fat} = \frac{340\ \text{kcal}}{780\ \text{kcal}} \times 100\% = 44\%$$

This answer is only an estimate for two reasons: The value of 9 kcal/g is approximate, and the 38 g of fat is known only to the nearest gram. A proper answer is about 44%.

■ EXERCISE 17.1A

A serving of two fried chicken thighs has 51 g of fat and furnishes 720 kcal. What percentage of the total calories comes from fat?

■ EXERCISE 17.1B

A lunch consists of a regular hamburger with 12 g of fat and 275 kcal, a serving of french fries with 12 g of fat and 240 kcal, and a chocolate milkshake with 9 g of fat and 360 kcal. What percentage of the total calories comes from fat?

Example 17.2 Fatty Acids

Following are line-angle structures of three fatty acids (see Section 9.1). Each corner and each end of a line is a carbon atom, and each carbon atom is attached to enough hydrogen atoms to give each carbon atom four bonds. **(a)** Which is a saturated fatty acid? **(b)** Which is a monounsaturated fatty acid? **(c)** Which is an omega-3 fatty acid?

I.  COOH

II. 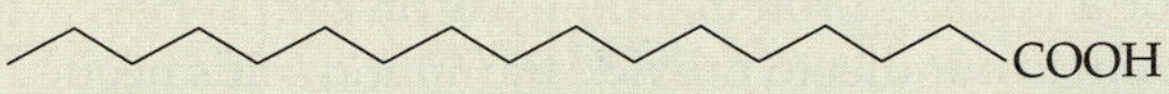 COOH

III. 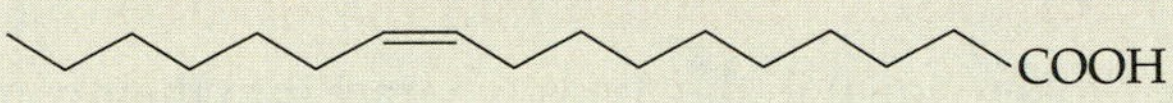 COOH

Solution

a. Fatty acid II has no carbon-to-carbon double bonds; it is a saturated fatty acid.

b. Fatty acid III has one carbon-to-carbon double bond; it is a monounsaturated fatty acid.

c. Fatty acid I has one of its carbon-to-carbon double bonds three carbons removed from the end farthest from the carboxyl group (the omega end); it is an omega-3 fatty acid.

■ EXERCISE 17.2A

Which of the fatty acids in Example 17.2 is polyunsaturated?

■ EXERCISE 17.2B

Is fatty acid III likely to be more similar physiologically to fatty acid II or to fatty acid I? Explain.

Self-Assessment Questions

1. Fats are
- **a.** esters of glycerol and fatty acids
- **b.** esters of cholesterol and fatty acids
- **c.** polymeric steroids
- **d.** polymers of amino acids

2. Among lipoproteins, LDLs are
- **a.** bad because they can block arteries
- **b.** the form that carries cholesterol to the liver for processing and excretion
- **c.** the good form because they can clear arteries
- **d.** the kind increased by exercise

Questions 3–5 refer to the following structures.
- **a.** $CH_3(CH_2)_{16}COOH$
- **b.** $CH_3(CH_2)_5CH{=}CH(CH_2)_7COOH$
- **c.** $CH_3(CH_2)_3(CH_2CH{=}CH)_2(CH_2)_7COOH$
- **d.** $CH_3(CH_2CH{=}CH)_3(CH_2)_7COOH$

3. Which is a saturated fatty acid?

4. Which is polyunsaturated but not an omega-3 fatty acid?

5. Which is polyunsaturated and an omega-3 fatty acid?

6. In shape, *trans* fatty acid molecules resemble
- **a.** cholesterol
- **b.** disaccharides
- **c.** other unsaturated fatty acids
- **d.** saturated fatty acids

7. According to most health professionals, what percentages of total calories should the total daily intake of fat and of saturated fat, respectively, not exceed?
- **a.** 30, 15
- **b.** 10, 30
- **c.** 30, 10
- **d.** 60, 20

Answers: 1, a; 2, a; 3, a; 4, c; 5, d; 6, d; 7, c

17.3 Proteins: Muscle and Much More

Learning Objectives › List the essential amino acids, and explain why they are essential. › Describe some protein deficiency diseases and their causes.

As we saw in Chapter 16, proteins are polymers of amino acids. A gene carries the blueprint for a specific protein, and each protein serves a particular purpose. We require protein in our diet to provide the amino acids needed to make muscles, hair, enzymes, and many other cellular components vital to life.

Protein Metabolism: Essential Amino Acids

Proteins are broken down in the digestive tract into their component amino acids.

$$\text{Proteins} + n\,H_2O \xrightarrow{\text{Proteases}} \text{Amino acids}$$

From these amino acids, our bodies synthesize proteins for growth and repair of tissues. When a diet contains more protein than is needed for the body's growth

Vegetarian Diets

Green plants trap a small fraction of the energy that reaches them from the Sun. They use some of this energy to convert carbon dioxide, water, and mineral nutrients (including nitrates, phosphates, and sulfates) to proteins. Cattle eat plant protein, digest it, and convert a small portion of it to animal protein. It takes 100 g of protein feed to produce 4.7 g of edible beef or veal protein, an efficiency of only 4.7%. People eat this animal protein, digest it, and reassemble some of the amino acids into human protein.

Some of the energy originally transformed by green plants is lost as heat at every step. If people ate the plant protein directly, one highly inefficient step would be skipped. A vegetarian diet conserves energy. Pork production, at a protein conversion efficiency of 12.1%, and chicken or turkey production (at 18.2%) are more efficient than beef production. Milk production (22.7%) and egg production (23.3%) are still more efficient but do not compare well with eating plant protein directly.

Vegetarians generally are less likely than meat eaters to have high blood pressure. Vegetarian diets that are low in saturated fat can help us avoid or even reverse coronary artery disease. These diets also offer protection from some other diseases. However, although complete proteins can be obtained by eating a carefully selected mixture of vegetable foods, total (*vegan*) vegetarianism can be dangerous, especially for young children. Even when the diet includes a wide variety of plant materials, an all-vegetable diet is usually short in several nutrients, including vitamin B_{12} (a nutrient not found in plants), calcium, iron, riboflavin, and vitamin D (required by children not exposed to sunlight). A modified vegetarian (*lacto-ovo*) diet that includes eggs, milk, and milk products without red meat can provide excellent nutrition.

A variety of traditional dishes supply relatively good protein by combining foods from plant sources, usually a cereal grain with a legume (beans, peas, peanuts, and so on). The grain is deficient in tryptophan and lysine, but it has sufficient methionine. The legume is deficient in methionine, but it has enough tryptophan and lysine. A few such combinations are listed in Table 17.2. Peanut butter sandwiches are a popular American example of a legume–cereal grain combination.

Table 17.2 Traditional Foods That Combine a Cereal Grain with a Legume

Group	Food[a]
Mexican	Corn tortillas and beans
Japanese	Rice and soybean curds (tofu)
English working class	Baked beans on toasted bread
Native American	Corn and beans (succotash)
Western African	Rice and peanuts (ground nuts)
Cajun (Louisiana)	Red beans and rice
Middle Eastern	Hummus and pita bread

[a]Cereal grains are in red, and legumes are in blue.

and repair, the excess protein is used as a source of energy, providing about 4 kcal per gram.

The adult human body can synthesize all but nine of the amino acids needed for making proteins. These nine are called **essential amino acids**—isoleucine, lysine, phenylalanine, tryptophan, leucine, methionine, threonine, arginine, and valine (see Table 16.3 for structures)—and must be included in our diet. Each of the essential amino acids is a **limiting reactant** in protein synthesis. When the body is deficient in one of them, it can't make proper proteins.

The distinction between essential and nonessential amino acids is somewhat ambiguous, because some amino acids can be produced from others. For example, both methionine and cysteine contain sulfur, and although methionine cannot be synthesized from other precursors, cysteine can partially meet the need for methionine. Similarly, tyrosine can partially substitute for phenylalanine. And histidine is essential for infants and children, but it is not essential for healthy adults.

An *adequate* (or *complete*) *protein* supplies all the essential amino acids in the quantities needed for the growth and repair of body tissues. Most proteins from animal sources contain all the essential amino acids in adequate amounts. Lean meat, milk, fish, eggs, and cheese supply adequate protein. Gelatin, a component of jellied candies and desserts, is one of the few inadequate animal proteins. It contains almost no tryptophan and has only small amounts of threonine, methionine, and isoleucine.

In contrast, most plant proteins are deficient in one or more amino acids. Corn protein has insufficient lysine and tryptophan, and people who subsist chiefly on corn may suffer from malnutrition even though they get adequate calories. Protein from rice is short of lysine and threonine. Wheat protein lacks enough lysine. Even soy protein, one of the best nonanimal proteins, is deficient in the essential amino acid methionine.

Protein Deficiency in Young and Old

Our daily requirement for protein is about 0.8 g per kilogram of body weight. Diets with inadequate protein are common in some parts of the world. A protein-deficiency disease called *kwashiorkor* (Figure 17.8) is rare in developed countries but is common during times of famine in parts of Africa where corn is the major food. In the United States, protein deficiency occurs mainly among elderly persons in nursing homes.

Nutrition is especially important during a child's early years. This is readily apparent from the fact that the human brain reaches nearly full size by the age of two. Early protein deficiency leads to both physical and mental retardation.

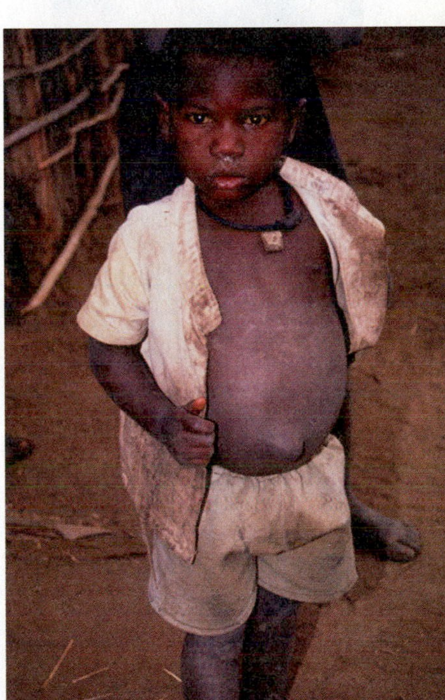

▲ **Figure 17.8** An extreme lack of proteins and vitamins causes a deficiency disease called *kwashiorkor*. The symptoms include retarded growth, discoloration of skin and hair, bloating, a swollen belly, and mental apathy.

Self-Assessment Questions

1. The numbers of kilocalories in 1 g of carbohydrate, fat, and protein, respectively, are
   a. 4, 7, 4 b. 4, 4, 7 c. 4, 9, 4 d. 4, 12, 6
2. The end products of the hydrolysis of a protein are
   a. amino acids b. fatty acids
   c. monosaccharides d. peptides
3. An essential amino acid is one that
   a. has more calories than other amino acids
   b. is needed in greater quantities than some others
   c. is synthesized in the body
   d. must be included in the diet
4. Which of the following foods furnishes complete protein?
   a. brown rice b. eggs
   c. gelatin with fruit d. tofu
5. The daily protein requirement for an 80-kg male is
   a. 0.8 g b. 48 g c. 64 g d. 100 g
6. One can get complete protein by eating whole wheat bread with
   a. butter b. jelly c. peanut butter d. corn chips
7. Strict vegetarian diets are often deficient in
   a. B vitamins and vitamin C b. magnesium and folic acid
   c. vitamin B_{12} and iron d. vitamin B_{12} and folic acid

Answers: 1, c; 2, a; 3, d; 4, b; 5, c; 6, c; 7, c

17.4 Minerals, Vitamins, and Other Essentials

Learning Objectives › Identify the vitamins and the bulk dietary minerals, and state their functions.

In addition to the three major foodstuffs—carbohydrates, fats, and proteins—humans require a variety of minerals and vitamins for good nutrition. We also need dietary fiber and adequate water. According to the World Health Organization (WHO), one of every three people in developing countries is affected by mineral and vitamin deficiencies. Let's consider some of the most important minerals and vitamins.

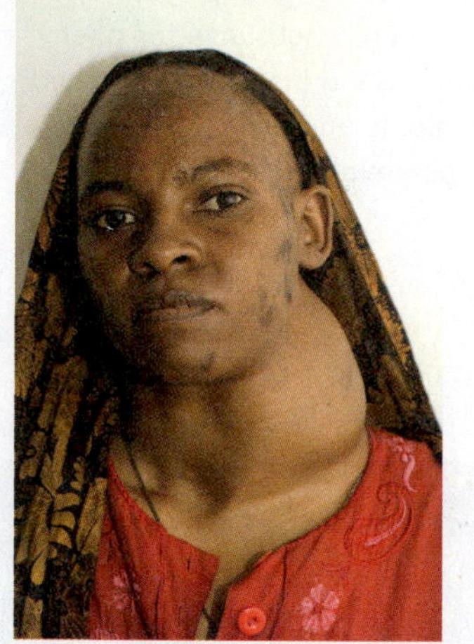

▲ **Figure 17.9** A person with goiter. The swollen thyroid gland in the neck results from a dietary deficiency of the trace element iodine.

Dietary Minerals

Thirty elements, listed in Table 17.3, are known to be essential to one or more living organisms. Among these are six structural elements found in organic compounds such as carbohydrates, fats, and proteins. Several inorganic substances, called **dietary minerals**, are vital to life. Minerals represent about 4% of the weight of the human body. Eleven elements that comprise the structural elements and the macrominerals make up more than 99% of all the atoms in the body. The 19 trace elements include iron, copper, zinc, and 16 others called *ultratrace elements.*

Minerals serve a variety of functions; that of iodine is quite dramatic. According to WHO, 740 million people suffer from iodine deficiency, and 50 million of them have some degree of mental impairment. A small amount of iodine is necessary for proper thyroid function. Greater deficiencies have dire effects, of which goiter is perhaps the best known (Figure 17.9). Pregnant women deficient in iodine can experience stillbirths or spontaneous abortions or have babies with congenital abnormalities. Iodine is available naturally in seafood, but to guard against iodine deficiency, a small amount of potassium iodide (KI) is often added to table salt. The use of iodized salt has greatly reduced the incidence of goiter.

Table 17.3 Elements Essential to Life

Element	Symbol	Form Used	Element	Symbol	Form Used
Bulk Structural Elements			**Ultratrace Elements**		
Hydrogen	H	Covalent	Manganese	Mn	Mn^{2+}
Carbon	C	Covalent	Molybdenum	Mo	Mo^{2+}
Oxygen	O	Covalent	Chromium	Cr	?
Nitrogen	N	Covalent	Cobalt	Co	Co^{2+}
Phosphorus[a]	P	Covalent	Vanadium	V	?
Sulfur[a]	S	Covalent	Nickel	Ni	Ni^{2+}
			Cadmium	Cd	Cd^{2+}
Macrominerals			Tin	Sn	Sn^{2+}
Sodium	Na	Na^+	Lead	Pb	Pb^{2+}
Potassium	K	K^+	Lithium	Li	Li^+
Calcium	Ca	Ca^{2+}	Fluorine	F	F^-
Magnesium	Mg	Mg^{2+}	Iodine	I	I^-
Chlorine	Cl	Cl^-	Selenium	Se	SeO_4^{2-}?
Phosphorus[a]	P	$H_2PO_4^-$	Silicon	Si	?
Sulfur[a]	S	SO_4^{2-}	Arsenic	As	?
			Boron	B	H_3BO_3
Trace Elements					
Iron	Fe	Fe^{2+}			
Copper	Cu	Cu^{2+}			
Zinc	Zn	Zn^{2+}			

[a]Note that phosphorus and sulfur each appear twice; they are structural elements and are also components of the macrominerals phosphate and sulfate.

Iron(II) ions (Fe^{2+}) are necessary for proper functioning of the oxygen-transporting compound hemoglobin. Without sufficient iron, the oxygen supply to body tissues is reduced, and anemia, a general weakening of the body, results. According to WHO, more than 30% of people worldwide, but especially in developing countries, suffer from anemia, which is often made worse by malaria and parasitic worm infections. Foods especially rich in iron compounds include red meat and liver. It appears that most adult males need very little dietary iron because iron is retained by the body and lost mainly through bleeding.

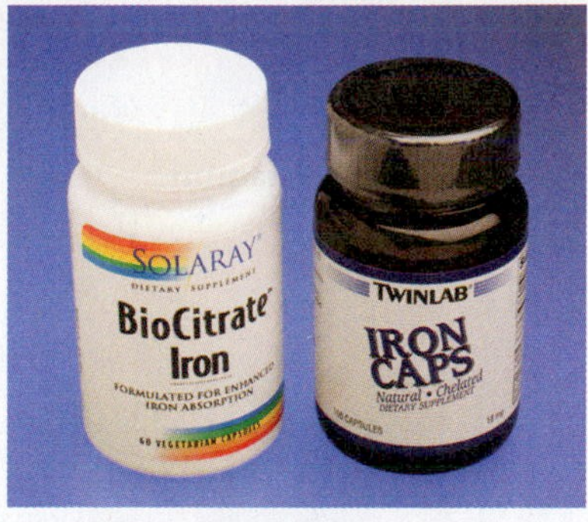

▲ **It DOES Matter!**
Iron is an example of a substance that can be both essential and toxic. The National Institutes of Health recommend a daily intake of 8 mg for adult males and 18 mg for adult females but also point out that a 200-mg dose of iron in children can cause death.

Calcium and phosphorus are necessary for the proper development of bones and teeth. Growing children need about 1.5 g of each of these minerals each day, which they can get from milk. The calcium and phosphorus needs of adults are less precisely known but are very real. For example, calcium ions are necessary for the coagulation of blood (to stop bleeding) and for maintenance of the rhythm of the heartbeat. Phosphorus occurs in phosphate units in adenosine triphosphate (ATP), the "energy currency" of the body. Phosphorus is necessary for the body to obtain, store, and use energy from foods. In phosphate units, phosphorus is also an important part of the backbone of the DNA and RNA chains (Section 16.6).

Sodium ions and chloride ions make up sodium chloride (salt). In moderate amounts, salt is essential to life. It is important to the exchange of fluids between cells and plasma, for example. However, the presence of salt increases water retention, and a high volume of retained fluids can cause swelling and high blood pressure (hypertension). Most physicians agree that our diets generally contain too much salt. About 65 million people in the United States suffer from hypertension, the leading risk factor for stroke, heart attack, kidney failure, and heart failure. Antihypertensives are among the most widely prescribed drugs in the United States.

Iron, copper, zinc, cobalt, manganese, molybdenum, calcium, and magnesium are *cofactors* (Section 16.5) essential to the proper functioning of many life-sustaining enzymes. A great deal remains to be learned about the role of inorganic chemicals in our bodies. Bioinorganic chemistry is a flourishing area of research.

The Vitamins: Vital, but Not All Are Amines

Why are British sailors called "limeys"? And what does this term have to do with food? Sailors on long voyages had been plagued since early times by *scurvy*. In 1747, Scottish navy surgeon James Lind showed that this disease could be prevented by including fresh fruit and vegetables in the diet. Fresh fruits that could conveniently be carried on long voyages (there was no refrigeration) were limes, lemons, and oranges. British ships put to sea with barrels of limes aboard, and sailors ate a lime or two every day. That is how they came to be known as "lime eaters," or simply "limeys."

In 1897, the Dutch scientist Christiaan Eijkman showed that polished rice lacked something found in the hull of whole-grain rice. Lack of that substance caused the disease *beriberi,* which was a serious problem in the Dutch East Indies (modern Indonesia) at that time. A British scientist, F. G. Hopkins, found that rats fed a synthetic diet of carbohydrates, fats, proteins, and minerals were unable to sustain healthy growth. Again, something was missing.

In 1912, Casimir Funk, a Polish biochemist, coined the word *vitamine* (from the Latin word *vita,* meaning "life") for these missing factors. Funk thought all these factors contained an amine group. In the United States, the final *e* was dropped after it was found that not all the factors were amines. The generic term became *vitamin.* Eijkman and Hopkins shared the 1929 Nobel Prize in Physiology and Medicine for their discoveries relating to vitamins.

Vitamins are specific organic compounds that are required in the diet (in addition to the usual proteins, fats, carbohydrates, and minerals) to prevent specific diseases. Some vitamins, along with their sources and deficiency symptoms, are listed in Table 17.4 on page 508. The role of vitamins in the prevention of deficiency diseases, such as those shown in Figure 17.10, has been well established.

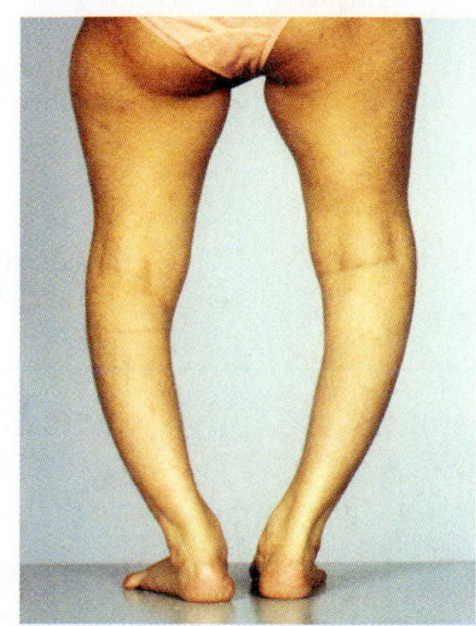

(a)

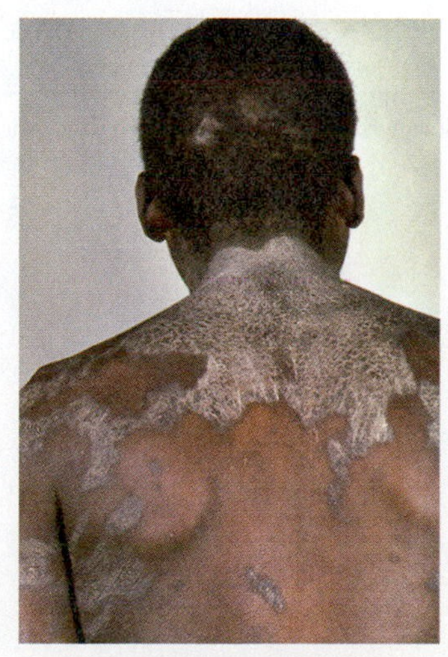

(b)

▲ **Figure 17.10** (a) Softened bones caused by vitamin D deficiency. (b) Inflammation and abnormal pigmentation characterize pellagra, caused by niacin deficiency.

Table 17.4 Some of the Vitamins

Vitamin[a]	Name	Sources	Deficiency results in
Fat-Soluble Vitamins			
A	Retinol	Fish, liver, eggs, butter, cheese; also (as β-carotene, a vitamin precursor) in carrots and other orange or red vegetables	Blindness in children; night blindness in adults
D_2	Calciferol	Cod liver oil, mushrooms, irradiated ergosterol (milk supplement)	Rickets
E	α-Tocopherol	Wheat germ oil, green vegetables, egg yolks, meat	Sterility, muscular dystrophy
K_1	Phylloquinone	Spinach, other green leafy vegetables	Hemorrhage
Water-Soluble Vitamins			
B_1	Thiamine	Germ of cereal grains, legumes, nuts, milk, and brewer's yeast	Beriberi—polyneuritis resulting in muscle paralysis, enlargement of heart, and ultimately heart failure
B_2	Riboflavin	Milk, red meat, liver, egg white, green vegetables, whole wheat flour (or fortified white flour), and fish	Dermatitis, glossitis (tongue inflammation)
B_3	Niacin	Red meat, liver, collards, turnip greens, yeast, and tomato juice	Pellagra—skin lesions, swollen and discolored tongue, loss of appetite, diarrhea, and various mental disorders (Figure 17.10)
B_6	Pyridoxine	Eggs, liver, yeast, peas, beans, and milk	Dermatitis, apathy, irritability, and increased susceptibility to infections; convulsions in infants
B_9	Folic acid	Liver, kidney, mushrooms, yeast, and green leafy vegetables	Anemias (folic acid is used to treat megaloblastic anemia, a condition characterized by giant red blood cells); neural tube defects in fetuses of deficient mothers
B_{12}	Cyanocobalamin	Liver, meat, eggs and fish (not found in plants)	Pernicious anemia
C	Ascorbic acid	Citrus fruits, tomatoes, green peppers, broccoli, strawberries	Scurvy

[a]Some vitamins exist in more than one chemical form. We name a common form of each here.

Vitamins do not share a common chemical structure. They can, however, be divided into two broad categories: *fat-soluble vitamins* (A, D, E, and K) and *water-soluble vitamins* (B vitamins and vitamin C). The fat-soluble vitamins incorporate a high proportion of hydrocarbon parts. They contain one or two oxygen atoms but are only slightly polar as a whole.

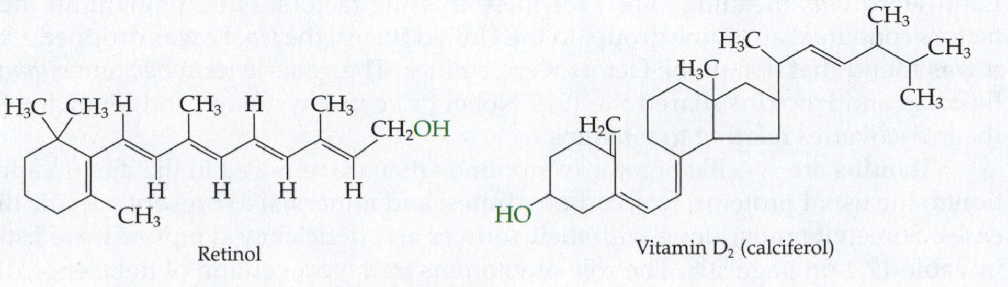

Retinol

Vitamin D_2 (calciferol)

Fat-soluble vitamins

In contrast, a water-soluble vitamin contains a high proportion of the electronegative atoms oxygen and nitrogen, which can form hydrogen bonds to water. Therefore, the molecule as a whole is soluble in water.

Ascorbic acid Nicotinic acid Nicotinamide

Water-soluble vitamins (sites for hydrogen bonding in color)

Fat-soluble vitamins dissolve in the fatty tissue of the body, where reserves can be stored for future use. An adult can store several years' supply of vitamin A. If the diet becomes deficient in vitamin A, these reserves are mobilized, and the adult remains free of the deficiency disease for quite a while. However, a small child who has not built up a store of the vitamin soon exhibits deficiency symptoms. WHO estimates that more than 100 million children in developing countries are deficient in vitamin A, and a quarter million to a half million become blind each year. Half the blinded children die within a year.

Because they are efficiently stored in the body, overdoses of fat-soluble vitamins can have adverse effects, although these are rarely encountered. Large excesses of vitamin A cause irritability, dry skin, and a feeling of pressure inside the head. Too much vitamin D can cause pain in the bones, hard deposits in the joints, nausea, diarrhea, and weight loss. Vitamins E and K are also fat soluble, but they are metabolized and excreted. They are not stored to the extent that vitamins A and D are, and excess intake seldom causes problems.

The body has a limited capacity to store water-soluble vitamins. It excretes anything over the amount that can be used immediately. Water-soluble vitamins are needed frequently, every day or so. Some foods lose their vitamin content when they are cooked in water and then drained. The water-soluble vitamins go down the drain with the water.

4. Are large doses of vitamins beneficial? Although there is some evidence that large doses of antioxidants such as vitamin C may have beneficial effects, "megadoses" of most vitamins have not generally been shown to have any significant benefit. In fact, some of the fat-soluble vitamins are toxic in large amounts. There are well-documented examples of polar explorers who suffered poisoning from eating the livers of polar bears or seals, which contain extremely high levels of vitamin A.

Other Essentials: Fiber and Water

We need carbohydrates, proteins, fats, minerals, and vitamins in our diets, but some other items are also important. One is *fiber;* another is *water.*

Dietary fiber may be soluble or insoluble. Insoluble fiber is usually cellulose; soluble fiber generally consists of sticky materials called *gums* and *pectins*, often used for gelling, thickening, and stabilizing foods such as jams, jellies, and dairy products such as yogurt. High-fiber diets prevent constipation and are an aid to dieters. Fiber has no calories because the body doesn't absorb it. Therefore, high-fiber foods such as fruits and vegetables are low in fat and often low in calories. Fiber takes up space in the stomach, making us feel full and, therefore, eat less food. Soluble fiber lowers cholesterol levels, perhaps by removing bile acids that digest fat. It may also help control blood sugar by delaying the emptying of the stomach, thus slowing sugar absorption after a meal. This may reduce the amount of insulin needed by a diabetic. These properties make dietary fiber beneficial to people with high blood pressure, diabetes, heart disease, and diverticulitis.

Many of the foods we eat are mainly water. It should come as no surprise that tomatoes are 90% water or that melons, oranges, and grapes are largely water. But water is one of the main ingredients in practically all foods, from roast beef and seafood to potatoes and onions.

In addition to the water we get in our food, we need to drink about 1.0–1.5 L of water each day. We could satisfy this need by drinking plain water, but we often choose other beverages—milk, coffee, tea, and soft drinks. Many people also drink beverages that contain ethanol, made by fermenting grains or fruit juices. Beer is usually made from malted barley, and wine from grape juice. Even these alcoholic beverages are mainly water. Water as a nutrient is discussed further in Chapter 19.

In 2009, worldwide consumption of beverages included an estimated 328 billion L of tea, 215 billion L of milk, 128 billion L of coffee, 196 billion L of soft drinks, 176 billion L of beer, and 240 billion L of bottled water.

It's a Drug! No, It's a Food! No, It's . . . a Dietary Supplement!

Almost every day, we see advertisements for products that are claimed to promote rapid weight loss, improve stamina, aid memory, or provide other seemingly miraculous benefits. (There are thousands of such products; see Collaborative Group Project 5 for some examples.) Although these products may appear to act as drugs, many are not classified as such. Legally, they are *dietary supplements.*

The Dietary Supplement Health and Education Act, enacted by the U.S. Congress in 1994, changed the law so that dietary supplements became regulated as foods, not as drugs. Manufacturers are permitted to describe some specific benefits that may be attributed to use of a supplement. However, they must also include a disclaimer, such as: "This statement has not been evaluated by the Food and Drug Administration. This product is not intended to diagnose, treat, cure, or prevent any disease."

Some supplements are simply combinations of various vitamins. Others contain minerals, amino acids, other nutrients, herbs or other plant materials, or extracts of animal or plant origin.

Should you take a particular supplement? Maybe, maybe not. A supplement containing omega-3 oils might well aid in reducing LDL cholesterol. But a tablespoon a day of a special preparation of vitamins and minerals is not likely to reverse the effects of aging, no matter how brightly colored the bottle, or how attractive the person in the advertisement. Perhaps a judicious application of the FLaReS principles (see this chapter's Critical Thinking Exercises) to the manufacturer's claims will provide insight.

Supplement Facts

Serving size 1 Tablet

Amount Per Serving	%DV
Vitamin B-6 (as pyridoxine HCl)......5 mg	250%
Folic Acid.................................400 mcg	250%
Vitamin B-12..........................1000 mcg	16666%

DIRECTIONS: As a dietary supplement, take 1 or 2 tablets daily. Allow tablet to dissolve under tongue. Conforms to USP <2091> for weight.

This statement has not been evaluated by the Food and Drug Administration. This product is not intended to diagnose, treat, cure, or prevent any disease.

▲ Most dietary supplements do not go through the rigorous testing that is required by law for all prescription drugs and over-the-counter drugs.

Self-Assessment Questions

1. About what percentage of our body weight is minerals?
   a. 1% b. 4% c. 10% d. 20%
2. A deficiency of iodine results in
   a. anemia b. goiter c. osteoporosis d. scurvy
3. Iron in red blood cells is part of the
   a. cytochromes b. hemoglobin c. myoglobin d. plasma
4. Iron is swiftly depleted from the body by
   a. blood loss b. energetic exercise
   c. inactivity d. weight loss
5. Most of the calcium and phosphorus in the body is in the
   a. blood b. bones and teeth
   c. liver d. muscle tissue
6. People with high blood pressure are usually told to restrict intake of
   a. Ca^{2+} b. Mg^{2+} c. Na^{+} d. SO_4^{2-}
7. Vitamins are
   a. compounds with a common functional group
   b. most effective when taken as supplements
   c. specific organic compounds required in the diet to prevent diseases
   d. vital (essential) amines
8. The water-soluble vitamins are the B vitamins and vitamin
   a. A b. C c. D d. E
9. Eating foods high in fiber
   a. can cause constipation b. helps build muscle
   c. helps to fill you up d. provides quick energy

10. Soluble dietary fiber
  a. acts in the same way as insoluble fiber
  b. may help lower cholesterol levels
  c. is not affected by food processing
  d. is a good source of trace elements

Answers: 1, b; 2, b; 3, b; 4, a; 5, b; 6, c; 7, c; 8, b; 9, c; 10, b

17.5 Starvation, Fasting, and Malnutrition

Learning Objective › Describe the effects of starvation, fasting, and malnutrition.

When totally deprived of food, whether voluntarily or involuntarily, the human body suffers **starvation**. Involuntary starvation is a serious problem in much of the world. Although starvation is seldom the sole cause of death, those weakened by malnutrition succumb readily to disease. Even a seemingly minor disease, such as measles, can become life threatening.

Metabolic changes like those that accompany starvation also occur during fasting. During total fasting, the body's glycogen stores are depleted in less than a day and the body calls on its fat reserves. Fat is first taken from around the kidneys and the heart. Then it is removed from other parts of the body, eventually even from the bone marrow.

Weight loss through diet and exercise is discussed in Chapter 19.

Increased dependence on stored fats as an energy source leads to *ketosis,* a condition characterized by the appearance of compounds called *ketone bodies* in the blood and urine (Figure 17.11). Ketosis rapidly develops into *acidosis*; the blood pH drops, and oxygen transport is hindered. Oxygen deprivation leads to depression and lethargy.

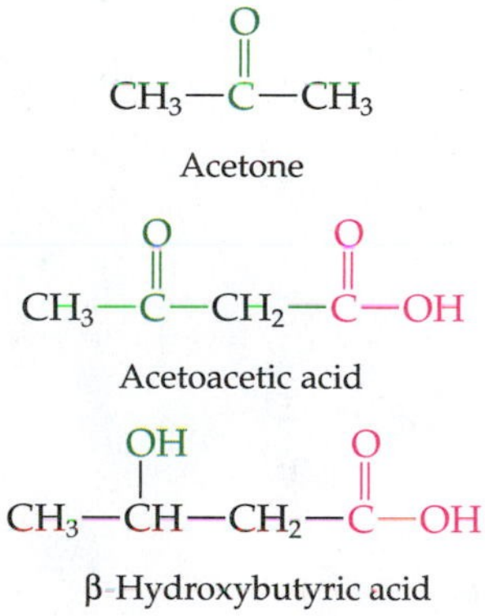

Acidosis is also associated with the insulin-deficiency disease diabetes. (See the essay on diabetes in Section 18.5.) Insulin enables the body's cells to take up glucose from the bloodstream. A lack of insulin causes the liver to act as though the cells are starving, and they start burning fat for energy while blood sugar levels rise. This fat metabolism leads to the production of ketone bodies and subsequent acidosis.

In the early stages of a *total* fast, body protein is metabolized at a relatively rapid rate. After several weeks, the rate of protein breakdown slows considerably as the brain adjusts to using the breakdown products of fatty acid metabolism for its energy source. When fat reserves are substantially depleted, the body must again draw heavily on its structural proteins for its energy requirements. The emaciated appearance of a starving individual is due to the depletion of muscle proteins.

$CH_3-C(=O)-CH_3$

Acetone

$CH_3-C(=O)-CH_2-C(=O)-OH$

Acetoacetic acid

$CH_3-CH(OH)-CH_2-C(=O)-OH$

β-Hydroxybutyric acid

▲ **Figure 17.11** The three ketone bodies produced in fat metabolism.

Q: *Identify the functional groups in each of the compounds. Which ketone body is not a ketone?*

Processed Food: Less Nutrition

Malnutrition need not be due to starvation or dieting. It can be the result of eating too much highly processed food.

Whole wheat is an excellent source of vitamin B_1 and other vitamins. To make white flour, the wheat germ and bran are removed from the grain. This greatly increases the storage life of the flour, but the remaining material has few minerals or vitamins and little fiber. We eat the starch and use much of the germ and bran for animal food. Cattle and hogs often get better nutrition than we do. Similarly, polished rice has had most of its protein and minerals removed, and it has almost no vitamins. The disease beriberi became prevalent when polished rice was introduced into Southeast Asia.

When many fruits and vegetables are peeled, they lose most of their vitamins, minerals, and fiber. The peels are often dumped (directly or through a garbage disposal) into a sewage system, where they contribute to water pollution (Chapter 14). The heat used to cook food also destroys some vitamins. If water is used in cooking, some of the water-soluble vitamins (vitamin C and B vitamins) and some of the minerals are often drained off and discarded with the water.

5. Are some foods really "super foods" or "miracle foods"? Some foods do provide special benefits. For example, flaxseed has cholesterol-reducing properties, cherries have been found to alleviate symptoms of gout in some people, and cranberries may aid in preventing some urinary tract infections. However, no single food or special combination of foods will magically bring perfect health, especially if the remainder of the diet is unhealthy. A few tablespoons of flaxseed with your breakfast cereal won't offset the adverse effects of a 500-kcal coffee drink laden with sugar and fat.

It is estimated that 90% of the food budget of an average family in the United States goes to buy processed foods. A diet of hamburgers, potato chips, and soft drinks is lacking in many essential nutrients. Highly processed convenience foods are making many people in developed nations obese but poorly nourished despite their abundance of food.

Self-Assessment Questions

1. During fasting or starvation, glycogen stores are depleted in about
   a. 1 hour b. 1 day c. 1 week d. 1 month
2. After glycogen stores are depleted, the body draws on its reserves of
   a. amino acids b. fat c. glycogen d. protein
3. When fat reserves have been used up, the body uses for its energy source
   a. adipose tissue b. amino acid reserves
   c. glycogen stores d. structural proteins
4. Which of the following is *not* a ketone body?
   a. CH_3COCH_3 b. $CH_3CHOHCH_2COCH_3$
   c. $CH_3CHOHCH_2CHOHCH_3$ d. CH_3COCH_2COOH

Answers: 1, b; 2, b; 3, d; 4, c

17.6 Food Additives

Learning Objective › List some common food additives and their purposes.

Food labels on processed foods are almost undecipherable. For example, a cake mix box may read "egg whites, vegetable oils, nonfat dry milk, lecithin, mono- and diglycerides, propylene glycol monostearate, xanthan gums, sodium citrate, aluminum sulfate, artificial flavor, iron phosphate, niacin, riboflavin, and irradiated ergosterol."

Ingredients on food labels are listed in decreasing order by weight, but often we can recognize only a few of the ingredients. Just what is in the food we eat? More than 3000 substances appear on a list on the FDA's Web site called "Everything Added to Food in the United States (EAFUS)." We examine some of those here.

Most of the substances listed on a label are **food additives**, substances other than basic foodstuffs that are put into food for various reasons related to production, processing, packaging, or storage. Because food processing removes certain essential substances, some additives are included in prepared food to increase its nutritional value. Other substances are added to enhance color and flavor, to retard spoilage, to provide texture, to sanitize, to bleach, to ripen or prevent ripening, to control moisture levels, or to control foaming. Sugar, salt, and corn syrup are used in the greatest amounts. These three, plus citric acid, baking soda, vegetable colors, mustard, and pepper, make up more than 98% (by weight) of all additives.

Some food additives, such as salt to preserve meat and fish and spices to flavor and preserve foods, have been used since ancient times. Throughout the centuries, other additives were found to be useful. Movement of much of the population from farms to cities increased the necessity for using preservatives. More widespread consumption of convenience foods has also led to greater use of additives.

In the United States, food additives are regulated by the Food and Drug Administration (FDA). The original Food, Drug, and Cosmetic Act was passed by Congress in 1938. Under this act, the FDA had to prove that an additive was unsafe before its use could be prevented. The Food Additives Amendment of 1958 shifted the burden of proof to the food industry. A company that wishes to use a food additive must first furnish proof to the FDA that the additive is safe for the intended use. The FDA can also regulate the quantity of additives that can be used.

6. Should the government prohibit food additives? Many additives provide useful improvements in food. For example, most people find that unsalted bread has little taste. Which soft drink would you prefer if they were all colorless? Canned tomatoes processed without calcium chloride may be soft and mushy.

Table 17.5 Your Breakfast—As Seen by a Chemist[a]

Chilled Melon	
Starches	Anisyl propionate
Sugars	Amyl acetate
Cellulose	Ascorbic acid
Pectin	Vitamin A
Malic acid	Riboflavin
Citric acid	Thiamine
Succinic acid	
Scrambled Eggs	
Ovalbumin	Lecithin
Conalbumin	Lipids (fats)
Ovomucoid	Fatty acids
Mucin	Butyric acid
Globulins	Acetic acid
Amino acids	Sodium chloride
Lipovitellin	Lutein
Livetin	Zeazanthin
Cholesterol	Vitamin A
Sugar-Cured Ham	
Actomyosin	Adenosine triphosphate (ATP)
Myogen	Glucose
Nucleoproteins	Collagen
Peptides	Elastin
Amino acids	Creatine
Myoglobin	Pyroligneous acid
Lipids (fats)	Sodium chloride
Linoleic acid	Sodium nitrate
Oleic acid	Sodium nitrite
Lecithin	Sodium phosphate
Cholesterol	Sucrose
Coffee	
Caffeine	Acetone
Essential oils	Methyl acetate
Methanol	Furan
Acetaldehyde	Diacetyl
Methyl formate	Butanol
Ethanol	Methylfuran
Dimethyl sulfide	Isoprene
Propionaldehyde	Methylbutanol

[a]The chemicals listed are those found normally in the foods. The chemical listings are not necessarily complete.
Source: Manufacturing Chemists Association, Washington, DC.

Some people express concern about the "chemicals in our food," but food itself consists of chemicals. Table 17.5 shows the chemical composition of a typical breakfast. Many of the chemicals in this breakfast might be harmful in large amounts but are harmless in the trace amounts that occur naturally in foods. Indeed, some make important contributions to delightful flavors and aromas.

Our bodies are also collections of chemicals. If broken down into its elements (Table 17.6), your body would be worth only a few dollars. It is the unique combination and arrangement of the elements in each human body that make each of us different from everyone else and each individual's worth beyond measure. Since food is chemical and we are chemical, we shouldn't worry about most of the chemicals in our food—perhaps just some specific ones.

Table 17.6 Approximate Elemental Analysis of the Human Body

Element	Percent by Weight
Oxygen	65
Carbon	18
Hydrogen	10
Nitrogen	3
Calcium	1.5
Phosphorus	1
Potassium	0.35
Sulfur	0.25
Chlorine	0.15
Sodium	0.15
Magnesium	0.05
Iron	0.004

Trace elements to make 100%

Additives That Improve Nutrition

The first nutrient supplement approved by the Bureau of Chemistry (which later became the FDA) of the U.S. Department of Agriculture was potassium iodide (KI), added to table salt in 1924 to reduce the incidence of goiter (recall Figure 17.9).

Several other chemicals are added to foods to prevent deficiency diseases. Addition of vitamin B_1 (thiamine) to polished rice is essential in the Far East, where beriberi is still a problem. The replacement of the B vitamins thiamine, riboflavin, folic acid, and niacin (which are removed in processing) and the addition of iron, usually ferrous carbonate ($FeCO_3$), to flour are referred to as **enrichment**. Enriched bread or pasta made from this flour still isn't as nutritious as bread or pasta made from whole wheat. It lacks vitamin B_6, pantothenic acid, zinc, magnesium, and fiber, nutrients usually provided by whole-grain flour. Despite these shortcomings, the enrichment of bread, corn meal, and cereals has almost eliminated pellagra, a disease that once plagued the southern United States.

The GRAS List

Some food additives have been used for many years without apparent harmful effects. In 1958, the U.S. Congress established a list of additives *generally recognized as safe* (*GRAS*). Many of the substances on the **GRAS** list are familiar spices, flavors, and nutrients. Some of the substances placed on the 1958 list have since been removed, including cyclamate sweeteners and some food colors. Some other substances have been added to the original list. About 7000 substances are now given GRAS status.

There were some deficiencies in the original testing procedures. The FDA has since reevaluated several of them based on new research findings—and greater consumer awareness. Improved instruments and better experimental designs have revealed the possibility of harm, though slight, from some additives previously thought safe. Most of the newer experiments involve feeding massive doses of additives to small laboratory animals, and these studies have been criticized for that reason.

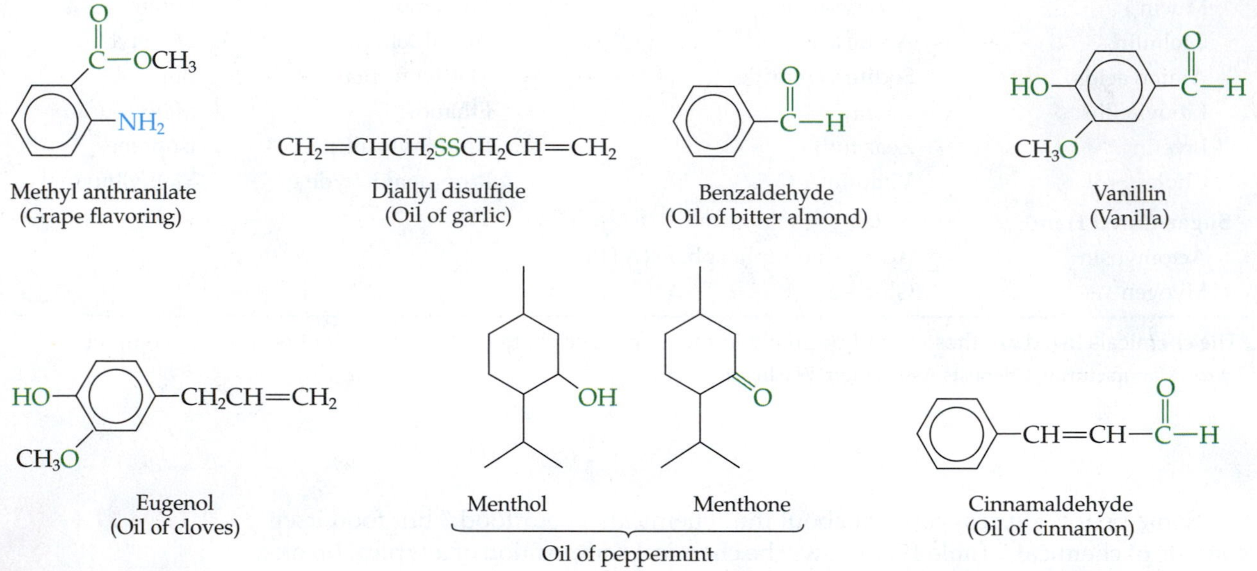

$C_6H_4(NH_2)-C(=O)-OCH_3$
Methyl anthranilate
(Grape flavoring)

$CH_2{=}CHCH_2SSCH_2CH{=}CH_2$
Diallyl disulfide
(Oil of garlic)

$C_6H_5-C(=O)-H$
Benzaldehyde
(Oil of bitter almond)

HO–C_6H_3(–OCH_3)–C(=O)–H
Vanillin
(Vanilla)

HO–C_6H_3(–OCH_3)–$CH_2CH{=}CH_2$
Eugenol
(Oil of cloves)

OH
Menthol

O
Menthone

Oil of peppermint

$C_6H_5-CH{=}CH-C(=O)-H$
Cinnamaldehyde
(Oil of cinnamon)

▲ **Figure 17.12** Some molecular flavorings. See Table 9.7 for others.

Q: *Which of the compounds shown here have aldehyde functional groups? Which are phenols? Ethers? Alkenes? Which is an ester? A ketone? An alcohol?*

Vitamin C (ascorbic acid) is frequently added to fruit juices, flavored drinks, and other beverages. Although our diets generally contain enough ascorbic acid to prevent scurvy, some scientists recommend a much larger intake than minimum daily requirements. Vitamin D is added to milk in developed countries, and consumption of fortified milk has led to the almost total elimination of rickets. Similarly, vitamin A, which occurs naturally in butter, is added to margarine so that the substitute more nearly matches butter in nutritional quality.

If we ate a balanced diet of fresh foods, we probably wouldn't need nutritional supplements. But many people choose to eat mainly processed foods and convenience foods. If their usual diet is composed mainly of highly processed foods, people may need the nutrients provided by vitamin and mineral food additives.

Additives That Taste Good

Spice cake, soda pop, gingerbread, sausage, and many other foods depend on spices and other additives for most of their flavor. Cloves, ginger, cinnamon, and nutmeg are examples of natural spices, and basil, marjoram, thyme, and rosemary are widely used herbs. Natural flavors are also extracted from fruits and other plant materials.

Some esters that serve as flavors are listed in Table 9.7. Other flavor compounds are shown in Figure 17.12. Chemists can analyze natural flavors and then synthesize components and make mixtures that resemble those flavors. Major components of natural and artificial flavors are often identical. For example, both vanilla extract

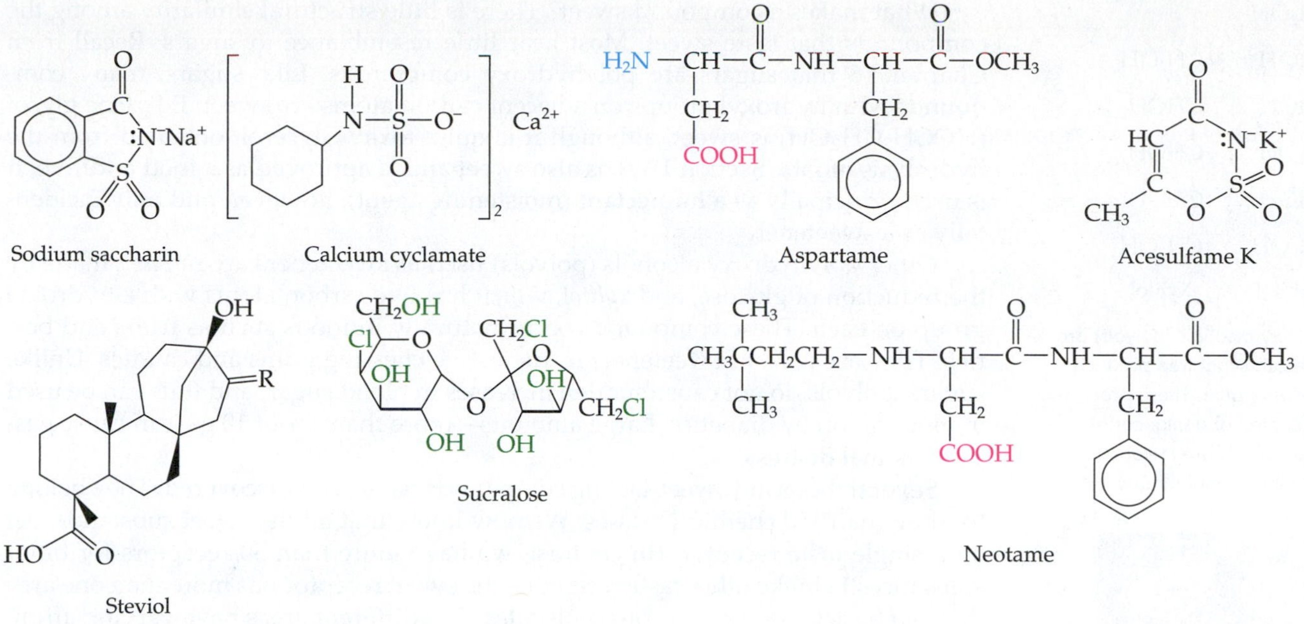

▲ **Figure 17.13** Seven artificial sweeteners. Note that sucralose (Splenda®) is a chlorinated derivative of sucrose. It is the only artificial sweetener actually made from sucrose. Steviol is a precursor of the natural sweetener stevia.

and imitation vanilla owe their flavor mainly to vanillin. The natural flavor is often more complex because vanilla extract contains a wider variety of chemicals than imitation vanilla does. Flavor additives, whether natural or synthetic, probably present little hazard when used in moderation, and they contribute considerably to our enjoyment of food.

Artificial Sweeteners

Obesity is a major problem in most developed countries. Presumably, people could reduce their intake of calories by replacing sugars with noncaloric sweeteners, but there is little evidence that artificial sweeteners are of value in controlling obesity. People eat more and more sugar; annual per capita consumption in the United States averages 150 lb.

For many years, the major artificial sweeteners were saccharin and cyclamates. Cyclamates were banned in the United States in 1970 after studies showed that they caused cancer in laboratory animals. (Subsequent studies have failed to confirm these findings, but the FDA has not lifted the ban.) In 1977, saccharin was shown to cause bladder cancer in laboratory animals. However, the move by the FDA to ban it was blocked by Congress because at that time saccharin was the only approved artificial sweetener. Its ban would have meant the end of diet soft drinks and other low-calorie products.

There are now five FDA-approved artificial sweeteners (Figure 17.13). *Aspartame* (the methyl ester of the dipeptide aspartylphenylalanine) was approved in 1981. A closely related compound, called *neotame*, has a 3,3-dimethylbutyl group $CH_3C(CH_3)_2CH_2CH_2—$ on the nitrogen atom of the aspartyl unit of the dipeptide. There are anecdotal reports of problems with aspartame, but repeated studies have shown it to be generally safe, except for people with phenylketonuria, an inherited condition in which phenylalanine cannot be metabolized properly. Other artificial sweeteners approved for use in the United States include acesulfame K (Sunette®) and sucralose (Splenda®); these sweeteners can survive the high temperatures of cooking processes, whereas aspartame is broken down by heat. Table 17.7 compares the sweetness of a variety of substances.

A natural product of note is *stevia*, a South American herb long used as a sweetener by the Guarani Indians of Paraguay. Leaves of this herb (*Stevia rebaudiana*) contain glycosides that provide a sweetness at least 30 times that of sucrose. Stevia, an approved food additive in Japan and South America, is available in the United States as a dietary supplement; it is on the FDA's GRAS list.

Table 17.7 Relative Sweetness of Some Compounds

Compound	Relative Sweetness[a]
Lactose	0.16
Maltose	0.33
Glucose	0.74
Sucrose	1.00
Fructose	1.73
Steviol glycoside	30
Cyclamate	45
Aspartame	180
Acesulfame K	200
Saccharin	300
Sucralose	600
Neotame	13,000

[a]Sweetness is relative to sucrose at a value of 1.

Sorbitol	Xylitol
CH_2OH	
CHOH	CH_2OH
CHOH	CHOH
CHOH	CHOH
CHOH	CHOH
CH_2OH	CH_2OH

▲ Polyhydroxy alcohols (polyols) are used to sweeten sugar-free products such as chewing gum. These products aid in control of dental caries because the polyols are metabolized slowly if at all in dental plaque.

What makes a compound sweet? There is little structural similarity among the compounds that taste sweet. Most bear little resemblance to sugars. Recall from Chapter 16 that sugars are polyhydroxy compounds. Like sugars, many compounds with hydroxyl groups on adjacent carbon atoms are sweet. Ethylene glycol ($HOCH_2CH_2OH$) is sweet, although it is quite toxic. Glycerol, obtained from the hydrolysis of fats (Section 17.2), is also sweet and is approved as a food additive. It is used principally as a **humectant** (moistening agent), however, and only incidentally as a sweetener.

Other polyhydroxy alcohols (polyols) used as sweeteners are *sorbitol*, made by the reduction of glucose, and *xylitol*, which has five carbon atoms with a hydroxyl group on each. These compounds occur naturally in foods such as fruits and berries. They are used as sweeteners in sugar-free chewing gums and candies. Unlike sugars, polyols do not cause sudden increases in blood sugar, and thus can be used in moderation by diabetics. Large amounts—more than about 10 g—can cause gastrointestinal distress.

Several thousand sweet-tasting compounds have been discovered. They belong to more than 150 chemical classes. We now know that all the sweet substances act on a single taste receptor. (In contrast, we have more than 30 receptors for bitter substances.) Unlike other taste receptors, the sweet receptor has more than one area that can be activated by various molecules. The different areas have varying affinities for certain molecules. For example, sucralose fits the receptor more tightly than sucrose does, partly because its chlorine atoms carry more negative charge than the oxygen atoms in the OH groups they replace. Neotame fits the receptor so tightly that it keeps the receptor firing repeatedly.

Flavor Enhancers

Some chemical substances, though not particularly flavorful themselves, are used to enhance other flavors. Common table salt (sodium chloride) is a familiar example. In addition to being a necessary nutrient, salt seems to increase sweetness and helps to mask bitterness and sourness.

Another popular flavor enhancer is monosodium glutamate (MSG). MSG is the sodium salt of glutamic acid, one of the 20 amino acids that occur naturally in proteins. It is used in many convenience foods.

$$HOOC{-}CH_2CH_2\underset{^{+}NH_3}{CH}{-}\overset{O}{\overset{\|}{C}}{-}O^-$$

Glutamic acid

$$HOOC{-}CH_2CH_2\underset{NH_2}{CH}{-}\overset{O}{\overset{\|}{C}}{-}O^-Na^+$$

MSG

Although glutamates are found naturally in proteins, there is evidence that huge excesses can be harmful. MSG can numb portions of the brains of laboratory animals. It may also be *teratogenic*, causing birth defects when eaten in large amounts by women who are pregnant.

Additives That Retard Spoilage

Food spoilage can result from the growth of molds, yeasts, or bacteria. Substances that prevent such growth are often called *antimicrobials*, and they include certain carboxylic acids and their salts. Propionic acid and its sodium and calcium salts are used to inhibit molding of bread and cheese. Sorbic acid, benzoic acid, and their salts are also used (Figure 17.14).

Some inorganic compounds can also be added to inhibit spoilage. Sodium nitrite ($NaNO_2$) is used to cure meat and to maintain the pink color of smoked hams, frankfurters, and bologna. It also contributes to the tangy flavor of processed meat products. Nitrites are particularly effective as inhibitors of *Clostridium botulinum*, the bacterium that produces botulism poisoning. However, only about 10% of the amount used to keep meat pink is needed to prevent botulism. Nitrites have

CH_3CH_2COOH

Propionic acid

$CH_3CH_2COO^-Na^+$

Sodium propionate

$CH_3CH{=}CHCH{=}CHCOOH$

Sorbic acid

$CH_3CH{=}CHCH{=}CHCOO^-K^+$

Potassium sorbate

$C_6H_5{-}COOH$

Benzoic acid

$C_6H_5{-}COO^-Na^+$

Sodium benzoate

▲ **Figure 17.14** Most spoilage inhibitors are carboxylic acids or salts of carboxylic acids.

been investigated as possible causes of cancer of the stomach. In the presence of the hydrochloric acid (HCl) in the stomach, nitrites are converted to nitrous acid.

$$NaNO_2 + HCl \longrightarrow HNO_2 + NaCl$$

This acid may then react with secondary amines (amines with two alkyl groups on nitrogen) to form *nitroso* compounds.

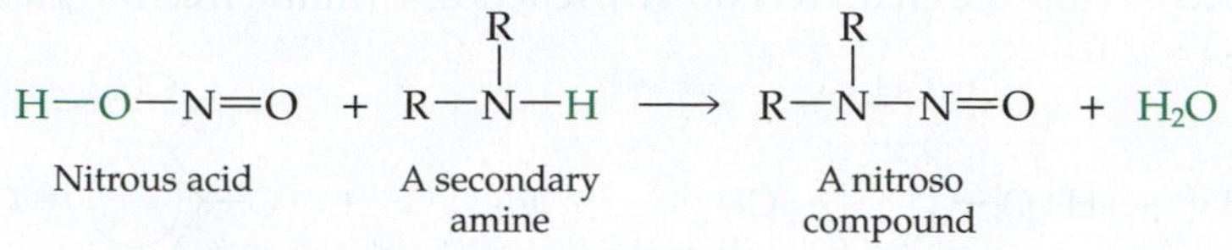

$$\underset{\text{Nitrous acid}}{H{-}O{-}N{=}O} + \underset{\text{A secondary amine}}{R{-}\overset{R}{\overset{|}{N}}{-}H} \longrightarrow \underset{\text{A nitroso compound}}{R{-}\overset{R}{\overset{|}{N}}{-}N{=}O} + H_2O$$

The R groups of nitroso compounds can be alkyl groups such as methyl (CH_3—), or ethyl (CH_3CH_2—), or they can be more complex. In any case, these compounds are among the most potent carcinogens known. The rate of stomach cancer is higher in countries where people use prepared meats than in developing nations, where people eat little or no cured meat. However, the incidence of stomach cancer is *decreasing* in the United States, perhaps because ascorbic acid (vitamin C) inhibits the reaction between nitrous acid and amines to form nitrosamines, and many people have orange juice with their breakfast bacon or sausage. Nevertheless, possible problems with nitrites have led the FDA to approve sodium hypophosphite (NaH_2PO_2) as a meat preservative.

Other inorganic food additives include sulfur dioxide and sulfite salts. A gas at room temperature, sulfur dioxide (SO_2) serves as a disinfectant and preservative, particularly for dried fruits such as peaches, apricots, and raisins. It is also used as a bleach to prevent the browning of wines, corn syrup, jellies, dehydrated potatoes, and other foods. Sulfur dioxide seems safe for most people when ingested with food, but it is a powerful irritant when inhaled and is a damaging ingredient of polluted air in some areas (Chapter 13). Sulfur dioxide and sulfite salts cause severe allergic reactions in some people. The FDA requires food labels to indicate the presence of these compounds in a food.

One person in a hundred has a strong allergic reaction to sulfur dioxide and related compounds called *sulfiting agents.* Common ones include sodium sulfite (Na_2SO_3), potassium sulfite (K_2SO_3), sodium bisulfite ($NaHSO_3$), potassium bisulfite ($KHSO_3$), sodium metabisulfite ($Na_2S_2O_5$), and potassium metabisulfite ($K_2S_2O_5$).

Antioxidants: BHA and BHT

One class of preservatives is composed of **antioxidants**, which inhibit the chemical spoilage of food that occurs in the presence of oxygen. These substances are added to foods (or their packaging) to prevent fats and oils from forming rancid products that make foods unpalatable. Antioxidants also minimize the destruction of some essential amino acids and vitamins. Packaged foods that contain fats or oils (such as bread, potato chips, sausage, and breakfast cereal) often have antioxidants added. Compounds commonly used as antioxidants include butylated hydroxytoluene (BHT), butylated hydroxyanisole (BHA), propyl gallate, and *tert*-butylhydroquinone (Figure 17.15).

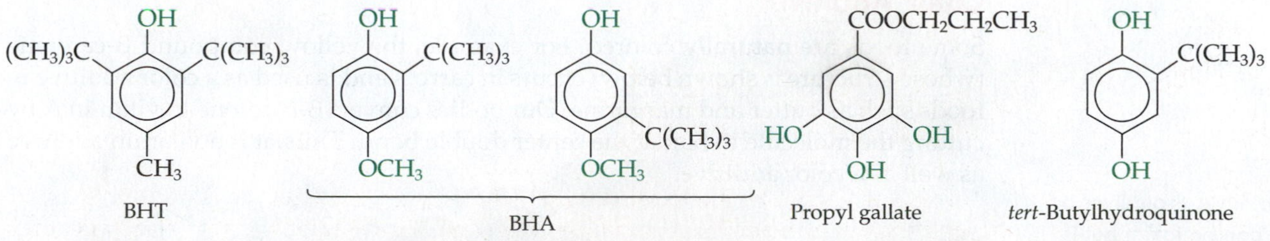

▲ **Figure 17.15** Four common antioxidants. BHA is a mixture of two isomers.

Q: *What functional group is common to all four compounds? What other functional group is present in BHA? In propyl gallate?*

Fats turn rancid, in part as a result of oxidation, a process that occurs through the formation of molecular fragments called **free radicals,** which have an unpaired electron as a distinguishing feature. (Recall from Section 4.6 that covalent bonds are shared *pairs* of electrons.) Without specifying the structures of radicals, we can summarize the process. First, a fat molecule reacts with oxygen to form a free radical.

$$\text{Fat} + O_2 \longrightarrow \text{Free radical}$$

The radical then reacts with another fat molecule to form a new free radical that can repeat the process. A reaction such as this, in which intermediates are formed that keep the reaction going, is called a **chain reaction**. One molecule of oxygen can lead to the decomposition of many fat molecules.

To preserve foods containing fats, processors package the products to exclude air. However, it cannot be excluded completely, so chemical antioxidants such as BHT are used to stop the chain reaction by reacting with the free radicals.

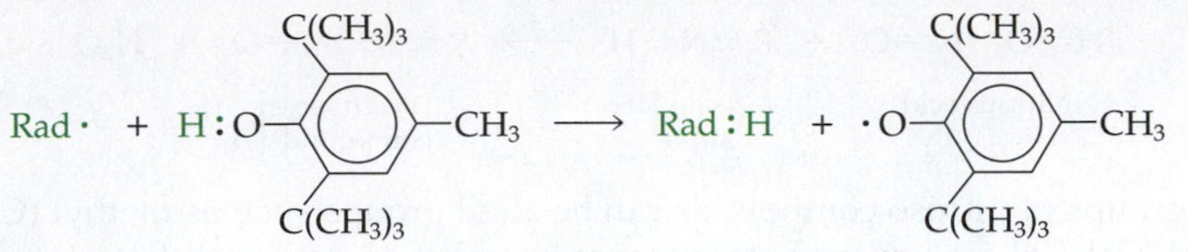

Rad· + H:O–(ring with two $C(CH_3)_3$ groups)–CH_3 ⟶ Rad:H + ·O–(ring with two $C(CH_3)_3$ groups)–CH_3

BHT

The new radical formed from BHT is rather stable. The unpaired electron doesn't have to stay on the oxygen atom but can move around in the electron cloud of the benzene ring. The BHT radical doesn't react with fat molecules, and the chain is broken.

Why are the butyl groups important? Without them, two phenol molecules (Section 9.5) would simply couple when exposed to an oxidizing agent.

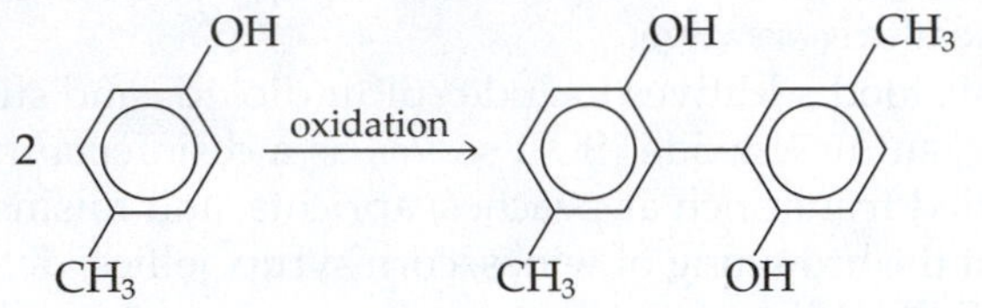

2 (OH, CH_3 phenol) —oxidation⟶ (coupled biphenyl with OH, CH_3, CH_3, OH)

With the bulky butyl groups attached, the rings can't get close enough together for coupling. They are free, then, to trap free radicals formed by the oxidation of fats.

Many food additives have been criticized as being harmful, and BHA and BHT are no exceptions. They have been reported to cause allergic reactions in some people. In one study, pregnant mice fed diets containing 0.5% BHA or BHT gave birth to offspring with brain abnormalities. On the other hand, when relatively large amounts of BHT were fed to rats daily, their life spans were increased by a human equivalent of 20 years. One theory about aging is that it is caused in part by the formation of free radicals. BHT retards this chemical breakdown in cells in the same way that it retards spoilage in foods.

BHA and BHT are synthetic chemicals, but antioxidants such as vitamin E and vitamin C occur naturally. Vitamin E (like BHT) is a phenol, with several substituents on the benzene ring. Presumably, its action as an antioxidant is quite similar to that of BHT. However, one recent study suggests that large doses of vitamin E may also be somewhat harmful.

Color Additives

Some foods are naturally colored. For example, the yellow compound β-carotene (whose structure is shown below) occurs in carrots and is used as a color additive in foods such as butter and margarine. Our bodies convert β-carotene to vitamin A by cutting the molecule in half at the center double bond. Thus, it is a vitamin additive as well as a color additive.

Too much vitamin A (from liver or supplements) can be toxic, but if too much β-carotene is consumed, the body merely stores it in fat, eventually using or excreting it. Very large amounts of β-carotene have been known to cause the skin to turn orange! The effect is temporary and harmless.

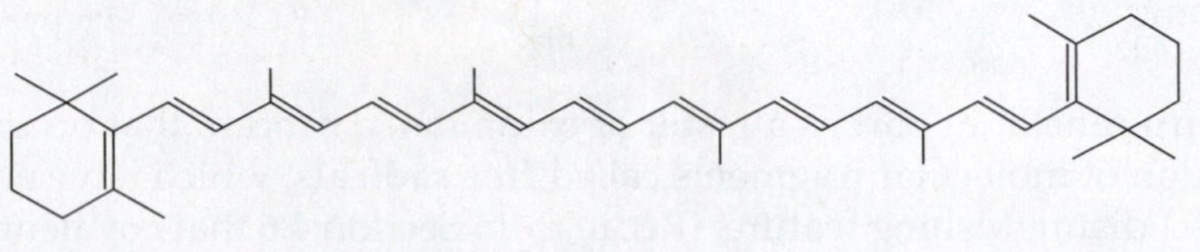

β-Carotene

Other natural food colors include beet juice, grape-hull extract, and saffron (from autumn-flowering crocus flowers).

Nanoscience in Foods

Nanoscience and nanotechnology involve the production and use of materials at a nanometer scale—billionths of a meter. The properties of nanomaterials differ from those of larger-scale materials, and nanotechnology has the potential to revolutionize many aspects of food quality and packaging in the future. For example, nanotechnology may be used to develop foods that can adjust in color, flavor, or nutrient content to accommodate each consumer's taste or health condition. Some possible food-related applications of nanoscience include the following:

- **Nano foods.** Several companies are exploring the use of nanotechnology to create drinks containing nanocapsules that can change color and flavor and to make ice cream with nanoparticle emulsions to improve texture. Scientists are also developing novel delivery systems that help protect nutrients and flavors and that improve control of the release of encapsulated compounds.
- **Nano packaging.** Nanomaterials are being developed that will extend food shelf life and change color to signal when the food spoils. Nanoparticles could be used in packaging film to yield a material with greater mechanical strength but lower permeability to oxygen and water. Such film could perhaps remove carbon dioxide or block out gases such as oxygen and ethylene that shorten the shelf life of food.
- **Nano security devices.** Nanosensors are being developed for pathogen and contaminant detection. Single-molecule sensors would detect changes in food quality and thus maintain food safety. Nanodevices are being investigated that would allow the tracking of individual shipments.

Nanotechnology centers around the world are developing an impressive body of research on new possibilities for food production—flavors, nutrition, colors, packaging, and much more. Nanotechnology offers enormous potential benefits to society, but health concerns associated with nanomaterials are surfacing. The same factors that enhance the usefulness of these materials also increase the potential for harm. Some nanoparticles can be absorbed into cells and move throughout the body and brain. Their small size may increase their potential toxicity.

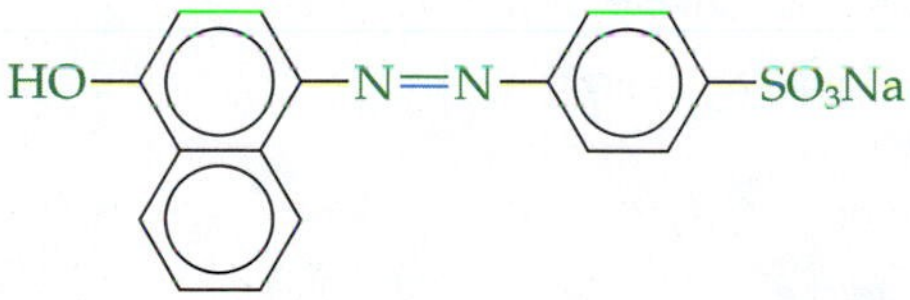

HO— —N=N— —SO_3Na

FD&C Orange No. 1

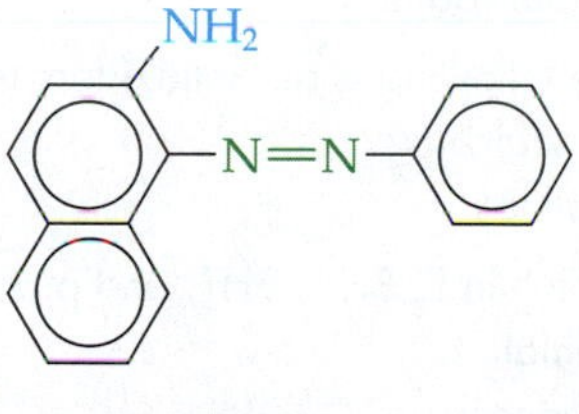

NH_2 —N=N—

FD&C Yellow No. 3

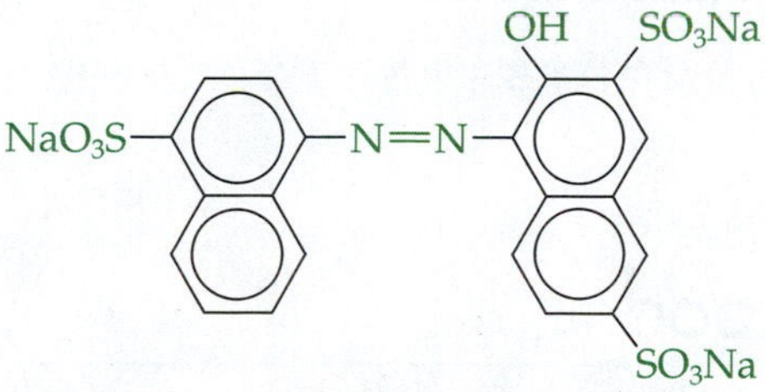

OH SO_3Na NaO_3S— —N=N— SO_3Na

FD&C Red No. 2

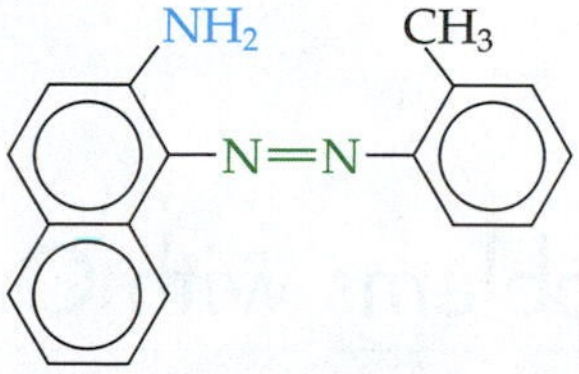

NH_2 CH_3 —N=N—

FD&C Yellow No. 4

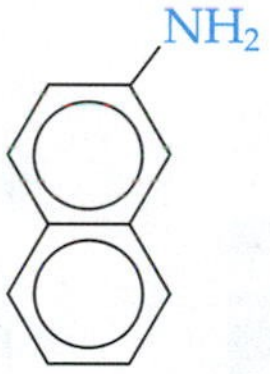

NH_2

β-Naphthylamine

▲ **Figure 17.16** Four synthetic food colorings that have been banned by the FDA (left). Note that the two yellow dyes are related to β-naphthylamine (right), a carcinogen.

We expect many foods to have characteristic colors. To increase the attractiveness and acceptability of its products, the food industry has used synthetic food colors for decades. Since the Food and Drug Act of 1906, the FDA has regulated the use of these chemicals and set limits on their concentrations. But the FDA is not infallible. Some colors once on the approved list were later shown to be harmful and were removed from the list. In 1950, Food, Drug, and Cosmetic (FD&C) Orange No. 1 in pumpkin-colored Halloween candy caused gastrointestinal upsets in several children and was then banned by the FDA.

In following years, other dyes were banned. FD&C Yellow No. 3 and No. 4 were found to contain small amounts of β-naphthylamine, a carcinogen that causes bladder cancer in laboratory animals. Furthermore, they reacted with stomach acids to produce more β-naphthylamine. FD&C Red No. 2 was also shown to be a weak carcinogen in laboratory animals. The structures of these dyes are given in Figure 17.16.

Food colors, even those that have been banned, present little risk. They have been used for years with apparent safety and are normally used in tiny amounts. Although the risk is low, however, the benefit is largely aesthetic. Any foods that contain artificial colors must say so on the label, so you can avoid them if you want to.

Self-Assessment Questions

1. To use a new food additive, a company must
   a. notify the FDA that it plans to use the additive
   b. pay the FDA to test the additive for safety
   c. provide the FDA with evidence that the additive is safe for the intended use
   d. submit an application to the FDA, but does not have to prove it safe and effective
2. Compared to synthetic flavors, natural flavors
   a. are chemical-free
   b. have different main ingredients
   c. come from the Spice Islands
   d. contain a wider variety of chemicals
3. The flavor enhancer MSG is related to a(n)
   a. amino acid b. fatty acid
   c. monosaccharide d. polyhydroxy alcohol
4. Calcium propionate is added to bread to
   a. act as an antioxidant b. enhance the flavor
   c. inhibit mold growth c. replace Ca^{2+} removed in processing
5. The food additive that inhibits formation of botulin toxin is sodium
   a. acetate b. ascorbate c. benzoate d. nitrite
6. Antioxidants
   a. aid in lipid transport b. aid in oxygen transport
   c. prevent color fading d. trap free radicals
7. Which of the following is an antioxidant used to prevent rancidity?
   a. ascorbic acid b. BHT
   c. sodium sulfite d. sugar
8. Vitamin C, vitamin E, BHA, BHT, and propyl gallate are
   a. antimicrobial b. antioxidants
   c. flavor enhancers d. unintentional additives

Answers: 1, c; 2, d; 3, a; 4, c; 5, d; 6, d; 7, b; 8, b

HO—C(=O)—C(=O)—OH

Oxalic acid

▲ Poisonous oxalic acid is found in rhubarb leaves.

17.7 Problems with Our Food

Learning Objective › Identify and describe some of the main problems with harmful substances in our food.

People have been trying to deal with poisons in their food for millennia. Early foragers learned—by the painful process of trial and error—that some plants and animals were poisonous. Rhubarb leaves contain toxic oxalic acid. Bruised celery produces *psoralens*, compounds that are powerful mutagens and carcinogens. The Japanese relish a variety of puffer fish that contains deadly poison in its ovaries and liver. Fifty or so Japanese people die each year from improperly prepared puffers.

One of the most toxic substances known is the toxin botulin that is produced by the bacterium *Clostridium botulinum*. This organism grows in improperly canned food. If the food isn't properly sterilized before it is sealed in jars or cans, the microorganism flourishes under anaerobic (without air) conditions. Botulin is so toxic that 1 g of it could kill more than a million people. The point is that a food is not inherently good simply because it is natural. Neither is it necessarily bad because a synthetic chemical substance has been added to it.

GREEN CHEMISTRY

Principles 5, 12

David M. Brown, *Davidson College*

Greener Ways to Isolate Nutrients from Food

The adoption of green chemistry principles has led to dramatic and exciting transformations in the field of molecular gastronomy. At one time, large-scale extractions of natural products, bioactive food components, and essential oils from plants relied on organic solvents, including diethyl ether, methylene chloride, chloroform, carbon tetrachloride, benzene, toluene, and others. Although these substances were once considered acceptable, we now know they are hazardous. Most of them are extremely flammable, highly volatile, carcinogenic, mutagenic, or teratogenic or show some combination of these risks. For these reasons, it is wise to avoid exposure to these hazardous solvents.

As a new generation of chemists evolves and applies the Twelve Principles of Green Chemistry, safer solvents (Principle 5) are being used with increasing frequency. Ethanol and supercritical carbon dioxide are currently the two solvents most widely used to extract natural products, bioactive food components, and essential oils. Ethanol extracts organic molecules of greater polarity. Supercritical carbon dioxide complements that by extracting organic molecules of lesser polarity. Mixtures of ethanol and supercritical carbon dioxide may be used to extract organic molecules of medium polarity. Now we don't have to use the more hazardous solvents.

Further, using more benign solvents such as ethanol and supercritical carbon dioxide instead of more hazardous solvents allows for safer reaction and processing conditions (for instance, flammability is less of a problem, Principle 12). Perhaps the most popular large-scale extraction is that of caffeine from coffee and tea, which was once performed using the carcinogenic and highly volatile solvent methylene chloride, but is now done using safer solvents such as supercritical carbon dioxide or water. The process is now safer and more effective due to green chemistry.

Spurred by the success of the caffeine-extraction process, greener technologies have been extended to the diverse fields of natural products, bioactive food components, and essential oils. It is now common to see bottles of concentrated extracts of dietary supplements, nutraceuticals, phytochemicals, and herbs on the shelves of pharmacies and health food stores as well as in "big-box" retailers. The potential health benefits and exact physiological function at the molecular level of these materials are subjects of research. Shown in the table below are some examples.

Similarly, essential oils from plants are extracted and concentrated from, for example, rosemary, hibiscus, and lavender. These concentrated oils are used as ingredients for fragrances and flavors (perfumes, herbal teas, soft drinks, and candies).

In the extraction of natural products, bioactive food components, and essential oils, green chemistry has played, and will continue to play, a crucial role in the reduction of hazardous solvents and protection of the environment.

Natural Product	Food Sources
Allicin	Garlic
Cyanidin	Dark pigmented berries
Beta-Carotene	Carrots, pumpkin, spinach
Capsaicin	Chili peppers
Epigallocatechin (EGC)	Green tea, pomegranate
Chlorophyll c_1	Algae and green vegetables
Curcumin	Turmeric (a component of curry)
EPA (an omega-3 fatty acid)	Fish
D-Limonene	Oranges, lemons, limes, cherries
Lycopene	Tomatoes, grapefruit, watermelon
Resveratrol	Plums, red grape skins

Botulin toxin (Botox®) is used in minute quantities for producing long-term (lasting for months) paralysis of muscles. Originally intended for the relief of unmanageable muscle spasms, Botox® is now widely used for cosmetic purposes, to paralyze facial muscles to conceal wrinkles. The treatment lasts only 4–6 months.

Carcinogens

There is little chance that we will suffer acute poisoning from approved food additives. But what about cancer? Could all these chemicals in our food increase our risk of developing cancer? The possibility exists, though the risk is low.

Carcinogens occur naturally in food. A charcoal-broiled steak contains 3,4-benzpyrene, a carcinogen also found in cigarette smoke and automobile exhaust fumes. Cinnamon and nutmeg contain *safrole*, a carcinogen that has been banned as a flavoring in root beer.

$CH_2CH{=}CH_2$

3,4-Benzpyrene Safrole

Among the most potent carcinogens are **aflatoxins**, compounds produced by molds growing on stored peanuts and grains (Figure 17.17). Aflatoxin B_1 is estimated to be 10 million times as potent a carcinogen as saccharin, and there is no way to keep it completely out of our food. The FDA sets a limit of 20 ppb for the maximum level of aflatoxins.

▶ **Figure 17.17** Aflatoxins, toxic and carcinogenic compounds, are produced by molds that grow on peanuts and stored grains.

Scientists estimate that our consumption of natural carcinogens is 10,000 times our consumption of synthetic carcinogens. Should we ban steaks, spices, peanuts, and grains because they contain naturally occurring carcinogens? Probably not. The risk is slight, and more serious risks face us in everyday life. Should we ban additives that have been shown to be carcinogenic? Certainly we should carefully weigh the risks against any benefits the additives might provide.

Food Contaminants

Food contamination can come from many sources and can occur at any step between producer and consumer. Pesticide residues, insect parts, hair from food workers, glass from broken containers, and antibiotics added to animal feeds are examples of contaminants. (See Collaborative Group Project 6.)

Antibiotics in animal feed are a troubling example of food contamination, because they often show up in the meat we eat. Antibiotics are added in low-level dosages to animal feed to promote weight gain. In fact, in 2009, 13.1 million kg of antibiotics were sold for use in animals in the United States. Residues of these antibiotics in meat may result in the sensitization of individuals who eat the meat, thus hastening the development of allergies. Scientists also fear that the use of antibiotics in animal feeds will hasten the process by which bacteria become drug resistant (Section 18.3).

Today's food contamination problems are usually biological, not chemical. For example, bacteria such as the O157:H7 strain of *Escherichia coli* (*E. coli*), a fecal contaminant sometimes found in raw meat or dairy products and occasionally in raw fruits and vegetables, can cause serious food poisoning. *E. coli* contamination has been responsible for many costly food recalls in recent years. *Salmonella* contamination of poultry, eggs, unprocessed milk, meat, or water can cause cramping, fever, dehydration, and diarrhea. *Salmonella* is also carried by pet turtles and birds. *Listeria monocytogenes* causes listeriosis, a food-borne illness marked by fever, muscle aches, nausea, and diarrhea.

Viruses such as hepatitis A, which causes a serious contagious disease of the liver, and the Norwalk virus, which causes about 50% of all outbreaks of food-borne gastroenteritis in the United States, can be spread when infected workers handle food products.

Parasites such as the roundworms *Trichinella spiralis*, which causes trichinosis, and *Anisakis simplex*, which causes anisakiasis, are relatively rare problems in developed countries but are fairly common in developing parts of the world. The few cases of trichinosis that occur in the United States result mainly from eating undercooked game meat or pork from home-raised pigs. Trichinosis is characterized by symptoms such as nausea, heartburn, and diarrhea. Anisakiasis results from eating raw or undercooked fish in dishes such as sushi and sashimi (Japan), cod livers (Scandinavia), fermented herrings (Netherlands), or ceviche, a citrus-marinated, raw seafood that is popular in Latin America.

Proper cooking and food handling procedures reduce the chance of contracting most food-borne diseases.

A World without Food Additives

Could we get along without food additives? Some of us could. But food spoilage might drastically reduce the food supply in some parts of an already hungry world, and diseases due to vitamin and mineral deficiencies might increase. Foods might cost more and be less nutritious. Food additives seem to be a necessary part of modern society. Use of some food additives poses potential hazards, but the major problem with our food supply is still contamination by harmful microorganisms, rodents, and insects. Indeed, according to the CDC, about 48 million illnesses and 3000 deaths result each year in the United States from food poisoning caused by bacteria, viruses, and parasites. Few, if any, deaths associated with the use of intentional food additives have been documented.

What should we do about food additives? We should be sure that the FDA is staffed with qualified personnel who can perform adequate testing of proposed food additives. People trained in chemistry are necessary for the control and monitoring of food additives and the detection of contaminants. Research on the analytical techniques necessary for the detection of trace quantities is vital to adequate consumer protection. We should demand laws to prevent the unnecessary and excessive use of pesticides and other agricultural chemicals that might contaminate our food. Above all, we should be alert and informed about these problems that are so vital to our health and well-being.

Self-Assessment Questions

1. Aflatoxins are
   a. antioxidants **b.** carcinogens **c.** on the GRAS list **d.** found only in peanuts
2. About how many people die from food poisoning in the U.S. each year?
   a. 100 **b.** 300 **c.** 3000 **d.** 30,000
3. The major problem with the food supply is contamination by
   a. aflatoxins **b.** chemicals **c.** microorganisms **d.** pesticides

Answers: 1, b; 2, c; 3, c

CRITICAL THINKING  EXERCISES

Apply knowledge that you have gained in this chapter and one or more of the FLaReS principles (Chapter 1) to evaluate the following statements or claims.

17.1 The author of a new diet book claims that he and many other people have been able to lose a substantial amount of weight by following a diet very low in carbohydrates (from bread, cereals, and pasta) but high in proteins (from meats).

17.2 An opponent of genetically modified (GM) foods suggests that the outcry against genetic modification occurred because the "public didn't want to eat food with 'genes' in it."

17.3 A Web site states that a chemical in marijuana, delta 1-tetrahydrocannabinol (delta 1-THC), is a fat-soluble vitamin called "vitamin M." The site claims that vitamin status is justified "because many of the properties of delta 1-THC are similar to those of the fat-soluble vitamins."

17.4 A Web site states that natural vitamins may be worth the extra cost because those vitamins occur within a family of "things like trace elements, enzymes, cofactors and other unknown factors that help them absorb into the human body and function to their full potential," whereas "synthetic vitamins are usually isolated into that one pure chemical, thereby leaving out some of the additional benefits that nature intended."

17.5 7-Day Detox is a unique detoxification supplement whose label states that it contains 34 different ingredients intended to flush toxins and fat out of your system.

17.6 A woman's doctor orders her to follow a strict low-fat diet. She makes a bowl of fat-free popcorn and then sprays it with a "flavor spray." The label of the spray lists the ingredients as canola oil, butter, and lecithin. It also indicates that a serving size of 1 spray (0.5 g) has 5 calories and 0 g of fat. (The FDA allows less than 0.5 g to be rounded to zero.) She sprays the popcorn about 40 times to give it a lot of flavor, pointing out that at zero grams of fat per spray, she is still adhering to the low-fat diet.

SUMMARY

Section 17.1—The three main classes of substances in foods are carbohydrates, fats, and proteins. We also need vitamins, minerals, fiber, and water in our diets. Carbohydrates include sugars, starches, and cellulose. Glucose, also called **blood sugar**, is the sugar used directly by cells for energy. Other sugars include fructose, sucrose (table sugar), and lactose. Sucrose and lactose are broken down during digestion. **Starch** is a polymer of α-glucose, and **cellulose** is a β-glucose polymer. Human beings can hydrolyze starch to glucose but cannot hydrolyze cellulose, which instead serves as dietary fiber. The liver and muscles store small amounts of carbohydrates as **glycogen**.

Section 17.2—Dietary fats are esters called **triglycerides**, which are broken down by enzymes to form fatty acids and glycerol. Fats are stored in **adipose tissue** located in **fat depots** and are hydrolyzed back to glycerol and fatty acids when needed. A **lipoprotein** is a cholesterol–protein combination transported in the blood. Low-density lipoproteins (LDLs) carry cholesterol to the cells for use and increase the risk of heart disease, while high-density lipoproteins (HDLs) carry it to the liver for excretion. Polyunsaturated fats (mostly from plants), *cis* fatty acids, and omega-3 fatty acids tend to lower LDL levels. Saturated fats (mostly from animals) and *trans* fatty acids made by hydrogenation of polyunsaturated fats have been implicated in cardiovascular disease.

Section 17.3—Proteins, polymers of amino acids, are broken down to amino acids during digestion. The **essential amino acids** must be included in the diet. Each essential amino acid is a **limiting reactant** in protein synthesis; a deficiency leads to an inability to make the proper proteins. Most animal proteins have these essential amino acids; plant proteins usually are deficient and must be combined with other plant proteins for complete nutrition. Protein deficiency is common in developing nations.

Section 17.4—**Dietary minerals** are inorganic substances vital to life. Bulk structural elements include carbon, hydrogen, and oxygen. Macrominerals include sodium, potassium, and calcium. We also need trace elements such as iron and ultratrace elements such as manganese, chromium, and vanadium. Minerals serve a variety of functions: Iodine is needed by the thyroid; iron is part of hemoglobin; and calcium and phosphorus are vital to the bones and teeth.

Vitamins are organic compounds that are required in the diet to prevent certain diseases. The B vitamins and vitamin C are water soluble and are needed frequently, whereas vitamins A, D, E, and K are all fat soluble and can be stored.

Dietary fiber may be soluble (gums and pectins) or insoluble (cellulose). It prevents digestion problems such as constipation. Drinking enough water is important, but it need not be plain water. Most drinks are mainly water.

Section 17.5—**Starvation** is deprivation of food that causes metabolic changes. The body first depletes its glycogen and then metabolizes fat and muscle tissue. Malnutrition can result from starvation, dieting, or eating too much highly processed food.

Section 17.6—**Food additives** are substances other than basic foodstuffs that are added to food to aid nutrition, inhibit spoilage, enhance color and flavor, provide texture, and so on. There are thousands of additives. The FDA regulates which additives, and how much of them, can be used.

The list of additives generally recognized as safe is the **GRAS list**, which is periodically reevaluated. Some additives have been found to be harmful; additives are usually banned if they are shown to cause cancer in laboratory animals.

Enrichment includes the replacement of B vitamins and the addition of iron to flour. Vitamin C is added to many beverages, and vitamin D to milk. Natural herbs and spices, or their synthetic counterparts, add flavor. Artificial sweeteners reduce sugar intake but do not appear to aid in controlling obesity. Glycerol is a sweet-tasting compound that is used primarily as a **humectant** or moistening agent. Salt and MSG are flavor enhancers.

Propionate, sorbate, and benzoate nitrite salts inhibit spoilage and bacterial growth. Fats may turn rancid partly from formation of **free radicals** with unpaired electrons. One free radical can cause a **chain reaction** that leads to decomposition of many fat molecules. BHT and BHA are **antioxidants** that react with free radicals and prevent rancidity.

Natural food colorings, such as β-carotene, and synthetic food colorings improve the appearance of food.

Section 17.7—Toxic substances occur naturally in foods, but occasionally are added in the form of pesticide residues or animal feed additives. Charcoal-broiled steak, cinnamon, and nutmeg contain carcinogens. **Aflatoxins** are produced by molds on peanuts and grain and are potent carcinogens. We may consume about 10,000 times as much of natural carcinogens as synthetic carcinogens. Most food contaminants are not chemicals but rather organisms such as bacteria, viruses, and parasites.

Without food additives, spoilage and disease would be likely to cause serious problems worldwide. Additives continue to be carefully scrutinized and regulated.

Green chemistry Green chemistry has revised extractions of natural products, bioactive food components, and essential oils from plants by substituting less hazardous solvents. For example, in decaffeination of coffee and tea, more benign supercritical carbon dioxide or water has replaced the volatile and carcinogenic solvent methylene chloride. Greener extraction technology is being extended to a large variety of dietary supplements and nutraceuticals derived from plants and other natural products.

Learning Objectives

› Identify dietary carbohydrates, and state their function.	Problems 1, 17–20
› Identify dietary lipids, and state their function.	Problems 2, 21–24, 55, 56
› List the essential amino acids, and explain why they are essential.	Problems 4, 25–27, 29, 30
› Describe some protein deficiency diseases and their causes.	Problem 28
› Identify the vitamins and the bulk dietary minerals, and state their functions.	Problems 3, 5, 11, 31–40, 63
› Describe the effects of starvation, fasting, and malnutrition.	Problem 6
› List some common food additives and their purposes.	Problems 7–9, 12, 13, 15, 16, 41, 42, 44, 46–48, 64, 67
› Identify and describe some of the main problems with harmful substances in our food.	Problems 47, 48
› Identify common molecules derived from food sources.	Problems 69, 71
› Distinguish polar molecules from nonpolar molecules and predict which can be extracted with ethanol or supercritical carbon dioxide.	Problem 70
› Describe how green chemistry has made the extraction of natural products, bioactive food components, and essential oils from plants safer and less hazardous.	Problems 71, 72

REVIEW QUESTIONS

1. What is the role of carbohydrates in the diet?
2. What functions do fats serve?
3. Which vitamins and minerals are organic and which are inorganic?
4. What is the role of proteins in the diet?
5. Is an excess of a water-soluble vitamin or an excess of a fat-soluble vitamin more likely to be dangerous? Why?
6. What is starvation?
7. What is a food additive?
8. What are the two major categories of food additives? Give an example of each.
9. What is MSG?
10. What is botulism? What are aflatoxins?
11. What fat-soluble vitamin serves as an antioxidant?

12. Name three artificial sweeteners. Which are approved for current use in the United States?
13. What is the chemical nature of aspartame?
14. List some contaminants that have been found in foods.
15. List five functions of food additives.
16. What U.S. government agency regulates the use of food additives? What must be done before a company can use a new food additive?

PROBLEMS

Carbohydrates

17. What are the chemical names of the following sugars?
    a. blood sugar
    b. table sugar
    c. fruit sugar
18. What is the main sugar in corn syrup? How is high-fructose corn syrup made?
19. What type of chemical reaction is involved in the digestion of starch?
20. What sugar is formed when starch is digested?

Fats and Cholesterol

21. What type of chemical reaction is involved in the digestion of fats? What products are formed?
22. Where is fat stored in the body?
23. How do animal fats differ from vegetable oils?
24. What is a *trans* fat? How are *trans* fats made?

Proteins

25. What is an adequate protein? List some foods that contain adequate proteins.
26. What is the limiting reactant in any protein synthesis?
27. Which essential amino acids are likely to be lacking in corn? In beans?
28. What is kwashiorkor? What age group in developed countries suffers a similar condition?
29. *Ezekiel* 4:9 describes a bread made from "wheat, and barley, and beans, and lentils, and millet, and spelt . . . ." Would the bread supply complete protein?
30. How do dietary proteins differ from dietary carbohydrates and fats in elemental composition?

Minerals

31. Give a biological function for the dietary mineral or a name to match the biological function.
    a. thyroid (regulating metabolism)
    b. iron
    c. bones and teeth, heartbeat rhythm
    d. phosphorus
32. Of the minerals Ca, Cl, Co, Mo, Na, P, and Zn, which is likely to be found in relatively large amounts in the human body? Explain.

Vitamins

33. Classify the following vitamins as water soluble or fat soluble.

Pantothenic acid

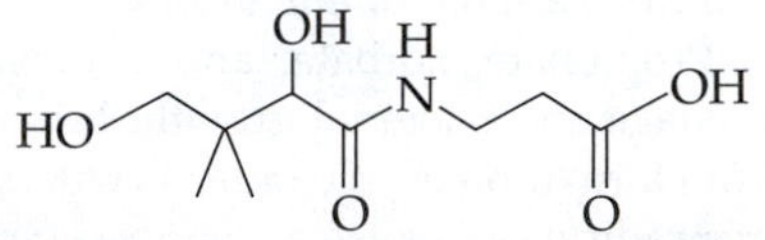

HO OH H N OH O O

Phyllloquinone

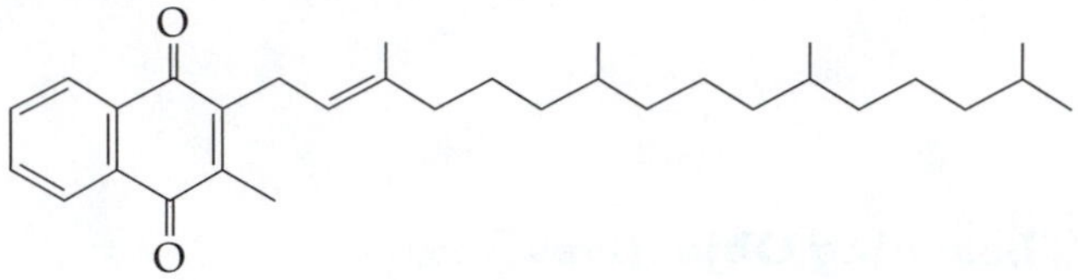

O O

Biotin

O N N H H OH S O

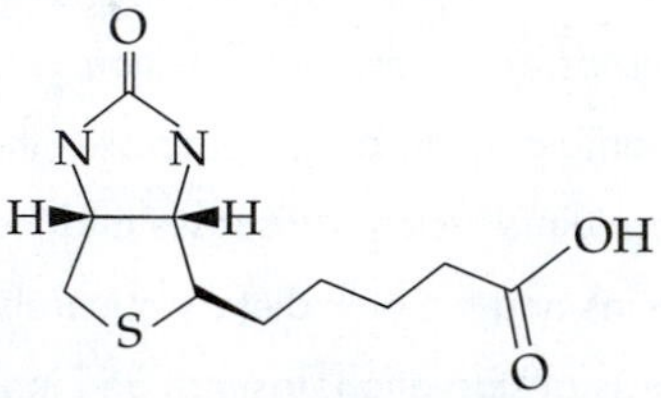

34. Coenzyme Q_{10} (CoQ_{10}; shown below) is claimed by some to have vitamin-like activity: It prevents oxidation of LDLs and may act as an antihypertensive, perhaps reducing the risk of cardiovascular disease. CoQ_{10} belongs to a family of substances called *ubiquinones* and is synthesized in the body. **(a)** Is CoQ_{10} a vitamin? **(b)** Is it fat soluble or water soluble?

CoQ_{10}

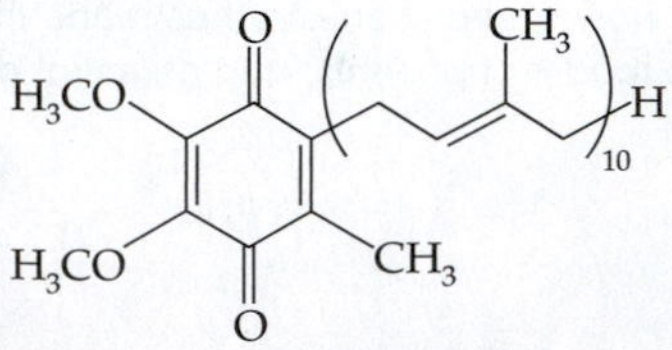

H_3CO O CH_3 H 10 H_3CO CH_3 O

35. Match the compound with its designation as a vitamin.

Compound	Designation
ascorbic acid	vitamin A
calciferol	vitamin B_{12}
cyanocobalamin	vitamin C
retinol	vitamin D
tocopherol	vitamin E

36. Which of the following are B vitamins?
a. niacin
b. phylloquinone
c. pyridoxine
d. calciferol
e. ascorbic acid

37. Name a vitamin that prevents the deficiency disease or a disease that the vitamin prevents.
a. pellagra
b. beriberi
c. cyanocobalamin (vitamin B_{12})

38. Name a vitamin that prevents the deficiency disease or a disease that the vitamin prevents.
a. scurvy b. retinol c. α-tocopherol

39. Identify each of the following vitamins as water soluble or fat soluble.
a. vitamin A
b. vitamin B_6
c. vitamin B_{12}
d. vitamin C
e. vitamin K

40. Identify each of the following vitamins as water soluble or fat soluble.
a. calciferol
b. niacin
c. riboflavin
d. tocopherol

Food Additives

41. Identify the function of the food additive or name a food additive that has the specified function.
a. $FeCO_3$
b. disinfectant and preservative
c. potassium sorbate

42. Identify the function of the food additive or name a food additive that has the specified function.
a. potassium iodide
b. vanillin
c. flavor enhancer
d. prevent botulism

43. What is the purpose of each of the following food additives?
a. BHA b. FD&C Yellow No. 5 c. saccharin

44. What is the purpose of each of the following food additives?
a. aspartame
b. vitamin D
c. sodium hypophosphite

45. Which of the following is true about a dietary supplement labeled "natural"? It is (a) mild acting; (b) without risk of side effects; (c) always safe to use with medications; or (d) none of the above.

46. Propyl gallate is made by esterification of gallic acid, which is obtained by the hydrolysis of tannins from pods of the tara tree. Is propyl gallate a natural antioxidant?

47. What are antioxidants? Name a natural antioxidant and two synthetic antioxidants.

48. What is a chain reaction? What is the action of an antioxidant on a chain reaction?

Calorie and Nutrient Calculations

49. The label on a can of vegetable beef soup indicates that each 1-cup portion supplies 120 kcal and has 8 g of protein, 16 g of carbohydrate, and 3 g of fat. Calculate the percentages of calories that come from carbohydrate, fat, and protein.

50. The label on a can of New-Orleans–style navy beans indicates that each ½-cup serving supplies 130 kcal and has 8 g of protein, 23 g of carbohydrate, and 1.5 g of fat. Calculate the percentages of calories that come from carbohydrate, fat, and protein.

51. A ¼-cup serving of Martha Rose Shulman's asparagus-and-herb lasagna provides 5 g of fat, 6 g of carbohydrate, and 3 g of protein. About how many kilocalories does a serving of lasagna provide? What percentage of the calories comes from fat?

52. A 3-oz grilled lamb chop provides about 170 kcal, 23.5 g protein, and 6 g fat. How much carbohydrate does the lamb provide?

53. An adult female goes on a diet that provides 1200 kcal per day with no more than 25% from fat and no more than 30% of that fat being saturated fat. How much saturated fat, in grams, is permitted in this diet?

54. A very active male teenager needs about 3000 kcal per day. If the guideline of 30% or less of total calories from fat is followed, how much fat, in grams, is permitted?

ADDITIONAL PROBLEMS

55. Omega-6 fatty acids are unsaturated fatty acids in which the double bond closest to the methyl (omega) end of the molecule occurs at the sixth carbon from that end. Which of the following are omega-6 fatty acids? Refer to Table 16.1 for structures not given here.
a. palmitoleic acid, $CH_3(CH_2)_5CH{=}CH(CH_2)_7CO_2H$
b. oleic acid
c. linoleic acid
d. linolenic acid
e. arachidonic acid

56. Following are line-angle formulas for two fats. **(a)** Which is a saturated fat and which is a polyunsaturated fat? **(b)** Identify the fatty-acid units in each.

(a)

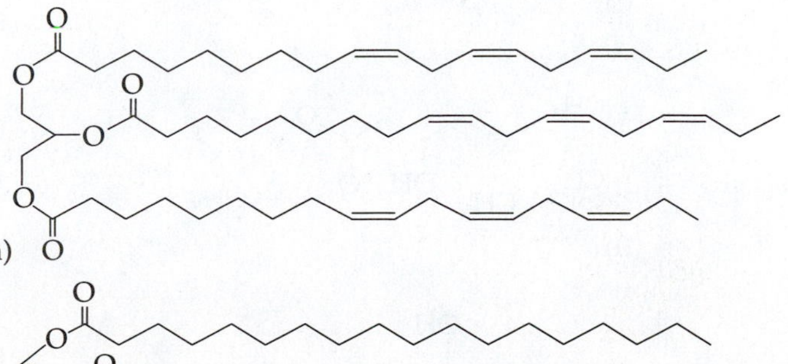

(b)

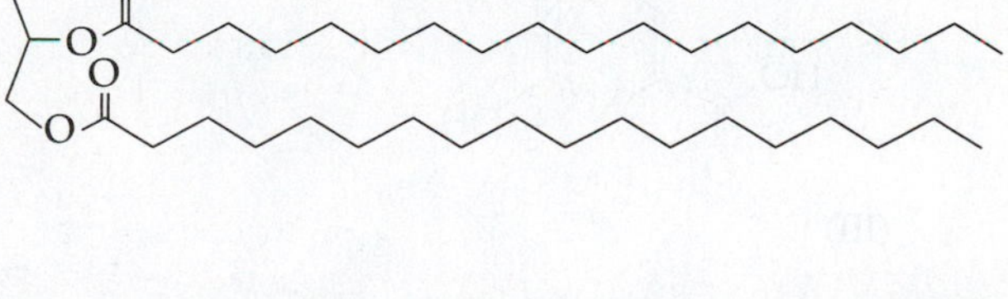

Use the nutritional labels shown below to answer Problems 57–61.

57. What percentage of the energy of whole milk comes from fat?

58. Based on a 2200-kcal diet, what percentage of the maximum daily amount of cholesterol does a cup of whole milk provide?

59. Based on a 2200-kcal diet, what percentage of the maximum daily amount of saturated fat does a cup of whole milk provide?

60. A student drinks 4 cups of fat-free milk in a day and wants to consume 60 g per day of protein. What percentage of that protein is obtained from the milk?

61. What percentage of the calories in fat-free milk comes **(a)** from sugars and **(b)** from protein?

62. Shown below are three substances sold as nutritional supplements. Pangamic acid (I) has not been shown to be required in the human diet. Dietary deficiency in pangamic acid is not associated with any disease. Carnitine (II) is synthesized in the body from the amino acids lysine and methionine. It is required for the transport of fatty acids from the cellular fluid into the mitochondria during the breakdown of fats. Orotic acid (III) Is manufactured in the body by intestinal microorganisms. For each substance: **(a)** Is it likely to be water soluble or fat soluble? **(b)** Is it a vitamin?

(I)

(II)

(III)

63. Of the vitamins calciferol, riboflavin, retinol, and cyanocobolamin, which are most likely to be needed on a daily basis? Explain.

64. Sodium saccharin and sucralose (Figure 17.13) are both readily soluble in water, but for somewhat different reasons. Explain.

65. Pioneers in the United States made heavy use of butter, beef tallow, and lard for their long treks across the country. One reason for this was the ready availability of these fats. But even if canola oil, soybean oil, and similar oils had been available, they probably would not have been used much. Consult Table 16.2 and suggest a chemical reason that is related to storage.

66. A diet that includes a lot of meat makes less efficient use of the energy originally captured by plants through photosynthesis than a vegetarian diet does. Explain.

67. When eating a thick canned soup such as beef vegetable soup, you may notice that the liquid in the soup becomes thinner as you eat. Suggest a reason for this phenomenon. (*Hint:* Starches are used as thickeners in some soups.)

68. What structural differences are there between sucrose (Figure 16.5) and sucralose (Figure 17.13)?

69. Match each natural product with the food(s) in which it can be found.

a. lycopene	1. algae and green vegetables
b. resveratrol	2. plums and red grapes
c. allicin	3. tomatoes, grapefruit, and watermelon
d. chlorophyll	4. garlic

70. Identify each of the following molecules as polar or nonpolar, and state whether the compound could be extracted efficiently by supercritical carbon dioxide.
    - **a.** cholesterol
    - **b.** sodium chloride
    - **c.** oxalic acid
    - **d.** limonene

71. List the advantages of supercritical carbon dioxide over methylene chloride (CH_2Cl_2) as a solvent for extraction of a substance from food.

72. List the advantages of supercritical carbon dioxide over methylene chloride as a solvent for extraction of a substance from food.

 COLLABORATIVE GROUP PROJECTS

Prepare a PowerPoint, poster, or other presentation (as directed by your instructor) to share with the class.

1. The Calorie Control Council lists several fat substitutes. Prepare a brief report on one of them.
2. Prepare a brief report on one of the minerals listed in Table 17.3. Identify principal dietary sources and uses of the mineral.
3. Prepare a brief report on one of the vitamins listed in Table 17.4. Identify principal dietary sources and uses of the vitamin.
4. Examine the label on each of the following. Make a list of the food additives in each. Try to determine the function of each additive. Do all the labels provide this information?
   a. a can of soft drink
   b. a can of beer
   c. a box of dried soup mix
   d. a can of soup
   e. a can of fruit drink
   f. a cake mix box
5. Prepare a brief report on one of the following dietary supplements. What is the presumed function of each?
   a. acidophilus
   b. androstenedione
   c. coenzyme Q_{10}
   d. diindolylmethane
   e. glucosamine
   f. L-arginine
   g. St. John's wort
   h. valerian
6. Prepare a brief report on one of the following chemical contaminants found in food in the past. Is the contaminant still found in food today?
   a. acrylamide
   b. bisphenol A
   c. DDT
   d. DES
   e. melamine
   f. perchlorates

Drugs

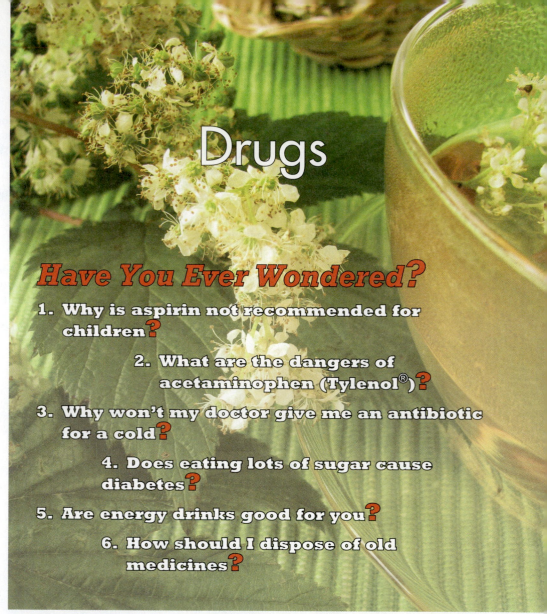

Learning Objectives

- Identify common drugs as natural, semisynthetic, or synthetic. (18.1)
- Define *chemotherapy*, and explain its origin. (18.1)
- List the common OTC analgesics, antipyretics, and anti-inflammatory drugs, and describe how each works. (18.2)
- Name several common narcotics, describe how each functions, and state its potential for addiction. (18.2)
- List the common antibacterial drugs, and describe the action of each. (18.3)
- Name the common antiviral drugs, and describe the action of each. (18.3)
- Describe the action of the common types of anticancer drugs. (18.4)
- Define the terms *hormone, prostaglandin,* and *steroid,* and explain the function of each. (18.5)
- List the three types of sex hormones, and explain how each acts and how birth control drugs work. (18.5)
- Describe the action of four types of drugs used to treat heart disease. (18.6)
- Explain how the brain amines norepinephrine and serotonin affect the mind and how various drugs change their action. (18.7)
- Identify some stimulant drugs, depressant drugs, and psychotropic drugs, and describe how they affect the mind. (18.7)
- Differentiate between drug abuse and drug misuse. (18.8)
- Differentiate between a placebo and a nocebo. (18.8)
- Explain how green chemistry can be applied to the manufacture of drugs.
- Identify green chemistry principles that contribute to improving the E-factor of a chemical synthesis.

Have You Ever Wondered?

1. Why is aspirin not recommended for children?
2. What are the dangers of acetaminophen (Tylenol®)?
3. Why won't my doctor give me an antibiotic for a cold?
4. Does eating lots of sugar cause diabetes?
5. Are energy drinks good for you?
6. How should I dispose of old medicines?

Chemical Cures, Comforts, and Cautions

The word *drug* originally referred to a dried plant (or plant part) used as a medicine, either directly or after extracting active ingredients as a tea. Today, a **drug** is defined as a chemical substance that affects the functioning of living things. Drugs are used to relieve pain, to treat illnesses, and to improve one's health or well-being. Many people literally owe their lives to drugs. Drugs can kill bacteria, lower blood pressure, prevent seizures, relieve allergies, and do many other remarkable things.

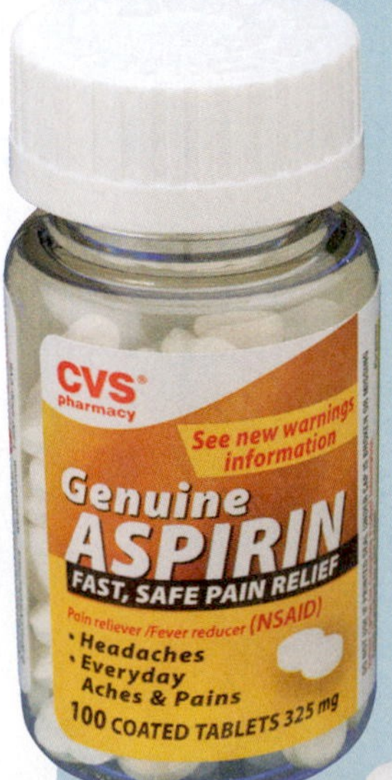

Spirea, or *meadowsweet,* contains salicylates, which became the basis for aspirin, the most widely used drug in the world. French chemist Charles Frédéric Gerhardt made crude acetylsalicylic acid (o-$CH_3COOC_6H_4COOH$) by reacting sodium salicylate (o-HOC_6H_4COONa) with acetyl chloride (CH_3COCl). *Aspirin,* Bayer's brand name, came from *acetylated Spirsäure,* the German name for salicylic acid, with the typical drug-naming ending *-in* added. In this chapter, we will look at natural and synthetic drugs that are intended to combat a wide range of ills, as well as those that see illicit use.

We still obtain many drugs from natural sources; the following examples are or have been obtained from plants.

- Quinine, the antimalarial drug, from the bark of *Cinchona* species
- Morphine, the analgesic, from the opium poppy
- Digoxin, for heart disorders, from *Digitalis purpurea* (page 561)
- Vinblastine and vincristine, anticancer agents from the Madagascar periwinkle *(Catharanthus roseus)*
- The anticancer drug paclitaxel (Taxol), first obtained from the bark of the Pacific yew tree *(Taxus brevifolia)*
- Tubocurarine, the muscle relaxant, from *Chondrodendron tomentosum*, used by Amazon natives in the arrow poison curare

Many other drugs are obtained from microorganisms, including the following important ones.

- Antibacterial agents (penicillins) and cholesterol-lowering agents (statins) from *Penicillium* species
- Immunosuppressants, such as cyclosporins, from *Streptomyces* species

A potential vast resource for new drugs is marine organisms. The following are some drugs from the sea.

- The anticancer drug dolastatin-10 from a sea hare
- An anti-inflammatory agent manoalide from the sponge *Luffariella variabilis*
- Ziconotide, a drug for treatment of severe pain, derived from cone snail venom

▲ Opium poppy.

▲ Madagascar periwinkle.

▲ Pacific yew tree *(Taxus brevifolia)*.

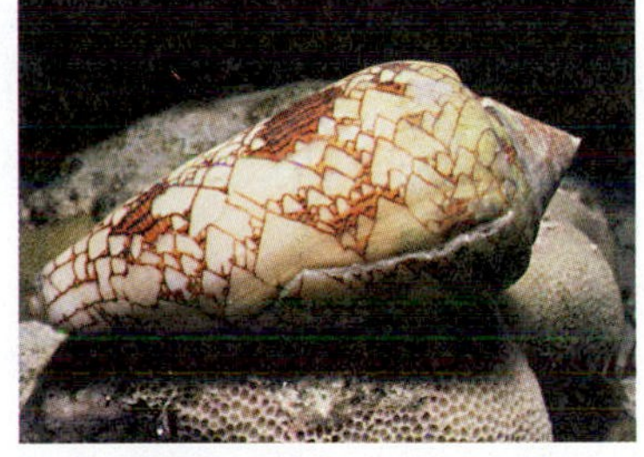

▲ Cone snail *(Conus textile)*.

18.1 Scientific Drug Design

Learning Objectives › Identify common drugs as natural, semisynthetic, or synthetic. › Define *chemotherapy*, and explain its origin.

Starting with molecules from natural sources, chemists make modifications to improve the substances' properties. These drugs are said to be *semisynthetic*. Many of the earliest science-based drugs were semisynthetic. Examples include the following.

- Salicylic acid (first obtained from willow bark) was converted to acetylsalicylic acid (aspirin).
- Morphine (from opium poppies) was converted to heroin.
- Lysergic acid (from ergot fungus) was converted to LSD.

There are now many completely synthetic drugs on the market. These substances are represented in nearly all categories, from antibacterial drugs to sleeping pills to narcotics such as methadone and fentanyl.

Drugs are used to treat, diagnose, and prevent diseases. People use drugs for many reasons—to relieve pain, to fight infections, to stay awake, to get to sleep, to calm anxiety, to prevent conception, and to treat various conditions from arthritis to heart disease to pneumonia to cancer. Many types of drugs can, however, do more harm than good, especially if used in the wrong amounts or for the wrong reasons.

Technically, there is no legal definition for "natural." The word is commonly used to describe those materials that are extracted directly from plant or animal sources by physical processes, as opposed to materials formed by chemical reactions.

▲ Some cults in ancient Greece worshiped opium. This Greek coin from that period shows an opium poppy capsule to the left of the head.

Humans have used drugs since prehistoric times, and drug use occurs in all cultures. Most societies have used alcohol, and the use of marijuana goes back to at least 3000 B.C.E. The narcotic effect of the opium poppy was known to the Greeks in the third century B.C.E, and the Indians of the Andes Mountains have long chewed leaves of the coca plant for the stimulating effect of the cocaine.

In 1904, Paul Ehrlich (1854–1915), a German chemist, found that certain dyes used to stain bacteria to make them more visible under a microscope could also be used to kill the bacteria. He used dyes to combat the organism that causes African sleeping sickness. He also prepared an arsenic compound that proved somewhat effective against the organism that causes syphilis. Ehrlich realized that certain chemicals were more toxic to disease organisms than to human cells and could therefore be used to control or cure infectious diseases. He coined the term **chemotherapy** (from "chemical therapy"). Ehrlich was awarded the Nobel Prize in Physiology or Medicine in 1908.

Drug industry sales worldwide in 2010 totaled more than $860 billion. In 2010, Americans had 4.0 billion prescriptions filled, an average of about 13 per person, and spent about $307 billion for prescription drugs.

The use of drugs is not new, but never before has there been such a vast array of them. There are dozens of pharmaceutical companies producing thousands of drugs. Their research laboratories spend huge sums to develop new drugs each year. According to a 2010 study by C. P. Adams, a Federal Trade Commission (FTC) economist, and V. V. Brantneran, an FTC research analyst, it costs an estimated $1 billion to develop a new drug. (The cost varies substantially depending on the kind of drug.) That cost means that companies must often charge high prices for the products they develop, at least for a while, making them unaffordable for many of the people who need them. After the patent rights expire, other companies can make generic versions of the same products and sell them at lower prices because they have incurred no research costs. Generic drugs must act identically to the original products.

Because many drugs are sold under generic names and several different brand names, there are thousands of prescription medicines on the market. Several hundred other medicines are available over the counter (OTC) under thousands of brand names and in many combinations. Some of these drugs are vital to the health of the people who take them. Other drugs are mainly recreational and can be quite destructive. Many of these are addictive, and most are also illegal. In this chapter, we look at some of the many drugs that are available today.

Self-Assessment Questions

For questions 1–3, match each drug in the left column with the correct category in the right column.

1. digitalis — a. natural
2. heroin — b. semisynthetic
3. morphine — c. synthetic
4. Chemotherapy is
   a. improving one's health by avoiding chemicals
   b. improving one's mind by studying chemistry
   c. treating cancer with radiation
   d. treating a disease with chemicals

Answers: 1, a; 2, b; 3, a; 4, d

18.2 Pain Relievers: From Aspirin to Oxycodone

Learning Objectives › List the common OTC analgesics, antipyretics, and anti-inflammatory drugs, and describe how each works. › Name several common narcotics, describe how each functions, and state its potential for addiction.

Acetylsalicylic acid, commonly called *aspirin* in the United States, is widely used around the world. About 40 million kg are consumed annually—enough to make 100 billion standard tablets. Its history goes back at least 2400 years to the time of

Hippocrates in ancient Greece, who knew that sick people could ease their pain and lower their fever by chewing willow leaves. Even earlier, the Old Testament (Leviticus 23:40) tells the Israelites to "take you on the first day the boughs of goodly trees, . . . and willows of the brook."

It was not until 1835 that chemists isolated the active ingredient, salicylic acid (page 255), an effective **analgesic** (pain reliever), **antipyretic** (fever reducer), and **anti-inflammatory** that, unfortunately, also caused considerable stomach distress and bleeding. Aspirin was introduced in 1893 by the Bayer Company in Germany. Acetylsalicylic acid had the desirable medicinal properties of salicylic acid, but it was gentler to the stomach.

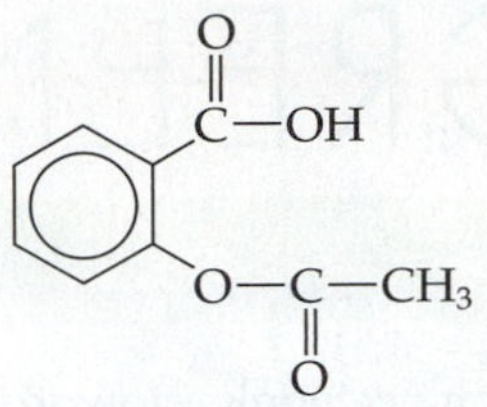

Aspirin tablets are sold under a variety of trade names and store brands. A standard aspirin tablet contains 325 mg of acetylsalicylic acid held together with an inert binder such as starch. "Extra strength" formulations usually contain 500 mg.

▲ Acetylsalicylic acid (aspirin).

Nonsteroidal Anti-Inflammatory Drugs (NSAIDs)

Aspirin is one of several substances called **nonsteroidal anti-inflammatory drugs (NSAIDs)**, a designation that distinguishes these drugs from the more potent steroidal anti-inflammatory drugs such as cortisone and prednisone (Section 18.5). Other NSAIDs include ibuprofen (Advil®, Motrin®), naproxen (Aleve®), and ketoprofen (Orudis®) (Figure 18.1). Acetaminophen, like aspirin, relieves minor aches and reduces fever but is not anti-inflammatory and is therefore not an NSAID.

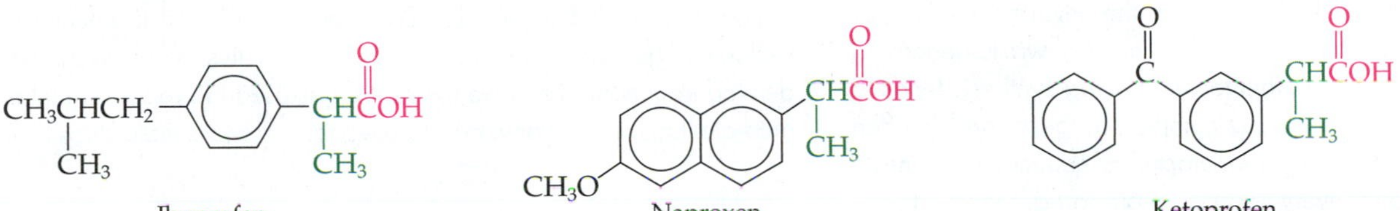

Ibuprofen

Naproxen

Ketoprofen

▲ **Figure 18.1** Three NSAIDs. Ibuprofen, naproxen, and ketoprofen are derivatives of propionic acid (CH_3CH_2COOH).

NSAIDs act to relieve pain and reduce inflammation by inhibiting the production of **prostaglandins**, hormone-like lipids that are derived from a fatty acid and are involved in sending pain messages to the brain (Section 18.5). Thus, NSAIDs don't cure whatever is causing the pain; they merely "kill the messenger." Inflammation is caused by an overproduction of prostaglandin derivatives, and inhibition of their synthesis reduces the inflammatory process.

Regrettably, for those who take NSAIDs regularly, prostaglandins also affect the blood platelets, the kidneys, and the stomach lining, leading to the side effects most often associated with taking NSAIDs: excessive bleeding and stomach pains. The anticoagulant effect (inhibition of the clotting of blood) of NSAIDs often leads to complications in patients taking NSAIDs for treatment of arthritis. About 1.5% of patients with rheumatoid arthritis taking NSAIDs for a year had a serious stomach complication. This is a small proportion, but it translates to a large number of people because of the vast number of patients taking NSAIDs.

Because NSAIDs act as anticoagulants, small daily doses seem to lower the risk of heart attack and stroke, presumably by the same anticoagulant action that causes bleeding in the stomach. Adult low-strength (usually 81 mg) aspirin tablets are now routinely used by people at risk for heart attack and stroke. NSAIDs should not be used by people facing surgery, childbirth, or some other hazard involving the possible loss of blood (they should be withheld for at least a week before the event).

NSAIDs also reduce body temperature. Fevers are induced by substances called *pyrogens*, compounds produced by and released from leukocytes (white blood cells) and other circulating cells. Pyrogens usually use prostaglandins as secondary mediators. Fevers therefore can be reduced by aspirin and other prostaglandin inhibitors. Pyrogens that do not work through prostaglandins are not affected by NSAIDs.

▲ **It DOES Matter!**
Almost every single-ingredient analgesic product sold today uses one of four active ingredients: acetaminophen, aspirin, ibuprofen, or naproxen. These drugs are available in generic forms, under dozens of brand names, and in many combinations, including cough/cold and allergy/sinus products. They are often combined with caffeine in OTC products and with codeine, hydrocodone, or oxycodone in prescription pain medicines. You can search the Internet for brand names, using the generic names as key words.

GREEN CHEMISTRY

Principles 1, 2, 5, 9

Joseph Fortunak, *Howard University*

Green Pharmaceuticals

This chapter discusses a common set of principles for finding new medicines—scientists investigate the pathway of a disease, then choose a molecular target to interrupt the progression of the disease. Since drugs must be selective and safe, newer drugs tend to be structurally complex and to require lengthy syntheses. Because companies spend about twice the amount of money on manufacturing as on new drug research and development, there is a powerful incentive to implement green chemistry to reduce waste and cost. Green chemistry essays in Chapters 4 and 9 discussed organic synthesis and drug manufacturing. Now that you have learned how drugs target bacterial infections, cancer, and pain, we'll discuss some examples of how green chemistry principles apply to the production of drugs.

In 1992, Roger Sheldon (University of Delft, Netherlands) coined the term *E-factor*, which stands for the environmental factor for chemical production. The E-factor is the mass of waste generated for each kilogram of product manufactured. Drug synthesis tends to use large amounts of solvents and complex reagents and is often energy intensive. In fact, drug manufacturers commonly generate over 100 kg of waste for every kg of drug prepared, for an E-factor greater than 100. Syntheses using aqueous reactions, enzymatic processes, catalysts that mimic biological processes, and without hazardous solvents are increasingly used to make drug synthesis more efficient and green (Principles 5 and 9).

Drugs that exist as stereoisomers (see Figure 18.18) almost always require dosage in a single isomeric form. An example is pregabalin (Lyrica®), used to treat fibromyalgia and neuropathic pain, which had sales of almost \$3 billion in 2010. Only one isomer of the molecule can bind to a subunit of the calcium-ion channels in the central nervous system and block abnormal pain signals. The original synthesis of pregabalin provided a mixture of mirror images that were separated, with the "wrong" isomer being discarded—a process that led to an E-factor greater than 85.

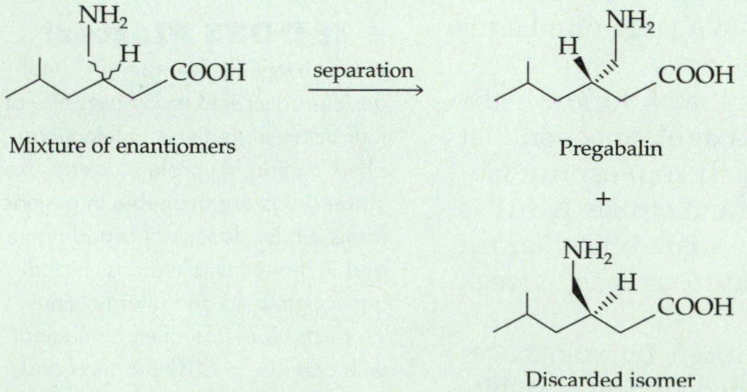

NH_2, H, COOH — Mixture of enantiomers —separation→ NH_2, H, COOH — Pregabalin + NH_2, H, COOH — Discarded isomer

A new synthesis of pregabalin was developed by the drug company Pfizer, which originally brought pregabalin to the market. It took advantage of an enzyme known as *lipolase*. In this powerful example of the use of *biocatalysis* for green chemistry, the wrong mirror image can be recycled and used instead of being discarded. This method reduced the E-factor to 12.

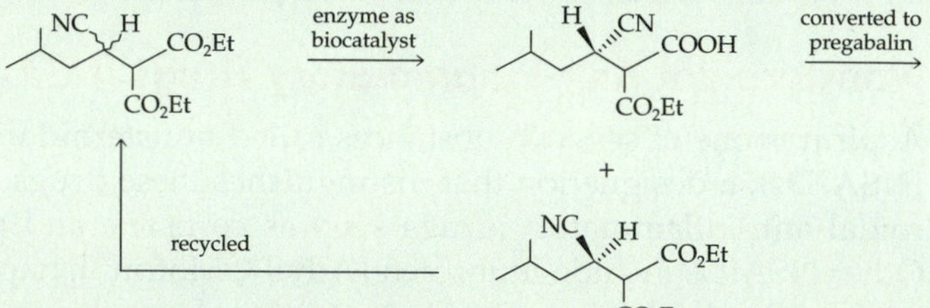

NC, H, CO_2Et, CO_2Et —enzyme as biocatalyst→ H, CN, COOH, CO_2Et —converted to pregabalin→
\+ NC, H, CO_2Et, CO_2Et (recycled)

An elegant synthesis of pregabalin that may turn out to be even more efficient was reported by the Tokyo University of Science. This method relies on an exciting development in biocatalysis—small amino acids and their simple derivatives were found to effectively replace larger, more expensive catalysts. In this case, a catalyst derived from natural proline (page 465) is used to prepare an intermediate that can be converted to pregabalin in two simple steps.

O, C, H —(N, H, Ph, Ph, $OSi(CH_3)_3$ (from proline)), CH_3NO_2→ NO_2, O, C, H — Easily converted to pregabalin

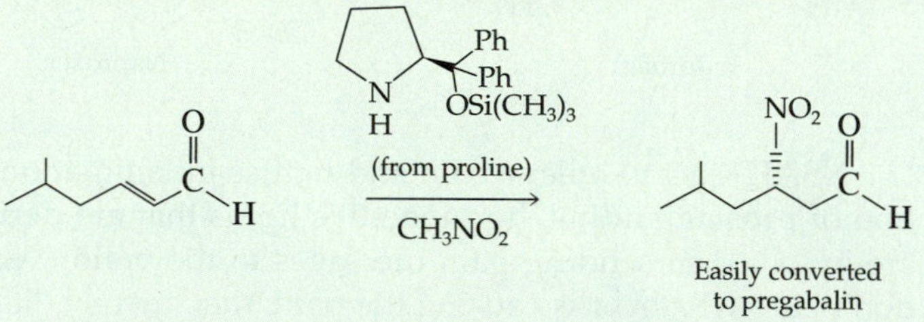

These methods of synthesis of a single drug illustrate Green Chemistry Principles 1, 2, 5, and 9. Subsequent iterations of a synthetic process demonstrate the evolutionary improvement of chemical manufacturing over time, as the success of a drug drives the need for improved chemistry.

Another interesting application of green chemistry in the synthesis of drugs is the development of biocatalytic evolution of enzymes. Most "wild" enzymes that catalyze reactions are imperfect. They often achieve low conversion, require high energy input, and do not work in the presence of organic solvents. Further, they can be costly and easily inactivated. The directed evolution of enzymes has led to catalysts that are many times more active than their natural precursors. An example is a biocatalyst developed by the company Codexis that is used to produce N-acetylneuraminic acid (NANA), an intermediate in the synthesis of several antiviral drugs. Codexis developed a "one-pot, two-enzyme" process to produce NANA.

Green chemistry has become more important as drug molecules have become increasingly complex and more difficult to produce with high chemical efficiency. The expense and high E-factors common to drug manufacturing have provided incentives for the development of a variety of green chemistry approaches. As detailed here, more efficient syntheses, use of enzymes, and biocatalysis are important components of these improvements.

The body tries to fight off infection by elevating its temperature. Mild fevers in adults (those below 39 °C, or 102 °F) are usually best left untreated. High fevers, however, can cause brain damage and require immediate treatment.

1. Why is aspirin not recommended for children? The use of aspirin in children suffering from the flu or chickenpox is associated with *Reye's syndrome*, a potentially fatal illness. For this reason, aspirin products carry a warning that they should not be used to treat children with fevers.

How NSAIDs Work

Prostaglandins are produced in the body from a cell membrane component called *arachidonic acid* (Section 18.5). Scientists have identified enzymes called *cyclooxygenases* (COX) that catalyze the conversion. Two of these are COX-1, found in stomach and kidney tissues where NSAID side effects occur, and COX-2, found in tissues where inflammation occurs. The older NSAIDs, such as aspirin, ibuprofen, ketoprofen, and naproxen, inhibit both COX-1 and COX-2, providing relief from pain and inflammation but also producing undesirable side effects. Newer NSAIDs preferentially inhibit COX-2. Three COX-2 inhibitors came onto the market as anti-inflammatory agents claiming to have fewer NSAID-type side effects than the older drugs. However, two of them—rofecoxib (Vioxx®) and aldecoxib (Bextra®)—were quickly removed from the market because they led to a higher risk of stroke and heart attacks.

NSAIDs marketed for use by children typically contain one-quarter of the normal adult dose per tablet, with fewer tablets per bottle than their adult counterparts. These measures significantly reduce the possibility of an accidental overdose.

Celecoxib (Celebrex®) (Figure 18.2) remains on the market but carries a new warning label, called a "black box" warning because it is the strongest warning that a medicine label can provide. The U.S. Food and Drug Administration (FDA) now requires labels on all prescription NSAIDs to include a boxed warning highlighting the potential for increased risk of heart problems, as well as information regarding allergic reactions and internal bleeding.

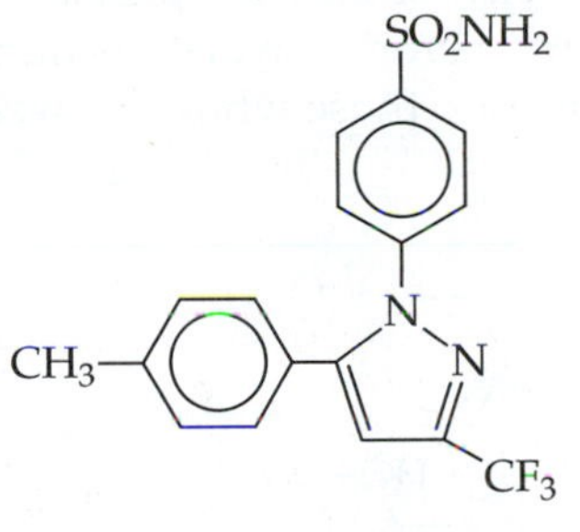

Celecoxib (Celebrex®)

◀ **Figure 18.2** Celecoxib is the only COX-2 inhibiting prescription NSAID that remains on the market.

Acetaminophen: A COX-3 Inhibitor

Acetaminophen, perhaps best known by the brand name Tylenol®, is the most widely used analgesic in the United States. It provides relief of pain and reduction of fever comparable to that of aspirin. The total world market for acetaminophen (called *paracetamol* in many countries) is about 110 million kg/year. Unlike NSAIDs, acetaminophen is not effective against inflammation, and it is not an anticoagulant. People allergic to aspirin or susceptible to bleeding can safely take acetaminophen, but it is of limited use to people with arthritis. Acetaminophen is often used to relieve the pain that follows minor surgery. Regular acetaminophen tablets contain 325 mg, and extra-strength forms 500 mg. Overuse of acetaminophen, especially when combined with alcohol, has been linked to liver and kidney damage.

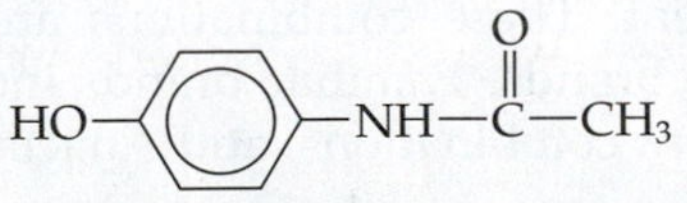

2. What are the dangers of acetaminophen (Tylenol®)? Although the normal dose of acetaminophen is safe, large doses are quite toxic, causing liver damage. This effect is synergistic with alcohol. As little as 4 g (eight extra-strength tablets) in 24 hours, coupled with recent alcohol use, can cause severe liver toxicity. Accidental overdose on acetaminophen is far too common, and it often occurs because acetaminophen is an ingredient in many OTC medicines for treatment of cold symptoms, allergies, insomnia, and other maladies. A careful review of the active ingredients in such medications can save a life!

Acetaminophen

Acetaminophen acts on a third variant of cyclooxygenase enzyme, COX-3. Inhibition of COX-3 may represent a mechanism by which acetaminophen decreases pain and fever. However, COX-3 appears to have no role in inflammation.

Chemistry, Allergies, and the Common Cold

Store shelves are stocked with a variety of cold and allergy medicines, which contain antihistamines, cough suppressants, expectorants, bronchodilators, or nasal decongestants. None cure the common cold, which is caused by as many as 200 related viruses; in fact, no drug provides a cure. Most cold remedies just treat the symptoms. An FDA advisory panel reviews these substances periodically for safety and effectiveness.

Many cold medicines contain an **antihistamine**, such as diphenhydramine or cetirizine (Figure 18.3). Antihistamines relieve the symptoms of allergies: sneezing, itchy eyes, and runny nose. They don't cure colds, but they can temporarily relieve some of the symptoms.

When an **allergen** (a substance that triggers an allergic reaction) binds to the surfaces of certain cells, it triggers the release of *histamine*, which causes the redness, swelling, and itching associated with allergies. An antihistamine inhibits the release of histamine. Many cough and cold products contain more than one ingredient (see Collaborative Group Project 1).

Other OTC cold medicines include *antitussives* (cough suppressants) and *expectorants* (substances that help bring up mucus from the bronchial passages). Codeine and hydrocodone (Table 18.1, page 538) are effective antitussives but are available only by prescription; both are narcotics. Should a cough really be suppressed? Ordinarily, a cough is functional; the respiratory tract uses the coughing mechanism to rid itself of congestion. When a cough is dry or interferes with needed rest, however, temporary cough suppression may be advisable.

Only one expectorant, glyceryl guaiacolate (guaifenesin), is rated safe and effective, and its effectiveness is not well documented.

Nasal *decongestants*, such as naphazoline, phenylephrine, oxymetazoline, and xylometazoline, seem to be safe and effective for occasional use, although repeated use leads to a *rebound effect* in which the nasal passages swell and make congestion seem worse.

How should you treat a common cold? First, you should drink plenty of liquids and get lots of rest. When you are in good physical condition and have a strong immune system, colds seem to strike less often. Frequent washing of the hands, especially when colds are prevalent, can dramatically reduce transmission of the virus. Many people claim to get cold relief by using some favorite over-the-counter drug. And, of course, there are those who still swear by chicken soup!

(a) Histamine — $CH_2CH_2NH_2$

(b) Diphenhydramine — $CH{-}OCH_2CH_2{-}N(CH_3){-}CH_3$

(c) Cetirizine — $HC{-}N \; N{-}CH_2CH_2OCH_2COOH$, Cl

▲ **Figure 18.3** Histamine (a) and two antihistamines: (b) diphenhydramine (Benadryl®) and (c) cetirizine (Zyrtec®). Diphenhydramine is also used as a cough suppressant.

Q: *To what family of organic compounds do these three substances belong?*

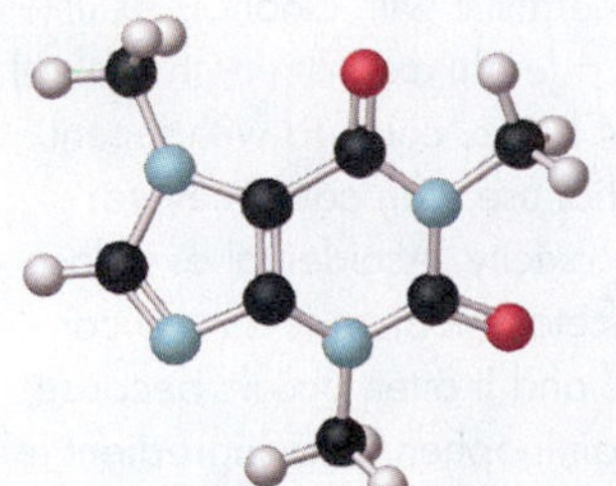

▲ Caffeine ($C_8H_{10}N_4O_2$) is a stimulant (Section 18.7) that is added to NSAIDs in some combination pain-relief formulation to speed the action of the NSAID.

Combination Pain Relievers

Many analgesic products are a combination of one or more NSAIDs, acetaminophen, caffeine, antihistamines, or other drugs. Acetaminophen, for example, is found in more than 70 combination products for pain relief, allergy symptoms, and cold and flu treatment. These combinations are available under various brand names and as store brands. Familiar brands include Excedrin, which can be purchased in six different combinations, and Anacin, which is available in five different formulations.

Many other combination pain relievers are available. Most claim some advantage over regular aspirin. However, such advantages are marginal at best. For occasional use by most people, plain aspirin may be the cheapest, safest, and most effective product.

Narcotics

When pain is too great to be relieved by OTC analgesics, stronger prescription drugs are available. Most such drugs are classified as **narcotics**, drugs that produce narcosis (stupor or general anesthesia) and analgesia (relief of pain). Many drugs produce these effects, but in the United States only those that are also *addictive* are legally classified as narcotics.

Several narcotics are products of opium, the dried, resinous juice of the unripe seeds of the opium poppy (*Papaver somniferum*) (Figure 18.4). Opium is a complex mixture of 20 or so alkaloids, plus sugars, resins, waxes, and water. The principal alkaloid, morphine, makes up about 10% of the weight of raw opium. Opium was used in many patent medicines during the nineteenth century. Laudanum, a solution of opium in alcohol, contained about 10 mg of morphine per mL of solution and was widely used during the Victorian era for everything from toothaches to tuberculosis. It was even used to quiet colicky babies. The English Romantic poets Samuel Taylor Coleridge (1772–1834), Percy Bysshe Shelley (1792–1822), and George Gordon Byron (Lord Byron) (1788–1824) were among the prominent users, along with the French poet Charles Baudelaire (1821–1867). Mary Todd Lincoln (1818–1882), wife of the sixteenth President of the United States, was prescribed laudanum for sleep problems, perhaps accounting for her anxiety and hallucinations. Paregoric, a much weaker solution that contained only 0.4 mg of morphine per mL, was also widely used, especially for diarrhea.

▲ **Figure 18.4** Opium poppy seed pod. The slits on the seed pod are exuding resinous juice, which is dried to form opium. About 10% of the weight of raw opium is morphine.

Morphine was first isolated in 1805 by Friedrich Sertürner, a German pharmacist. With the invention of the hypodermic syringe in the 1850s, a new method of administration became available. Injection of morphine directly into the bloodstream was more effective for the relief of pain, but this method also seriously escalated the problem of addiction.

Morphine was used widely during the American Civil War (1861–1865) for relief of pain due to battle wounds. One side effect of morphine use is constipation. Noting this, soldiers came to use morphine as a treatment for that other common malady of men on the battlefront—dysentery. More than 100,000 soldiers became addicted to morphine while serving in the war. The affliction was so common among veterans that it came to be known as "soldier's disease."

Morphine and other narcotics were placed under control of the federal government by the Harrison Act of 1914. Morphine is still used by prescription for the relief of severe pain. It also induces lethargy, drowsiness, confusion, euphoria, chronic constipation, and depression of the respiratory system. Morphine is addictive, which becomes a problem when it is administered in amounts greater than the prescribed dose or for a period longer than the prescribed time.

Changes in the morphine molecule alter its physiological properties. Replacement of the phenolic hydroxyl group (—OH) by a methoxy group ($-OCH_3$) produces codeine (see Additional Problem 55). Codeine is present in opium at about 0.7–2.5%, but it is usually synthesized by methylating the more abundant morphine molecules. Codeine is similar to morphine in its action, but it is less potent, has less tendency to induce sleep, and is less addictive. For relief of moderate pain, codeine is often combined with acetaminophen (for example, in Tylenol 2 and Tylenol 3) or with aspirin (in Empirin Codeine). For cough suppression, codeine is given in liquid preparations that are regulated less stringently than stronger narcotics.

Conversion of both the —OH groups of the morphine molecule to acetate ester groups produces heroin (see Additional Problem 56). This semisynthetic morphine derivative was first prepared by chemists at the Bayer Company in Germany in 1874. It received little attention until 1890, when it was proposed as an antidote for morphine addiction. Shortly thereafter, Bayer widely advertised heroin as a sedative for coughs, often in the same ads describing aspirin. However, it was soon found that heroin induced addiction more quickly than morphine and that heroin addiction was harder to cure.

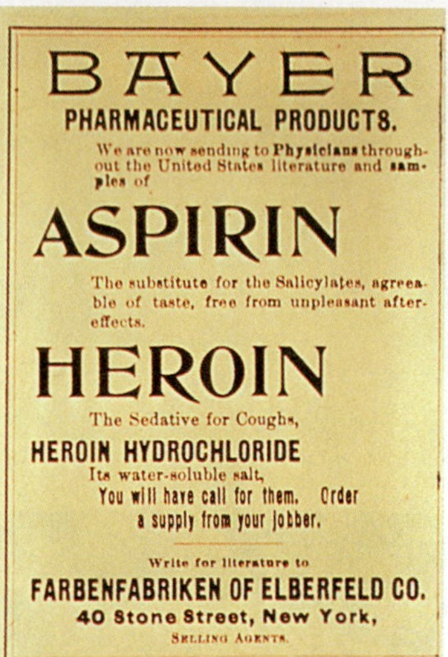

▲ Heroin was regarded as a safe medicine in 1900 and was widely used as a cough suppressant. It was also thought to be a nonaddictive substitute for morphine.

The physiological action of heroin is similar to that of morphine. Heroin is less polar than morphine. Heroin enters the fatty tissues of the brain more rapidly and seems to produce a stronger feeling of euphoria than morphine. Heroin is not legal in the United States, even by prescription. It has, however, been advocated for use in the relief of pain in terminal cancer patients and has been so used in Britain.

Addiction probably has three components: psychological dependence, physical dependence, and tolerance. Psychological dependence is evident in the uncontrollable desire for the drug. Physical dependence is shown by acute withdrawal symptoms such as convulsions. Tolerance for the drug is evidenced by the fact that increasing dosages are required to produce in an addict the same degree of narcosis and analgesia.

Deaths from heroin and other narcotics are usually attributed to overdoses, but the situation is not always clear. The problem is often a matter of quality control. Street drugs vary considerably in potency, and a particular dose can be much higher in potency than expected.

Much research has gone into developing a drug that would be as effective as morphine for the relief of pain but would not be addictive. Several synthetic narcotics are available. Some common ones are listed in Table 18.1. Structures of some of these and other narcotics are given in Figure 18.5.

Table 18.1 Some Synthetic Narcotics

Substance	Duration of Action (h)	Approximate Oral Dose (mg) Equivalent to 30 mg of Morphine
Meperidine (Demerol®)	2–4	300
Hydrocodone	4–8	20
Fentanyl	1–2[a]	< 1
Oxycodone	4–6[b]	20
Hydromorphone (Dilaudid®)	4–5	7.5
Methadone	4–6[c]	Not applicable

[a]Used in transdermal patches for chronic pain.

[b]Often dispensed in a time-release form (OxyContin®) that allows 12 h between doses.

[c]Used for treatment of heroin addiction; not usually given for pain relief.

▶ **Figure 18.5** Structural formulas of some synthetic narcotics: (a) meperidine (Demerol®), (b) methadone, (c) pentazocine (Talwin®), and (d) naloxone.

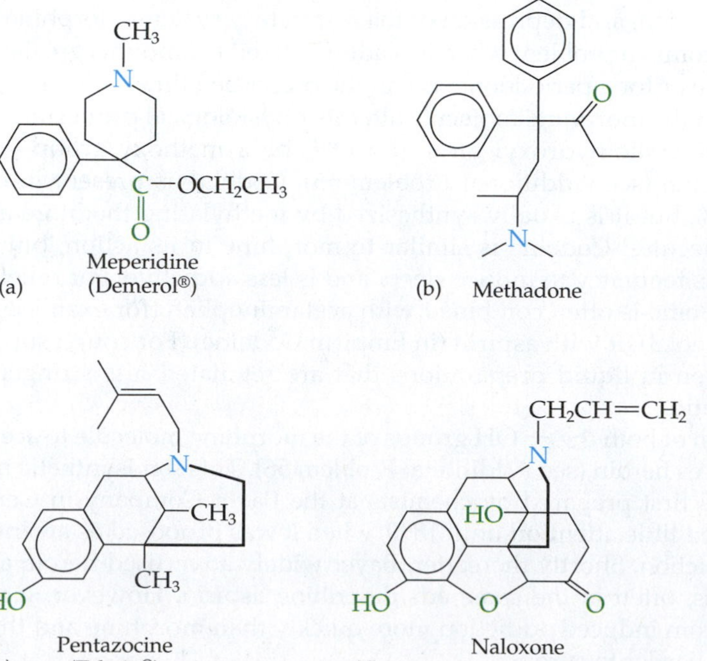

Oxycodone is a semisynthetic opioid related to codeine (see Additional Problem 57). It is used for relief of moderate to severe pain. It is available alone and in combinations with acetaminophen, ibuprofen, or aspirin. A sustained-release form of oxycodone is called OxyContin®. Abused for its euphoric effects, OxyContin and its generic equivalents are widely available illegally.

Hydrocodone, another synthetic narcotic, is always combined with acetaminophen or another medication. Sold as HYCD/APAP (hydrocodone/acetaminophen), this combination was the most prescribed drug in the United States in 2010, with 131.2 million prescriptions.

Hydrocodone

The synthetic narcotic methadone is widely used to treat heroin addiction. Like heroin, methadone is highly addictive. However, when taken orally, it does not induce the sleepy stupor characteristic of heroin intoxication. Unlike a heroin addict, a person on methadone maintenance is usually able to hold a productive job. If an addict who has been taking methadone reverts to heroin, the methadone in his or her system effectively blocks the euphoric rush normally produced by heroin and so reduces the addict's temptation to use heroin.

Morphine Agonists and Antagonists

Chemists have synthesized many morphine analogs, but relatively few have shown significant analgesic activity, and most of those are addictive. Morphine acts by binding to receptors in the brain. A morphine receptor is shaped with a flat hole that binds to the benzene ring, a cavity that binds two carbon atoms, and an anionic site that binds the nitrogen atom. A molecule that has morphine-like action is called a morphine **agonist**. A morphine **antagonist** inhibits the action of morphine by blocking morphine receptors. Some molecules have both agonist and antagonist effects. An example is pentazocine, Figure 18.5(c), which is less addictive than morphine and is effective for the relief of pain.

Pure antagonists such as naloxone, Figure 18.5(d), are used to treat opiate addicts. An addict who has overdosed can be brought back from death's door by an injection of naloxone.

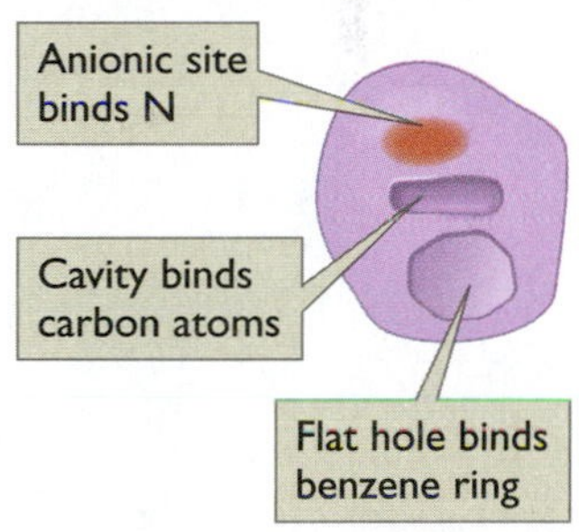

▲ Diagram of a morphine receptor.

Natural Opiates: Endorphins and Enkephalins

Morphine acts by binding to specific receptor sites in the brain. Why should the human brain have receptors for a plant-derived drug such as morphine? Scientists concluded that the body must produce its own substances that fit these receptors. Actually, it produces several morphine-like substances, called **endorphins** (from "endogenous morphines"). Each endorphin is a short peptide chain composed of amino-acid units. Those with five amino-acid units are called *enkephalins*. There are two enkephalins, which differ only in the amino acid at the end of the chain. *Leu*-enkephalin has the sequence Tyr-Gly-Gly-Phe-Leu, and *Met*-enkephalin has the sequence Tyr-Gly-Gly-Phe-Met. Other endorphins have chains of 30 or more amino acids.

Some enkephalins have been synthesized and shown to be potent pain relievers. Their use in medicine is quite limited, however, because they are rapidly broken down in the body by the enzymes that hydrolyze proteins. Researchers have sought to make analogs that are more resistant to hydrolysis and can be employed as morphine substitutes for the relief of pain. Unfortunately, both natural enkephalins and their analogs, such as morphine, seem to be addictive.

It appears that endorphins are released during strenuous exercise and in response to pain. Capsaicin (the active compound in chili peppers) can also stimulate endorphin release. Some evidence indicates that acupuncture causes the release of brain "opiates" that relieve pain. The long needles stimulate deep sensory nerves, which release peptides that then block pain signals for a brief time.

Endorphin release has also been used to explain other phenomena once thought to be largely psychological. A soldier, wounded in battle, may feel no pain until the skirmish is over. His body has secreted its own painkiller.

Self-Assessment Questions

1. An antipyretic is a(n)
   a. appetite suppressant
   b. fever reducer
   c. fire retardant
   d. gum treatment
2. NSAIDs act by inhibiting the production of
   a. endorphins
   b. ketone bodies
   c. norepinephrine
   d. prostaglandins
3. Which of the following is not an anticoagulant?
   a. acetaminophen
   b. aspirin
   c. ibuprofen
   d. naproxen
4. Allergens trigger the release of
   a. endorphins
   b. histamines
   c. prostaglandins
   d. pyrogens
5. Which of the following cures the common cold?
   a. antibiotics
   b. antihistamines
   c. nothing yet discovered
   d. vitamin C
6. An active ingredient in opium that is less abundant and less powerful than morphine is
   a. caffeine
   b. codeine
   c. methadone
   d. pentazocine
7. A semisynthetic opiate produced by adding acetyl groups to morphine molecules is
   a. heroin
   b. MDMA
   c. meperidine
   d. methadone
8. Methadone used to treat addiction is intended to
   a. act as an opiate antagonist
   b. detoxify the patient during withdrawal
   c. satisfy addicts' craving yet leave them able to function in society
   d. treat the underlying causes of addiction
9. Substances produced in the body that resemble the opiates in their effects are called
   a. endorphins
   b. oxytocins
   c. placebos
   d. thyroxins

Answers: 1, b; 2, d; 3, a; 4, b; 5, c; 6, b; 7, a; 8, c; 9, a

18.3 Drugs and Infectious Diseases

Learning Objectives › List the common antibacterial drugs, and describe the action of each. › Name the common antiviral drugs, and describe the action of each.

A century ago, infectious diseases were the main cause of death in the United States (Figure 18.6). At the time of the American Civil War, thousands of wounded soldiers required amputations of wounded arms or legs, and nearly 80% of the patients died after coming to a hospital, mostly from infections. Today, infectious disease categories have moved toward the bottom of the list of the top ten leading causes of death. (These ten causes account for more than three-quarters of all deaths in the United States.) Many diseases have been brought under control through the use of *antibacterial drugs*.

Antibacterial Drugs

The first antibacterial drugs were *sulfa drugs*, whose prototype was discovered in 1935 by the German chemist Gerhard Domagk (1895–1964). Sulfa drugs were used extensively during World War II to prevent wound infections. Many soldiers who would have died in earlier wars lived.

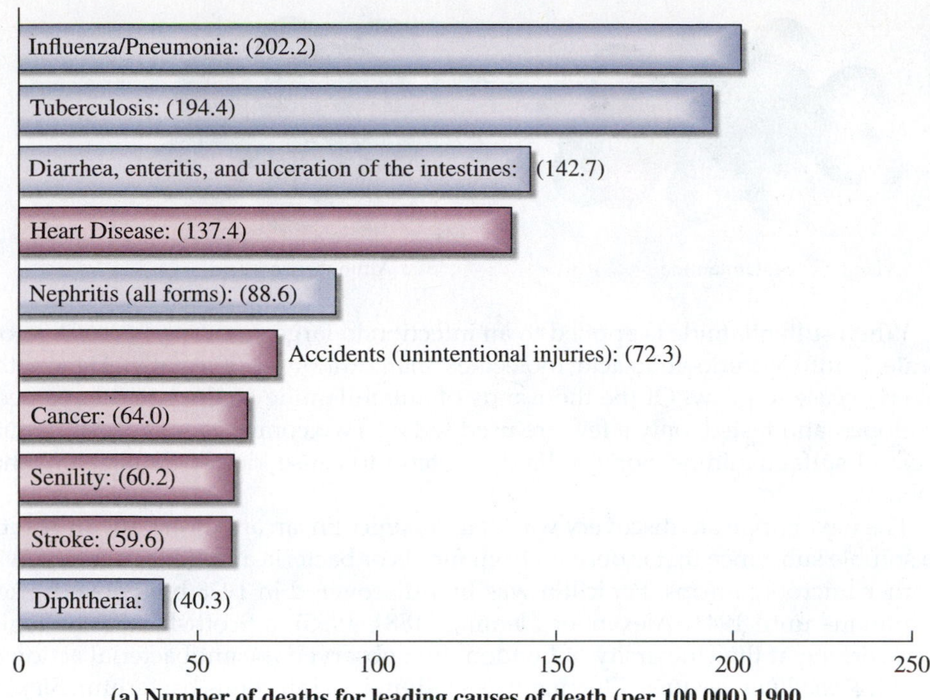

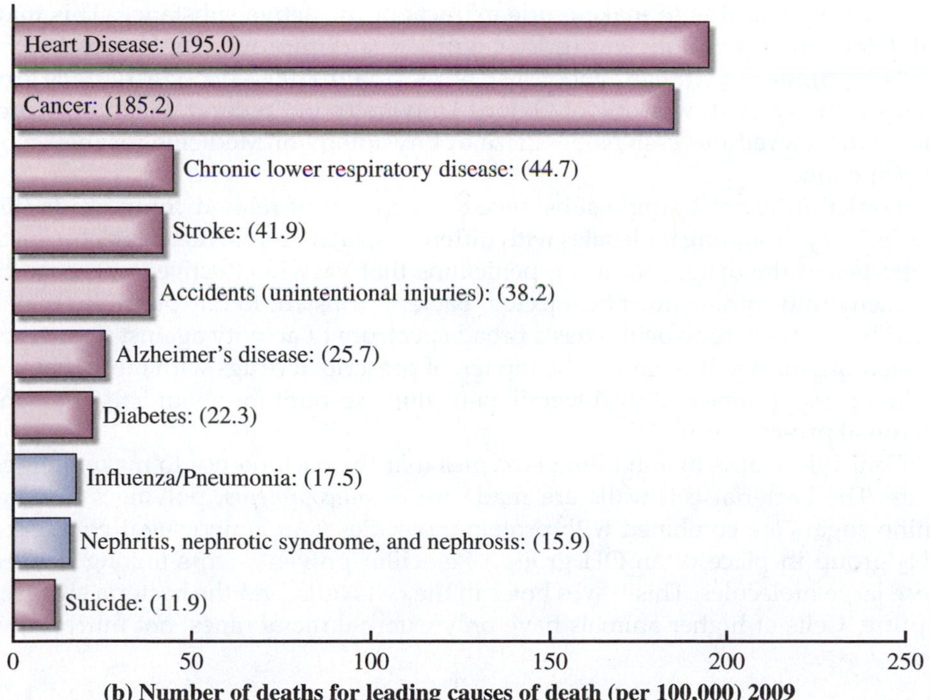

◀ **Figure 18.6** (a) In 1900, five of the ten leading causes of death—responsible for three-fifths of all deaths—in the United States were infectious diseases. (b) The leading causes of death in 2009 were so-called lifestyle diseases: heart disease, stroke, and diabetes, related in part to our diets; cancer and lung diseases, to cigarette smoking; and accidents, often to excessive consumption of alcohol.

Sulfanilamide, the simplest sulfa drug, was one of the first to have its action understood at the molecular level. Its effectiveness is based on a case of mistaken identity. Bacteria need *para*-aminobenzoic acid (PABA) to make folic acid, which is essential for the formation of certain compounds the bacteria require for proper growth. But bacterial enzymes can't tell the difference between sulfanilamide and PABA because their molecules are so similar.

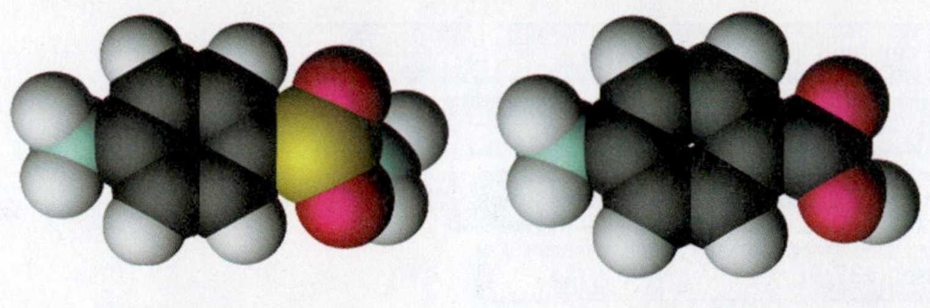

Sulfanilamide   *para*-Aminobenzoic acid

Sulfathiazole

Sulfaguanidine

When sulfanilamide is applied to an infection in large amounts, bacteria incorporate it into pseudo–folic-acid molecules that cannot act normally. Hence, the bacteria cease to grow. Of the thousands of sulfanilamide analogs that have been developed and tested, only a few are used today. Two common ones are sulfathiazole and sulfaguanidine. Some sulfa drugs tend to cause kidney damage or other problems.

The next important discovery was that of penicillin, an antibiotic. An **antibiotic** is a soluble substance that is derived from molds or bacteria and inhibits the growth of other microorganisms. Penicillin was first discovered in 1928 but was not tried on humans until 1941. Alexander Fleming (1881–1955), a Scottish microbiologist then working at the University of London, first observed the antibacterial action of a mold, *Penicillium notatum*. Fleming was studying an infectious bacterium, *Staphylococcus aureus*, and one of his cultures became contaminated with a blue mold. Contaminated cultures generally are useless. Most investigators probably would have destroyed the culture and started over, but Fleming noted that bacterial colonies had been destroyed in the vicinity of the mold.

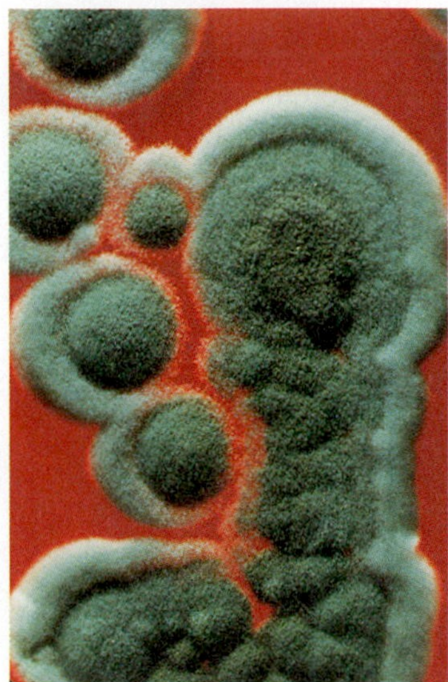

▲ Penicillin molds. These symmetrical colonies of mold are *Penicillium chrysogenum*, a mutant form of which produces nearly all commercial penicillin.

Fleming was able to make crude extracts of the active substance. This material, later called *penicillin*, was further purified and improved by Howard Florey (1898–1968), an Australian, and Ernst Boris Chain (1906–1979), a refugee from Nazi Germany, both working at Oxford University in England. Fleming, Florey, and Chain shared the 1945 Nobel Prize in Physiology or Medicine for their work on penicillin.

Penicillin is not a single substance but a group of related compounds (Figure 18.7). By designing molecules with different structures, chemists can change the properties of the drug, producing penicillins that vary in effectiveness. Some can be taken orally; others must be injected. Bacteria resistant to one penicillin may be killed by another. Amoxicillin has a broad spectrum of activity against many types of microorganisms. It is among the top ten of prescribed drugs with more than 52.3 million prescriptions in 2010. Overall, penicillins account for about half of all antimicrobial prescriptions.

Penicillin works by inhibiting enzymes that the bacteria use to make their cell walls. The bacterial cell walls are made up of *mucoproteins*, polymers in which amino sugars are combined with protein molecules. (An amino sugar contains an NH_2 group in place of an OH group.) Penicillin prevents cross-linking between these large molecules. This leaves holes in the cell walls, and the bacteria swell and rupture. Cells of higher animals have only external membranes, not mucoprotein

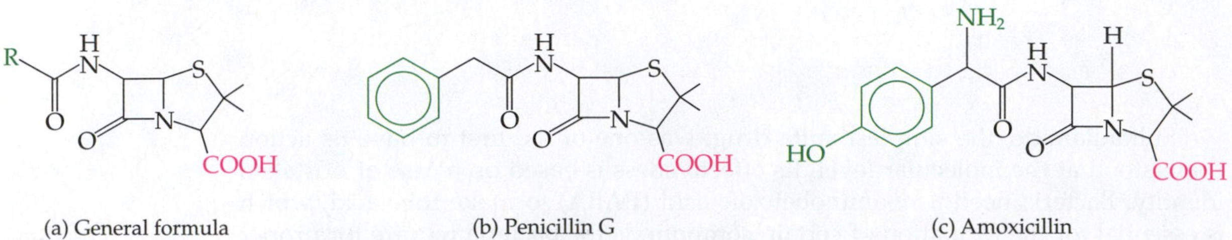

(a) General formula   (b) Penicillin G   (c) Amoxicillin

▲ **Figure 18.7** Penicillins. (a) A general formula where R is a variable side chain. (b) Penicillin G is generally considered the most effective penicillin but can only be given by injection. (c) Amoxicillin can be administered orally.

walls, and are therefore not affected by penicillin. Thus, penicillin can destroy bacteria without harming human cells. However, some people can't take penicillin because they are allergic to it.

In their early days, antibiotics were known as miracle drugs. The number of deaths from blood poisoning (septicemia), pneumonia, and other infectious diseases was reduced substantially by the use of antibiotics. Before 1941, a person with a major bacterial infection almost always died. Today, such deaths are rare except for those ill with other conditions such as AIDS. Six decades ago, pneumonia was a dreaded killer of people of all ages. Today, it kills mainly the elderly and those with AIDS.

Antibiotics have indeed worked miracles in our time, but even miracle drugs are not without problems. It wasn't long after antibiotics were first used that disease organisms began to develop strains resistant to them. One strain can spread antibiotic resistance to another by sharing genes, and the emergence of more and more resistant strains of bacteria is a serious threat to world health. For example, tuberculosis had been almost completely wiped out in developed countries, but a drug-resistant strain has become rampant in Russia and among AIDS patients everywhere.

3. Why won't my doctor give me an antibiotic for a cold? Colds are the result of many different viruses. Not only are antibiotics ineffective against viruses, but the indiscriminate use of antibiotics increases the likelihood that antibiotic-resistant strains of bacteria will develop.

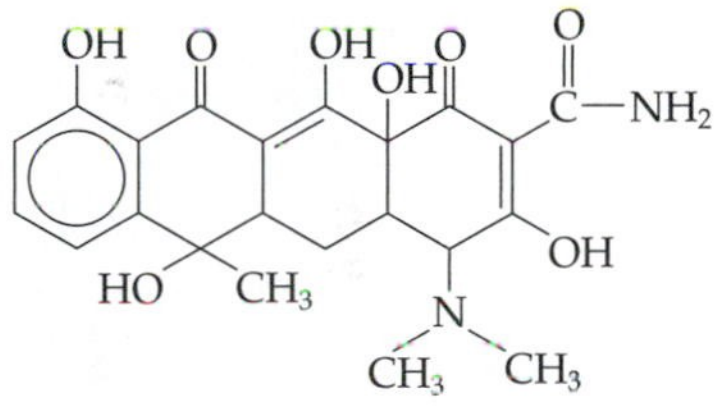

Another example of the development of resistance involves erythromycin, an antibiotic obtained from *Streptomyces erythreus*. As long as it had only limited use, erythromycin could handle all strains of staphylococci. After it was put into extensive use, resistant strains of these bacteria began to appear. Staph infections are now a serious problem in hospitals. People who are admitted to a hospital for treatment sometimes develop serious bacterial infections. Some even die of these staph infections. The CDC estimated in 2007 that staph infections cause more than 94,000 serious illnesses and about 19,000 deaths each year. Later studies have shown a decline in staph infections, but no more precise data are available.

In a race to stay ahead of resistant strains of bacteria, scientists continue to seek new antibiotics. Penicillins have been partially displaced by related compounds called *cephalosporins* such as cephalexin (Keflex®). Unfortunately, some strains of bacteria are resistant to cephalosporins.

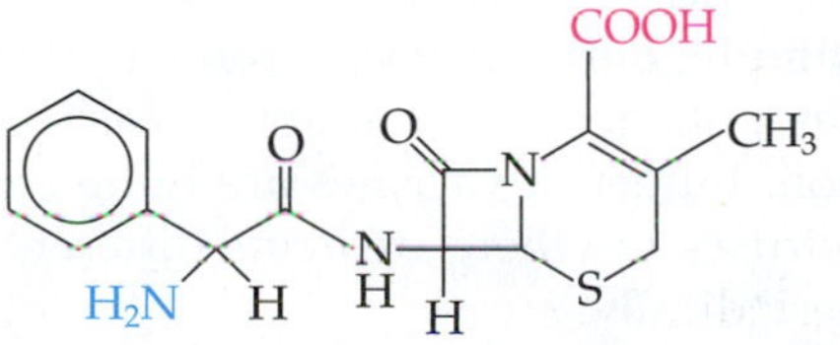

Cephalexin

Another important development in the field of antibiotics was the discovery of a group of compounds called *tetracyclines*. The first of these four-ring compounds to be isolated was chlortetracycline (Aureomycin®), by Benjamin Duggor (1872–1956) in 1948 from *Streptomyces aureofaciens*. Scientists at Pfizer Laboratories isolated oxytetracycline (Terramycin®) from *Streptomyces rimosus* in 1950, and both drugs were later found to be derivatives of tetracycline, a compound now obtained from *Streptomyces viridifaciens*. All three compounds (Figure 18.8) are **broad-spectrum antibiotics**, so called because they are effective against a wide variety of bacteria.

Tetracyclines bind to bacterial ribosomes, inhibiting bacterial protein synthesis and blocking growth of the bacteria. Tetracyclines do not bind to mammalian ribosomes and thus do not affect protein synthesis in host cells. Several disease-causing organisms have developed strains resistant to tetracyclines.

When given to young children, tetracyclines can cause the discoloration of permanent teeth, even though the teeth may not appear until several years later. Women are told to avoid tetracyclines during pregnancy for the same reason. This probably results from the interaction of tetracyclines with calcium during the period of tooth development. Calcium ions in milk and other foods combine with hydroxyl groups on tetracycline molecules.

Tetracycline

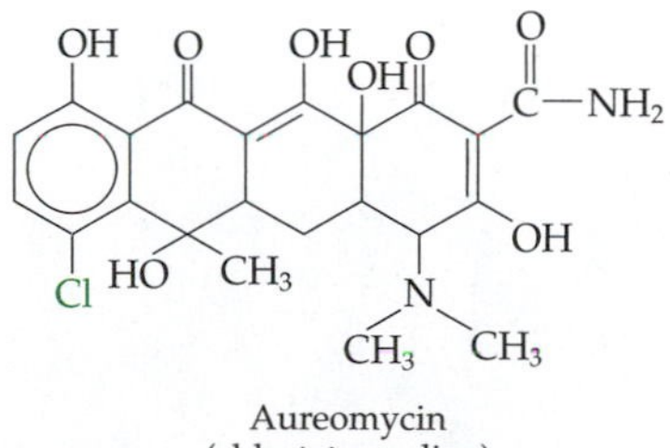

Aureomycin (chlortetracycline)

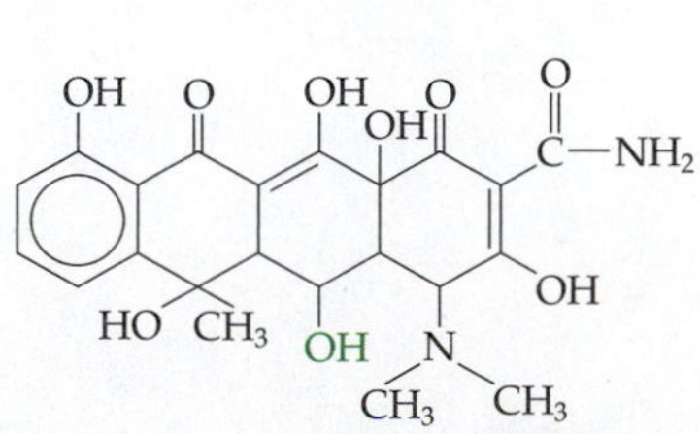

Terramycin (oxytetracycline)

▲ **Figure 18.8** Three tetracycline antibiotics. Subtle structural differences are highlighted by color.

Structure–Function Relationships

Fluoroquinolones are of particular interest to chemists and pharmacologists because many of their structural features correlate with their activity, making possible a rational, logical approach to synthesis of new drugs in this class.

The basic skeletal structure for fluoroquinolones is

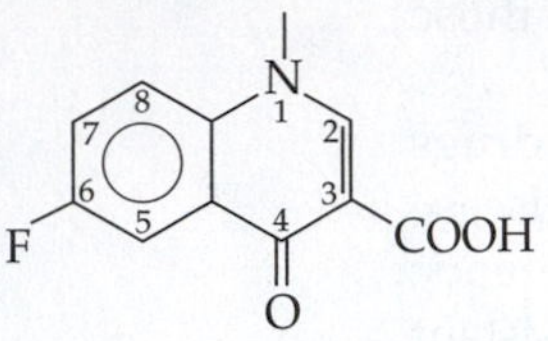

The fluorine atom at position 6 is essential for broad antimicrobial activity when taken orally. Effectiveness depends on the carboxyl group at position 3 and the carbonyl oxygen at position 4, which are responsible for binding to the bacterial DNA complex. A nitrogen-containing ring structure at position 7 or a methoxy group at position 8 broadens the range of bacteria affected. If position 7 has a bulky substituent, the drug has fewer side effects on the nervous system.

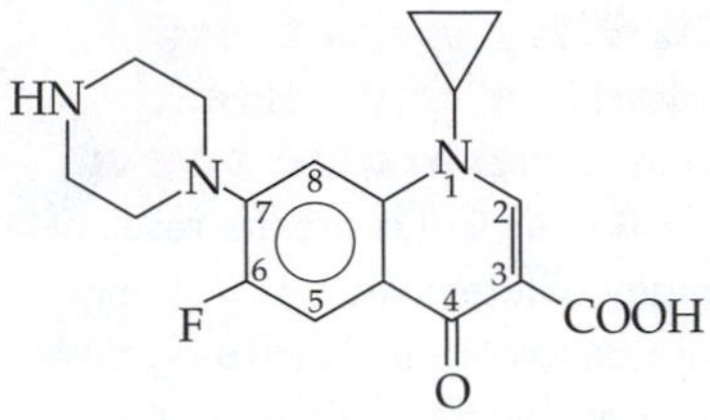

Ciprofloxacin (Cipro®)

Fluoroquinolone antibiotics were first introduced in 1986 and now represent about one-third of the $32 billion global antibiotics market. They act against a broad spectrum of bacteria and seemingly have few side effects. A major use is against bacteria with penicillin resistance. Fluoroquinolones act by inhibiting DNA replication in bacteria through interference with the action of an enzyme called DNA gyrase. Humans do not have this enzyme, so fluoroquinolones do not harm human cells. Because their mechanism of action differs from that of other antibiotics, it was hoped that resistance to fluoroquinolones would be slow to emerge. However, such resistance has already been observed.

Viruses and Antiviral Drugs

For most of us, antibiotics have eliminated the terror of bacterial infections such as pneumonia and diphtheria. We worry about resistant strains of bacteria, but for most people these problems are not insurmountable. However, viral diseases cannot be cured by antibiotics, and viral infections, from colds and influenza to herpes and **acquired immune deficiency syndrome (AIDS)**, still plague us. Some viral infections—such as poliomyelitis, mumps, measles, and smallpox—can be prevented by vaccination. Influenza vaccines are quite effective against common recurrent strains of flu viruses, but there are many different strains of these viruses, and new ones appear periodically.

DNA Viruses and RNA Viruses

Viruses are composed of nucleic acids and proteins (Figure 18.9). They have an external coat that shows a repetitive pattern of protein molecules. Some coats also include a lipid membrane, and others have sugar–protein combinations called *glycoproteins*. The genetic material of a virus is either DNA or RNA. A *DNA virus* moves to the location in a host cell where the DNA is replicated, and it directs the host cell to produce viral proteins. The viral proteins and viral DNA assemble into new viruses that are released by the host cell. These new viruses can then invade other cells and continue the process.

Most *RNA viruses* use their nucleic acids in much the same way. The virus penetrates to where the RNA strands of a host cell are replicated and induces the synthesis of viral proteins. The new RNA strands and viral proteins are then assembled into new viruses. Some RNA viruses, called **retroviruses**, synthesize *DNA* in the host cell. This process is the opposite of the transcription of DNA into RNA (Section 16.7) that normally occurs in cells (the term *retro* implies working backward). The synthesis of DNA from an RNA template is catalyzed by an enzyme called *reverse transcriptase*. The human immunodeficiency virus (HIV) that causes AIDS is a retrovirus. HIV invades and eventually destroys *T cells*, white blood cells that normally help protect the body from infections. Once the T cells are destroyed, the AIDS victim often succumbs to pneumonia or some other infection.

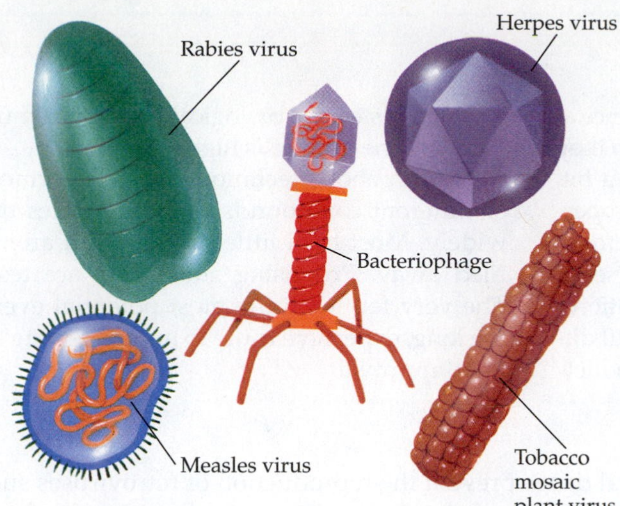

◀ **Figure 18.9** Viruses come in a variety of shapes, which are determined by their protein coats.

Worldwide, 33.3 million people were living with AIDS in 2009. More than 25 million are already dead from AIDS, and 1.8 million more died in 2009. Some 2.6 million people became infected with HIV in 2009. In the United States, more than 1.0 million persons are living with HIV/AIDS, and about 40,000 new HIV infections occur each year.

Antiviral Drugs

Scientists have developed a variety of drugs that are effective against some viruses. None provide cures. Structures of some common antiviral agents are given in Figure 18.10. Another antiviral agent, acyclovir (Zovirax®), is used to treat chickenpox, shingles, cold sores, and the symptoms of genital herpes.

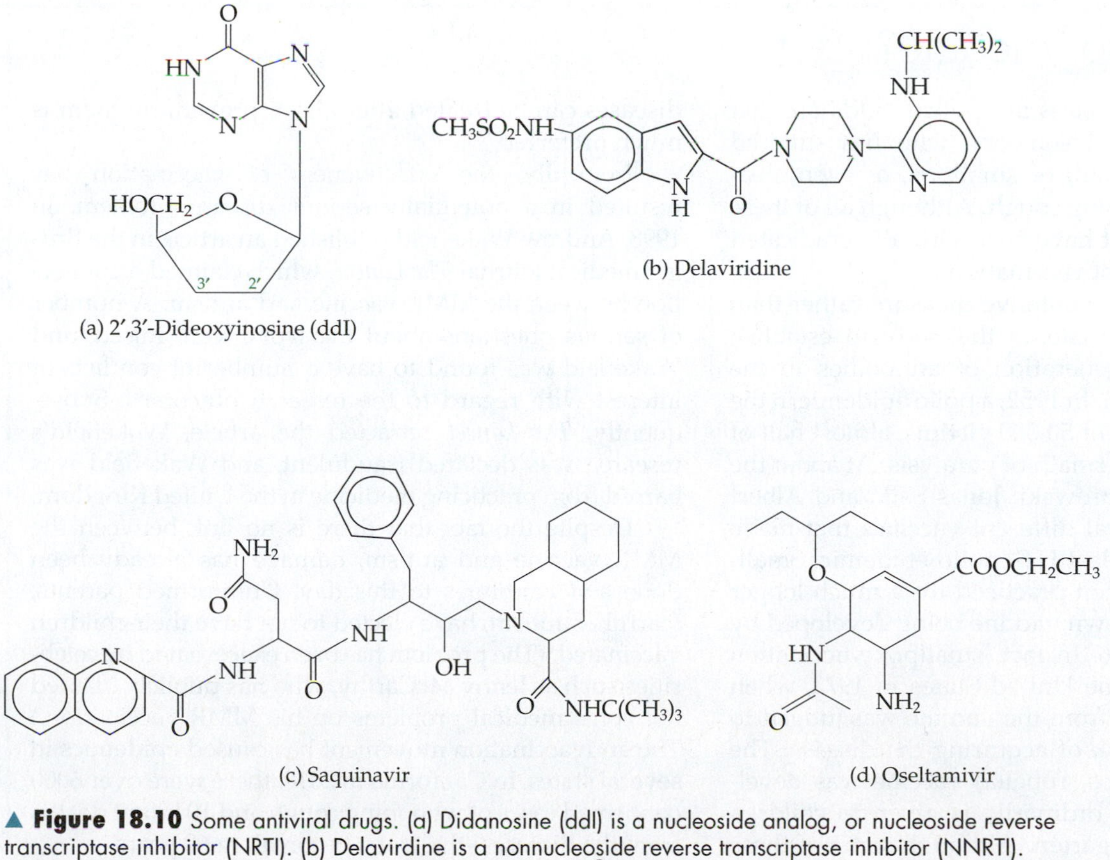

(a) 2′,3′-Dideoxyinosine (ddI)

(b) Delaviridine

(c) Saquinavir

(d) Oseltamivir

▲ **Figure 18.10** Some antiviral drugs. (a) Didanosine (ddI) is a nucleoside analog, or nucleoside reverse transcriptase inhibitor (NRTI). (b) Delavirdine is a nonnucleoside reverse transcriptase inhibitor (NNRTI). (c) Saquinavir is a protease inhibitor. (d) Oseltamivir (Tamiflu®) can prevent influenza if it is given in early stages.

Combinatorial Chemistry

For a century, chemists have synthesized one substance at a time and then tested it for biological activity. Then they made a new compound by varying the structure a bit, hoping to obtain a substance with more desirable properties and less undesirable attributes. Now many chemists use *combinatorial chemistry*, a technique in which a set of starting chemicals is reacted in all possible combinations. For example, a set of 10 compounds reacted with 10 different reagents gives 100 possible products. The products are then tested for biological activity in much the same manner. The process is highly automated.

Such robotic techniques yield enormous numbers of different compounds with properties that can vary widely. Most hold little promise and are discarded or filed away. Promising substances are tested further. The very few with the most potential eventually start the long, expensive route to human testing and possible FDA approval.

Antiretroviral drugs prevent the reproduction of retroviruses such as HIV and are used against AIDS. The following are three important kinds of antiretrovirals.

- *Nucleoside analogs*, or nucleoside reverse transcriptase inhibitors (NRTIs), include didanosine (ddI, Videx®), lamivudine (3TC, Epivir®), stavudine (d4T, Zerit®), zalcitabine (ddC, Hivid®), zidovudine (AZT, Retrovir®), and tenofovir (part of the combination drug Atripla®). Substitution of an analog for a nucleoside in viral DNA cripples the retrovirus, slowing down its replication.
- *Nonnucleoside reverse transcriptase inhibitors (NNRTIs)* stop the reverse transcriptase from working properly to make more of the retrovirus. NNRTIs include delavirdine (Rescriptor®), efavirenz, rilpivirine, and nevirapine (Viramune®).
- *Protease inhibitors* block the enzyme protease so that new copies of the retrovirus can't infect new cells. Protease inhibitors include ritonavir (Norvir®), darunavir, atazanavir, and saquinavir (Invirase®).

Vaccine or No Vaccine?

If the students in your class are polled, odds are that none have encountered someone who has suffered from poliomyelitis (polio) or smallpox, or even measles, mumps, or whooping cough. Although all of these are viral diseases, most have been virtually eradicated by the simple method of vaccination.

Vaccination is a preventative measure rather than a treatment; a vaccine causes the body to establish immunity, often by generation of antibodies to the virus or microorganism. In 1952, a polio epidemic in the United States struck over 50,000 victims, almost half of whom suffered the aftermath of paralysis. At about the same time, Hilary Koprowski, Jonas Salk, and Albert Sabin developed several different vaccines that made the 1952 outbreak the last U.S. polio epidemic. Smallpox vaccination has been practiced for a much longer time, with the best-known vaccine being developed by Edward Jenner in 1796. In fact, smallpox vaccination was discontinued in the United States in 1972, when the tiny statistical risk from the vaccine was judged to be greater than the risk of acquiring the disease. The MMR (measles, mumps, rubella) vaccine was developed in the 1970 and ordinarily is given to children before entering kindergarten. Although some of these diseases can be treated after onset, preventing them is much preferred.

Ironically, the effectiveness of vaccination has resulted in a potentially serious disease problem. In 1998, Andrew Wakefield published an article in the British medical journal *The Lancet*, which claimed a connection between the MMR vaccine and autism. A number of serious questions about the work were raised, and Wakefield was found to have a number of conflicts of interest with regard to the research outcomes. Subsequently, *The Lancet* retracted the article, Wakefield's research was declared fraudulent, and Wakefield was barred from practicing medicine in the United Kingdom.

Despite the fact that there is no link between the MMR vaccine and autism, damage has already been done and continues to this day. Uninformed parents, fearful of autism, have elected to not have their children vaccinated. (The problem has been exacerbated by celebrities such as Jenny McCarthy, who has publicly blamed her son's medical problems on his MMR vaccination.) The antivaccination movement has caused epidemics in several states. In California in 2010, there were over 6000 confirmed cases of whooping cough and 10 infant deaths from the disease—the worst outbreak in 60 years.

Combinations of AIDS drugs seem to be more effective than any one of them alone. For example, Atripla® contains efavirenz, emtricitabine, and tenofovir. It provides a once daily single-pill treatment that can control HIV for long periods of time.

Basic Research and Drug Development

Scientists had to understand the normal biochemistry of cells before they could develop drugs to treat diseases caused by viruses. Gertrude Elion and George Hitchings of Burroughs Wellcome Research Laboratories in North Carolina and James Black of Kings College in London did much of the basic biochemical research that led to the development of antiviral drugs and many anticancer drugs (Section 18.4). They determined the shapes of cell membrane receptors and learned how normal cells work. They and other scientists were then able to design drugs to block receptors in infected cells. Elion, Hitchings, and Black shared the 1988 Nobel Prize in Physiology or Medicine for their work.

Drug design in its early days was often a hit-or-miss procedure. Today, scientists use powerful computers to design molecules to fit receptors, making drug design a more precise science.

Self-Assessment Questions

1. Sulfathiazole is selectively toxic to bacteria because mammals can obtain a certain compound from the diet, while bacterial cells must synthesize it. That compound is
   a. *para*-aminobenzoic acid **b.** ascorbic acid
   c. folic acid **d.** uracil
2. Penicillins act by inhibiting the synthesis of
   a. bacterial cell walls **b.** folic acid
   c. β-lactams **d.** viral RNA
3. Antibiotics kill
   a. all living cells **b.** bacteria but not viruses
   c. both viruses and bacteria **d.** neither bacteria nor viruses
4. Taking antibiotics for a stomach virus will
   a. cure the illness
   b. increase the chance that drug-resistant bacteria will develop
   c. lessen the symptoms
   d. shorten the duration of the illness
5. Viruses consist of a protein coat surrounding a core of
   a. lipids
   b. nucleic acids
   c. polysaccharides
   d. proteins
6. Most RNA viruses replicate in host cells by replicating RNA strands and synthesizing
   a. host-cell lipids **b.** host-cell proteins
   c. viral polysaccharides **d.** viral proteins
7. Retroviruses replicate in host cells by
   a. replicating RNA strands and synthesizing viral proteins
   b. replicating RNA strands and synthesizing host-cell proteins
   c. synthesizing DNA and forming new viruses
   d. synthesizing DNA and replicating host cells
8. What HIV enzyme catalyzes the synthesis of viral DNA inside the host cell?
   a. DNA polymerase **b.** protease
   c. reverse transcriptase **d.** RNA polymerase
9. The best treatment for viral diseases such as diphtheria, mumps, and smallpox is
   a. antibacterial drugs **b.** antiviral drugs
   c. tetracyclines **d.** vaccinations

Answers: 1, a; 2, a; 3, b; 4, b; 5, b; 6, d; 7, c; 8, c; 9, d

18.4 Chemicals Against Cancer

Learning Objective › Describe the action of the common types of anticancer drugs.

Despite decades of "war" on cancer, it remains a dread disease. Each year in the United States, more than 1.5 million new cases are diagnosed and cancer kills about 570,000 people. Scientists have made progress, but much remains to be done. A major problem is that the drugs that kill cancer cells damage normal cells as well. Thus, a main aim of cancer research is to find a way to kill cancerous tissue without killing too many normal cells.

Chemotherapy to treat cancer affects any body cells that undergo rapid replacement, not just cancer cells. Included are the cells that line the digestive tract and those that produce hair. Side effects of chemotherapy therefore include nausea and loss of hair.

Treatment with drugs, radiation, and/or surgery yields a high rate of cure for some kinds of cancer. For example, with treatment, early-stage prostate cancer has an overall five-year survival rate of nearly 100%. For other types, such as lung and bronchus cancer, the overall five-year survival rate is only 15.0%, mainly because lung cancer is often advanced at the time of diagnosis. The five-year survival rate for all cancers is about 68%.

Several categories of anticancer drugs are used widely, and we look at some of them here.

Antimetabolites: Inhibition of Nucleic Acid Synthesis

An **antimetabolite** is a compound that closely resembles a substance essential to normal body metabolism, which allows it to interfere with physiological reactions involving that substance. Rapidly dividing cells, characteristic of cancer, require an abundance of DNA. Cancer antimetabolites block DNA synthesis and therefore block the increase in the number of cancer cells. Because cancer cells are undergoing rapid growth and cell division, they are generally affected to a greater extent than normal cells. Research over the last two decades has led to refinements in how antimetabolites are administered, increasing their effectiveness.

Gertrude Elion and George Hitchings patented 6-mercaptopurine (6-MP) in 1954. This compound can substitute for adenine in nucleotides, the phosphate–sugar–base units of both DNA and RNA (Section 16.6), and the pseudonucleotides then inhibit the synthesis of nucleotides incorporating adenine and guanine. This slows DNA synthesis and cell division, thus inhibiting the multiplication of cancer cells. Prior to 6-MP, half of all children with acute leukemia died within a few months. Combined with other medications, 6-MP was able to cure approximately 80% of child leukemia patients.

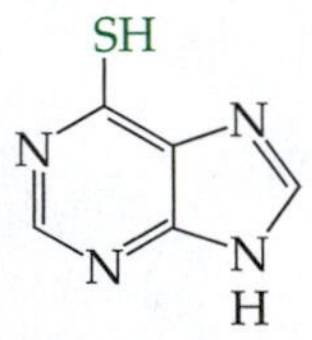

SH N N N N H

6-Mercaptopurine

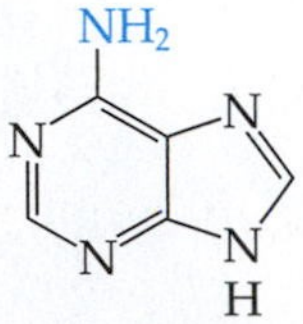

NH_2 N N N N H

Adenine

Another prominent antimetabolite is 5-fluorouracil (5-FU), which blocks synthesis of the thymine-containing nucleotide thymidine, an essential component for DNA replication. 5-FU is employed against a variety of cancers, especially those of the breast and the digestive tract.

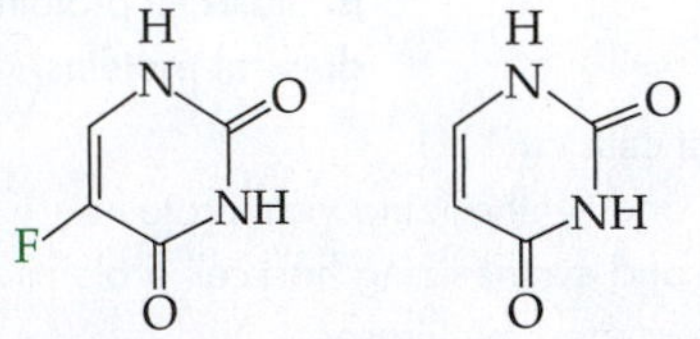

H N O NH F O

5-Fluorouracil

H N O NH O

Uracil

The antimetabolite methotrexate acts somewhat differently. It is a folic-acid antagonist that interferes with cellular reproduction. Note the similarity between its structure and that of folic acid. Like the pseudo-folic acid formed from sulfanilamide, methotrexate competes successfully with folic acid for an essential enzyme but cannot perform the growth-enhancing function of folic acid. Again, cell division is slowed and cancer growth is retarded. Methotrexate is used frequently against leukemia. It is also used in the treatment of psoriasis and certain inflammatory diseases such as rheumatoid arthritis.

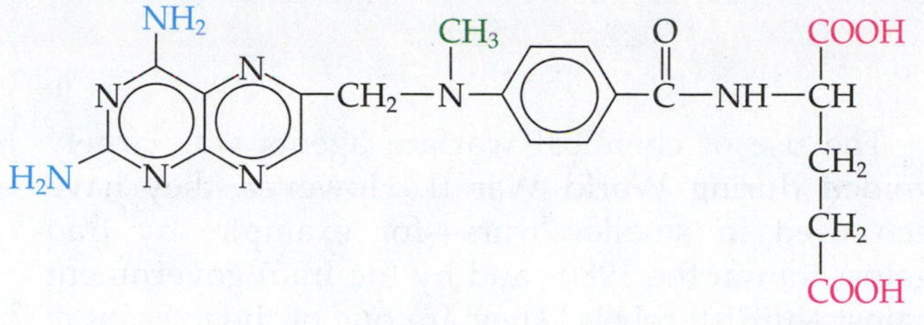

Methotrexate

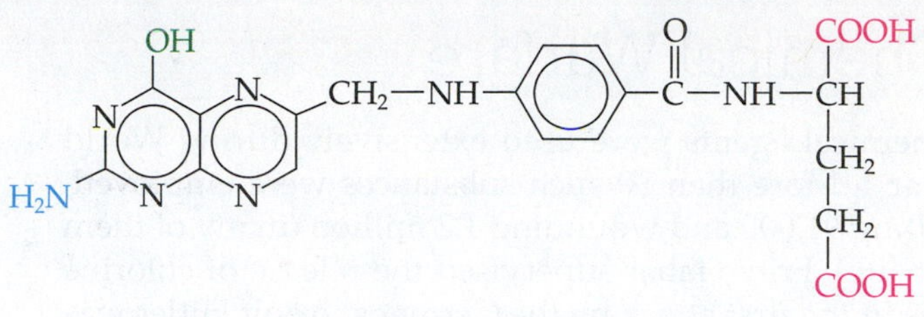

Folic acid

Alkylating Agents: Turning Old Weapons into Anticancer Drugs

Alkylating agents are highly reactive compounds that can transfer alkyl groups to compounds of biological importance. These introduced alkyl groups then block the usual action of the biological molecules. Some alkylating agents are used against cancer. Typical among these are nitrogen mustards, compounds that arose out of chemical warfare research.

The original mustard gas was a sulfur-containing blister agent used during World War I. Contact with either the liquid or the vapor causes blisters that are painful and slow to heal. It is easily detected, however, by its garlic or horseradish odor. Mustard gas is denoted by the military symbol H.

$$Cl{-}CH_2CH_2{-}S{-}CH_2CH_2{-}Cl$$

Mustard gas (H)

Nitrogen mustards (symbol HN) were developed about 1935. Though not quite as effective overall as mustard gas, nitrogen mustards produce greater eye damage and don't have an obvious odor. Structurally, nitrogen mustards are chlorinated amines.

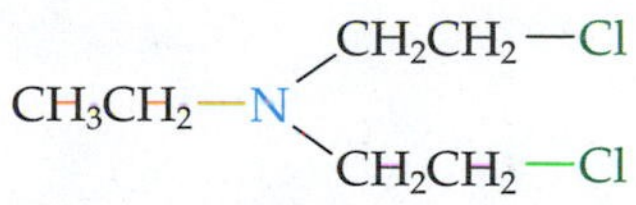

$$CH_3CH_2{-}N(CH_2CH_2{-}Cl)_2 \qquad CH_3{-}N(CH_2CH_2{-}Cl)_2 \qquad Cl{-}CH_2CH_2{-}N(CH_2CH_2{-}Cl)_2$$

HN_1 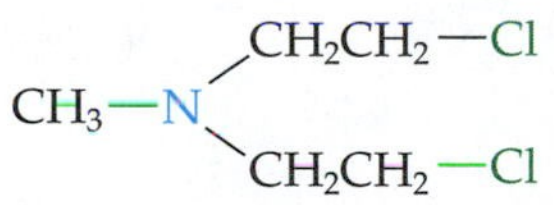 $\quad$ HN_2 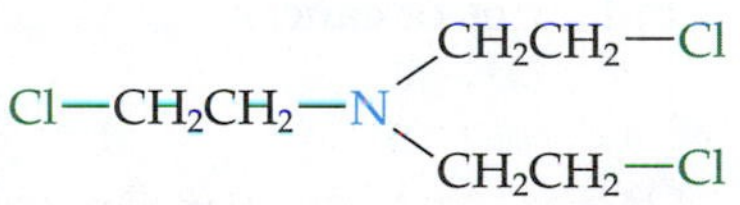 $\quad$ HN_3

Cisplatin: The Platinum Standard of Cancer Treatment

The platinum-containing compound cisplatin $[PtCl_2(NH_3)_2]$ is a prominent anticancer drug. Cisplatin was first synthesized in 1844. Its biological effect was discovered by accident in 1965 by Barnett Rosenberg at Michigan State University. Rosenberg was using inert platinum electrodes in an experiment designed to measure the effect of electrical currents on cell division. He found that *E. coli* were growing in length but failing to divide, reaching 300 times their normal length. After much further study, Rosenberg and his team found that the electric current had caused a chemical reaction between the platinum in the electrodes and nutrients in the solution containing the bacteria. The reaction produced a new compound, later called cisplatin. Because the compound inhibited cell division, Rosenberg reasoned that it might be effective as an anticancer drug. It is. Cisplatin, an alkylating agent, binds to DNA and blocks its replication. It is widely used to treat cancers of the ovaries, testes, uterus, head, neck, breast, and lungs and advanced bladder cancers.

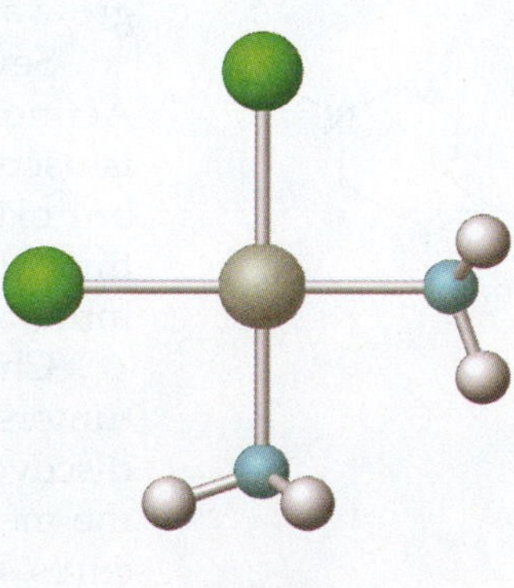
Cisplatin

Chemical Warfare

Chemical agents were used extensively during World War I. More than 30 such substances were employed, killing 91,000 and wounding 1.2 million (many of them for life). Fritz Haber supervised the release of chlorine gas in the first attack by the Germans. Adolf Hitler was among those wounded when the British retaliated with phosgene a few days later. Haber considered gas warfare to be "a higher form of killing." Fortunately, his views have not become widely accepted.

The use of chemical warfare agents was largely avoided during World War II. However, they have been used in smaller wars—for example, by Iraq against Iran in the 1980s and by the Iraqi government against Kurdish rebels. They are one of the *weapons of mass destruction (WMDs)* that can kill huge numbers of people and might be used by a rogue nation or a terrorist group. (The other WMDs are nuclear devices and biological agents such as anthrax and botulism.)

In cancer treatment, nitrogen mustards, which are bifunctional alkylating agents (that is, agents with two functional groups), act by cross-linking two DNA strands. Cross-linking prevents or hinders replication and thus impedes growth of cancer cells. Knowledge gained through science is neither good nor evil. The same knowledge—in this case, the ability to make nitrogen mustards—can be used either for our benefit or for our destruction.

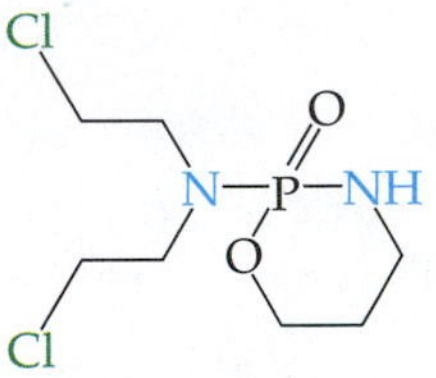

The nitrogen mustard often used for cancer therapy is a compound called cyclophosphamide (Cytoxan®). It is used to treat Hodgkin's disease, lymphomas, leukemias, and other cancers.

Cl
O
N—P—NH
O
Cl
Cyclophosphamide

Alkylating agents can cause cancer as well as cure it. For example, the nitrogen mustard HN_2 causes lung, mammary, and liver tumors when injected into mice, yet it can be used with some success in the management of certain human tumors. There is still a lot of mystery—and seeming contradiction—regarding the causes and cures of cancer.

Other Anticancer Agents

There are many other anticancer agents in use today. Alkaloids from vinca plants have been shown to be effective against leukemia and Hodgkin's disease. Paclitaxel (Taxol®), first obtained from the Pacific yew tree, is effective against cancers of the breast, ovary, and cervix.

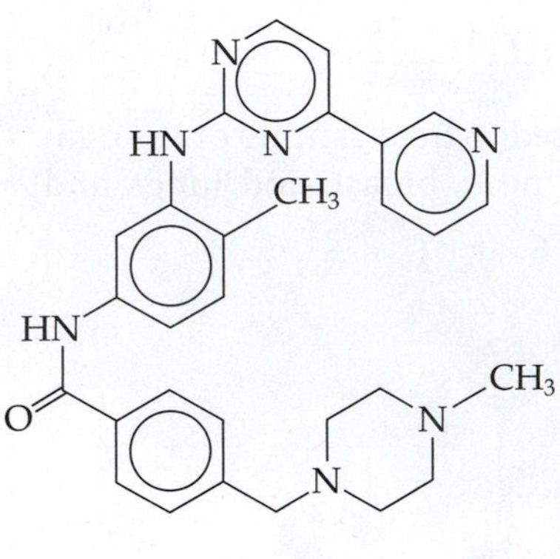

Imatinib (Gleevec®) is a synthetic drug that is particularly effective against chronic myeloid leukemia. Cell growth is controlled by substances called *growth factors*, which act by attaching to receptor proteins on the surface of certain types of cells. People with chronic myeloid leukemia produce cells with damaged receptors that send grow-and-divide signals to the cells even with no growth factor present. Imatinib inhibits the faulty receptors, preventing them from stimulating the cells to grow and divide; the cancer cells cannot multiply.

N
HN N N
CH_3
HN
CH_3
O N
N
Imatinib

Several antibiotics have been found to kill cancer cells as well as bacteria. Actinomycin, obtained from the molds *Streptomyces antibioticus* and *S. parvus*, is used against Hodgkin's disease and other types of cancer. It is quite effective but extremely toxic. Actinomycin acts by binding to the double helix of DNA, thus blocking the replication of RNA on the DNA template. Protein synthesis is inhibited.

Chemotherapy is only part of the treatment for cancer. Surgical removal of tumors and radiation treatment remain major tools. It is unlikely that research will discover a single agent that can cure all cancers. Active research is under way on the mechanisms of carcinogenesis, and a better understanding will lead to better cures. Prevention of cancer is a greater hope. Deaths from smoking-related cancers account for at least 30% of all cancer deaths. Reducing cigarette smoking can significantly reduce cancer deaths.

Self-Assessment Questions

1. 5-Fluorouracil inhibits the formation of nucleotides containing the base
   a. adenine b. cytosine c. guanine d. thymine
2. 6-Mercaptopurine mimics the base adenine, forming a pseudonucleotide and thus slowing
   a. cell-mediated immune reactions b. DNA synthesis
   c. RNA transport d. viral replication
3. Methotrexate is a folic-acid antagonist that slows
   a. cell division
   b. cell-mediated immune reactions
   c. transport of nutrients to the cancer cell
   d. viral replication
4. Cisplatin inhibits cell division by
   a. being incorporated in RNA
   b. binding to DNA and blocking its replication
   c. halting viral replication
   d. substituting for cytosine in a nucleotide
5. Which of the following anticancer drugs was once used as a chemical warfare agent?
   a. cisplatin b. methotrexate
   c. nitrogen mustards d. vinblastine
6. Cyclophosphamide acts by
   a. being incorporated in RNA
   b. cross-linking two DNA strands and blocking replication
   c. halting viral replication
   d. substituting for cytosine in a nucleotide

Answers: 1, d; 2, b; 3, a; 4, b; 5, c; 6, b

18.5 Hormones: The Regulators

Learning Objectives › Define the terms *hormone*, *prostaglandin*, and *steroid*, and explain the function of each. › List the three types of sex hormones, and explain how each acts and how birth control drugs work.

Before we discuss the next group of drugs, we need to take a brief look at the human endocrine system and some of the chemical compounds, called *hormones*, this system manufactures. A **hormone** is a chemical messenger produced in the endocrine glands (Figure 18.11). Hormones released in one part of the body send signals for profound physiological changes in other parts of the body. By causing reactions to speed up or slow down, hormones control growth, metabolism, reproduction, and many other functions of body and mind. Some of the important human hormones and their physiological effects are listed in Table 18.2 (see page 554). Still other hormones are formed in tissues of the heart, liver, kidney, gut, and placenta.

Prostaglandins: Hormone Mediators

A *prostaglandin* is a hormone-like lipid derived from a fatty acid. Each prostaglandin molecule has 20 carbon atoms, including a 5-carbon ring. Prostaglandins function similarly to hormones in that they act on target cells. However, they differ from hormones in that they (1) act near the site where they are produced, (2) can have different effects in different tissues, and (3) are rapidly metabolized. Prostaglandins are synthesized in the body from arachidonic acid (Figure 18.12). There are six primary prostaglandins, which are widely distributed throughout the body. Extremely small doses of these potent biological chemicals can elicit marked changes. In addition to the six primary prostaglandins, many others have been identified.

▶ Figure 18.11 The approximate locations of the eight major endocrine glands in the human body.

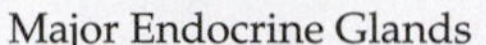

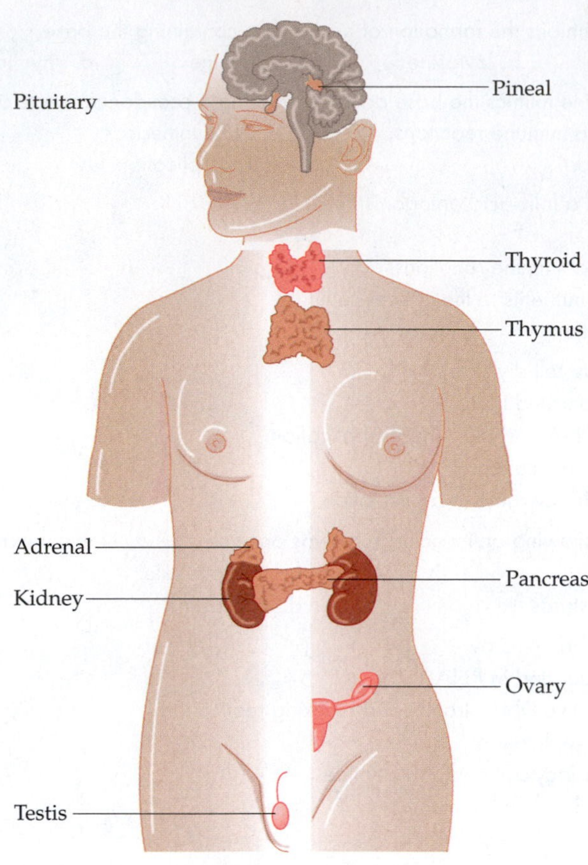

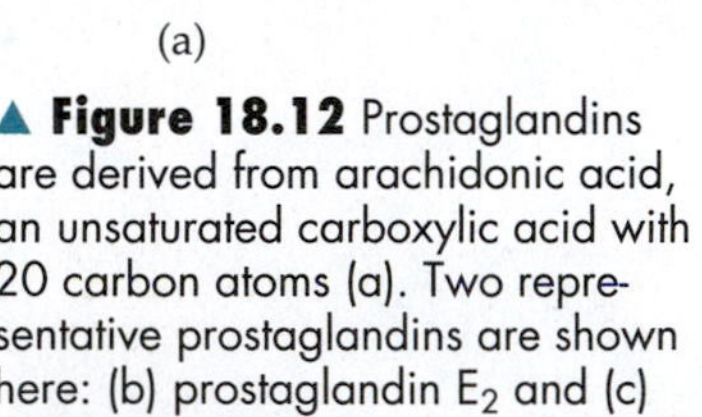

(a)

O
COOH
CH_3
HO
OH
PGE_2

(b)

HO
COOH
CH_3
HO
OH
$PGF_{2\alpha}$

(c)

▲ Figure 18.12 Prostaglandins are derived from arachidonic acid, an unsaturated carboxylic acid with 20 carbon atoms (a). Two representative prostaglandins are shown here: (b) prostaglandin E_2 and (c) prostaglandin $F_{2\alpha}$.

Prostaglandins act as mediators of hormone action. They regulate such things as blood pressure, blood clotting, pain sensation, smooth muscle activity, and secretion of substances related to reproduction. A single prostaglandin can have different, even opposite, effects in different tissues. This range of physiological activity has led to the synthesis of hundreds of prostaglandins and analogs. Prostaglandin E_2 (PGE_2), also known as dinoprostone (Cervidil®), is used to induce labor. PGE_1 can lower blood pressure. A PGE_1 analog called misoprostol is used to help prevent peptic ulcers, a common side effect of large doses of NSAIDs. Other prostaglandins can be used clinically to relieve nasal congestion, to provide relief from asthma, to treat glaucoma, to treat pulmonary hypertension, and to prevent formation of the blood clots associated with heart attacks and strokes.

$PGE_{2\alpha}$ is used in cattle to synchronize breeding. It is also used in the artificial insemination of prize cows. Injection of $PGE_{2\alpha}$ along with a hormone into a prize cow will induce the release of many ova, which are then fertilized with sperm from a champion bull. The developing embryos are implanted in less valuable cows, enabling a farmer to get several calves a year from one outstanding cow.

4. Does eating lots of sugar cause diabetes? Not directly. However, high sugar intake contributes greatly to obesity, and obesity is strongly linked to Type 2 diabetes.

Diabetes

The pancreas produces the hormone *insulin*, with which the body increases cellular usage of glucose. *Diabetes* arises when the pancreas does not produce enough insulin (Type 1) or when the insulin is not properly used by the body (Type 2). In both cases, elevated blood glucose levels are the result. Most Americans diagnosed with diabetes suffer from Type 2. Type 2 has a strong genetic component and is also closely tied to lifestyle. Poor diet, obesity, and lack of exercise all appear to be contributing factors to Type 2. Paralleling the increase in obesity, Type 2 diabetes has become increasingly common, even among children and adolescents.

People who suffer from Type 1 diabetes ordinarily must take insulin, injected in some fashion. (Insulin taken orally is broken down by the body's digestive system before it can reach the bloodstream.) Type 2 diabetics may be able to control their disease with careful diet, exercise, and loss of weight. When these measures aren't enough, a biguanide such as metformin (Glucophage®) is often prescribed. Metformin works by reducing the production of glucose in the liver. It is one of the most widely prescribed medications, with over 25 million prescriptions annually. Sulfonylureas, which increase the production of insulin from the pancreas, are also used to treat Type 2 diabetes. Sometimes these oral drugs are not enough to maintain glucose levels in individuals with Type 2 diabetes, and insulin must be administered.

$$CH_3-N(CH_3)-C(=NH)-NH-C(=NH)-NH_2$$

Metformin

A number of complications can arise from diabetes, including blindness, cardiovascular disease, kidney disease, and nerve damage. Thus, diagnosis and control of diabetes is very important. About 24 million Americans have the disease—and almost a quarter of them aren't aware of it.

Steroids

A **steroid** is a compound with a four-ring skeletal structure. Steroids occur widely in living organisms, and not all are hormones (Figure 18.13). Cholesterol, for example, is a steroid component of all animal tissues. About 10% of the brain is cholesterol; it is a vital part of the membranes of nerve cells. Cholesterol is also found in deposits in hardened arteries and is a major component of certain types of gallstones. Cortisol, another natural steroid, is an adrenal hormone (Table 18.2). Prednisone is a synthetic steroid used to reduce inflammation in arthritis sufferers and to treat injuries.

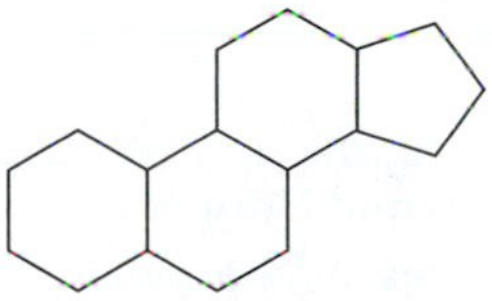

▲ Skeletal structure of steroids.

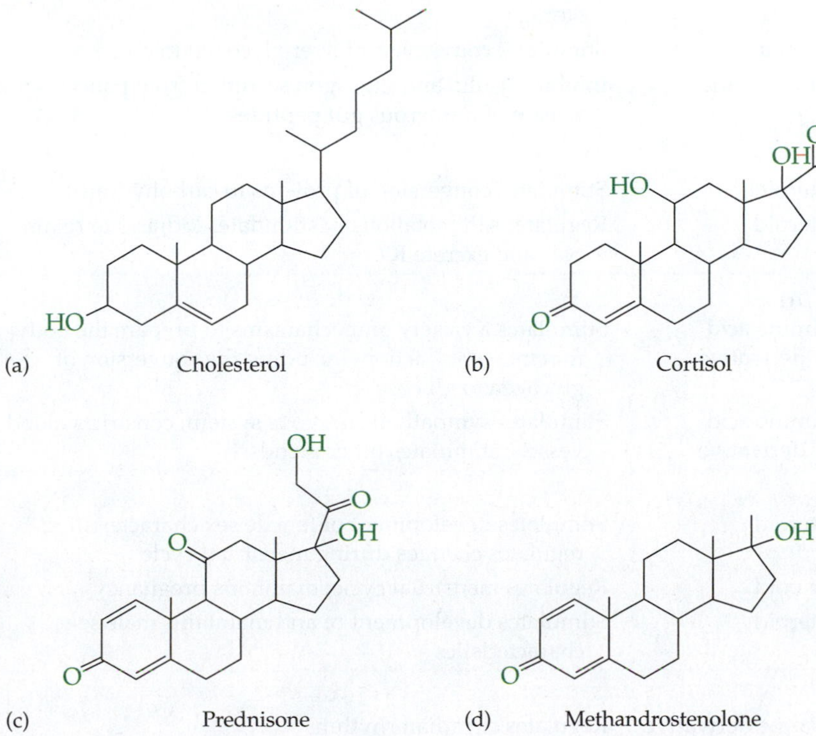

HO (a) Cholesterol

HO OH O OH O (b) Cortisol

OH O OH O O (c) Prednisone

OH O (d) Methandrostenolone

◀ **Figure 18.13** Formulas of four steroids. (a) Cholesterol is an essential component of all animal cells. (b) Cortisol is a hormone secreted by the adrenal glands in response to physical or psychological stress. (c) Prednisone is a synthetic anti-inflammatory substance. (d) Methandrostenolone (Dianabol®) is an anabolic steroid (Chapter 19). Note that all have the same basic four-ring structure.

Table 18.2 Some Human Hormones and Their Physiological Effect

Name	Chemical Nature	Function(s)
Pituitary Hormones		
Vasopressin (antidiuretic hormone)	Nonapeptide	Stimulates contractions of smooth muscle; regulates water retention and blood pressure
Oxytocin	Nonapeptide	Stimulates contraction of the smooth muscle of the uterus; stimulates secretion of milk
Growth hormone (GH) (or somatotropin)	Protein	Stimulates body growth and bone growth
Thyroid-stimulating hormone (TSH)	Protein	Stimulates growth of the thyroid gland and production of thyroid hormones
Melanocyte-stimulating hormones (MSHs)	Peptides	Controls skin pigmentation
Adrenocorticotrophic hormone (ACTH)	Protein	Stimulates growth of the adrenal cortex and production of cortical hormones
Follicle-stimulating hormone (FSH)	Protein	Stimulates maturation of egg follicles in ovaries of females and of sperm cells in testes of males
Luteinizing hormone (LH)	Protein	Stimulates female ovulation and male secretion of testosterone
Prolactin	Protein	Maintains the production of estrogens and progesterone; stimulates the formation of milk
Hypothalamic Hormones		
Corticotropin-releasing factor (CRF)	Protein	Acts on corticotrope to release ACTH and β-endorphin (lipotropin)
Gonadotropin-releasing factor (GnRF)	Decapeptide	Acts on gonadotrope to release LH and FSH
Somatostatin release inhibiting factor (SIF)	Polypeptide	Inhibits GH and TSH secretion
Thyrotropin-releasing factor (TRF)	Tripeptide	Stimulates TSH and prolactin secretion
Thyroid Hormone		
Thyroxine	Amino acid derivative	Increases rate of cellular metabolism
Parathyroid Hormone		
Parathyroid hormone	Protein	Regulates Ca^{2+} level in blood
Pancreatic Hormones		
Insulin	Protein	Increases cellular usage of glucose; increases glycogen storage
Glucagon	Protein	Stimulates conversion of liver glycogen to glucose
Somatostatin	Polypeptide	Inhibits insulin and glucagon secretion from pancreas and release of numerous gut peptides
Adrenal Cortical Hormones		
Cortisol	Steroid	Stimulates conversion of proteins to carbohydrates
Aldosterone	Steroid	Regulates salt metabolism; stimulates kidneys to retain Na^{+} and excrete K^{+}
Adrenal Medullary Hormones		
Epinephrine (adrenaline)	Amino acid derivative	Stimulates a variety of mechanisms to prepare the body for emergency action, including the conversion of glycogen to glucose
Norepinephrine (noradrenaline)	Amino acid derivative	Stimulates sympathetic nervous system; constricts blood vessels; stimulates other glands
Gonadal Hormones		
Estradiol	Steroid	Stimulates development of female sex characteristics; regulates changes during menstrual cycle
Progesterone	Steroid	Regulates menstrual cycle; maintains pregnancy
Testosterone	Steroid	Stimulates development of and maintains male sex characteristics
Pineal Hormone		
Melatonin	Amine derivative	Regulates circadian rhythms

Many drugs, both natural and synthetic, are based on steroids, including the notorious anabolic steroids (Chapter 19) that are abused by athletes and body builders. Some steroid drugs are anti-inflammatories used to treat arthritis, bronchial asthma, dermatitis, and eye infections. Some are sex hormones that are active ingredients in birth control pills.

Serendipity often plays a role in the discovery of new drugs. Percy Julian, a grandson of slaves, was a chemist at the Glidden Paint Company doing research on soybeans when his work led to the development of new steroid-based drugs. It often happens that new drugs are discovered by chemists who are not really looking for them.

▲ Percy Lavon Julian (1899–1975) was involved in the synthesis of a variety of steroids, including physostigmine, a drug used to treat glaucoma. Untreated, glaucoma causes blindness. Julian is shown here on a 1992 U.S. postage stamp.

Sex Hormones

Sex hormones are steroids (Figure 18.14). Note that male sex hormones differ only slightly in structure from female sex hormones. In fact, the female hormone progesterone can be converted to the male hormone testosterone by a simple biochemical reaction. The physiological actions of these structurally similar compounds, however, are markedly different.

An **androgen** is any compound that stimulates the development or controls the maintenance of masculine characteristics. These male sex hormones are secreted by the testes. In males, the pituitary hormones FSH and LH (Table 18.2) are required for the continued production of sperm and of androgens. These hormones are responsible for development of the sex organs and for secondary sexual characteristics, such as voice and hair distribution. The most important androgen is testosterone.

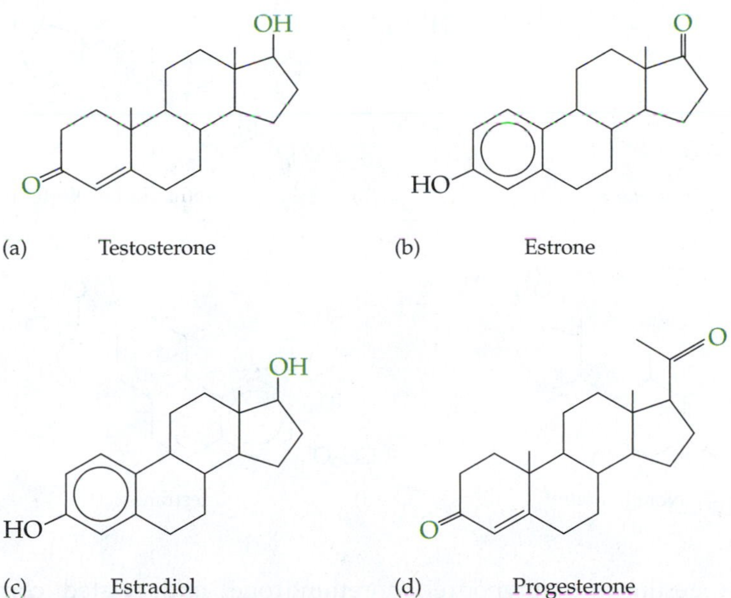

◀ **Figure 18.14** Structural formulas of the principal sex hormones. Testosterone (a) is the main male sex hormone (androgen). Estrone (b) and estradiol (c) are female sex hormones (estrogens). Progesterone (d), also produced by females, is essential to the maintenance of pregnancy.

An **estrogen** is a compound that controls female sexual functions, such as the menstrual cycle, the development of breasts, and other secondary sexual characteristics. The two important estrogens are estradiol and estrone. These female sex hormones are produced mainly in the ovaries. Another female sex hormone is progesterone, which prepares the uterus for pregnancy and prevents the further release of eggs from the ovaries during pregnancy. A related type of compound, called a **progestin**, is any steroid hormone that has the effect of progesterone. In females, the pituitary hormones FSH and LH (Table 18.2) are required for the production of ova and of estrogens and progesterone.

Sex hormones—both natural and synthetic—are sometimes used therapeutically. For example, a woman who has passed menopause may be given hormones to compensate for those no longer being produced by her ovaries. Hormone replacement therapy provides benefits but also has risks, and its use is quite controversial.

Chemistry and Social Revolution: The Pill

When administered by injection, progesterone serves as an effective birth control drug. It fools the body into acting as if it were already pregnant. The structure of progesterone was determined in 1934 by Adolf Butenandt (1903–1995), who received the Nobel Prize in Chemistry in 1939. Other chemists began to try to design a contraceptive that would be effective when taken orally.

In 1938, Hans Inhoffen (1906–1992) synthesized the first oral contraceptive, ethisterone, by incorporating an ethynyl group (—C≡CH). (The ethynyl group is derived from ethyne, HC≡CH, also called acetylene.) However, ethisterone had to be taken in large doses to be effective and was not widely used.

In 1951, Carl Djerassi synthesized 19-norprogesterone, which is simply progesterone with one of its methyl groups missing. It was four to eight times as effective as progesterone as a birth control agent. However, like progesterone itself, 19-norprogesterone had to be given by injection, an undesirable property. Djerassi then combined the two improvements: remove a methyl group to make the drug more effective, and add an ethynyl group to allow oral administration. Djerassi synthesized norethindrone (Norlutin®), which proved effective when taken in small doses (Figure 18.15), and patented it in 1956. Working at about the same time as Djerassi, Frank Colton synthesized norethynodrel, another progestin, for which G. D. Searle was awarded patents in 1954 and 1955. Norethynodrel, a progestin, was used in Enovid, the first birth control pill approved by the FDA (1960).

▲ In 1951, Carl Djerassi (b. 1923), a professor of chemistry at Stanford University at the time, synthesized Norlutin, a progestin.

▶ **Figure 18.15** Formulas of some synthetic sex hormones: ethisterone (a), norethindrone (b), norethynodrel (c), and mestranol (d). In 1960, G. D. Searle's Enovid, which contained 9.85 mg of norethynodrel and 150 mg of mestranol, became the first birth control pill approved by the FDA. Djerassi's norethindrone and Colton's norethynodrel differ only in the position of a double bond.

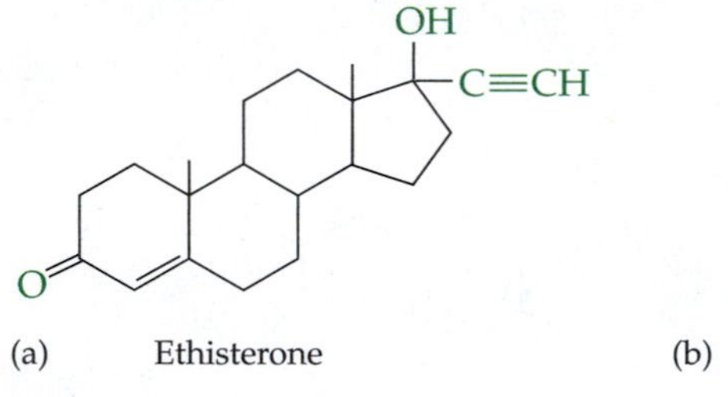

(a) Ethisterone

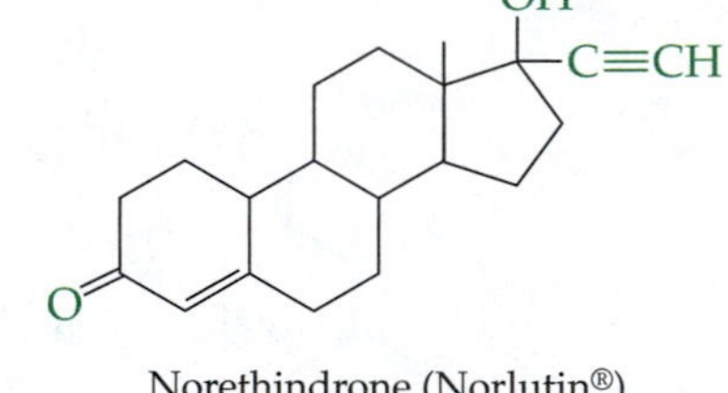

(b) Norethindrone (Norlutin®)

OH
C≡CH
O

(c) Norethynodrel

OH
C≡CH
CH_3O

(d) Mestranol

The progestins—norethynodrel, norethindrone, and related compounds—mimic the action of progesterone. Mestranol, a synthetic estrogen, regulates the menstrual cycle and the progestin establishes a state of false pregnancy. A woman does not ovulate when she is pregnant or in the state of false pregnancy established by a progestin, and because she does not ovulate, she cannot conceive.

Emergency Contraceptives

Several products, called *emergency contraceptives* or *morning-after pills*, can be used to prevent pregnancy after unprotected intercourse. There are two kinds of emergency contraception pills (ECPs): combination pills with both estrogen and progestin (synthetic analogs of the natural substances), and pills containing only progestin. Given in high doses, ECPs disrupt hormone functions on which pregnancy depends. ECPs halt development of the uterine lining and inhibit ovulation and fertilization.

One brand of ECP, called Previn®, contains both an estrogen (ethinyl estradiol) and a progestin (levonorgestrel). Another ECP, called Plan B®, available

▲ Frank Colton (1923–2003).

over the counter, contains only levonorgestrel. ECPs are taken as two doses, 12 hours apart. They are 75–89% effective in preventing pregnancy after unprotected sexual intercourse, and they work best if taken as soon as possible after intercourse. Only one woman out of 100 will become pregnant after taking progestin-only ECPs.

(a) Levonorgestrel (b) Ethinyl estradiol

An intrauterine device (IUD), the Copper T 380A IUD (ParaGard®), is also used for emergency contraception. IUD insertion reduces the incidence of pregnancy by 99.9% if done within three to five days of unprotected intercourse. Copper(II) ions in the IUD interfere with sperm transport and fertilization. The copper IUD probably causes an inflammation that makes the endometrium unsuitable for implantation.

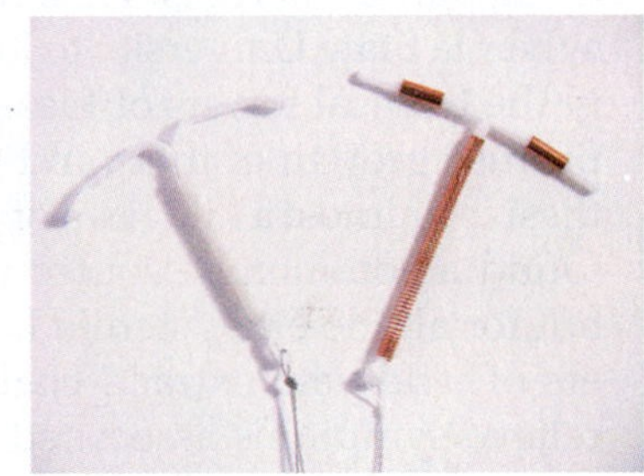
▲ The Copper T 380A IUD (ParaGard®).

ECPs are not the same as the so-called medical abortion pills such as mifepristone (or RU-486). Mifepristone (Mifeprex®), which inhibits the action of progesterone, works after a woman becomes pregnant and the fertilized egg has attached to the wall of the uterus. It causes the uterus to expel the egg, ending the pregnancy. ECPs prevent pregnancy after sexual intercourse, while mifepristone ends an unwanted pregnancy at an early stage.

Mifepristone

People who believe that human life begins when the ovum is fertilized by the sperm equate the use of mifepristone with abortion and oppose the use of the drug. Others consider the drug another method of birth control and see its use as being safer than a surgical abortion.

Risks of Taking Birth Control Pills

Oral contraceptives are currently used by more than 100 million women worldwide and by about 12 million women in the United States. Most women report no side effects. Of the side effects that are reported, almost all are minor. Some women experience hypertension, acne, or abnormal bleeding. These pills increase the risk of blood clotting in some women, but so does pregnancy. Blood clots can clog arteries and cause death by stroke or heart attack. The death rate associated with birth control pills is about 3 in 100,000, only one-tenth as high as the death rate associated with childbirth. For smokers, however, the risks are much higher. For women over 40 who smoke 15 cigarettes per day and take an oral contraceptive, the risk of death from stroke or heart attack is 1 in 5000. The FDA advises all women who smoke, especially those over 40, to use some other method of contraception.

Chemical Treasure in the Rainforest

In 1940, progesterone was one of the most expensive compounds in the world. Obtained with great difficulty from animals, it sold for $200 per gram—equivalent to about $1600 in today's dollars. American chemist Russell Marker (1902–1995) wondered if progesterone could be made from a plant steroid. He took diosgenin, which occurs in various plants, and converted it to progesterone.

He examined more than 400 plants from all over the world, looking for a more abundant source of this plant steroid, finally identifying a Mexican wild yam, *Dioscorea villosa*, that contained a significant quantity of diosgenin in its roots. He left his faculty post at Pennsylvania State University to look for more of these vines in the tropical forests of Mexico. Eventually he found a profuse growth of them and within a few months synthesized almost a kilogram of progesterone. Marker had found a commercial source not only for progesterone but for all the other steroid hormones as well. (Marketers of wild yam extracts claim that these extracts may relieve symptoms associated with menopause, but the yam as such does not contain progesterone or anything else that acts like progesterone.)

Tropical rainforests are warm, moist, and fertile areas that contain more different kinds of plants and animals than anyplace else on Earth. These forests are living chemical factories full of valuable and irreplaceable natural resources. Unfortunately, the world's rainforests are rapidly disappearing.

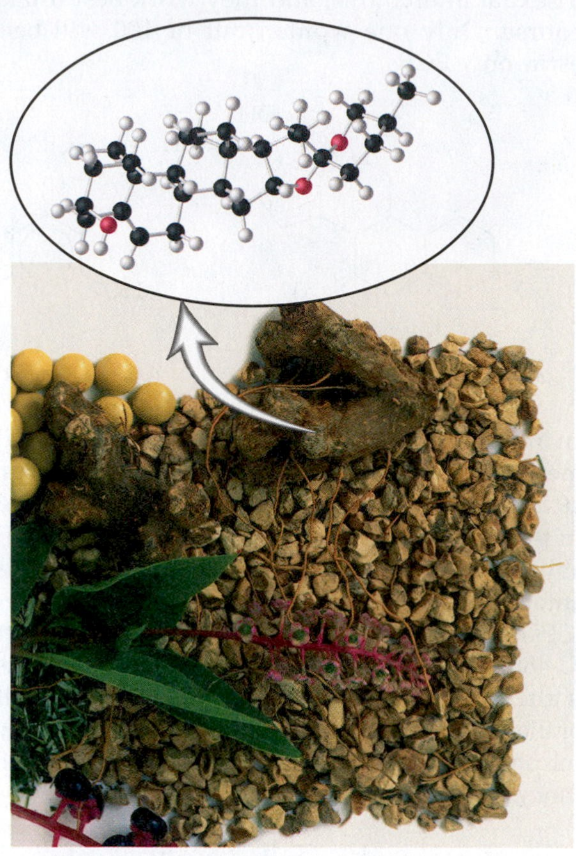

▲ The Mexican wild yam is a source of diosgenin, from which progesterone is made.

The Minipill

Because most of the side effects of oral contraceptives are associated with the estrogen component, the amount of estrogen in birth control pills has been greatly reduced over the years. Today's pills contain only a fraction of a milligram of estrogen. "Minipills" are now available that contain only small amounts of progestin and no estrogen at all. Minipills are not quite as effective as the combination pills, but they have fewer side effects.

A Pill for Males?

Why should females have to bear all the responsibility for contraception? Why not a pill for males? Many men are willing to share the risks and the responsibility of contraception, but condoms and vasectomies are the only effective forms of contraception available to them. There are biological reasons for females to bear the burden. Women are the ones who get pregnant when contraception fails, and in females contraception has to interfere with only one monthly event: ovulation. Males produce sperm continuously.

In males, the pituitary hormones FSH and LH (Table 18.2) are required for the continued production of sperm and of the male hormone testosterone. Several research groups have developed what may be a safe, effective, and reversible contraceptive for males. The pill has a progestin—the same key ingredient as is used in pills for women—combined with the male sex hormone testosterone.

The progestin seems to function much as it does in the women's pill: It suppresses the rate of sperm production and the quantity of sperm produced. When will such male birth control pills be available to the public? Optimistic projections estimate a wait of several years; others say there will be no male pill in our lifetimes.

Self-Assessment Questions

1. Hormones are produced in the endocrine glands and act
   a. on the brain only
   b. on nearby cells only
   c. on sex organs only
   d. throughout the body
2. Prostaglandins are synthesized in the body from
   a. arachidonic acid
   b. ascorbic acid
   c. cholesterol
   d. progesterone
3. Which of the following is *not* a steroid?
   a. prednisone
   b. progesterone
   c. prolactin
   d. testosterone
4. The gonads are stimulated to produce sex hormones and eggs or sperm by
   a. ACTH and LH
   b. FSH and LH
   c. LH and CRF
   d. TRF and GH
5. The hormone that maintains pregnancy is
   a. estradiol
   b. estrone
   c. progesterone
   d. prolactin
6. The functional group that makes a birth control drug effective orally is
   a. $CH_3CH_2—$
   b. $CH_2{=}CH—$
   c. $HC{\equiv}C—$
   d. $CH_3CO—$

Answers: 1, d; 2, a; 3, c; 4, b; 5, c; 6, c

18.6 Drugs for the Heart

Learning Objective › Describe the action of four types of drugs used to treat heart disease.

The heart is a muscle that beats virtually every second of every day for as long as we live. Diseases of the cardiovascular system are responsible for one-third of deaths in the United States and more than one-fifth of deaths worldwide. Four of the top ten prescription drugs worldwide are for treating cardiovascular disease. These drugs prolong life and improve its quality.

Major diseases of the heart and blood vessels include

- ischemic ("lacking oxygen") coronary artery disease,
- heart arrhythmias (abnormal heartbeat),
- hypertension (high blood pressure), and
- congestive heart failure.

Atherosclerosis (buildup of fatty deposits in the lining of the arteries) is the primary cause of coronary artery disease, which in turn causes myocardial infarction (heart attack). Thus, most drug treatments for the heart aim to increase its supply of blood (and oxygen), to normalize its rhythm, to lower blood pressure, or to prevent accumulation of lipid plaque deposits in blood vessels.

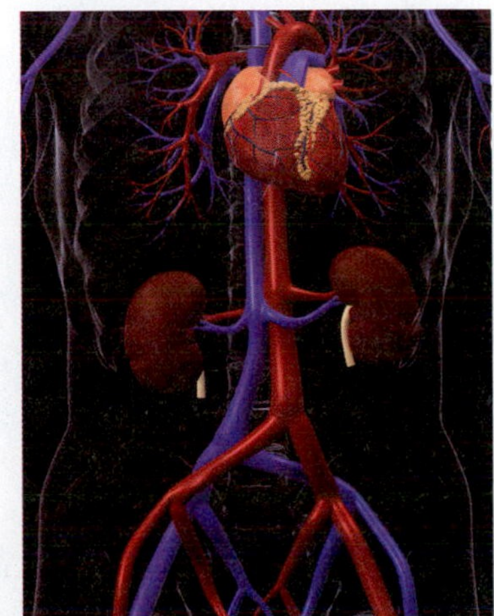

▲ The cardiovascular system. Over the course of 24 h, the heart pumps more than 8000 L of blood through nearly 100,000 km of blood vessels.

Lowering Blood Pressure

Hypertension, or high blood pressure, is defined as pressure, in millimeters of mercury (mmHg), above 140/90. Normal blood pressure is defined as less than 120/80. Hypertension is the most common cardiovascular disease, affecting more than one

NO—A Messenger Molecule

The simple nitrogen monoxide molecule (NO), notorious as an air pollutant (Chapter 13), was found in 1986 to act as a *messenger molecule* that carries signals between cells in the body. All previously known messenger molecules are complex substances such as norepinephrine and serotonin (Section 18.7) that act by fitting specific receptors in cell membranes. Commonly called nitric oxide, NO is essential to maintaining blood pressure and establishing long-term memory. It also aids in the immune response to foreign invaders in the body and mediates the relaxation phase of intestinal contractions in the digestion of food.

NO is formed in cells from arginine, a nitrogen-rich amino acid (Section 16.4), in a reaction catalyzed by an enzyme. NO kills invading microorganisms, probably by deactivating iron-containing enzymes in much the same way as carbon monoxide destroys the oxygen-carrying capacity of hemoglobin (Section 13.4).

Louis Ignarro, Robert F. Furchgott, and Ferid Murad, who discovered the physiological role of NO, were awarded a 1998 Nobel Prize in Physiology or Medicine. This award has a fortuitous link to Alfred Nobel, whose invention of dynamite made him wealthy and provided the financial basis of the Nobel prizes. Nitroglycerin, the explosive ingredient of dynamite, relieves the chest pain of heart disease. In his later years, Nobel refused to take nitroglycerin for his heart disease because it causes headaches, and he did not think it would relieve his chest pain. Murad showed that nitroglycerin acts by releasing NO.

NO also dilates the blood vessels that allow blood flow into the penis to cause an erection. Research on this role of NO led to the development of the anti-impotence drug sildenafil (Viagra®). One of the physiological effects of sildenafil is the production of small quantities of NO in the bloodstream. Related research has led to drugs for treating shock and a drug for treating high blood pressure in newborn babies.

Further research indicates that two other gases, carbon monoxide (CO) and hydrogen sulfide (H_2S), also act as messenger molecules. Research into the development of heart medicines based on these substances is under way.

in four adults in the United States. Because it seldom produces symptoms, many people have hypertension without realizing it. There are four major categories of drugs for lowering blood pressure.

- *Diuretics* [for example, hydrochlorothiazide (HCT)] cause the kidneys to excrete more water and thus lower the blood volume.
- *Beta blockers*, (for example, propranolol and metoprolol; see Section 18.7) slow the heart rate and reduce the force of the heartbeat.
- *Calcium channel blockers* (for example, amlodipine) are powerful vasodilators, inducing muscles around the blood vessels to relax.
- *Angiotensin-converting enzyme (ACE) inhibitors* (for example, lisinopril) inhibit the action of an enzyme that causes blood vessels to contract.

Studies show that diuretics, the oldest, simplest, and cheapest of the blood-pressure–lowering drugs, may also be the most effective for treating hypertension in most people. However, both a diuretic and one of the other medications are often prescribed.

Normalizing Heart Rhythm

An *arrhythmia* is an abnormal heartbeat. Some arrhythmias exhibit no symptoms and are discovered only during a physical examination, but others can be life threatening. The electrical properties of nerves and muscles arise from the flow of ions across cell membranes, and drugs for arrhythmia alter this flow. There are several types of such drugs, with different mechanisms of action, but all of them tend to have a narrow margin between the therapeutic dose and a harmful amount. A change in the heart's rhythm can have serious consequences. A too-rapid heartbeat, known as *fibrillation*, is so common that defibrillator devices are now available on many airplanes and in various other public places.

Treating Coronary Artery Disease

A common symptom of coronary artery disease is chest pain, called *angina pectoris*. This pain is caused by an insufficient supply of oxygen to the heart, usually due to partial blockage of the coronary arteries by lipid-containing plaque (arteriosclerosis). When the blockage is complete, a heart attack occurs, and some of the heart muscle dies. Medical treatment for coronary artery disease usually involves dilation (widening) of the blood vessels to the heart to increase the blood flow and slowing of the heart rate to decrease its workload and its demand for oxygen. Some of the drugs used are the same as those used to lower high blood pressure (beta blockers, for example). Several organic nitro compounds, especially amyl nitrite ($CH_3CH_2CH_2CH_2CH_2ONO$) and nitroglycerin, have a long history in the treatment of angina pectoris. These compounds act by releasing nitric oxide (NO), which relaxes the constricted vessels that are reducing the supply of blood and oxygen to the heart.

$H_2C-O-NO_2$
$HC-O-NO_2$
$H_2C-O-NO_2$

Nitroglycerin

Although many new drugs are being used to treat heart failure, one that has been used for centuries still plays an important role. The foxglove plant was used by the ancient Egyptians and Romans. The plant contains a mixture of glycosides that yield carbohydrates and steroids on hydrolysis. Hydrolysis of digoxin (one of those glycosides) yields the steroid digitoxigenin, which affects the rhythm and strength of the heart muscles' contractions. Digoxin is still used to treat patients with heart failure.

Self-Assessment Questions

1. Which of the following is a treatment for hypertension (high blood pressure)?
   a. acetaminophen **b.** a diuretic **c.** nitroglycerin **d.** prednisone
2. Drugs called beta blockers
   a. lessen blood flow to the kidneys
   b. lessen the damage due to beta particles
   c. prevent the hydrolysis of beta linkages
   d. slow the rate of the heartbeat
3. Drugs such as amyl nitrite and nitroglycerin act by releasing a substance that relaxes the smooth muscles in blood vessels. That substance is
   a. an amino acid **b.** digitalis
   c. nitric oxide **d.** a steroid

Answers: 1, b; 2, d; 3, c

18.7 Drugs and the Mind

Learning Objectives › Explain how the brain amines norepinephrine and serotonin affect the mind and how various drugs change their action. › Identify some stimulant drugs, depressant drugs, and psychotropic drugs, and explain how they affect the mind.

A **psychotropic drug** is one that affects the human mind. The first drugs used by primitive peoples probably were mind-altering substances. Alcoholic beverages, marijuana, opium, coca leaves, peyote, and other plant materials have been used for their psychotropic effects for thousands of years. Generally, only one or two of these were used in any given society. Today, thousands of psychotropic drugs are readily available. Some still come from plants, but many are synthetic.

There is no clear distinction between drugs that affect the mind and those that affect the body. Most drugs probably affect both mind and body. It can still be helpful, however, to distinguish between drugs that act mainly on the body and drugs that affect mainly the mind.

Psychotropic drugs are divided into three classes.

- A **stimulant drug**, such as cocaine or an amphetamine, increases alertness, speeds mental processes, and generally elevates the mood.
- A **depressant drug**, such as alcohol, almost any anesthetic, an opiate, a barbiturate, or any of certain tranquilizers, reduces the level of consciousness and

the intensity of reactions to environmental stimuli. In general, depressants dull emotional responses.

- A **hallucinogenic drug**, such as lysergic acid diethylamide (LSD) or marijuana, alters qualitatively the perception of one's surroundings.

We will examine some of the major drugs in each category, but first we need to look at some chemistry of the nervous system.

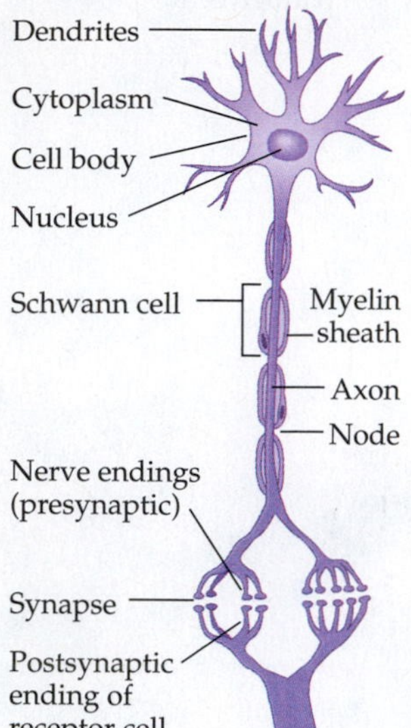

▲ **Figure 18.16** Diagram of a human nerve cell.

Chemistry of the Nervous System

The nervous system is made up of about 12 billion **neurons** (nerve cells) with 10^{13} connections between them. The brain has the capacity to handle about 10 trillion bits of information. Nerve cells vary a great deal in shape and size. One type is shown in Figure 18.16. The essential parts of each cell are the cell body, the axon, and the dendrites. We discuss here only the nerves that make up the involuntary (autonomic) nervous system. These nerves carry messages between organs and glands that act involuntarily (such as the heart, the digestive organs, and the lungs) and the brain and spinal column.

The axon on a nerve cell may be up to 60 cm long, but there is no continuous pathway from an organ to the central nervous system. Messages must be transmitted across tiny, fluid-filled gaps, or **synapses** (Figure 18.17). When an electrical signal from a nerve cell in the brain reaches the end of an axon of a presynaptic nerve cell, chemicals called **neurotransmitters** are released from tiny vesicles into the synapse. Receptors on the postsynaptic cell bind the neurotransmitter, causing changes in that receiving cell. After a brief interval, the neurotransmitters are released from the receptor site and carried back to the presynaptic cell by substances called *transporters*.

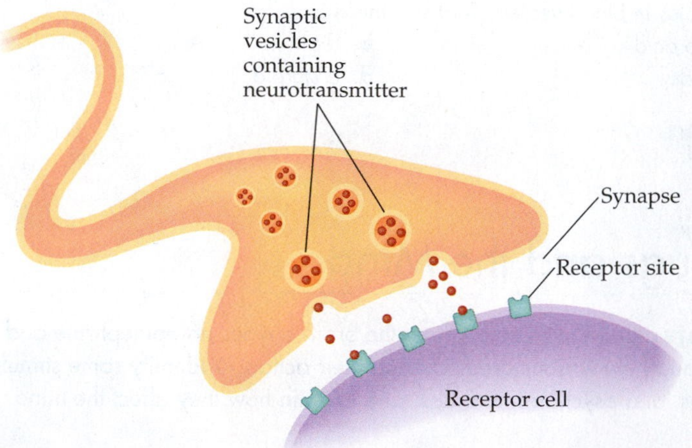

▶ **Figure 18.17** Diagram of a synapse. When an electrical signal reaches the presynaptic nerve ending, neurotransmitter molecules are released from the vesicles. They migrate across the synapse to the postsynaptic nerve cell, where they fit specific receptor sites.

There are many neurotransmitters (Table 18.3 lists some of them). Substances that act as neurotransmitters include amino acids, peptides, and monosubstituted amines (monoamines). For example, glutamate, the carboxylate anion of the amino acid glutamic acid, is the most common neurotransmitter in the brain. More than 50 peptides function as neurotransmitters. Messages are carried to other nerve cells, to muscles, and to the endocrine glands (such as the adrenal glands). Each neurotransmitter fits one or more receptor sites on the receptor cell. For example, nerve impulses trigger release of glutamate from the presynaptic cell. Glutamate receptors in the postsynaptic cell bind glutamate and are activated. Neurotransmitters determine to a large degree how you think, feel, and move about. If there are problems with their synthesis or uptake, things can go quite wrong. Many drugs (and some poisons) act by mimicking the action of a neurotransmitter. Others act by blocking the receptor sites and preventing neurotransmitter molecules from acting on them.

Table 18.3 Selected Neurotransmitters[a]

Transmitter Molecule	Precursor Molecule	Site of Synthesis
Dopamine	Tyrosine	Central nervous system (CNS)
Norepinephrine	Tyrosine	CNS
Epinephrine	Tyrosine	Adrenal medulla, some CNS cells
Serotonin [5-Hydroxy-tryptamine (5-HT)]	Tryptophan	CNS, gut
Acetylcholine	Choline	CNS, parasympathetic nerves
GABA	Glutamate	CNS
Glutamate		CNS
Aspartate		CNS
Glycine		Spinal cord
Histamine	Histidine	Hypothalamus
Adenosine	ATP	CNS, peripheral nerves
ATP		Sympathetic, sensory and enteric nerves
Nitric oxide (NO)	Arginine	CNS, gastrointestinal tract

[a]Not all of these are discussed in this text.

Biochemical Theories of Brain Diseases

Like other organs, the brain can suffer from disease. Normal brain activity involves many chemical substances. Problems arise when an imbalance of these substances develops. We all have ups and downs in our lives. These moods probably result from multiple causes, but it is likely that a variety of compounds formed in the brain are involved. Before we consider these ups and downs, however, let's take a look at epinephrine, an amine formed in the adrenal glands and in some central nervous system cells (Figure 18.18).

Epinephrine is secreted by the adrenal glands—and is thus often called *adrenaline*—when a person is under stress or is frightened. A tiny amount of epinephrine causes a large increase in blood pressure, and its flow prepares the body for fight or flight. Because culturally imposed inhibitions prevent fighting or fleeing in most modern situations, the adrenaline-induced supercharge is often not used. This sort of frustration has been implicated in some forms of mental illness.

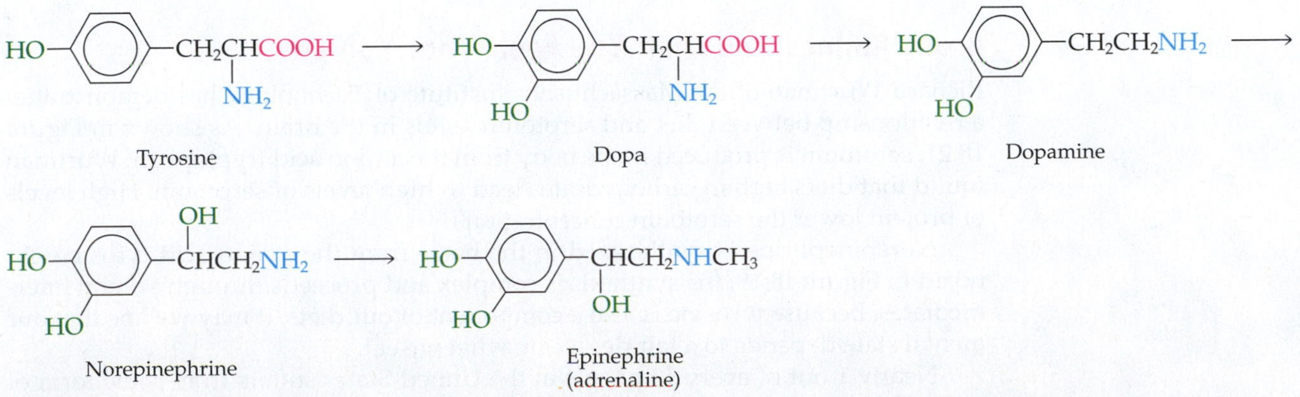

▲ **Figure 18.18** The biosynthesis of epinephrine and norepinephrine from tyrosine. L-Dopa, the left-handed form of the compound (see the box on page 565), is used to treat Parkinson's disease, which results from inadequate dopamine production. Dopamine cannot be used directly to treat the disease because it is not absorbed into the brain. Schizophrenia has been attributed to an overabundance of dopamine in nerve cells.

Biochemical theories of mental illness usually involve chemical imbalances of brain amines, which can be improved with medication. One such brain amine is norepinephrine (NE), a relative of epinephrine. NE is a neurotransmitter formed in the brain (Figure 18.18). When produced in excess, NE causes euphoria. In large excess, NE induces a manic state.

Another brain amine is the neurotransmitter *serotonin*. Serotonin is involved in sleep, appetite, memory, learning, sensory perception, mood, sexual behavior, and regulation of body temperature. This brain amine is also involved in behaviors such as eating, sleeping, and aggression. Serotonin inhibits the nervous system in ways that calm, soothe, and generate feelings of contentment and satisfaction. The main metabolite of serotonin, 5-hydroxyindoleacetic acid (5-HIAA), is found in unusually low levels in the cerebrospinal fluid of severely depressed patients with a history of suicide attempts; this finding indicates that abnormal metabolism of serotonin plays a role in depression. Some research suggests that a reduced flow of serotonin through the synapses in the frontal lobe of the brain causes depression. Cerebrospinal fluid levels of 5-HIAA are also low in murderers and other violent offenders. However, they are higher than normal in people with obsessive–compulsive disorder, sociopaths, and people with guilt complexes.

NE and related compounds fall into several general categories. NE *agonists* (drugs that enhance or mimic the action of NE) are stimulants. NE *antagonists* (drugs that block the action of NE) slow down various processes. For example, beta blockers (Figure 18.19) reduce the stimulant action of epinephrine and NE on various kinds of cells. Propranolol (Inderal®) is used to treat cardiac arrhythmias, angina, and hypertension by slightly lessening the force of the heartbeat. Unfortunately, it also causes lethargy and depression. Metoprolol (Lopressor®) acts selectively on the cells of the heart. It can be used by hypertensive patients who have asthma because it does not act on receptors in the bronchi.

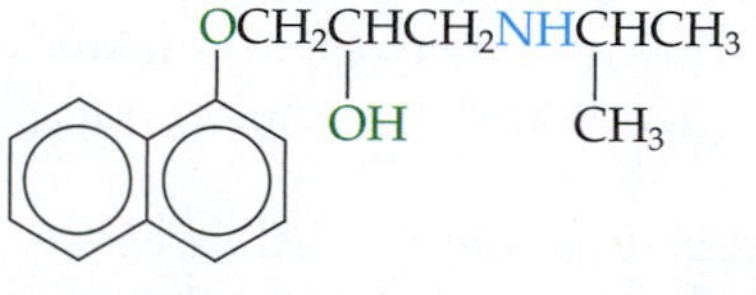

▶ **Figure 18.19** Propranolol and metoprolol are beta blockers, widely used to treat high blood pressure.

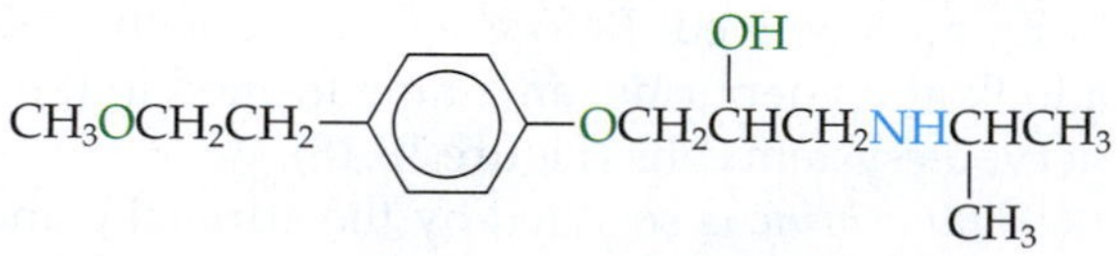

Propranolol: $OCH_2CH(OH)CH_2NHCH(CH_3)CH_3$ (on a naphthalene ring)

Metoprolol: $CH_3OCH_2CH_2-C_6H_4-OCH_2CH(OH)CH_2NHCH(CH_3)CH_3$

Serotonin agonists are used to treat depression, anxiety, and obsessive–compulsive disorder. Serotonin antagonists are used to treat migraine headaches and to relieve the nausea caused by cancer chemotherapy.

Brain Amines and Diet: You Feel What You Eat

Richard Wurtman of the Massachusetts Institute of Technology has demonstrated a relationship between diet and serotonin levels in the brain. As shown in Figure 18.21, serotonin is produced in the body from the amino acid tryptophan. Wurtman found that diets high in carbohydrates lead to high levels of serotonin. High levels of protein lower the serotonin concentration.

Norepinephrine is synthesized in the body from the amino acid tyrosine. As noted in Figure 18.18, the synthesis is complex and proceeds through several intermediates. Because tyrosine is also a component of our diets, it may well be that our mental state depends to a fair degree on what we eat.

Nearly 1 out of every 10 people in the United States suffers from some form of mental illness. More than half the patients in hospitals are there because of mental problems. When the biochemistry of the brain is more fully understood, mental illness may be cured (or at least alleviated) by the administration of drugs—or by adjusting the diet.

Right-Handed and Left-Handed Molecules

Like people, molecules can be either right-handed or left-handed. Ball-and-stick models of two structures for the amino acid alanine [$CH_3CH(NH_2)COOH$] are shown in Figure 18.20. These structures are **stereoisomers**, isomers having the same structural formula but differing in the arrangement of atoms or groups of atoms in three-dimensional space. Models of the two stereoisomers of alanine are as alike—and as different—as a pair of gloves. If you place one of the models in front of a mirror, the image in the mirror will be identical to the other model. Molecules that are nonsuperimposable (nonidentical) mirror images of each other are stereoisomers of a specific type called **enantiomers** (Greek *enantios*, "opposite").

Enantiomers have a **chiral carbon**, a carbon atom to which four different groups are attached. For example, the central carbon of alanine has four groups (H, CH_3, COOH, and NH_2) joined to it. If a molecule contains one or more chiral carbons, it is likely to exist as two or more stereoisomers. In contrast, propane ($CH_3CH_2CH_3$), for example, does not contain a chiral carbon and thus does not exist as a pair of stereoisomers.

Stereoisomerism is quite common in organic chemicals of biological importance. The simple sugars (Section 16.2) are all right-handed. While 19 of the 20 amino acids that make up proteins are left-handed, the other, glycine (H_2NCH_2COOH), has no handedness.

A right-hand glove doesn't fit on a left hand, or vice versa. Similarly, enantiomers fit enzymes differently, and they have different effects. As an example, consider atorvastatin (Lipitor®), the best-selling drug in the world, with U.S. sales of \$7.2 billion in 2010, which is used to lower blood cholesterol. Initial research on this drug in 1989 was promising but not outstanding. Later it was found that only the left-handed isomer is active; thus, it is much more effective when separated from its right-handed form. The development of drugs that consist of only one enantiomer is becoming increasingly important in the pharmaceutical industry.

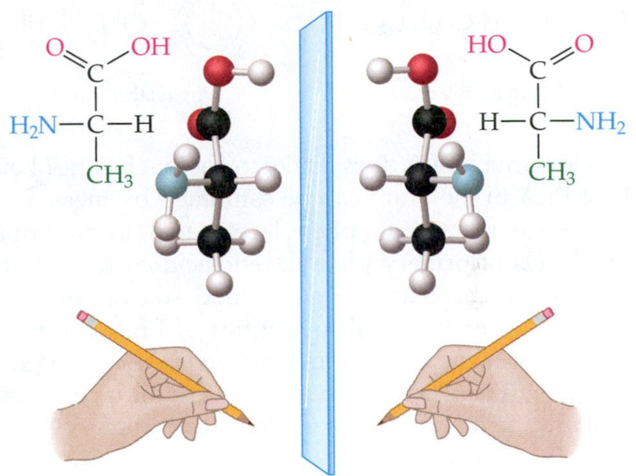

▲ **Figure 18.20** Ball-and-stick models and structural formulas of D- and L-alanine. The molecules are *enantiomers*, mirror images of one another. Like right and left hands, enantiomers cannot be superimposed on one another.

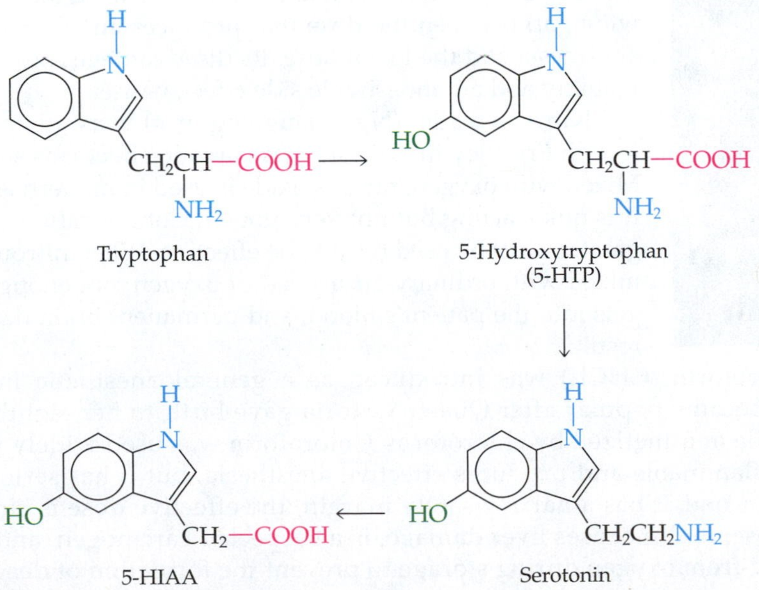

Tryptophan → 5-Hydroxytryptophan (5-HTP) → Serotonin → 5-HIAA

◀ **Figure 18.21** Serotonin is produced in the brain from the amino acid tryptophan. The synthesis involves several steps; some are omitted here for simplicity. 5-HIAA is a metabolite of serotonin.

Anesthetics

An **anesthetic** is a substance that causes lack of feeling or awareness. A **general anesthetic** acts on the brain to produce unconsciousness and a general insensitivity to pain. A local anesthetic causes loss of feeling in a part of the body. Diethyl ether

Love, Trust, Sexual Fidelity, and Chemistry

The notion that such emotions as love and trust might be chemical in origin is unsettling. However, emotions that trigger romantic relationships seem to be governed in part by a substance called β-*phenylethylamine (PEA).* PEA functions as a neurotransmitter in the human brain. It seems to create excited, alert feelings and aggressive moods. Increased levels of PEA produce a feeling much like "being in love." The chemical structure of PEA resembles that of norepinephrine (page 563).

C_6H_5—$CH_2CH_2NH_2$

β-Phenylethylamine

C_6H_5—CH_2—COOH

Phenylacetic acid

How much PEA does it take to get that feeling? Levels of PEA in the brain can be estimated by measuring levels of its metabolite, phenylacetic acid, in the urine. Low levels of urinary phenylacetic acid correlate with depression. There are no good food sources of PEA. Chocolate contains small quantities of PEA, but most of the PEA in chocolate is metabolized before it reaches the brain. PEA releases dopamine (it is a dopamine agonist), producing an antidepressant effect. Some research has shown that oral doses of PEA relieve depression in some people.

Oxytocin (Table 18.2), sometimes called the "cuddling chemical," increases the bond between lovers. It also induces contractions during childbirth and lactation afterward. Swiss scientists have shown that oxytocin increases trust in people. People playing a trust game were more trusting after taking one sniff of oxytocin.

If oxytocin equals love, vasopressin may keep couples together. Few mammals are monogamous, mating and bonding with one partner for life. The prairie vole is one such mammal. Montane voles, a closely related species, are polygamous. Scientists have found that within 24 hours after mating, the male prairie vole is hooked for life. Postcoital production of vasopressin in the male is responsible for this monogamous behavior. Male montane voles, which have a different pattern of vasopressin receptors than prairie voles, did not react significantly to female voles when injected with vasopressin. When given a compound to suppress the effect of vasopressin, the prairie voles lose their devotion to each other. Perhaps the solution to the high divorce rate is a few sniffs of vasopressin.

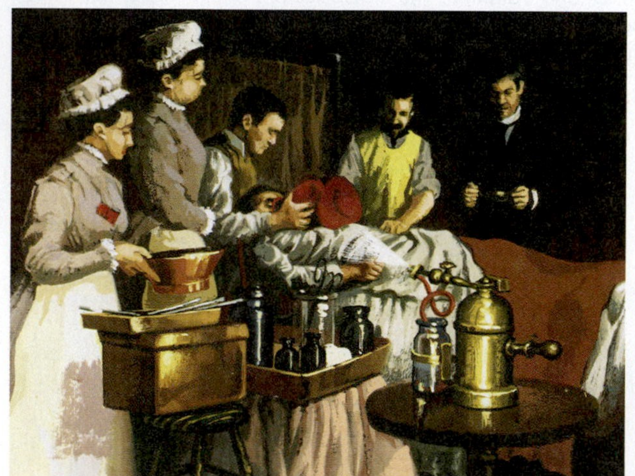

▲ This painting shows an operation in Boston in 1846, during which ether was used as an anesthetic.

($CH_3CH_2OCH_2CH_3$), the first general anesthetic, was introduced into surgical practice in the 1840s. Inhalation of ether vapor produces unconsciousness by depressing the activity of the central nervous system. Ether is relatively safe because there is a fairly wide gap between the dose that produces an effective level of anesthesia and the lethal dose. Its disadvantages are high flammability and an undesirable side effect, nausea.

Nitrous oxide (N_2O, laughing gas) was discovered by Joseph Priestley in 1772, and its narcotic effect was soon noted. Mixed with oxygen, nitrous oxide is used in modern anesthesia. It is quick acting but not very potent. Concentrations of 50% or greater must be used for it to be effective. When nitrous oxide is mixed with ordinary air instead of oxygen, not enough oxygen gets into the patient's blood, and permanent brain damage can result.

Chloroform ($CHCl_3$) was introduced as a general anesthetic in 1847. It quickly became popular after Queen Victoria gave birth to her eighth child in 1853 while anesthetized by chloroform. Chloroform was used widely for years. It is nonflammable and produces effective anesthesia, but it has serious drawbacks. For one, it has a narrow safety margin; the effective dose is close to the lethal dose. It also causes liver damage, is a suspected carcinogen, and must be protected from oxygen during storage to prevent the formation of deadly phosgene gas.

Modern inhalant anesthetics include fluorine-containing compounds (Table 18.4). These compounds are nonflammable and relatively safe for patients. Their safety for operating room personnel, however, has been questioned. For example, female operating room workers suffer a higher rate of miscarriages than women in the general population.

Solvent Sniffing: Self-Administered Anesthesia

Nearly all gaseous and volatile liquid organic compounds exhibit anesthetic action, and this leads to their abuse. The sniffing of glue solvents, gasoline, aerosol propellants, and other inhalants is perhaps the deadliest form of drug abuse. The dose required for intoxication is often close to the dose that will stop the heart. And it is difficult to measure the dose inhaled from the plastic or paper bag normally used in sniffing. Also, as with nitrous oxide, sublethal doses can cause permanent brain damage by cutting down the oxygen supply to the brain.

Table 18.4 Inhaled Anesthetic Agents

Generic or Chemical Name	Formula	Commercial Name	Year Introduced	Currently in Use?
Diethyl ether	$CH_3CH_2OCH_2CH_3$	Ether	1842	No
Nitrous oxide	N_2O	Nitrous oxide	1844	Yes
Chloroform	$CHCl_3$	Chloroform	1847	No
Isoflurane	$CHF_2OCHClCF_3$	Forane®	1980	Yes
Desflurane	$CHF_2OCHFCF_3$	Suprane®	1992	Yes
Sevoflurane	$CH_2FOCH(CF_3)_2$	Ultane®	1995	Yes

Modern surgical practice usually makes use of a variety of drugs. Generally, a patient is given

- a tranquilizer such as a benzodiazepine (Valium® or Versed®; page 571) to decrease anxiety,
- an intravenous anesthetic such as thiopental (page 570) to produce unconsciousness quickly,
- a narcotic pain medication (such as fentanyl; Table 18.1) to block pain,
- an inhalant anesthetic (Table 18.4) to provide insensitivity to pain and to keep the patient unconscious, often combined with oxygen and nitrous oxide to support life, and
- a relaxant such as pancuronim bromide to relax the muscles and make it easier to insert the breathing tube.

General anesthetics reduce nerve transmission at the synapses by inhibiting the excitatory effect of certain neurotransmitters on central nervous system receptors. The anesthetics bind only weakly, and it is difficult to determine their exact mode of action.

Local Anesthetics

Local anesthetics are used to render a part of the body insensitive to pain. They block nerve conduction by reducing the permeability of the nerve cell membrane to sodium ions. The patient remains conscious during dental work or minor surgery.

The first local anesthetic to be used successfully was cocaine, a drug first isolated in 1860 from the leaves of the coca plant (Figure 18.22). Its structure was determined by Richard Willstätter in 1898. Scientists have made many attempts to develop synthetic compounds with similar properties. Cocaine is a powerful stimulant whose abuse is discussed on page 574.

Because local anesthetics are weak bases (amines), they are usually used in the form of hydrochloride salts, which are water-soluble. Some of the local anesthetics (Figure 18.23) are amine–esters (cocaine, procaine, and chloroprocaine), and others are amine–amides (lidocaine, mepivacaine, prilocaine, bupivacaine, and etidocaine). The amine–esters cause allergic reactions in some people; the amine–amides do not. The ethyl and butyl esters of *para*-aminobenzoic acid (PABA) are topical

▲ **Figure 18.22** Coca leaves contain the alkaloid cocaine, a local anesthetic and stimulant.

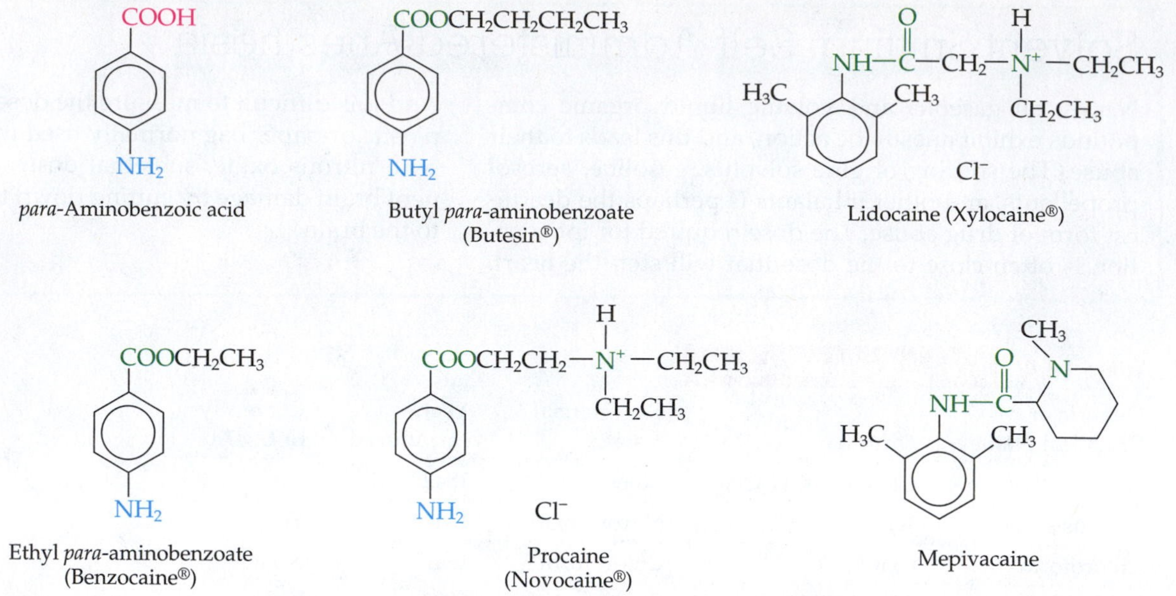

COOH
NH_2
para-Aminobenzoic acid

$COOCH_2CH_2CH_2CH_3$
NH_2
Butyl *para*-aminobenzoate (Butesin®)

Lidocaine (Xylocaine®)

$COOCH_2CH_3$
NH_2
Ethyl *para*-aminobenzoate (Benzocaine®)

Procaine (Novocaine®)

Mepivacaine

▲ **Figure 18.23** Some local anesthetics. They are often used in the form of a hydrochloride or picrate salt, which is more soluble in water than the free base.

Q: *Which of these are derived from para-aminobenzoic acid? Which have amide functional groups? Which are esters?*

anesthetics, usually used in the form of picrate salts in ointments that are applied to the skin to relieve the pain of burns and open wounds.

Introduction of a second nitrogen atom in the alkyl group of the ester produces a more powerful anesthetic (Table 18.5). Perhaps the best known of these is procaine (Novocaine®), first synthesized in 1905 by Alfred Einhorn (1865–1917), who had worked with Willstätter on the structure of cocaine. Procaine takes a fairly long time to take effect, wears off very quickly, and causes allergic reactions. It is no longer used in dentistry, having been replaced largely by the amine–amide anesthetics.

Table 18.5 Substances Commonly Used as Local Anesthetics

Substance	Duration of Action
Procaine (Novocain®)	Short
Lidocaine (Xylocaine®)	Medium (30–60 min)
Mepivacaine (Carbocaine®)	Fast (6–10 min)
Bupivacaine (Marcaine®)	Moderate (8–12 min)
Prilocaine (Citanest®)	Medium (30–90 min)
Chloroprocaine (Nesacaine®)	Short (15–30 min)
Cocaine	Medium
Etidocaine (Duranest®)	Long (120–180 min)

Lidocaine was introduced in the 1940s and is still the most widely used local anesthetic. It takes effect quickly. When combined with a small quantity of epinephrine, it acts for an hour or more. (See Collaborative Group Project 12.)

Dissociative Anesthetics: Ketamine and PCP

Ketamine, an intravenous anesthetic, is called a *dissociative anesthetic* because it disconnects a person's perceptions from his or her sensations. It reduces or blocks signals to the conscious mind from parts of the brain that are associated with the senses. Ketamine induces hallucinations like those reported by people who have had near-death experiences. They seem to remember observing their rescuers from a vantage point above the scene or moving through a dark tunnel toward a bright light.

Ketamine acts as an NMDA-receptor antagonist. N-methyl-D-aspartate, or NMDA, is an amino acid derivative that mimics the action of the neurotransmitter glutamate (Table 18.3). Because ketamine acts by binding to receptors in the body, it is assumed that the body produces its own chemicals that fit these receptors. These compounds may be synthesized or released only in extreme circumstances—such as in near-death experiences.

Ketamine is used widely in veterinary medicine. Because it suppresses breathing much less than most other available anesthetics, ketamine is sometimes used as an anesthetic for humans with unknown medical histories and for children and persons of poor health.

Phencyclidine, commonly known as PCP, is closely related to ketamine. PCP was formerly used as an animal tranquilizer and for a brief time as a general anesthetic for humans. It is now fairly common on the illegal drug scene. PCP, which is soluble in fat and has no appreciable water solubility, is stored in fatty tissue and released when the fat is metabolized, accounting for the "flashbacks" commonly experienced by users. Many users experience bad "trips" with PCP, and about 1 in 1000 develops a severe form of schizophrenia. High doses cause illusions and hallucinations and can also cause seizures, coma, and death. However, death of PCP users more often results from an accident or suicide during a "trip."

O NHCH3 Cl

Ketamine

N

Phencyclidine (PCP)

Depressant Drugs

We start our exploration of depressant drugs by reconsidering ethyl alcohol, discussed in some detail in Chapter 9, because it is by far the most used and abused depressant drug in the world.

In nature, sugars in fruit are often fermented into alcohol by airborne yeasts, but purposeful production of ethanol probably did not begin until people began to farm. As early as 3700 B.C.E., the Egyptians fermented fruit to make wine and the Babylonians made beer from barley. People have been fermenting fruits and grains ever since, but relatively pure ethanol was first produced by Muslim alchemists who invented distillation in the eighth or ninth century.

People often think they are stimulated ("get high") when they drink, but ethanol is actually a depressant. It slows down both physical and mental activity. Nearly two-thirds of adults in the United States drink alcohol, and nearly one-third have five or more drinks on at least one day each year. There are at least 15 million alcoholics in the United States, and alcoholism costs \$185 billion a year. Approximately 30% of current drinkers in the United States drink to excess. According to the CDC, excessive drinking of alcohol kills about 79,000 people each year in the United States, and underage drinking causes about 5000 deaths of people under 21 each year. For 15- to 24-year-olds, the three leading causes of death are automobile accidents, homicides, and suicides, and alcohol is a leading factor in all three.

For some, there is a positive side to drinking alcohol. Longevity studies indicate that those who use alcohol moderately (no more than a drink or two a day) live longer than nondrinkers. This may result from alcohol's relaxing effect. Heavier drinking, however, can cause many health problems. Alcoholism shortens the life span of alcoholics by 10 to 12 years.

Alcoholic beverages are generally high in calories. Pure ethanol furnishes about 7 kcal/g. Ethanol is metabolized by oxidation to acetaldehyde at a rate of about 1 oz (about 30 mL) per hour, and the buildup of ethanol concentration in the blood caused by drinking at a rate faster than this results in intoxication.

Oxidation of ethanol uses up a substance called NAD^+, the oxidized form of nicotinamide adenine dinucleotide; the reduced form is represented as NADH, where the H is a hydrogen atom:

$$\underset{\text{Ethanol}}{CH_3CH_2OH} + NAD^+ \longrightarrow \underset{\text{Acetaldehyde}}{CH_3CHO} + NADH + H^+$$

Because NAD^+ is usually employed in the oxidation of fats, drinking too much alcohol causes fat to be deposited—mainly in the abdomen—rather than metabolized. This results in the familiar "beer gut" of many heavy drinkers.

Just how ethanol intoxicates is still somewhat of a mystery. Researchers have found that ethanol disrupts receptors for two neurotransmitters (Table 18.3): *gamma*-aminobutyric acid (GABA), which inhibits impulsiveness, and glutamate, which excites certain nerve cells. Long-term drinking changes the balance of GABA and glutamate, disrupting the brain's control over muscle activity and causing the drinker to stagger and fall. Ethanol also raises dopamine levels in the brain; dopamine is associated with the pleasurable aspects of alcohol and other drugs.

Excessive drinking over time changes the levels of some of the brain chemicals, causing a craving for ethanol in order to bring back good feelings or to avoid bad feelings. Studies on twins raised separately show that there is undoubtedly a genetic component to alcoholism. There are also emotional, psychological, social, and cultural factors. We still have much to learn about this ancient drug.

Barbiturates

A family of depressants, the barbiturates display a wide range of properties. They can be employed to produce mild sedation, deep sleep, or even death. More than 2500 barbiturates have been synthesized over the years, but only a few have found widespread use in medicine (Figure 18.24).

(a)

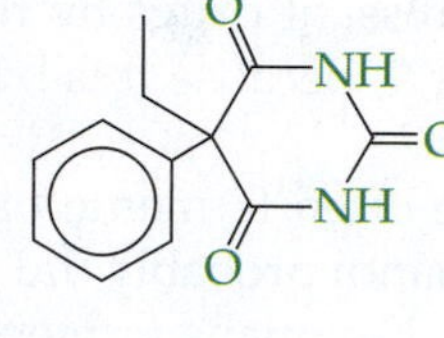

(b)

(c)

▶ **Figure 18.24** Formulas of some barbiturate drugs. (a) Pentobarbital (Nembutal®), (b) phenobarbital (Luminal®), and (c) thiopental (Pentothal®). These drugs, derived from barbituric acid, are often used in the form of their sodium salts; for example, thiopental is used as sodium pentothal.

- Pentobarbital is employed as a short-acting hypnotic drug. Before the discovery of modern tranquilizers, it was used widely to calm anxiety.
- Phenobarbital is a long-acting drug. It is employed as an anticonvulsant for people suffering from seizure disorders such as epilepsy.
- Thiopental, which differs from pentobarbital only in having a sulfur atom on the ring in place of one of the oxygen atoms, is used as an anesthetic (page 567).

Barbiturates were once used in small doses (a few milligrams) as sedatives. In larger doses (about 100 mg), barbiturates induce sleep. They were once widely prescribed as sleeping pills but have been replaced by drugs such as benzodiazepines (page 571), which have less potential for abuse and are less likely to be lethal.

Barbiturates are especially dangerous when ingested along with ethyl alcohol. This combination produces an effect perhaps ten times greater than the sum of the effects of two depressants. In the past, many people died by accident or through suicide by ingesting this combination. The phenomenon, in which two chemicals bring about an effect greater than that from each individual chemical, is called a **synergistic effect** (Section 12.2). Synergistic effects can be deadly, and they are not limited to alcohol–barbiturate combinations. Two drugs should never be taken at the same time without competent medical supervision.

Barbiturates, like ethanol, are intoxicating, and they are strongly addictive. Habitual use leads to the development of a tolerance, meaning that ever-larger doses are required to produce the same degree of intoxication. The side effects of barbiturates are similar to those of alcohol: hangovers, drowsiness, dizziness, and headaches. Withdrawal symptoms are often severe, including convulsions and delirium, and withdrawal can cause death.

Barbiturates are cyclic amides. The mechanism of their action is similar in some respects to that of alcohol: They act on GABA receptors.

Antianxiety Agents

The hectic pace of life in the modern world causes some people to seek rest and relaxation in chemicals. Many turn to ethyl alcohol. The drink before dinner—to "unwind" from the tensions of the day—is a part of the way of life for many people. This search for relief from stress and anxiety has made antidepressant drugs highly popular. According to the CDC, antidepressants are now the most commonly prescribed drugs, with 164 million prescriptions in the United States in 2008.

One class of antianxiety drugs (anxiolytics) is the *benzodiazepines*, compounds that feature seven-member heterocyclic rings (Figure 18.25). Three common ones are diazepam (Valium®), a classic antianxiety agent; clonazepam, an anticonvulsant as well as antianxiety drug; and lorazepam, used to treat insomnia. Antianxiety agents—sometimes called *minor tranquilizers*—make people feel better simply by making them feel dull and insensitive, but they do not solve any of the underlying problems that cause anxiety. They are thought to act on GABA receptors, dampening neuron activity in parts of the brain associated with cognitive functioning.

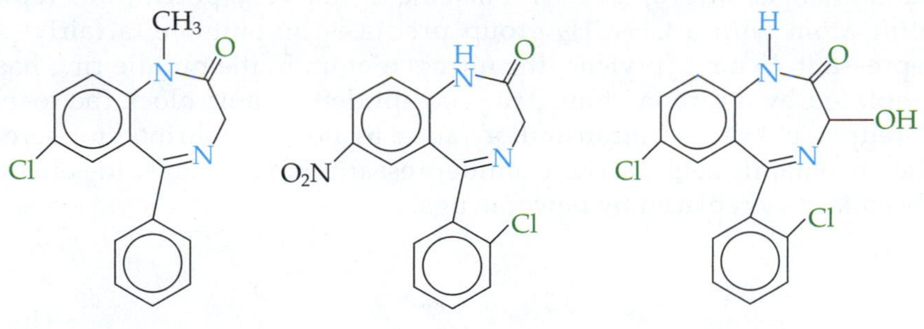

Diazepam　　Clonazepam　　Lorazepam

Figure 18.25 Three benzodiazepines: diazepam (Valium®), clonazepam (Klonopin®), and lorazepam (Ativan®).

The first antipsychotic drugs—sometimes referred to as *major tranquilizers*—were compounds called *phenothiazines*. In 1952, chlorpromazine (Thorazine®) was administered as a tranquilizer to psychotic patients in the United States. The drug had been tested in France as an antihistamine, and medical workers there had noted that it calmed mentally ill patients being treated for allergies. Found to be helpful in controlling the symptoms of schizophrenia, chlorpromazine revolutionized therapy for mental illness. Chlorpromazine is one of several phenothiazines used as antipsychotics. Promazine (chlorpromazine without the chlorine atom on one of the rings) is much less potent than chlorpromazine.

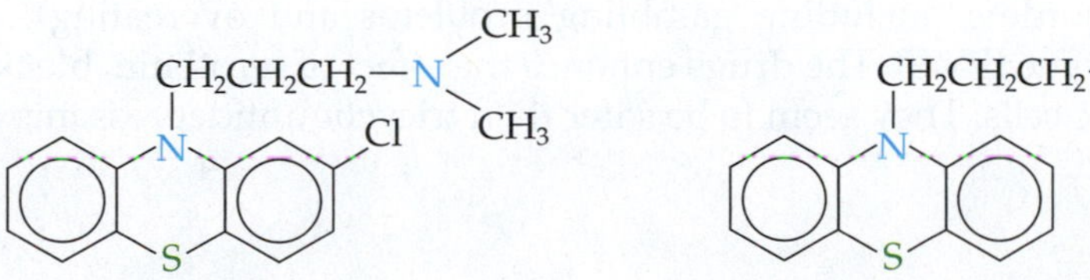

Chlorpromazine (Thorazine®)　　Promazine

Phenothiazines act in part as dopamine antagonists. They block postsynaptic receptors for dopamine, a neurotransmitter important in the control of detailed motion (such as grasping small objects), in memory and emotions, and in exciting the cells of the brain. Some researchers think schizophrenic patients produce too much dopamine, whereas others think that they have too many dopamine receptors. In either case, blocking the action of dopamine relieves the symptoms of schizophrenia.

A second generation of antipsychotics, called *atypical antipsychotics*, includes aripiprazole (Abilify®), risperidone (Risperdal®), clozapine (Clozaril®), and

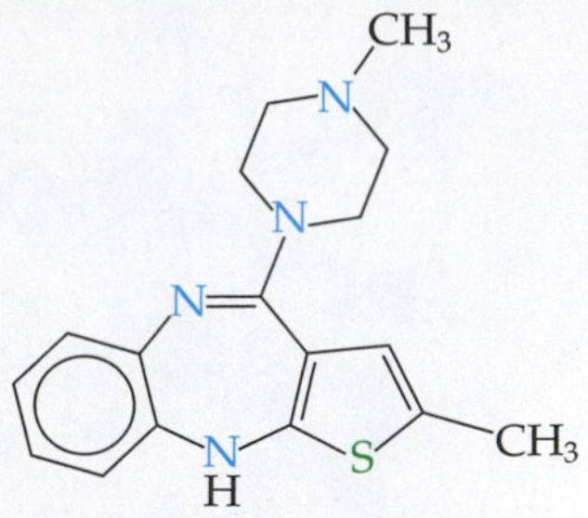

Olanzapine (Zyprexa®)

olanzapine (Zyprexa®). These drugs are thought to act on a type of serotonin receptor that loosens the binding of dopamine receptors, allowing more dopamine to reach the neurons. Aripiprazole is used to treat schizophrenia, acute manic episodes of bipolar disorder, and depression. Risperidone is used to treat schizophrenia. Clozapine, the first of the atypical antipsychotics to be developed, has been shown to be the most effective drug for treating schizophrenia, but its severe side effects—such as destruction of white blood cells—cause it to be used only if other antipsychotic drugs have failed. Olanzapine is used to treat psychotic disorders, such as schizophrenia and acute manic episodes, and to stabilize bipolar disorder.

Antipsychotic drugs have served to reduce greatly the number of patients confined to mental hospitals. They do not cure schizophrenia but control its symptoms well enough that 95% of all schizophrenics no longer need hospitalization. Patients who stop taking these medications relapse.

The oldest class of antidepressant drugs consists of the tricyclic (three-ring) antidepressants. Examples are imipramine (Tofranil®) and amitriptyline (Elavil®). Note that slight changes in the structure of a molecule can result in profound changes in properties. Promazine is not very potent, but replacing its sulfur atom with a CH_2CH_2 group produces imipramine, a fairly potent antidepressant. In amitriptylene, the nitrogen atom in the middle ring has also been replaced by a carbon atom. Tricyclic antidepressants block the reabsorption ("reuptake") of neurotransmitters such as norepinephrine and serotonin into the presynaptic neuron. These antidepressants have serious side effects and have been largely replaced by newer drugs.

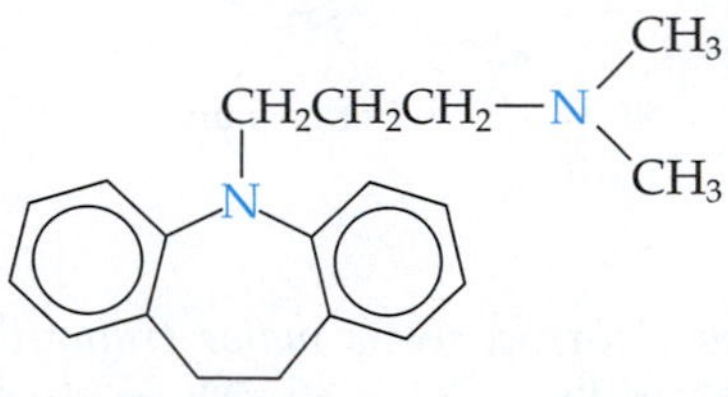

Imipramine (Tofranil®)

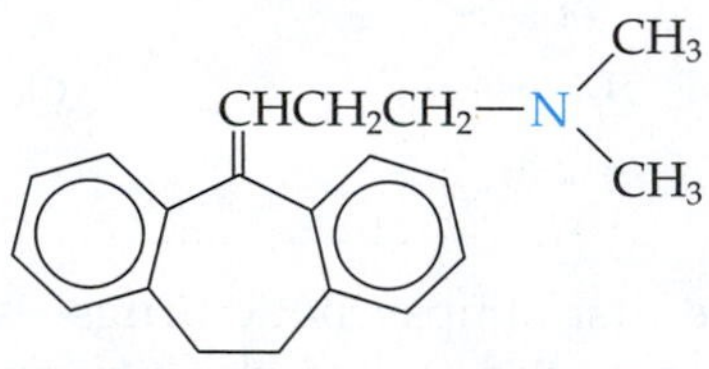

Amitriptylene (Elavil®)

Antidepressants commonly prescribed today include drugs called *selective serotonin-reuptake inhibitors* (SSRIs). Three major ones are shown in Figure 18.26. Doctors prescribe these drugs to help people cope with a wide variety of psychological disorders, including anxiety syndromes such as panic disorder, obsessive-compulsive disorders (including gambling problems and overeating), and premenstrual syndrome (PMS). The drugs enhance the effect of serotonin, blocking its reuptake by nerve cells. They seem to be safer than tricyclic antidepressants and more easily tolerated.

▶ **Figure 18.26** Three selective serotonin reuptake inhibitors (SSRIs): fluoxetine (Prozac®), paroxetine (Paxil®), and sertraline (Zoloft®).

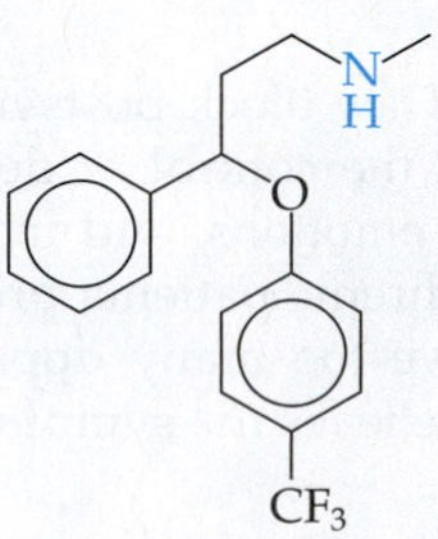

Fluoxetine

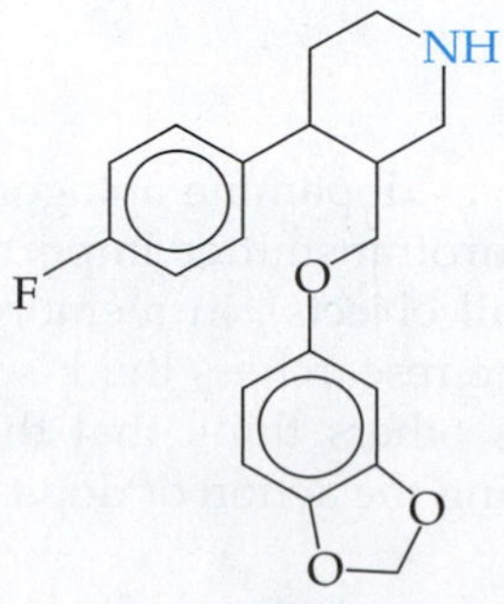

Paroxetine

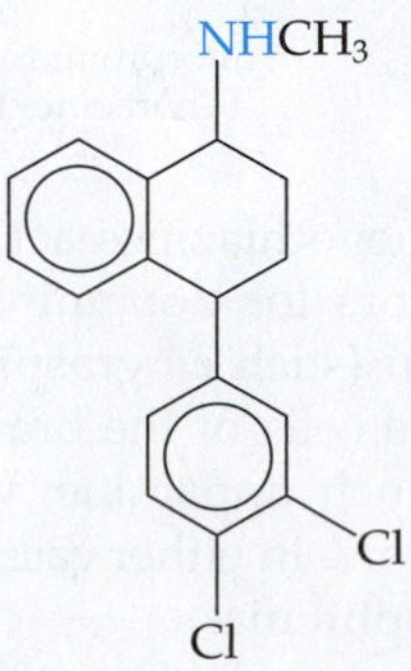

Sertraline

Stimulant Drugs

Among the more widely known stimulant drugs are a variety of synthetic amines related to β-phenylethylamine (Figure 18.27). These drugs, called **amphetamines**, are similar in structure to epinephrine and norepinephrine (page 563). They seem to act by increasing levels of norepinephrine, serotonin, and dopamine in the brain.

◀ **Figure 18.27** β-Phenylethylamine (a) and related compounds. (b) Amphetamine, (c) methamphetamine, (d) methylphenidate, and (e) phenylpropanolamine.

Amphetamine and methamphetamine are inexpensive and have been widely abused. Amphetamine was once used as a diet drug, but it had little long-term effect. Amphetamine induces excitability, restlessness, tremors, insomnia, dilated pupils, increased pulse rate and blood pressure, hallucinations, and psychoses.

Methamphetamine has a more pronounced psychological effect than amphetamine. Methamphetamine is made readily from an antihistamine and household chemicals. Illegal "meth labs" have operated in all parts of the United States. Like other amine drugs, amphetamines are often distributed as hydrochloride salts. The free-base form (the basic amine form that has not been neutralized by an acid) of methamphetamine is smoked because it vaporizes more readily than the salts. Long-term effects of methamphetamine use include severe mental problems, loss of memory, and serious dental problems.

Either methylphenidate (Ritalin®) or a mixture of amphetamines is used to treat attention deficit hyperactivity disorder (ADHD) in children. Although they are stimulants, these drugs seem to calm children who otherwise can't sit still. This use has received criticism that it "leads to drug abuse" and "solves the teacher's problem, not the kid's."

Like many other drugs, amphetamine exists as mirror-image isomers (enantiomers). Benzedrine® is a mixture of the two isomers in equal amounts. The dextro (right-handed) isomer is a stronger stimulant than the levo (left-handed) isomer. The pure dextro isomer is sold under the trade name Dexedrine®.

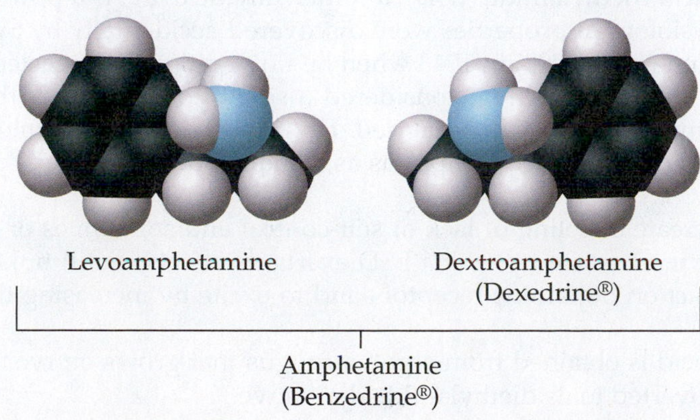

◀ Benzedrine® is a mixture of Dexedrine® and its enantiomer, levoamphetamine. As is often the case, the two isomers differ greatly in their biological activity.

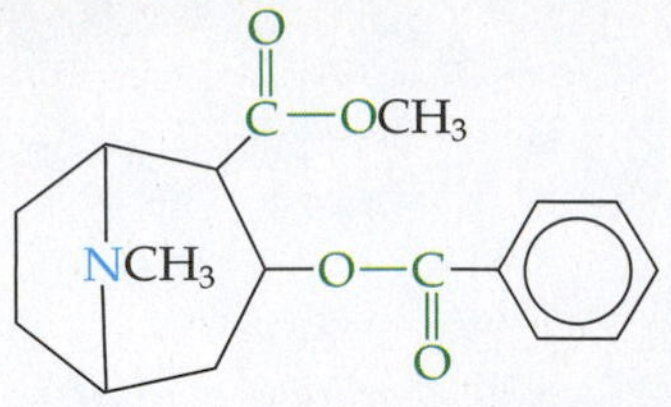

Cocaine

According to the CDC, drug overdoses killed more than 33,000 people in 2005. Contrary to popular belief, most were not caused by cocaine or heroin, but by OxyContin and other pain killers diverted into the illegal drug trade. More than 15 million Americans admitted to using prescription drugs for nonmedical reasons.

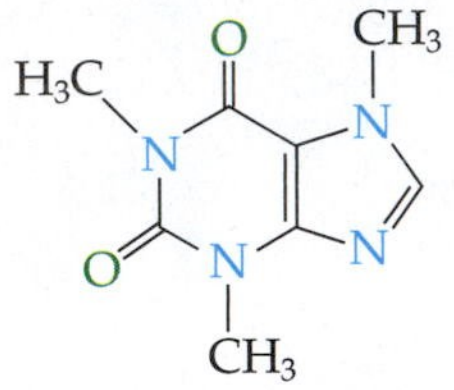

Caffeine

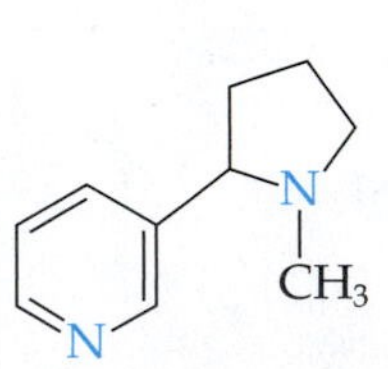

Nicotine

Table 18.6 Caffeine in Soft Drinks	
Brand	**Caffeine**[a]
5-Hour Energy (2 oz)	138
Red Bull (8.2 oz)	80
Sun Drop	63
Mountain Dew	55
Mello Yello	53
Diet Coke	46
Dr Pepper	41
Diet Sunkist Orange	41
Pepsi-Cola	38
Diet Pepsi	36

[a]Milligrams per 12-oz serving.
Sources: National Soft Drink Association, FDA.

Cocaine, Caffeine, and Nicotine

Three plant alkaloids have long been used as stimulants. Cocaine, first used as a local anesthetic (page 567), is also a powerful stimulant. The drug is obtained from the leaves of a shrub that grows almost exclusively on the eastern slopes of the Andes Mountains. Many of the Indians living in and around the area of cultivation chew coca leaves—mixed with lime and ashes—to experience the stimulant effect. Cocaine used to arrive in the United States as the salt cocaine hydrochloride, but now much of it comes in the form of broken lumps of the free base, a form called *crack cocaine.*

Cocaine hydrochloride is readily absorbed through the mucous membrane of the nose, and this is the form used by those who "snort" cocaine. Those who smoke cocaine use crack, which readily vaporizes at the temperature of a burning cigarette. When smoked, cocaine reaches the brain in 15 seconds. It acts by preventing the reuptake of dopamine after it is released by nerve cells, leaving high levels of dopamine to stimulate the pleasure centers of the brain. After the binge, dopamine is depleted in less than an hour, leaving the user in a pleasureless state and (often) craving more cocaine. The use of cocaine increases stamina and reduces fatigue, but the effect is short lived. Stimulation is followed by depression.

Coffee, tea, and cola soft drinks naturally contain the mild stimulant caffeine. Caffeine is also added to many other soft drinks (Table 18.6) and is the source of the "lift" provided by many so-called energy drinks. An effective dose of caffeine is about 200 mg. This is about the amount in one 10-oz cup of strong drip coffee or three to five cups of tea.

Is caffeine addictive? The "morning grouch" syndrome suggests that it is mildly so. Overall, the hazards of caffeine ingestion seem to be slight.

Another common stimulant is nicotine. This drug is taken by smoking or chewing tobacco. Nicotine is highly toxic to animals and has been used in agriculture as a contact insecticide. It is especially deadly when injected. The lethal dose for a human is estimated to be about 50 mg. Nicotine seems to have a rather transient effect as a stimulant, with the initial response followed by depression. Most smokers keep a near-constant level of nicotine in their bloodstreams by indulging frequently.

Nicotine is powerfully addictive. Consider the 1972 memorandum from a Philip Morris scientist who noted that "no one has ever become a cigarette smoker by smoking cigarettes without nicotine." He suggested that the company "think of the cigarette as a dispenser for a dose unit of nicotine."

Hallucinogenic Drugs

Hallucinogenic drugs are consciousness-altering substances that induce changes in sensory perception, qualitatively altering the way users perceive things. Common hallucinogenic drugs include natural products from psilocybin mushrooms and peyote cactus, synthetic chemicals such as MDMA ("Ecstasy"), dimethyltryptamine (DMT), and PCP and ketamine (page 568), and semisynthetic drugs such as LSD and mescaline. Marijuana is sometimes considered a mild hallucinogen.

Lysergic acid diethylamide (LSD), a semisynthetic drug, is a powerful hallucinogen. Its physiological properties were discovered accidentally by Swiss chemist Albert Hofmann (1906–2008) in 1943 when he unintentionally ingested some LSD. He later took 250 mg, which he considered a small dose, to verify that LSD had caused the symptoms he had experienced. Hofmann had a rough time for the next few hours, experiencing such symptoms as visual disturbances and schizophrenic behavior.

LSD can create a feeling of lack of self-control and sometimes of extreme terror. The exact mechanism by which LSD exerts its effects is still unknown, but it is thought to act on dopamine receptors and to excite by increasing the release of glutamate.

Lysergic acid is obtained from ergot, a fungus that grows on rye. This carboxylic acid is converted to its diethylamide derivative.

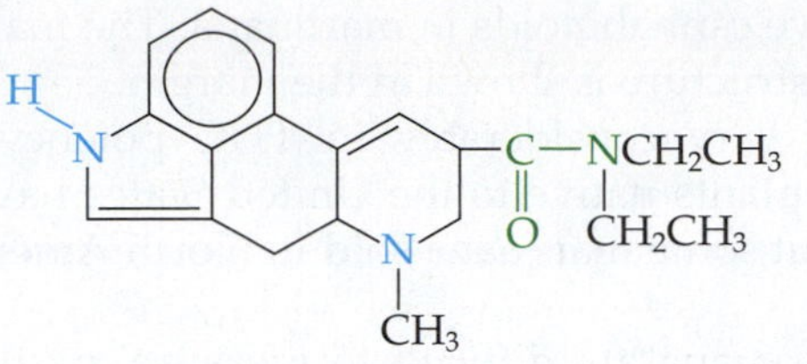

Lysergic acid diethylamide (LSD)

The potency of LSD is indicated by the small amount required for a person to experience its extraordinary effects. The usual dose is probably about 10–100 μg (no wonder Hofmann had a bad time after taking 250 mg). To give you an idea of how small this is, a portion of LSD the size of an aspirin tablet could provide up to 30,000 doses.

Many kinds of plants produce hallucinogenic compounds; the following are two examples.

- Psilocybin, a hallucinogenic alkaloid of the tryptamine family, is found in several species of mushrooms, including *Psilocybe cubensis*. Its effects resemble those of LSD but are of shorter duration.
- Mescaline (3,4,5-trimethoxyphenylethylamine) is a hallucinogenic drug related to phenylethylamine (see Figure 18.27). It is found in the peyote cactus, *Lophophora williamsii*, which is used in the religious ceremonies of some Indian tribes, and in other species. Mescaline is also made synthetically. The effects last for up to 12 hours.

5. Are energy drinks good for you? Energy drinks aren't easily classified as either good or bad for you. Most energy drinks contain herbs and extracts that are purported to improve physical and mental ability. However, almost all contain caffeine, up to 400 mg in a single serving (twice as much as in a large cup of strong coffee). The caffeine is thought to be responsible for most of the effects of such drinks. As with any other caffeine-containing beverage, consumption in moderation is recommended. Well-known effects of excessive caffeine consumption include nervousness, headache, and sleeping problems. More dramatic (and unpleasant) effects may occur with consumption of large amounts of caffeine over a long period.

Marijuana

The plant *Cannabis sativa*, commonly known as marijuana, has long been useful. The plant stems yield tough fibers (hemp) for making ropes. *Cannabis* has been used as a drug in tribal religious rituals and also has a long history as a medicine, particularly in India. In the United States, marijuana is the most commonly used illegal drug.

The term **marijuana** refers to a mixture made by gathering the leaves and flower buds of the plant (Figure 18.28), which are generally dried and smoked.

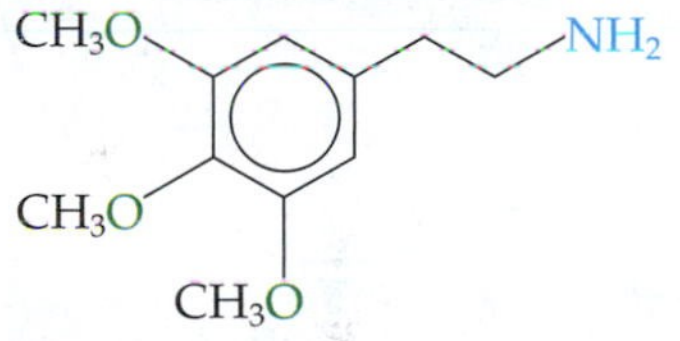

Mescaline

Club Drugs: Raves and Rapes

Club drugs are substances used by teenagers and young adults at all-night dance parties called "raves." These drugs include 3,4-methylenedioxymethamphetamine (MDMA, or Ecstasy), *gamma*-hydroxybutyrate ($HOCH_2CH_2CH_2COOH$; GHB), Rohypnol® (flunitrazepam), ketamine, methamphetamine, and LSD. Use of such drugs can cause serious health problems, especially in combination with alcohol.

Especially troubling are substances known as *date rape drugs*: Rohypnol, ketamine, and GHB have been used to facilitate sexual assault because they render the victim incapable of resisting. Events that happen while a person is under the influence of these drugs often cannot be remembered. The GHB analogs *gamma*-butyrolactone (GBL), and 1,4-butanediol ($HOCH_2CH_2CH_2CH_2OH$) have similar effects. (See Additional Problems 59 and 60.)

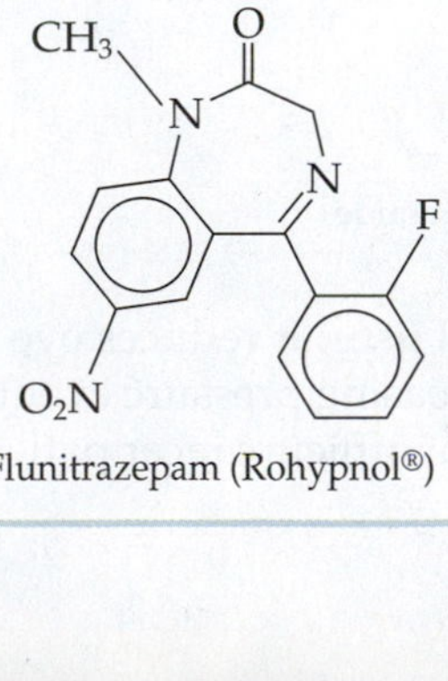

Flunitrazepam (Rohypnol®)

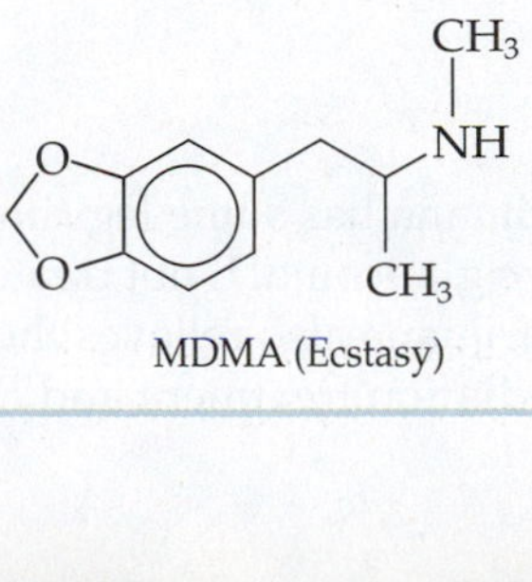

MDMA (Ecstasy)

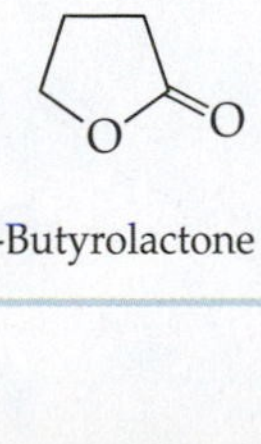

gamma-Butyrolactone (GBL)

Several medical drugs are obtained from the ergot fungus. Because ergotamine shrinks blood vessels in the brain, it is used to treat migraine headaches. Ergonovine induces uterine contractions and can reduce bleeding after childbirth. Like LSD, both of these compounds are lysergic acid amides.

There are several active cannabinoids in marijuana. The main one is *tetrahydrocannabinol (THC)*, whose structure is shown in the margin.

Tetrahydrocannabinol (THC)

Marijuana plants vary considerably in THC potency, depending on their genetic variety. Wild plants native to the United States have a low THC content, usually about 0.1%, but some marijuana sold in North America has a THC content approaching 6%.

The effects of marijuana are difficult to measure, partly because of the variable amount of THC in different samples. Smoking marijuana increases the pulse rate, distorts the sense of time, and impairs some complex motor functions. Other possible effects include a euphoric floating sensation, a feeling of anxiety, a heightened enjoyment of food, and a false impression of brilliance. Although studies have shown no mind-expanding effects, users sometimes experience hallucinations. Because it is fat-soluble, THC is stored in the body. Stress and dieting can produce a positive THC test long after the drug was last used.

The long-term effects of marijuana, such as causing psychotic symptoms that persist beyond temporary intoxication, are unclear. There is some evidence of increased risk of psychotic problems in people who have used marijuana, with the greatest increase (50–200%) observed in people who used the drug most frequently. People who use marijuana heavily are often lazy, passive, and mentally sluggish, but it is difficult to prove that marijuana is the cause. Even if it is, the damage is less extensive than that caused by heavy use of alcohol.

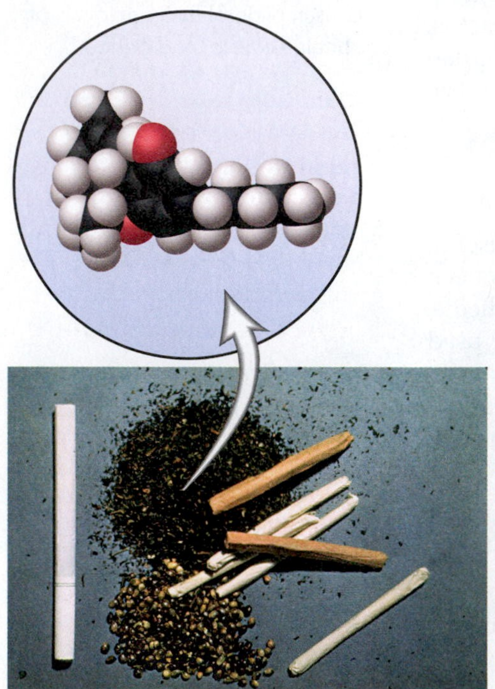

▲ **Figure 18.28** Prepared marijuana.

When a person smokes marijuana, THC rapidly passes from the lungs into the bloodstream and is carried to the brain, where it binds to specific sites called *cannabinoid receptors* on nerve cells. Some regions of the brain have many such receptors; other areas have few or none. The parts of the brain that influence pleasure, memory, thought, concentration, judgment, and sensory and time perception and that regulate movement are rich in receptors. As THC enters the brain, it activates the brain's reward system in the same way that food and drink do. Like nearly all drugs of abuse, THC causes a euphoric feeling by stimulating the release of dopamine.

The location of receptors in movement control centers in the brain explains the loss of coordination seen in those intoxicated by the drug. The presence of receptors in memory and cognition areas of the brain explains why marijuana users do poorly on tests. That few receptors are present in the brainstem, where breathing and heartbeat are controlled, is probably why it is hard to get a lethal dose of pure marijuana.

The fact that THC binds to receptors in the brain indicates that the brain produces a THC-like substance. This substance is *anandamide*, derived from arachidonic acid, which is the precursor of prostaglandins.

Voters in several states and cities have approved the medical use of marijuana and some other drugs. Still illegal under federal law, synthetic THC can legally be proscribed for this use.

Anandamide

Marijuana has some legitimate medical uses. It reduces eye pressure in people who have glaucoma. If not treated, this increasing pressure eventually causes blindness. Marijuana also relieves the nausea that afflicts cancer patients who are undergoing radiation treatment and chemotherapy.

Self-Assessment Questions

1. Neurotransmitters are
   a. chemicals that carry messages across the synapses between nerve cells
   b. electrical signals that move along an axon
   c. implantable diagnostic devices that measure brain-wave activity
   d. nerve cells that send sensory messages
2. Serotonin is produced in the body from the dietary amino acid
   a. cysteine b. serine c. tryptophan d. tyrosine
3. Depression may result from abnormal metabolism of
   a. acetylcholine b. GABA c. nitric oxide d. serotonin
4. A hazard of the use of nitrous oxide as an anesthetic is that it
   a. can cause brain damage if not combined with O_2
   b. has too long a recovery time
   c. induces anesthesia that is too deep
   d. is flammable
5. Ethyl alcohol is a(n)
   a. analgesic b. depressant c. narcotic d. stimulant
6. Which of the following classes of drugs is commonly used to treat anxiety?
   a. amphetamines b. benzodiazepines
   c. opiates d. steroids
7. Several stimulant drugs are derivatives of
   a. *para*-aminobenzoic acid b. caffeine
   c. ketamine d. β-phenylethylamine
8. Dextroamphetamine is composed of molecules that
   a. differ from amphetamine by a $-CH_3$ group
   b. are a mixture of left- and right-handed isomers
   c. are all the left-handed isomer
   d. are all the right-handed isomer
9. LSD acts on the receptors for the neurotransmitter
   a. acetylcholine b. dopamine c. GABA d. serotonin
10. The THC-like substance produced in the brain is
    a. anandamide b. an endorphin c. LSD d. morphine

Answers: 1, a; 2, c; 3, d; 4, a; 5, b; 6, b; 7, d; 8, d; 9, d; 10, a

▲ **It DOES Matter!**
University of California, Irvine, researchers Daniele Piomelli, Nicholas DiPatrizio, and colleagues have found that when rats tasted fatty foods, such as potato chips or french fries, a signal was generated that stimulates the production of anandamide and other natural compounds similar to THC. These compounds trigger the desire for more fatty foods, making it hard to resist eating more chips or fries.

18.8 Drugs and Society

Learning Objectives › Differentiate between drug abuse and drug misuse. › Differentiate between a placebo and a nocebo.

Illegal drugs cause enormous problems. Their marketing is covert, with sellers failing to report their income or pay taxes on it, making the illicit drug business enormously lucrative. Annual revenues for drug dealers amount to at least $400 billion, about half of which comes from the United States. Worldwide, people spend more money for illegal drugs than for food. The large amounts of money involved make illegal drugs a dangerous business in which crimes are frequent, murders are common, and corrupt politicians abound. **Drug abuse** (using drugs for their intoxicating effects) is a serious problem, not only for the abusers but for society in general.

The illegal drug user is the biggest loser. Street drugs are expensive, and most are addictive. Many addicted users steal to pay for drugs and eventually end up in jail. One study found that 16% of convicted jail inmates admitted that they committed their offense to get money for drugs. In the workplace, 50–80% of all accidents and personal injuries are drug related. Drug users are absent from work over twice as often as nonusers, and they are five times as likely to file claims for worker's

Placebo and Nocebo Effects

An interesting phenomenon associated with the testing of drugs is the **placebo effect**. A placebo is an inactive substance given in the form of medication to a patient.

A common way to evaluate a new drug is to administer it to one group of patients and to give a placebo to a similar "control" group. In a double-blind study, which is the type most accepted by the medical community, neither the patients nor the doctors know who is receiving the real drug and who is receiving the placebo.

Sometimes people who think they are receiving a certain drug expect positive results and may actually experience such results, even though they have not been given the actual drug. In one study of a new tranquilizer, 40% of the patients who had been given placebos reported that they felt much better and rated the drug as highly effective. The psychological effect of a placebo can be very powerful.

The placebo effect confers health benefits from a treatment that should have no effect. Conversely, patients can experience a nocebo effect. A *nocebo* is a substance that is harmless but that produces harmful effects because the person involved thinks it harmful. The patient presumes a bad outcome, and that presumption becomes a self-fulfilling prophecy. In layperson's terms, this is being "worried sick" or "scared to death." Perhaps the most extreme example is the voodoo hex, a notion so powerful that those who are "cursed" and believe in it may die of fright.

6. How should I dispose of old medicines? The Substance Abuse and Mental Health Services Administration recommends that old medicine be mixed with coffee grounds, cat litter, or similar material, then bagged and disposed of in the trash. This minimizes the possibility of abuse (especially if used cat litter is employed!). Alternatively, some communities now provide periodic disposal services. There are environmental concerns about flushing medications down the sink or toilet. Some medications may affect fish and wildlife even in very low doses.

compensation. They are a drain on their employers' income, and they often have trouble keeping a job.

Illegal drugs are not always what their sellers claim they are. Buyers simply have to trust the information sellers give them about the identity and quality of the products they buy. In fact, crime labs have generally found that nearly two-thirds of all drugs (other than marijuana) brought in for analysis are something other than what the dealers said they were.

There can be difficulties even with legal drugs that have been approved and tested. Problems range from faulty prescriptions written by physicians to pharmacies' errors in filling prescriptions, and patients' mistakes in taking medications. Some drugs have undesirable side effects that are worse than the condition being treated. Some drugs (both prescription and over the counter) have such similar names that they are easily confused. **Drug misuse**—for example, using penicillin, which has no effect on viruses, to treat a viral infection—is all too common. Such overuse of penicillin has led to strains of bacteria that are now immune to penicillin.

Many drugs have supplied enormous benefits to society: longer and healthier lives, relief from pain, and more. Sometimes drugs can create problems: addiction, dangerous side effects, even death. We must use them wisely.

Self-Assessment Questions

1. Using an antibiotic to treat a cold is an example of
   a. appropriate therapy
   b. drug abuse
   c. drug misuse
   d. a placebo effect
2. Using the narcotic OxyContin for its intoxicating effect is an example of
   a. appropriate recreation
   b. drug abuse
   c. drug misuse
   d. legal intoxication
3. A placebo is
   a. an alcohol solution of an active drug
   b. an inactive substance that looks like real medication
   c. a PCB
   d. a platinum/cesium/boron drug
4. In a double-blind study, some patients are given the drug being tested and others are given
   a. acupuncture
   b. a homeopathic formulation
   c. morphine
   d. a placebo

Answers: 1, c; 2, b; 3, b; 4, d

CRITICAL THINKING  EXERCISES

Apply knowledge that you have gained in this chapter and one or more of the FLaReS principles (Chapter 1) to evaluate the following statements or claims.

18.1 A television advertisement featured Dr. Robert Jarvik, inventor of the artificial heart, encouraging consumers to "talk to their doctor" about using the cholesterol-lowering drug Lipitor. (The advertisement was pulled from the air in February 2008.)

18.2 Researchers at the Centre for Complementary Medicine in Munich, Germany, reviewed 29 studies of patients with depression that compared treatment with St. John's wort (*Hypericum perforatum*) with treatment with a placebo or with standard antidepressant medications. They concluded, "Overall … the St. John's wort extracts … were superior to placebos and as effective as standard antidepressants, with fewer side effects." They also noted that studies in German-speaking countries, where the herbal remedy has long been used, were more favorable to St. John's wort than were studies from other countries and that products on the market vary in composition and can sometimes compromise the effects of other medications.

18.3 A nurse claims to be able to help patients by "therapeutic touch," a technique that she says allows her to sense a patient's energy fields by moving her hands above the patient's body.

18.4 A television advertisement shows an actor taking a medicine that inhibits the production of stomach acid, then eating a large meal of rich, spicy food.

18.5 A television advertisement shows an actor taking an antihistamine and then joyously walking through a grassy, flower-filled meadow without experiencing the usual allergy symptoms.

18.6 A Web site recommends S-adenosylmethionine (SAMe) for treatment of depression, arthritis, and liver disease.

18.7 A Web site claims that red wine is good for your heart.

SUMMARY

Section 18.1—A **drug** is a substance that relieves pain, treats illness, or improves one's health or well-being. Many drugs are obtained from natural sources. Paul Ehrlich established **chemotherapy**, based on the fact that some chemicals were more toxic to disease organisms than to human cells.

Section 18.2—Aspirin is a **nonsteroidal anti-inflammatory drug (NSAID)**. It is an **analgesic** (pain reliever), **antipyretic** (fever reducer), and **anti-inflammatory** (reduces inflammation). NSAIDs inhibit the production of **prostaglandins**, hormone-like lipids that are derived from a fatty acid and send pain messages to the brain. Ibuprofen, ketoprofen, and naproxen are also NSAIDs. Acetaminophen is an analgesic and antipyretic but does not reduce inflammation. Many analgesic products are combinations of one or more NSAIDs with other drugs. Cold medicines often contain an **antihistamine** to relieve symptoms caused by **allergens**. An allergen triggers the release of histamine, causing sneezing, itchy eyes, and runny nose. No treatment cures a cold.

A **narcotic** relieves pain and produces stupor or anesthesia but is addictive. Opium contains morphine, a natural narcotic. Codeine is made from morphine; it is less potent and less addictive. Codeine is often combined with acetaminophen for pain relief, and it is used to suppress coughs. Heroin is a much more potent and highly addictive derivative of morphine. Several synthetic narcotics have been prepared. A morphine **agonist** has morphine-like action; a morphine **antagonist** blocks morphine receptors. The body produces morphine-like substances called **endorphins** in response to extreme pain.

Section 18.3—Sulfa drugs were the first antibacterial drugs; they mimic compounds essential for bacterial growth. An **antibiotic** is a soluble substance that is derived from mold or bacteria and inhibits the growth of other microorganisms. Penicillins prevent bacteria from forming their mucoprotein cell walls but do not harm animal cells, which do not have mucoprotein walls. Tetracyclines and fluoroquinolones are **broad-spectrum antibiotics**, which are effective against a wide variety of bacteria. Antibiotic-resistant bacteria often develop after an antibiotic has been in use for a while.

Viral diseases cannot be cured with antibiotics. Some, such as measles, mumps, and smallpox, are usually prevented by vaccination, but vaccines are not available for all viral diseases. Herpes and **acquired immune deficiency syndrome (AIDS)** are viral infections. Viruses are composed of nucleic acids—either DNA or RNA—and proteins. A **retrovirus** such as the AIDS virus is an RNA virus that synthesizes DNA in the host cell. Antiviral drugs are used to treat some viral diseases.

Section 18.4—Many anticancer drugs are **antimetabolites**, which inhibit DNA synthesis and thus slow the growth of cancer cells. Alkylating agents transfer alkyl groups to biological molecules, blocking their usual action. Nitrogen mustards, which arose from chemical warfare research, are alkylating agents.

Section 18.5—A **hormone** is a chemical messenger that is produced in the endocrine glands and signals physiological changes in other parts of the body. Prostaglandins act as mediators of hormone action. There are six primary prostaglandins. Some hormones are **steroids**, compounds with a four-ring skeletal structure. Cholesterol and cortisol are steroids, as are sex hormones. An **androgen** stimulates the development or controls the maintenance of masculine characteristics, and an **estrogen** controls female sexual functions. Estradiol, estrone, and progesterone are estrogens. A **progestin** is a steroid hormone that has the effect of progesterone.

Birth control pills contain a synthetic estrogen or a progestin, which acts by creating a state of false pregnancy, preventing ovulation and conception. Birth control pills are safer than childbirth for nonsmokers but are much less safe for smokers.

Section 18.6—Diseases of the cardiovascular system include coronary artery disease, arrhythmias, hypertension, and congestive heart failure. Drugs for hypertension include diuretics, beta blockers, calcium channel blockers, and ACE inhibitors. Drugs for arrhythmia alter the flow of ions across cell membranes. Treatment for coronary artery disease can be the same as for hypertension; however, organic nitro compounds are also used.

Section 18.7—**Psychotropic drugs** are drugs that affect the mind. They can be divided into three classes: **stimulant drugs** such as cocaine and amphetamines; **depressant drugs** such as alcohol, anesthetics, opiates, barbiturates, and tranquilizers; and **hallucinogenic drugs** such as LSD.

The **neurons** (nerve cells) of the nervous system have tiny gaps called **synapses** between them. **Neurotransmitters** are chemicals that are released into the synapses during nerve transmissions and cause changes in the receiving cells.

Mental illness is thought to involve brain amines such as norepinephrine (NE) and serotonin. NE agonists enhance or mimic the action of NE. NE antagonists block its action and slow down various processes. Some brain amines appear to be affected by diet. Agonist and antagonist molecules must have the proper shapes. Many compounds exist as **stereoisomers**, which have the same formula but different arrangements of atoms. Stereoisomers that are not superimposable on their mirror images are called **enantiomers** and usually have one or more **chiral carbons** (carbon atoms with four different groups attached).

An **anesthetic** is a substance that causes lack of feeling or awareness. A **general anesthetic** produces unconsciousness and general insensitivity to pain. A local anesthetic causes loss of feeling in a part of the body.

Alcohol is the most common depressant used worldwide. It appears to disrupt the functioning of two neurotransmitters that control muscle activity. Barbiturates such as pentobarbital and thiopental are used as sedatives and anesthetics. Ingesting alcohol and a barbiturate together produces a **synergistic effect**, with the action of one enhancing the other; the result can be deadly.

Phenothiazines are one type of tranquilizer that act as dopamine antagonists and relieve symptoms of schizophrenia. Commonly prescribed antidepressants are SSRIs, which enhance the effect of serotonin.

Amphetamines are stimulants, similar in structure to epinephrine and NE. Amphetamine exists as enantiomers, one of which is much more potent than the other. Methamphetamine is even more potent than amphetamine and is easy to make. Caffeine in coffee, tea, and soft drinks and nicotine in tobacco are widely used legal stimulants.

Hallucinogenic drugs induce changes in sensory perception. The best-known hallucinogenic drugs are LSD and **marijuana**. Psilocybin from certain mushrooms and mescaline from peyote cactus are natural hallucinogens.

Section 18.8—**Drug abuse**, or using drugs for their intoxicating effects, is a serious problem for abusers and society. **Drug misuse**, in which legal drugs are used incorrectly or by mistake, is also a problem. New drugs must be tested properly to avoid the **placebo effect**, in which an inactive substance, given as medication, produces results in patients for psychological reasons.

Green chemistry Drugs have contributed substantially to improvements over the last century in both the quality of life and the reduction of mortality. Many drug molecules are complex and are produced with very low chemical efficiency (high E-factors). The expense and difficulty of drug manufacturing provide incentives for the development of green chemistry approaches. More efficient syntheses, use of enzymes, and biocatalysis are important components of these improvements.

Learning Objectives

› Identify common drugs as natural, semisynthetic, or synthetic.	Problem 10
› Define *chemotherapy*, and explain its origin.	Problems 1–14
› List the common OTC analgesics, antipyretics, and anti-inflammatory drugs, and describe how each works.	Problems 15–20
› Name several common narcotics, describe how each functions, and state its potential for addiction.	Problems 9, 21–24
› List the common antibacterial drugs, and describe the action of each.	Problems 1, 25–28
› Name the common antiviral drugs, and describe the action of each.	Problems 29, 30
› Describe the action of the common types of anticancer drugs.	Problems 31, 32, 61, 62, 67
› Define the terms *hormone*, *prostaglandin*, and *steroid*, and explain the function of each.	Problems 2, 3, 5, 41, 45
› List the three types of sex hormones, and explain how each acts and how birth control drugs work.	Problems 4, 5, 33–36
› Describe the action of four types of drugs used to treat heart disease.	Problem 44 and Collaborative Group Project 8
› Explain how the brain amines norepinephrine and serotonin affect the mind and how various drugs change their action.	Problems 11, 37, 38

› Identify some stimulant drugs, depressant drugs, and psychotropic drugs, and describe how they affect the mind.	Problems 6, 7, 10, 13, 14, 37–40
› Differentiate between drug abuse and drug misuse.	Problems 37, 38, 54–57
› Differentiate between a placebo and a nocebo.	Collaborative Group Project 10
› Explain how green chemistry can be applied to the manufacture of drugs.	Problem 69
› Identify green chemistry principles that contribute to improving the E-factor of a chemical synthesis.	Problems 68, 70

REVIEW QUESTIONS

1. What is an antibiotic?
2. What is a hormone?
3. What is cortisol? Prednisone?
4. How do birth control pills work?
5. What are prostaglandins? How do prostaglandins differ from hormones?
6. Describe two medical uses of barbiturates, and state the relative doses for these purposes. What are the hazards of long-term barbiturate use?
7. Name two dissociative anesthetics.
8. Describe a synergistic effect involving drugs.
9. What is a narcotic?
10. Classify the following drugs as natural, semisynthetic, or synthetic: paclitaxel, heroin, morphine, penicillin, cisplatin.
11. How may a person's mental state be related to his or her diet?
12. What are psychotropic drugs?
13. Are tranquilizers a cure for schizophrenia?
14. What are the effects of a hallucinogenic drug?

PROBLEMS

NSAIDs and Related Drugs

15. What is the chemical name for aspirin?
16. In what ways do aspirin and acetaminophen act similarly? Why is aspirin preferred over acetaminophen for the treatment of arthritis?
17. Why is acetaminophen used instead of aspirin for the relief of pain associated with surgical procedures?
18. What is a COX-2 inhibitor?
19. What two functional groups are present in the acetaminophen molecule?
20. What two functional groups are present in the aspirin (acetylsalicylic acid) molecule?

Narcotics

21. How does heroin differ from morphine in its physiological effects? In what ways are their physiological effects similar?
22. How does codeine differ from morphine in its physiological effects? In what ways are their physiological effects similar?
23. How are endorphins related to **(a)** the anesthetic effect of acupuncture and **(b)** the absence of pain in a wounded soldier?
24. What is an agonist? What is an antagonist?

Antibacterial Drugs

25. Look at the molecular models of sulfanilamide and *para*-aminobenzoic acid on page 542, and write structural formulas for the two compounds.
26. What are penicillins? How do they kill bacteria?
27. Tetracyclines are broad-spectrum antibiotics. What does this mean?
28. What are fluoroquinolones? How do they kill bacteria?

Antiviral Drugs

29. Do antiviral drugs cure viral diseases? What is the best way to deal with viral diseases?
30. What are the three classes of antiviral drugs? How does each work?

Anticancer Drugs

31. List two major classes of anticancer drugs.
32. Do anticancer drugs sometimes cause cancer? Explain.

Hormones and Birth Control Drugs

33. What is an estrogen? What is an androgen?
34. How does mifepristone (RU-486) work?
35. What molecular structural feature makes a contraceptive steroid effective orally?
36. What are emergency contraceptives? How do they work?

Drugs and the Mind

37. What is a psychotropic drug?
38. What is a hallucinogenic drug?

Anesthetics

39. Which of these anesthetics is dangerous because of flammability?
   a. diethyl ether b. halothane
   c. chloroform d. isoflurane

40. For each of the following anesthetics, identify a disadvantage other than flammability that is associated with its use.
   a. nitrous oxide
   b. halothane
   c. diethyl ether

ADDITIONAL PROBLEMS

41. Which of the following compounds are classified as steroids?
   a. cholesterol b. prednisone
   c. progesterone d. prostaglandin E_2

42. Review the boxed feature "Structure–Function Relationships" (page 544), and then draw the structure of a fluoroquinolone drug, which should be similar to ciprofloxacin in action but does not have the large nitrogen-containing ring at position 7.

43. A 140-lb patient was treated with the antibiotic ampicillin for a urinary tract infection. The daily dose was 40 mg/kg divided into three doses per day. **(a)** What was the daily dose, in grams, for the patient? **(b)** Each ampicillin capsule contains 500 mg of active ingredient. How many capsules did the patient have to take every 8 hours?

44. What kind of disease is a diuretic used to treat? How does it work?

45. What structural feature is shared by all steroids?

46. Ephedrine hydrochloride has the chemical formula $C_{10}H_{16}NO^+Cl^-$. Is it water soluble or fat soluble? Explain.

47. Diphenhydramine (Benadryl®) has the chemical formula $C_{17}H_{21}NO$. Is it water soluble or fat soluble? Explain.

48. What structural feature is common to all barbiturate molecules? How is this structure modified to change the properties of individual barbiturate drugs?

49. The dissociative anesthetics ketamine and PCP are classified as derivatives of cyclohexylamine. Write the structural formula for cyclohexylamine.

Problems 50–53 use the concept of an LD_{50} value, which is discussed more fully in Chapter 22. The LD_{50} of a substance is the dose (in mg substance per kg body mass) that would be lethal to 50% of a population of test animals.

50. When administered orally to rats, ibuprofen and naproxen have LD_{50} values of 1000 mg/kg and 534 mg/kg, respectively. Which is more toxic? Explain.

51. When administered subcutaneously to rats, the LD_{50} values of the toxins of the Southern copperhead snake and the timber rattlesnake are 25.6 mg/kg and 3.1 mg/kg, respectively. Which is more toxic? Explain.

52. When administered orally to rats, aspirin has an LD_{50} value of 1500 mg/kg of body weight. If the toxicity is the same for humans, how many 325-mg tablets would kill a typical 10.0-kg child?

53. When administered intravenously to rats, the LD_{50} of procaine is 50 mg/kg, and that of nicotine is 1.0 mg/kg. Which drug is more toxic? What is the approximate lethal dose of each for a 50-kg human?

54. If the minimum lethal dose (MLD) of amphetamine is 5 mg/kg, what is the MLD for a 70-kg person? Can toxicity studies on animals always be extrapolated to humans?

55. As noted in Section 18.2, replacement of the phenolic —OH group of the morphine molecule by a methoxy (—OCH_3) group produces codeine. Draw the structure of the codeine molecule.

56. As noted in Section 18.2, conversion of both —OH groups of the morphine molecule to acetate esters produces heroin. Draw the structure of the heroin molecule.

57. As noted in Section 18.2, oxycodone is related to codeine, differing only in that the hydroxyl group of codeine has been oxidized to a carbonyl group (as in ketone synthesis, Chapter 9). Draw the structure of the oxycodone molecule.

58. Nalorphine, a morphine antagonist, is related to morphine in that the methyl group on the N atom of morphine is replaced by a propenyl group (—$CH_2CH{=}CH_2$). Draw the structure of the nalorphine molecule.

Problems 59 and 60 are based on the boxed feature "Club Drugs" (page 575). You may need to review some topics in Chapter 9.

59. What kind of compound is the GHB analog *gamma*-butyrolactone (GBL)? What kind of reaction would convert GBL to GHB?

60. What kind of compound is the GHB analog 1,4-butanediol? What kind of reaction would convert 1,4-butanediol to GHB?

61. What compound does the following formula represent? To which class of anticancer drugs does it belong?

SH
N N
N N
H

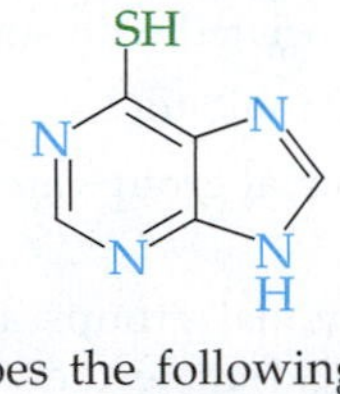

62. What compound does the following formula represent? To which class of anticancer drugs does it belong?

Cl Cl
N
O=P–NH
O

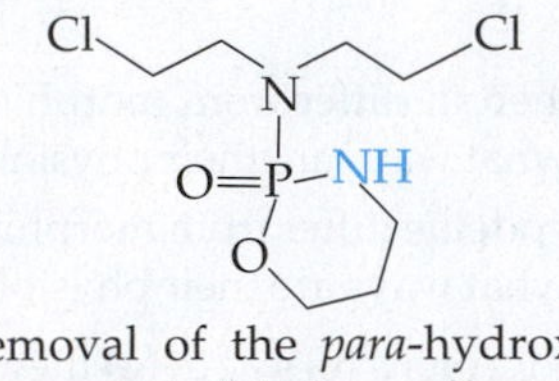

63. How would removal of the *para*-hydroxyl group from the molecule represented below affect its solubility in **(a)** water and **(b)** fat?

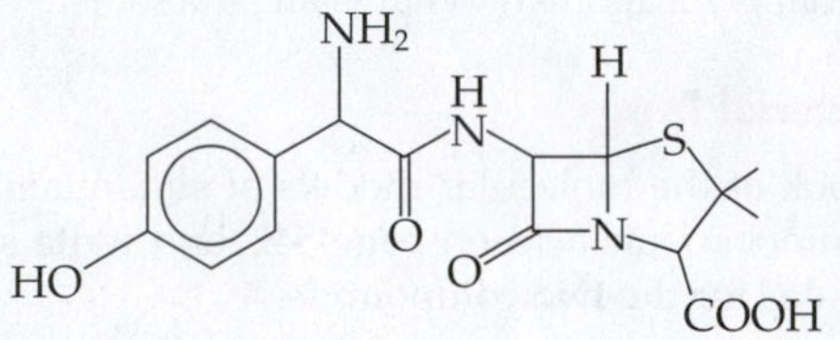

NH₂ H
H
N S
HO O N
O COOH

64. Which NSAID does the following formula represent? To what aromatic hydrocarbon is it related? Name the two oxygen-containing functional groups.

O, C, CH, H_3C, COOH

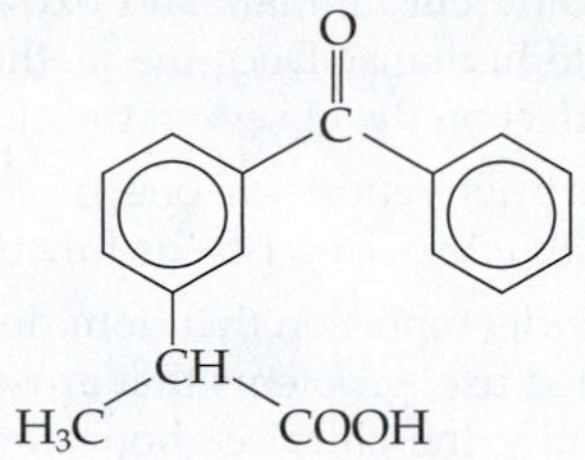

65. Chloramphenicol (Exercise 1.1A) is a broad-spectrum antibiotic that acts by inhibiting bacterial protein synthesis. It is soluble in water to the extent of 2.5 mg/mL. How would conversion of chloramphenicol (R = —H) to **(a)** its palmitate ester [R = $—CO(CH_2)_{14}CH_3$] and **(b)** its sodium succinate (R = $—COCH_2CH_2COONa$) derivative affect its solubility? Explain.

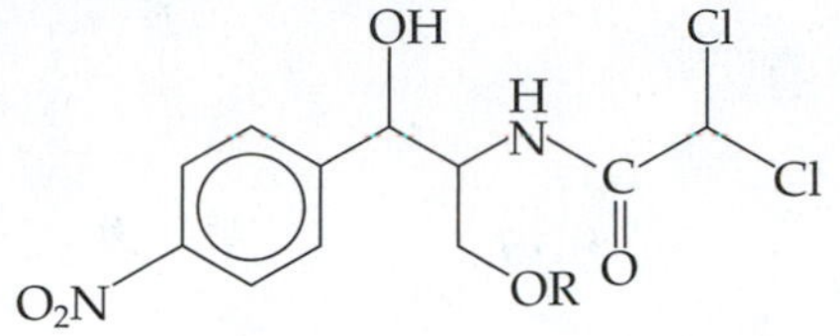

OH, Cl, H, N, C, Cl, O, OR, O_2N

66. What type of drug does the following formula represent? Name the three types of oxygen-containing functional groups present.

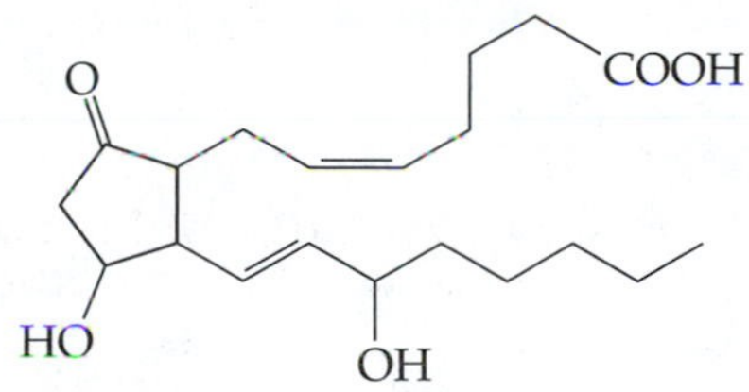

O, COOH, HO, OH

67. What type of drug is megestrol acetate (shown below), used for the treatment of some cancers?

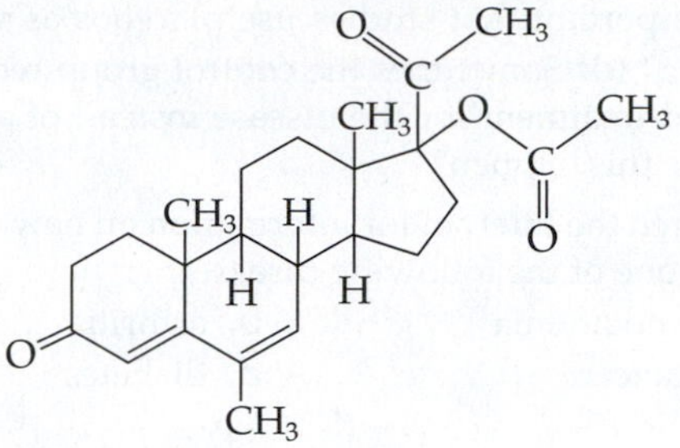

O, CH_3, C, CH_3, O, CH_3, C, CH_3, H, O, H, H, O, CH_3

a. phencyclidine
b. prostaglandin
c. steroid
d. tetracycline

68. Which of the following is a reason why syntheses of most drugs have high E-factors?
a. Biocatalysis is used.
b. Single-step syntheses are common.
c. Recycling of inactive isomers is always possible.
d. Large amounts of solvent and complex reagents are used.

69. Identify two ways in which the synthesis of pregabalin was improved through the application of green chemistry.

70. Which green chemistry principles can improve the E-factor in the manufacture of a drug?
a. synthesis without solvent (Principle 5)
b. use of a catalyst (Principle 9)
c. reducing the amount of waste generated (Principle 1)
d. all of the above

COLLABORATIVE GROUP PROJECTS

Prepare a PowerPoint, poster, or other presentation (as directed by your instructor) to share with the class. For Projects 1–7, give the chemical structure, medical use, toxicity, and (if possible) side effects of each substance.

1. Prepare a brief report, including a list of the ingredients and their amounts, on a combination product such as Advil® Cold & Sinus, Aleve® Cold & Sinus, Dimetapp® Cold & Flu, Theraflu®, Excedrin PM®, Alka-Seltzer® Plus, DayQuil®, or NyQuil.
2. Prepare a brief report on an antihistamine, such as azatadine, fexofenadine, cyproheptadine, cetirizine, dexchlorpheniramine, loratadine, promethazine, or tripelennamine.
3. Prepare a brief report on one of the narcotics listed in Table 18.1.
4. Prepare a brief report on an antibiotic, such as vancomycin, gramicidin, erythromycin, ciprofloxacin, trimethoprim, cefoxitin, cefoperazone, or azithromycin.
5. Prepare a brief report on an anticancer drug, such as bleomycin, fludarabine, hydroxyurea, levamisole, procarbazine, tamoxifen, or vinblastine.
6. Prepare a brief report on an antiviral drug, such as cefoperazone, azithromycin, ganciclovir, indinavir, ribavirin, rimantadine, ritonavir, or valacyclovir.
7. Prepare a brief report on an antidepressant, such as sertraline, paroxetine, citalopram, desipramine, isocarboxazid, phenelzine, fluvoxamine, or nortriptyline.
8. Four major drug categories for lowering blood pressure are listed on page 560. Give the chemical structure, toxicity, and side effects of each of the examples listed.
9. Do a cost analysis of five brands of plain aspirin, calculating the cost per gram of each. Compare the cost per gram of an extra-strength aspirin formulation with that of plain aspirin.
10. Search the Internet to learn about drug trials, and answer the following questions. **(a)** Why might a person who is

gravely ill not want to participate in a placebo-controlled drug study? **(b)** What are the advantages and disadvantages of participating in such a drug study? **(c)** Why is it important that studies use placebos as well as the test drug? **(d)** Sometimes the control group receives the standard treatment for the disease instead of a placebo. Why does this happen?

11. Search the Internet for information on new drugs for treating one of the following diseases.

a. pneumonia **b.** arthritis
c. cancer **d.** diabetes

12. Use *The Merck Index* or a similar reference work to look up the toxicities of cocaine, procaine, lidocaine, mepivacaine, and bupivacaine. Is it always accurate to compare toxicities in different animals and extrapolate those animal toxicities to humans? Does the method of administration have an effect on the observed toxicity?

13. Prepare a brief report on one of the neurotransmitters listed in Table 18.3. Describe its function and site of action.

14. Prepare a brief report on thalidomide—its structure, original intended use, problems that arose, and proposed new uses. Identify the chiral carbon atom(s) on thalidomide that were the source of the problems.

Fitness and Health

Have You Ever Wondered?

1. **Do large doses or special combinations of vitamins, improve physical fitness?**
2. **Does vitamin C help to cure cancer?**
3. **Which diet pill will help me lose the most weight?**
4. **If I stop exercising, will the muscle I've developed turn to fat?**

Learning Objectives

- List the recommendations (sources and percentages) for calories from fats and other sources in the American diet. (19.1)
- Describe the special dietary requirements of athletes. (19.1)
- Describe the dietary requirements for vitamins, minerals, and water. (19.2)
- Explain how weight is lost through diet and exercise. (19.3)
- Calculate weight loss due to calorie reduction and to exercise. (19.3)
- Describe several ways to measure fitness. (19.4)
- Calculate BMI values. (19.4)
- Differentiate between aerobic exercise and anaerobic exercise, and describe the chemistry that occurs during each. (19.5)
- Describe how muscles are built and how they work. (19.5)
- Describe the physiological effects of restorative drugs, stimulant drugs, and anabolic steroids. (19.6)
- Explain how endorphins, neurotrophins, and tobacco can affect the brain and body. (19.6)
- Explain how green chemistry principles can help us make transportation choices.
- Describe the relationship between walking or biking and personal health, especially the implications for weight loss.

The Chemistry of Wellness

For much of human history, the main concern of most people was obtaining enough food to stay alive. How the world has changed! Especially in developed countries, people now have scores of labor-saving devices and abundant food. Most people earn their daily bread with little physical exertion. So much food is available, and so little physical effort required to obtain it, that many people eat more than they should and get much less exercise than they need.

Obesity has become a major epidemic. According to the Centers for Disease Control and Prevention (CDC), 68% of American adults are either

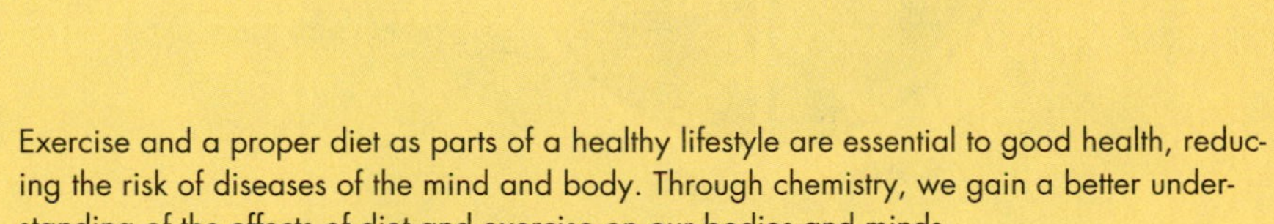

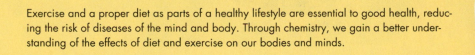

Exercise and a proper diet as parts of a healthy lifestyle are essential to good health, reducing the risk of diseases of the mind and body. Through chemistry, we gain a better understanding of the effects of diet and exercise on our bodies and minds.

overweight or obese; half of those are considered obese. The International Obesity Task Force estimates that 1.5 billion people worldwide are overweight, with 500 million of those being obese.

How do we stay healthy and physically fit? By some special diet or kind of exercise? In this chapter, we examine nutrition, electrolyte balance, muscle action, drugs, and other topics related to well-being and physical fitness.

19.1 Calories: Quantity and Quality

Learning Objectives › List the recommendations (sources and percentages) for calories from fats and other sources in the American diet. › Describe the special dietary requirements of athletes.

Although obesity is rampant in the developed world, many people still struggle daily just to obtain enough food to survive. In fact, research shows that undereating is healthier than overeating. Large studies have shown that mice given 40% less food than a control group live longer and have fewer tumors.

Total calorie intake is important, but the distribution of calories is even more important. The *2010 Dietary Guidelines for Americans* from the U.S. Departments of Agriculture (USDA) and Health and Human Services (HHS) include some recommendations, presented as a food plate in Figure 19.1.

A food plan based on these general recommendations should be tailored to the individual. For the average 2000-calorie-a-day diet, the guidelines suggest

- Enjoy your food, but eat less.
- Avoid oversized portions.
- Make half of your plate fruits and vegetables.
- Whole grains should be at least half of total grains.
- Switch to fat-free or low-fat (1%) milk.
- Compare the sodium content of foods like soup, bread, and frozen meals, and choose the foods with lower amounts.
- Drink water instead of sugary drinks.

The 2000-calorie-per-day diet is an average. You should follow a diet that takes into account your weight, age, and level of activity. Then you should adjust it to include

The Department of Health and Human Services (HHS) and the Department of Agriculture (USDA) jointly publish *Dietary Guidelines for Americans* every 5 years. Find this document on the Internet using the title as key words.

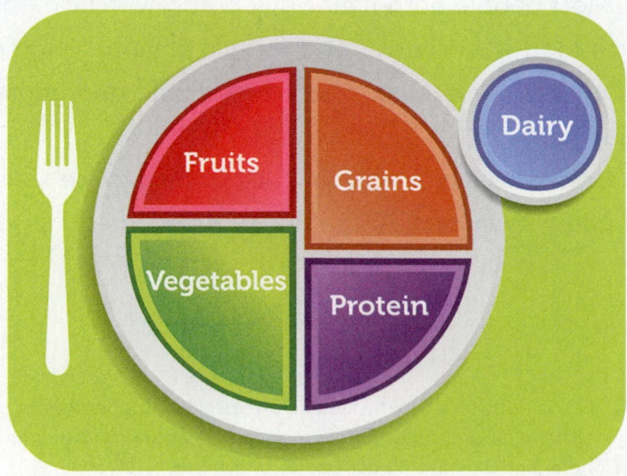

▶ **Figure 19.1** A daily food guide presented as a plate of food. More detailed recommendations in *Dietary Guidelines for Americans* are based on an individual's age, sex, activity level, and general health.

fewer calories if you want to lose weight or more calories if you want to gain weight. Calorie intake calculators available on the Internet might be of some help.

A key recommendation for adults is to keep fat intake between 20% and 35% of all calories. Most fats should be made up of polyunsaturated and monounsaturated fatty acids. Only 7–10% of calories should come from saturated fats, and intake of synthetic *trans* fatty acids should be kept to a minimum. Also, the diet should contain less than 300 mg/day of cholesterol.

The "good" fats come from sources such as fish, nuts, and vegetable oils. Olive oil and canola oil are rich in monounsaturated fatty acids, and fish oils contain beneficial omega-3 fatty acids. A study of people living on the Greek island of Crete showed that they had an amazingly low incidence of cardiovascular disease, in spite of their diet, which averaged about 40% fat. This result is thought to be due to the high percentage of olive oil in their diet.

More than half the fats in the typical American diet are animal fats, and 70% of saturated fat comes from animal products. Saturated fats and cholesterol are implicated in artery clogging. They are found in animal products such as butter, lard, red meats, and fast-food hamburgers. We should choose meat, poultry, milk, and milk products that are lean, low in fat, or fat free.

Trans fats, produced when vegetable oils are hydrogenated (for example, to produce margarine), are high in *trans* fatty acids (Section 17.2). As the name implies, *trans* fatty acids contain carbon-to-carbon double bonds with the *trans* configuration, so that they behave more like saturated fatty acids (Figure 17.7). Unless margarine has been specially treated to remove the *trans* fat, it has about the same health effects as butter.

The *percentage* of fat in the American diet has dropped from 40% in 1990 to about 34% today, but the absolute quantity of fat consumed has increased because Americans are eating more total calories. Also, 34% is an average figure; for some people, the percentage is as high as 45%.

A healthy diet can help us avoid disease. Harvard Medical School studies indicate that correct dietary choices, regular exercise, and avoidance of smoking would prevent about 82% of heart attacks, about 70% of strokes, over 90% of Type 2 diabetes, and over 70% of colon cancer. In contrast, the most effective drugs against cholesterol buildup, called *statins*, only reduce heart attacks by about 20–30%.

Nutrition and the Athlete

The recommended ranges for energy nutrients for most people are 20–35% of calories from fat, 45–65% of calories from carbohydrates, and 10–35% of calories from protein. (Recall from Chapter 17 that each gram of carbohydrate or protein provides about 4 kcal; a gram of fat provides about 9 kcal.) Athletes generally need more calories because they expend more energy than the average sedentary individual. Those extra calories should come mainly from carbohydrates. Foods rich in carbohydrates, especially starches, are the preferred source of energy for the healthy body.

Fatty and protein-rich foods also supply calories, but protein metabolism produces more toxic wastes that tax the liver and kidneys. The pregame steak dinner consumed by some athletes in the past was based on a myth that protein builds muscle. It doesn't. Although athletes do need the **Dietary Reference Intake (DRI)**, quantity of protein (0.8 g protein/kg body weight), with few exceptions, they do not need an excess. DRIs are nutrient-based reference values established by the Food and Nutrition Board of the U.S. National Academy of Sciences for use in planning and assessing diets. They have replaced the Recommended Dietary Allowances (RDAs) that were published since 1941 by the National Academy of Sciences. Protein consumed in amounts greater than that needed for synthesis and repair of tissue only makes an athlete fatter (as a result of excessive calorie intake)—not more muscular.

Muscles are built through exercise, not through eating excess protein. When a muscle contracts against a resistance, an amino acid called *creatine* is released. Creatine stimulates production of the protein myosin, thus building more muscle tissue. If the exercise stops, the muscle begins to shrink after about two days. After about two months without exercise, muscle built through an exercise program is almost completely gone.

$$NH_2-\underset{\underset{NH}{\|}}{C}-\underset{\underset{CH_3}{|}}{N}-CH_2COOH$$

Creatine

Self-Assessment Questions

1. The two major requirements for good health and fitness are
   a. food and entertainment
   b. food and medicine
   c. good nutrition and exercise
   d. nutrition and steroids
2. Which of the following has been shown to extend the life span of mice?
   a. amino acid supplements
   b. low-fat diets
   c. undereating
   d. vitamin supplements
3. The fats most detrimental to health are
   a. all unsaturated fats
   b. monounsaturated fats
   c. polyunsaturated fats
   d. saturated and *trans* fats
4. What is the maximum amount of fat that a diet providing 2200 kcal per day should include?
   a. 22 g
   b. 86 g
   c. 198 g
   d. 220 g
5. What is the maximum amount of saturated fat that a diet providing 2000 kcal per day should include?
   a. 11 g
   b. 22 g
   c. 50 g
   d. 200 g
6. Most of the saturated fats in our diets come from
   a. animal products
   b. cooking oils
   c. candies
   d. vegetables
7. Dietary Reference Intakes (DRIs) are nutrient-based reference values that are
   a. appropriate for undernourished and ill people
   b. guarantees of good health for everyone
   c. useful for planning and assessing diets
   d. minimum daily requirements
8. About how much protein does a 66-kg athlete require per day?
   a. 6.6 g
   b. 8.3 g
   c. 53 g
   d. 2.5 kg

Answers: 1, c; 2, c; 3, d; 4, b; 5, b; 6, a; 7, c; 8, c

19.2 Vitamins, Minerals, Fluids, and Electrolytes

Learning Objective › Describe the dietary requirements for vitamins, minerals, and water.

Good nutrition requires sufficient carbohydrates, fats, and proteins; proper proportions of essential minerals and vitamins; and adequate water. *Vitamins* are organic substances that the human body needs but cannot manufacture in sufficient quantities. Unlike hormones and enzymes, which the body can synthesize, vitamins must be included in the diet. *Minerals*, inorganic elements that the body needs, must also be present in the diet. Table 19.1 lists DRIs of vitamins and minerals for young adult women and men. A more complete list for various ages and with a number of qualifications is available from the Food and Nutrition Board.

Many medical professionals say that vitamin and mineral supplements are unnecessary when the diet is well balanced and includes the DRI for each nutrient. However, for those who choose to take such supplements, reasonable doses of vitamins and minerals from tablets and capsules are not likely to cause harm and can be beneficial in some cases. For example, the body has an increased demand for vitamins and minerals during periods of rapid growth, during pregnancy and lactation, and during periods of trauma and recovery from disease. A study of people aged 65 years and older showed that a daily dose of 18 vitamins and minerals seems to strengthen the immune system. The number of infections in the study group was 50% less than that in a control group, which received no supplements.

Vitamins and minerals are discussed in Chapter 17. See Table 17.3 for a list of essential minerals and trace minerals. Table 17.4 lists most vitamins along with food sources and deficiency symptoms.

The DRI values for vitamins and minerals set by the Food and Nutrition Board are quite modest, and they are readily supplied by any well-balanced diet. The DRI values for vitamins are the amounts that will prevent deficiency

Table 19.1 Dietary Reference Intakes of Vitamins and Minerals for Young Adults

Nutrient	Females	Males
Vitamins		
Vitamin A	700 μg[a]	900 μg[a]
Vitamin C	75 mg[b]	90 mg[b]
Vitamin D	200 IU[c]	200 IU[c]
Vitamin E	30 IU	30 IU
Thiamine (B_1)	1.1 mg	1.2 mg
Riboflavin (B_2)	1.1 mg	1.3 mg
Niacin	14 mg	16 mg
Pyridoxine (B_6)	1.5 mg	1.7 mg
Cyanocobalamin (B_{12})	3 μg	3 μg
Folacin (folic acid)	400 μg	400 μg
Pantothenic acid	5 mg	5 mg
Biotin	100–200 μg	100–200 μg
Minerals		
Calcium	1200 mg	1200 mg
Phosphorus	700 mg	700 mg
Magnesium	320 mg	420 mg
Iron	15 mg	10 mg
Zinc	12 mg	15 mg
Iodine	150 μg	150 μg
Fluoride	3 mg	4 mg
Selenium	55 μg	70 μg
Potassium	2 g	2 g

[a]To the extent that the vitamin A requirement is met by β-carotene, multiply these by 6.

[b]Smokers should add 35 mg.

[c]IU (for "international unit") is a measure of the biological activity of many vitamins, hormones, and drugs. See also the margin note on page 590.

diseases such as beriberi, pellagra, and scurvy. Some scientists believe that *optimum* intakes of some vitamins are somewhat higher than the DRI values. For example, they think that the current DRIs for vitamins C, D, and E are too low. If you eat a well-balanced diet and you are in good health, you probably do not need vitamin supplements. Small doses of vitamins are not toxic; some of the fat-soluble vitamins (A and D) are toxic in large doses, however, so caution is warranted.

Vitamin A is essential for good vision, bone development, and skin maintenance. There is some evidence that it may confer resistance to certain kinds of cancer. This may help to explain the anticancer activity that has been noted for cruciferous vegetables such as broccoli, cauliflower, Brussels sprouts, and cabbage. Most cruciferous vegetables are rich in β-carotene, which is converted to vitamin A in the body.

Vitamin A is a fat-soluble vitamin stored in the fatty tissues of the body and especially in the liver. Large doses can be toxic. The recommended upper limit for intake of vitamin A is 3000 μg/day. Studies in affluent countries have shown that ingesting vitamin A from supplements and in fortified foods at levels even slightly above the DRI leads to an increased risk of bone fractures later in life.

Larger quantities of β-carotene can be taken safely because excess β-carotene is not converted to vitamin A. It may have important functions other than as a precursor of vitamin A. Some nutritionists argue that β-carotene is needed in

1. Do large doses or special combinations of vitamins improve physical fitness? Vitamins should not be thought of as fuel, like food or water or oxygen. Although a daily vitamin tablet may be good insurance for many people, vitamin doses in large excess of the DRIs have not been found to have any special fitness benefit. Nor do special combinations provide improved stamina or strength. In fact, megadoses of some vitamins can have deleterious effects.

▲ Dorothy Crowfoot Hodgkin (1910–1994) used X-rays to determine the structures of several important organic compounds, including vitamin B_{12}, penicillin, and cholesterol.

People with low levels of vitamin C are more likely to develop cataracts and glaucoma, as well as gingivitis and periodontal disease. Some suggest that very large doses of vitamin C may cure or prevent colds, but there is little evidence for this.

2. Does vitamin C help to cure cancer? A 2008 study by the National Institutes of Health found that *injected* vitamin C does appear to slow brain, ovarian, and pancreatic tumor growth in mice. However, these studies have not yet been extended to human beings. Also, the body precisely regulates the amount of vitamin C in the blood when it is taken orally, so oral doses of the vitamin do not provide these benefits.

An international unit (IU) measures the biological activity of many vitamins, hormones, and drugs. For each substance to which the IU applies, an international agreement specifies the biological effect expected from a dose of 1 IU. The IU is used to measure comparative potency of a substance such as a vitamin because the vitamin may exist in more than one form. For example, 1 IU of vitamin A is the biological equivalent of 0.3 μg retinol or 0.6 μg β-carotene.

quantities greater than those needed to meet the vitamin A requirement. However, a single ½-cup serving of carrots is sufficient to provide the DRI of vitamin A from β-carotene. Consuming foods that contain β-carotene is probably the safest way to obtain the proper quantity of vitamin A.

The B family of vitamins has eight members. Because they are all water soluble, excess intake is excreted in the urine. Little or no toxicity is connected with B vitamins, with the possible exceptions of vitamin B_6 and folic acid, both of which apparently can cause neurological damage in some people if taken in extremely large daily doses. Several B vitamins serve as coenzymes (Section 16.5). In addition to preventing the skin lesions of pellagra, niacin (vitamin B_3) offers some relief from arthritis and helps in lowering the blood cholesterol level.

Vitamin B_6 (pyridoxine) has been found to help people with arthritis by shrinking the connective tissue membranes that line the joints. Vitamin B_6 is a coenzyme for more than 100 different enzymes.

Vitamin B_{12} (cyanocobalamin) is not found in plants, and vegetarians are apt to be deficient in this vitamin. That deficiency can lead to pernicious anemia. The molecular formula of vitamin B_{12} is $C_{63}H_{88}CoN_{14}O_{14}P$, giving it a molecular mass of 1355.38 u. Its very complicated structure was determined by Dorothy Hodgkin of Oxford University in 1956 using X-ray crystallography, a technique in which an X-ray beam is used to bombard a crystal. The beam is scattered in a definite pattern determined by the crystal structure. No one had ever attempted to establish the structure of a molecule of this size and complexity before. Hodgkin received the 1964 Nobel Prize in Chemistry for this work.

Another B vitamin is folic acid, which is critical in the development of the nervous system of a fetus. Its presence in a pregnant woman's diet prevents spina bifida in her baby. Folic acid also helps prevent cardiovascular disease. An upper limit of 1000 μg has been set; more than that can cause nerve damage.

Vitamin C is ascorbic acid, the component in citrus fruits that combats scurvy. About 60–80 mg daily will prevent scurvy, but vitamin C does more than that. It promotes the healing of wounds, burns, and lesions such as gastric ulcers. It also seems to play an important role in maintaining collagen, the body's major structural protein. Like vitamin E, it is an antioxidant, and these two vitamins, along with β-carotene, are included in many antioxidant formulations. Antioxidants may act as anticarcinogens. About 200 mg of vitamin C per day is probably optimal, and an upper limit of 2000 mg/day has been set.

Vitamin C seems to be essential for efficient functioning of the immune system. *Interferons*, large molecules formed by the action of viruses on their host cells, are agents in the immune system. By producing an interferon, one virus can interfere with the growth of another. An increased level of vitamin C has been shown to increase the body's production of interferons.

Vitamin D is a steroid hormone that protects children against rickets. It promotes the absorption of calcium and phosphorus from foods to produce and maintain healthy bones. Too much vitamin D can lead to excessive calcium and phosphorus absorption, with subsequent formation of calcium deposits in various soft body tissues, including those of the heart. The DRI for vitamin D increases with age, from 200 international units (IU) for adults aged 20–50 to reaching 600 IU for those over 70. The recommended upper limit is 2000 IU.

Vitamin E is a mixture of *tocopherols,* phenols with hydrocarbon side chains. Its antioxidant activity may have value in maintaining the cardiovascular system, and it has been used to treat coronary heart disease, angina, rheumatic heart disease, high blood pressure, arteriosclerosis, varicose veins, and a number of other cardiovascular problems. As an antioxidant, vitamin E can inactivate free radicals. It is generally believed that much of the physiological damage from aging is a result of the production of free radicals. Indeed, vitamin E has been called the "antiaging vitamin." However, studies of these effects are often contradictory and far from conclusive. Vitamin E is also an anticoagulant that has been useful in preventing blood clots after surgery.

Rats deprived of vitamin E become sterile. Vitamin E deficiency can also lead to muscular dystrophy, a disease of the skeletal muscles. A lack of vitamin E can lead to a deficiency in vitamin A. This occurs because vitamin A can be oxidized to an inactive form when vitamin E is not present to act as an antioxidant. Vitamin E also collaborates with vitamin C in protecting blood vessels and other tissues against oxidation. Vitamin E is the fat-soluble antioxidant vitamin, and vitamin C the water-soluble one. Oxidation of unsaturated fatty acids in cell membranes can be prevented or reversed by vitamin E, which is itself oxidized in the process. Vitamin C can then restore vitamin E to its unoxidized form. The upper limit for vitamin E is 800 IU/day or 400 IU/day, depending on side effects. And, according to a study published in October 2011, even 400 IU/day may increase the risk of prostate cancer in men.

LDL cholesterol is oxidized before it is deposited in arteries, and vitamin E prevents the oxidation of cholesterol. Some think this is the mechanism by which vitamin E helps to protect against cardiovascular disease.

Body Fluids and Electrolytes

Another aspect of the relationship of chemistry and nutrition is the balance between fluid intake and electrolyte intake. An **electrolyte** is a substance that conducts electricity when dissolved in water. In the body, electrolytes are ions required by cells to maintain their internal and external electric charge and thus control the flow of water molecules across the cell membrane. The main electrolytes are sodium ions (Na^+), potassium ions (K^+), and chloride ions (Cl^-). Others include calcium ions (Ca^{2+}), magnesium ions (Mg^{2+}), sulfate ions (SO_4^{2-}), hydrogen phosphate ions (HPO_4^{2-}), and bicarbonate ions (HCO_3^-).

Water is an essential nutrient, a fact obvious to anyone who has been deprived of it. Many people seem to prefer to meet the body's need for water by consuming soft drinks, coffee, beer, fruit juice, energy drinks, and other beverages. Some of these beverages actually impair the body's use of the water they contain. Alcoholic drinks promote water loss by blocking the action of *antidiuretic hormone* (*ADH*), also known as *vasopressin*. Caffeine has a diuretic effect on the kidneys, promoting urine formation and consequent water loss.

The best way to replace water lost through respiration, sweat, tears, and urination is to drink water. Unfortunately, thirst is often a *delayed* response to water loss, and it may be masked by such symptoms of dehydration as exhaustion, confusion, headache, and nausea. Sweat is about 99% water, but a liter of sweat typically contains 1.15 g Na^+, 1.48 g Cl^-, 0.02 g Ca^{2+}, 0.23 g K^+, 0.05 g Mg^{2+}, and minute amounts of urea, lactic acid, and body oils. Most people consume too much sodium chloride (Na^+ and Cl^-), and only traces of the other electrolytes are lost. Thus, it makes the most sense to replace the water component of lost sweat with plain water.

Commercial beverages such as sports drinks, energy drinks, vitamin waters, protein waters, and fitness waters usually contain one or more ingredients that are more effective as advertising gimmicks than as aids to athletic performance. Sports drinks usually contain sweeteners and electrolytes. Energy drinks usually have sugars and often contain caffeine as a mild stimulant. The ingredients in vitamin waters and protein waters are obvious, but there are far better and less expensive sources of both. Although these drinks are quite popular with both serious and weekend athletes, they are so concentrated (a hazard that can lead to diarrhea) that they are of marginal value except for endurance athletes (Figure 19.2).

▲ **Figure 19.2** The best replacement for fluids lost during exercise generally is plain water. Sports drinks help little, except when engaging in endurance activities lasting for 2 hr or more. At that point, carbohydrates in the drinks delay the onset of exhaustion by a few minutes.

How do you know if you are drinking enough water and are in a proper state of hydration? The urine is a good indicator of hydration. When you are properly hydrated, your urine is clear and almost colorless. When you are dehydrated, your urine gets cloudy or dark because your kidneys are trying to conserve water so as to keep the blood volume from shrinking and to prevent shock.

Dehydration can be quite serious, even deadly. We become thirsty when total body fluid volume decreases by 0.5–1.0%. Beyond that, things get worse

Improving Athletic Performance through Chemistry

Chemistry has transformed athletic performance in recent decades. New materials have been used to make protective gear such as plastic helmets and foam padding for football, ice hockey, skateboarding, and other sports. Improved equipment has changed the nature of most sports events. Baseball, football, and other sports are quite different when played on artificial turf or under a dome than when played outdoors on grass. Traction changes, the ball bounces differently, and so on. Skateboards of the 1950s consisted of metal roller-skate wheels on a flat wooden board. Today's skateboards have wide urethane wheels, specially shaped composite-construction boards, and shock-absorbing wheel mounts that make incredible stunts almost commonplace. Several decades ago, running shoes had thin leather soles and little or no foot support. Now these shoes have thick, shock-absorbing soles and built-in support for arches and ankles.

▲ Sometimes technology can be *too* beneficial. Specially designed full-length swimsuits dramatically reduce drag. So many swimming world records were set immediately afterward that the suits were banned in 2010.

Biochemistry has brought a better understanding of the human body and the way it works. Chemistry has helped to provide better nutrition. Today's athletes are bigger, faster, and stronger than their predecessors. More than 30 new world records were set at the 2008 Olympic Games in Beijing.

(Table 19.2). Muscles tire and cramp. Dizziness and fainting may follow, and brain cells shrink, resulting in mental confusion. Finally, the heat regulatory system fails, causing *heat stroke*, which can be fatal without prompt medical attention.

Table 19.2 Effects of Varying Degrees of Dehydration

Percentage of Body Weight Lost as Sweat	Physiological Effect
2%	Performance impaired
4%	Muscular work capacity declines
5%	Heat exhaustion
7%	Hallucinations
10%	Circulatory collapse and heat stroke

Self-Assessment Questions

1. Which of the following cannot be synthesized by the body and therefore must be included in the diet?
   a. enzymes b. hormones
   c. unsaturated fats d. vitamins
2. Which of the following is a precursor of vitamin A?
   a. β-carotene b. cholesterol
   c. pyridoxine d. tryptophan
3. For which of the following are large doses most likely to be harmful?
   a. β-carotene b. niacin
   c. vitamin A d. vitamin C
4. All B vitamins
   a. are synthetic
   b. are water soluble
   c. have the same functional group
   d. have molecular masses above 1000 u

5. Vitamin C is a(n)
   a. antimetabolite
   b. fat-soluble antioxidant
   c. oxidizing agent
   d. water-soluble antioxidant
6. The major electrolytes in body fluids are
   a. Ca^{2+}, Fe^{2+}, and Cl^-
   b. Ca^{2+}, Na^+, and $HSO4^-$
   c. Na^+, K^+, and Cl^-
   d. Na^+, K^+, and HCO_3^-
7. The best replacement for water lost except in prolonged exercise is
   a. beer
   b. non-fat milk
   c. plain water
   d. soft drinks
8. What is the minimal percentage of body weight lost in fluids that can cause reduced performance?
   a. 2%
   b. 4%
   c. 6%
   d. 10%

Answers: 1, d; 2, a; 3, c; 4, b; 5, d; 6, c; 7, c; 8, a

19.3 Weight Loss: Diets and Exercise

Learning Objectives › Explain how weight is lost through diet and exercise. › Calculate weight loss due to calorie reduction and to exercise.

With obesity an epidemic and so many people overweight, dieting is a major U.S. industry. It is possible to lose weight through dieting alone, but it isn't easy. One pound of adipose (fatty) tissue stores about 3500 kcal of energy. If you reduce your intake by 100 kcal/day and keep your activity level constant, you will burn off a pound of fat in 35 days. Unfortunately, people are seldom patient enough, and they resort to more stringent diets. To achieve their goals more rapidly, they exclude certain foods and reduce the amounts of others. Such diets can be harmful. Diets with fewer than 1200 kcal/day are likely to be deficient in necessary nutrients, particularly in B vitamins and iron. Further, dieting slows down metabolism. Weight lost through dieting is quickly regained when the dieter resumes old eating habits.

Example 19.1 Weight Loss through Dieting

If you ordinarily expend 2000 kcal/day and you go on a diet limited to 1500 kcal/day, about how long will it take to lose 1.0 lb of fat?

Solution

You will use 2000 − 1500 = 500 kcal/day more than you consume. There are about 3500 kcal in 1.0 lb of fat, so it will take

$$3500 \text{ kcal} \times \frac{1 \text{ day}}{500 \text{ kcal}} = 7 \text{ days}$$

Keep in mind, however, that your weight loss will not be all fat. You will probably lose more than 1 lb, but it will be mostly water with some protein and a little glycogen.

■ EXERCISE 19.1A

A person who expends 1800 kcal/day goes on a diet limited to 1200 kcal/day without a change in activities. Estimate how much fat she will lose if she stays on this diet for 3 weeks.

■ EXERCISE 19.1B

A person who expends 2200 kcal/day goes on a diet limited to 1800 kcal/day and adds exercise activities that use 220 kcal/day. Estimate how much fat he will lose if he stays on this program for 6 weeks.

Biochemistry of Hunger

Scientists are just beginning to understand the complex biochemistry of hunger mechanisms. Several molecules that regulate body weight have been identified. Some determine whether we want to eat now or stop eating. Others control long-term fat balance. Much of what we now know is disappointing for people who want to lose weight: The hunger mechanisms protect against weight loss and favor weight gain.

Two peptide hormones, known as *ghrelin* and *peptide YY (PYY)*, are produced by the digestive tract and are linked to short-term eating behaviors. Ghrelin, a modified peptide, is an appetite stimulant produced by the stomach. PYY acts as an appetite suppressant. Studies at Imperial College, London, found that people ate about 30% less after they were given a dose of PYY. The research also found that obese people had lower natural levels of PYY, which may explain why these people feel hungrier and overeat.

The hormone insulin and a substance called *leptin*, which is produced by fat cells, determine longer-term weight balance. When insulin levels go up, glucose levels go down, and we experience hunger. Conversely, when glucose levels are high, the activity of brain cells sensitive to glucose is lessened, and we feel satiated.

Leptin, a protein consisting of 146 amino-acid units, is produced by fat cells. It causes weight loss in mice by decreasing their appetite and increasing their metabolic rates. Levels of leptin tell the hypothalamus (a regulatory center in the brain) how much fat is in the body. Humans also produce leptin, and scientists hoped it would be the route to a cure for the ever-growing obesity problem. That hope is largely unrealized. Only a few cases of severe human obesity, caused by defects in leptin production, have been helped by leptin treatment. As it turns out, most obese humans have *higher* than normal blood levels of leptin and are resistant to its actions. Leptin's main role seems to be to protect against weight loss in times of scarcity rather than against weight gain in times of plentiful food.

3. Which diet pill will help me lose the most weight? Most of the so-called diet pills on the market are actually classified as *dietary supplements* (page 510) and have not been demonstrated to aid in weight loss. A few diet aids have limited use, but most of those are prescription drugs. *Orlistat* (Alli®) was approved for over-the-counter sales in 2007. It has been tested and shown to reduce the amount of fat absorbed from food, but it may have unpleasant side effects including diarrhea.

Other substances involved in weight control include *cholecystokinin (CCK)*, a peptide formed in the intestine that signals that we have eaten enough food and a class of compounds called *melanocortins*, which act on the brain to regulate food intake.

It remains to be seen whether this new knowledge about the body's weight-control systems will pay off in better obesity treatments. A complication is that many social factors are also involved in eating behavior. Some people are motivated by environmental cues to eat. A family gathering, the sight or smell of food, and a stressful situation can all trigger the hunger mechanism.

Crash Diets: Quick = Quack

Any weight-loss program that promises a loss of more than a pound or two a week is likely to be dangerous quackery. Most quick-weight-loss diets depend on factors other than fat metabolism to hook prospective customers. The diets often include a **diuretic**, such as caffeine, to increase the output of urine. Weight loss is water loss, and that weight is regained when the body is rehydrated.

Other quick-weight-loss diets depend on depleting the body's stores of glycogen. On a low-carbohydrate diet, the body draws on its glycogen reserves, depleting them in about 24 hours. Recall that glycogen is a polymer of glucose (Section 16.2). Glycogen molecules have lots of hydroxyl (—OH) groups that can form hydrogen bonds to water molecules. We can store at most about 1 lb of glycogen. Each pound of glycogen carries about 3 lb of water held to it by these hydrogen bonds. Depleting the pound of glycogen results in a weight loss of about 4 lb (1 lb glycogen + 3 lb water). No fat is lost, and the weight is quickly regained when the dieter resumes eating carbohydrates.

If your normal energy expenditure is 2400 kcal/day, the most fat you can lose by *total fasting* for a day is 0.69 lb (2400 kcal/day divided by 3500 kcal/lb of adipose tissue). This assumes that your body burns nothing but fat—which does not occur. The brain runs on glucose, and if that glucose isn't supplied in the diet, it is obtained from protein. Any diet that restricts carbohydrate intake results in a loss of muscle mass as well as fat. When you gain the weight back (as 90% of all dieters do), you gain mostly fat. People who diet without exercising will replace metabolically active tissue (muscle) with inactive fat when they gain back the lost weight. Weight loss becomes harder with each subsequent attempted diet.

Many crash diets are also deficient in minerals such as iron, calcium, and potassium. A deficiency of these minerals can disrupt nerve-impulse transmissions to muscles, which impairs athletic performance. Nerve-impulse transmission to vital organs may also be impaired in cases of severe restriction, and death can result from cardiac arrest.

There is little evidence that commercial weight-loss programs are effective in helping people drop excess pounds and keep them off. Almost no rigorous studies of the programs have been carried out, and U.S. Federal Trade Commission officials say that companies are unwilling to conduct such studies.

Exercise for Weight Loss

Studies consistently show that people who exercise regularly live longer. They are sick less often and have fewer signs of depression. They can move faster, and they have stronger bones and muscles. Although there are dozens of good reasons for regular exercise, many people begin exercise programs for one simple reason: They want to lose weight.

People who do not increase their food intake when they begin an exercise program lose weight. Contrary to a common myth, exercise (for up to an hour a day) does not cause an increase in appetite. Most of the weight loss from exercise results from an increase in metabolic rate during the activity, but the increased metabolic rate continues for several hours after completion of the exercise. Exercise helps us maintain both fitness and proper body weight.

4. If I stop exercising, will the muscle I've developed turn to fat? Muscle does not turn into fat, although without regular exercise muscles become flabby and will lose mass.

Example 19.2 Weight Loss through Exercise

A 135-lb person doing high-impact aerobics burns about 6.9 kcal/min. How long does a person have to do such exercise to lose 1.0 lb of adipose (fat) tissue?

Solution

One pound of adipose tissue stores 3500 kcal of energy. To burn it at 6.9 kcal/min requires

$$3500\ \text{kcal} \times \frac{1\ \text{min}}{6.9\ \text{kcal}} = 500\ \text{min}$$

It takes about 500 min (more than 8 hr) to burn 1 lb of fat, even doing high-impact aerobics.

■ EXERCISE 19.2A

Walking a mile uses about 100 kcal. About how far do you have to walk to burn 1.0 lb of fat?

■ EXERCISE 19.2B

A moderately active person can calculate the calories needed each day to maintain a desired weight by multiplying the desired weight (in pounds) by 15 kcal/lb. How many calories per day does such a person need to maintain a weight of 180 lb?

The most sensible approach to weight loss is to adhere to a balanced low-calorie diet that meets the DRI for essential nutrients and to engage in a reasonable, consistent, individualized exercise program. This approach applies the principles of weight loss by decreasing intake and increasing output.

Weight loss or gain is based on the law of conservation of energy (Section 15.3). When we take in more calories than we use up, the excess calories are stored as fat. When we take in fewer calories than we need for our activities, our bodies burn some of the stored fat to make up for the deficit. One pound of adipose tissue requires 200 mi of blood capillaries to serve its cells. Excess fat therefore puts extra strain on the heart.

On a weight-loss diet (without exercise), about 65% of the weight lost is fat and about 11% is protein (muscle tissue). The rest is water and a little glycogen.

Fad Diets

Weight loss diets are often lacking in balanced nutrition and can be harmful to one's health. In the more extreme low-carbohydrate diets, ketosis (Section 17.5) is deliberately induced, and possible side effects include depression and lethargy. In the early stages of a diet deficient in carbohydrates, the body converts amino acids to glucose that the brain requires. If there are enough adequate proteins in the diet, tissue proteins are spared.

Even low-carbohydrate diets high in adequate proteins are hard on the body, which must rid itself of the nitrogen compounds—ammonia and urea—formed by the breakdown of proteins. This puts an increased stress on the liver, where the waste products are formed, and on the kidneys, where they are excreted.

Contrary to a popular notion, fasting does not "cleanse" the body. Indeed, quite the reverse occurs. A shift to fat metabolism produces ketone bodies (Section 17.5), and protein breakdown produces ammonia, urea, and other wastes. You can lose weight by fasting, but the process should be carefully monitored by a physician.

Self-Assessment Questions

1. How many kilocalories of energy are stored in 1.0 lb of adipose tissue?
   a. 454 kcal **b.** 1000 kcal **c.** 3500 kcal **d.** 10,000 kcal
2. To lose 1.0 lb per week, how many more kilocalories must you burn each day than you take in?
   a. 100 **b.** 300 **c.** 500 **d.** 1000
3. Which of the following hormones acts as an appetite stimulant?
   a. ADH **b.** ghrelin **c.** leptin **d.** PYY
4. Blood glucose levels are lowered by the hormone
   a. cholecystokinin **b.** glucagon **c.** insulin **d.** oxytocin
5. Which of the following seems to tell the brain it is time to stop eating?
   a. cholecystokinin (CCK) **b.** ghrelin
   c. leptin **d.** oxytocin
6. About how much glycogen can the adult body store?
   a. 100 g **b.** 1 lb
   c. 4 lb **d.** an almost unlimited quantity
7. Crash diets
   a. are a good way to lose weight and keep it off
   b. depend on glycogen depletion for quick weight loss
   c. result in a decrease in the number of fat cells
   d. lead to a depletion of adipose tissue

Answers: 1, c; 2, c; 3, b; 4, c; 5, a; 6, b; 7, b

▲ **It DOES Matter!**
In Europe during the Middle Ages—and even later—people accused of crimes were often tried by some kind of ordeal. In trial by water, the innocent sank and the guilty floated. Suspected witches were tied hand to foot and thrown into the water. The guilty floated, were fished out, dried off, and executed. In those days, body density was *really* important!

19.4 Measuring Fitness

Learning Objectives › Describe several ways to measure fitness. › Calculate BMI values.

Measuring fitness is basically the same as measuring fatness. How much fat is enough? The male body requires about 3% body fat, and the average female body needs 10–12%. It is not easy to measure percent body fat accurately. Weight alone does not indicate degree of fitness. A tall 200-lb man may be much more fit than a 160-lb man with a smaller frame. Skinfold calipers are sometimes used, but they are quite inaccurate and measure water retention as well as fat.

One way to estimate body fat is by measuring a person's density. Mass is determined by weighing, and volume is calculated with the help of a dunk tank like the one shown in Figure 19.3. The difference between a person's weight in air and when submerged in water corresponds to the *mass* of the displaced water. When this mass is divided by the density of water and then corrected for air in the lungs, it gives a reasonable value for the person's volume. Mass divided by volume yields the person's density, although results can vary with the amount of air in the lungs. Fat is less dense (0.903 g/mL) than the water (1.00 g/mL) that makes up most of the body's mass. The higher the proportion of body fat a person has, the lower the density and the more buoyant that person is in water.

A simpler way to estimate degree of fatness is by measuring the waist and the hips. The waist should be measured at the narrowest point and the hips should be measured where the circumference is the largest. The waist measurement should then be divided by the hip measurement. This ratio should be less than 1 for men and should be 0.8 or less for women. (Because the units cancel out, the measurements can be made in inches or centimeters, as long as the same units are used for both.)

Some modern scales provide a measure of body fat content, using *bioelectric impedance analysis*. The person stands on the scale in bare feet, and a small electric current is sent through the body. Fat has greater impedance (resistance to varying current) than does muscle. By measuring the impedance of the body, the percentage of body fat can be calculated based on height and weight. However, there are many other variables, such as bone density, water content, and location of fat. Although such scales are not very accurate, they may be useful for monitoring *changes* in body fat content.

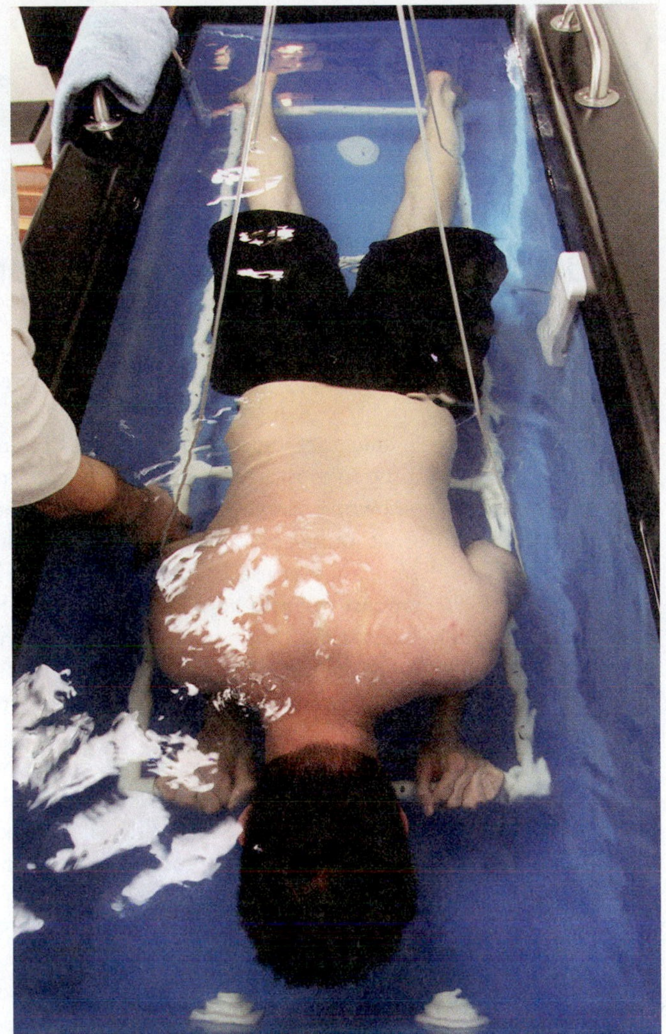

▲ **Figure 19.3** When submerged in water, a body displaces its own volume of water. The difference between a person's weight in air and when submerged in water corresponds to the *mass* of the displaced water. Because the density of water is 1.00 g/mL, the mass of water displaced (in grams) equals the person's volume (in milliliters).

Q: *What is the volume, in liters, of a person who displaces 48.5 kg of water?*

Body Mass Index

Body mass index (BMI) is a commonly used measure of fatness. It is defined as weight (in kilograms) divided by the square of the height (in meters). For a person who is 1.6 m tall and weighs 62 kg, the body mass index is $62/(1.6)^2 = 24$. A BMI below 18.5 indicates that a person is underweight. A BMI from 25 to 29.9 indicates that a person is overweight, and a BMI of 30 or more indicates obesity. When measurements are in pounds and inches, the equation is

$$\text{BMI} = \frac{705 \times \text{body weight (lb)}}{[\text{height (in.)}]^2}$$

In other words, a person who is 5 ft 10 in. tall (70 in.) and weighs 140 lb has a BMI of

$$\frac{705 \times 140}{70 \times 70} = 20$$

which is within the ideal range.

Example 19.3 Body Mass Index

What is the BMI for a person who is 6 ft 1 in. tall and weighs 205 lb?

Solution

The person's height is $(6 \times 12) + 1 = 72 + 1 = 73$ in.

$$\text{BMI} = \frac{705 \times 205}{73 \times 73} = 27$$

The body mass index is 27.

GREEN CHEMISTRY

Principles 3, 6, 7, 9

Doris Lewis, *Suffolk University*

Your Fitness Benefits the Planet

How do you get to class each day? Do you walk, bike, drive, or take public transportation? You might be surprised to learn that green chemistry principles can apply to your personal transportation.

According to green chemistry ideals, we should limit our use of the fossil fuels that support most transport, such as gasoline, because they are nonrenewable resources (Principle 7). Further, burning of these materials produces greenhouse gases including CO_2. Principle 3 suggests that use of fossil fuels should be reduced because this process releases harmful substances to the environment, including gases that have been linked to destructive climate change. As shown in the equation in Section 13.4, the combustion of 1 mol of octane, a component of gasoline, releases 8 mol of CO_2.

Although the chemical reactions that power your body when you walk or bike produce CO_2, they are based on renewable fuels—the carbohydrates in your food (Section 17.1). The reaction of carbohydrates with oxygen powers your body and leads to CO_2 as a byproduct. The plants that produced the carbohydrates you eat incorporated CO_2 from the atmosphere through photosynthesis (Section 15.1) and thus decreased the amount of this greenhouse gas. Your energy source, therefore, is carbon-neutral because the carbon dioxide that you produce is balanced by the carbon dioxide used up to make the fuel your body uses. Because the plants you consume use the energy of the Sun to power photosynthesis, it is fair to say that you, too, are powered by renewable solar energy. Although the carbon compounds in fossil fuels came originally from plants, those plants died millions of years ago, so their removal of CO_2 does not help our atmosphere today.

Unlike internal combustion engines that burn at high temperatures, your body is able to fuel your motion at the temperature of 98.6 °F, or 37.0 °C. Therefore, walking or biking is consistent with Principle 6, design for energy efficiency. How does your body perform this feat? Its energy reactions involve enzymes, or selective biochemical catalysts, as prescribed by Principle 9.

Walking and biking are healthier not only for the planet but also for you. Studies have shown that an average of two or more walking trips per week results in an yearly projected weight loss of 0.9–1.8 lb—approximately the yearly weight gain of the average American. A 150-lb person walking only 20 min at 4 mi/h burns 114 calories that would be deposited as fat were the same amount of time spent sitting in a car (Section 19.3). Walking has been shown to provide protection from heart attack, stroke, and diabetes. It also triggers release of endorphins, the body's stress-relieving and mood-lifting chemicals (Section 19.6).

Prefer biking to walking? Riding a bicycle instead of driving a car saves an average of $8000 per year, and biking 10 mi per day burns 110,000 kcal a year. This choice can keep off more than 30 lb of fat each year and save a whopping 3500 lb of greenhouse gas emissions. Bike riders have banded together to promote commuting by bike and safer bike routes and to sponsor Bike-to-Work days in many cities. Riding a bike to work can change your entire day. You arrive at work refreshed and less stressed.

Universities in Boston co-sponsor "Hub on Wheels," a city-wide bike ride and festival, aided by student activists in environmental clubs who promote bikes as alternative transportation. What does your college do to encourage biking? How are students and student groups involved? Students at Suffolk University created a YouTube video as a service project to promote biking.

On Earth Day 2010, the U.S. Department of Transportation released a study that recommends improved biking and walking transport networks as a way of reducing greenhouse emissions. Simply making it easier to walk or bike would reduce greenhouse gases by 0.2–0.6% by 2030, at a relatively low cost (less than $200 per ton of CO_2). Since walking or biking is less expensive than other modes of transportation, there would be a net overall savings. Green chemistry can improve your health and the planet's health, while saving us money.

▲ Bicycling to work or school is an all-win proposition. Even an elaborate bicycle is much less expensive than a car. Bicycling provides healthy exercise, it does not generate pollution, and operating cost is nil.

■ EXERCISE 19.3A
What is the BMI for a person who is 5.0 ft tall and weighs 120 lb?

■ EXERCISE 19.3B
What is the maximum weight, in pounds, that a person who is 5 ft 10 in. tall can maintain and have a BMI that does not exceed 25.0?

V_{O_2} max: A Measure of Fitness

As we increase exercise intensity, our uptake of oxygen must also increase. For example, the faster we run, the more oxygen we need to sustain the pace. However, the body reaches a point at which it simply cannot increase the amount of oxygen it consumes even if the intensity of exercise increases. The V_{O_2} max is the maximum amount (in milliliters per kilogram of body weight) of oxygen that a person can use in 1 minute.

V_{O_2} max is therefore a measure of fitness. The higher the V_{O_2} max, the greater is an athlete's fitness. A person with a high V_{O_2} max can exercise more intensely than those who are less fit. The V_{O_2} max can be increased by working out at an intensity that raises the heart rate to 65–85% of its maximum for at least 20 minutes three to five times a week. Limitations on V_{O_2} max include the ability of muscle cells to use oxygen in metabolizing fuels and the ability of the cardiovascular system and lungs to transport oxygen to the muscles.

Direct testing of V_{O_2} max requires expensive equipment, including a gas analyzer to measure O_2 taken in and exhaled. Percent V_{O_2} max can be estimated indirectly from percent maximum heart rate (%MHR), where MHR is the highest number of beats the heart makes in a minute of exercising.

$$\%\text{MHR} = (0.64 \times \%V_{O_2}\text{ max}) + 37$$

The relationship holds quite well for both males and females of all ages and activity levels. For example, 80% MHR corresponds to a $\%V_{O_2}$ max of

$$80 = (0.64 \times \%V_{O_2}\text{ max}) + 37$$
$$\%V_{O_2}\text{ max} = 67$$

Equations for determining MHR values and tables for evaluating fitness levels can be found in exercise physiology textbooks and on the Internet (see Collaborative Group Project 2).

▲ **It DOES Matter!**
Extreme-endurance athletes, such as triathletes and ultramarathoners, may need a bit more protein than the DRI. However, nearly all Americans eat 50% more protein than they need, so even these athletes seldom need protein supplements. Weightlifters and bodybuilders need no extra protein.

Self-Assessment Questions

1. Body mass index (BMI) is calculated as
   a. percentage of body fat × waist circumference (in.)
   b. (height ÷ weight) × 100
   c. [705 × weight (lb)] ÷ [height (in.)]
   d. weight (kg) ÷ [height (m)]^2
2. A person with a BMI of 35 is
   a. obese
   b. overweight but not obese
   c. quite fit
   d. underweight
3. The maximum amount of oxygen used in a minute of exercise is the
   a. aerobic threshold
   b. lactate threshold
   c. oxygen debt
   d. V_{O_2} max

Answers: 1, d; 2, a; 3, d

19.5 Some Muscular Chemistry

Learning Objectives › Differentiate between aerobic exercise and anaerobic exercise, and describe the chemistry that occurs during each. › Describe how muscles are built and how they work.

The human body has about 600 muscles. Exercise makes these muscles larger, more flexible, and more efficient in their use of oxygen. Exercise strengthens the heart because the heart is an organ comprised mainly of muscle. With regular exercise, resting pulse and blood pressure usually decline. A person who exercises regularly is able to do more physical work with less strain. Exercise is an art, but it is also increasingly a science—a science in which chemistry plays a vital role.

Energy for Muscle Contraction: ATP

When cells metabolize glucose or fatty acids, only part of the chemical energy in these substances is converted to heat. Some of the energy is stored in the high-energy phosphate bonds of adenosine triphosphate (ATP) molecules.

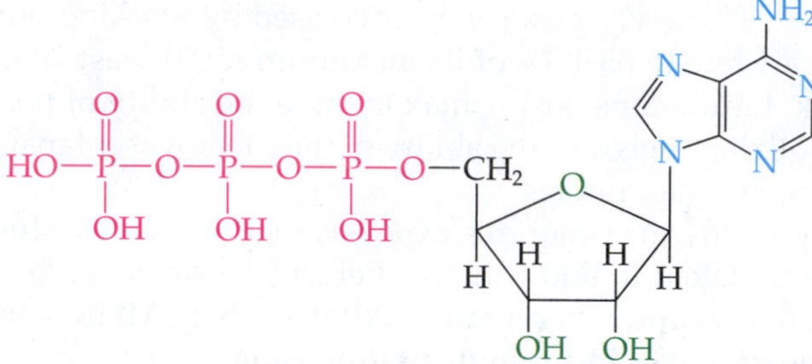

Adenosine triphosphate

Stimulation of muscles causes them to contract. This contraction is *work*, and it requires energy that the muscles get from the molecules of ATP. The energy stored in ATP powers the physical movement of muscle tissue. Two proteins, actin and myosin, play important roles in this process. Together they form a loose complex called *actomyosin*, the contractile protein that makes up muscles (Figure 19.4).

When ATP is added to actomyosin in the laboratory, the protein fibers contract. Myosins turn the chemical energy of ATP into motion. Myosin molecules "walk" along the actin filaments. It takes about 2×10^{12} myosin molecules acting in unison in the arm to lift a 40-g spoonful of sugar. Not only does myosin serve as part of the structural complex in muscles, it also acts as an enzyme for the removal of a phosphate group from ATP. Thus, it is directly involved in liberating the energy required for muscle contraction.

In a resting person, muscle activity (including that of the heart muscle) accounts for only about 15–30% of the body's energy requirements. Other activities, such as cell repair, transmission of nerve impulses, and maintenance of body temperature, account for the remaining energy needs. During intense physical activity, the energy requirements of muscle may be more than 200 times the resting level.

Aerobic Exercise: Plenty of Oxygen

The ATP in muscle tissue is sufficient for activities lasting for at most a few seconds. Fortunately, muscles have a more extensive energy supply in the form of glycogen, a starchlike form of dietary carbohydrate that has been ingested, digested to glucose, absorbed, and stored.

When muscle contraction begins, glycogen is converted to pyruvic acid by muscle cells, in a series of steps.

$$\underset{\text{Glycogen}}{(C_6H_{10}O_5)_n} \longrightarrow \underset{\text{Pyruvic acid}}{2n\ CH_3\overset{\overset{O}{\|}}{C}-\overset{\overset{O}{\|}}{C}OH}$$

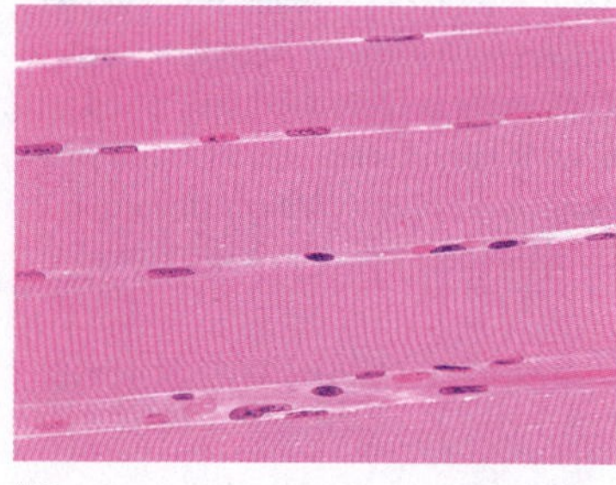

(a)

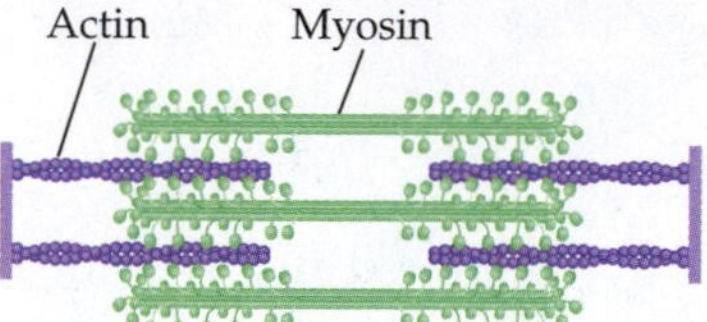

Extended muscle fibers

Resting fibers

Partially contracted fibers

(b)

▲ **Figure 19.4** Skeletal muscle tissue has a banded, or *striated*, appearance, shown here in a micrograph at 180× magnification (a). The diagram of the actomyosin complex in muscle (b) shows extended muscle fibers (top), resting fibers (middle), and partially contracted fibers (bottom).

◀ **Figure 19.5** Aerobic exercise is performed at a pace that allows us to get enough oxygen to our muscle cells to oxidize pyruvic acid to carbon dioxide and water. Aerobic dance is a popular form of aerobic exercise.

Because acids in biological systems are usually ionized at the pH of cellular fluids, biochemists usually refer to them by the names of their anions. For example, lactic acid becomes lactate, and pyruvic acid becomes pyruvate.

Then, if sufficient oxygen is readily available, the pyruvic acid is oxidized to carbon dioxide and water in another series of steps.

$$2\,CH_3\overset{\overset{\displaystyle O}{\|}}{C}-\overset{\overset{\displaystyle O}{\|}}{C}OH + 5\,O_2 \longrightarrow 6\,CO_2 + 4\,H_2O$$

Muscle contractions that occur under these circumstances—that is, in the presence of oxygen—constitute **aerobic exercise** (Figure 19.5).

Anaerobic Exercise and Oxygen Debt

When sufficient oxygen is not available, pyruvic acid is reduced to lactic acid.

$$CH_3COCOOH + [2\,H] \longrightarrow CH_3CHOHCOOH$$

[2 H] represents hydrogen atoms from one of several biochemical reducing agents.

If **anaerobic exercise** (muscle activity with insufficient oxygen) persists, an excess of lactic acid builds up in the muscle cells. This lactic acid ionizes, forming lactate ions and hydronium ions.

$$CH_3CHOHCOOH + H_2O \longrightarrow CH_3CHOHCOO^- + H_3O^+$$

Muscle fatigue correlates well with lactate levels, which were long thought to be its cause. However, studies have shown that muscle tiredness is related to calcium ion flow. Ordinarily, muscle contractions are managed by the ebb and flow of Ca^{2+} ions. As muscles grow tired, tiny channels in muscle cells start leaking Ca^{2+}, which weakens contractions. At the same time, the leaked Ca^{2+} ions stimulate an enzyme that breaks down muscle fibers, further contributing to the muscle fatigue. Levels of several other products of muscle metabolism, including phosphocreatine (the phosphorylated form of creatine, page 587), ATP, and ions such as Na^+, K^+, and $H_2PO_4^-$, change during fatigue. These changes may also contribute to muscle tiredness.

$$H_2O_3PNH-\underset{\underset{\displaystyle NH}{\|}}{C}-\underset{\underset{\displaystyle CH_3}{|}}{N}-CH_2COOH$$

Phosphocreatine

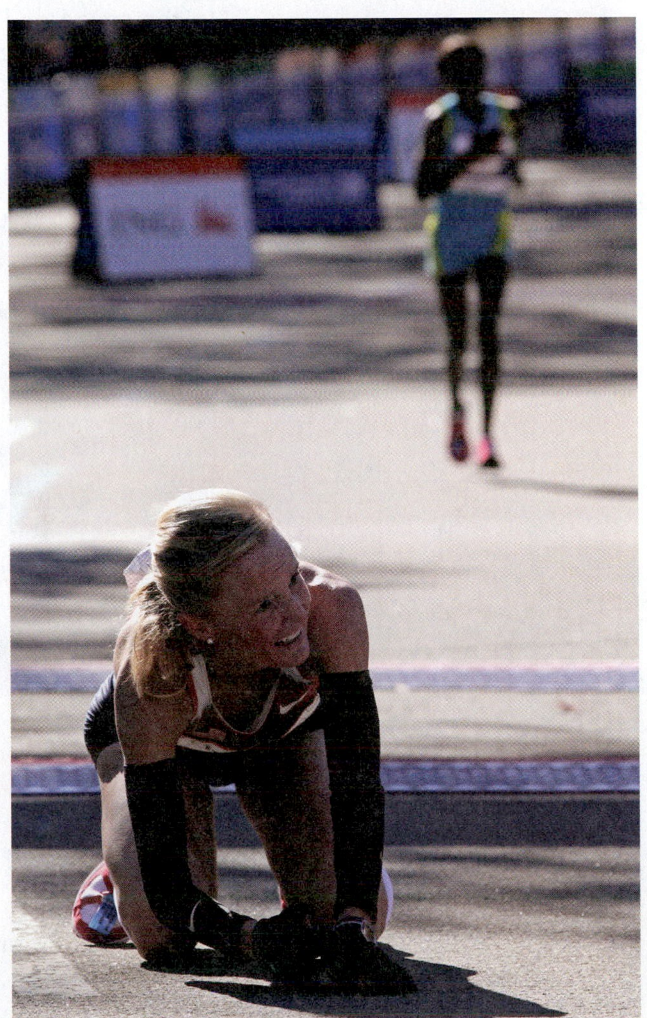

▲ **Figure 19.6** After a race, the metabolism that fueled the effort continues. The athlete gulps air to repay her oxygen debt.

Well-trained athletes can continue for a while after muscle fatigue sets in, but most people quit. At this point, the **oxygen debt** starts to be repaid (Figure 19.6). After exercise ends, the cells' demand for oxygen decreases, making more oxygen available to oxidize the lactic acid resulting from anaerobic metabolism back to pyruvic acid. This acid is then converted to carbon dioxide, water, and energy.

Most athletes emphasize one type of exercise (anaerobic or aerobic) over the other. For example, an athlete training for a 60-m dash does mainly anaerobic exercising, but one planning to run a 10-km race does mainly aerobic exercising. Sprinting and weightlifting are largely anaerobic activities. A marathon run (42 km) is largely aerobic. During a marathon, athletes must set a pace to run for more than 2 hours. Their muscle cells depend on slow, steady aerobic conversion of carbohydrates to energy. During anaerobic activities, however, muscle cells use almost no oxygen. Rather, they depend on the quick energy provided by anaerobic metabolism.

After glycogen stores are depleted, muscle cells can switch over to fat metabolism. Fats are the main source of energy for sustained activity of low or moderate intensity, such as the last part of a marathon run.

Muscle Fibers: Twitch Kind Do You Have?

Muscles are tools with which we do work. The quality and type of muscle fibers that an athlete has affect his or her athletic performance, just as the quality of machinery influences how work is done. For example, we can remove snow from a driveway in more than one way. We can do it in 10 min with a snowblower, or we can spend 50 min shoveling. Muscles are classified according to the speed and effort required to accomplish this work. The two classes of muscle fibers (Figure 19.7) are **fast-twitch fibers** (which are stronger and larger and most suited for anaerobic activity) and **slow-twitch fibers** (which are best for aerobic work). Table 19.3 lists some characteristics of these two types of muscle fibers.

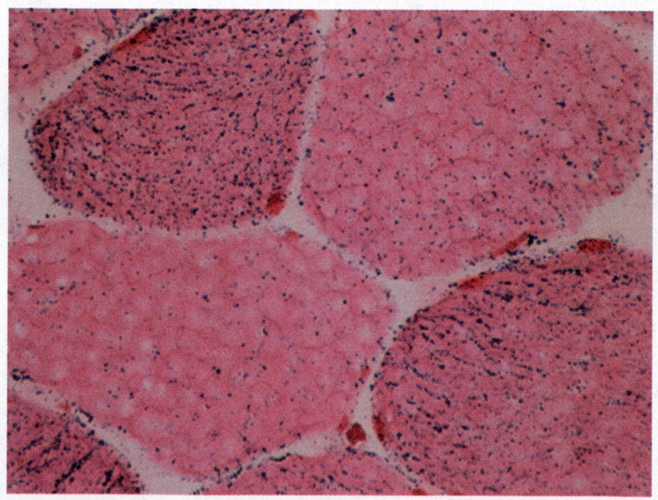

▶ **Figure 19.7** Slow-twitch muscle fibers have more mitochondria (elongated violet dots) than fast-twitch fibers do.

Myoglobin is a red, heme-containing protein in muscle that stores oxygen (similar to the way hemoglobin stores and transports oxygen in the blood).

Table 19.3 A Comparison of Two Types of Muscle Fibers

Characteristic	Type I	Type IIB[a]
Category	Slow twitch	Fast twitch
Color	Red	White
Respiratory capacity	High	Low
Myoglobin level	High	Low
Catalytic activity of actomyosin	Low	High
Capacity for glycogen use	Low	High

[a]There is a type IIA fiber (not considered here) that resembles type I in some respects and type IIB in others.

Type I (slow-twitch) fibers are called on during activity of light or moderate intensity. The respiratory capacity of these fibers is high, which means that they can provide a large amount of energy via aerobic pathways. The myoglobin level is also high. Aerobic oxidation requires oxygen, and muscle tissue rich in slow-twitch fibers is supplied with high levels of oxygen.

Type I muscle fibers have a low capacity to use glycogen and thus are not geared to anaerobic generation of energy. Their action does not require the hydrolysis of glycogen. The catalytic activity of the actomyosin complex is low. Remember that actomyosin not only is the structural unit in muscle that undergoes contraction but also is responsible for catalyzing the hydrolysis of ATP to provide energy for the contraction. Low catalytic activity means that the energy is parceled out more slowly. Slow energy output is not good if you want to lift 200 kg, but it is great for a 15-km run.

Type IIB (fast-twitch) fibers have characteristics opposite those of type I fibers. Low respiratory capacity and low myoglobin levels do not bode well for aerobic oxidation. A high capacity for glycogen use and a high catalytic activity of actomyosin allow tissue rich in fast-twitch fibers to generate ATP rapidly and also to hydrolyze this ATP rapidly during intense muscle activity. Thus, this type of muscle tissue has the capacity to do short bursts of vigorous work but fatigues rather quickly. A period of recovery, during which lactic acid is cleared from the muscle, is required between the brief periods of activity.

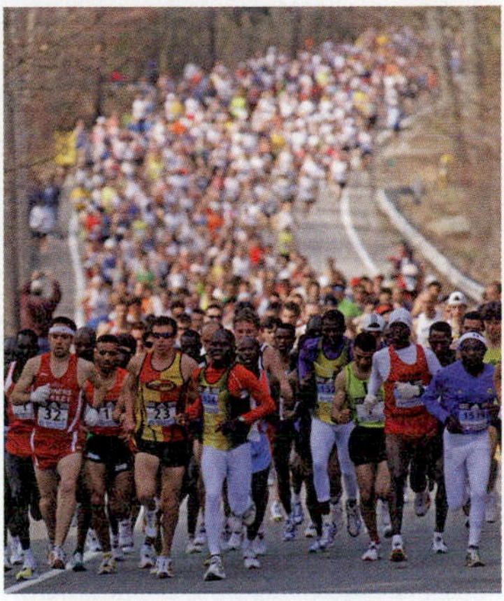

▲ **Figure 19.8** The New York City Marathon attracts more than 30,000 runners each year.

Q: *What is the predominant muscle type in the elite runners in this race? Do their muscles have high or low aerobic capacity?*

Building Muscles

Endurance exercise increases myoglobin levels in skeletal muscles. The increased myoglobin provides faster oxygen transport and increased respiratory capacity (Figure 19.8), and these changes usually are apparent within 2 weeks. Endurance training does not necessarily increase the size of muscles.

If you want larger muscles, try weightlifting. Weight training (Figure 19.9) develops fast-twitch muscle fibers. These fibers increase in size and strength with repeated anaerobic exercise. Weight training does *not* increase respiratory capacity.

Muscle-fiber type seems to be inherited. Research shows that world-class marathon runners may possess as high as 80–90% slow-twitch fibers, while championship sprinters may have up to 70% fast-twitch muscle fibers. Some exceptions have been noted, however, and factors such as training and body composition are important in athletics, as are other factors, including nutrition, fluid and electrolyte balance, and drug use or misuse.

▲ **Figure 19.9** Weightlifting is a popular activity in many gyms and fitness centers.

Q: *What is the predominant muscle type in elite weightlifters? Do their muscles have high or low aerobic capacity?*

Self-Assessment Questions

1. The high-energy compound used directly by muscles when contracting is
   a. an amino acid **b.** ATP **c.** a fatty acid **d.** glucose
2. When muscle contraction begins, glycogen is converted to
   a. creatine **b.** creatinine **c.** lactic acid **d.** pyruvic acid
3. During aerobic exercise, pyruvic acid is converted to
   a. CO_2 and H_2O **b.** glycogen **c.** lactic acid **d.** phosphocreatine
4. During anaerobic exercise, pyruvic acid is converted to
   a. CO_2 and H_2O **b.** glycogen **c.** lactic acid **d.** phosphocreatine
5. When produced during exercise, which of the following results in oxygen debt?
   a. ATP **b.** glycogen **c.** lactic acid **d.** pyruvic acid
6. Fast-twitch muscle fiber is classified as
   a. type I **b.** type IIA **c.** type IIB **c.** type III
7. The reddish color of slow-twitch muscle fibers is due to the presence of
   a. actomyosin **b.** creatine **c.** myoglobin **d.** pyruvic acid

Answers: 1, b; 2, d; 3, a; 4, c; 5, c; 6, c; 7, c

19.6 Drugs, Athletic Performance, and the Brain

Learning Objectives › Describe the physiological effects of restorative drugs, stimulant drugs, and anabolic steroids. › Explain how endorphins, neurotrophins, and tobacco can affect the brain and body.

Muscle chemistry and metabolism, aerobic and anaerobic exercise, and nutrition and fluid balance all rely on normal internal processes. It would seem that hard work and proper nutrition are the best answers to improved performance. However, many athletes turn instead to drugs, such as the stimulants amphetamine and cocaine, to improve performance and to anabolic steroids to build muscles.

Like most other people, athletes use drugs to alleviate pain or soreness that results from overuse and to treat injuries. These **restorative drugs** include analgesics (painkillers), such as aspirin and acetaminophen (Section 18.2), and anti-inflammatory drugs, such as aspirin, ibuprofen, ketoprofen, and cortisone. Cortisone derivatives are often injected to reduce swelling in damaged joints and tissues. Relief is often transitory, however, and side effects can be severe. Prolonged use of cortisone derivatives can cause fluid retention, hypertension, ulcers, disturbance of the sex-hormone balance, and other problems. Other substances that can be bought over the counter and applied externally include oil of wintergreen (methyl salicylate) and capsaicin (the active ingredient in hot peppers). These substances are usually one ingredient of an ointment or cream. When applied to the skin, they cause a mild burning sensation, thus serving as a counterirritant for sore muscles. Methyl salicylate is also an aspirin derivative and acts as an analgesic.

Stimulant Drugs

Some athletes use *stimulant drugs* (Section 18.7) to try to improve performance. The caffeine in a strong cup of coffee may be of some benefit. Caffeine triggers the release of fatty acids. Metabolism of these compounds may conserve glycogen, but any such effect is small. Caffeine also increases the heart rate, speeds metabolism, and increases urine output. The latter effect could lead to dehydration.

Other athletes resort to stronger stimulants, including amphetamines and cocaine. These drugs stimulate the central nervous system, increasing alertness, respiration, blood pressure, muscle tension, and heart rate. They also mask symptoms of fatigue and give an athlete a sense of increased stamina.

Anabolic Steroids

Many strenuous athletic performances depend on well-developed muscles. Muscle mass depends on the level of the male hormone *testosterone* (Section 18.5). When boys reach puberty, testosterone levels rise, and the boys become more muscular if they exercise. Men generally have larger muscles than women because they have more testosterone.

Testosterone and some of its semisynthetic derivatives are taken by athletes in an attempt to build muscle mass quicker. Steroid hormones used to increase muscle mass are called **anabolic steroids**. These chemicals aid in the building (anabolism) of body proteins (Section 16.4) and thus of muscle tissue.

There are no reputable controlled studies demonstrating the effectiveness of anabolic steroids. They do seem to work—at least for some people—but the side effects are many. In males, side effects include testicular atrophy and loss of function, impotence, acne, liver damage that may lead to cancer, edema (swelling), elevated cholesterol levels, and growth of breasts.

Anabolic steroids act as male hormones (androgens), making women more masculine. They help women build larger muscles, but they also result in balding, extra body hair, a deep voice, and menstrual irregularities. What price will athletes pay for improved performance?

Drugs, Athletic Performance, and Drug Screening

The use of drugs to increase athletic performance not only is illegal and physically dangerous but also can be psychologically damaging. Stimulant drugs give users a false sense of confidence by affecting their ego, giving the delusion of invincibility. Such a feeling of "greatness" often ends as the competition begins, however, because the stimulant effect is short lived (it lasts for only half an hour to an hour for cocaine). Exhaustion and extreme depression usually follow. More stimulants are needed to combat these "down" feelings, and the user then runs the risk of addiction or overdose.

Because drug use for the enhancement or improvement of performance is illegal, chemists play an important role in sports: screening blood and urine samples for illegal drugs. Using sophisticated instruments, chemists can detect minute amounts of illegal drugs. Drug testing has been used at the Olympic Games since 1968, and it is rapidly becoming standard practice for athletes in college and professional sports.

Drugs are used at great risk of health (and legal!) problems. The use of illegal drugs violates the spirit of fair athletic competition. Let's work toward a world in which events and medals are won by drug-free athletes who are highly motivated, well-nourished, and well-trained.

Exercise and the Brain

Hard, consistent training improves athletic performance. Few drugs help, but athletes' own bodies manufacture a variety of substances that aid performance. Examples are the pain-relieving **endorphins** (Section 18.2).

After vigorous activity, athletes have an increased level of endorphins in their blood. Stimulated by exercise, deep sensory nerves release endorphins to block the pain message. Exercise extended over a long period of time, such as distance running, sometimes causes in an athlete many of the same symptoms experienced by opiate users. Athletes get a euphoric high during or after a hard run. Unfortunately, both natural endorphins and their analogs, such as morphine, seem to be addictive. Athletes, especially runners, tend to suffer from withdrawal: They feel bad when they don't get the vigorous exercise of a long, hard run. This can be positive because exercise is important to the maintenance of good health. It can be negative if the person exercises when injured or to the exclusion of family or work obligations. Athletes also seem to develop a tolerance to their own endorphins. They have to run farther and farther to get that euphoric feeling.

Exercise also directly affects the brain by increasing its blood supply and by producing **neurotrophins**, substances that enhance the growth of brain cells. Exercises that involve complex motions, such as dance movements, lead to an increase in the connections between brain cells. Both our muscles and our brains work better when we exercise regularly.

No Smoking

If you want to stay healthy and fit, one thing you certainly should *not* do is use tobacco. Tobacco use and smoking are dangerous addictions that cause a wide variety of diseases, including cancer, heart disease, and emphysema, and often result in death. More than 400,000 children become regular smokers each year. Almost a third will eventually die from smoking.

Cigarette smoking is the chief preventable cause of premature death in the United States. One in five deaths in the United States is smoking related. According to the CDC, cigarette smoking is associated with death from 24 different diseases, including heart disease, stroke, and lung diseases such as cancer, stroke, emphysema, and pneumonia. Smoking causes diseases of the gums and mouth, chronic hoarseness, vocal cord polyps, and premature aging and wrinkling of the skin. Lung cancer is not the only malignancy caused by cigarette smoking. Cancers of the pancreas, bladder, breast, kidney, mouth and throat, stomach, larynx, and cervix are also associated with smoking. In fact, smoking kills more

A study of military veterans, conducted at Harvard University, concluded that smokers are 4.3 times as likely as nonsmokers to develop Alzheimer's disease. Heavy smokers get Alzheimer's 2.3 years sooner, on average, than nonsmokers.

people than AIDS, alcohol, illegal drugs, car accidents, murders, and suicides combined.

We fear cancer, but heart attack and stroke are the major causes of disability and death of smokers. Cigarette smokers have a 70% higher risk of heart attack than nonsmokers. When they are also overweight, with high blood pressure and high cholesterol, their risk is 200% higher. At every age, the death rate is higher among smokers than among nonsmokers.

Women who smoke during pregnancy have more stillborn babies, more premature babies, and more babies who die before they are a month old. Women who take birth control pills and also smoke have an abnormally high risk of stroke. Women who smoke are advised to use some other method of birth control.

One of the gases in cigarette smoke is carbon monoxide, which ties up about 8% of the hemoglobin in the blood. Smokers therefore breathe less efficiently. They work harder to breathe, but less oxygen reaches their cells. It is no wonder that fatigue is a common problem for smokers. More than 4700 chemicals have been identified in cigarette smoke, including many that are quite poisonous and 63 that are known or suspected carcinogens. Some of these are listed in Table 19.4.

Table 19.4 Some Potential Carcinogens[a] and Teratogens[b] Identified in Cigarette Smoke

Acetone	*Chromium*	*Hydrazine*	*Nitropropane*
Acrylonitrile	*Chrysene*	*Indeno(1,2,3-c,d)pyrene*	*Nitrosamines*
Aminobiphenyl	Copper	*Lead*	*Nitrosonornicotine*
Aniline	*Crotonaldehyde*	Mercury	*Polonium-210*
Anthracenes	DDT	*N-Nitrosoanabasine*	*Quinoline*
Arsenic	*Dibenz(a,h)acridine*	*N-Nitrosodiethanolamine*	Styrene
Benz(a)anthracene	*Dibenz(a,h)anthracene*	*N-Nitrosodiethylamine*	Titanium
Benzene	*Dibenz(a,j)acridine*	*N-Nitrosodimethylamine*	Toluene
Benzo(a)pyrene	*Dibenzo(a,l)pyrene*	*N-Nitrosoethylmethylamine*	*Toluidine*
Benzo(b)fluoranthene	*Dibenzo(c,g)carbazole*		*Urethane*
Benzo(j)fluoranthene	Dieldrin	*N-Nitrosomorpholine*	*Vinyl chloride*
Butadiene	*Dimethylhydrazine*	*N-Nitrosopyrrolidine*	
Cadmium	*Ethylcarbamate*	*Naphthylamine*	
Carbon monoxide	*Formaldehyde*	Nickel	

[a]Proven or suspected of causing cancer; in italics.
[b]Proven or suspected of causing birth defects; in green.

In the linings of the lungs are *cilia* (tiny, hairlike processes) that help to sweep out particulate matter breathed into the lungs. In smokers, the tar from cigarette smoke forms a sticky coating that keeps the cilia from moving freely. The reduced action of the cilia may explain the smoker's cough. Pathologists claim that during an autopsy it is usually easy to tell if the body was that of a smoker. Lungs are normally pink. A smoker's lungs are black.

Unfortunately, cigarette smoke also harms nonsmokers. Secondhand smoke contains more than 7000 chemicals, of which hundreds are toxic and about 70 are carcinogens. Secondhand smoke causes an estimated 3000 premature deaths each year in the United States and causes up to 300,000 children to suffer from lower respiratory tract infections. Children of smokers miss twice as much school time because of respiratory infections as do children of nonsmokers.

Efforts to lessen indoor pollution caused by smoking have led many restaurants, bars, and public buildings to be declared nonsmoking areas. About half of the U.S. population now lives under a ban on smoking covering all workplaces, restaurants, and bars. Smoking has never been a smart or a healthy thing to do, but now it isn't even fashionable.

Chemistry of Sports Materials

The athlete's world is shaped by chemicals. The ability to perform reflects biochemistry within the athlete. Chemicals taken by athletes may hinder or enhance their performance. Yet another chemical dimension to the sports world is that chemicals are used to enhance athletic clothing and equipment (Table 19.5). Athletic clothing depends on chemicals for its shape and protective qualities.

Swimsuits, ski pants, and elastic support clothing stretch because of synthetic fibers. Undergarments made of polypropylene or polyester fibers wick perspiration away from the skin and keep the athlete dry even during vigorous exercise. Outdoor enthusiasts work and play in rain and winds wearing suits made of materials that have billions of tiny holes too small to pass drops of water but that readily pass water vapor. Raindrops falling on the outside are held together by surface tension and run off rather than penetrating the fabric. Water vapor from sweating skin, however, can pass from the warm area inside the suit where vapor concentration is high to the cooler area outside the suit where the vapor concentration is lower. The runner stays relatively dry.

Athletes of all sorts are aided by equipment made of materials developed by the chemical industry. Football, hockey, and baseball players are protected by polycarbonate helmets and protective pads of synthetic foamed rubbers. Brightly dyed nylon uniforms with synthetic colors add to the glamour of amateur and professional teams. Many sports events are played on artificial turf, a carpet of nylon or polypropylene with an underpad of synthetic foamed polymers. Stadiums are protected from the weather by Teflon covers reinforced with glass fibers and held aloft by air pressure.

The dramatic effect of new materials is perhaps best illustrated in pole vaulting (Figure 19.10). The sport probably originated with the use of wooden poles to vault over streams or other obstacles. It became a sport in the early nineteenth century when the Germans introduced the vertical vault form of competition. The record using a wooden pole was set at 3.48 m in 1887. Bamboo poles were introduced in 1879 and were popular for decades, with the record set at 4.77 m in 1942. Metal poles came into use in the 1950s with records set in 1957 at 4.78 m using an aluminum pole and in 1960 at 4.80 m with a steel pole. Fiberglass poles were introduced in 1952, but it took several years for athletes to learn how to use these highly flexible poles effectively. The first world record using a fiberglass pole was 4.83 m, set in 1961. Carbon fiber, stronger for its weight than glass fiber, was introduced in 1990. Modern poles are constructed from composites of either fiberglass or carbon fiber and fiberglass in several layers. Today, the world-record pole vault is 6.14 m.

From the soles of sports shoes and the wax used on cross-country skis to titanium golf clubs and tennis sweaters that stretch and yet retain their shape, the sports world is thoroughly immersed in chemicals.

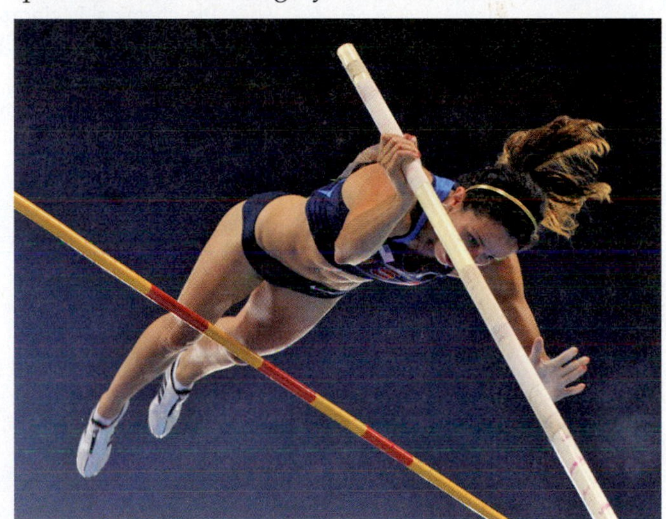

▲ **Figure 19.10** U.S. silver medalist Jennifer Stuczynski Suhr makes an attempt in the women's pole vault final during the Beijing 2008 Olympic Games.

Table 19.5 Some Sports and Recreational Items Made from Chemicals Derived from Petroleum

Wet suits	Motorcycle helmets	Darts	Fishing nets
Golf-cart bodies	Dune-buggy bodies	Tents	Hiking boots
Warm-up suits	Checkers	Stadium cushions	Frisbees
Ping-Pong paddles	Chess boards	Foul-weather gear	Fishing boots
Rafts	Shorts	Foot pads	Diving masks
Uniforms	Tennis shoes	Visors	Guitar picks
Track shoes	Paddles	Basketballs	Beach balls
Dominoes	Decoys	Canoes and kayaks	Sunglasses
Windbreakers	Volleyballs	Ice chests	Dog leashes
Sails	Sleeping bags	Life jackets	Dice
Football helmets	Tennis balls	In-line skates	Pole-vaulting poles
Swimsuits	Insect repellents	Artificial turf	Aquariums
Bicycle tires, seats, and handles	Swimming-pool liners	Golf club impact surfaces	

Self-Assessment Questions

1. Which of the following, as used by athletes, is a restorative drug?
   a. aspirin b. caffeine c. creatinine d. testosterone
2. Caffeine is thought to aid endurance athletes by
   a. conserving creatine
   b. conserving stored O_2
   c. stimulating the release of free amino acids
   d. stimulating the release of fatty acids
3. Anabolic steroids
   a. build muscles without exercise b. increase sexual drive
   c. help build larger muscles d. make female athletes more feminine
4. Endorphins are
   a. chemicals produced by the body that are similar to morphine
   b. chemicals produced by the body that carry pain messages
   c. chemicals produced by the body that stimulate muscle growth
   d. synthetic drugs similar to morphine
5. Exercise is thought to help the brain work better by
   a. acting as a stimulant b. increasing aerobic capacity
   c. increasing levels of neurotrophins d. inhibiting production of endorphins
6. The chemical in cigarette smoke that makes breathing less efficient is
   a. CO b. CO_2 c. nicotine d. NO
7. About how many chemicals have been identified in cigarette smoke?
   a. 20 b. 60 c. 360 d. 7000

Answers: 1, a; 2, d; 3, c; 4, a; 5, c; 6, a; 7, d

CRITICAL THINKING  EXERCISES

Apply knowledge that you have gained in this chapter and one or more of the FLaReS principles (Chapter 1) to evaluate the following statements or claims.

19.1 An advertisement in an American sports magazine claims that an amino-acid supplement helps build muscle mass.

19.2 In the past, Inuit peoples ate an all-meat diet and seemed to thrive. We should eat a meat-only diet for maximum health.

19.3 The right nutrients from whole foods will keep your memory sharp and your mind agile as you grow older.

19.4 The various ways by which performance can be improved are called *ergogenic aids*. These include mechanical, physiological, psychological, pharmacological, and nutritional aids. Unfortunately, many of the claims for these aids have not been substantiated by rigorous scientific trials. Here are several claims:
   a. A creatine supplement "makes muscles much less prone to fatigue and the capacity to undertake strenuous exercise is increased."
   b. Sodium bicarbonate reduces the acidity of the blood and "may be able to draw more of the acid produced within the muscle cells out into the blood and thus reduce the level of acidity within the muscle cells themselves. This could delay the onset of fatigue."
   c. Two factors that limit prolonged exercise are depletion of the body's carbohydrate stores and dehydration. Consuming sports drinks containing carbohydrates and electrolytes before, during, and after exercise will help prevent blood glucose levels falling too low, help maintain the body's glycogen stores, and replace electrolytes lost through perspiration.

19.5 An online advertisement says, "I cut down 47 lbs of stomach fat in a month by obeying this one old rule."

19.6 An advertisement for a weight-loss pill claims that the substance in the pill "melts fat from your body."

SUMMARY

Section 19.1—Good health and fitness require a nutritious diet and regular exercise. Today's dietary guidelines emphasize nutrient-dense foods and a balanced eating program. A balanced diet consists largely of fruits, vegetables, whole grains, and dairy products in the proper proportions. Total fats intake should not exceed 35% of calories; saturated fats (mostly of animal origin) should account for less than 10% of calories. Athletes generally need more calories, which should come mostly from carbohydrates—especially starches. Exercise, not extra protein, builds muscle tissue. The **Dietary Reference Intakes (DRIs)** for protein and other nutrients are established by the U.S. Academy of Sciences for planning and assessing diets.

Section 19.2—Organic substances (vitamins) and inorganic substances (minerals) that the body cannot produce must be supplied by the diet. Vitamin and mineral supplements may not be necessary with a well-balanced diet, but they do no harm and may be beneficial. Vitamin A is essential for vision and skin maintenance. There are several B vitamins; B_3 and B_6 may help arthritis patients; B_{12} is not found in plants, and a lack can cause anemia. Vitamin C prevents scurvy, promotes healing, is needed for the immune system, and is an antioxidant. Vitamin D promotes absorption of calcium and phosphorus. Vitamin E is an antioxidant and an anticoagulant, and a deficiency of it can lead to muscular dystrophy. An **electrolyte** is a substance that conducts electricity in a water solution. The main electrolytes in the body are ions of sodium, potassium, chlorine, calcium, and magnesium, as well as sulfate, hydrogen phosphate, and bicarbonate ions. Water is an essential nutrient.

Section 19.3—Drastic diets are unlikely to be permanently successful, and the weight lost is usually regained. One pound of adipose tissue stores about 3500 kcal of energy. A variety of chemical substances that are produced in the body are regulators of body weight. Quick-weight-loss diets often include a **diuretic** to increase urine output, which results in temporary weight loss. Low-carbohydrate diets cause quick weight loss by depleting glycogen and water.

Exercise aids in weight loss, because the increase in metabolic rate that it causes continues after it ends. The most sensible approach to weight loss involves a balanced low-calorie diet and a consistent exercise program.

Section 19.4—The male body requires about 3% body fat; the female body, 10–12%. The percentage of body fat can be estimated by several methods. Density measurement is probably the most accurate. Body mass index (BMI) indicates fatness, and V_{O_2} max is a measure of fitness.

Section 19.5—Exercise makes muscles larger, more flexible, and more efficient. Energy for muscular work comes from ATP. A protein complex called *actomyosin* contracts when ATP is added to it. ATP provides energy for just a few seconds, after which glycogen is metabolized. If metabolism occurs with plenty of oxygen—during **aerobic exercise**—CO_2 and H_2O are formed. With insufficient oxygen—during **anaerobic exercise**—lactic acid is formed and muscle fatigue occurs. When exercise ends, the **oxygen debt** is repaid; the cells' oxygen demand decreases, and the lactic acid can be oxidized to CO_2 and H_2O. There are two classes of muscle fibers. **Fast-twitch fibers** are larger and stronger and good for short bursts of vigorous exercise, while **slow-twitch fibers** are geared for steady exercise of long endurance. Weight training develops fast-twitch muscles but does not increase respiratory capacity. Long-distance running develops slow-twitch muscles and increases respiratory capacity.

Section 19.6—Athletes sometimes use **restorative drugs**, such as aspirin, ibuprofen, or cortisone, to alleviate pain and treat injuries. They may use stimulant drugs such as caffeine and cocaine. **Anabolic steroids** appear to increase muscle mass, but they have many bad effects, including impotence and liver cancer.

The body can manufacture pain-relieving **endorphins** that may help performance, but it appears that some athletes can become addicted to them. Exercise also directly affects the brain by producing **neurotrophins**, substances that enhance the growth of brain cells. Smoking reduces athletic performance, causes diseases, and leads to earlier death, and athletes should avoid it. From modern sports clothing and equipment to artificial turf, chemistry has contributed greatly to the world of sports.

Green chemistry Walking or biking instead of driving is not only healthy and enjoyable but follows green chemistry principles. Your body's energy comes from renewable plant carbohydrate sources rather than nonrenewable fossil fuels whose use in most transportation options leads to harmful carbon dioxide buildup in the atmosphere.

Learning Objectives

› List the recommendations (sources and percentages) for calories from fats and other sources in the American diet.	Problems 1,12
› Describe the special dietary requirements of athletes.	Problems 6, 11, 45
› Describe the dietary requirements for vitamins, minerals, and water.	Problems 13–22
› Explain how weight is lost through diet and exercise.	Problems 3, 9, 23, 24, 31, 32, 60
› Calculate weight loss due to calorie reduction and exercise.	Problems 25–30, 58
› Describe several ways to measure fitness.	Problems 7, 56, 59
› Calculate BMI values.	Problems 33, 34, 57, 59, 61
› Differentiate between aerobic exercise and anaerobic exercise, and describe the chemistry that occurs during each.	Problems 38, 39, 41–44

› Describe how muscles are built and how they work.	Problems 35–46, 62
› Describe the physiological effects of restorative drugs, stimulant drugs, and anabolic steroids.	Problems 10, 47, 48, 51
› Describe how endorphins, neurotrophins, and tobacco can affect the brain and body.	Problems 31, 32, 49, 50, 53, 54
› Explain how green chemistry principles can help us make transportation choices.	Problems 64, 67
› Describe the relationship between walking or biking and personal health, especially the implications for weight loss.	Problems 65, 66

REVIEW QUESTIONS

1. What kinds of foods are the main dietary source of saturated fats?
2. Why are the federal dietary guidelines (Figure 19.1) not the same for everyone?
3. How might you lose 5 lb in just 1 week? Would it be a useful way to lose weight and keep it off?
4. Do you think it is likely that obesity is inherited?
5. List three ways in which chemistry has had an impact on sports.
6. How do the nutritional needs of an athlete differ from those of a sedentary individual? How is this extra need best met?
7. List two ways to determine percent body fat. Describe a limitation of each method.
8. Why does excess body fat put a strain on the heart?
9. List some problems that result from low-calorie diets.
10. What are the effects of anabolic steroids on females?

PROBLEMS

Nutrition

11. Do athletes need more protein than other people? Explain.
12. What are two good reasons for not going on a high-protein diet?

Vitamins and Minerals

13. What benefit is derived from vitamin B_{12}?
14. In addition to preventing pellagra, what does vitamin B_3 (niacin) do?
15. What kinds of problems are helped by vitamin B_6 (pyridoxine)?
16. What are some of the benefits of vitamin A?
17. What are the benefits of vitamin D? Is taking a daily megadose of vitamin D a good idea?
18. Vitamins C and E are antioxidants. What does this mean?

Electrolytes

19. What is a diuretic? Describe the function of antidiuretic hormone (ADH).
20. How is the appearance of urine related to dehydration?
21. Is thirst a good indicator of dehydration? Are you always thirsty when dehydrated?
22. What are some of the effects of dehydration? What is heat stroke?

Diet and Exercise

23. List two ways in which fad diets can produce quick weight loss. Why is the weight rapidly regained?
24. Why does a diet that restricts carbohydrate intake lead to loss of muscle mass as well as fat?
25. A quarter-pound burger provides 420 kcal of energy. How long would a 130-lb person have to walk to burn those calories if 1 h of walking uses about 210 kcal?
26. One kilogram of fat tissue stores about 7700 kcal of energy. An average person burns about 40 kcal while walking 1 km. If such a person walks 5 km each day, how much fat will be burned in 1 year?
27. The DRI for protein is about 0.8 g/kg body weight. How much protein is required each day by a 253-lb football player?
28. How much protein is required each day by a 110-lb gymnast? (See Problem 27.)
29. A 70-kg man can store about 2000 kcal as glycogen. How far could such a man run on this stored starch if he expends 100 kcal/km while running and the glycogen is his only source of energy?
30. A 70-kg man can store about 100,000 kcal of energy as fat. How far could such a man run on this stored fat if he expends 100 kcal/km while running and the fat is his only source of energy?
31. Describe the role of each of the following substances involved in the control of body weight.
    a. leptin
    b. ghrelin
32. Describe the role of each of the following substances involved in the control of body weight.
    a. cholecystokinin
    b. PYY

Body Mass Index

33. What is the body mass index (BMI) for a 6-ft 9-in. baseball player who weighs 182 lb?

34. What is the BMI for a 5-ft 11-in. football player who weighs 224 lb?

Muscles

35. How many muscles do humans have?

36. What two proteins make up the actomyosin complex?

37. Muscles are made of protein. Does eating more protein result in larger muscles?

38. What is aerobic exercise? What is anaerobic exercise?

39. Which type of metabolism (aerobic or anaerobic) is primarily responsible for providing energy for **(a)** intense bursts of vigorous activity and **(b)** prolonged low levels of activity?

40. What are the two functions of the actomyosin protein complex?

41. Explain why high levels of myoglobin are appropriate for muscle tissue geared to aerobic oxidation.

42. Categorize type I and type IIB muscle fibers as suited to aerobic oxidation or to anaerobic use of glycogen.

43. Why does the high catalytic activity of actomyosin in type IIB fibers suggest that these are the muscle fibers engaged in brief, intense physical activity?

44. Which type of muscle fiber is most affected by endurance training exercises? What changes occur in the muscle tissue?

45. Muscle is protein. Does an athlete need extra protein (above the DRI) to build muscles? What is the best way to build muscles?

46. Describe the biochemical process by which muscles are built.

Drugs

47. How are cortisone derivatives used in sports medicine? What are some of the side effects of their use?

48. What are anabolic steroids? List some side effects of the use of anabolic steroids **(a)** in males and **(b)** in females.

49. Give a biochemical explanation of the "runner's high."

50. What evidence indicates that long-distance running is addictive? Give a biochemical explanation of addiction to long-distance running.

51. Does cocaine enhance athletic performance? Explain fully. What happens when the effect of cocaine wears off?

52. What is the role of chemists in the control of drug use by athletes?

Smoking and Health

53. What are some of the health problems related to smoking?

54. Why is it important for pregnant women not to smoke?

ADDITIONAL PROBLEMS

55. If you are moderately active and want to maintain a weight of 160 lb, about how many calories do you need each day?

56. An athlete can run a 400-m race in 45 s. Her maximum oxygen intake is 4 L/min, but working muscles at their maximum exertion requires about 0.2 L of oxygen per minute for each kilogram of body weight. If the athlete weighs 50 kg, what oxygen debt will she incur?

57. Fat tissue has a density of about 0.90 g/mL, and lean tissue a density of about 1.1 g/mL. Calculate the density of a person who has a body volume of 80 L and weighs 85 kg. Is the person fat or lean?

58. The British measure body weight by the stone (1 stone = 14 lb). By how many kilocalories would you have to overeat each day to gain 1.0 stone over the course of a year?

59. Following is a table of data used to determine an individual's percentage of body fat. Make a graph of the data.
   a. Estimate the percent body fat for person A, who has a body density of 1.037 g/cm^3.
   b. Estimate the percent body fat for person B, who weighs 165 lb in air and 14 lb when submerged in water.
   c. Which person is more likely to be a well-trained athlete?
   d. A 20-year-old male weighs 89.34 kg on land and 5.30 kg underwater. The water has a density of 0.9951 kg/L. The male's residual lung volume is 1.57 L, and his maximum lung volume is 6.51 L. Calculate his body density. Why does a person float in spite of the fact that his or her body density is greater than that of water?

Body Density (g/cm^3)	Body Fat (%)
1.010	38.3
1.030	29.5
1.050	21.0
1.070	12.9
1.090	5.07

60. An athlete gains 40 lb after retiring. What is the likely explanation?

61. What is the body mass index (BMI) for **(a)** the tallest man in medical history, who was 8 ft 11 in. tall and weighed 199 kg, and **(b)** one of the heaviest men in history, who weighed 486 kg and stood 184 cm tall?

62. Birds use large, well-developed breast muscles for flying. Pheasants can fly at 80 km/h, but only for short distances. Great blue herons can fly at about 35 km/h but can cruise great distances. What kind of fibers predominate in the breast muscles of each?

63. A 100-mL sample of blood contains 15 g of hemoglobin (Hb). Each gram of Hb can combine with 1.34 mL of $O_2(g)$ at body temperature and pressure. How much O_2 is in **(a)** 100 mL of blood and **(b)** the approximately 6.0 L of blood in an average adult?

64. Give two examples of green chemistry principles that support healthy choices about transportation.

65. If you weigh 155 lb and bike at a moderate rate of 12–13.9 mi/h, you burn about 45 k cal/mi. If you live 1 mi from campus and commute round trip 80 days per semester, how many pounds lighter will you be at the end of the semester than if you had driven to class?

66. Endorphins are
a. toxic auto emissions
b. mood-enhancing chemicals
c. renewable fuels
d. biochemical catalysts

67. Carbon dioxide is an undesirable byproduct because
a. it inhibits photosynthesis
b. it creates fossil fuels
c. it leads to conditions for climate change
d. it decreases engine efficiency

COLLABORATIVE GROUP PROJECTS

Prepare a PowerPoint, poster, or other presentation (as directed by your instructor) to share with the class.

1. Popular diets are often based on books, such as the following:

   YOU: On a Diet: The Owner's Manual for Waist Management by Michael F. Roizen and Mehmet Oz

   The Fat Smash Diet: The Last Diet You'll Ever Need by Ian Smith

   The Sonoma Diet: Trimmer Waist, Better Health in Just 10 Days! by Connie Guttersen

   The South Beach Diet: The Delicious, Doctor-Designed, Foolproof Plan for Fast and Healthy Weight Loss by Arthur Agatston

   The Good Mood Diet: Feel Great While You Lose Weight by Susan M. Kleiner

   Search the Internet or print publications such as *Consumer Reports* for characteristics and views of each diet. Prepare a brief report, pro or con, on one of the diets.

2. Equations for determining maximum heart rate (MHR) and tables for evaluating fitness levels can be found in exercise physiology textbooks and online. Use these resources to calculate your V_{O_2} max. How does your fitness level compare with that of your classmates? With that of each of the following athletes: **(a)** endurance runner or bicyclist, 75 mL/kg/min; **(b)** volleyball (female), 50 mL/kg/min; **(c)** football (male), 60–65 mL/kg/min; and **(d)** baseball (male), 50 mL/kg/min?

3. Choose one or more of the chemicals in Table 19.4. Use a reference such as *The Merck Index* to determine the formula and properties of the substance.

4. Choose one or more of the sports or recreational items in Table 19.5, and try to determine what synthetic materials are used in it.

5. Only four Nobel Prizes in Chemistry have been awarded to women: Marie Curie (1911), her daughter Irène Joliot-Curie (1935), Dorothy Crowfoot Hodgkin (1964), and Ada E. Yonath (2009). Write a brief essay about Hodgkin or Yonath based on information from the library or the Internet.

6. Search the Internet or sources from the library for information on the various drugs that athletes use to enhance their performance. Use a reference such as *The Merck Index* to determine the formula and function of one or more of these drugs.

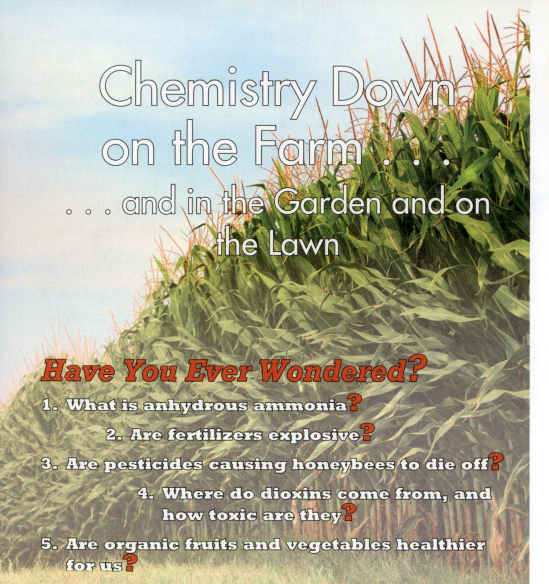

20 Chemistry Down on the Farm . . .

. . . and in the Garden and on the Lawn

Have You Ever Wondered?

1. What is anhydrous ammonia?
2. Are fertilizers explosive?
3. Are pesticides causing honeybees to die off?
4. Where do dioxins come from, and how toxic are they?
5. Are organic fruits and vegetables healthier for us?

Learning Objectives

- List the three primary plant nutrients as well as several secondary nutrients and micronutrients, and describe the function of each. (20.1)
- Differentiate between organic fertilizers and conventional fertilizers. (20.1)
- Name and describe the action of the main kinds of pesticides. (20.2)
- List several biological pest controls, and explain how they work. (20.2)
- Name and describe the action of the major herbicides and defoliants. (20.3)
- Describe sustainable agriculture and organic farming. (20.4)
- Calculate the doubling time for a population using the rule of 72. (20.5)
- Identify the benefits of pesticides to humans and the challenges in their use.
- Give examples of pesticides that have been designed to reduce the hazards to humans and the environment.

The earliest humans obtained their food by hunting and gathering. The dawn of the agricultural revolution about 10,000 years ago led to a rapid increase in population, which in turn created a need for more organized ways to obtain food and sparked the development of modern agriculture, with all of its benefits and drawbacks. The most dramatic changes in agricultural chemistry have happened over the last century. In this chapter, we examine chemical aspects of past, present, and potential future agricultural practice.

Our food comes ultimately from green plants. All organisms can transform one type of food into another, but only green plants can use sunlight to convert carbon dioxide and water to the sugars that directly or indirectly fuel all living things.

$$6\ CO_2 + 6\ H_2O \xrightarrow{\text{sunlight}} C_6H_{12}O_6 + 6\ O_2$$

This reaction also replenishes the oxygen in the atmosphere and removes carbon dioxide (Section 13.2). Using other nutrients, particularly compounds

Modern agriculture produces abundant food for much of Earth's growing population, but it has led to many problems, both economic and environmental. Many people are turning to sustainable practices.

of nitrogen and phosphorus, plants can convert the sugars produced by photosynthesis to proteins, fats, and other chemicals that we use as food.

The structural elements of plants—carbon, hydrogen, and oxygen—are derived from air and water. Other plant nutrients are taken from the soil, and energy is supplied by the Sun. In early agricultural societies, people grew plants for food and obtained energy from the food. Much of this energy was reinvested in the production of food, although a portion went into making clothing and building shelter. Figure 20.1 shows a simplified diagram of the energy flow in such a society. A real society is much more complicated than indicated here. Some plants, for example, might be fed to animals, and some human energy would then be obtained from animal flesh or animal products such as milk and eggs.

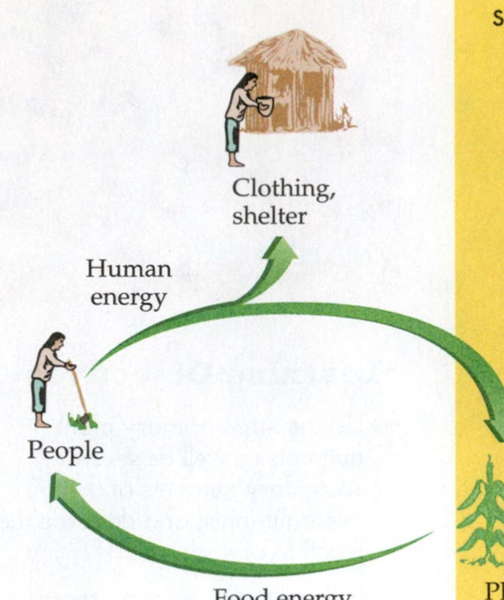

▲ **Figure 20.1** Energy flow in an early agricultural society.

In early societies, nearly all the energy came from renewable resources. One unit of human work energy, supplemented liberally by energy from the Sun, might produce ten units of food energy. The surplus energy could be used to grow crops for cloth, to make clothing, and to provide shelter. It also might be used in games or cultural activities.

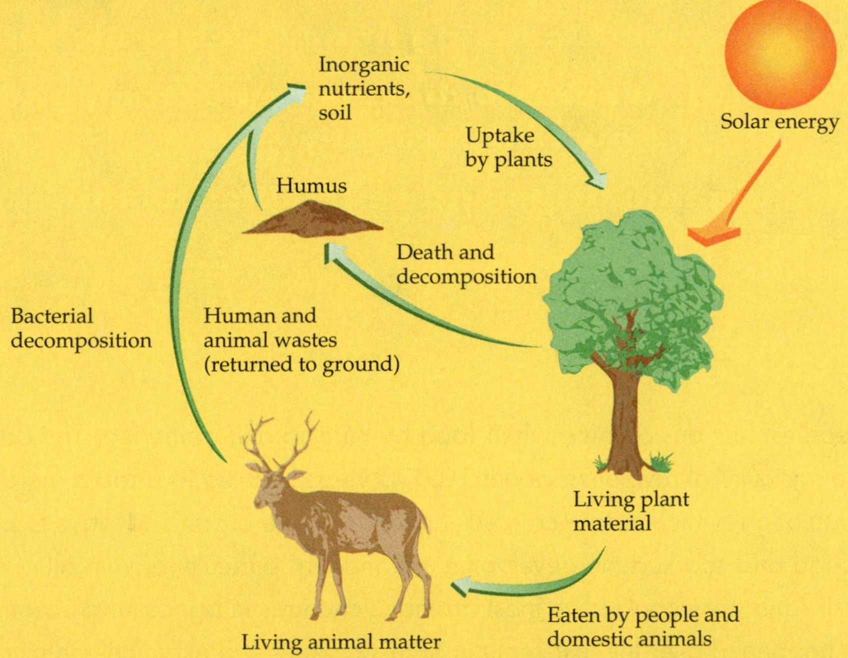

► **Figure 20.2** Flow of nutrients in a simple system.

▲ Soil consists of rock broken down by weathering, plus various types of decaying plant and animal matter. To build even a few millimeters of soil from rock takes many years. The United States loses 5 billion tons of soil each year to erosion. Developing countries often suffer far greater soil losses as more land is cleared for farming in an attempt to feed an increasing population.

The flow of nutrients is also rather simple. Unused portions of plants as well as human and animal wastes are returned to the soil. These are broken down by microorganisms to provide nutrients for the growth of new plants (Figure 20.2) and maintain the humus content of the soil. Properly practiced, this kind of agriculture could be continued for centuries without seriously depleting the soil, but farming at this level supports relatively few people. By making use of fertilizers, pesticides, and energy from fossil fuels, modern high-production farming has greatly expanded yields. Many people use materials and methods similar those of modern farming to maintain green lawns and sustain productive vegetable and flower gardens.

20.1 Farming with Chemicals: Fertilizers

Learning Objectives › List the three primary plant nutrients as well as several secondary nutrients and micronutrients, and describe the function of each. › Differentiate between organic fertilizers and conventional fertilizers.

To replace nutrients lost from the soil and to increase crop production, modern farmers use a variety of chemical fertilizers. The three **primary plant nutrients** are nitrogen, phosphorus, and potassium. Let's consider nitrogen first.

Nitrogen Fertilizers

Nitrogen, although present in air in the elemental form (N_2) is not generally available to plants. Some bacteria are able to *fix* nitrogen—that is, to convert it to a combined, soluble form. Colonies of bacteria that can perform this vital function grow in nodules on the roots of legumes (plants such as clovers and peas) (Figure 20.3). Thus, farmers are able to restore fertility to the soil by crop rotation. A nitrogen-fixing crop (such as clover) is alternated with a nitrogen-consuming crop (such as corn).

◄ **Figure 20.3** Bacteria in nodules on the roots of legumes fix atmospheric nitrogen by converting it to soluble compounds that plants can use as nutrients.

Legumes are still used to some extent to supply nitrogen to the soil. But the modern high-yield methods of production demand chemical fertilizers. With the application of fertilizers, farmers don't have to alternate crops to restore soil fertility. Why raise a corn crop every other year if you can raise one every year?

Plants usually take up nitrogen in the form of nitrate ions (NO_3^-) or ammonium ions (NH_4^+). These ions are combined with carbon compounds from photosynthesis to form the amino acids that make up proteins, compounds essential to all life processes. For years, farmers were dependent on manure as a source of nitrates. After the discovery of deposits of sodium nitrate (called *Chile saltpeter*) in the deserts of northern Chile, this substance was widely used as a source of nitrogen.

A rapid rise in population growth during the late nineteenth and early twentieth centuries put increasing pressure on the available food supply, which led to an increasing demand for nitrogen fertilizers. The atmosphere offered a seemingly inexhaustible supply of nitrogen—if only it could be converted to a form useful to humans. Every flash of lightning forms some nitric acid in the air (Figure 20.4). Lightning contributes about a billion tons of fixed nitrogen each year—more than is provided by nitrogen-fixing bacteria.

▲ **Figure 20.4** The intense heat in a lightning flash fixes nitrogen into nitric acid, which then falls to Earth and enriches the soil.

The first real breakthrough in nitrogen fixation came in Germany on the eve of World War I. A process developed by Fritz Haber and transformed into a large-scale method using a catalyst and high pressure by Carl Bosch made possible the combination of nitrogen and hydrogen to make ammonia.

$$3\,H_2 + N_2 \longrightarrow 2\,NH_3$$

By 1913, one nitrogen-fixation plant was in production and several more were under construction. The Germans were interested in ammonium nitrate mainly as an explosive, but it turned out to be a valuable nitrogen fertilizer as well. The Germans were able to make ammonium nitrate (NH_4NO_3), an explosive, by oxidizing some ammonia to nitric acid.

$$NH_3 + 2\,O_2 \longrightarrow HNO_3 + H_2O$$

Fritz Haber: A Faustian Bargain

Fritz Haber was awarded the Nobel Prize in Chemistry in 1918 for his discovery of the process for large-scale nitrogen fixation. It is ironic, because Alfred Nobel originally endowed the Nobel Prizes out of bitter disappointment that the explosives he had developed for excavation and mining were put to such destructive uses in war. Yet Haber's process was adapted by the Germans to make explosives that were used in World War I. Haber also advocated the use of poison gas in war, and he even supervised, from the front lines, the release of chlorine in the first poison-gas attack. Also ironic is that despite his work for his native land, he was exiled from Germany in 1933. Nazi racial laws forced the Jewish-born Haber out of his position as director of the Kaiser Wilhelm Institute of Physical Chemistry. He accepted a post at Cambridge University in England but died of a stroke less than a year later.

▲ Fritz Haber (1868–1934), a German chemist, invented a process for manufacturing ammonia from N_2 and H_2.

The nitric acid was then reacted with more ammonia to produce ammonium nitrate.

$$HNO_3 + NH_3 \longrightarrow NH_4NO_3$$

A gas at room temperature, ammonia is easily compressed into a liquid that can be stored and transported in tanks. It is applied directly to the soil as fertilizer (Figure 20.5). This form of ammonia [NH_3(l)] is not the same as household ammonia [NH_3(aq)], which usually contains detergents and other ingredients as well as NH_3.

Some ammonia is reacted with carbon dioxide to form urea, an organic compound that releases nitrogen into the soil slowly (rather than all at once as inorganic forms do). Urea is a natural component of urine. Human urine can be used as a fertilizer if it is kept separate from feces, diluted with five times its weight in water 5:1, and used fresh.

$$2\,NH_3 + CO_2 \longrightarrow \underset{\text{Urea}}{NH_2{-}\overset{\overset{\displaystyle O}{\|}}{C}{-}NH_2} + H_2O$$

1. What is anhydrous ammonia?

Anhydrous ammonia is simply gaseous ammonia that has been compressed until it liquefies (*anhydrous* means "without water"; ammonia used in laboratories and home cleaning is ammonia gas dissolved in water). Anhydrous ammonia is easily applied, partly because strong hydrogen bonds form between ammonia and water in the soil. Unfortunately, it is probably best known for its use in the illegal manufacture of methamphetamine (Section 18.7).

◀ **Figure 20.5** A farmer applies anhydrous ammonia, a source of the plant nutrient nitrogen, to his fields.

Some solids made from ammonia for application as fertilizers are listed in Table 20.1. These products can be applied separately or combined with other plant nutrients to make a more complete fertilizer.

Table 20.1 Various Nitrogen Fertilizers Made from Ammonia

Reagent	Product Fertilizer	Formula
None	Anhydrous ammonia	NH_3
Carbon dioxide	Urea	NH_2CONH_2
Sulfuric acid	Ammonium sulfate	$(NH_4)_2SO_4$
Nitric acid	Ammonium nitrate	NH_4NO_3
Phosphoric acid	Ammonium hydrogen phosphate	$(NH_4)_2HPO_4$

The atmosphere has vast amounts of nitrogen, but current industrial methods of fixing it require a lot of energy and use nonrenewable resources. (The hydrogen needed for the synthesis of ammonia is made from natural gas.) Genes for nitrogen fixation have been transferred from bacteria into non-legume plants. Perhaps someday soon we will see the development of transgenic corn and cotton capable of producing their own nitrogen fertilizer the way clovers and peas do.

2. Are fertilizers explosive? Ammonium nitrate consists of an oxidizing anion (NO_3^-) and a reducing cation (NH_4^+), and it has been used as a high explosive. However, it is rather difficult to set off; doing so generally requires either extreme conditions or a second, more sensitive explosive. Fertilizers such as potassium nitrate contain oxidizing agents but do not contain a reducing cation and are not explosive. Ammonia is combustible but is not explosive.

Phosphorus Fertilizers

The limiting factor in plant growth is often the availability of phosphorus. Plants incorporate phosphates into DNA and RNA (Chapter 16) and other compounds essential to plant growth. Phosphates have probably been used as fertilizers since ancient times—in the form of bone, guano (bird droppings), and fish meal. However, phosphates as such were not recognized as plant nutrients until 1800. Following this discovery, the great battlefields of Europe were dug up and bones were shipped to chemical plants for processing into fertilizer.

Animal bones are rich in phosphorus, but the phosphorus is tightly bound and not readily available to plants. In the 1840s, chemists learned how to treat animal bones with sulfuric acid to convert them to a more soluble form called *superphosphate*. In 1843, John Bennett Lawes patented a process for treating coprolites (fossilized dung) with sulfuric acid to produce the first commercially available superphosphate. Within two decades, the same treatment was being applied to phosphate rock to produce thousands of tons a year. The crucial reaction for forming superphosphate is

$$\underset{\text{Phosphate rock or bone (insoluble)}}{Ca_3(PO_4)_2} + 2\,H_2SO_4 \longrightarrow \underbrace{Ca(H_2PO_4)_2 + 2\,CaSO_4}_{\text{Superphosphate (more soluble)}}$$

▲ **Figure 20.6** Phosphate fertilizers are obtained from an ore called *rock phosphate*, which is largely the skeletal remains of ancient sea creatures. This phosphate ore sample, from Morocco, contains a tooth from a shark of the Paleozoic era, between 200 and 500 million years ago.

Modern phosphate fertilizers are often produced by treating phosphate rock with phosphoric acid to make water-soluble calcium dihydrogen phosphate.

$$Ca_3(PO_4)_2 + 4\,H_3PO_4 \longrightarrow 3\,Ca(H_2PO_4)_2$$

More commonly used today is ammonium monohydrogen phosphate [$(NH_4)_2HPO_4$], which supplies both nitrogen and phosphorus.

Phosphates are common in the soil, but often at concentrations too low for adequate support of plant growth. Fortunately, there are more concentrated deposits. The presence of bones and teeth from early fish and other animals in these ore deposits indicates that they are largely the skeletal remains of sea creatures of ages past (Figure 20.6). Unfortunately, fluorides are often associated with phosphate ores, and they can cause a serious pollution problem during the production of phosphate fertilizers.

About 90% of all phosphates produced are used in agriculture. China is the leading producer and user, with the United States second. The rich phosphate deposits in the United States may be depleted within 30 years. Worldwide, Morocco has about one third of the reserves. Our use of phosphates scatters them irretrievably throughout the environment.

Potassium Fertilizers

The third major element necessary for plant growth is potassium. Plants use it in the form of the simple ion K^+. Generally, potassium is abundant, and there are no problems with solubility. Potassium ions, along with Na^+ ions, are essential to the fluid balance of cells. They also seem to be involved in the formation and transport of carbohydrates and may be necessary for the assembly of proteins from amino acids. Uptake of potassium ions from the soil leaves the soil acidic. Each time a positive potassium ion enters the root tip, a positive hydronium ion must leave for the plant to maintain electrical neutrality (Figure 20.7).

The usual chemical form of potassium in commercial fertilizers is potassium chloride (KCl). Vast deposits of this salt occur in and around Stassfurt, Germany, and for years this source supplied nearly all the world's potassium fertilizer. With the coming of World War I, the United States sought supplies within its own borders. Deposits at Searles Lake, California, and Carlsbad, New Mexico, now supply most U.S. needs. Canada has vast deposits in Saskatchewan and Alberta. Beds of potassium chloride up to 200 m thick lie about 1.5 km below the Canadian prairies (Figure 20.8). Although the reserves are large, potassium salts are a nonrenewable resource that we should use wisely.

▲ **Figure 20.7** When a root tip takes up K^+ ions from the soil, H_3O^+ ions are transferred to the soil. The uptake of potassium ions therefore tends to make soil acidic.

▶ **Figure 20.8** Mining potassium chloride about 1.5 km below the prairies of Saskatchewan, Canada.

Other Essential Elements

In addition to the three major nutrients (nitrogen, phosphorus, and potassium), a variety of other elements are necessary for proper plant growth. Three **secondary plant nutrients**—magnesium, calcium, and sulfur—are needed in moderate amounts. Calcium, in the form of lime (calcium oxide), is used to neutralize acidic soils.

$$CaO(s) + 2\,H^+(aq) \longrightarrow Ca^{2+}(aq) + H_2O(l)$$

Calcium ions are also necessary plant nutrients. Magnesium ions (Mg^{2+}) are incorporated into chlorophyll molecules and therefore are necessary for photosynthesis. Sulfur is a constituent of several amino acids and is necessary for protein synthesis.

Plants need eight other elements, called **micronutrients**, in small amounts. These elements are summarized in Table 20.2. Many soils contain these trace elements in sufficient quantities, but some are deficient in one or more, and their productivity can be markedly increased by adding small amounts of the needed elements.

Table 20.2 Eight Micronutrients Necessary for Proper Plant Growth

Element	Form Used by Plants	Function	Symptoms of Deficiency
Boron	H_3BO_3	Required for protein synthesis; essential for reproduction and for carbohydrate metabolism	Death of growing points of stems, poor growth of roots, poor flower and seed production
Chlorine	Cl^-	Increases water content of plant tissue; involved in carbohydrate metabolism	Shriveling
Copper	Cu^{2+}	Constituent of enzymes; essential for reproduction and for chlorophyll production	Twig dieback, yellowing of newer leaves
Iron	Fe^{2+}	Constituent of enzymes; essential for chlorophyll production	Yellowing of leaves, particularly between veins
Manganese	Mn^{2+}	Essential for redox reactions and for the transformation of carbohydrates	Yellowing of leaves, brown streaks of dead tissue
Molybdenum	$MoO_4{}^{2-}$	Essential to nitrogen fixation by legumes and to reduction of nitrates for protein synthesis	Stunting, pale-green or yellow leaves
Nickel	Ni^{2+}	Required for iron absorption; constituent of enzymes	Failure of seeds to germinate
Zinc	Zn^{2+}	Essential for early growth and maturing	Stunting, reduced seed and grain yields

Plants may also require other elements, including sodium, silicon, vanadium, chromium, selenium, cobalt, fluorine, and arsenic. Most of these elements are present in soil, but it is not known whether they are necessary for plant growth.

▲ In 1912, American farmers produced an average of 26 bushels of corn per acre. In 2007, the yield per acre was 151 bushels. The fivefold increase is mainly due to the increased use of fertilizers.

Fertilizers: A Mixed Bag

Farmers and gardeners often buy *complete fertilizers*, which, despite the name, usually contain only the three main nutrients. The three numbers—for example, 5-10-5—on fertilizer bags (Figure 20.9) indicate the proportions of nitrogen, phosphorus, and potassium (NPK). The first number represents the percentage of nitrogen (N); the second, the percentage of phosphorus (calculated as P_2O_5); and the third, the percentage of potassium (calculated as K_2O). So, 5-10-5 means that a fertilizer contains the equivalent of 5% N, 10% P_2O_5, and 5% K_2O; the rest is inert material.

Fertilizers must be water soluble to be used by plants. When it rains, though, nutrients from fertilizers can be washed into streams and lakes, where they can stimulate growth of algae. These chemicals, particularly nitrates, also enter the groundwater.

▲ **Figure 20.9** The numbers on this box of fertilizer indicate that the fertilizer is 18% N, 18% P_2O_5, and 21% K_2O. Actually, there is no K_2O or P_2O_5 in fertilizer; these formulas are used merely as a basis for calculation. The actual form of potassium in fertilizers is nearly always KCl, although any potassium salt can furnish the needed K^+ ions. Phosphorus is supplied as one of several salts.

Organic Fertilizers

Recall from Chapter 9 that the word *organic* has several meanings. Most of the fertilizers we have discussed so far are inorganic in the chemical sense. They are simple molecules, such as the NH_3 of anhydrous ammonia, or ionic compounds such as NH_4NO_3, $Ca(H_2PO_4)_2$, and KCl.

Urea is organic in the chemical sense: It is a carbon compound. People engaged in organic farming and gardening use the word *organic* not to refer to carbon-containing compounds but to imply the use of natural plant and animal products such as cottonseed meal, blood meal, fish emulsion, manure, and sewage sludge. Rock phosphate is sold as an organic fertilizer even though it is clearly inorganic in the chemical sense.

Organic fertilizers generally must be broken down by soil organisms to release the actual nutrients that the plants use. Whether from cow manure or a chemical factory, nitrogen is taken up by plants as NO_3^- ions. Your garden plants don't care if the nitrogen they need came from a compost pile or a chemical factory. Nutrient release from organic fertilizers generally takes some time. Usually, slow release over a long growing period is desirable, but organic materials may not release sufficient nutrients when needed by the plants.

Organic materials also have the advantage in that they provide humus, a dark-colored substance consisting of partially decayed plant or animal matter. Humus improves the texture of soils, thus improving water retention, reducing the loss of nutrients through leaching, and helping to resist erosion. It also provides a better environment for beneficial soil organisms such as earthworms.

If sold as fertilizers, organic products have an NPK ratio on the package label, just as synthetic fertilizers do. However, some organic materials, such as composted manure and sewage sludge, are sold as soil conditioners. These products have no claim as to nutrient content on the package, although they do furnish some nutrients.

Fresh human manure should not be used to fertilize fruits and vegetables to avoid the possibility of transmitting human pathogens, such as *E. coli*, a common fecal bacterium. The variant *E. coli* O157:H7 causes a food-borne illness that has increasingly been linked to contaminated vegetables. In Germany in 2011, *E. coli* contaminated bean sprouts killed 22 people and infected over 2400 more. The illness can cause severe problems in susceptible people, particularly children and the elderly. Pig, dog, and cat feces should not be used as fertilizers as they can carry internal parasitic worms from those animals to humans.

Organic fertilizers are often inexpensive or even free, if you can find the right source. [For example, the NPK ratio of urine (page 616) is about 18:2:5.] In contrast, manufactured nitrogen fertilizers are usually made using natural gas and require a high energy input. Intelligent use of organic fertilizers can save money and be environmentally friendly. Unwise use can be expensive or even disastrous.

Example 20.1 Fertilizer Production Equations

Write an equation to show the formation of ammonium sulfate (Table 20.1) from ammonia. What other compound is needed?

Solution

We have seen that ammonium nitrate is made by reacting ammonia with nitric acid. Ammonium sulfate should therefore be formed by reacting ammonia with sulfuric acid. We write the equation.

$$NH_3 + H_2SO_4 \longrightarrow (NH_4)_2SO_4 \qquad \text{(not balanced)}$$

Balancing the equation requires the coefficient 2 for NH_3.

$$2\,NH_3 + H_2SO_4 \longrightarrow (NH_4)_2SO_4$$

■ EXERCISE 20.1A

Write an equation to show the formation of ammonium monohydrogen phosphate (Table 20.1) from ammonia.

■ EXERCISE 20.1B

The micronutrient zinc is often applied in the form of zinc sulfate. Write the equation for the formation of zinc sulfate from zinc oxide.

▲ **It DOES Matter!**

Some soil additives are used for purposes other than fertilization. Calcium hydroxide [$Ca(OH)_2$, slaked lime] brings the acidity of soil to a better range for most plants. Vermiculite (above) is made from mica, in a process similar to that used in making puffed rice cereal. It lightens the soil and increases its ability to hold moisture. The backyard farmer may obtain vermiculite from packages in which it is used as cushioning material.

Self-Assessment Questions

1. Nitrogen is taken up by plants in the form of
   - **a.** N_2
   - **b.** NO_2
   - **c.** NO_2^-
   - **d.** NO_3^-
2. On fertilizer labels, NPK means
   - **a.** nitre, potash, and kalium
   - **b.** nitrogen, phosphorus, and krypton
   - **c.** nitrogen, phosphorus, and potassium
   - **d.** nitrogen, potassium, and krypton
3. The third number in 24-5-10 on a fertilizer label represents 10%
   - **a.** active ingredients
   - **b.** inert ingredients
   - **c.** K_2O
   - **d.** P_2O_5
4. Which of the following furnishes two primary plant nutrients?
   - **a.** NH_4NO_3
   - **b.** $(NH_4)_2HPO_4$
   - **c.** $(NH_4)_2SO_4$
   - **d.** NH_2CONH_2
5. Anhydrous ammonia is made from
   - **a.** H_2 and N_2
   - **b.** N_2 and O_2
   - **c.** NH_4NO_3
   - **d.** urea
6. To make phosphates more available to plants, phosphate rock is treated with
   - **a.** CO_2
   - **b.** H_2O
   - **c.** H_2SO_4
   - **d.** NH_3
7. The secondary plant nutrients are
   - **a.** C, H, and O
   - **b.** Ca, Mg, and S
   - **c.** N, P, and K
   - **d.** Zn, Cu, and Fe
8. The plant nutrient essential to the function of chlorophyll is
   - **a.** Ca^{2+}
   - **b.** Co^{2+}
   - **c.** Fe^{2+}
   - **d.** Mg^{2+}

Answers: 1, d; 2, c; 3, c; 4, b; 5, a; 6, c; 7, b; 8, d

▲ Organic farmers use animal manure as fertilizer.

▲ **It DOES Matter!**
Locust plagues have devastated crops throughout history. Desert locusts (*Schistocerca gregaria*) are usually solitary insects, but under certain environmental conditions, they change to a swarm-forming "gregarious" phase and can devastate crops. A neurochemical mechanism underlies this change, which also includes a change in body color from green to yellow. The key is the neurotransmitter serotonin, which in humans modulates anger, body temperature, mood, sleep, appetite, and metabolism (Section 18.7). In locusts, serotonin is synthesized in response to increased numbers and increased social contacts, and perhaps other factors.

20.2 The War against Pests

Learning Objectives › Name and describe the action of the main kinds of pesticides. › List several biological pest controls, and explain how they work.

People have always been plagued by insect pests. Three of the ten plagues of Egypt (described in the book of *Exodus*) were insect plagues—lice, flies, and locusts. The decline of Roman civilization has been attributed in part to malaria, a disease carried by mosquitoes and that destroys vigor and vitality when it does not kill. Bubonic plague, carried by fleas from rats to humans, swept through the Western world repeatedly during the Middle Ages. One such plague during the 1660s is estimated to have killed 25 million people, 25% of the population of Europe at that time. The first attempt (by the French during the 1880s) to dig a canal across Panama was defeated by outbreaks of yellow fever and malaria.

The use of modern chemical **pesticides** (substances that kill organisms that we consider pests) may be all that stands between us and some of these insect-borne plagues. Pesticides also prevent the consumption of a major portion of our food supply by insects and other pests.

In earlier days, people tried to control insect pests by draining swamps, pouring oil on ponds (to kill mosquito larvae), and using various chemicals. Most of these chemicals were compounds of arsenic. Lead arsenate [$Pb_3(AsO_4)_2$] is a particularly effective poison because both the lead and the arsenic in it are toxic. A few pesticides, such as pyrethrum (used in mosquito control) and nicotine sulfate (Black Leaf 40), are obtained from plant matter.

However, only a few insect species are harmful. Many are directly beneficial, and others play important roles in ecological systems and are indirectly beneficial. Most poisons are indiscriminate. They kill all insects, not just those we consider pests. Many of those poisons are also toxic to humans and other animals. Some say we should call such poisons *biocides* (because they kill living things) rather than **insecticides** (substances that kill insects). Table 20.3 lists the acute toxicities (from short-term exposures) of some insecticides. Effects of long-term exposure are more difficult to measure. Toxic substances in general are discussed in Chapter 22.

Example 20.2 Pesticide Toxicity

What quantity of the pesticide lindane, an ingredient in shampoos for the treatment of scabies and head lice, could lead to the death of a 15-kg (33-lb) child if the lethal dose is the same as it is for male rats (Table 20.3)?

Solution

The lethal dose is given as 88 mg of lindane per kilogram of body weight, and the child's body weight is 15 kg.

$$\text{Lethal dose} = 15\ \cancel{\text{kg}} \times \frac{88\ \text{mg}}{1\ \cancel{\text{kg}}} = 1300\ \text{mg}$$

The lethal dose is 1300 mg, or 1.3 g.

■ EXERCISE 20.2

How much parathion should it take to kill a 75-kg (165-lb) farm worker if the lethal dose is the same as it is for rats (Table 20.3)?

DDT: The Dream Insecticide

Shortly before World War II, Swiss scientist Paul Müller (1899–1965) found that DDT (dichlorodiphenyltrichloroethane), a chlorinated hydrocarbon, is a potent insecticide. DDT was soon used effectively against grapevine pests and against a particularly severe potato beetle infestation.

Table 20.3 Approximate Acute Toxicity of Insecticidal Preparations Administered Orally to Rats

Pesticide	LD_{50}[a]	Category of Acute Toxicity	Selected Uses
Pyrethrins[b]	200–2600	Slightly toxic	Food crops; pest control (flea, tick, fly)
Malathion	1000 (1375)	Slightly toxic	Crops (alfalfa, lettuce)
Lead arsenate	825	Slightly toxic	Banned in 1988
Diazinon	285 (250)	Moderately toxic	Crops (lettuce, almonds, broccoli)
Carbaryl	250	Moderately toxic	Crops (apples, pecans, grapes, citrus fruits)
Nicotine[c]	230	Moderately toxic	Restricted to use by certified applicators
DDT[d]	118 (113)	Moderately toxic	Most uses banned; malaria-carrying mosquito control
Lindane	91 (88)	Moderately toxic	Crops (cotton); see also Example 20.2
Methyl parathion	14 (24)	Highly toxic	Crops (cotton, rice, fruit trees)
Parathion	3.6 (13)	Highly toxic	Crops (alfalfa, barley, corn, cotton)
Carbofuran[e]	2	Highly toxic	Field crops, some fruits and vegetables
Aldicarb	1	Highly toxic	Crops (cotton)

[a]Dose in milligrams per kilogram of body weight that will kill 50% of a test population. Values in parentheses are for male rats. (LD_{50} is discussed in more detail in Chapter 22.)

[b]Active ingredients of pyrethrum; LD_{50} depends on variability of concentration of active components in the formulation.

[c]Oral in mice. Nicotine is much more toxic by injection.

[d]Estimated LD_{50} for humans is 500 mg/kg.

[e]In mice.

Sources: O'Neill, Maryadele J., Patricia E. Heckelman, Cherie B. Koch, Kristin J. Roman, and Catherine M. Kenny, *The Merck Index*, 14th ed. (Whitehouse Station, NJ: Merck & Co., 2006), and the Extension Toxicology Network.

When the war began, supplies of pyrethrum, a major insecticide of the time, were cut off by the Japanese occupation of Southeast Asia and the Dutch East Indies (now Indonesia). Lead, arsenic, and copper that were used in insecticides were diverted for armaments and other military purposes.

The Allies, desperately needing an insecticide to protect soldiers from disease-bearing lice, ticks, and mosquitoes, obtained a small quantity of DDT and quickly tested it. Combined with talcum, DDT was an effective delousing powder. Clothing was impregnated with DDT, and it seemed to have no harmful effects even on those exposed to large doses. Allied soldiers were nearly free of lice, but German troops were heavily infested and many were sick with typhus. (In earlier wars, more soldiers probably died from typhus than from bullets.)

DDT is easily synthesized from cheap, readily available chemicals. Chlorobenzene (C_6H_5Cl) and chloral hydrate [$Cl_3CCH(OH)_2$] are warmed in the presence of sulfuric acid. When the reaction is complete, the mixture is poured into water, and the DDT separates out because, like other chlorinated hydrocarbons, it is almost insoluble in water.

$$2\ \text{Cl–}C_6H_5 + \text{HO–CH(OH)–}CCl_3 \xrightarrow{H_2SO_4} \text{Cl–}C_6H_4\text{–CH(}C_6H_4\text{–Cl)–}CCl_3 + 2\ H_2O$$

Chlorobenzene   Chloral hydrate   DDT

A cheap insecticide that is effective against a variety of insect pests, DDT came into widespread use after the war (Figure 20.10, page 625). Other chlorinated hydrocarbons were synthesized, tested, and used against insects. Although invaluable to farmers in the production of food and fiber, chlorinated hydrocarbons won

GREEN CHEMISTRY

Principles 3, 4, 5, 6, 9, 10

Amy S. Cannon, *Beyond Benign*

Safer Pesticides through Green Chemistry

The practice of agriculture has been largely responsible for the growth of human civilization, allowing humans to settle in societies and raise food to sustain their communities. Population growth brought the challenge of producing enough food, in a sustainable manner, to feed the world's population. This challenge is one of the toughest that humans have faced in history. The solution involves global issues such as clean water, population growth, land use, energy use, genetic modification, and pesticide and fertilizer use.

From a scientific point of view, the chemicals we use on the farm and in the garden can have a drastic impact on our food production and the sustainability of agricultural practices. Pesticide use in agriculture has led to a drastic reduction in crop failure and increased crop yields, but pesticides often are toxic to more than just the target organisms. How do we ensure that pesticides target pest organisms and do not harm beneficial ones?

The need for more specifically targeted pesticides has been addressed by green chemists. Green Chemistry Principle 4 encourages the design of safer, more benign products and processes without compromising on efficacy or cost. This is perhaps the most important application of green chemistry in the production and use of pesticides. Generally, a safer pesticide means higher selectivity toward the pest organism and fewer effects on the surrounding environment and on beneficial organisms.

In creating selectively targeted pesticides, scientists focus on the relationships between the structure and function of a molecule. The goal is to find specific modes of action that are unique to the target pest. New research is tapping into naturally inspired, or *biomimetic*, methods for repelling or thwarting pests. New pesticides employ other principles of green chemistry as well. Chemists are aiming to reduce the environmental impact of processes for making the pesticides, including less hazardous chemical synthesis (Principle 3) through the use of catalytic reagents (Principle 9), energy-efficient processes (Principle 6), and safer solvents (Principle 5). Many pesticides are also designed to be biodegradable (Principle 10).

The EPA's Presidential Green Chemistry Challenge Award (PGCCA) program has presented awards for several alternative pesticides for plant and crop protection, including the following:

- The 2001 Small Business Award was given to Eden Bioscience Corporation for Messenger®, a product based on naturally occurring proteins that trigger a plant's natural defense system much like the immune response in animals. The protein also enhances natural plant growth. Messenger® is produced with a water-based process that uses no harsh chemicals, is low energy, and generates no hazardous waste; the product is readily biodegradable.
- The 2003 Small Business Award was given to AgraQuest, Inc., for the creation of Serenade®, a fungicide for fruits and vegetables. Serenade® takes advantage of a naturally occurring strain of bacteria to prevent the growth of damaging fungi and is nontoxic to beneficial and nontarget organisms. It does not generate any hazardous chemical residues and is safe for workers and the groundwater.
- Two awards (1999 and 2008) went to Dow AgroSciences LLC for technologies based on an innovative pest-control approach called *spinosad pesticides*. The first award recognized the insect-control products Tracer®, Naturalyte® Insect Control, and Precise®, which are effective against pests on vegetables and exhibit low toxicity to nontarget beneficial organisms. The active ingredient in these products is generated from naturally occurring bacteria, and contact or ingestion is harmful to the nervous system of certain insects. The second award was for the design of a new type of insect-control products called *spinetoram* that are modifications of the original spinosad pesticides. These products, Radiant® and Delegate®, are useful for addressing pest problems in tree fruits and nuts and are dramatically less toxic than the traditional organophosphate pesticides.
- The Clarke company received an award in 2010 for using one of Dow's 1999 award-winning spinosad-based pesticides to create a pesticide that is effective at controlling mosquito larvae and that replaces organophosphates and other traditional toxic pesticides. The new product, branded as Natular™, was created by encapsulating the spinosad in a plaster matrix, allowing the active ingredient to be stable in water. The product slowly releases the spinosad over time in aquatic environments and results in effective mosquito control. This new product is certified for use in organic farming.

▲ Most of today's pesticides require workers to wear the bulky, uncomfortable environmental suits shown here. Greener pesticides may eventually permit pest control without protective clothing.

their most dramatic victories in the field of public health. According to the World Health Organization (WHO), approximately 25 million lives have been saved and hundreds of millions of illnesses prevented by the use of DDT and related pesticides.

DDT seemed to be a dream come true. It would at last free the world from insect-borne diseases. It would protect crops from the ravages of insects and thus increase food production. In recognition of his discovery, Müller was awarded the Nobel Prize in Physiology and Medicine in 1948.

▲ **Figure 20.10** Insecticides are often applied by aerial spraying. Winds can spread the pesticide over a wide area.

Even before Müller received his prize, however, there were warnings that all was not well. Houseflies resistant to DDT were reported as early as 1946, and DDT's toxicity to fish was documented by 1947. Such early warnings were largely ignored, and it was also assumed that the toxicity would disappear soon after the chemical was discharged into the environment. DDT was used extensively to protect crops and control mosquitoes and to try to prevent Dutch elm disease. By 1962, the year Rachel Carson's book *Silent Spring* (Section 1.2) appeared, U.S. production of DDT had reached 76 million kg/year.

Today, in developed countries, DDT is known mostly for its harmful environmental effects. Birds were threatened because DDT causes their eggs to have shells that are thin, poorly formed, and easily broken. Even a few parts per billion of DDT interfere with the growth of plankton and the reproduction of crustaceans such as shrimp.

Chlorinated hydrocarbons generally are unreactive. This lack of reactivity was a major advantage of DDT. Sprayed on a crop, DDT stayed there and killed insects for weeks. This *pesticide persistence* also turned out to be a major disadvantage: The substance did not break down readily in the environment. Although not very toxic to humans and other warm-blooded creatures, DDT is highly toxic to cold-blooded organisms, which include insects, of course, and fish. DDT's lack of reactivity toward oxygen, water, and components of the soil led to its buildup in the environment, where it threatened fish, birds, and other wildlife.

Biological Magnification: Concentration in Fatty Tissues

Chlorinated hydrocarbons are good solvents for fats, and fats are good solvents for chlorinated hydrocarbons such as DDT. When these compounds are ingested as contaminants in food or water, they are concentrated in fatty tissues. Because they are fat-soluble, chlorinated hydrocarbons tend to become concentrated in animals higher on the food chain.

This *biological magnification* was graphically demonstrated in California in 1957. Clear Lake, about 100 miles north of San Francisco, was sprayed with DDT in an effort to control gnats. After spraying, the water contained only 0.02 ppm of DDT, but the microscopic plant and animal life contained 5 ppm—250 times as much. Fish feeding on these microorganisms contained up to 2000 ppm. Grebes, the diving birds that ate the fish, died by the hundreds (Figure 20.11).

DDT and other chlorinated hydrocarbons such as PCBs (Section 10.7) are nerve poisons. They are concentrated in the fatlike compounds that make up nerve sheaths. DDT also interferes with calcium metabolism essential to the formation of healthy bones and teeth. Although harm to humans has never been conclusively demonstrated, the disruption of calcium metabolism in birds was disastrous for some species. The shells of their eggs, composed mainly of calcium compounds, were thin and poorly formed. The Bald Eagle, Peregrine Falcon, Brown Pelican, and other species became endangered but have made dramatic recoveries since DDT was banned in the United States and other industrialized countries in the 1970s.

DDT is still used in some countries where malaria and typhus are great health problems. It is applied mainly on the inside walls of houses, so the environmental

Development of Insect Resistance

In the six decades or so in which pesticides have been widely used, hundreds of insect species have become resistant to one or more of these poisons. Resistance has resulted in increases in crop losses and in insect-transmitted diseases. Some insect species such as the cotton bollworm, the Colorado potato beetle, malaria-transmitting *Anopheles* mosquitoes, and the German cockroach exhibit resistance to all commercially available pest control agents.

Insects develop resistance to a pesticide by natural selection. A genetic mutation for resistance can spread quickly: For example, if a farmer uses a new pesticide on a field with 10.0 billion pest insects, perhaps 9.9 billion are killed. Resistant insects survive and pass the gene for resistance to the next generation. The resistant insect group becomes a larger percentage of the whole. Through repetition of this process over several generations, the resistant insects become the predominant form and the pesticide is no longer effective.

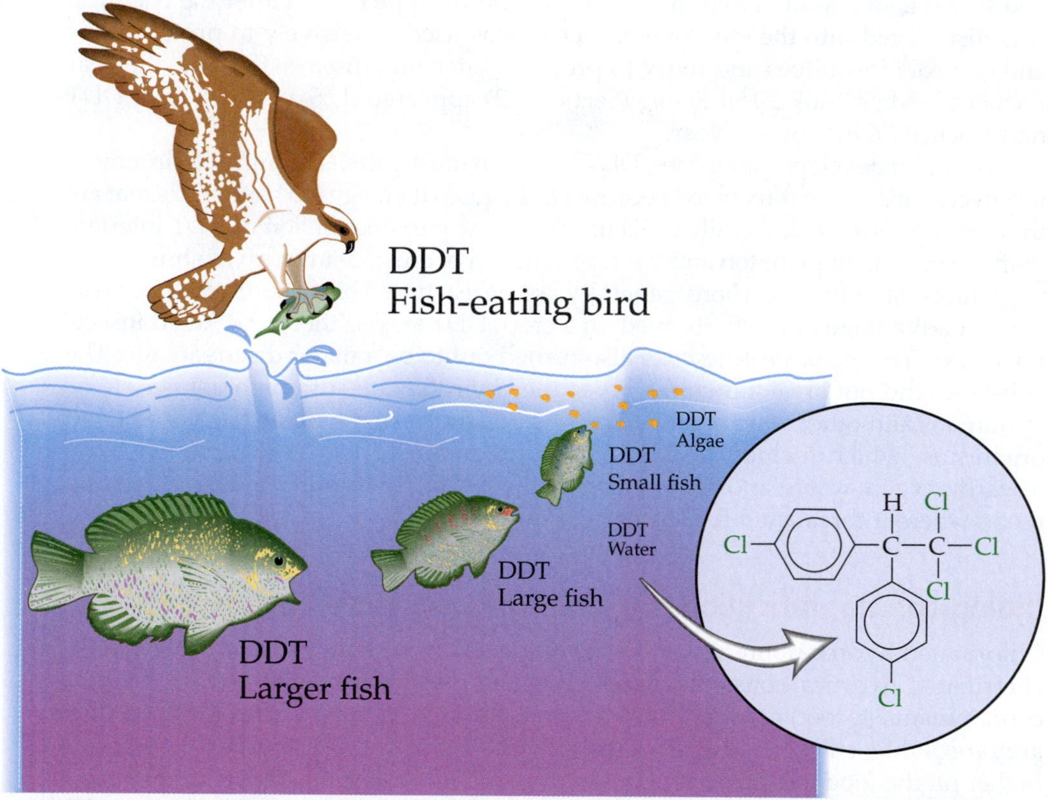

Figure 20.11 Concentration of DDT going up a food chain. Animals at the top of the food chain have the highest concentrations of the pesticide. DDT dissolves in the fatty membranes of cells. The wedge-shaped DDT molecules open channels in the membranes, causing them to leak.

impact is much less than that of the earlier widespread use of DDT in agriculture. Malaria infects between 300 million and 500 million people and kills 1 million every year. About 90% of the deaths occur in Africa, and most of the victims are children under 5.

In 2000, more than 120 countries signed a treaty to phase out *persistent organic pollutants (POPs)*, a group of chemicals, many of them chlorinated hydrocarbons, that includes DDT. This treaty has the goal of reducing and ultimately eliminating the use of DDT, but individual countries may continue to use it for controlling malaria. As bad as DDT may sound, it may have saved the lives of more people than any other chemical substance.

Organophosphorus Compounds

Bans and restrictions on chlorinated hydrocarbon insecticides have led to increased use of *organophosphorus* compounds (containing carbon and phosphorus) such as malathion, diazinon, and parathion (Figure 20.12). More than two dozen of these

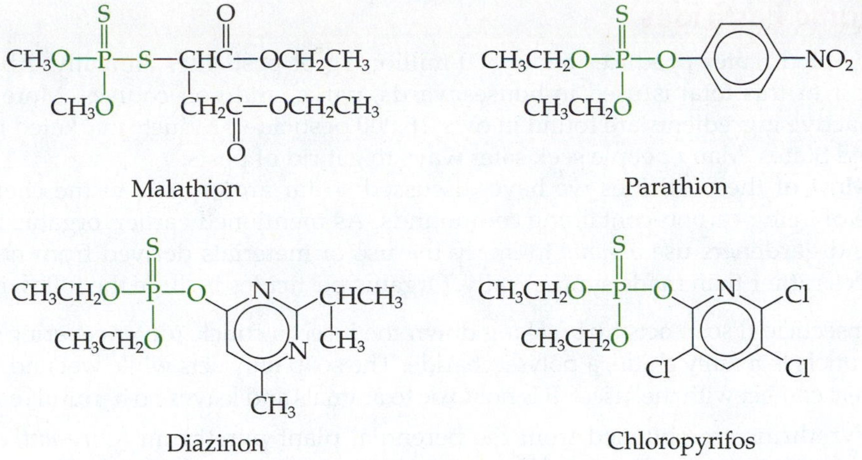

Malathion

Parathion

Diazinon

Chloropyrifos

◀ **Figure 20.12** Four organic phosphorus compounds used as insecticides.

insecticides are available commercially. They have been extensively studied and evaluated for effectiveness against insects and for toxicity to people, laboratory animals, and farm animals.

Organophosphorus compounds are nerve poisons (Chapter 22); they interfere with the conduction of nerve signals in insects. At high levels of exposure, they do the same in humans. Most are more toxic to mammals than chlorinated hydrocarbons (Table 20.3). Malathion is a notable exception; it is less toxic than DDT. Like chlorinated hydrocarbons, organophosphorus pesticides concentrate in fatty tissues. However, the phosphorus compounds are less persistent in the environment. They break down in days or weeks, whereas chlorinated hydrocarbons often persist for years. Residues of organophosphorus compounds are seldom found in food.

3. Are pesticides causing honeybees to die off? Although pesticides such as carbaryl are quite toxic to honeybees, it appears that the *colony collapse disorder* that first appeared in 2006 may have any number of causes. The USDA Agricultural Research Service has indicated that mites, viruses, pesticides, environmental stresses, and nutrition may be individually or jointly responsible. Honeybees are important pollinators, and their declining numbers could affect some crop yields by 30% or more in years to come if the problem is not solved.

Carbamates: Targeting the Pest

Another widely used family of insecticides is the carbamates. Examples are carbaryl (Sevin®), carbofuran (Furadan®), and aldicarb (Temik®) (Figure 20.13). Like the phosphorus compounds, carbamates are nerve poisons, but they act over a shorter span of time. Most carbamates are *narrow-spectrum insecticides* directed specifically at one, or a few, insect pests. In contrast, chlorinated hydrocarbons and organophosphorus compounds kill many kinds of insects and are called *broad-spectrum insecticides*. Carbaryl has a low toxicity to mammals, but carbofuran and aldicarb have toxicities similar to that of parathion. Carbaryl is particularly effective against wasps but unfortunately is also quite toxic to honeybees. Millions of these valuable insects have been wiped out by spraying crops with carbaryl.

The carbamate insecticide carbaryl was being made at a chemical plant in Bhopal, India, in 1984 when an explosion released 40 t of the toxic gas methyl isocyanate ($CH_3N{=}C{=}O$). More than 3000 people were killed immediately, and there were perhaps as many as 20,000 deaths in all.

Carbamates are characterized by the presence of the carbamate group:

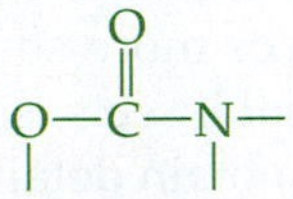

$$-O-\overset{\overset{\displaystyle O}{\|}}{C}-\underset{|}{N}-$$

Many variations can be obtained by changing the groups attached to the O and the N. Generally, carbamates break down fairly rapidly in the environment and do not accumulate in fatty tissue, which gives these insecticides an advantage over chlorinated hydrocarbons and organic phosphorus compounds.

Carbaryl (Sevin®)

Aldicarb (Temik®)

Carbofuran (Furadan®)

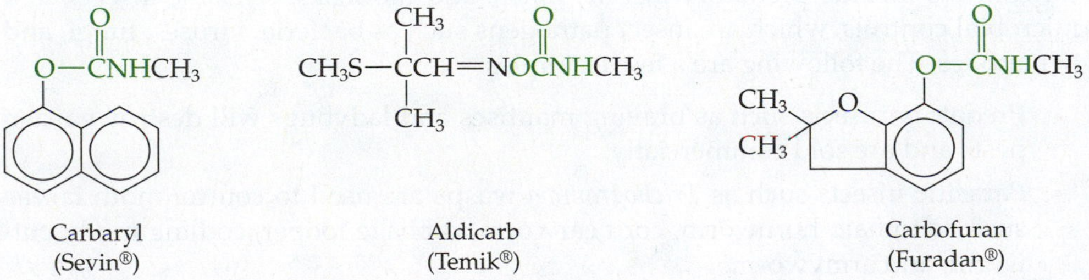

◀ **Figure 20.13** Three carbamate insecticides.

To protect themselves from being eaten, some plants produce their own pesticides, which often make up 5–10% of their dry weight. Nicotine protects tobacco plants. Pyrethrins are also plant-produced pesticides. Physostigmine is a naturally occurring carbamate. Our consumption of natural pesticides is probably 10,000 times our consumption of synthetic ones.

Organic Pesticides

The United States produces about 500 million kg of pesticides annually. About a quarter of this total is used in houses, yards, parks, and golf courses. More than 1000 active ingredients are found in over 16,000 pesticide products marketed in the United States. Many people seek safer ways to get rid of pests.

Most of the pesticides we have discussed so far are organic in the chemical sense of being carbon-containing compounds. As mentioned earlier, organic farmers and gardeners use *organic* to imply the use of materials derived from natural sources rather than made synthetically. Organic pesticides include the following.

- Insecticidal soap acts by breaking down the insect's cuticle (outer covering). The cuticle is mainly chitin, a polysaccharide. The soap only acts while wet and in direct contact with the insect. It is not toxic to animals and leaves no harmful residue.
- Pyrethrins are obtained from the perennial plant pyrethrum (*Chrysanthemum cinerariaefolium*). (Pyrethroids are synthetic derivatives of the natural pyrethrins.) Pyrethrins are low in toxicity to mammals because they are quickly broken down into inactive forms by mammalian liver enzymes. (Some of the pyrethroids are moderately toxic to mammals and quite toxic to fish and tadpoles.) Insects, which have no liver, are much more susceptible to pyrethrins.
- Rotenone is a natural product obtained from the roots and stems of several tropical and subtropical plant species. It is slightly toxic to mammals, but extremely toxic to insects and fish.
- Boric acid (H_3BO_3), usually applied as a bait, dust, or powder, is mainly used for control of ants and cockroaches. It acts as a stomach poison and as a desiccant by abrading the wax from the insect's cuticle. Boric acid is moderately toxic to humans.
- Cryolite (Na_3AlF_6) is used on food crops and ornamental plants. It blocks caterpillars and other grazing insects from feeding. Toxicological hazards, if any, are very slight.
- Diatomaceous earth is the fossilized remains of diatoms, a type of algae whose shells consist largely of silica. The shells are ground to a fine powder with sharp-edged particles that cut the insects' cuticles and absorb oils, causing the insects to dehydrate and die. If ingested, the particles cause the same sort of damage to the digestive system. Diatomaceous earth is harmless to people.
- Ryania is a botanical insecticide obtained from *Ryania speciosa*, a tropical plant. The active principle is an alkaloid called *ryanodine*. Ryania is highly toxic to the caterpillars of fruit moths, codling moths, and corn earworms. It has a very low toxicity to mammals but is very toxic to fish.

Just because a product is considered organic doesn't mean it is safe. Some organic pesticides are as toxic as or more so than some synthetic pesticides. They can also be quite toxic to beneficial insects, such as honeybees. To use these products most effectively, you should obtain detailed directions from a university cooperative extension office, located in most counties.

Biological Insect Controls

The use of natural enemies is another method for controlling pests. These biological controls include predatory insects, mites, and mollusks; parasitic insects; and microbial controls, which are insect pathogens such as bacteria, viruses, fungi, and nematodes. The following are a few examples.

- Predatory insects such as praying mantises and ladybugs will destroy garden pests and are sold commercially.
- Parasitic insects such as *Trichogramma* wasps are used to control moth larvae such as tomato hornworm, corn earworm, cabbage looper, codling moth, cutworm, and armyworm.

- *Bacillus thuringiensis (Bt)*, sold under trade names such as Dipel®, is widely used by home gardeners against cabbage loopers, hornworms, and other moth caterpillars. Bt is also used against Colorado potato beetles, mosquito larvae, black flies, European corn borers, grape leaf rollers, and gypsy moths.
- Naturally occurring nuclear polyhedrosis virus (NPV) is present at low levels in many insect populations. These viruses can be grown in culture and applied to crops. NPV is highly selective, affecting only *Heliothis* caterpillars. Natural viral pesticides appear to be harmless to humans, wildlife, and beneficial insects. They are completely biodegradable but are generally quite expensive to produce.

Microbial controls such as Bt are host-specific: They don't harm organisms other than the targeted ones. The gene for the toxin produced by Bt has been inserted into cotton, corn, potato, and other plants. These genetically modified (GM) cotton plants are protected from damage by cotton bollworms. However, the pests are already developing resistance to the toxin. Also, some people fear that the introduced genes will spread to wild relatives of the cultivated species, leading to the development of "super weeds." People also fear that proteins produced in GM plants will cause allergic reactions in susceptible individuals. For example, introduction of a gene for a peanut protein into another food plant could cause a dangerous reaction in people allergic to peanuts.

A highly successful biological approach is the breeding of insect- and fungus-resistant plants. Yields of corn (maize), wheat, rice, and other grains have been increased substantially in this manner. Not all such research is successful, however. Plant breeders produced a potato that is insect resistant, but it had to be taken off the market because it is also toxic to people. Public fears about foods from genetically modified plants have slowed developments, particularly in Europe.

Sterile Insect Technique

A *sterile insect technique (SIT)* is a method of insect control that involves rearing large numbers of males, sterilizing them with radiation or chemicals or by cross-breeding, and then releasing them in areas of infestation. These sterile males, which far outnumber the local fertile males, mate with wild females. If a female mates with a sterile male, no offspring are produced, thus reducing the reproductive potential of the insect population and controlling its growth.

Successful SIT programs have been conducted against screwworm, a pest that seriously affects cattle in the southern United States, Mexico, and Central America, as well as in Libya. SIT programs have also been employed against the Mediterranean fruit fly (medfly) in Latin America and against the codling moth in Canada. The great expense and limited applicability of SIT probably mean that it will not become a major method of insect control.

Pheromones: The Sex Trap

Substances called *pheromones* are increasingly important in insect control. A **pheromone** is a chemical that is secreted externally by an insect to mark a trail, send an alarm, or attract a mate. Insect **sex attractants** are usually secreted by females to attract males (Figure 20.14).

▲ **Figure 20.14** A male gypsy moth uses its large antennae to detect pheromones from a female.

Chemical research has identified pheromones of hundreds of insect species. Most are blends of two or more chemicals that must be present in exactly the right proportions to be biologically active. Chemists can synthesize these compounds, and workers can use them to lure male insects into traps, allowing a determination of which pests are present and the level of infestation. The workers can then undertake measures, including the use of conventional pesticides, to minimize damage to the crops.

If the attractant is exceptionally powerful and the insect population level is very low, a pheromone trap technique called "attract and kill" may achieve sufficient control. Otherwise, the attractant can be used in quantities sufficient to confuse and disorient males, who detect a female in every direction but can't find one to mate with. Mating disruption has been used successfully in controlling some insect pests. Many grape growers in Germany and Switzerland use this technique, allowing them to produce wine without using conventional insecticides.

Some sex attractants have relatively simple structures. The sex attractant for the codling moth, which infests apples, is an alcohol with a straight chain of 12 carbon atoms and two double bonds.

OH

However, most sex attractants have complicated structures, and all are secreted in extremely tiny amounts. This can make research on these attractants difficult and tedious. For example, a team of U.S. Department of Agriculture researchers had to use the tips of the abdomens of 87,000 female gypsy moths to isolate a minute amount of a powerful sex attractant.

Yet pheromones are effective at extremely low levels. A male silkworm moth can detect as few as 40 molecules per second. If a female releases as little as 0.01 mg, she can attract every male within 1 km. Gypsy moth larvae have defoliated great areas of forest, mainly in the northeastern United States, and have now spread over much of the country. The gypsy moth pheromone has been used mainly in traps to monitor insect populations.

Pheromones are usually too expensive to play a huge role in insect control, though the use of recombinant DNA methods (Section 16.18) to synthesize them holds promise for future work. For now, the cost is high, and research is painstaking and time-consuming. Workers must be careful not to get the attractants on their clothes. Who wants to be attacked on a warm summer night by a million sex-crazed gypsy moths?

Juvenile Hormones

Some insects can be controlled by the use of *juvenile hormones*. Hormones are the chemical messengers that control many life functions in plants and animals, and minute quantities produce profound physiological changes. In the insect world, a **juvenile hormone** controls the rate of development of the young. Normally, production of the hormone is shut off at the appropriate time to allow proper maturation to the adult stage.

Chemists have been able to isolate insect juvenile hormones and determine their structures. With knowledge of the structure, they can synthesize a hormone or one of its analogs. The application of juvenile hormones to ponds where mosquitoes breed keeps the mosquitoes in the harmless preadult stage. Because only adult insects can reproduce, juvenile hormones appear to be a nearly perfect method of mosquito control.

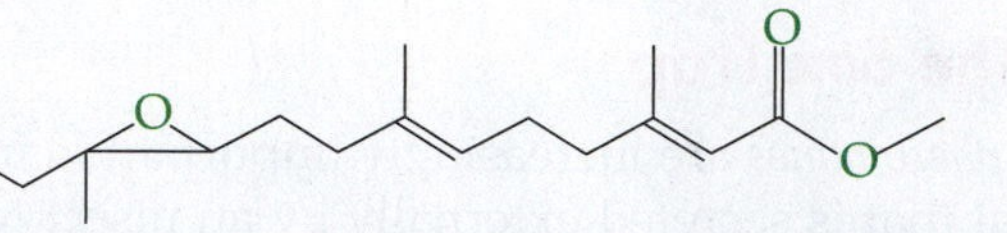

O O O

A natural juvenile hormone

Methoprene, a juvenile hormone analog, is approved by the EPA for use against mosquitoes and fleas.

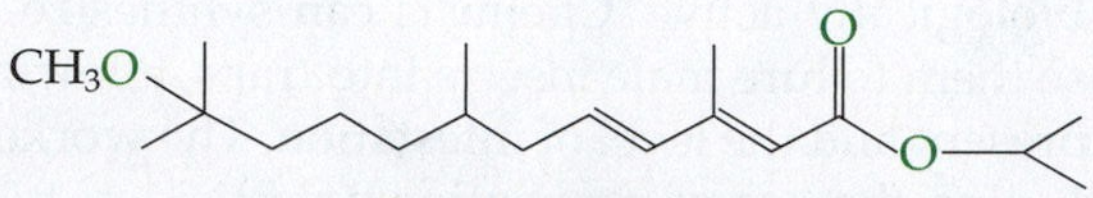

CH_3O O O

Methoprene

The synthesis of juvenile hormones is difficult and expensive, and they can only be used against insects that are pests at the adult stage. Little would be gained by keeping a moth or a butterfly in the caterpillar stage for a longer period of time. Caterpillars have voracious appetites and do a lot of damage to crops.

Self-Assessment Questions

1. A pesticide is a product that kills
   a. insects and weeds only
   b. mice and rats only
   c. other organisms as well as the target
   d. ticks and fleas only
2. Spraying of pesticides on crops
   a. affects only the sprayed crops
   b. has no effect on the food chain
   c. is necessary if farmers are to grow crops
   d. may result in pesticides ending up in rivers and lakes
3. If pesticides that can be stored in body fat get into a lake, which organism will show the highest level in its fat?
   a. fish　　b. microscopic animals
   c. microscopic plants　　d. osprey (fish hawk)
4. Compared to DDT, organic phosphorus compounds are generally
   a. less persistent and less toxic
   b. less persistent and more toxic
   c. more persistent and less toxic
   d. more persistent and more toxic
5. The SIT method of insect control works best when
   a. there is a large target insect population
   b. the females mate repeatedly
   c. the males of the pest species can be reared in mass
   d. the males mate with related species
6. A substance produced by an organism to influence the behavior of another member of the same species is a(n)
   a. agonist　　b. inducer　　c. marker　　d. pheromone
7. The use of ladybugs and praying mantises to control insect pests is an example of
   a. biocidal control　　b. biological control
   c. abiotic control　　d. exploitation of insect pests

Answers: 1, c; 2, d; 3, d; 4, b; 5, c; 6, d; 7, b

20.3 Herbicides and Defoliants

Learning Objective › Name and describe the action of the major herbicides and defoliants.

The United States produces about 225 million kg of herbicides annually. **Herbicides**, four of which are shown in Figure 20.15, are chemicals used to kill weeds. Some herbicides are **defoliants**, which cause leaves to fall off plants.

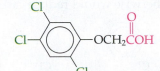

▲ Dandelions, introduced into North America from Europe because of their attractive flowers and their uses as a salad vegetable and a folk medicine, are now generally considered a lawn weed. About half of all homeowners treat their lawns with herbicides such as 2,4-D (Weed-B-Gon®) and glyphosate (Roundup®). More than 10 million pounds of 2,4-D are used on lawns in the United States each year.

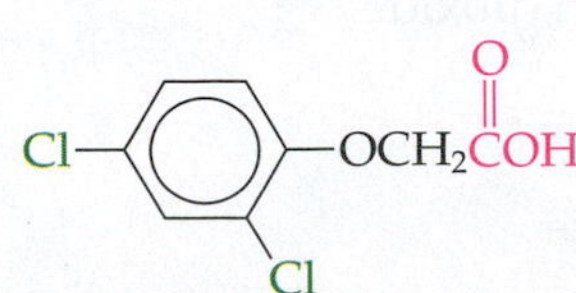

2,4-Dichlorophenoxyacetic acid (2,4-D)

2,4,5-Trichlorophenoxyacetic acid (2,4,5-T)

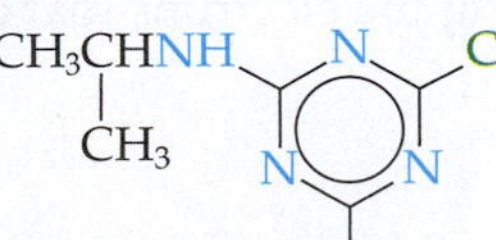

Atrazine

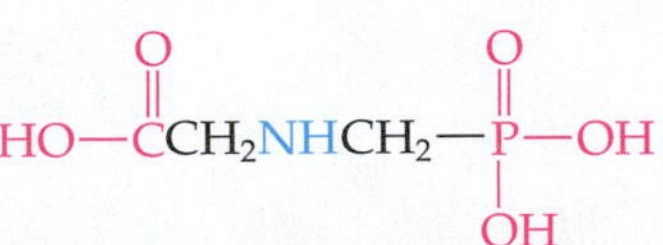

Glyphosate

▲ **Figure 20.15** Four common herbicides: 2,4-dichlorophenoxyacetic acid (2,4-D), 2,4,5-trichlorophenoxyacetic acid (2,4,5-T), atrazine, and glyphosate.

Q: *What are the alkyl groups on the atrazine molecule?*

2,4-D and 2,4,5-T

Crop plants that have no competition from weeds produce more abundant harvests. Weeds cause crop losses of billions of dollars a year in the United States. Removing weeds by hand or hoe is tedious, backbreaking work, so chemical herbicides are used to kill unwanted plants.

Early herbicides included solutions of copper salts, sulfuric acid, and sodium chlorate ($NaClO_3$). It wasn't until the introduction of 2,4-D (2,4-dichlorophenoxyacetic acid) in 1945 that the use of herbicides became common. 2,4-D and its derivatives are growth-regulator herbicides, which are especially effective against newly emerged, rapidly growing broad-leaved plants. One derivative of 2,4-D is 2,4,5-T (2,4,5-trichlorophenoxyacetic acid), which is especially effective against woody plants and works by defoliation.

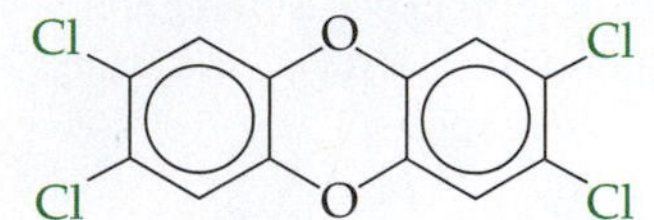

2,3,7,8-Tetrachlorodibenzo-*para*-dioxin (a dioxin)

Combined in a formulation called **Agent Orange**, 2,4-D and 2,4,5-T were used extensively in Vietnam to remove enemy cover and to destroy crops that maintained enemy armies. Agent Orange caused vast ecological damage and is suspected of causing birth defects in children born to both American soldiers and Vietnamese exposed to the herbicides. Laboratory studies show that 2,4-D and 2,4,5-T, when pure, do not cause abnormalities in fetuses of laboratory animals. Extensive birth defects are caused, however, by **dioxins**, contaminants of 2,4,5-T frequently found in the herbicide. The most toxic dioxin is 2,3,7,8-tetrachlorodibenzo-*para*-dioxin, abbreviated 2,3,7,8-TCDD, or just TCDD. Continuing concern about dioxin contamination led the EPA to ban 2,4,5-T in 1985.

4. Where do dioxins come from, and how toxic are they? In addition to being contaminants in 2,4-T, dioxins are formed in small quantities when certain plastics, notably polyvinyl chloride (PVC), are burned. Although the exact nature and degree of their toxicity in humans is still under debate, dioxins have been classified as a carcinogen based on animal studies. It appears that very low levels of dioxins are sufficient to cause tumors in animals.

Atrazine and Glyphosate

The most widely used herbicides in the United States are atrazine and glyphosate. Atrazine binds to a protein in the chloroplasts of plant cells, shutting off the electron-transfer reactions of photosynthesis. Atrazine is often used on corn crops. Corn plants deactivate atrazine by removing the chlorine atom. Weeds cannot deactivate the compound and are killed. Some studies indicate that atrazine interferes with the hormone system, disrupting estrogen function. Atrazine has been linked to sexual abnormalities in frogs.

Glyphosate, a derivative of the amino acid glycine, is used to control perennial grasses. It is not selective, however, and kills all vegetation by inhibiting the function of a certain plant enzyme. Glyphosate is metabolized by bacteria in the soil, so that other plants can be sown or transplanted into treated areas shortly after spraying. It is sold under several trade names, including Roundup®. Genetically modified soybeans, corn, alfalfa, and other plants that are resistant to glyphosate have been developed. When glyphosate is applied to a field, the weeds are killed but the crop plants remain unharmed. However, widespread use of glyphosate has resulted in many glyphosate-resistant weeds.

Paraquat: A Preemergent Herbicide

A **preemergent herbicide** is one used to kill weed plants before crop seedlings emerge. Paraquat, an ionic compound that is toxic to most plants but is rapidly broken down in the soil, is a notable example. Paraquat inhibits photosynthesis by accepting the electrons that otherwise would reduce carbon dioxide.

$CH_3—{}^{+}N$ ... $N^{+}—CH_3$ Cl^- Cl^-

Paraquat

Organic Herbicides

There are a number of methods for killing weeds other than using synthetic herbicides. The manual labor of hoeing and other cultivation practices such as mulching have been used for millennia. These practices are readily applied to small areas

Pesticides and Herbicides—Risks and Benefits

The EPA estimates that physicians diagnose 10,000–20,000 pesticide poisonings each year among agricultural workers. Many agricultural poisoning cases are never reported, and many other incidents affect people who have used pesticides in their home, lawn, or garden. The WHO estimates that pesticide poisonings kill some 300,000 agricultural workers yearly worldwide and adversely affect the health of 2 million to 5 million more. Many of the deaths are suicides caused by despair.

Pesticides are usually poisonous because their purpose is to kill—usually harmful insects. About 67 million pounds of pesticides are used each year on lawns in the United States, and lawns and gardens usually receive heavier pesticide applications per acre than agricultural land.

Do we really need to use pesticides? Insect pests cause billions of dollars of damage each year, and weeds can greatly reduce yields, but can we really justify adding so much toxic material to our environment to get rid of them? Consider the case of DDT, which was banned because it had done so much environmental damage. It was used to kill mosquitoes, but it also killed birds. It is true that DDT kills mosquitoes that spread malaria, but is malaria really a health problem today? Worldwide, the answer is yes. Worldwide, at least 100 million people have the disease, and each year it causes more than a million deaths, mostly among young children.

What about herbicides? Except for problems with dioxin contamination of 2,4,5-T, herbicides seem to have a better safety record than insecticides. Roadsides, vacant lots, and industrial areas have been kept free of weeds, and the value of agricultural crops has been increased by billions of dollars. People who suffer from allergies to ragweed, poison ivy, or other noxious weeds have been helped greatly by the use of herbicides. But we still don't know the ultimate effect on the environment of their long-term use.

▲ Many pesticides are used in homes against insect infestations and on gardens and lawns to prevent plant damage and to kill weeds. But less toxic alternatives are available. For example, diatomaceous earth is quite effective against snails and slugs.

such as lawns and gardens. There are also herbicides made from natural ingredients. The following are some examples.

- Oil of cloves (in which eugenol is the active ingredient) helps control young broadleaf weeds.
- Acetic acid, often combined with citric acid, helps kill young grasses. (Some preparations contain both oil of cloves and acetic acid, making them useful against a broad assortment of weeds.)
- Soap-based herbicides cause clogging of plants' *stomata*, the respiratory organs of the leaves.
- Gluten meal, a by-product of the wet-milling process for corn, acts as a pre-emergent herbicide by inhibiting the root formation of germinating plant seeds.

These types of organic herbicides do not work as rapidly or as well as synthetic herbicides. For instance, corn gluten meal often requires 4 years of repeated applications to achieve good weed control. And some organic herbicides are effective only at fairly high concentrations, making them quite expensive for widespread use.

Self-Assessment Questions

1. Agent Orange, a mixture of 2,4-D and 2,4,5-T used as a defoliant by the U.S. military during the Vietnam War, was harmful mainly due to
a. 2,4-D **b.** 2,4,5-T
c. dioxin impurity in 2,4-D **d.** dioxin impurity in 2,4,5-T

2. The herbicide atrazine acts by inhibiting
a. amino-acid synthesis **b.** cell division
c. lipid synthesis **d.** photosynthesis

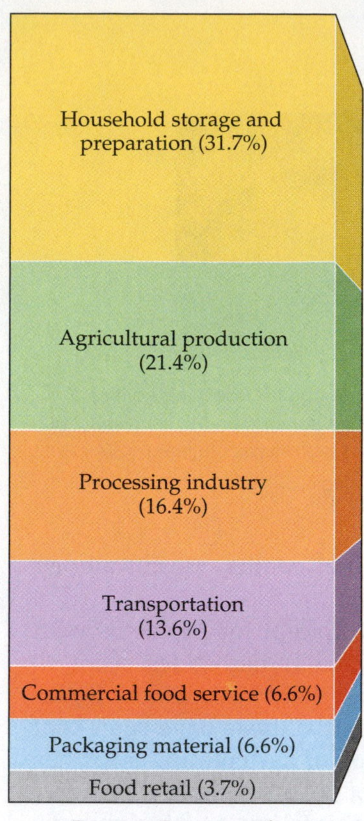

▲ **Figure 20.16** Energy usage in modern agriculture and food production. (Data from the University of Michigan Center for Sustainable Systems.)

3. Glyphosate can be used to kill grasses shortly before other plants are sown because
   a. it is not toxic to other plants
   b. it is metabolized by soil bacteria
   c. other plants are resistant to it
   d. it is a preemergent

Answers: 1, c; 2, d; 3, b

20.4 Sustainable Agriculture

Learning Objective › Describe sustainable agriculture and organic farming.

Agriculture changed dramatically in the twentieth century. Mechanization and increased use of pesticides, synthetic fertilizers, and fossil fuel energy led to vastly increased production. With reduced labor demands, fewer and fewer farmers could produce more and more food and fiber.

These changes also brought problems which have led to calls for alternatives to conventional farming. Most prominent among these alternatives is **sustainable agriculture**, which is the ability of a farm to produce food and fiber indefinitely, without causing irreparable damage to the ecosystem. Sustainable agriculture has three main goals: a healthy environment, farm profitability, and social and economic equity. Much of sustainable agriculture is similar to the practices that organic farmers and gardeners have followed for generations.

Modern agriculture is energy intensive. Nonrenewable petroleum energy is required for the production of fertilizers, pesticides, and farm machinery. Energy is also required to run the machinery needed to till, harvest, dry, and transport the crops, to process and package the food, and to preserve and prepare the food in consumers' households. A breakdown of the energy used in agriculture and food production is presented in Figure 20.16.

A 21-year Swiss study compared conventional plots that used synthetic fertilizers and synthetic pesticides to organic plots that were fertilized with manure and treated only occasionally with a copper fungicide. Crops of potatoes, winter wheat, grass clover, barley, and beets were grown under otherwise identical conditions. The organic method appeared to be more efficient, with yields only 20% less even though the nutrient input had been reduced by 50%. The organic method was said to use 20–56% less energy than the conventional approach, when the energy required for production of fertilizers and pesticides was taken into account.

Organic farming is carried out without the use of synthetic fertilizers or pesticides. As was mentioned earlier, organic farmers (and gardeners) use manure from farm animals for fertilizer, and they rotate other crops with legumes to restore nitrogen to the soil. They control insects by planting a variety of crops, alternating the use of fields. (A corn pest has a hard time surviving during the year that its home field is planted in soybeans.) Organic farming is also less energy intensive. According to a study by the Center for the Biology of Natural Systems at Washington University, comparable conventional farms used 2.3 times as much energy as organic farms. Production on organic farms was 10% lower, but costs were comparably lower. Organic farms require 12% more labor than conventional ones. Human labor is a renewable resource, though, whereas petroleum is not. Compared with conventional methods, organic farming uses less energy and leads to healthier soils.

In addition to organic practices, sustainable agriculture involves buying local products and using local services when possible, thus avoiding the cost of transportation while getting fresher food and strengthening the economy of the local community. Sustainable agriculture promotes independent farmers and ranchers producing good food and making a good living while protecting the environment.

Conventional agriculture can result in severe soil erosion and is the source of considerable water pollution. No doubt we should practice organic farming to the limit of our ability to do so. But we should not delude ourselves. Abrupt banning of synthetic fertilizers and pesticides would likely lead to a drastic drop in food production.

5. Are organic fruits and vegetables healthier for us?

Organically grown fruits and vegetables do not contain the pesticides and fertilizer residues found in foods grown by conventional methods, but they can contain natural toxins or contaminants such as *E. coli* from organic fertilizer. It is worth noting that most applied pesticides are concentrated on the surfaces of fruits or vegetables. Organic bananas, oranges, and grapefruit may be no better than the conventionally grown fruits because their peels are not eaten.

Transportation's share of food costs soared as fuel prices rose dramatically in 2008. Half the cost of broccoli in New York City may well be freight costs.

Nanoscience and Food Production

Nanoscience and nanotechnology involve the production and use of materials on a scale of nanometers—billionths of a meter. These materials have properties different from those exhibited by materials at a larger scale. Such nanoscale materials have the potential to revolutionize many aspects of food production in the future. Developments in nanoscience and nanotechnology may lead to applications such as the following.

- **Nanoparticle pesticides.** Industries are developing pesticides made up of nanoparticles. These pesticides are more readily taken up by plants. They can also be designed in time-release forms. Nanoparticle pesticides have the advantage that far less of the substance needs to be applied, reducing both cost and potential for environmental damage.
- **Nanoscale fertilizers.** Nanoscale application increases the efficacy of some fertilizer and micronutrient formulations. *Zeolites* are silicate minerals with nanosized pores. Incorporating fertilizers into zeolites with pores of various sizes can ensure slow and efficient release of the fertilizers.
- **Nanoparticle medications.** Researchers are feeding chickens bioactive polystyrene nanoparticles that bind with bacteria as a substitute for antibiotics. Others are adding nanoparticle vaccines to trout ponds to be taken up by fish.
- **Nanoscale security devices.** Nanosensors that can detect pathogens and contaminants are being developed. These sensors can detect pathogens in plants at an early stage, leading to prevention of crop diseases, and thus to healthier crops and improved food production. Scientists at Pacific Northwest National Laboratory, in Richland, Washington, have developed an electrochemical sensor that uses zirconium oxide (ZrO_2) nanoparticles for detection of organophosphate pesticides and nerve agents. Nanodevices that would allow tracking of individual shipments, leading to quicker detection of sources of contaminated foods, are also being investigated.

The same factors that enhance the usefulness of nano materials also increase the potential for harm. Some nanoparticles can be absorbed into cells and can move throughout the body and brain, where they may cause damage. Their small size may increase their potential toxicity.

Nanotechnology centers around the world are producing an impressive body of research. Scientists will build many new technologies for food production on this research. Economists estimate that the global market for nanotechnology could be $1 trillion within a decade. Nanotechnology offers enormous potential benefits to the economy and to society, but it also presents the possibility of risks that have not been fully evaluated.

As far as human energy is concerned, U.S. agriculture is enormously efficient. Each farmworker produces enough food for about 80 people. But this productivity is based on fossil fuels. About 10 units of petroleum energy are required to produce 1 unit of food energy. In terms of production per hectare, modern farming is marvelously efficient. But, in terms of the energy used in relation to the energy produced, it is remarkably inefficient. It should be noted, however, that in energy-efficient early agricultural societies, nearly all human energy went into food production. In modern societies, only about 10% of human energy is devoted to producing food. The other 90% is used to provide the materials and services that are so much a part of our civilization. We should try to make our food production more energy-efficient, but it is unlikely that we will want to return to an outmoded way of life.

Self-Assessment Questions

1. Farming that meets human needs without degrading the environment or depleting resources is called
   - **a.** corporate farming
   - **b.** industrial farming
   - **c.** local farming
   - **d.** sustainable agriculture
2. Organic farming differs from conventional agriculture in that organic farmers use no
   - **a.** animal manure
   - **b.** crop rotation
   - **c.** legumes
   - **d.** synthetic pesticides

Answers: 1, d; 2, d

20.5 Some Malthusian Mathematics

Learning Objective › Calculate the doubling time for a population using the rule of 72.

In 1830, Thomas Robert Malthus, an English clergyman and political economist, made the statement that population would increase faster than the food supply. Unless the birthrate was controlled, he said, poverty and war would have to serve as restrictions on the increase.

Malthus's prediction was based on simple mathematics: Population grows geometrically, while the food supply increases arithmetically. In **arithmetic growth**, a constant amount is added during each growth period. As an example, consider a child who starts to save money in a piggy bank. The first week, the child puts in 25¢. Each week thereafter, she adds 25¢. The growth of her savings is *arithmetic*, and it increases by a constant amount (25¢) each week. At the end of the first week, she will have 25¢; at the end of the second, 50¢; the third, 75¢; the fourth, $1.00; the fifth, $1.25; the sixth, $1.50; and so on.

In **geometric growth**, the increment increases in size for each growth period. Again, let's use a child's bank as an example. The first week she puts in 25¢. The second week she puts in another 25¢ to double the amount saved (to 50¢). The third week she puts in 50¢ to double this amount again. Each week she puts in an amount equal to what is already there and doubles the amount in the bank. At the end of the first week, she has 25¢; the second, 50¢; the third, $1.00; the fourth, $2.00; the fifth, $4.00; the sixth, $8.00; and so on. Before long, she will have to start robbing banks to keep up her geometrically growing deposits!

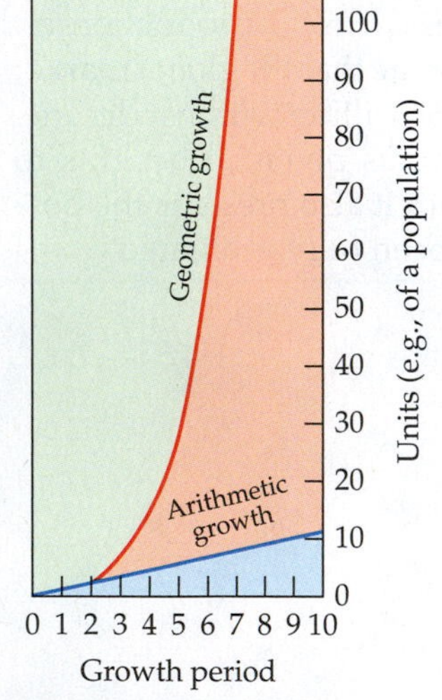

▲ **Figure 20.17** Arithmetic growth and geometric growth through ten periods, each starting with one unit.

Table 20.4 compares arithmetic and geometric growth through ten growth periods. These data are shown graphically in Figure 20.17. Note that arithmetic growth is slow and steady. Geometric growth starts slowly and then shoots up like a rocket.

For a population growing geometrically, we can calculate the **doubling time** using the **rule of 72**. Simply divide 72 by the percentage of annual growth. For example, Earth's population was 7.0 billion in 2011 and growing by 1.092% per year. If it continues to grow at this rate, it will double to 14 billion in 66 years.

Table 20.4 Arithmetic and Geometric Growth through Ten Periods[a]

	Growth Period										
	0	1	2	3	4	5	6	7	8	9	10
Arithmetic growth	1	2	3	4	5	6	7	8	9	10	11
Geometric growth	1	2	4	8	16	32	64	128	256	512	1024

[a]Starting with one unit.

Example 20.3 Population Growth

The population of the United States was 313 million in 2011 and was growing at a rate of 0.963% per year. If growth continues at the same rate, when will the population have doubled to 626 million?

Solution

We divide 72 by the annual growth rate.

$$\text{Doubling time} = \frac{72}{0.963/\text{yr}} = 75\ \text{yr}$$

If its growth continues at 0.963% per year, the U.S. population will double to 626 million people in 75 years, that is, by 2086. Many factors will affect the growth rate. It will change as the birthrate changes and as immigration laws and their enforcement change. An epidemic or other catastrophe might also change the death rate.

■ EXERCISE 20.3A

The population of Albania was estimated to be 3.00 million in 2011 and was growing at a rate of 0.267% per year. If growth continues at the same rate, when will the population have doubled to 6.00 million?

■ EXERCISE 20.3B

The population of Bulgaria was estimated to be 7.09 million in 2008 and was declining at a rate of 0.781% per year. If the decline continues at this rate, when will the population have been halved to 3.55 million?

The World Factbook, an annual publication of the U.S. Central Intelligence Agency, is available online and in most libraries. It offers population data, growth rates, and much more.

Earth's population has grown enormously since the time of Malthus, reaching 7 billion in 2011. Famine has brought suffering and death to millions in war-ravaged areas around the world (Figure 20.18), while modern farming often produces surpluses in developed countries. Even developing nations

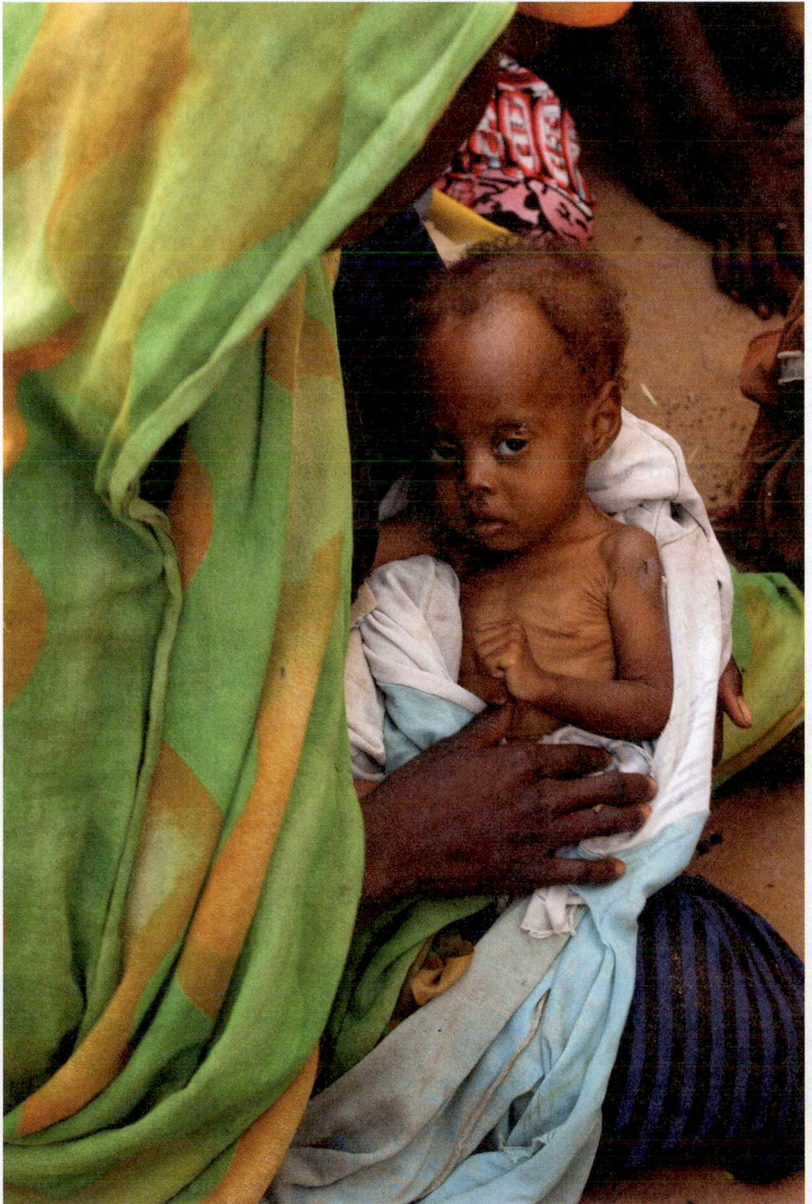

◀ **Figure 20.18** In developed countries, science has thwarted the Malthusian prediction of hunger. But starvation is still a fact of life for many people in developing countries. In 2008, according to the United Nations, more than 2 million people faced death from starvation and disease in the Darfur region of Sudan.

have made great progress in food production, with many of them becoming self-sufficient. Despite surpluses in some parts of the world, an estimated 800 million people are seriously malnourished. Half are children under five years old, who will carry the physical and mental scars of this deprivation for the rest of their lives.

Scientific developments, such as those outlined in this chapter, have brought abundance to many, but millions still go hungry.

Can We Feed a Hungry World?

The United Nations Population Division projects that Earth's population will reach 9 billion in 2045. Can we feed all those people?

An alliance between science and agriculture has increased food supplies beyond the imagination of people of a few generations ago. As a result of irrigation, synthetic fertilizers, pesticides, and improved genetic varieties of plants and animals, most people of the world have abundant food.

Food production can be further increased through genetic engineering (Section 16.8). Scientists are designing plants that produce more food, that are resistant to disease and insect pests, and that grow well in hostile environments. They can design animals that grow larger and produce more meat or milk. Such efforts may someday provide us with food in unimaginable abundance. But the hungry are with us now, and 75 million more people come to dinner each year. Further, many people oppose the genetic modification of food crops, which may hamper the use of this approach.

Even quadrupling current food production would meet our needs for only a few decades. Virtually all the world's available arable land is now under cultivation, and we lose farmland every day to housing, roads, erosion, encroaching deserts, and the increasing salt content of irrigated soils. Growing corn, soybeans, and other crops for the production of biofuels (Section 15.9) has already diverted land from food production and led to increased food prices. It will be difficult to keep food production ahead of the rate of population growth, particularly in developing countries. Fortunately, the rate of growth has slowed in many of these nations.

Despite a growing movement toward sustainable agriculture, we are still greatly dependent on a high-energy form of agriculture that uses synthetic fertilizers, pesticides, and herbicides and depends on machinery that burns fossil fuels. Ultimately, the only solution to the problem is to stabilize population. Obviously, that will come someday. The only questions are when and how. Population control could be accomplished through decreasing the birthrate, which is happening in almost all developed countries and in many developing ones. A few nations still have populations growing at explosive rates that far outstrip their food supplies. Birth control isn't the only way to limit population growth. Another possibility is an increase in the death rate—through catastrophic war, famine, pestilence, or the poisoning of the environment by the wastes of an ever-expanding population. The ghost of Thomas Malthus haunts us yet.

Use a Web browser to find a population clock. Several of these are accessible, including a world clock, a U.S. clock, and clocks for several other countries. Some clocks also show the decline of arable land.

Self-Assessment Questions

1. The rapid population growth that occurred in the late nineteenth and early twentieth centuries was due in large part to
   a. conservation of natural resources
   b. global peace
   c. use of scientific agricultural practices
   d. equitable distribution of wealth
2. Uganda's estimated population in 2009 was 32.7 million, and it is growing at a rate of 3.59% per year. If that growth rate continues, the population will have doubled in about
   a. 10 yr b. 20 yr c. 40 yr d. 80 yr

Answers: 1, c; 2, b

CRITICAL THINKING  EXERCISES

Apply knowledge that you have gained in this chapter and one or more of the FLaReS principles (Chapter 1) to evaluate the following statements or claims.

20.1 An advertisement claims that a certain cereal made from organically grown grains provides a "life energy" that cannot be obtained from ordinary processed cereals.

20.2 An advertisement implies that rotenone is safer than synthetic pesticides because it is obtained from natural sources.

20.3 A newspaper claims that certain genetically modified crops may become weeds if not properly controlled.

20.4 Many people claim that vegetables grown in backyard gardens are more nutritious than those grown on commercial farms.

20.5 A Web site states that nitrate ions from synthetic fertilizers such as ammonium nitrate are less effective as plant nutrients than nitrate ions from the breakdown of organic fertilizers by soil bacteria, and thus nonorganic foods are less nutritious.

20.6 A newspaper article suggests, "Try out tobacco 'sun tea' as a nontoxic pesticide." In the article is this claim: "This special tea can help you eliminate most garden pests without any unwanted toxicity."

SUMMARY

Section 20.1—The three **primary plant nutrients** are nitrogen, phosphorus, and potassium. Atmospheric nitrogen is fixed naturally by soil bacteria and by lightning. Artificial fixation of nitrogen produces ammonia and nitrates that can be added to the soil. Phosphorus can be made available by treating phosphate rock. Potassium, as potassium chloride, is usually mined. The **secondary plant nutrients** are calcium, magnesium, and sulfur. Eight other **micronutrients** are needed in small amounts. The three numbers on commercial fertilizers indicate the percentages of N, percentages of P_2O_5, and percentages of K_2O in the fertilizer. Organic fertilizers include composted manure and sewage sludge.

Section 20.2—Pests can cause plagues and ruin food supplies. **Pesticides** are used to kill organisms that we consider pests, including many insects. Most **insecticides** kill all insects they come in contact with, not just the harmful ones. The insecticide DDT saved millions of lives during and after World War II, yet its persistence in the environment caused problems. The fat-soluble chlorinated hydrocarbon became concentrated at higher levels of the food chain and led to birds producing easily broken eggshells. Widely banned, DDT continues to be used in some developing countries for malaria control. Organic phosphorus compounds are nerve poisons. Although they accumulate in fatty tissues, they are less persistent in the environment than chlorinated compounds like DDT. Carbamates are mostly narrow-spectrum insecticides, harmful to just a few insect pests. They neither accumulate in fatty tissue nor persist in the environment. Organic pesticides include pyrethrins, rotenone, boric acid, and diatomaceous earth. Some pests can be controlled biologically, using praying mantises, ladybugs, and pest-specific bacteria and viruses. Some insects can be controlled by SIT, or sterilization and release of males. A **pheromone** is a chemical secreted by an insect to mark a trail, send an alarm, or, in the case of a **sex attractant**, attract a mate. **Juvenile hormones** can be used to keep insect pests in an immature stage, in which they cannot reproduce. Pheromones and juvenile hormones have proved useful to some extent in monitoring and control of insect pests but are difficult to produce and expensive to use.

Section 20.3—**Herbicides** kill weeds and **defoliants** cause leaves to fall off plants. The herbicide 2,4-D and the defoliant 2,4,5-T were combined in **Agent Orange**, used to remove ground cover in Vietnam. Highly toxic **dioxins** that were contaminants in this mixture caused birth defects, resulting in a ban on 2,4,5-T. Atrazine and glyphosate are the most widely used herbicides in the United States. Paraquat is a **preemergent herbicide** that kills weed plants before crop seedlings emerge. Organic herbicides include oil of cloves, acetic acid, and gluten meal.

Section 20.4—Sustainable agriculture is the ability of a farm to produce food and fiber indefinitely, without causing irreparable damage to the ecosystem. **Organic farming** avoids the use of synthetic fertilizers and pesticides. It is less energy intensive and less productive than conventional farming but costs less and uses renewable resources.

Section 20.5—According to Malthus, food production shows a steady increase called **arithmetic growth**. Because population increase occurs as **geometric growth**, with the rate of increase itself increasing, food production cannot keep up with population. The **doubling time** can be calculated with the **rule of 72**; the doubling time equals 72 divided by the percentage of annual growth. Additional scientific and technical advances may help increase food production or control population in years to come, but Malthus's prediction still hangs over us.

Green chemistry Applying green chemistry principles to the design of new pesticides, scientists have been able to create effective pest-control products that target only the pest and not the surroundings or beneficial organisms. These new pesticides are produced with more benign reagents and processes that require less energy. Some have been designed so that they biodegrade, leaving behind no harmful residues.

Learning Objectives

› List the three primary plant nutrients as well as several secondary nutrients and micronutrients, and describe the function of each.	Problems 7–14
› Differentiate between organic fertilizers and conventional fertilizers.	Problems 10, 12, 33, 34
› Name and describe the action of the main kinds of pesticides.	Problems 15–22
› List several biological pest controls, and explain how they work.	Problems 19–21, 37, 38
› Name and describe the action of the major herbicides and defoliants.	Problems 3, 22, 34, 40, 42
› Describe sustainable agriculture and organic farming.	Problems 2, 4, 33, 34
› Calculate the doubling time for a population using the rule of 72.	Problems 25–30, 39
› Identify the benefits of pesticides to humans and the challenges in their use.	Problems 45, 46
› Give examples of pesticides that have been designed to reduce the hazards to humans and the environment.	Problem 47

REVIEW QUESTIONS

1. Where does most of the matter of a growing plant come from?
2. List the three main goals of sustainable agriculture.
3. What is a preemergent herbicide?
4. Compare organic farming with conventional farming. Consider energy requirements, labor, profitability, and crop yields.
5. What did Thomas Malthus predict in his famous 1830 statement?
6. Why has Malthus's prediction not come true?

PROBLEMS

Fertilizers

7. List the three structural elements of plants.
8. What is the role of nitrogen in plant nutrition?
9. List several ways that nitrogen can be fixed.
10. How is ammonia made?
11. What is anhydrous ammonia? How is it used?
12. What is urea? From what components is synthetic urea made?
13. What is the source of phosphate fertilizers? What is the role of phosphorus in plant nutrition?
14. Why does soil become acidic when potassium ions are absorbed by plants?

Pesticides

15. List the advantages and disadvantages of DDT as an insecticide.
16. Why is DDT especially harmful to birds?
17. Describe how chlorinated hydrocarbons become concentrated in a food chain.
18. Define and give an example of **(a)** a narrow-spectrum insecticide and **(b)** a broad-spectrum insecticide.
19. How are pheromones used in insect control?
20. How are juvenile hormones used against insect pests?
21. Describe SIT as a method for controlling insects. Why is it not more widely used?
22. Define and give an example of **(a)** a herbicide and **(b)** a defoliant.

Toxicity

23. How much DDT would it take to kill a person weighing 70 kg if the lethal dose is 0.50 g per kilogram of body weight?
24. How much parathion should it take to kill the person in Problem 23 if the lethal dose is 5 mg per kilogram of body weight?

Growth

25. What is arithmetic growth? Give an example.
26. What is geometric growth? Give an example.
27. You start a savings account, planning to add \$50 each month. How many months will it take you to save \$1000? Do your savings grow arithmetically or geometrically?
28. You are raising rabbits. Starting with two, you have four at the end of 2 months, eight at the end of 4 months, and so on. The rabbit population doubles every 2 months. How many rabbits will you have at the end of 24 months? Is the rabbit population growing arithmetically or geometrically?

29. The population of India was estimated to be 1.19 billion in 2010 and was growing at the value of 1.344% a year. At this rate, how many years will it take for the population to double to 2.38 billion? What factors are likely to change this rate of growth?

30. The population of China was estimated to be 1.34 billion in 2011 and was growing at an annual rate of 0.493%. At this rate, how many years will it take for the population to double to 2.68 billion? What factors are likely to change this rate of growth?

ADDITIONAL PROBLEMS

31. Give the overall chemical equation for photosynthesis.

32. Give the chemical equation for the synthesis of ammonia.

33. Indicate whether each of the following pesticides is organic (a) in the chemical sense only, (b) in the sense used in organic farming only, (c) in both senses, or (d) in no way at all.
   1. boric acid
   2. diatomaceous earth
   3. lead arsenate
   4. malathion
   5. rotenone

34. Indicate whether each of the following herbicides is organic (a) in the chemical sense only, (b) in the sense used in organic farming only, (c) in both senses, or (d) in no way at all.
   1. acetic acid
   2. atrazine
   3. 2,4-D
   4. gluten meal
   5. glyphosate

35. The compound ammonium monohydrogen phosphate is frequently used as a fertilizer. **(a)** What two plant nutrients does it supply? **(b)** Write the equation for the formation of this compound from ammonia and an appropriate acid.

36. The micronutrient copper is often applied in the form of copper(II) sulfate. Write the equation for the formation of copper sulfate(II) from copper(II) oxide and an appropriate acid.

37. Referring to Section 20.2, identify the functional group(s) in **(a)** the sex attractant for the codling moth, **(b)** the juvenile hormone molecule, and **(c)** the methoprene molecule.

38. The pheromones that act as recognition signals for both the queen honeybee and the worker bees are hydroxycarboxylic acids with the molecular formula $C_{10}H_{18}$ and a double bond between the second and third carbon atoms. These acids differ only in the position of the —OH group, which is on the ninth carbon of the queen bee molecule and on the tenth carbon of the worker bee molecule. Draw structural formulas for the two molecules.

39. Suppose you are given a penny on January 1 and that amount is doubled on every subsequent day of the 31-day month. That is, you get 1¢ on the first day, 2¢ on the second day, 4¢ on the third, 8¢ on the fourth day, and so on. How much money do you receive on January 31?

40. Oil of cloves, used as an organic herbicide, has eugenol as its principal active component. Name the functional groups in the eugenol molecule.

CH_3O

HO

Eugenol

41. Potassium bicarbonate, usually combined with horticultural oil (a highly refined petroleum product), is often sold as an organic pesticide. Potassium bicarbonate is made by reacting potassium carbonate with carbon dioxide and water. The potassium carbonate is produced by electrolysis of potassium chloride to form potassium hydroxide. The potassium hydroxide is then treated with carbon dioxide to form potassium carbonate. Write equations for the three reactions. Is potassium carbonate organic? Explain.

42. The herbicide dicamba (Banvel®), widely used to control broadleaf weeds, has the systematic name 2-methoxy-3,6-dichlorobenzoic acid. The methoxy group is $—OCH_3$. Draw the structure of dicamba.

43. The population of Zimbabwe, which is growing faster than that of any other country in the world, was estimated to be 12.1 million in 2011 and increasing at an annual rate of 4.31%. At this rate, how many years will it take for the population to double to 24.2 million? What factors are likely to change this rate of growth?

44. How much urea, in kilograms, can be made from 88.4 kg of ammonia, assuming excess CO_2? The equation is

$$2\,NH_3 + CO_2 \longrightarrow CO(NH_2)_2 + H_2O$$

45. Which two of the following are benefits of using pesticides on food crops?
   a. increased yield of food production
   b. reduced crop failure
   c. identification of new pests
   d. improved taste of foods

46. Give two potential drawbacks of using pesticides on food crops.

47. What are some potential benefits of applying green chemistry principles during the design of pesticides?
   a. safer, less toxic pesticides that are more selective for the pest organism and are harmless to other organisms
   b. pesticides that biodegrade after their useful lifetime and leave behind no toxic residues
   c. reductions in waste, energy use, and exposure to harmful reagents during the synthesis of pesticides
   d. all of the above

 COLLABORATIVE GROUP PROJECTS

Prepare a PowerPoint, poster, or other presentation (as directed by your instructor) to share with the class.

1. Prepare a brief report on one of the insecticides listed in Table 20.3. List its principal advantages and disadvantages.
2. Prepare a brief report on one of the following alternative methods of insect control. List its principal advantages and disadvantages.
   a. Bt
   b. a viral agent
   c. SIT
   d. sex attractants
   e. a juvenile hormone
3. Examine the label on a bag of fertilizer. What is its composition?
4. Examine the label on a package of yard or garden pesticide. List its trade name and active ingredients.
5. Prepare a brief report on one of the following scientists.
   a. Fritz Haber
   b. F. G. Hopkins
   c. Justus von Liebig
   d. Ellen Swallow Richards
6. Look for several Web sites with different viewpoints on the use of fertilizers and pesticides. Defend one side of an issue involving the use of these substances.
7. Use data from Problems 29 and 30 to predict when the population of India will be greater than that of China.
8. Look for several Web sites with different perspectives on factory farms, also called *confined animal feeding operations (CAFOs)*. Choose one perspective and defend it.

Household Chemicals

Have You Ever Wondered?

1. Is there a benefit to using homemade soap?
2. Why can't hand dishwashing liquid be used in a dishwasher?
3. Does putting more fabric softener in the washer make fabrics even softer?
4. What is the difference between paint and lacquer?
5. Is thick shampoo better for my hair?
6. Can I make my own household cleaners instead of buying them?

Learning Objectives

- Describe the structure of soap, and explain how it is made and how it works to remove greasy dirt. (21.1)
- Explain the reasons for the advantages and disadvantages of soap. (21.1)
- List the advantages and disadvantages of synthetic detergents. (21.2)
- Classify surfactants as amphoteric, anionic, cationic, and nonionic, and describe how they are used in various detergent formulations. (21.2)
- Identify a fabric softener from its structure, and describe its action. (21.3)
- Name two types of laundry bleaches, and describe how they work. (21.3)
- List the major ingredient(s) (and their purposes) of some all-purpose cleaning products and some special-purpose cleaning products. (21.4)
- Identify compounds used in solvents and paints, and explain their purposes. (21.5)
- Identify waxes by their structure. (21.5)
- Identify the principal ingredients in various cosmetic products. (21.6)
- Describe the chemical nature of skin, hair, and teeth. (21.6)
- Use green chemistry principles to help select greener household products.

Helps and Hazards

If someone offered you a job in a place where poisonous chemicals were used every day, where toxic vapors and harmful dusts and molds were common, where corrosive acids and alkalis were often used, and where highly flammable liquids and vapors posed a fire hazard, would you take the job? You probably have, many times. This is a description of a typical American home.

People tend to be careful in a chemistry laboratory because they know it can be dangerous there. They often are much less cautious in their homes, even though some of the chemicals on the shelves can be just as toxic and hazardous as those in a laboratory—and many are exactly the same substances. There are perhaps a half million chemical products available for use in the American home. They include waxes, wax removers, paints,

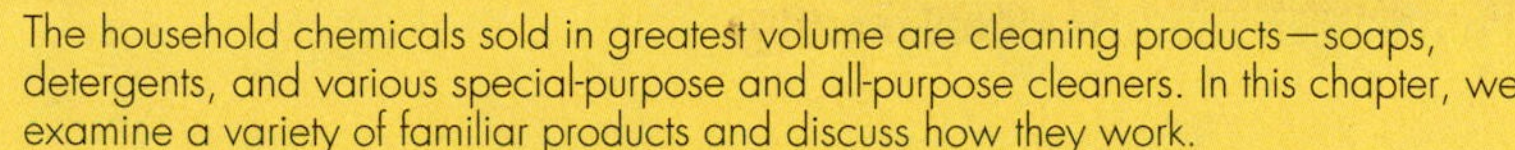
The household chemicals sold in greatest volume are cleaning products—soaps, detergents, and various special-purpose and all-purpose cleaners. In this chapter, we examine a variety of familiar products and discuss how they work.

According to the Chemical Abstracts Service (CAS) of the American Chemical Society, there are nearly 50,000,000 commercially available chemicals. A typical U.S. supermarket offers perhaps 40,000 different consumer products. An online superstore may offer a million or more.

paint removers, bleaches, insecticides, rodenticides, spot removers, solvents, disinfectants, detergents, toothpastes, shampoos, perfumes, lotions, shaving creams, deodorants, hair sprays, and many others (Figure 21.1). Some of these products are quite harmless, but others contain corrosive or toxic chemicals or present fire hazards. Some cause environmental problems when they are used or discarded.

Extensive use of chemicals in the home has resulted in many accidents. Studies show that chemicals are often used without regard to the directions or precautions given on their labels. Frequently the labels aren't read at all, and *misuse* of household chemicals can sometimes end in tragedy.

We discussed the chemical composition of food and the chemicals that are used in producing it in Chapter 17. Some agricultural chemicals are also used around the home, especially in the yard and garden. We discussed the polymers used in our clothing and home furnishings in Chapter 10 and the fuels burned in our furnaces and automobiles in Chapter 15. We discussed the chemistry of our bodies in Chapter 16. But there are many other chemicals around the house—cleaning products, personal care supplies, and an assortment of other things. In this chapter, we look at some household chemicals. Let's begin with cleaning agents, which make up the largest volume of household chemicals.

▲ **Figure 21.1** A modern home is stocked with a variety of chemical products.

21.1 Cleaning with Soap

Learning Objectives › Describe the structure of soap, and explain how it is made and how it works to remove greasy dirt. › Explain the reasons for the advantages and disadvantages of soap.

Personal Cleanliness

The history of the cleanliness of the body and clothing is rather spotty. The Romans, with their great public baths, probably did not use any sort of soap. They covered their bodies with oil, worked up a sweat in a steam bath, and then wiped off the oil. A dip in a pool of fresh water completed the "cleansing."

During the Middle Ages, bodily cleanliness was prized in some cultures, but not in others. For example, twelfth-century Paris, with a population of about 100,000, had many public bathhouses. In contrast, the Renaissance, a revival of learning and art that lasted from the fourteenth to the seventeenth centuries, was not noted for cleanliness. Queen Elizabeth I of England (1533–1603) bathed once a month, a habit that caused many to think her overly fastidious. A common remedy for unpleasant body odor back then was the liberal use of perfume.

And today? Perhaps we have gone too far in the other direction. With soap, detergent, body wash, shampoo, conditioner, deodorant, antiperspirant, aftershave, cologne, and perfume, we may add more during and after a shower than we remove in the shower.

▲ Queen Isabella of Castile (1451–1504), who supported the 1492 voyage of Columbus to the New World, is reported to have bathed only twice in her life.

In developing societies, clothes were cleaned by beating them with rocks in the nearest stream. Sometimes plants, such as the soapworts of Europe or the soapberries of tropical America, were used as cleansing agents. The leaves of soapworts and soapberries contain *saponins*, chemical compounds that produce a soapy lather. These saponins may have been the first detergents.

Ashes of plants contain potassium carbonate (K_2CO_3) and sodium carbonate (Na_2CO_3). The carbonate ion present in both these compounds reacts with water to form an alkaline solution that has detergent properties. These alkaline plant ashes were used as cleansing agents by the Babylonians at least 4000 years ago. Europeans used plant ashes to wash their clothes as recently as 100 years ago. Sodium carbonate is still sold today as washing soda.

Fat + Lye → Soap

The first written record of soap is found in the writings of Pliny the Elder (C.E. 23–79), a Roman scholar who described the Phoenicians' synthesis of soap using goat tallow and ashes. By the second century C.E., sodium carbonate (produced by the evaporation of alkaline water) was heated with lime (from limestone or seashells) to produce sodium hydroxide (lye).

$$Na_2CO_3 + Ca(OH)_2 \longrightarrow 2\,NaOH + CaCO_3$$

The sodium hydroxide was heated with animal fats or vegetable oils to produce soap (Figure 21.2). Note that a **soap** is a salt of a long-chain carboxylic acid (Chapter 9). An example is sodium myristate (sodium tetradecanoate), $CH_3CH_2CH_2CH_2CH_2CH_2CH_2CH_2CH_2CH_2CH_2CH_2CH_2COO^- Na^+$. To save space, the CH_2 groups can be lumped together within parentheses to give a shorter formula, $CH_3(CH_2)_{12}COO^- Na^+$.

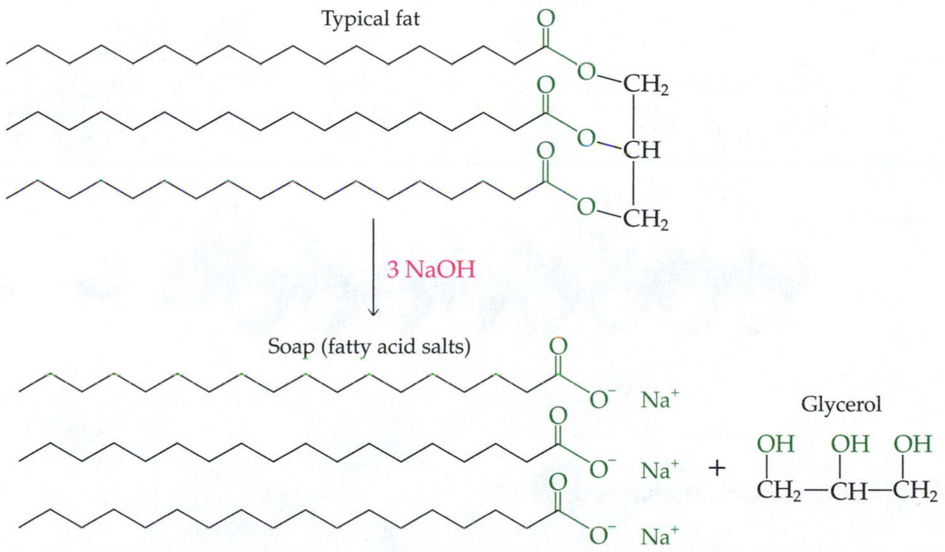

Typical fat

3 NaOH

Soap (fatty acid salts)

Glycerol

◀ **Figure 21.2** Soap can be made by reacting animal fat or vegetable oil with sodium hydroxide. Vegetable oils, with unsaturated carbon chains, generally produce softer soaps. Coconut oil, with shorter carbon chains, yields soap that is more soluble in water.

Q: *Write the structure of triolein, the oil in which all three fatty acid residues are from oleic acid.*

Although soap has been known for hundreds of years, it was first used mainly as a medicine. The discovery of disease-causing microorganisms increased interest in cleanliness and improved public health practices during the eighteenth century. By the middle of the nineteenth century, soap was in common use.

American pioneers made soap in a process similar to that used by ancient people. Lye, or potash, was added to animal fat in a huge iron kettle, and the mixture was cooked over a wood fire for several hours. The soap rose to the surface and, on cooling, solidified. The glycerol remained as a liquid on the bottom of the pot. Both the glycerol and the soap often contained unreacted alkali, which eroded the skin. The harshness of Grandma's lye soap is not just a myth.

In modern commercial soapmaking, fats and oils are often hydrolyzed to fatty acids and glycerol with superheated steam. The fatty acids are then neutralized to make soap. Hand soaps usually contain additives such as dyes, perfumes, creams, and oils. Scouring soaps contain abrasives such as silica and pumice. Some soaps have air blown in before they solidify to lower their density so that they float.

Early settlers did not have lye (sodium hydroxide) for soapmaking. Instead, they filled a large pot with wood ashes and allowed water to trickle down through the ashes, dissolving the basic compounds in the ash. These compounds were mostly potassium carbonate and potassium hydroxide. Using a pot of ashes gave rise to the term *potash* for these compounds.

1. Is there a benefit to using homemade soap? Soapmaking is a popular hobby, and it is not difficult to make many kinds of soap at home. There is some benefit to homemade soap, because it contains only the ingredients you wish to add. Allergies to perfumes and other additives can be avoided. However, it is probably easier to find a commercial soap that "works" for you.

Some bath bars contain synthetic detergents. Their action is similar to that of soap, and consumers seldom make a distinction between soap and synthetic detergents.

Potassium soaps are softer than sodium soaps and produce a finer lather. They are used alone, or in combination with sodium soaps, in liquid soaps and shaving creams. However, most liquids for hand cleaning contain synthetic detergents. Soaps can also be made by reacting fatty acids with triethanolamine. These substances are used in shampoos and other cosmetics.

How Soap Works

Dirt and grime usually adhere to skin, clothing, and other surfaces because they are combined with greases and oils—body oils, cooking fats, lubricating greases, and other similar substances—that act a little like sticky glues. Because oils are not miscible with water, washing with water alone does little good.

Soap is not really composed of molecules. Soap is ionic. However, it is convenient to refer to the pair of ions as a "soap molecule."

A soap molecule has a dual nature. One end is ionic and therefore polar and **hydrophilic** (water attracting). The rest of the molecule is a hydrocarbon chain and therefore nonpolar and **hydrophobic** (water repelling). Figure 21.3 shows a typical soap. The hydrophilic "head" dissolves in water, while the hydrophobic "tail" dissolves in nonpolar substances, such as oils.

(a) $CH_3CH_2CH_2CH_2CH_2CH_2CH_2CH_2CH_2CH_2CH_2CH_2CH_2CH_2CH_2COO^- Na^+$

Hydrocarbon tail Ionic head

(b) O, O^- Na^+

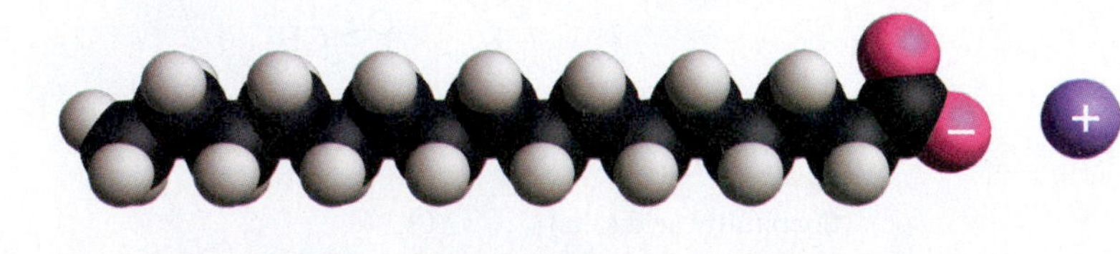

(c)

(d)

▶ **Figure 21.3** Representations of sodium palmitate, a soap. (a) Condensed formula. (b) Structural formula. (c) Space-filling model. (d) Schematic representation of the palmitate anion.

The cleansing action of soap is illustrated in Figure 21.4. A spherical collection of molecules like that shown in the figure is called a **micelle**. The hydrocarbon tails stick in the oil, with their ionic heads remaining in the aqueous phase. The formation of micelles breaks the oil into tiny droplets and disperses them throughout the solution. The droplets don't coalesce because of the repulsion of the charged groups (the carboxyl anions) on their surfaces. The oil and water form an *emulsion*, with soap acting as the *emulsifying agent*. Because the oil no longer is "gluing" it to the surface, the dirt can be removed easily. Any agent, including soap, that stabilizes the suspension of nonpolar substances—such as oil and grease—in water is called a **surface-active agent** (or **surfactant**). If not mixed into the water, soap tends to act at the liquid surface. The ionic heads interact with the water, while the hydrocarbon tails stick up out of the water.

When we mix oil and vinegar to make mayonnaise, we need an emulsifying agent. Because soaps are not noted for their flavor, we use instead the proteins found in an egg yolk.

Disadvantage and Advantages of Soap

A major disadvantage of soap is that it doesn't work well in hard water. Hard water contains calcium, magnesium, and iron ions. Soap anions react with these

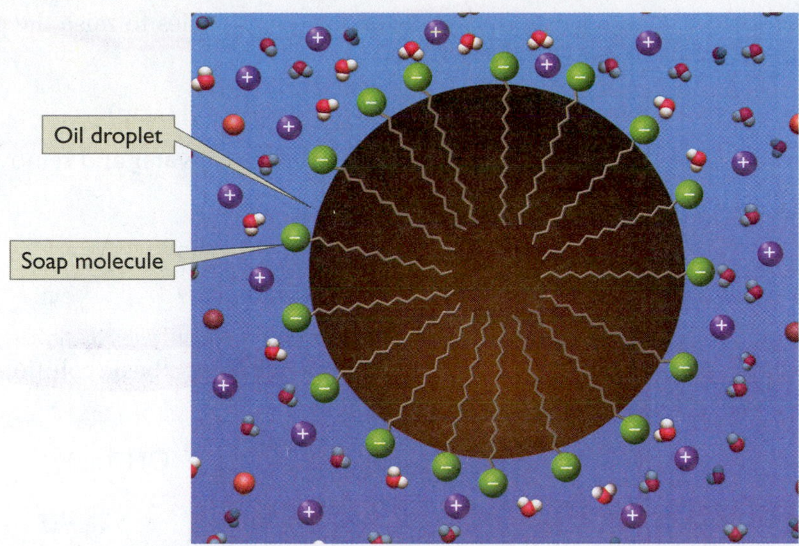

◀ **Figure 21.4** The cleaning action of soap is visualized in this diagram of a soap micelle. A tiny oil droplet is suspended in water because the hydrophobic hydrocarbon tails of soap molecules are immersed in the oil, while their hydrophilic ionic heads extend into the water. Attraction between the water and the ionic ends of the soap molecules carries the oil droplet into the water.

metal ions to form greasy, insoluble curds (Figure 21.5). With calcium ions, the reaction is

$$2\ CH_3CH_2CH_2CH_2CH_2CH_2CH_2CH_2CH_2CH_2CH_2CH_2CH_2CH_2CH_2CH_2COO^-\ Na^+(aq) + Ca^{2+}(aq) \longrightarrow$$
A sodium soap (soluble)

$$(CH_3CH_2CH_2CH_2CH_2CH_2CH_2CH_2CH_2CH_2CH_2CH_2CH_2CH_2CH_2CH_2COO^-)_2Ca^{2+}(s) + 2\ Na^+(aq)$$
A calcium soap (insoluble)

These deposits make up the familiar ring around the bathtub. They leave freshly washed hair sticky and are responsible for the "tattletale gray" of laundry. For cleaning clothes and for many other purposes, soap has been largely replaced by synthetic detergents.

Soap does have some advantages. It is an excellent cleanser in soft water, it is relatively nontoxic, it is derived from renewable resources (animal fats and vegetable oils), and it is biodegradable.

◀ **Figure 21.5** Sudsing quality of hard water versus soft water. *From left*: Detergent in hard water, soap in hard water, detergent in soft water, and soap in soft water. Note that the sudsing of the detergent is about the same in both hard and soft water. Note also that there is little sudsing and that insoluble material is formed when soap is used in hard water.

Q: *In acidic solutions, soaps are converted to free fatty acids, which not only have no detergent action but are insoluble in water and separate as a greasy scum. Write the equation for this reaction, using sodium stearate as the soap.*

Water Softeners

To aid the action of soaps, various water-softening agents and devices are used. Water softeners are used to remove ions of calcium, magnesium, and iron, the ions that make water hard. An effective water softener is washing soda, sodium carbonate

A substance that produces hydroxide ions in water is a base (Chapter 7). Carbonate and phosphate ions are bases because they react with water to form hydroxide ions. Bases are also defined as proton acceptors, and carbonate and phosphate ions accept protons from water molecules.

($Na_2CO_3 \cdot 10H_2O$). Carbonate ions react with water molecules to raise the pH and thus prevent the precipitation of fatty acids.

$$CO_3^{2-}(aq) + H_2O(l) \longrightarrow HCO_3^{-}(aq) + OH^{-}(aq)$$

The carbonate ions also react with the ions that cause hard water and remove them as insoluble salts.

$$Mg^{2+}(aq) + CO_3^{2-}(aq) \longrightarrow MgCO_3(s)$$
$$Ca^{2+}(aq) + CO_3^{2-}(aq) \longrightarrow CaCO_3(s)$$

Sodium phosphate (Na_3PO_4, commonly called *trisodium phosphate*, or *TSP*) is another water-softening agent. Like washing soda, it makes a basic solution in water and precipitates calcium and magnesium ions.

$$PO_4^{3-}(aq) + H_2O(l) \longrightarrow HPO_4^{2-}(aq) + OH^{-}(aq)$$
$$2\,PO_4^{3-}(aq) + 3\,Mg^{2+}(aq) \longrightarrow Mg_3(PO_4)_2(s)$$

Phosphates seem to aid in the cleaning process in some other way that is not yet well understood.

Water-softening tanks are widely used in homes and businesses. These tanks contain an insoluble polymeric resin that attracts and holds calcium, magnesium, and iron ions to its surface, replacing them with sodium ions and thus softening the water (Figure 21.6). After a period of use, the resin becomes saturated with hard-water ions and must be regenerated by adding salt (NaCl) to replace its sodium ions. (Water filters such as Brita® that attach to a faucet usually contain activated carbon, which absorbs dissolved organic substances that give water an off taste; most do not remove hard-water ions.)

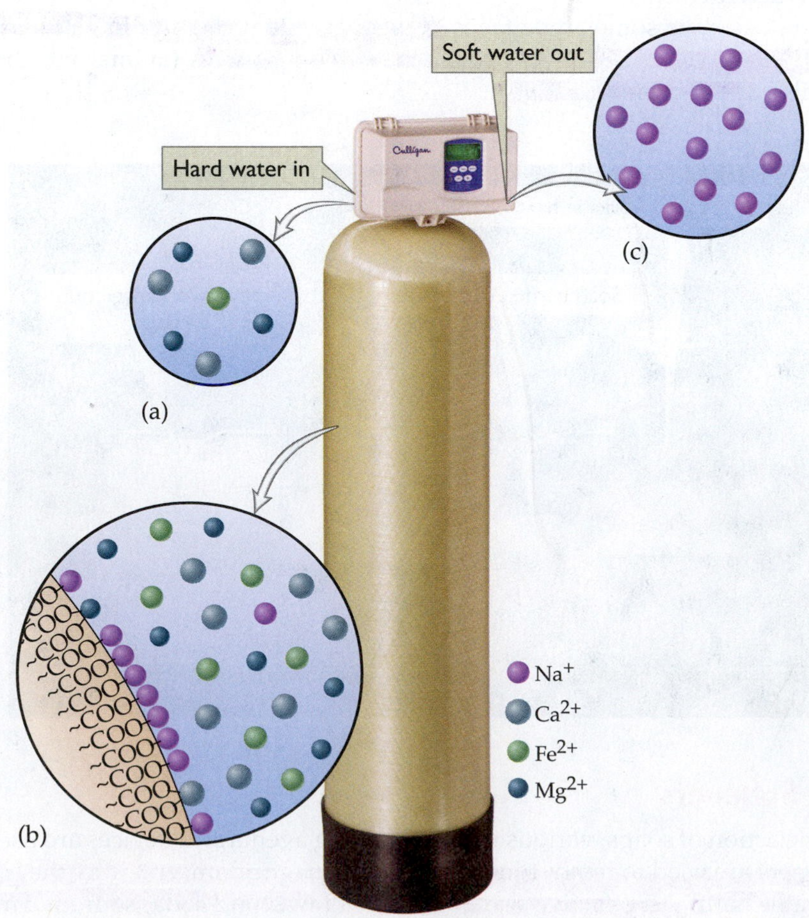

▶ **Figure 21.6** Water softeners work by *ion exchange*. Hard water going into the softener contains doubly charged cations—Ca^{2+}, Mg^{2+}, and Fe^{2+}. Those ions attach to the ion-exchange resin, and Na^+ (violet) ions are released. The water leaving the softener contains mostly Na^+ ions.

Q: *If one mole each of Ca^{2+}, Mg^{2+}, and Fe^{2+} is present in hard water, how many moles of Na^+ will be released from the ion-exchange resin?*

Self-Assessment Questions

1. Saponins are
   a. micelles
   b. plant materials that produce lather in water
   c. synthetic detergents
   d. water softeners
2. Which of the following is a soap formula?
   a. $CH_3(CH_2)_{12}CH_2OH$
   b. $CH_3(CH_2)_{12}COOH$
   c. $CH_3(CH_2)_{14}COONa$
   d. $CH_3(CH_2)_{10}SO_3Na$
3. Reaction of tripalmitin, a fat containing three palmitic acid parts, with NaOH gives glycerol plus three molecules of
   a. $CH_3(CH_2)_{14}CH_2OH$
   b. $CH_3(CH_2)_{14}COOH$
   c. $CH_3(CH_2)_{14}COONa$
   d. $CH_3(CH_2)_{14}COOCH_3$
4. The formula for sodium stearate is
   a. $CH_3(CH_2)_{12}COONa$
   b. $CH_3(CH_2)_{14}COONa$
   c. $CH_3(CH_2)_{16}COONa$
   d. $CH_3(CH_2)_7CH{=}CH(CH_2)_7COONa$
5. The hydrocarbon portion of a soap molecule is
   a. hydrophilic
   b. hydrophobic
   c. ionic
   d. polar covalent
6. Soap removes oily dirt by forming
   a. an acidic solution
   b. curds
   c. fat globules
   d. micelles
7. In the cleansing action of soap, the hydrocarbon tail
   a. intermingles with the oily dirt, while the ionic head interacts with the water
   b. intermingles with the water, while the ionic head interacts with the oily dirt
   c. remains inert and takes no part in the process
   d. separates from the ionic head and dissolves in the oily dirt
8. Which of the following ions does not contribute to making water hard?
   a. Ca^{2+}
   b. Fe^{2+}
   c. Mg^{2+}
   d. Na^+
9. In hard water, metal ions combine with soap anions, and the soap
   a. cleans about as well as in soft water
   b. dissolves but doesn't clean
   c. forms suds but doesn't clean
   d. precipitates and doesn't clean

Answers: 1, b; 2, c; 3, c; 4, c; 5, b; 6, d; 7, a; 8, d; 9, d

21.2 Synthetic Detergents

Learning Objectives › List the advantages and disadvantages of synthetic detergents. › Classify surfactants as amphoteric, anionic, cationic, and nonionic, and describe how they are used in various detergent formulations.

A technological approach to the problems associated with soap was the development of new synthetic detergents. Molecules of synthetic detergents are enough like those of soap to have the same cleaning action but different enough to resist the effects of acids and hard water. The raw materials for soap manufacture were scarce and expensive during and immediately after World War II. The synthetic detergent industry developed rapidly in the postwar period.

ABS Detergents: Nonbiodegradable

Within a few years of the war's end, cheap synthetic detergents, made from petroleum products, were widely available. Alkylbenzenesulfonate (ABS) detergents were made from propylene ($CH_2{=}CHCH_3$), benzene (C_6H_6), and sulfuric acid

(H_2SO_4). The resulting sulfonic acid (RSO_3H) was neutralized with a base, usually sodium carbonate, to yield the final product.

$-SO_3^- Na^+$

Sales of ABS detergents soared. For a decade or more, nearly everyone was happy, but suds began to accumulate in sewage treatment plants. Foam piled high in rivers, and, in some areas, a head of foam even appeared on drinking water (Figure 21.7). The branched-chain structure of ABS molecules was not readily broken down by the microorganisms in sewage treatment plants, and the groundwater supply was threatened. Public outcries caused laws to be passed and industries to change their processes. Biodegradable detergents were quickly put on the market, and nonbiodegradable detergents were banned.

(a)

(b)

▶ **Figure 21.7** ABS detergents do not degrade in nature. Their use led to foam on rivers such as that on the Bogotá River in Colombia (a). They also caused contaminated water from a groundwater source to foam as it came from the tap (b).

LAS Detergents: Biodegradable

Biodegradable detergents called *linear alkylsulfonates (LASs)* have a linear chain of carbon atoms.

$-SO_3^- Na^+$

Microorganisms can break down LAS molecules by producing enzymes that degrade the molecule two (and only two) carbon atoms at a time (Figure 21.8). The branched chain of ABS molecules blocks this enzyme action, preventing their degradation. Thus, technology solved the problem of foaming rivers.

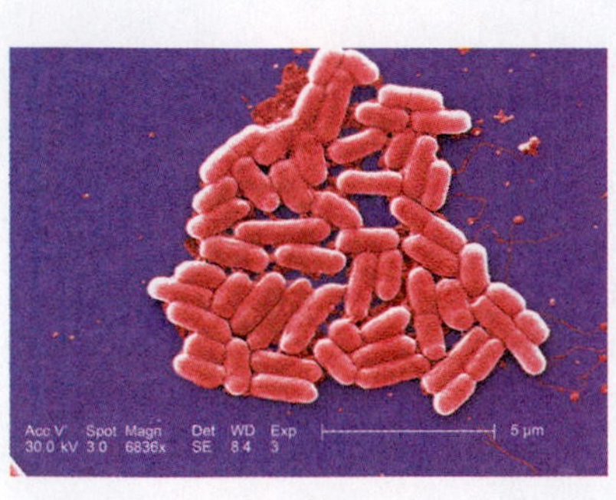

(a)

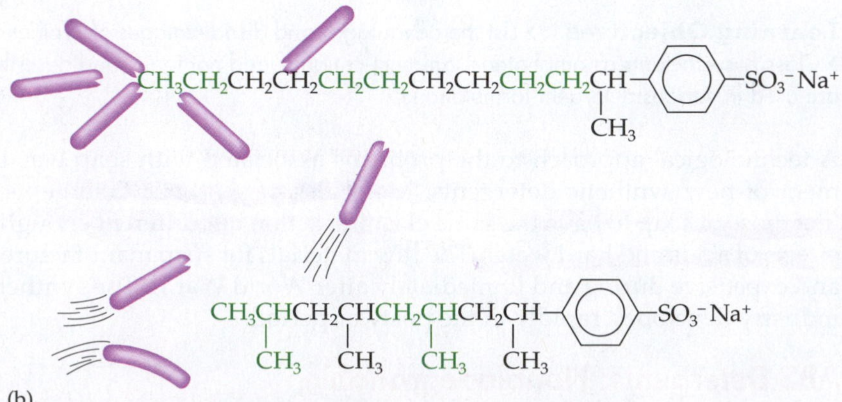

(b)

▲ **Figure 21.8** Microorganisms such as *Escherichia coli*, shown in (a) magnified 42,500 times by scanning electron microscopy, are able to degrade LAS detergents. They can readily metabolize these detergents (b), removing two carbon atoms at a time from each molecule. It takes them much longer to break down the branched chains of the ABS molecules.

The cleansing action of synthetic detergents is quite similar to that of soaps. However, detergents work better than soap in acidic solution and in hard water. Their calcium and magnesium salts, unlike those of soaps, are soluble and do not separate out, even in extremely hard water. As Figure 21.5 shows, the cleansing action of a synthetic detergent is little affected by hard water.

Laundry Detergent Formulations

Detergent products used in homes and commercial laundries usually contain a variety of ingredients. The main component is a surfactant, but other substances are added to provide a variety of functions, such as increasing cleaning performance for specific soils or surfaces. Some additives ensure product stability. Others are intended to supply a unique identity to a particular product. Common additives include builders, brighteners, fabric softeners, and other substances that lessen the redeposition of dirt or simply reduce the cost.

Surfactants are used in thousands of products, not just in cleaning products. A small amount of lecithin, an edible surfactant, is often added to chocolate in the manufacturing process. The lecithin helps the chocolate disperse on the tongue more easily. The chocolate tastes "more chocolatey."

Surfactants enable the cleaning solution to wet the surface to be cleaned. They loosen and remove soil, usually with the aid of mechanical action. Surfactants also emulsify oily soils and keep them dispersed and suspended so that they do not settle back on the surface (Figure 21.4). Many cleaning products include two or more surfactants.

Surfactants are generally classified according to the ionic charge, if any, on their active part. An ionic detergent is always associated with a small ion of opposite charge, called a *counter ion*. Soaps and ABS and LAS detergents are all **anionic surfactants**; they have a negative charge on the active part. Other common categories of anionic surfactants are the alkyl sulfates, such as sodium dodecyl sulfate, and the alcohol ethoxysulfates (AESs). The counter ion for most anionic surfactants is Na^+.

$CH_3(CH_2)_nOSO_3^-\ Na^+$	$CH_3(CH_2)_mO(CH_2CH_2O)_nSO_3^-\ Na^+$
An alkyl sulfate	An alcohol ethoxysulfate (AES)
$n = 11$ to 13	$m = 6$ to 13, $n = 7$ to 13

Anionic surfactants are used in laundry and hand dishwashing detergents, household cleaners, and personal cleansing products. They have excellent cleaning properties and generally make a lot of suds.

As the name indicates, **nonionic surfactants** have no electrical charge. They are low sudsing and not affected by water hardness. They work well on most soils and are typically used in laundry and automatic dishwasher formulations. The most widely used nonionic surfactants are the *alcohol ethoxylates*.

$$CH_3(CH_2)_mO(CH_2CH_2O)_nH$$

An alcohol ethoxylate

$m = 6$ to 13, $n = 7$ to 13

Cationic surfactants have a positive charge on the active part. These surfactants are not particularly good detergents, but they have a germicidal action. They are therefore used as cleansers and disinfectants in the food and dairy industries and as the sanitizing ingredient in some household cleaners. The most common cationic surfactants are *quaternary ammonium salts* (or *quats*), so called because they have four hydrocarbon groups attached to a nitrogen atom that bears a positive charge.

$$CH_3(CH_2)_nCH_2N^+(CH_3)_3\ Cl^-$$

A quaternary ammonium salt

$n = 10$ to 16

Sometimes cationic surfactants are used along with nonionic surfactants. Cationic surfactants are seldom used with anionic ones because the ions of opposite charge tend to clump together and precipitate from solution, destroying the detergent action of both.

Amphoteric surfactants carry both a positive and a negative charge. They react with both acids and bases and are noted for their mildness, sudsing, and stability.

They are used in personal cleansing products such as shampoos for babies and in household cleaning products such as liquid handwashing soaps. Typical amphoteric surfactants are compounds called *betaines*.

$$CH_3(CH_2)_nCH_2NH_2^+\ CH_2COO^-$$

A betaine

$n = 10$ to 16

CONCEPTUAL Example 21.1 Classification of Surfactants

Classify each of the following surfactants as anionic, cationic, nonionic, or amphoteric.

a. $CH_3(CH_2)_{14}CH_2N^+(CH_3)_3\ Cl^-$
b. $CH_3(CH_2)_{13}O(CH_2CH_2O)_7SO_3^-\ Na^+$
c. $CH_3(CH_2)_{12}CH_2NH_2^+\ CH_2COO^-$
d. $CH_3(CH_2)_{12}CON(CH_2CH_2OH)_2$

Solution

a. The N atom of the active part bears a positive charge, making this a cationic surfactant. (The counter ion is Cl^-.)
b. There is a negative charge on the $—SO_3$ group of the active part, making this an anionic surfactant. (The counter ion is Na^+.)
c. This substance has both a positive charge (on the N atom) and a negative charge (on the $—COO^-$ group), making this an amphoteric surfactant.
d. This substance has neither a positive charge nor a negative charge, so it is a nonionic surfactant.

■ EXERCISE 21.1

Classify each of the following surfactants as anionic, cationic, nonionic, or amphoteric.

a. $CH_3(CH_2)_8—C_6H_4—O(CH_2CH_2O)_9H$
b. $CH_3(CH_2)_{14}COO^-\ K^+$
c. $CH_3(CH_2)_9—C_6H_4—SO_3^-\ Na^+$
d. $CH_3(CH_2)_{12}CH_2N^+(CH_3)_3\ Cl^-$

Any substance added to a surfactant to increase its detergency is called a **builder**. Most builders are water softeners that reduce water hardness. Sodium citrate ($Na_3C_6H_5O_7$) and complex phosphates such as sodium tripolyphosphate ($Na_5P_3O_{10}$) and sodium hexametaphosphate [$(NaPO_3)_6$)] tie up Ca^{2+} and Mg^{2+} ions in soluble complexes, a process called *sequestration*. The complex phosphates also enhance detergency through a synergistic effect. For example, if a wash solution contains 1.00 g/L of an alkyl sulfate detergent, it will have a certain cleaning action. Similarly, a wash solution with 1.00 g/L of sodium tripolyphosphate will have a certain detergency. But a solution that has 0.50 g/L of alkyl sulfate detergent and 0.50 g/L of sodium tripolyphosphate will clean clothes better than either of the first two solutions.

Phosphates speed the eutrophication of lakes (Chapter 14). In some areas, phosphates from detergents contribute somewhat to this process. Several state and local governments have banned the sale of detergents containing phosphates.

Sodium carbonate acts by reacting with hard-water ions to form an insoluble substance (Section 21.1). Automatic washing machines can be harmed by the $CaCO_3$ and $MgCO_3$ precipitates. These builders also produce a mild alkalinity, which assists cleaning, especially of acidic soils and stains.

Complex aluminosilicates called *zeolites* are often used as builders. Zeolite anions act through *ion exchange*, trapping calcium ions by exchanging them for their own sodium ions.

$$Ca^{2+}(aq) + Na_2Al_2Si_2O_8(s) \longrightarrow 2\ Na^+(aq) + CaAl_2Si_2O_8(s)$$

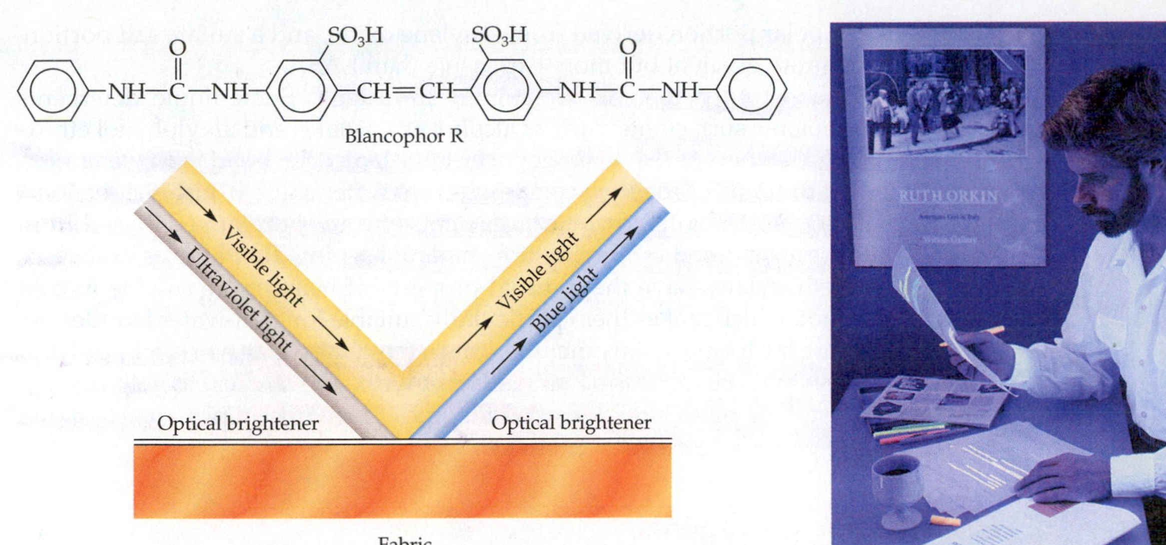

▲ **Figure 21.9** (a) An optical brightener, called a *blancophor* (or colorless dye), converts invisible ultraviolet light to visible blue light, making the fabric look brighter and masking any yellowish color. (b) A shirt washed in a detergent formulation that includes an optical brightener glows in the light from an ultraviolet lamp (black light).

Calcium and magnesium ions are held in suspension by the zeolites (rather than being precipitated).

Almost all detergent formulations include fluorescent dyes called **optical brighteners.** After white clothing is worn a few times, it often looks yellowish and drab. Optical brighteners absorb ultraviolet rays in sunlight and transmit them as blue light. This blue light both camouflages the yellowish color and increases the amount of visible light reaching the eye, giving the garment the appearance of being "whiter than white" (Figure 21.9). Brighteners are also used in cosmetics, paper, soap, plastics, and other products.

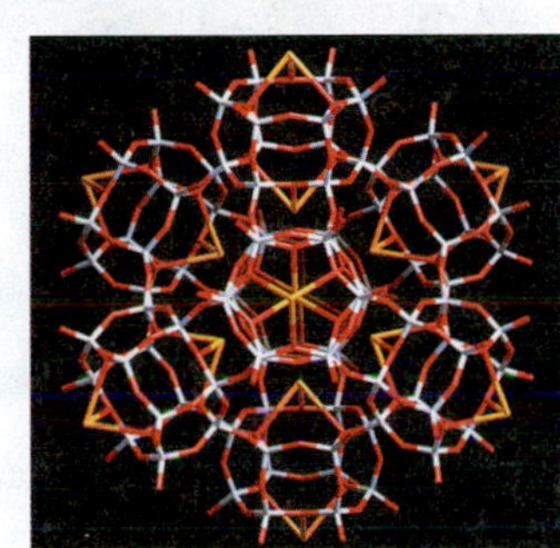

▲ Zeolites used in detergent formulations trap positive ions such as Ca^{2+} and Mg^{2+} in their cagelike structures and hold the ions in suspension in the wash water.

Optical brighteners appear to have low toxicity to humans, although they cause skin rashes in some people. They may have developmental and reproductive effects, but additional testing is needed to confirm or refute this. Their effect on lakes and streams is largely unknown, despite the large amounts entering our waterways. The only benefit of these compounds is cosmetic.

Early laundry detergent preparations were powders, but liquid laundry detergent formulations now command much of the market. In general, powders are more concentrated and clean better, but many consumers find liquids to be more convenient. Laundry detergent formulations two or three times more concentrated than in the past, often called "ultra" detergents, allow use of a smaller volume of a product. Liquid products may also have a solvent such as ethanol, isopropyl alcohol, or propylene glycol to help prevent separation of the other components and to help dissolve greasy soils. Some liquid laundry detergents use sodium citrate, sodium silicate, sodium carbonate, or zeolites as builders. Some formulations are *unbuilt*—high in surfactants but containing no builders.

Linear alkylbenzene sulfonate (LAS) surfactants are the cheapest surfactants used in liquid laundry detergents. In unbuilt formulations, they usually are in the form of the sodium salt (page 650) or the triethanolamine $[N(CH_2CH_2OH)_3]$ salt.

$$CH_3(CH_2)_9CH(CH_3){-}C_6H_4{-}SO_3^-\ HN^+(CH_2CH_2OH)_3$$

Triethanolamine salt of an LAS

In built varieties, LAS surfactants are often present as the potassium salt.

$$CH_3(CH_2)_9CH(CH_3){-}C_6H_4{-}SO_3^-\ K^+$$

Potassium salt of an LAS

Other popular surfactants for liquid formulations are alcohol ethoxysulfonates (AESs). AES surfactants have a hydrocarbon portion derived from an alcohol or an

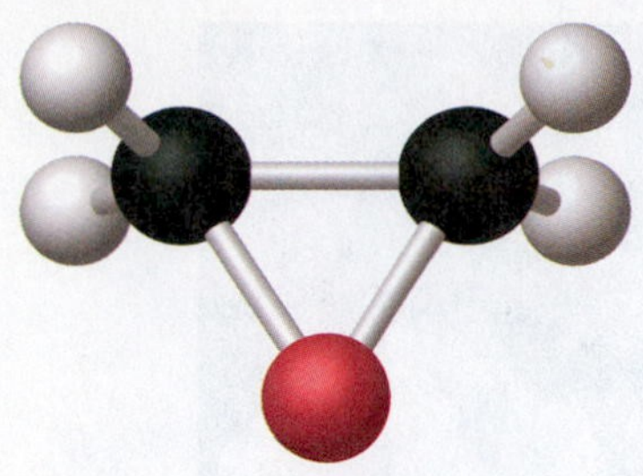

▲ Ethylene oxide.

alkylphenol, a polar portion derived from ethylene oxide, and a sulfate salt portion. AES surfactants are efficient but more expensive than LAS.

Both AES and LAS detergents are anionic surfactants. Some liquid detergents also contain nonionic surfactants, such as alcohol ethoxylates and alkylphenol ethoxylates. The oxygen atoms of the nonionic surfactants hydrogen bond with water molecules, making the ends of the surfactant molecules water soluble, just like the ionic end of an anionic surfactant. Nonionic surfactants effectively remove oily soil from fabrics. They are not as good as anionic surfactants at keeping dirt particles in suspension. Alcohol ethoxylates have the unusual property of being more soluble in cold water than in hot, which makes them particularly suitable for cold-water laundering.

Some detergent formulations include *lipases* (enzymes that work on lipids) to help remove fats and oils, *amylases* (enzymes that work on starches) to help remove starchy stains such as pasta, and *proteases* (enzymes that work on proteins) to aid in the removal of protein stains such as blood.

Dishwashing Detergents

Liquid detergents for washing dishes by hand generally contain one or more surfactants as the main active ingredients. Like liquid laundry detergents, these formulations most often include the surfactant LAS as the sodium or the triethanolamine salt. Some use nonionic surfactants such as cocamido DEA, an amide made from a fatty acid and diethanolamine [$HN(CH_2CH_2OH)_2$].

$$CH_3(CH_2)_nCON(CH_2CH_2OH)_2$$

Cocamido DEA

$$n = 8 \text{ to } 12$$

Few dishwashing liquids contain builders; those that do usually have only small amounts. These detergents may also contain enzymes to help remove greases and protein stains, fragrances, preservatives, solvents, bleaches, and other ingredients. Most liquid dishwashing detergents differ significantly only in the concentration or effectiveness of the surfactant.

Detergents for automatic dishwashers are quite different from dishwashing liquids. They are often strongly alkaline and should never be used for hand dishwashing. They contain sodium tripolyphosphate ($Na_5P_3O_{10}$), sodium carbonate, sodium metasilicate (Na_2SiO_3), sodium sulfate, a chlorine or oxygen bleach, and only a small amount of surfactant, usually a nonionic type. Some contain sodium hydroxide. They depend mainly on their strong alkalis, heat, and the vigorous agitation of the machine for cleaning. Dishes that are washed repeatedly in an automatic dishwasher may be permanently etched by these strong alkalis, which is why delicate crystal stemware is often washed by hand.

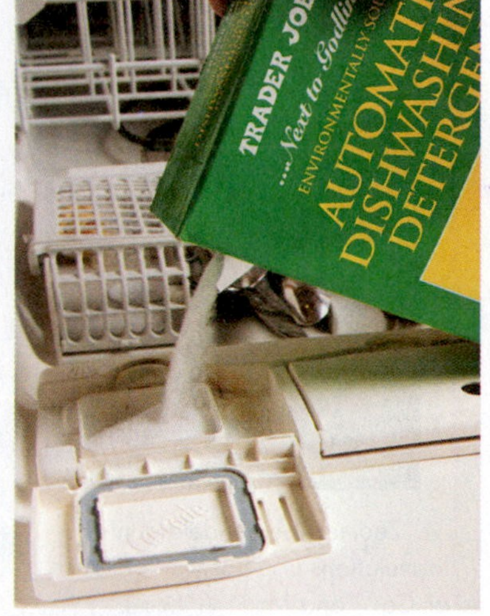

▲ **It DOES Matter!**
Using more than the recommended amount of dishwasher detergent generally does not result in cleaner dishes. Moreover, the higher pH leads to faster etching of the glass in the washer.

2. Why can't hand dishwashing liquid be used in a dishwasher? The surfactants in hand dishwashing liquid generally form lots of suds. In a dishwasher, those suds would fill the chamber and inhibit the sprays of water that do much of the cleaning. The suds can also make something of a mess.

Self-Assessment Questions

1. The hydrocarbon chain of ABS detergents is
   a. branched and readily biodegraded
   b. branched and resistant to biodegradation
   c. unbranched and readily biodegraded
   d. unbranched and resistant to biodegradation
2. Which of the following is an LAS detergent?
   a. $CH_3(CH_2)_{10}CH_2N^+(CH_3)_3\ Cl^-$
   b. $CH_3(CH_2)_{11}OSO_3^-\ Na^+$
   c. $CH_3(CH_2)_9CH(CH_3)C_6H_4SO_3^-Na^+$
   d. $CH_3(CH_2)_8O(OCH_2CH_2)_9H$
3. Carbonate ions react with water to form
   a. $Ca(OH)_2(s)$
   b. $HCO_3^-(aq)$ and $OH^-(aq)$
   c. $Na_2CO_3(s)$
   d. soaps
4. Hard-water ions react with carbonate ions to form products such as
   a. $CaCO_3(s)$
   b. $Ca(OH)_2(s)$
   c. $Na_2CO_3(s)$
   d. soap curds

5. When it softens water, an ion exchange resin retains
   a. chloride ions b. hardness ions
   c. hydroxide ions d. sodium ions
6. An optical brightener converts ultraviolet light to
   a. black light b. blue light
   c. heat d. yellow light

For items 7–9, match the enzyme type in the left column with type of stain it acts on, listed in the right column.

7. amylase (a) fats and oils
8. lipase (b) blood and egg
9. protease (c) potatoes, pasta, and rice
10. What kind of surfactant is cocamido DEA, $CH_3(CH_2)_{10}CON(CH_2CH_2OH)_2$, used in hand dishwashing detergents?
    a. amphoteric b. anionic
    c. cationic d. nonionic
11. Which of the following is the most likely to irritate the skin?
    a. detergent for automatic dishwashers b. liquid handwashing soap
    c. liquid dishwashing detergent d. powdered laundry detergent

Answers: 1, b; 2, c; 3, b; 4, a; 5, b; 6, b; 7, c; 8, a; 9, b; 10, d; 11, a

21.3 Laundry Auxiliaries: Softeners and Bleaches

Learning Objectives › Identify a fabric softener from its structure, and describe its action. › Name two types of laundry bleaches, and describe how they work.

Section 21.2 discussed cationic surfactants, whose active part is a positive ion and which are often quaternary ammonium salts. The cations have four hydrocarbon groups attached to a nitrogen atom that bears a positive charge. One of the hydrocarbon groups is a long chain with 12 to 18 carbon atoms. The other three are small, usually methyl groups. An example of such a cationic surfactant is octadecyltrimethylammonium chloride. The Cl^- counter ion is not shown.

$$CH_3CH_2CH_2CH_2CH_2CH_2CH_2CH_2CH_2CH_2CH_2CH_2CH_2CH_2CH_2CH_2CH_2CH_2\overset{\displaystyle CH_3}{\underset{\displaystyle CH_3}{N^+}}{-}CH_3$$

Fabric Softeners

Another kind of quaternary salt with *two* long carbon chains and two smaller groups on a nitrogen is used as a fabric softener. An example is dioctadecyldimethylammonium chloride. These compounds are strongly adsorbed by the fabric, forming a film one molecule thick on the surface. The long hydrocarbon chains lubricate the fibers, imparting increased flexibility and softness to the fabric.

3. Does putting more fabric softener in the washer make the fabrics even softer? A very small amount of fabric softener gives a soft feeling to the laundry. Too much produces a coating that can make the laundry feel damp or waxy.

$$\begin{array}{r}CH_3\quad\\ CH_3CH_2CH_2CH_2CH_2CH_2CH_2CH_2CH_2CH_2CH_2CH_2CH_2CH_2CH_2CH_2CH_2CH_2{-}N^+{-}CH_3\\ CH_3CH_2CH_2CH_2CH_2CH_2CH_2CH_2CH_2CH_2CH_2CH_2CH_2CH_2CH_2CH_2CH_2CH_2\quad\quad\quad\end{array}$$

Laundry Bleaches: Whiter Whites

Bleaches are oxidizing agents (Chapter 8) that remove colored stains from fabrics. There are two main types of laundry bleaches: chlorine bleaches and oxygen bleaches. Most familiar liquid chlorine laundry bleaches (such as Clorox® and

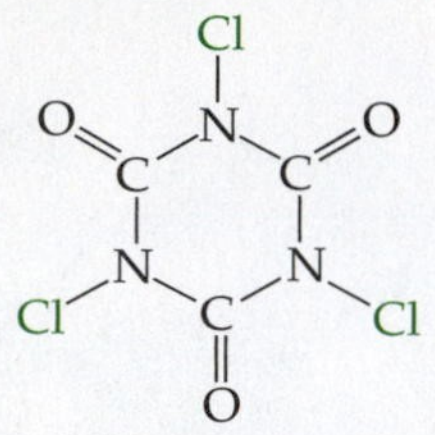

Symclosene

Purex®) are dilute solutions of sodium hypochlorite (NaOCl) that differ mainly in price. "Ultra" chlorine bleaches have a higher concentration of NaOCl. Hypochlorite bleaches release chlorine rapidly, and high concentrations of chlorine can damage fabrics. These bleaches do not work well on polyester fabrics, often causing yellowing rather than the desired whitening.

Other bleaches are available in solid forms that release chlorine slowly in water to minimize damage to fabrics. Trichloroisocyanuric acid, also known as trichlor or symclosene, is an example of a cyanurate-type bleach.

Oxygen bleaches usually contain sodium percarbonate ($2Na_2CO_3 \cdot 3H_2O_2$) or sodium perborate ($NaBO_2 \cdot H_2O_2$). As indicated by the formulas, these compounds are complexes of Na_2CO_3 or $NaBO_2$ and hydrogen peroxide (H_2O_2). In hot water, the hydrogen peroxide is liberated and acts as a strong oxidizing agent.

Borates are somewhat toxic. Perborate bleaches are less active than chlorine bleaches and require higher temperatures, higher alkalinity, and higher concentrations to do an equivalent job. They are used mainly for bleaching white, resin-treated, polyester–cotton fabrics. These fabrics last much longer with oxygen bleaching than with chlorine bleaching. Percarbonate bleaches act like a combination of hydrogen peroxide and sodium carbonate. Less toxic than the perborate bleaches, percarbonate bleaches are rapidly becoming the predominant type of oxygen bleach. Properly used, oxygen bleaches make fabrics whiter than do chlorine bleaches.

Bleaches work by acting on certain light-absorbing chemical groups, called *chromophores*, that cause a substance to be colored. Most chromophores have a number of carbon-to-carbon double bonds. With a chromophore represented as $-CH{=}CH-C({=}O)-CH_2$, its oxidation can be written as

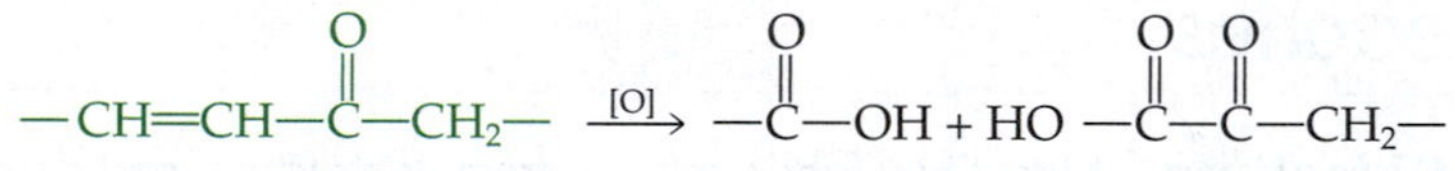

$$\underset{\text{Chromophore (colored)}}{-CH{=}CH-\overset{O}{\overset{\|}{C}}-CH_2-} \xrightarrow{[O]} \underset{\text{Fragments (colorless)}}{-\overset{O}{\overset{\|}{C}}-OH + HO-\overset{O}{\overset{\|}{C}}-\overset{O}{\overset{\|}{C}}-CH_2-}$$

Thus, the bleach attacks the color-producing groups, not the soil itself. It does not actually remove the stain, but merely changes it to a colorless form. Sometimes not all of the stain is oxidized, and a very faint ghost of the original stain can be seen.

Self-Assessment Questions

1. Which of the following could serve as a fabric softener?
   a. $CH_3(CH_2)_{10}CON(CH_2CH_2OH)_2$
   b. $CH_3(CH_2)_{10}CH_2N^+(CH_3)_3\ Cl^-$
   c. $CH_3(CH_2)_{16}CH_2N^+(CH_3)_3\ Cl^-$
   d. $CH_3(CH_2)_{16}CH_2N^+(CH_3)_2CH_2(CH_2)_{16}CH_3\ Cl^-$
2. To what class of compounds do most fabric softeners belong?
   a. amphoteric detergents b. anionic detergents
   c. nonionic detergents d. quaternary ammonium salts
3. Bleaches are
   a. bases b. builders
   c. oxidizing agents d. surfactants
4. The main component of household bleach, often called chlorine bleach, is
   a. HCOCl b. KOCl c. NaOCl d. NaOH
5. Which of the following is a key component of oxygen bleach?
   a. $H_3C_6O_7$ b. $KMnO_4$ c. $NaBO_2 \cdot H_2O_2$ d. $NaClO_4$
6. Bleaches act by
   a. enhancing surfactant action b. opening active sites
   c. sequestering hard-water ions d. oxidizing chromophores

Answers: 1, d; 2, d; 3, c; 4, c; 5, c; 6, d

21.4 All-Purpose and Special-Purpose Cleaning Products

Learning Objective › List the major ingredient(s) (and their purposes) of some all-purpose cleaning products and some special-purpose cleaning products.

All-Purpose Cleaners

Various all-purpose cleaning products are available for use on walls, floors, countertops, appliances, and other tough, durable surfaces. Those for use in water solution may contain surfactants, sodium carbonate, ammonia, solvent-type grease cutters, disinfectants, bleaches, deodorants, and other ingredients. Some are great for certain jobs but not as good for others. They damage some surfaces but work especially well on others. Most important, they may be harmful when used improperly. Reading the labels is important.

The physical and chemical processes that clean a surface take some time. An often overlooked technique in cleaning is allowing the surface to soak. Plain water or dilute soap solution is an amazingly effective, cheap, and nonpolluting cleaner when it is simply sprayed on a surface and allowed to stand for a few minutes.

Household ammonia solutions, straight from the bottle, are effective for loosening baked-on grease or burned-on food. Diluted with water, these solutions clean mirrors, windows, and other glass surfaces. Mixed with detergent, ammonia rapidly removes wax from vinyl floor coverings. Ammonia vapors are highly irritating, so this cleanser should not be used in a closed room. Ammonia should not be used on asphalt tile, wood surfaces, or aluminum because it may stain, pit, or erode these materials.

Baking soda (sodium bicarbonate, $NaHCO_3$) straight from the box is a mild abrasive cleanser. It absorbs food odors to some extent, making it good for cleaning the inside of a refrigerator.

Vinegar (acetic acid) cuts grease film. Vinegar should not be used on marble, though, because it reacts with and dissolves the marble, pitting the surface.

$$\underset{\text{Marble}}{CaCO_3(s)} + 2\ \underset{\text{Vinegar}}{CH_3COOH(aq)} \longrightarrow Ca^{2+}(aq) + 2\ CH_3COO^-(aq) + CO_2(g) + H_2O(l)$$

▲ Vinegar reacts with marble, pitting the surface. Carbon dioxide gas is given off, forming bubbles.

Hazards of Mixing Cleaners

Mixing bleach with other household chemicals can be quite dangerous. For example, mixing a hypochlorite bleach with hydrochloric acid produces poisonous chlorine gas.

$$2\ HCl(aq) + ClO^-(aq) \longrightarrow Cl^-(aq) + H_2O(l) + Cl_2(g)$$

Mixing bleach with toilet bowl cleaners that contain HCl is especially dangerous. Most bathrooms are small and poorly ventilated, so generating chlorine in such a limited space is hazardous. Chlorine can do enormous damage to the throat and the entire respiratory tract. If the concentration of chlorine in the air is high enough, it can kill.

Mixing bleach with ammonia is also extremely hazardous. Two of the gases produced are chloramine (NH_2Cl) and hydrazine (NH_2NH_2), both of which are quite toxic. *Never* mix bleach with other chemicals without specific directions to do so. In fact, it is a good rule not to mix any chemicals unless you know exactly what you are doing.

Special-Purpose Cleaners

Many highly specialized cleaning products are on the market. For metals, there are chrome cleaners, brass cleaners, copper cleaners, and silver cleaners. There are lime removers, rust removers, and grease removers. There are cleaners specifically for wood surfaces, for vinyl floor coverings, and for ceramic tile. Let's look at just a few of the special-purpose cleaners found in almost any home.

GREEN CHEMISTRY

Principles 1–12

Marty Mulvihill, *University of California–Berkeley*

Practicing Green Chemistry at Home

The Twelve Principles of Green Chemistry help chemists to design and use chemicals more safely and more efficiently. These principles can also guide the use of chemical products in our own homes. While we don't often get the opportunity to design the products found in our homes, we do control which ones we buy and how we use them. You will see how we can become greener consumers by combining these principles with an understanding of the chemistry found in this chapter.

1. **Buy and use only what you need.** Principles 1, 2, 8, and 9 are all strategies that help chemists avoid unnecessary waste. You can avoid waste at home by buying and using only the products that you need.
2. **Choose safer products.** Principles 3, 4, and 5 all remind chemists to choose the safest ingredients possible that will still provide the desired function. The same is true at home. Consult reliable sources to determine which products are the safest.
3. **Choose products that minimize depletion of resources.** Principle 7 encourages chemists to use renewable feedstock chemicals, and Principle 6 promotes energy efficiency. You can minimize depletion of resources by choosing products that are energy efficient or made from renewable resources.
4. **Reusable, recyclable, or readily degradable materials are preferable.** Principle 10 tells chemists to design chemicals that degrade in the environment. Look for products that readily degrade in the environment. Also buy items in packaging that can be reused or recycled.
5. **Stay informed.** Principle 11 encourages chemists to monitor their reactions in real time so that they can avoid hazards and waste. As consumers, we should monitor new developments in product safety and regulations so that we can choose the best products.
6. **Prevent Accidents.** Principle 12 reminds chemists that they should strive to prevent accidents by using inherently safer chemistry. You can prevent accidents by reading product labels, using proper protective gear, maximizing ventilation, and choosing the safest products.

This chapter introduces many of the chemical ingredients found in household products and helps you understand what functions they perform. You should identify the function of as many ingredients as possible in the products that you buy. Avoid items with too many additional ingredients. This is how chemists think about buying and using only what they need. For example, soap improves hygiene by destroying microorganisms and removing oils. This means that all soap is antibacterial and that adding antibacterial agents may be unnecessary.

Training yourself to identify and understand product ingredients will also help you choose safer products. For example, paints contain more than pigment (Section 21.5). They also have solvents that allow them to spread before drying. Traditional solvents were volatile hydrocarbons, often called VOCs (Section 13.4). These chemicals have low boiling points and high vapor pressures. Many VOCs can irritate the respiratory track and cause health problems. Greener paint products have some or all of the hydrocarbon solvents replaced by water. These usually have "low-VOC" or "VOC-free" on their labels.

We can ensure a healthier environment by minimizing depletion of resources. For example, concentrated, cold-water detergents improve energy efficiency by removing the need to heat wash water. Also, many products are now made from renewable resources. For example, many of the fragrances mentioned in this chapter are naturally occurring chemicals. There are also plastics and fuels that are made from plants.

Products made from plant materials help reduce reliance on petroleum and often are more degradable. Degradability is controlled by chemical structure. Molecules that are linear and contain only carbon, hydrogen, and oxygen degrade more quickly than complicated molecules that contain many rings, branches, or halogen atoms. Molecules that degrade quickly are less likely to cause harm when they are released into the environment. Understanding basic chemistry and the importance of green chemistry helps us become greener, better informed consumers.

▲ Some products are labeled or certified, by Green Seal, for example, to help consumers make greener choices.

Toilet bowl cleaners are acids that dissolve the "lime" buildup that forms in toilet bowls. The residue is mainly calcium carbonate ($CaCO_3$), deposited from hard water, and often discolored by such things as iron compounds and fungal growth. Calcium carbonate is readily dissolved by acid. The solid crystalline cleaners usually contain sodium bisulfate ($NaHSO_4$), and the liquid cleaners include hydrochloric acid (HCl), citric acid, or some other acidic material.

$$\begin{array}{l} \quad H_2C-COOH \\ \quad\quad | \\ HO-C-COOH \\ \quad\quad | \\ \quad H_2C-COOH \end{array}$$

Citric acid

Most scouring powder cleansers contain an abrasive such as silica (SiO_2) that scrapes soil from hard surfaces and a surfactant to dissolve grease. Some include a bleach. Scouring powders are mainly intended for removing stains from porcelain tubs and sinks. Such abrasive cleansers may scratch the finish on appliances, countertops, and metal utensils. They may even scratch the surfaces of sinks, toilet bowls, and bathtubs. Dirt gets into the scratches and makes cleaning even more difficult.

Glass cleaners are volatile liquids that evaporate without leaving a residue. A common glass cleaner is simply isopropyl alcohol (rubbing alcohol) diluted with water. Most commercial glass cleaners contain ammonia or vinegar for greater cleaning power.

You can make your own glass cleaner. Put about 1.6 L of cold water into a 1-gal bucket. Carefully add 60 mL of sudsy ammonia and 240 mL of isopropyl (rubbing) alcohol. Mix well and pour the solution into clean spray bottles. Add 1 or 2 drops of blue food coloring if you want your cleaner look like a popular name-brand window cleaner. (Adapted from *How to Clean and Care for Practically Anything*, Yonkers, NY: Consumer Reports Special Publications, 2002.)

When a kitchen drain becomes clogged, it is usually because the pipe has been blocked by grease. Drain cleaners often contain sodium hydroxide, either in the solid form or as a concentrated liquid. The sodium hydroxide reacts with the water in the pipe to generate heat, which melts much of the grease. The sodium hydroxide then reacts with some of the grease, converting it to soap, which is easier to remove than the grease. Some products also contain bits of aluminum metal that react with the sodium hydroxide solution to form hydrogen gas, which bubbles out of the clogged area of the drain, creating a stirring action.

Many liquid drain cleaners contain bleach (NaOCl) as well as concentrated sodium hydroxide. Bathtub or shower drains are often clogged with hair, so the bleach degrades the hair, helping to unplug the drain. The best drain cleaner is prevention: Don't pour grease down the kitchen sink, and try to keep hair out of the bathtub drain. If a drain does get plugged, a mechanical device such as a plumber's snake is often a better choice than a chemical drain cleaner.

6. Can I make my own household cleaners instead of buying them? It is possible to make almost any household cleaner, or a substitute, at home. Sometimes the homemade product is as good as or better than the store-bought product; an example is window cleaner. In other cases, the commercial product is superior. On the Internet, you can find directions for making dishwasher detergent and laundry detergent, but the cleaning agent is usually sodium carbonate (washing soda), which is much less effective than carefully formulated commercial detergents.

The active ingredient in most oven cleaners is sodium hydroxide. Several popular products are dispensed as an aerosol foam. The greasy deposits on oven walls are converted to soaps when they react with the sodium hydroxide. The resulting mixture can then be washed off with a wet sponge. (Wear rubber gloves, because sodium hydroxide is extremely caustic and damaging to the skin.)

A hand sanitizer is useful when there is no water available for hand washing. Most hand sanitizers contain a high concentration of alcohol, which kills bacteria and evaporates rapidly during use, leaving the hands clean and dry. A surfactant, often a quaternary ammonium salt, provides additional germicidal properties, and a thickening agent makes the sanitizer easier to spread over the hands.

The combination of alcohol and surfactant makes hand sanitizers effective against a variety of bacteria. However, the high concentration of alcohol means that many of these preparations are flammable, so care should be taken around flames. Also, hand sanitizers protect for a limited time. They must be applied several times during the day to continue to kill bacteria. Nonetheless, using a hand sanitizer is a convenient way to minimize exposure during cold and flu season.

Do-it-yourselfers and garage mechanics often use a waterless hand cleaner to remove grease and grime from their hands. Like hand sanitizers, these hand cleaners do not need water to work. In fact, they work best if applied without water at first. Most waterless hand cleaners contain lanolin (Section 21.5), plus an oil such as oil of lemons or oranges and a surfactant that thickens the mixture into a creamy emulsion. Pumice (powdered volcanic ash) is often added to help loosen the dirt from the creases and folds of the skin. The oil acts as a solvent for the grease on the hands, and the surfactant keeps the oil and grease suspended so that it can be wiped off with a towel.

Green Cleaners

Many cleaning products marketed for home use are claimed to be "natural" or "green" and thus "safer to use" than traditional products. Consumer choices are hampered by lack of a standard definition or federal oversight of green cleaners.

You can make your own hand sanitizer. To 175 mL of 70% isopropyl alcohol (rubbing alcohol), add 80 mL of aloe vera gel. If you want a scent, add a few drops of an essential oil such as oil of cinnamon, peppermint oil, or oil of cloves. Mix the ingredients, and put the mixture in an emptied and cleaned liquid soap or hand sanitizer bottle.

Manufacturers do not have to list all the ingredients because doing so could disclose trade secrets. There are 84,000 chemical compounds in the EPA's inventory, and the EPA requires manufacturers to provide only a caution of toxicity. Products claiming to be green can contain harmful substances. For example, a solvent made with a natural compound called *limonene*, derived from orange peels, is combustible and can irritate the skin and eyes.

In general, green products have more ingredients derived from plants. If scented, they usually employ a natural scent such as citrus or lavender. Green substances derived from corn or soy are common. One useful example is the ester ethyl lactate ($CH_3CHOHCOOCH_2CH_3$); both the alcohol (ethanol) and the carboxylic acid (lactic acid) from which the ester is made can be produced from corn. Ethyl lactate dissolves many different substances and has a low volatility, thus contributing little to air pollution. It also degrades readily in the environment.

You can evaluate green cleaners yourself; see Collaborative Group Project 6.

Self-Assessment Questions

1. Household ammonia can be used safely for all of the following *except*
   a. cleaning aluminum
   b. loosening baked-on grease
   c. polishing mirrors
   d. wax removal

2. Vinegar can be used safely for all of the following *except*
   a. cutting grease
   b. dissolving mineral deposits
   c. polishing marble surfaces
   d. removing soap scum

3. Baking soda (sodium bicarbonate) can be used safely for all of the following *except*
   a. deodorizing a carpet
   b. deodorizing a refrigerator
   c. neutralizing acids
   d. neutralizing bleach

4. Both vinegar and ammonia are effective for cleaning certain surfaces. Mixing the two together forms a(n)
   a. effective bleach
   b. more effective cleaner
   c. salt
   d. toxic gas

5 Mixing hypochlorite bleach and an acid forms
   a. a more effective cleaner
   b. a more powerful bleach
   c. a surfactant
   d. toxic Cl_2 gas

6. Mixing hypochlorite bleach and ammonia produces
   a. ammonium hypochlorite
   b. a more effective cleaner
   c. a surfactant
   d. toxic gases

7. Lime ($CaCO_3$) deposits in toilet bowls can be removed by treatment with
   a. HCl   **b.** NaCl
   c. NaOCl   **d.** NaOH

8. The most effective way to keep drains open is to
   a. avoid letting grease and hair get in them
   b. convert grease to soap before putting it down a drain
   c. treat them once a week with NaOCl
   d. treat them twice a month with NaOH

Answers: 1, a; 2, c; 3, d; 4, c; 5, d; 6, d; 7, a; 8, a

21.5 Solvents, Paints, and Waxes

Learning Objectives › Identify compounds used in solvents and paints, and explain their purposes. › Identify waxes by their structure.

Of the thousands of chemicals available for use in the home, three common categories are solvents, paints, and waxes.

▲ **Figure 21.10** Cleansers that contain petroleum distillates have labels warning of their combustibility and of the hazard of swallowing them.

Solvents

Solvents are used in the home to remove paint, varnish, adhesives, waxes, and other materials. Petroleum solvents, called petroleum distillates on labels, are also added to some all-purpose cleansers as grease cutters (Figure 21.10). They dissolve grease readily but, like gasoline, are highly flammable and deadly when swallowed. The lungs become saturated with hydrocarbon vapors, fill with fluid, and fail to function.

Most organic solvents used around the home are volatile and flammable. Many have toxic fumes, and nearly all are narcotic at high concentrations. Such solvents should be used only with adequate ventilation and never around a flame. Be sure to read—and heed—all precautions before you use any solvent. Gasoline should not be used for cleaning. It is too hazardous in too many ways.

A troubling problem connected with household solvents is the practice of inhaling fumes to get "high." The popularity of solvent sniffing seems to be related mainly to peer pressure, especially among young teenagers. Long-term sniffing can cause permanent damage to vital organs, especially the lungs. There can be irreversible brain damage, and some individuals have died of heart failure while sniffing solvents.

4. What is the difference between paint and lacquer? Paint, whether it is enamel, oil-based, or latex, hardens by a chemical reaction. Oil-based paints commonly use linseed oil that oxidizes to a hard surface. Lacquer contains a polymer in a solvent, and it hardens by evaporation of the solvent. There is no chemical reaction. After it hardens, lacquer can be removed with lacquer solvent.

Paints

Paint is a broad term often used to cover a wide variety of products—lacquers, enamels, varnishes, oil-base coatings, and a number of different water-base finishes. Any or all of these materials can be found in any home. A paint contains three basic ingredients: a pigment, a binder, and a solvent. "White lead" [basic lead carbonate, $2PbCO_3 \cdot Pb(OH)_2$] was the pigment of choice for most paints until the 1970s. Its use was banned in 1977, and it has been replaced by titanium dioxide (TiO_2).

Titanium dioxide is a brilliant white nontoxic pigment with great stability and excellent hiding power. All ordinary paints are pigmented with titanium dioxide. For colored paints, small amounts of colored pigments or dyes are added to the white base mixture.

▲ Addition of colored pigments or dyes to a white base mixture produces a great variety of colored paints.

The binder, or film former, is the substance that binds the pigment particles together and holds them on the painted surface. In oil paints, the binder is usually tung oil or linseed oil. In water-based paints, it is a latex-based polymer. Most interior paints have polyvinyl acetate as the binder. Exterior water-based paints use viscous acrylic polymers, called *resins*, as binders. Acrylic latex paints are much more resistant to rain and sunlight.

The solvent in paint keeps the paint fluid until it is applied to a surface. The solvent might be an alcohol, a hydrocarbon, an ester, a ketone (or some mixture thereof), or water.

Paint may also contain additives: a drier (or activator) to make the paint dry faster, a fungicide to act as a preservative, a thickener to increase the paint's viscosity, an antiskinning agent to keep the paint from forming a skin inside the can, and a surfactant to stabilize the mixture and keep the pigment particles separated.

Waxes

Chemically, a **wax** is an ester of a long-chain organic acid (fatty acid) with a long-chain alcohol. Waxes are produced by plants and animals mainly as protective coatings. (These compounds are not to be confused with paraffin wax, which is made up of hydrocarbons.)

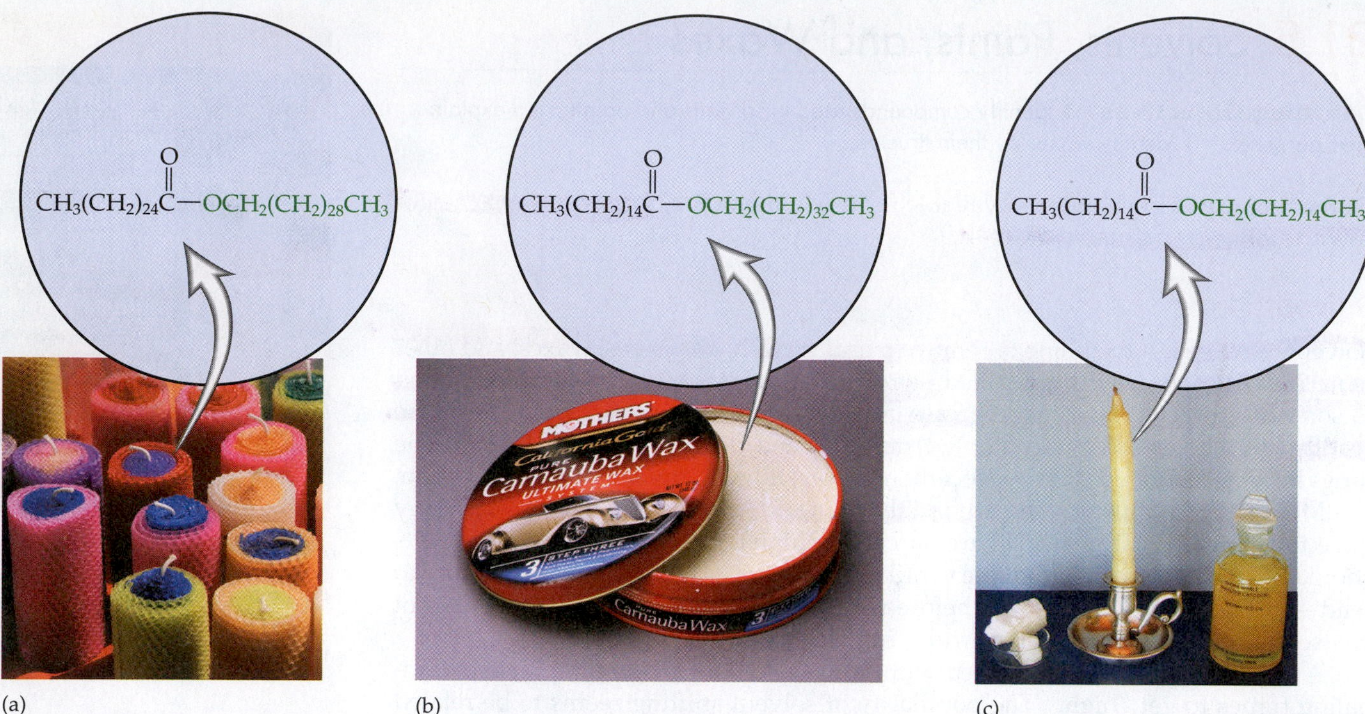

▲ **Figure 21.11** The molecular views show the esters that are typical components of (a) beeswax, (b) carnauba wax, and (c) spermaceti.

Three typical waxes are shown in Figure 21.11. Beeswax is the material with which bees build honeycombs and is used in such household products as candles and shoe polish. Carnauba wax is a coating that forms on the leaves of certain palm trees in Brazil. It is a mixture of esters similar to those in beeswax and is used in making automobile wax, floor wax, and furniture polish. Spermaceti wax, which is extracted from the head of a sperm whale, is largely cetyl palmitate. Once widely used in making cosmetics and other products, spermaceti wax is now in short supply because the sperm whale was hunted almost to extinction. It is now protected by international treaties.

Lanolin, the grease in sheep's wool, is also a wax. Because it forms stable emulsions with water, it is used in various skin creams and lotions.

Many natural waxes have been replaced by synthetic polymers such as silicones (Section 10.5), which are often cheaper and more effective.

Self-Assessment Questions

1. Which is *not* a property of organic solvents in household and commercial products?
   a. They are nonflammable.
   b. They can be abused as inhalant drugs.
   c. They dissolve greases.
   d. They remove paints and varnishes.
2. The three basic components of a paint are a binder, a solvent, and a
   a. builder
   b. surfactant
   c. pigment
   d. wax
3. Which of the following is a wax?
   a. $CH_3(CH_2)_{14}COOCH_3$
   b. $CH_3(CH_2)_{28}CH_2OH$
   c. $CH_3(CH_2)_{28}COOCH_3$
   d. $CH_3(CH_2)_{14}COOCH_2(CH_2)_{28}CH_3$

Answers: 1, a; 2, c; 3, d

21.6 Cosmetics: Personal Care Chemicals

Learning Objectives › Identify the principal ingredients in various cosmetic products. › Describe the chemical nature of skin, hair, and teeth.

Ages ago, people used materials from nature for cleansing, beautifying, and otherwise altering their appearance. Evidence indicates that 7000 years ago, Egyptians used powdered antimony and the green copper ore *malachite* as eye shadow. Egyptian pharaohs used perfumed hair oils as far back as 3500 B.C.E. Claudius Galen, a Greek physician of the second century C.E., is said to have invented cold cream. Fashion-conscious gentlemen of seventeenth-century Europe used cosmetics lavishly, often to cover the fact that they seldom bathed. Ladies of eighteenth-century Europe whitened their faces with lead carbonate ($PbCO_3$), and many died from lead poisoning.

The use of cosmetics has a long and interesting history, but past usage doesn't even come close to the amounts and varieties of cosmetics used by people in the modern industrial world. Each year, we spend billions of dollars on everything from hair sprays to nail polishes, from mouthwashes to foot powders. Combined sales of the world's 100 largest cosmetics companies were more than $125 billion in 2008.

What is a cosmetic? The U.S. Food, Drug, and Cosmetic Act of 1938 defined **cosmetics** as "articles intended to be rubbed, poured, sprinkled or sprayed on, introduced into, or otherwise applied to the human body or any part thereof, for cleansing, beautifying, promoting attractiveness or altering the appearance." Soap, although obviously used for cleansing, is specifically excluded from coverage by the law. Also excluded are substances that affect the body's structure or functions. Antiperspirants, products that reduce perspiration, are legally classified as drugs, as are antidandruff shampoos.

The main difference between drugs and cosmetics is that drugs must be proven safe and effective before they are marketed while cosmetics generally do not have to be tested before being marketed. Most brands of a given type of cosmetic contain the same (or quite similar) active ingredients. Thus, advertising is usually geared toward selling a name, a container, or a fragrance rather than the actual product itself.

The Food, Drug, and Cosmetic Act states that if a product has drug properties, it must be approved as a drug. Nevertheless, the cosmetics industry uses the term *cosmeceutical* to refer to cosmetic products that allegedly have medicinal or druglike benefits. We will discuss several such products in the following sections.

About 8000 different chemicals are used in cosmetics. They are sold in tens of thousands of different combinations.

Skin Creams and Lotions

Skin is the body's largest organ, with an area of about 18 ft^2. It encloses the body, forming a barrier to keep harmful substances out and moisture and nutrients in (Figure 21.12). The outer layer of skin, the *epidermis*, is divided into two parts: dead cells on the outside (the corneal layer), and living cells on the inside, continually replacing corneal cells, which are then sloughed off.

The corneal layer is composed mainly of a tough, fibrous protein called **keratin**. Keratin has a moisture content of about 10%. Below 10% moisture, the human skin is dry and flaky. Above 10%, conditions are ideal for the growth of harmful microorganisms. Skin is protected from loss of moisture by **sebum**, an oily secretion of the sebaceous glands. Exposure to sun and wind can leave the skin dry and scaly, and too frequent washing removes natural skin oils.

Cosmetics are applied to the dead cells of the corneal layer. Most of the preparations applied to the skin consist mainly of lotions and creams. A **lotion** is an emulsion of tiny oil droplets dispersed in water. A **cream** is the opposite, having tiny water droplets dispersed in oil (Figure 21.13). The essential ingredient of either is a fatty or oily substance that forms a protective film over the skin and helps hold moisture in. Typical substances used for this purpose are mineral oil and petroleum jelly, both mixtures of alkanes obtained from petroleum. Others are natural fats

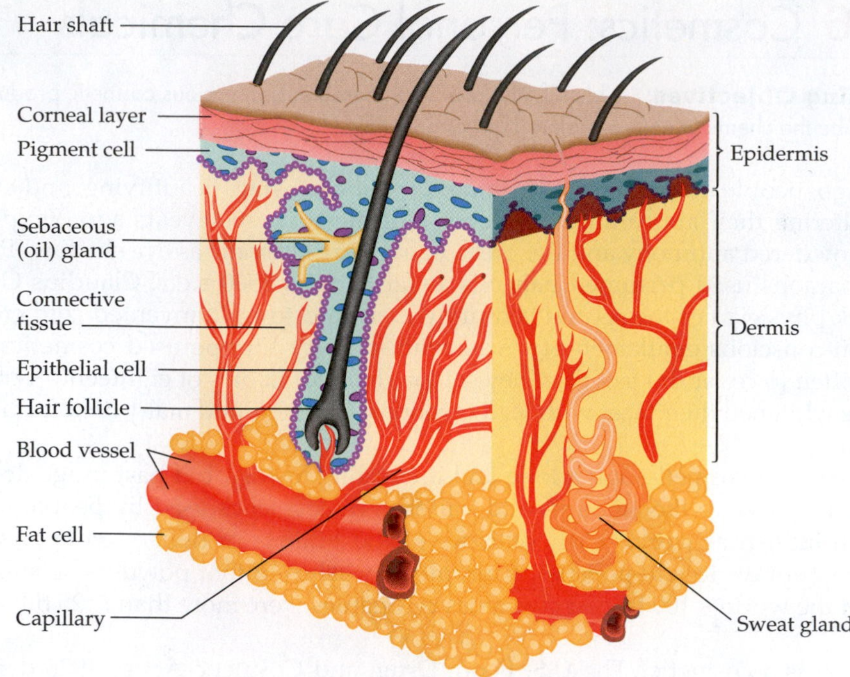

▶ **Figure 21.12** Cross section of skin. Skin has two main layers: Each square inch of the dermis contains about 1 m of blood vessels, 4 m of nerves, 100 sweat glands, several oil glands, more than 3 million cells, and the active part of hair follicles. The epidermis, laying over the dermis, consists of a thin layer of cells that divide continuously. These cells move upward to the corneal layer, dying as they do so. Cosmetics generally affect only the outer corneal layer of dead cells.

and oils, propylene glycol, glycerol, and waxes. Lanolin, an oily substance obtained from sheep's wool, aloe vera gel, olive oil, and palm oil are also used, and beeswax is often added to harden the product. Lotions and creams often contain reforms and emulsifiers (compounds that keep the oily portions from separating from the water).

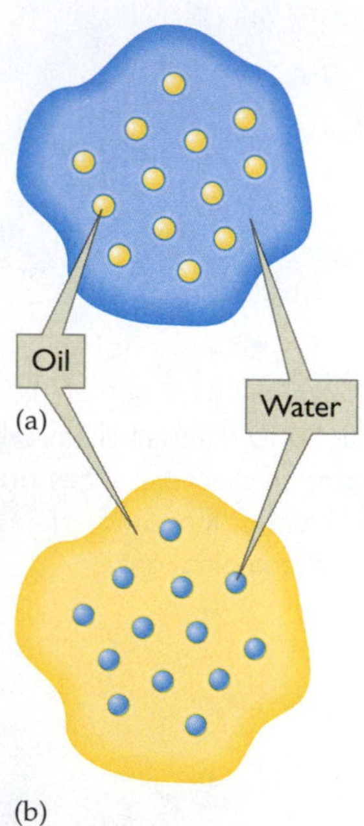

▲ **Figure 21.13** A lotion is an emulsion of oil in water (a). A cream is an emulsion of water in oil (b). A lotion feels cool because evaporating water removes heat from the skin. A cream feels greasy.

Some creams have been formulated with hormones, vitamins, and other unusual ingredients. Few, if any, have been found to confer any particular benefit. [The vitamin A derivative, isotretinoin (Accutane®; Section 22.6), used to treat acne, is a medicine, not a cosmetic.]

Creams and lotions protect the skin by coating and softening it. Such skin softeners are called **emollients**. Petroleum jelly (such as Vaseline®) or a good grade of mineral oil (baby oil) works as well for most people as fancy creams or lotions.

As in other industries, cosmetic companies are moving toward greener products. Sales of natural cosmetics were about $27 billion worldwide in 2009. Made from renewable plant, animal, and mineral products, these cosmetics may be better for the environment, but there is little evidence that they work better than traditional cosmetics. In fact, natural components may be more likely to cause allergic reactions than the synthetic ingredients. Natural is not necessarily better: Think of poison ivy as an extreme example.

It may seem strange that gasoline, a mixture of alkanes, dries out the skin but the higher alkanes in mineral oil and petroleum jelly soften it. Keep in mind, however, that gasoline is a thin, free-flowing liquid. It dissolves natural skin oils and carries them away. Higher alkanes are viscous, staying right on the skin and serving as emollients.

Moisturizers hold moisture to the skin. They work best when applied while the skin is still wet from a bath or shower. Moisturizers don't actually add moisture to skin. Rather, they form a physical barrier that hinders evaporation of water. Moisturizers are often substances such as lanolin. Collagen (the protein in connective tissue) is an effective moisturizer in skin lotions.

Some cosmetics contain *humectants* such as glycerol, lactic acid, or urea. Glycerol, with its three hydroxyl groups, holds water by hydrogen bonding. Urea actually binds water below the surface of the epidermis, right down to the skin-building cells. Urea and lactic acid also act as *exfoliants*, causing the dead cells to fall off more rapidly, leaving new, fresher-looking skin exposed.

Antiaging Creams and Lotions

Some cosmetics are claimed to reduce wrinkles, spots, and other signs of aging skin. Prominent among them are products containing alpha hydroxy acids (AHAs), derived from fruit and milk sugars. An alpha hydroxy acid is a carboxylic acid that has a hydroxyl group on the carbon atom next to the carboxyl carbon. Glycolic acid and lactic acid are typical examples. Consumers spend billions of dollars each year for cosmetics containing AHAs. There is some scientific evidence that they may work.

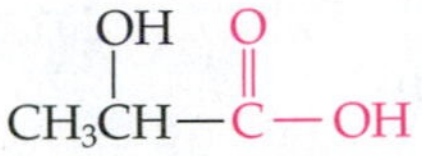

$$CH_3CH(OH)-C(=O)-OH$$

Lactic acid

AHAs and related substances act as exfoliants (page 664). They cause dead skin cells to be sloughed off, to be replaced by newer, fresher-looking skin. They seem to be relatively safe. They do cause redness, swelling, burning, blistering, bleeding, rash, itching, and skin discoloration in some people. People who use AHA-containing products have greater sensitivity to sun, perhaps putting them at greater risk of skin cancer.

The best treatment for wrinkling of the skin is prevention, accomplished largely by avoiding excessive exposure to the Sun and by not smoking cigarettes. Cigarette smoking leads to premature aging of the skin. Nicotine causes constriction of the tiny blood vessels that feed the skin. Repeated constriction over the years causes the skin to lose its elasticity and become wrinkled.

Sunscreens

Ultraviolet rays in sunlight turn light skin darker by triggering production of the pigment **melanin**. The dark melanin then protects the deeper layers of the skin from damage. Excessive exposure to ultraviolet radiation causes premature aging of the skin and leads to skin cancer. Our quest for tanned skin has resulted in an epidemic of skin cancer. Shorter-wavelength ultraviolet rays (UV-B) are more energetic and are especially harmful.

Sunscreens offer either physical or chemical protection from UV rays. Physical sunscreens, or sunblocks, are opaque films that prevent UV rays from reaching the skin, thus protecting against both UV-A and UV-B. Most contain zinc oxide (ZnO) or titanium dioxide (TiO_2) pigments, Chemical sunscreens absorb UV rays before they can cause any damage. Typical ingredients include avobenzone or oxybenzone, which protect against UV-A.

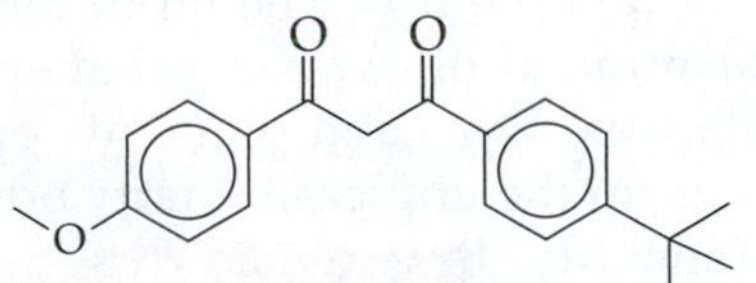

Avobenzone 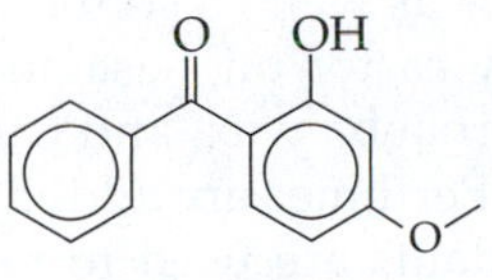 Oxybenzone

For many years, the active ingredient in many sunscreen lotions was *para*-aminobenzoic acid (PABA) or one of its esters. In rare cases, PABA-based ingredients cause skin problems, including burning, rashes, swelling, and tightening of the skin.

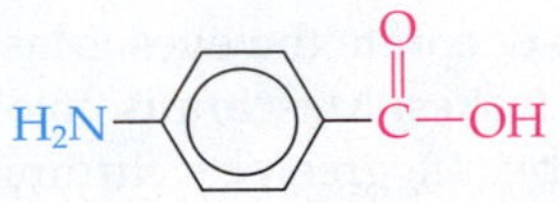

$$H_2N-C_6H_4-C(=O)-OH$$

para-Aminobenzoic acid

PABA derivatives generally are water soluble and thus wash off when swimming. They provide only partial UV-B protection and no UV-A protection and are therefore seldom used today. Octyl methoxycinnamate (OMC) is now used as a UV-B filter in many sunscreen lotions.

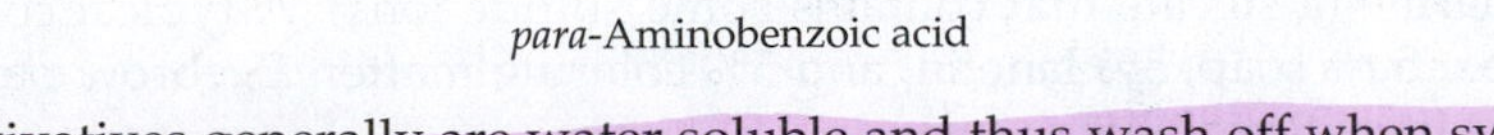

$$CH_3O-C_6H_4-CH{=}CHCOOCH_2CH(CH_2CH_3)CH_2CH_2CH_2CH_3$$

Octyl methoxycinnamate (OMC)
(2-ethylhexyl-4'-methoxycinnamate)

Nanoparticles in Cosmetics

Nanoparticles are a hot research topic, and they have received a lot of attention in the popular media. It is no surprise that nanoparticles are showing up in consumer products, including cosmetics such as lip gloss and sunscreens. However, an exciting research finding does not necessarily lead to a better consumer product. It is difficult for consumers to separate the new scientific discovery from the marketing claims about it.

Physical sunscreens, typically opaque white creams with titanium dioxide or zinc oxide pigments, are often considered unattractive. Reducing the pigment particles to nanoscale size makes the creams transparent, but they still provide protection from the Sun's UV rays. Unfortunately, the nanoparticles also present possible risks. Because of their minute size, the particles don't just sit on the skin but can penetrate deeper. Once inside the body, they can be absorbed by cells, tissues, and organs that larger particles can't get into.

Whether or not nanoparticles pose health risks to users of these cosmetics has yet to be determined. We lack enough information to make a good decision. Nanoparticle toxicity is an active area of research.

The eight-carbon alkyl group helps make this compound insoluble in water and less likely to wash off while swimming.

The **skin protection factor (SPF)** is a rating that depends on the type and concentration of a sunscreen's ultraviolet-absorbing substances. SPF values range from 2 to 45 or more. An SPF of 15, for example, indicates that the product should allow you to stay in the sun without burning 15 times as long as you could with unprotected skin.

Lipsticks and Lip Balms

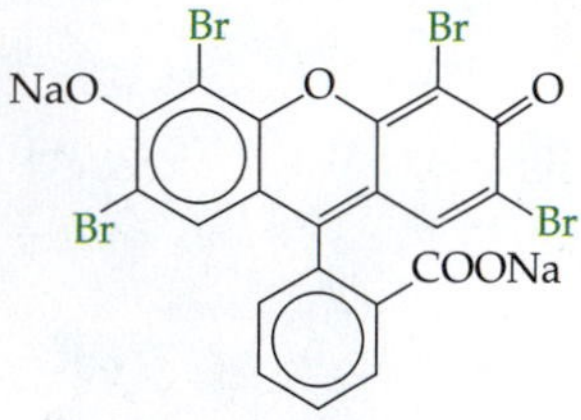

Tetrabromofluorescein

Lipsticks and lip balms are quite similar to skin creams in composition and function. They are made of an oil and a wax, with a higher proportion of wax than in creams. Because it has little in the way of protective oils, the skin of the lips dries out easily, leading to chapped lips. Lipsticks and lip balms prevent moisture loss as well as soften and brighten the lips. The oil in these products is frequently castor oil, sesame oil, or mineral oil. Waxes often employed are beeswax, carnauba wax, and candelilla wax. Dyes and pigments provide color to lipsticks. Perfumes are added to cover up the unpleasant fatty odor of the oil, and antioxidants are used to retard rancidity. Bromo acid dyes such as tetrabromofluorescein, a bluish-red compound, are responsible for the color of most lipsticks.

Eye Makeup

Various chemicals are used to decorate the eyes. Mascara, to darken eyelashes, has a base of soap, oils, fats, and waxes. Mascara is colored brown by iron oxide pigments, black by carbon (lampblack), green by chromium(III) oxide (Cr_2O_3), or blue by ultramarine (a silicate that contains some sulfide ions). A typical composition is 40% wax, 50% soap, 5% lanolin, and 5% coloring matter. Eyebrow pencils have about the same ingredients.

Eye shadow creams have a base of petroleum jelly with the usual fats, oils, and waxes. Powdered eye shadows have talc [a hydrated magnesium silicate, $Mg_3Si_4O_{10}(OH)_2$] or corn silk as a base. Eye shadows are colored by dyes or made white with zinc oxide or titanium dioxide pigments.

Some people have allergic reactions to ingredients in eye makeup. A more serious problem is eye infection caused by bacterial contamination. It is recommended that eye makeup be discarded after 3 months. Mascara is of special concern because of the wand applicator, which can easily scratch the cornea.

Deodorants and Antiperspirants

Deodorants are products that have perfume to mask body odor and a germicide to kill odor-causing bacteria. Bacteria act on perspiration residue and sebum (natural body oil) to produce malodorous compounds such as short-chain fatty acids and amines. The germicide is usually a long-chain quaternary ammonium salt (Section 21.2) or a phenol such as triclosan.

Triclosan

Antiperspirants are usually deodorants as well, but they also retard perspiration. The active antiperspirant ingredient is a variable complex of chlorides and hydroxides of aluminum and zirconium. Aluminum chlorohydrate [$Al_2(OH)_5Cl \cdot 2\ H_2O$] is a typical compound found in many antiperspirants. Zirconium and aluminum chlorides and hydroxides function as **astringents**, which constrict the openings of the sweat glands and thus restrict the amount of perspiration that can escape. Antiperspirants can be formulated into creams or lotions, or they can be dissolved in alcohol and applied as sprays.

Sweating is a natural, healthy body process, and to stop it routinely is probably not wise. Regular bathing and changing of clothes make antiperspirants unnecessary for most people. But if you still feel the need for underarm protection, a deodorant product should suffice.

Toothpaste: Soap with Grit and Flavor

After soap (which doesn't count officially, because the law says it isn't a cosmetic), toothpaste is the most important cosmetic product. Its only essential components are a detergent and an abrasive. Soap and sodium bicarbonate could do the job quite well but would be rather unpalatable. The ideal abrasive should be hard enough to clean teeth but not hard enough to damage tooth enamel. Abrasives frequently used in toothpaste are listed in Table 21.1. Some have been criticized as being too harsh.

Table 21.1 Abrasives Commonly Used in Toothpastes

Name	Chemical Formula
Precipitated calcium carbonate	$CaCO_3$
Insoluble sodium metaphosphate	$(NaPO_3)_n$
Calcium hydrogen phosphate	$CaHPO_4$
Titanium dioxide	TiO_2
Tricalcium phosphate	$Ca_3(PO_4)_2$
Calcium pyrophosphate	$Ca_2P_2O_7$
Hydrated alumina	$Al_2O_3 \cdot nH_2O$
Hydrated silica	$SiO_2 \cdot nH_2O$

$HO-C_6H_4-C(=O)-OCH_3$

Methyl *para*-hydroxybenzoate (Methylparaben)

Typical detergents are alkyl sulfates, such as sodium dodecyl sulfate [sodium lauryl sulfate, $CH_3(CH_2)_{11}OSO_3^-\ Na^+$]. Any pharmaceutical grade of soap or detergent would probably work satisfactorily. Most toothpastes have flavors, colors, aromas, and sweet tastes. Ingredients include sweeteners such as sorbitol, glycerol (glycerin), and saccharin (Section 17.6); flavors such as wintergreen and peppermint; thickeners such as cellulose gum and polyethylene glycols; and preservatives such as methyl *para*-hydroxybenzoate.

Tooth decay is caused primarily by bacteria that convert sugars to *plaque*, a biofilm that is composed of thousands of bacteria, small particles, proteins, and mucus and is deposited on the teeth when they are not cleaned adequately. These bacteria convert sugars to acids such as lactic acid ($CH_3CHOHCOOH$). Acids dissolve tooth enamel. If not removed, plaque can harden into *calculus*, also known as *tartar*. Brushing and flossing remove plaque and thus prevent decay. Decay can be minimized by eating sugars only at meals rather than in snacks and by brushing immediately after eating. Acids such as lactic acid in beer and phosphoric acid

You can make your own toothpaste. Stir together 360 cm^3 of sodium bicarbonate (baking soda) and 120 cm^3 of sodium chloride (table salt). To this dry mixture, add 30 mL of glycerol (glycerin). Stir in just enough water to make a thick paste. Add a few drops of peppermint oil to improve the taste. Store in a closed container.

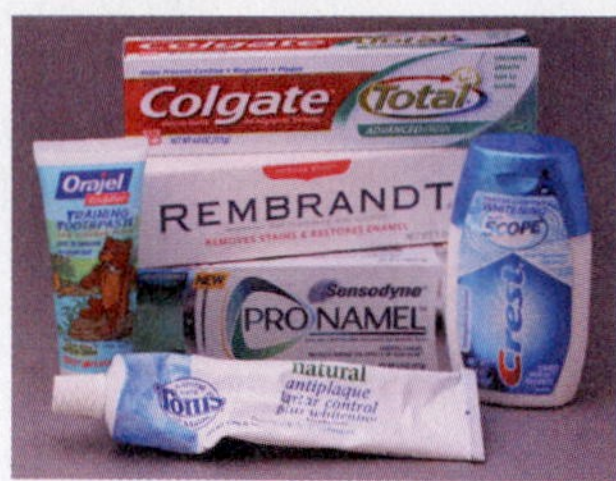

▲ Toothpastes are available under many brand names and in various formulations. Some contain baking soda (sodium bicarbonate) and/or hydrogen peroxide as ingredients, but there is only marginal evidence of their effectiveness. The only essential ingredients in a toothpaste are a detergent and an abrasive.

(H_3PO_4) in soft drinks may also erode the tooth enamel of people who consume these beverages in large amounts.

Many modern toothpastes contain fluorine compounds, such as stannous fluoride (SnF_2), shown to be effective in reducing the incidence of tooth decay. The enamel of teeth is composed mainly of hydroxyapatite [$Ca_5(PO_4)_3OH$]. Fluoride from toothpaste (or drinking water) converts part of the enamel to fluorapatite [$Ca_5(PO_4)_3F$]. Fluorapatite is stronger and more resistant to decay than hydroxyapatite.

The main cause of tooth loss in adults is gum disease. Toothpaste formulations with baking soda ($NaHCO_3$) and hydrogen peroxide (H_2O_2) as ingredients are purported to prevent gum disease, but there seems to be little evidence that they do.

Popular teeth whiteners often include hydrogen peroxide as a bleaching agent. The peroxide works on colored compounds in teeth in much the same way as bleaches work on stained clothing. However, the action of the H_2O_2 is slow. In toothpaste, the peroxide is not in contact with the teeth long enough to have a significant effect. Most of the successful teeth whiteners require application for 30 minutes or more. Dentists' preparations often use higher concentrations of peroxide along with ultraviolet light, which speeds the reaction. Caution is advised concerning teeth-whitening preparations. If used too often, they can cause teeth to become brittle. Broken white teeth are not as attractive.

Perfumes, Colognes, and Aftershaves

Note that fragrance molecules (Table 21.2) are fat soluble. They dissolve in skin oils and can be retained for hours.

Perfumes are among the most ancient and widely used cosmetics. Originally, all perfumes were extracted from natural sources such as fragrant plants. Their chemistry is exceedingly complex, but chemists have identified many of the components of perfumes and synthesized them in the laboratory, allowing the production of many synthetic perfumes. The best perfumes are probably still made from natural materials because chemists have so far been unable to identify all the many important, but minor, ingredients.

A good perfume may have a hundred or more constituents. The components are divided into three categories, called *notes*, based on differences in volatility. The

Table 21.2 Compounds with Flowery and Fruity Odors Used in Perfumes

Name	Structure[a]	Odor	Molecular Formula	Molecular Mass (u)
Citral		Lemon	$C_{10}H_{16}O$	152.24
Irone		Violet	$C_{14}H_{22}O$	206.33
Jasmone		Jasmine	$C_{11}H_{16}O$	164.25
Phenylacetaldehyde		Lilac, hyacinth	C_8H_8O	120.15
2-Phenylethanol		Rose	$C_8H_{10}O$	122.17

[a]Note that each compound has only 1 oxygen atom and 10 or more carbon atoms.

most volatile fraction (the one that vaporizes most readily) is called the **top note.** This fraction, made up of relatively small molecules, is responsible for the odor when a perfume is first applied. Common top notes include citrus and ginger scents and chemical compounds such as phenylacetaldehyde (Table 21.2), which has a lilac or hyacinth odor.

The **middle note** (or *heart note*) is intermediate in volatility. This fraction is responsible for the lingering aroma after most of the top-note compounds have vaporized. Typical middle notes include lavender and rose scents and chemical compounds such as 2-phenylethanol, which has the aroma of roses. Some top- and middle-note compounds are synthesized in large quantities for use in perfumes.

The **end note** (or *base note*) is the low-volatility fraction and is made up of compounds with large molecules, often with musky odors. Essential oils—volatile oily compounds from plants with pleasant aromas—such as those from sandalwood and patchouli are typically used to supply base notes.

Odors vary with dilution. A concentrated solution of a compound may have an unpleasant odor, yet a dilute solution of it will have a pleasant aroma. Such compounds include musks (Table 21.3), which are often added to perfumes to moderate the odors of flowery or fruity top and middle notes. The Ethiopian civet cat, from which the compound civetone is obtained, is a skunklike animal. Its secretion, like that of the skunk, is a defensive weapon. The secretion from musk deer is probably a pheromone (Chapter 18) that serves as a sex attractant for the deer. Synthetic civetone and muscone have been produced, but many upscale perfume makers still prefer natural civetone. Almost all muscone used in perfumes today is synthetic.

Are there sex attractants for humans? The evidence is scanty, but some perfume makers add α-androstenol to their products. α-Androstenol is a steroid that occurs naturally in human hair and urine. Some studies hint that it may act as a sex attractant for human females, but this seems more likely to be just an advertising ploy. Even if there are human sex attractants, it is doubtful that they have much influence on human behavior because we probably have overriding cultural constraints. Anyway, we seem to prefer the sex attractant of the musk deer.

CH_3 CH_3 HO

α-Androstenol

A perfume usually consists of 10–25% fragrant compounds and fixatives dissolved in ethyl alcohol. **Colognes** are perfumes diluted with ethyl alcohol or an alcohol–water mixture. They are only about one-tenth as strong as perfumes, usually containing only 1–2% perfume essence.

OH

Menthol

Aftershave lotions are similar to colognes. Most are about 50–70% ethanol, the remainder being water, perfume, and food coloring. Some have menthol added for a cooling effect on the skin. Others contain an emollient to soothe chapped skin.

Table 21.3 Unpleasant Compounds Used to Fix Delicate Odors in Perfumes

Compound	Structure	Natural Source	Molecular Formula	Molecular Mass (u)
Civetone	=O	Civet cat	$C_{17}H_{30}O$	250.42
Muscone	O, CH_3	Musk deer	$C_{16}H_{30}O$	238.41
Indole	NH	Feces	C_8H_7N	117.15

Aromatherapy

Aromatherapy is the practice of using essential oils as a purported way to promote health and well-being. The aromas from these oils are supposed to have a positive effect on the nervous system. Aromatherapy includes the use of soap, bath additives, shower gels, and cosmetic products containing essential oils, along with accessories such as car scenters, candles, room fragrances, oil burners, and sprays for bed linens.

Commonly used essential oils are those from marigold, lemon, orange, grapefruit, geranium, lavender, jasmine, and bergamot. The essential oils are diluted by carrier oils, which are vegetable oils such as sweet almond oil, apricot kernel oil, and grapeseed oil, before being applied to the skin.

Some aromas seem to have a positive psychological effect on people. It may be as simple as a pleasant feeling caused when a scent recalls a pleasant experience. The U.S. aromatherapy market is valued at $800 million a year and accounts for most of worldwide sales. Home fragrance products account for nearly half the aromatherapy sales in the United States. It is difficult to evaluate the claims of aromatherapy's proponents through scientific experiments. Most of the reported effects are highly subjective.

▲ Shampoos are available in many forms and under many brand names. The only essential ingredient in any shampoo is a detergent.

Perfumes are the source of many allergic reactions associated with cosmetics and other consumer products. **Hypoallergenic cosmetics** are those that purport to cause fewer allergic reactions than regular products. The term has no legal meaning, but most of these cosmetics do not contain perfume.

Some Hairy Chemistry

Like skin, hair is composed mainly of the fibrous protein keratin. Recall (Chapter 16) that protein molecules are made up of amino-acid chains held together by four types of forces: hydrogen bonds, salt bridges, disulfide linkages, and dispersion forces. Of these, hydrogen bonds and salt bridges are important to understanding the actions of shampoos and conditioners. Hydrogen bonds between protein chains are disrupted by water (Figure 21.14); salt bridges are destroyed by changes in pH (Figure 21.15). Disulfide linkages are broken and restored when hair is permanently waved or straightened.

Shampoo

The keratin of hair has five or six times as many disulfide linkages as the keratin of skin. When hair is washed, the keratin absorbs water and is softened and made more elastic. The water disrupts hydrogen bonds and some of the salt bridges. Acids and bases are particularly disruptive to salt bridges, making control of pH important in hair care. The number of salt bridges is maximized at a pH of 4.1.

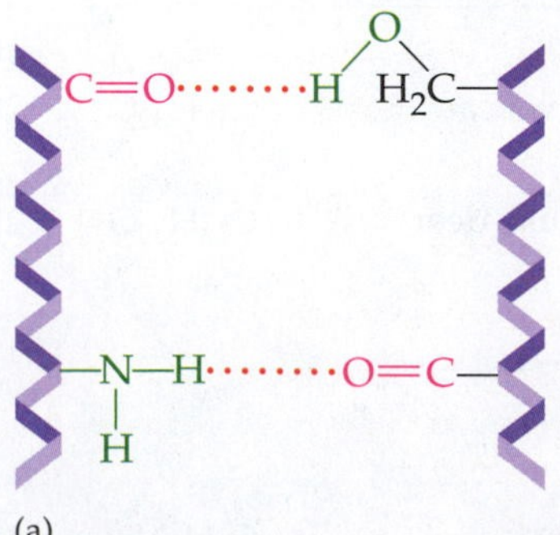

(a)

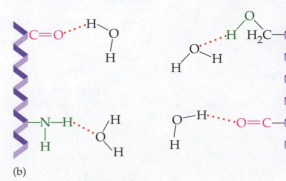

(b)

▲ **Figure 21.14** In a strand of hair, adjacent protein chains are held together by hydrogen bonds that link the carbonyl group of one chain to the amide group of another (a). When hair is wet, these groups can hydrogen bond with water rather than with each other (b), disrupting the hydrogen bonds between chains.

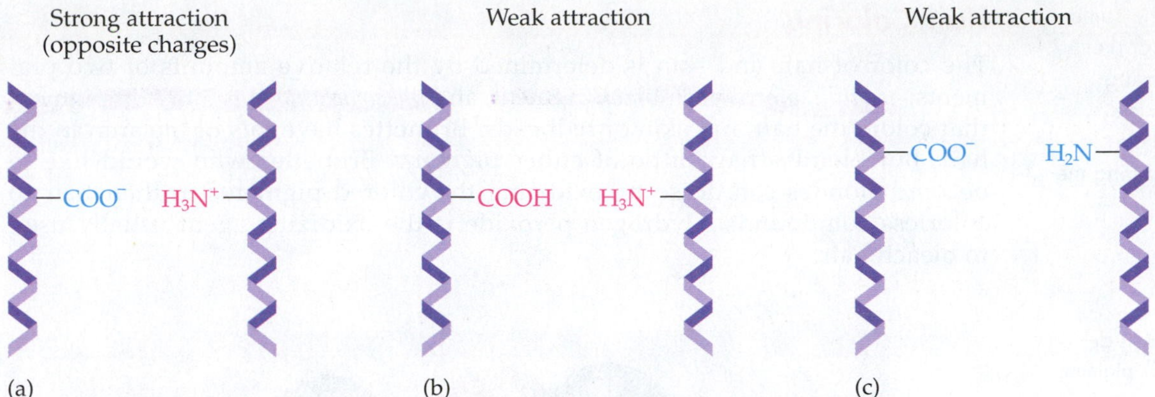

▲ **Figure 21.15** Strong electrostatic forces between an ionized carboxyl group on one protein chain and an ionized amino function on another hold the chains together (a). A change in pH can disrupt this salt bridge. If the pH drops, the carboxyl group takes on a proton and loses its charge (b). If the pH rises, a proton is removed from the amino group and it is left uncharged (c). In either case, the forces between the protein chains are weakened considerably.

The visible portion of hair is dead. Only the root is alive. The hair shaft is lubricated by sebum. Washing the hair removes this oil and any dirt adhering to it.

Before World War II, the cleansing agent in shampoos was soap. Soap-based shampoos worked well in soft water but left a dulling film on hair in hard water. People often removed the film by using a rinse containing vinegar or lemon juice. Such rinses are usually not needed with today's products.

Modern shampoos use a synthetic detergent as a cleansing agent. In shampoos for adults, the detergent is often an anionic type such as sodium dodecyl sulfate, the same detergent used in many toothpastes. In shampoos used for babies and children, the detergent is often an amphoteric surfactant (Section 21.2) that is less irritating to the eyes. Amphoteric surfactants react with both acids and bases. In an acidic solution, the surfactant can accept a proton on its negatively charged oxygen. In a basic solution, it can give up one of the protons from the nitrogen.

The only essential ingredient in shampoo is a detergent of some sort. What, then, is all the advertising about? You can buy shampoos that are fruit or herb scented, protein enriched, and pH balanced or made especially for oily or dry hair. Shampoos for oily, normal, and dry hair seem to differ primarily in the concentration of the detergent. Shampoo for oily hair is more concentrated; shampoo for dry hair is more dilute.

Because hair is protein, a protein-enriched shampoo does give it more body. The protein (usually keratin or collagen) coats the hair and literally glues split ends together. Protein is often added to conditioners, too. Conditioners are mainly long-chain alcohols or long-chain quaternary ammonium salts. These quats are similar to the compounds used in fabric softeners (Section 21.3), and they work in much the same way to coat hair fibers.

Because there are acidic and basic groups on the protein chains in hair, the acidity or basicity of a shampoo affects hair. Hair and skin are both slightly acidic. Highly basic (high-pH) or strongly acidic (low-pH) shampoos would damage hair, and such products would also irritate the skin and eyes. Most shampoos have pH values between 5 and 8, close to neutral or very slightly acidic.

How about all those flavors and fragrances? Ample evidence indicates that such "natural" ingredients as milk, honey, strawberries, herbs, cucumbers, and lemons add nothing to the usefulness of shampoos or other cosmetics. Why are they there? Smells sell, and such ingredients also appeal to those interested in a more natural lifestyle. There is one hazard in the use of such fragrances: bees, mosquitoes, and other insects like certain fruit and flower odors, too. Using such products before going on a picnic or a hike could lead to a bee in your bonnet.

5. Is thick shampoo better for my hair? Shampoo is thickened with fine silica or a polymer. A thicker shampoo simply has more of the thickening agent added and is not better for your hair.

What turns hair gray? The same substance that bleaches darker hair blonde. With increasing age, the hydrogen peroxide concentration in hair follicles builds up, ultimately inhibiting the production of melanin.

Hair Coloring

The color of hair and skin is determined by the relative amounts of two pigments: *melanin*, a brownish-black pigment, and *phaeomelanin*, a red-brown pigment that colors the hair and skin of redheads. Brunettes have lots of melanin in the hair, but blondes have little of either pigment. Brunettes who would like to become blondes can do so by oxidizing the colored pigments in their hair to colorless compounds. Hydrogen peroxide is the oxidizing agent usually used to bleach hair.

▶ Brown or black hair color is determined by the brownish-black pigment melanin; red hair color by the red-brown pigment phaeomelanin; and blonde hair color by scarcity of both pigments.

It DOES Matter!

Why does the type of melanin in your skin matter? It is not just cosmetic. People with dark skin are perhaps a hundred times less likely to get melanoma or other skin cancers. Melanin is a good sunblock. How easily someone gets sunburn or how hard it is for some people to get a tan depends on the amount and kind of melanin in their skin. Having predominantly phaeomelanin is a major risk factor for most forms of skin cancer.

Hair dyeing is more complicated than bleaching. The color may be temporary, from water-soluble dyes that can be washed out, or more permanent, from dyes that penetrate the hair and remain there. Such dyes are often used in the form of a water-soluble, often colorless, precursor that soaks into the hair and then is oxidized by hydrogen peroxide to a colored compound. Permanent dyes affect only the dead outer portion of the hair shaft. New hair, as it grows from the scalp, has its natural color.

Permanent dyes are often derivatives of an aromatic amine called *para*-phenylenediamine (Figure 21.16). Variations in color can be obtained by placing substituents on this molecule. The *para*-phenylenediamine molecule produces a black color, and the derivative *para*-aminodiphenylaminesulfonic acid is used in blonde formulations. Intermediate colors can be obtained by the use of other derivatives. One derivative, *para*-methoxy-*meta*-phenylenediamine (MMPD), has been shown to be carcinogenic when fed to rats and mice, but the hazard to those who use it as hair dye is not yet known. It is interesting to note that one substitute

$H_2N-C_6H_4-NH_2$
para-Phenylenediamine
(a)

$H_2N-C_6H_4-NH-C_6H_4-SO_3H$
para-Aminodiphenylaminesulfonic acid
(b)

H_2N, NH_2, OCH_3
MMPD
(c)

H_2N, NH_2, OCH_2CH_3
EMPD
(d)

▲ **Figure 21.16** Most hair dyes are derivatives of *para*-phenylenediamine (a). These include *para*-aminodiphenylaminesulfonic acid (b), *para*-methoxy-*meta*-phenylenediamine (MMPD) (c), and *para*-ethoxy-*meta*-phenylenediamine (EMPD) (d).

for MMPD was its homolog, *para*-ethoxy-*meta*-phenylenediamine (EMPD). Screening revealed that EMPD causes mutations in bacteria. Such mutagens are often also carcinogens.

The chemistry of colored oxidation products is quite complex. These products probably include quinones and nitro compounds, among others, which are produced by the oxidation of aromatic amines.

H_2N–(ring)–NH_2 $\xrightarrow{\text{oxidation}}$ O=(ring)=O

A diamine — A quinone

(ring)–NH_2 $\xrightarrow{\text{oxidation}}$ (ring)–NO_2

An amine — A nitro compound

Hair treatments that develop color gradually, such as Grecian Formula®, use rather simple chemistry. A solution containing colorless lead acetate $[Pb(CH_3COO)_2]$ is rubbed on the hair. As it penetrates the hair shaft, Pb^{2+} ions react with sulfur atoms in the hair to form black lead(II) sulfide (PbS). Repeated applications produce darker colors as more lead sulfide is formed.

Permanent Waving: Chemistry to Curl Your Hair

The chemistry of curly hair is interesting. Hair is protein, and adjacent protein chains are held together by disulfide linkages. Permanent wave lotion contains a reducing agent such as thioglycolic acid ($HSCH_2COOH$). This wave lotion ruptures the disulfide linkages (Figure 21.17), allowing the protein chains to be pulled apart as the hair is held in a curled position on rollers. The hair is then treated with a mild oxidizing agent such as hydrogen peroxide. Disulfide linkages are formed in new positions to give shape to the hair.

The same chemical process can be used to straighten naturally curly hair. The change in curliness depends only on how the hair is arranged after the disulfide bonds have been reduced and before the linkages have been restored. As in the case of permanent dyes, permanent curls grow out as new hair is formed.

▲ **Figure 21.17** Permanent waving of hair is accomplished by breaking disulfide bonds between protein chains and then reforming them in new positions.

Q: *Write a balanced equation for the reaction of a thiol, RSH, with hydrogen peroxide to form a disulfide.*

Hair Sprays

Hair can be held in place by **resins**, solid or semisolid organic materials that form a sticky film on the hair. Common resins used on hair are polyvinylpyrrolidone (PVP) and its copolymers.

$$\cdots CH{-}CH_2{-}CH{-}CH_2{-}CH{-}CH_2{-}CH{-}CH_2{-}CH{-}CH_2 \cdots$$

(each CH bears a pyrrolidone ring, N attached, with C=O)

The resin is dissolved in a solvent, and the mixture is sprayed on the hair, where the solvent evaporates. The propellants in hair sprays are usually volatile hydrocarbons, which are flammable.

Holding resins are also available as mousses. A **mousse** is simply a foam or froth. The active ingredients, like those of hair sprays, are resins such as PVP. Coloring agents and conditioners are also available as mousses. Silicone polymers are often used to impart a sheen to the hair.

Hair Removers

Chemicals that remove unwanted hair are called **depilatories**. Most of them contain a soluble sulfur compound, such as sodium sulfide or calcium thioglycolate [$Ca(OOCCH_2SH)_2$], formulated into a cream or lotion. These strongly basic mixtures destroy some of the peptide bonds in the hair so that it can be washed off. Remember that skin is made of protein, too, and so any chemical that attacks the hair can also damage the skin.

Hair Restorers

For years, men have been searching for a way to make hair grow on bald spots. Women suffer from baldness, too, but seem to consider wigs more acceptable than men do.

Minoxidil was first introduced as a drug for treating high blood pressure. It acts by dilating the blood vessels. When people who were taking the drug started growing hair on various parts of their bodies, it was applied to the scalps of people who were becoming bald. Minoxidil can produce a growth of fine hair anyplace on the skin where there are hair follicles. Minoxidil is sold under the trade name Rogaine®, although generic versions are now available. To be effective, it must be used continuously, and the cost can be several hundred dollars a year or more.

The FDA cannot ban a cosmetic without proof of harm, but testing a product for carcinogenicity (Chapter 22) would cost at least $500,000 and take 2 years.

The Well-Informed Consumer

This chapter cannot even attempt to tell you everything about the many chemical products you have in your home. Books have been written about some of them, and there are many volumes in the library that can help you if you want to know more. There is also much information available on the Internet, but much of it is little more than advertising hype; read it with caution! We hope that the knowledge you have gained here and the information you read on product labels will make you a better-informed consumer.

When you are faced with many different brands of a product at the supermarket or drugstore, remember that the most expensive one is not necessarily better than the others. Consider the soap and detergent industry, which does a lot of advertising. Each laundry powder and shampoo is claimed to be superior to all its competitors, but most brands are much alike. Advertising is expensive, so the brands that are the most widely advertised probably cost the most. Of course, sometimes one brand really is somewhat better than another, but the better product might be the less expensive one.

If you are unhappy with a product you have bought, tell the company that made it. The cosmetic industry gets thousands of complaints from customers every year. In addition, you can complain to the FDA. Many reports are presented each year to the FDA regarding adverse effects of cosmetic products: makeup products, skin care products, fragrances, and various kinds of hair care products.

Most cosmetics are made from inexpensive ingredients, and yet many highly advertised cosmetics have extremely high price tags. Are they worth it? This is a judgment that lies beyond the realm of chemistry. The $100 product inside that fancy little bottle with the famous label may have cost the manufacturer less than $5 to produce. On the other hand, if the product makes you look better or feel better, perhaps the price is not important. Only you can decide.

Self-Assessment Questions

1. To market a new cosmetic, a manufacturer
   a. does not have to prove that it is safe and effective for its intended use
   b. must pay the FDA to test it for safety
   c. must provide the FDA with evidence that the ingredients are safe for the intended use
   d. must submit an application to the FDA showing that the product is not a cosmeceutical

2. Which type of ultraviolet radiation is most responsible for sunburn?
   a. UV-A b. UV-B c. UV-C d. UV-X
3. Lipsticks usually contain a colored pigment,
   a. a fat, and a surfactant
   b. an oil, and a soap
   c. an oil, and a wax
   d. a wax, and a surfactant
4. The basic ingredients of any toothpaste are a detergent (or soap) and a(n)
   a. abrasive b. fluoride c. sweetener d. whitener
5. Sugar contributes to tooth decay by
   a. being converted by bacteria into acid that erodes tooth enamel
   b. directly attacking tooth enamel
   c. mechanically abrading tooth enamel
   d. triggering the release of stomach acid
6. Which of the fractions of a perfume is made up of the smallest molecules?
   a. end note b. middle note c. base note d. top note
7. The main ingredient in most aftershave lotions is
   a. ethanol b. menthol c. an emollient d. perfume
8. If a cosmetic is labeled as hypoallergenic, it
   a. is all natural
   b. is dermatologist tested
   c. probably has no perfume in it
   d. still may contain substances that can cause allergic reactions
9. When hair is wetted, what type of force is disrupted?
   a. hydrogen bonds
   b. disulfide linkages
   c. salt bridges
   d. peptide bonds
10. The essential ingredient in a shampoo is
   a. a conditioner b. a fragrance c. a detergent d. protein
11. What chemical forces are disrupted during home permanents?
   a. hydrogen bonds b. disulfide linkages
   c. salt bridges d. peptide bonds

Answers: 1, a; 2, b; 3, c; 4, a; 5, a; 6, d; 7, a; 8, c; 9, a; 10, c; 11, b

CRITICAL THINKING  EXERCISES

Apply knowledge that you have gained in this chapter and one or more of the FLaReS principles (Chapter 1) to evaluate the following advertising claims.

21.1 A laundry detergent "leaves clothes 50% brighter, 50% whiter [and is] 100% new & improved."

21.2 A product is claimed to be an odor-removing spray.

21.3 A shampoo brand is claimed to be "SLS [sodium lauryl sulfate] free."

21.4 A cosmetics advertisement states, "Most mineral-based cosmetics have synthetic preservatives such as parabens, dyes, and fillers which may be harmful. Our brand uses bismuth oxychloride, a natural ingredient."

21.5 A new skin cream "reduces wrinkles and prevents or reverses damage caused by aging and sun exposure."

21.6 A vitamin in a skin cream "nourishes the skin."

21.7 ". . . products that contain artificial ingredients do not provide true aromatherapy benefits."

21.8 "Laundry balls contain no chemicals [and yet are] reusable indefinitely [in the washing machine to] clean, deodorize, sterilize, bleach and soften clothes."

SUMMARY

Section 21.1—Some plants contain saponins, which produce lather. Plant ashes contain K_2CO_3 and Na_2CO_3, which are alkaline and have detergent properties. A **soap** is a salt of a long-chain carboxylic acid, traditionally made from fat and lye (NaOH). A soap molecule has a **hydrophobic** hydrocarbon tail (soluble in oil or grease) and a **hydrophilic** polar head (soluble in water). Soap molecules disperse oil or grease in water by forming **micelles**, tiny spherical oil droplets in which the hydrocarbon tails of soap molecules are embedded. Agents that stabilize suspensions in this way are called **surface-active agents (surfactants)**. Soaps do not work well in hard water (water containing Ca^{2+}, Fe^{2+}, or Mg^{2+} ions) because they form insoluble salts.

Section 21.2—A synthetic detergent usually has a long hydrocarbon tail and a polar or ionic head. ABS detergents have branched-chain structures and are not easily biodegraded. LAS detergents have a linear chain of carbon atoms that can be broken down by microorganisms. Soaps, ABS detergents, and LAS detergents are **anionic surfactants** that have a negative charge on the active part. A **nonionic surfactant** has no charge. A **cationic surfactant** such as a quaternary ammonium salt (quat) has a positive charge. An **amphoteric surfactant** carries both a positive and a negative charge. Detergent formulations often include **builders** such as complex phosphates to increase detergency. **Optical brighteners**, which are fluorescent dyes, are often added to detergents to make whites "whiter." Other components such as bleaches, fragrances, and fabric softeners may be included. Liquid dishwashing detergents contain mainly surfactants as the active ingredients. Detergents for automatic dishwashers are often strongly alkaline and should not be used for hand dishwashing.

Section 21.3—Cationic surfactants include quaternary ammonium salts, and those with two long hydrocarbon chains are used as fabric softeners. **Bleaches** are oxidizing agents. Hypochlorite bleaches release chlorine. Oxygen bleaches usually contain perborates or percarbonates. Bleaches act by oxidizing colored chromophores to colorless fragments.

Section 21.4—All-purpose cleaners may contain surfactants, ammonia, disinfectants, and other ingredients. Reading the label is imperative, so that a cleaner may be used properly and safely. Household ammonia, sodium bicarbonate (baking soda), and vinegar are good cleaners for many purposes. Special-purpose cleaners have specific purposes. Toilet bowl cleaners usually contain an acid. Scouring powders contain an abrasive. Glass cleaners contain ammonia. Drain cleaners contain NaOH and sometimes bleach. The active ingredient in oven cleaners is NaOH.

Section 21.5—Solvents are used to remove paint and other materials. Many organic solvents are volatile and flammable. **Paint** contains a pigment, a binder, and a solvent. Titanium dioxide is the most common pigment. Water-based paints contain a polymer as the binder; oil-based paints use tung oil or linseed oil. A **wax** is an ester of a fatty acid with a long-chain alcohol. Beeswax and carnauba wax are commonly used waxes. **Lanolin**, from sheep's wool, is also a wax, used in skin creams and lotions.

Section 21.6—A **cosmetic** is something applied to the body for cleansing, promoting attractiveness, or a similar purpose, but cosmetics do not have to be proven safe and effective like drugs. Skin has an outer layer made of a tough, fibrous protein called **keratin. Sebum**, an oily secretion, protects skin from loss of moisture. A **lotion** is an emulsion of oil droplets in water; a **cream** is an emulsion of water droplets in oil. Each of these is a **moisturizer** that forms a protective physical barrier over the skin to hold in moisture. Creams and lotions also soften skin; such skin softeners are called **emollients**. Humectants such as glycerol hydrogen bond to water and hold it to the skin. Ultraviolet rays trigger the production of the pigment **melanin**, which darkens the skin. **Sunscreens** block or absorb ultraviolet (UV) radiation, of which UV-B rays are more harmful than UV-A rays. The **skin protection factor (SPF)** indicates how effective a sunscreen's UV-absorbing substances are. Eye makeup and lipstick are mainly blends of oil, waxes, and pigments. **Deodorants** mask body odor and kill odor-causing bacteria. **Antiperspirants** also retard perspiration. Their most common ingredients act as **astringents**, constricting the openings of the sweat glands. Toothpaste contains a detergent and an abrasive, as well as a thickener, flavoring, and often an added fluoride compound. The fragrance of a **perfume** is due to three fractions: the **top note** (which is the most volatile), the **middle note** (of intermediate volatility), and the **end note** (of lowest volatility). **Colognes** are diluted perfumes. **Hypoallergenic cosmetics** purport to cause fewer allergic reactions than regular products, but the term has no legal meaning. Shampoos are synthetic detergents blended with perfume and sometimes with a protein or other conditioners added to give the hair more body. Dark hair contains the pigment melanin, red hair contains phaeomelanin, and blonde hair contains very little of either pigment. Many hair dyes are based on *para*-phenylenediamine. Permanent waving of the hair uses a reducing agent to break the disulfide linkages between protein chains and then an oxidizing neutralizer to reform the linkages in different positions. Hair sprays contain **resins**, organic materials that form a sticky film on the hair. Such resins are also available in foam form as **mousses**. Chemicals that remove hair are called **depilatories**, and most such chemicals can also damage the skin.

Green chemistry Consumers can apply the principles of green chemistry to make greener choices when selecting and using household products.

Learning Objectives

› Describe the structure of soap, and explain how it is made and how it works to remove greasy dirt.	Problems 9–16
› Explain the reasons for the advantages and disadvantages of soap.	Problems 1, 61
› List the advantages and disadvantages of synthetic detergents.	Problems 2, 4, 62

› Classify surfactants as amphoteric, anionic, cationic, and nonionic, and describe how they are used in various detergent formulations.	Problems 25–32, 64
› Identify a fabric softener from its structure, and describe its action.	Problems 33, 34
› Name two types of laundry bleaches, and describe how they work.	Problems 35, 36
› List the major ingredient(s) (and their purposes) of some all-purpose cleaning products and some special-purpose cleaning products.	Problems 3, 5–7, 70, 71, 74
› Identify compounds used in solvents and paints, and explain their purposes.	Problems 37–40, 75
› Identify waxes by their structure.	Problems 72, 73
› Identify the principal ingredients in various cosmetic products.	Problems 41–46, 51–56, 63, 65, 68
› Describe the chemical nature of skin, hair, and teeth.	Problems 47, 49, 50, 57–60
› Use green chemistry principles to help select greener household products.	Problems 75–77

REVIEW QUESTIONS

1. What are some advantages and disadvantages of soaps?
2. What are some advantages and disadvantages of synthetic detergents?
3. Match the formula in the left column with the description or use in the right column.

(1) CH_3COOH	**(a)** ingredient in vinegar
(2) $Na_2Al_2Si_2O_8$	**(b)** mild abrasive cleaner
(3) $NaHCO_3$	**(c)** used as bleach
(4) $NaOCl$	**(d)** used to make soap
(5) $NaOH$	**(e)** water softener
(6) Na_3PO_4	**(f)** zeolite

4. What ingredients are used in liquid dishwashing detergents (for hand dishwashing)? How do detergents for automatic dishwashers differ from those used for hand dishwashing?
5. List some uses of diluted household ammonia. What safety precautions should be followed when using ammonia?
6. What sorts of surfaces should not be cleaned with ammonia? Why?
7. List two properties of baking soda that make it useful as a cleaning agent.
8. What is the legal definition of a cosmetic? Is soap a cosmetic?

PROBLEMS

Soaps

9. How does a potassium soap differ from a sodium soap?
10. Why does soap fail to work in hard water?
11. What ingredient is added to scouring soaps?
12. How does soap (or detergent) clean a dirty surface?
13. What products are formed when tripalmitin reacts with lye (sodium hydroxide)?
14. Give the structural formula for each of the following.
    a. potassium stearate
    b. sodium palmitate
15. Give the structures of the products formed in the following reaction.

$$\begin{array}{l} CH_2O-\overset{O}{\overset{\|}{C}}(CH_2)_{10}CH_3 \\ | \\ CH-O-\overset{O}{\overset{\|}{C}}(CH_2)_{10}CH_3 \quad + \; 3\,NaOH \longrightarrow \\ | \\ CH_2O-\overset{O}{\overset{\|}{C}}(CH_2)_{10}CH_3 \end{array}$$

16. Give the structures of the products formed in the following reaction.

$$\begin{array}{l} CH_2O-\overset{O}{\overset{\|}{C}}(CH_2)_6CH_3 \\ | \\ CH-O-\overset{O}{\overset{\|}{C}}(CH_2)_4CH_3 \quad + \; 3\,NaOH \longrightarrow \\ | \\ CH_2O-\overset{O}{\overset{\|}{C}}(CH_2)_8CH_3 \end{array}$$

Water Softeners

17. Describe how trisodium phosphate softens water.
18. How does a water-softening tank work?
19. Write the equations that show how **(a)** phosphate ions and **(b)** carbonate ions react with water to form basic solutions.
20. Write the equations that show how **(a)** carbonate ions and **(b)** phosphate ions react with hard-water ions. Use M^{2+} to represent a hard-water ion.

Builders

21. What is a (detergent) builder?
22. How does sodium tripolyphosphate aid the cleaning action of a detergent?
23. How do zeolites aid the cleaning action of a detergent?
24. What advantage do zeolites have over carbonates as builders?

Detergents: Structures and Properties

25. What is an amphoteric surfactant?
26. Classify each of the following surfactants as anionic, cationic, nonionic, or amphoteric.
    a. $CH_3(CH_2)_9CH_2CH_2OSO_3^-\ Na^+$
    b. $CH_3{-}C_6H_4{-}(CH)_{10}N^+(CH_3)_3\ Cl^-$
27. Cationic surfactants are not particularly good detergents, yet they are widely used, especially in the food industry. Why?
28. Cationic surfactants are often used with nonionic surfactants but are seldom used with anionic surfactants. Why not?

Problems 29 through 32 refer to compounds I, II, and III below; C_6H_4 represents a 1, 4-disubstituted benzene ring.

I. $CH_3(CH_2)_9CH(CH_3){-}C_6H_4{-}SO_3^-\ Na^+$
II. $CH_3(CH_2)_{11}OSO_3^-\ Na^+$
III. $CH_3(CH_2)_{15}N^+(CH_3)_3\ Br^-$

29. Which are biodegradable?
30. Which is an LAS detergent?
31. Which is an alkyl sulfate?
32. Which are anionic surfactant? Which is a cationic surfactant?

Fabric Softeners

33. Give an example of a compound that acts as a fabric softener.
34. How do fabric softeners work?

Bleaches

35. How do cyanurate-type bleaches work?
36. How do sodium percarbonate and sodium perborate work as bleaches?

Solvents

37. List some uses of organic solvents in the home.
38. What are the main hazards of using solvents in the home?
39. List two hazards of cleansers that contain petroleum distillates.
40. Should gasoline be used as a cleaning solvent? Why or why not?

Skin Treatments

41. What is an emollient?
42. What is a skin moisturizer?
43. Name one advantage of OMC over PABA in sunscreen lotions.
44. Name two compounds and one element used in some types of eye makeup.

Lipsticks

45. How does lipstick differ from skin cream?
46. What materials are used to color lipsticks?

Toothpastes

47. What is the principal cause of tooth decay?
48. What is the purpose of **(a)** glycerol, **(b)** titanium dioxide, and **(c)** sodium dodecyl sulfate in toothpaste?
49. How do fluorides strengthen tooth enamel?
50. What are the best ways to prevent tooth decay?

Perfumes and Colognes

51. What is a perfume? What is a cologne?
52. What is a musk? Why are musks added to perfumes?
53. What is the function of menthol in some aftershave lotions?
54. Differentiate between a deodorant and an antiperspirant.

Hair and Hair Care

55. What is the difference between a temporary and a permanent hair dye? Why is a permanent dye not really permanent?
56. What are resins? How are resins used in hair care?
57. What kind of chemical reagent is used to break disulfide linkages in hair? What kind of chemical reaction is involved?
58. What kind of chemical reagent is used to restore disulfide linkages in hair? What kind of chemical reaction is involved?
59. What kind of chemical reaction is involved in the bleaching of hair?
60. What kind of chemical reaction is involved when a colorless precursor compound is converted to a colored dye in hair?

ADDITIONAL PROBLEMS

Problems 61 through 64 refer to structures I through IV below.

I. $CH_3(CH_2)_{15}N^+H_2CH_2COO^-$
II. $CH_3(CH_2)_{10}COO^-$
III. $CH_3(CH_2)_9CH(CH_3){-}C_6H_4{-}SO_3^-\ Na^+$
IV. $CH_3(CH_2)_{11}{-}C_6H_4{-}N^+(CH_3)_3\ Cl^-$

61. Which are soaps?
62. Which are synthetic detergents?
63. Which is a principal ingredient in baby shampoo?
64. Which is an amphoteric surfactant?

65. Write the structure for isopropyl palmitate, an ingredient in skin creams.

66. The hardness of water is reported as milligrams of calcium carbonate per liter of water. Calculate the quantity of sodium carbonate needed to soften 10.0 L of water with a hardness of 295 mg/L. (*Hint:* How much Ca^{2+} is present in the water?)

67. Tin(II) fluoride (listed as stannous fluoride on labels) is the active ingredient in fluoride toothpastes. What mass of SnF_2 can be prepared by reaction of 10.0 g SnO with excess HF?

$$SnO + 2\,HF \rightarrow SnF_2 + H_2O$$

68. Phenylacetaldehyde and 2-phenylethanol have similar molecular masses, but phenylacetaldehyde is a top-note component and 2-phenylethanol is a middle-note component of perfumes. Referring to Table 21.2, explain why this is so.

69. When you search the Internet for information about the composition of a particular industrial detergent mixture, you find that it contains quats. What type of surfactant are these ingredients?

70. Sodium hydroxide performs several functions in a drain cleaner. Name two of these functions.

71. Optical brighteners make fabric appear to reflect more light (energy) than strikes the fabric. Do optical brighteners violate the law of conservation of energy? Explain.

72. Referring to Figure 21.11, describe how the esters of carnauba wax and spermaceti are similar and how they are different.

73. Review Figure 21.11(a) and Section 9.7. Draw the condensed structure of **(a)** the carboxylic acid and **(b)** the alcohol that is formed when the ester in beeswax undergoes hydrolysis.

74. Write equations for the dissolution of the calcium carbonate buildup in a toilet bowl by each of the following toilet bowl cleaners.
   a. hydrochloric acid
   b. sodium bisulfate
   c. citric acid ($HC_6H_7O_7$)

75. Which of the following molecules is *not* a volatile organic compound?
   a. hexane
   b. ether
   c. water
   d. acetone

76. Which of the following molecules would be degraded by microorganisms in the environment?

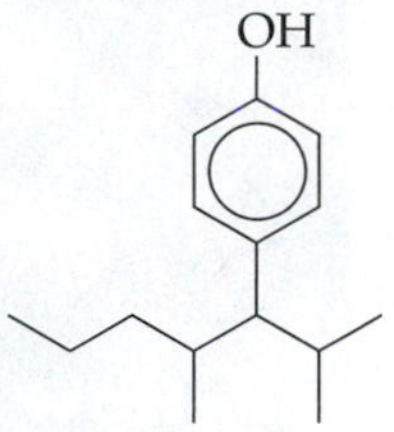

OH
(a)

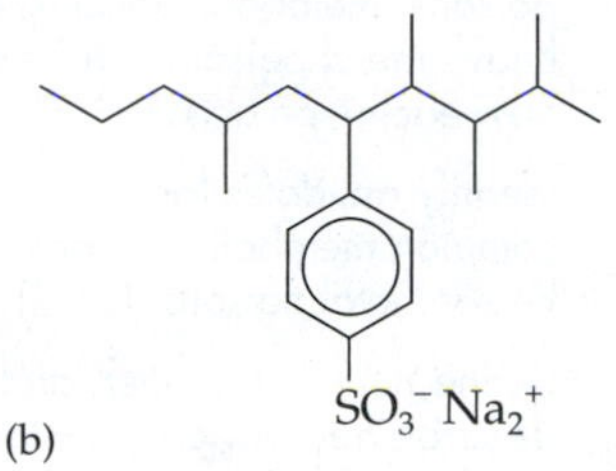

$SO_3^-\ Na_2^+$
(b)

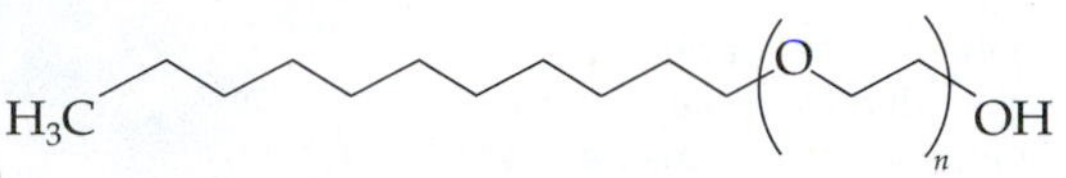

H_3C O OH n
(c)

77. Match each chemical formula with its classification in household products.

a. NaOCl	1. soap
b. $CH_3(CH_2)_{14}COO^-\ Na^+$	2. wax
c. $Na_5P_3O_{10}$	3. bleach
d. $CH_3(CH_2)_{14}COOCH_2-(CH_2)_{28}CH_3$	4. detergent builder

COLLABORATIVE GROUP PROJECTS

Prepare a PowerPoint, poster, or other presentation (as directed by your instructor) for presentation to the class.

1. Read the poem, "Watching the Mayan Women," by Luisa Villani, in *Hayden's Ferry Review*, issue 26 (Spring/Summer 2000, Arizona State University, Tempe, AZ; http://www.loc.gov/poetry/180/067.html). Relate its content to the material in this chapter.

2. Examine the label on several brands of one or more of the following household or personal care products. Identify the essential ingredients in each type of product. Use a reference such as *The Merck Index* to determine the formula and function of each ingredient.
   a. scouring cleaner
   b. window cleaner
   c. oven cleaner
   d. toilet bowl cleaner
   e. liquid drain cleaner
   f. solid drain cleaner
   g. paint remover
   h. toothpaste
   i. skin lotion
   j. shampoo

3. The Clearwater Chemical Company has announced that it has developed a biodegradable detergent. Describe what tests, if any, should be done before the detergent is marketed. Should Clearwater be allowed to market the detergent until it is proven harmful? Can a product ever be proven safe?

4. Maxisuds, Inc., has announced that it has developed a replacement for phosphate builders in detergents. Describe what tests, if any, should be done before the builder is used in detergent formulations. Should Maxisuds be allowed to market the builder until it is proven harmful? Can a product ever be proven safe?

5. Consult an industry-sponsored Web site about soaps and detergents. Then find a site sponsored by an environmental organization that presents information on how these materials affect the environment. Compare and contrast the two viewpoints.

6. A Web site lists the following as green cleaners (see the essay on page 658). In what sense is each one green? Are any of them not green? If so, in what sense? Consider whether each substance is natural or synthetic, whether it comes from a renewable or nonrenewable source, its toxicity, and its effect on the environment.
   a. baking soda
   b. borax
   c. cat litter
   d. cornstarch
   e. hydrogen peroxide
   f. isopropyl alcohol
   g. lemon
   h. lemon juice
   i. olive oil
   j. vinegar (acetic acid)

22 Poisons

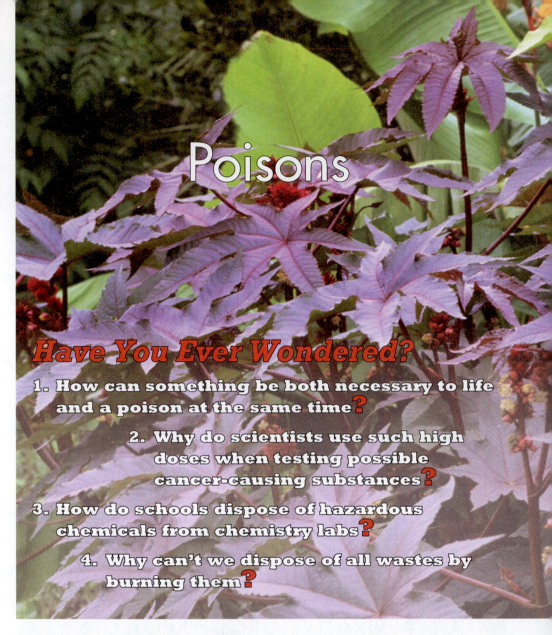

Learning Objectives

- Name some natural poisons and their sources. (22.1)
- Distinguish among corrosive poisons, metabolic poisons, and heavy metal poisons, and explain how each type acts. (22.2)
- Identify antidotes for some common metabolic poisons and heavy metal poisons. (22.2)
- Define *neurotransmitter*, and describe how various substances interfere with the action of neurotransmitters. (22.3)
- Explain the concept of an LD_{50} value, and list some of its limitations as a measure of toxicity. (22.4)
- Calculate lethal doses from LD_{50} values and body weights. (22.4)
- Describe how the liver is able to detoxify some substances. (22.5)
- Describe how cancers develop. (22.6)
- List some chemical carcinogens and anticarcinogens. (22.6)
- Name and describe three ways to test for carcinogens (22.6)
- Define *hazardous waste*, and list and give an example of the four types of such wastes. (22.7)
- Identify new approaches for testing the toxicity of synthetic chemicals.
- Discuss the importance of toxicity screening in the manufacture of safe chemicals.

Have You Ever Wondered?

1. How can something be both necessary to life and a poison at the same time?
2. Why do scientists use such high doses when testing possible cancer-causing substances?
3. How do schools dispose of hazardous chemicals from chemistry labs?
4. Why can't we dispose of all wastes by burning them?

Toxicology: What Makes a Poison?

What is a poison? Perhaps a better question is: How much is a poison? A substance may be harmless in one amount but injurious—or even deadly—in another. It was probably Paracelsus who first suggested around 1500 C.E. that "the dose makes the poison." Even a common substance such as table salt or sugar can be poisonous if eaten in abnormally large amounts.

A **poison** is a substance that causes injury, illness, or death of a living organism. We usually think of a substance as poisonous if it can kill or

We tend not to think of *poisons* and *natural* in the same context. But when it comes to poisons, nature has outperformed human beings for millennia. Even today, the most toxic substances come from nature, not scientific laboratories. The seeds of ornamental castor bean plants contain a deadly poison called *ricin*. Ricin is composed of two peptide chains linked by a disulfide bond. One microgram of ricin, an amount the size of a single grain of table sugar, is enough to kill three average adult human beings. In this chapter we will examine both natural and man-made poisons. We will learn what those poisons do to the body and how various poisonings are treated.

injure at a low dosage. The toxic dose need not be the same for everyone. An amount of salt that is safe for an adult could be deadly for a tiny infant. An amount of sugar that is all right for a healthy teenager might be quite harmful to her diabetic father.

Of course, some compounds are much more toxic than others. It would take a massive dose of salt to kill a healthy adult, whereas a few nanograms of botulin could be fatal. How the substance is administered also matters. Nicotine given intravenously is more than 50 times as toxic as when taken orally. Pure fresh water that is delightful to drink can be deadly if inhaled in large quantity.

In this chapter we take a look at poisons. **Toxicology** is the study of the effects of poisons, their detection and identification, and their antidotes. This chapter covers only a few of the many toxic substances that are known, giving priority to those that are more likely to be encountered in everyday life.

Recall from Chapter 17 that vitamin A is essential to health but that it can build to toxic levels in the body's fatty tissues.

1. How can something be both necessary to life and a poison at the same time? There are many substances that, at low doses, carry out a needed function in the body. At high doses, the same substances cause a detrimental biochemical reaction. For example, iron ions are needed to make red blood cells. But an excess of iron can be absorbed by other cells, causing cellular death. Iron can also interfere with liver function.

22.1 Natural Poisons

Learning Objective › Name some natural poisons and their sources.

When Socrates was accused of corrupting the youth of Athens in 399 B.C.E., he was given the choice of exile or death. He chose death by drinking a cup of hemlock. A **toxin** is a poison that is naturally produced by a plant or animal. Toxins were well known in the ancient world; in fact, poisoning was an official means of execution in many ancient societies. Hemlock was the official Athenian poison. Snake and insect venoms as well as plant alkaloids were widely used. Today many aboriginal tribes still use various natural poisons for hunting and warfare. Curare, used by certain South American tribes to poison their arrows, is a notorious example.

Within the past 150 years, we have learned much more about these natural poisons. The hemlock taken by Socrates was probably prepared from the unripe fruit of *Conium maculatum* (poison hemlock), dried and brewed into a tea (Figure 22.1). That fruit contains coniine, which causes, nausea, weakness, paralysis, and—as in the case of Socrates—death.

Alkaloids are heterocyclic amines (Section 9.8) that occur naturally in plants. In addition to coniine and the toxins in curare, alkaloids include caffeine, nicotine, morphine, and cocaine (Section 19.6). One of the most poisonous alkaloids is strychnine, which occurs in the seeds of several varieties of trees in the species *Strychnos*. A dose of only 30 mg can be fatal.

◄**Figure 22.1** Poison hemlock *(Conium maculatum)*, the plant whose unripe fruit was probably the source of the hemlock taken by Socrates. The main alkaloid in poison hemlock is coniine.

▲ Lucrezia Borgia (1480–1519).

Toxins are produced by animals—snakes, lizards, frogs, and others—as well as by plants. Many insects and lots of microorganisms also produce poisons. For example, each year about 20,000 Americans get *E. coli* infections, and approximately 1% of them die. Perhaps the most poisonous bacterial toxin of all is *botulin*, the nerve poison that causes botulism (Section 22.3).

Renaissance Poisoners

Despite a lack of historical evidence, Lucrezia Borgia has become legendary in the annals of poisoning. The illegitimate daughter of Pope Alexander VI, this Italian Renaissance woman is considered to be one of the most evil women to have ever lived. She has been portrayed in that role in many works of art, novels, and films. She is accused of poisoning husbands and lovers with a mixture of arsenic, phosphorus, and copper, prepared in the abdomen of a decaying hog. Borgia is also thought to have worn a hollow ring that carried poison she put in victims' drinks. Her reputation for evil may be undeserved, based in part on propaganda from her enemies and on the very real crimes of her brother Cesare, who is known to have killed several foes.

▲ Oleander blossoms are beautiful—but all parts of the plant are poisonous.

Poisonous Plants in the Garden and Home

Because many natural poisons are alkaloids that occur in plants, it is not surprising that poisons are found in gardens and on farms or ranches. In addition to the toxic pesticides that might be found on a shelf (Chapter 20), some of the plants themselves are toxic. For example, oleander (*Nerium oleander*), a beautiful shrub, contains several types of poison, including the potent cardiac glycosides *oleandrin* and *neriine*. (Cardiac glycosides are compounds that have a steroid part and a sugar part and that increase the heart's force of contraction.) Oleander's poisons are so strong that one can be poisoned by eating the honey made by bees that have fed on oleander nectar.

Iris, azaleas, and hydrangeas all are poisonous. So are holly berries, wisteria seeds, and the leaves and berries of privet hedges. Indoor plants can also be poisonous. Philodendron, one of the most popular, is quite toxic. The rosary pea (*Abrus precatorius*) has beautiful seeds that are often used to make jewelry. However, the seeds contain *abrin*. Like ricin (page 680), abrin is composed of two peptide chains that act together to inhibit protein synthesis by shutting down ribosomes. The amount of poison in one pea seed, about 3 μg, is enough to kill a person. Fortunately, the seeds present little danger when swallowed whole. However, if the coating is broken, the toxin is released.

▲ Rosary peas are often used to make necklaces and have been used for rosaries.

Self-Assessment Questions

1. The study of poisons is called
   - a. oncology
   - b. pharmacology
   - c. proctology
   - d. toxicology
2. A poison is
   - a. any alkaloid
   - b. any chemical
   - c. best defined by dose
   - d. a synthetic chemical
3. Many natural poisons are heterocyclic amines called
   - a. alkaloids
   - b. botulism
   - c. purines
   - d. reducing agents
4. The active ingredient in the poison that Socrates took was
   - a. arsenic
   - b. an alkaloid
   - c. botulin
   - d. ricin

Answers: 1, d; 2, c; 3, a; 4, b

22.2 Poisons and How They Act

Learning Objectives › Distinguish among corrosive poisons, metabolic poisons, and heavy metal poisons, and explain how each acts. › Identify antidotes for some common metabolic poisons and heavy metal poisons.

Poisons act in many ways. We examine the action of a few prominent poisons here. Recall from Chapter 7 that strong acids and strong bases have corrosive effects on human tissue. These substances indiscriminately destroy living cells. Corrosive chemicals in lesser concentrations can exhibit more subtle effects.

Strong Acids and Bases as Poisons

Both acids and bases catalyze the hydrolysis of amides, including proteins (polyamides).

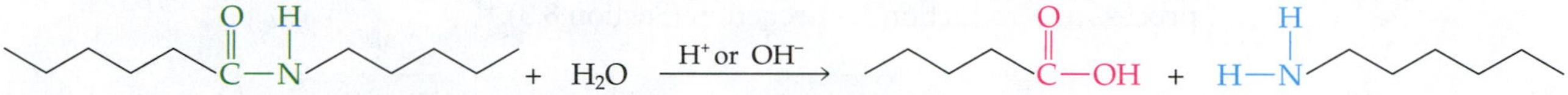

$$\sim\sim C(=O)-N(H)\sim\sim + H_2O \xrightarrow{H^+ \text{ or } OH^-} \sim\sim C(=O)-OH + H-N(H)\sim\sim$$

Intact protein molecule — Fragments

Shape is vital to the function of a protein, and the hydrolysis products cannot carry out the functions of the original protein. For example, if the protein is an enzyme, it is deactivated by hydrolysis. In cases of severe exposure, fragmentation continues until the tissue is completely destroyed.

Acids in the lungs are particularly destructive. In Chapter 13, we saw how sulfuric acid is formed when sulfur-containing coal is burned. Acids are also formed when certain plastics and other wastes are burned. These acid air pollutants cause the breakdown of lung tissue.

Oxidizing Agents as Poisons

Other air pollutants also damage living cells. Ozone, peroxyacetyl nitrate (PAN), and the other oxidizing components of photochemical smog probably do their main damage through the deactivation of enzymes. The active sites of enzymes often incorporate the sulfur-containing amino acids cysteine and methionine. Cysteine is readily oxidized by ozone to cysteic acid.

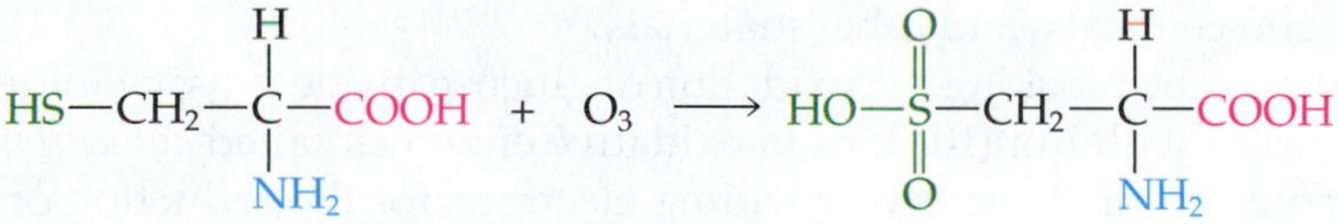

$$HS-CH_2-CH(NH_2)-COOH + O_3 \longrightarrow HO-S(=O)_2-CH_2-CH(NH_2)-COOH$$

Cysteine — Cysteic acid

Methionine is oxidized to methionine sulfoxide.

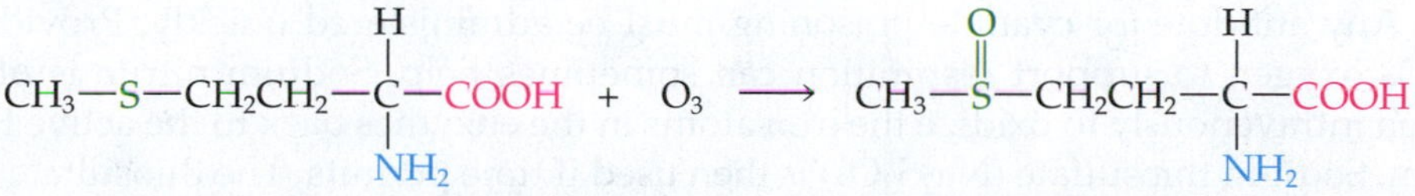

$$CH_3-S-CH_2CH_2-CH(NH_2)-COOH + O_3 \longrightarrow CH_3-S(=O)-CH_2CH_2-CH(NH_2)-COOH$$

Methionine — Methionine sulfoxide

Tryptophan also reacts with ozone. This amino acid does not contain sulfur, but it undergoes a ring-opening oxidation at the double bond.

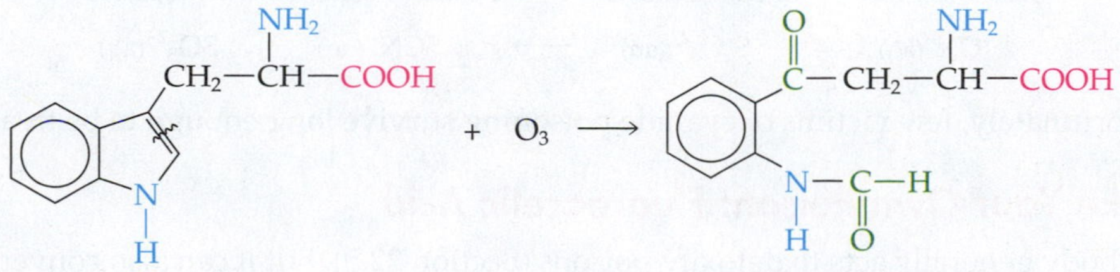

$$\text{Tryptophan (indole ring with } CH_2-CH(NH_2)-COOH\text{)} + O_3 \longrightarrow \text{Oxidation product (benzene ring with } C(=O)-CH_2-CH(NH_2)-COOH \text{ and } N(H)-C(=O)-H\text{)}$$

Tryptophan — Oxidation product

No doubt oxidizing agents can break bonds in many other chemical substances in a cell. Such powerful agents as ozone are more likely to make an indiscriminate attack than to react in a highly specific way.

Metabolic Poisons

Hemoglobin is bright red and is responsible for the red color of blood. Methemoglobin is brown. During cooking, red meat turns brown because hemoglobin is oxidized to methemoglobin. Dried bloodstains turn brown for the same reason.

Certain chemical substances prevent cellular oxidation of metabolites by blocking the transport of oxygen in the bloodstream or by interfering with oxidative processes in the cells. These chemicals act on the iron atoms in complex protein molecules. Probably the best known of these metabolic poisons is carbon monoxide. Recall (Section 13.4) that CO blocks the transport of oxygen by binding tightly to the iron atom in hemoglobin.

Nitrate ions, found in dangerous amounts in the groundwater in some agricultural areas (Section 14.5), also diminish the ability of hemoglobin to carry oxygen. Microorganisms in the digestive tract reduce nitrates to nitrites. We can write the process as a reduction half-reaction (Section 8.3).

$$\underset{\text{Nitrate ion}}{2\,H^+(aq) + NO_3^-(aq)} + 2\,e^- \longrightarrow \underset{\text{Nitrite ion}}{NO_2^-(aq)} + H_2O$$

Deaths that occur in house fires are often actually caused by toxic gases. Smoldering fires produce carbon monoxide, but hydrogen cyanide (formed by burning plastics and fabrics; Chapter 10) is also important. Some fire department rescue crews carry spring-loaded hypodermic syringes filled with sodium thiosulfate solution for emergency treatment of victims of smoke inhalation.

The nitrite ions oxidize the Fe^{2+} in hemoglobin to Fe^{3+}, forming *methemoglobin*, which is incapable of carrying oxygen. The resulting oxygen-deficiency disease is called *methemoglobinemia*, known when it affects infants as "blue-baby syndrome."

Cyanides, compounds that contain a C≡N group, are among the most notorious poisons in both fact and fiction. They include salts such as sodium cyanide (NaCN) and the covalent compound hydrogen cyanide (H—C≡N). Cyanides act quickly and are powerful. It takes only about 50 mg of HCN or 200–300 mg of a cyanide salt to kill. Cyanide exposure occurs frequently in victims of smoke inhalation from house fires. Experts use HCN gas to exterminate pests in ships, warehouses, and railway cars, and on citrus and other fruit trees. Sodium cyanide (NaCN) is employed to extract gold and silver from ores and in electroplating baths.

Worldwide, about 1.1 billion kg of hydrogen cyanide is produced annually. About 150 million kg is used to produce sodium cyanide for gold processing. The rest is used industrially in the production of plastics, adhesives, fire retardants, cosmetics, pharmaceuticals, and other materials.

In the World War II Nazi death camps, both carbon monoxide and hydrogen cyanide were used to murder 6 million Jews, gypsies, Poles, and others. Treblinka, Belzec, and Sobibor used CO from internal combustion engines in closed chambers. Auschwitz/Birkenau, Stutthof, and other camps used HCN in the form of *Zyklon-B* (HCN absorbed in a carrier, typically wood pulp or diatomaceous earth).

Cyanides act by blocking the oxidation of glucose inside cells; cyanide ions form a stable complex with iron(III) ions in oxidative enzymes called *cytochrome oxidases*. These enzymes normally act by providing electrons for the reduction of oxygen in the cell. Cyanide blocks this action and brings an abrupt end to cellular respiration, causing death in minutes. Cyanides are sometimes used to commit suicide, particularly by health-care and laboratory workers.

Any antidote for cyanide poisoning must be administered quickly. Providing 100% oxygen to support respiration can sometimes help. Sodium nitrite is often given intravenously to oxidize the iron atoms in the enzymes back to the active Fe^{3+} form. Sodium thiosulfate ($Na_2S_2O_3$) is then used if time permits. The thiosulfate ion transfers a sulfur atom to the cyanide ion, converting it to the relatively innocuous thiocyanate ion.

$$\underset{\text{Cyanide ion}}{CN^-(aq)} + \underset{\text{Thiosulfate ion}}{S_2O_3^{2-}(aq)} \longrightarrow \underset{\text{Thiocyanate ion}}{SCN^-(aq)} + \underset{\text{Sulfite ion}}{SO_3^{2-}(aq)}$$

Unfortunately, few victims of cyanide poisoning survive long enough to be treated.

```
      CH2—COOH
      |
  HO—C—COOH
      |
      CH2—COOH
```

Citric acid

```
   F—CH—COOH
      |
  HO—C—COOH
      |
      CH2—COOH
```

Fluorocitric acid

Make Your Own Poison: Fluoroacetic Acid

The body generally acts to detoxify poisons (Section 22.5), but it can also convert an essentially harmless chemical to a deadly poison. Fluoroacetic acid (FCH_2COOH) is one such compound. Our cells use acetic acid to produce citric acid, which is then broken down in a series of steps, most of which release energy. When fluoroacetic acid is ingested, it is incorporated into fluorocitric acid. The latter effectively blocks the citric acid cycle by tying up the enzyme that acts on citric acid. Thus, the energy-producing mechanism of the cell is shut off, and death comes quickly.

Sodium fluoroacetate (FCH_2COONa), a salt of fluoroacetic acid and also known as *Compound 1080*, is used to poison rodents and predatory animals. It is not selective, making it dangerous to humans, pets, and other animals.

Fluoroacetic acid occurs in nature in an extremely poisonous South African plant called *gifblaar*. Natives have used this plant to poison the tips of their arrows.

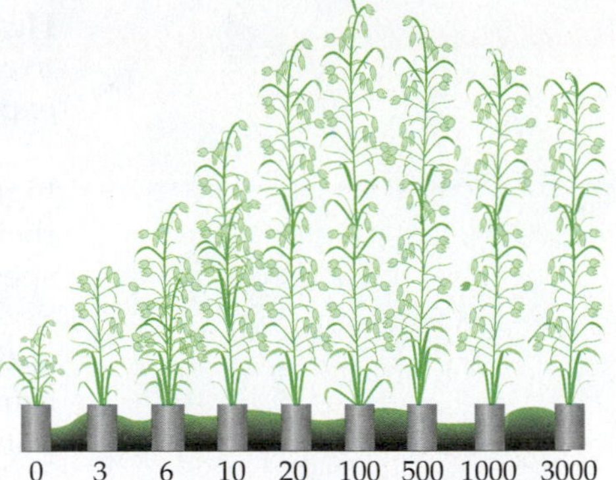

▲ **Figure 22.2** The effect of copper ions on the height of oat seedlings. From left to right, the concentrations of Cu^{2+} are 0, 3, 6, 10, 20, 100, 500, 2000, and 3000 μg/L. The plants on the left show varying degrees of deficiency; those on the right show copper ion toxicity. The optimum level of Cu^{2+} for oat seedlings is therefore about 100 μg/L.

Heavy Metal Poisons

Metals with densities at least five times that of water are called *heavy metals*. Many heavy metals are toxic, but lead, mercury, and cadmium are especially notable. Of course, metals need not be dense to be toxic. One especially toxic metal is beryllium, a very light metal. All beryllium compounds are poisonous and can cause a painful and usually fatal disease known as *berylliosis*.

People have long used a variety of metals in industry and agriculture and around the home. Most metals and their compounds show some toxicity when ingested in large amounts. Even essential mineral nutrients can be toxic when taken in excessive amounts. In many cases, too little of a metal ion (a deficiency) can be as dangerous as too much (toxicity). This effect is illustrated in Figure 22.2.

Some metal ions are critical to human health—in the right amounts. The average adult requires 10–18 mg of iron every day. When less is taken in, the person suffers from anemia. Yet an overdose can cause vomiting, diarrhea, shock, coma, and even death. As few as 10–15 tablets, each containing 325 mg of $FeSO_4$ (65 mg Fe per tablet) have been fatal to children. Large excesses of Fe^{2+} can damage the intestinal lining. Iron poisoning occurs when the concentration of circulating Fe^{2+} is more than the iron-binding proteins in the blood can take up.

Other heavy metals exert their action primarily by inactivating enzymes. In simple laboratory chemical reactions, heavy metal ions react with hydrogen sulfide to form insoluble sulfides.

$$Pb^{2+}(aq) + H_2S(g) \rightarrow PbS(s) + 2\,H^+(aq)$$
$$Hg^{2+}(aq) + H_2S(g) \rightarrow HgS(s) + 2\,H^+(aq)$$

Most enzymes have amino acids with sulfhydryl (—SH) groups. These groups bind with heavy metal ions in the same way that H_2S does, rendering the enzymes inactive (Figure 22.3).

Mercury (Hg) is a most unusual metal. It is the only common metal that is a liquid at room temperature. People have long been fascinated by this bright, silvery, dense liquid, once known as *quicksilver*. Children sometimes play with the mercury from a broken thermometer.

Mercury metal has many uses. It is used in thermometers and barometers. Dentists use it to make amalgams for filling teeth. It is used as a liquid metal electrical contact in switches. These uses are now restricted in many areas.

In the United States, about 140,000 kg of mercury is released each year into the air, about 40% from coal-fired power plants. (Although mercury occurs in only trace amounts in coal, we burn a billion metric tons of coal a year.) Other sources of mercury are waste incinerators and factories that produce chlorine and sodium hydroxide (chlor-alkali plants). The mercury returns to the land and water.

Mercury presents a hazard to those who work with it because its vapor is toxic. Mercury vapor is quite hazardous when inhaled, particularly when exposure takes place over a long period of time. An open container of mercury or a spill on the floor can release enough mercury vapor into the air to exceed the established maximum safe level by a factor of 200.

Hazardous chronic exposure usually occurs with regular occupational use of the metal, such as in mining or extraction. The body converts the inhaled mercury to

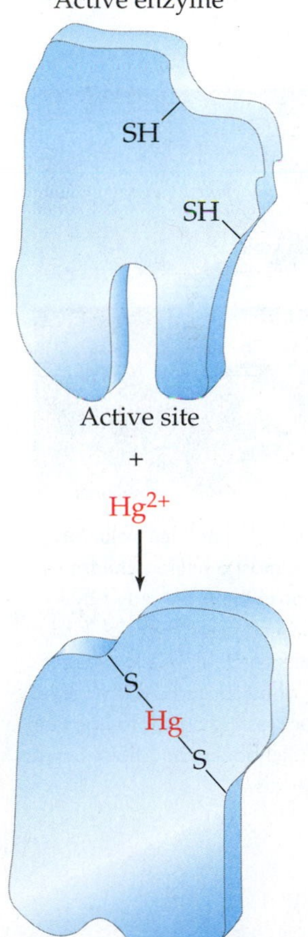

▲ **Figure 22.3** Mercury poisoning. Enzymes catalyze reactions by binding a reactant molecule at the active site (Section 16.5). Mercury ions react with sulfhydryl groups to change the shape of the enzyme and destroy the active site.

Hg^{2+} ions. Because mercury is a cumulative poison (it takes the body about 70 days to rid itself of *half* of a given dose), chronic poisoning is a threat to those continually exposed.

In aquatic systems, mercury vapor is converted by anaerobic organisms to highly toxic methylmercury ions (CH_3Hg^+). Fish tend to concentrate CH_3Hg^+ in their bodies. People in 46 states have been warned to limit consumption of certain species of fish—particularly swordfish and shark—or to avoid them entirely.

Fortunately, there are antidotes for mercury poisoning. While searching for an antidote for the arsenic-containing war gas lewisite (page 687), British scientists came up with a compound for treating heavy metal poisoning as well. The compound, a derivative of glycerol, is called *British antilewisite (BAL)*. It acts by *chelating* (from the Greek *chela* meaning "claw") Hg^{2+} ions, surrounding the ions so that they are tied up and cannot attack vital enzymes.

CH_2—CH—CH_2
OH SH SH
BAL

[CH_2—CH—CH_2; S S OH; Hg; OH S S; CH_2—CH—CH_2]$^{2-}$
Mercury atom chelated by two BAL molecules

The bad news is that the effects of mercury poisoning may not show up for several weeks. By the time the symptoms—loss of equilibrium, sight, feeling, and hearing—are recognizable, extensive damage has already been done to the brain and nervous system. Such damage is largely irreversible. BAL and similar antidotes are effective only when a person knows that he or she has been poisoned and seeks treatment right away.

All compounds of mercury, except those that are virtually insoluble in water, are poisonous no matter how they are administered. However, metallic mercury does not seem to be very toxic when ingested (swallowed). Most of it passes through the system unchanged. Indeed, there are numerous reports of mercury being given orally in the eighteenth and nineteenth centuries as a remedy for obstruction of the bowels. Doses varied from a few ounces to a pound or more!

▲ In 2007, Fisher-Price voluntarily recalled almost a million children's toys because the paint may have contained excessive levels of lead. Less extensive children's toy recalls in 2011 affected particular varieties of memory testing cards, toy garden rakes, sketchbooks, and ESI-R Screening Materials.

Lead is widespread in the environment, reflecting the many uses we have for this soft, dense, corrosion-resistant metal and its compounds. Lead (as Pb^{2+} ions) is present in many foods, generally in concentrations of less than 0.3 ppm. Lead ions also get into our drinking water (up to 0.1 ppm) from lead-sealed pipes. Lead compounds were once widely used in house paints, and tetraethyllead was used in most gasolines. Since those two uses were banned, exposure to lead has decreased dramatically, from about 15 μg/dL in the 1970s to less than 2 μg/dL today. The CDC sets a blood lead level above 10 μg/dL as an unacceptable health risk, but adverse health effects can occur at lower concentrations. Effects include lower intelligence and poor school performance.

Lead and its compounds are quite toxic. Metallic lead is generally converted to Pb^{2+} in the body. Lead can damage the brain, liver, and kidneys. Extreme cases can be fatal.

Lead poisoning is especially harmful to children. Some children develop a craving that causes them to eat unusual things, and children with this syndrome (called *pica*) eat chips of peeling lead-based paints. These children probably also pick up lead compounds from the streets, where they were deposited by automobile exhausts. They also ingest lead from food and even from toys coated with lead-containing paint. Large amounts of Pb^{2+} in a child's blood can cause mental retardation, behavior problems, anemia, hearing loss, developmental delays, and other physical and mental problems.

Adults can excrete about 2 mg of lead per day. Most people take in less than that from air, food, and water, and thus generally do not accumulate toxic levels.

Arsenic Poisoning

Arsenic is not a metal, but it has some metallic properties. In commercial poisons, arsenic is usually found as arsenate (AsO_4^{3-}) or arsenite (AsO_3^{3-}) ions. Like heavy metal ions, these ions render enzymes inactive by tying up sulfhydryl groups.

$$^{-}O-As(O^{-})_2 + (HS)_2\text{-Enzyme} \longrightarrow {}^{-}O-As(S)_2\text{-Enzyme} + 2\,OH^{-}$$

Arsenite ion　Enzyme　Enzyme (inactive)

There are numerous organic compounds containing arsenic. One such compound, *arsphenamine*, was the first antibacterial agent and was once used widely in the treatment of syphilis.

$$HO-C_6H_3(NH_2)-As{=}As-C_6H_3(NH_2)-OH$$

Arsphenamine

Another arsenic compound, *lewisite*, first synthesized by (and named for) W. Lee Lewis, was developed as a blister agent for use in chemical warfare. The United States started large-scale production of lewisite in 1918, but fortunately World War I came to an end before this gas could be employed.

$$ClCH{=}CH-AsCl_2$$

Lewisite

If intake exceeds excretion, however, lead builds up in the body and chronic irreversible lead poisoning can result.

Lead poisoning is usually treated with a combination of BAL and another chelating agent called *ethylenediaminetetraacetic acid* (*EDTA*).

$$(HOOC-CH_2)_2N-CH_2CH_2-N(CH_2-COOH)_2$$

EDTA

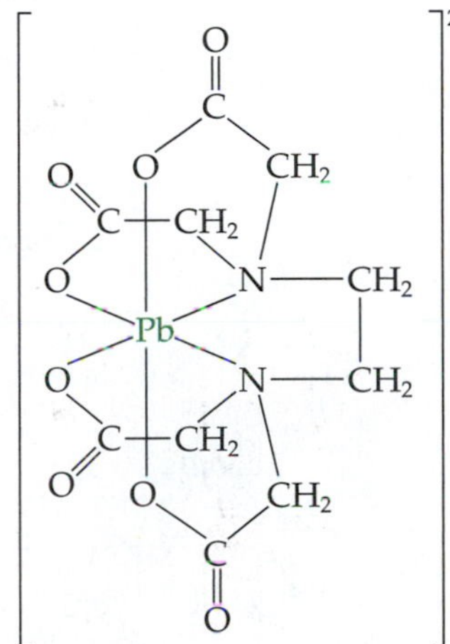
Lead–EDTA complex

The calcium salt of EDTA is administered intravenously. In the body, calcium ions are displaced by lead ions, to which EDTA binds more tightly.

$$CaEDTA^{2-} + Pb^{2+} \longrightarrow PbEDTA^{2-} + Ca^{2+}$$

The lead–EDTA complex is then excreted.

As with mercury poisoning, the neurological damage caused by lead compounds is irreversible. Treatment must begin early to be effective.

Cadmium is another useful but troublesome heavy metal. It is used in alloys, in the electronics industry, in nickel–cadmium rechargeable batteries, and in many other applications. Cadmium (as Cd^{2+} ions) is quite toxic. Cadmium poisoning leads to loss of calcium ions (Ca^{2+}) from the bones, leaving them brittle and easily broken. It also causes severe abdominal pain, vomiting, diarrhea, and a choking sensation.

The most notable cases of cadmium poisoning occurred along the upper Zintsu River in Japan, where cadmium ions entered the water in milling wastes from a mine. Downstream, farm families used the water to irrigate their rice fields and for drinking, cooking, and other household purposes. Many of these people soon began to suffer from a strange, painful malady that became known as *itai-itai*, the "ouch-ouch" disease. Over 200 people died, and thousands were disabled.

▲ After importation of Chinese toys was restricted because they contained lead, some overseas manufacturers substituted cadmium. Unfortunately, cadmium ions are even more toxic than lead ions.

Self-Assessment Questions

1. Which of the following is *not* a corrosive poison?
a. HCN　**b.** HNO_3　**c.** O_3　**d.** NaOH

2. What type of poisons are carbon monoxide and cyanides?
a. catalytic　**b.** heavy metal
c. hemolytic　**d.** metabolic

3. Nitrites poison by
   a. blocking the action of cytochrome oxidase
   b. blocking the action of acetylcholinesterase
   c. displacing O_2 from oxyhemoglobin
   d. oxidizing Fe^{2+} in hemoglobin

4. Cyanides poison by
   a. blocking the action of cytochrome oxidase
   b. blocking the action of acetylcholinesterase
   c. displacing O_2 from oxyhemoglobin
   d. oxidizing Fe^{2+} in hemoglobin

5. The most important toxic heavy metals are
   a. gold, platinum, and silver
   b. iron, calcium, and mercury
   c. lead, silver, and gold
   d. lead, mercury, and cadmium

6. The main source of mercury in the environment is
   a. broken thermometers
   b. dental fillings
   c. the burning of coal
   d. chlor-alkali plants

7. One reason for the dramatic decrease in lead found in the environment is the banning of
   a. leaded gasoline
   b. lead in pencils
   c. lead solder for copper pipes
   d. lead alloys

8. Lead poisoning can be treated with
   a. a chelating agent
   b. an oxidizing agent
   c. a reducing agent
   d. a strong acid

9. Cadmium compounds
   a. are used in some dental fillings
   b. act as blister agents in warfare
   c. cause "ouch-ouch" disease
   d. are found in high concentrations in fish

Answers: 1, a; 2, d; 3, c; 4, a; 5, d; 6, c; 7, a; 8, a; 9, c

22.3 More Chemistry of the Nervous System

Learning Objective › Define *neurotransmitter*, and describe how various substances interfere with the action of neurotransmitters.

Some of the most toxic substances known act on the nervous system. Signals are shuttled across synapses between nerve cells by chemical messengers called *neurotransmitters* (Section 18.7). Neurotoxins can disrupt the action of a neurotransmitter in several ways: by interfering with its synthesis or transport, by occupying its receptor site, or by blocking its degradation.

One such chemical messenger is *acetylcholine* (*ACh*). It activates the postsynaptic nerve cell by fitting into a specific receptor and thus changing the permeability of the cell membrane to certain ions. Once ACh has carried the impulse across the synapse, it is rapidly hydrolyzed to acetic acid and relatively inactive choline in a reaction catalyzed by an enzyme, acetylcholinesterase.

$$\underset{\text{Acetylcholine}}{CH_3\overset{O}{\overset{\|}{C}}OCH_2CH_2{-}\overset{CH_3}{\overset{|}{\underset{\underset{CH_3}{|}}{N^+}}}{-}CH_3} \;\; 1 \;\; H_2O \xrightarrow{\text{acetylcholinesterase}} \underset{\text{Acetic acid}}{CH_3\overset{O}{\overset{\|}{C}}OH} + \underset{\text{Choline}}{HOCH_2CH_2{-}\overset{CH_3}{\overset{|}{\underset{\underset{CH_3}{|}}{N^+}}}{-}CH_3}$$

The postsynaptic cell releases the hydrolysis products and is then ready to receive further impulses. Other enzymes, such as acetylase, convert the acetic acid and choline back to acetylcholine, completing the cycle (Figure 22.4).

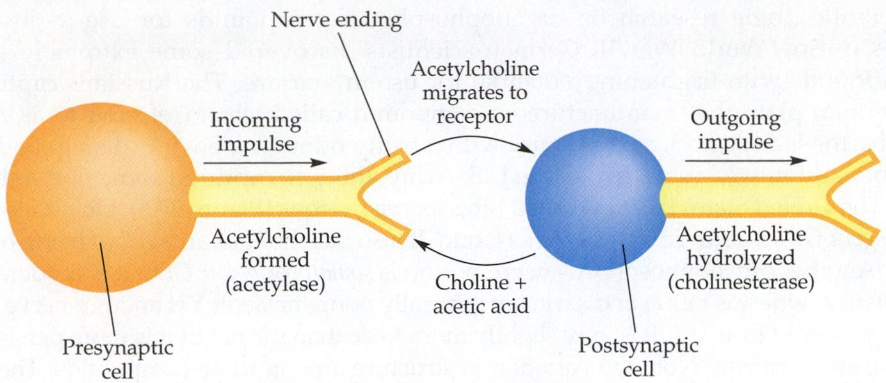

Figure 22.4 The acetylcholine cycle.

People with Alzheimer's disease are deficient in the enzyme acetylase. They produce too little acetylcholine for proper brain function. Drugs to treat the disease, such as donepezil (Aricept®), inhibit the action of acetylcholinesterase, thus helping to prevent the decline of ACh levels. These drugs are only moderately effective.

Nerve Poisons and the Acetylcholine Cycle

Various substances can disrupt the acetylcholine cycle at three different points, as illustrated by the following examples.

- Botulin, the deadly toxin produced by *Clostridium botulinum* (an anaerobic bacterium) found in improperly processed canned food, is a powerful ACh antagonist; it blocks the synthesis of ACh. When no messengers are formed, no messages are carried. Paralysis sets in and death occurs, usually from respiratory failure.
- Curare, atropine, and some local anesthetics act by blocking ACh receptor sites. In this case, the message is sent but not received. Local anesthetics use this mechanism to provide pain relief in a limited area, but these drugs, too, can be lethal in sufficient quantity.
- Anticholinesterase poisons act by inhibiting the enzyme cholinesterase.

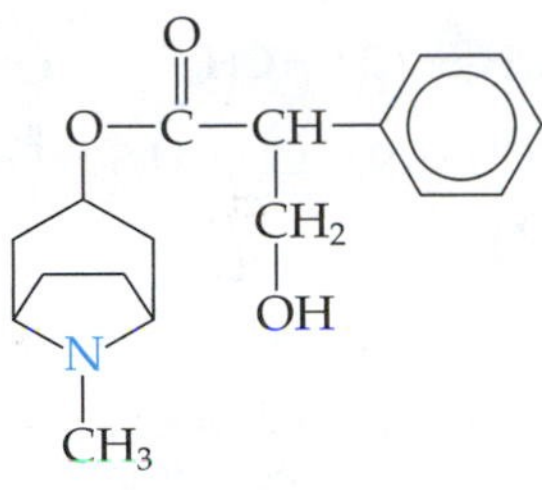

Atropine

Organophosphorus Compounds as Insecticides and Weapons of War

Organic phosphorus insecticides (Section 20.2) are well-known nerve poisons. The phosphorus–oxygen linkage is thought to bond tightly to acetylcholinesterase, blocking the breakdown of acetylcholine (Figure 22.5). Acetylcholine therefore builds up, causing postsynaptic nerve cells to fire repeatedly. This overstimulates the muscles, glands, and organs. The heart beats wildly and irregularly, and the victim goes into convulsions and dies quickly.

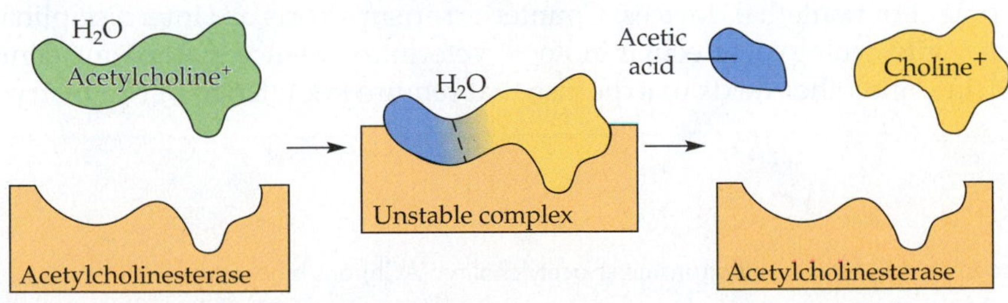

(a) Normal catalysis of acetylcholine

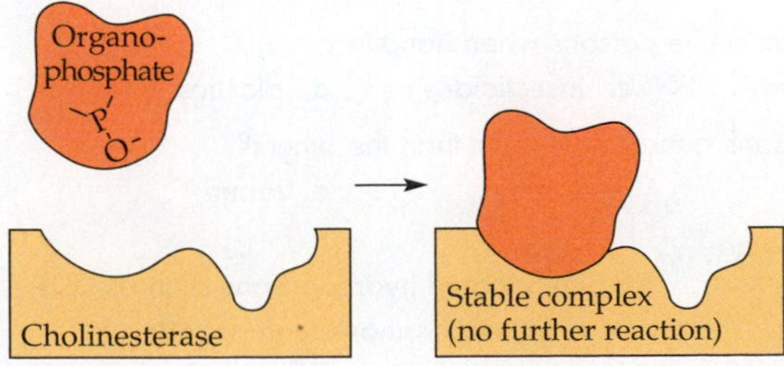

(b) Catalysis inhibited by organophosphate toxin

Figure 22.5 (a) Acetylcholinesterase catalyzes the hydrolysis of acetylcholine to acetic acid and choline. (b) An organophosphate ties up acetylcholinesterase, preventing it from breaking down acetylcholine.

Q: *What functional group is split in the hydrolysis of acetylcholine?*

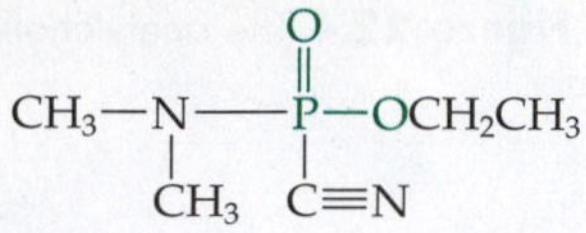

$CH_3{-}N(CH_3){-}P(=O)(C{\equiv}N){-}OCH_2CH_3$

Tabun
(agent GA)

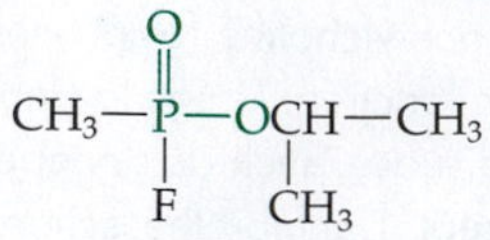

$CH_3{-}P(=O)(F){-}OCH(CH_3){-}CH_3$

Sarin
(agent GB)

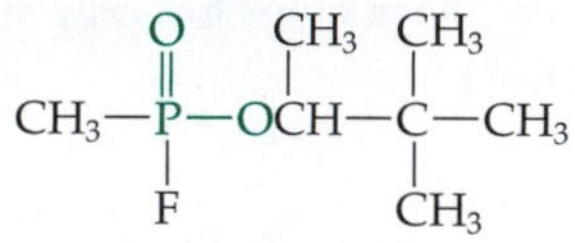

$CH_3{-}P(=O)(F){-}OCH(CH_3){-}C(CH_3)_2{-}CH_3$

Soman
(agent GD)

$CH_3{-}CH(CH_3){-}N(CH(CH_3){-}CH_3){-}CH_2CH_2S{-}P(=O)(CH_2CH_3){-}OCH_3$

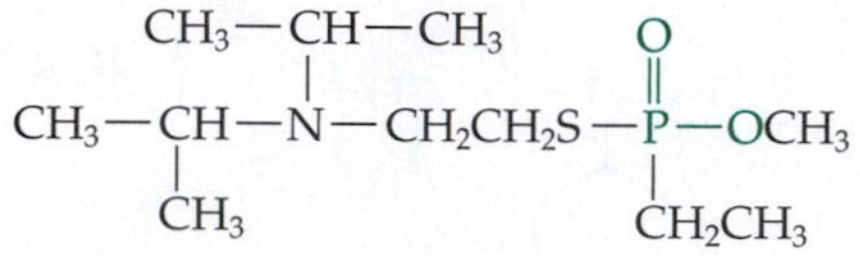

VX

▲ **Figure 22.6** Four organophosphorus compounds used as nerve poisons in chemical warfare. Compare these structures with those of the insecticides malathion and parathion (Figure 20.12).

While doing research on organophosphorus compounds for use as insecticides during World War II, German scientists discovered some extremely toxic compounds with frightening potential for use in warfare. The Russians captured a German plant that manufactured a compound called *tabun* (referred to as *agent GA* by the U.S. Army), a compound with a fruity odor. The Soviets dismantled the factory and moved it to Russia. The U.S. Army, though, captured some of the stock.

The United States has developed other nerve poisons (Figure 22.6). One, called *sarin* (*agent GB*), is four times as toxic as tabun. It also has the "advantage" of being odorless. Another organophosphorus nerve poison is *soman* (or *agent GD*). It is moderately persistent, whereas tabun and sarin are generally nonpersistent. Yet another nerve poison is referred to as *VX*. It is only slightly more toxic than sarin, but it is more persistent in the environment. Note the variation in structure among these compounds. The approach to developing chemical warfare agents is much the same as that for developing drugs—find one that works, then synthesize and test structural variations.

These nerve poisons are among the most toxic synthetic chemicals known (although still not nearly as toxic as the natural toxin botulin). They are inhaled or absorbed through the skin, causing a complete loss of muscular coordination and subsequent death by cessation of breathing. The usual antidote is atropine injection and artificial respiration. Without an antidote, death usually occurs in 2–10 min depending on the dose absorbed.

The phosphorus-based insecticides malathion and parathion (Section 20.2) are similar to the nerve poisons used as chemical warfare agents but far less toxic. Nonetheless, they and other insecticides like them should be used with great caution.

Nerve poisons have helped us gain an understanding of the chemistry of the nervous system. This knowledge enables scientists to design antidotes for nerve poisons, to better understand diseases of the nervous system, and to develop new drugs to treat pain and diseases such as Alzheimer's disease and Parkinson's disease.

Chemistry and Counterterrorism

When people think of terrorism, they often think of the negative role of chemistry, associating it with chemical weapons and chemical warfare. However, there are many applications of chemistry in counterterrorism. Chemistry plays an important role in countering the proliferation of chemical weapons and in detecting and defending against them in case of an attack. Knowledge of chemistry is essential in the evaluation of a threat. Chemistry can also help in the development of nonlethal devices. Counterterrorism efforts are interdisciplinary, involving toxicology, molecular biology, veterinary science, pathology, clinical medicine, and other fields of expertise that require knowledge of chemistry.

Self-Assessment Questions

1. Receptor sites for the neurotransmitter acetylcholine (ACh) are blocked by
a. atropine **b.** choline **c.** opiates **d.** naloxone

2. Botulin acts on the acetylcholine (ACh) cycle by
a. blocking the synthesis of ACh **b.** inhibiting acetylcholinesterase
c. inhibiting cholinesterase **d.** inhibiting reverse transcriptase

3. Most people are likely to encounter nerve poisons when handling
a. fertilizers **b.** explosives **c.** insecticides **d.** plastics

4. Which of the following nerve poisons is much less toxic than the others?
a. malathion **b.** sarin **c.** soman **d.** tabun

5. The most hazardous nerve poisons are
a. alkaloids such as cocaine **b.** chlorinated hydrocarbons such as DDT
c. hydrocarbons such as gasoline **d.** organophosphorus compounds

Answers: 1, a; 2, a; 3, c; 4, a; 5, d

22.4 The Lethal Dose

Learning Objectives › Explain the concept of an LD_{50} value, and list some of its limitations as a measure of toxicity. › Calculate lethal doses from LD_{50} values and body weights.

Some substances are much more poisonous than others. To quantify toxicity, scientists use the $\mathbf{LD_{50}}$ (lethal dose for 50%) value, which specifies the dosage that kills 50% of a population of test animals. This statistic is used because animals vary in strength and in their susceptibility to toxins. The dose that kills 50% is the average lethal dose.

Usually, LD_{50} values are given in terms of mass of poison per unit of body weight of the test animal (for example, milligrams of poison per kilogram of animal). Tested substances are most often given orally. (Values for intravenous administration can differ greatly from those for oral ingestion.) Although LD_{50} values are useful in comparing the relative toxicities of various substances, the values for test animals are not necessarily the same values that would be measured for humans.

Table 22.1 lists LD_{50} values for a variety of substances. The larger the LD_{50} value, the less toxic the substance. In general, substances with oral LD_{50} values greater than 15,000 mg/kg are considered nearly nontoxic. Substances with LD_{50} values from 7500 to 15,000 mg/kg are considered to be of low toxicity; those with values from 500 to 7500 mg/kg, moderately toxic; and those with values less than 500 mg/kg, highly toxic.

Table 22.1 Approximate LD_{50} Values for Selected Substances

Substance	Test Animal	Route	LD_{50} (mg/kg)	Use or Occurrence
Sucrose	Rat	Oral	29,700	Table sugar
Sodium chloride	Rat	Oral	3000	Table salt
Ethyl alcohol	Rat	Oral	2080	Beverage alcohol
Aspirin	Rat	Oral	1500	Analgesic
Acetaminophen	Mouse	Oral	340	Analgesic
Nicotine	Mouse	Oral (intravenous)	230 (0.3)	Tobacco component, insecticide
Caffeine	Rat	Oral	192	Coffee and cola ingredient
Rotenone	Rat	Oral (intravenous)	132 (6)	Insecticide
Sodium cyanide	Rat	Oral	15	Gold extraction
Arsenic trioxide	Rat	Oral	15	Manufacture of insecticides and drugs
Ethylene glycol	Rat	Oral	6.86	Antifreeze
Ketamine	Rat	Oral	0.229	Veterinary anesthetic
Sarin	Human	Skin contact	0.01	Chemical warfare agent
Agent VX	Human	Skin contact	0.01	Chemical warfare agent
Tetanus toxin	Human	Puncture wound	0.0000025	In soil
Ricin	Mice	Oral	0.000005	Castor beans
Botulin toxin	Human	Inhalation Oral	0.000003 0.0000002	Possible biological warfare agent Food poisoning

The Botox Enigma

Botulin is the most toxic substance known, with a median lethal dose of only about 0.2 ng/kg of body weight. (Recall that 1 nanogram is one-billionth of a gram.) Yet botulin, in a commercial formulation called Botox®, is used medically to treat intractable muscle spasms and is widely used in cosmetic surgery to remove wrinkles. When a muscle contracts over a long period of time without relaxing, it can cause severe pain. Tiny amounts of Botox can be injected into the muscle, where it binds to receptors on nerve endings. This stops the release of acetylcholine, and the signal for the muscle to contract is blocked. The muscle fibers that were pulling too hard are paralyzed, providing relief from the spasm.

▶ Botox is a purified and extremely dilute preparation of the botulin toxin that causes the food poisoning known as *botulism*. When Botox is injected into specific muscles, it blocks the signals that cause muscles to contract. Because the muscles can't constrict, the skin levels out and appears less wrinkled.

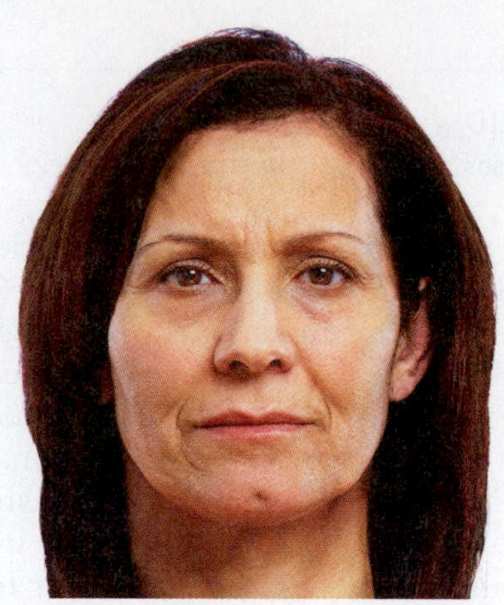

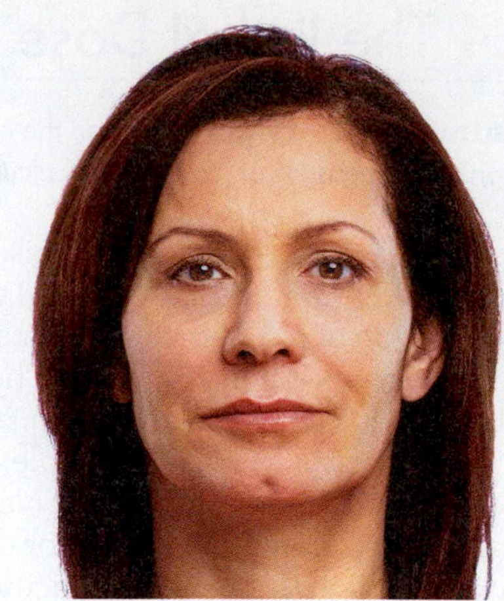

Botox is also used to treat afflictions such as uncontrollable blinking, crossed eyes, and Parkinson's disease. In the case of crossed eyes, for example, the optic muscles cause the eyeballs to be drawn to focus inward. Treatment with botulin prevents the muscles from doing so, and repeated treatments correct the problem.

Botox curbs migraine headache pain in some people, probably by blocking nerves that carry pain messages to the brain and by relaxing muscles, making them less sensitive to pain. It is also used to treat excessive sweating, most likely by blocking the release of acetylcholine, the chemical that stimulates the sweat glands. Botox injections are used to treat bladder problems in which the patients are suffering from involuntary contractions of the bladder muscles. These contractions can cause incontinence or make it impossible to completely empty the bladder. Botox blocks the contractions.

In cosmetic surgery, small, carefully delivered amounts of Botox inactivate small facial muscles, markedly reducing "surprise wrinkles" in the forehead, frown lines between the eyebrows, and crow's feet at the corners of the eyes. These Botox treatments wear off in a few months.

Self-Assessment Questions

1. Toxicity is often reported in terms of an LD_{50} value, which is the
   a. dose that kills half of a tested population
   b. lowest dose that kills an average 50-year-old person
   c. lowest dose likely to kill a 50-month-old child
   d. portion of the tested population killed by a 50-mg dose
2. According to Table 22.1, which of the following substances is most toxic?
   a. aspirin **b.** caffeine **c.** ketamine **d.** sodium cyanide

Answers: 1, a; 2, c

22.5 The Liver as a Detox Facility

Learning Objective › Describe how the liver is able to detoxify some substances.

A traditional antidote for methanol or ethylene glycol poisoning is ethanol, administered intravenously. This "loads up" the liver enzymes with ethanol, blocking oxidation of methanol until the compound can be excreted. A safer antidote, the drug *fomepizole*, inhibits the liver enzyme that catalyzes the oxidation of alcohols.

The human body can handle moderate amounts of some poisons. The liver is able to detoxify some compounds by oxidation or reduction or by coupling them with amino acids or other normal body chemicals.

Perhaps the most common route is oxidation. Ethanol (Section 9.5) is detoxified by oxidation to acetaldehyde, which in turn is oxidized to acetic acid and then to carbon dioxide and water.

$$CH_3CH_2OH \longrightarrow CH_3CHO \longrightarrow CH_3COOH \longrightarrow CO_2 + H_2O$$

Highly toxic nicotine from tobacco is detoxified by oxidation to cotinine.

Nicotine $\xrightarrow{\text{liver enzymes}}$ Cotinine

Cotinine is less toxic than nicotine, and the added oxygen atom makes it more water soluble, and thus more readily excreted in the urine, than nicotine.

The liver has a system of iron-containing enzymes called *P-450* enzymes. The iron atoms are able to transfer oxygen to compounds that are otherwise highly resistant to oxidation. The P-450 enzymes catalyze the oxidation of fat-soluble substances (which are otherwise likely to be retained in the body) into water-soluble ones that are readily excreted. These enzymes also conjugate compounds with amino acids. For example, toluene is virtually insoluble in water. P-450 enzymes oxidize toluene to the more soluble benzoic acid, and then couple the benzoic acid with the amino acid glycine to form hippuric acid, which is even more soluble and is readily excreted.

$$C_6H_5{-}CH_3 \xrightarrow{\text{oxidation}} C_6H_5{-}\overset{\overset{\large O}{\|}}{C}{-}OH \xrightarrow[\text{(Glycine)}]{H_2N{-}CH_2{-}COOH} C_6H_5{-}\overset{\overset{\large O}{\|}}{C}{-}NHCH_2\overset{\overset{\large O}{\|}}{C}{-}OH$$

Toluene — Benzoic acid — Hippuric acid

Note that liver enzymes simply oxidize, reduce, or conjugate. The end product is not always less toxic. For example, as was noted in Section 9.5, methanol is oxidized to more toxic formaldehyde, which then reacts with proteins in the cells to cause blindness, convulsions, respiratory failure, and death.

The liver enzymes that oxidize alcohols also deactivate the male hormone testosterone. Buildup of these enzymes in a chronic alcoholic leads to a more rapid destruction of testosterone. This is the mechanism underlying alcoholic impotence, one of the well-known characteristics of the disease.

Benzene, because of its general inertness in the body, does not react until it reaches the liver. There it is slowly oxidized to an epoxide.

Benzene $\xrightarrow{\text{oxidation in the liver}}$ An epoxide (carcinogen)

The epoxide is a highly reactive molecule that can attack certain key proteins. The damage done by this epoxide sometimes results in leukemia.

Carbon tetrachloride (CCl_4) is also quite inert in the body. But when it reaches the liver, it is converted to the reactive trichloromethyl free radical ($Cl_3C\cdot$), which in turn attacks the unsaturated fatty acids in the body. This action can trigger cancer.

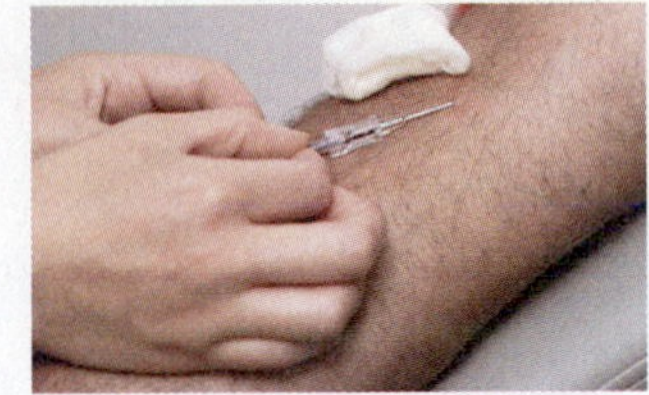

▲ It DOES Matter!

Before prescribing certain drugs such as statins, doctors will often perform a blood test for liver enzymes. It is essential that the liver function properly for these drugs to work; if the liver is damaged, some of these drugs can worsen the damage. "Leakage" of liver enzymes into the bloodstream indicates a problem that must be rectified before the drug is administered.

Getting Rid of "Toxins"

Two thousand years ago, Greek physicians applied the theory of the four *humors*—blood, phlegm, black bile, and yellow bile—to diagnose illnesses. They held that people in good health had a balance of these fluids and that too much or too little of one or more of them caused disease. A person who is positive and happy is still said to be "in a good humor." For a patient short of a humor, treatment included bed rest, a change in diet, or medicines. For those with too much of a humor, treatment included sweating, purging, and bloodletting. Today, some people believe that sweating gets rid of "toxins." And there is a rather large business built on the idea that laxatives and other "colon cleansers" somehow purify the body. Erroneous beliefs often persist for centuries.

▲ In the Middle Ages, bloodletting was often the treatment for inflammation from infection.

Self-Assessment Questions

1. In the human body, which of the following statements is *not* true?
   a. Benzene is inert and thus nontoxic.
   b. Mercury vapor is converted to Hg^{2+}.
   c. Some nontoxic substances can be converted to toxic forms.
   d. Some poisons can be converted to nontoxic forms.
2. What substance is oxidized to cotinine in the liver?
   a. benzene b. methanol c. nicotine d. toluene

Answers: 1, a; 2, c

22.6 Carcinogens and Teratogens

Learning Objectives › Describe how cancers develop. › List some chemical carcinogens and anticarcinogens. › Name and describe three ways to test for carcinogens.

A **carcinogen** is something that causes the growth of tumors. A *tumor* is an abnormal growth of new tissue and can be either benign or malignant. *Benign tumors* are characterized by slow growth. They often regress spontaneously, and they do not invade neighboring tissues. *Malignant tumors*, often called *cancers*, can grow slowly or rapidly and can invade and destroy neighboring tissues.

Actually, cancer is not a single disease. Rather, the term is a catchall for about 200 different afflictions, many of them not even closely related to each other. We worry about carcinogens because half of the men and one-third of the women in the United States will develop cancer at some point in their lives.

What Causes Cancer?

Most people seem to believe that synthetic chemicals are a major cause of cancer, but the facts indicate otherwise. Like deaths in general (Section 18.3), most cancers are caused by lifestyle factors. Nearly two-thirds of all cancer deaths in the United States are linked to diet, tobacco, or a lack of exercise (Figure 22.7).

The U.S. Occupational Safety and Health Administration (OSHA) has a National Toxicology Program (NTP) that compiles ongoing lists of carcinogens in two categories. The 2010 list titled "Known Human Carcinogens" has 58 entries. For these, the NTP thinks there is sufficient evidence of carcinogenicity from studies in humans to establish a causal relationship between exposure to the agent, substance, or mixture, and human cancer. Another 188 entries are included in the list titled "Reasonably Anticipated to Be Human Carcinogens." These suspected carcinogens often are structurally related to substances that are known to be carcinogens, or there is limited evidence of their carcinogenicity from studies in humans or in experimental animals.

Some carcinogens, such as sunlight, radon, and safrole in sassafras, occur naturally. Some scientists estimate that 99.99% of all carcinogens that we ingest are natural

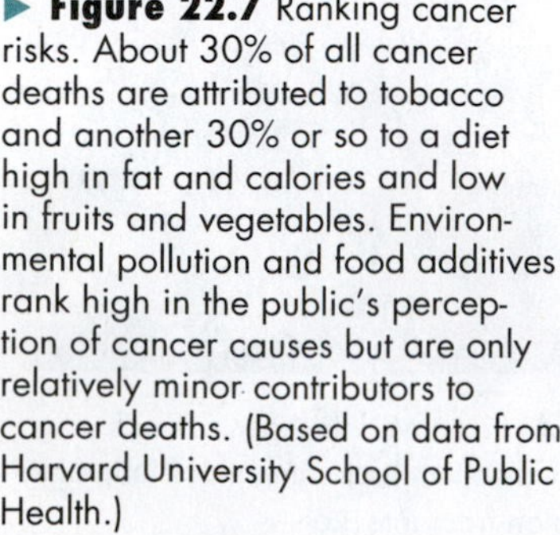

▶ **Figure 22.7** Ranking cancer risks. About 30% of all cancer deaths are attributed to tobacco and another 30% or so to a diet high in fat and calories and low in fruits and vegetables. Environmental pollution and food additives rank high in the public's perception of cancer causes but are only relatively minor contributors to cancer deaths. (Based on data from Harvard University School of Public Health.)

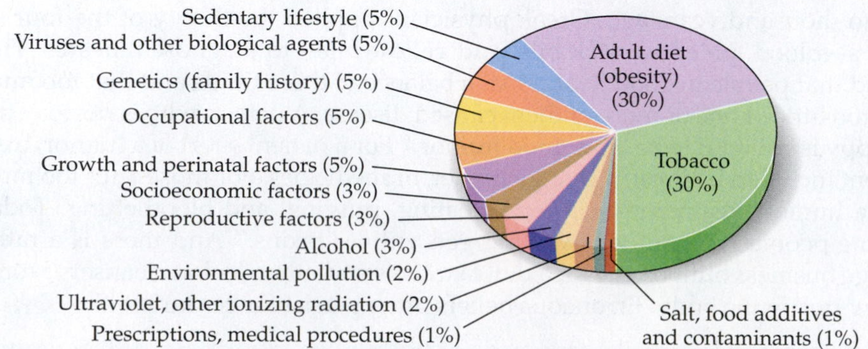

How Cigarette Smoking Causes Cancer

The association between cigarette smoking and cancer has been known for decades, but the precise mechanism was not determined until 1996. The research scientists who found the link focused on a tumor-suppressor gene called *P53*, a gene that is mutated in about 60% of all lung cancers, and on a metabolite of benzpyrene, a carcinogen found in tobacco smoke.

In the body, benzpyrene is oxidized to an active carcinogen (an epoxide) that binds to specific nucleotides in the gene—sites called "hot spots"—where mutations frequently occur. It seems quite likely that the benzpyrene metabolite causes many of the mutations.

ones. Plants produce compounds to protect themselves from fungi, insects, and higher animals, including humans. Some of these compounds that are carcinogens are found in mushrooms, basil, celery, figs, mustard, pepper, fennel, parsnips, and citrus oils—almost every place that a curious chemist looks. Carcinogens are also produced during cooking and as products of normal metabolism. Because carcinogens are so widespread, we must have some way of protecting ourselves from them.

How Cancers Develop

How do chemicals and physical factors cause cancer? Their mechanisms of action are probably quite varied. Some carcinogens chemically modify DNA, thus scrambling the code for its replication and for the synthesis of proteins. For example, aflatoxin B, produced by molds on foods, is known to bind to guanine residues in DNA. Just how this initiates cancer, however, has not yet been determined.

Genetics plays a role in the development of many forms of cancer. Certain genes, called *oncogenes*, seem to trigger or sustain the processes that convert normal cells to cancerous ones. There are about 100 known oncogenes, which develop from ordinary genes that regulate cell growth and cell division. Chemical carcinogens, radiation, or perhaps some viruses can activate oncogenes. It seems that more than one oncogene must be turned on, perhaps at different stages of the process, before a cancer develops. There are also *suppressor genes* that ordinarily prevent the development of cancers. These genes must be inactivated before a cancer develops. Suppressor gene inactivation can occur through mutation, alteration, or loss. In all, several mutations may be required in a cell before it turns cancerous.

A hereditary form of breast cancer that usually develops before age 50 results from a mutation in a tumor-suppressor gene called *BRCA1*. Women who have a mutant form of *BRCA1* have an 82% risk of developing breast cancer, compared with most women in the United States, who have about a 10% risk.

Chemical Carcinogens

A variety of widely different chemical compounds are carcinogenic. We will concentrate on only a few major classes here.

Polycyclic aromatic hydrocarbons (PAHs), of which 3,4-benzpyrene (Section 13.7) is perhaps the best known, are among the more notorious carcinogens. These hydrocarbons are formed during the incomplete burning of nearly any organic material. They have been found in charcoal-grilled meats, cigarette smoke, automobile exhausts, coffee, burnt sugar, and many other materials. Not all polycyclic aromatic hydrocarbons are carcinogenic. There are strong correlations between carcinogenicity and certain molecular sizes and shapes.

Aromatic amines make up another important class of carcinogens. Two prominent ones are β-naphthylamine (Section 17.6) and benzidine. Once widely used in the dye industry, these compounds were responsible for a high incidence of bladder cancer among workers whose jobs brought them into prolonged contact with them.

Not all carcinogens are aromatic compounds. Two prominent aliphatic (nonaromatic) ones are dimethylnitrosamine (Section 17.6) and vinyl chloride (Section 10.3). Other nonaromatic carcinogens include three- and four-membered heterocyclic rings containing nitrogen or oxygen, such as epoxides and derivatives of ethyleneimine, as well as cyclic esters called *lactones* (Figure 22.8).

$H_2N-C_6H_4-C_6H_4-NH_2$

Benzidine

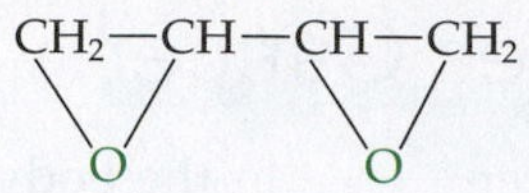

Bis(epoxy)butane 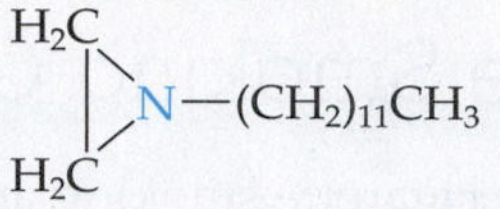 N-Laurylethyleneimine 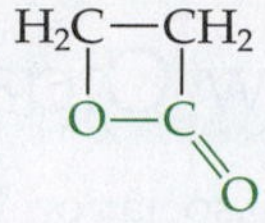 β-Propiolactone

▶ **Figure 22.8** Three small-ring heterocyclic carcinogens.

Q: *To what family of compounds does each compound belong?*

This list of carcinogens is far from all-inclusive. Its purpose is to give you an idea of some of the kinds of compounds that have tumor-inducing properties.

Anticarcinogens

If the food we eat has many natural carcinogens, why don't we all get cancer? Probably because other substances in our food act as **anticarcinogens**. Antioxidant vitamins are believed to protect against some forms of cancer, and the food additive butylated hydroxytoluene (BHT) may give protection against stomach cancer. Certain vitamins have also been shown to have anticarcinogenic effects.

Antioxidant vitamins include vitamin C, vitamin E, and β-carotene, a precursor of vitamin A. A diet rich in cruciferous vegetables (cabbage, broccoli, Brussels sprouts, kale, and cauliflower) has been shown to reduce the incidence of cancer both in animals and in human population groups. The evidence for the anticarcinogenicity of the vitamins taken as supplements is less conclusive and, in the case of β-carotene, even contradictory. Yellow, red, or blue plant pigments called *flavonoids* are thought to be anticarcinogens. Good sources of flavonoids are citrus fruits, berries, red onions, green tea, and dark chocolate.

There are probably many other anticarcinogens in our food that have not yet been identified.

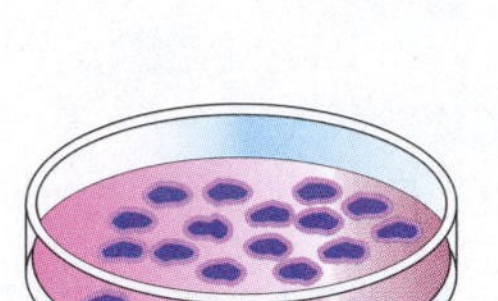

Mutant induced revertants

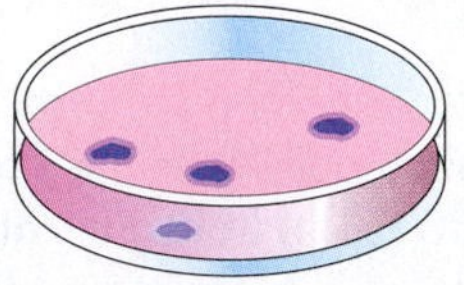

Spontaneous revertants

▲ **Figure 22.9** The Ames test. Both petri dishes contain a modified strain of *Salmonella* bacteria. A chemical added to the upper petri dish has caused the *Salmonella* to revert back to their unmodified form, indicating that mutations have occurred and the chemical is a mutagen. The bottom dish is a control that shows only a few spontaneous mutations and little reversion.

Three Ways to Test for Carcinogens

How do we know that a chemical causes cancer? Obviously, we can't experiment on humans to see what happens. That leaves us with no way to prove absolutely whether a chemical causes cancer in humans. Three ways to gain evidence against a substance are bacterial screening for mutagenesis, animal tests, and epidemiological studies.

The quickest and cheapest way to find out whether or not a substance may be carcinogenic is to use a screening test such as that developed by Bruce N. Ames of the University of California at Berkeley. The **Ames test** is a simple laboratory procedure that can be carried out in a petri dish (Figure 22.9). It assumes that most carcinogens are also mutagens, altering genes in some way. This usually seems to be the case. About 90% of the chemicals that appear on a list of either mutagens or carcinogens are found on the other list as well.

The Ames test uses a special strain of *Salmonella* bacteria that have been modified so that they require histidine as an essential amino acid. The bacteria are placed in an agar medium containing all nutrients except histidine. Incubating the mixture in the presence of a mutagenic chemical causes the bacteria to mutate so that they no longer require histidine and can grow like normal bacteria. Cancer is an uncontrolled growth of cells, so growth of bacterial colonies in a petri dish means that the chemical added was a mutagen, and probably also a carcinogen.

Chemicals suspected of being carcinogens can be tested on animals. Tests involving low dosages and millions of rats would cost too much, so tests are usually done by using large doses and a few dozen rats. An equal number of rats serve as controls; these are exposed to the same diet and environment but not given the suspected carcinogen. A higher incidence of cancer in the experimental animals than in the controls indicates that the compound is carcinogenic.

2. Why do scientists use such high doses when testing possible cancer-causing substances? The validity of some animal tests is sometimes questioned in the media. However, it has been observed repeatedly that a substance that is not a carcinogen will not cause cancer even in high doses. The high doses often used in animal testing simply make positive results appear sooner.

Animal tests are not conclusive. Humans are not usually exposed to comparable doses; there may be a threshold below which a compound is not carcinogenic. Further, human metabolism is somewhat different from that of the test animals. A carcinogen might be active in rats but not in humans (or vice versa). There is only a 70% correlation between the carcinogenesis of a chemical in rats and that in mice. The correlation between carcinogenesis in either rodent and that in humans is probably less.

What Kills You? What Makes You Sick?

Media reports often focus on "toxic chemicals." You might even think that chemicals are a leading cause of death and injury. True, some chemicals are quite toxic. Misused, they can make you sick or even kill you. However, if you look again at Figure 18.6, you'll find it difficult to associate any of the leading causes of death directly with chemicals. In developed countries, most of the causes of premature death are related to lifestyle. Nearly half are due to cardiovascular diseases, and another 20% or so are due to cancer. In these countries, it is "sociologicals," not "chemicals," that kill people.

Accidents and suicides often involve automobile crashes and guns. More than 15,000 people are murdered each year in the United States, most with guns, knives, or clubs of some sort. The physical force of a moving projectile, not its chemical nature, does the damage. It is these "physicals" that kill.

Worldwide, the main causes of premature death are infectious and parasitic diseases, "biologicals" that account for nearly one-third of total deaths. Every day in some of the world's poorest countries,

- 24,000 people die from hunger;
- 14,000 people die from lack of access to clean water and sanitation; and
- 22,000 people die from illnesses that could easily be prevented, such as diarrheal dehydration, acute respiratory infections, measles, and malaria.

Even in the United States, food poisoning, caused by *Escherichia coli*, *Cyclospora*, *Listeria*, *Salmonella*, and other microorganisms, sickens thousands each year. Chicken, meat, and eggs are sometimes contaminated with *Salmonella*. *E. coli* is a common inhabitant of cow intestines. People who eat beef that is carelessly slaughtered or eat foods exposed to water contaminated with cow manure are often infected.

In all these cases, of course, chemistry is involved at some level. We can identify the toxins produced by bacteria and work out the molecular mechanisms by which viruses invade and destroy cells. Nicotine is the chemical—a natural one, but a chemical no less—that makes tobacco addictive. Perfectly natural ethanol is the most dangerous of the chemicals in alcoholic beverages.

Chemicals can be dangerous, but we can use them to our advantage if we are careful. As far as being threats to our lives and health, though, chemicals are far down the list. Even more likely to kill us than chemicals are "geologicals"—earthquakes, floods, storms, and extremely hot or cold weather.

Animal studies are expensive. In cancer studies, animal tests of a single substance may take 4–8 years and cost hundreds of thousands of dollars. Further, animal testing is controversial. Supporters and opponents argue over both the ethics and the value of the tests.

The best evidence that a substance causes cancer in humans comes from *epidemiological studies*. A population that has a higher than normal rate for a particular kind of cancer is studied for common factors in the individuals' backgrounds. Studies of this sort showed that cigarette smoking causes lung cancer, that vinyl chloride causes a rare form of liver cancer, and that asbestos causes cancer of the lining of the pleural cavity (the body cavity containing the lungs). These studies sometimes require sophisticated mathematical analyses, and there is always the chance that some other (unknown) factor is involved in the carcinogenesis.

More recently, epidemiological studies were carried out to determine whether or not electromagnetic fields, such as those surrounding high-voltage power lines, certain electric appliances, and cellular phones could cause cancer. The results so far indicate that if there is such an effect, it is exceedingly small.

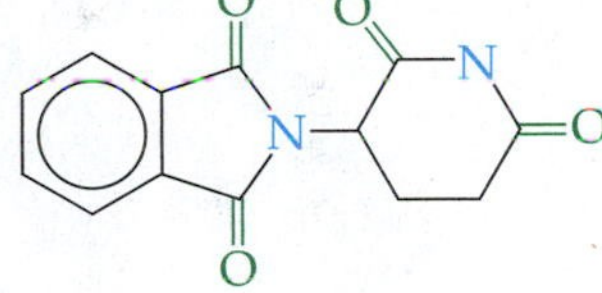

Thalidomide

▲ Above: Structure of thalidomide.
▼ Below: Frances O. Kelsey (in dark hat) of the FDA receives a Distinguished Federal Civilian Service Award from President John Kennedy for her refusal to approve thalidomide for use in the United States.

Birth Defects: Teratogens

A **teratogen** is a substance that causes birth defects. Perhaps the most notorious teratogen is the tranquilizer *thalidomide*. Fifty years ago, thalidomide was considered so safe, based on laboratory studies, that it was often prescribed for pregnant women. In Germany, it was available without a prescription. It took several years for the human population to provide evidence that laboratory animals had not provided.

Thalidomide is now being used for treating certain conditions, with strict restrictions in place to prevent its use by pregnant women. It has a unique anti-inflammatory action against a debilitating skin condition that often occurs with leprosy. Thalidomide is also being studied for use in the treatment of *wasting*, the severe weight-loss condition that often accompanies AIDS. Scientists are also studying thalidomide derivatives, hoping to enhance the beneficial effects while reducing the harmful properties.

The drug had a disastrous effect on developing human embryos. About 12,000 women who had taken the drug during the first 12 weeks of pregnancy had babies who suffered from *phocomelia*, a condition characterized by shortened or absent arms and legs and other physical defects. The drug was used widely in Germany and Great Britain, and these two countries bore the brunt of the tragedy. The United States escaped relatively unscathed because Frances O. Kelsey of the FDA believed that there was evidence to doubt the drug's safety and therefore did not approve it for use in the United States. Kelsey received the Distinguished Federal Civilian Service Award from President John F. Kennedy in 1962.

Other chemicals that act as teratogens include isotretinoin (Accutane®), a prescription medication approved for use in treating severe acne. When taken by women during the first trimester of pregnancy, it can cause multiple major malformations. Educational materials provided to physicians and to patients have prevented all but a few tragedies associated with the use of isotretinoin.

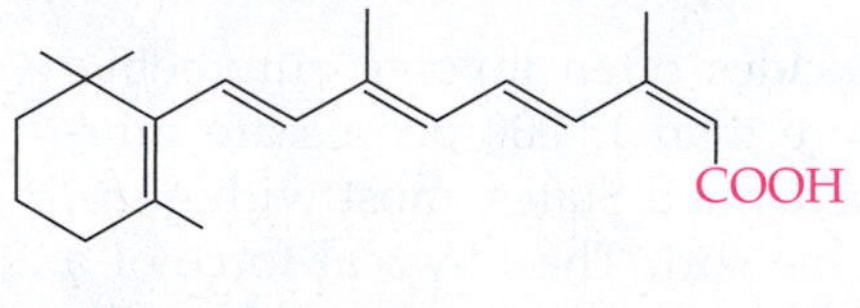

COOH

Isotretinoin
(13-*cis*-retinoic acid)

By far the most hazardous teratogen, in terms of the number of babies born with birth defects, is ethyl alcohol, which causes fetal alcohol syndrome.

Self-Assessment Questions

1. Some genes that are involved in cancer development when they are switched on are called
   a. DNA repair genes b. oncogenes
   c. P53 d. suppressor genes
2. Some genes are involved in preventing the development of cancers. These genes, when switched off, allow cancerous cells to grow. They are called
   a. DNA repair genes b. oncogenes
   c. BRCA1 genes d. suppressor genes
3. Which of the following is *not* a naturally occurring carcinogen?
   a. sunlight b. radon
   c. benzidine d. safrole
4. Many polycyclic aromatic hydrocarbons (PAHs) are known carcinogens. Sources of PAHs include
   a. artificial flavorings b. automobile exhausts
   c. pesticides d. plastics
5. A prominent aliphatic carcinogen is
   a. arachidonic acid b. butane
   c. valine d. vinyl chloride
6. Which of the following is an anticarcinogen?
   a. benzidine b. bis(epoxy)butane
   c. butylated hydroxytoluene d. vinyl chloride
7. The fastest way to determine whether a substance is likely to be a carcinogen is to use
   a. the Ames test b. animal tests
   c. epidemiological studies d. metabolic testing
8. The Ames test is a(n)
   a. evaluation of new compounds for hepatotoxicity
   b. immunological test for melanoma
   c. standardized final exam for introductory chemistry courses
   d. test for mutagenicity used as a screen for potential carcinogens
9. A teratogen is a substance that causes
   a. birth defects b. skin, eye, and respiratory irritation
   c. panic attacks d. tetanus

10. The teratogen that causes damage to the greatest number of fetuses is
a. ethanol **b.** isotretinoin
c. malathion **d.** thalidomide

Answers: 1, b; 2, d; 3, c; 4, b; 5, d; 6, c; 7, a; 8, d; 9, a; 10, a

22.7 Hazardous Wastes

Learning Objective › Define *hazardous waste*, and list and give an example of the four types of such wastes.

The public has become increasingly concerned in recent years about hazardous wastes in the environment. Problems created by chemical dumps made household words out of Love Canal in New York and Valley of the Drums in Kentucky. Although often overblown in the news media, serious problems do exist. Hazardous wastes can cause fires or explosions. They can pollute the air, and they can contaminate our food and water. Occasionally, they poison by direct contact. As long as we want the products that industries produce, however, we will have to deal with the problems of hazardous wastes (Table 22.2).

Table 22.2 Industrial Products and Hazardous Waste By-Products

Product	Associated Waste
Plastics	Organic chlorine compounds
Pesticides	Organic chlorine compounds, organophosphate compounds
Medicines	Organic solvents and residues, heavy metals (for example, mercury and zinc)
Paints	Heavy metals, pigments, solvents, organic residues
Oil, gasoline	Oil, phenols and other organic compounds, heavy metals, ammonium salts, acids, strong bases
Metals	Heavy metals, fluorides, cyanides, acid and alkaline cleaners, solvents, pigments, abrasives, plating salts, oils, phenols
Leather	Heavy metals, organic solvents
Textiles	Heavy metals, dyes, organic chlorine compounds, solvents

The first step in dealing with any problem is to understand the problem. A **hazardous waste** is one that can cause or contribute to death or illness or that threatens human health or the environment when improperly managed. For convenience, hazardous wastes are divided into four types: reactive, flammable, toxic, and corrosive.

A **reactive waste** tends to react spontaneously or to react vigorously with air or water. Such wastes can generate toxic gases, such as hydrogen cyanide (HCN) or hydrogen sulfide (H_2S), or explode when exposed to shock or heat. Explosives such as trinitrotoluene (TNT) and nitroglycerin obviously are reactive wastes. Examples of household wastes that can explode include improperly handled propane tanks and aerosol cans. Another example of a reactive waste is sodium metal. It reacts with water to form hydrogen gas, which can then explode when ignited in air.

$$2\,Na(s) + 2\,H_2O(l) \longrightarrow 2\,NaOH(aq) + H_2(g)$$

$$2\,H_2(g) + O_2(g) \longrightarrow 2\,H_2O(g)$$

Reactive wastes can usually be deactivated before disposal. Propane tanks and aerosol cans can be thoroughly emptied and properly discarded. Sodium can be treated with isopropyl alcohol, with which it reacts slowly, rather than being dumped without treatment.

A **flammable waste** is one that burns readily on ignition, presenting a fire hazard. An example is hexane, a hydrocarbon solvent. Hexane (presumably dumped

GREEN CHEMISTRY

Principles 3, 11, 12

Siba Das and Robert L. Tanguay, *Oregon State University*

Fishing for a Greener World

As inhabitants of the industrialized world, we are exposed daily to thousands of natural and synthetic chemicals in the air we breathe, the food we eat, the water we drink, and the many consumer products and pharmaceuticals that we depend on. As we have learned in this chapter, any chemical can be toxic if the exposure is large enough. Chemicals designated as toxic produce injury at low concentrations, and nontoxic compounds produce no adverse responses even at fairly high concentrations (Sections 22.4 and 22.6). Toxicology is the discipline that studies the toxicity of chemicals in hopes of protecting human and environmental health.

You may think that the remarkable advances of modern science would provide a rapid means to determine if chemicals are toxic, and to a great extent, they have. The pace of synthetic chemical discovery and commercialization, however, still outruns our ability to evaluate the toxicity of this constantly changing sea of chemicals. Many reasons for the lag in toxicity testing exist, perhaps the most important being the need for reliable evaluation of toxicity. The burden of proof for chemical safety seldom lies with the chemical manufacturer. More commonly, it is the responsibility of the federal government, which requires expertly generated experimental evidence from tests on animals that respond much like human beings.

For these reasons, the "gold standard" for chemical toxicity testing is laboratory rats and mice. Rodent studies are very expensive and fairly slow to complete. Furthermore, much of the rodent testing in the past used chemical concentrations that were too high to simulate the exposures that human beings might receive (Section 22.6). Finally, although rodents resemble human beings, they have metabolic and physiological differences that often do not translate into a realistic assessment of chemical hazard to human beings.

To apply green chemistry approaches efficiently, it is necessary to know the toxic potential of existing chemicals. With the traditional approach, testing one chemical at a time using rodents, we will remain largely blind to the safety of our chemical innovations. The National Academy of Sciences recommends that we make bold moves to develop new inexpensive testing strategies that can investigate many compounds, using thousands of tests in a day, and will enable us to identify chemical hazards quickly. Clearly, doing so many assays would be too expensive and slow if we tested on rodents, so that approach has to be retired. Such a high volume of tests can be completed using isolated cells grown in plastic dishes.

By testing thousands of chemicals in a number of different cells isolated from distinct organs, it may be possible to predict hazards to live animals. A persistent obstacle to relying on cultured cell testing, though, is that cells lack the physiologic, metabolic, and developmental complexity of the whole animal. Therefore, although more rapid and less expensive than animal testing, cell studies are still far from being fully predictive.

One solution is faster, predictive animal tests that lend themselves to automation. The study of embryonic zebrafish has emerged as the choice for such an approach. No other vertebrate is better suited to fast chemical screening. Therefore, zebrafish have been used to study the toxicity of organophosphates, lead, arsenic, ethanol, nicotine, and many other common toxicants.

One application of green chemistry principles to fast, extensive zebrafish testing is in green nanotechnology. Nanotechnology is a swiftly emerging field that focuses on manipulating matter at the molecular level. This submicroscopic control over synthesis enables the production of fantastic new materials with wide-ranging uses in energy production, construction, aerospace, consumer products, and medicine. In response to the fast-paced development of these newly produced nanomaterials, zebrafish toxicity screening is under way to evaluate the toxicity of each starting material, the waste materials, and the final products before the nanoparticles reach large-scale, commercial production (abiding by Green Chemistry Principles 3, 11, and 12).

This frontloaded approach to toxicology can guide chemical development so that structures can be subtly altered for improved consumer safety before millions of dollars have been invested in production and marketing. We can reduce the load of poisons in the environment and, consequently, our interaction with them by following the principles of green chemistry.

▲ The zebrafish is an excellent candidate for testing toxins and toxicity. Zebrafish have a rapid growth cycle, they are widely applicable to many areas of biology, and there are a number of transgenic modifications that have proven useful in various studies.

accidentally by Ralston-Purina) was ignited in the sewers of Louisville, Kentucky, in 1981, causing explosions that blew up several blocks of streets.

$$2\,C_6H_{14}(l) + 19\,O_2(g) \longrightarrow 12\,CO_2(g) + 14\,H_2O(g)$$

Examples of flammable household wastes include gasoline, lighter fluid, many solvents, and nail polish.

A **toxic waste** contains or releases toxic substances in quantities sufficient to pose a hazard to human health or to the environment. Most of the toxic substances discussed in this chapter would qualify as toxic wastes if they were improperly dumped in the environment. Some toxic wastes can be incinerated safely. For example, PCBs (Section 10.7) are burned at high temperatures to form carbon dioxide, water, and hydrogen chloride. If the hydrogen chloride is removed by scrubbing or is safely diluted and dispersed, this is a satisfactory way to dispose of PCBs. Some toxic wastes cannot be incinerated, however, and must be contained and monitored for years. Examples of household toxic wastes include paint, pesticides, motor oil, medicines, and cleansers.

A **corrosive waste** is one that requires a special container because it corrodes conventional container materials. Acids cannot be stored in steel drums because they react with and dissolve the iron.

$$Fe(s) + 2\,H^+(aq) \longrightarrow Fe^{2+}(aq) + H_2(aq)$$

Acid wastes can be neutralized (Chapter 7) before disposal, and lime (CaO) is an inexpensive base for this neutralization.

$$2\,H^+(aq) + CaO(s) \longrightarrow Ca^{2+}(aq) + H_2O(l)$$

Examples of household corrosive wastes include battery acid, drain cleaners, and oven cleaners.

The best way to handle hazardous wastes is not to produce them in the first place. This is a major focus of green chemistry. Many industries have modified manufacturing processes to prevent wastes (Green Chemistry Principle 1) and maximize atom economy (Principle 2), and some wastes can be reprocessed to recover energy or materials. Hydrocarbon solvents such as hexane can be purified and reused or burned as fuels. Often the waste from one industry can become raw material for another industry. For example, waste nitric acid from the metals industry can be converted to fertilizer.

If a hazardous waste cannot be used or incinerated or treated to render it less hazardous, it must be stored in a secure landfill. Unfortunately, landfills often leak, contaminating the groundwater. We clean up one toxic waste dump and move the materials to another, playing a rather macabre shell game. The best current technology for treating organic wastes, including chlorinated compounds, is incineration (Figure 22.10). At 1260 °C, greater than 99.9999% destruction is achieved.

Biodegradation is another method that shows great promise. Scientists have identified microorganisms that degrade hydrocarbons such as those in gasoline.

3. How do schools dispose of hazardous chemicals from chemistry labs? Schools generally produce much smaller amounts of waste than industries do. A common method of disposal is the *lab pack*. A number of sealed waste containers are placed in a drum filled with material, such as vermiculite, that will absorb leakage. The drum is then sealed and buried in a secure landfill.

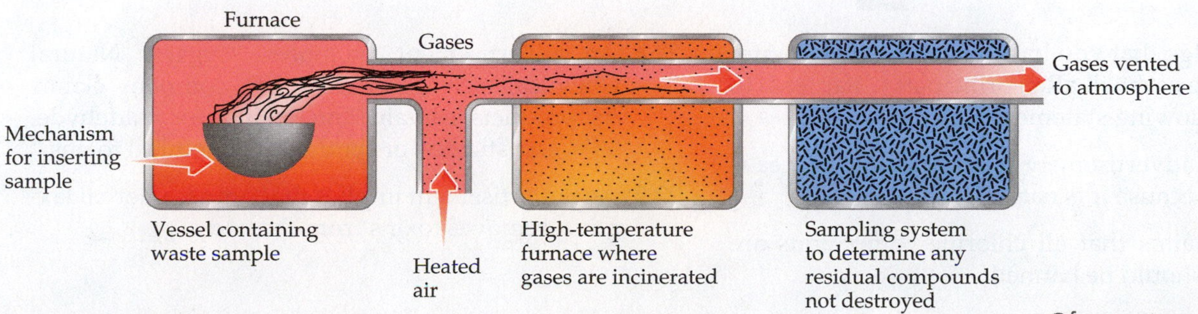

▲ **Figure 22.10** A schematic diagram of an incinerator for hazardous wastes.

Q: *PCBs are burned in air at high temperatures, forming carbon dioxide, water, and hydrogen chloride. Write the equation for the incineration of the PCB component* $C_6H_2Cl_3$—$C_6H_3Cl_2$.

Often an issue with incineration is finding a place to build the incinerator. No one wants a hazardous waste incinerator nearby.

4. Why can't we dispose of wastes like PCBs, lead, and dioxins by burning them? PCBs, nerve gases, and other organic materials usually can be disposed of by incineration (Figure 22.10), because they are oxidized to simple compounds like CO_2 and H_2O. However, toxins such as lead, mercury, and arsenic are elements. If a waste containing lead compounds is incinerated, the lead will still be present in some form, such as PbO or elemental Pb, after incineration.

Other bacteria, when provided with proper nutrients, can degrade chlorinated hydrocarbons. Certain bacteria in the soil can even break down TNT and nitroglycerin. Through genetic engineering, scientists are developing new strains of bacteria that can decompose a great variety of wastes.

What Price Poisons?

We use so many poisons in and around our homes and workplaces that accidents are bound to happen. Poison control centers have been established in many cities to help physicians deal with emergency poisonings. Are insecticides, medicines, cleansers, and other chemicals worth the price we pay in terms of accidental poisonings? That is for you to decide. Generally, it is the misuse of these chemicals that leads to tragedy.

Perhaps it is easy to be negative about chemists and chemistry when you think of such horrors as nerve gases, carcinogens, and teratogens. But keep in mind that many toxic chemicals are of enormous benefit to us and that they can be used safely despite their hazardous nature. The plastics industry was able to control vinyl chloride emissions once the hazard was known. We are still able to have valuable vinyl plastics even though the vinyl chloride from which they are made causes cancer.

Increasingly, we have to decide whether the benefits we gain from hazardous substances are worth the risks we assume by using them. Many issues involving toxic chemicals are emotional. Most of the decisions regarding them are political. Yet possible solutions to such problems lie mainly in the field of chemistry.

We hope that the chemistry you have learned here will help you make wise decisions. Most of all, we hope that you will continue to learn more about chemistry throughout the rest of your life, because chemistry affects nearly everything you do. We wish you success and happiness, and may the joy of learning go with you always.

Self-Assessment Questions

For items 1–4, match the waste described or named in the left column with the category in the right column.

1. tends to react vigorously with water — (a) corrosive
2. common strong acids and bases — (b) flammable
3. discarded unused pesticides — (c) reactive
4. sodium metal — (d) toxic
5. The best way to deal with hazardous wastes is to
   - **a.** burn them in an incinerator
   - **b.** bury them in a landfill
   - **c.** compost them
   - **d.** minimize or eliminate their use

Answers: 1, c; 2, a; 3, d; 4, c; 5, d

CRITICAL THINKING  EXERCISES

Apply knowledge that you have gained in this chapter and one or more of the FLaReS principles (Chapter 1) to evaluate the following statements or claims.

22.1 An online advertisement implies that echinacea is nontoxic because it is natural.

22.2 A book claims that all chlorine compounds are toxic and should be banned.

22.3 A natural foods enthusiast contends that no food that contains a carcinogen should be allowed on the market.

22.4 An advertisement promotes "Organic Natural Chemical-Free Mattresses." The company claims its products contain "no toxins, formaldehyde, VOCs, pesticides, or synthetic or chemical foams."

22.5 An advertisement implies that senna, a herbal laxative, removes toxins from the body.

SUMMARY

A **poison** is a substance that causes injury, illness, or death. **Toxicology** is the branch of pharmacology that deals with poisons.

Section 22.1—A **toxin** is a poison that is naturally produced by a plant or animal. Many natural poisons exist, including curare, strychnine, and botulin. Many plants, including hemlock, holly berries, iris, azalea, and hydrangea, are toxic.

Section 22.2—Poisons act in different ways. Strong acids and strong bases are toxic because they are corrosive. They cause hydrolysis of proteins. Strong oxidizing agents such as ozone and PAN damage largely by deactivating enzymes. Carbon monoxide and nitrite ions are toxic because they interfere with the transport of oxygen by the blood. Cyanide is a poison because it shuts down cell respiration. Several substances, including fluoroacetic acid, are not highly toxic themselves, but in the body they form substances that are toxic. Heavy metal poisons such as lead and mercury inactivate enzymes by tying up their —SH groups. Cadmium leads to loss of calcium ions from bones. Heavy metal poisoning can be treated with chelating agents that tie up the metal ions so that they can be excreted.

Section 22.3—Nerve poisons, such as organophosphorus compounds, interfere with the acetylcholine cycle. Nerve poisons are among the most toxic synthetic chemicals known.

Section 22.4—An **LD_{50}** value indicates a dosage that kills 50% of a population of test animals. Many substances not ordinarily thought of as poisons do have some toxicity, indicated by a high LD_{50} value. Botulism toxin has the lowest LD_{50} value and is the most toxic substance known.

Section 22.5—The liver can detoxify substances by oxidizing or reducing them or by coupling them with other chemicals normally found in the body. The liver's P-450 enzymes carry out many such detoxifying reactions. Sometimes liver enzymes convert a less toxic substance, such as benzene or CCl_4, into one that is more toxic.

Section 22.6—A **carcinogen** causes the growth of tumors. A benign tumor grows slowly and does not invade neighboring tissues. A malignant tumor, or cancer, can invade and destroy neighboring tissues. Some carcinogens are natural, but most cancer deaths are linked to tobacco, diet, and obesity. Oncogenes appear to trigger processes that convert normal cells to cancer, and suppressor genes act to prevent the development of cancers. Some substances in our food, including antioxidant vitamins, act as **anticarcinogens**.

The **Ames test** screens substances for carcinogenicity by observing bacterial growth. Animal testing is often necessary but is not conclusive. Epidemiological studies appear to be most useful for identifying carcinogens.

A **teratogen** is a substance that causes birth defects.

Section 22.7—**Hazardous wastes** can be classified as **reactive waste**, which tends to react spontaneously or to react vigorously with air or water; **flammable waste**, which burns readily on ignition; **toxic waste**, which contains or releases toxic substances; and **corrosive waste**, which destroys conventional container materials. The best way to handle hazardous wastes is not to produce them in the first place. Wastes may be stored in a landfill or incinerated, and biodegradation shows promise for disposing of some wastes.

Green chemistry Industries seeking to market new products and technologies are increasingly faced with consumer demand that chemicals and processes be green. Thus, there is a need for an approach to chemical testing that provides high-quality data quickly. New testing methods, including a rapid, inexpensive, automated approach involving zebrafish, have improved the ability to assess the toxicity of chemicals being developed.

Learning Objectives

› Name some natural poisons and their sources.	Problems 45, 47
› Distinguish among corrosive poisons, metabolic poisons, and heavy metal poisons, and explain how each type acts.	Problems 4, 5, 9–15, 17–19, 22
› Identify antidotes for some common metabolic poisons and heavy metal poisons.	Problems 16, 20, 21
› Define *neurotransmitter*, and describe how various substances interfere with the action of neurotransmitters.	Problems 23–26
› Explain the concept of an LD_{50}, and list some of its limitations as a measure of toxicity.	Problems 7, 33, 34, 45–48
› Calculate lethal doses from LD_{50} values and body weights.	Problems 33, 34, 45–48, 52–54, 57
› Describe how the liver is able to detoxify some substances.	Problems 27–32, 55, 56
› Describe how cancers develop.	Problems 35, 36
› List some chemical carcinogens and anticarcinogens.	Problems 7, 38, 41, 55
› Name and describe three ways to test for carcinogens	Problems 39, 40, 42, 49
› Define *hazardous waste*, and list and give an example of the four types of such wastes.	Problems 43, 44
› Identify new approaches for testing the toxicity of synthetic chemicals.	Problems 58–60
› Discuss the importance of toxicity screening in the manufacture of safe chemicals.	Problems 60, 61

REVIEW QUESTIONS

1. Is sucrose (table sugar) poisonous? Explain.
2. How can a substance be more harmful to one person than to another? Give an example.
3. How does the toxicity of a substance depend on the route of administration?
4. How does fluoroacetic acid exert its toxic effect?
5. List some sources of mercury poisoning and of lead poisoning.
6. What are the two leading causes of cancer?
7. Name several natural carcinogens.
8. How does cigarette smoking cause cancer?

PROBLEMS

Corrosive Poisons

9. Which of the following are corrosive poisons?
   a. octane
   b. nitric acid
   c. trinitrotoluene
   d. potassium hydroxide
10. How do dilute solutions of acids and bases damage living cells?
11. What kind of reaction is involved when acids break down protein molecules? What is the role of the acid in the reaction?
12. How does ozone damage living cells?

Poisons Affecting Oxygen Transport and Oxidative Processes

13. What is a metabolic poison? List two such poisons.
14. What is methemoglobin? How is it formed?
15. How do cyanides exert their toxic effect?
16. How does sodium thiosulfate act as an antidote for cyanide poisoning?

Heavy Metal Poisons

17. Which of the following are heavy metals?
   a. lead
   b. lithium
   c. magnesium
   d. tellurium
18. Iron (as Fe^{2+}) is a necessary nutrient. What are the effects of too little Fe^{2+}? Of too much?
19. How does mercury (as Hg^{2+}) exert its toxic effect?
20. How does BAL act as an antidote for mercury poisoning?
21. How does EDTA act as an antidote for lead poisoning?
22. How does cadmium (as Cd^{2+}) exert its toxic effect? What is *itai-itai*?

Chemistry of the Nervous System

23. List three nerve poisons developed for use in warfare.
24. What is acetylcholine? Describe its action.
25. What are anticholinesterase poisons? How do they act on the acetylcholine cycle?
26. Describe some uses of botulin in medicine.

Detoxification

27. How does the liver detoxify ethanol?
28. What is the P-450 system? What is its function?
29. Do the P-450 enzymes always detoxify foreign substances? Explain.
30. List two steps in the detoxification of ingested toluene. What is the effect of these steps?
31. List two reasons why the conversion of nicotine to cotinine in the liver lessens the risk of nicotine poisoning.
32. How does ethanol work as an antidote for methanol poisoning?

Lethal Dose

33. The LD_{50} value for methyl isocyanate (orally in rats), the substance that caused the Bhopal tragedy, is 140 mg/kg. Estimate the lethal dose for a 125-lb human.
34. The LD_{50} value for carbaryl (Sevin®), given orally to rats, is 307 mg/kg. If this value could be extrapolated to humans, what would be the lethal dose for an 18-kg child?

Carcinogens, Mutagens, and Teratogens

35. What are oncogenes? How are they involved in the development of cancer?
36. What are suppressor genes? How are they involved in the development of cancer?
37. List some conditions under which polycyclic hydrocarbons are formed.
38. Name **(a)** two aromatic amines and **(b)** two aliphatic compounds that are carcinogens.
39. List some of the limitations involved in testing compounds for carcinogenicity by using laboratory animals.
40. What is an epidemiological study? Can such a study prove absolutely that a substance causes cancer?
41. What is a mutagen? A teratogen?
42. Describe the Ames test for mutagenicity. What are its limitations as a screening test for carcinogens?

Hazardous Wastes

43. Define and give an example of a flammable waste.
44. Which of the following are reactive wastes?
   a. NaCN, which reacts with water to form toxic HCN gas
   b. Sr metal, which reacts with water to form flammable H_2 gas
   c. trinitrotoluene, an explosive
   d. phosphoric acid, which dissolves steel drums

ADDITIONAL PROBLEMS

45. Botulin toxin has an estimated LD_{50} value of 200 pg/kg of body weight and an estimated molar mass of 150,000 g/mol. About how many molecules comprise a lethal dose for a 66-kg human?

46. Refer to Problem 45. How much botulin would it take to kill **(a)** a 60-kg person and **(b)** all 7.0 billion people on Earth, assuming an average body weight of 60 kg?

47. Absinthe, a wormwood-flavored liqueur that was highly popular in France from about 1880 to 1914, contains thujone, a neurotoxin with an LD_{50} value (orally in mice) of 87.5 mg/kg. Absinthe was the subject of famous artworks by Degas, Van Gogh, and others. Banned in 1912 in the United States, the liqueur became legal again in 2007, with levels in the commercially distilled product limited to 10 mg/L or less. **(a)** Determine the molecular formula of thujone from the structure below. **(b)** Estimate the lethal dose for a 55-kg person. **(c)** What is the maximum mass of thujone that a 0.50-L bottle of absinthe can contain?

CH_3, O, H_3C, CH_3

Thujone

48. Phosphorus comes in two forms, or *allotropes*. Red phosphorus is used in manufacture of matches and is only mildly toxic. White phosphorus, a waxy yellow solid, is highly toxic, with an orally ingested lethal dose of just 70 mg for a 55-kg person. **(a)** What is the LD_{50} (in milligrams/kilogram) for white phosphorus? **(b)** Where does white phosphorus fall in Table 22.1?

49. A British study more than 50 years ago involved 1357 people with lung cancer. Of these, 1350 were smokers and 7 were nonsmokers. A control group without cancer, matched in age and other characteristics, consisted of 1296 smokers and 61 nonsmokers. **(a)** Calculate the percentage of cancer sufferers who smoked and the percentage of controls who smoked. What can you infer from these proportions? **(b)** Calculate the odds of smoking for the cancer sufferers and the odds of smoking for the controls. **(c)** Calculate the odds ratio. Interpret this result.

50. Which of the nutrients listed in Table 17.3 are heavy metals?

51. How is the statement "The dose makes the poison" related to Table 22.1?

52. Plutonium is an extremely hazardous heavy metal, mainly because it is radioactive. In one set of experiments, the LD_{50} value for plutonium (injected into rats) was found to be somewhat more than 200 μg per/kg. Where in Table 22.1 should plutonium be placed?

53. Refer to Problem 52, and determine whether either of the following doses of plutonium would be considered lethal for a 55-kg female: **(a)** a 1.5-mg dose and **(b)** a 20-mg dose.

54. Referring to Table 22.1, determine whether the following would be expected to be lethal to a 60-kg male: **(a)** a 25-mg dose of arsenic trioxide and **(b)** a 15-mg dose of ketamine.

55. Justify the following statement: "Benzene itself is not toxic; the body makes it toxic."

56. Why does the added oxygen atom in cotinine make it more soluble in water? Why is this important?

57. The LD_{50} value for ethyl alcohol given orally to rats is 10.3 g/kg. **(a)** What volume in milliliters of 100 proof vodka (50% ethanol) would kill a typical 395-g rat? **(b)** Assuming that the rat's mass is 67% water, what would its blood alcohol level be, in milligrams per milliliter? (Density of 100 proof vodka = 0.92 g/mL.)

58. A chemical can be classified as toxic if it causes injury to cells only at high concentrations. (Answer true or false.)

59. What is the current "gold standard" for chemical toxicity testing?
    a. cultured cell testing
    b. rodent testing
    c. human testing
    d. nanotechnology testing

60. Which of the following are reasons to develop new methods for automated toxicity screening?
    a. increased speed of testing
    b. reduced cost of testing
    c. ability to test more compounds
    d. all of the above

61. What are the benefits of applying green chemistry principles to toxicity testing of chemicals before they are manufactured on a large scale?

COLLABORATIVE GROUP PROJECTS

Prepare a PowerPoint, poster, or other presentation (as directed by your instructor) to be shared with the class.

1. Prepare a brief report on one of the following pesticides. Include chemical formula, uses, toxicity, and possible carcinogenicity.

a. alachlor	**b.** fenoxycarb
c. propoxur	**d.** propachlor
e. tribufos	**f.** trichlorfon

2. Propose a disposal method for each of the following wastes. Be as specific as possible, and justify your choice.
    a. hydrochloric acid contaminated with iron salts
    b. picric acid (an explosive)
    c. soybean oil contaminated with PCBs

3. Choose one of the following arguments, and be prepared to support either side (for or against).

a. Carcinogens that occur naturally in foods should be subjected to the same tests used to evaluate synthetic pesticides.
b. Substances should be tested for toxicity or carcinogenicity on laboratory animals.
c. Nerve gases are less humane than bullets in warfare.

4. Search the Internet for information on brownfields. What are they? What is being done about them? Are there any near you?

5. Many tooth fillings consist of amalgams containing mercury, and the safety of these amalgams is a recurring controversy. Using your favorite search methods, find some Web sites dealing with this issue and write a brief analysis of the opposing points of view.

6. Search the Internet for information on the effects of cadmium in the environment and do a risk–benefit analysis (Chapter 1) of cadmium use.

Appendix REVIEW OF MEASUREMENT AND MATHEMATICS

Accurate measurements are essential to science. As noted in Chapter 1, measurements can be made in a variety of units, but most scientists use the International System of Units (SI). The data they record often has to be converted from one kind of unit to another and otherwise manipulated mathematically. This appendix extends the discussion of metric measurement and reviews some of the mathematics that you may find useful in this course.

A.1 The International System of Units

As noted in Chapter 1, the standard SI unit of length is the *meter*. This distance was once defined as 0.0000001 of Earth's quadrant—that is, of the distance from the North Pole to the equator measured along a meridian. The quadrant proved difficult to measure accurately, and today the meter is defined precisely as the distance light travels in a vacuum during 1/299,792,458 of a second.

The SI unit of mass is the *kilogram* (1 kg = 1000 g). It is based on a standard platinum–iridium cylinder kept at the International Bureau of Weights and Measures. The *gram* is a more convenient unit for many chemical operations.

The derived SI unit of volume is the *cubic meter*. The units more frequently employed in chemistry, however, are the *liter* (1 L = 0.001 m^3) and the *milliliter* (1 mL = 0.001 L). Other SI units of length, mass, and volume are derived from these basic units. Table A.1 lists some metric units of length, mass, and volume and illustrates the use of prefixes.

A.2 Exponential (Scientific) Notation

Scientists often use numbers that are inconceivably large or small. For example, light travels at about 300,000,000 m/s. There are 602,200,000,000,000,000,000,000 carbon atoms in 12.01 g of carbon. On the small side, the diameter of an atom is about 0.0000000001 m, and the diameter of an atomic nucleus is about 0.000000000000001 m. Because it is difficult to keep track of the zeros in such numbers, scientists find it convenient to express them in exponential notation.

Table A.1 Some Metric Units of Length, Mass, and Volume

Length	
1 kilometer (km)	= 1000 meters (m)
1 meter (m)	= 100 centimeters (cm)
1 centimeter (cm)	= 10 millimeters (mm)
1 millimeter (mm)	= 1000 micrometers (μm)
Mass	
1 kilogram (kg)	= 1000 grams (g)
1 gram (g)	= 1000 milligrams (mg)
1 milligram (mg)	= 1000 micrograms (μg)
Volume	
1 liter (L)	= 1000 milliliters (mL)
1 milliliter (mL)	= 1000 microliters (μL)
1 milliliter (mL)	= 1 cubic centimeter (cm^3)

A number is in *exponential notation* when it is written as the product of a coefficient and a power of 10. (Such a number is called *scientific notation* when the coefficient has a value between 1 and 10). Two examples are

$$4.18 \times 10^3 \qquad \text{and} \qquad 6.57 \times 10^{-4}$$

Expressing numbers in exponential form generally serves two purposes.

1. We can write very large or very small numbers in a minimum of space and with a reduced chance of typographical error.
2. We can convey explicit information about the precision of measurements: The number of significant figures (Section A.4) in a measured quantity is stated unambiguously.

In the expression 10^n, n is the exponent of 10, and the number 10 is said to be raised to the nth power. If n is a *positive quantity*, 10^n has a value *greater than 1*. If n is a *negative quantity*, 10^n has a value *less than 1*. We are particularly interested in cases where n is an integer. For example,

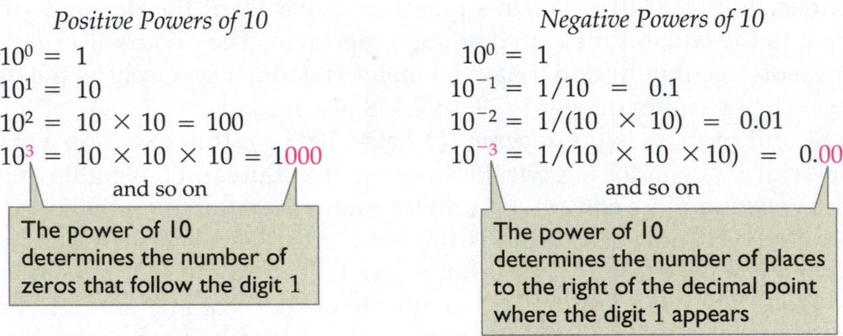

We express 612,000 in scientific notation as follows:

$$612{,}000 = 6.12 \times 100{,}000 = 6.12 \times 10^5$$

We express 0.000505 in scientific notation as

$$0.000505 = 5.05 \times 0.0001 = 5.05 \times 10^{-4}$$

We can use a more direct approach to converting numbers to scientific notation.

- Count the number of places a decimal point must be moved to produce a coefficient having a value between 1 and 10.
- The number of places counted then becomes the power of 10.
- The power of 10 is *positive* if the decimal point is moved to the *left*.

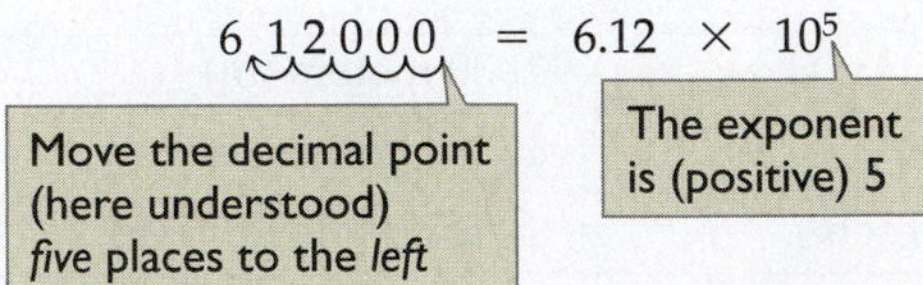

- The power of 10 is *negative* if the decimal point is moved to the *right*.

$$0.000505 = 5.05 \times 10^{-4}$$

Move the decimal point *four* places to the *right*

The exponent is (negative) 4

To convert a number from exponential form to the conventional form, move the decimal point in the opposite direction.

$$3.75 \times 10^6 = 3.750000$$

The exponent is 6 — Move the decimal point *six* places to the *right*

$$7.91 \times 10^{-7} = 0.000000791$$

The exponent is –7 — Move the decimal point *seven* places to the *left*

It is easy to handle exponential numbers on most calculators. A typical procedure is to enter the number, hit the key [EE] or [EXP], and then enter the exponent of 10. The keystrokes required for the number 2.85×10^7 are [2] [.] [8] [5] [EE] [7].

For the number 1.67×10^{-5}, the keystrokes are [1] [.] [6] [7] [EXP] [5] [±]; the last keystroke changes the sign of the exponent. Many calculators can be set to convert all numbers and calculated results to the exponential form, regardless of the form in which the numbers are entered. Most scientific and graphing calculators can also be set to display a fixed number of digits in the results.

Addition and Subtraction

To add or subtract numbers in exponential notation using a scientific or graphing calculator, simply enter the numbers as usual and perform the desired operations. However, to add or subtract numbers *by hand* in exponential notation, it is necessary to express each quantity as the *same power of 10*. In calculations, this approach treats the power of 10 in the same way as a unit—it is simply "carried along." For example, we express each quantity in the following calculation with the power 10^{-3}.

$$(3.22 \times 10^{-3}) + (7.3 \times 10^{-4}) - (4.8 \times 10^{-4}) =$$
$$(3.22 \times 10^{-3}) + (0.73 \times 10^{-3}) - (0.48 \times 10^{-3}) = (3.22 + 0.73 - 0.48) \times 10^{-3}$$
$$= 3.47 \times 10^{-3}$$

Multiplication and Division

To multiply numbers expressed in exponential form by hand, *multiply* all coefficients to obtain the coefficient of the result and *add* all exponents to obtain the power of 10 in the result. Generally, most calculators perform these operations automatically, and no intermediate results need to be recorded.

To divide two numbers in exponential form, *divide* the coefficients to obtain the coefficient of the result and *subtract* the exponent in the denominator from the exponent in the numerator to obtain the power of 10. In the example below, multiplication and division are combined. First, the rule for multiplication is applied to the numerator and to the denominator, and then the rule for division is used.

Rewrite in exponential form

$$\frac{0.015 \times 0.0088 \times 822}{0.092 \times 0.48} = \frac{(1.5 \times 10^{-2})(8.8 \times 10^{-3})(8.22 \times 10^{2})}{(9.2 \times 10^{-2})(4.8 \times 10^{-1})}$$

Apply the rule for multiplication to the numerator and denominator

Apply the rule for division

$$= \frac{1.1 \times 10^{-1}}{4.4 \times 10^{-2}} = 0.25 \times 10^{-1-(-2)} = 0.25 \times 10^{1} = 2.5$$

Raising a Number to a Power and Extracting the Root of an Exponential Number

To raise an exponential number to a given power, raise the coefficient to that power and multiply the exponent by that power. For example, we can cube a number (that is, raise it to the *third* power) in the following manner.

Rewrite in exponential form | Cube the coefficient | Multiply the exponent by 3

$$(0.0066)^3 = (6.6 \times 10^{-3})^3 = (6.6)^3 \times 10^{(-3 \times 3)}$$

$$= (2.9 \times 10^2) \times 10^{-9} = 2.9 \times 10^{-7}$$

To extract the root of an exponential number, we raise the number to a fractional power—one-half power for a square root, one-third power for a cube root, and so on. Most calculators have keys designed for extracting square roots and cube roots. Thus, to extract the square root of 1.57×10^5, enter the number 1.57×10^5 into a calculator, and use the [$\sqrt{\ }$] key.

$$\sqrt{1.57 \times 10^{-5}} = 3.96 \times 10^{-3}$$

Some calculators allow you to extract roots by keying the root in as a fractional exponent. For example, we can take a cube root as follows.

$$(2.75 \times 10^{-9})^{1/3} = 1.40 \times 10^{-3}$$

Self-Assessment Questions

For items 1–4, express the number in scientific notation, and then select the correct answer.

1. 35,400
a. 3.54×10^{-4} **b.** 35.4×10^{-3} **c.** 3.54×10^{4} **d.** 35.4×10^{4}

2. 43,600,000
a. 436×10^{4} **b.** 43.6×10^{-6} **c.** 4.36×10^{7} **d.** 4.36×10^{-7}

3. 0.000000000000312
a. 3.12×10^{-15} **b.** 3.12×10^{-13} **c.** 3.12×10^{-12} **d.** 3.12×10^{13}

4. 0.000438
a. 4.38×10^{-3} **b.** 4.38×10^{-4} **c.** 4.38×10^{4} **d.** 4.38×10^{6}

For items 5–6, express the number in decimal (ordinary) notation, and then select the correct answer.

5. 7.1×10^4
a. 0.00071 **b.** 0.000071 **c.** 71,000 **d.** 710,000

6. 2.83×10^{-4}
a. 0.000283 **b.** 0.00283 **c.** 2830 **d.** 28,300

For items 7–14, perform the indicated operation, and then select the correct answer.

7. $(3.0 \times 10^4) \times (2.1 \times 10^5) = ?$
a. 5.1×10^{9} **b.** 6.3×10^{1} **c.** 6.3×10^{9} **d.** 6.3×10^{20}

8. $(6.27 \times 10^{-5}) \times (4.12 \times 10^{-12}) = ?$
a. 2.58×10^{-17} **b.** 2.58×10^{-16}
c. 2.58×10^{-59} **d.** 2.58×10^{59}

9. $\dfrac{4.33 \times 10^{-7}}{7.61 \times 10^{22}} = ?$
a. 5.69×10^{-30} **b.** 5.69×10^{-15}
c. 5.69×10^{15} **d.** 5.69×10^{30}

10. $\dfrac{9.37 \times 10^{9}}{3.79 \times 10^{27}} = ?$
a. 2.47×10^{-36} **b.** 2.47×10^{-35}
c. 2.47×10^{-18} **d.** 2.47×10^{36}

11. $\dfrac{2.21 \times 10^{5}}{9.80 \times 10^{-7}} = ?$

a. 2.26×10^{-12} **b.** 2.26×10^{-11}
c. 2.26×10^{11} **d.** 4.43×10^{12}

12. $\dfrac{4.60 \times 10^{-12}}{2.17 \times 10^{3}} = ?$

a. 2.12×10^{-15} **b.** 2.12×10^{-14}
c. 2.12×10^{14} **d.** 2.12×10^{15}

13. $(2.19 \times 10^{-6})^2 = ?$

a. 4.80×10^{-12} **b.** 4.80×10^{-6}
c. 4.80×10^{6} **d.** 4.80×10^{12}

14. $\sqrt{1.74 \times 10^{-7}} = ?$

a. 1.32×10^{-7} **b.** 4.17×10^{-7}
c. 4.17×10^{-4} **d.** 1.32×10^{-4}

Answers: 1, c; 2, c; 3, b; 4, b; 5, c; 6, a; 7, c; 8, b; 9, a; 10, c; 11, c; 12, a; 13, a; 14, c

A.3 Unit Conversions

Chapter 1 discusses conversions within the metric system. Because we live in a world in which almost all countries except the United States use metric measurements, we sometimes need to convert between common and metric units. Suppose that an American applies for a job in another country and the job application asks for her height in centimeters. She knows that her height is 66.0 in. Her height is the same, whether we express it in inches, feet, centimeters, or millimeters. Thus, when we measure something in one unit and then convert it to another, we must not change the measured quantity in any fundamental way. We can use equivalencies (given here to three significant figures; Section A.4) such as those in Table A.2 to derive conversion factors.

A variety of conversion calculators are available on the Internet. Use the key words *conversion calculator.*

In mathematics, multiplying a quantity by 1 does not change its value. We can therefore use a factor equivalent to 1 to convert between inches and centimeters. We find our factor in the definition of the inch in Table A.2.

$$1 \text{ in.} = 2.54 \text{ cm}$$

Table A.2 Some Conversions between Common and Metric Units

Length
1 mile (mi) = 1.61 kilometers (km)
1 yard (yd) = 0.914 meter (m)
1 inch (in.) = 2.54 centimeters (cm)[a]
Mass
1 pound (lb) = 454 grams (g)
1 ounce (oz) = 28.4 grams (g)
1 pound (lb) = 0.454 kilogram (kg)
Volume
1 U.S. quart (qt) = 0.946 liter (L)
1 U.S. pint (pt) = 0.473 liter (L)
1 fluid ounce (fl oz) = 29.6 milliliters (mL)
1 gallon (gal) = 3.78 liters (L)

[a]This conversion is exact. The other conversions are available with more significant digits if needed; see any edition of the *CRC Handbook of Chemistry and Physics.*

Notice that if we divide both sides of this equation by 1 in., we obtain a ratio of quantities that is equal to 1.

$$1 = \frac{1\ \text{in.}}{1\ \text{in.}} = \frac{2.54\ \text{cm}}{1\ \text{in.}}$$

If we divide both sides of the equation by 2.54 cm, we also obtain a ratio of quantities that is equal to 1.

$$\frac{1\ \text{in.}}{2.54\ \text{cm}} = \frac{2.54\ \text{cm}}{2.54\ \text{cm}} = 1$$

The two ratios, one shown in red and the other in blue, are conversion factors. A *conversion factor* is a ratio of terms, equivalent to the number 1, used to change the unit in which a quantity is expressed. We call this process the *unit conversion method* of problem solving. Because we set up calculations by examining the *dimensions* associated with the given quantity, those associated with the desired result, and those needed in the conversion factors, the process is sometimes called *dimensional analysis*.

What happens when we multiply a known quantity by a conversion factor? The original unit cancels out and is replaced by the desired unit. Thus, our general approach to using conversion factors is

Desired quantity and unit = given quantity and unit × conversion factors

Now let's return to the question about the woman's height, a measured quantity of 66.0 in. To get an answer in centimeters, we must use the appropriate conversion factor (in blue). Note that the desired unit (cm) is in the numerator and the unit to be replaced (in.) is in the denominator. Thus, we can cancel the unit in. so that only the unit cm remains.

$$66.0\ \cancel{\text{in.}} \times \frac{2.54\ \text{cm}}{1\ \cancel{\text{in.}}} = 168\ \text{cm (rounded off from 167.64)}$$

You can see why the other conversion factor (in red) won't work. No units cancel. Instead, we get a nonsensical unit.

$$66.0\ \text{in.} \times \frac{1\ \text{in.}}{2.54\ \text{cm}} = \frac{26.0\ \text{in.}^2}{\text{cm}}$$

Following are some examples and exercises to give you some practice in this method of problem solving.

Example A.1 Unit Conversions

a. Convert 0.742 kg to grams.
b. Convert 0.615 lb to ounces.
c. Convert 135 lb to kilograms.

Solution

a. This is a conversion from one metric unit to another. We simply use our knowledge of prefixes to convert from kilograms to grams.

We start here
This converts kg to g
Our answer: the number and the unit

$$0.742\ \cancel{\text{kg}} \times \frac{1000\ \text{g}}{1\ \cancel{\text{kg}}} = 742\ \text{g}$$

b. This is a conversion from one common unit to another. Here we use the fact that 1 lb = 16 oz to convert from pounds to ounces. Then we proceed as in part (a), arranging the conversion factor to cancel the unit lb.

$$0.615\ \cancel{\text{lb}} \times \frac{16\ \text{oz}}{1\ \cancel{\text{lb}}} = 9.84\ \text{oz}$$

c. This is a conversion from a common unit to a metric unit. We need data from Table A.2 to convert from pounds to kilograms. Then we proceed as in part (b), arranging the conversion factor to cancel the unit lb.

$$135\ \text{lb} \times \frac{0.454\ \text{kg}}{1\ \text{lb}} = 61.3\ \text{kg}$$

(Our answers have the proper number of significant figures. If you do not understand significant figures and wish to do so, they are discussed in Section A.4. This text uses three significant figures for most calculations.)

■ EXERCISE A.1

a. Convert 16.3 mg to grams.

b. Convert 24.5 oz to pounds.

c. Convert 12.5 fl oz to milliliters.

Quite often, to get the desired unit, we must use more than one conversion factor. We can do so by arranging all the necessary conversion factors in a single setup that yields the final answer in the desired unit.

Example A.2 Unit Conversions

What is the length, in millimeters, of a 3.25-ft piece of tubing?

Solution

No relationship between feet and millimeters is given in Table A.2, and so we need more than one conversion factor. We can think of the problem as a series of three conversions.

1. Use the fact that 1 ft = 12 in. to convert from feet to inches.
2. Use data from Table A.2 to convert from inches to centimeters.
3. Use our knowledge of prefixes to convert from centimeters to millimeters.

We could solve this problem in three distinct steps by making one conversion in each step, but it is just as easy to combine three conversion factors into a single setup. Then we proceed as indicated below.

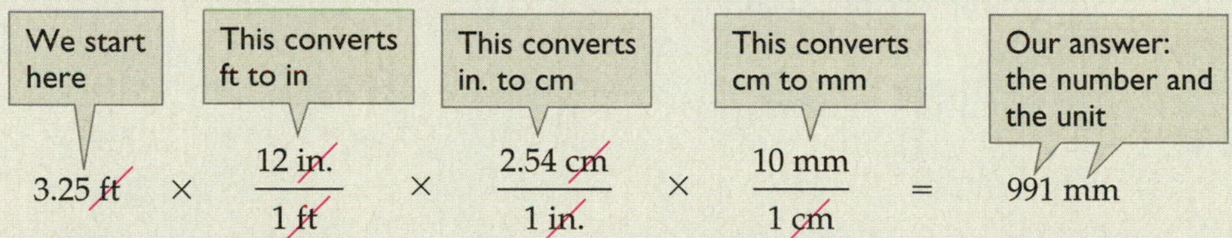

$$3.25\ \text{ft} \times \frac{12\ \text{in.}}{1\ \text{ft}} \times \frac{2.54\ \text{cm}}{1\ \text{in.}} \times \frac{10\ \text{mm}}{1\ \text{cm}} = 991\ \text{mm}$$

■ EXERCISE A.2

Carry out the following conversions.

a. 90.3 mm to meters

b. 729.9 ft to kilometers

c. 1.17 gal to fluid ounces

Sometimes we need to convert two or more units in the measured quantity. We can do this by arranging all the necessary conversion factors in a single setup so that the starting units cancel and the conversions yield the final answer in the desired units.

Example A.3 Unit Conversions

A saline solution has 1.00 lb of salt in 1.00 gal of solution. Calculate the concentration in grams per liter of solution.

Solution

First, let's identify the measured quantities. They can be expressed in the form of a ratio of mass of salt in pounds to a volume in gallons.

$$\frac{1.00 \text{ lb (salt)}}{1.00 \text{ gal (solution)}}$$

This ratio must be converted to one expressed in grams per liter. We must convert from pounds to grams in the numerator and from gallons to liters in the denominator. The following set of equivalent values from Table A.2 can be used to formulate conversion factors.

$$1 \text{ lb} = 454 \text{ g} \qquad 1 \text{ gal} = 3.78 \text{ L}$$

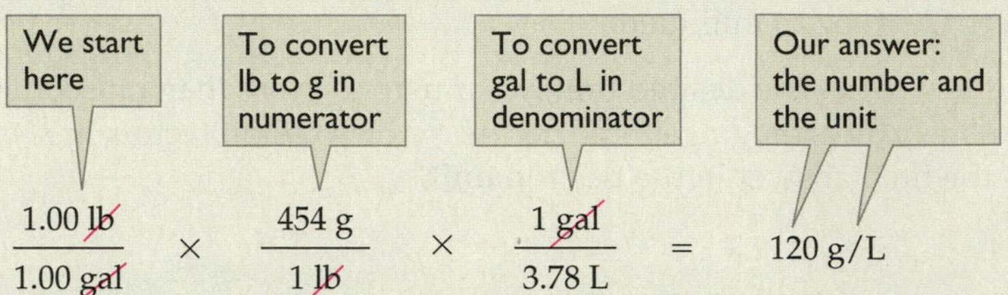

$$\frac{1.00 \text{ lb}}{1.00 \text{ gal}} \times \frac{454 \text{ g}}{1 \text{ lb}} \times \frac{1 \text{ gal}}{3.78 \text{ L}} = 120 \text{ g/L}$$

Note that we could also do the conversions in the numerator and denominator separately and then divide the numerator by the denominator.

$$\text{Numerator:} \quad 1.00 \text{ lb} \times \frac{454 \text{ g}}{1 \text{ lb}} = 454 \text{ g}$$

$$\text{Denominator:} \quad 1.00 \text{ gal} \times \frac{3.78 \text{ L}}{1 \text{ gal}} = 3.78 \text{ L}$$

$$\text{Division:} \quad \frac{454 \text{ g}}{3.78 \text{ L}} = 120 \text{ g/L}$$

Both methods give the same answer to three significant figures.

■ EXERCISE A.3

Carry out the following conversions.

a. 88.0 km/h to meters per second

b. 1.22 ft/s to kilometers per hour

c. 4.07 g/L to ounces per quart

Self-Assessment Questions

For items 1–5, perform the indicated conversion, and then select the correct answer. You may need data from Table A.2 for some of the items.

1. 645 μs to seconds
a. 6.45×10^{-6} s **b.** 6.45×10^{-4} s **c.** 6.45×10^{-2} s **d.** 6.45×10^{8} s

2. 1445 oz to grams
a. 50.9 g **b.** 90.3 g **c.** 144.5 g **d.** 4.10×10^4 g

3. 1.24×10^5 mm to feet
a. 10.3 ft **b.** 103 ft **c.** 407 ft **d.** 4.88×10^3 ft

4. 12.0 fl oz to milliliters
a. 0.405 mL **b.** 240 mL **c.** 355 mL **d.** 3.55×10^5 mL

5. 343 m/s to miles per hour
a. 0.0592 mi/h **b.** 12.8 mi/h **c.** 767 mi/h **d.** 1220 mi/h

Answers: 1, b; 2, d; 3, c; 4, c; 5, c

A.4 Precision, Accuracy, and Significant Figures

Counting can give exact numbers. For example, we can count exactly 24 students in a room. Measurements, on the other hand, are subject to error. One source of error is the measuring instruments themselves. For example, an incorrectly calibrated thermometer may consistently yield a result that is 0.2 °C too low. Other errors may result from the experimenter's lack of skill or care in using measuring instruments. But even the most careful measurement will have some uncertainty associated with it. For example, a meter stick can be used to measure to the nearest millimeter or so. But there is no way for a meter stick to give a measurement that is correct to the nearest 0.001 mm.

Precision and Accuracy

Suppose that five students were asked to measure a person's height using a meter stick marked off in millimeters. The five measurements are recorded in Table A.3. The *precision* of a set of measurements refers to how closely individual measurements agree with one another. We say that the precision is good if each of the measurements is close to the average or poor if there is a wide deviation from the average value.

Table A.3 Five Measurements of a Person's Height

Student	Height (m)
1	1.827
2	1.824
3	1.826
4	1.828
5	1.829
Average	1.827

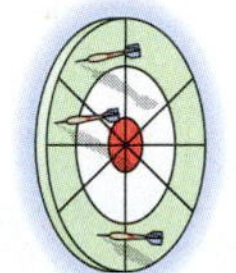

(a) Low accuracy Low precision

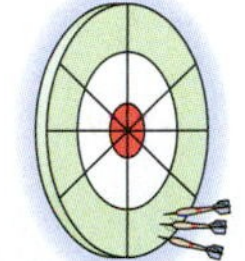

(b) Low accuracy High precision

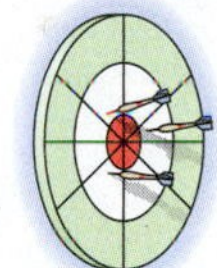

(c) High accuracy Low precision

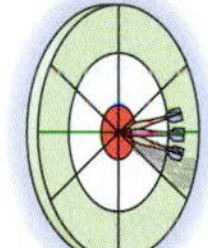

(d) High accuracy High precision

▲ Comparing precision and accuracy: a dartboard analogy. (a) The darts are both scattered (low precision) and off-center (low accuracy). (b) The darts are in a tight cluster (high precision) but still off-center (low accuracy). (c) The darts are somewhat scattered (low precision) but evenly distributed about the center (high accuracy). (d) The darts are in a tight cluster (high precision) and well centered (high accuracy).

How would you describe the precision of the data in Table A.3? Examine the individual data, note the average value, and determine how much the individual data differ from the average. Because the maximum deviation from the average value is 0.003 m, the precision is quite good.

The *accuracy* of a set of measurements refers to the closeness of the average of the set to the "correct," or most probable, value. Measurements of high precision are more likely to be accurate than are those of poor precision, but even highly precise measurements are sometimes inaccurate. For example, what if the meter sticks used to obtain the data in Table A.3 were actually 1005 mm long but still had 1000-mm markings? The accuracy of the measurements would be rather poor, even though the precision would remain good.

Sampling Errors

No matter how accurate an analysis, it will not mean much unless it is performed on valid, representative samples. Consider determining the level of glucose in the blood of a patient. High glucose levels are associated with diabetes, a debilitating disease. Results vary, depending on several factors such as the time of day and what and when the person last ate. Glucose levels are much higher soon after a meal high in sugars. They also depend on other factors, such as stress. Medical doctors usually take blood for analysis after a night of fasting. These fasting glucose levels tend to be more reliable, but physicians often repeat the analysis when high or otherwise suspicious results are obtained. Therefore, there is no one true value for the level of glucose in a person's blood. Repeated samplings provide an average level. Similar results from several measurements give much more confidence in the findings. For example, a diagnosis of diabetes is usually based on two consecutive fasting blood glucose levels above 120 mg/dL.

Significant Figures

Look again at Table A.3. Notice that the five measurements of height agree in the first three digits (1.82); they differ only in the fourth digit. We say that the fourth digit is uncertain. All digits known with certainty, plus the first uncertain one, are called *significant figures*. The precision of a measurement is reflected in the number of significant figures—the more significant figures, the more precise the measurement. The measurements in Table A.3 have four significant figures. In other words, we are quite sure that the person's height is between 1.82 m and 1.83 m. Our best estimate of the average value, including the uncertain digit, is 1.827 m.

The number 1.827 has four digits; we say it has four significant figures. In any properly reported measurement, all nonzero digits are significant. Zeros, however, may or may not be significant because they can be used in two ways: as a part of the measured value or to position a decimal point.

- Zeros between two other significant digits are significant. *Examples*: 4807 (four significant figures); 70.004 (five).
- The lone zero preceding a decimal point is there for aesthetic purposes; it is not significant. *Example*: 0.352 (three significant figures).
- Zeros that precede the first nonzero digit are also not significant. *Examples*: 0.000819 (three significant figures); 0.03307 (four).
- Zeros at the end of a number are significant if they are to the right of the decimal point. *Examples*: 0.2000 (four significant figures); 0.050120 (five).

We can summarize these four situations with a general rule: When we read a number from left to right, all the digits starting with the first nonzero digit are significant. Numbers without a decimal point that end in zeros are a special case, however.

- Zeros at the end of a number may or may not be significant if the number is written without a decimal point. *Example*: 700. We do not know whether the number 700 was measured to the nearest unit, ten, or hundred. To avoid this confusion, we can use exponential notation (Section A.2). In exponential notation, 700 is recorded as 7×10^2 or 7.0×10^2 or 7.00×10^2 to indicate one, two, or three significant figures, respectively. The only significant digits are those in the coefficient, not in the power of 10.

We use significant figures only with measurements—quantities subject to error. The concept does not apply to a quantity that is

1. inherently an integer, such as 3 sides to a triangle or 12 items in a dozen;
2. inherently a fraction, such as the radius of a circle equals $\frac{1}{2}$ of the diameter;
3. obtained by an accurate count, such as 18 students in a class; or
4. a defined quantity, such as 1 km = 1000 m.

In these contexts, the numbers 3, 12, $\frac{1}{2}$, 18, and 1000 can have as many significant figures as we want. More properly, we say that each is an *exact value*.

Example A.4 Significant Figures

In everyday life, common units are often used with metric units in parentheses (or vice versa), but significant figures are not always considered. Which of the following has followed proper significant figure usage?

a. A popular science magazine reports: "Peregrine falcons are the world's fastest animals, reaching speeds of up to 200 mi/h (322 km/h)."

b. A urinal is rated at "1.0 gpf (gallons per flush) or 3.8 lpf (liters per flush)."

Solution

a. The quantity "322 km/h" has three significant figures but "200 mi/h" has only one; significant figure rules were not followed.

b. Each quantity has two significant figures; significant figure rules were followed.

■ EXERCISE A.4

Which of the following has followed proper significant figure usage?

a. A Web site states: "fats and ethanol have the greatest amount of food energy per mass, 9 and 7 kcal/g (38 and 30 kJ/g) respectively."

b. A set of exercise room weights are rated at "12 lb (26 kg)."

Significant Figures in Calculations: Multiplication and Division

If we measure a sheet of notepaper and find it to be 14.5 cm wide and 21.7 cm long, we can find the area of the paper by multiplying the two quantities. A calculator gives the answer as 314.65. Can we conclude that the area is 314.65 cm^2? That is, can we know the area to the nearest hundredth of a square centimeter when we know the width and length only to the nearest tenth of a centimeter? It just doesn't seem reasonable—and it isn't. A calculated quantity can be no more precise than the data used in the calculation, and the reported result should reflect this fact.

A strict application of this principle involves a fairly complicated statistical analysis that we will not attempt here, but we can do a fairly good job by using a practical rule involving significant figures:

> In multiplication and division, the reported result should have no more significant figures than the factor with the fewest significant figures.

In other words, a calculation is only as precise as the least precise measurement that enters into the calculation.

To obtain a numerical answer with the proper number of significant figures often requires that we round off numbers. In rounding, we drop all digits that are not significant and, if necessary, adjust the last reported digit. We use the following rules in rounding.

- If the leftmost digit to be dropped is *4 or less*, drop it and all following digits. *Example*: If we need four significant figures, 69.744 rounds to 69.74, or if we need three significant figures, to 69.7.
- If the leftmost digit to be dropped is *5 or greater*, increase the final retained digit by 1. *Example*: 538.76 rounds to 538.8 if we need four significant figures. Similarly, 74.397 rounds to 74.40 if we need four significant figures or to 74.4 if we need three.

Example A.5 Unit Conversions

What is the area, in square centimeters, of a rectangular gauze bandage that is 2.54 cm wide and 12.42 cm long? Use the correct number of significant figures in the answer.

Solution

The area of a rectangle is the product of its length and width. In the result, we can show only as many significant figures as there are in the least precisely stated dimension, the width, which has three significant figures.

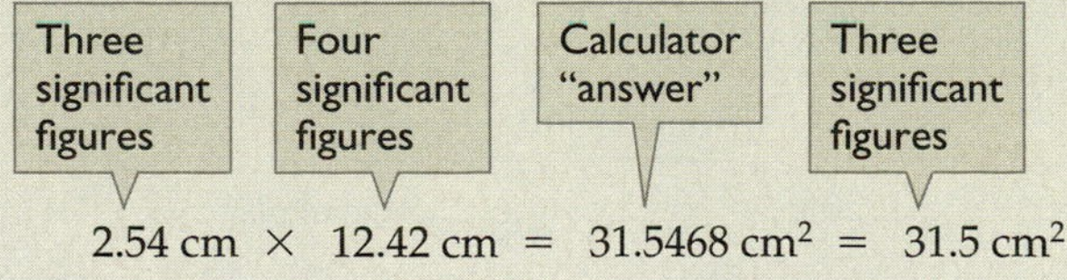

We use the rules for rounding off numbers as the basis for dropping the digits 468.

■ EXERCISE A.5

Calculate the volume, in cubic meters, of a rectangular block of foamed plastic that is 1.827 m long, 1.04 m wide, and 0.064 m thick. Use the correct number of significant figures.

Example A.6 Significant Figures

For a laboratory experiment, a teacher wants to divide all of a 226.8-g sample of glucose equally among the 18 members of her class. How many grams of glucose should each student receive?

Solution

The number 18 is a counted number, that is, an exact number that is not subject to significant figure rules. The answer should carry four significant figures, the same as in 226.8 g.

$$\frac{226.8 \text{ g}}{18 \text{ students}} = 12.60 \text{ g/student}$$

In this calculation, a calculator displays the result 12.6. We add the digit 0 to emphasize that the result is precise to four significant figures.

■ EXERCISE A.6

A dozen eggs has a mass of 681 g. What is the average mass of one of the eggs, expressed with the appropriate number of significant figures?

Significant Figures in Calculations: Addition and Subtraction

In addition or subtraction, we are concerned not with the number of significant figures but with the number of digits to the right of the decimal point. When we add or subtract quantities with varying numbers of digits to the right of the decimal point, we need to note the one with the fewest such digits. The result should contain the same number of digits to the right of its decimal point. For example, if you are adding several masses and one of them is measured only to the nearest gram, the total mass cannot be stated to the nearest milligram no matter how precise the other measurements are.

We apply this idea in Example A.7. Note that in a calculation involving several steps, we need round off only the final result.

Example A.7 Significant Figures

Perform the following calculation and round off the answer to the correct number of significant figures.

$$2.146 \text{ g} + 72.1 \text{ g} - 9.1434 \text{ g}$$

Solution

In this calculation, we add two numbers and subtract a third from the sum of the first two.

2.146 g	three decimal places
+ 72.1 g	one decimal place
74.246 g	
− 9.1434 g	four decimal places
65.1026 g = 65.1 g	one decimal place

Note that we do not round off the intermediate result (74.246). When using a calculator, you generally don't need to write down an intermediate result.

■ EXERCISE A.7

Perform the indicated operations and give answers with the proper number of significant figures. Note that in addition and subtraction all terms must be expressed in the same unit.

a. 48.2 m + 3.82 m + 48.4394 m

b. 15.436 L + 5.3 L − 6.24 L − 8.177 L

c. (51.5 m + 2.67 m) × (33.42 m − 0.124 m)

d. $\dfrac{125.1 \text{ g} - 1.22 \text{ g}}{52.5 \text{ mL} + 0.63 \text{ mL}}$

Self-Assessment Questions

1. A measurement has good precision if it

a. is close to an accepted standard

b. is close to similar measurements

c. has few significant figures

d. is the only value determined

2. Following is data for the length of a pencil as measured by students X, Y, and Z. The length is known to be 11.54 cm.

	Trial 1	Trial 2	Trial 3
X	11.8	11.1	11.5
Y	11.7	11.2	11.6
Z	11.3	11.4	11.5

Which of the following best characterizes the data?

a. Y has the most precise data, X the most accurate

b. Y has the most precise data, Z the most accurate

c. Z has the most precise data, X the most accurate

d. Z has the most precise data, Y the most accurate

3. 725.8055 rounded to three significant figures is

a. 725.806 **b.** 725.81 **c.** 725.8 **d.** 726

For items 4–6, determine the number of significant figures, and then select the correct answer.

4. 0.0000073

a. 2 **b.** 5 **c.** 6 **d.** 8

5. 0.04000

a. 2 **b.** 4 **c.** 5 **d.** 6

6. 80.0040

a. 2 **b.** 4 **c.** 5 **d.** 6

For items 7–16, perform the indicated calculation, and then select the correct answer, with the proper number of significant figures.

7. 7.20 + 3.013 + 0.04327 = ?

a. 10.26 **b.** 10.256 **c.** 10.2563 **d.** 10.25627

8. 4.702 − 0.4123 = ?

a. 4.2897 **b.** 4.29 **c.** 4.290 **d.** 4.30

9. 10.03 + 4.555 = ?

a. 14 **b.** 14.59 **c.** 14.6 **d.** 15

10. 15.3 − 4.001 = ?

a. 11 **b.** 11.2 **c.** 11.299 **d.** 11.3

11. 4.602 ÷ 0.0240 = ?

a. 191 **b.** 191.75 **c.** 191.8 **d.** 192

12. 40.625 × 0.0028 = ?
a. 0.11 **b.** 0.11375 **c.** 0.1138 **d.** 0.114

13. 8.64 ÷ 0.1216 = ?
a. 71.1 **b.** 71.05 **c.** 71.0526 **d.** 71.053

14. (10.30)(0.186) ÷ 0.085 = ?
a. 23 **b.** 22.5 **c.** 22.5388 **d.** 2.254

15. (42.5 + 0.459) ÷ 28.45 = ?
a. 1.510 **b.** 1.5103 **c.** 1.51 **d.** 1.510

16. (7.06 ÷ 0.084) − (29.6 × 0.023) = ?
a. 83 **b.** 83.3 **c.** 83.4 **d.** 83.369

Answers: 1. b; 2. d; 3. d; 4. a; 5. b; 6. d; 7. a; 8. c; 9. b; 10. d; 11. d; 12. d; 13. a; 14. a; 15. c; 16. a

A.5 Calculations Involving Temperature and Heat

As noted in Chapter 1, we sometimes need to make conversions from one temperature scale to another or from one energy unit to another.

Temperature

On the Fahrenheit scale, the freezing point of water is 32 °F and the boiling point is 212 °F; on the Celsius scale, the freezing point of water is 0 °C and the boiling point is 100 °C. A 100° temperature interval (100 – 0) on the Celsius scale therefore equals a 180° interval (212 – 32) on the Fahrenheit scale. From these facts, we can derive two equations that relate temperatures on the two scales. One of these requires multiplying the degrees of Celsius temperature by the factor 1.8 (that is, 180/100) to obtain the degrees of Fahrenheit temperature, followed by adding 32 to account for the fact that 0 °C = 32 °F.

In everyday life, the following ditty will often suffice to assess the meaning of a Celsius temperature.
THE CELSIUS SCALE
Thirty is hot,
Twenty is pleasing,
Ten is quite cool,
And zero is freezing.

$$°F = (1.8 \times °C) + 32$$

In the other equation, we subtract 32 from the Fahrenheit temperature to get the number of degrees Fahrenheit above the freezing point of water. Then this quantity is divided by 1.8.

$$°C = \frac{°F - 32}{1.8}$$

The SI unit of temperature is the kelvin (Chapters 1 and 6). Recall that to convert from °C to K, we simply add 273.15. And to convert from K to °C, we subtract 273.15.

$$K = °C + 273.15 \quad \text{and} \quad °C = K - 273.15$$

Example A.8 illustrates a practical situation where conversion between Celsius and Fahrenheit temperatures is necessary.

Example A.8 Temperature Conversion

At home, you keep your thermostat set at 68 °F. When traveling, you have a room with a thermostat that uses the Celsius scale. What Celsius temperature will give you the same temperature as at home?

Solution

$$°C = \frac{°F - 32}{1.8} = \frac{68 - 32}{1.8} = 20\ °C$$

■ EXERCISE A.8

a. Convert 85.0 °C to degrees Fahrenheit.

b. Convert −12.2 °C to degrees Fahrenheit.

c. Convert 355 °F to degrees Celsius.

d. Convert −20.8 °F to degrees Celsius.

Heat

Chapter 1 introduced the SI unit of energy, the *joule*. A joule (J) is the work done by a force of 1 newton* acting over a distance of 1 meter. Chapter 1 also introduced the more familiar unit, the calorie.

$$1 \text{ cal} = 4.184 \text{ J}$$

$$1 \text{ kcal} = 1000 \text{ cal} = 4184 \text{ J}$$

A calorie (cal) is the amount of heat required to raise the temperature of 1 g of water by 1 °C. (This quantity varies slightly with temperature; a calorie is defined more precisely as the amount of heat required to raise the temperature of 1 g of water from 14.5° to 15.5 °C.)

Some substances gain or lose heat more readily than others (Table A.4). The *specific heat* of a substance is the amount of heat required to raise the temperature of 1 g of the substance by 1 °C. The definition of a calorie indicates that the specific heat of water is 1.00 cal/g °C. In SI, the specific heat of water is 4.184 J/g °C. Note that metals all have much lower values of specific heat than does water. This means that a sample of water must absorb much more heat to raise its temperature than a sample of a metal of similar mass does. The metal sample may become red hot after absorbing a quantity of heat that makes the water sample only lukewarm.

We can use the following equation, in which ΔT is the change in temperature (in either °C or K), to calculate the quantity of heat absorbed or released by a system.

$$\text{Heat absorbed or released} = \text{mass} \times \text{specific heat} \times \Delta T$$

Table A.4 Specific Heats of Selected Substances

	Specific Heat	
Substance	**cal/g °C**	**J/g °C**
Aluminum (Al)	0.216	0.902
Copper (Cu)	0.0921	0.385
Ethyl alcohol (CH_3CH_2OH)	0.588	2.46
Iron (Fe)	0.106	0.443
Ethylene glycol ($HOCH_2CH_2OH$)	0.561	2.35
Magnesium (Mg)	0.245	1.025
Mercury (Hg)	0.0332	0.139
Sulfur (S)	0.169	0.706
Water (H_2O)	1.000	4.182

*A *newton* (N) is the basic SI unit of force. A newton is the force required to give a 1-kg mass an acceleration of 1 m/s^2. That is, $1 \text{ N} = 1 \text{ kg m/s}^2$. Therefore, $1 \text{ J} = 1 \text{ N m} = 1 \text{ kg m}^2/\text{s}^2$.

Example A.9 Heat Absorbed

How much heat, in calories, kilocalories, and kilojoules, does it take to raise the temperature of 225 g of water from 25.0 °C to 100.0 °C?

Solution

First, we list the quantities we need for the calculations.

$$\begin{aligned}\text{Mass of water} &= 225\text{ g}\\ \text{Specific heat of water} &= 1.00\text{ cal/(g °C)}\\ \text{Temperature change} &= (100.0 - 25.0)\text{ °C} = 75.0\text{ °C}\end{aligned}$$

Then we use the equation for the quantity of heat absorbed.

$$\begin{aligned}\text{Heat absorbed} &= \text{mass} \times \text{specific heat} \times \Delta T\\ &= 225\text{ g} \times 1.00\text{ cal/g °C} \times 75.0\text{ °C}\\ &= 16{,}900\text{ cal}\end{aligned}$$

We can then convert the unit cal to the units kcal and kJ.

$$16{,}900\ \cancel{\text{cal}} \times \frac{1\text{ kcal}}{1000\ \cancel{\text{cal}}} = 16.9\text{ kcal}$$

$$16.9\ \cancel{\text{kcal}} \times \frac{4.184\text{ kJ}}{1\ \cancel{\text{kcal}}} = 70.7\text{ kJ}$$

▪ EXERCISE A.9

How much heat, in calories, kilocalories, and kilojoules, is released by 975 g of water as it cools from 100.0 °C to 18.0 °C?

Table A.5 Some Conversion Units for Energy

1 calorie (cal) = 4.184 joules (J) (defined; exact)
1 British thermal unit (Btu) = 1055 joules (J) = 252 calories (cal)
1 food Calorie = 1 kilocalorie (kcal) = 1000 calories (cal) = 4184 joules (J)

Self-Assessment Questions

For items 1–10, perform the indicated conversion, and then select the correct answer.

1. 25 °C to kelvins
   a. −298 K **b.** −248 K **c.** 248 K **d.** 298 K
2. 373 K to degrees Celsius
   a. −73 °C **b.** 0 °C **c.** 73 °C **d.** 100 °C
3. 301 K to degrees Celsius
   a. −72 °C **b.** 28 °C **c.** 128 °C **d.** 374 °C
4. 473 °C to kelvins
   a. 100 K **b.** 200 K **c.** 300 K **d.** 746 K
5. 37.0 °C to degrees Fahrenheit
   a. −20.6 °F **b.** −38.3 °F **c.** 69.0 °F **d.** 98.6 °F
6. 5.50 °F to degrees Celsius
   a. −20.8°C **b.** −14.7 °C **c.** 3.06 °C **d.** 6.31 °C
7. 273 °C to degrees Fahrenheit
   a. 152 °F **b.** 491 °F **c.** 523 °F **d.** 549 °F
8. 98.2 °F to degrees Celsius
   a. 36.8 °C **d.** 54.6 °C **c.** 72.3 °C **d.** 177 °C

9. 2175 °C to degrees Fahrenheit
a. 1190 °F **b.** 1208 °F **c.** 1226 °F **d.** 3947 °F

10. 25.0 °F to degrees Celsius
a. −31.6 °C **b.** −13.9 °C **c.** −3.89 °C **d.** 42.8 °C

11. Of each of the following pairs, which is the larger unit: °C or °F? cal or Cal?
a. °C, cal **b.** °C, Cal **c.** °F, cal **d.** °F, Cal

12. The temperatures, 0 K, 0 °C, and 0 °F, arranged from coldest to hottest, are
a. 0 °C, 0 °F, 0 K **b.** 0 °C, 0 K, 0 °F **c.** 0 °F, 0 °C, 0 K **d.** 0 K, 0 °F, 0 °C

For items 13–20, perform the indicated conversion, and then select the correct answer. You may need data from Table A.5 for some of the items.

13. 0.820 kcal to calories
a. 0.000820 cal **b.** 8.20 cal **c.** 820 cal **d.** 820,000 cal

14. 65,500 cal to kilocalories
a. 0.0655 kcal **b.** 0.655 kcal **c.** 6.55 kcal **d.** 65.5 kcal

15. 0.359 kJ to joules
a. 0.000359 J **b.** 0.00359 J **c.** 35.9 J **d.** 359 J

16. 0.741 kcal to joules
a. 0.000741 J **b.** 3.10 J **c.** 741 J **d.** 3100 J

17. 8.63 kJ to calories
a. 2.06 cal **b.** 20.6 cal **c.** 86.3 cal **d.** 2060 cal

18. 1.36 kcal to kilojoules
a. 1.36 kJ **b.** 5.69 kJ **c.** 325 kJ **d.** 5690 kJ

19. 345 cal to joules
a. 0.345 J **b.** 1.44 J **c.** 82.5 J **d.** 1440 J

20. 873 kJ to kilocalories
a. 0.873 kcal **b.** 209 kcal **c.** 873 kcal **d.** 2090 kcal

21. How much heat, in calories, is required to raise the temperature of 50.0 g of water from 20.0 °C to 50.0 °C?
a. 30.0 kcal **b.** 50.0 kcal **c.** 1500 cal **d.** 2500 kcal

22. How much heat, in kilojoules, is required to raise the temperature of 131 g of iron from 15.0 °C to 95.0 °C?
a. 0.058 kJ **b.** 1.11 kJ **c.** 4.65 kJ **d.** 4650 kJ

Answers: 1, d; 2, d; 3, b; 4, d; 5, d; 6, b; 7, c; 8, a; 9, d; 10, c; 11, b; 12, d; 13, c; 14, d; 15, d; 16, d; 17, d; 18, b; 19, d; 20, b; 21, c; 22, c

Glossary

absolute zero The lowest possible temperature, 0 K or −273.15 °C or −459.7 °F.
absorb Gather a substance on a surface in a condensed layer.
acid A substance that, when added to water, produces an excess of hydrogen ions; a proton donor.
acid–base indicator A substance that is one color in acid and another color in base.
acidic anhydride A substance, such as a nonmetal oxide, that reacts with water to form an acid.
acid rain Precipitation having a pH less than 5.6.
acquired immune deficiency syndrome (AIDS) A disease caused by a retrovirus (HIV) that weakens the immune system.
activated sludge method A technique for secondary sewage treatment in which the sewage is aerated and some sludge is recycled.
activation energy The minimum quantity of energy that must be available before a chemical reaction can take place.
active site The region on an enzyme or a catalyst where a reaction occurs.
addition polymerization A polymerization reaction in which all the atoms of the monomer molecules are included in the polymer.
addition reaction A reaction in which the single product contains all the atoms of two reactant molecules.
adipose tissue Connective tissue where fat is stored.
advanced treatment Sewage treatment designed to remove phosphates, nitrates, other soluble impurities, and metals and other contaminants; also called tertiary treatment.
aerobic exercise Physical activity in which muscle contractions occur in the presence of oxygen.
aerobic oxidation An oxidation process occurring in the presence of oxygen.
aerosol Particles of 1 μm diameter or less, dispersed in air.
aflatoxins Toxins produced by molds growing on stored peanuts and grains.
Agent Orange A combination of 2,4-D and 2,4,5-T used extensively in Vietnam to remove forest cover and destroy crops that maintained enemy armies.
agonist A molecule that fits and activates a specific receptor.
AIDS See **acquired immune deficiency syndrome**.
alchemy A mixture of chemistry and magic practiced in Europe during the Middle Ages (500 to 1500 C.E.).
alcohol (ROH) An organic compound composed of an alkyl group and a hydroxyl group.
aldehyde (RCHO) An organic compound with a carbonyl group that has a hydrogen atom attached to the carbonyl carbon.
aldose A monosaccharide with an aldehyde functional group.
aliphatic compound A nonaromatic substance. *See* also **aromatic compound.**
alkali metal A metal in group 1A in the customary U.S. arrangement of the periodic table or in group 1 of the IUPAC-recommended table.
alkaline earth metal An element in group 2A in the customary U.S. arrangement of the periodic table or in group 2 of the IUPAC-recommended table.
alkaloid A physiologically active nitrogen-containing organic compound that occurs naturally in a plant.
alkalosis A physiological condition in which the pH of the blood is too high.
alkane A hydrocarbon with only single bonds; a saturated hydrocarbon.
alkene A hydrocarbon containing one or more double bonds.
alkyl group (—R) The group of atoms that results when a hydrogen atom is removed from an alkane.
alkyne A hydrocarbon containing one or more triple bonds.
allergen A substance that triggers an allergic reaction.
allotropes Different forms of the same element in the same physical state.
alloy A mixture of two or more elements, at least one of which is a metal; an alloy has metallic properties.
alpha decay Emission of an alpha particle (^4_2He) by a radioactive nucleus.
alpha helix A secondary structure of a protein molecule in which the chains coil around one another in a spiral arrangement.
alpha (α) particle A cluster of two protons and two neutrons; a helium nucleus.
Ames test A laboratory test that screens for mutagens, which are usually also carcinogens.
amide group (—CON—) A functional group in which a carbon is joined to an oxygen atom by a double bond and to a nitrogen atom by a single bond.
amine A nitrogen compound derived from ammonia by replacing one or more hydrogen atoms with alkyl or aromatic group(s).
amino acid An organic compound that contains both an amino group and a carboxyl group; amino acids combine to produce proteins.
amino group ($-NH_2$) A functional group comprised of a nitrogen atom bonded to two hydrogen atoms.
amphetamines Stimulant drugs that are similar in structure to epinephrine and norepinephrine.
amphoteric surfactant A surfactant whose active part bears both a negative charge and a positive charge.
anabolic steroid A drug that aids in the building (anabolism) of body proteins and thus of muscle tissue.
anabolism The building up of molecules through metabolic processes.
anaerobic decay Decomposition in the absence of oxygen.
anaerobic exercise Physical activity that takes place without sufficient oxygen.
analgesic A substance that provides pain relief.
androgen A male sex hormone.
anesthetic A substance that causes loss of feeling or awareness.
anion A negatively charged ion.
anionic surfactant A surfactant whose active part (water-soluble head) bears a negative charge.
anode A positive electrode at which oxidation occurs.
antagonist A molecule that prevents the action of an agonist by blocking its receptor.
antibiotic A soluble substance, produced by a mold or bacterium, which inhibits growth of other microorganisms.
anticarcinogen A substance that inhibits the development of cancer.
anticholinergic A drug that acts on nerves using acetylcholine as a neurotransmitter.
anticoagulant A substance that inhibits the clotting of blood.
anticodon The sequence of three adjacent nucleotides in a tRNA molecule that is complementary to a codon on mRNA.
antihistamine A substance that relieves the symptoms caused by allergens: sneezing, itchy eyes, and runny nose.
anti-inflammatory A substance that inhibits inflammation.
antimetabolite A compound that inhibits the synthesis of DNA and thus slows the growth of cancer cells.
antioxidant A reducing agent that retards damaging oxidation reactions in living cells or reacts with free radicals to prevent rancidity in foods.
antiperspirant A formulation that retards perspiration by constricting the openings of sweat glands.
antipyretic A fever-reducing substance.
apoenzyme The pure protein part of an enzyme.
applied research An investigation aimed at creating a useful product or solving a particular problem.
aqueous solution A solution in which the solvent is water.

arithmetic growth A process in which a constant quantity is added during each period of time.
aromatic compound A compound that has a ring structure and properties like those of benzene.
asbestos A fibrous silicate mineral composed of chains of SiO_4 tetrahedra.
astringent A substance that constricts the openings of sweat glands, thus reducing the amount of perspiration that escapes.
atmosphere The thin blanket of air surrounding Earth.
atmosphere (atm) A unit of pressure equal to 760 mmHg.
atom The smallest characteristic particle of an element.
atomic mass unit (u) The unit of relative atomic masses, equal to $\frac{1}{12}$ the mass of a carbon-12 atom.
atomic number (Z) The number of protons in the nucleus of an atom.
atomic theory A model that explains the law of multiple proportions and the law of constant composition by stating that all elements are composed of atoms.
Avogadro's hypothesis Equal volumes of gases, regardless of their compositions, contain equal numbers of molecules when measured at a given temperature and pressure.
Avogadro's law At a fixed temperature and pressure, the volume of a gas is directly proportional to the amount (number of moles) of gas.
Avogadro's number The number of atoms (6.022×10^{23}) in exactly 12 g of pure carbon-12.

background radiation Constantly occurring radiation from cosmic rays and from natural radioactive isotopes in air, water, soil, and rocks.
base A substance that, when added to water, produces an excess of hydroxide ions; a proton acceptor.
base triplet The sequence of three bases on a tRNA molecule that determine which amino acid it can carry.
basic anhydride A substance, such as a metal oxide, that reacts with water to form a base.
basic research The search for knowledge for its own sake.
battery A series of two or more connected electrochemical cells.
becquerel (Bq) A measure of the rate of radioactive decay; 1 becquerel (Bq) = 1 disintegration/s.
beta decay Emission of a beta particle by a radioactive nucleus.
beta (β) particle An electron emitted by a radioactive nucleus.
beta pleated sheet A secondary protein structure in which arrays of chains form a zigzag sheet.
binary ionic compound A compound consisting of cations of a metal and anions of a nonmetal.
binding energy The energy that holds the nucleons together in an atom's nucleus.
biochemical oxygen demand (BOD) The quantity of oxygen required by microorganisms to remove organic matter from water.
biochemistry The study of the chemistry of living things and life processes.
biomass Dry plant material used as fuel.
bitumen A hydrocarbon mixture obtained from tar sands by heating.
bleach An oxidizing agent used to remove unwanted color from fabric or other material.
blood sugar Glucose, a simple sugar that is circulated in the bloodstream and used directly by cells for energy.
boiling point The temperature at which a substance changes state from a liquid to a gas throughout the bulk of the liquid.
bond See **chemical bond**.
bonding pair A pair of electrons shared by two atoms, forming a chemical bond.
Boyle's law For a given mass of gas at constant temperature, the volume varies inversely with the pressure.
breeder reactor A nuclear reactor that converts nonfissionable isotopes to nuclear fuel.
broad-spectrum antibiotic An antibiotic that is effective against a wide variety of microorganisms.
bronze An alloy of copper and tin.
buffer solution A mixture of a weak acid and its conjugate base or a weak base and its conjugate acid that maintains a nearly constant pH when a small amount of strong acid or strong base is added.
builder Any substance (often a complex phosphate) added to a surfactant to increase its detergency.

calorie (cal) The amount of heat required to raise the temperature of 1 g of water by 1 °C.
carbohydrate A compound consisting of carbon, hydrogen, and oxygen; a starch or sugar.
carbon-14 dating A radioisotopic technique for determining the age of artifacts, based on the half-life of carbon-14.
carbonyl group (C═O) A functional group consisting of a carbon atom joined to an oxygen atom by a double bond.
carboxyl group (—COOH) A carbon atom with a double bond to one oxygen atom and a single bond to a second oxygen atom, which in turn is bonded to a hydrogen atom; the functional group of carboxylic acids.
carboxylic acid (RCOOH) An organic compound that contains the carboxyl functional group.
carcinogen A substance or physical entity that causes the growth of tumors.
catabolism Any metabolic process in which complex compounds are broken down into simpler substances.
catalyst A substance that increases the rate of a chemical reaction without itself being used up.
catalytic converter A device that uses catalysts that oxidize carbon monoxide and hydrocarbons to carbon dioxide and reduce nitrogen oxides to nitrogen gas.
catalytic reforming A process that converts straight-chain alkanes to aromatic hydrocarbons.
cathode A negative electrode at which reduction occurs.
cathode ray A stream of high-speed electrons emitted from a cathode in an evacuated tube.
cation A positively charged ion.
cationic surfactant A surfactant whose active part (water-soluble head) bears a positive charge.
celluloid Cellulose nitrate, a synthetic material derived from natural cellulose by treating it with nitric acid.
cellulose A polymer comprised of glucose units joined by beta linkages.
Celsius scale A temperature scale on which water freezes at 0° and boils at 100°.
cement A complex mixture of calcium and aluminum silicates made from limestone and clay; mixed with water to make concrete.
ceramic A hard, solid product made by heating clay and other minerals to fuse them.
chain reaction A self-sustaining reaction in which one or more products of one event cause one or more new events.
charcoal filtration Filtration of water through charcoal to adsorb organic compounds.
Charles's law For a given mass of gas at constant pressure, the volume varies directly with the absolute temperature.
chelating Tying up metal ions by surrounding them.
chemical bond The force of attraction that holds atoms or ions together in compounds.
chemical change A change in chemical composition.
chemical equation A shorthand representation of a chemical change that uses symbols and formulas instead of words.
chemical property A characteristic of a substance that describes the way in which the substance reacts with another substance to change its composition.
chemical symbol An abbreviation, consisting of one or two letters, that stands for an element.
chemistry The study of matter and the changes it undergoes.
chemotherapy The use of chemicals to control or cure diseases.
chiral carbon A carbon atom that has four different groups attached to it.
coal A solid fossil fuel that is rich in carbon.
codon A sequence of three adjacent nucleotides in an mRNA molecule that specifies one amino acid.
coenzyme An organic molecule (often a vitamin) that combines with an apoenzyme to make a complete, functioning enzyme.
cofactor An ion or molecule that combines with an apoenzyme to make a complete, functioning enzyme.
cologne A diluted perfume.
combined gas law The single relationship that incorporates the simple gas laws.

compound A substance made up of two or more elements combined in a fixed ratio.
concentrated solution A solution that has a relatively large amount of solute per unit volume of solution.
concrete A building material made from cement, sand, gravel, and water.
condensation The reverse of vaporization; a change from the gaseous state to the liquid state.
condensation polymerization A polymerization reaction in which not all the atoms in the starting monomers are incorporated in the polymer because water (or other small) molecules are formed as by-products.
condensed structural formula A chemical formula for an organic compound that omits the bonds joining hydrogens to carbons.
conjugate acid–base pair Two molecules or ions that differ by one proton.
copolymer A polymer formed by the combination of two (or more) different monomers.
core electrons Electrons in any shell of an atom except the outermost shell.
corrosive waste A hazardous waste that requires a special container because it destroys conventional container materials.
cosmetics Substances defined in the 1938 U.S. Food, Drug, and Cosmetic Act as "articles intended to be rubbed, poured, sprinkled or sprayed on, introduced into, or otherwise applied to the human body or any part thereof, for cleaning, beautifying, promoting attractiveness or altering the appearance."
cosmic rays Extremely high-energy radiation from outer space.
covalent bond A bond formed when two atoms share one or more pairs of electrons.
cream An emulsion of tiny water droplets in oil.
critical mass The minimum amount of fissionable material required to achieve a self-sustaining chain reaction.
crystal A solid, regular array of ions.
cyclic hydrocarbon A ring-containing hydrocarbon.

daughter isotope An isotope formed by the radioactive decay of another isotope.
defoliant A substance that causes premature dropping of leaves by plants.
density The amount of mass per unit volume.
deodorant A product that contains perfume to mask body odor; some have a germicide to kill odor-causing bacteria.
deoxyribonucleic acid (DNA) The type of nucleic acid found primarily in the nuclei of cells; contains the sugar deoxyribose.
depilatory A hair remover.
deposition The direct formation of a solid from a gas without passing through the liquid state; the reverse of sublimation.
depressant drug A drug that slows both physical and mental activity.
detergent A cleansing agent, usually a synthetic surfactant.
deuterium An isotope of hydrogen with a proton and a neutron in the nucleus (mass of 2 u).
dextro isomer A "right-handed" isomer.
dietary mineral An inorganic substance required in the diet for proper health and well-being.
Dietary Reference Intakes (DRIs) A set of reference values for nutrients established by the U.S. Academy of Sciences for planning and assessing diets.
dilute solution A solution that has a relatively small amount of solute per unit volume of solution.
dioxins Highly toxic chlorinated cyclic compounds produced by burning wastes containing chlorinated compounds; once found as contaminants in the defoliant 2, 4, 5-T.
dipole A molecule that is polar.
dipole–dipole forces The attractive forces that exist among polar covalent molecules.
disaccharide A sugar that on hydrolysis yields two monosaccharide molecules per molecule of disaccharide.
dispersion forces The momentary, usually weak, attractive forces between molecules resulting from electron motions that create short-lived dipoles.
dissociative anesthetic A substance that causes gross personality disorders, including hallucinations similar to those in near-death experiences.
dissolved oxygen Oxygen dissolved in water; provides a measure of the water's ability to support fish and other aquatic life.
disulfide linkage A covalent linkage between cysteine units through two sulfur atoms.
diuretic A substance that increases the output of urine.
double bond The sharing of two pairs of electrons between two atoms.
doubling time The time it takes a population to double in size.
drug A substance that affects the functioning of living things; used to relieve pain, to treat illness, or to improve health or well-being.
drug abuse The use of a drug for its intoxicating effect.
drug misuse The use of a drug in a manner other than its intended use.

elastomer A polymeric material that returns to its original shape after being stretched.
electrochemical cell A device that produces electricity by means of a chemical reaction.
electrode A carbon rod or a metal strip inserted into an electrochemical cell, at which oxidation or reduction occurs.
electrolysis The process of using electricity to cause chemical change.
electrolyte A compound that conducts an electric current in water solution.
electron The subatomic particle that bears a unit of negative charge.
electron capture (EC) A type of radioactive decay in which a nucleus absorbs an electron from the first or second shell of the atom.
electron configuration The arrangement of an atom's electrons in its energy levels.
electron-dot symbol See **Lewis symbol.**
electronegativity The attraction of an atom in a molecule for a bonding pair of electrons.
electrostatic precipitator A device that removes particulate matter from smokestack gases by creating an electric charge on the particles, which are then removed by attraction to a surface of opposite charge.
element A substance composed of atoms that have the same number of protons.
emollient An oil or grease used as a skin softener.
emulsion A suspension of submicroscopic particles of fat or oil in water.
enantiomers Isomers that are not superimposable on their mirror image.
end note The fraction of a perfume that has the lowest volatility; composed of large molecules.
endorphins Naturally occurring peptides that bond to the same receptor sites as morphine.
endothermic Absorbing energy from the surroundings.
energy The ability to do work.
energy levels (shells) The specific, quantized values of energy that an electron can have in an atom.
enrichment (of food) Replacement of B vitamins and addition of iron to flour.
enrichment (of an isotope) The process by which the proportion of one isotope of an element is increased relative to those of the others.
entropy A measure of the dispersal of energy among the possible states of a system.
enzyme A biological catalyst.
essential amino acid An amino acid that is not produced in the body and must be included in the diet.
ester (RCOOR′) A compound derived from a carboxylic acid and an alcohol; the —OH of the acid is replaced by an —OR group.
estrogen A female sex hormone.
ether (ROR′) A molecule with two hydrocarbon groups attached to the same oxygen atom.
eutrophication The excessive growth of algae in a body of water, which causes some of the plants to die because of a lack of light; the water becomes choked with vegetation, depleted of oxygen, and useless as a fish habitat or for recreation.
excited state A state in which an atom has at least one electron that has moved from a lower to a higher energy level.
exothermic Releasing energy (usually heat) to the surroundings.

fast-twitch fibers The stronger, larger muscle fibers that are suited for short bursts of vigorous exercise.
fat An ester formed by the reaction of glycerol with three fatty-acid units; a triglyceride or triacylglycerol.

fat depots Storage places for fats in the body.
fatty acid A carboxylic acid that contains 4 to 20 or more carbon atoms in a chain.
first law of thermodynamics (law of conservation of energy) Energy cannot be created or destroyed, only transformed.
flammable waste A hazardous waste that burns readily on ignition, presenting a fire hazard.
FLaReS An acronym representing four rules used to test a claim: falsifiability, logic, replicability, and sufficiency.
flocculent A substance that causes particles to clump together and settle out.
food additive Any substance other than a basic foodstuff that is added to food to aid nutrition, enhance color or flavor, or provide texture.
formula A representation of a chemical substance in which the component chemical elements are represented by their symbols.
formula mass The sum of the masses of the atoms represented in the formula of a substance, expressed in atomic mass units (u).
fossil fuels Natural fuels derived from once-living plants and animals; especially coal, petroleum, and natural gas.
free radical A highly reactive chemical species that contains an unpaired electron.
freezing The reverse of melting; a change from the liquid to the solid state.
fuel A substance that burns readily with the release of significant energy.
fuel cell A device that produces electricity directly from continuously supplied fuel and oxygen.
functional group An atom or group of atoms that confers characteristic properties to a family of organic compounds.
fundamental particle An electron, proton, or neutron.

gamma decay Emission of a gamma ray ($^{0}_{0}\gamma$) by a radioactive nucleus.
gamma (γ) rays Radiation that is emitted by radioactive substances and has higher energy and is more penetrating than X-rays.
gas The state of matter in which the substance takes both the shape and volume of a container that it occupies.
gasoline The fraction of petroleum that consists of hydrocarbons, mainly alkanes, with five to twelve carbons and is used as automotive fuel.
gene The segment of a DNA molecule that contains the information necessary to produce a protein; the smallest unit of hereditary information.
general anesthetic A depressant that acts on the brain to produce unconsciousness and insensitivity to pain.
geometric growth A process in which the rate of growth itself increases during each period of time.
geothermal energy Energy derived from the heat of Earth's interior.
glass A noncrystalline solid material obtained by melting sand with soda, lime, and various other metal oxides.
glass transition temperature (T_g) The temperature above which a polymer is rubbery and tough and below which the polymer is brittle.
global warming An increase in Earth's average temperature.
globular protein A protein whose molecules are folded into compact spherical or ovoid shapes.
glycogen A polymer of glucose with alpha linkages and branched chains; stored in the liver and muscles.
GRAS list A list, established by the U.S. Congress in 1958, of food additives generally recognized as safe.
green chemistry An approach that uses materials and processes that are intended to prevent or reduce pollution at its source.
greenhouse effect The retention of the Sun's heat energy by Earth's atmosphere as a result of excess carbon dioxide and other gases in the atmosphere.
ground state The state of an atom in which all of its electrons are in the lowest possible energy levels.
group The elements in a column in the periodic table; a family of elements.

half-life The length of time required for one-half of the radioactive nuclei in a sample to decay.
hallucinogenic drug A drug that produces visions and sensations that are not part of reality.
halogen An element in group 7A in the customary U.S. arrangement of the periodic table or in group 17 of the IUPAC-recommended table.
hard water Water containing excessive concentrations of ions of calcium, magnesium, and/or iron.
hazardous waste A waste that, when improperly managed, can cause or contribute to death or illness or threaten human health or the environment.
heat Energy transfer that occurs as a result of a temperature difference.
heat of vaporization The amount of heat involved in the evaporation or condensation of a fixed amount of a substance.
heat stroke A failure of the body's heat regulatory system; unless the victim is treated promptly, the rapid rise in body temperature will cause brain damage or death.
herbicide A material used to kill weeds (plants classified as pests).
heterocyclic compound A cyclic compound in which one or more atoms in the ring is not carbon.
homogeneous Completely uniform; a property of a sample that has the same composition in all parts.
homologous series A series of compounds whose adjacent members differ by a fixed unit of structure.
hormone A chemical messenger secreted into the blood by an endocrine gland.
humectant A moistening agent added to food.
hydrocarbon An organic compound that contains only carbon and hydrogen.
hydrogen bomb A bomb based on the nuclear fusion of isotopes of hydrogen.
hydrogen bond A type of intermolecular force in which a hydrogen atom covalently bonded in one molecule is attracted to a nonmetal atom in a neighboring molecule; both the atom to which the hydrogen atom is bonded and the one to which it is attracted are small, highly electronegative atoms, usually N, O, or F.
hydrolysis The reaction of a substance with water; literally, a splitting by water.
hydrophilic Attracted to polar solvents such as water.
hydrophobic Not attracted to water; attracted to oil or grease.
hypoallergenic cosmetics Cosmetics claimed to cause fewer allergic reactions than regular products.
hypothesis A tentative explanation of observations that can be tested by experiment.

ideal gas law The volume of a gas is proportional to the amount of gas and its Kelvin temperature and inversely proportional to its pressure.
induced radioactivity Radioactivity caused by bombarding a stable isotope with elemental particles, forming a radioactive isotope.
industrial smog (sulfurous smog) Polluted air associated with industrial activities, characterized by sulfur oxides and particulate matter.
inorganic chemistry The study of the compounds of all elements other than carbon.
insecticide A substance that is used to kill insects.
iodine number The number of grams of iodine that reacts with 100 g of a fat or oil; an indication of the degree of unsaturation.
ion A charged atom or group of atoms.
ionic bond The chemical bond that results when electrons are transferred from a metal to a nonmetal; the electrostatic attraction between ions of opposite charge.
ionizing radiation Radiation that produces ions as it passes through matter.
isoelectronic Having the same electron configuration.
isomers Compounds that have the same molecular formula but different structures.
isotopes Atoms that have the same number of protons but different numbers of neutrons.

joule (J) The SI unit of energy (1 J = 0.239 cal).
juvenile hormone A hormone that controls the rate of development of young organisms; used to prevent insects from maturing.

kelvin (K) The SI unit of temperature; zero on the Kelvin scale is absolute zero.
keratin The tough, fibrous protein that comprises most of the outermost layer of the epidermis.
kerogen The complex material found in oil shale; has an approximate composition of $(C_6H_8O)_n$, where *n* is a large number.

ketone (RCOR′) An organic compound with a carbonyl group between two carbon atoms.
ketose A monosaccharide with a ketone functional group.
kilocalorie (kcal) A unit of energy equal to 1000 cal; one food calorie.
kilogram (kg) The SI unit of mass, a quantity equal to about 2.2 lb.
kinetic energy The energy of motion.
kinetic–molecular theory An explanation of the behavior of gases based on the motion and energy of particles.

lanolin A natural wax obtained from sheep's wool.
law of combining volumes The volumes of gaseous reactants and products are in a small whole-number ratio when all measurements are made at the same temperature and pressure.
law of conservation of energy See **first law of thermodynamics.**
law of conservation of mass Matter is neither created nor destroyed during a chemical change.
law of definite proportions A compound always contains the same elements in exactly the same proportions by mass; also called the *law of constant composition*.
law of multiple proportions Elements may combine in different proportions to form more than one compound—for example, CO and CO_2.
LD_{50} The dosage that is lethal to 50% of a population of test animals.
levo isomer A "left-handed" isomer.
Lewis formula A structural formula of a molecule or polyatomic ion that shows the arrangement of atoms, bonds, and lone pairs.
Lewis symbol A symbol consisting of the element's symbol surrounded by dots representing the atom's valence electrons; also referred to as an *electron-dot symbol*.
limiting reactant The reactant that is used up first in a reaction, after which the reaction ceases no matter how much remains of the other reactants.
line-angle formula A representation of a molecule in which the corners and ends of lines are understood to be carbon atoms and each carbon atom is understood to be attached to enough hydrogen atoms to give it four bonds.
line spectrum The pattern of colored lines emitted by an element.
lipid A substance from animal or plant cells that is soluble in solvents of low polarity and insoluble in water.
lipoprotein A protein combined with a lipid, such as a triglyceride or cholesterol.
liquid The state of matter in which the substance assumes the shape of its container, flows readily, and maintains a fairly constant volume.
liter (L) A unit of volume equal to a cubic decimeter.
local anesthetic A substance that renders part of the body insensitive to pain while leaving the patient conscious.
lone pair A pair of unshared electrons in the valence shell of an atom; also called a *nonbonding pair*.
lotion An emulsion of tiny oil droplets dispersed in water.

main group elements The elements in the A groups of the customary U.S. arrangement of the periodic table or in groups 1, 2, and 13–18 of the IUPAC-recommended table.
marijuana A hallucinogenic drug consisting of the leaves, flowers, seeds, and small stems of the *Cannabis* plant.
mass A measure of the quantity of matter.
mass–energy equation Einstein's equation $E = mc^2$, in which E is energy, m is mass, and c is the speed of light.
mass number (A) The sum of the numbers of protons and neutrons in the nucleus of an atom; also called the *nucleon number*.
matter The stuff of which all materials are made; anything that has mass and occupies space.
melanin A brownish-black pigment that determines the color of the skin and hair.
melting point The temperature at which a substance changes from the solid to the liquid state.
messenger RNA (mRNA) The type of RNA that contains the codons for a protein; travels from the nucleus of the cell to a ribosome.
metabolism The set of coordinated chemical reactions that keep the cells of an organism alive.
metalloid An element with properties intermediate between those of metals and those of nonmetals.
metals The elements that are to the left of the heavy, stepped line in the periodic table.
meter (m) The SI unit of length, slightly longer than a yard.
mica A mineral composed of SiO_4 tetrahedra arranged in a two-dimensional, sheetlike array.
micelle A tiny spherical oil droplet in which the hydrocarbon tails of soap molecules are embedded, with their hydrophilic heads lying along the outer surface.
micronutrient A substance needed by a plant or animal in only tiny amounts.
middle note The fraction of a perfume that is intermediate in volatility and is responsible for the lingering aroma after most top-note compounds have vaporized.
mineral (dietary) An inorganic substance required in the diet for good health.
mineral (geological) A naturally occurring inorganic solid with a definite composition.
mixture Matter with a variable composition.
moisturizer A substance that acts to retain moisture in the skin by forming a protective physical barrier.
molarity (M) The concentration of a solution in moles of solute per liter of solution.
molar mass The mass of one mole of a substance expressed in units of grams/mole.
molar volume The volume occupied by 1 mol of a substance (usually a gas) under specified conditions.
mole (mol) The amount of a substance that contains 6.022×10^{23} elementary units (atoms, molecules, or formula units) of the substance.
molecular mass The mass of a molecule of a substance; the sum of the atomic masses as indicated by the molecular formula, expressed in atomic mass units (u).
molecule An electrically neutral unit of two or more atoms joined by covalent bonds; the smallest fundamental unit of a molecular substance.
monomer A substance of relatively low molecular mass; monomer molecules are the building blocks of polymers.
monosaccharide A carbohydrate that cannot be hydrolyzed into simpler sugars.
mousse A foamy hair care product composed of resins and used to hold hair in place.
mutagen Any entity that causes changes in genes without destroying the genetic material.

narcotic A depressant, analgesic drug that induces narcosis (sleep).
natural gas A mixture of gases, mainly methane, found in underground deposits.
natural philosophy Philosophical speculation about nature.
neuron A nerve cell.
neurotransmitter A chemical that carries an impulse across a synapse from one nerve cell to the next.
neurotrophin A substance produced during exercise that promotes the growth of brain cells.
neutralization The combination of H^+ and OH^- to form water or the reaction of an acid and a base to produce a salt and water.
neutron A nuclear particle with a mass of approximately 1 u and no electric charge.
nitrogen cycle The various processes by which nitrogen is cycled among the atmosphere, soil, water, and living organisms.
nitrogen fixation A process that combines nitrogen with one or more other elements.
noble gases Generally unreactive elements that appear in group 8A of the customary U.S. arrangement of the periodic table or in group 18 of the IUPAC-recommended table.
nonbonding pair See **lone pair.**
nonionic surfactant A surfactant whose active part bears no ionic charge.
nonmetals The elements to the right of the heavy, stepped line in the periodic table.
nonpolar covalent bond A covalent bond in which there is equal sharing of the bonding pair of electrons.
nonsteroidal anti-inflammatory drug (NSAID) A type of anti-inflammatory drug that is milder than the more potent steroidal anti-inflammatory drugs such as cortisone and prednisone.

nuclear fission The splitting of an atomic nucleus into two smaller ones.
nuclear fusion The combination of two small atomic nuclei to produce one larger nucleus.
nuclear reactor A power plant that produces electricity using nuclear fission reactions.
nucleic acid A nucleotide polymer, DNA or RNA.
nucleon A proton or a neutron.
nucleon number See **mass number**.
nucleotide A combination of an amine base, a sugar unit, and a phosphate unit; the monomer unit of nucleic acids.
nucleus The tiny core of an atom, composed of protons and neutrons and containing all the positive charge and most of the mass of the atom.

octane rating The comparison of the antiknock quality of a gasoline to that of pure isooctane (with a rating of 100).
octet rule Atoms tend to have eight electrons in the outermost shell.
oil (food) A substance formed from glycerol and fatty acids, which is liquid at room temperature.
oil shale Fossil rock from which oil can be obtained at high cost.
optical brightener A compound that absorbs the invisible ultraviolet component of sunlight and reemits it as visible light at the blue end of the spectrum; added to detergents to make whites "whiter."
orbital A volume of space in an atom that is occupied by one or two electrons.
organic chemistry The study of the compounds of carbon.
organic farming Farming without using synthetic fertilizers or pesticides.
oxidation An increase in oxidation number; combination of an element or compound with oxygen; loss of hydrogen; loss of electrons.
oxidizing agent A substance that causes oxidation and is itself reduced.
oxygen cycle The various processes by which oxygen is cycled among the atmosphere, soil, water, and living organisms.
oxygen debt The demand for oxygen in muscle cells that builds up during anaerobic exercise.
ozone layer The layer of the stratosphere that contains ozone and shields living creatures on Earth from the Sun's ultraviolet radiation.

paint A surface coating that contains a pigment, a binder, and a solvent.
particulate matter (PM) An air pollutant composed of solid and liquid particles whose size is greater than that of a molecule.
peptide bond The amide linkage that joins amino acids in chains of peptides, polypeptides, and proteins.
percent by mass The concentration of a solution, expressed as (mass of solute ÷ mass of solution) × 100%.
percent by volume The concentration of a solution, expressed as (volume of solute ÷ volume of solution) × 100%.
perfume A fragrant mixture of plant extracts and other chemicals dissolved in alcohol.
period A horizontal row of the periodic table.
periodic table A systematic arrangement of the elements in columns and rows; elements in a given column have similar properties.
pesticide A substance that kills some kind of pest (weeds, insects, rodents, and so on).
petroleum A thick liquid mixture of (mostly) hydrocarbons occurring in various geologic deposits.
pH The negative logarithm of the hydronium ion concentration, which indicates the degree of acidity or basicity of a solution.
pharmacology The study of the response of living organisms to drugs.
phenol A compound with an OH group attached to a benzene ring.
pheromone A chemical secreted by an insect or other organism to mark a trail, send out an alarm, or attract a mate.
photochemical smog Smog created by the action of sunlight on hydrocarbons and nitrogen oxides, which come mainly from automobile exhaust.
photon A unit particle of energy.
photosynthesis The chemical process used by green plants to convert solar energy into chemical energy by reducing carbon dioxide and producing glucose.
photovoltaic cell A solar cell; a cell that uses semiconductors to convert sunlight directly to electric energy.
physical change A change in physical state or form.
physical property A quality of a substance that can be demonstrated without changing the composition of the substance.
phytoremediation A method of wastewater treatment that allows plants in a lagoon to remove metals and other contaminates.
placebo effect The phenomenon in which an inactive substance produces results in recipients for psychological reasons.
plasma A state of matter similar to a gas but composed of isolated electrons and nuclei rather than discrete whole atoms or molecules.
plasticizer A substance added to some plastics to make them more flexible and easier to work with.
poison A substance that causes injury, illness, or death of a living organism.
polar covalent bond A covalent bond in which the bonding pair of electrons is shared unequally by the two atoms, giving each atom a partial positive or negative charge.
polar molecule A molecule that has a separation between centers of positive and negative charge; a dipole.
pollutant A chemical that causes undesirable effects by being in the wrong place and/or in the wrong concentration.
polyamide A polymer that has monomer units joined by amide linkages.
polyatomic ion A charged particle consisting of two or more covalently bonded atoms.
polyester A polymer that has monomer units joined by ester linkages.
polymer A molecule with a large molecular mass that is formed of repeating smaller units (monomers).
polymerase chain reaction (PCR) A process that reproduces many copies of a DNA fragment.
polypeptide A polymer of amino acids, usually of lower molecular mass than a protein.
polysaccharide A carbohydrate, such as starch or cellulose, that consists of many monosaccharide units linked together.
polyunsaturated fat A fat containing fatty-acid units that have two or more carbon-to-carbon double bonds.
positron (β^+ or ${}^{0}_{+1}e$) A positively charged particle with the mass of an electron.
potential energy Energy due to position or composition.
preemergent herbicide A herbicide that is rapidly broken down in the soil and can therefore be used to kill weed plants before crop seedlings emerge.
primary plant nutrients Nitrogen, phosphorus, and potassium.
primary sewage treatment Treatment of wastewater in a holding pond to allow some of the sewage solids to settle out as sludge.
primary structure The amino-acid sequence in a protein.
product A substance produced by a chemical reaction; product formulas follow the arrow in a chemical equation.
progestin A steroid hormone that mimics the action of progesterone.
prostaglandin One of several hormone-like lipids that are derived from the fatty acid arachidonic acid; involved in increased blood pressure, the contractions of smooth muscle, and other physiological processes.
protein An amino acid polymer with a molecular weight exceeding about 10,000 u.
proton (H^+) The hydrogen ion in acid–base chemistry.
proton (nuclear) The unit of positive charge in the nucleus of an atom.
psychotropic drugs Drugs that affect the mind.
purine A heterocyclic amine base with two fused rings, found in nucleic acids.
pyrimidine A heterocyclic amine base with one ring, found in nucleic acids.

quantum A discrete unit of energy; one photon.
quartz A silicate composed of SiO_4 tetrahedra arranged in a three-dimensional array.
quaternary structure An arrangement of protein subunits in a particular pattern.

radiation therapy Use of radioisotopes to destroy cancer cells.
radioactive decay The disintegration of an unstable atomic nucleus with spontaneous emission of radiation.
radioactive fallout Radioactive debris produced by explosion of a nuclear bomb.

radioactivity The spontaneous emission of particles (for example, alpha or beta) or rays (gamma) from unstable atomic nuclei.
radioisotopes Atoms or ions with radioactive nuclei.
reactant A starting material in a chemical change; reactant formulas precede the arrow in a chemical equation.
reactive wastes Hazardous wastes that tend to react spontaneously or to react vigorously with air or water.
Recommended Daily Allowance (RDA) The recommended level of a nutrient necessary for a balanced diet.
reducing agent A substance that causes reduction and is itself oxidized.
reduction A decrease in oxidation number; a gain of electrons; a loss of oxygen; a gain of hydrogen.
replication Copying or duplication; the process by which DNA reproduces itself.
resin A polymeric organic material, usually a sticky solid or semisolid.
restorative drug A drug used to relieve the pain and reduce the inflammation resulting from overuse of muscles.
retrovirus An RNA virus that synthesizes DNA in a host cell.
reverse osmosis A method of pressure filtration through a semipermeable membrane; water flows from an area of high salt concentration to an area of low salt concentration.
ribonucleic acid (RNA) The form of nucleic acid found mainly in the cytoplasm but also present in all other parts of the cell; contains the sugar ribose.
risk–benefit analysis A technique for estimating a desirability quotient by dividing the benefits by the risks.
rule of 72 A mathematical formula that gives the doubling time for a population growing geometrically; 72 divided by the annual rate of growth expressed as a percentage equals the doubling time.

salt An ionic compound produced by the reaction of an acid with a base.
saponins Natural compounds in some plants that produce a soapy lather.
saturated fat A triglyceride composed of a large proportion of saturated fatty acids esterified with glycerol.
saturated hydrocarbon An alkane; a compound of carbon and hydrogen with only single bonds.
science An accumulation of knowledge about nature and the physical world.
scientific law A summary of experimental data; often expressed in the form of a mathematical equation.
scientific model A representation of an invisible process that uses tangible items or pictures.
sebum An oily secretion that protects the skin from moisture loss.
second law of thermodynamics The entropy of the universe increases in any spontaneous process.
secondary plant nutrients Magnesium, calcium, and sulfur.
secondary sewage treatment Passing effluent from primary sewage treatment through gravel and sand filters to aerate the water and remove suspended solids.
secondary structure The arrangement of a protein's polypeptide chains—for example, helix or pleated sheet.
sex attractant A pheromone released by an organism to attract a mate.
shell One of the specific, quantized energy levels that an electron can occupy in an atom.
significant figures Those measured digits that are known with certainty plus one uncertain digit.
silicone A polymer whose chains consists of alternating silicon and oxygen atoms.
single bond A pair of electrons shared between two atoms.
SI units (International System of Units) A measuring system that is used by scientists worldwide and has seven base quantities with their multiples and submultiples.
skin protection factor (SPF) The rating of a sunscreen's ability to absorb or block ultraviolet radiation.
slag A relatively low-melting product of the reaction of limestone with silicate impurities in iron ore.
slow-twitch fibers Muscle fibers suited for steady exercise of long duration.
smog The combination of smoke and fog; polluted air.
soap A salt (usually a sodium salt) of a long-chain carboxylic acid.
solar cell A device used for converting sunlight to electricity; a photoelectric cell.
solid A state of matter in which the substance has a definite shape and volume.
solute The substance that is dissolved in another substance (solvent) to form a solution; usually present in a smaller amount than the solvent.
solution A homogeneous mixture of two or more substances.
solvent The substance that dissolves another substance (solute) to form a solution; usually present in a larger amount than the solute.
specific heat The amount of heat required to raise the temperature of 1 g of a substance by 1 °C.
standard temperature and pressure (STP) Conditions of 0 °C and 1 atm pressure.
starch A polymer of glucose units joined by alpha linkages; a complex carbohydrate.
starvation The withholding of nutrition from the body, whether voluntary or involuntary.
steel An alloy of iron containing small amounts of carbon and usually another metal such as manganese, nickel, or chromium.
stereoisomers Isomers having the same formula but differing in the arrangement of atoms or groups of atoms in three-dimensional space.
steroid A molecule that has a four-ring skeletal structure, with one cyclopentane and three cyclohexane fused rings.
stimulant drug A drug that increases alertness, speeds up mental processes, and generally elevates the mood.
stoichiometric factor A factor that relates the numbers of moles of two substances through their coefficients in a chemical equation.
stoichiometry The quantitative relationship between reactants and products in a chemical reaction.
strong acid An acid that ionizes completely in water; a potent proton donor.
strong base A base that dissociates completely in water; a potent proton acceptor.
structural formula A chemical formula that shows how the atoms of a molecule are arranged, to which other atom(s) they are bonded, and the kinds of bonds.
sublevel See **subshell**.
sublimation Conversion of a solid directly to the gaseous state without going through the liquid state.
subshell A set of orbitals in an atom that are in the same shell and have the same energy; also called a *sublevel*.
substance A sample of matter that always has the same composition, no matter how it is made or where it is found.
substituent An atom or group of atoms substituted for a hydrogen atom on a hydrocarbon.
substrate The substance that attaches to the active site of an enzyme and is then acted upon.
sulfurous smog See **industrial smog**.
sunscreen A substance or mixture that blocks or absorbs ultraviolet (UV) radiation.
supercritical fluid An intermediate state having properties of both gases and liquids.
surface-active agent (surfactant) Any substance that stabilizes the suspension in water of a nonpolar substance such as oil.
surroundings Everything that is not part of the system being observed in a thermochemical study.
sustainable agriculture Farming practices that can produce food and fiber indefinitely, without causing irreparable damage to the ecosystem.
sustainable chemistry An approach designed to meet the needs of the present generation without compromising the needs of future generations.
synapse A tiny gap between nerve cells.
synergistic effect An effect greater than the sum of the effects expected from two or more phenomena.
system The part of the universe under consideration in a thermochemical study.

tar sands Sands that contain bitumen, a thick hydrocarbon material.
technology The practical application of knowledge by which humans modify the materials of nature to better satisfy their needs and wants.

temperature A measure of heat intensity, or how energetic the particles of a sample are.
temperature inversion A warm layer of air above a cool, stagnant lower layer.
teratogen A substance that causes birth defects when introduced into the body of a pregnant female.
tertiary structure The folding pattern of a protein.
tetracyclines Antibacterial drugs with four fused rings.
theory A detailed explanation of a phenomenon that is based on experimentation and may be revised if new data warrant.
thermochemistry The study of energy changes that occur during chemical reactions.
thermonuclear reactions Nuclear fusion reactions that require extremely high temperatures and pressures.
thermoplastic polymer A kind of polymer that can be heated and reshaped.
thermosetting polymer A kind of polymer that cannot be softened and remolded.
top note The fraction of a perfume that vaporizes most quickly, is composed of relatively small molecules, and is responsible for the odor when the perfume is first applied.
toxicology The branch of pharmacology that deals with the effects of poisons on the body, their identification and detection, and remedies for them.
toxic waste A waste that contains or releases poisonous substances in amounts large enough to threaten human health or the environment.
toxin A poisonous substance produced by a living organism.
tracers Radioisotopes used to trace the movement of substances or locate the sites of activity in physical, chemical, and biological systems.
transcription The process by which a segment of DNA transfers its information to a messenger RNA (mRNA) molecule during protein synthesis.
transfer RNA (tRNA) A small molecule that contains anticodon nucleotides; the RNA molecule that bonds to and carries an amino acid.
transition elements Metallic elements in the B groups of the customary U.S. arrangement of the periodic table or in groups 3–12 of the IUPAC-recommended table.
translation The process by which the information contained in the codon of an mRNA molecule is converted to a protein structure.
transmutation The conversion of one element into another.
triglyceride An ester of glycerol with three fatty-acid units; also called a triacylglycerol.
triple bond The sharing of three pairs of electrons between two atoms.
tritium A radioactive isotope of hydrogen with two neutrons and one proton in the nucleus (hydrogen-3).

unsaturated hydrocarbon An alkene, alkyne, or aromatic hydrocarbon; a hydrocarbon containing one or more double or triple bonds or aromatic rings.

valence electrons Electrons in the outermost shell of an atom.
valence shell electron pair repulsion theory (VSEPR theory) A theory of chemical bonding useful in determining the shapes of molecules; it states that valence shell electron pairs around a central atom locate themselves as far apart as possible.
vaporization The process by which a substance changes from the liquid to the gaseous (vapor) state.
variable A factor that changes during an experiment.
vitamin An organic compound that is required in the diet to protect against some diseases.
volatile organic compounds (VOCs) Compounds that cause pollution because they vaporize readily.
VSEPR theory See **valence shell electron pair repulsion theory**.
vulcanization The process of making naturally soft rubber harder by reacting it with sulfur.

wax An ester of a long-chain fatty acid with a long-chain alcohol.
weak acid An acid that ionizes only slightly in water; a poor proton donor.
weak base A base that ionizes only slightly in water; a poor proton acceptor.
weight A measure of the force of attraction between Earth (or another planet) and an object.
wet scrubber A pollution control device that uses water to remove pollutants from smokestack gases.

X-rays Radiation similar to visible light but of much higher energy and much more penetrating.

zwitterion A molecule that contains both a positive charge and a negative charge; a dipolar ion.

Brief Answers to Selected Problems

Answers are provided for *all in-chapter exercises*. Brief answers are given for *odd-numbered Review Questions*; more complete answers can be obtained by reviewing the text. Answers are provided for *all odd-numbered Problems and Additional Problems.*

NOTE: For numerical problems, your answer may differ slightly from ours because of rounding and the use of significant figures (see Appendix).

Chapter 1

1.1 **A. a.** DQ would probably be small.
b. DQ would probably be large.
B. a. DQ would be uncertain.
b. DQ would probably be large.

1.2 **A. a.** 1.00 kg
b. 179 lb

1.3 **A.** physical: a, c; chemical: b
B. physical: b, d; chemical: a, c

1.4 **A.** elements: He, No, Os; compounds: CuO, NO, KF
B. 8

1.5 **a.** 7.24 kg
b. 4.29 μm
c. 7.91 ms
d. 2.29 cg
e. 7.90 Mm

1.6 **a.** 7.45×10^{-9} m
b. 5.25×10^{-6} s
c. 1.415×10^{3} m
d. 2.06×10^{-3} m
e. 6.19×10^{3} m

1.7 **A.** 500 cm^2
B. 1600 cm^3

1.8 **a.** 7.55×10^{2} mm
b. 0.2056 L
c. 2.06×10^{5} μg
d. 73.8 mm

1.9 **A.** Ice
B. Padauk floats, and ebony sinks. Both sink in ethyl alcohol.

1.10 **A.** 1.11 g/mL
B. 11.8 g/cm^3

1.11 **A.** 316 g
B. 47.7 kg

1.12 **A.** 14.8 cm^3
B. No (1.33 L)

1.13 **A.** 351 K
B. 77 K

1.14 **A.** 1799 kcal
B. 34 kcal

1. Science is testable, reproducible, explanatory, predictive, and tentative. Testability best distinguishes science.
3. These problems usually involve too many variables to be treated by scientific methods.
5. Risk–benefit analysis compares benefits of an action with risks of that action.
7. A desirability quotient (DQ) is benefits divided by risks. A large DQ means that risks are minimal compared with benefits.
9. liter; milliliter
11. **(a)** applied; **(b)** applied; **(c)** basic.
13. Penicillin has saved thousands of lives, causing harm to a very few. The DQ for penicillin is large.
15. **(a)** high; **(b)** high, but lower than (a).
17. Food producers benefit through increased profits. The consumer assumes the greatest risk.
19. 100 g, 2 kg
21. Yes
23. 250 mL
25. 1.46×10^{9} km^3
27. Yes; the 26.3-mm i.d. tube is larger than 25.4 mm (1 inch).
29. physical property: a, c, d; chemical property: b.
31. physical change: a, c; chemical change: b
33. substance: a, c, d; mixture: b
35. homogeneous: a, b, c; heterogeneous: d
37. a substance
39. elements: a, b, d; compound: c
41. **a.** aluminum; **b.** calcium; **c.** chlorine; **d.** silver
43. f
45. **a.** 8.01 μg **b.** 7.9 mL **c.** 1.05 km
47. **a.** 0.0374 L **b.** 1.55×10^{5} m **c.** 198 mg **d.** 1.19×10^{4} cm^2 **e.** 0.078 ms
49. **a.** cm **b.** kg **c.** dL
51. 10.0 mm; 1830 mm
53. **a.** 1.17 g/mL **b.** 1.26 g/mL
55. **a.** 120 g **b.** 490 g
57. **a.** 344 mL **b.** 495 cm^3
59.

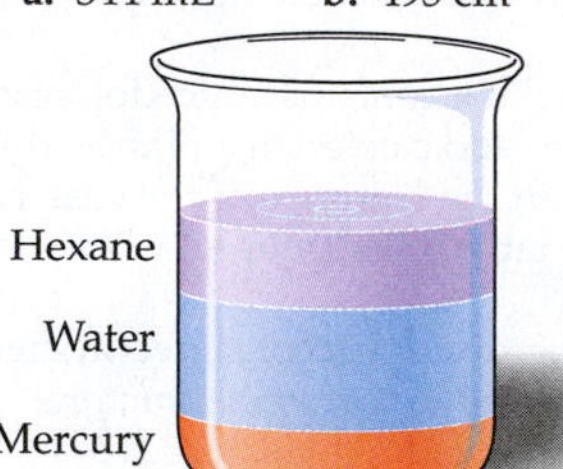

61. Yes
63. 14.8 cm
65. −78 °C
67. 38.5 kcal
69. 52.6 min
71. b.
73. 5.7 y
75. 1, d; 2, e; 3, b; 4, a; 5, d
77. 600 g
79. Cabbage (lightest) < potatoes < sugar (heaviest)
81. 5.23 g/cm^3
83. 6.73×10^{-6} cm
85. 0.908 metric ton
87. **a.** 1.3 g/cm^3; **b.** 5.4 g/cm^3; **c.** 0.688 g/cm^3; Jupiter and Earth are more dense than water; Saturn is less dense and would float (in a large enough ocean!).
89. Green chemistry is an approach that uses materials and processes that are intended to prevent or reduce pollution at its source.
91. a

Chapter 2

2.1 **A.** 2.19 g nitrogen **B.** 63.0 g nitrogen
2.2 3 atoms hydrogen/1 atom phosphorus
2.3 average Cl + I is 81.2; actual Br is 79.9.

1. **a.** atomic: matter is made of discrete particles; continuous: matter is infinitely divisible.
b. Greek: four elements, no atoms; modern: each element has its own kind of atom.

3. discrete: a, c, e; continuous: b, d
5. An element is a substance that could not be broken down into simpler substances.
7. Different elements can combine in two or more different sets of proportions, each set corresponding to a different compound.
a. 2:1 **b.** 3:1 **c.** 3:5
9. C has 15 oxygen atoms; the initial mixture has only 14.
11. **a.** conservation of mass: no atoms are created or destroyed.
b. definite proportions: only whole atoms combine.
c. multiple proportions; 1 C atom can combine with 1 O atom to make CO, or 1 C atom can combine with 2 O atoms to make CO_2.
13. Law of multiple proportions
15. No. In the open vessel, a gas has escaped and is not part of the weight after reaction.
17. No. The elements have only been mixed; they have not reacted chemically.
19. 6.60 g
21. The mass of titanium(IV) oxide formed cannot be greater than the masses of titanium and oxygen together.
23. (b)
25. **a.** 86.9 g hydrogen. **b.** 688 g oxygen
27. 3.8 kg carbon
29. C:O ratio for carbon suboxide is 1.000:0.888. Ratio of 1.332:0.888 = 3:2; 2.664:0.888 = 3:1.
31. SnO_2
33. The S:F ratios are (T) 1.00:2.37 and (U) 1.00:3.56. 3.56:2.37 = 1.50:1 or 3:2.
35. **a.** Yes; Dalton assumed that atoms of different elements had different masses.
b. No; Dalton assumed that atoms of one element differ (in mass) from atoms of any other element.
37. Contradict. Dalton regarded atoms as indivisible.
39. (d)
41. Yes; the ratio of carbon to hydrogen is the same for the different samples.
43. 0.4467 g nitrogen
45. Six fluorine atoms
47. Conservation of mass
49. 108.0 g of mercury oxide
51. 1.334:1.000 or 4:3
53. (1) Lead compounds, once used in paints, have been replaced with titanium dioxide, a much safer material. (2) Metal salts with lower toxicity now substitute for the lead stabilizers in plastics.

Chapter 3

3.1 **A.** 33 neutrons **B.** 131; iodine-131
3.2 **A.** $^{90}_{37}X$ and $^{88}_{37}X$; $^{88}_{38}X$ and $^{93}_{38}X$ **B.** three
3.3 **A.** 32 electrons **B.** 3
3.4 **a.** (Be) 2 2
b. (Mg) 2 8 2; both have the same number of outer electrons.
3.5 **A. a.** $1s^22s^22p^5$
b. $1s^22s^22p^63s^23p^5$ (Both have the valence configuration ns^2np^5.)
B. a. $1s^22s^22p^63s^23p^63d^24s^2$
b. $1s^22s^22p^63s^23p^63d^{10}4s^24p^1$
3.6 **A. a.** (Rb) $5s^1$
b. (Se) $4s^24p^4$
c. (Ge) $4s^24p^2$
B. a. (Ga) $4s^24p^1$
b. (In) $5s^25p^1$
1. **a.** Crookes invented the gas discharge tube.
b. Goldstein discovered positive particles.
c. Faraday developed electrolysis.
d. Thomson determined mass-to-charge ratio of the electron.
3. Both are forms of radiation; gamma rays are more energetic.
5. A and B, no; A and C, no; A and D, yes; B and C, yes
7. A and B
9. Sc; scandium; 45.0 u
11. The atom in which the electron moves from the first to the third shell.
13. **a.** 3 **b.** 12 **c.** 17 **d.** 9 **e.** 13 **f.** 15
15. **a.** $^{42}_{20}Ca$, calcium-42
b. $^{51}_{23}V$, vanadium-51
17. 4
19. **a.** 7 **b.** 13 **c.** 19
21. **a.** Excited state; one electron has been raised to the 2*p* subshell.
b. Incorrect; a *p* subshell can only hold at most 6 electrons.
c. Excited state; two electrons have been raised to the 2*p* subshell.
d. Ground state; all six electrons are in the lowest possible subshell.
23. neon
25. Si has two 3*p* electrons; Ge has two 4*p* electrons; germanium is a much larger atom.
27. metal, a, b, and c; nonmetal, d
29. Ne and Kr
31. Four
33. **a.** 15 **b.** phosphorus **c.** 15 **d.** 6 **e.** 0
35.

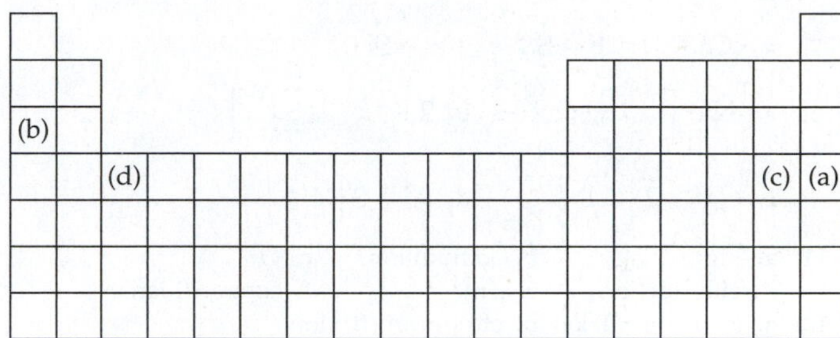

37. **a.** $1s^22s^22p^63s^23p^63d^64s^2$
b. $1s^22s^22p^63s^23p^63d^{10}4s^24p^64d^{10}5s^25p^2$
c. $1s^22s^22p^63s^23p^63d^{10}4s^24p^64d^{10}4f^{14}5s^25p^65d^{10}6s^26p^2$
39. The period 5 elements are in group 2A (only *s* electrons) and group 3B (*d* electrons). Therefore, the elements are strontium (Sr) and yttrium (Y).
41. b
43. d

Chapter 4

4.1 **a.** :Ar: **b.** ·Ca· **c.** :F· **d.** :N· **e.** K· **f.** :S·
4.2 **A.** Li· + :F· ⟶ Li^+ + $:F:^-$
B. Rb· + :I· ⟶ Rb^+ + $:I:^-$
4.3 2 ·Al· + 3 :O· ⟶ 2 Al^{3+} + 3 $:O:^{2-}$
4.4 **A. a.** CaF_2 **b.** Li_2O
B. $FeCl_2$ and $FeCl_3$
4.5 **a.** K_2O **b.** Ca_3N_2 **c.** CaS
4.6 **a.** calcium fluoride **b.** copper(II) bromide
4.7 **a.** bromine trifluoride
b. bromine pentafluoride
c. dinitrogen monoxide
d. dinitrogen pentoxide
4.8 **a.** PCl_3 **b.** Cl_2O_7
c. NI_3 **d.** S_2Cl_2
4.9 **a.** :Br· + ·Br: ⟶ :Br:Br:
b. H· + ·Br: ⟶ H:Br:
c. :I· + ·Cl: ⟶ :I:Cl:
4.10 **A. a.** polar covalent **b.** ionic **c.** nonpolar covalent
B. a. polar covalent **b.** polar covalent **c.** nonpolar covalent
4.11 **A. a.** $Ca(C_2H_3O_2)_2$ **b.** K_2O **c.** $Al_2(SO_4)_3$
B. a. 3 **b.** 4
4.12 **A. a.** calcium carbonate **b.** magnesium phosphate
c. potassium chromate

B. a. ammonium sulfate
b. potassium dihydrogen phosphate
c. copper(II) dichromate

4.13 A. a. :F̤—Ö—F̤: b. $H-C(H)(H)-Cl$:

B. a. $[:N=N=N:]^-$ b. :Ö=N̈—Ö—F̤:

4.14 A. a. pyramidal b. triangular
B. a. triangular b. bent (at both O)

1. Sodium metal is quite reactive; sodium ions (as in NaCl) are quite unreactive.
3. a. 1+ b. 2− c. 3− d. 2+
5. a. 1 b. 1 c. 2 d. 1
e. 3 f. 3
7. a. ·Ca· b. :S̤: c. ·Si·
9. a. $Na^+[:\ddot{I}:]^-$ b. $2\,K^+[:\ddot{S}:]^{2-}$
c. $Ca^{2+}\ 2[:\ddot{Cl}:]^-$ d. $Al^{3+}\ 3[:\ddot{F}:]^-$
11. a. Mg^{2+} b. sodium ion c. O^{2-}
d. chloride ion e. Zn^{2+} f. copper(I) ion
13. a. chromium(II) ion b. chromium(III) ion
c. chromium(VI) ion
15. a. V^{2+} b. Ti^{2+} c. Ti^{4+}
17. a. NaI b. potassium chloride
c. Cu_2O d. magnesium fluoride
e. $FeBr_2$ f. iron(III) bromide
19. Cr_2O_3, chromium(III) oxide, and CrO_3, chromium(VI) oxide
21. a. KOH b. magnesium carbonate
c. $Fe(CN)_3$ d. FeC_2O_4
e. copper(II) sulfate f. sodium dichromate
23. H· + ·F̤: ⟶ H:F̤:
25. ·P̤· + 3 H· ⟶ H:P̤:H (with H below P)
27. ·C̣· + 4 :C̤l· ⟶ :C̤l:C(:C̤l:)(:C̤l:):C̤l:
29. a. N_2O_4 b. $BrCl_3$
c. oxygen difluoride d. NI_3
e. carbon tetrabromide f. dinitrogen tetrasulfide
31. a. $H-Si(H)(H)-H$ b. :N(:F̤:)(:F̤:)—N(:F̤:)(:F̤:):
c. $H-C(H)(H)-N(H)(H)$: d. $H-C(=O)-H$ (:O: with two lone pairs)
e. :N(H)(H)(H)—Ö: (with H on each) f. H—Ö—P(—Ö—H)—Ö—H

33. a. $[:\ddot{Cl}-\ddot{O}:]^-$ b. $[H-\ddot{O}-P(:\ddot{O}:)(:\ddot{O}:)-\ddot{O}:]^{2-}$
c. $[:\ddot{O}-\ddot{Br}(:\ddot{O}:)-\ddot{O}:]^-$
35. a. polar b. polar c. polar
37. a. H—O (arrow toward O) b. N—F (arrow toward F) c. Cl—B (arrow toward Cl)
39. a. $\overset{\delta+}{Si}-\overset{\delta-}{O}$
b. is not polar
c. $\overset{\delta-}{F}-\overset{\delta+}{N}$
41. a. ionic b. nonpolar covalent
c. ionic d. nonpolar covalent
43. a. tetrahedral b. bent
c. pyramidal d. tetrahedral
e. bent f. triangular
45. Nonpolar; the two polar Be—F bonds cancel.
47. a. nonpolar bonds; 109.5°; nonpolar molecule
b. nonpolar bonds; 109.5°; nonpolar molecule
c. nonpolar bonds; 109.5°; nonpolar molecule
d. polar bonds; 109.5°; nonpolar molecule
e. polar bonds; 109.5°; polar molecule
f. polar bonds; 120°; polar molecule
49. a, c
51. a. Al(:B̤r:)(:B̤r:)—B̤r: b. H—Be—H c. H—B(H)—H
53. Neon has an octet of valence electrons (a full outer shell).
55. AlP; Mg_3P_2
57. Polar covalent
59. No; a potassium salt, to avoid having the mouth catch fire!
61. a. Ca^{2+}: $1s^22s^22p^63s^23p^6$
b. Rb^+: $1s^22s^22p^63s^23p^63d^{10}4s^24p^6$
c. S^{2-}: $1s^22s^22p^63s^23p^6$
d. I^-: $1s^22s^22p^63s^23p^63d^{10}4s^24p^64d^{10}5s^25p^6$
e. N^{3-}: $1s^22s^22p^6$
f. Se^{2-}: $1s^22s^22p^63s^23p^63d^{10}4s^24p^6$
63. The halogens have seven valence electrons. Forming single bonds by sharing a bond with one other atom gives them an octet of electrons.
65. $Al_2(WO_4)_3$
67. $Q_3(ZX_4)_2$
69. Molecular recognition
71. Medicinal chemists design new drug molecules to resemble biological molecules that bind to enzymes which recognize the molecules by shapes and partial charges.

Chapter 5

5.1 A. $3\,H_2 + N_2 \longrightarrow 2\,NH_3$
B. $2\,Fe_2O_3 + 3\,C \longrightarrow 3\,CO_2 + 4\,Fe$
5.2 A. 1.48 L CO_2
B. propane; 8 L
5.3 A. a. 65.0 u b. 98.0 u
c. 147.0 u d. 234.1 u
5.4 a. 13.8% N b. 41.1% N
5.5 A. a. 2.04 g Si b. 1000 g H_2O
c. 17.0 g $Ca(H_2PO_4)_2$
B. a. 0.0664 mol Fe b. 2.84 mol C_4H_{10}
c. 0.000674 mol $Mg(NO_3)_2$

5.6 *Molecular:* 2 molecules H_2S react with 3 molecules O_2 to form 2 molecules SO_2 and 2 molecules H_2O
Molar: 2 mol H_2S react with 3 mol O_2 to form 2 mol SO_2 and 2 mol H_2O
Mass: 68.2 g H_2S react with 96.0 g O_2 to form 128.1 g SO_2 and 36.0 g H_2O

5.7 **A. a.** 1.59 mol CO_2 **b.** 0.168 mol CO_2
B. propane; 15 mol

5.8 **A.** 0.763 g O_2
B. a. 2130 g CO_2 **b.** 2350 g CO_2

5.9 **A.** 0.00870 M
B. 0.968 M

5.10 **A. a.** 9.00 M **b.** 1.26 M
B. 0.274 M

5.11 **a.** 673 g KOH **b.** 5.61 g KOH

5.12 **A.** 29.7 mL
B. 6.30×10^{-4} g HNO_3

5.13 **A.** 90.7% ethanol
B. 34.8% toluene

5.14 **A.** 2.81% H_2O_2
B. 51.3% NaOH

5.15 **A.** Dissolve 5.62 g glucose in enough water to make 125 g solution.
B. Dissolve 15.6 g NaCl in enough water to make 1750 g solution.

1. a. The smallest repeating unit of a substance
b. The sum of the atomic masses of a chemical compound
c. The amount of a substance that contains 6.022×10^{23} formula units of the substance
d. The number of atoms (6.022×10^{23}) in exactly 12 g of pure carbon-12
e. The formula mass of a substance expressed in grams; mass of one mole
f. The volume occupied by 1 mol of a gas under specified conditions

3. Avogadro's hypothesis states that equal volumes of all gases contain the same number of molecules at fixed temperature and pressure. It explains why volumes of gaseous reactants and products combine in small whole-number ratios.

5. a. A homogeneous mixture of two or more substances
b. The substance that dissolves another substance (solute) to form a solution
c. The substance that is dissolved in another substance (solvent) to form a solution
d. A solution in which the solvent is water.

7. a. 12 **b.** 3 **c.** 6

9. 6 N; 3 P; 27 H; 12 O

11. a. Two molecules of H_2O_2 decompose to give two molecules of H_2O and one molecule of O_2.
b. 2 mol H_2O_2 decompose to give 2 mol H_2O and 1 mol O_2.
c. 68 g H_2O_2 decompose to give 36 g H_2O and 32 g O_2.

13. a. $2\,Mg + O_2 \rightarrow MgO$
b. $C_3H_8 + 5\,O_2 \rightarrow 3\,CO_2 + 4\,H_2O$
c. $3\,H_2 + Ta_2O_3 \rightarrow 2\,Ta + 3\,H_2O$

15. a. $N_2 + O_2 \rightarrow 2\,NO$
b. $2\,O_3 \rightarrow 3\,O_2$
c. $UO_2 + 4\,HF \rightarrow UF_4 + 2\,H_2O$

17.

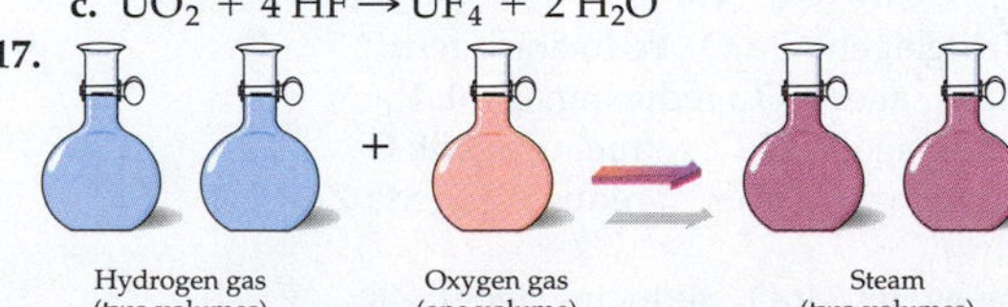

19. a. 124 L **b.** 3.05 mL

21. 6:1 or 6 times

23. a. 6.02×10^{23} S_8 molecules **b.** 4.82×10^{24} S atoms

25. c

27. a. 169.9 g **b.** 127.2 g **c.** 447.2 g **d.** 104.1 g

29. a. 1770 g $BaSO_4$ **b.** 6.35 g $CuCl_2$ **c.** 85.6 g $C_{12}H_{22}O_{11}$

31. a. 0.0195 mol Sb_2S_3 **b.** 0.133 mol MoO_3
c. 3.56 mol $AlPO_4$

33. a. 16.5% **b.** 26.2%

35. a. 32.5 mol CO_2 **b.** 20.3 mol O_2

37. a. 2480 g NH_3 **b.** 193 g H_2

39. a. 2.34 M HCl **b.** 0.138 M Li_2CO_3

41. a. 70.0 g NaOH **b.** 17.0 g $C_6H_{12}O_6$

43. a. 0.416 L **b.** 0.900 L

45. a. 9.28% water by vol **b.** 10.5% methanol by vol

47. Add 277 g NaCl to 3098 g water.

49. Add 40.0 mL acetic acid to enough water to make 2.00 L of solution.

51. Charge is not balanced in the equation $Al(s) + 2\,H^+(aq) \rightarrow Al^{3+}(aq) + H_2(g)$.

53. a. $Hg(NO_3)_2(s) \longrightarrow Hg(l) + 2\,NO_2(g) + O_2(g)$
b. $Na_2CO_3(aq) + 2\,HCl(aq) \longrightarrow H_2O(l) + CO_2(g) + 2\,NaCl(aq)$

55. a. yes **b.** 0.50 mol C_2H_2

57. 2.65×10^9 g CaO

59. 0.418 mol H_2O_2

61. a. 90.7% ethanol **b.** 0.800% acetone

63. a. 2.38×10^{-22} g U **b.** 602 atoms!

65. 0.00825 L (8.25 mL)

67. There are about 2000 times as many molecules in a cup of water as there are cups of water in Earth's oceans. The statement is valid.

69. 53,000 kg

71. 55.5 mol H_2O

73. a. (1) $C_6H_{12}O_6 \rightarrow 2\,C_2H_5OH + 2\,CO_2$; (2) $C_2H_4 + H_2O \rightarrow C_2H_5OH$
b. (1) 51.1%; (2) 100%
c. (1) CO_2 is a byproduct ("waste"); (2) no byproduct
d. (1) sustainable; (2) not sustainable
e. reaction (1) does produce a byproduct, but is sustainable and does not consume valuable, non-renewable petroleum.

75. a. 67.1% **b.** 30.6 g CO_2 **c.** 83.0%

Chapter 6

6.1 400 mm Hg

6.2 **A.** 1800 mL **B.** 503 mm Hg

6.3 **A. a.** 2.98 L **b.** 234 L
B. −167 °C

6.4 **A.** 5.86 g/L
B. 1.29 g/L; only 0.22 times that of Xe

6.5 921 mL

6.6 **A. a.** 0.0526 atm **b.** 9.99 L
B. 112 L

1. Both solids and liquids are difficult to compress because the particles are close together. Liquids flow because their particles are free to move; solids have fixed shapes because their particles have fixed positions.

3. Dispersion forces in helium; dipole-dipole interactions in HCl; hydrogen bonding in water; ionic bonds in NaCl

5. Volume is inversely proportional to pressure, directly proportional to absolute temperature.

7. b, d

9. HBr

11. No. Hexane is nonpolar; it has no dipole to attract the K^+ and NO_3^- ions of KNO_3.

13. a. 1740 mL **b.** 3790 mm Hg

15. a. 9730 L **b.** 1620 min (27 h)

17. 6.93 L

19. 819 K (546 °C)

21. a. 22.4 L **b.** 39.2 L **c.** 5.04 L

23. 9.91 g/L

25. a. 47.5 g/mol **b.** 66.5 g/mol

27. a. decrease **b.** decrease **c.** increase

29. a. temperature decreases **b.** pressure decreases

31. a. 0.172 L **b.** 1.04 atm

33. 0.0208 mol Kr

35. 3.00 g He

37. b, c, and d
39. d; one mole of each occupies the same volume; PF_3 has the largest molar mass.
41. 0.394 L
43. a. All three flasks contain the same number of atoms.
b. flask Z
c. flask X
d. All three flasks still have the same number of moles.
45. 1.25 atm
47. C_4H_{10}
49. e
51. Perchloroethylene and methylene chloride

Chapter 7

7.1 A. a. $HBr(aq) \xrightarrow{H_2O} H^+(aq) + Br^-(aq)$
b. $Ca(OH)_2(s) \xrightarrow{H_2O} Ca^{2+}(aq) + 2\,OH^-(aq)$
B. $CH_3COOH(aq) \xrightarrow{H_2O} H^+(aq) + CH_3COO^-(aq)$
7.2 A. $HBr(aq) + H_2O \longrightarrow H_3O^+(aq) + Br^-(aq)$
B. $HBr(aq) + CH_3OH \longrightarrow CH_3OH_2^+(aq) + Br^-(aq)$
7.3 A. H_2SeO_3 B. HNO_3
7.4 A. $Sr(OH)_2$ B. KOH
7.5 A. $NaOH(aq) + HC_2H_3O_2(aq) \longrightarrow NaC_2H_3O_2(aq) + H_2O$
B. $2\,HCl(aq) + Mg(OH)_2(aq) \longrightarrow MgCl_2(aq) + 2\,H_2O$
7.6 A. pH = 11 B. pH = 3
7.7 A. 1.0×10^{-2} M (0.010 M) B. 1.0×10^{-3} M (0.0010 M)
7.8 (c)
7.9 Beaker III: HNO_3; Beaker II: KOH
1. a. Arrhenius: forms H^+ in water; Brønsted–Lowry: proton donor
b. Arrhenius: forms OH^- in water; Brønsted–Lowry: proton acceptor
c. Ionic compound from acid-base neutralization
3. An acid turns litmus red, tastes sour, dissolves active metals, and neutralizes bases. A base turns litmus blue, tastes bitter, feels slippery, and neutralizes acids.
5. A strong base in water ionizes to a much greater extent than does a weak base.
7. Acidic anhydrides react with water to form acids. Basic anhydrides react with water to form bases.
9. $Mg(OH)_2$ is insoluble in water, so that few $OH^-(aq)$ ions form.
11. A condition in which the blood is too alkaline
13. $HClO_4(aq) \xrightarrow{H_2O} H^+(aq) + ClO_4^-(aq)$
15. $RbOH(s) \xrightarrow{H_2O} Rb^+(aq) + OH^-(aq)$
17. base: a, b, c; acid: none
19. $HCl(g) + H_2O \longrightarrow H_3O^+(aq) + Cl^-(aq)$; hydrochloric acid
21. $NH_3(aq) + H_2O \longrightarrow NH_4^+(aq) + OH^-(aq)$
23. a. hydrochloric acid b. $Sr(OH)_2$
c. potassium hydroxide d. H_3BO_3
25. a. phosphoric acid (an acid)
b. cesium hydroxide (a base)
c. carbonic acid (an acid)
27. a. HNO_2 b. H_3PO_3
29. a. H_2SO_4 (an acid) b. $Mg(OH)_2$ (a base)
31. strong acid
33. weak base
35. a. strong base b. strong acid
c. weak acid d. salt
37. highest: a; lowest, b
39. a. $HNO_2(aq) \xrightarrow{H_2O} H^+(aq) + NO_2^-(aq)$
b. $Ba(OH)_2(s) \xrightarrow{H_2O} Ba^{2+}(aq) + 2\,OH^-(aq)$
c. $HBr(aq) \xrightarrow{H_2O} H^+(aq) + Br^-(aq)$
41. a. $HClO(aq) + H_2O \rightleftharpoons H_3O^+(aq) + ClO^-(aq)$
b. $HNO_2(aq) + H_2O \rightleftharpoons H_3O^+(aq) + NO_2^-(aq)$
c. $H_2S(aq) + H_2O \rightleftharpoons H_3O^+(aq) + HS^-(aq)$
43. a. $KOH(aq) + HCl(aq) \longrightarrow KCl(aq) + H_2O$
b. $LiOH(aq) + HNO_3(aq) \longrightarrow LiNO_3(aq) + H_2O$
45. $H_2SO_3(aq) + Mg(OH)_2(aq) \longrightarrow MgSO_3(aq) + 2\,H_2O$
47. acidic: a, c; basic: d; neutral: b
49. pH = 5
51. 1.0×10^{-3} M H^+
53. 10 and 11
55. a. acid: HNO_3; base: NH_3
b. NO_3^-
c. NH_4^+
57. $3\,HCl(aq) + Al(OH)_3(s) \longrightarrow AlCl_3(aq) + 3\,H_2O$
$2\,HCl(aq) + Mg(OH)_2(s) \longrightarrow MgCl_2(aq) + 2\,H_2O$
59. No. Covalent OH-containing compounds do not produce OH^- ions in water.
61. a. weak base b. strong base
63. a. 3 b. 2
65. $HPO_4^{2-}(aq) + H_2O \longrightarrow H_3O^+(aq) + PO_4^{3-}(aq)$
$HPO_4^{2-}(aq) + H_2O \longrightarrow OH^-(aq) + H_2PO_4^-(aq)$
67. $Al_2(CO_3)_3(s) + 6\,HCl(aq) \longrightarrow 2\,AlCl_3(aq) + 3\,CO_2(g) + 3\,H_2O(l)$
69. $HS^-(aq) + H_2O \longrightarrow H_2S(g) + OH^-(aq)$
71. Decrease
73. $HC_{16}H_{31}O_2(s) + KOH(aq) \longrightarrow KC_{16}H_{31}O_2 + H_2O(l)$; a soap

Chapter 8

8.1 oxidation: a, b, d; reduction: c
8.2 reduction: a; oxidation: b
8.3 reduction: a; oxidation: b, c, d
8.4 a. oxidizing agent: O_2; reducing agent: Se
b. oxidizing agent: CH_3CN; reducing agent: H_2
c. oxidizing agent: V_2O_5; reducing agent: H_2
d. oxidizing agent: Br_2; reducing agent: K
8.5 oxidation: $Al \longrightarrow Al^{3+} + 3\,e^-$; reduction: $Br_2 + 2\,e^- \longrightarrow 2\,Br^-$
8.6 A. Half-reactions: $Fe \longrightarrow Fe^{3+} + 3\,e^-$; $Mg^{2+} + 2\,e^- \longrightarrow Mg$
Overall: $2\,Fe + 3\,Mg^{2+} \longrightarrow 2\,Fe^{3+} + 3\,Mg$
B. Half-reactions:
$Pb \longrightarrow Pb^{2+} + 2\,e^-$; $Ag(NH_3)_2^+ + e^- \longrightarrow Ag + 2\,NH_3$
Overall: $Pb + 2\,Ag(NH_3)_2^+ \longrightarrow Pb^{2+} + 2\,Ag + 4\,NH_3$
8.7 A. $2\,Zn + O_2 \longrightarrow 2\,ZnO$
B. $Se + O_2 \longrightarrow SeO_2$
8.8 A. $2\,PbS + 3\,O_2 \longrightarrow 2\,PbO + 2\,SO_2$
B. $C_2H_5OH + 3\,O_2 \longrightarrow 2\,CO_2 + 3\,H_2O$
1. Oxidation: oxidation number increases; reduction: oxidation number decreases
3. To allow ions to flow from one compartment to the other and thus keep the solutions electrically neutral
5. Zinc; it is the anode; oxidized to Zn^{2+}
7. $PbSO_4$ is converted to Pb and PbO_2.
9. Iron is oxidized to iron(III) hydroxide; salt water acts as an electrolyte.
11. Silver is oxidized by hydrogen sulfide to (black) silver sulfide; use aluminum to reduce the silver sulfide back to metallic silver.
13. a. oxidized (Fe loses e^-)
b. oxidized (H_2O loses H)
c. oxidized (Sr loses e^-)
d. reduced (P_4 gains e^-)
e. oxidized (CH_4O loses H)
15. a. $Ca \longrightarrow Ca^{2+} + 2\,e^-$
b. $Al \longrightarrow Al^{3+} + 3\,e^-$
c. $Cu \longrightarrow Cu^+ + e^-$; $Cu \longrightarrow Cu^{2+} + 2\,e^-$
17. a. oxidizing agent: Fe_2O_3; reducing agent: C
b. oxidizing agent: O_2; reducing agent: P_4
c. oxidizing agent: H_2O; reducing agent: C
d. oxidizing agent: H_2SO_4; reducing agent: Zn
19. Cu
21. oxidizing agent: MnO_2; reducing agent: Zn
23. a. oxidation: $Fe \longrightarrow Fe^{2+} + 2\,e^-$; reduction: $2\,H^+ + 2\,e^- \longrightarrow H_2$
b. oxidation: $Al \longrightarrow Al^{3+} + 3\,e^-$ reduction: $Cr^{2+} + 2\,e^- \longrightarrow Cr$
25. a. oxidation: $2\,H_2O_2 \longrightarrow 2\,O_2 + 4\,H^+ + 4\,e^-$ reduction: $Fe^{3+} + e^- \longrightarrow Fe^{2+}$
overall: $2\,H_2O_2 + 4\,Fe^{3+} \longrightarrow 2\,O_2 + 4\,Fe^{2+} + 4\,H^+$

b. oxidation: $C_2H_6O \longrightarrow C_2H_4O + 2\,H^+ + 2\,e^-$
reduction: $WO_3 + 6\,H^+ + 6\,e^- \longrightarrow W + 3\,H_2O$
overall: $3\,C_2H_6O + WO_3 \longrightarrow 3\,C_2H_4O + W + 3\,H_2O$

27. **a.** SO_2 is oxidized; HNO_3 is the oxidizing agent
b. HI is oxidized, CrO_3 is the oxidizing agent

29. Reduced; ethylene gains hydrogen.

31. Ta_2O_5 is reduced; the reducing agent is Na.

33. Zr was oxidized; water was the oxidizing agent.

35. Nitrite ion is reduced; ascorbic acid is the reducing agent.

37. **a.** SO_2 **b.** $CO_2 + H_2O$ **c.** $CO_2 + H_2O$

39. Indoxyl is oxidized; O_2 is the oxidizing agent.

41. $2\,Al(s) + 3\,Cu^{2+}(aq) \longrightarrow 2\,Al^{3+}(aq) + 3\,Cu(s)$

43. $H_2S + Pb^{2+} \longrightarrow PbS + 2\,H^+$
$S^{2-} + 4\,H_2O_2 \longrightarrow SO_4^{2-} + 4\,H_2O$

45. 160 L O_2

47. **a.** V^{2+} is oxidized; it loses an electron when forming V^{3+}.
b. neither; there are two O atoms per N atom in both NO_2 and N_2O_4.
c. CO is reduced; C gains H.

49. $H_2 + Cl_2 \longrightarrow 2\,HCl$; Cl_2 is the oxidizing agent.

51. $2\,Al(s) + 6\,H_2O(l) \longrightarrow 2\,Al(OH)_3 + 3\,H_2$; H_2O is the oxidizing agent and Al is the reducing agent.

53. **a.** $NAD^+ + H^+ + 2\,e^- \longrightarrow NADH$; $CH_3CH_2OH \longrightarrow CH_3CHO + 2\,H^+ + 2\,e^-$
b. $NADH \longrightarrow NAD^+ + H^+ + 2\,e^-$; $CH_3COCOOH + 2\,H^+ + 2\,e^- \longrightarrow CH_3CHOHCOOH$
Overall: $NADH + CH_3COCOOH + H^+ \longrightarrow NAD^+ + CH_3CHOHCOOH$

55. **a.** industrial **b.** specialty
c. specialty **d.** industrial

57. Organic parts may undergo oxidation, inactivating the catalyst.

Chapter 9

9.1 **a.** molecular: C_6H_{14}; complete structural:

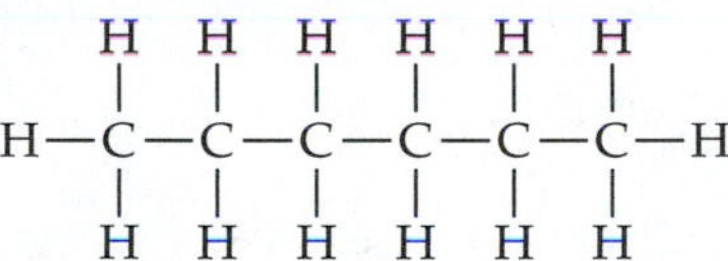

condensed structural: $CH_3CH_2CH_2CH_2CH_2CH_3$

b. molecular: C_8H_{18}; complete structural:

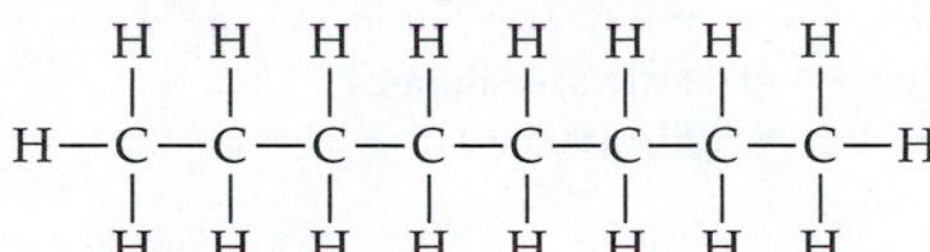

condensed structural: $CH_3CH_2CH_2CH_2CH_2CH_2CH_2CH_3$

9.2 **A.**
```
     CH2
   /     \
 CH2     CH2
  |       |
 CH2 --- CH2
```

B. C_nH_{2n}

9.3 **a.** C_6H_{12} **b.** C_7H_{12}

9.4 **a.** $CHCl_3$ **b.** CCl_4

9.5 **a.** $CH_3CH_2CH_2CH_2OH$
b.
```
   H  H  H  H
   |  |  |  |
H—C—C—C—C—H
   |  |  |  |
   H  H  |  H
        O—H
```

9.6 **a.** alcohol **b.** ether
c. ether **d.** phenol
e. ether

9.7 **A.** $CH_3OCH_2CH_2CH_3$ **B.** $CH_3CH_2OC(CH_3)_3$

9.8 **a.** ketone **b.** aldehyde **c.** aldehyde

9.9 **a.** $CH_3CH_2CH_2COOH$
b. CH_3CHO
c. $CH_3CH_2COCH_2CH_3$
d. $CH_3CH_2COCH_2CH_2CH_2CH_2CH_3$
e. $CH_3CH_2CH_2CH_2CH_2CH_2CHO$
f. $CH_3CH_2CH_2CH_2CH_2COOH$

9.10 **a.** $CH_3CH_2CH_2CH_2NH_2$
b. $CH_3CH_2NHCH_2CH_3$
c. $CH_3NHCH_2CH_2CH_3$
d. $(CH_3)_2CHNHCH_3$

9.11 **a.** amine (NH) **b.** amide (CONH)
c. amine (N) **d.** both (NH and $CONH_2$)

9.12 heterocyclic compounds: (a) and (d)

1. Carbon atoms can bond strongly to each other; can bond strongly to other elements; can form chains, rings, and other kinds of structures.

3. Isomers have the same molecular formula but different structural formulas.

5. A set of six delocalized electrons

7. 1–4 C, gases; 5–16 C, liquids; >18 C, solids

9. **a.** ethanol **b.** 2-propanol **c.** methanol

11. Historical use: anesthetic; modern use: solvent

13. **a.** alcohol **b.** ketone **c.** ester
d. ether **e.** carboxylic acid **f.** aldehyde

15. organic: a, b; inorganic: c, d

17. **a.** 6 **b.** 10 **c.** 5 **d.** 5

19. **a.** C_9H_{20} **b.** $C_{13}H_{28}$

21. **a.** butane **b.** ethylene (ethene) **c.** acetylene (ethyne)

23. **a.** C_5H_{12}; $CH_3CH_2CH_2CH_2CH_3$
b. C_9H_{20}; $CH_3CH_2CH_2CH_2CH_2CH_2CH_2CH_2CH_3$

25. **a.** methyl **b.** *sec*-butyl

27. **a.** methanol **b.** propyl alcohol (1-propanol)
c. CH_3CH_2OH
d. $CH_3CH_2CH_2CH_2CH_2CH_2CH_2OH$

29. (benzene ring with OH and CH_3 on adjacent carbons) I—(benzene ring)—OH

31. **a.** $CH_3CH_2CH_2OCH_2CH_2CH_3$
b. $CH_3CH_2CH_2CH_2OCH_2CH_3$

33. **a.**
```
      O
      ‖
CH3—C—CH3
```
b. HCHO
c. butyraldehyde (butanal)
d. butyl ethyl ketone (3-heptanone)

35. **a.** acetic acid (ethanoic acid)
b. pentanoic acid
c. HCOOH
d. $CH_3CH_2CH_2CH_2CH_2CH_2CH_2COOH$

37. **a.** $CH_3COOCH_2CH_3$
b. $CH_3CH_2CH_2COOCH_3$
c. ethyl propionate (ethyl propanoate)

39. **a.** CH_3NH_2 **b.** $CH_3CH_2NHCH_3$
c. propylamine **d.** ethylmethylamine

41. same: a, b; isomers, c

43. **a.** homologs **b.** none of these

45. **a.** unsaturated; alkene **b.** saturated; alkane

47. **a.** ester **b.** aldehyde **c.** amine
d. ether **e.** ketone **f.** carboxylic acid

49. **a.** heterocyclic, amine **b.** not heterocyclic, amine

51. $C_{18}H_{27}NO_3$; ether, phenol, amide

53. **a.** $CH_3CH_2C{\equiv}CCH_3 + 2\,H_2 \xrightarrow{Ni} CH_3CH_2CH_2CH_2CH_3$
b. $CH_3CH{=}C(CH_3)CH_2CH_2CH_2CH_3 + H_2 \xrightarrow{Ni} CH_3CH_2CH(CH_3)CH_2CH_2CH_2CH_3$

55. **a.** $CH_3CH_2CH_2CH_2OH$ **b.** $CH_3CH_2CH(OH)CH_2CH_3$
c. $(CH_3)_2CHCH(OH)CH_3$ **d.** $C_6H_5CH_2OH$

57. isomerism

59. Equation is balanced as is. 731 g

61. **a.** dispersion and (weak) dipole-dipole

b. hydrogen bonds. The stronger hydrogen bonds cause ethanol to remain a liquid at room temperature.

63. a. HO— —OH b. O= =O

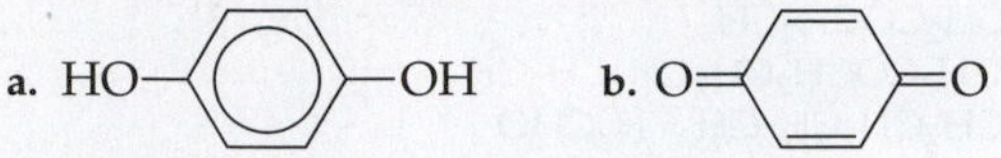

65. a. 0.000655 g/mL
b. 0.001250 g/mL
c. 0.001830 g/mL
d. 0.002410 g/mL. Grams per liter would be more appropriate.

67. b

69. Solvent is renewable and less toxic, and less solvent is used.

71. Less energy is used; molecules absorb energy directly so less energy is lost to the surroundings.

Chapter 10

10.1 $-CH_2CH(C{\equiv}N)-$

10.2 A. $\lbrack CH_2CH(COCH_3)CH_2CH(COCH_3)CH_2CH(COCH_3)CH_2CH(COCH_3) \rbrack$

B. $\lbrack CH_2CH(OCOCH_3)CH_2CH(OCOCH_3)CH_2CH(OCOCH_3)CH_2CH(OCOCH_3) \rbrack$

10.3 a. $\lbrack OCH_2COOCH_2COOCH_2COOCH_2CO \rbrack$
b. $\lbrack OCH_2(C{=}O) \rbrack_n$

1. PVC has a Cl atom on alternate C atoms.

3. Polymerization in which all the monomer atoms are incorporated in the polymer; a double bond

5. styrene

7. The first synthetic polymer; phenol and formaldehyde

9. Synthetic fibers; they are cheaper and have a wider range of properties.

11. For many applications, plastics must be separated by type, melted, and formed into new objects.

13. LDPE has highly branched molecules—a loosely packed, amorphous structure that makes it soft and flexible compared with HDPE.

15. a. $CH_2{=}CH_2$ b. $CH_2{=}CH{-}C{\equiv}N$

17. a. $\lbrack CH_2CHClCH_2CHClCH_2CHClCH_2CHCl \rbrack$
b. $\lbrack CH_2CF_2CH_2CF_2CH_2CF_2CH_2CF_2 \rbrack$

19. a. $\lbrack CH_2CH(CH_2CH_2CH_3)CH_2CH(CH_2CH_2CH_3)CH_2CH(CH_2CH_2CH_3) \rbrack$
b. $\lbrack CH_2CH(CN)(COOCH_3)CH_2CH(CN)(COOCH_3)CH_2CH(CN)(COOCH_3)CH_2CH(CN)(COOCH_3) \rbrack$

21. $CH_2{=}CH{-}CH{=}CH_2$

23. When stretched, rubber's coiled molecules are straightened. When released, the molecules coil again.

25. SBR is made by copolymerization of styrene and butadiene.

27. $\lbrack CO(CH_2)_6CONH(CH_2)_8NHCO(CH_2)_6CONH(CH_2)_8NH \rbrack$

29. $\lbrack OCH_2COOCH_2COOCH_2COOCH_2CO \rbrack$

31. The long chains can entangle with one another; intermolecular forces are greatly multiplied in large molecules; large polymer molecules move more slowly than do small molecules.

33. The temperature at which the properties of the polymer change from hard, stiff, and brittle to rubbery and tough; rubbery materials such as automobile tires should have a low T_g; glass substitutes, a high T_g.

35. Monomer: a; repeating unit: b; polymer: c. addition polymerization

37. $CH_2{=}CHCl$ and $CH_2{=}CCl_2$

39. $n\ CH_2{=}C(C{\equiv}N)(C{=}O)OC_8H_{17} \longrightarrow \lbrack CH_2{-}C(C{\equiv}N)(C{=}O)OC_8H_{17} \rbrack_n$

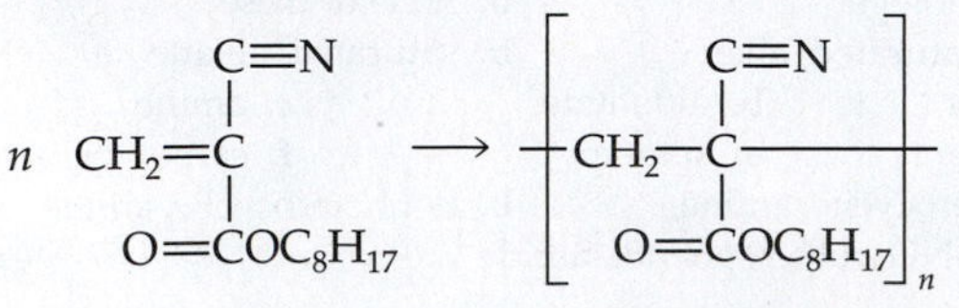

41. $\sim CH_2C(CH_3)_2CH_2C(CH_3)_2CH_2C(CH_3)_2CH_2C(CH_3)_2\sim$

43. $CH_3CH(OH)CH_2COOH$

45. There are only two C atoms in a backbone segment of polypropylene; the CH_3 is a pendant group.

47. Elastomer; the golf ball

49. A simple diester, dibutylterephthalate, rather than a polymer

51. $\lbrack O{-}Si(CH_2CH_3)(CH(CH_3)_2){-}O{-}Si(CH_2CH_3)(CH(CH_3)_2){-}O{-}Si(CH_2CH_3)(CH(CH_3)_2){-}O{-}Si(CH_2CH_3)(CH(CH_3)_2) \rbrack$

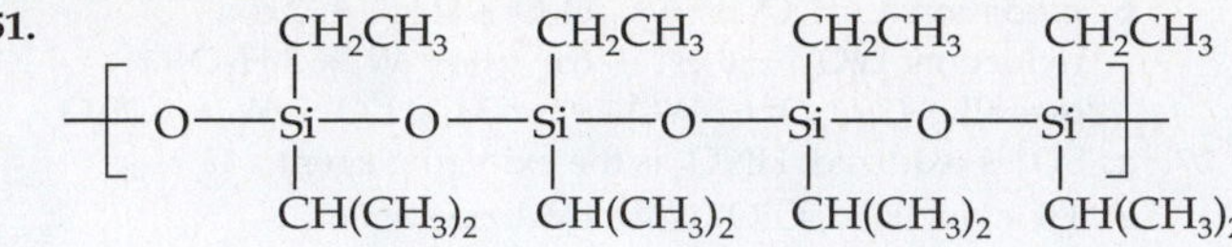

53. a. $\lbrack CH_2CH_2OCH_2CH_2OCH_2CH_2OCH_2CH_2O \rbrack$
b. $\lbrack CH_2CH_2SCH_2CH_2SCH_2CH_2SCH_2CH_2S \rbrack$

55. b

57. c

Chapter 11

11.1 a. ${}^{235}_{92}U \longrightarrow {}^{4}_{2}He + {}^{231}_{90}Th$ b. ${}^{210}_{82}Pb \longrightarrow {}^{0}_{-1}e + {}^{210}_{83}Bi$
c. ${}^{18}_{9}F \longrightarrow {}^{0}_{+1}e + {}^{18}_{8}O$ d. ${}^{13}_{8}O + {}^{0}_{-1}e \longrightarrow {}^{13}_{7}N$

11.2 A. 6.25% B. 500 Bq; 4 Bq

11.3 a. yes (3 Bq left) b. no (4.0×10^{10} Bq remain)

11.4 a. 11,460 y; b. 49 y

11.5 a. A neutron (${}^{1}_{0}n$) b. Thorium-232 (${}^{232}_{90}Th$)

11.6 Silicon-30 (${}^{30}_{14}Si$)

11.7 Higher; the gas can be absorbed by inhalation and decay in the body.

1. (i), (b); (ii), (a); (iii), (c)

3 ${}^{1}_{1}H$, ${}^{2}_{1}H$, ${}^{3}_{1}H$

5. a. ${}^{60}_{27}Co$ b. ${}^{127}_{53}I$ c. ${}^{22}_{11}Na$ d. ${}^{42}_{20}Ca$

7. Isotopes: b, c

9. 155

11. a. *A*, down 4; *Z*, down 2 b. no change in either
c. *A*, down 1; *Z*, down 1

13. a. alpha b. gamma

15. more massive; energy dissipated over a short distance

17. Fission is the splitting of large atoms. Fusion is the joining of small atoms. Both liberate energy because, in each case, the nuclei formed have greater nuclear stability than the reacting nuclei (Fig. 11.10).

19. a. ${}^{250}_{98}Cf \longrightarrow {}^{4}_{2}He + {}^{246}_{96}Cm$
b. ${}^{210}_{83}Bi \longrightarrow {}^{210}_{84}Po + {}^{0}_{-1}e$
c. ${}^{117}_{53}I \longrightarrow {}^{117}_{52}Te + {}^{0}_{+1}e$

21. a. ${}^{179}_{79}Au \longrightarrow {}^{175}_{77}Ir + {}^{4}_{2}He$
b. ${}^{12}_{6}C + {}^{2}_{1}H \longrightarrow {}^{13}_{6}C + {}^{1}_{1}H$
c. ${}^{154}_{62}Sm + {}^{1}_{0}n \longrightarrow 2\ {}^{1}_{0}n + {}^{153}_{62}Sm$

23. beta particle; ${}^{99}_{42}Mo \longrightarrow {}^{99m}_{43}Tc + {}^{0}_{-1}e$

25. ${}^{24}_{12}Mg + {}^{1}_{0}n \longrightarrow {}^{1}_{1}H + {}^{24}_{11}Na$; sodium-24

27. ${}^{215}_{85}At \longrightarrow {}^{4}_{2}He + {}^{211}_{83}Bi$; astatine-215

29. ${}^{210}_{87}Fr$

31. 156 h (6.5 d)

33. b

35. 26 s

37. 2 counts/min

39. 5730 y

41. 5730 y; 11,460 y

43. a. ${}^{121}_{51}Sb + {}^{4}_{2}He \longrightarrow {}^{124}_{53}I + {}^{1}_{0}n$ b. ${}^{124}_{53}I \longrightarrow {}^{124}_{52}Te + {}^{0}_{+1}e$

45. ${}^{247}_{97}Bk + {}^{48}_{20}Ca \longrightarrow {}^{293}_{117}117 + 2\ {}^{1}_{0}n$; ${}^{247}_{97}Bk + {}^{48}_{20}Ca \longrightarrow {}^{294}_{117}117 + {}^{1}_{0}n$

47. ${}^{223}_{88}Ra \longrightarrow {}^{219}_{86}Rn + {}^{4}_{2}He$; ${}^{223}_{88}Ra \longrightarrow {}^{209}_{82}Pb + {}^{14}_{6}C$

49. 853 cm^3; 131 cm^3; smaller than a baseball (~200 cm^3)

51. a. 1900 y b. 14,400 y

53. the neutron, ${}^{1}_{0}n$

55. a. 2.2×10^{13} cal; 2.2×10^{10} kcal
b. 2.0×10^{8} bowls

57. 7.5×10^{17} atoms

59. false

61. The presence of two amides increases the ability to bind to metal ions without losing the benefits of using this type of molecule.

Chapter 12

1. One substance enhances the effect of another; asbestos fibers and cigarette smoke

3. Mining operations, particulate matter from crushing, high energy consumption

5. Copper and tin are easier to obtain from ores than is iron.
7. Most aluminum is found in aluminum-containing clays and is too widely scattered to be mined.
9. The problem is keeping the metal in a usable form and not dispersed through the environment.
11. Lithosphere: solid portion of Earth; hydrosphere: watery portion; atmosphere: gaseous mass surrounding Earth
13. Al, Fe, Ca; differences in atomic mass
15. $PbS(s) + 2\,HCl(aq) \longrightarrow PbCl_2(aq) + H_2S(g)$
17. SiO_2; the SiO_4 tetrahedra are arranged in a three-dimensional array.
19. The SiO_4 tetrahedra are arranged in flat two-dimensional arrays.
21. Sand (silicon dioxide), soda (sodium carbonate), and limestone (calcium carbonate)
23. Other metal oxides are substituted for silica, soda, or lime.
25. Limestone and clay
27. Iron ore or scrap iron (source of iron), limestone (removes impurities), and coke or coal (reducing agent)
29. Reduction; $Fe_2O_3 + 3\,CO \longrightarrow 2\,Fe + 3\,CO_2$.
31. The limestone reacts with impurities to form slag.
33. Iron drawn off a blast furnace; phosphorus, silicon, and excess carbon
35. $V_2O_5 + 5\,Ca \longrightarrow 2\,V + 5\,CaO$;
 a. V_2O_5 b. Ca c. Ca d. V_2O_5
37. $Al_2O_3 + 3\,C + 3\,Cl_2 \longrightarrow 2\,AlCl_3 + 3\,CO$;
 a. Cl_2 b. C c. C d. Cl_2
39. 102 g Nd
41. 133 million kg Al_2O_3; 279 million kg bauxite
43. 20.4 m
45. 1.7×10^7 kg ore per day
47. 282,000 cubic feet, 28 feet deep
49. a. $Fe_2O_3 + 3\,H_2 \longrightarrow 2\,Fe + 3\,H_2O$
 b. $Fe_2O_3 + 3\,CO \longrightarrow 2\,Fe + 3\,H_2O$
51. 69.0% (paper, cardboard, yard wastes, plastics, and wood)
53. a. 3.4×10^9 kg b. 7.7 km c. 5.7×10^{10} km
55. a. 46%
 b. less than either route to Fe from magnetite (49% and 70%)
57. Saves material (Al) and saves energy

Chapter 13

13.1 A. 3790 g H_2O B. 4940 kg CO_2
1. Refrigerant; molding of plastic foams
3. Solid mineral matter left behind after burning coal is bottom ash. Fly ash goes out the smokestack.
5. Gases that trap heat in the atmosphere; CO_2, CH_4, H_2O
7. A combination of smoke and fog; polluted air
9. Conversion of N_2 to a form usable by plants; increases the food supply
11. Thermosphere
13. a. $4\,Fe(s) + 3\,O_2(g) \longrightarrow 2\,Fe_2O_3(s)$
 b. $4\,Cr(s) + 3\,O_2(g) \longrightarrow 2\,Cr_2O_3(s)$
15. Cold, damp, still
17. $S + O_2 \longrightarrow SO_2$
19. $SO_2 + 2\,H_2S \longrightarrow 3\,S + 2\,H_2O$
21. The lime reacts with SO_2 to form an easily collected solid.
 $CaCO_3(s) \xrightarrow{heat} CaO(s) + CO_2(g)$;
 $CaO(s) + SO_2(g) \longrightarrow CaSO_3(s)$.
23. High temperatures; $N_2 + O_2 \longrightarrow 2\,NO$
25. Peroxyacetylnitrate; hydrocarbons, oxygen, and nitrogen dioxide; makes breathing difficult and causes the eyes to smart and itch
27. a, c
29. NO
31. By hindering O_2 transport and thus adding to the workload of the heart
33. Allotropes
35. Global warming
37. HNO_3: H_2SO_4
39. $2\,Fe(s) + 6\,HNO_3(aq) \longrightarrow 3\,H_2(g) + 2\,Fe(NO_3)_3(aq)$
41. Carbon monoxide from poorly ventilated heaters indoors; from automobiles outdoors
43. The crawl space allows gaseous radon to dissipate through vents; the concrete slab traps it inside.
45. A gas; it can escape from rocks and enter houses, and is readily inhaled.
47. The warming of Earth caused by gases absorbing infrared radiation
49. Some waste heat is formed in every process (second law of thermodynamics).
51. 6900 μg (6.9 mg)
53. Water vapor will form clouds and might even lead to cooling by reflecting sunlight back to space.
55. There would be about two air molecules from the Buddha's breath in a breath you take today.
57. $3\,NO_2 + H_2O \longrightarrow 2\,HNO_3 + NO$; $2\,NO + O_2 \longrightarrow 2\,NO_2$
59. a
61. 54 million metric tons

Chapter 14

14.1 A. a. 0.1 ppb b. 100 ppt
 B. 1×10^{-9} M
1. The crude oil would not dissolve; it would float.
3. Microorganisms that cause disease
5. VOCs from fueling and dry cleaning, nitrates from farms and lawns, illegal dumping, many other sources
7. Chlorinated hydrocarbons are unreactive and do not break down readily.
9. Water expands when it freezes because it forms a rigid hydrogen-bonded structure with relatively large holes. The ice floats, protecting the deeper water from freezing.
11. 3.0×10^4 cal
13. Vaporization of water (sweat) cools our bodies.
15. Water evaporates from the skin, removing heat.
17. Dust, dissolved atmospheric gases such as carbon dioxide and oxygen, nitric acid from lightning storms; various pollutants
19. 51 mg/L
21. Acid rain and mine runoff
23. The limestone that neutralizes the acid leaves calcium ions in the water.
25. It mobilizes toxic (to fish) Al^{3+} ions from clays.
27. About 1 ppm
29. Yes. Ultraviolet light kills microorganisms.
31. Sewage is collected in a pond; it removes solids that are allowed to settle.
33. Organic molecules and inorganic ions such as nitrates and phosphates
35. tertiary: a; secondary: c; primary: b
37. $2\,HNO_3(aq) + CaCO_3(s) \longrightarrow$
 $Ca^{2+}(aq) + 2\,NO_3^-(aq) + CO_2(g) + H_2O(l)$
39. a. 11 ppb b. 140 ppm
41. No, the levels (0.009 mg Cu/L, 8 mg NO_3^-/L) are below the standards.
43. a. $CHCl_3$ b. NaCl, phosphate ion, sand c. sand
45. Boiling water; to boil water the molecules must be separated to relatively large distances.
47. Cl_2 is reduced; it is the oxidizing agent. SO_2 is the reducing agent.
49. A positron ($^{0}_{+1}e$)
51. a. 9120 kcal b. 687 g c. 33.9 ft^3 d. 38 cents
53. c
55. a
57. Microporous: pores less than 2 nm in diameter; mesoporous: between 2 nm and 50 nm; macroporous; larger than 50 nm

Chapter 15

15.1 A. 39,000 J B. 6.1 ¢
15.2 A. 183 kJ B. 2700 kJ
15.3 A. 2210 kJ B. 1.43 kcal
1. Nuclear fusion
3. Coal; petroleum

5. a, b
7. a. $C_6H_{12}O_6(s) + 6\,O_2(g) \longrightarrow 6\,CO_2(g) + 6\,H_2O(l)$
b. $C_3H_8(g) + 5\,O_2(g) \longrightarrow 3\,CO_2(g) + 4\,H_2O(l)$
9. $C(s) + O_2(g) \longrightarrow CO_2(g)$
11. $CH_4(g) + 2\,O_2(g) \longrightarrow CO_2(g) + 2\,H_2O(l)$
13. Yes. Both H_2 and CO are readily oxidized (will burn), forming water and CO_2, respectively.
15. A reaction goes faster at a higher temperature.
17. 19,700 kJ
19. 4.44 kJ
21. 803 kJ
23. Energy is conserved.
25. A measure of the degree of distribution of energy in a system; increased
27. It is not possible to create energy.
29. Coal is plentiful and a good fuel, but burning it leads to significant air pollution from particulates, SO_x, and CO.
31. 43.2 y
33. 60.3 y
35. $2\,C_2H_6 + 7\,O_2 \longrightarrow 4\,CO_2(g) + 6\,H_2O(l)$
37. Ancient marine animals
39. Molecules in kerosene have higher molecular masses than do molecules in gasoline.
41. Asphalt is a residue left from petroleum distillation.
43. 19.3%
45. No; the uranium is enriched to only about 3% uranium-235; to explode, it would have to be enriched to about 90%.
47. No; reactor grade uranium is enriched to only about 3% uranium-235; to make a bomb, it would have to be enriched to about 90%.
49. By converting nonfissionable uranium-238 to fissile plutonium-239. No, the plutonium-239 is simply an easier-to-use source of energy than uranium-238.
51. Little radioactivity produced; plentiful fuel (deuterium). Plasma is a hot, gaseous mixture of positive and negative ions.
53. ${}^{232}_{90}Th + {}^{1}_{0}n \longrightarrow {}^{233}_{90}Th$
${}^{233}_{90}Th \longrightarrow {}^{0}_{-1}e + {}^{233}_{91}Pa$
${}^{233}_{91}Pa \longrightarrow {}^{0}_{-1}e + {}^{233}_{92}U$
55. 2.24×10^7 mol CH_4; 360 t CH_4
57. An electronic device that produces electricity directly from light
59. 12 m^2; it works only when the sun shines; energy storage is needed for nighttime and very cloudy days.
61. Plant material used directly as fuel
63. Oxidizing and reducing agents are fed into a fuel cell continuously; the cell does not go "dead" as long as reactants are supplied.
65. $C(s) + 2\,H_2(g) \longrightarrow CH_4(g)$;
$C(s) + H_2O(g) \longrightarrow CO(g) + H_2(g)$
67. Endothermic; the reaction absorbs heat, cooling the treated area.
69. 100 watts; 1 hp = 7.45 human power
71. a. 99 W b. 5.9×10^8 W
c. They provide the same energy. The grenade provides more power so you wouldn't want to eat a hand grenade.
73. a. Removal by photosynthesis
b. Animal respiration
c. Converted to insoluble carbonates.
75. 29 metric tons SO_2; no, there would be 260 $\mu g\ SO_2/m^3$.
77. a. 75 y b. 19 y
c. Rate of energy use will likely grow instead of remain the same, and so reserves might not last the 75 y calculated in part (a). Worldwide use is unlikely to reach the U.S. level anytime soon, if ever, and so the estimate in (b) is not at all realistic.
79. d

Chapter 16

16.1 Mannose differs from glucose in configuration about C-2 only.
16.2 A. a. H-P-V-A b. histidylprolylvalylalanine
B. a. Thr-Gly-Ala-Ala-Leu b. T-G-A-A-L
16.3 A. 3 B. 24
16.4 A. Sugar: ribose; base: uracil; RNA
B. Neither; thymine occurs only in DNA, ribose only in RNA.
1. Photosynthesis converts solar energy to carbohydrates, which provide energy to plants and to organisms that eat plants.
3. In every cell; muscles, skin, hair, nails
5. Polyamides
7. If the molar mass of a polypeptide exceeds about 10,000 g, it is called a protein.
9. Hydrogen bonds
11. DNA is a double helix; RNA is a single helix with some loops.
13. A process that produces millions of copies of a specific DNA sequence
15. Step 1: isolation and amplification
Step 2: gene is spliced into a plasmid
Step 3: plasmid is inserted into a host cell
Step 4: plasmid replicates, making copies of itself
17. A carbohydrate that cannot be further hydrolyzed; glucose, fructose, and galactose
19. Glycogen is animal starch. Amylose is a plant starch with glucose units joined in a continuous chain. Amylopectin is a plant starch with branched chains of glucose units.
21. c, d
23. Sucrose and lactose
25. a. glucose b. glucose
27. Ketone and alcohol (hydroxyl)
29. Aldehyde and alcohol (hydroxyl); in configuration about C-4
31. Structurally, oils have more C-to-C double bonds than fats have. At room temperature, fats are solids, and oils are liquid.
33. saturated: a, d; unsaturated: b, c
35. a. 18 b. 16
c. 18
37. Liquid oil (right); it is unsaturated.
39. An amino group and a carboxyl group; a zwitterion is a molecule that carries both a positive and a negative charge.
41. lysine and leucine
43. a. H_3N^+—CH(—CH_3)—C(=O)—O^- b. H_3N^+—CH(—CH_2SH)—C(=O)—O^-
45. a. $H_3N^+\ CH_2CO$—NH C(—CH_3) $HCOO^-$
b. $H_3N^+\ CH_2CO$—NH C $HCOO^-$ (with CH_3 under CH_2CO and CH_2OH under C)
47. Aspartylphenylalanine
49. Hydrogen bonds, ionic bonds, disulfide linkages, and dispersion forces
51. DNA: a; RNA: b, c
53. Ribose; uracil
55. a. guanine b. thymine
c. cytosine d. adenine
57. Each strand of the parent DNA double helix remains associated with the newly synthesized DNA strand.
59. a. DNA and mRNA b. mRNA and tRNA
61. 3′-TACTCGCTGAAACGCCCTAAT-5′
63. 5′-AGGCTA-3′
65. a. 3′-AAC-5′ b. 3′-CUU-5′ c. 3′-AGG-5′
67. a. glutamine b. phenylalanine c. glycine
69. a. primary b. secondary
71. a. pyrimidine b. pyrimidine
73. a. purine b. RNA
75. a. ~Thr-Ser-Met-Ala~
b. ~Thr-Ser-Ala-Ala~
77. 3′-AUG-5′ (The sequences must be antiparallel.)
79. Water
81. d

Chapter 17

17.1 **A.** About 64% **B.** About 34%

17.2 **A.** Fatty acid I

B. Fatty acid I, because fatty acid III is a cis fatty acid and not a trans fatty acid

1. Energy source

3. All vitamins are organic; all minerals are inorganic.

5. Fat soluble; an excess is stored and accumulated; excess water-soluble vitamins are excreted.

7. Substances other than basic foodstuffs that are put into food for various reasons related to production, processing, packaging, or storage

9. Monosodium glutamate, a flavor enhancer

11. α-Tocopherol (vitamin E)

13. The methyl ester of the dipeptide aspartylphenylalanine

15. Add nutritional value, enhance flavor or color, retard spoilage, provide texture, sanitize (and others)

17. a. glucose **b.** sucrose **c.** fructose

19. Hydrolysis

21. Hydrolysis; fatty acids, glycerol, mono- and diglycerides

23. Most animal fats are solids; most vegetable oils are liquids; animal fats generally have fewer C-to-C double bonds than vegetable oils.

25. An adequate protein provides all the essential amino acids in sufficient quantities; meat, eggs, milk.

27. Corn: lysine and tryptophan; beans: methionine

29. Yes; it has grains and beans.

31. a. iodine **b.** hemoglobin (oxygen transport) **c.** calcium **d.** nucleic acids, ATP (obtaining, storing, and using energy from foods), bones, teeth

33. Water soluble: pantothenic acid, biotin; fat soluble: phylloquinone

35. Ascorbic acid, vitamin C; calciferol, vitamin D; cyanocobalamin, vitamin B_{12}; retinol, vitamin A; tocopherol, vitamin E

37. a. niacin (vitamin B_3) **b.** thiamine (vitamin B_1) **c.** pernicious anemia

39. Water soluble: b, c, d; fat soluble: a, e

41. a. improve nutrition **b.** SO_2 **c.** inhibit spoilage

43. a. antioxidant **b.** color **c.** artificial sweetener

45. d

47. Reducing agents, usually free-radical scavengers added to foods to prevent fats and oils from becoming rancid; vitamin E; BHT, and BHA

49. About 53% from carbohydrates; 23% from fat; 27% from protein

51. About 81 kcal; about 56% from fat

53. About 11 g saturated fat

55. c, e

57. About 45%

59. About 23%

61. a. about 60% **b.** about 40%

63. Riboflavin and cyanocobolamin; they are water soluble and not easily stored.

65. Double bonds in unsaturated fats are more reactive than single bonds in saturated fats; unsaturated fats and oils would have spoiled more readily than saturated fats.

67. The thick polymeric starch is broken down to smaller, more soluble molecules by enzymes in saliva.

69. a. 3 **b.** 2 **c.** 4 **d.** 1

71. Less toxic; easily removed.

Chapter 18

1. A drug that kills or slows the growth of bacteria; originally limited to formulations derived from living organisms

3. Cortisol: a hormone released in the body during stressed or agitated states; prednisone: a semisynthetic hormone similar to cortisone

5. Mediators of hormone action; prostaglandins act near where they are produced; hormones act throughout the body.

7. Ketamine, PCP

9. A drug that produces stupor and relief of pain

11. Brain amines are made from dietary amino acids; for example, high-carbohydrate diets produce high serotonin levels in the brain.

13. No; they help control some symptoms.

15. Acetylsalicylic acid

17. Acetaminophen does not promote bleeding.

19. Amide, phenol

21. Both are analgesics and addictive; heroin is more potent and more addictive.

23. a. Acupuncture needles may stimulate nerves that trigger release of endorphins, peptides that block pain signals.

b. The wounds cause the body to secrete pain-killing endorphins.

25. H_2N—⟨benzene ring⟩—COOH H_2N—⟨benzene ring⟩—SO_2NH_2

27. They are effective against a wide variety of bacteria.

29. No; vaccination

31. Antimetabolites and alkylating agents

33. A female sex hormone; a male sex hormone

35. An ethynyl group, H—C≡C—

37. One that changes the way we perceive things

39. a

41. a, b, c

43. a. 2.55 g **b.** 1.7 (about 2)

45.

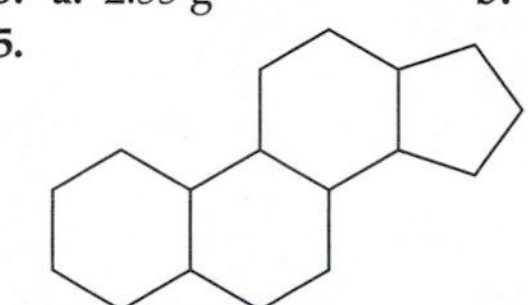

47. Fat soluble; 17 C atoms with only 1 O atom, 1 N atom

49. ⟨cyclohexane ring⟩—NH_2

51. Timber rattlesnake; its lower LD_{50} means that less of its toxin is required in a fatal dose.

53. Nicotine, because it takes a smaller amount to kill the rat—2500 mg procaine; 50 mg nicotine.

55. CH_3 N CH_3O O OH

57. CH_3 N CH_3O O O

59. Ester; hydrolysis

61. 6-mercaptopurine; antimetabolite

63. a. Removing the polar —OH group would make the compound less soluble in water.

b. Removing the polar —OH group would make the compound more soluble in fat.

65. a. The long hydrocarbon chain would make the drug much less soluble in water.

b. The ionic and polar groups of the sodium succinate derivative would make the drug more soluble in water.

67. c

69. Use of lipolase allows the wrong enantiomer to be recycled and used instead of being discarded. Also, small, amino acid catalysts are being used as replacements for larger expensive enzymes.

Chapter 19

19.1 **A.** 3.6 lb **B.** 7.4 lb
19.2 **A.** 35 mi **B.** 2700 kcal
19.3 **A.** 23.5 **B.** 174 lb

1. Meat and other animal products
3. Deplete glycogen stores and dehydrate yourself; no, it would be mostly water loss.
5. Better understanding of muscle physiology; drugs; improved equipment
7. Skinfold calipers (inaccurate and measure water retention as well as fat); displacement of water (cannot get all of the air out of the lungs)
9. Often deficient in B vitamins, iron, and other nutrients; slows metabolism, making future dieting more difficult and weight gain easier
11. Most do not.
13. Avoid pernicious anemia
15. Arthritis; B_6 is a cofactor for more than 100 enzymes.
17. Promotes absorption of calcium and phosphorus. The upper limit is 2000 IU; more than that can be toxic.
19. Promotes production of urine; ADH acts to retain urine.
21. No. Thirst is often a delayed response.
23. Depletion of glycogen and water loss
25. 2.0 h
27. 92 g
29. 20 km
31. **a.** Leptin protects against weight loss. **b.** Ghrelin is an appetite stimulant.
33. 19.6
35. About 600
37. No
39. **a.** anaerobic **b.** aerobic
41. Store needed oxygen
43. ATP can be generated rapidly and hydrolyzed rapidly.
45. No; the best way to build muscles is by exercise.
47. Anti-inflammatory; fluid retention, hypertension, ulcers, disturbance of sex hormone balance
49. The body releases endorphins that have much the same effect as some narcotics.
51. The athlete might perform better briefly, but fatigue follows quickly.
53. Heart disease; stroke; lung cancer; emphysema; pneumonia; cancers of the pancreas, bladder, breast, kidney, and cervix
55. 2400 kcal
57. 1.06 g/mL; lean
59. **a.** 26.7% **b.** 3.61% **c.** Person B **d.** 1.077 g/cm^3
61. **a.** 27 **b.** 144
63. **a.** 20 mL O_2 **b.** 1200 mL O_2
65. 2 lb lighter
67. c

Chapter 20

20.1 **A.** $2\,NH_3 + H_3PO_4 \longrightarrow (NH_4)_2HPO_4$
B. $ZnO + H_2SO_4 \longrightarrow ZnSO_4 + H_2O$
20.2 980 mg
20.3 **A.** In 270 y; by 2281
B. In 92 y; by 2103

1. CO_2 and H_2O
3. Kills weed plants before crop seedlings emerge
5. Population would increase faster than the food supply unless the birthrate were controlled; poverty and war would serve as restrictions.
7. C, H, O
9. Lightning, bacteria, the Haber process
11. Ammonia without water; as fertilizer
13. Phosphate rock is treated with phosphoric acid to make calcium dihydrogen phosphate; plays a role in the energy transfer processes of photosynthesis.
15. DDT is effective against many insects, but it remains toxic long after initial use.
17. They are fat soluble and become concentrated in fats moving up the food chain.
19. Mostly to bait traps and monitor infestations to determine when best to use a pesticide
21. Male insects are sterilized by radiation, chemicals, or cross-breeding, and then released for nonproductive breeding. Expensive and time consuming.
23. 35 g DDT
25. Addition of a constant amount each growth period; adding $10 to a savings account each week
27. 20 months; arithmetically
29. 53.6 y; changes in birthrate or death rate (war, famine, . . .)
31. $6\,CO_2 + 6\,H_2O \longrightarrow C_6H_{12}O_6 + 6\,O_2$
33. (1), b; (2), b; (3), d; (4), a; (5), c
35. **a.** N, P **b.** $2\,NH_3 + H_3PO_4 \longrightarrow (NH_4)_2HPO_4$
37. **a.** alkene, alcohol **b.** ester, alkene, ether (epoxide) **c.** ether, alkene, ester
39. $10,737,418.24
41. $K_2CO_3 + CO_2 + H_2O \longrightarrow 2\,KHCO_3$
$2\,KCl + 2\,H_2O \longrightarrow 2\,KOH + H_2 + Cl_2$
$2\,KOH + CO_2 \longrightarrow K_2CO_3 + H_2O$
not organic
43. 16.7 y; changes in birthrate or death rate (war, famine, . . .)
45. a and b
47. d

Chapter 21

21.1 **a.** nonionic **b.** anionic **c.** anionic **d.** cationic

1. An excellent cleanser in soft water, relatively nontoxic, derived from renewable sources, biodegradable; doesn't work well in hard water or acidic water
3. 1, a; 2, f; 3, b; 4, c; 5, d; 6, e
5. Loosens baked-on grease and burned-on food, excellent glass cleaner; vapors are irritating, toxic; don't mix with chlorine bleaches
7. Mildly abrasive and absorbs odors
9. It is softer and produces a finer lather.
11. Abrasives
13. Sodium palmitate and glycerol
15. $3\,CH_3(CH_2)_{10}COO^-Na^+ + HOCH_2CHOHCH_2OH$ (glycerol)
17. Precipitates hard water ions; makes the water more alkaline
19. $PO_4^{3-} + H_2O \longrightarrow HPO_4^{2-} + OH^-$
$CO_3^{2-} + H_2O \longrightarrow HCO_3^- + OH^-$
21. A substance added to a surfactant to increase its detergency
23. By binding Ca^{2+} and Mg^{2+} in soluble complexes
25. A surfactant molecule that carries both a positive and a negative charge
27. Cationic surfactants have germicidal action.
29. All three
31. II
33. Hexadecyltrimethylammonium chloride
35. They slowly release chlorine in water.
37. To remove paint, varnish, adhesives, waxes, etc.
39. Flammability, toxic fumes
41. A skin softener
43. OMC is insoluble in water and does not wash off as easily as PABA from sweat or while swimming.
45. Lipstick is harder, contains more wax, and is usually colored with pigments.
47. Bacteria
49. Enamel is converted from hydroxyapatite to fluorapatite, a harder substance.

51. A complex mixture of compounds used as a fragrance; cologne is diluted perfume.
53. Makes the face feel cool
55. Temporary dyes are water soluble and can be washed out; permanent dyes last until the hair is cut off or falls out.
57. A reducing agent; redox reaction
59. Oxidation
61. II
63. I
65. $CH_3(CH_2)_{14}COOCH(CH_3)_2$
67. 11.6 g SnF_2
69. Cationic (quaternary ammonium compounds)
71. No. Brighteners convert energy in the form of ultraviolet light into visible light, but no energy is destroyed.
73. **a.** $CH_3(CH_2)_{24}COOH$ **b.** $CH_3(CH_2)_{28}CH_2OH$
75. c
77. **a.** 3 **b.** 1 **c.** 4 **d.** 2

Chapter 22

1. In a sense; enormous amounts of sugar can be harmful; large amounts for a diabetic.
3. The route of administration determines the speed of the poison's action, the rate at which it is detoxified, etc.
5. Mercury: occupational exposure; eating contaminated fish, etc. Lead: leaded paint chips; soldered pipes (water) and cans (food).
7. Sunlight, radon, safrole, PAHs
9. b, d
11. Hydrolysis of amides; catalyst
13. A substance that blocks the transport of oxygen in the bloodstream; CO, nitrate ions
15. By blocking the oxidation of glucose inside the cell
17. a, d
19. By tying up sulfhydryl groups, thus deactivating enzymes
21. By chelating Pb^{2+} ions, thus enhancing their excretion
23. Sarin, tabun, soman
25. Poisons that block cholinesterase
27. By oxidizing ethanol to acetaldehyde, then to acetic acid, and finally to carbon dioxide and water
29. No. Some are oxidized to more toxic substances.
31. Cotinine is less toxic and is more water soluble (more readily excreted) than nicotine.
33. 7.94 g
35. Genes that regulate cell growth; they sustain the abnormal growth characteristic of cancer.
37. Incomplete burning of almost any organic material
39. Humans are not exposed to comparable doses; human metabolism is different from test-animal metabolism.
41. A mutagen causes mutations; a teratogen causes birth defects.
43. A waste that burns readily on ignition, presenting a fire hazard; hexane, gasoline
45. 5.3×10^{10} molecules
47. **a.** $C_{10}H_{16}O$ **b.** 4800 mg **c.** 5 mg
49. **a.** 99.48%; % smokers in control group: 95.50% **b.** 0.9948:1 for cancer cases; 0.9550:1 for controls **c.** 0.96:1
51. Some substances are harmless or even necessary at low levels; toxic at high levels.
53. **a.** No **b.** Yes
55. The body converts inert benzene to a carcinogenic epoxide.
57. **a.** 38.8 mL vodka **b.** 15.4 mg/mL
59. b
61. Saving millions of dollars, improved consumer safety, and reducing the load of poisons in the environment.

Appendix

A.1 **a.** 0.0163 g **b.** 1.53 lb **c.** 370 mL
A.2 **a.** 0.0903 m **b.** 0.2224 km **c.** 150 fl oz
A.3 **a.** 24.4 m/s **b.** 1.34 km/h **c.** 0.136 oz/qt
A.4 **a.** No **b.** No
A.5 0.12 m^3
A.6 56.8 g
A.7 **a.** 100.5 m **b.** 6.3 L **c.** 1800 m^2 (1.80×10^3 m^2) **d.** 2.33 g/mL
A.8 **a.** 185 °F **b.** 10.0 °F **c.** 179 °C **d.** −29.3 °C
A.9 80,000 cal; 80.0 kcal; 334 kJ

Credits

Chapter 1 Page 1 (TL): Arne Naevra. Page 1 (TR): Tomukas/Shutterstock. Page 1 (B): Armin Rose/Shutterstock. Page 2 (T): Jupiter Images/Creatas. Page 2 (B): Stephen Denness/Shutterstock. Page 3 (T): Getty Images/Photos.com/Jupiterimages. Page 3 (B): Hieronymus Brunschwig. Page 4 (T): Library of Congress. Page 4 (B): HANDOUT/MCT/Newscom. Page 6: James Steidl/Shutterstock. Page 8: iofoto/Shutterstock. Page 11: Everett Collection/Alamy. Page 12: AP photo/Karen Tam. Page 13: NASA. Page 14 (R): Pearson Education/Tom Bochsler. Page 14 (L): Charles D. Winters/Photo Researchers, Inc. Page 18 (L to R): US Mint; jmatzick/Shutterstock; Theasis/iStockphoto; bryngelzon/iStockphoto. Page 20: Richard Megna/Fundamental Photographs. Page 26: Pearson Education/Eric Schrader. Page 30 (L): niderlander/Shutterstock. Page 30 (R): Dhoxax/Shutterstock. Page 31: Dmitrijs Bindemanis/Shutterstock. Page 36: Terry McCreary. Page 37: Buquet Christophe/Shutterstock. Page 38: David Anderson/iStockphoto. Page 39 (T): Yana Petruseva/Shutterstock. Page 39 (B): David A. Aguilar/Harvard-Smithsonian Center for Astrophysics. Chapter 2 Page 41 (TL): Viennaphoto/allOver photography/Alamy. Page 41 (TR): Stockbyte/Getty Images, Inc. Page 41 (B): Wilson Ho. Page 42 (T): Haydn Hansell/Alamy. Page 42 (B): konradlew/iStockphoto. Page 42 (inset): Susumu Nishinaga/Photo Researchers, Inc. Page 44: Jacques-Louis David. Page 45 (T, L to R): Morozova Tatyana/Shutterstock; Katharina Wittfeld/Shutterstock; Richard Megna/Fundamental Photographs. Page 45 (B): C. Marvin Lang. Page 47: PRISMA/Visual & Written/The Image Works. Page 48: Mat Meadows/Peter Arnold/Alamy. Page 51: Library of Congress. Page 53: Drs. Ali Yazdani & Daniel J. Hornbaker/Photo Researchers, Inc. Page 54 (T, L to R): Harry Taylor/Dorling Kindersley; Mark Wragg/iStockphoto; Sieto/iStockphoto; Tammy Peluso/iStockphoto. Page 54 (B, L to R): Harry Taylor/Dorling Kindersley; Michael Shake/Shutterstock; Joe Potato Photo/iStockphoto; Lya Cattel/iStockphoto. Page 55: © Libby Welch/Alamy. Page 59 (both): Richard Megna/Fundamental Photographs. Chapter 3 Page 61 (TL): Gary718/Dreamstime. Page 61 (B): Angelo Cavalli/SuperStock. Page 62: Getty Images/Photos.com/Jupiter Images. Page 63: Richard Megna/Fundamental Photographs. Page 65: Otto Glasser/Images from the History of Medicine/National Library of Medicine. Page 66: Photos 12/Alamy. Page 67: STR/AFP/Getty Images/Newscom. Page 73 (T): Shutterstock. Page 73 (BA): Richard Megna/Fundamental Photographs. Page 74 (TL): David Parker/Science Photo Library/Photo Researchers, Inc. Page 74 (TR): Wabash Instrument Corp./Fundamental Photographs. Page 74 (ML): Gary J. Shulfer/C. Marvin Lang. Page 82 (both): Richard Megna/Fundamental Photographs. Page 83 (T): Yuriko Nakao/REUTERS. Page 83 (B): Dorling Kindersley/Colin Keates. Chapter 4 Page 89 (TL): Phase4Photography/Shutterstock. Page 89 (TR): moodboard/Alamy. Page 89 (B): Fotocrisis/Shutterstock. Page 91: Lawrence Berkeley National Laboratory/Photo Researchers, Inc. Page 93 (A): Richard Megna/Fundamental Photographs. Page 94 (T): Charles D. Winters/Photo Researchers, Inc. Page 94 (B): Richard Megna/Fundamental Photographs. Page 96: Alexander Dvorak/Shutterstock. Page 99: Pearson Education/Eric Schrader. Page 112: Pearson Education/Eric Schrader. Chapter 5 Page 125 (TL): STR/AFP/Getty Images/Newscom. Page 125 (TR): andibyte/Shutterstock. Page 125 (B): Summit Oxygen International Ltd. Page 130: Gary J. Shulfer/C. Marvin Lang. Page 135: Richard Megna/Fundamental Photographs. Page 136: GENT SHKULLAKU/AFP/Getty Images/Newscom. Page 141: Lynnea Kleinschmidt. Page 143: Pearson Education/Eric Schrader. Page 144 (T): Pearson Education/Eric Schrader. Page 144 (B): Pearson Education/Nathan Eldridge. Chapter 6 Page 152 (TL): Josh Resnick/Shutterstock. Page 152 (TR): Shutterstock. Page 152 (B): Juliya_strekoza/Shutterstock. Page 153 (L): GTS Production/Shutterstock. Page 153 (R): Eric Skiff, used under a Creative Commons License. http://creativecommons.org/licenses/by-sa/2.0/deed.en. Page 154: Nikita Tiunov/Shutterstock. Page 156 (TL): Ariel Bravy/Shutterstock. Page 156 (ML): Richard Megna/Fundamental Photographs. Page 156 (MR): Richard Megna/Fundamental Photographs. Page 160 (L): Tony Freeman/PhotoEdit Inc. Page 160 (M): George Mattei/Photo Researchers, Inc. Page 160 (R): Liv Friis-Larsen/Shutterstock. Page 166 (both): Richard Megna/Fundamental Photographs. Page 167: Oleksiy Mark/Shutterstock. Chapter 7 Page 175 (TL): Image Source/Alamy. Page 175 (TR): schankz/Shutterstock. Page 175 (B): Valentyn Volkov/Shutterstock. Page 176 (T): Lajos Repasi/iStockphoto. Page 176 (BA): Pearson Education/Eric Schrader. Page 177 (TL): Pearson Education/Eric Schrader. Page 177 (TR): Tyler Boyes/Shutterstock. Page 177 (MR): Denise Kappa/Shutterstock. Page 177 (BR): Richard Megna/Fundamental Photographs. Page 178: Science and Society/SuperStock. Page 182: a11/ZUMA Press/Newscom. Page 184: Everett Collection. Page 187 (A): Richard Megna/Fundamental Photographs. Page 189: Richard Megna/Fundamental Photographs. Page 193: Pearson Education/Creative Digital Vision. Page 194: Pearson Education/Eric Schrader. Page 195 (T): Michael Page Gadomski/Photo Researchers, Inc. Page 195 (B): Tom McNemar/Shutterstock. Chapter 8 Page 201 (TL): Evoken68/Dreamstime. Page 201 (TR): eyecraveeyecrave/iStockphoto. Page 201 (B): Ben Willmore/Digital Mastery. Page 202 (both): Paul Silverman/Fundamental Photographs. Page 208 (both): Peticolas/Megna-Fundamental Photographs. Page 210 (both): Spencer Grant/PhotoEdit. Page 211: Marianne de Jong/Shutterstock. Page 212: Rkasprzak/Dreamstime. Page 214: Rich Chartier/Walter Drake Company. Page 216 (T): Kzenon/Shutterstock. Page 216 (B): NASA/Jim Grossmann. Page 217: Richard Megna/Fundamental Photographs. Page 218: Pearson Education/Eric Schrader. Page 219: Paul Reid/Shutterstock. Page 221: Pearson Education/Eric Schrader. Page 222 (L): SuperStock/SuperStock. Page 222 (R): Karl R. Martin/Shutterstock. Page 223: vovan/Shutterstock. Page 227 (T): Sherri R. Camp/Shutterstock. Page 227 (B): Jacob Kearns/Shutterstock. Chapter 9 Page 229 (TL): The Scoville Food Institute. Page 229 (TR): Paul Paladin/Shutterstock. Page 229 (B): Abel Tumik/Shutterstock. Page 231: VladimirB/Shutterstock. Page 233: naphtalina/iStockphoto. Page 236: Richard Megna/Fundamental Photographs. Page 237: Bon Appetit/Alamy. Page 238: Clive Freeman/The Royal Institution/SPL/Photo Researchers, Inc. Page 241: Pearson Education/Eric Schrader. Page 245: Pearson Education/Eric Schrader. Page 246: Pearson Education/Eric Schrader. Page 247: Southern Illinois University/Photo Researchers, Inc. Page 252: Pearson Education/Eric Schrader. Chapter 10 Page 266 (TL): Konkolas/Shutterstock. Page 266 (TR): BALDUCCI/SINTESI/SIPA/Newscom. Page 266 (B): BALDUCCI/SINTESI/SIPA/Newscom. Page 267: Shutterstock. Page 269: Richard Megna/Fundamental Photographs. Page 271 (T): AP Photo/Joe Appel. Page 271 (B): Richard Megna/Fundamental Photographs. Page 273 (TR): Dennis McDonald/PhotoEdit. Page 273 (ML): Shutterstock. Page 273 (M): James Edward Bates/Biloxi Sun-Herald/MCT/Newscom. Page 273 (MR): Inara Prusakova/Shutterstock. Page 273 (BR): Shutterstock. Page 274 (T): Shutterstock. Page 274 (B): Zoonar/richterfoto/age footstock. Page 276: Geoff Tompkinson/Photo Researchers, Inc. Page 278 (T): Shutterstock. Page 278 (B): Shutterstock. Page 282 (T): Pearson Education/Eric Schrader. Page 282 (B): Mar Photographics/Alamy. Page 283 (T): Shutterstock. Page 283 (B): REUTERS/Toshiyuki Aizawa. Page 285: Amoco Fabrics & Fibers Co. Page 286: Ambient Images Inc./Alamy. Page 287: Xinhua/Photoshot/Newscom. Chapter 11 Page 295 (TL): Scott Camazine/Alamy. Page 295 (TR): Steven Needell, MD/Custom Medical Stock Photo. Page 295 (B): SergeyIT/Shutterstock. Page 298: Nora D. Volkow, MD/National Institute of Health. Page 308: Bain News Service/Library of Congress. Page 309 (T): William Paul Quick. Page 309 (B): Richard Megna/Fundamental Photographs. Page 310: Simon Fraser/SPL/Photo Researchers, Inc. Page 311 (A): Bristol Myers Squibb Medical Imaging MA. Page 312 (L): Olivier Voisin/Photo Researchers, Inc. Page 312 (R): Wellcome Dept. of Cognitive Neurology/Science Photo Library/Photo Researchers, Inc. Page 315: SuperStock/agefotostock. Page 316 (T): Pictorial Press Ltd/Alamy. Page 316 (B): Robert R. Davis, AIP Emilio Segre Visual Archives, Physics Today Collection. Page 320: Lawrence Berkeley National Lab. Page 321: US Air Force. Page 322: JIJI PRESS/AFP/Getty Images/Newscom. Page 323 U.S. Department of Energy. Page 324: GeoEye Inc. Chapter 12 Page 331 (TL): holgs/iStockphoto. Page 331 (TR): cardiae/Shutterstock. Page 331 (B): Monkey Business Images/Shutterstock. Page 333: Galyna Andrushko/Shutterstock. Page 334 (L): Dr. Richard Busch/American Geological Institute, AGI. Earth Science World Image Bank. Page 334 (R): AIRMAN MELODY A. WEISS/US Air Force. Page 335 (T): Chip Clark. Page 335 (B): From *Asbestos and Other Fibrous Materials: Mineralogy, Crystal Chemistry, and Health Effects* by H. Catherine W. Skinner, Malcolm Ross, and Clifford Frondel. New York: Oxford University Press, 1988. Page 336 (L): Lee Prince/Shutterstock. Page 336 (R): Lebazele/iStockphoto. Page 337 (T): nikkytok/Shutterstock. Page 337 (B): Bruce C. Murray/Shutterstock. Page 338: polat/iStockphoto. Page 342 (T): Arturo Limon/Shutterstock. Page 342 (M): ITAR-TASS/Alexander Kolbasov/Newscom. Page 342 (B): Charles D. Winters/Photo Researchers, Inc. Page 345: Mike Morley/iStockphoto. Page 348: Photolibrary, Inc. Chapter 13 Page 350 (R): Yellowj/Shutterstock. Page 350 (L): frescomovie/Shutterstock. Page 351: Mario Babiera/Alamy. Page 355: NASA. Page 356: EcoSphere Associates, Inc. 2006. Page 357 (T): Tim Graham/Alamy. Page 357 (B): Sergei Butorin/Shutterstock. Page 358 (T): AP Photo. Page 358 (B): Dr. Gerald L. Fisher/Science Photo Library/Photo Researchers, Inc. Page 359: Tennessee Valley Authority. Page 362: Jens Peermann/Shutterstock. Page 366: Richard Megna/Fundamental Photographs. Page 369: ITAR-TASS/Alexei Filippov/Newscom. Page 370: bluebird13/iStockphoto. Page 371: Susan Solomon. Page 372: NASA. Page 376: Johnathan Patz/Center for Sustainability and the Global Environment (SAGE). Chapter 14 Page 385 (TL): Jonutis/Shutterstock. Page 385 (TR): Mclek/Shutterstock. Page 385 (B): ifong/Shutterstock. Page 386: NASA. Page 387: NASA. Page 388: age fotostock/SuperStock. Page 389: Ieva Geneviciene/Shutterstock. Page 391: U.S. Environmental Protection Agency Headquarters/H.D.A. Linquist, U.S. EPA. Page 392 (T): ZUMA Press/Newscom. Page 392 (M): Peter Arnold, Inc./Alamy. Page 392 (B): monap/iStockphoto. Page 393: Robert Brook/Alamy. Page 396: Pearson Education/Eric Schrader. Page 397: AP Photo/EyePress. Page 398 (T): U.S. Geological Survey, Denver. Page 398 (B): Mike Segar/Reuters.

Page 401: AP Photo/Pavel Rahman. Page 403: National Institute of Dental Research. Chapter 15 Page 411 (TL): Elena Elisseeva/Shutterstock. Page 411 (TR): Shi Yali/Shutterstock. Page 411 (B): Rafa Irusta/Shutterstock. Page 412: European Space Agency. Page 413: U.S. Consumer Product Safety Commission. Page 415 (T): Mark Phillips/Alamy Images. Page 415 (M): Tony Freeman/PhotoEdit. Page 415 (BL): Richard Megna/Fundamental Photographs. Page 415 (BR): Richard Megna/Fundamental Photographs. Page 417 (L): Greenshoots Communications/Alamy Images. Page 417 (R): Richard Megna/Fundamental Photographs. Page 419: D&D Photos/Shutterstock. Page 420 (T): Pearson Education/Eric Schrader. Page 420 (B): Richard Megna/Fundamental Photographs. Page 421: Attila JANDI/Shutterstock. Page 423: Dorling Kindersley. Page 425 (TL): U.S. Department of the Interior. Page 425 (TR): U.S. Department of the Interior. Page 425 (B): Tennessee Valley Authority. Page 426: Patsy Michaud/Shutterstock. Page 430: BackyardProduction/iStockphoto. Page 434: Larry Lee Photography/Corbis. Page 436: U.S. Department of Energy. Page 437: AP Photo/Tokyo Electric Power Co. via Kyodo News. Page 438: EFDA-JET. Page 440: Shutterstock. Page 442: Logan Buell/iStockphoto. Page 443: Martin Bond/Photo Researchers, Inc. Page 444: MAD/JDP/Reuters. Page 445: Videowokart/Shutterstock. Page 446: Bob Strong/Reuters. Page 447: STEVE ALLEN/Photo Researchers, Inc. Page 452: Pearson Education/Eric Schrader. Chapter 16 Page 454 (TR): Zeamonkey Images/Shutterstock. Page 454 (TL): Tiago Sá Brito/Shutterstock. Page 454 (B): picturepartners/Shutterstock. Page 457: Pearson Education/Eric Schrader. Page 459 (L): Biophoto Associates/Photo Researchers, Inc. Page 459 (R): CNRI/Photo Researchers, Inc. Page 462: Shutterstock. Page 464: Richard Megna/Fundamental Photographs. Page 467: UCLA Henry Samueli School of Engineering and Applied Science. Page 475: Klaudia Steiner/iStockphoto. Page 478: A. Barrington Brown/Photo Researchers, Inc. Page 479: Science Photo library/Photo Researchers, Inc. Page 482: Angela Waye/Shutterstock. Page 486: Golden Rice. Page 490 (A): Pearson Education/Eric Schrader. Chapter 17 Page 494 (TL): Alex Jackson/Shutterstock. Page 494 (TR): Chris Ryan/Alamy. Page 494 (B): Anna Kucherova/Shutterstock. Page 496 (T): Richard Megna/Fundamental Photographs. Page 496 (M): Jenny Mie Lau King/Shutterstock. Page 496 (B): ranplett/iStockphoto. Page 497: Marianna Day Massey/Newscom. Page 498: Pearson Education/Eric Schrader. Page 499 (L): Martin M. Rotker/Photo Researchers, Inc. Page 499 (R): Peter Arnold, Inc./Alamy. Page 500: Pearson Education/Eric Schrader. Page 501: Pearson Education/Eric Schrader. Page 505: Andy Crump/Photo Researchers, Inc. Page 506: Medicimage/Photolibrary. Page 507 (T): Pearson Education/Eric Schrader. Page 507 (M): Biophoto Associates/Photo Researchers, Inc. Page 507 (B): National Medical Slide/Custom Medical Stock Photo. Page 516: GraÃ§a Victoria/Shutterstock. Page 520: Komar Maria/Shutterstock. Page 522: HO/AP Wide World Photos. Page 528: Pearson Education/Eric Schrader. Chapter 18 Page 530 (TL): Radu Razvan/Shutterstock. Page 530 (TR): Heike Rau/Shutterstock. Page 530 (B): Pearson Education/Eric Schrader. Page 531 (T to B): Karel Gallas/Shutterstock; mce128/iStockphoto; Jeff Rotman/Photo Researchers, Inc. Page 532: John Hill. Page 533: Mike Kemp/Alamy Images. Page 537: Nigel Cattlin/Alamy Images. Page 538: Drug Enforcement Administration. Page 542: Dr. Jeremy Burgess/SPL/Photo Researchers, Inc. Page 555: Gary J. Shulfer/C. Marvin Lang. Page 556 (T): Carl Djerassi. Page 556 (B): Pfizer/Pharmacia Corporation. Page 557: Custom Medical Stock Photo/Newscom. Page 558: Steve Gorton/Dorling Kindersley Media Library. Page 559: Sebastian Kaulitzki/Shutterstock. Page 566: Prisma Archivo/Alamy Images. Page 567: Ildi Papp/Shutterstock. Page 576: Drug Enforcement Administration. Page 577: Monkey Business Images/Shutterstock. Chapter 19 Page 585 (TL): Aleksandr Markin/Shutterstock. Page 585 (TR): Foodpics/Shutterstock. Page 585 (B): Rido/Shutterstock. Page 586: U.S. Department of Agriculture. Page 590: Helen Fagan/John Olive. Page 591: Christopher Edwin Nuzzaco/Shutterstock. Page 592: A3390 Kay Nietfeld Deutsch Presse Agentur/Newscom. Page 596: Everett Collection. Page 597: Steve Zylius/Photoshot. Page 598: Bikesbelong.org. Page 599: ROBYN BECK/AFP/Getty Images/Newscom. Page 600: Nina Zanetti/Pearson Education. Page 601 (T): Andresr/Shutterstock. Page 601 (B): AP Photo/Kathy Willens. Page 602: Dr. William McDonald, MD. Page 603 (T): AP Photo/Greg M. Cooper. Page 603 (B): AP Photo. Page 607: AP Photo/Thomas Kienzle. Chapter 20 Page 613 (TR): JIANG HONGYAN/Shutterstock. Page 613 (TL): Jorge Moro/Shutterstock. Page 613 (B): design56/Shutterstock. Page 614: Stephanie Coffman/Shutterstock. Page 615 (L): Pearson Education/Eric Schrader. Page 615 (R): clintspencer/iStockphoto. Page 616: INTERFOTO/Alamy. Page 617: Anonymous. Page 618 (T): Martin Land/Photo Researchers, Inc. Page 618 (B): National Archives and Records Administration. Page 619: Shutterstock. Page 620: Pearson Education/Eric Schrader. Page 621 (T): Dorling Kindersley. Page 621 (B): Michaela Steininger/Shutterstock. Page 622: Duan yang-Imaginechina/Newscom. Page 624: David T. Gomez/iStockphoto. Page 625: U.S. Department of Agriculture. Page 629: U.S. Department of Agriculture. Page 631: Yellowj/Shutterstock. Page 633: Jonathan Pearson/Alamy. Page 637: Christine Nesbitt/afrphotos/Newscom. Chapter 21 Page 643 (TL): Katrina Brown/Shutterstock. Page 643 (TR): YuriyZhuravov/Shutterstock. Page 643 (B): Atiketta Sangasaeng/Shutterstock. Page 644 (T): Richard Megna/Fundamental Photographs. Page 644 (B): Ken Welsh/Alamy. Page 647: Richard Megna/Fundamental Photographs. Page 648: Culligan International Company. Page 650 (TL): Inc/Shutterstock. Page 650 (TR): Richard Megna/Fundamental Photographs. Page 650 (B): Janice Haney Carr/Centers for Disease Control and Prevention. Page 653 (T): Richard Megna/Fundamental Photographs. Page 653 (B): Alfred Pasieka/Photo Researchers, Inc. Page 654: Pearson Education/Eric Schrader. Page 657: Pearson Education/Eric Schrader. Page 658: Green Seal, Inc. Page 661 (T): Richard Megna/Fundamental Photographs. Page 661 (B): GWImages/Shutterstock. Page 662 (L): ChandraPhoto/Shutterstock. Page 662 (M): Pearson Education/Eric Schrader. Page 662 (R): Genevieve Anderson. Page 668: Pearson Education/Eric Schrader. Page 670: Pearson Education/Eric Schrader. Page 672 (L): Tracy Whiteside/Shutterstock. Page 672 (R): Elena Yakusheva/Shutterstock. Chapter 22 Page 680 (TL): Jerry Ballard/Alamy. Page 680 (TR): olmes Garden Photos/Alamy. Page 680 (B): blickwinkel/Alamy. Page 681: Photolibrary, Inc. Page 682 (T to B): Stadelsches Kulturinstitut, Frankfurt am Main, Germany/SuperStock; Sufi/Shutterstock; Photolibrary, Inc. Page 686: AP Photo/Kevin Wolf. Page 687: AP Photo. Page 692 (both): ALLERGAN/Newscom. Page 693 (T): Picsfive/Shutterstock. Page 693 (B): New York Public Library/Photo Researchers, Inc. Page 697: U.S. Food and Drug Administration. Page 700: Andrew Ilyasov/iStockphoto.

Section 1.12: Lett, James, "A Field Guide to Critical Thinking" from THE SKEPTICAL INQUIRER, Winter 1990, pages 153–160. Copyright © 1990. Used by permission. Front endpaper: "Twelve Principles of Green Chemistry" from GREEN CHEMISTRY: THEORY AND PRACTICE by Paul Anastas and John Warner (1999), Page 30, Fig 4.1. By permission of Oxford University Press. Green essay (chapter 14): From the British Zeolite Association, www.bza.org. Used by permission.

Index

A

ABC (atmospheric brown cloud), 355
Abilify®, 571
Abortion pills, 557
Abrin, 682
Abrus precatorius, 682
ABS detergents, 649–50
Absinthe, 705
Absolute scale, 28–29
Absolute zero, 164
Accuracy, of measurements, A9
Accutane®, 664, 698
ACE inhibitors, 560
Acesulfame K, 515
Acetaldehyde, 249, 250
Acetaminophen, 533, 535, 536, 537, 691
Acetic acid, 252, 462, 657
Acetone, 249, 250
Acetylcholine, 563, 688–89
Acetylene, 236, 237
Acetylsalicylic acid, 532–33. *See also* Aspirin
Acid–base indicator, 177
Acid rain, 176, 183, 193, 365–66, 392
Acid waters, 392
Acidic anhydrides, 183–84, 193
Acidosis, 511
Acids, 175–200
  acidic anhydrides as, 183–84, 193
  Arrhenius theory of, 178–80
  bases compared with, 176–77
  Brønsted-Lowry acid–base theory of, 180–81, 183, 191
  buffer solutions and, 191–92
  conjugate acid–base pairs, 191
  as corrosive, 176
  defined, 176–77, 178, 181
  examples of, 175, 176, 178
  hydrogen and hydroxide ions in, 190
  in industry and daily life, 192–95
  ionization of, 178, 179, 180, 185
  neutralization reaction and, 179, 186–88
  pH scale and, 188–90
  as poisons, 683
  as proton acceptor, 180–81
  safety alert concerning, 176, 195
  stomach acid, 193–94
  strong and weak, 178, 185
  sustainability and, 182
  uses of, 178
  vitamins as, 185
Acne, 218, 664, 698
Acquired immune deficiency syndrome (AIDS), 9, 36, 543, 544–47
Acrilan, 275
Acrylic fibers, 285
ACTH (adrenocorticotrophic hormone), 554
Actinomycin, 550
Activated sludge method, 405
Activation energy, 219
Active site, 473
Actomyosin, 600
Acyclovir, 545
Adams, C. P., 532
Addiction, 537–39
Addition polymerization, 272–76
Adenosine, 563
Adenosine monophosphate (AMP), 476–77
Adenosine triphosphate (ATP), 563, 600
Adequate (or complete) protein, 505
ADH (antidiuretic hormone), 591
ADHD (attention deficit hyperactivity disorder), 573
Adhesives, 281
Adipose tissue, 499
Adrenal cortical hormones, 554
Adrenal medullary hormones, 554
Adrenaline, 554, 563
Adrenocorticotrophic hormone (ACTH), 554
Advanced sewage treatment, 405
Advil®, 533
Aerobic exercise, 216, 600–601
Aerobic oxidation, 392–93
Aerosol, 358
AESs (alcohol ethoxysulfates), 651, 653–54
Aflatoxins, 10, 522
Aftershave lotions, 669
Agent GA, 690
Agent Orange, 632
Agent VX, 690, 691
Agonists, 539, 564
AgraQuest, Inc., 624
Agriculture, 613–42
  air pollution and, 379
  Carver's contributions to, 11–12
  energy used in, 604, 634–35
  factory farms and, 642
  fertilizers and, 615–21
  global warming and, 376
  herbicides and defoliants, 631–33
  irrigation for, 396, 406
  nanoscience and food production, 635
  organic farming, 621, 624, 634
  organic herbicides in, 632–33
  ozone damage to, 370
  pesticides and, 622–30
  population growth and, 636–38
  primary plant nutrients and, 615–18
  radioisotopes used in, 308–9
  secondary plant nutrients and, 619
  soil loss and, 614
  sustainable agriculture, 634–35
Agriculture Department (USDA), 473, 495, 513, 586, 627, 630
AHAs (alpha hydroxy acids), 665
AIDS/HIV, 9, 36, 543, 544–47
Air, 350–84. *See also* Air pollution; Atmosphere
  as essential for human life, 350
Air cleaners, 368
Air pollution, 355–84
  acid rain, 176, 183, 193, 365–66, 392
  ambient air quality standards for criteria air pollutants, 378
  atmospheric brown cloud (ABC), 355
  automobiles and, 139
  carbon dioxide and climate change, 373–77, 442
  carbon monoxide, 360, 361, 378–79
  in China, 356, 357, 367, 384
  cigarette smoke, 367–68
  coal burning as source of, 425
  concentrations of urban pollutants at different times during sunny day, 363
  costs of, 379
  deaths from, 350–51, 358, 368, 370
  electronic air cleaners, 368
  EPA on, 358, 361, 366, 367, 368, 378
  EPA's criteria pollutants, 378
  free radicals and, 112
  global nature of, 355–56
  green chemistry and, 369
  health and environmental effects of, 350–51, 358–62, 367–69, 379
  historical survey of, 355–60
  industrial smog, 356–60
  from kerosene or natural gas heaters, 368
  in London smog, 358
  major air pollutants, 378–79
  from microwave ovens, 356
  from mold, 368
  motor vehicle emissions and, 360–64, 378, 379
  nitrogen oxides, 360, 361
  nuclear energy to minimize, 435–36
  ozone, 362, 370–72
  from petroleum, 427
  photochemical smog, 362–65
  prevention and alleviation of industrial smog, 359–60
  radon and daughter isotopes, 368
  smog, 356–65
  volatile organic compounds (VOCs) as, 360, 361–62, 369
  wood smoke and, 367
Air purifier, 91
Air quality standards, 361, 368, 378
Airplane accidents, 10
Alanine, 565
Alchemy, 3, 307
Alcohol ethoxysulfates (AESs), 651, 653–54
Alcoholic beverages
  absinthe, 705
  alcoholism and, 569
  calories in, 569
  as depressant, 569
  ethanol in, 150, 244, 245, 569, 697
  fetal alcohol syndrome and, 245
  historical use of, 532
  intoxication from, 150, 245, 569–70
  lethal dose of, 691
  percentage of alcohol in, 141
  proof of, 245
  statistics on drinking, 569
  warning labels on, 245
Alcohols. *See also* Ethyl alcohol (ethanol)
  classification of, 247–48
  denatured alcohol, 244
  formulas of, 246
  functional group of, 242
  methyl alcohol (methanol), 204, 220, 244
  models of, 244
  multifunctional alcohols, 245–46
  toxicity of, 245, 246
Aldecoxib, 535
Aldehydes, 220, 242, 249–51, 362, 363
Aldicarb, 623, 627
Aldose, 457, 458
Aldosterone, 554
Aleve®, 533
Aliphatic hydrocarbons
  alkanes, 230–31
  alkenes, 236–37, 242
  alkynes, 236–37
  condensed structural formulas for, 231–33
  cyclic hydrocarbons, 235
  defined, 230
  homologous series, 232
  isomers, 232–33
  properties of alkanes, 234
  safety alert concerning, 234
Alka-Seltzer®, 193
Alkali formers, 53
Alkali metals, 81–82
Alkaline batteries, 211
Alkaline earth metals, 82
Alkaloids, 258–59, 681
Alkalosis, 194
Alkanes
  condensed structural formulas for, 231–33
  cycloalkanes, 235
  defined, 230–31
  homologous series of, 232
  isomers of, 232–33
  properties of, 234
  as saturated hydrocarbons, 231, 236
  structural formulas for, 231, 233
  uses and occurrences of, 234
Alkenes, 236, 237, 242
Alkyl groups, 241, 243
Alkylating agents, 549–50
Alkylation, 429
Alkylbenzenesulfonate (ABS) detergents, 649–50
Alkynes, 236, 237, 242
Allergens, 536
Allergies, 10, 536, 670
Allergy medicines, 536
Alli®, 594
Allosteric site, 473
Allotropes, 370, 705
Alloys, 338, 339
Alpha (α), 470
Alpha carbon, 463
Alpha decay, 298–99, 301
Alpha hydroxy acids (AHAs), 665
Alpha linkage, 459
Alpha particles, 66–67, 302, 313–14
Alternative fuels, 430–31
Aluminum
  corrosion and, 214
  in Earth's crust, 332, 345
  electron configuration for, 79
  environmental costs of production of, 340
  green chemistry for production of, 345
  ion of, 97
  production of, 339, 345
  protection for, 214, 339–40
  recycling of, 340
  scarcity of, as scrap metal, 338
  specific heat of, 387, A15
  steel versus, 339–40, 345

Aluminum hydroxide, 194
Alzheimer's disease, 486, 541, 606, 690
American Health Association, 500
American Lung Association, 370, 384
Ames test, 696
Amide group, 257
Amides, 242, 257–58, 323
Amine isomers, 256–57
Amines, 181, 186, 242, 256–57
Amino acids
  defined, 179, 463
  essential, in diet, 504–5
  proteins as polymers of, 257, 267, 293, 463–68
  sequencing of, 468
Amino group, 257
Amitriptyline, 572
Amlodipine, 560
Ammonia
  anhydrous ammonia, 606–7
  as base, 179, 180–81, 186
  as cleaning product, 657
  different representations of molecule of, 119
  nitrogen fertilizers and, 219, 617
  as polyatomic molecule, 106
  as pyramidal molecule, 116, 117
  uses of, 179, 219
Ammonium ions, 615
Ammonium nitrate, 214, 215, 617
Amonton's law, 173–74
Amorphous polymers, 284
Amount of substance, measurement of, 20
AMP (adenosine monophosphate), 476–77
Ampere, 20
Amphetamines, 573, 604
Amphiprotic, 186
Amphoteric surfactants, 651–52
amu (atomic mass unit), 51
Amyl nitrite, 561
Amylases, 654
Amylopectin, 459, 460
Amylose, 459, 460
Anabolic steroids, 555, 604
Anabolism, 456
Anacin, 536
Anaerobic decay, 392, 393
Anaerobic exercise, 601–2
Analgesic (pain reliever), 255, 530–33, 535–39
Anandamide, 576, 577
Ancient Greeks. *See* Greeks
Androgen, 555, 604
Anemia, 485, 507, 590, 685
Anesthetics, 240, 247, 565–69, 689
ANFO, 214–15
Angina pectoris, 560–61
Angiotension-converting enzyme (ACE) inhibitors, 560
Anhydrides, 183–84, 193
Anhydrous ammonia, 606–7
Aniline, 257
Animals
  antibiotics in feed for, 522–23
  artificial insemination of, 552
  carcinogens tested on, 696–97
  cells of, 456
  feed for, 474
  grass as food for, 459
  nanoparticle medications for, 635
  proteins in, 464
  sex attractants for, 629–30, 669
  smell of, when dead, 257
  zebrafish in tests for toxicity, 700
Anionic surfactants, 651
Anions
  acids and, 178, 601
  defined, 62
  names of, 98
Anisakiasis, 523
Anisakis simplex, 523
Anode, 62, 64, 209
Antacids, 193–94
Antagonists, 539, 564
Antiaging creams and lotions, 665
Antianxiety agents, 571–72
Antibacterial drugs, 9, 540–44
Antibiotics
  in animal feed, 522–23
  broad-spectrum, 543
  for cancer treatment, 550
  for infectious diseases, 542–44
Anticancer drugs, 531, 548–50
Anticarcinogens, 696
Antidepressants, 254, 571, 572
Antidiuretic hormone (ADH), 591
Antifreeze, 246, 247
Antihistamine, 536
Antihypertensives, 507, 559–60
Anti-inflammatory drugs, 531, 533, 535
Antimetabolites, 548
Antimicrobials, 516
Antioxidants, 219, 517–18
Antiperspirants, 667
Antipsychotics, 571–72
Antipyretic (fever reducer), 255, 533
Antiseptics, 217
Antitussives, 536
Antiviral drugs, 544, 545–47
Apoenzyme, 473
Applied research, 11–12
Aqueous solutions, 141
Aquifers, 389
Arachidonic acid, 535, 551, 552
Area, measurement of, 23
Argon, 79, 351, 373
Aripiprazole, 571, 572
Aristotle, 2, 3, 43
Arithmetic growth, 636
Aromatherapy, 670
Aromatic amines, 695
Aromatic compounds, 238–39, 695
Arrhenius, Svante, 178
Arrhenius theory, 178–80
Arrhythmia, 560
Arsenic poisoning, 687, 691, 702
Arsphenamine, 687
Arteriosclerosis, 499, 560–61
Artificial sweeteners, 8, 515–16
Artificial transmutation, 307–8
Asbestos, 334, 335, 697
Asbestosis, 335
Ascorbic acid. *See* Vitamin C (ascorbic acid)
Aspartame, 8, 515
Aspartate, 563
Asphyxia, 234
Aspirin, 255, 530–33, 535, 537, 691
Asthma, 362, 367, 368, 370
Astringents, 667
Astronauts, 13
Atazanavir, 546
Atherosclerosis, 559
Athletes. *See also* Exercise
  anabolic steroids and, 604
  drug screening of, 605
  drugs and, 604–7
  nutrition for, 587, 599
  oxygen debt in, 601–2
  restorative drugs and, 604
  sports materials for, 592, 607
  stimulant drugs and, 604
  water and electrolytes for, 591–92
Atmosphere. *See also* Air; Air pollution
  chemistry of, 352–54, 373
  composition of, 351
  defined, 351
  diagram of structural regions of, 332
  layers of, 351
  mass of, 384
  nitrogen cycle and, 352–53
  oxygen cycle and, 353, 354
  temperature inversions in, 353–54
Atmospheric brown cloud (ABC), 355
Atom economy, 140
Atom ratios, 50
Atomic bombs. *See* Nuclear bombs
Atomic mass unit (amu), 51
Atomic masses, 48, 51
Atomic number, 70
Atomic structure, 61–88. *See also* Atoms
  atomic number and, 70
  Bohr model of, 73–76
  cathode-ray tubes and, 63
  electrical properties of atoms and, 62–64
  electrolysis and, 62–63
  electron configurations and periodic table, 81–83
  electrons in, 69, 73–80
  fireworks and flame tests and, 73
  Goldstein's experiment and, 64
  green chemistry and, 55, 84
  isotopes, 70–72
  main-shell electron configurations, 76
  Millikan's oil-drop experiment and, 64
  neutron, 69–70
  nuclear model of atom, 68–69
  nucleus, 68, 69–72, 296
  proton, 69, 70
  quantum model of, 77–80
  radioactivity and, 66–67
  stable electron configurations, 90–91
  Thomson's experiment and, 63
  X-rays and, 65–66
Atomic theory of matter, 47–50
Atomic weights, 48
Atoms, 41–60. *See also* Atomic structure
  ancient Greeks' ideas about, 42–43, 53
  Dalton's atomic theory and, 47–50, 62
  defined, 19
  green chemistry and, 55
  ions compared with, 94
  magnetic properties of nuclei of, 12
  molecules compared with, 53–54
  size of, 41–42, 296
  spin of nuclei of, 12
Atorvastatin, 565
ATP (adenosine triphosphate), 563, 600
Atrazine, 631, 632
Atripla®, 546
Atropine, 689
Attention deficit hyperactivity disorder (ADHD), 573
Atypical antipsychotics, 571–72
Aureomycin®, 543
Autism, 546
Automobiles. *See also* Gasoline
  air pollution and, 139
  alternative fuels for, 430–31
  alternator of, 212
  antifreeze for, 246, 247
  biodiesel fuels for, 182, 441, 442
  catalytic converters in, 364
  diesel fuel for, 430
  electric-only, 365
  emissions from, 360–64, 378, 379
  flexible fuel vehicles (FFVs), 430
  hybrid, 364
  hydrogen as fuel for, 444, 445
  lead storage batteries in, 211
  recycling of, 340
  risk of death from, 10
  smog testing of, 378
  statistics on energy uses by, 412
Avobenzone, 665
Avogadro, Amedeo, 39, 130, 131, 167
Avogadro's hypothesis, 130, 131, 167
Avogadro's law, 167–68
Avogadro's number, 131
AZT, 546

B

Bacillus thuringiensis, 486, 629
Background radiation, 10, 296–97
Bacon, Francis, 3–4
Baekeland, Leo, 280
Bag filtration, 359
Bakelite, 267, 280
Baking soda, 193–94, 657, 668
BAL (British antilewisite), 686, 687
Balancing chemical equations, 126–28
Balancing nuclear equations, 301–2
Bangladesh, 401
Banvel®, 641
Barbiturates, 570
Barium, 74
Base note, of perfume, 669
Bases, 175–200
  acids compared with, 176–77
  Arrhenius theory of, 178–80
  basic anhydrides, 184
  Brønsted-Lowry acid–base theory of, 180–81, 183, 191
  buffer solutions and, 191–92
  conjugate acid–base pairs, 191
  defined, 176–77, 178, 181
  examples of, 175, 176, 178
  hydrogen and hydroxide ions in, 190
  in industry and daily life, 192–95
  ionization of, 179, 180
  neutralization reaction and, 179, 186–88
  pH scale and, 188–90
  as poisons, 683
  as proton acceptors, 180–81
  safety alert on, 176, 195
  strong and weak, 179, 185–86
  sustainability and, 182
  uses of, 179
BASF–Dow Chemical Company, 220
Basic anhydrides, 184
Basic copper carbonate, 45
Basic oxygen process, 340
Basic research, 12
Batteries, 211–12
  solar, 441
  voltage of, 209
Baudelaire, Charles, 537
Bauxite, 339
Bayer Company, 537
Becquerel, Antoine Henri, 66
Becquerel (Bq), 303
Beeswax, 662
Benadryl®, 536
Benefits, defined, 8
Benign tumors, 694
Benzaldehyde, 250
Benzedrine®, 573
Benzene, 155, 238–39, 397, 693
Benzidine, 695
Benzodiazepines, 567, 571
Benzoic acid, 252
Benzoyl peroxide, 218
Benzpyrene, 695
Bergius method, 433
Beriberi, 507, 589
Berylliosis, 685
Beryllium, 79
Berzelius, J. J., 45, 51
Beta (β) pleated sheet, 470
Beta blockers, 560, 561

Beta decay, 299, 301
Beta linkage, 459
Beta particles, 66–67, 302, 313–14
Betaines, 652
Beverages. *See also* Alcoholic beverages; Drinking water
  caffeine in soft drinks, 574
  decaffeinated coffee and tea, 155, 521
  energy drinks and sports drinks, 575, 591
  milk, 8, 144
  worldwide consumption of, 509
Bextra®, 535
BHA (butylated hydroxyanisole), 517–18
BHT (butylated hydroxytoluene), 517, 518, 696
Bicarbonate ions, in water, 390
Bile salts, 500
Binary ionic compounds
  crossover method for determining formulas of, 98–99
  defined, 98
  formulas and names of, 98–100
Binder, in paint, 278
Binding energy, 315
Biocatalysis, 467, 534
Biochemical oxygen demand (BOD), 392–93
Biochemistry, 454–93
  carbohydrates as storehouse of energy, 457–60
  defined, 454, 455
  energy and living cell, 455–56
  fats and other lipids, 460–62
  nucleic acids, 476–80
  proteins, 463–66, 468–75
Biodegradable plastics, 287
Biodegradation, 701–2
Biodiesel fuels, 182, 441, 442
Bioelectric impedance analysis, 597
Biomass, 441, 443
Biosphere, 414
Biotin (vitamin B_7), 589
Biphenyl, 288
Bipolar disorder, 572
Birth control, 556–59
Birth defects, 9, 516, 606, 697–98
Bis(epoxy)butane, 696
Bisphenol-A (BPA), 282
Black, James, 547
Black copolymer, 278
Blancophor, 653
Bleached versus unbleached flour, 112
Bleaches, 218, 655–56, 659
Bleaching powder, 218
Bloch, Felix, 12
Blood
  hemoglobin in, 97, 361, 466, 507, 684
  lipoproteins in, 500
  nutrients circulating in, 161
  pH of, 192, 195
Blood-alcohol levels, 150, 245
Blood sugar, 495
Blow molding, 274, 275
Blue baby syndrome, 397, 684
BMI (body mass index), 597
BOD (biochemical oxygen demand), 392–93
Body, human. *See* Human body
Body mass index (BMI), 597
Bohr, Niels, 74–77, 316
Boiling point
  of alkanes, 234
  defined, 154
  of liquids, 154
  of water, 159
Bombs. *See* Dirty bombs; Nuclear bombs
Bonding pairs, 101
Borates, 218, 656
Borgia, Lucrezia, 682
Boric acid, 628
Boron, 79, 619
Bosch, Carl, 616
Botox®, 691–92
Bottled water, 404, 405
Bottom ash, 358
Botulin, 681, 689, 691–92
Botulism poisoning, 516, 520, 682
Bouwman, Elisabeth, 227
Bovine spongiform encephalopathy (BSE), 473
Boyle, Robert, 5–6, 44, 162
Boyle's law, 6, 162–64
BPA (bisphenol-A), 282
Bq (becquerel), 303
Brain
  diet and brain amines, 564
  drugs' effects on, 561–76
  exercise and, 605
  nervous system and, 562–65
Brantneran, V. V., 532
BRCA1 gene, 695
Breast cancer, 695
Breeder reactors, 437
British antilewisite (BAL), 686, 687
Broad-spectrum antibiotics, 543
Broad-spectrum insecticides, 627
Bromine ion, 97
Brønsted, J. N., 180
Brønsted-Lowry acid–base theory, 180–81, 183, 191
Bronze, 338
Brunschwig, Hieronymus, 3
BSE (bovine spongiform encephalopathy), 473
Buckminsterfullerene, 270
Buffer solutions, 191–92
Builders, 652
Bupivacaine, 567, 568
Burning
  of hydrocarbons, 237
  of PCBs, 701, 702
  of plastics, 273, 286
  of PVC, 273, 286, 632
  of radioactive waste, 304
  of solid wastes, 343
Burroughs Wellcome Research Laboratories, 547
Butane, 233, 234, 243
Butenandt, Adolf, 556
Button batteries, 212
Butylated hydroxyanisole (BHA), 517–18
Butylated hydroxytoluene (BHT), 517, 518, 696
Butyraldehyde (butanal), 250
Butyric acid, 252
Byron, George Gordon (Lord Byron), 537

C

Cadmium, 74, 687
Caffeine
  athletes' use of, 604
  chemical structure of, 536, 574
  in decaffeinated coffee and tea, 155, 521
  diuretic effect of, 591
  in energy drinks, 575
  lethal dose of, 691
  as mildly addictive, 574
  in NSAIDs (nonsteroidal anti-inflammatory drugs), 536
  in soft drinks, 574
Calcium
  as dietary mineral, 507
  in Earth's crust, 332, 345
  electron configuration of, 79
  flame test for, 73
  ion of, 94, 97
  line spectrum of, 74
Calcium carbonate, 194, 333
Calcium channel blockers, 560
Calcium cyclamate, 515
Calcium hydroxide, 179, 621
Calcium hypochlorite, 217, 218
Calcium ions, in water, 390
Calcium oxide, 183, 195
Calculus, 667
Calorie (cal), 29, 416, A15
Calories
  in alcoholic beverages, 569
  for athletes, 587
  daily food plan and, 586–87
  from fats, 498, 502, 587
  Recommended Dietary Allowances (RDAs) for, 587
Cancer. *See also* Carcinogens
  air pollution and, 367
  angiosarcoma, 273
  anticancer drugs and, 531, 548–50
  breast cancer, 695
  causes of, 694–95
  colon cancer, 587
  deaths from, 495, 541, 548, 550
  diet linked with, 495
  glioma, 298
  liver cancer, 697
  lung cancer, 335, 368, 548, 695, 697, 705
  melanoma, 298, 486
  mesothelioma, 335
  process for development of, 695
  prostate cancer, 548, 591
  risk of death from, 10, 694–95
  risk of, from different causes, 694
  secondhand smoke and, 367–68
  skin cancer, 298, 371
  smoking-related cancers, 335, 550, 605, 694–95, 697
  statistics on, 548
  survival rate for, 548
  thyroid cancer, 310–11, 436
  treatment of, 486, 548, 550, 576
  ultraviolet light and, 298, 371
  vitamin C in treatment of, 590
Candela (cd), 20
Cannabinoid receptors, 576
Cannabis sativa, 575–76
Capsaicin, 229, 264, 539
Carbamates, 627
Carbaryl, 623, 627
Carbocaine®, 568
Carbofuran, 623, 627
Carbohydrases, 474
Carbohydrates
  defined, 457
  in diet, 495–97
  digestion and metabolism of, 496
  disaccharides, 458
  monosaccharides, 457–58
  photosynthesis and, 84, 223, 455
  polysaccharides, 458–60
  simple sugars, 457–58, 495–96
  starch and cellulose as, 458–60, 496–97
  as storehouse of energy, 457–60
Carbolic acid, 246
Carbon
  chemical properties of, 15, 230
  electron configuration of, 79
  forms of, 270
Carbon cycle, 424
Carbon dioxide
  acid rain and, 193
  chemical properties of, 48
  climate change and, 373–77, 442
  in Earth's atmosphere, 351, 373, 375, 376
  as greenhouse gas, 139, 373–75, 384
  per capita emission of, 453
  in rainwater, 389, 390
  as supercritical fluid, 155
Carbon disulfide, 217
Carbon-14 dating, 305
Carbon monoxide
  chemical properties of, 15
  in cigarette smoke, 606
  as deadly gas, 48, 136, 286, 360, 361, 379, 684
  EPA guidelines on, 368, 378
  health and environmental effects of, 379
  indoor air pollution and, 368
  as messenger molecule, 560
  sources of emissions of, 360, 361, 379
Carbon monoxide detectors, 22, 361, 368
Carbon sequestration, 377
Carbon tetrachloride, 240, 397, 693
Carbonate minerals, 333
Carbonyl group, 249
Carboxyl group, 251–52
Carboxylic acids, 242, 251–53
Carcinogens, 695–96
  aflatoxins as, 522
  Ames test of, 696
  animal studies on, 696–97
  anticarcinogens, 696
  aromatics as, 379
  artificial sweeteners as, 515
  asbestos as, 335, 697
  benzene as, 155, 239
  chloroform as, 566
  in cigarette smoke, 606, 695
  defined, 694
  epidemiological studies of, 697
  in food, 522
  food colorings as, 36
  MTBE as, 430
  particulate matter as, 379
  in process for development of cancers, 695
  radon as, 368
  ranking of, 694–95
  tests for, 696–97
  vinyl chloride as, 273
Cardiac glycosides, 682
Cardiovascular disease. *See* Heart disease
Cargill Dow LLC, 287
Caries, dental, 402–3, 496, 516, 667–68
Carlisle, Anthony, 46, 62, 105
Carlsbad Caverns National Park, 333
Carnauba wax, 662
Carnitine, 528
Carothers, Wallace, 280
Carson, Rachel, 4, 625
Carver, George Washington, 11–12
Cast iron, 339
Catabolism, 456
Catalysts
  in biocatalysis, 467, 534
  defined, 192n, 219
  enzymes as, 474
  green oxidation, 220
  oxidation, 364
  rate of chemical reactions and, 415
  in redox reactions, 220
  reduction, 364
  TAML®, 220
Catalytic converters, 364
Catalytic reforming, 430
Cathode, 62, 64, 209
Cathode ray, 63
Cathode-ray tubes, 63
Cationic surfactants, 651
Cations, 62, 98
Causality versus correlation, 7
Cavendish, Henry, 46
CCK (cholecystokinin), 594

CDC. *See* Centers for Disease Control (CDC)
Celebrex®, 535
Celecoxib, 535
Cell membrane, 455
Cell phones, 298
Cells (biological)
  animal, 456
  respiration in, 223
  energy and, 455–56
  neurons as, 562
  nucleus of, 455
  parts of, 455
  plant, 455
  radiation damage to, 297
  in skin, 664
Cellular respiration, 223
Cellulases, 474
Celluloid, 267
Cellulose, 458–60, 496–97, 509
Cellulose nitrate, 267
Celsius scale, 28–29, 164–165, A14–A15
Cement, 337
Centers for Disease Control (CDC), 495, 523, 543, 585–86, 686
Centimeter (cm), 22, 23, A1, A5
Central Intelligence Agency (CIA), 637
Cephalexin, 543
Cephalosporins, 543
Ceramics, 336
Cervidil®, 552
Cesium-137, 321
Cetirizine, 536
CFCs (chlorofluorocarbons), 240–41, 371–72, 375, 420
Chadwick, James, 69–70, 329
Chain, Ernst Boris, 542
Chain reaction, 518
  for nuclear bomb, 317–19
Chain-reaction polymerization, 272–76
Charcoal filtration, 405
Charles, Jacques, 164–65
Charles's law, 164–67
Chelating, 686
Chemical bonds, 89–124
  in compounds, 89–90
  covalent, 100–102
  defined, 89, 153
  green chemistry and, 118
  HONC rules and, 105
  important consequences of, 90
  intramolecular forces in, 153, 157–59
  ionic, 93
  Lewis formulas and, 108–12
  multiple, 101
  number of, formed by selected elements, 111
  octet rule and, 96–97
  polar covalent, 102–5
  shapes of molecules and, 113–17
  single, 101
  stable electron configurations and, 90–91
  valence shell electron pair repulsion (VSEPR) theory and, 113–15
Chemical carcinogens, 695–96
Chemical change, defined, 14–15
Chemical equations, 125–51
  atom economy and, 140
  balancing of, 126–28
  defined, 126
  mass relationships in, 137–39
  molar relationships in, 137
  mole and mass relationships in, 135–36
  nuclear equations versus, 298, 302
  products in, 126
  reactants in, 126
  volume relationships in, 129–31
Chemical industry, 10, 31
Chemical properties, 14, 15
Chemical symbols, 18, 19
Chemical warfare, 549, 550, 687, 690, 691
Chemicals. *See also* Household chemicals; *specific chemicals*
  defined, 2
  use of, as good or bad, 2, 4
Chemistry. *See also* Biochemistry; Electrochemistry; Green chemistry; Nuclear chemistry; Organic chemistry
  central role of, 1–2, 10–11
  combinational, 546
  defined, 13
  historical roots of, 2–4
  vocabulary of, 119
Chemistry labs, in schools, 701
Chemotherapy, 532, 548, 550
Chernobyl, Ukraine, nuclear disaster, 295, 297, 436
Chernousenko, Vladimir, 297
Chile saltpeter, 615
Chili peppers, 229, 264, 539
China
  air pollution in, 356, 357, 367, 384
  carbon dioxide emission in, 384
  groundwater contamination in, 397
  industry in, 338, 356, 357, 377
  nuclear power plants in, 435
  rare earths in, 340, 341, 342
Chiral carbon, 565
Chloral hydrate, 623
Chloramphenicol, 9, 583
Chloride ions, in water, 390
Chlorinated hydrocarbons, 239–41, 625, 627, 702
Chlorination, of drinking water, 402, 404
Chlorine
  as disinfectant, 217
  electron configuration of, 79
  ion of, 97
  odor of, 93
  as plant nutrient, 619
  reaction of sodium and, 92–94
  safety alert on, 657
Chlorine bleaches, 218
Chlorine dioxide, 112
Chlorobenzene, 623
Chlorofluorocarbons (CFCs), 240–41, 371–72, 375, 420
Chloroform, 240, 397, 405, 566, 567
Chloroplasts, 455
Chloroprocaine, 567, 568
Chloropyrifos, 626–27
Chlorpromazine, 571
Chlortetracycline, 543
Cholecystokinin (CCK), 594
Cholera, 391–92
Cholesterol, 499–503, 553, 565, 591
Cholinesterase, 689
Chromium, 342
Chromophores, 656
Chromosomes, 479
Chrysanthemum cinerariaefolium, 628
Chrysotile asbestos, 334, 335
CIA (Central Intelligence Agency), 637
Cigarette smoking
  air pollution from, 367–68
  birth control pills and, 557
  deaths and risk of death from, 10, 605–6
  diseases caused by, 335, 550, 605–6, 694–95, 697
  health problems from secondhand smoke, 367–68, 606
  lethal dose of nicotine, 691
  pregnant women and, 606
  premature aging of skin due to, 665
  statistics on, 605
Cilia, in lungs, 606
Cis fatty acids, 501–2
Cisplatin, 549
Citanest®, 568
Citral, 668
Civetone, 669
Clarke company, 624
Clausius, Rudolf, 39
Clean Water Act, 406
Cleaning products
  all-purpose cleaners, 657
  detergents, 247, 475, 492, 649–55
  dishwashing detergents, 654
  drain cleaners, 659
  glass cleaners, 659
  green cleaners, 559–60, 658
  hand sanitizers, 659, 660
  hazards of mixing, 657
  homemade household cleaners, 659
  laundry bleaches, 655–56
  laundry detergents, 475, 492, 651–54
  oven cleaners, 659
  scouring powders, 659
  soaps, 182, 246, 644–48
  special-purpose cleaners, 657, 659
  supercritical fluids and, 155
  synthetic detergents, 649–54
  toilet-bowl cleaners, 187, 194, 657, 659
Climate change
  carbon dioxide and, 373–77, 442
  defined, 376
  and global warming, 375–77
  greenhouse effect and, 373–75
  weather and, 376
Clonazepam, 571
Cloning, 484
Clorox®, 218, 655
Closed ecosystem, 356
Clostridium botulinum, 516, 520, 689
Clozapine, 571, 572
Clozaril, 571
Club drugs, 575
Cm (centimeter), 22, 23, A1, A5
Coal
  carbon cycle and, 424
  composition and energy content of typical grades of, 423
  conversion of, to liquid fuels, 8
  defined, 423
  as energy source, 423–25
  gasification and liquefaction of, 432–33
  mining of, 424–25
  pollution from burning of, 425
  reserves and consumption rates of, 422
Cocaine, 532, 567, 568, 574, 604
Cocaine hydrochloride, 574
Codeine, 537
Codexis company, 467, 534
Codon, 481–82
Coenzyme Q_{10}, 526
Coenzymes, 473, 526
Cofactors, 473, 507
Coffee. *See* Caffeine
Coke, 219
Cold medicines, 536
Coleridge, Samuel Taylor, 537
Collins, Terry, 220
Colognes, 669
Colon cancer, 587
Colony collapse, 627
Color additives, 518–20
Colton, Frank, 556
Combinational chemistry, 546
Combined gas law, 169
Combining volumes, law of, 129–30
Comet water, 389
Complete protein, 505
Composite materials, 281
Composition of matter, 15
Compound 1080, 685
Compounds. *See also specific compounds*
  binary ionic, 98–100
  chemical bonds in, 89–90
  covalent (or molecular), 101–2
  defined, 47–48
  elements compared with, 47–48
  ionic, 94–97
  reaction of oxygen with, 216–17
Compression molding, 274
Computer chips, 25
Computers, 8–9, 25, 396
Concentrated solutions, 141
Concrete, 337
Condensation, 154
Condensation polymers, 279–83
Condensed structural formulas. *See also* Structural formulas
  of alkanes, 231–33
  of alkyl groups, 243
  defined, 231
  of polymers, 283
Conducting polymers, 276
Confined animal feeding operations, 642
Conium maculatum, 681
Conjugate acid–base pairs, 191
Conjugated system, 276
Conservation of energy, law of, 418–19, 595
Conservation of mass, law of, 43–44, 48
Continuous spectrum, 73–74
Contraceptives, 556–59
Control rods, in nuclear power plant, 435
Convenient energy, 432–33
Conversion factor, A6
Cookware, 273, 275, 283
Copolymer, 271
Copper
  chemical symbol for, 19
  density of, 25, 26
  ions of, 97
  native, 342
  physical properties of, 14
  as plant nutrient, 619
  production of, 338
  scarcity of, as scrap metal, 338
  specific heat of, 387, A15
  uses of, 338
Copper ion toxicity, 685
Copper T 380A IUD, 557
Core electrons, 90
Coronary artery disease, 560–61
Correlation versus causality, 7
Corrosion, 213–14
Corrosive waste, 701
Corticotropin-releasing factor (CRF), 554
Cortisol, 553, 554
Cortisone, 533
Cosmetics
  aftershave lotions, 669
  antiaging creams and lotions, 665
  colognes, 669
  consumer information on, 674
  defined, 663
  deodorants and antiperspirants, 667
  eye makeup, 666
  hair coloring, 672–73
  hair removers, 674
  hair restorers, 674
  hair sprays, 673

history of, 663
hypoallergenic, 670
lipsticks and lip balms, 666
nanoparticles in, 666
perfumes, 155, 250, 253, 521, 668–70
permanent waving, 673
sales of, 663, 664
shampoos, 189, 670–71
skin creams and lotions, 234, 246, 663–65
sunscreens, 665–66
toothpastes, 667–68
Cosmetology, 176
Cosmic rays, 296, 297
Cotton, 285
Counter ion, 651
Counterterrorism, 690
Covalent bonds
bonding pairs in, 101
defined, 100–101
double, 101
electronegativity and, 103–5
Lewis symbols and, 103
polar covalent, 102–5
triple, 101
Covalent (or molecular) compounds, 101–2
COX (cyclooxygenases), 535
Crack cocaine, 574
Cram, Donald J., 118
Crash diets, 594–95, 596, 612
Creams, 663–65
Creatine, 587
Creslan, 275
CRF (corticotropin-releasing factor), 554
Crick, Francis H. C., 478
Critical mass, 319
Critical thinking, 32–33
Crookes, William, 63
Crossover method, for formulas of binary ionic compounds, 98–99
CRT displays, 369
Cryolite, 628
Cryptosporidium, 391, 392
Crystal of sodium chloride, 93
Crystalline polymers, 284
Cubic meter, A-1
Curare, 689
Curie, Marie Sklodowska, 66
Curie, Pierre, 66
Cyanides, 684
Cyanoacrylates, 293
Cyanocobalamin (vitamin B_{12})
deficiency of, 508
Dietary Reference Intake (DRI) value for, 589
food sources of, 508
functions of, 590
health problems from deficiency of, 590
Cyclamates, 515
Cyclic ethers, 247
Cyclic hydrocarbons, 235
Cycloalkanes, 235
Cyclone separator, 359
Cyclooxygenases (COX), 535
Cyclophosphamide, 550
Cyclopropane, 235
Cyclospora, 697
Cysteine, 683
Cytochrome oxidases, 684
Cytoxan®, 550

D

2,4-D (2,4-dichlorophenoxyacetic acid), 631–32
Dalton, John, 47–51, 62, 129
Dandelions, 631
Darunavir, 546
Date rape drugs, 575
Daughter isotopes, 368
Davy, Humphrey, 62
DBP (dibutyl phthalate), 289
DDT, 240, 288, 622–23, 625–26, 633
De Broglie, Louis, 77
Death
from AIDS, 545
from air pollution, 350–51, 358, 368, 370
from alcohol use, 569
from cancer, 495, 541, 548, 550
from cholera, 392
from cigarette smoking, 605–6
of coal miners, 424–25
from contaminated water, 389, 697
diet linked with, 495
from drug overdoses, 574
from food poisoning, 520, 523, 697
from heart disease, 495, 541, 559
in house fires, 684
from hunger, 494–95, 697
from infectious diseases, 540, 541, 543, 697
leading causes of, 495, 541
lifetime risk of, from different causes, 10, 697
from malaria, 626
from narcotics, 538
in Nazi death camps, 684
from nerve poisons, 690
from nuclear accidents, 436–37
from pesticide poisoning, 633
from radiation sickness, 436–37
from staph infections, 543
from typhoid, 392
from whooping cough, 546
Decimeter (dm), 23
Decongestants, 536
Deduction, 90–91
Definite proportions, law of, 44–46, 48
Defoliants, 486, 631–33
Degradable plastics, 286
Dehydration, 591–92
Delavirdine, 545, 546
Delegate®, 624
Demerol®, 538
Democritus, 42–43, 53
Denature, 195
Denatured alcohol, 244
Density
of alkanes, 234
of common substances, at specified temperatures, 26
defined, 25
equations for, 25–28
from mass and volume, 27
Deodorants, 667
Deoxyribonucleic acid (DNA), 159, 267, 297, 476–80, 507
Depilatories, 674
Deposition, 154
Depressant drugs, 561–62, 569–70
Depression, 572. *See also* Antidepressants
Desflurane, 567
Desirability quotient (DQ), 8–9
Detergents
ABS, 649–50
dishwashing, 654
enzymes in, 475, 492
LAS, 650–51
laundry, 475, 492, 651–54
production of, 247
synthetic, 649–54
Deuterium, 70
Deuterium–tritium reaction, 437–38
Dexedrine®, 573
Dextrin, 460
Dextroamphetamine, 573
Dextrose. *See* Glucose
DHA (docosahexaenoic acid), 501
Diabetes
artificial sweeteners and, 516
deaths from, 495, 541
drugs for, 467, 553
healthy diet for prevention of, 587
insulin for, 484, 486, 511
sugar intake and, 552
test strips for monitoring of, 474
Diacetyl, 264
Diacylglycerol, 498–99
Diamond, 6, 270
Diatomaceous earth, 628
Diazepam, 571
Diazinon, 623, 626–27
Dibutyl phthalate (DBP), 289
Dicamba, 641
2,4-Dichlorophenoxyacetic acid (2,4-D), 631–32
Didanosine, 545, 546
Diesel fuel, 430
Diet. *See* Food
Diet pills, 594
Dietary Guidelines for Americans, 586
Dietary minerals, 506–7, 510, 588–89
Dietary Reference Intake (DRI), 587, 588–89
Dietary Supplement Health and Education Act, 510
Dietary supplements, 94, 99, 510, 528, 588, 594
Diethyl ether, 247, 565–66, 567
Dieting, 593–96, 612
Digitoxigenin, 561
Diglycerides, 461, 498–99
Digoxin, 531, 561
Dilaudid®, 538
Dilute solutions, 141
Dimethoxyethyl phthalate (DMEP), 289
Dimethylamine, 256
Dimethylnitrosamine, 695
Dimethyltryptamine (DMT), 574
Dinoprostone, 552
Dioctyl phthalate (DOP), 289
Dioxins, 632
DiPatrizio, Nicholas, 577
Dipel®, 629
Dipeptide, 466
Diphenhydramine, 536
Dipole, 116–17, 157–58
Dipole–dipole forces, 157–58
Direct reduction process, 349
Dirty bombs, 324
Disaccharides, 458
Disease. *See* Cancer; Diabetes; Health problems; Heart disease; Stroke; *specific diseases*
Dishwashing detergents, 654
Disinfectants, 217, 218
Dispersion forces, 158, 472
Dissociative anesthetics, 568–69
Dissolved oxygen (DO), 392
Disulfide linkage, 472
Diuretics, 560
Djerassi, Carl, 556
dm (decimeter), 23
DMEP (dimethoxyethyl phthalate), 289
DMT (dimethyltryptamine), 574
DNA
hydrogen bonds and, 159
parts, structure, and function of, 476–80, 507
as polymer, 267
protein synthesis and, 481–82
radiation damage to, 297
recombinant, 484–86
template strand of, 481
DNA fingerprinting, 484
DNA polymerases, 483
DNA viruses, 544–45
DO (dissolved oxygen), 392
Dobereiner, Johann, 53
Docosahexaenoic acid (DHA), 501
Dolastatin-10, 531
Domagk, Gerhard, 540
DOP (dioctyl phthalate), 289
Dopamine, 563, 570–74
Double bonds, 101
Doubling time, 636
Dow AgroSciences LLC, 624
Dow Chemical Company, 220, 254
DQ (desirability quotient), 8–9
DRI (Dietary Reference Intake), 587, 588–89
Drinking water
for athletes, 591–92
in Bangladesh and West Bengal, 401
bottled, 404, 405
chemical disinfection of, 402
chlorination of, 402, 404
contaminant concentrations in, 399–400
daily use of and need for, 396
in diet, 509, 591
EPA standards on, 395, 399–400, 406
fluorides in, 402–3
groundwater contamination and, 397–98
mineral water, 404
as nutrient, 509
ozone for treatment of, 402, 404
purification of small quantities of, in emergencies, 402
Safe Drinking Water Act, 399
UV irradiation of, 402
water treatment for production of, 401–3
worldwide consumption of, 509
Drug abuse, 573–78, 604–5. *See also specific illegal drugs*
Drug misuse, 578
Drug screening, 605
Drugs, 530–84
acetaminophen, 535
alkylating agents, 549–50
anesthetics, 240, 247, 565–69, 689
antianxiety agents, 571–72
antibacterial drugs, 540–44
anticancer drugs, 531, 548–50
antidepressants, 254, 571, 572
anti-inflammatory drugs, 531, 533, 535
antimetabolites, 548
antipsychotics, 571–72
antiviral drugs, 544, 545–47
athletic performance and, 604–7
barbiturates, 570
basic research on purines and, 12
for birth control, 556–59
brain affected by, 561–76
caffeine as, 574
for cholesterol, 565
club, 575
cocaine, 532, 567, 568, 574
cold and allergy medicines, 536
cost for development of, 532
date rape drugs, 575
defined, 530
depressants, 561–62, 569–70
for diabetes, 467, 553
diet pills, 594
disposal of old medicines, 578
E-factor for production of, 534
green pharmaceuticals, 534
hallucinogenic drugs, 562, 574–75
hazardous wastes from manufacture of, 699
for heart disorders, 531, 559–61, 564
historical development of, 37, 532–33, 540–42
hormones, 551–59

Drugs (*continued*)
for hypertension, 507, 559–60
immunosuppressants, 531
marijuana, 532, 562, 575–76
from marine organisms, 531
from microorganisms, 531
muscle relaxants, 531
nanoparticle medications for animals, 635
narcotics, 537–39
natural sources for, 531
nicotine as, 574
nocebo effect and, 578
nonsteroidal anti-inflammatory drugs (NSAIDs), 533, 535
pain relievers, 255, 530–33, 535–39
placebo effect and, 578
psychotropic, 561
restorative, 604
risk-benefit analysis of, 9
scientific drug design, 531–32
semisynthetic, 531
society and, 577–78
steroids, 553, 555, 604
stimulants, 561, 573, 604
in surgical practice, 567
synthetic, 254
tranquilizers, 567, 571
vasodilators, 246
Dry cells, 211
Dry cleaning, 155, 240, 398
DSM Engineering Plastics, 293
Ductile, 83
Duggor, Benjamin, 543
Duranest, 568
Dust, in water, 390
Dying lakes, 392–94
Dynel, 275
Dysentery, 392

E

E-factor, 534
Earth, 331–49
age of, 304–5
ancient people on, 333
atmosphere of, 332, 351–54
as closed ecosystem, 356
core of, 332
crust of, 332
dwindling resources of, 342–45
elements in crust of, 55, 216, 221, 332–33, 345
green chemistry and, 345
hydrosphere of, 332
lithosphere of, 332, 333
mantle of, 332
metals and ores in, 338–41
minerals in, 333, 345
oxygen in outermost structure of, 216
population of, 332, 344, 636–38
silicates in, 334–37
size of, 331
structural regions of, 332–33
Easel Biotechnologies, 467
EC (electron capture), 300, 301
Ecosphere®, 356
ECPs (emergency contraceptives), 556–57
"Ecstasy" (MDMA), 574, 575
Eden Bioscience Corporation, 624
EDTA (ethylenediaminetetraacetic acid), 687
Efavirenz, 546
Ehrlich, Paul, 532
Eicosapentaenoic (EPA), 501
Einhorn, Alfred, 568
Einstein, Albert, 315, 329
Ejkman, Christian, 507
Elastomers, 277–78. *See also* Rubber
Elavil®, 572
Electric current, measurement of, 20
Electric vehicles, 365
Electricity
from coal-burning power plants, 432, 433
convenience of, 432
generation of, 433
from hydroelectric plants, 445
from nuclear power plants, 434–35
static, 62
Electrochemical cell, 208–9, 212
Electrochemistry
of dry cells, 211
of electrochemical cell, 208–9, 212
historical development of, 62
of lead storage batteries, 211
photochromic glass and, 210
redox reactions and, 208–12
Electrodes, 62, 209
Electrolysis
apparatus for, 62
batteries and, 211, 212
defined, 62
in industry, 212
of water, 46
Electrolytes, 62, 181, 591
Electromagnetic radiation, 298
Electron capture (EC), 300, 301
Electron cloud, 77
Electron configurations
of first twenty elements, 79
main-shell, 76
order-of-filling chart for determining, 79
periodic table and, 81–83
stable, 90–91
valence-shell, 82–83
Electron-dot symbols. *See* Lewis (electron-dot) symbols
Electron orbitals, 77–78
Electron sets, 113
Electron-shell capacity, 75
Electronegativity, 103–5
Electronic air cleaners, 368
Electronics
computer chips and, 25
gold-plating and gold wires in, 8–9
Electrons
in Bohr model, 73–77
characteristics of, 70
core, 90
in covalent bonds, 100–102
defined, 63
electron-shell capacity for, 75
energy level of, 74–75
excited state of, 75
ground state of, 75
mass-to-charge ratio of, 63
Millikan's oil-drop experiment on charge of, 64
orbitals and, 77–79
as particles and waves, 77
periodic table and configurations of, 81–83
quantum model of arrangement of, 77–80
redox reactions as gain or loss of, 205–6
in Rutherford's nuclear theory of the atom, 69, 307
stable configurations of, 90–91
subshells (sublevels) for, 78, 80
symbol for, 302
valence, 81, 82, 90
valence-shell configurations of, 82–83
in valence shell electron pair repulsion (VSEPR) theory, 113–15
Electrostatic precipitator, 359
Elementary Treatise on Chemistry (Lavoisier), 44
Elements. *See also specific elements*
ancient Greeks' ideas about, 42–43, 53
Boyle's definition of, 44
chemical symbols for, 18–19
compounds compared with, 47–48
Dalton's symbols for, 49
defined, 17, 44
in Earth's crust, 55, 216, 221, 332–33, 345
essential to life, 506
green chemistry and, 55
in human body, 513
number of, 17
periodic table of, 51–52, 324–25
properties of, 51–52
reaction of oxygen with, 216
ultratrace, 506
Elion, Gertrude, 12, 547, 548
Emergency contraceptives (ECPs), 556–57
Emollients, 664
Emotions, 566
EMPD (*para*-ethoxy-*meta*-phenylenediamine), 672–73
Emulsifying agent, 646
Emulsions, 500, 646
Enantiomers, 565
End note, of perfume, 669
Endocrine glands, 552, 554. *See also* Hormones
Endonuclease, 484
Endorphins, 539, 598, 605
Endothermic chemical reactions, 416–17
Energy, 411–53
in agriculture and food production, 614, 634
in biological systems, 455–56
biomass as source of, 441, 443
carbohydrates as storehouse of, 457–60
chemical reactions and, 415–18
coal as source of, 423–25
conservation of, 447–48
convenient, 432–33
conversions, 30
defined, 28, 50, 412
Earth's energy ledger, 413
Einstein's equivalence of mass and, 315, 329
energy return on energy invested (EROEI), 431, 442
entropy and, 420–21
fuel cells as source of, 443, 445
future and, 447–48
geothermal, 446, 447
green chemistry and, 442
historical development of, 421
home usage of, 413
hydrogen as source of, 443, 444, 445
kinetic, 413–14
kinetics and, 415
law of conservation of, 418–19, 595
laws of thermodynamics and, 418–21
life-support system and, 414
matter compared with, 412
natural gas as source of, 426
nuclear, 322–25, 434–38
from nucleus, 296, 315–18
ocean thermal, 447
petroleum as source of, 426–28
potential, 413–14
power and energy conversion, 413
quantum of, 74–75
recycling for saving of, 344
renewable sources of, 439–48
shortage of, 422
solar cells as source of, 440–41
solar, 84, 411, 439–42
statistics on U.S. use of, 412
from Sun, 411–14
thermochemistry and, 416–18
total primary consumption of, per capita, 448
waterpower as source of, 421, 445, 446
wind, 411, 421, 431, 441, 445, 446
Energy consumption, 422
Energy drinks, 575
Energy level, 74–75
Energy production, 422
Energy return on energy invested (EROEI), 431, 442
Enkephalins, 539
Enovid, 556
Enrichment, 513
Entropy, 420–21
Environment. *See* Air pollution; Green chemistry; Pollution; Recycling; Water pollution
Environmental Protection Agency (EPA)
on air pollution, 358, 361, 366, 367, 368, 378
air quality standards of, 361, 368, 378
drinking water standards of, 395, 399–400, 406
on indoor air pollution, 367, 368
inventory of chemical compounds by, 660
on land pollution, 342
Office of Wastewater Management (OWM), 287, 410
on paper production, 396
Presidential Green Chemistry Challenge Award, 31, 140, 220, 254, 467, 624
Superfund sites and, 410
Enzymes, 472–75, 534, 693
EPA. *See* Environmental Protection Agency (EPA)
EPA (eicosapentaenoic), 501
Epichlorohydrin, 254
Epidemiological studies, 697
Epinephrine, 554, 563, 573
Epivir®, 546
EPO (erythropoietin), 485
Epoxies, 281
Equations. *See* Chemical equations; Nuclear equations
Ergogenic aids, 608
Ergotamine, 576
EROEI (energy return on energy invested), 431, 442
Erythromycin, 543
Erythropoietin (EPO), 485
Erythrulose, 457
Escherichia coli, 484, 523, 620, 650, 682, 697
Essential amino acids, 504–5
Essential oils, 669, 670
Esters, 242, 253, 255
Estimation, 23–24
Estradiol, 554, 555
Estrogen, 555, 556, 558
Estrone, 555
Ethane
addition reaction in production of, 237
models of, 231
physical properties, uses, and occurrences of, 234
structural formula for, 236
Ethanol. *See* Ethyl alcohol (ethanol)
Ethene, 236
Ethers, 242, 247–48
Ethisterone, 556
Ethyl alcohol (ethanol). *See also* Alcoholic beverages
density of, 26

energy return on energy invested (EROEI) for, 435
as green solvent, 254, 521
models of, 244
as motor vehicle fuel, 430
as octane booster in gasoline, 430
oxidation of, 569
specific heat of, 387, A15
toxicity of, 245
uses of, 150, 244–45
Ethyl lactate, 660
Ethyl methyl ketone, 250
Ethylamine, 256
Ethylene, 236, 237
Ethylene glycol, 245–246, 691, A15
Ethylene oxide, 247, 654
Ethylenediaminetetraacetic acid (EDTA), 687
Ethyne, 236
Etidocaine, 567, 568
Eugenol, 641
Eutrophication, 393, 652
Evaporation, 6
Excedrin, 536
Excited state, 75
Exercise
aerobic, 600–601
anaerobic, 601–2
biking and walking as, 598
brain and, 605
for building muscles, 587, 603
endorphins and, 598, 605
green chemistry and, 598
hydration for and dehydration from, 591–92
oxygen debt and, 216, 601–2
sports and recreational items for, 607
for weight loss, 595
weightlifting as, 603
Exons, 480
Exothermic chemical reactions, 416, 417
Expectorants, 536
Explosion, 213, 214–15
Exponential notation, 21–22, A1–A4
addition and subtraction and, A3
conversion of number from exponential form to conventional form, A2–A3
defined, 21, A-2
extracting root of exponential number, A4
multiplication and division and, A3
negative quantity of *n*, A-2
positive quantity of *n*, A-2
raising number to power, A4
Extremophiles, 474
Extrusion molding, 275
ExxonMobile, 395
Eye makeup, 666
Eyeglasses, with photochromic lenses, 210

F

Fabric softeners, 655
Fabrics. *See* Fibers
Factor VIII, 485
Factory farms, 642
Fahrenheit temperature scale, 29, 30, A14–A15
Falsifiability, 32
Faraday, Michael, 62–63, 238
Farming. *See* Agriculture
Fast-twitch muscle fibers, 602–3
Fasting, 511, 594–95, 596
Fat depots, 499
Fat-soluble vitamins, 508–9
Fats
biochemistry of, 460–62
calories from, in diet, 498, 502, 587
defined, 461
in diet, 498–503, 577, 587
fatty acids in, 462
iodine numbers for, 462
metabolism of, 498–99, 511
monounsaturated, 461–62, 501–2
polyunsaturated, 461–62
saturated, 237, 461–62, 499
trans, 502, 587
unsaturated, 237, 461–62
Fatty acid spiral, 499
Fatty acids, 460–62, 499–503
FDA. *See* Food and Drug Administration (FDA)
Federal Trade Commission (FTC), 532, 595
Fentanyl, 538, 567
Fermi, Enrico, 316, 319
Fertilizers
complete, 619
groundwater contamination from, 397
labels of, 620
micronutrients and, 619
nanoscale, 635
nitrogen, 219, 615–17
nonexplosive, 617
organic, 230, 620, 621
phosphorus, 617–18
potassium, 618
primary plant nutrients and, 615–18
production equations for, 621
secondary plant nutrients and, 619
Fetal alcohol syndrome, 245
Fevers, 533, 535
FFVs (flexible fuel vehicles), 430
Fiber (dietary), 509
Fibers
acrylic, 285
asbestos, 334, 335
in cotton, 285
in flame-retardant fabrics, 286
formation of, 285
microfibers, 285
in nylon fabrics, 285, 287
optical, 337
in permanent-press fabrics, 285
polyester, 247, 280, 285
in silk fabrics, 285
Fibrillation, 560
FiLCHeRS criteria, 32n
Fire, ancient people's discovery of, 333
Fire extinguishers, 240
Fire hazards
flame-retardant fabrics as, 286
flammable waste as, 699, 701
of plastics, 286
Fireworks, 73
First law of thermodynamics, 418–19
Fischer-Tropsch method, 433
Fitness and health, 585–612. *See also* Exercise
acids and bases affecting, 195
bioelectric impedance analysis and, 597
body fluids and electrolytes and, 591–92
body mass index (BMI), 597
cholesterol level and, 145
crash diets and fad diets and, 594–95, 596, 612
Dietary Guidelines for Americans, 586
Dietary Reference Intake (DRI), 587, 588–89
dietary sodium limits and, 133
dietary supplements and, 94, 99, 510, 528, 588, 594
dieting for weight loss and, 593–96, 612
fluorides in drinking water and, 402–3
green chemistry and, 598
low-sodium diet and, 93
measuring fitness, 596–97, 599
obesity and, 495, 515, 553, 585–86, 593–96
Recommended Dietary Allowances (RDAs), 587
vitamins and minerals and, 507–11, 588–91
V_{O2} max, 599
weight loss and, 593–96
Flame tests, 73
Flammable waste, 699, 701
FLaReS criteria, 32–33
Flavonoids, 696
Flavors and flavor enhancers, 253, 514–15, 516
Fleming, Alexander, 542
Flexible fuel vehicles (FFVs), 430
Flocculent, 402
Flocs, 405
Florey, Howard, 542
Fluids. *See* Liquids
Flunitrazepam, 575
Fluorapatite, 403
Fluorescence, 66
Fluorides, 402–3, 668
Fluorine, 76, 79, 97
Fluoroacetic acid, 684–85
Fluorocarbons, 241
Fluoroquinolones, 544
5-fluorouracil (5-FU), 548
Fluoxetine, 572
Fly ash, 358, 359, 425
Folic acid (vitamin B_9)
chemical structure of, 548–549
deficiency of, 508
Dietary Reference Intake (DRI) value for, 589
food sources of, 508
functions of, 590
Follicle-stimulating hormone (FSH), 554, 555, 558
Food, 494–529. *See also* Beverages; Food additives
as anticarcinogens, 696
antioxidants in, 219
artificial sweeteners in, 8
bleached versus unbleached flour, 112
brain amines and diet, 564
butter versus margarine, 501
calories in, 586–87
carbohydrates in, 495–97
carcinogens in, 522
cellular respiration for metabolism of, 223
chemicals in breakfast foods, 513
chocolate, 651
cholesterol and, 499–503, 591
contaminants in, 522–23
cost of, 634
dietary minerals in, 506–7
Dietary Reference Intake (DRI), 587, 588–89
digestion and metabolism of carbohydrates from, 496
digestion and metabolism of fats from, 498–99
fasting from, 511, 594–95, 596
fats in, 498–503, 577
fiber in, 509
genetically modified (GM), 486, 487, 638
green chemistry and, 521
hunger and, 494–95, 594, 637, 638
irradiated, 309
isolation of nutrients from, 521
Italian dressing, 160
labels for, 99
lacto-ovo diet and, 504
low-carbohydrate, 497
low-sodium diet and, 93
malnutrition and, 511–12
nanoscience and, 519
nutrient calculations for, 502
organic, 230
oxidation of, 112
popcorn, 264
problems with, 520, 522–23
processed, 511–12
proteins in, 504–5
Recommended Dietary Allowances (RDAs), 587
rice ("golden rice"), 486
salad dressings, 462
saturated versus unsaturated fats in 237, 461–62
smell of fresh versus rotting fruit, 253
starvation and, 511, 637
"super foods" or "miracle foods," 512
traditional foods that combine cereal grain with legume, 504
vegan diet and, 504
vegetarian diets and, 504
weight-loss diets and, 593–96
Food additives
antioxidants, 517–18
artificial sweeteners, 8, 515–16
color additives, 518–20
defined, 512
FDA regulation of, 512, 514, 515, 517, 519, 523
flavor enhancers, 253, 516
food colorings, 36
for good taste, 514–15
GRAS (generally recognized as safe) list of, 514
for improved nutrition, 513–14
for popcorn, 264
for retarding spoilage, 252, 516–17
vitamins as, 514
Food Additives Amendment, 512
Food and Drug Act, 519
Food and Drug Administration (FDA)
on artificial sweeteners, 515
on birth control pills, 556, 557
on bottled water, 404
on cold and allergy medicines, 536
cosmetics and, 674
on dietary supplements, 510
on fat calories, 498
on food additives, 512, 514, 515, 517, 519, 523
on food labels, 502
on phthalate plasticizers, 288
on prescription drugs, 535
on supercritical water and carbon dioxide, 155
on thalidomide, 697, 698
Food colorings, 36
Food, Drug, and Cosmetic Act, 663
Food poisoning, 520, 523, 697
Formaldehyde, 204, 245, 249–50, 281, 367
Formatin, 249
Formic acid, 252
Formula (or molecular) mass, 132–34
Formulas. *See also* Structural formulas
of alcohols, 246
chemical symbols in, 18
of ethers, 248
of hydrocarbons, 231–33, 235, 237, 240, 243, 246, 248, 252–53, 256–57
law of definite proportions and, 46
of polymers, 283

Fossil fuels, 421–25
Fracking, 426, 442
Fractional electrolysis, 437–38
Fragrances, 155, 250, 253, 521, 668–71. *See also* Perfumes
Franklin, Rosalind, 478
Free radicals
- antioxidants and, 517–18
- chain reaction for, 518
- defined, 110, 517
- Lewis formulas of, 110–11
- radiation damage to cells and, 297
- useful applications of, 112
- Vitamin E and, 590

Freezing, 154
Frisch, Otto, 316
Fructose, 457, 458, 474, 495–96, 515
FSH (follicle-stimulating hormone), 554, 555, 558
FTC. *See* Federal Trade Commission (FTC)
Fuel cells, 212, 443, 445
Fuels
- alternative, 430–31
- biodiesel, 182, 441, 442
- convenience of, in various physical states, 423
- conversion of coal to liquid, 8
- defined, 421
- diesel, 430
- ethanol as, 430
- fossil, 421–25
- gasoline as, 233, 234, 244–45, 360, 378, 397, 427–30
- hydrocarbons in, 233, 234, 467
- hydrogen as, 222
- natural gas as, 426
- nonfuels compared with, 422
- oxygen and, 216
- petroleum-derived, 427
- propane and butanes as, 233

Fukushima, Japan, nuclear disaster at, 67, 295, 436–37
Fuller, R. Buckminster, 270
Functional groups, 241–43
Funk, Casimir, 507
Furadan®, 627
Furchgott, Robert F., 112, 560

G

g (gram), A1, A5
GABA, 563, 570, 571
Galactose, 457, 458
Galileo Galilei, 4
Gamma-aminobutyric acid (GABA), 563, 570, 571
Gamma decay, 299, 301
Gamma-hydroxybutyrate (GHB), 575
Gamma rays, 66–67, 302, 309, 313–14
Gamma-ray imaging, 311
Garbage, 342–44, 349
Gas heaters, 368
Gas laws
- Amonton's law, 173–74
- Avogadro's law on molar volume, 167–68
- Boyle's law on pressure–volume relationship, 162–64
- Charles's law on temperature–volume relationship, 164–67
- combined gas law, 169
- ideal gas law, 169–70
- simple gas laws, 162–68, 173–74

Gases
- Amonton's law and, 173–74
- Avogadro's hypothesis on, 130, 131, 167
- Avogadro's law on molar volume of, 167–68
- Boyle's law on pressure–volume relationship for, 162–64
- change from liquid to, 154
- change from solid to, 154
- change to liquid from, 154
- change to solid from, 154
- Charles's law on temperature–volume relationship for, 164–67
- combined gas law and, 169
- condensation of, 154
- defined, 16
- greenhouse, 139, 373–75
- ideal gas law and, 169–70
- kinetic-molecular theory of, 17, 161–62
- molar volume of, 167–68
- noble, 82, 90
- properties of, 153–54
- simple gas laws and, 162–68, 173–74
- volume relationships of, 129–31

Gasoline
- conversion of automobile emissions to, 360
- defined, 429
- ethanol in, 244–45
- as fraction of petroleum, 427–28, 429
- hazardous waste from production of, 699
- hydrocarbons in, 233, 234
- octane ratings of, 429–30
- straight-run, 429
- tetraethyllead in, 378
- volatile organic compounds (VOCs) in, 397

Gastroenteritis, 523
Gay-Lussac, Joseph Louis, 39, 129–30
Geiger, Hans, 68
Geim, Andre, 270
Gene therapy, 486–87
General anesthetics, 565–67
Genes, 479–83
Genetic code, 481–82
Genetically modified (GM) foods and plants, 486, 487, 629, 638
Genetics, 478–82, 695
Genome
- defined, 479
- human, 483–87

Geometric growth, 636
Geothermal energy, 446, 447
Gerlach, Walther, 12
Germanium, 52
Germicides, 247
GH (growth hormone), 554
GHB (*gamma*-hydroxybutyrate), 575
Ghrelin, 594
Giardia, 392
Gifblaar, 685
Glass, 336–37
Glass transition temperature, 284–85
Gleevec®, 550
Glidden Pain Company, 555
Glioma, 298
Global warming, 375–77
Globular protein, 471
Glucagon, 554
Glucophage®, 553
Glucose
- as blood sugar, 495
- cyclic structure for, 458
- in diet, 495
- metabolism of, 23
- photosynthesis of, 455
- relative sweetness of, 515
- as simple sugar, 457, 495
- structure of, 458

Glucose oxidase, 474
Glutamate, 563, 570
Gluten, 39
Glycerol, 182, 245–46, 254, 498–99, 516
Glyceryl guaiacolate, 536
Glycine, 257, 563
Glycogen, 460, 497, 594
Glycoproteins, 544
Glyphosate, 631, 632
GM (genetically modified) foods and plants, 486, 487, 629, 638
GnRF (gonadotropin-releasing factor), 554
Goiter, 506, 513
Gold, 17, 18
- chemical symbol for, 19
- density of, 26
- 14K versus 18K, 143
- impossibility of changing lead into, 18
- mining of, 342, 348
- in production of catalytic converters, 364

Gold-plating and gold wires, 8–9
Goldstein, Eugen, 64, 307
Gonadal hormones, 554
Gonadotropin-releasing factor (GnRF), 554
Goodyear, Charles, 277
Grain alcohol. *See* Ethyl alcohol (ethanol)
Gram, A1, A5
Graphene, 270
Graphite, 270
GRAS (generally recognized as safe) list, 514
Gravity, 13
Grecian Formula®, 673
Greeks
- four humors theory of, 693
- historical roots of chemistry and, 2, 3, 43
- on matter, 42–43, 53

Green chemistry
- air pollution and, 369
- aluminum and iron production and, 345
- atom economy and, 140
- atoms and atomic structure and, 55, 84
- awards for, 31
- chemical bonds and, 118
- defined, 4, 31
- elements and, 55
- energy and, 442
- enzymes and, 474, 534
- fitness and health and, 598
- food and, 521
- hazardous elements and, 55
- household chemicals and, 658, 659–60
- nuclear waste remediation and, 323
- organic synthesis and, 254
- oxidation catalysts and, 220
- pesticides and, 624
- pharmaceuticals and, 534
- polymers and, 287
- porous materials in water remediation and, 395
- principles and goals of, 31
- risk-benefit analysis and, 31
- scarce elements and, 55
- scientific method and, 31
- solar energy and, 84
- supercritical fluids and, 155
- sustainability and, 182
- toxicity and, 700

Greenhouse gases and greenhouse effect, 139, 373–75
Ground state, 75
Groundwater contamination, 390, 397–98
Group (or family) in periodic table, 81–82
Growth factors, 550
Growth hormone (GH), 554
Guaifenesin, 536
Gulf of Mexico oil spill, 387
Gums, 509

H

Haber, Fritz, 550, 616
Hahn, Otto, 316
Hair, 670–74
Hair coloring, 672–73
Hair removers, 674
Hair restorers, 674
Hair sprays, 673
Half-life, 303–4
Hall, Charles Martin, 339
Hallucinogenic drugs, 562, 574–75
Halogens, defined, 82
Hand sanitizer, 659, 660
Hard water, 390, 646–48
Harrison Act, 537
Hazardous elements, 55
Hazardous wastes, 47, 699, 701–2
HCT (hydrochlorothiazide), 560
HDLs (high-density lipoproteins), 500
HDPE (high-density polyethylene), 269–71, 286, 287
Health. *See* Fitness and health; Health problems; Medicine
Health and Human Services Department (HHS), 586
Health problems. *See also* Cancer; Diabetes; Heart disease; Stroke; *other specific diseases*
- from air pollution, 350–51, 358–62, 367–70, 379
- from cigarette smoking, 10, 335, 367–68, 550, 557, 605–6
- from contaminated water, 389
- genetic components of diseases, 483, 484
- from groundwater contamination, 397
- healthy diet for prevention of, 587
- heavy metal poisons and, 685–87
- from industrial smog, 359
- infectious diseases, 540–47, 697
- mental illness, 311, 563–64, 571–72
- obesity and, 495, 515, 553, 585–86, 593
- from pathogenic microorganisms, 391–92
- pesticide poisonings, 633
- radiation sickness, 312, 436–37
- vitamin deficiencies and, 507–8, 588–90
- waterborne diseases, 391–92, 406

Heart disease
- air pollution and, 379
- arrhythmia in, 560
- birth control pills and, 557
- cholesterol and, 500, 501
- coronary artery disease, 560–61
- deaths from, 495, 541, 559
- diet and, 462, 495, 500, 501
- drugs for, 246, 474, 485, 531, 552, 559–61, 564
- gamma-ray imaging and, 311
- healthy diet for prevention of, 587
- hypertension and, 507, 559–60
- risk of death from, 10
- types of, 559

Heart note, of perfume, 669
Heat. *See also* Temperature
- defined, 28
- measurement of, A15–A16
- specific heat, 387, A15

Heat of vaporization, 387
Heat stroke, 592
Heavy metal poisons, 685–87, 702
Heavy water, 71
Helen (unit of beauty), 38
Helicobacter pylori (H. pylori), 194

Heliothi caterpillars, 629
Helium, 76, 78, 79
Helix structure
  of DNA, 478
  of proteins, 470
  of RNA, 478, 479, 480
Hematite, 54
Hemlock, 681
Hemoglobin, 97, 361, 466, 507, 684
Hemophilia, 474, 485
Henry, William, 38
Hepatitis A, 523
Hepatitis B, 486
Herbicides and defoliants, 486, 631–33
Heredity, 478–82
Heroin, 9, 531, 537–39
Héroult, Paul, 339
Heterocyclic compounds, 258–59
Heterogeneous mixtures, 17, 18
Hexane, 26, 699, 701
Hexylresorcinol, 247
HFCS (high-fructose corn syrup), 496
HFCs (hydrofluorocarbons), 372
HGH (human growth hormone), 485
HHS. *See* Health and Human Services Department (HHS)
High-density lipoproteins (HDLs), 500
High-density polyethylene (HDPE), 269–71, 286, 287
High-fructose corn syrup (HFCS), 496
High-level liquid waste (HLLW), 323
Hindenburg airship, 222
Hippocrates, 533
Histamine, 536, 563
Hitchings, George, 12, 547, 548
Hitler, Adolf, 550
HIV/AIDS, 9, 36, 543, 544–47
Hivid®, 546
HLLW (high-level liquid waste), 323
Hodgkin, Dorothy Crawford, 590
Hofmann, Albert, 574–75
Homeopathic remedies, 150
Homogeneous mixtures, 17, 18
Homologous series, 232
HONC rules, 105
Honeybees, 627, 641
Hoover Dam, 445
Hopkins, F. G., 507
Hormone replacement therapy, 555
Hormones
  birth control and, 556–59
  defined, 551
  endocrine glands and, 552, 554
  functions of, 554
  juvenile, 630
  prostaglandins as mediators of, 551–52
  sex, 555–59, 604
  steroid, 553, 555
Household chemicals, 643–79
  all-purpose cleaners, 657
  cosmetics, 663–74
  detergents, 247, 475, 492, 649–55
  dishwashing detergents, 654
  fabric softeners, 655
  green, 658, 659–60
  laundry bleaches, 655–56
  laundry detergents, 475, 492, 651–54
  misuse of, 644
  paints, 661
  soap, 182, 246, 644–48
  solvents, 661
  special-purpose cleaners, 657, 659
  synthetic detergents, 649–54
  variety of, 643–44
  warning labels for, 660, 661
  water softeners, 647–48
  waxes, 661–62
Housekeeping genes, 480
Human body. *See also* Biochemistry; Brain; Fitness and health; Health problems
  acids and bases in blood, 195
  artificial parts for, 282–83, 289
  body odor, 252
  bone density in, 311
  cellular respiration in, 223
  chromosomes in, 479
  cilia in lungs of, 606
  elemental analysis of, 513
  endocrine glands of, 552, 554
  endorphins in, 539, 598, 605
  eye color, 482
  hair, 670–74
  heart, 559–61
  hemoglobin in blood, 97, 361, 466, 507, 684
  hormones in, 551–59
  liver as detox facility for, 692–93
  MRI scans of, 12, 295
  muscles and muscular chemistry, 587, 595–603
  nervous system and brain, 562–65, 688–90
  nitric oxide in cardiovascular system of, 112
  normal body temperature, 30
  nutrients circulating in blood in, 161
  oxidation of foods by, 112
  oxygen in, 215
  PET scans of, 295, 311–12
  pH of blood, 192, 195
  proteins and, 257
  sense of taste, 176
  skin, 663, 664, 665, 672
  stomach acid, 193–94
  sweating, 591, 667
  tooth pain from biting on aluminum foil, 209
  water in, 215, 385
Human genome, 483–87
Human growth hormone (HGH), 485
Humectants, 516, 664
Hunger, 494–95, 511, 594, 637, 638, 697
Hyatt, John Wesley, 267
Hybrid, 238
Hybrid vehicles, 364
HYCD/APAP, 539
Hydrations, 264
Hydraulic fracturing (fracking), 426, 442
Hydrocarbon fuels, 467
Hydrocarbons
  aliphatic, 230–37
  alkanes, 230–31, 234, 242
  alkenes, 236–37
  alkynes, 236–37, 242
  aromatic, 238–39
  benzene, 238–39
  burning of, 237
  chlorinated, 239–41, 625
  condensed structural formulas for, 231–33, 243
  cyclic, 235
  defined, 230
  formulas for, 231–33, 235, 237, 240, 243, 246, 248, 252–53, 256–57
  functional groups on, 241–43
  green chemistry and, 254
  health and environmental effects of, 379
  heterocyclic, 258–59
  homologous series of, 232
  isomers of, 232–33
  ring-containing, 235
  safety alerts on, 234, 240
  saturated, 231, 236
  as solvents, 363
  structural formulas for, 231–33, 235, 243
  unsaturated, 236–37
Hydrochloric acid
  industrial uses of, 194
  molar solution of, 188
  reagent grade, 144
  in stomach, 193–94, 517
  as strong acid, 178, 180, 185
  in toilet-bowl cleaner, 187, 194, 657, 659
Hydrochlorothiazide (HCT), 560
Hydrocodone, 538, 539
Hydroelectric plants, 445
Hydrofluorocarbons (HFCs), 372
Hydrogen
  in Earth's crust, 332–33, 345
  electron configuration of, 76, 78, 79
  energy cycle of, 84
  as fuel, 222, 444, 445
  industrial production of, 222
  isotopes of, 70, 71
  laboratory use of, 221
  Lavoisier's naming of, 46
  line spectrum of, 74
  properties and uses of, 221–22, 444
  as reducing agent, 219, 221–22
  redox reactions as gain or loss of, 204–5, 206
  as renewable energy source, 443, 444, 445
  states of, 158
Hydrogen bonds, 158–59
Hydrogen chloride, 103–4, 157–58, 180, 185, 188, 286
Hydrogen cyanide, 185, 286, 684, 699
Hydrogen fluoride, 158–59
Hydrogen ions
  acids and, 178
  pH and, 188, 189–90
  production of, from hydrogen cyanide, 185
  symbol of, 97
Hydrogen–oxygen fuel cell, 443, 445
Hydrogen peroxide, 217, 220, 415, 668, 672
Hydrogen sulfide, 50, 216, 560, 699
Hydrogenations, 264
Hydromorphone, 538
Hydronium ions, 179–80
Hydrophilic, 646
Hydrophobic, 646
Hydroquinone, 264
Hydrosphere, 332. *See also* Water
Hydroxides, 179, 185, 186, 190
Hydroxyapatite, 403
Hydroxyl radicals, 112
Hyperacidity, 193
Hypertension, 507, 559–60
Hypoallergenic cosmetics, 670
Hypochlorous acid, 217
Hypothalamic hormones, 554
Hypotheses, 5

I

Ibuprofen, 533
Ice, 386–88
Icebergs, 386
Ideal gas law, 169–70
Ignarro, Louis J., 112, 560
Illegal drugs. *See* Drug abuse; *specific illegal drugs*
Illness. *See* Cancer; Diabetes; Health problems; Heart disease; Stroke; *specific illnesses*
Imatinib, 550
Imipramine, 572
Immunosuppressants, 531
Incineration of solid wastes, 343, 701, 702
Inderal®, 564
India, 338, 340, 377, 401, 435
Indigo dye, 227
Indium, 341
Indole, 669
Induced-fit model, 473
Industrial smog, 356–60
Industry. *See also* Technology
  acids and bases used in, 194–95
  applied research and, 11–12
  chemical, 10, 31
  in China, 338, 356, 357, 377
  electrolysis in, 212
  enzymes used by, 474–75
  ethanol used by, 244
  green chemistry and, 31
  hazardous wastes from, 47, 699, 701–2
  hydrogen used by, 222
  manufacture of plastics and rubber, 271
  metals used in, 340–41
  oxygen used by, 216
  radioisotopes used in, 308–9
  smog from, 356–60
  statistics on energy uses by, 412
  water pollution from, 393–94, 396
  water quantities used by, to produce various materials, 394, 396
Infectious diseases, 540–47, 697
Infrared radiation (IR), 375
Inhoffen, Hans, 556
Injection molding, 275
Inorganic chemicals, defined, 229–30
Insecticides, 239, 240, 288, 622–23, 625. *See also* Pesticides
Inside air pollution, 367–68, 606
Insoluble versus soluble, 141
Insulin, 484, 486, 491, 511, 553, 554, 594
Interferons, 486, 590
Intergovernmental Panel on Climate Change (IPCC; United Nations), 375–76
Intermolecular forces, 153, 156
International System of Units (SI units), 20, 22–24, 28–29, A1
International Union of Pure and Applied Chemistry (IUPAC), 81, 252
International unit (IU), 590
Intramolecular forces, 153, 157–59
Intrauterine device (IUD), 557
Introns, 480
Invirase®, 546
Iodine
  as antiseptic, 217
  deficiency in, for humans, 506
  ion of, 97
  physical properties of, 14
Iodine numbers, 462
Iodine-131, 321
Ion–dipole interactions, 160–61
Ionic bonds, 93, 472
Ionic compounds
  formulas and names of binary, 98–100
  Lewis symbols for, 94–97
Ionic liquids, 174
Ionic substances
  ion–dipole interactions in, 160–61
  molecular substances compared with, 156–57
Ionization, of acids and bases, 178, 179, 180, 185
Ionizing radiation, 297, 298, 310
Ions
  atoms compared with, 94
  defined, 62
  electron transfer to form, 95–96
  hydronium, 179–80
  negative, 91, 156
  periodic relationships of simple, 96

Ions (*continued*)
polyatomic, 106–8
symbols and names of simple, 97
IPCC. *See* Intergovernmental Panel on Climate Change (IPCC; United Nations)
IR (infrared radiation), 375
Iridium, 364
Iron
alloys of, 339
blast furnace for production of, 339
chemical properties of, 14, 15
chemical symbol for, 19
as dietary mineral, 507, 685
in Earth's crust, 332, 345
environmental costs of production of, 340
green chemistry for production of, 345
ions of, 94, 97
as plant nutrient, 619
production of, 338–39, 345, 349
recycling of, 54, 340
rusting of, 96, 194, 213–14
specific heat of, 387, A15
Iron ions, 390, 507
Iron ore, 54
Irone, 668
Irradiated foods, 309
Irrigation, 396, 406
Isobutane, 233, 243
Isobutyl methyl ketone, 250
Isocyanate, 36
Isoelectronic, 91
Isoflurane, 567
Isomerases, 474
Isomerization, 429
Isomers, 232–33
Isopropyl alcohol, 245
Isotopes. *See also* Radioisotopes
defined, 48–49, 70
of hydrogen, 70, 71
isotopic signatures of, 307
in nuclear equations, 298
photosynthesis and, 88
stability of, 305
symbols for, 71–72
Isotopic enrichment, 319
Isotopic signatures, 307
Isotretinoin, 664, 698
Itai-itai, 687
IU (international unit), 590
IUD (intrauterine device), 557
IUPAC. *See* International Union of Pure and Applied Chemistry (IUPAC)

J

J (joule), 29, 412, 416, A15
Januvia, 467
Japan, 67, 295, 435, 436–37, 687
Jasmone, 668
Jeffreys, Alec, 484
Jenner, Edward, 546
Joule (J), 29, 412, 416, A15
Julian, Percy Lavon, 555
Jupiter, 331
Juvenile hormones, 630

K

K (kelvin), 20, 28–29
Karat (K), 143
kcal (kilocalorie), 29
Keflex®, 543
Kekulé, August, 238
Kelly, Walt, 379
Kelsey, Frances O., 697, 698
Kelvin, Lord, 165
Kelvin (K), 20, 28–29, 165
Kelvin scale, 28–29, 165
Kennedy, John F., 697, 698
Kepler, Johannes, 75
Keratin, 663, 670
Kerosene heaters, 368
Ketamine, 568–69, 574, 575, 691
Ketone bodies, 511, 596
Ketones, 242, 249, 250–51
Ketoprofen, 533
Ketose, 457, 458
Ketosis, 511
Kevlar, 271, 292
kg (kilogram), 20, 22, A1, A5
Kidney disease, 485, 495, 507
Kilocalorie (kcal), 29
Kilogram (kg), 20, 22, A1, A5
Kilometer (km), 22, A5
Kilowatt hour (kWh), 412
Kinetic energy, 413–14
Kinetic-molecular theory, 6, 17, 161–62
Kinetics, 415
km (kilometer), 22, A5
Koprowski, Hilary, 546
Kornberg, Arthur, 12
Kuru, 473
Kwashiorkor, 505
kWh (kilowatt hour), 412

L

L (liter), 23, A1, A5
Laboratory chemicals, toxicity of, 176
Lacquer, 661
Lacto-ovo diet, 504
Lactones, 695
Lactose, 457, 458, 515
Lactose intolerance, 8
Lakes, dying, 392–94
Lamivudine, 546
Land pollution, 342–44
Lanolin, 662
Lanthanide elements, 340, 341
LAS detergents, 650–51, 653, 654
Laudanum, 537
Laundry bleaches, 655–56
Laundry detergents, 475, 492, 651–54
N-Laurylethyleneimine, 696
Lauterbur, Paul, 12
Lavoisier, Antoine, 37, 43–44, 47
Law of combining volumes, 129–30
Law of conservation of energy, 418–19, 595
Law of conservation of mass, 43–44, 48
Law of definite proportions, 44–46, 48
Law of multiple proportions, 47, 48, 49
Laws of thermodynamics, 418–21
LCD monitors, 369
LD_{50}, 691
LDLs (low-density lipoproteins), 500–501, 591
LDPE (low-density polyethylene), 269–71
Lead
ambient air quality standard for, 378
chemical symbol for, 19
as hazardous element, 55, 336, 379, 686–87, 702
impossibility of changing into gold, 18
specific heat of, 387
uses of, 686
Lead arsenate, 623
Lead dioxide, 203
Lead poisoning, 336, 686–87
Lead storage batteries, 211
Leather, 699
Lecithin, 651
Lehn, Jean-Marie, 118
Length
conversions between common and metric units of, A5–A8
measurement of, 20, 22, A1
Leptin, 594
Lethal dose of poisons, 691–92
Lett, James, 32n
Leucippus, 42, 53
Leukemia, 239, 297, 550
Levoamphetamine, 573
Lewis, G. N., 91
Lewis formulas
of free radicals, 110–11
rules for writing, 108–12
Lewis (electron-dot) symbols, 92
covalent bonds and, 103
defined, 91
for ionic compounds, 94–97
for main group elements, 92
periodic table and, 92
Lewisite, 687
LH (luteinizing hormone), 554, 555, 558
Liao, James, 467
Liber de arte distillandi (Brunschwig), 3
Lidocaine, 567, 568
Light, as energy, 50
Lime, 184, 194–95, 402
Limestone, 333
Limiting reactant, 505
Limonene, 660
Lincoln, Mary Todd, 537
Lindane, 623
Line spectra, 73–75
Linear alkylsulfonates (LAS) detergents, 650–51, 653, 654
Linear low-density polyethylene (LLDPE), 271
Lipases, 475, 498, 654
Lipids, 460–62
Lipitor®, 565
Lipolase, 534
Lipoproteins, 500
Lipsticks and lip balms, 666
Liquid crystal display (LCD) monitors, 369
Liquid-metal fast breeder reactors, 437
Liquid oxygen, 216, 415
Liquids. *See also* Alcoholic beverages; Beverages; Drinking water; Water
boiling point of, 154
change from gas to, 154
change from solids to, 154
change to gas from, 154, 155
defined, 16
freezing of, 154
ionic, 174
kinetic-molecular theory and, 17
properties of, 153–54
supercritical fluids, 155, 521
vaporization of, 154
Lister, Joseph, 247
Listeria monocytogenes, 523, 697
Listeriosis, 523
Liter (L), 23, A1, A5
Lithium
in batteries, 212
electron configuration of, 76, 78, 79
flame test of, 73
ion of, 97
sources, uses, and production of, 341
Lithium hydroxide, 179
Lithosphere, 332, 333
Liver, 692–93
LLDPE (linear low-density polyethylene), 271
Local anesthetics, 567–68, 689
Locust plagues, 622
Logic, 32
London smog, 358
Lone pairs, 101
Lophophora williamsii, 575
Lopressor®, 564
Lorazepam, 571
Lotions, 663–65
Love, 566
Love Canal, N.Y., chemical dump, 398, 699
Low-density lipoproteins (LDLs), 500–501, 591
Low-density polyethylene (LDPE), 269–71
Low-sodium diet, 93
Lowry, T. M., 180
LSD, 531, 562, 574–75
Lucite, 275
Lucretius, 43
Luffariella variabilis, 531
Luminous intensity, measurement of, 20
Lung cancer, 335, 368, 548, 695, 697, 705
Luteinizing hormone (LH), 554, 555, 558
Lye, 185, 645
Lyrica®, 534
Lysergic acid, 531
Lysergic acid diethylamide (LSD), 531, 562, 574–75

M

m (meter), 20, 22, 23, A1, A5
Maalox®, 194
Mad cow disease, 473
Magnesium
density of, 26
in Earth's crust, 332, 345
electron configuration of, 79
ion of, 97
specific heat of, A15
Magnesium hydroxide, 179
Magnesium ions in water, 390
Magnetic properties of atomic nuclei, 12
Magnetic resonance imaging (MRI), 12, 295
Main group elements in periodic table, 81
Major tranquilizers, 571
Malachite, 663
Malaria, 625–26
Malathion, 623, 626–27
Malignant tumors, 694. *See also* Cancer
Malleable, 83
Malnutrition, 511–12
Malthus, Thomas Robert, 636
Malthusian mathematics, 636–38
Manganese, 619
Manhattan Project, 319–21, 323
Mannose, 457
Mansfield, Peter, 12
Marcaine®, 568
Marijuana, 532, 562, 574, 575–76
Marker, Russell, 558
Mars, 331, 386
Marsden, Ernest, 68
Mass
conversions between common and metric units of, A5–A8
defined, 13
from density and volume, 27
Einstein's equivalence of, to energy, 315, 329
formula, 132–34
law of conservation of, 43–44, 48
mass relationships in chemical equations, 137–39
measurement of, 20, 22, A1
molar, 134–39
and mole relationships in chemical equations, 135–36
molecular, 132–33
percent composition by, 133–34
percent concentrations and, 144–45

Mass–energy equation, 315, 329
Mass number, 71
Mass ratios, 49
Mass-to-charge ratio of electrons, 63
Mass-to-mole conversions, 134–39
Mathematics, Malthusian, 636–38
Matter. *See also* Compounds; Elements; Gases; Liquids; Solids
- ancient Greeks' ideas on, 42–43, 53
- classification of, 16–19
- composition of, 15
- Dalton's atomic theory of, 47–50, 62
- defined, 13
- energy and, 28–30
- energy compared with, 412
- measurement of, 20–25
- states of, 16–17, 152–74, 385–88
- structure of, 15
- as substances and mixtures, 17, 18

Maximum contaminant levels (MCLs), 399
Maxwell, James Clerk, 39
McCarthy, Jenny, 546
MCLs (maximum contaminant levels), 399
MDMA ("Ecstasy"), 574, 575
Measles, 546
Measurement
- estimation in, 23–24
- exponential numbers and, 21–22, A1–A4
- of fitness, 596–97, 599
- IU (international unit) as, 590
- of matter, 20–25
- metric system for, 20–24, A1
- numerical prefixes and, 21–22
- precision and accuracy of, A9
- sampling errors and, A9–A10
- scientific notation and, 21–22
- SI units for, 20, 22–24, 28–29, A1
- significant figures and, A10–A13
- of temperature, 28–29, A14–A15
- unit conversions and, 24, A5–A8

Medicinal chemistry, 118
Medicine. *See also* Drugs; *specific medications*
- antacids, 193–94
- antipyretics (fever reducers), 255
- antiseptics for surgery, 247
- blood extenders, 241
- Botox®, 691–92
- enzymes used in, 474
- gamma-ray imaging in, 311
- gene therapy, 486–87
- homeopathic remedies, 150
- intravenous solutions, 144
- marijuana used in, 576
- mouthwashes and sore-throat remedies, 246
- nuclear medicine, 297, 309–12
- PET (positron emission tomography) in, 295, 311–12
- photoscan of thyroid in, 310–11
- radiation therapy, 310
- radioisotopes in, 295, 309–12, 325
- recombinant DNA for production of materials used by, 484–86
- salts used in, 181
- X-rays and, 65–66, 295, 310

Meitner, Lise, 316
Melanin, 665, 672
Melanocortins, 594
Melanocyte-stimulating hormones (MSHs), 554
Melanoma, 298, 486
Melatonin, 554
Melting point
- of alkanes, 234
- defined, 154
- of solids, 154
- of water, 159

Mendeleev, Dmitri Ivanovich, 51–52
Mental illness, 311, 563–64, 571–72
Meperidine, 538
Mepivacaine, 567, 568
6-mercaptopurine (6-MP), 548
Merck, 467
Mercury (element)
- chemical symbol for, 19
- density of, 26
- as hazardous element, 55, 685–86, 702
- specific heat of, A15
- uses of, 685

Mercury (planet), 13, 331
Mercury poisoning, 685–86
Mescaline, 574, 575
Mesoporous materials, 395
Mesothelioma, 335
Messenger®, 624
Messenger molecules, 560
Messenger RNA (mRNA), 481–82
Mestranol, 556
Metabolic poisons, 684
Metabolism
- of carbohydrates, 496
- defined, 456
- of fats, 498–99, 511
- of glucose, 23
- of proteins, 504–5

Metabolix, Inc., 287
Metal oxides, 184
Metalloids, 83
Metals
- alkali metals, 81–82
- alkaline earth metals, 82
- aluminum, 339–40
- copper and bronze, 338
- defined, 83
- hazardous waste from production of, 699
- high prices of, 344
- iron and steel, 338–40
- recycling of, 343–44
- reduction of, 219
- scarcity of scrap, 338
- technologically important, 340–41

Meter (m), 20, 22, 23, A1, A5
Metformin, 553
Methadone, 538, 539
Methamphetamine, 573, 575
Methandrostenolone, 553
Methane
- asphyxia from breathing pure, 234
- decomposition of, to form hydrogen gas, 49
- greenhouse effect and, 375
- models of, 231
- physical properties, uses, and occurrences of, 234
- as polyatomic molecule, 106
- redox reaction and, 203, 204
- as tetrahedral molecule, 116, 231

Methanol. *See* Methyl alcohol (methanol)
Methemoglobin, 684
Methemoglobinemia (blue baby syndrome), 397, 684
Methionine, 683
Methoprene, 630
Methotrexate, 548–49
Methyl alcohol (methanol)
- models of, 244
- as octane booster in gasoline, 430
- as oxidation catalyst, 220
- production of, 244
- redox reaction and, 204
- toxicity of, 245
- uses of, 244

Methyl chloride, 240
Methyl ethyl ketone peroxide, 112
Methyl group, 241–42
Methyl parathion, 623
Methyl salicylate, 255
Methyl *tert*-butyl ether (MTBE), 397, 430
Methylamine, 256
Methylene chloride, 155, 240, 397
Methylphenidate, 573
Metoprolol, 560, 564
Metric system
- conversions between common units and, A5–A8
- units of length, mass, and volume in, 20–24, A1

mg (milligram), 22, A1
Micas, 335
Micelle, 646
Microfibers, 285
Microgram (μg), 22
Micrometer (μm), 22, 25
Micronutrients, 619
Microporous materials, 395
Microsecond (μs), 23
Microstates, 420
Microwave ovens, 356
Microwaves, 254, 298
Middle note, of perfume, 669
Mifeprex®, 557
Mifepristone, 557
Milk, 8
Milk of magnesia, 194
Milligram (mg), 22, A1
Millikan, Robert A., 64
Milliliter (mL), 23, A1, A5
Millimeter (mm), 22, 23, A1
Millisecond (ms), 23
Mineral oil, 234
Mineral spirits, 234
Mineral water, 404
Minerals, 333, 345, 390
Minerals, dietary, 506–7, 510, 588–89
Mining of coal, 424–25
Minipills, 558
Minor tranquilizers, 571
Minoxidil, 674
Misoprostol, 552
Mitochondria, 455
Mixtures, 17, 18
mL (milliliter), 23, A1, A5
mm (millimeter), 22, 23, A1
MMPD (*para*-methoxy-*meta*-phenylenediamine), 672
MMR vaccination, 546
Mobil, 395
Moderator in nuclear power plant, 435
Moisturizers, 664
Molar mass, 134–36
Molar volume, 167–68
Molarity
- defined, 141
- mass and, in solution concentration, 142
- moles and, in solution concentration, 141–42
- moles from molarity and volume, 143
- solution concentration and, 141–43
- solution preparation and, 142–43

Mold, 368
Molding of polymers, 274–75
Mole
- defined, 20, 131–32
- and mass relationships in chemical equations, 135–36
- molar relationships in chemical equations, 137

Mole-to-mass conversion, 134–39
Molecular formulas of hydrocarbons, 233, 237
Molecular (or covalent) compounds, 101–2
Molecular (or formula) mass, 132–34
Molecular recognition, 118
Molecular substances, 156–57
Molecules
- atoms compared with, 53–54
- defined, 15, 19, 53
- dipole, 116–17
- polar and nonpolar, 116–17
- polyatomic, 105–6
- shapes of, 113–17

Molina, Mario, 371
Molybdenum, 619
Monoacylglycerol, 498
Monoglyceride, 498–99
Monomers, 267, 287
Monosaccharides, 457–58, 495–96
Monosodium glutamate (MSG), 516
Monounsaturated fatty acids/fats, 461–62
Monsanto Corporation, 288
Montreal Protocol, 372
Moon, 13, 331
Morning-after pills, 556–57
Morphine, 531, 537, 539
Moses, 391
Mosquitoes, 31
Motor oil, 158
Motor vehicles. *See* Automobiles
Motrin®, 533
Mousse, 673
Mouthwashes and sore-throat remedies, 246
MRI (magnetic resonance imaging), 12, 295
mRNA, 481–82
ms (millisecond), 23
MSG, 516
MSHs (melanocyte-stimulating hormones), 554
MSWs (municipal solid wastes), 342–43
MTBE (methyl tert-butyl ether), 397, 430
Mucin, 194
Mucoproteins, 542
Müller, Paul, 622, 625
Multifunctional alcohols, 245–46
Multiple proportions, law of, 47, 48, 49
Mumps, 546
Municipal solid wastes (MSWs), 342–43
Murad, Ferid, 112, 560
Muriatic acid, 194
Murphy, Cullen, 39
Muscle relaxants, 531
Muscles
- aerobic exercise and, 600–601
- anaerobic exercise and oxygen debt in, 601–2
- building of, 587, 603
- energy for contraction of, 600
- from exercise, 587, 595
- striated appearance of, 600
- types of fibers in, 602–3

Muscone, 669
Muscovite mica, 334
Mustard gas, 549
Mutations, 309
Mylanta®, 194
Mylar®, 280

N

N-acetylneuraminic acid (NANA), 534
N-type semiconductor, 440–41
Naloxone, 538, 539
Naming
- of acids in biological systems, 601
- of anions, 98
- of binary ionic compounds, 98–100
- of carboxylic acids, 252
- of cations, 98
- of covalent bonds, 101–2

Naming (*continued*)
of hydrocarbons, 232
of ions, 97
of organic molecules, 232
of peptides, 466
NANA (*N*-acetylneuraminic acid), 534
Nano foods, 519
Nano packaging, 519
Nano security devices, 519
Nanogram (ng), 22
Nanometer (nm), 22, 25
Nanoparticle medications, 635
Nanoparticle pesticides, 635
Nanoscale fertilizers, 635
Nanoscale security devices, 635
Nanoscience and nanotechnology
cosmetics and, 666
defined, 25
food production and, 635
foods and, 518
Nanosecond (ns), 23
Nanotubes, 3, 25, 270, 335
Naphazoline, 536
Naphthalene, 239
β-Naphthylamine, 695
Napoleon III, 339
Naproxen, 533
Narcotics, 537–39
Narrow-spectrum insecticides, 627
National Academy of Sciences, 587
National Cancer Institute (NCI), 368, 486
National Institutes of Health, 507, 590
National Research Council, 371
Natular™, 31, 624
Natural gas
air pollution from heaters using, 368
composition of, 426
defined, 426
as energy source, 426
hydraulic fracturing (fracking) for production of, 426, 442
limited supply of, 289, 422
reserves and consumption rates of, 422
Natural philosophy, 3
Natural Resources Defense Council (NRDC), 410
Naturalyte® Insect Control, 624
NatureWorks, 182, 287
Nazi death camps, 684
NCI. *See* National Cancer Institute (NCI)
NE (norepinephrine), 554, 563, 564, 572
Negative ions, 91, 156
Neon, 15, 76, 79
Neoprene, 278
Neotame, 515
Neriin, 682
Nerium oleander, 682
Nerve poisons, 689–90
Nervous system, 562–65, 688–90
Nesacaine, 568
Neurons, 562
Neurotransmitters, 562–64, 570, 572, 688
Neurotrophins, 605
Neutralization, 179, 186–88
Neutrons
characteristics of, 70
defined, 69
isotopes and, 70–71
symbol for, 302
Nevirapine, 546
New System of Chemical Philosophy, A (Dalton), 51
ng (nanogram), 22
Niacin (vitamin B_3)
deficiency of, 507, 508
Dietary Reference Intake (DRI) value for, 589
food sources for, 508
NiCad cells, 212
Nicholl, Whitlock, 62
Nicholson, William, 46, 62, 105
Nickel, 219, 619
Nickel-metal hydride cell, 212
Nicotine. *See also* Cigarette smoking
as addictive drug, 574
as carcinogen, 697
in cigarettes, 574, 665, 697
lethal dose of, 691
in pesticides, 623, 628
Nitrate ions, 615, 684
Nitrates, 397, 398
Nitric acid, 384, 390, 615
Nitric oxide (NO), 112, 193, 203, 366, 560, 563
Nitrites, 516–17
Nitrogen
in Earth's atmosphere, 351, 352–53, 373
electron configuration of, 78, 79
ion of, 97
in water, 390
Nitrogen cycle, 352–53
Nitrogen dioxide, 183, 193, 378
Nitrogen fertilizers, 219, 615–17
Nitrogen fixation, 252
Nitrogen monoxide. *See* Nitric oxide (NO)
Nitrogen oxides, 360, 361, 378–79, 392
Nitrogen trifluoride, 369
Nitrogen-containing compounds
alkaloids, 258–59
amides, 242, 257–58
amines, 242, 256–57
heterocyclic compounds, 258–59
Nitroglycerin, 15, 214, 246, 560, 561, 699
Nitroso compounds, 517
Nitrous oxide, 566, 567
nm (nanometer), 22, 25
NMR (nuclear magnetic resonance), 12
NNRTIs (nonnucleoside reverse transcriptase inhibitors), 546
NO (nitric oxide), 112, 193, 203, 366, 560, 563
Nobel, Alfred, 560
Nobel Prize, 12, 63, 64, 66, 75, 112, 118, 254, 270, 316, 321, 371, 478, 507, 542, 547, 556, 560, 616, 625
Noble gases, 82, 90
Nocebo effect, 578
Nomex, 286
Nonionic surfactants, 651, 654
Nonmetal oxides, 183–84
Nonmetals, 83
Nonnucleoside reverse transcriptase inhibitors (NNRTIs), 546
Nonpolar covalent bonds, 104
Nonpolar molecules, 116–17
Nonsteroidal anti-inflammatory drugs (NSAIDs), 533, 535
Nonstick coating, 273
Noradrenaline, 554
Norepinephrine (NE), 554, 563, 564, 572, 573
Norethindrone, 556
Norethynodrel, 556
Norlutin®, 556
North Korea nuclear power plant, 324
Norvir®, 546
Notes, of perfumes, 668–69
Novocaine®, 568
Novoselov, Konstantin, 270
NPV (nuclear polyhedrosis virus), 629
NRDC. *See* Natural Resources Defense Council (NRDC)
NRTIs (nucleoside reverse transcriptase inhibitors), 546
ns (nanosecond), 23
NSAIDs (nonsteroidal anti-inflammatory drugs), 533, 535
Nuclear accidents, 67, 295, 297, 436–37
Nuclear Age, 324–25
Nuclear bombs
construction of, 320
isotopic enrichment for, 319
Manhattan Project and, 319–21, 323
radioactive fallout from, 320–21
sustainable chain reaction for, 319
synthesis of plutonium for, 319–20
Nuclear chain reaction, 317–19
Nuclear chemistry, 295–330
artificial transmutation in, 307–8
binding energy in, 315
cell phones and, 298
chemical reactions versus nuclear reactions, 302
energy from nucleus and, 315–18
half-life in, 303–4
isotopes in, 305
isotopic signatures and, 307
microwaves and, 298
and natural radioactivity, 296–97, 318
nuclear fission, 315–17, 435, 436
nuclear fusion, 315, 318, 437–38
penetrating power of radiation, 313–14
and radiation damage to cells, 297
and radioisotopic dating, 304–6
thermonuclear reactions, 318
uses of radioisotopes, 308–12
Nuclear energy
advantage of, 435–36
breeder reactors for, 437
disadvantages of, 436–37
nuclear fission and, 435, 436
nuclear fusion and, 437–38
nuclear power plants and, 434–35
nuclear proliferation and, 324
nuclear reactors for, 434, 453
risk-benefit analysis of, 9
uses of, 296, 322–25
Nuclear equations, 298–302, 307–8
Nuclear fission, 315–17, 435, 436
Nuclear fusion, 315, 318, 437–38
Nuclear magnetic resonance (NMR), 12
Nuclear medicine, 297, 309–12
Nuclear model of atom, 68–69
Nuclear polyhedrosis virus (NPV), 629
Nuclear power plants, 322–24, 434–35
Nuclear proliferation, 324
Nuclear reactors, 434, 453
Nuclear waste
burning of, 304
green remediation of, 323
statistics on, 436
tailings, 436
Nucleic acids
components of, 476
constituents of, 259
defined, 476
DNA, 476–80
genetic information and, 267
parts, structure, and function of, 476–80
RNA, 478, 479, 481–82
Nucleon number, 71
Nucleons, 71, 298
Nucleoside analogs, 546
Nucleoside reverse transcriptase inhibitors (NRTIs), 546
Nucleotides, 476–77
Nucleus of atom
atomic number and, 71
defined, 68
density of, 296
energy from, 296, 315–18
isotopes of, 71–72
size of, 296
subatomic particles in, 68–70, 302
Nucleus of cell, 455
Nuclides, 323
Numerical prefixes, 21–22
Nutrition. *See* Fitness and health; Food
Nylon, 279–80, 285, 287

O

Obesity, 495, 515, 553, 585–86, 593–96
Occupational Safety and Health Administration (OSHA), 694
Ocean thermal energy, 447
Octane rating, 429–30
Octet rule, 96–97
Odor. *See* Smell
Oil-drop experiment on electron charge, 64
Oil of cloves, 641
Oil of wintergreen, 255
Oil spills, 386–87
Oils
defined, 461
emulsions and, 500
hydrogenation of vegetable oils, 501
iodine numbers for, 462
salad dressings, 462
water and, 160, 500
Olanzapine, 572
Oleander, 682
Oleandrin, 682
Oleic acid, 501
Omega-3 fatty acids, 501
On the Nature of Things (Lucretius), 43
"On water" reactions, 254
Oncogenes, 695
Opium, 531, 532, 537
Oppenheimer, J. Robert, 320
Optical brighteners, 653
Optical fibers, 337
Orbitals, 77–79
Ores, 338–42
Organic chemistry, 229–65
alcohols, 242, 244–46
aldehydes, 242, 249–50
aliphatic hydrocarbons, 230–37
alkaloids, 258–59
alkanes, 230–37, 242
alkenes, 236–37
alkynes, 236–37, 242
amides, 242, 257–58
amines, 242, 256–57
aromatic compounds, 238–39
benzene, 238–39
carboxylic acids, 242, 251–53
chlorinated hydrocarbons, 239–41
defined, 230
esters, 242, 253, 255
ethers, 242, 247–48
functional groups, 241–43
green chemistry and, 254
heterocyclic compounds, 258–59
inorganic chemistry versus, 229–30
ketones, 242, 249, 250–51
nitrogen-containing compounds, 256–59
phenols, 246–47, 262
salicylates, 255
stems for names of molecules in, 232
Organic farming, 621, 624, 634
Organic fertilizers, 230, 620, 621
Organic food, 230

Organic herbicides, 632–33
Organic pesticides, 628
Organic synthesis, 254
Organophosphorus compounds, 626–27, 689–90
Orlistat, 594
Orotic acid, 528
Orudis®, 533
Oseltamivir, 545
OSHA. *See* Occupational Safety and Health Administration (OSHA)
Osteoporosis, 311
Oxalic acid, 246, 520
Oxidants, 215
Oxidation, 96
Oxidation catalyst, 364
Oxidation-reduction (redox) reactions, 201–28
  balancing equations for, 209–10
  catalysts in, 220
  in cells and batteries, 208–12
  corrosion and, 213–14
  definition of, 202–3
  different views of, 203–6
  in electrochemistry, 208–12
  examples of, 201–2
  explosions and, 213, 214–15
  as gain or loss of electrons, 205–6
  as gain or loss of hydrogen atoms, 204–5, 206
  as gain or loss of oxygen atoms, 203–4, 206
  green chemistry and, 220
  half–reactions in, 209
  living things and, 223
  oxidizing agents in, 206–7, 215–18
  photochromic glass and, 210
  photosynthesis and, 223
  and protection of aluminum, 214
  reducing agents in, 206–7, 218–19, 221–22
  and rusting of iron, 213–14
  and silver tarnish, 214
Oxide minerals, 333
Oxidizing agents, 206–7, 215–18, 683–84
Oxybenzone, 665
Oxycodone, 538, 539
OxyContin®, 539, 574
Oxygen
  in common oxidizing agents, 217–18
  dissolved oxygen (DO), 392
  in Earth's atmosphere, 351, 353, 354, 373
  in Earth's crust, 332–33, 345
  electron configuration of, 79
  ion of, 97
  Lavoisier's naming of and experiments on, 43–44, 46
  liquid, 216, 415
  occurrence and properties of, 215–16
  as oxidizing agent, 215–18
  ozone as form of, 217, 370
  production of, 216
  reactions of, with compounds, 216–17
  reactions of, with other elements, 216
  redox reactions as gain or loss of, 203–4, 206
  in water, 390
Oxygen bleaches, 218, 656
Oxygen cycle, 353, 354
Oxygen debt, 216, 601–2
Oxygenates, 430
Oxymetazoline, 536
Oxytetracycline, 543
Oxytocin, 554, 566
Ozone
  as air pollutant, 362, 370–72, 378–79
  as allotrope as oxygen, 217, 370
  ambient air quality standard for, 378
  chlorofluorocarbons and, 371–72
  defined, 217
  depletion of atmospheric layer of, 241
  for drinking water treatment, 402, 404
  global warming and, 377
  health and environmental effects of, 378–79, 683
  international cooperation on depletion of, 372
  stratospheric ozone shield, 370–71

P

P53 gene, 695
P-450 enzymes, 693
P-type semiconductor, 440–41
PABA (*para*-aminobenzoic acid), 541, 567–68, 665
Paclitaxel, 531, 550
PAHs (polycyclic aromatic hydrocarbons), 695
Pain relievers, 255, 530–33, 535–39
Paints, 278, 281, 661, 699
Palladium, 219, 341
PAN (peroxyacetyl nitrate), 357, 360, 362, 363, 683
Pancreatic hormones, 554
Pancuronim bromide, 567
Pangamic acid, 528
Pantothenic acid (vitamin B_5), 589
Paper production, 396
Paper versus plastic bags, 343
Para-aminobenzoic acid (PABA), 541, 567–68, 665
Para-aminodiphenylaminesulfonic acid, 672
Para-ethoxy-*meta*-phenylenediamine (EMPD), 672–73
Para-methoxy-*meta*-phenylenediamine (MMPD), 672
Para-phenylenediamine, 672
Paracelsus, 680
Paracetamol, 535
ParaGard®, 557
Paraquat, 632
Parathion, 623, 626–27
Paregoric, 537
Parkinson's disease, 690, 692
Paroxetine, 572
Particulate matter (PM), 358, 378
Pathogenic microorganisms, 391–92
Pauling, Linus, 104, 321
PCBs, 240, 288, 474, 625, 701, 702
PCP (phencyclidine), 569, 574
PCR (polymerase chain reaction), 483
PEA (β-phenylethylamine), 566, 573
Pectins, 509
Pedersen, Charles J., 118
Pellagra, 507, 589
Penicillins, 531, 542–43
Penicillium species, 531, 542
Pentazocine, 538
Pentobarbital, 570
Pepcid AC™, 194
Peptide YY (PYY), 594
Peptides and peptide bond, 464, 466, 468
Percent by mass, 144–45
Percent by volume, 143–44
Percent composition by mass, 133–34
Percent concentrations, 143–45
Perchloroethylene, 155
Perfluorocarbons, 241
Perfluorooctanoic acid (PFOA), 397
Perfumes, 155, 250, 253, 521, 668–70
Period, in periodic table, 81
Periodic table
  electron configurations and, 81–83
  group (or family) in, 81–82
  Lewis symbols and, 92
  main group elements in, 81
  Mendeleev's version of, 51–52
  metals and nonmetals in, 83
  modern version of, 52
  new elements in, 324–25
  outer electron configurations and, 81, 82
  period in, 81
  predicting periodical properties from, 53
  transition elements in, 81
Permanent-press fabrics, 285
Permanent waving of hair, 673
Peroxyacetyl nitrate (PAN), 357, 360, 362, 363, 683
Persistent organic pollutants (POPs), 626
Pesticide resistance, 625–26
Pesticides, 622–30
  biological insect controls, 628–29
  biological magnification and, 625–26
  broad-spectrum insecticides, 627
  carbamates, 627
  DDT, 240, 288, 622–23, 625–26, 633
  defined, 622
  green chemistry and, 624
  hazardous wastes from manufacture of, 699
  honeybee deaths and, 627
  juvenile hormones as, 630
  nanoparticle, 635
  narrow-spectrum, 627
  organic, 628
  organophosphorus compounds, 626–27, 689–90
  pesticide resistance and, 625–26
  pheromones as, 629–30
  risks and benefits of, 633
  spinosad, 624
  sterile insect technique (SIT), 629
  toxicity of, 4, 622–23, 625, 633
PET (polyethylene terephthalate), 220, 280, 285, 286, 287, 404
PET (positron emission tomography), 295, 311–12
Petroleum
  defined, 426
  as energy source, 426–28
  fractions and fractional distillation of, 427–28
  limited supply of, 269, 289, 422, 427
  obtaining and refining of, 427–28
  reserves and consumption rates of, 422
  sports and recreational items made from, 607
Petroleum distillates, 233, 234
Petroleum jelly, 234, 664
Peyote cactus, 574, 575
Pfizer Laboratories, 534, 543
PFOA (perfluorooctanoic acid), 397
pg (picogram), 22
PGCCA (Presidential Green Chemistry Challenge Award), 31, 140, 220, 254, 467, 624
pH
  of acid rain, 365
  approximate values of, for common solutions, 189
  of blood, 192, 195
  of buffer solutions, 191–92
  hydrogen ion concentration and, 188, 189–90
  of soil for plants, 177, 195
  of solutions, 188–90
pH-balanced shampoos, 189
pH meter, 189
pH scale, 188–90
Phaeomelanin, 672
Pharmaceuticals. *See* Drugs
PHAs (polyhydroxyalkanoates), 287
Phase diagram, 155
Phencyclidine (PCP), 569, 574
Phenobarbital, 570
Phenol-formaldehyde, 280–81
Phenols, 246–48, 262
Phenothiazines, 571
Phenyl salicylate, 255
Phenylacetaldehyde, 668, 669
Phenylephrine, 536
2-Phenylethanol, 668, 669
β-phenylethylamine (PEA), 566, 573
Pheromones, 629–30, 641
Phlogiston theory, 60
Phocomelia, 698
Phosphates, 652
Phosphorus, 79, 507, 705
Phosphorus fertilizers, 617–18
Photochemical smog, 362–65
Photochromic glass, 210
Photography, 264
Photons, 420
Photosynthesis
  carbohydrates and, 84, 223, 455
  chemical bonds and, 118
  defined, 414
  isotopes and, 88
  light reaction and dark reaction in, 227
  process of, 613–14
  redox reactions in, 223
Photovoltaic cells, 440–41
Phthalate esters, 288
Phthalic acid, 289
Physical activity, 216. *See also* Exercise
Physical change, 14
Physical fitness. *See* Fitness and health
Physical properties, 14, 153
Physostigmine, 628
Phytoremediation, 405
Picogram (pg), 22
Picometer (pm), 22, 25
Picosecond (ps), 23
Pig iron, 339
Pineal hormone, 554
Piomelli, Daniele, 577
Pituitary hormones, 554
PLA (polylactic acid), 182, 282, 287
PLA plastic, 282, 287
Placebo effect, 578
Plan B®, 556–57
Planets, 13, 331–32
Plants. *See also* Agriculture; Photosynthesis
  cells of, 455
  essential oils from, 521
  micronutrients for, 619
  pH of soil for, 177, 195
  poisonous, 682
  primary nutrients for, 615–18
  proteins in, 464
  secondary nutrients for, 619
Plaque, 667
Plasma (nuclear fusion), 438
Plasmid, 484
Plasticizers, 288
Plastics
  advantages of, 285
  biodegradable, 287
  burning of, 273, 286
  defined, 274
  degradable, 286
  environment and, 285–89
  fire hazards of, 286
  free radicals and, 112
  future and, 288–89
  granular polymeric resins for, 274
  green chemistry and, 287

Plastics (*continued*)
 hazardous wastes from manufacture of, 699
 manufacture of, 271
 molding of, 274–75
 versus paper, for bags, 343
 PLA, 182
 pollution by plasticizers used in production of, 288
 recycling of, 269, 286, 287, 343, 404
 resin identification codes for, 287
 as solid waste, 285–86
 uses of, 266
Platinum, 219, 341, 342
Pleated sheet structure, of proteins, 470
Plexiglas, 275
Pliny the Elder, 645
Plunkett, Roy, 273
Plutonium, 319–20, 323–25, 437, 705
Plutonium-239, 437
PM. *See* Particulate matter (PM)
pm (picometer), 22, 25
Poisons, 680–706. *See also* Toxicity
 botox as, 691–92
 carcinogens, 694–97
 defined, 680–81
 fluoroacetic acid as, 684–85
 green chemistry on testing for, 700
 hazardous wastes as, 47, 699, 701–2
 heavy metal, 685–87, 702
 history of, 681, 682
 lethal dose of, 691–92
 metabolic, 684
 natural, 680–82
 nerve, 689–90
 nervous system chemistry and, 688–90
 organophosphorus compounds as, 689–90
 oxidizing agents as, 683–84
 in plants found in garden and home, 682
 risks and benefits of, 702
 strong acids and bases as, 683
 teratogens, 697–98
 zebrafish in testing for, 700
Polar covalent bonds, 102–5
Polar molecules, 116–17
Polio vaccination, 546
Pollutants. *See also* Air pollution; Pollution; Water pollution
 ambient air quality standards for, 378
 concentrations of urban pollutants at different times during sunny day, 363
 defined, 356
 EPA's criteria list of, 378
 persistent organic pollutants (POPs), 626
Pollution. *See also* Air pollution; Pollutants; Water pollution
 enzymes in clean-up of, 474
 of land, 342–44
 from metal production, 340
 plasticizers and, 288
 sulfurous, 357, 362
 thermal, 436
Polyacetylene, 276
Polyacrylonitrile, 275, 285
Polyamides, 279–80
Polyatomic ions, 106–10
Polyatomic molecules, 105–6, 108–10
Polybutadiene, 278
Polycarbonates, 281
Polychlorinated biphenyls (PCBs), 240, 288, 474, 625, 701, 702
Polychloroprene (Neoprene), 278
Polycyclic aromatic hydrocarbons (PAHs), 695
Polyesters, 247, 280, 285
Polyethylene
 formula for, 268–69
 high-density polyethylene (HDPE), 269–71, 286, 287
 linear low-density polyethylene (LLDPE), 271
 low-density polyethylene (LDPE), 269–71
 models of, 269
 types of, 269–71
 ultra-high-molecular-weight polyethylene (UHMWPE), 271
 uses of, 269, 275, 287
Polyethylene terephthalate (PET), 220, 280, 285, 286, 287, 404
Polyhydroxy alcohols, 516
Polyhydroxyalkanoates (PHAs), 287
Polylactic acid (PLA), 182, 282, 287
Polymerase chain reaction (PCR), 483
Polymerization
 addition polymerization, 272–76
 condensation polymerization, 279
 defined, 267
Polymers, 266–94
 amorphous, 284
 biodegradable, 287
 celluloid, 267
 condensation, 279–83
 condensed structural formulas of, 283
 conducting, 276
 copolymers, 271
 crystalline, 284
 defined, 267
 fiber formation and, 285
 formation of, 237
 glass transition temperature and, 284–85
 greener, 287
 natural, 267
 nylon and other polyamides, 279–80
 in paints, 278
 polyethylene, 268–71
 polyethylene terephthalate and other polyesters, 280, 285
 polypropylene, 272
 polystyrene, 272–73
 processing of, 274–75
 properties of, 284–85
 proteins as, 267, 463–66, 468
 PTFE as, 241, 273
 recycling of, 269, 286, 287
 repeat units in, 268, 274
 rubber and other elastomers, 276–78
 structure of, 274
 synthetic, 289
 thermoplastic, 271
 thermosetting, 271
 uses of, 266, 275, 288–89
 vinyl, 273
Polymethyl methacrylate, 275
Polyols, 516
Polypeptide, 466
Polypropylene, 272, 275
Polysaccharides, 458–60
Polystyrene, 272–73, 275
Polytetrafluoroethylene (PTFE), 241, 273, 275
Polyunsaturated fatty acids/fats, 461–62
Polyurethanes, 281
Polyvinyl acetate, 275
Polyvinyl chloride (PVC), 240, 273, 275, 286, 288, 289, 632
Polyvinylidene chloride, 275
POPs (persistent organic pollutants), 626
Population growth, 332, 344, 636–38
Positive hole, 440
Positive particles, 64
Positron, 300, 302
Positron emission, 300, 301
Positron emission tomography (PET), 295, 311–12
Potable water, 389, 399–403
Potassium
 chemical symbol for, 19
 in Earth's crust, 332
 electron configuration of, 79
 flame test of, 73
 ion of, 97
Potassium bicarbonate, 641
Potassium carbonate, 645
Potassium chloride, 618
Potassium dichromate, 218
Potassium hydroxide, 179, 185, 645
Potassium iodide, 513
Potassium ions, in water, 390
Potassium nitrate, 187
Potential energy, 413–14
Power
 defined, 412
 energy conversion and, 413
Powers of ten, 21–22
Precision, of measurements, A9
Prednisone, 533, 553
Preemergent herbicide, 632
Prefixes
 for covalent compounds, 101
 numerical, 21–22
Pregabalin, 534
Prescription drugs. *See* Drugs
Presidential Green Chemistry Challenge Award (PGCCA), 31, 140, 220, 254, 467, 624
Pressure
 Boyle's law on relationship with volume, 162–64
 standard temperature and pressure (STP), 167
Previn®, 556
Priestley, Joseph, 37, 43, 149, 566
Prilocaine, 567, 568
Prilosec, 194
Primary sewage treatment, 404–5
Primary structure, of proteins, 469–70
Prions, 473
Procaine, 567, 568
Products, in chemical equations, 126
Progesterone, 554–58
Progestin, 556, 558–59
Prolactin, 554
Promazine, 571, 572
Propane
 alkyl groups derived from, 242, 243
 as fuel, 233
 model of, 231
 physical properties, uses, and occurrences of, 234
 structural formula of, 231
Propane torch, 231
β-Propiolactone, 696
Propionaldehyde (propanal), 250
Propionic acid, 252
Propranolol, 560, 564
Propylene glycol, 245–46
Propylene oxide, 220
Prostaglandins, 533, 535, 551–52
Prostate cancer, 548, 591
Protease inhibitors, 546
Proteases, 474, 654
Protein deficiency, 505
Protein hydrolysis experiment, 475
Proteins
 adequate (or complete), 505
 deficiency of, 505
 defined, 466
 in diet, 504–5
 enzymes as, 472–75
 globular, 471
 helix structure of, 470
 linking of chains of, 472
 metabolism of, 504–5
 peptide bonds in, 464, 466
 pleated sheet structure of, 470
 as polymers of amino acids, 257, 267, 293, 463–68
 RNA and synthesis of, 481–82
 sequence of amino acids in, 468
 structure and function of, 464, 469–75
 synthesis of, in ribosomes, 455
Protium, 70
Protons
 atomic number and, 70
 in Brønsted-Lowry acid–base theory, 180–81
 characteristics of, 70
 defined, 69
 hydrogen ion as, 178
 symbol for, 302
Proust, Joseph Louis, 45, 47
ps (picosecond), 23
Psilocybe cubensis, 575
Psilocybin mushrooms, 574, 575
Psoralens, 520
Psychotropic drugs, 561, 569–76
PTFE (polytetrafluoroethylene), 241, 273, 275
Purcell, Edward M., 12
Purex®, 218, 656
Purines, 12, 259, 476
PVC, 273, 275, 286, 288, 289, 632
Pyrethrins, 623, 628
Pyridoxine (vitamin B_6)
 deficiency of, 508
 Dietary Reference Intake (DRI) value for, 589
 food sources for, 508
 functions of, 590
Pyrimidines, 259, 476
Pyrite, 384
Pyrogens, 533
PYY (peptide YY), 594

Q

Quantum, 74
Quantum mechanics, 77
Quantum model of electron arrangement, 77–80
Quartz, 334, 335
Quaternary ammonium salts (quats), 651
Quaternary structure of proteins, 469, 471
Quats, 651
Quicksilver, 685
Quinine, 531

R

Rabi, Isidor Isaac, 12
Radiant®, 624
Radiation. *See also* Radioactivity
 alpha decay and, 298–99, 301
 background, 10, 296–97
 beta decay and, 299, 301
 damage to cells from, 297
 electromagnetic, 298
 electron capture (EC) and, 300, 301
 gamma decay and, 299, 301
 hydroxyl radicals in body from, 112
 infrared radiation (IR), 375
 ionizing, 297, 298, 310
 medical uses of, 309–12
 microwaves as, 254
 penetrating power of, 313–14
 positron emission and, 300, 301
 protection from, 313–14
 smoke detectors and, 314

Radiation sickness, 312, 436–37
Radiation therapy, 310–11
Radioactive fallout, 320–21
Radioactive waste, 323
Radioactivity
  alpha particle and, 66–67
  beta particle and, 66–67
  defined, 66
  discovery of, 66
  gamma rays and, 66–67, 302, 309, 313
  types of, 66–67
Radioisotopes
  half-life of, 303–4
  and harm to human body, 310
  in industry and agriculture, 308–9
  in medicine, 295, 309–12, 325
  as tracers, 308–9, 325
  use of, in radioactive dating, 306
Radioisotopic dating, 304–6
Radon, 10, 297, 298–99, 368, 390
Rainbow of colors, 73–74
Rainwater. *See* Acid rain; Water
Ralston-Purina, 701
Rare earths, 340, 341, 342
RDAs (Recommended Dietary Allowances), 587
Reactants, defined, 126
Reactive waste, 699
Reagent grade concentrated hydrochloric acid, 144
Rebound effect, 536
Recombinant vaccines, 486
Recommended Dietary Allowances (RDAs), 587
Recreation. *See* Exercise; Fitness and health
Recycling
  of aluminum and iron, 54, 340
  of automobiles, 340
  of metals, 343–44
  paper production and, 396
  of plastic bags, 343
  of plastic bottles, 404
  of plastics, 269, 286, 287, 343, 404
  of scarce elements, 55
Redox reactions. *See* Oxidation-reduction (redox) reactions
Reducing agents, 206–7, 218–19, 221–22
Reduction, 96. *See also* Oxidation-reduction (redox) reactions
Reduction catalyst, 364
Reforming process, 444
Relativity, special theory of, 315
Renewable energy sources
  biomass as, 441, 443
  fuel cells as, 443, 445
  geothermal energy as, 446, 447
  hydrogen as, 443
  ocean thermal energy as, 447
  solar cells as, 440–41
  solar energy as, 84, 411, 439–42
  waterpower as, 421, 445, 446
  wind as, 411, 421, 431, 441, 445, 446
Repeat units, in polymers, 268, 274
Replicability, 5, 32
Replication, of DNA molecules, 479
Rescriptor®, 546
Research. *See* Scientific research
Resin identification codes, 287
Resins, 280–81, 673
Respiratory illnesses, 370, 379, 541, 606
Restorative drugs, 604
Restriction sites, 484
Retrovir®, 546
Retroviruses, 544, 546
Reverse osmosis, 405
Reverse transcriptase, 544
Riboflavin (vitamin B_2), 508, 589
Ribonucleic acid (RNA), 478, 479, 481–482, 507
Ribose, 457
Ribosomes, 455
Ricin, 691
Rilpivirine, 546
Ring-containing hydrocarbons, 235
Risk-benefit analysis, 8–10, 31
Risks
  of birth control pills, 557
  of cancer from different causes, 694
  of death from different causes, 10, 697
  defined, 8
  of nuclear energy production, 9
  of pesticides, 633
  of poisons, 702
  reduction of, by green chemistry, 31
Risperdal®, 571
Risperidone, 571, 572
Ritalin®, 573
Ritonavir, 546
RNA, 478, 479, 481–82, 507
RNA viruses, 544–45
Rock phosphate, 618
Roentgen, Wilhelm Conrad, 65–66
Rofecoxib, 535
Rogaine®, 674
Rohypnol®, 575
Rolaids®, 194
Roosevelt, Franklin D., 319
Rosenberg, Barnett, 549
Rotenone, 628, 691
Roundup®, 631, 632
Rowland, F. Sherwood, 371
RU-486, 557
Rubber
  manufacture of, 271
  natural, 276–77
  synthetic, 278
  vulcanization of, 277
Rubbing alcohol, 143, 245
Rubella, 546
Rule of 72, 636
Rushton, W.A.H., 38
Rusting, of iron, 96, 194, 213–14
Rutherford, Ernest, 66–69, 73, 307, 308
Ryania, 628
Ryania speciosa, 628
Ryanodine, 628

S

s (second), 20, 23
Sabin, Albert, 546
Saccharin, 515
Safe Drinking Water Act, 399
Safety alerts. *See also* Poisons; Toxicity
  on acids and bases, 176, 195
  on alcohols, 245
  on asbestos, 335
  on carbon monoxide, 48, 136, 286, 360, 361, 379
  on chlorinated hydrocarbons, 240
  on hazards of mixing cleaners, 657
  on hydrocarbons, 234
  on hydrogen peroxide, 217
  on laboratory chemicals, 176
Salicylates, 255
Salicylic acid, 255
Salk, Jonas, 546
Salmonella contamination, 523, 696, 697
Salol, 255
Salt bridges, 472
Salt lamp, 156
Saltpeter, 187
Salts. *See also* Sodium chloride; *specific compounds*
  defined, 179, 181, 187
  medical uses of, 181
  soap as, 182
  uses of, 181
Sampling errors, A9–A10
Sanitary landfills, 342–43
Saquinavir, 545, 546
Saran®, 275
Sarin, 690, 691
Sasol company, 433
Saturated fatty acids/fats, 237, 461–62
Saturated hydrocarbons, 231–37. *See also* Alkanes
Saturated versus unsaturated fats, 237
Saturn, 331
SBR (styrene-butadiene rubber), 278
SBS (styrene-butadiene-styrene), 278
Scanning tunneling microscope (STM), 53, 61
Scarce elements, 55
Sceptical Chymist, The (Boyle), 44
Scheele, Carl Wilhelm, 43
Schistocerca gregaria, 622
Schizophrenia, 311, 571, 572
School chemistry labs, 701
Schrödinger, Erwin, 77, 78
SCID (severe combined immunodeficiency disease), 486
Science. *See also* Chemistry; Scientific research
  characteristics of, 5–7
  correlation versus causality in, 7
  critical thinking and, 32–33
  deduction in, 90–91
  defined, 2
  limitations of, 7
  natural philosophy and, 3
  process diagram of, 6
  risk–benefit analysis in, 8–10
  serendipity in, 65–66
Scientific laws, 5–6
Scientific models, 6–7
Scientific notation, 21–22, A1–A4
Scientific research
  applied, 11–12
  basic, 12
  green chemistry and, 31
  need for further, 5
Scientific theories. *See* Theories
Scurvy, 507, 589, 590
Seaborg, Glenn T., 319, 320
Searle, G. D., 556
Sebum, 663
Second law of thermodynamics, 419–20
Second (s), 20, 23
Secondary plant nutrients, 619
Secondary sewage treatment, 405
Secondary structure, of proteins, 469, 470–71
Segrè, Emilio, 316
Selective serotonin–reuptake inhibitors (SSRIs), 572
Semimetals, 83
Semisynthetic drugs, 531
Septic tanks, 406
Sequestration, 652
Serenade®, 624
Serendipity, 65–66
Serotonin, 563, 564, 565, 572, 573, 622
Sertraline®, 254, 572
Sertürner, Friedrich, 531, 537
Severe combined immunodeficiency disease (SCID), 486
Sevin®, 623, 627
Sevoflurane, 567
Sewage and sewage treatment, 392–94, 404–6
Sex attractants, 629–30, 669
Sex hormones, 555–59, 604
Sexuality fidelity, 566
Shampoo, 189, 670–71
Shapes of molecules, 113–17
Sharpless, K. B., 254
Sheldon, Roger, 534
Shelley, Percy Bysshe, 537
Shells, 75–76
Short tandem repeats (STRs), 484
Shroud of Turin, 306, 325
SI units, 20, 22–24, 28–29, A1
SIDS (sudden infant death syndrome), 368
SIF (somatostatin release inhibiting factor), 554
Significant figures
  addition and subtraction and, A12–A13
  defined, 24, A10
  multiplication and division and, A11–A12
Sildenafil, 560
Silent Spring (Carson), 4, 625
Silicates, 333, 334–37
Silicon
  chain formation by, 230
  in Earth's crust, 332–33, 345
  electron configuration of, 79
  silicone versus, 282
Silicon crystals, 440–41
Silicones, 281–83
Silk fabrics, 285
Silly Putty, 282
Silver
  chemical properties of, 15
  chemical symbol for, 19
  ion of, 97
  mining of, 342
  specific heat of, 387
  tarnishing of, 214
Single bonds, 101
SIT (sterile insect technique), 629
Skin, 663, 664, 665, 672
Skin cancer, 298, 371
Skin creams and lotions, 234, 246, 663–65
Skin protection factor (SPF), 666
Slag, 339
Slaked lime, 184, 195, 402, 621
Slow-twitch muscle fibers, 602–3
Smallpox vaccination, 546
Smell
  aromatherapy and, 670
  body odor and, 252
  of dead animals, 257
  fragrances and, 155, 250, 253, 521, 668–71
  of fresh versus rotting fruit, 253
  of perfumes, 250, 253, 668–70
  of shampoos, 671
Smog
  automobile emissions and, 361–62
  industrial, 356–60
  London, 358
  photochemical, 362–65
  sulfurous, 357, 362
Smog testing of vehicles, 378
Smoke detectors, 314
Smoking. *See* Cigarette smoking
Soap
  benefit of homemade, 646
  cleaning action of, 646, 647
  disadvantage and advantages of, 646–47
  history of, 644–45
  production of, 246, 645–46
  as salt, 182
  in shampoos, 671
  structure of, 645
  water softeners and, 647–48
Socrates, 681

Sodium
chemical symbol for, 19
dietary limits for intake of, 93, 133
in Earth's crust, 332, 345
electron configuration of, 76, 79
flame test of, 73
ion of, 97
line spectrum of, 74
reaction of chlorine and, 92–94
Sodium bicarbonate, 193–94
Sodium carbonate, 652
Sodium chloride
as dietary mineral, 507
as flavor enhancer, 516
lethal dose of, 691
in salt lamp, 156
source of, 331
as table salt, 181, 187
Sodium cyanide, 684, 691
Sodium dodecyl sulfate, 651
Sodium fluoroacetate, 685
Sodium hydroxide, 179, 185, 645
Sodium hypochlorite, 218, 656
Sodium ions in water, 390
Sodium nitrate, 615
Sodium nitrite, 516
Sodium palmitate, 646
Sodium perborate, 218
Sodium percarbonate, 218
Sodium saccharin, 515
Soft water, 390
Solar cells, 440–41
Solar energy, 84, 411, 439–42
Solar heating, 439–40
Solid wastes, 342–44, 349. *See also* Hazardous wastes
Solids
change from gas to, 154
change of liquids to, 154
change to gas from, 154
change to liquid from, 154
defined, 16
kinetic–molecular theory and, 17
melting point of, 154
properties of, 153–54
sublimation of, 154
Solomon, Susan, 371
Soluble versus insoluble, 141
Solutes, 141, 159, 160
Solutions
aqueous, 141
buffer, 191–92
concentrated, 141
concentrations of, 141
defined, 141, 159
dilute, 141
forces in, 159–61
molarity of, 141–43
of nonpolar solutes in nonpolar solvents, 160
percent by mass and, 144–45
percent by volume and, 143–44
percent concentrations of, 143–45
pH of, 188–90
Solvent sniffing, 567
Solvents
defined, 141, 159
designation of, in chemical formulas, 178
green, 254, 521
as household chemicals, 661
hydrocarbons as, 363
ketones as, 250
nonpolar, 160
supercritical fluids as, 155, 521
toxic, 155, 254
water as, 155, 160–61
Soman, 690
Somatostatin, 554
Somatostatin release inhibiting factor (SIF), 554
Somatotropin, 554
Sorbitol, 516
Sørensen, S. P. L., 188
Specific heat, 387, A15
Spermaceti wax, 662
SPF (skin protection factor), 666
Spin, of atomic nuclei, 12
Spinosad pesticides, 624
Splenda®, 515
Spodumene, 334
Spontaneous process, 419–20
SSRIs (selective serotonin–reuptake inhibitors), 572
Stain removal, 218
Standard temperature and pressure (STP), 167
Staph infections, 543
Staphylococcus aureus, 542
Starch, 458–60, 496–97
Starvation, 511, 637
States of matter, 16–17, 152–74, 385–88. *See also* Gases; Liquids; Solids
Statins, 531, 587, 693
Stavudine, 546
Stearic acid, 501, 502
Steel and steelmaking, 338–40, 345
Stereoisomers, 534, 565
Sterile insect technique (SIT), 629
Stern, Otto, 12
Steroids, 553, 555, 604
Stevia, 515
Steviol, 515
Stimulant drugs, 561, 573, 604
STM (scanning tunneling microscope), 53, 61
Stoichiometric factor, 137
Stoichiometry, 137, 374
Stone, Edward, 255
STP (standard temperature and pressure), 167
Straight-run gasoline, 429
Stratosphere, 351
Streptomyces species, 531, 543, 550
Strip mining, 425
Stroke
arteriosclerosis and, 499
birth control pills and, 557
cholesterol and, 500
cigarette smoking and, 605
deaths from, 495, 541, 605
drugs for, 485, 533, 535, 552
healthy diet for prevention of, 587
hypertension and, 507
Strong acids, 178, 185
Strong bases, 179, 185
Strontium, 73, 74
Strontium-90, 321
STRs (short tandem repeats), 484
Structural formulas. *See also* Condensed structural formulas
of alkyl groups, 243
of amine isomers, 256–57
of cyclic hydrocarbons, 235
defined, 231
of oxygen-containing organic compounds, 252–53
Structure of matter, 15
Strychnine, 681
Strychnos species, 681
Styrene-butadiene rubber (SBR), 278, 287
Styrene-butadiene-styrene (SBS), 278
Styrofoam, 273
Sublimation, 154
Subshells (sublevels), 78, 80
Substance Abuse and Mental Health Services Administration, 578
Substances, defined, 17
Substituent, 239
Substrate, 473
Sucralose, 515
Sucrose, 458, 496, 515, 691
Sudden infant death syndrome (SIDS), 368
Sufficiency, 32
Sugars
blood sugar, 495
diabetes and, 552
in diet, 495–96
disaccharides, 458
monosaccharides, 457–58, 495–96
in nucleic acids, 476–77
per capita consumption of, 496
relative sweetness of, 515
simple, 457–58, 495–96
Suhr, Jennifer Stuczynski, 607
Sulfa drugs, 540–42
Sulfaguanidine, 542
Sulfanilamide, 541–42
Sulfate ions in water, 390
Sulfathiazole, 542
Sulfide minerals, 333
Sulfite salts, 517
Sulfur
chemical properties of, 14–15
electron configuration of, 79
ion of, 97
specific heat of, 387, A15
Sulfur dioxide, 183, 193, 366, 378–79, 517
Sulfur oxides, 379, 392
Sulfuric acid, 178, 183, 185, 195, 199, 359, 366, 425, 683
Sulfurous pollution, 357, 362
Sun
energy of, 411–14, 614
radiation from, 296, 373
as renewal energy source, 439–41
thermonuclear reactions of, 318, 437
wrinkling of skin from exposure to, 665
Sunette®, 515
Sunscreens, 665–66
Super-glues, 293
Superconducting ceramics, 336
Supercritical fluids, 155, 521
Superfund Act, 430
Superfund sites, 410
Suppressor genes, 695
Surface-active agent, 646
Surfactants, 646, 651–52
Surgeon General of the United States, 367
Surroundings, 416
Sustainability, 182. *See also* Green chemistry
Sustainable agriculture, 634–35
Sustainable chain reaction, 319
Sustainable chemistry, 4
Sweating, 591, 667
Sweeteners, artificial, 8, 515–16
Symclosene, 656
Synapses, 562
Synergistic effects, 335, 359, 570
Synthetic detergents, 649–54
Synthetic polymers, 289
System, 416
Szilard, Leo, 317–18, 320

T

2,4,5-T (2,4,5-trichlorophenoxyacetic acid), 631–32
T cells, 544
Table salt. *See* Sodium chloride
Tabun, 690
Tagamet HB™, 194
Tailings, 436
Talwin®, 538
Tamiflu®, 545
TAML®, catalysts, 220
Tannins, 391
Tantalum, 341
Tartar, 667
Taxol®, 531, 550
Technology. *See also* Industry; Nanoscience and nanotechnology
applied research and, 11–12
in chemical industry, 10, 31
defined, 2
green chemistry and, 31
metals used in, 340–41
risk-benefit analysis in, 8–10
Teeth
dental caries, 402–3, 496, 516, 667–68
pain in, from biting on aluminum foil, 209
Teflon®, 273, 275
Temik®, 627
Temperature
absolute zero, 164
Charles's law on relationship with volume, 164–67
chemical reactions and, 415
conversions of, 29
defined, 28
extremes of heat and cold, 164
glass transition temperature and polymers, 284–85
and global warming, 375–77
measurement of, 20, 28–29, 164–165, A14–A15
normal body, 30
and specific heat, 387, A15
standard temperature and pressure (STP), 167
Temperature inversion, 353–54
Template strand, 481
Tenofovir, 546
10W40 motor oil, 158
Teratogens, 9, 516, 606, 697–98
Terramycin®, 543
Terrorist attacks, 10
Tert-butyl alcohol, 430
Tertiary sewage treatment, 405
Tertiary structure, of proteins, 469, 471
Testosterone, 554, 555, 558, 604
Tetanus toxin, 691
Tetracyclines, 543
Tetraethyllead, 378, 430
Tetrahydrocannabinol (THC), 576
Textiles, 699
Thales, 386
Thalidomide, 9, 697–98
THC (tetrahydrocannabinol), 576
Theories, 2, 6. *See also specific theories*
Thermal inversion, 353–54
Thermal pollution, 436
Thermochemistry, 416–18
Thermodynamics, laws of, 418–21
Thermonuclear reactions, 318, 437
Thermoplastic polymers, 271
Thermosetting polymers, 271
Thermosetting resins, 281
Thermosphere, 351
Thiamine (vitamin B_1), 508, 589
Thioglycolic acid, 673
Thiopental, 567, 570
Thomson, Joseph John, 63
Thomson, William, Lord Kelvin, 165
Thorazine®, 571
Thorium-232, 437
Three Mile Island nuclear disaster, 295, 436
Thujone, 705
Thyroid cancer, 310–11, 436
Thyroid hormone, 554
Thyroid-stimulating hormone (TSH), 554
Thyrotropin-releasing factor (TRF), 554
Thyroxine, 554
Time, measurement of, 20, 23
Tin, 19, 342

Tincture of iodine, 217
Tissue plasminogen activator (TPA), 485
Titanium dioxide, 661, 665
TNT, 214, 699
Tobacco. *See* Cigarette smoking; Nicotine
Tocopherols, 590
Tofranil®, 572
Tokamak, 438
Toluene, 239, 397
Toothpaste, 667–68
Top note, of perfume, 669
Total fasting, 594–95, 596
Toxic waste, 701
Toxicity. *See also* Poisons; Safety alerts
  of alcohols, 245, 246
  of DDT, 623, 625–26, 633
  of laboratory chemicals, 176
  of lead, 379
  of pesticides, 4, 622–23, 625, 633
  of solvents, 155, 254
  variables regarding, 244
  zebrafish in testing for, 700
Toxicology, 681, 700
Toxin, 681. *See also* Poisons; Toxicity
TPA (tissue plasminogen activator), 485
Tracer®, 624
Tracers, 308–9, 325
Tranquilizers, 567, 571
Trans fatty acids, 502, 587
Transcription, 481
Transfer molding, 274
Transfer RNA (tRNA), 481–82
Transition elements, in periodic table, 81
Translation, 481
Transmutation, 307–8
Transportation Department, 598
Transporters, 562
Trash. *See* Garbage
TRF (thyrotropin-releasing factor), 554
Trichinella spiralis, 523
Trichinosis, 523
Trichlor, 656
2,4,5-Trichlorophenoxyacetic acid (2,4,5-T), 631–32
Trichloroethylene, 398
Trichloroisocyanuric acid, 656
Trichogramma wasps, 628
Triglycerides, 182, 461, 489–99
Trimethylamine, 256
Trinitrotoluene (TNT), 214, 699
Tripeptide, 466
Triple bonds, 101
Tritium, 70, 299
tRNA, 481–82
Troposphere, 351
Trost, Barry, 140
Truman, Harry, 319, 320
Trust, 566
Tryptophan, 564, 683
TSH (thyroid-stimulating hormone), 554
Tuberculosis, 543
Tubocurarine, 531
Tumors, 694
Tums®, 194
Tylenol®, 535, 537
Typhoid, 392
Tyrosine, 564

U

Ubiquinones, 526
UHMWPE (ultra-high-molecular-weight polyethylene), 271
Ulcers, 194
Ultra-high-molecular-weight polyethylene (UHMWPE), 271
Ultratrace elements, 506
Ultraviolet (UV) light
  as carcinogen, 298, 371
  stratospheric ozone shield as protection from, 370–71, 377
  sunscreens for protection from, 665
  for water treatment, 402
Unbuilt, 653
Underground storage tanks (USTs), 398
UNICEF, 401
Unit conversion method, A6
Unit conversions, 24, A5–A8
United Nations, 372, 375–76, 637, 638
Units. *See specific units*
Unsaturated fatty acids/fats, 237, 461–62, 501–2
Unsaturated hydrocarbons, 236–37
Uranium, 319–24, 437
Uranium-235 isotope, 437, 452
Urea, 230, 257, 281, 617, 620
Urine, density of, 26
USDA. *See* Agriculture Department (USDA)
USTs (underground storage tanks), 398
UV light. *See* Ultraviolet (UV) light

V

Vaccination, 546
Valence electrons, 81, 82, 90
Valence-shell electron configurations, 82–83
Valence shell electron pair repulsion (VSEPR) theory, 113–15
Valium®, 567, 571
Vaporization, 154, 420
Variables, 7
Vaseline®, 234, 664
Vasopressin, 554, 566, 591
Vegan diet, 504
Vegetarian diets, 504
Vehicles. *See* Automobiles
Venus, 13, 331
Vermiculite, 621
Versed®, 567
Very-low-density lipoproteins (VLDLs), 500
Viagra®, 112, 560
Videx®, 545, 546
Vietnam War, 632
Vinblastine, 531
Vincristine, 531
Vinegar, 252, 462, 657
Vinyl chloride, 240, 273, 286, 695, 697
Vinyl polymers, 273
Vioxx®, 535
Viramune®, 546
Virent Energy Systems, 467
Viruses, 544–47
Vitalism, 265
Vitamin A
  as anticarcinogen, 696
  deficiency of, 508, 591
  Dietary Reference Intake (DRI) value for, 589
  as fat-soluble vitamin, 508–9
  food sources for, 508, 589
  functions of, 589–90
Vitamin B family, 508–9, 589, 590
Vitamin C (ascorbic acid)
  as acid, 185, 227
  as anticarcinogen, 696
  chemical structure of, 509
  deficiency of, 507, 508, 589, 590
  Dietary Reference Intake (DRI) value for, 589, 590
  food sources of, 508
  functions of, 227, 590
  as water-soluble vitamin, 508–9
Vitamin D
  chemical structure of, 508
  deficiency of, 507, 508
  Dietary Reference Intake (DRI) value for, 589, 590
  as fat-soluble vitamin, 508–9
  food sources for, 508
  functions of, 590
Vitamin E
  as anticarcinogen, 696
  deficiency of, 508, 591
  Dietary Reference Intake (DRI) value for, 589, 591
  as fat-soluble vitamin, 508–9
  food sources for, 508
  functions of, 590–91
Vitamin K, 508
Vitamins. *See also specific vitamins*
  acid nature of Vitamin C, 185, 227
  as anticarcinogens, 696
  deficiencies of, 507–8, 588–90
  defined, 507, 588
  descriptions and functions of, 589–91
  Dietary Reference Intake (DRI) values for, 588–89
  as dietary supplements, 510, 588
  fat-soluble, 508–9
  as food additives, 514
  food sources of, 508, 511, 518, 589–90
  IU (international unit) for measurement of, 590
  large doses of, 589
  loss of, in processed foods, 511
  water-soluble, 508–9
Vitrification, 330
VLDLs (very-low-density lipoproteins), 500
V_{O_2} max, 599
Volatile organic compounds (VOCs)
  air pollution from, 360, 361–62, 369
  in household chemicals, 658
  water pollution from, 397–98
Volta, Alessandro, 46, 62
Volume
  Avogadro's hypothesis on, 130, 131, 167
  Boyle's law on relationship with pressure, 162–64
  Charles's law on relationship with temperature, 164–67
  in chemical equations, 129–31
  conversions between common and metric units of, A5–A8
  of gases, 129–31
  law of combining, 129–30
  from mass and density, 27
  measurement of, 23, A1
  molar, 167–68
  percent concentrations and, 143–44
VSEPR (valence shell electron pair repulsion) theory, 113–15
Vulcanization, 277

W

W (watt), 412
Wakefield, Andrew, 546
Warfare. *See* Chemical warfare; *specific wars*
Warhol (unit of fame), 39
Washington University, Center for the Biology of Natural Systems, 634
Wastewater treatment, 404–5
Water, 385–410. *See also* Drinking water; Water pollution
  acidification of, 376
  alkaline (basic), 176, 391
  amphiprotic nature of, 186
  as bent molecule, 116–17
  boiling point of, 159
  Clean Water Act and, 406
  from comets, 389
  density of, 26, 234, 386–87
  dissolved minerals in, 390
  electrolysis of, 46
  evaporation of, 6
  gases in, 389–90
  green chemistry and, 395
  hard, 390, 646–48
  heat of vaporization of, 387
  heavy, 71
  in human body, 215, 385
  hydrogen bonds and, 159
  melting point of, 159
  molecule of, 19, 387–88
  in Moses story, 391
  natural contaminants of, 389–91
  in nature, 388–91
  oil and, 160, 500
  organic matter in, 390
  as polyatomic molecule, 105–6
  potable, 389, 399–403
  radon in groundwater, 390
  salt dissolving in, 160–61
  sea rise experiment and, 376
  soft, 390
  as solvent, 155, 160–61, 385, 389
  source of Earth's, 389
  specific heat of, 387, A15
  states of, 152, 385–88
  as substance, 17, 18
  supercritical, 155
  unique properties of, 386–88
  uses of and quantities used, 394, 396
  vaporization of, 420
Water cycle, 389–91
Water pollution
  acid waters, 392
  chemical and biological contamination and, 391–94
  in China, 397
  Clean Water Act for, 406
  filter to remove, 386
  future and, 406
  green chemistry and, 395
  groundwater contamination and, 397–98
  from leaking underground storage tanks, 398
  natural contaminants and, 389–91
  from nitrates, 397, 398
  oil spills and, 386–87
  from sewage, 392–94
  solubility principles and, 161
  substances formed in water by breakdown of organic matter, 393
  TAML® catalysts for treatment of, 220
  from volatile organic compounds (VOCs), 397–98
  and waterborne diseases, 391–92, 406
Water softeners, 647–48
Water-soluble vitamins, 508–9
Water vapor, 384
Waterborne diseases, 391–92, 406
Waterpower, 421, 445, 446
Watson, James D., 478, 479
Watt (W), 412
Waxes, 661–62
Weak acids, 178, 185
Weak bases, 179, 185–86
Weapons of mass destruction (WMDs), 550
Weather, climate change and, 376
Weed-B-Gon®, 631

Weight, defined, 13
Weight loss, 593–96, 612. *See also* Dieting; Obesity
Weighting, 48
West Bengal, India, 401
Wet scrubber, 359–60
Whewell, William, 62
WHO. *See* World Health Organization (WHO)
Whooping cough, 546
Wilkins, Maurice, 478
Wind energy, 411, 421, 431, 441, 445, 446
Wind turbines, 411, 446
WMDs (weapons of mass destruction), 550
Wöhler, Friedrich, 230
Woo-suk, Hwang, 32
Wood alcohol. *See* Methyl alcohol (methanol)
Wood smoke, 367
World Bank, 401
World Factbook, 637
World Health Organization (WHO), 298, 350, 357, 370, 379, 495, 506, 507, 625, 633
World War I, 549, 550, 687
World War II, 319–21, 323, 550, 623, 684, 690
Wunderlich, Carl, 30
Wurtman, Richard, 564

X

X-rays, 65–66, 295, 310
Xylenes, 239
Xylitol, 516
Xylocaine®, 568
Xylometazoline, 536

Y

Young, John W., 13
Yttrium, 341

Z

Zalcitabine, 546
Zantac™, 194
Zebrafish testing, 700
Zeolites, 395, 635, 652–53
Zerit®, 546
Ziconotide, 531
Zidovudine, 546
Zinc, 97, 619
Zinc-air cells, 212
Zinc oxide, 665
Zirconium, 364
Zirconium oxide, 635
Zirconium silicate, 334
Zoloft®, 254
Zovirax®, 545
Zwitterion, 464
Zyprexa®, 572
Zyrtec®, 536
Zytec®, 536